Chicago Tribune

THE RISE OF A GREAT
AMERICAN NEWSPAPER

Chicago Tribune

THE RISE OF A GREAT AMERICAN NEWSPAPER

by Lloyd Wendt

RAND McNALLY & COMPANY
Chicago   New York   San Francisco

PERMISSIONS

The author gratefully acknowledges permission to quote from the following books:

American Economic History by Harold U. Faulkner, copyright © 1931. Reprinted by permission of the publisher, Harper & Row, Publishers, Inc.

Barbarians in Our Midst by Virgil Peterson, copyright © 1952. Published by Little, Brown and Company. Reprinted by permission of the author.

The Dry and Lawless Years by John H. Lyle, copyright © 1960. Reprinted by permission of the publisher, Prentice-Hall, Inc.

The Growth of the American Republic by Samuel Eliot Morison and Henry Steele Commager, copyright © 1930, 1962. Reprinted by permission of the publisher, Oxford University Press.

Horace White, Nineteenth Century Liberal by Joseph Logsdon, copyright © 1971. Reprinted by permission of the publisher, Greenwood Press.

James Keeley, Newspaperman by James Weber Linn, copyright © 1937, renewed 1965. Reprinted by permission of the publisher, The Bobbs-Merrill Company, Inc.

Lincoln's Herndon by David Donald, copyright © 1948. Reprinted by permission of the publisher, Alfred A. Knopf, Inc.

The Man Who Elected Lincoln by Jay Monaghan, copyright © 1956. Reprinted by permission of the publisher, The Bobbs-Merrill Company, Inc.

The Rise of the City by Arthur M. Schlesinger (vol. 10 of *A History of American Life*), copyright © 1933. Published by The Macmillan Company. Reprinted by permission of Arthur Schlesinger, Jr.

The Territorial Imperative by Robert Ardrey, copyright © 1966. Reprinted by permission of the publisher, Atheneum Publishers.

PHOTO CREDITS

Except where otherwise noted, all photographs and other illustrations are from the Chicago Tribune Reference Library or Tribune Company Archives.

Library of Congress Cataloging in Publication Data
Wendt, Lloyd.
   Chicago tribune.

   Bibliography: p.
   Includes index.
   1. Chicago tribune.   I.   Title.
PN4899.C4T87   071'.73'11   79-19815
ISBN 0-528-81826-0

To Helen, Bette, and Julie,
Brooks and Win

OTHER BOOKS BY LLOYD WENDT

Bright Tomorrow
Gunners Get Glory

WITH HERMAN KOGAN

Bet a Million!
Big Bill of Chicago
Chicago: A Pictorial History
Give the Lady What She Wants!
Lords of the Levee

**Congress shall make no law
respecting an establishment of religion,
or prohibiting the free exercise thereof;
or abridging the freedom of speech,
or of the press;
or the right of the people peaceably to assemble,
and to petition the Government
for a redress of grievances.**

First Amendment to the
Constitution of the United States

**When judgment is brought to bear upon an event,
the event is weighed up as it is, and not as it might be,
if it were not as it is.**

Benedetto Croce
History as the Story of Liberty

CONTENTS

PREFACE

The metropolitan newspaper never sleeps, never rests, but writes its autobiography in daily book-length segments. This book makes no attempt to abridge what the *Chicago Tribune* has said for itself over its first 130 years, from the edition of June 10, 1847, through mid-1977. Rather, it tells the story of the paper's movers and shakers, as philosopher Henri Bergson called those who give to institutions and society that shake which moves them forward. It is especially the story of the strong individuals who stamped their personalities on the pages of the newspaper. Of abolitionists Joseph Medill and Charles Ray, and their later compatriot William Bross, who shaped the *Tribune* while they helped to shape up their wild frontier town of Chicago; of Henry Demarest Lloyd, first and perhaps greatest of the muckrakers; of gentle reformer Medill McCormick, who preferred politics to newspapering; of disciplinarian James Keeley, who won for the *Tribune* some of its most memorable scoops; of Joseph Patterson, who took his flair for pleasing readers to New York to found the country's highest circulation newspaper; and of Robert R. McCormick, Progressive turned archconservative, but either way a fit antagonist for the likes of Big Bill Thompson and Al Capone in the battle for Chicago.

Like individuals, most newspapers are more diligent in recalling their correct decisions and judgments than their errors. I have sought to review both the triumphs and the mistakes of the *Tribune*, casting its story in the context of the times, against a background of history, and with some awareness of the changing ethos. There were adversary and activist journalists in the 1850s as there have been in the 1970s, for example, but they cannot be evaluated by precisely the same criteria.

I have been concerned not only with news and opinion, but also with people and their times, and with the rise of the *Tribune* from struggling daily journal to one of the world's most successful newspaper enterprises. As the institution grew, so did its thrust and influence in the affairs of the city, the state, and the nation. The way that influence was applied depended on the goals and motivations of the movers and shakers, although the consequences were not always what they might have desired. Joseph Medill led the *Tribune* to the brink of bankruptcy in the struggle to elect Abraham Lincoln president, and Robert R. McCormick's long fight against the New Deal won the paper worldwide enmity. Yet the *Tribune* has endured.

11

In preparing this history, I am fortunate to have had first access to the letters, memoirs, fragmented diaries, and manuscripts that were gathered together over the years but organized for study only recently by Harold Hutchings, Tribune Company's first archivist, and his assistant and successor, Lee Major. The documents include an enormous treasury of Medill, McCormick, and Patterson papers. It has been possible through the expanded and organized Tribune Company Archives to trace additional letters of Joseph Medill, Charles Ray, William Rand, William Bross, and others in libraries and collections about the country. Also, in the past several years, many documents believed lost in the Chicago Fire have been discovered, and generous persons have given to various Chicago libraries copies of missing editions of the city's newspapers. Gifts to Tribune Company Archives, such as the recently discovered Albert Bodman Papers, have made it possible to fill in gaps in the *Tribune*'s Civil War report and other prefire news; they are a genuine boon to anyone who is seeking to complete the record of the press in Chicago.

The editing and production of a metropolitan newspaper is a highly complex process, requiring the skilled services of thousands of persons who are vital to its operations but who receive little or no mention in the newspaper. Nor is a history of this kind the work of a single individual. I regret that I cannot publicly thank all those who have helped me, but I can acknowledge my indebtedness to a few, most especially my wife, Helen, who has aided in the research and has encouraged me with great understanding. Stanton R. Cook long before he became a high official of Tribune Company suggested that I write a biography of Colonel McCormick, which became instead this book; as chief executive officer he has opened Tribune Company Archives, libraries, and corporate records to me in complete freedom. I am grateful to Herman Kogan, my collaborator on five books of history and biography relating to Chicago, for his advice and help; to Carl Guldager, knowledgeable in literature and the somewhat arcane field of business history; to Harold Finley, for assistance in the area of economic history; and to Don H. Reuben, expert in the law of the press, for useful counsel.

I am thankful to the research professionals who find joy in aiding those in need: archivist Hutchings, a former executive editor of the *Tribune*; archivist Major; Mabel Johnson, manager of library services, Chicago Tribune Company; Norma Ebright, *Chicago Tribune* librarian; Al Wykel and Barbara Newcombe, managers of the paper's reference rooms; Athena Robbins, formerly of the *Tribune*'s advertising department. Thanks are due also to Kenan Heise, editor of the paper's "Action Line," collector of Chicagoana, and author of books on Chicago history, who helped with special research problems; to Gus Hartoonian and Dale

Larson, of the *Tribune*, who assisted in the selection of art and photographs; to Thomas Dean, attorney with Kirkland and Ellis, who helped me with law firm history.

To the editors of Rand McNally & Company, who attended the manuscript with awesome devotion, advising me on organizational problems, rechecking the extensive historical data involved, and meticulously guiding my revisions, I owe much. I am particularly grateful to the late Stephen P. Sutton, senior editor, who before his untimely death made useful suggestions, and to Peggy Leith Anderson, associate editor, who superbly executed the arduous tasks of research verification, historical guidance, and copy revision. I am indebted also to Mildred Morrison, formerly associated with me at *Chicago Today* and now secretary to the director of the McCormick Charitable Trust, who aided with research and manuscript preparation, and Mary Newman and Milli Backus, who typed much of the manuscript.

I am grateful to directors and staffs of libraries and institutions cited in the Bibliography and to scores of persons who provided information from their own experience, from newspaper morgues, from private collections. While I was on the staff of the *Tribune* and working on earlier books, I interviewed managing editor E. S. Beck and Colonel McCormick. After these books appeared, Colonel McCormick in particular talked to me often about early days in Chicago and his experiences. I have drawn on my memory and notes and memos relating to these conversations, as well as various personal observations, or involvements in the *Tribune* scene. Mrs. Maryland McCormick, widow of Colonel McCormick, also shared her recollections in lengthy interviews with me.

Persons who sat for formal interviews in some depth, all now retired from the *Tribune* or who left the paper for other work unless otherwise noted, include: Fred J. Byington, liaison, Canadian operations, director of transportation, and later secretary of Tribune Company and subsidiaries; Levering Cartwright, reporter and later editorial writer in the 1920s, and since a publisher and investment counselor; Harry Cohen, employed by the advertising department, 1908–1912, later proprietor of his own advertising firm; Paul Fulton, advertising manager; the late William J. Fulton, New York, London, and UN correspondent, successively; John Goldrick, currently secretary of Tribune Company and its subsidiaries and assistant to the publisher of the *Tribune*; Harold F. Grumhaus, president and chairman of Tribune Company and publisher, *Chicago Tribune*; the late Harry Hirsch, assistant director of circulation; Charles B. Jordan, assistant to the president, Chicago Tribune Company, and formerly assistant advertising director; Edward L. Kaiser, of the *Tribune* advertising department and Chicago Tribune–New York News Syndicate; A. M. Kennedy, former Sunday editor and secretary of Tribune Company; Harry King, manager of company relations, advertising; Clayton Kirkpatrick, currently president of Chicago Tribune Company and formerly editor, *Chicago Tribune*; John S. Knight, Knight-Ridder Newspapers, former president and publisher, *Chicago Daily News*; Al Madsen, chief photographer, *Chicago Tribune*; the late J. Loy Maloney, managing editor and executive editor; the late W. D. Maxwell, editor, and vice-president of Tribune Company; Gwen Morgan, foreign correspondent; Frederick A. Nichols, president, Tribune Company, and formerly of the *Tribune* advertising department; E. R. Noderer, foreign correspondent and chief, London bureau; James G. Paddock, manager, classified advertising; John Park, production manager; James Patterson, a former director of Tribune Company and assistant managing editor, *New York News*; Wayne Perry, currently production director, *Chicago Tribune*; Walter Simmons, war correspondent, chief of the Tokyo bureau, and Sunday editor; Eugene Strusacker, manager, New York advertising office; Wayne Thomis, aviation editor of the *Tribune* and personal pilot for Colonel McCormick; Dr. Theodore Van Dellen, *Tribune* medical director and columnist; Arthur Veysey, war correspondent and chief, London bureau, currently co-director with Gwen Morgan (Mrs. Veysey) of the Cantigny Museum; J. Howard Wood, chairman and president of Tribune Company and publisher, *Chicago Tribune*.

I am indebted to the late Joseph Garrett, whose index of early *Tribunes* has been most helpful; and to the late Philip Kinsley, veteran reporter and writer for the paper, whose three-volume history, *The Chicago Tribune: Its First Hundred Years,* has proved highly useful to me and with whom I discussed *Tribune* history long before I considered such a project for myself.

As a member of the *Tribune*'s staff for many years, and as editor and publisher of a satellite, yet competing, daily and Sunday paper, I have been quite aware of the controversial nature of the *Tribune* over the years. In a book of this scope, it is inevitable that some events of importance have been omitted, while other events have been given what may seem to be undue or insufficient value. I have tried to document the facts and to focus on those areas in which, in my opinion, the paper made a significant, or at least novel contribution. At the same time, I have also attempted to follow the main traces of history, which any worthy newspaper must itself traverse.

L.W.

SARASOTA, FLORIDA

SEPTEMBER, 1979

Chicago Tribune

THE RISE OF A GREAT AMERICAN NEWSPAPER

JOSEPH MEDILL
OF THE <u>TRIBUNE</u>

1

They walked briskly in the dreary midmorning drizzle of a February day in 1865, the tall, gaunt man ever so slightly ahead, almost loping on tender feet, showing a glint of good humor for the first time since greeting his three visitors two hours before. He turned to the younger man beside him. "You never liked our Washington weather, Medill," he stated, his smile a flicker of understanding. He knew well enough Joseph Medill's opinions of Washington, D.C., weather and all; he had read them almost daily when he practiced law in Springfield, Illinois, sometimes aloud for Billy Herndon's benefit. Medill's gray-blue eyes smiled, too. He had hated Washington and never hesitated to say so in print.

"No, sir, Mr. President." Medill walked near Abraham Lincoln's side, equal but deferential, a few inches shorter and many years younger; a man of 42 who told the president of the United States often enough, in the pages of the *Chicago Tribune,* how to run the country and how to run the war. So? It was the right of any citizen to criticize and advise. It was his duty, especially if he possessed a printing press and the means of distribution. And Medill felt particularly responsible and qualified, since he and Dr. Charles Ray and their *Tribune* had elected Lincoln, or so they believed, and Lincoln had publicly agreed that the *Tribune* had done more for him than any other paper in the Northwest, the fulcrum of political power. Some observers went even further, asserting that the *Tribune* had started the war, a compliment the proprietors were disinclined to accept.

They were still friends, Lincoln's sideways glance told him, but not precisely in the old way. Medill almost blushed remembering that time years before, when he had come hot from the composing room where an entire chase of type had been pied, to find Lincoln comfortably sprawled with his dusty boots across the editor's desk. Medill snapped, "Dammit, Abe, get your feet off my desk!" and that black look flared. Then they both smiled and shook hands warmly as Lincoln's boots struck the floor.

Now, Medill worried for his friend, though he had written recently that Lincoln's health was good. The president appeared so haggard, his tired eyes sunken, weary. Yet he pushed ahead with old-time vigor into the freshening wind, enjoying the moment of freedom in the outside air; and the young editor beside him, still clean-shaven and nonconformist in a nation of whiskered men, was happy that he had written just a few days before: "We will follow Father Abraham to victory. The noblest, the purest in character, the most unambitious and patriotic of any president since our first. . . . Honest Old Abe, beloved by all of us."

Lincoln had not read the editorial—he no longer read any newspapers—but John Nicolay or John Hay or Sen. Lyman Trumbull would have told him how the *Tribune* really felt. Lincoln knew that Medill was in full charge of the paper now, so he knew those were Medill's own sentiments. Even so, the friendship had been strained in the two-hour interview in Lincoln's office, where the president listened until at last, nettled, he exclaimed: "I cannot do it! But I will go with you to Stanton and hear the arguments on both sides." So now, they were heading for the office of the secretary of war, Edwin M. Stanton, Lincoln stepping gingerly in his new, custom-made New York boots.

Behind them trudged Col. R. M. Hough, the bristly, hot-tempered adjutant general to Gov. Richard Oglesby of Illinois. The third delegate from Chicago was S. S. Hayes, the rotund city comptroller, whose scrubby black beard glistened against his pale face—a lethargic, sedentary man, but a man of courage. The unreasonable number of men required of Illinois and especially Cook County by the latest call for troops had led Chicago citizens to select a committee to carry their protest to Washington. Several of the men first chosen declined to serve, and Medill himself was reluctant to undertake the delicate mission. But when he was persuaded that he could best represent Chicago, Cook County, and Illinois, he was pleased to have the support of Hough, designated by Governor Oglesby, and Hayes, who represented Mayor Francis Sherman.

They were calling on an angry Stanton, a gruff, self-righteous, belligerent man. Hours earlier, the secretary of war had glared through thick-lensed spectacles with his myopic, owl-like eyes at the Chicago delegation and rejected their arguments. He had no intention of changing the enrollment plan. Rhode Island had asked for it to be changed; a dozen states were asking, though the president only the week before had supported the formula, and there was no way it could be altered. Even so,

Medill, Hough, and Hayes had gone to plead their case with Lincoln. Now, in the company of the president, they were on their way back to the War Department to settle an issue that Medill knew well enough had been settled weeks before.

Medill had first met Stanton when they were yearling lawyers back in Ohio, friends then, along with Salmon Portland Chase, who was now chief justice of the U.S. Supreme Court. But Stanton was a breed apart, tough, taciturn, a curmudgeon seemingly disliked by all in Washington, a man who openly had called Lincoln "the Illinois ape." Yet he had been appointed secretary of war, because able men of cabinet stature who were honest and worked diligently were as hard to come by as a fighting general. Medill and Dr. Ray and their *Chicago Tribune* had helped bring that about, with their insistent editorials demanding the ouster of Simon Cameron, Lincoln's first war secretary. The *Tribune*'s effort was ironic, for Lincoln blamed Medill and Ray, along with Norman Judd and Judge David Davis, for the deal that had given Cameron the cabinet post in the first place, though Medill had no part in it. It was five years, a generation of anguish, ago, when they were the young movers and shakers, determined to make their hero the first Republican president, who would suppress slavery without resorting to war and keep the Union together.

The War Department's blue-uniformed sentries came rigidly to attention as the president appeared. Lincoln nodded a friendly "at ease" and led his visitors to the second floor and into the chattering telegraph operations room en route to Stanton's office. Again officers came to attention. Chairs scraped and creaked as operators and cipher clerks, without turning from their work, tensed up in response to the president's arrival and then quickly relaxed. Lincoln knew them all, many by name, from countless prior visits. After introducing his guests to Maj. Thomas Eckert, he led them to the freshest bulletins being posted by the cipher clerks as the young operators listened to their clicking instruments and called out the words. President Lincoln turned to Medill and softly said, "From General Grant." He was glancing at a brief message signed "Juno," seeming to understand the sounds and ciphers before they could be decoded. Medill felt warm with pleasure at Lincoln's trust.

Lincoln nodded to Major Eckert and they passed Eckert's office and entered Stanton's vast cave of maps and charts, where the big, glowering, asthmatic secretary sat beneath the dark oils of Gen. Henry Knox and Gen. Henry Dearborn, resplendent in dress uniform, and other portraits of Stanton's predecessors. Provost Marshal General James B. Fry stood stiffly beside him. Stanton rose and seemed to bristle again, whether more at the sight of Lincoln or the unwelcome delegation no one could tell.

After a few renewed civilities, Lincoln nodded to Medill, who argued the Illinois, Cook County, and Chicago position. Illinois had raised 150 regiments, in the field or in training. No state in the North had sent up more men in proportion to population. Medill quoted from his own *Tribune* of February 18: "The whole number of men put into the army by Illinois exclusive of re-enlisted soldiers, between July 1, 1864, and December 31, 1864, was 16,182, of which number Cook county furnished 2,679 men. . . . No other Congressional district put in so many men." The enrollment formula was wrong for Illinois, Medill insisted, and especially for Cook County. Chicago was a Federal factory, a vast supply depot vital to the war effort, which attracted hundreds of alien workers as young men were drained away into the military services. These aliens, unless they volunteered, could not be put into uniform. But the enrollment formula was based upon total male population of military age. The formula, said Medill, looking straight at General Fry, who had contrived it, would require 6,000 more men of Cook County, twice the number that would be fair. "There are now not more than 18,000 men left in the entire county capable of carrying arms, and as for Chicago itself, during the course of this war the city has sent up 22,000 men! If the enrollment is delayed, Cook County will at once provide 2,600 more men—the others to await a new roll call." It was clear from General Fry's emboldened look, and Stanton's glare of cold fury, and the blackening frown on Lincoln's haggard face, that the argument, conducted for days in the columns of the *Chicago Tribune* and in citizens' mass meetings, had at last come to an end.

*   *   *

For months the *Tribune* had acknowledged to its readers that after four years of the most brutal fighting known to man, even greater sacrifices would be required. The armies were devouring men on a scale not known before in military history, as new weapons outmarched generals' old tactics. When conscription became a possibility, the draft riots, especially those in New York, had provided warning that the carnage was no longer docilely accepted. Chicago shuddered when the *Tribune* required an entire supplemental page to list only the Illinois casualties among the more than 13,000 suffered by Union forces at the Battle of Shiloh, and continued to be no less shocked as other reports came in, especially those of battles fought by Grant. Even Chicago had a small draft riot, though Chicago was zealously loyal. And now the system of bonus payments, running as high as $420 a man, was diminishing in effectiveness, and Chicago needed time to get more men, or to force the government to give Cook County credit for the excess volunteers in the early years of the war.

The *Tribune* questioned the fairness of the enrollment formula, but not the need for men, especially when its hero, Gen. Ulysses S. Grant, needed them. Said the paper on February 18: "Gen. Grant . . . tells the country that 100,000 fresh men would terminate the existence of the Confederate Government by the first of May. The people are rapidly furnishing those men. . . . The same Providence, in harmony with whose eternal laws of justice and righteousness we are fighting, has guided us to success hitherto, and still guides us."

On this note Medill and his two committeemen departed, to arrive in Washington as the *Tribune* published good news and a cry for vengeance. "VICTORY. JOHN BROWN'S SOUL IS MARCHING ON!" exulted the headlines on February 21, as the paper announced the fall of Charleston, "the birth-place of Treason—the cradle of Secession—the nursery of rebellion." A small Union flag was printed on page one to mark the victory. "It would be an act of retributive justice to raze [*Charleston*] to the ground . . . or like the fate of Sodom and Gomorrah, leave a pile of ashes as the only memento of what was once the home of treason," said the *Tribune*. "We do righteously glory therefore in the fall of this nest of vipers, coupling our rejoicings with profound gratitude to God, who is at once the God of Battle and the Prince of Peace."

*   *   *

Medill had finished. Stanton nodded to Fry, who read the sanguinary statistics of four years of fighting in a loud, sonorous voice, Lincoln listening with head bowed. Then Stanton summed up: There could be no question of the need for more troops, there could be no city nor section nor state asking for special favor, not even Illinois. A cruel thrust, but none risked a glance at Lincoln. Medill, who after the meeting joined his delegation in a pledge to remain silent about it so long as the war lasted and Lincoln should be president, remembered the scene 30 years later:

> I shall never forget how he suddenly lifted his head and turned on us a black and frowning face. "Gentlemen," he said, in a voice full of bitterness, "after Boston, Chicago has been the chief instrument in bringing this war on the country. The Northwest has opposed the South as New England has opposed the South. It is you who are largely responsible for making blood flow as it has. You called for war until we had it. You called for Emancipation, and I have given it to you. Whatever you have asked you have had. Now you come here begging to be let off from the call for men which I have made to carry out the war you have demanded. You ought to be ashamed of yourselves. I have a right to expect better things of you. Go home, and raise your 6,000 extra men.
>
> "And you, Medill, you are acting like a coward. You and your *Tribune* have had more influence than any [*other*] paper in the Northwest in making this war. You can influence great masses, and yet you cry to be spared at a moment when your cause is suffering. Go home and send us those men."

"I couldn't say anything," Medill remembered. "It was the first time I ever was whipped, and I didn't have an answer. . . . [We raised] 6,000 men—making 28,000 in the war from a city of 156,000. But there might have been crape on every door almost in Chicago, for every family had lost a son or a husband. I lost two brothers. It was hard for the mothers."

On March 1, a few days after Medill's trip to Washington, the Tribune reported the Cook County deficit at 3,254, after an intense campaign for bonus payments to volunteers; Cook County was preparing to implement the draft. Said the paper editorially:

> There seems to be nothing left for the people of Cook county to do but fill the quota assessed to them, and to rely upon a future enrollment to prove the injustice of the call now made upon them and a future draft (if there be one) to relieve them from their disproportionate share of the burden. The reasons assigned by the President for refusing to order a new enrollment immediately are founded upon considerations of the public safety, to which all local considerations must succumb. The people of Cook county can appreciate these reasons. They can and will fill the quota which they are required to face, notwithstanding the manifest and glaring injustice of the enrollment.

But the end was mercifully approaching. On March 23, the Tribune reported: "Sherman and Grant, like the opposing jaws of a terrible vise, are nearing one another. . . . Richmond will be ours by surrender or by evacuation. . . . The end is near." And, on April 10, headlines, and four columns of page one bulletins: "THE END: THE OLD FLAG VINDI-CATED. LEE AND HIS WHOLE ARMY SURRENDERED YESTER-DAY. . . . The sun in his course on this blessed tenth of April, 1865, beholds a Union restored, inseparable, indivisible, eternal!" For North and South, no more bloodshed, no more drafts.

Medill, too, was war weary. A rheumatic spine and a hearing defect had kept him out of the military, but he had served in a hundred ways in addition to his long hours on the newspaper, and he had lost two brothers, William and James, in the war. Had he and radicals like him really brought on the conflict?

*   *   *

Lincoln was not alone in fixing heavy responsibility for the nation's trauma upon the Chicago Tribune; others among its friends and almost all its enemies concurred. Yet, astonishingly, only a decade earlier the Tribune had been near death. Spawned in the mudflats of pestilential Chicago, a town of 16,000 souls, on June 10, 1847, the Tribune had briefly done well but by 1855 had come down with that usually terminal newspaper illness, constricted paid circulation. Then, under the direction of Joseph Medill and Dr. Charles Ray, and by singularly unorthodox means, it began its rise to wealth, power, and national influence, and by 1860 it could claim to have elected Lincoln president.

Had the *Tribune* merely been carried along on the coattails of Chicago, the most swiftly growing city in America? But why should the *Tribune,* a common scold always attacking the city government, be singled out for special favor? After all, John Wentworth's *Daily Democrat* was the oldest of the city's newspapers and was for years loyal to the Democrats, who ruled the town. Yet it was absorbed by the *Tribune* in 1861. And there was the *Evening Journal,* also older, and now rivaling the *Tribune* in its espousal of the new Republicanism. Chicago's phenomenal spurt to greatness did not appear to have an unusual effect upon the *Journal,* nor upon the *Chicago Times,* founded in 1854 by supporters of Stephen A. Douglas, the man who would be bitterly opposed by Medill and Ray's *Tribune.* Ironically, it may have been Senator Douglas himself who rejuvenated the *Tribune,* who raised up Abe Lincoln for president, and who precipitated civil war—Douglas and his infernal Kansas-Nebraska Act. For that was the legislation that reopened the struggle between the North and the South, that turned the thoughts of Joseph Medill, editor of the *Cleveland Morning Leader,* and Dr. Charles Ray, editor of the *Galena Jeffersonian,* toward Chicago and the faltering *Chicago Daily Tribune* in the winter of 1854–55.

The newspaper Joseph Medill represented in Washington that February day in 1865 began in a third-floor loft at LaSalle and Lake streets in Chicago on June 10, 1847. Its originators, said the paper in 1864, were James Kelly, "now a successful leather dealer," John E. Wheeler, "now proprietor of the *Dial* at Kewanee," and Joseph K. C. Forrest, Washington correspondent at the time the first history of the paper was written. Kelly was the owner of the *Gem of the Prairie,* a literary weekly, and he desired to have a daily paper from which the weekly *Gem,* turning to news instead of the essays and stories that had been its fare, could cull type, a practice of most combined weekly and daily newspapers at the time. The first issue was 400 copies, not many for the thriving lake-port town of 16,000. Forrest claimed to have suggested the name *Tribune.* Since he was investing $600 in the venture, his views were given respectful attention. Wheeler, a former employee of Horace Greeley's *New York Tribune* who had come west for his health, also favored the name.

In the early days of newspapers, reporting of the news was guided by the party affiliations of the editors or publishers, who obtained readers by adhering to the terms of a "prospectus," published annually or semiannually, which in effect contracted with the subscribers to report the news and to express opinion from a particular viewpoint. Chicago's first newspaper was the *Chicago Democrat,* launched by John Calhoun on November 26, 1833, a few months after Chicago's incorporation as a village. Calhoun, a 25-year-old Jacksonian Democrat from New York

State, promised that his weekly paper would adhere strictly to Democratic principles. When the *Tribune* appeared, the *Democrat* was a daily paper edited by John Wentworth, but it remained faithful to its founder's word. Chicago's second paper also began as a weekly, in the spring of 1835, when T. O. Davis established the *Chicago American,* inking a June dateline into his masthead when he missed his intended May publication date. Davis promised to support the viewpoint of the Whigs, led by the revered Henry Clay. In 1839 the *American* became a daily paper, but it ceased publication in 1842 when Chicago Whigs became dissatisfied with Davis's efforts. It was succeeded by the *Chicago Express,* a campaign newspaper supporting Clay's presidential hopes. After Clay's defeat in the 1844 elections, the campaign publication was replaced by the staunchly Whig *Daily Journal.*

The *Chicago Daily Tribune* was thus one of three major dailies then being published in Chicago. Only the *Journal* acknowledged the arrival of the *Tribune,* welcoming it to "the stormy sea" of Chicago journalism and commending the proprietors on their new paper's appearance, though it was an afternoon competitor.

The *Tribune*'s Prospectus, for the benefit of new readers who might subscribe, stated the policy of the editors, who also were the printers and circulators: "Our views, in all probability, will sometimes be coincident with the conservatives; sometimes we may be found in the ranks of the radicals; but shall at all times be faithful to humanity—to the whole of humanity—without regard to race, sectional divisions, party lines, or parallels of latitude or longitude." Beneath this leader appeared the new *Tribune*'s poetic exhortation:

> Men of thought! be up and stirring,
>   Night and day;
> Sow the seed—withdraw the curtain;
>   Clear the way,
> Men of action! aid and cheer them
>   As ye may.

Despite their high purposes, the editors found the sea of journalism to be choppy if not stormy. Within a month, Kelly's failing eyesight forced him to sell his interest in the *Tribune;* it was purchased by Thomas A. Stewart, who had at one time been associated with the *Gem of the Prairie.* While Kelly's departure was amicable, Forrest's, in September, was not. Forrest added to the injury caused by his resignation by taking his talents and capital to Wentworth's *Democrat* (thereby precipitating a feud that endured until the *Tribune* absorbed the *Democrat* in 1861, thus getting Forrest back). Wheeler, whose health was not improving, became the editor, and he brought to the *Tribune* a youthful teacher who was to become one of the city's ablest journalists.

John Locke Scripps was born near Cape Girardeau, Missouri, but soon was taken by his family to Rushville, Illinois, where he worked in a print shop while completing his early schooling. He entered McKendrie College in Lebanon, Illinois, and stayed on to become a teacher of philosophy, as was his namesake, John Locke, whose ideas on the rights of man had inspired the American colonials toward rebellion. Scripps was a fervent abolitionist, but also a pragmatist. He saw, as a college teacher whose courses included commercial geography, that Chicago was a city of enormous growth potential and opportunity. Fond of writing, he decided to make himself a specialist in reporting and writing business and commercial news, and he convinced Wheeler that such a department should be added to the *Tribune*.

Scripps's desire to be a commercial reporter could not have evolved at a better time. Chicago was booming—new business houses were opening, and shipments of grain and beef had doubled. A system of plank roads was paying 32 percent on investment, and the *Tribune* gave support to the proposed Galena and Chicago Union Railroad for which former mayor William B. Ogden sought subscribers. Cyrus Hall McCormick came to town, looking for capital and a site for his reaper plant. He found both; Ogden loaned him $100,000 and McCormick and his brothers, William and Leander, built a steam-powered factory north of the Chicago River near Pine Street (later Michigan Avenue). He soon employed 120 men, who turned out hundreds of McCormick reapers a year.

On April 16, 1848, the Chicago dream of a water connection between the Great Lakes and the Mississippi River and thence the Gulf of Mexico became a reality with the opening of the Illinois and Michigan Canal, connecting the Illinois River with the Chicago River and thus with Lake Michigan. Louis Joliet had proposed such a canal in 1673 after he and Jacques Marquette had portaged to the site of Chicago, "on the Lake of the Illinois," as they returned from their journey down the Mississippi. On the opening day, 16 vessels passed through the canal, and Chicago celebrated, for now the city was the midpoint of a continuous navigable waterway from New York Harbor to the mouth of the Mississippi. Grain from Illinois could be shipped to New York via the Great Lakes and the Erie Canal, while sugar from New Orleans and cotton from Memphis would arrive by barge up the Mississippi and Illinois rivers and through the canal to the port of Chicago. The canal trustees put on sale 45,620 acres of farmland along the waterway, and 2,244 town lots, which were snapped up. (Judge David Davis, a friend and supporter of Lincoln, recalled that he was not a believer in the Chicago boom and was much annoyed when he was forced to accept $800 of such lots in settlement of an account. He didn't inspect his 80 acres on the southwest side of Chicago but did pay the taxes. Sixteen years later a land developer sought him out and paid more than $1 million for the $800 lots.)

Despite its rapid growth, Chicago in 1848 remained essentially a shantytown sprawling on a sea of mud. Many plank roads were built on stringers laid on the marshy soil along the Chicago River. In wet weather, green and black slime spurted up between the planks, dousing unwary passersby. In downtown areas signs stuck in the muddy holes where planks had given way under traffic announced, "No Bottom Here," "Shortest Road to China," "Gone, but Not Forgotten." Clerks in a dry goods store near the *Tribune* put a man's hat and coat on a pole thrust into a sustaining bit of muck and attached a sign, "Gone to the Lower Regions." Only two buildings were made of stone, one of them the city hall; the rest were "balloon frame" buildings of lumber, which was plentiful. Bookseller and later publisher William Bross bought a lot and cottage on the lake near Michigan Avenue and Van Buren Street, and helped sustain his family by raising a garden and keeping a cow. Boatmen brought in clean water in barrels. It also could be had through a system of hollow logs connected to James H. Woodworth's pumping station at Lake Street near the lake, but new resident Bross suspected, probably correctly, that the logged water carried cholera. The boom roared on as boosters and developers responded to rumors that Chicago would soon be linked by rail to the East, which could cut to two days the time needed to bring passengers and freight from the East Coast. A New York traveler to Chicago in 1848 described his prerailroad ordeal: Steamer to Albany; railway cars to Buffalo; steamer to Detroit; strap-iron railroad to Kalamazoo; box wagon to St. Joseph, Michigan, walking beside it most of the way; steamer to Chicago. Elapsed time, nearly a week.

On November 20, 1848, Chicago did get a railroad, Ogden's Galena and Chicago Union, the first section of which ran west a few miles to the banks of the Des Plaines River. Chicago was jubilant as the secondhand locomotive "Pioneer" drew a train of secondhand cars, packed with Chicago officials and civic leaders, over the strap-iron rails. In only its second week of operation it was remarkably successful, hauling 30 wagonloads of grain that had been teamed to the railhead by farmers. Within three years the new railroad exceeded the Illinois and Michigan Canal in tonnage. Although many more miles of track were laid, the Galena and Chicago Union never reached Galena; but it carried millions of tons of grain to Chicago over the next 15 years and continued to do so as part of the Chicago and North Western Railway Company, which absorbed it in 1864.

Under Wheeler's capable direction, the *Tribune* added to its services and circulation. The paper was aggressive in seeking out arriving stages, boats, and Wabash trace caravans for news to be had from travelers, commercial visitors, and potential new residents. On March 22, 1848, the *Tribune* received its first telegraphic dispatch, which covered news of revolution in France and the dethronement of Louis Philippe. In December it announced triumphantly that henceforth it would receive news via O'Reilly's Line, thus becoming the first paper in the West to receive news by wire regularly. This service, the *Tribune* assured its readers, would provide reports of the sessions of Congress direct from Washington.

Scripps obtained a one-third interest in the paper in August, 1848, and the firm of Wheeler, Stewart, and Scripps launched a weekly edition in February, 1849. But the *Tribune* was not particularly prosperous. The small office moved frequently. The paper gave its address as 159 Lake Street on April 23, 1849, the earliest issue extant. On May 22, 1849, the *Tribune* lost most of its printing equipment in a fire. Publication was suspended for two days while temporary facilities were located, but since the plant was fully insured, the fire seemed almost providential. In June the *Tribune* moved to new quarters at the corner of Lake and Clark streets and soon after acquired new type, announcing with pride its "new dress." Since the *Tribune* did not solicit advertising its revenues continued sparse, but it had extensive readership in the business community. When Scripps wrote his annual review of Chicago's trade and commerce, he was given the entire front page for his report. Circulation increased steadily and by the end of 1849 was near 1,000.

The *Tribune*'s political judgments were not marked by similar success. In the presidential campaign of 1848, Wheeler backed Martin Van Buren, the candidate of the antislavery Free Soil party, against Democrat Lewis Cass and Whig Zachary Taylor, "Old Rough and Ready," a slave owner and hero of the recently concluded war with Mexico. Taylor won, the last time the Whigs would win a presidential election. In local politics Wheeler did no better, and the *Tribune*'s opposition did not prevent the election of a series of Democratic candidates for mayor.

*   *   *

The year 1850 began auspiciously for the nation, which had of late appeared on the verge of disintegrating as the debate grew ever more acrimonious over whether slavery should be permitted in the vast stretches of land acquired at the close of the Mexican War. In January, Henry Clay, the aging patriarch of the Whigs, offered the first of a series of resolutions that would result in what came to be called the Compromise of 1850. Though the resolutions moved slowly through Congress, the country was relieved, for it appeared that the threat of civil war had been averted.

The *Tribune* seemingly was lulled by the talk of compromise and in May, 1850, abandoned its Free Soil position. The scattered files are inconclusive as to the paper's continuing policy, but an occasional editorial in praise of the Whigs is to be found, indicating that Clay's efforts were effective, at least so far as the *Tribune* editors were concerned. Yet the telegraphic dispatches of the day reflected the bitter battle in Congress as Clay, with the aid of Daniel Webster of Massachusetts and Stephen A. Douglas of Illinois, fought his way through ambushes laid by both Southern radicals threatening secession and Northern extremists promising civil war. At last, in September, the Congress passed five statutes based on Clay's resolutions. Senator Clay's purpose, "to settle and adjust amicably all existing questions of controversy arising out of the institution of slavery," was only superficially achieved, but the country breathed easier, despite dire predictions by the radicals on each side, who insisted that the seeds of war had been sown.

Under the Compromise of 1850, California was granted its request to enter the Union as a free state. The territories of New Mexico and Utah were organized without direct mention of slavery, but a "popular sovereignty" clause provided that states formed from these territories would settle the issue by plebiscite when they applied for statehood. Texas was paid $10 million to drop a claim for part of the New Mexico Territory. The slave trade, yet not slave ownership, was barred from the District of Columbia. But then came the statute that aroused the North to an angry pitch—the Fugitive Slave Law.

A fugitive slave act had been passed in 1793, but the Northern states had ignored it. Now, under the provisions of the new statute, special federal commissioners would be appointed to restore slaves to masters who could claim them simply by presenting an affidavit of ownership. All citizens were required to aid in enforcement of the law. Anyone harboring or concealing a fugitive would be subject to a fine of $1,000, six months' imprisonment, and liability for civil damages. The legislatures of many Northern states passed resolutions condemning the act. The Chicago City Council passed such a resolution on October 1, adding that the Fugitive Slave Law need not be enforced by Chicago police. The Underground Railroad, a secret network of antislavery groups that aided escaping slaves, vastly expanded and Chicago became a major station.

While Northerners condemned the Fugitive Slave Law, Southerners denounced the other compromise measures, and secessionist advocates demanded that Southern states leave the Union. Scattered copies of the *Tribune* available indicate that the paper, perhaps influenced by Scripps's strong abolitionist views, swung away from initial acceptance of compromise efforts and moved toward a Know-Nothing position. The Native American or American party, as it was officially known during its brief career, was a fervently nationalistic group formed in the East from a number of anti-Catholic, antiforeign secret societies, composed mostly of radical Whigs. (The members' "I know nothing" response to questions about their organization gave the party its popular name.) The Know-Nothings were now emerging from secrecy and were beginning to attract abolitionists who were dissatisfied with the Whigs and Democrats.

On the subject of Senator Douglas, the *Tribune,* like the other Chicago newspapers, was ambivalent. Douglas was in good part responsible for the passage of the Compromise, including the Fugitive Slave Law. Yet he had also introduced in the Senate legislation that would enormously aid the growth and prosperity of Illinois, a bill authorizing federal land grants for a central railroad that would stretch from far northwestern Illinois to the Gulf of Mexico. Chicago editors were quite pleased when the bill was amended to include a branch line with its northern terminus at the port of Chicago. On September 20, 1850, only a few days after passage of the last of the compromise measures, Senator Douglas's railroad bill, ultimately creating the Illinois Central Railroad, also became law.

Chicagoans were elated, for in the meantime the Erie Railroad had connected the Great Lakes to New York, and the Michigan Central and Michigan Southern were known to be making plans for extensions westward to Chicago. With a railroad link to the South also certain, the queen city of the Northwest was about to come into its own. Douglas hoped his railroad would bind the North and South together, as it did when the southern sections were completed after the Civil War. But in the 1850s, railroads running east to west largely controlled the destiny of the country, linking Chicago and the Northwest to the northeastern states.

Senator Douglas, angry at the North's criticism of his role in securing passage of the Compromise and dissatisfied with the ambivalence of the Chicago press, confided to friends that he desired to acquire his own newspaper. He requested Chicago associates to look into the possibility of buying the *Chicago Daily Tribune.* Such a move would bring him into direct confrontation with another powerful and flamboyant Illinois Democrat, Congressman "Long John" Wentworth, a flame-haired opportunist who stretched over his six-and-a-half-foot frame as much political shrewdness and showmanship as Douglas could compress into his five-and-a-quarter. The *Tribune* proprietors, unaware that their paper might become a pawn, albeit a lucrative one, in a power struggle between two politicians, went happily along with coverage of commercial news, the addition of another telegraph service, Speed's Line, and special articles for the ladies, taking only occasional potshots at Douglas and at Wentworth's *Daily Democrat.*

Business was the *Tribune*'s primary concern. Chicago was growing, expanding south to 12th Street, site of the new Southern Hotel, and Charles Cleaver was moving workmen's homes from within the city to a point as far as what is now 38th Street, where he was building a slaughterhouse on the lake. Harbor traffic continued to increase, and plank roads, extending like spokes of a wheel from downtown Chicago, were bringing the traffic of the rural areas to the city. By the end of the year, there were 50 miles of such roads.

On December 28, 1850, Scripps was given an entire four-page special edition for his annual commercial report. (Scripps's reputation grew so that Dr. Charles H. Ray wrote from Galena, asking his advice on business news reporting.) He summarized the railroad outlook—Ogden's Galena and Chicago Union showing 22 percent returns, almost equal to the plank roads; the central railroad authorized; the Michigan Central, Michigan Southern, and Northern Indiana expected within two or three years; the Rock Island also to arrive then or soon after. The great boon of the Erie and Illinois and Michigan canals, already demonstrated, would be augmented by the opening of the Sault Ste. Marie, which would enable Chicago to tap the copper resources of Lake Superior. It was predicted that Chicago soon would be the nation's foremost lumber market and a leading grain and beef market. There were, in growing Chicago, six exchange dealers and banks, 32 forwarding and commission houses, 14 wholesale grocers, 50 lumber dealers. Docks and warehouses were being built along the river and its north and south branches. During the year 6.99 miles of plank streets were built, bringing Chicago's total to 9.59 miles, and gas lighting was introduced, including street and bridge lamps. Chicago's population stood at 28,269, not counting some residents on the fringes, 18th largest in the nation, with Cincinnati, 115,435, and St. Louis, 77,860, leading in the West.

Though 1850 was another boom year for Chicago, the *Tribune*'s growth was modest. In May, 1850, the paper moved to 171½ Lake Street, over the Masonic Hall, where it shared space and presses with two religious weeklies, *Prairie Herald* and *Watchman of the Prairies,* published by J. Ambrose Wight and William Bross. The press they shared was an Adams power press, driven by an old black Canadian pony tramping on a revolving platform. In December, 1850, the paper reckoned its daily circulation at 1,200, an increase of about 200 over the year.

Competition was keen. Alfred Dutch's *Commercial Advertiser* was providing especially strong rivalry on business news, and Wentworth's *Daily Democrat* gave the *Tribune* proprietors cause for concern not only for financial reasons, but because Wentworth was moving away from support of Douglas and the Democrats and toward a political milieu already being divided between the *Tribune* and Charles L. Wilson's *Daily Journal.* Congressman Wentworth, the only Illinois Democrat to vote against the Compromise of 1850, was an ambitious and able man, if a vainglorious one. His enemies charged that half the content of his *Democrat* concerned his own activities. Instrumental in moving Douglas's central railroad bill through the House of Representatives, Wentworth asserted that he was responsible for the Chicago terminus of the railroad. He applied his influence on the railroad's behalf in the Illinois legislature and the Chicago City Council and claimed to have powered through the council the ordinances needed to give the Illinois Central a right-of-way along the lakefront.

Wentworth had enjoyed phenomenal success as a Chicago editor and politician from the time he arrived penniless in the city in 1836, walking from Detroit since he lacked stage fare. He carried with him a letter from Isaac Hill, Democratic governor of his home state of New Hampshire, to Horatio Hill, the governor's brother. Wentworth, a scrawny, grinning, red-haired youth, six feet six inches tall and weighing 150 pounds, had recently graduated from Dartmouth College and spent some months teaching English in his hometown of Sandwich. Horatio Hill had just arranged to purchase Chicago's first paper, the *Democrat,* from its founder, John Calhoun. Calhoun was in ill health and weary of fighting his creditors, especially the dour banker Ebenezer Peck, who, Calhoun complained, sought to dictate his editorial policies. Hill intended to go east to solicit funds to complete his purchase; meantime, he required an editor to keep the *Democrat* going. When Wentworth showed up—a personable string bean, eager and hungry, professing a knowledge of English and bearing a letter of reference—Hill asked him to take charge of the paper. Wentworth accepted, and communicated the good news to his family in the East. The fact that he knew nothing about the newspaper business did not frighten the brash 21-year-old. "After all," he noted candidly, "I have nothing else to do." Wentworth learned fast and was a better businessman than Calhoun. By the time Hill dejectedly reported to his Chicago associates that he could not raise $2,300 to pay for control of the paper, pleased Chicago Democrats decided they liked Wentworth's editing so much that they would advance him the money. Several of them did so, including the ubiquitous Peck, who plagued Wentworth for the next few years as he had Calhoun. The deal was made, and by 1840 Wentworth had paid off the loan, totaling $2,800, including interest.

The other aggressive editor-proprietor in brisk competition with the *Tribune* was Charles Wilson, brother of Richard, founder of the *Daily Journal.* When Richard Wilson was made Chicago postmaster, Charles took charge of the *Journal* and determined to make it the outstanding Whig paper in Illinois. Charles, a grocery clerk before he joined the staff of his brother's paper, was a hardworking bachelor who learned the newspaper trade well, and especially enjoyed politics. He became a friend of William H. Seward—U.S. senator, Whig leader, and perennial candidate for the presidency—and of Abraham Lincoln. While the *Tribune* under Wheeler, Scripps, and Stewart supported the Free Soilers, then leaned toward the Whigs, then flirted with the Know-Nothings, Charles Wilson drove the *Journal* ahead to dominate the Whig party in Chicago.

In July, 1851, Wheeler sold his interest in the *Tribune* to 22-year-old Thomas J. Waite, who became business manager. A year later Scripps disposed of his share to a Whig syndicate represented by Gen. William Duane Wilson and departed to join bookseller William Bross in establishing the *Democratic Press*. General Wilson took the title of political editor of the *Tribune*, and Stewart was local and commercial editor. Waite died of cholera in August, 1852, and in October Henry Fowler purchased Waite's interest, joining Wilson and Stewart as proprietors. Meantime, on July 26, the *Tribune*, which had been an afternoon paper issued at 11 A.M., changed its publication time from afternoon to morning and raised its subscription price to 15¢ a week.

The *Tribune* now had to arrange for its own presses, since the Wight and Bross equipment would print the *Democratic Press*. The new proprietors moved to the Evans Block, 51 Clark Street, "first door south of the post office," where they installed both a Richard Hoe cylinder press, the most modern available, and an Adams flatbed press. The *Tribune* proudly described its commodious new offices, composing room, and pressroom and especially invited the ladies to come to view the presses in operation. The paper came out in a new type dress, expanded to seven, then nine columns, and filled most of page one and part of the other three pages with advertising as circulation increased. The new staff seemed to be more than usually conscious of women readers, possibly because of an increase of dry goods store advertising addressed primarily to them, and a prevalence of women's rights crusaders visiting the city from time to time. On December 13, 1852, it expanded its women's columns to a women's department, "Edited by a Lady." She endured the anonymity enjoined upon all editorial personnel except proprietors and top editors, who used their names over departments or signed their contributions with an initial. The lady editor discussed homemaking interests and also expressed her opinions about the disreputable conditions of Chicago streets, which spurted mud onto ladies' gowns when they went calling or shopping. She urged the city to establish "wash houses" for the poor, a boon granted some generations later.

In 1853, *Tribune* policy changed from a political orientation to one primarily directing readers to lead better moral and religious lives. In January, the paper promised in its Prospectus that it would support Whig principles and a protective tariff. Nothing was said about slavery. The paper declared that it was going to give much attention to the regenerative benefits of Christianity, news of churches, the evils of Popery, the wickedness of drinking, and the merits of the Temperance movement. But the editors swiftly demonstrated that their capabilities were not limited to psalm singing and benign exhortation when they disposed of the *Tribune* enemy, John Wentworth, with a succinct sentence and an apt quotation from Proverbs. "Long John Wentworth of the *Democrat* is briefly departing Chicago," the paper noted. "'The wicked flee when no man pursueth. . . .'" Later in the year, the paper moved into Wentworth's favorite territory, crusading against wildcat currency, especially attacking the notes issued by George Smith & Company, one of the town's 14 banking houses. Alfred Dutch, proprietor of the *Commercial Advertiser*, Chicago's first paper devoting itself totally to commercial news, defended the Smith bank, asserting that other bankers had paid the *Tribune* to bring its charges. The *Tribune* sued Dutch for libel, its first action in the courts. The outcome is not recorded, however. Soon after the filing of the suit, *Tribune* type was smashed by intruders, causing a delay in publication. A group of prominent citizens offered a $100 reward for information, matching a sum offered by the paper, but the vandals were never apprehended.

In March, youthful proprietor-editor Henry Fowler, backed by two wealthy and devout Presbyterians, Timothy Wright and Capt. J. D. Webster, took over the paper, buying Wilson's share. Wright and Webster were silent partners, and the firm was known as Henry Fowler & Company. Fowler was editor-in-chief with Wilson temporarily remaining as his assistant. Though his name was removed from the masthead, Thomas Stewart stayed on as an editor and part-owner. Fowler continued the increased coverage of religious and Temperance news, but the "Whig principles" he supported were those of the extremist Native Americans, or Know-Nothings. He went to New York to report on the sermons of a preacher winning wide acclaim, Henry Ward Beecher, and wrote an extensive series of articles on him. Texts of sermons, disputations of a religious nature, and the activities of religious and benevolent organizations crowded the paper. Fowler's churchly bias entered into his commentary on mundane news. The city was excited by the new railroad lines that had entered Chicago in 1852, but Fowler dourly noted that one of them, the Rock Island (which was open as far as La Salle by March, 1853), was indulging in desecration of the Sabbath. "On the last Lord's day the cars of the Rock Island made a trip to La Salle and back," he recorded in his *Tribune* leader. "This is a profanation of the Sabbath on the part of the manager of the road and seems more wanton and inexcusable as there was no real necessity for it." Fowler observed that Harriet Beecher Stowe's novel *Uncle Tom's Cabin* was popular among his readers, but he warned them that the book was highly emotional and cautioned them against some of the more lurid passages. "The moral virtues of the book's depiction of slavery cannot be doubted," he wrote, "but the arousal of base passions could do more harm than good."

The arrival of the railroads from the East brought social and economic changes, and also big news of a violent nature. The Michigan

Southern, Michigan Central, and Northern Indiana (later the New York Central) were all in a hot race to be the first to enter Chicago from the East. In February, 1852, the Michigan Southern became the first eastern line to reach Chicago, running from the Indiana border into the city on tracks built by the Rock Island Railroad. The Michigan Central, using Illinois Central tracks, and the Northern Indiana (which was consolidated with an Illinois company and thus could build its own tracks in Illinois) both entered Chicago in May of the same year. By 1853 the trains were racing against the clock daily to Chicago, and on April 25, 1853, occurred the country's worst railroad wreck as the Michigan Central and Michigan Southern trains crashed at Grand Crossing. Eighteen persons were killed, 40 injured. There was an uproar from newspapers, preachers, and the public, but the craze for speed was on and tragic railroad wrecks would continue to be big news.

Fowler's bigoted editorials soon drove readers from the *Tribune*. Circulation, which was reported as high as 1,800 early in 1852, in time fell below 1,400. The paper began to publish the work of noted authors, including Charles Dickens, and launched an attack on Senator Douglas, not so much for his stand on slavery, but for his failure to do anything about a railroad route from Chicago to the Pacific. It also attacked Ald. William Bross, an editor-proprietor of the *Democratic Press* and a leader in the Presbyterian church, charging that he was using his City Hall connections to obtain profitable municipal printing contracts for his paper. But soon the *Tribune* slipped back into its preoccupation with religious and moral topics. It extolled the benefits of Temperance, religion, and pure thoughts, yearned for the good old days before the election of Andrew Jackson, and sternly admonished women that their place was in the home. Fowler stated that the paper opposed slavery, but also it was against the fanaticism of the abolitionists.

*   *   *

Slavery had been a cancer in American life from the day the Republic was born. When the Northwest Ordinance finally passed on July 13, 1787, it appeared that the disease had been contained, since slavery was proscribed forever from the territory "Northwest of the River Ohio." Although vast new lands were opened for settlement following the Louisiana Purchase in 1803, the slavery question did not arise until Missouri began petitioning Congress for statehood. The bitter debate that followed alarmed the nation, but attempts to prohibit slavery in Missouri were abandoned when Maine asked to enter the Union as a free state, since the existing numerical balance between slave and free states would be maintained. The Missouri Compromise of 1820 permitted Missouri to enter the Union as a slave state and Maine as a free state. In addition, to avoid future controversy, slavery was prohibited in the rest of the region of the Louisiana Purchase north of 36° 30′ north latitude. The problem seemed to have been resolved until 1848, when the Mexican War yielded new territories. Though the admission of California as a free state upset the balance between slave and free states, the Compromise of 1850 apparently settled the sectional question by applying the principle of popular sovereignty to the new territories.

But the truce was an uneasy one and was extremely short-lived. Senator Stephen Douglas of Illinois, desiring to facilitate construction of a transcontinental railroad along a northern route, began working on a bill for the political organization of the territories west of Iowa and Missouri. As part of the Louisiana Purchase, these lands were subject to provisions of the Missouri Compromise. Douglas, however, soon found that the South, favoring a southern route for a railroad to the Pacific, would not support his legislation unless it called specifically for repeal of the Missouri Compromise boundary. Thus, in January, 1854, Douglas presented to the Senate the Kansas-Nebraska Bill, which repealed the Missouri Compromise and provided that popular sovereignty would decide which states would be slave and which would be free. The North was outraged by the repeal of the near-sacred Missouri Compromise, and the outcry against Douglas's perfidy could be heard from Maine to Iowa. Nonetheless, the bill became law in May, 1854, and it loosed hellish forces. Southern slave owners and Northern abolitionists rushed to colonize the border area of Kansas, and there was civil war in Kansas Territory long before there was a war between the states.

Amid the hysteria sweeping the North as the Kansas-Nebraska Bill worked its way through Congress, Chicago and Illinois newspapers seemed united in their determination to halt the spread of slavery and in their revulsion for Senator Douglas. Even the *Tribune* was shaken out of its absorption with Temperance and religion. After publishing the strong speech of Sen. William H. Seward of New York opposing the Nebraska Bill, the paper said: "We love the South but we love the North more. Between slavery and liberty we cannot hesitate. If we must choose, we choose where humanity stands upright and free. The Nebraska Bill opens a great highway for the onward march of slavery. We will give no quarter to traitors, but follow to his political grave every man who betrays freedom." The paper declared its opposition to the enforcement of the Fugitive Slave Law and urged antislavery immigrants to settle in Kansas to help it organize as a free state. Charles Wilson's *Daily Journal,* of course, led the attacks on Douglas; the *Democratic Press* declared that it could no longer fully support the Democratic party; and even John Wentworth's

Democrat, long the official organ of the Democratic party in Chicago, adopted a neutral stance. Senator Douglas felt compelled to make good his threat to start still another Chicago newspaper. In August, 1854, he brought James W. Sheahan from Washington to establish the *Chicago Daily Times.* Sheahan, Jesuit-educated, had worked for a press service in Washington while attending law school, and had written a biography of Douglas. The new paper quickly supplanted the *Democrat* as the organ of the Democratic party.

The *Tribune* did not stray far from its extensive coverage of church events, and Fowler stepped up his antiforeign, anti-Catholic campaign. In the spring of 1854, the paper supported Amos G. Throop, the "Maine Law" (prohibition of liquor sales) candidate for mayor, linking "Rum, Slavery and Democracy" as the triple evils menacing Chicago. Democratic candidate Isaac L. Milliken was overwhelmingly elected. Scripps and Bross, in their *Democratic Press,* berated Fowler's *Tribune* for referring to Irish voters as "whiskey drinking, gambling, ignorant, Irish Democrats." Even in faraway Galena, Dr. Charles Ray, who was disgusted with the Democrats' Nebraska position himself, felt called upon to support his party in Chicago, and his *Jeffersonian* scolded the *Tribune* for its "insane" attacks on Irish and Catholics.

Fowler left the *Tribune* in the summer of 1854, pleading ill health. He soon entered a seminary to complete his theological studies; later he became a minister in Auburn, New York. Timothy Wright and Captain Webster bought his stock but remained silent partners. The editor was Tom Stewart, and the firm name became T. A. Stewart & Co. Stewart was a capable newspaperman but had problems with his fellow owners, and his health was beginning to suffer. Wright continued to favor the Fowler policies, while Webster began looking for a new editor, calling on Joseph Medill in Cleveland among others. Stewart withdrew somewhat from Fowler's extremes. He continued to attack Douglas and adopted many of the views of the Know-Nothing party, yet he welcomed the efforts of abolitionists to organize a Republican party in Illinois. The antislavery radicals were led by Owen Lovejoy, brother of abolitionist newspaperman Elijah Lovejoy, who had been murdered by a proslavery mob in 1837. When the *Democratic Press* sneered at the attempts to form a new party, the *Tribune* challenged "our timid and cautious friends [*to*] come out from among that foul [*Democratic*] party and take a stand with us for the Republican platform."

In September a meeting of Free Soilers and Anti-Nebraska Democrats and Whigs was set up in Aurora to organize a new Republican party. Stewart praised this move and urged people of any ethnic origin or political persuasion to attend. "The only safety for the cause of freedom," the *Tribune* said, "lies in abandonment of old party distinctions and enlisting every lover of freedom in the ranks of the Republican party."

The effectiveness of Stewart's campaign against Douglas was evident when the "Little Giant" returned to Chicago to defend his support of the Kansas-Nebraska Act on September 1. An unruly crowd of 8,000 awaited Douglas at North Market Hall, and the meeting erupted into a near riot that shocked the country, or at least the Eastern newspapers. The *Tribune* headlined its story "GROANS FOR DOUGLAS—CHEERS FOR THE TRIBUNE," and produced a highly colored report of the meeting. The paper asserted that the only supporters of Douglas present were members of his bodyguard and the Irish, who were paid 25¢ apiece. Douglas, lambasted by almost every Chicago paper save his own, singled out the *Tribune* for reply. The Market Hall gathering was a mob, he declared. "The tone of it was produced and regulated by the influence of that organ of the Whig and Free Soil parties, the *Chicago Tribune*." The *Tribune* was pleased: "He laid the result of the meeting at our door, where we are very well content to leave it lie."

*   *   *

On October 4, Abraham Lincoln, who was campaigning as a Whig for the state legislature and who had hesitated to comment on the Nebraska Act previously, spoke out in Springfield, in reply to an address by Douglas. (Because the speech was not reported in its entirety until he repeated it on October 16 in Peoria, it is known as his Peoria speech.) "Slavery," he said, "is founded in the selfishness of man's nature—opposition to it in his love of justice. These principles are an eternal antagonism, and when brought into collision so fiercely as slavery extension brings them, shocks, and throes, and convulsions must ceaselessly follow." In Ohio, Joseph Medill reprinted parts of this speech and commented favorably upon it in his *Cleveland Leader*.

Like Medill, Tom Stewart was impressed by Lincoln's Peoria speech and published much of it, which may have been the version Medill reprinted. "It would be impossible in these limits to give an idea of the strength of Mr. Lincoln's argument," the *Tribune* said. It went on:

> We deemed it by far the ablest effort of the campaign from any source whatever. The occasion was a great one and the speaker was in every way equal to it. The effect he produced on his listeners was magnetic. No one who was present will ever forget the power and vehemence of the following: "Stand with anyone that stands *right*. Stand with him while he is right and *part* with him when he goes wrong. . . . Stand *with* the Abolitionist in restoring the Missouri Compromise; and stand *against* him when he attempts to repeal the fugitive slave law. . . . I object to the *new* position which the avowed principle of this Nebraska law gives to slavery in the body politic. . . . I object to it because it assumes there can be a Moral Right in the enslaving of one man by another."

The same day that Lincoln spoke in Springfield, October 4, the antislavery radicals led by Owen Lovejoy and Ichabod Codding were to meet at the statehouse to organize their own version of a Republican party. Since Lincoln was speaking, they decided to delay their convention 24 hours so that they might hear him. That evening Lincoln's friend and law partner, Billy Herndon, told him that the abolitionists were hoping he would join them. Early on the morning of October 5, Lincoln hitched up "Old Bob" to a buggy and left town. He was seeking votes against Douglas, but he wanted no association with the radicals.

CHICAGO,
THE MEETING PLACE

2

Joseph Meharry Medill was a decade into the newspaper business by the time he considered a move to Chicago in the winter of 1854–55, and he had a failure or two behind him. Journalism had not been his first choice, not until he met Katherine Patrick, who worked for her father's country weekly, the *Tuscarawas Advocate*, in New Philadelphia, Ohio. She taught him the craft of typesetting and turned his thoughts from teaching and the law, in which he was trained and had experience.

Medill was born in New Brunswick, Canada, on April 6, 1823. His Scotch-Irish parents had emigrated in 1819 from the Ulster area of Ireland, where his father, William, was a Belfast shipwright and a Presbyterian, and his mother, Margaret Corbett, a communicant of the Church of England. William Medill assumed that the small farm upon which he settled, near what is now St. John's, would be a part of the state of Maine, but before the Webster-Ashburton Treaty would decree otherwise, William moved his family, including Joseph and his younger brother James, to a farm in Stark County, Ohio, near Massillon.

Joseph and his siblings—he eventually had three brothers and two sisters—attended the district school, where it developed that the gangling, red-haired older brother had a special aptitude for reading and writing. Books were few among the families of the frontier community, but young Joseph discovered that A. C. Wales, a farmer living three miles distant, had a collection of books he was willing to lend. After chores, Medill frequently walked to the Wales farm, eating cold chicken on the way for his supper, to borrow another book or two. He was especially fond of history, biography, and travel, and his favorite boyhood books were Gibbon's *Decline and Fall of the Roman Empire,* Humboldt's *Travels,* and Goldsmith's *Animated Nature.* From Gibbon, Medill conceived a fondness for Roman order that he was never to lose. As a newspaper editor, he supported a strong central government, Roman style, rather than the loose confederation favored in Greek democracy. He became fond of the name *Tribune* also, since it was the tribune of the Romans who had the power to speak out for the common people against injustices by the rulers. While a farm boy, Medill read the weekly edition of Horace Greeley's *New York Tribune* and earned a bit of money organizing reader clubs and soliciting subscriptions for that newspaper.

When William Medill perceived that his eldest son would never be content with farming, he gave the boy permission to enroll with a Canton clergyman who taught Latin, logic, and natural philosophy. Canton was five miles from the farm, and Medill walked there and back to his classes each Saturday. In addition to his farm chores and schoolwork, he wrote letters on political subjects, which he sent to editors of the newspapers in his area. Some were published. They earned him little money, mostly a limited transitory fame. Medill decided to study law, and in 1844 he entered the law offices of Hiram Griswold and Seymour Belden, in Canton, to read for the bar. He was admitted to practice in 1846, and formed a partnership in New Philadelphia with George McIlvaine, who later became chief justice of Ohio. Along the circuit, Medill became acquainted with other young lawyers who would attain national prominence in later years, among them Salmon Portland Chase, John A. Bingham, and Edwin M. Stanton.

Medill's law practice was meager, however, and urgently needing income, he agreed to teach the village school for a few months. Among his pupils was Katherine Patrick, and Medill found himself dallying at the offices of the *Tuscarawas Advocate,* where Katherine helped her father and brother get out the paper. Judge James Patrick had founded the paper, the county's first weekly, in 1819, and he jealously guarded it as well as his lovely auburn-haired daughter. In addition to being an editor and a judge, James Patrick was also Indian agent for the area, a leader in the Whig party, and an elder in the Presbyterian church. At first Patrick viewed dimly the visits of the tall, lean, square-jawed teacher to his print shop. Young Medill, so far as Judge Patrick was concerned, was simply an unsuccessful lawyer turned itinerant schoolteacher who was taking advantage of the fact that Katherine was his pupil—though it was in the young man's favor that he was interested in learning printing. When the judge discovered the newcomer to be not only discernibly intelligent, responsible, and persistent, but also abstinent and a Whig and a Presbyterian, he no longer wished to thwart the determination of his headstrong

Katherine to accept Medill's proposal of marriage. Besides, the young man had decided to take up newspapering, a career denigrated by some people but not, of course, by Judge Patrick. So Joseph Medill and Katherine Patrick had an "understanding." But the early abrasions between her father and his prospective son-in-law never fully healed. In more than ten years Medill did not write a letter to Judge Patrick, nor did he return to visit New Philadelphia.

*   *   *

In 1849 Joseph told his father that he would like to take two years from his law practice to prove to himself that he had the qualities of a newspaper editor. He astutely pointed out that as proprietor of a weekly newspaper he would be able to provide employment for his three brothers, who showed no more affinity for farm work than he did. He promised also to steadfastly follow his favorite maxim, which he frequently wrote down and committed to type: "All wealth is produced by labor— actual muscular effort, directed by brains. Nature furnishes the materials of labor, man shapes them for utility and luxury." It was not difficult for him to convince Katherine that he soon would be economically self-sustaining and they could marry. She promised to wait.

Medill arranged to purchase the *Coshocton Democratic Whig*, founded by Dr. William Maxwell but owned by J. C. Ricketts, who, it developed, not only was insolvent but was not completely candid about his affairs, so that Medill was plagued for years by Ricketts's creditors. However, with a loan of $500 from his father, the promise of temporarily free services from his three brothers in exchange for printing instruction, the blessing of Judge Patrick, the prayerful confidence of Katherine, and more self-assurance than most people thought the shy young man possessed, Medill entered into journalism, with brothers William, James, and Samuel comprising his staff. Joseph Medill knew precisely what needed to be done to rehabilitate the *Democratic Whig*.

First, he purchased new type, had the press repaired, and paid the newsprint bill. The *Democratic Whig* had not been issued for some weeks, and when Medill was ready to print, he renamed his paper the *Coshocton Republican*. There was no Republican party at the time, and Medill made it clear his paper would be Whig, the party that had supported the American Revolution and had fought against royalty and privilege in England. But at the same time he urged the Whigs to take a stand against slavery, the position advocated by the Free Soil party in the 1848 election. "On you [*Whigs*]," Medill wrote in a draft for an editorial, "rest the hopes of the Goddess of Liberty, on you depend the future greatness, happiness and liberty of unborn millions. Why then exhibit such indifference, such unjustifiable apathy? Arouse to action! Union and harmony is all that is wanting. Enough patriotism remains yet in the land if rightly exerted to avert the storm and turn aside the shaft that threatens the very existence of this Republic."

Medill's writing may have aroused some of the apathetic Whig readers in Coshocton, but it did not arouse the advertisers. Most proprietor-editors of the time considered it beneath their dignity to solicit advertising, and Medill was of that persuasion. Such advertising revenue that did find its way to the *Republican* was usually not in the form of cash. Medill complained that he got only chickens, ducks, and lengths of dry goods. He induced his parents to move to Coshocton so that he and his brothers could live as a family with them and thus use some of the produce, an arrangement the brothers were required to accept, since Medill had no money with which to pay them. These difficulties, however, did not keep the young editor from proffering profound concepts to his readers. On the subject of the tariff, he wrote: "Free traders only look at one side of the matter. They see that the tariff increases the apparent cost of manufacture. They refuse to see that the wages of the mechanic are increased in equal ratio, must be, else the goods would not be advanced in price. They refuse to see that, but for the tariff, the farmer would get less for his produce, at least in proportion to the tariff."

Medill did not totally change his tariff position in his lifetime, though it was almost exactly opposite that of several of his later associates at the *Chicago Tribune*, including two chief editors, bringing about a major schism and requiring Medill to leave the paper for nearly nine years. In addition to supporting a protective tariff, a Whig policy of limited popularity among Ohio farmers, Medill lashed out against an array of contemporary ills, including "Dorrism, repudiation, Gerrymandering, horde money, slavery annexation, falsehoods, and Locofocoism."

Joseph Medill was possibly ahead of his time in his editorial stands, and certainly ahead of his community. By late 1851 he had had enough of the practice of journalism in Coshocton. Medill disposed of the *Republican*, briefly owned a paper in Newark, Ohio, then, with his own money and funds loaned to him by Hiram Griswold, with whom he had studied law, and friends in New Philadelphia and Massillon, he established the *Daily Forest City* in Cleveland. Outlining his enterprise to the Cleveland postmaster, Medill said his new paper would firmly support Whig policies and would cost subscribers $3 a year daily, $2 triweekly, or $1 weekly. Medill sought to enlist the help of the postmaster in his venture, a not uncommon practice, offering him a commission of 10 percent on all subscriptions directly obtained. In addition, the young editor asked for a list of all Whigs in the area and suggested to the postmaster that he should prepare for a glut of mail once the presses of the *Daily Forest City* started.

There was more work to be done before Medill's project could get under way. A new press to be installed, new type distributed, and his printers prepared to meet Medill's high standards—such mechanical preparations would mark Medill's publishing style as long as he lived. His three brothers, loyal despite the fact that he had not paid them any cash in 18 months, joined him in Cleveland to help get out the paper and to operate the job shop. In addition to the money supplied to him by friends, Medill was able to extend his credit with C. Foster & Bros., Cincinnati, for his new printing equipment.

At last the four-page *Daily Forest City,* a Whig morning newspaper, appeared in April, 1852, its Prospectus stating: "The *Forest City* will furnish the latest and best summary of current events of the day at home and abroad and the fullest and most reliable report of Produce, Cattle and Money Markets of any paper in Cleveland. . . . Politically, the *Forest City* will be liberal, courteous and will use all honorable means to effect the greatest amount of practicable good." On April 10, editor Medill announced that his paper, "in common with a large majority of the American people," favored for president, "the scar-covered hero of Lundy's Lane." The scar-covered hero, of course, was Gen. Winfield Scott, who had been severely wounded in the Battle of Lundy's Lane in Canada on July 25, 1814, a fight in which the British were badly mauled. Scott was also a veteran of the Mexican War, as was his opponent, Franklin Pierce, who beat out Sen. Stephen A. Douglas for the Democratic nomination.

Throughout the summer and fall Medill fought hard for his Whig hero, and for Whig party principles. *"General Scott is omnipotent,"* he exulted in a letter to a friend. So far as eastern Ohio was concerned any other candidate would be *"utter madness and insanity. . . . We can rally on a man pledged to let the [Missouri] Compromise alone."* Medill took time out from the campaign to wed Katherine on September 2, 1852. Scott and the Whigs went down to disastrous defeat in November, getting only 42 electoral votes to 254 for Pierce.

The young Cleveland editor was dismayed by the Whig debacle. The party lost, he concluded, because its leaders did not espouse the principles that had distinguished Whigs in the past, and, worse, they lacked the courage to stand firm against the surrender to slavery embodied in the Compromise of 1850 and most especially in the Fugitive Slave Law. Medill undertook to carry on the needed Whig reform in Ohio. He was 29, a quiet-spoken but intense young man who had a temper and could be stubborn. Ordinarily he would not push himself into the attention of others, but now he was determined that Whig mistakes must be corrected. He began a series of editorials in the *Daily Forest City* offering explanations for the defeat and concluding that although the Whig party, and no other, represented the desire of the people of Ohio to stand against slavery, it could not do so because of failing leadership. He began to suggest to his friends, to political leaders with whom he corresponded, to other editors, and finally to his readers, that a new party, to be called the Republican party, should be started. There were among the Whigs, Free Soilers, and Democrats, Medill thought, enough friends of liberty to strike the needed blows for freedom in the next presidential election. Medill looked to the *New York Tribune,* owned and edited by his hero, Horace Greeley, but found little comfort there. Greeley admitted that the Whigs were annihilated and doubted that the party could be reconstituted. Yet he declared in the *New York Tribune,* "We mean to stay in the Whig party." At the same time Greeley wrote his friend Schuyler Colfax of Indiana, "*I have ceased to expect wisdom from the Whig party.*" And to another friend he confided, "*I have had enough of party politics. . . . I am not going to stump the country again in the interest of any party or candidate.*"

Medill accepted no such defeatism, and his efforts continued through 1853. His editorials extolled the idea of a party uniting diverse factions that could come together against the evil of slavery, a party favoring a strong central government, a protective tariff, and attention to the rivers and harbors of the country. He censured J. Watson Webb, editor of the *New York Courier and Enquirer,* for affixing the foreign name of Whig to a party in the first place, when it was launched in opposition to Jacksonian Democracy in 1830. Webb responded: "The name Whig is a good enough standard. It is the standard under which the best battles for liberty have been won among the English-speaking people, and especially I see no reason for assuming the name under which Imperial Rome fell."

The introduction of the Nebraska Bill before the U.S. Senate in January, 1854, gave Medill new resolve and increased the number of approving replies to his letters and editorials. Greeley finally wrote Medill:

> Go ahead, *my friend, with your proposed Republican party, and God bless you. I hope you will have the best of luck. The time has indeed come to bury our beloved [Whig] party; it is dead. But we have many fool friends who insist it is only in a comatose state and will recover, but I tell them it is dead—still, I dare not yet in New York announce the demise of the party and call for the organization of a new one. . . . I like the name for it. . . . If you can get the name Republican started in the West it will grow in the East. I fully agree to the new name and the new christening.*

Medill persisted. Editor Joseph Warren of the *Detroit Tribune* cheered his efforts. His old friend U.S. Sen. Salmon Chase supported him but cautioned him to "go slow"; John D. Defrees, editor of the *Indianapolis Morning Journal,* wrote that the Whigs in his state were "too blue" to consider any plan. Others who were powerful in the Whig party— Benjamin F. Wade, Schuyler Colfax, and Joshua R. Giddings—gave

Medill restrained encouragement, as did the editors of the *Buffalo Express,* the *Pittsburgh Gazette,* and the *Cincinnati Gazette.*

Meantime, Medill was expanding his newspaper business. He took Edwin Cowles as a partner, agreeing at Cowles's insistence to change the name of the paper to the *Cleveland Morning Leader,* a change that became effective on March 16, 1854. He also had acquired, sometime during 1853, his other partner, John Champion Vaughan. Born in Charleston, South Carolina, and reputedly once the owner of slaves, Vaughan had become a flaming abolitionist, associated, it was said, with the Lovejoy faction in Illinois. He had owned the *True Democrat,* which claimed to be the leading Free Soil paper in Ohio.

Now Cowles and Vaughan supported Medill in summoning leading politicians of Ohio to a meeting during March, 1854, in the *Leader* offices. Among those promising to attend was Salmon Chase, but he failed to appear for the good and highly acceptable reason that he was helping to lead a Senate fight against the Kansas-Nebraska Bill. Some 20 men from the Whig, Free Soil, and Democratic parties attended to hear Medill, Vaughan, and Rufus Spaulding describe the principles of the proposed new Republican party. Forty-five years later, Medill summarized the results of the meeting, saying, "Name of the new party: National Republican. Platform: No more slave States; no more slave territory; resistance to proslavery aggression; slavery is sectional; liberty is national. The platform was written in part by myself and in part by Rufus Spaulding, and the last two clauses were by John C. Vaughan."

In the fall of 1854, Medill was visited by Capt. J. D. Webster, one of the proprietors of the *Chicago Tribune.* Webster invited the young editor to Chicago, where, after an extensive inspection of the rude town and a study of the *Tribune*'s printing facilities, he declined a job as managing editor. Much of the paper's equipment was old, and the proprietors were evidently not interested in investing more capital. Though the *Tribune* was properly antislavery and anti-Democrat, its other Know-Nothing policies were abhorrent to Medill. Nonetheless, the rough city had an almost palpable aura of enthusiasm that Medill found exhilarating, and he returned to Cleveland with Chicago much on his mind. Cowles, especially, could not understand Medill's growing determination to go into the wild Northwest, particularly considering their success in Cleveland, with their *Morning Leader* prospering and their job shop doing well. Their call for a Republican party had been rebuffed originally, but now, after the passage of the Kansas-Nebraska Act, they were almost heroes. Chicago, of all places, wild and rude and cholera-scourged, a town denounced often enough in their own *Leader* for its wicked, sinful, and pestilential ways! What about his family? Little Katherine, born July 11, 1853, was not yet 18 months old, and Kitty was expecting another child soon. Why not stay in elegant, civilized Cleveland, enjoying the hard-earned respect of the community and his new prosperity?

At times during the winter of 1854–55, items about Chicago appeared in the *Leader* as Medill contemplated his course. He commended Chicago businessmen for their enlightened merchandising and financial methods, and suggested that Cleveland and other merchants might well copy them. "The action of Chicago merchants, in banding together, regardless of party, is worthy of note in these days of banking panics. . . . Is this not businesslike? Is this not common sense?" He published the remarks made in Peoria by a Springfield lawyer, Abraham Lincoln, in reply to Senator Douglas, the man responsible for the Kansas-Nebraska Act, and expressed his satisfaction with Lincoln's views. He noted that the tonnage of Chicago's lake port had passed that of Cleveland, Toledo, and Buffalo, once its chief rivals, and that a branch of the Illinois Central Railroad was indeed bound into the heart of Chicago. By the end of 1855, Medill observed, the state of Illinois would have nearly 3,000 miles of railroad, including the nation's longest line, the Illinois Central, and Chicago would be served by ten trunk lines and 11 branch lines. One railroad, the Michigan Central, boasted that it had carried 3,400 immigrants into Chicago on a single day. "Chicago, unlike Cleveland and other lake ports, uniquely joins many railroads with water transportation to reach a vast area swiftly opening to agricultural settlement," the *Leader* said.

By the spring of 1855, Medill had made up his mind to move his family, now including daughter Elinor, born January 30, to Chicago. He had confided his Chicago dream to Greeley in New York, and had been encouraged. Go to Chicago and start a penny paper, advised the editor who would later be credited with advising all young men to go west. Greeley even suggested a partner for Medill, Dr. Charles Ray, an Illinois Democrat, editor of the *Galena Jeffersonian,* who had become disenchanted with Stephen Douglas following passage of the Kansas-Nebraska Act, and who also looked with interest upon Chicago.

* * *

Traveling by a train of cars across the flat, black farm country of Ohio and Indiana, Joseph Medill had 11 hours of daylight to contemplate the vast resources of that northwest area to which he was about to commit himself and his family, and to study again the facts and figures. Dr. Charles Ray, whose letter had put him on the train to Chicago, was awaiting him, and a quick decision would be made. Buy the *Chicago Tribune*? Start a penny paper? Medill carried with him a copy of the Chicago paper he most admired, the *Democratic Press,* published by William Bross and John Scripps. Bross had enticed Scripps to leave the *Tribune,* where he had been editing the best commercial pages of any paper in the West, except, of course, the *Cleveland Leader*. As a pioneer himself in the reporting of business news, Medill could admire professional perfection. The *Democratic Press* would be a competitor to reckon with. Senator Douglas's *Daily Times* had a brilliant editorial page, produced by the newcomer from Washington, James Sheahan, but was involved almost entirely in politics, while Congressman John Wentworth's *Democrat* seemed mostly concerned with Long John Wentworth himself. Bross and Scripps were the ones to watch.

It was difficult to see how the purchase of the *Tribune* at a good price could be wrong, even though much of the equipment would need replacing. Chicago was a wide-open market, and with good business management and a more forward-looking political attitude, the paper should soon improve its financial situation and even begin to play an important role in influencing the city's destiny. Medill remembered what he himself had written: "Compared with Cleveland, Chicago is a quagmire on the lake, but it is clear this prairie metropolis will become a great city."

Chicago's population had grown from 60,000 to 85,000 in only two years, 1853 to 1855. The city doubled its shipment of grain in one year, from 6 million to 12 million bushels, and now expected to double that figure by 1856. Chicago's future was clear enough, though only in recent months would Eastern bankers make loans to its businessmen. As Bross and the other boosters incessantly pointed out, in 20 years Chicago had grown from a spraddling village among the sand dunes to America's busiest inland port, the world's greatest lumber market, the second-biggest pork packer—and pushing Cincinnati for first—the fastest-growing railroad center, and the unique maker of McCormick reaping machines. But also, Medill knew well enough, Chicago was the dirtiest, dreariest, muddiest collection of yellow-pine and tarpaper shacks, balloon buildings, and deal storefronts ever gathered together on the American continent. Yet there were the bright aspects, too, an exciting new downtown section, with five-story pink marble stores along Lake Street and a new five-story brick hotel.

Medill had been told on his prior visit that in spring hundreds, perhaps thousands of barges, ferryboats, lake schooners, and even oceangoing vessels would arrive to bring in manufactured products and carry away the produce of the Northwest's farms, forests, and mines. Boosters were predicting that in 1855 Chicago would be shipping more pork, beef, and grain to Europe than any other American port, and he could believe it. It was more difficult to believe that in summer the pleasant, attractive river would become one of the vilest streams in the universe, reeking from sewage and packers' offal, its stench rivaling that of the town's stinking mosquito marshes along the lakefront. Medill respected Kitty's fears of Chicago. Its cholera record was abominable. But he resolved to keep away from the lake and the river, to the westerly high ground, when they acquired their Chicago home.

The long trip from Cleveland, aboard the new train of cars, was a pleasant one on the relatively warm day, with a refreshing breeze coming in through the open windows. The coaches were packed with immigrants, who had brought aboard such household goods as they could carry, as well as crates of chickens, ducks, and squealing pigs. There were frequent stops at tiny way stations along the Northern Indiana Railroad where the passengers could alight to help the fireman get wood, or to "jerk" water from the creek in leather buckets. Medill joined in these activities despite his rheumatic spine. He mixed well with the other passengers. Somewhat aloof and soft-spoken, he could be aggressive, and now he was out to make friends with the drummers and merchants who were among the passengers. These merchants and salesmen, bound for Chicago, were eager enough to discuss their favorite town.

They told him that Chicago was booming this spring of 1855, but there were a few problems, too: lack of federal attention to the Chicago River, for one; and Mayor Levi Boone, a Know-Nothing just elected with the support of the *Chicago Tribune,* for another. Boone was attempting to enforce Sunday closing of the saloons and beer gardens. This, in a wide-open town, a town that had more Irish than any other city except New York and Boston, more Germans than any other American town save Cincinnati and Milwaukee! If the Irish and the Germans ever got together, and they were joined by the Scandinavians, then, look out! The Know-Nothings ought to realize that Chicago was a workingman's town. When a man worked 11 or 12 hours a day, six days a week, he should have the right to a glass of beer with friends in his favorite saloon or beer garden on a Sunday. Medill could warmly agree with their point of view. He knew the Know-Nothings well enough—the Native American party, which had arisen from secret societies formed in Boston and New York to vent their hostility to the foreign-born, especially Catholics. Since the disastrous Whig defeat in 1852, the Know-Nothings had grown in popularity and were spreading through the West, supplanting the Whigs, the earlier representatives of conservatism and nationalism. In his editorials in the *Leader,* Medill had frequently pointed out the futility of a political course that rejected or ignored the foreign-born, and Greeley had declared that the Republican party, to succeed, would have to capture at least the German vote since the Democrats already had the Irish. Medill resolved to change the *Tribune*'s political position as swiftly as possible, should he and Ray get the paper.

There were many facts to be gleaned from the merchants and traveling salesmen. Chicago now had seven daily newspapers, two published in

German, and more than a dozen weeklies. The city had received 107,000 immigrants in 1854; many found jobs in construction and the machine shops, while other thousands went farther west to build railroads and seek out farmland. A merchant returning from a trip east to buy and to visit relatives proudly told Medill that Chicago now had one dry goods store to every 92 inhabitants. This was possible because most stores' customers came equally from Chicago and the country areas, and there was constantly increasing travel from towns along the new rail lines. The development appealed to Medill, who had successful weekly and tri-weekly editions for the country trade in the Cleveland area.

The turmoil of the station astonished Medill, even though he had been to Chicago before and was accustomed to busy Cleveland. Steve-dores descended on the cars to unload boxes and bales of merchandise and pile them on drays, bound for the Lake Street stores. Railroad agents bawled out for companies of immigrant "colonizers," who were to take omnibuses to their westbound trains for a look at farmlands and town sites in Illinois, Iowa, or Kansas. Hackies and omnibus drivers vied for the baggage of the business travelers. Medill found a bus for the new Tremont House handy and was soon aboard with his carpetbag. Within an hour he had sponged and shaved in his elegant room. Then, re-sponding to the knock of a callboy, he was led to the office of John B. Drake, assistant to the owner of the Tremont House. "Come with me, Mr. Medill," Drake cried happily as he led the way to the rotunda. "I have someone waiting for you—Dr. Charles Ray, of Springfield and Galena."

*   *   *

Dr. Charles Henry Ray was an intense yet hearty man, nearly as tall as Medill himself, pate and jowls covered by curling brown hair. He was smiling, flashing white teeth as his blue eyes fixed on his visitor, and he firmly grasped and shook Medill's hand. Medill was impressed. A doctor's gaze, an editor's inquisitorial assessment, a politician's greeting. Medill was pleased to discover that the Greeley comments about Dr. Ray were quite correct. Ray had once edited the *Galena Jeffersonian* in keeping with his firm Democratic principles, but now he was an ardent abolitionist, a staunch opponent of the Kansas-Nebraska Act, and an implacable enemy of Senator Douglas. He was not a Republican but was interested. The two men accepted an invitation to one of Drake's celebrated game dinners, compliments of the Tremont House, then talked eagerly through much of the night.

It was clear from the beginning that Dr. Ray, two years senior to Medill and completely knowledgeable in Illinois politics, had no intention of taking second place in any newspaper partnership they might form. That was awkward, because it developed that Medill would put in more money. Medill suggested that he could get additional money, as well as talent, from John Vaughan, a co-proprietor of the *Leader,* and Alfred Cowles, the younger brother of Edwin Cowles, his other Cleveland associate. Also, Medill wished to bring his brothers into the job shop; they would work almost without pay until the venture was earning its way. Dr. Ray was unconcerned about such details. His interest lay in finding in Chicago the proper medium for disseminating his political views as widely and speedily as possible.

Medill learned in the next few days that in Dr. Ray he had acquired a formidable partner with great powers of articulation, both oral and written. Ray was fiery, incisive, opinionated, and enormously persuasive. Medill regarded himself as a plodder, one who always played safe. Ray, on the other hand, was ready to take spectacular chances. He confided to Medill that he had rarely been free of debt until he received his inheritance three years before. Sure that Galena was the Northwest's city of the future, he had invested his patrimony in the *Jeffersonian.* When he realized that Chicago offered a better forum for his ideas, he sold his interest in the paper. Recently he had used part of the proceeds to purchase some land near Cairo, Illinois, where developers assured him a rival city would soon spring up. Dr. Ray was erratic and moody, either in a state of elation or depressed. Yet it was clear that he had a quality that touched human hearts, and the poise and diplomacy to appeal to political leaders.

The prospective partners had little trouble deciding that Dr. Ray would have the title of editor-in-chief and hold the ultimate responsibility for the editorial columns. Medill would be managing editor and superintendent of editorial, concerned with the day-to-day functioning of the enterprise. Medill was pleased to allocate the business of leading public opinion to a man with the verve and imagination of Charles Ray. And, considering Ray's freely confessed financial vagaries, he would be even more pleased to have jurisdiction of the counting room.

Dr. Ray's life story fascinated Medill. Ray had sailed before the mast, while Medill had merely written unpublished fiction about such a dream. Ray was born in Norwich, New York, on March 12, 1821, the second son of Levi Ray, an operator of forges and machine shops from Massachusetts. Levi Ray, though an employer of workmen in his shops, was a staunch Democrat, first as a supporter of Andrew Jackson, then as an adherent of the somewhat radical "Locofoco" wing of the party. Charles Ray had little interest in his father's business. He desired to be a doctor, and, following graduation from the Norwich schools, worked with a local practitioner until he joined the 105th New York Infantry, in which he served for two years, first as surgeon's mate and then as surgeon. After this service, Ray signed on the brig *Newton* to sail out of New Bedford on

June 19, 1841, on a two-year whaling cruise in the Indian Ocean.

At sea Charles had plenty of time to read and reflect, and to talk politics with the crew. His father's teachings evidently surfaced, for Ray described himself as "the crack Locofoco in the ship's company." At the end of the two-year trip, Ray said, he had little to show for it except the experience and the price of a splendid suit of clothes, which he promptly bought and wore to Norwich to bedazzle Jane PerLee, the sweetheart who had been waiting for him. Ray lived at home that winter, pursuing his medical studies with another local physician, and in 1844 he received his New York State medical diploma. Dr. Ray then departed for the West, after promising Jane he would send for her as soon as he had paid his debts. In Buffalo, he visited a family friend, former congressman Millard Fillmore, a powerful leader in the Whig party who would later become 13th president of the United States. Fillmore suggested there ought to be opportunity for a bright young doctor in Springfield, Illinois. He knew a couple of good Whigs there—John Todd Stuart, who had been a congressional colleague of Fillmore, and Abraham Lincoln, who had served in the Illinois legislature and was once Stuart's law partner. Fillmore provided Ray with a letter of introduction to Stuart. It described Dr. Ray as a man who had come to him *"highly recommended for his scientific and professional attainments."*

Dr. Ray passed through Chicago in the spring of 1845, after arriving on a passenger steamer from New Buffalo, Michigan. He was not impressed with the sprawling shantytown on the lake, though, as a doctor, he should have been, since Chicago at the time had the country's highest incidence of ague and cholera. Both emanated, it was believed, from the "miasma" arising from the swamps bordering the mouth of the Chicago River. Dr. Ray gladly paid out $12 to take the Frink & Walker stage to Springfield, a comparatively beautiful city of more than 3,000, dominated by the graceful new state capitol. In Springfield, Dr. Ray learned there was no longer a Lincoln and Stuart partnership, but Lincoln and Herndon. He found Stuart, however, and through him met the Lincolns and their friends. Dr. Ray was not fond of any of them. He disliked their Whig politics, and he resented their superior ways. Lincoln's wife, the former Mary Todd, put on airs, it was said, because she came from a leading Kentucky family. And here in Springfield her brother-in-law was State Sen. Ninian W. Edwards, himself the son of a former Illinois governor and U.S. senator. In any event, these social connections evidently did Dr. Ray's medical practice little good, for soon he joined a new friend, Tench S. Fairchild, in publishing a Temperance newspaper.

Ray and Fairchild hoped to enjoy the popularity of the powerful Temperance movement sweeping across the country, led by evangelistic speakers, mostly reformed drunkards, who declaimed against the evils of drink. The Temperance meetings rivaled those of the emotional revival meetings conducted by itinerant preachers. One of the lecturers, John B. Gough, a former actor, was particularly effective in his dramatic descriptions of liquor-induced delirium tremens and attracted huge crowds. Fairchild followed Gough about the country attempting to sell subscriptions to the Temperance tract that Dr. Ray was writing and editing in Springfield. He sold few subscriptions, however, and when Gough went on a drunken spree and could not appear to describe the horrors of drink, the enterprise failed.

Dr. Ray had barely broken even during his year in Springfield. He moved to the village of Mackinaw, 60 miles northeast, to practice medicine there. Jane PerLee came at last from New York State to marry him, and the Rays remained in Mackinaw for five years, becoming parents of a daughter, Maria, and the owners of a two-room brick house. Dr. Ray at last was a respected citizen, and though he was often in debt he was able to support his wife and daughter and even to help others from time to time.

During the period in Mackinaw, Dr. Ray's political instincts began to assert themselves. He became interested in the slavery question and at one time hoped to run for Congress, but he lacked the needed funds. As the national debate over slavery intensified and parts of the South threatened secession, Dr. Ray, as a Democrat, at first accepted the reasoning of Senator Douglas, who declared that compromise measures such as those brought before the Senate in January, 1850, by Henry Clay were needed to save the Union. Yet he yearned to speak his own thoughts about slavery and other matters important to the nation and to Illinois, and he found Mackinaw increasingly dull and confining.

Ray was aware of the efforts of Sen. Sidney Breese and now of Senator Douglas to get federal support for a railroad to extend across the Illinois prairies from Cairo, at the junction of the Mississippi and Ohio rivers, to Galena, in the far northwest corner of the state. Surely this augured well for Galena, already one of the Northwest's most important towns. Dr. Ray was therefore pleased to learn that in Galena he could work with a Dr. George E. Robinson and at the same time obtain an editorial job with the *Galena Jeffersonian,* the Democratic newspaper. Such an opportunity was almost beyond his dreams. He could write, he could edit, he could practice medicine in a city certain to be one of the dominant cities in Illinois if not the entire Northwest.

In the winter of 1851–52, Dr. Ray, now established in Galena, was informed that his father had died, leaving him a modest inheritance. He decided to invest the money in the *Jeffersonian.* He had worked for the paper a year and knew he had found his true vocation. Despite the revelation that Galena had been double-crossed by Douglas's Illinois

Central Railroad Bill—the final version provided for a major branch to Chicago and made Galena a mere way station by establishing the main road's northwestern terminus at Dubuque—Ray was still sanguine about Galena's prospects. Many railroads had failed, but water transportation was certain. Besides, the Galena and Chicago Union would give the city all the railroad connections it really needed.

By February, 1852, Dr. Ray had acquired a share of the *Jeffersonian*. He was determined to become an influential voice in northwestern Illinois, and the energy of his thought and expression soon brought his editorial leaders wide recognition. They were often reprinted by other papers in the state. "We belong to no clique, no faction, no sect, no man or party of men," Ray declared. "There is no question that we dare not examine, when examination is necessary, no man whom we dare not censure when censure is deserved. We shall beg no man's patronage, nor shall we change an opinion, alter a line or erase a word to secure it."

Though the uproar aroused by the passage of the Compromise of 1850 had nearly died away by the time Ray gained control of the *Jeffersonian*, his own interest in the slavery question increased. The Fugitive Slave Law had caused the Underground Railroad in northern Illinois to step up its activities, and Dr. Ray became concerned about the plight of runaway slaves. Like most other Northerners, he was shocked by *Uncle Tom's Cabin*, which he considered to be a realistic depiction of life under the slave system. Dr. Ray, a faithful Democrat who was loath to abandon his party despite its proslavery tendencies, found a new hero, Salmon Chase. Chase had been sent to the U.S. Senate by Ohio Free Soilers and Democrats, had opposed the 1850 Compromise, and was beginning to encourage Democrats to renounce the proslavery elements in their ranks.

The short period of seeming tranquillity for the nation came to a close early in 1854, when Senator Douglas moved to end the Missouri Compromise by permitting each new state to decide whether to be slave or free. This was too much for Dr. Ray. Like Joseph Medill and other editors, Ray branded Douglas's Nebraska Bill as divisive and sure to precipitate a quarrel that could lead to civil war. In Cleveland, Medill called more urgently for the formation of a new Republican party. Ray reprinted an appeal written by Chase and other opposition congressmen asking the people to unite against the spread of slavery. Later in the year, Springfield lawyer Abraham Lincoln would re-enter politics, campaigning for the re-election of U.S. Congressman Richard Yates, a firm opponent of the Kansas-Nebraska Act, while Lincoln himself stood for the state legislature in an effort to reunite the shattered Whig party. Old political parties broke down, with men like Medill leaving the Whigs because they despaired that the Whigs could solve the great national problems of division and slavery, and men like Ray leaving the Democrats for similar reasons. Medill, once asked if he should be credited with starting the new Republican party, responded wryly that perhaps Senator Douglas had a better claim.

Five Northern legislatures voted to denounce the Kansas-Nebraska Bill, and a special session of the Illinois legislature was called for February, 1854, to debate the measure. Dr. Ray, quite aware of proslavery strength in southern and central Illinois, and of the power and skill of Douglas, knew he must attend the session to report the proceedings for the *Jeffersonian*. Also he hoped to induce Horace Greeley to accept his letters for the *New York Tribune*. The route to Springfield was now through Chicago, via stagecoach and the Galena and Chicago Union. Dr. Ray saw a new city of almost 70,000, grown from the town of 12,000 he had visited nine years before. The arrival of the railroads from the East in 1852 had brought Chicago unrivaled prosperity.

Dr. Ray realized at last that he had made a mistake in choosing Galena. Even Springfield had grown and had changed. Illinois was no longer so powerfully dominated by the settlers from the South, who had arrived via the rivers. Now the legislature was being filled by New Englanders, and by representatives of the foreign-born farmers and tradesmen who had fled the mid-century European revolutions and were being distributed by railroads and barge lines throughout the northern and central parts of the state. There was a strong element of Free Soilers, ready to censure Douglas. In Washington, the Little Giant defended himself against the rising storm. Why not decide the slavery question by popular sovereignty? What could be more democratic than to allow each new state to decide whether to be slave or free? Douglas had long proclaimed that America's mission was to achieve unchallenged dominance in the Western Hemisphere. But first the country must solve its internal problems. Slavery should not be allowed to shatter the Union. "We calmly look the storm in the face," Douglas told the Senate, "defy its mutterings and howlings about our heads, and hold on firmly to the Union and to the Constitution as the surest and only means of preserving it."

But in the Illinois legislature, the Free Soilers pointed to the Northwest Ordinance and the Missouri Compromise, both limiting the extension of slavery into new territories. They denounced Douglas and his Democrats as betrayers of the Constitution, the Union, and all decent people. In his boardinghouse, Dr. Ray heard other details and allegations concerning Douglas—his land purchases in Chicago, his wife's inherited slaves in Mississippi, and his ambitions for the presidency. When a vote was called in the legislature, Ray watched, appalled, as the Douglas political machine smashed the Free Soil opposition, then cynically rammed through a resolution actually commending the Nebraska Bill! Ray was furious. He wrote to Elihu Washburne, the Harvard-trained Whig congressman from Galena, that he was finished with Douglas, President Pierce, and the Democratic party: *"I have but just begun to hate them, and to fight."*

Ray returned to Galena to write on the Springfield fiasco. He disputed the Douglas assertion that popular sovereignty would have to decide the slavery question in the several states because it was the only way to prevent civil war. "Civil war?" cried Ray. "Civil war, indeed. Give the South everything it asks and establish slavery in the North because the Southerners threaten trouble! Has the Senator no feelings of wrong about slavery?" Throughout 1854, Ray's editorials continued to berate the Little Giant, calling him "Little Whelp," and denounced the Democrats who "worshipped Douglas as a Democratic Christ." Loyal Galena Democrats stopped the paper, and Ray himself was beginning to feel he should seek a wider forum for his ideas. When his associates at the *Jeffersonian* demanded that he sell out, Ray yielded, providing he could retain his editorship long enough to permit him to attend January's legislative sessions in Springfield, at which a U.S. senator to succeed James Shields would be elected. It was agreed.

Ray's wife, Jane, had gone east to be with her parents during the last weeks of pregnancy, and in December Ray went to visit her following the birth of their son. On his return he looked in at the *Chicago Tribune*. He was shocked by its Know-Nothing policies, antiforeign, anti-Catholic, antiliquor. They seemed incomprehensible in a city rapidly filling up with foreign-born, mostly Catholic. Sooner or later those Irish, Germans, and Scandinavians would be qualified to vote, and they ought not be handed over to the proslavery Democrats. The Whigs, Ray felt, would be helpless against the Democrats. He heard talk of the Whig hero, Abraham Lincoln, and, remembering his brief acquaintance with him in Springfield, was unimpressed. He wrote his friend Washburne: *"I am afraid of 'Abe.' He is Southern by birth, Southern in his associations and Southern, if I mistake not, in his sympathies. . . . His wife, you know, is a Todd, of a proslavery family, and so are all his kin. . . . But give us a Salmon Chase in Illinois. . . ."* Then, concluding, Ray weakened, *"After all, Abe may be the man. At all events I will take your advice and see him as soon as I get to Springfield."*

*   *   *

In Springfield in January, 1855, Dr. Ray still possessed his editorial trappings. When he sought the position of clerk of the Senate, he promptly won the support of State Sen. Norman B. Judd, a leader of the Anti-Nebraskans and attorney-lobbyist for the Rock Island Railroad. Ray suggested to Judd that William H. Bissell, who had been elected to

Congress in 1852 as an antislavery Democrat, would be an excellent candidate for the Senate, but Judd disagreed. He proposed instead Abraham Lincoln, the Whig who had taken no unequivocal slavery position, or Lyman Trumbull, of Belleville, an Anti-Nebraska Democrat and former Illinois secretary of state. The disagreement did not affect Ray's own arrangements at all. The following day he was nominated for clerk of the Senate by Judd and elected to the job, which paid $6 a day and gave him a position of importance and a front-row seat for covering the news. Elated by this turn of fortune, Ray took some of the money received from the sale of his *Jeffersonian* interest and invested it in land not far from Cairo, Illinois, where a new city was to be built. His investment would soon be lost.

Ray found time at last to make his promised call on Abe Lincoln, who had resigned the seat he had recently won in the state legislature in order to make himself eligible for the U.S. Senate. Lincoln and Herndon were established in new offices, which seemed as casual and untidy as the ones Ray remembered from nearly ten years before. Lincoln had aged; he seemed even more gaunt and somber, but his lively eyes bespoke his keen interest in what the editor of the *Jeffersonian* had to say. After a few pleasantries, Ray suggested to Lincoln that his only chance to win the U.S. Senate seat was to take a strong stand against slavery. Lincoln was noncommittal. He told a funny story, one that Ray, in his annoyance, promptly forgot. Dr. Ray concluded that Lyman Trumbull might really be the best candidate. But in the succeeding days, he had cause to change his mind. He watched Lincoln working smoothly among the state senators, composing quarrels, preparing the way for Whigs and Anti-Nebraska Democrats to get together. Ray told Judd that Lincoln was winning votes.

Lincoln indeed was. The first ballot was cast on February 8, 1855. Dr. Ray intoned the vote: Abraham Lincoln, 44 votes, seven short of election; James Shields, 41; Trumbull, five. The next few ballots produced little change, but Ray, from his vantage position, thought he saw through the Democrats' plan. They would switch their votes at the right moment from Shields to Gov. Joel A. Matteson. Could Lincoln counter such a move? On the seventh ballot, Democratic support shifted from Shields to Matteson. Lincoln lost nearly 30 votes on the next two ballots, Trumbull's total rose to 35, and Matteson received 47 votes, just four short of victory. Lincoln called upon his followers to support Trumbull on the tenth ballot, and the Anti-Nebraska Democrat was elected. The day following, Lincoln wrote Elihu Washburne: *"I regret my defeat moderately. . . . On the whole, it is perhaps as well for the general cause that Trumbull is elected. The* [Nebraska] *men confess that they hate it worse than any thing that could have happened."*

Charles Ray felt he understood Abraham Lincoln at last. Selflessly, Lincoln had given up his possible chance of election to avoid any risk that a proslavery Democrat might be sent to the Senate. Lincoln had given the North a Free Soil, Anti-Nebraska Democrat in a time of dire need. Ray had learned also that the lean, joke-cracking lawyer with the high-pitched voice was no political neophyte. Lincoln could not win for himself, but he could and did win for the cause. And he had obtained from the victorious Trumbull forces a promise of support should he choose to run against Senator Douglas in three years.

Dr. Ray was ready to begin working to unite the Whig and Anti-Nebraska forces that had given Trumbull the senatorship so nearly won by Lincoln. On his way back to Galena to wrap up his affairs there, Ray passed through Chicago and stopped in at the offices of the *Tribune*, where he learned the paper was for sale. The proprietors had been unable to engage a suitable managing editor and were now hoping to find a buyer for their floundering business. Ray wrote to Washburne, confiding his hope that he could buy a share in a Chicago paper, and hinting his need of a loan. He wrote also to Horace Greeley, asking advice. Greeley responded promptly. He was coming west. If Dr. Ray could meet him in Chicago or Freeport, they could discuss the matter. Late in March, Greeley and Ray did meet to discuss the matter; Greeley told Ray about Joseph Medill, whom he had stopped to visit in Cleveland en route, and urged him to contact Medill immediately. Greeley himself wrote "a friend in Ohio" praising Ray. Greeley's letter evidently was addressed to Medill, though Ray did not say so in relating the incident in a jubilant letter to Jane.

*   *   *

Charles Ray and Joseph Medill left the Tremont House to walk to the *Tribune* offices to look into the condition of the equipment. The two men had agreed that should they acquire the paper each would take $1,200 a year as salary, the amount being paid the governor of Illinois at the time. They would, of course, share the profits according to their holdings. As editor-in-chief, Dr. Ray would have final responsibility for the editorial page, but each proprietor would have one vote on general policy decisions. Medill, as managing editor and superintendent of editorial, would be responsible for news-gathering operations as well as the mechanical departments, circulation, and advertising. Though neither man was really concerned about soliciting advertising, Medill did insist that they abolish the $15-a-year rate for a business "card," a space about an inch deep and a column wide, substituting a rate of 50¢ weekly, and eliminate the free subscription to the advertiser. This was acceptable to Ray, who had charged $15 a year at Galena and was glad to get it. Under Medill's plan, advertisers would pay $26 a year if they were in the paper consistently, and they would be able to change their "copy" once a week—a costly process, but that would be Medill's responsibility.

As the two men neared the Clark Street address, Ray told Medill again of his concern about the Know-Nothing policies of the paper. The prospective proprietors knew that an immediate change in editorial policy would be required. But Medill's interest now was in the presses and type. While Ray asked questions of the paper's editors about the readers—who were they, what were their aspirations, their politics, their religion—Medill went through the composing, press, and counting rooms. According to Ray's biographer, Medill "inspected the building, tallied the stocks of paper, checked the subscription lists and looked critically at the presses." Dr. Ray watched impatiently, puffing on his cigar. When Medill emerged from the composing room, he had a sheaf of papers covered with figures. They would have to buy new type and new presses. Unfortunately, there wouldn't be enough money. Medill could furnish one-third of the funds, Ray one-fourth. But Captain Webster, Timothy Wright, and Thomas Stewart, present *Tribune* owners, were willing to remain in the venture, at least for a time. It would mean less editorial freedom for Ray and Medill, but they had no choice.

Medill had severed his ties with the *Cleveland Leader,* effective April 11, and Ray had no further resources. Medill, his wife indicated in a letter to her father, was worried about the arrangements he had made. But the die was cast. The termination of Medill's Cleveland career was amicable, without ceremony. The *Leader* masthead read "Medill and Cowles" on April 11, and "Cowles and Pinkerton" the following day. Ray's plea to Congressman Washburne produced no added funds, nor could John Vaughan provide more. The new proprietors could not yet take full control.

NEW LIFE
FOR THE TRIBUNE

3

Strong antislavery sentiment sweeping the North in the spring of 1855 turned an increasing number of voters away from the Whigs and Democrats, toward the Native American (Know-Nothing) party, which in Chicago also attracted abolitionists and Free Soil Democrats. The *Chicago Tribune,* financially ailing, found itself politically powerful for the first time as the coalition of antislavery and antiforeign voters, with *Tribune* support, carried into City Hall Dr. Levi Boone, the Know-Nothing mayoral candidate, and a Know-Nothing city council. It was the first time in nine years that a Democrat had not been elected mayor. As Joseph Medill and Dr. Charles Ray arrived in Chicago to negotiate for the purchase of the *Tribune,* they found the proprietors glorying in their newfound political strength.

The *Tribune* in April stepped up its criticisms of the foreign-born and its antiliquor policy, insisting that Mayor Boone act at once to increase the saloon license rate and at the same time enforce the long-ignored municipal ordinance that required all saloons and beer gardens to be closed on Sunday, a proposal especially repugnant to the Germans, who numbered nearly 20 percent of the population of the city. The paper also urged support of a strict "Maine Law" (Prohibition) in an upcoming statewide referendum.

Dr. Ray had already seen the disastrous result of such a blue-nosed stand among the city's foreign population when he visited the *Tribune* offices in March and was present the night of Dr. Boone's election as enraged "foreigners" marched against the *Tribune.* The angry demonstrators, led by German and Irish bands and marching societies, swept down upon the paper, jeering its political victory and threatening it with extinction. Dr. Ray volunteered his services and responded with a defiant editorial, but it was clear that such policies could win no friends, nor spread influence among the foreign-born. Now, a few weeks later, Joseph Medill would have his opportunity to learn the intensity of popular feeling.

Mayor Boone, a grandnephew of frontiersman Daniel Boone, was panting for action and needed little urging from the *Tribune*. In mid-April he rammed through the city council a measure raising the saloon and beer garden license fee from $50 to $300 a year. At the same time Boone ordered his police to close the saloons and beer gardens on Sundays. Howls went up, not only from saloonkeepers, brewers, and distillers, but from thousands of workingmen, who insisted they were being deprived of the "poor men's clubs" to which they could repair only on Sunday, since they worked ten to 12 hours a day, six days a week. It was easy for the liquor interests to organize the workingmen's neighborhoods for a protest march on April 21, when the saloonkeepers and beer garden operators were to appear in court to respond to their citations. Hundreds of demonstrators, especially from the German neighborhoods, paraded in Clark Street, where they could shout insults at the *Chicago Tribune* on their way to the courthouse. They were led by a fifer and drummer, who turned them into Randolph Street and to the courthouse. Some of the demonstrators broke free, rushing into the courthouse and courtrooms and halting the hearings. The mob hesitated when rumor spread that Mayor Boone had deputized 150 special police and was ordering out two companies of militia, with the intention of storming the building. The angry demonstrators fled the courthouse, retreating back into Clark Street, and north across the Chicago River.

Mayor Boone, it developed, was indeed preparing for military action. He deputized 150 men and disclosed that state militiamen would arrive shortly to mount cannon and to aid in the defense of the courthouse. By afternoon, however, there was no sign of Boone's reinforcements, and the mob grew bold again. A frontal contingent, again howling hatred of the *Tribune,* as well as of Mayor Boone and adherents of law and order in general, moved back across the Clark Street bridge. A second and larger brigade also moved southward, uglier than the first, since many of the men carried guns, knives, clubs, and bricks. On signal from the police, the Clark Street bridgetender swung his span to midstream, checking the march of the rear guard. There were shouts of rage from both sides of the river at this perfidy. Men threatened to swim out to throttle the bridgetender. The span swung back.

Now the reinforced mob moved forward, toward police ranks just south of *Tribune* offices in the Evans Block. Someone in the mob fired a shotgun, tearing into the left arm of Officer George Hunt. The police opened fire and Peter Marten, in the crowd of rioters, fell dead, halting the advance. The police charged, wielding clubs and gunstocks. Eighty men were arrested and taken to jail. By evening, after 14 were charged with inciting a disturbance, all were released.

Chicago was shocked. The Lager Beer Riots were the second demonstration within months. Back in September a vast crowd had hooted down Senator Douglas when he attempted to defend his Nebraska Bill and pelted him with rotten fruit. But no one was killed or injured. Now the *Tribune* blamed the vested liquor interests for organizing the beer riots, and pointed out that the mob had been led by a German, Peter Marten, the man slain. Eleven days later two convicted rioters were granted a new trial, and the cases were dropped.

The newspapers and the citizens turned to other matters. The annual cholera epidemic, beginning in April, was worse than usual, and the dispatches from Kansas and Missouri showed that area to be near a state of civil war. The slavery issue was indeed polarizing the Northern population and causing a realignment of political parties, as Medill had predicted when he called for the organization of the Republican party in Ohio. Now it appeared that other Chicago newspapers might outshine the *Tribune* in leading the way to the kinds of reform Medill, Ray, and Vaughan had intended to demand. Long John Wentworth's *Democrat* joined the *Chicago Daily Journal,* the Whig publication edited by Charles Wilson, in attacking the Kansas-Nebraska Act. "We want no more slave territory! No more! Not an inch!" cried Wentworth. "We must unite against the Nebraska act . . . Free Democrats, Free Soil Whigs, the abolitionist Americans." Almost exactly the words Medill had used in his *Cleveland Leader.* But Wentworth wanted no part of a Republican party. It was a name "generally used to designate a Whig of Know Nothing and Maine Law proclivities," he said, a reference to the *Tribune*'s support of the Maine Law.

And that was the Medill, Ray, and Vaughan dilemma. They knew that Chicago and the rest of Illinois were ready for Republicanism and needed leaders to show the way. Someone should unite under the banner of freedom the thousands who had shouted down Douglas in September and the people who had marched in the beer demonstrations. But so long as they could not gain total control of the paper, the antiliquor campaign of the *Tribune* would seriously hamper the plan of Medill and Ray to win over the foreign-born to the antislavery effort. The potential proprietors could not alter *Tribune* policies while the purchase negotiations were under way. Stewart, Wright, and Webster would retain their interests until Ray and Vaughan could provide funds to buy them out. Stewart had shown himself a friend of the antislavery movement, but his health was suffering and he was anxious to retire. Wright was of staunch Presbyterian stock and was completely sincere in his antiforeign, antiliquor bias, and Webster, though ready for a change, would not abandon his friends. Changes in editorial policy would have to be gradual in any case, since the buyers would have some obligation to the subscription list they were acquiring and would have to adhere to the terms of their predecessors' Prospectus, at least until they had acquired sufficient dominance of the paper to publish their own Prospectus.

Joseph Medill was able to move in other directions, however. He brought Alfred Cowles from Cleveland to become bookkeeper in the counting room, and sent John Vaughan to New York to oversee the shipment of press and composing room equipment. While Medill was busy with physical and financial reorganization tasks, his brothers William, James, and Samuel arrived to take jobs in the *Tribune* composing room and to organize a job printing shop. Dr. Ray, meantime, could only fume and follow the editorial line laid down by Stewart, Wright, and Captain Webster, despite the fact that on April 27, 1855, an agreement was reached assuring Medill and his associates that they would ultimately gain full ownership of the *Tribune* for $40,000.

On May 4, 1855, the *Tribune* was forced to take cognizance of rumors concerning upcoming changes in the paper's proprietorship. It sought a light touch:

> Rumor hath it that the *Tribune* has changed hands and that its name is to be altered and its present principles and policies to be abandoned. The only semblance of truth is that the number of proprietors and editors is to be increased and the establishment put on a basis of magnitude and strength not exceeded by any other paper west of New York.
>
> This will be accomplished in due time and in the meantime the friends of the *Tribune* may be assured that it will remain true and consistent in support and advocacy of all measures calculated to advance the interests of Temperance, Morality and Religion and to increase the strength of the Republican party.

Conforming to its May 4 statement, the paper maintained its support of the Maine Liquor Law in the upcoming referendum, but without great enthusiasm. With the balloting scheduled for June 11, the paper said on June 4 that the voting would decide "whether *[Illinois]* shall remain free of the slavery of Rum, the dominion of the tyrant Intemperance." The Illinois voters evidently did not object to besotted slavery, for on June 12 it was found that the Prohibition proposal had been decisively defeated. The *Tribune* wasted no words mourning this moral lapse in Illinois, but instead called for a crusade on a higher level: "Unite," the paper urged. "Unite! Unite! There is a common cause, a common enemy. Why cannot all who fight for freedom be marshalled under one banner?" The time of change was near, and the keynote of new *Tribune* policy had been sounded. Henceforth all policies were subsidiary to the main objective, the halting or extirpation of slavery.

*   *   *

At last, on June 18, 1855, a formal announcement of a new ownership arrangement appeared in the paper. Timothy Wright, a silent partner in the *Tribune* for two years, now stepped forward as one of the proprietors, and Joseph Medill's participation in the paper's management was publicly acknowledged for the first time. Charles Ray would not actually purchase his share in the *Tribune* until August, and this was possibly the reason his name was not mentioned in the announcement. Similar circumstances may also account for John Vaughan's name being omitted. Both Ray and Vaughan, however, were already active on the editorial staff. Despite Medill and Ray's anxious concern to restore relations with the foreign-born, support the antislavery cause, and report the unrest in Kansas, there was no Prospectus discussing the slavery issue or the events in Kansas. The June 18 statement simply said:

> The *Chicago Tribune* daily, weekly and bi-weekly, will henceforth be published by a new firm by the name of Wright, Medill & Co. The proprietors had hoped to present the *Tribune* to its readers in an entirely new dress, but the press for the use of the office could not by any possibility be finished by Messrs. Hoe & Co. in time to meet the needs of the occasion. In the meantime, with the material at their command and now in use here, they will endeavor to make such minor improvements as will be satisfactory to the readers. Important changes in the editorial staff of the *Tribune* will be announced in their proper season.

The statement also introduced the new proprietors:

> Timothy Wright—Joe Medill.
> Mr. Wright, whose name appears this morning as one of the publishers of the *Tribune,* is one of the oldest and most respected citizens of Chicago. His interest is now and has been for many years identified with the Northwest and this city, and his connection with our paper will, while it affords an ample guarantee of its pecuniary responsibility, be an earnest that it will continue to be as it has heretofore been, a staunch advocate and defender of Western men and measures. . . .
> Mr. Medill, who will have the more immediate charge of the business of the office, is from Cleveland, lately one of the proprietors of the *Daily Leader* of that city. Our friends will find him a thorough business man—and an amiable and intelligent gentleman—one whose integrity and fair dealing are beyond question. We commend him to the good offices of our citizens generally and to friends of the *Tribune* particularly.

Thomas Stewart sold his interest in the *Tribune* to his associates and announced his retirement on June 21: "In rural pursuits, beyond and above the life of responsibility and excitement which the conductor of a permanent public journal must assume, I hope to regain, to some extent at least, health and strength." Stewart had been a proprietor of the paper since July 24, 1847, and with his departure the final direct link to the *Tribune*'s first days was gone.

On September 24, the *Tribune* was at last ready to announce new editors, a new Hoe press, and the new "dress" made possible by the fonts of gleaming copper-clad type. The paper was nine columns wide, in clear, easy-to-read, organized format. John C. Vaughan and Charles H. Ray were now proclaimed the new editors, with William W. Peck named the editor of local news. The paper shortly published its Prospectus: "Believing that the spread of Liberty, and not of Bondage, is the saving principle of the Republic, the *Tribune* has enlisted in the ranks of National Republicans, not for a campaign, but during the war, believing that slavery or involuntary servitude is inconsistent with all principles, civil or religious. . . . Slavery must be excluded from the National Territories, and the influence of the National Government must be on the side of freedom." Having thus stated its basic policy, the *Tribune* went on to declare its support of education, good morals, Temperance, progress, and reform, the statement at this point reflecting many ideas previously expressed by Medill in his *Cleveland Leader*.

The *Tribune* also declared that it would be a good newspaper, a commercial paper, and an agricultural paper. The advertising cards previously on the front page in three right-hand columns were moved inside to make way for news and special articles, expanding on the practice of Medill in Cleveland. The news was not only separated from the "Homes" column and other features, but was departmentalized into foreign, national, and local categories, instead of the hodgepodge of dispatches previously used. Other typical Medill touches indicate that the managing editor was responsible for both news and feature content while the two editors listed on the editorial page were chiefly involved in elucidating policy: There were popular science articles on colored daguerreotypes and Chinese kite flying; home articles, "Golden Rule for Wives," and the day following, "Hints for Husbands"; and sensational accounts from Eastern and Southern papers, "Witchcraft in Connecticut," detailing a recent murder case, and "Horrid Story of Negro Burned to Death," another recent event in Kentucky. The antiforeign, anti-Catholic, and antisaloon campaigns were ended.

One of the first *Tribune* readers to be impressed by the changes was a tall, spare lawyer from Springfield, who climbed the stairs to the Wright and Medill offices at 51 Clark Street, seeking Dr. Ray, who was out. So he

asked a young man he met upstairs: "Are you the new editor from
Cleveland, McDill, or Medill, or something?" "I am Medill," the editor
answered. "Whom have I the pleasure of addressing?" "Well, down on
the Sangamon River they used to call me Abraham Lincoln. Now they
generally call me Old Abe, and I ain't so old either." Lincoln then said he
had run up to subscribe to the paper, adding that he had been reading
borrowed copies, and he pulled from the pocket of his jeans a pocket-
book, untied a strap, and counted out $4. "I like your paper," Lincoln
said. "I didn't like it before you boys took hold of it, it was too much of a
Know-Nothing sheet." Lincoln and Medill chatted about politics for a
while, and Lincoln allowed that he was a "Seward Whig." Medill told him
of the Republican party as organized in Ohio.

*   *   *

Civil war threatened in Kansas from the day the House of Representatives approved the Kansas-Nebraska Act. The new editors of the *Tribune*
gave the harrowing events ample coverage. In the beginning the paper
relied upon various correspondents who were already in the field and
had submitted their letters, plus reports from the *New York Herald,* the
New York Times, the *New York Independent,* and the *Herald of Freedom,*
published in Kansas Territory. Correspondents signed themselves "L,"
"D," "T," and "Literal," but the correspondent who exceeded the rest in
colorful prose and shocking detail of murder, mayhem, bushwhacking,
and burning in "Bleeding Kansas" was "JR." James Redpath, a 22-year-
old Scot, first came to the attention of the *Tribune* editors while he was
reporting Kansas events for the *Missouri Democrat.* He was designated the
Chicago Tribune correspondent in 1855 and also sent his letters to Horace
Greeley's *New York Tribune.* More than any other newspaperman, Redpath
brought the events of Kansas home to Northern readers in vivid, angry,
exasperated terms. His earliest dispatches may have been unsigned, many
in the paper being without designation, but after the "JR" signature
began to appear, Free Soil and abolitionist readers knew that someone
was telling the story of Kansas as they desired to read it—repeated
invasions of unprincipled proslavery "border ruffians" (a term said to
have been invented by Redpath) from Missouri, who burned, pillaged,
and killed when they were not destroying ballot boxes and stealing
elections.

Up to the time of the passage of Senator Douglas's Kansas-Nebraska
Bill, Kansas was an unorganized territory and sparsely settled. But as
soon as it became evident that Douglas's popular sovereignty proposal
would enable Southern settlers to convert new territories into slave states,
the antislave forces in the North began to organize colonizers. In New
England, Eli Thayer formed the Emigrant Aid Company, which not only

dispatched settlers and mules to Kansas, but shipped Sharps rifles and ammunition in boxes labeled "Bibles" and "Hardware." Such Northern action aroused the South, and the struggle was on. The slave owners in Missouri formed guerrilla organizations, supplied them with guns and whiskey, and invaded Kansas Territory.

By early 1855 a census by Territorial Gov. Andrew H. Reeder showed the number of settlers in Kansas had grown to nearly 8,500 (of whom some 250 were slaves), sufficient to call for the election of a territorial legislature. On the appointed date, March 30, 1855, border ruffians from Missouri invaded in military formation, with guns, cannon, banners, and, as usual, ample supplies of corn liquor. Although Reeder's census had registered only 2,900 men of voting age, there were 6,310 votes cast in the "election." A subsequent federal investigation concluded that 4,908 votes were fraudulent. But the Pierce administration recognized the proslavery legislature, which met at Shawnee Mission and proceeded to enact proslavery laws. Soon, friction between Governor Reeder and the legislature caused his removal by President Pierce, who appointed Wilson Shannon in Reeder's place.

Enraged Free State settlers, refusing to recognize what they termed the "bogus" legislature, organized a constitutional convention, which met in Topeka in October and November. In a popular ballot held on December 15, 1855, Free Soil voters approved the Topeka Constitution, and on January 5, 1856, they elected their own "governor," Charles Robinson.

Redpath's dispatches to the *Tribune* regarding these and other events in Kansas were often sensational and at the very least were provided with titillating headlines. The "Wakarusa War," for example, was an incursion into Kansas by a large Missouri guerrilla band, which camped on the Wakarusa River near the Free State town of Lawrence for nearly two weeks in early December, then departed without fighting. "LAWRENCE PEOPLE NOT SUBDUED . . . BLOODY WORK IN KANSAS," read the *Tribune* headline over an account of the raid by "Missouri banditti and border ruffians stimulated by whiskey." Mexican War veteran James Henry Lane, formerly an Indiana politician and now a leader of the Kansas Free State forces, was described as a hero for organizing the Lawrence defenses, although it was subsequently learned that Territorial Governor Shannon had talked the Missourians out of attacking. The correction was provided later by JR, who was called upon to increase his supply of news.

Though the Wakarusa War was a war without a battle, the struggle for Kansas continued. The *Tribune* joyfully reported that mass meetings in support of the Free Staters were being held throughout the Midwest. The paper pleaded with workingmen to attend their own special mass meeting in South Market Hall: "Laborers of Chicago, it is your turn to be felt. The hand which seeks to enslave Kansas would fetter you." In other editorials the paper attacked the "slave oligarchy" and its "squatter legislature" and lambasted President Pierce as "a poor, weak, vacillating tool of the slave power." This language both laborers and farmers understood. Their position on slavery was not entirely idealistic, nor altruistic. The immigrants had come to America seeking freedom, and wanted it for all men, but even more they wanted jobs, homes, and land. The workmen saw danger in the competition of slave labor, and the farmers feared the competition of the plantation system.

In February, 1856, President Pierce felt obliged to announce that he would act against both alleged proslavery invaders and Free State usurpers to prevent an outbreak of civil war. The *Tribune* did not doubt that Pierce would use the U.S. Army against the Free State men. "President Pierce leaps into the pro-slavery current as if it were his natural element," the paper said. "Doubtless he means to swim upon it into office again."

The *Chicago Times* accused the *Tribune* of wickedly supporting a Kansas government known to be fraudulent and asserted that the new editors of the *Tribune* were secret members of a Know-Nothing lodge. The *Tribune* denied any Know-Nothing association, but admitted proudly that it indeed supported Jim Lane and all other God-fearing Kansas men who favored freedom.

Dispatches from Redpath and other sources in Kansas frequently filled three to six columns of the *Tribune,* in addition to Kansas news from Washington and that culled from Eastern newspapers, both North and South. "If we disappoint any of our readers by the space we devote to the affairs of Kansas," the paper said on February 19, "we beg them to remember, that just now we are at the beginning of great events of which that Territory is to be the theatre; and that a CIVIL WAR for the extension of Slavery and the subjugation of a free people, is a danger most imminent and pressing." The paper helped to sponsor a benefit which raised $2,000 to aid the Kansas cause, and the *Tribune* sent it care of the *Herald of Freedom*. "We will send more," the *Tribune* promised, "and when spring comes you may look for a large number of emigrants who will handle an axe or a Sharpe's [*sic*] rifle as the occasion may require."

The North was aroused, and other Chicago papers, excepting Douglas's *Times,* adopted the *Tribune*'s line. Long John Wentworth's *Democrat* led the rest in excoriating President Pierce. William Bross and John Scripps, in their *Democratic Press,* called openly for a Northern expedition to aid the outnumbered Free State settlers. Said the *Tribune,* somewhat smugly: "We are not unfrequently told that we crowd the *Tribune* with anti-slavery matter to the exclusion of other topics . . . we plead guilty."

Kansas even determined the *Tribune*'s choice in the March mayoral contest. The paper called for a mass meeting backing hotel owner Francis Sherman, once a prime enemy of the former *Tribune* proprietorship, who now had turned Anti-Nebraska Democrat and was deemed worthy of support. "FREEDOM IN KANSAS! LIBERTY FOREVER! MASS MEETING IN METROPOLITAN!" cried the editorial page headlines, over a leader which urged all Chicagoans to attend. Some 3,000 did, but not many of them bothered to vote the following Tuesday, and Thomas Dyer, the candidate of the Douglas Democrats, was elected Chicago's mayor. "The grog-shop vote," the *Tribune* sniffed on March 6.

In Kansas, the Free State legislature met in March and elected two U.S. "senators," Andrew Reeder and James Henry Lane. "Senator" Lane left for Washington with a memorial from the Free State legislature asking that Congress admit Kansas to statehood under the Topeka Constitution. Lane's arrival would throw new fuel on the fiery Senate debates over which was the legitimate territorial government of Kansas, and the *Tribune* would send its own correspondent to cover the story— Joseph Medill.

*   *   *

Late in 1855 Paul Selby, editor of the *Morgan Journal* of Jacksonville, Illinois, proposed that Anti-Nebraska editors should meet to discuss and agree upon a policy to be pursued during the approaching campaign. Among a number of Illinois papers that endorsed Selby's suggestion was the *Chicago Tribune*, which admitted, "The Anti-Nebraska party is wholly without an organization, and every newspaper is a law unto itself; and though all are contending for a common object, they are going divers ways to accomplish it. What we need is a full and free conference, a general concurrence in some system of policy . . . which all may embrace and for which all may contend."

The sessions of the editors' conference were scheduled for February 22, 1856, in Decatur. They attracted a prominent noneditor, Abraham Lincoln, who was at last prepared to identify himself with Republicanism. The important work of the conference was done by the resolutions committee, of which Dr. Charles Ray, representing the *Tribune*, was the chairman. Also influential on the committee were George Schneider, of the German newspaper *Illinois Staats-Zeitung*, and Lincoln. Although the word "Republican" did not appear in the editors' platform, many Illinois historians consider the Decatur gathering as the beginning of the Republican party in Illinois.

The editors disavowed any intention of interfering with slavery where it already existed in the states (a position Lincoln was always careful to maintain) but demanded the restoration of the Missouri Compromise, resolving to "strive by all legal means to restore to Kansas and Nebraska, a legal guarantee against Slavery, of which they were deprived at cost of the violation of the plighted faith of the Nation." The Decatur platform also opposed Know-Nothingism, saying in part, "In regard to office we hold merit, not birth place to be the test. . . . We should welcome the exiles and emigrants from the Old World, to homes of enterprise and of freedom in the New."

The final formal action of the Decatur conference was to call for Anti-Nebraska forces from all over the state to gather in Bloomington on May 29. "To your posts, men of Illinois," cried the *Tribune* on March 1. "Organize and prepare for action. Act in 1856 as the fathers acted in 1776, and so help save the republic and its liberties."

*   *   *

Despite the ominous news from Kansas, Chicago was in an optimistic mood that spring. The city's population had grown to 86,000 and there was no limit in sight. Chicago was now the railroad capital of America, served by ten trunk lines and 11 branch lines totaling 2,933 miles of track. The Rock Island Railroad's bridge over the Mississippi, an engineering marvel, opened on April 23. Suburban train service was initiated from the village of Hyde Park, south of Chicago, to the new Illinois Central Railroad station, described as the world's largest and most magnificent, at South Water Street and the lake in downtown Chicago.

The Board of Sewage Commissioners had authorized a drainage and sewage disposal system in 1855, requiring the grade of downtown streets to be raised as much as eight feet. Horrified citizens protested this absurdity—first floors of elegant business buildings would become basements by such a plan! Indeed, they did, and the famous Tremont House soon appeared to be situated in a deep ditch. But a young engineer named George M. Pullman showed Chicago the way. He had been raising houses on jackscrews along the Erie Canal. He successfully raised the Erie Hotel in Chicago and was given the Tremont job. Pullman promised that he would raise the five-story brick hotel six and a half feet "without breaking a plate or cracking a cup." Using 5,000 jackscrews and scores of men, who gave each screw a half turn on signal, Pullman lifted the Tremont out of the cellar. His accomplishment, for which he received $45,000, was hailed throughout the world. "We work miracles in Chicago," the *Tribune* noted modestly.

A small miracle was being worked by the proprietors of the paper themselves. Within months after rehabilitating the *Tribune*, they achieved their initial merger, the absorption of the abolitionist weekly *Free West*, edited by Zebina Eastman. The *Tribune*'s revitalized news coverage and its changed editorial tone—it now urged that Catholics should be admitted

as delegates to a Know-Nothing national convention, and it ran a laudatory history of the German *Turnverein* (athletic clubs)—gained encouraging response from the Illinois public. Its circulation, the paper said,
increased by 1,200 subscribers from July to October, 1855, and by the
end of the year passed 3,000 for the first time! The success of the daily
Tribune was being matched by the popularity of the triweekly and weekly
editions, which circulated in the rural areas of Illinois, Wisconsin, Iowa,
and Minnesota, the triweekly going to the close-in towns and farms along
the railroad lines, the weekly servicing the remoter areas by stage and
pony. In the early months of 1856, circulation figures were reported to be
increasing at the rate of 100 a week, and revenues were up by 30 percent,
as dispatches from "Bleeding Kansas" and six-column texts of the Kansas
debate in the Senate were being mingled with fiction such as *Love Story,*
Butterfield at the Ball, and *The Gun-Makers of Moscow,* a novel by Sylvanus
Cobb, Jr.

"THE WAR HAS
BEGUN IN KANSAS"

4

In April, 1856, the time came for Joseph Medill to go to Washington as special correspondent for his paper. He was reluctant, but the proprietors felt that the *Tribune* should have its own Washington news, and a representative in the capital would be helpful to the cause of the antislavery movement and the Republican party. The *Tribune*'s reputation and influence were spreading fast. The *Chicago Times,* the *Democrat,* and the *Illinois Register* railed at "the *Tribune* clique," while Free Soil editors hailed its editorial leadership. To establish its preeminence in the Northwest, the paper needed now to have its own report on the Kansas struggle in Congress. Medill had recently settled his young wife, Katherine, and their daughters, Katherine and Elinor, in a home on tree-lined Washington Boulevard at Morgan Street, far from the cholera-spreading miasma of the river and lakefront. He and Kitty and the girls had been separated for months in 1855, a sufficient sacrifice, Kitty thought. But Washington was a task Medill set for himself.

"*Tomorrow I hope to be housekeeping,*" Katherine wrote her father, James Patrick, from Chicago. "*Have a German girl who can't speak a word of English to help me. Chicago is certainly the oddest looking place to be called a city I ever saw. . . . It looks like fifty little wooden towns huddled all up together. There are few brick houses, all wood. People live over stores and groceries. Houses are scarce and rents are high.*"

Dr. Ray, too, had established his family in Chicago, renting a comfortable house north of the river for Jane and the two babies. They thought the rent reasonable, $350 a year, and the Rays were able to afford two servant girls on his $1,200-a-year salary. Dr. Ray felt strongly that he was needed in Chicago, and Medill agreed.

There were business decisions to be made before Medill could go east. He was pleased with the work of Alfred Cowles, the 23-year-old book-keeper he had brought from Cleveland, who was proving to be a genius not only in the management of the counting room, but in the mechanical departments as well. Cowles, a descendant of John Cowles, who had come to Massachusetts in 1634, was born the son of an Ohio physician in Mantua, Ohio, on May 13, 1832. He learned the printing trade as a boy in the shop owned by his brother, Edwin. Alfred, like Edwin, attended the Grand River Institute of Ohio. Alfred went on to the University of Michigan, and entered the office of the *Cleveland Leader* in 1853 when Edwin joined Medill to form Medill, Cowles & Company, publisher of the *Leader*. Young Cowles, with his university training in business affairs and his experience in the mechanical area, was exactly the kind of assistant Medill required, and he did not hesitate now to recommend the young man for the position of *Tribune* business manager. It was a position Alfred Cowles would hold for more than 30 years, until his death in 1889. During this time he created one of the most efficient newspaper business systems in the country, and for a time he owned over 30 percent of the company's stock, his holdings exceeding those of any other proprietor, even Medill.

Although the business affairs of the paper were in top-notch condition, rifts were being felt in the editorial department. Dr. Ray apparently believed that his excellent editorials and news judgment were alone responsible for the popularity of the *Tribune*. Ray was in charge of the editorial page, but all the proprietors voted on editorial policy, and the news and features policies of the paper were so similar to those of the *Cleveland Leader* as to strongly suggest a profound Medill influence. Ray, much more assertive and better known among Illinois politicians than Medill, was regarded by many as the mover and shaker of the company, but Medill was then the principal proprietor and exerted considerable leverage on policy decisions. Nonetheless, Ray, in his determination to push ahead with his antislavery campaign, was inclined to be impatient and somewhat arrogant with his fellow proprietors.

John Vaughan, who worked with Ray on the editorial page, was of little help in the delicate situation. His strong abolitionist tendencies caused him to side frequently with Dr. Ray in his disagreements with Medill. Yet his radicalism was often embarrassing to both Ray and Medill, who rejected it as impractical if a coalition was to be created that would include Whigs, Anti-Nebraska Democrats, antislavery Know-Nothings, and those natural enemies of the Know-Nothings, the Catholics and foreign-born.

For the most part, though, Ray and Medill were in essential agreement on the direction the *Tribune* must take. So Medill felt no special anxiety about leaving the editorial page in Ray's hands when he went to Washington to cover the Kansas debates. But he was moody and unhappy in the capital, where he lived in a boardinghouse. *"My office is in my hat,"* he wrote Kitty. He disliked the hot, muggy Washington weather, as well as the town's activities. Aside from politics, he told *Tribune* readers,

> Washington is an exceedingly dull place. It is full of idle people who, in some way or other, live upon Uncle Sam's bounty, and spend their money in gambling, drinking and other alike useful occupations. The feelings between Members of Congress from the Southern and Northern sections of the country, I am told, are very harsh and bitter, and growing daily more so. Every one seems to feel that matters are fast coming to a crisis. Well, the sooner they do come, the better. Let it be for once settled, whether the policy of the country is to be freedom or slavery. That will be *the* issue in the next Presidential campaign. All other questions are lost sight of.

Medill wrote his first impressions of the Senate on April 29, summarizing his attitude succinctly in his first sentence: "The Senate is a body of very respectable looking men, rather old fogyish than otherwise." In a further dispatch, Medill discussed presidential candidates. He thought the Republican nomination would go to John C. Frémont or John McLean. "I should very cheerfully vote for Salmon P. Chase," he wrote, "and he would certainly make a very good president. But it is evident that he cannot be elected. We must succeed in electing our president, if Kansas is to be free, and be careful how we commit ourselves to a man. The cause must be kept ahead. The one committed to the cause and who can concentrate the greatest number of votes is the man."

On May 15, the *Tribune* devoted two and a half columns on page one and an equal amount of space on page two to reports from James Redpath in Kansas Territory. The reports detailed a memorial which the Free State government intended to present to Congress and summarized the many accounts Redpath and others had written of atrocities by proslavery men, which would be sent along in support of the memorial. The *Tribune* for the first time signed correspondence with the reporter's full name, an unusual tribute since not even Medill's dispatches were signed at that time. In its leader editorial on page two, the paper said: "We surrender the greater part of our paper, to-day, to our own Kansas correspondent, whose accounts of . . . that unhappy and ruffian-ridden territory . . . are entirely reliable, we believe, in every particular. The ingenuity of the Pro-Slavery press has been exercised to invalidate his testimony; but to this day, his evidence stands unimpeached."

The dispatch on May 20 was grim:

> The telegraph brings us startling news from Kansas. The General Government is resolved on driving the Free State men to unconditional submission to the black laws passed by the Border Ruffians, and in case of resistance, to murder them by U.S. soldiery, burn up their habitations, and deliver the Territory over to the slave-holding invaders. At present the Administration is engaged in arresting every prominent Free State man in Kansas on a charge of TREASON! to be tried by packed juries of Missourians, under the direction of an Alabama Judge. . . . Where will this thing end? Will the North stand tamely and idly looking on while their noble kinsmen are being sacrificed to the Moloch of Slavery? Will not their blood call for vengeance like the blood of Abel?

The *Tribune*'s fears were justified. Later it reported many Free Soil leaders arrested, including "Governor" Robinson. On May 25, the paper reported that Abolitionist John Brown and his sons had attacked "a pro-slavery force" along Pottawatomi Creek, and five "Missouri invaders" were killed. Southern newspapers declared the men were unarmed settlers. John Brown acted, the *Tribune* said, in revenge for the seizing and burning of Lawrence by proslavery men on May 21. A reign of terror began in Kansas.

*   *   *

The Anti-Nebraska convention in Bloomington on May 29 was of such importance that Medill returned from Washington to attend. The convention brought into Bloomington a motley collection of delegates, described by the *Illinois State Journal* as "Old line Whigs, Jefferson and Jackson Democrats, Republicans, Americans [*Know-Nothings*] and foreign-born citizens, laying aside all party differences, united together there in one common brotherhood to war against the allied forces of nullification, disunion, slavery propagandism, ruffianism, and gag law, which make up the present administration party of the country." The Chicago press was well represented, by men serving either as delegates or as reporters. There were Medill and Ray from the *Tribune;* John Locke Scripps from the *Democratic Press;* George Schneider, editor of the *Staats-Zeitung;* Charles Wilson, editor of the *Daily Journal;* and, astonishingly, Long John Wentworth, of the *Democrat.* Wentworth had declined to attend the Decatur conference but came to Bloomington a rabid Anti-Nebraska Democrat.

The delegates to the convention assembled in the Pike House headquarters the morning of May 29. There was great talk of the events in Kansas, and a shocking dispatch from Jacksonville. Paul Selby, whose call for the Decatur conference of editors had launched all the Bloomington excitement, could not attend. Political enemies had given him such a beating he was unable to leave Jacksonville. It was reported that Free State "Senator" Reeder, driven from Kansas by proslavery men, would speak in Bloomington that night. Abraham Lincoln, gaunt and tall, was there, looking for a few moderates and finding at least one, Norman Judd of Chicago. Lincoln was expected to speak, but Medill's attempt to get an advance copy of his talk from Billy Herndon was unsuccessful. Lincoln had not written even an outline of what he intended to say, and Medill was brushed aside. Both Lincoln and Herndon were too busy trying to keep peace among the various factions to have time for the needs of the press.

Dr. Ray, who was there as a delegate, met with convention leaders, including Lincoln and Judd, to select candidates for the coming state elections and to draft the party's platform. Ray cautioned against alienating the German vote, which he estimated at 20,000 in Illinois. Lincoln insisted that the platform be conservative and urged choice of William Bissell, Anti-Nebraska Democrat, as the nominee for governor.

The convention assembled in Major's Hall on the afternoon of the 29th and proceeded to endorse the slate of candidates, headed by Bissell, and to approve the platform, which was modeled after that of the Decatur editors' conference. Then came the time for speechmaking, and after several other men had had their say, there were calls for Lincoln to speak.

Lincoln had brooded long over the course the nation must take. He was eager to make sure that the divergent elements in the convention should be held together long enough for effective political action. He had worked hard as a conciliator, and now seemed to be the time for an emotional sealing of the compact, a call for action. The spare, dark-eyed lawyer tried on the spectacles he had purchased only that morning, removed them, evidently remembering he had no text, and surveyed the vast crowd of bearded men packed into a hall overheated by bodies and the sun on an unseasonably warm day. He began in his high-pitched voice, and a kind of mass hypnosis settled over the crowd. Years later, men who had heard Lincoln speak many times said it was his greatest speech. When he finished, the applause and shouts rocked the hall and the crowd rose to honor Lincoln with a standing ovation, a rarity on the frontier. No doubt of it, the audience was totally one emotionally with the earnest, raw-boned man from Springfield. In fact, points out Lincoln biographer Ida M. Tarbell, the fascination of the speech was such that "under the emotion and sweep of it no reporter kept his head sufficiently to take a note."

Medill sent no account of the text to his paper, nor did John Scripps, nor did any other reporter present, and their descriptive material reached the morning papers late. It was days afterward that the writers and editors, veterans like Medill and Scripps among them, began to recover from the astonishing impact of the man, the mystical aspect of the speech, which came to be called Lincoln's lost speech. In subsequent years Medill recalled the occasion in several interviews, among them an account in detail for Tarbell:

> At first his voice was shrill and hesitating. There was a curious introspective look in his eyes, which lasted for a few moments. Then his voice began to move steadily and smoothly forward. . . . He warmed up as he went on and spoke more rapidly; he looked a foot taller as he straightened himself to his full height and his eyes flashed fire; his countenance became wrapped in intense emotion; he rushed along like a thunderstorm. He . . . poured forth hot denunciations upon the slave power. . . .
>
> There stood Lincoln in the forefront . . . hurling thunderbolts at the foes of freedom, while the great convention roared its indorsement! I never witnessed such a scene before or since. As he described the aims and aggressions of the unappeasable slaveholders and the servility of their Northern allies . . . and the grasping after the rich prairies of Kansas and Nebraska to blight them with slavery and to deprive free labor of this rich inheritance, and exhorted the friends of freedom to resist them to the death—the convention went fairly wild.

Scripps, representing the *Democratic Press,* agreed. "There never was an audience more completely electrified by human eloquence," he recalled. "Again and again during its delivery, they sprang to their feet and upon benches and testified by long continued shouts and waving of hats, how deeply the speaker had wrought upon their minds and hearts. It fused the mass of hitherto incongruous elements into one perfect homogeneity."

"I well remember," Medill went on to tell Tarbell, "that after Lincoln had sat down and calm had succeeded the tempest, I waked out of a sort of hypnotic trance and then thought of my report for the *Tribune.* There was nothing written but an abbreviated introduction. It was some sort of satisfaction to find that I had not been 'scooped,' as all the newspaper men present had been equally carried away."

Medill expressed the belief that "after Mr. Lincoln cooled down he was rather pleased that his speech had not been reported, as it was too radical . . . on the slavery question for the digestion of Central and Southern Illinois . . . and that he preferred to let it stand as a remembrance in the minds of his audience." It was Medill's opinion that the Bloomington speech raised Lincoln to leadership in the Republican party in Illinois, even though he was still not ready to use or accept the name Republican. "On that occasion," said Medill, with the benefit of hindsight, "he planted the seed which germinated into a Presidential candidacy."

The *Tribune* editors expressed themselves as well satisfied with the Bloomington convention. Even Wentworth accepted it. "John Wentworth roars like a bull whenever the Republican party is mentioned," a friend noted, but Wentworth, like Trumbull and other Anti-Nebraska Democrats, was ready to vote Republican if, as Medill had written, the Republicans could find the man "committed to the cause and who can concentrate the greatest number of votes." It could not be Seward or Fillmore, Trumbull warned.

On June 2, the Democratic party met in Cincinnati and nominated James Buchanan of Pennsylvania for president and John C. Breckinridge of Kentucky for vice-president. Antislavery Know-Nothings met in New York and selected John C. Frémont, "the Pathfinder," who had helped to bring California into the Union as a free state, with W. F. Johnston of Pennsylvania as his running mate. The American party (conservative Know-Nothings) nominated former president Fillmore, the friend who had provided Dr. Ray with an introduction into Springfield society, and Andrew J. Donelson of Tennessee for vice-president. Medill continued to favor Frémont, and Ray agreed. When the Republicans held their first national convention, at Philadelphia, Frémont was also their man. Abraham Lincoln received 110 votes for vice-president on the first ballot, but the nomination went to a better-known candidate, William L. Dayton of New Jersey.

The *Tribune* and the other two pro-Republican papers in Chicago, the *Staats-Zeitung* and the *Journal,* immediately plumped for Frémont, and Long John Wentworth's *Democrat* soon followed. Though Senator Douglas had hoped to be the Democratic nominee, both Douglas and his *Chicago Times* remained loyal to their party and supported Buchanan. But editor Wentworth, in his new enthusiasm, went on the stump for Frémont, as did Lincoln. The two tallest men in Illinois politics covered many of the Republican meetings together, amusing each other with stories while candidates spoke. One evening a Chicago reporter covering a rally in Ogle County found both Lincoln and Wentworth intently studying the crowd throughout the meeting, then comparing notes. He learned what they were tallying—mothers breast-feeding their young. Lincoln counted 71, Wentworth 73. Wentworth passed a note to Lincoln, commenting that such vigorous people had no business voting for a "superannuated old bachelor" like Buchanan.

*   *   *

Returning to Chicago from the Bloomington convention, Dr. Ray learned that Kansas Free State "Senator" Jim Lane was in town. Ray invited him to address a mass meeting. Despite the short notice, thousands of Chicagoans packed Metropolitan Hall and the streets in front of it on

May 31, 1856, so Lane spoke from an outside balcony. He was a handsome, rugged, red-faced man, a spellbinder, rousing the crowd to a frenzy with his lurid descriptions of proslavery atrocities, election thefts, barn burnings, and the jailing and killing of Northern men. According to the *Tribune*, "As he detailed the series of infamous outrages inflicted upon the freemen of Kansas, the people were breathless with mortification and anger, or wild with enthusiasm to avenge those wrongs." When Lane called for contributions to send guns and men to Kansas, hundreds responded, and Lane collected over $15,000 as well as numerous rifles and six-shooters, a horse, and some gunpowder. Opined the *Tribune:* "It was the most remarkable meeting ever held in the State. We believe it will inaugurate a new era in Illinois. We believe it is the precursor of the liberation of Kansas from the hand of the oppressor, and of an all-pervading political revolution at home."

The strife in Kansas continued through the summer and into the fall. On July 4, the *Tribune*'s JR reported, a pitched battle was narrowly averted when four companies of U.S. Dragoons confronted 500 armed Free Staters, both sides having cannon loaded with grapeshot. When ordered to disperse, the Free Staters reluctantly did so. "It is the first scene of this kind in the history of the Republic," said the *Tribune*. "May it be the last." Later, in August, the Free Staters attacked and burned Fort Titus, a proslavery stronghold near Lecompton, capturing 26 men and 400 rifles. "The war has begun in Kansas," said the *Tribune* on August 22. "Freemen must fight or fall."

The results of the November election gave strong encouragement to Illinois Republicans. The apportionment of seats had enabled the Democrats to retain control of the legislature, but the Republicans, led by gubernatorial candidate William Bissell, won overwhelmingly in northern Illinois and captured all the state offices being contested. Nationally, however, antislavery forces had failed to unite behind a presidential candidate, and Democrat James Buchanan was elected. Though his popular vote was 400,000 less than the combined total for Frémont and Fillmore, Buchanan received 174 electoral votes while Frémont received 114 and Fillmore eight.

Meantime, on August 29, 1856, in order to comply with laws governing the partnership arrangement under which the *Tribune* was organized, the name of the firm was changed from Wright, Medill & Company to Vaughan, Ray & Medill. At the same time, Alfred Cowles became a member of the firm, of which Wright and Webster continued to be partners. Several months later, in late March, 1857, the firm's name changed again, to Ray, Medill & Company. Friction among the principal proprietors had apparently reached the flash point, for the radically abolitionist Vaughan departed the paper to study law, selling his interest in the *Tribune* to Alfred Cowles.

* * *

On March 6, 1857, two days after the inauguration of President Buchanan, Chief Justice Roger B. Taney announced a series of U.S. Supreme Court adjudications that were to become known as the Dred Scott decision. Dred Scott, a slave, had sued for his freedom, asserting he had become free when he was taken into free territory. The majority opinion read by Taney in essence said that Scott could not sue in the first place, since a Negro could not be a citizen of the United States, and, furthermore, the part of the Missouri Compromise barring slavery from certain territories was unconstitutional. Scott was soon freed by his owners, despite the decision, but the North was aroused.

On March 16, the *Tribune* published a famous editorial: "Is Illinois a Free State?" The editor answered his rhetorical question:

> She was one up to March 6th, 1857. On that day the five Slave-holders and one doughface [*easily influenced person*] of the United States Supreme Court, constituting a majority of the National Tribunal, solemnly decided
> First—That black men, whose ancestors came from Africa, were not and could not be citizens of the United States.
> Second—That black men *had no rights* which white men were bound to respect.
> Third—That black men, whose ancestors were brought to this country as slaves, are *property,* exactly the same as oxen or sheep.
> Fourth—That the Constitution of the United States recognizes *slaves as property,* and makes no difference whatever between them and horses, wagons, and any other kind of property. . . . It is a bad law . . . it is a false interpretation of the Constitution . . . it does not represent the judicial or legal opinion of the nation.

The editorial analyzed the implications of the decision in extended detail, and concluded:

> Under this decision, Douglas may bring his plantation negroes, in North Carolina and Mississippi, into Illinois, and set them to farming his lands in this State, with the Editor of the *Chicago Times* for his overseer, and no law of the State of Illinois can interfere to prevent him. We really can see nothing in the law, as interpreted by Taney & Co., to prevent opening a Slave pen and an auction block for the sale of black men, women and children right here in Chicago. . . . Slavery is now national. Freedom has no local habitation nor abiding place save in the hearts of Freemen. Illinois in law, *has ceased to be a free State!*

On following days the *Tribune* published the full text of the Supreme

Court opinion and the dissenting opinions, a major journalistic feat. Medill and Ray called upon the free people of the North to be ready for any contingency. Kansas was doomed, further editorials said. Douglas's popular sovereignty plan had now been made legally meaningless, and his continuing defense of his position on Kansas was described as "concatenation of falsehoods, a tissue of lies vomitted out." But the paper did not propose violent resistance. "The remedy," it said on March 19, "is union and action; the ballot box. . . . Let the next President be a Republican and 1860 will mark an era kindred with that of 1776 and the country and Constitution will be ruled and considered by men kindred in American principles with Washington, Jefferson and the Fathers." The *Tribune* editors suggested that all citizens who wished to oppose the spread of slavery and the machinations of proslavery politicians could best do so if they were well informed by reading the *Chicago Tribune*. New subscribers came in by the hundreds, one agent, C. D. Hay in central Illinois, boasting in a letter to Senator Trumbull that he had obtained more than 1,000 subscriptions for the *Chicago Tribune* and *Missouri Democrat* within a few weeks.

The general effect of the developments in the slavery issue was suggested in a letter from Katherine Medill to her father in November, 1857: *"I am getting to be so much of a Republican I can't conceive of an honest man honestly voting a Democratic ticket and sustaining the Dred Scott decision, the Fugitive Slave Law and all the affairs that have followed in their train. Chicago is getting to be a kind of Free Soil headquarters and it is impossible to live here and not get infected with this anti-slavery sentiment."* But not even Katherine would be welcome at the political meetings. "Women don't go," her husband told her. Chicago was unlike downstate Illinois, where many farmwives insisted on accompanying their husbands, even if they were not allowed to vote.

The furor over Kansas and the Dred Scott decision worried the followers of Senator Douglas. Northern Illinois was now strongly Republican, and even central Illinois was becoming alienated from the Douglas Democrats. The foreign vote in Chicago, except for the Irish, was turning Republican. When Lincoln wrote Charles Ray to ask for an assessment of the Chicago German vote, he was reassured. The efforts of the *Tribune* to attract the foreign-born were proving highly successful. The excesses of the proslavery forces were harming both the Democratic party and its newspaper supporters. Senator Douglas was beginning to understand that he must turn against the proslavery extremists in his party or risk losing the support of central Illinois in the upcoming senatorial election.

Joseph Medill also understood the situation. *"Things look bloody and belligerent* [in Kansas]," he wrote in December to Indiana's Schuyler

Colfax, who was in Washington. *"I hope claret may be drawn. The thing will never be well settled until the free state party men thoroughly thresh the Border Ruffians, troops and all. Public sentiment is such in this state that if the necessity comes the Governor can call the legislature together and it will vote men and money to support the people of Kansas in their right of self government. . . . I say, let the thing be fought out and now is as good a time as any."* Then, turning specifically to Douglas's problem, *"If Douglas falters in this crisis, he is a dead man. Now is his time to make a ten strike and redeem the great blunder he made three years ago. Tell him and rub in the idea."* Medill's purpose was still to advance the cause, rather than any man. If Douglas followed this advice successfully and managed to dissociate himself from the extremists without totally alienating the Democrats, he might again be elected senator, by a coalition that could include the Republicans. If he followed such counsel with some lack of success, the Democrats would be split, thus insuring a Republican senator in 1858 and, if the split were profound, a Republican president in 1860.

Whatever the source of his decision, Douglas in December, 1857, did opt for a ten strike. In direct opposition to President Buchanan, he publicly repudiated the Lecompton Constitution, recently framed by proslavery forces in Kansas as the constitution under which they would apply for statehood. Douglas viewed the Lecompton document as a patent betrayal of the principle of popular sovereignty, for the full constitution was not to be submitted to the voters of Kansas for approval. Rather, they would be permitted only to decide whether to accept the constitution "with slavery" or "without slavery." Since the constitution provided for slavery in Kansas, by choosing "without slavery" a voter was merely rejecting the importation of slaves. All slaves then living in Kansas and their descendants would continue in bondage. Despite opposition from Douglas and other Democratic leaders, Buchanan had nevertheless recommended to Congress that Kansas be admitted to statehood under the Lecompton Constitution. The Democrats were indeed split, and the Republicans rejoiced. Horace Greeley's *New York Tribune* hailed the selfless decision of Douglas, who was placing his devotion to popular sovereignty above his own interest and party loyalty. Greeley suggested that Douglas ought to be the next Republican U.S. senator from Illinois, and the cry was taken up by other Eastern newspapers.

Medill, Ray, and their friends were dismayed by the warmth of Greeley's acceptance of Douglas, and at the enthusiasm of those who echoed him. They had no intention of giving Douglas too much advantage in the senatorial campaign, since it appeared certain that Abraham Lincoln would oppose him. It was necessary to encourage Buchanan men to stay loyal to the president if the party split were to carry through to the election. Medill proposed such strategy to Sen. Lyman Trumbull. *"It is our policy to nurse the Buckmen along until they become strong enough to stand up and fight us,"* he wrote. *"We shall be able to knock them down at any time easily enough. The prospect is now that each faction will run separate tickets in every county—thereby giving us an easy victory and a United States Senator in place of Douglas."*

*   *   *

More than slavery and national policies occupied the *Tribune* editors in 1857. Long John Wentworth yearned for a renewal of his political life. Following the success of the Republican campaign in Chicago and northern Illinois, Wentworth was no longer asserting that there was no such thing as a Republican. In the campaigns of late 1856, his *Democrat* had referred to "the new or Republican Democracy" and "the great Democratic Republican party." Now, in January, his paper designated the new party as "Republican" without equivocation, and Wentworth disclosed his availability for the mayoralty on a Republican reform ticket. The *Tribune* editors shuddered. If Wentworth could successfully change his spots, would not Douglas be sure to follow? But Douglas's *Times* calmed their fears. Taking note that Wentworth was giving a series of parties for his precinct captains and other followers, the *Times* said: "The drunken revelries in which for several nights he has indulged in low brothels and in large saloons, leave no doubt that he has commenced campaigning." Clearly editor James Sheahan of the *Times* had no orders from Douglas, his proprietor, to encourage Wentworth in testing the waters.

The wily Wentworth, now weighing nearly 300 pounds and puffing a bit on his campaign jaunts, found it ridiculously easy to take over the Republican city apparatus. At a city convention on February 28, 1857, he was nominated by acclamation. His fellow editors were not utterly pleased. "For the first time Mr. Wentworth acknowledged on Saturday night that he belonged to the Republican party," said the *Tribune*. It noted with satisfaction that Lincoln had addressed the convention. "A. Lincoln made, as he always makes, a sensible and excellent speech. He was most enthusiastically welcomed." When Wentworth was elected on March 3 as Chicago's first Republican mayor, the *Tribune* gamely approved: "It shows that Chicago is sound to the core."

That spring the *Tribune* had been attacking the wildcat currency issued by many of the country's banking firms and leveling criticism at business establishments using lumber in their new construction. "R. Brown and Sons are building a new warehouse of lumber. They should use brick," said a typical item. The paper also assailed the criminals and vice mongers, who appeared to increase even faster than Chicago's booming population. Mayor Wentworth responded on April 20 by personally leading a police raid on the Sands, an area of brothels and gambling shacks on the north bank of the Chicago River near what is now Michigan Avenue. Wentworth, along with 30 officers in boats, crossed the river, drove out the gamblers, madams, girls, and pimps, and razed and burned the buildings. Some critics said Wentworth was clearing the land for former mayor Ogden, who had recently purchased the site, and others asserted that he had merely driven the prostitutes into other parts of the city. The *Tribune,* however, approved the drastic action, and a reporter asserted that 70 percent of the prostitutes had gone to Milwaukee, which appeased many of the Wentworth critics. A few weeks later, Wentworth staged another raid, in Gamblers' Alley, locking up the town's big-time crooks. He was becoming nationally famous for his fearless enforcement of the law, but he went a step too far. His third raid was against merchants and vendors who disobeyed his order to keep crates and signs off the sidewalks, and this time he was denounced as a tyrant.

Early in July, the business panic raging in the rest of the country hit Chicago. Hinckly & Co., one of the banks under attack from the *Tribune,* closed its doors on July 3, and other private banks followed. Before the year ended, there would be nearly 5,000 business failures in the country, 117 occurring in Chicago. Construction work halted, ships were idled, merchants reduced their inventories and sought desperately for loans. In October there was a fire, such as the *Tribune* had been warning against, that swept South Water and Lake streets. Razing elegant stores, warehouses, rooming houses, and a few upstairs brothels, it caused the deaths of 21 persons. An epidemic of cholera struck during the summer months. By year's end, fire, disease, and financial panic had diminished the city's population by 3,000, including those who died and those who fled.

Despite the troubled economic environment, which brought about a decline in circulation and advertising revenue, the *Tribune* continued efforts to improve its news-gathering services. The paper hired Robert R. Hitt, a Freeport phonographic reporter—also called a stenographer—to cover trials, major speeches, and significant meetings. Medill wanted no more "lost speech" experiences. One of Hitt's first assignments was to cover the *Effie Afton* case in the federal court in September, 1857. The steamboat *Effie Afton* had crashed into the Rock Island Railroad's bridge over the Mississippi. The Rock Island's general counsel, Norman Judd, employed Abraham Lincoln to represent the railroad against the steamboat company's claim that the bridge was a hazard to navigation. Because it pitted the old river transportation system, running north and south, against the new east-west railroad system, the case aroused great interest in the Northwest. Hitt provided exhaustive details of the trial, almost the text of Lincoln's defense. There was a hung jury, in effect giving Lincoln and the Rock Island the verdict.

Bad as the economic panic was, it left Chicago much better off than most cities. During 1857, the port of Chicago shipped 10 million bushels of wheat and 7 million bushels of corn. McCormick Reaper Works made 4,000 reapers and sold them throughout the Northwest, due in part to Cyrus McCormick's special credit arrangements for the farmers. The Lake Street merchants, some calling for capital at 18 and 20 percent, began rebuilding their stores, and new entrepreneurs arrived, seeking sites for shops and factories. The outlook for the remarkable "Windy City" on Lake Michigan seemed excellent. Of the 17,000 miles of railroad built in the United States in a decade, most was north of the Ohio River and linked to Chicago by trunk lines. In 1858, Chicago would welcome another railroad, the Pittsburgh, Ft. Wayne and Chicago. Although corn was down to 30¢ a bushel, wheat to 58¢, and eggs brought 10¢ a dozen wholesale, the immigrants continued to pour in, seeking jobs or heading for the farmlands of the West.

Amid such an improving environment, Joseph Medill had no intention of allowing his beloved *Chicago Tribune* to fail, despite its financial problems. He grew increasingly irked by Dr. Ray's apparent lack of concern about the paper's costs. As the crisis worsened and Medill learned that the *Democratic Press* was also in serious trouble, he convinced Ray and Cowles that drastic action was needed. Conversations were begun with William Bross, John Locke Scripps, and Barton W. Spears, proprietors of the *Democratic Press*. A merger of the two papers would reduce costs while creating a powerful morning newspaper. Medill had long admired both Bross and Scripps. But Spears, the business manager of the *Democratic Press,* was not entirely candid about the financial affairs of his paper in early conversations, and Medill was dismayed when he finally learned the extent of its debt. Yet the talks continued.

Meantime Horace Greeley sent Congressman Elihu Washburne, friend of Ray from Galena days and a longtime correspondent of Medill, to urge that Senator Douglas be taken into the Republican fold. Ray did not agree with the somewhat Machiavellian strategy Medill favored, which consisted of showing some friendship to the Little Giant to further the split with Buchanan. Ray wrote to Senator Trumbull, *"Tell our friends . . . who may be more zealous than discreet, that we in Illinois have not delegated our powers to them and that we may not ratify bargains that they make."* Yet, Ray confided, *"we are almost confounded by* [Douglas's] *anomalous position and we do not know how to treat him and his overtures to the Republican Party. Personally, I am inclined to give him the lash, but I want to do nothing that damages our cause or hinders emancipation in Kansas."*

The *Tribune* was much less hesitant about giving the lash to Long John Wentworth, who smelled no better as a Republican than he did as a Democrat. In addition to the seething hatred of Douglas's *Times,* which regarded Wentworth as a traitor, and the darts of Wilson's *Journal,*

Wentworth was now required to endure the scalding wrath of the increasingly influential *Tribune*. "The height of Mr. Wentworth's ambition," said that paper in one of its more respectful comments, "is the seat Douglas holds in the U.S. Senate. All his moves have been made to win that darling prize. He wants to control a balance of power in the next legislature and compel the Republican members to choose between him and Douglas." Wentworth's *Democrat* responded that his senatorial ambitions existed only in the "malignant brain" of his longtime tormentor, Ebenezer Peck. Peck's son William, it was pointed out, was the *Tribune*'s city editor. "It will be time enough," said the *Democrat*, "to discuss who shall be United States Senator when it shall be ascertained that Douglas cannot be."

Long John Wentworth was truly a mayor to inspire personal malice. The *Times* accused him of dishonesty, drunkenness, lechery, and habitual use of vile language, and made sneering references to the fact that his wife, Roxanna, declined to live in Chicago. (Wentworth's wife preferred to remain with her parents in Troy, New York, where her husband visited her regularly. This arrangement endured through five offspring and 26 years of marriage.) The *Tribune* declared that "Johannes Elongatus" failed to cope with the financial panic, and that criminality flourished following his quixotic raids. Doubtless convinced that it would be futile to seek renomination as mayor, Wentworth resolved to step aside at least temporarily. Shortly after "His Lengthiness" directed the purchase of Chicago's first steam fire engine, the voters in March, 1858, chose John C. Haines, also a Republican, as mayor. Wentworth hurried to New York, where his five-month-old son had suddenly died. When he returned to Chicago, it was rumored that he would run for governor with Lincoln's help, a report both Lincoln and a dispirited Wentworth denied.

Having disposed of Wentworth, at least for a time, Medill and Ray returned to the task of making Abraham Lincoln a U.S. senator. Greeley's *Tribune* and other Eastern papers were continuing their nefarious campaign to accomplish the nomination of Douglas, as a reward for his forthright stand on the Lecompton Constitution. The *Chicago Tribune* responded with dripping scorn:

> There seems to be a considerable notion pervading the brains of political wet-nurses at the East, that the barbarians of Illinois cannot take care of themselves. . . . If the Republicans of Illinois should now sink all party differences and re-elect Mr. Douglas, their party would be so disintegrated that the State would be lost to freedom in 1860, or if saved, saved only because he allowed it to be saved. The Republican party would be wholly at his mercy.

Lincoln, in town on a patent case, climbed the stairs to the *Tribune* offices at 51 Clark Street to consult with Medill, Ray, and the other editors. Lincoln thought Long John Wentworth too valuable to the

Republican cause to be driven from politics by the constant sniping of the *Tribune*. He obtained a truce of sorts for Wentworth, and the newspaper attacks slackened. Lincoln also appeared concerned that Greeley's activities might weaken the Republican cause. He told the group that Billy Herndon was going east to look over conditions there. Herndon planned to do more than that. He hoped to improve the situation for his partner by calling on Greeley, Seward, and other leaders to "straighten out" the Douglas matter. For good measure, while in Washington, Herndon called on Douglas himself, who was noncommittal on whether he would run as a Democrat or a Republican.

Dr. Ray, meantime, wrote Senator Trumbull, *"I take it that it is a foregone conclusion that Abraham Lincoln will be the next Republican candidate for Mr. Douglas' seat and that he will occupy it if we have a majority. The war here among the partisans of Douglas and Buchanan has commenced in good earnest. It is my conviction that in six months Douglas will not have 1,000 followers in Chicago."* Yet there was worry at the *Tribune*, for on May 27, Lincoln wrote to his friend Washburne, *"This morning my partner, Mr. Herndon, received a letter from Mr. Medill of the* Chicago Tribune, *showing the writer to be in great alarm at the prospect of Republicans going over to Douglas."* Lincoln, however, appeared less concerned: *"Unless* [Douglas] *plays his double game more successfully than we have ever seen done, he cannot carry many Republicans north without at the same time losing a larger number of his old friends south."*

*   *   *

On July 1, 1858, it was jointly announced that the *Chicago Daily Tribune* and the *Democratic Press* would be consolidated into a paper to be called the *Chicago Daily Press and Tribune*. The *Democratic Press* had done business totaling $111,508 during 1857. It about equaled the *Tribune*'s circulation of 4,000, printing its own and other newspapers on ten power presses in its establishment at 45 Clark Street. The merger was effected, said the *Tribune*, "to put an end to the expensive rivalry which has heretofore been kept up; to lay the foundations deep and strong of a public journal, which will become one of the established institutions of Chicago; to enable us to combat more powerfully, and, we trust, more successfully, public abuses; to give us a wider influence in public affairs, in behalf of sound morality and a just Government." The first issue of the consolidated paper promised that the editors would give "steady, zealous and consistent support . . . to the great cardinal doctrines of the Republican party."

John Scripps was named senior editor of the *Press and Tribune;* James F. Ballantyne, of the *Democratic Press,* became the commercial editor; and Henry Martyn Smith, Amherst graduate, lawyer, and former *Journal* and *Democratic Press* staff member, was made city editor. The arrangement of *Tribune* staff members was not announced, nor were the responsibilities of the proprietors described. Timothy Wright and Captain Webster had departed the *Tribune* earlier in the year, so that the proprietors having a vote each in the newly formed Press and Tribune Company consisted of Medill, Ray, and Cowles from the *Tribune* and Scripps, Spears, and Bross from the *Democratic Press*. Both Medill and Ray were quite aware that in Bross they had obtained one of the country's most remarkable talents, as a businessman, a journalist, and a Chicago booster. But Bross had made clear that he desired limited newspaper responsibilities, so that he could pursue a political career. He soon was writing regularly for the paper, nevertheless.

William Bross, a fervent Presbyterian, a scholar and a venturesome traveler, an editor and politician, was widely known as "Deacon" Bross, and the Second Presbyterian Church that he attended was often simply called "Bross church." Stocky, gray-eyed, and fierce-looking with his bushy russet beard and thick beetling brows, Bross was formidable in appearance and in manner, but a gentleman who grew really angry only when his town of Chicago was besmirched or impugned. Since the founding of the *Democratic Press* in 1852, Bross had used its pages, and a stream of pamphlets and booklets from its presses, to extoll Chicago's economic and geographic glories. He even insisted that Chicago was a healthful place in which to live, though all but one of his eight sons and daughters would die before attaining adulthood there.

Bross was born in Sussex County, New Jersey, in a log house on November 4, 1813. His family moved to Pennsylvania when he was nine, and he worked with his father in the lumber business. After attending Milford Academy and Williams College, he taught in eastern academies for ten years. Based on his studies of geography, and following a fact-finding tour, Bross decided that Chicago was the city of the future, and in 1848 he "removed thither, to the Garden City." He sold books for a few months, then joined the Reverend J. Ambrose Wight in the publication of the *Prairie Herald,* a religious newspaper. Bross and Scripps started the *Democratic Press* on the *Prairie Herald* presses on September 16, 1852. It was the year, said Bross, "when Chicago's prosperity really began."

Though Ballantyne had been named commercial editor, it was Bross who wrote the leading commercial reports for the *Press and Tribune*. Scripps specialized in political writing, and Dr. Ray continued as editor of the editorial page. Alfred Cowles was business manager, with Spears reporting to him, and both reporting to Medill when he was in Chicago. Medill happily described the new arrangement as a "cooperative" one. Troubles lay ahead, but it appeared in the beginning that a more brilliant and congenial group of leaders could not be found, though Medill continued to distrust Spears.

Enlarged by the addition of a column to its width, the *Chicago Daily Press and Tribune* promptly displayed editorial excellence but little economic improvement. Costs were rising, circulation revenues no longer earned adequate profits, and the obligations of the *Democratic Press* were greater than had first been contemplated. Yet the *Press and Tribune* declined to put advertising solicitors into the field, a demeaning practice engaged in only by the *Times,* whose solicitors were described as "bummers" by the *Press and Tribune.*

While reporting the news and continuing the Medill practice of a special feature or serial story on page one, the new paper bent to its task of improving the Republican political situation. Senator Douglas was regaining strength; it was clear that there would be a struggle for his senatorial seat and Lincoln might be the underdog even among Republicans. The debate over the Lecompton Constitution still raged in Washington, and a showdown in Kansas seemed imminent. Deacon Bross, never one for false modesty, would later attribute the *Tribune*'s growing influence during this critical period to the paper's principal editors:

> The course of the *Tribune* during and before the [*Civil*] war was the result of the matured opinions of four independent thinkers, and hence it was always right. With two such honest, able, patriotic and scholarly men as Mr. Scripps and Dr. Ray, not to mention Mr. Medill, with his sharp, discriminating mind, his wide acquaintance with men and things, and his acute journalistic and broad common sense, and with whatever I could contribute to the common stock, is it any wonder the *Tribune* achieved a national reputation?

THE GREAT DEBATES

5

While Joseph Medill and William Bross labored to create a newspaper consolidation that would dominate Chicago and the Northwest, Dr. Ray of the *Tribune* and John Scripps of the *Democratic Press* had been busy with their mutual political project, the candidacy of Abraham Lincoln and the ascendancy of the Republican party. Although 95 Republican county conventions declared for Lincoln during the spring and early summer of 1858—"the natural and expected remonstrance against outside inter-meddling," said the *Tribune*—the editors continued to be apprehensive. The Eastern press was thumping loudly for Senator Douglas, with Horace Greeley in particular calling for Illinois Republicans to support him for reelection. Though Medill had favored muted praise for Douglas as a means of nurturing a split in the Democratic party, Ray began to fear that Douglas might indeed capture enough Republican support in the next few months to keep Lincoln from being elected senator. Ray informed Lincoln of his qualms, and a secret meeting was arranged. Present in addition to Lincoln and Ray were William Bross and Norman Judd, the Illinois state chairman of the Republican party. Meeting in the Springfield state library prior to the Illinois Republican convention, the men approved plans to take the convention by storm.

The Republican gathering on June 16, 1858, was "the best and biggest ever held in Illinois," according to its partisans, including the *Chicago Tribune*. As scheduled, Judd nominated Richard Yates for chairman and the necessary committees were promptly named. Then Charles Wilson of the *Chicago Journal* moved that the convention endorse Abraham Lincoln as the "first and only choice" of Illinois Republicans for the Senate seat of Stephen A. Douglas. This was a signal to the Cook County delegation to rise and march through the hall behind Chicago's Anthony C. Hesing, a partner in the *Staats-Zeitung,* who carried a huge banner reading: "Cook County is for Abraham Lincoln." On this cue, a Peoria delegate arose to move that the Cook County slogan be amended to read: "Illinois is for Abraham Lincoln." The chairman, somewhat liberally applying the rules of order, decreed that motion carried as cheers and seconding shouts boomed about the hall. The delegates voted on Wilson's motion, and Lincoln was unanimously approved.

Not a formal nomination—the nominating and electing of U.S. senators was still the prerogative of the state legislatures—the endorsement of a senatorial candidate by a party convention was without precedent in American politics. By this step, the Republicans of Illinois had registered their ire with the meddling of Eastern Republicans and made it clear that if Douglas were reelected, it would be without Republican support. Lincoln emerged from the convention an avowed aspirant for the senatorship; he would have to undertake a statewide canvass against one of the toughest and ablest campaigners in the nation, but he could campaign openly for himself rather than on behalf of candidates for the Illinois legislature. And at least one historian contends that only the fact that Douglas thus knew well in advance who his opponent would be when the legislature convened convinced him to share the platform with Lincoln in their famous series of debates.

Lincoln had been expecting the endorsement of the convention and had for days been planning his acceptance address. He read it one night to Billy Herndon and asked for his criticism. Years later Herndon recalled that he answered: "It is true, but is it wise or politic to say so?" Two days later Lincoln assembled several of his friends in the State House and tried it on them. Most feared it was too radical, but Herndon, the last called upon, now said, "By God, deliver it just as it reads. . . . The speech is true—wise and politic; and will succeed—now as in the future. Nay, it will aid you—if it will not make you president of the United States." Lincoln concluded that he would give the speech as written. When he arose in the convention hall the evening of June 16, the huge throng seemed crazed with delight. Joseph Medill, one of those present, had no concern about a lost speech this time, for copies of the text would be made available to the press. In addition, covering the proceedings for the *Tribune* was a new reporter and special writer, Horace White, an active Illinois Republican and an ardent young abolitionist who had at one time sent the paper a few letters from Kansas.

As the din continued, Lincoln donned his spectacles, then began to read, and the crowd calmed.

> If we could first know *where* we are, and *whither* we are tending, we could then better judge *what* to do, and *how* to do it. We are now far into the *fifth* year, since a policy was initiated, with the *avowed* object, and *confident* promise, of putting an end to slavery agitation. Under the operation of that policy, that agitation has not only, *not ceased,* but has *constantly augmented.* In *my* opinion, it *will* not cease, until a *crisis* shall have been reached, and passed. "A house divided against itself cannot stand." I believe this government cannot endure, permanently half *slave* and half *free.* I do not expect the Union to be *dissolved* — I do not expect the house to *fall* — but I *do* expect it will cease to be divided. It will become *all* one thing, or *all* the other.

Lincoln continued his address by attacking Douglas's policy and his fitness to serve another term. He finished a bit late for the *Tribune* editions, so that the text of his remarks would not appear until later, but White caught the excitement of the day, and jubilantly opened his account with a quotation from a hymn by Thomas Moore:

> Sound the loud timbrel o'er Egypt's dark sea.
> Jehovah has triumphed; His people are free.

The *Tribune* headline read: "THE GREAT REPUBLICAN STATE CONVENTION! EVERY MAN FOR LINCOLN!" White described the proceedings, and concluded: "As I close this letter Mr. Lincoln is addressing an immense audience. I will send a full report of his speech." The text of the "House Divided" speech, published on June 19, was hailed by the *Tribune* as "logical and masterly" and "a powerful summing up of the issues before the people." The paper urged all loyal Republicans to "make the campaign one worthy of the principles of the party by overthrowing the one man responsible for disrupting national affairs." In Washington, Stephen Douglas, the man thus held responsible, told his friends, "I shall have my hands full. He is the strong man of his party . . . and the best stump speaker, with his droll ways and dry jokes, in the West."

Horace Greeley, in New York, was outraged by Lincoln's nomination and wrote to his former friend Medill at the *Chicago Tribune:*

> *You have taken your own course — don't try to throw the blame on others. You have repelled Douglas, who might have been conciliated, and attached to our side. . . . You have thrown a load upon us that may probably break us down. You knew what was the almost unanimous desire of the Republicans of other states, and you spurned and insulted them. Now go ahead and fight it through. You are in for it, and it does no good to make up wry faces.*

Though it railed against Greeley and other Eastern Republicans for meddling in Illinois politics, the *Tribune* was not above some meddling of its own from time to time. Within days of the Springfield convention, Lincoln became infuriated with his newspaper ally. Dr. Ray wrote an editorial that, in addition to dealing with Illinois problems and his fantasy about Wentworth's plotting, also probed party wounds in the Indiana segment of Republicanism, causing Lincoln to vent formal and bitter sarcasm upon him. *"My Dear Sir,"* he began:

> How, in God's name, do you let such paragraphs into the Tribune, *as the enclosed cut from that paper of yesterday? Does* Sheahan *write them? How can you have failed to perceive that in that short paragraph you have completely answered all your own well put complaints of Greeley and* [Anson] *Burlingame? What right have you to interfere in Indiana, more than they in Illinois? And what possible argument can be made why all Republicans shall stand out of Hon. John G. Davis' way, in his district in Indiana, that can not be made why all Republicans in Illinois shall stand out of Hon. S. A. Douglas' way?*
>
> *The part in larger type is plainly editorial, and your editorial at that, as you do not credit it to any other paper—I confess it astonishes me.*

Sheahan, of course, was editor of the pro-Douglas *Times* and a detested enemy of the *Chicago Tribune*.

That Lincoln's anger was soon appeased became evident when the candidate paid a visit to Chicago in early July. He saw several of his advisors, including Norman Judd, and had lunch with George Schneider, editor of the *Staats-Zeitung*. Schneider suggested that Lincoln should have a new picture taken, and when Lincoln agreed, they called in an itinerant daguerreotypist. Lincoln posed for him, holding, in position where its masthead could be read clearly, a copy of the newly established *Chicago Daily Press and Tribune*.

The *Press and Tribune* was ready to play an enthusiastic part in Lincoln's campaign, practicing superlatively well the activist journalism customary to the period. The paper made clear to readers its partisan bias and goals and expected them to judge its accomplishments on the basis of its involvement, polemics, and prejudices. There was no such thing as objective journalism, nor was there even a pretense of objectivity. The paper's readers were quite aware of the editorial slant, as outlined in the Prospectus. The *Press and Tribune* editors counseled Lincoln, provided him with strategic advice, afforded tactical intelligence on the enemy, and blasted foes in the news columns as well as on the editorial page. No reader was deceived. Nonpolitical news was reported with accuracy and in detail, political news was reported with bias and prejudice. While the readers did not know it, Medill, Ray, Bross, and their associates were about to court bankruptcy in their partisan support of Lincoln; meantime, they intended to publish the best Republican newspaper in the Northwest, and if a reader didn't like it, he could always subscribe to the *Chicago Times*.

*   *   *

The campaign in Illinois opened formally on the night of July 9, with Douglas scheduled to address a huge mass meeting from the balcony of the Tremont House. He had been hooted down in Chicago for his Kansas-Nebraska Act, but his stand since on the Lecompton Constitution had somewhat rehabilitated him in northern Illinois. Douglas supporters expected no further difficulties for him in the northern tiers of counties, though he had been read out of the Democratic party south of Springfield. The Chicago meeting proved them right. It was a tremendous demonstration for the Little Giant, who was bringing home to Chicago his new wife, a 23-year-old Southern girl of beauty and charm. For Adele, it had been reported, Senator Douglas had given up chewing tobacco, moderated his drinking, and donned tailored clothes. Chicago whooped it up for the resplendent new Douglas and his lovely Adele. There was a huge procession, bands, red fire, a horse militia, and such a throng of spectators that the marchers had difficulty reaching the Tremont House.

Douglas was in superb form as he defended his popular sovereignty position and insisted that it alone would solve America's problems of westward expansion, the "Manifest Destiny" of the United States. He attacked Lincoln's "House Divided" speech. Lincoln, Douglas said, would simply perpetuate sectionalism. Why not continue part slave and part free? The nation had done so for 82 years.

The *Press and Tribune* printed three and a half columns detailing the reception of the senator and his wife, including the full text of his remarks as provided by Robert Hitt. Not even Senator Douglas's own *Chicago Times* equaled this feat, so its rival announced that it would have extra copies of the July 10 paper for sale "to any non-subscribers who did not have the full text." At the same time, the *Press and Tribune* advertised the upcoming rebuttal: "The Hon. A. Lincoln will reply to Senator Douglas this evening. His speech will be a masterly dissection and exposure of the many sophistries and misrepresentations crowded into that of Judge Douglas. Let everybody turn out to hear him."

The *Chicago Times* declared that a crowd of 30,000 had heard Douglas, while the *Press and Tribune* estimated 12,000. Both papers agreed that Lincoln's crowd was smaller when the Republican candidate appeared on the Tremont House balcony. But the *Press and Tribune* insisted the Lincoln supporters were much more enthusiastic. The parade was as long, the bands as loud. There were flares and burning tar barrels, and several horses became frightened and ran through the crowd. But there was an added touch that must have delighted Medill and Ray as much as Lincoln. The crowd gasped in astonishment as a German *Turnverein* marching club and band, from Chicago's Seventh Ward, tramped in through the crowd to a special spot reserved beneath the balcony. The German vote was indeed being wooed, as Medill and Ray had promised.

Lincoln attacked Senator Douglas's pretensions to leadership of the force that had defeated the Lecompton Constitution in the House of Representatives. Douglas and his followers had provided 20 votes against Lecompton, Lincoln conceded, but it was a trivial contribution compared to the Republicans' 90 votes. He declared that Douglas's popular sovereignty solution had been vitiated by the Dred Scott decision. He repeated his position on slavery: "I have said a hundred times" that the people of the North should not meddle with slavery where it existed, but should demand that slavery be confined to its present boundaries, which would lead to its ultimate extinction. This was the intention of the founding fathers, Lincoln said. "Let us then turn this government back into the channel in which the framers of the Constitution originally placed it. . . . Let us discard all this quibbling about . . . this race and that race and the other race being inferior . . . and unite as one people throughout this land, until we shall once more stand up declaring that all men are created equal."

The *Press and Tribune* published the Lincoln text the day following, and both the Douglas and Lincoln addresses appeared in the next issue of the triweekly and weekly papers. A comparison of the speeches would show Lincoln's "masterly refutations" of Douglas's points, the paper said. The *Press and Tribune,* in effect, had instituted the Lincoln-Douglas debates, which it would shortly propose in its columns. Meantime, it angrily attacked the New York Associated Press, an organization unrelated to the Associated Press of today, charging that it had sent out a half-column, laudatory report of the Douglas speech, and only five lines on Lincoln's. "The agent is utterly worthless," the paper raged. "We wish to know how long this pro-slavery partisan of Douglas and the Union line is to be imposed on the Newspapers Association." It was the beginning of a feud that endured for years, until the Western newspapers, led by Medill, formed their own association and eventually obtained a reorganization of the Associated Press.

Following his July address, Lincoln remained in Chicago to confer with Norman Judd and other supporters, including the editors of the *Press and Tribune*. It was noted that Senator Douglas was planning to travel throughout the state in a private railroad car, to be accompanied by his wife, two secretaries, and, following his Chicago experience, a stenographer—he liked what Robert Hitt had done for the *Press and Tribune*. It was even rumored that a railroad flatcar mounting a brass cannon would accompany the senator, to salute his arrival in each town, and that at some points he would be escorted by a band of music. So a strategy was devised whereby Lincoln, traveling as an ordinary citizen in modest contrast to the Douglas splendor, would follow Douglas about the state and offer his own political speech as soon after Douglas's as he could. Lincoln followed the Little Giant to Bloomington and to Springfield, and was roundly ridiculed by the Douglas press.

After speaking in Springfield on July 17, Lincoln went to Chicago to again confer with state chairman Judd and other advisors. This time a new idea emerged, possibly from the *Press and Tribune*'s juxtaposition of the two Chicago speeches. Why not actual debates? Why not challenge Douglas and force him to share the platform with Lincoln? It was agreed that a written challenge should be prepared and that Norman Judd would present it to Douglas at the proper time. On July 22 an item in the *Press and Tribune* gave a hint of what was to come: "We have a suggestion to make. . . . Let Mr. Douglas and Mr. Lincoln agree to canvass the State together, in the usual western style. . . . In this way the people can make up their minds as to which candidate is *right*. If Mr. Douglas shall refuse to be a party to such arrangement, it will be because he is a coward."

Douglas and his friends did not care to be trapped into this kind of situation. It was Douglas who would attract the crowds, not Lincoln. Douglas's newspaper supporters denounced the Republican strategy as a dirty trick. In Chicago, Judd presented Douglas with the formal challenge in Lincoln's behalf on July 24:

Hon. S. A. Douglas

> *MY DEAR SIR: Will it be agreeable to you to make an arrangement for you and myself to divide time, and address the same audiences during the present canvass? Mr. Judd, who will hand you this, is authorized to receive your answer, and, if agreeable to you, to enter into the terms of such arrangement. Your obedient servant,*

A. Lincoln

Douglas had already announced his list of speaking dates, but he felt compelled to accept the challenge. He consented to meet Lincoln once in each congressional district, except in Springfield and Chicago, where both had already spoken. Seven towns were named: Ottawa, Freeport, Jonesboro, Charleston, Galesburg, Quincy, and Alton. Lincoln, of course, found the arrangements agreeable. The first meeting, at Ottawa, was scheduled for August 21.

*   *   *

There was other news in Chicago that summer. The economic recovery was clearly in evidence along Lake Street, where the landlords and merchants were rebuilding on a grander scale than before. Potter Palmer leased the five-story marble-fronted building at 112–116 Lake Street for an opening early in September. "It is the biggest dry goods store in the West," said the *Press and Tribune* in a report doubtless written by William Bross. "It is one of the finest and most costly business blocks in the United States." The west portion of the first floor, said the paper, "is a magnificent sales room fitted up tastefully and well, and after the manner of first class stores and with perfect system," while "at the rear of the carpet hall is a gem of an apartment which the fair shopper will readily appreciate as a shawl and mantilla room."

Palmer took advantage of the Medill policy of charging 50¢ a week for a business card but allowing the advertiser to change his copy. His announcements told of the goods available, heralding the arrival of new wares—English carpeting, velvet from Brussels, fine silks and embroideries, Balmoral mantle shawls. His own references to his new palace store were subdued, compared to Bross's prose: "Possessing facilities not enjoyed by any other firm in the trade, I am prepared to offer *dry goods* at less price than any other house in the city." Palmer's announcements were one column wide and six or seven inches long, less than W. M. Ross and T. B. Carter and other merchants had been using prior to 1857, but more than the rest of Lake Street seemed able to afford in 1858. Ultimately other dry goods stores would emulate Palmer in changing their advertising copy frequently, a practice made possible by Joseph Medill's rate system. The new approach to advertising would eventually help the *Tribune* and all other papers to prosper, but in 1858 the advertising outlook continued grim.

Cyrus H. Field completed laying his telegraph cable across the Atlantic Ocean floor during the summer, and the *Press and Tribune,* which had arranged for transoceanic dispatches, led the city in celebration. More than 60,000 persons joined in the festivities, sponsored by the various Chicago newspapers and civic organizations. Within a few months, however, the cable ceased to function, and service would not be restored until 1866.

That summer of 1858 the first horse railroad ran in State Street, and George Pullman paused in his task of lifting Chicago out of the mud on jackscrews to build his first sleeping car. It was tried on the Alton Railroad and called a success, even though the passengers insisted on sleeping in the curtained booths with their muddy boots on. Train arrivals tripled that summer, aiding the *Press and Tribune*'s financial situation by a slight increase in railroad advertising and ticket printing contracts for the job shop; grain shipments doubled, and Chicago moved to a close second to New Orleans in general cargo shipments and continued to challenge Cincinnati's preeminence in pork packing.

There was bad news that summer, too, mostly for Long John Wentworth. Late in August, a grand jury investigation disclosed that the police department had employed one George P. Brown to frequent the city's brothels and obtain evidence against the inmates. When "Beast" Brown was thus exposed, there was an uproar from press and pulpit, and Mayor Haines attributed the employment of Brown to his predecessor, John

Wentworth. Long John, who was visiting his wife in Troy, New York, came storming back to Chicago, insisting that Haines alone was responsible for what the *Press and Tribune* solemnly described as an "undercover" system. Judge Robert S. Wilson, in his instructions to the grand jury, in effect indicted both Wentworth and his *Democrat* and demanded that the jurors concur. Instead, the jury refused to return indictments, but it reprimanded Wentworth and other officials involved. "The days of Johannes Elongatus in politics are over," chortled the *Press and Tribune*, as Wentworth slipped back to the safety of Troy.

The proprietors of the *Press and Tribune* focused their attention upon the senatorial campaign. Since the state legislature would choose the winner, and legislative politics involved all of Illinois at every political level, the paper made elaborate preparations to inform the entire electorate about the issues. According to Illinois historian and Lincoln scholar Paul Angle, the Illinois senatorial contest of 1858 was "the first to be reported in modern fashion" and saw two important journalistic innovations: "For the first time correspondents traveled with candidates, and for the first time a series of political speeches was reported stenographically."

Both the *Press and Tribune* and the pro-Douglas *Chicago Times* engaged shorthand reporters, and, despite accusations made by each side, there is no evidence that either stenographer allowed partisan politics to affect the accuracy of his verbatim reports. The articles by some of the correspondents were an entirely different matter. On August 13, Douglas gave a speech in Havana, Illinois, which was described in a dispatch published in the *Press and Tribune:*

> The Pro-Slavery ringleader of the North-West has visited us and made a speech, which has cruelly disappointed his friends, and lost him a hundred votes in Mason County, at the very least. . . . My candid opinion is that Mr. Douglas can do nothing so *certain* to elect Abe Lincoln to the Senate, as to deliver the speech which he gave us today, in every county seat in the State. If I might prescribe a judicious course for the Little Giant, for the balance of the campaign, I should just tell him to *be sick.* . . . It would be difficult for me to give an adequate idea of the littleness, meanness and foulness of Douglas' harangue here today. . . . For instance, he called Lincoln a liar, a coward(!), a wretch and a sneak, and he called Trumbull a sneak, a wretch and a coward and a liar.

The *Times* correspondent in Havana on August 13 had this to say about Lincoln, who had come by steamer to the town:

> As Lincoln was about leaving the boat, the American flag was run up on board, but, as if indignant at being raised in honor of such a man, it displayed itself at mast head Union Jack down, and this little circumstance, together with his forgetting his carpet bag and umbrella, and being obliged to go back for them, seemed to affect Lincoln so much that it was with

difficulty that the committee could convey him ashore over the plank, which in fact they did not succeed in doing until a gentleman relieved him of his umbrella, which he manifested a determination to carry between his legs, and which it was with the greatest difficulty he could be extricated from. . . .

Lincoln is failing rapidly, but he has lost none of his awkwardness. He is all legs and arms, and his constant efforts to hide the extreme length of these members by keeping them twisted up when not in use, makes his movements very kinky and uncertain. His gestures when speaking, are positively painful, and while listening to him we are constantly uncomfortable, because you cannot divest yourself of the idea that he is suffering from an attack brought on by an imprudent indulgence in unripe fruit.

The *Press and Tribune* engaged Robert Hitt to provide verbatim reports of each of the seven debates and some other important speeches as well. In addition, the proprietors agreed that at least one of them would attend each debate, and Horace White was assigned to accompany Lincoln throughout the campaign, for Lincoln, like Douglas, had dozens of other speaking engagements. Provisions were made for most of the *Press and Tribune* staff to aid Lincoln as needed, and the company presses were at the disposal of the Republican party. The paper acquired an elaborate network of correspondents who reported on the campaign from their various towns. It announced that it would sell campaign editions at cost, and it made its stenographic reports available to other newspapers without charge. It became, in effect, a Lincoln campaign organization, working closely with Norman Judd and Lincoln himself. The costs were great, but the proprietors decreed that Lincoln and the Republicans must win, the march of slavery must be stopped.

To Joseph Medill, the course Lincoln should follow was clear, and he offered the candidate some advice:

> Douglas has great power—I may say, the secret of his strength lies in his tact of keeping his opponents on the defensive. He kept our party on it all thru the campaign of 1856, and seeks to play the same game on you. It is your chief point because the true policy is to pitch into him, charge him with being in a conspiracy with the South to enslave the North, that he helped put up the Dred Scott scheme which enslaves the territories and if pushed to its consequence carries slavery into free states. Charge him with being pro-slavery all over. . . . Charge him with deliberately laying his plans to strike down popular sovereignty after tying the hands of Congress, etc., etc. I need not enumerate. But charge home on him, force him into the defensive. Shoot into his hull between wind and water.

On August 21, the day of the first debate, the paper said:

> The gallant Lincoln will enter the lists at Ottawa today with Douglas. The meeting will be a memorable one. . . . A large delegation will be in attendance from this city, leaving here by 8 A.M. train, Chicago and Rock Island

railway and returning this evening. Let there be a good attendance of our Republicans. The *Tribune* of Monday will contain a full stenographic verbatim report on the speeches of Lincoln and Douglas. Let all who can be present to hear the champions, and all who can't should read and judge for themselves.

To ensure widespread circulation among the electorate, the paper announced an evening edition, much to the consternation of Charles Wilson, who was enjoying an evening monopoly with his *Journal*.

There were 10,000 in the crowd at Ottawa. Farmers in their wagons with their families, and others on horseback or in buggies, began arriving on the 16th. Mostly the farm families slept on the ground, or in their carts, but the Ottawa hotels were filled with politicians and city visitors. Special trains, such as that sponsored by the *Press and Tribune* from Chicago, and canalboats carried crowds, and Douglas's train snorted in covered with banners, a band aboard, and the brass cannon booming. Ottawa was festive with bunting. The streets throbbed to the music of visiting brass bands, and the crowds milled about in warm sunshine, patronizing the street vendors and crying out as some were preyed upon by pickpockets and strong-arm thugs. The candidates spoke from a decorated stand in a downtown grove, with steaming thousands packed around them. Douglas, as the man challenged, fixed the rules. In this first meeting he would have the first hour of debate, Lincoln an hour and a half, then Douglas a half hour for rebuttal. At their next meeting Lincoln would open, and so the candidates would alternate through the series. At a table up front, Hitt bent over his stenographic reports, and an official timekeeper checked his watches. There were five other reporters from Chicago and Springfield, but only the *Press and Tribune* would carry the full text.

Senator Douglas scored a major point with the Ottawa crowd when he accused Lincoln of aiding the passage of radical abolitionist resolutions at a meeting in Springfield in 1854. Shouting to make sure that every word was heard in the farthest recesses of the crowd, Douglas read out the resolutions. Hitt, knowing a copy of the complete document would be in the *Press and Tribune* files, wrote down only the first few lines of the resolutions. When his turn came, Lincoln faltered in reply. He denied being at the meeting, but he failed to disavow the accusation of radicalism.

Back in the *Press and Tribune* office in Chicago that night, Hitt prepared his transcription for the printer. When he got out the file on the Springfield resolutions, he discovered they were not what Douglas had quoted. Hitt hurried to show the discrepancy to Dr. Ray. Sputtering indignantly, Ray dashed off a headline for a special "side story": "DOUGLAS' OTTAWA SPEECH PROVED TO BE A LIE AND A

FRAUD." The story provided the Springfield resolutions and those Douglas had read, which had in fact come from a meeting of radicals held in Aurora.

Horace White's account of the debate was headed, "DRED SCOTT CHAMPION PULVERIZED," while Douglas's own paper, the *Times,* headlined, "LINCOLN BREAKS DOWN. DOUGLAS SKINS THE LIVING DOG" (an allusion to the biblical quotation, "A living dog is better than a dead lion," which Lincoln had used in his "House Divided" speech, implying that Douglas was the dead lion and he, Lincoln, the living dog). The *Times* also offered what it claimed was a verbatim report. Dr. Ray compared the *Times* and *Press and Tribune* texts and announced that he had found 100 errors of omission and commission in the *Times*'s version of the debate. Editor Sheahan of the *Times* chose to ignore Ray's charges, but he did not claim to provide the complete text of the subsequent debates.

Dr. Ray felt he had scored decisively with his forgery charges, though it was never shown that Douglas was aware that he was reading something other than the Springfield resolutions. For a time Ray insisted that Republican strategists should base the entire campaign on the forgery issue. He wrote his friend Congressman Washburne: *"Howl on that Douglas forgery, fraud and lie at Ottawa. We have got him on that sure, and we must make it a sufficient answer to all his charges during the campaign. . . . When you see Abe at Freeport, for God's sake tell him to 'Charge Chester! Charge!' . . . They (the Ruffians) feel like hell to-day. That forgery has cowed them."*

The *Press and Tribune* arranged for a special train of 17 cars to run from Chicago to the Freeport debate, and specials from other parts of the state were also scheduled. The round trip fare from Chicago aboard the Galena and Chicago Union train was $4.85, and more than 1,000 supporters made the trip. Lincoln himself came in on August 27 from Amboy, where he had spoken the previous night, arriving aboard a special train at 10:00 A.M. Senator Douglas arrived the night before with his wife, his band, secretaries, a stenographer, and the brass cannon. He was escorted to the Brewster House by a torchlight procession—"not much of a procession," observed the *Press and Tribune*—whereas Lincoln was met by 2,000 supporters who gave him "six deafening cheers" as he descended from the train of cars.

At some time during the day Joseph Medill spoke to Lincoln about his speech for that afternoon, which would open the debate. Medill recalled, in a *Tribune* article published on May 19, 1895, that he met with Lincoln aboard a train "going north" to Freeport, which would indicate that he had gone to hear the candidate at Amboy the night before. According to Medill's recollection, he strenuously objected to the second of a series of questions Lincoln proposed to ask of Judge Douglas, a question of crucial importance: "Can the people of a United States Territory, in any lawful way, against the wishes of citizens of the United States, exclude slavery from its limits prior to the formation of a State Constitution?"

Medill believed that Douglas would reply affirmatively and that this would help solidify his support from antislavery elements, which had been growing since his opposition to the Lecompton Constitution. The question could cost Lincoln the election, Medill concluded. Lincoln quietly pondered Medill's objections but indicated he still intended to put the question to Douglas. When the train arrived in Freeport, Medill, much agitated, sought help in dissuading Lincoln. But Lincoln persisted because, implied Medill, he knew full well that though a Douglas affirmative might return him to the Senate, it would cost him Southern support should he become a candidate for president in 1860.

Years later, when Medill recalled that August 27 day, he also referred to an occasion a few days after the 1860 election, when he went to Springfield to congratulate the president-elect.

> Mr. Lincoln . . . extended his hand and gave me a very cordial grip. . . . He bent his head down to my ear and said in low tones, something like this: "Do you recollect the argument we had on the way up to Freeport two years ago . . . ?" I replied that I recollected it very well. "Now," said he, "don't you think I was right in putting that question to him?" I said, "Yes, Mr. Lincoln, you were, and we were both right. Douglas' reply to that question undoubtedly hurt him badly for the Presidency, but it elected him to the Senate. . . . " Lincoln then gave me a broad smile and said: "And I have won the place he was playing for."

Medill's version of events surrounding the Freeport Question was accepted by historians for more than 50 years, until the Robert Todd Lincoln Collection was opened in 1947, revealing advice to the candidate written in Medill's hand and probably, according to historian Don E. Fehrenbacher, hand-delivered to Lincoln by Medill at Freeport. Prior to the debate, Medill, Ebenezer Peck, and Norman Judd had conferred on strategy and had in fact proposed to Lincoln that second question along with several others. Far from exhorting Lincoln to be careful, Medill had been as aggressive as usual. *"Employ your best hour in pitching into Dug,"* he implored. *"Make your assertions dogmaticall and unqualified. Be saucy . . . in other words give him h—l."* Medill had actually urged the candidate to ask the question that fetched Douglas's affirmative—which the Lincoln camp felt would highlight the contradictions in Douglas's stand on slavery and thus win the senatorial election for Lincoln. As Fehrenbacher points out, surely neither Lincoln nor his advisors were looking ahead to 1860 in the way Medill later recalled, since clearly the best way to advance Lincoln and the Republican cause was to retire Douglas from the U.S. Senate.

By two o'clock on Friday, August 27, a clouded, drizzling afternoon, more than 15,000 persons crowded about the speakers' stand in the town grove a short distance from the Brewster House. "Old Abe," as he was popularly being called, rose slowly, surveyed the huge crowd that filled the entire square, and lifted his arms to still the cheering. There was a booming voice from the back as a fierce, auburn-bearded man shouted: "Hold on Lincoln, you can't speak yet! Hitt isn't here and there is no use of your speaking unless the *Chicago Tribune* has a report."

It was Deacon Bross. Lincoln cast a sardonic smile upon him, for he knew that a newspaper needed advertising as much as a politician. "Ain't Hitt here?" Lincoln asked innocently. "Where is he?"

"Is Hitt in the crowd?" Bross yelled. "If he is tell him Mr. Bross of the *Chicago Press and Tribune* wants him to come to the stand and make a verbatim report for the only newspaper in the Northwest that has enterprise enough to publish these speeches in full."

There were cries from the crowd, "Hitt can't get through." Then a cheer, and a man was being passed over the heads of the people toward the speakers' stand.

Bross's promotional efforts, at Freeport and elsewhere, paid off in prestige and circulation for the *Press and Tribune*, and Lincoln would later say that the paper's efforts lifted intolerable campaign burdens from his shoulders. There was an endless issue of pamphlets, broadsides, and verbatim reports from the combined *Tribune* and *Democratic Press* batteries of presses. And, the more the *Press and Tribune* published and circulated, the more money it lost, so that Medill, Ray, and Bross were soon scurrying about looking for loans. But the proprietors clearly felt that their fortunes must be risked. Costly coverage and expensive special issues continued. The debates were attracting widespread attention, and the *Press and Tribune* proprietors continued to respond to all campaign requests. The candidates, too, were aware of the importance of their meetings. As Lincoln may have anticipated, Southern newspapers picked up Douglas's reply to his question, which, in effect, was yes. By refusing to enact friendly legislation, said Douglas, a territory could in essence exclude slavery. Though there was really nothing new in the "Freeport Doctrine," the answer, writes Douglas biographer Robert W. Johannsen, caused a sensation in the nation's newspapers and "was interpreted as a final and crushing blow to the rights of the South."

Through that extremely hot autumn, the debates continued, drawing eager town dwellers from their sweltering homes and thousands of farmers from their late harvests to hear the two ablest stump speakers of their time. Lincoln, spare and long and grimly earnest, his high-pitched voice carrying in the open air to the farthest extension of the crowd, ultimately soothing the sturdy farmers and townsfolk who stood more often than they sat, weaving an almost hypnotic spell broken occasionally by dry, wry humor; his gestures awkward, halting, but dramatically effective, especially, reports his biographer Thomas, when, to "give a point special emphasis, he would bend his knees, crouch slightly, then shoot upward to his tiptoes," his finger spearing skyward, the crowd responding with a gasp of emotional release. Beside him Douglas, dynamic, cocksure, a resplendent little man with a magnificently large head and voice, usually chomping a cigar now that he abjured chewing tobacco, a florid, perspiring, but always fascinating political performer who was at last beginning to tire, who was growing hoarse, who was increasingly inclined to lose his temper, yet, despite the steaming heat, despite Lincoln's ducking and taunting, and all that the Republicans or the ubiquitous *Press and Tribune* could do, this little striving man was beginning to win.

In the fourth debate, in Charleston, Lincoln himself wavered under the thrusts of the Little Giant and shocked his Northern abolitionist supporters by saying:

> I am not, nor ever have been in favor of bringing about in any way the social and political equality of the white and black races—that I am not nor ever have been in favor of making voters or jurors of Negroes, nor of qualifying them to hold office, nor to intermarry with white people; and I will say in addition to this that there is a physical difference between the white and black races which I believe will forever forbid the two races living together on terms of social and political equality.

But while Douglas grew increasingly weary and arrogant and resentful of criticism as the campaign wore on (he made over 100 speeches during the campaign), Lincoln gained his second wind and appeared fresher.

All of the debates, through to Alton on October 15, were given full coverage and added distribution by the *Press and Tribune,* while Alfred Cowles grimly studied his account books. "The defeat which Douglas has sustained on the stump will be equalled only by the overthrow which awaits him at the polls," the paper had said after the Galesburg debate. The editors soon knew differently, for ominous reports were coming in, and on October 30, a more correct assessment was printed. "Lincoln has made a splendid national reputation. His fame is secure. It cannot, it must not be that the scheme to stifle the voice of the people of Illinois through the ballot box will be suffered to succeed." The paper was referring to its own published report that Eastern Democrats were sending "colonizers" to Illinois to cast fraudulent ballots.

Election day was cold and wet and many farmers stayed home. The first election returns, printed on November 3, indicated that the Republicans had carried Chicago, and probably northern Illinois. On November 4, it was reported that 125,430 voters had backed Republican candidates, thus insuring Republican control of the state administration, against 121,609 votes for the Douglas Democrats and 5,071 for the Buchanan Democrats. Had the senatorial election been decided by popular vote, Lincoln would have won. But the Democrats still controlled the Illinois legislature, and on January 6, 1859, Douglas received 54 votes to Lincoln's 46 and was reelected U.S. senator.

Said the *Press and Tribune* on November 5:

> We are beaten, but not disheartened or overawed. The principles and policy for which we have contended and shall still continue to contend, commend themselves with such convincing power to our judgment and conscience that we cannot be false to them if we would. . . . Now is the time to put the elements of the next and the great campaign in motion. . . . We promise nothing, except to be true to our professions, and to leave nothing undone that will make the *Press and Tribune* worthy of your continued support.

In Springfield, Abraham Lincoln was disappointed, but not depressed. *"I am glad I made the late race,"* he wrote his friend Dr. A. G. Henry. *"It gave me a hearing on the great and durable question of the age, which I could have had in no other way; and though I now sink out of view, and shall be forgotten, I believe I have made some marks which will tell for the cause of civil liberty long after I am gone."* Lincoln also wrote to Dr. Ray: *"I believe . . . you are 'feeling like h—l yet.' Quit that. You will soon feel better. Another 'blow-up' is coming; and we shall have fun again. Douglas managed to be supported both as the best instrument to* put down *and to* up-hold *the slave power; but no ingenuity can long keep these antagonisms in harmony."*

*　　*　　*

The next "blow-up" had been anticipated for months by the proprietors of the *Press and Tribune.* They had frantically attempted to avert financial catastrophe by seeking new funds during the months of the senatorial campaign. The alternative, to curtail campaign activity, was rejected. Special campaign editions sold at cost or lower, speakers for doubtful areas, special trains, and elaborate staffing of the debates and other major campaign events—all of this, coupled with the poor economic climate and obligations assumed from the *Democratic Press,* had run the *Press and Tribune* deep into debt. Lincoln owed $1,000 when the campaign ended. The proprietors of the *Press and Tribune* owed $65,000. Barton Spears evidently had had enough of the uncertainties of newspapering; he sold his interest in the paper to his partners and retired. The remaining proprietors called together their creditors, said they could not meet their next mortgage payments, and asked for an extension. The creditors inspected the plant and equipment, the circulation lists, and the retrenchment program drawn up by Medill, Bross, and Cowles and agreed to renew the mortgage for three years at 10 percent interest. Dr. Ray, at least, was elated by this solution. Three years! Sufficient time to win the antislavery campaign by putting a Republican in the White House! (In fact, only 21 months later, the final payment was made and the bill books, in the words of the *Tribune,* were "kicked out of the office, never, it is to be hoped, again to have an abiding place in the establishment. . . . And thus when the Presidential campaign of 1860 had been fairly inaugurated the Tribune Company found themselves freed from every pecuniary obligation.")

Dr. Ray wrote the editorial restating the *Press and Tribune* position, breathing defiance. Said the paper on November 5, 1858:

> We shall be very sorry, very sorry indeed to believe that Illinois is a pro-slavery State; but whether it be or not, we owe to our fathers, our country and posterity, a war against the pro-slavery Democracy, here and elsewhere, to be terminated only with our lives—and we mean to discharge the debt with such power as has been given us. . . . The cause which animates [*Republicans*]—will outlive the mountains. . . . As said [*John*] Paul Jones, of heroic memory, when asked if he had struck his colors: WE HAVE ONLY BEGUN TO FIGHT.

Senator Douglas, having won the campaign, was inclined to be magnanimous. He sought an interview with Dr. Ray and Medill and told them he had no present intention of seeking the Democratic nomination for the next presidential election. He also stated that he would not seek peace with President Buchanan. Medill described the interview with Douglas in a letter to Congressman Schuyler Colfax. According to Medill, Douglas had gone on to say he was *"still a young man, only 45 years old and could wait until the signs came right, that his friends who were throwing up their caps for him as the next President were a set of jackasses. . . . Douglas will never be re-instated in the Democratic church,"* Medill concluded. *"He will gradually drift toward our side and finally be compelled to act with us in 1860."*

Dr. Ray and Medill were showing some signs of estrangement. Ray appeared unconcerned about costs, leaving it to Medill to rescue the paper from its debts, while Ray himself, according to Katherine Medill, was "hateful and arrogant." Ray had acquired a ready ally in young abolitionist Horace White, whom he had brought into the paper and later restored to duty after he had been let go for lack of funds. Yet, despite this friction, Medill and Ray remained in agreement on the antislavery, pro-Republican, anti-Douglas posture of the paper. Douglas "has a perilous ropewalk before him," the *Press and Tribune* said. "Therefore Mr. Douglas must cast his lot decisively this winter, either with the Republicans or the pro-slavery Democracy. There is no middle ground." The editors obviously hoped Douglas would tumble from the rope and into the morass.

Following a public demonstration in his behalf, Senator Douglas and Adele left for Washington, by way of New Orleans and Cuba. In his final Chicago statement, he declared again that the nation should reject the "fatal heresy" that it could not endure half slave and half free. Douglas said his trip was being made to test the voice of the South, but his political enemies declared that he was promoting his presidential candidacy and suggested he should visit the slave plantations his wife had inherited. Returning to the North, the senator was greeted as a hero in New York, where he was given a civic banquet attended by 3,000 guests, and in Philadelphia, where there was a torchlight procession, a fireworks display, and a 200-gun salute. The debates had benefited Douglas almost as much as Lincoln.

The *Press and Tribune* editors had not decided on a presidential candidate early in 1859, but they were united in their rejection of Douglas. They consistently jabbed at the Little Giant and clucked anxiously over "Honest Old Abe" and his future. When the *New York Tribune* sent out a questionnaire to the country's leading politicians but failed to print Lincoln's response, the *Press and Tribune* upbraided the New York paper: "Sufficient for us is the omission, a part and parcel of the policy which the *New York Tribune* has pursued toward one of the ablest and purest Republicans in the Union, since he dared oppose the nominee of that sheet for United States Senator in Illinois."

On June 15 Lincoln, who was back at his law business in Springfield, wrote a note to the *Press and Tribune* proprietors:

> *Herewith is a little draft to pay for your Daily another year from today. I suppose I shall take the Press & Tribune so long as it, and I both live, unless I become unable to pay for it. In its devotion to our cause always, and to me personally last year, I owe it a debt of gratitude, which I fear I shall never be able to pay.*
>
> Yours very truly,
> A. Lincoln

Despite the close relationship between his paper and Lincoln, during that summer Medill was writing his friend Salmon Chase that his aspirations for the presidency, which were great, would get proper consideration: "*Before long I propose to write one or more leading articles in favor of nominating a Western Candidate without espousing the claims of any man or attacking Seward. We do not think it policy thus early to commit our paper publicly to any candidate, but to work underground for you and openly for a Western man.*" In August, Medill wrote Chase that if Edward Bates of Missouri did not gain strength, "*I consider you have a pretty sure thing of the nomination.*" But a month later he wrote again, to say that Lincoln was forging ahead as a possible candidate for the Republicans in Illinois and Indiana.

In interviews granted 40 years later, such as one for the *Saturday Evening Post* in 1899, Joseph Medill recalled that the Lincoln presidential strategy was devised in the *Press and Tribune* offices in the summer of 1859 at a meeting of the Republican State Central Committee. According to his recollection, the *Press and Tribune* was to stand aside to permit the clamor for Lincoln's nomination to arise in downstate Illinois. Whether there was such a meeting is not of record, but events did follow the line Medill remembered, although the call for Lincoln began spontaneously and preceded the committee meeting by several months. A few days after Lincoln's Senate canvass, on November 4, 1858, the *Illinois Gazette* of Lacon, Illinois, urged Lincoln for president, a position echoed on November 19 by the downstate *Olney Times*. Nearly a year later, on October 25, 1859, the *Press and Tribune* noted, "The *Aledo Record* and the *Rock Island Register* favor the nomination of Abraham Lincoln for the presidency," probably the beginning of the planned campaign Medill spoke of. John Wentworth's *Democrat* declared for Sam Houston of Texas for president and Lincoln for vice-president.

That some sort of plan existed is indicated by the fact that two of Lincoln's closest newspaper confidants and most loyal supporters, the *Chicago Press and Tribune* and the *Springfield Journal,* for which Lincoln often wrote, kept silent as to whom they favored for the nomination. But when Charles Wilson's *Chicago Journal,* a longtime Republican paper, urged New York's Senator Seward, asserting that he was a favorite of the Eastern seaboard, the *Press and Tribune* disagreed: Seward's nomination "would be the signal of a union of Americans [*Know-Nothings*] with Democrats to beat him. Would it be wise to nominate a candidate however great his talents, or sincere his free soilism, who, instead of attracting the conservatives to his support would repel them?"

While knocking down potential strong adversaries, the *Press and Tribune* continued to withhold its own endorsement. This fit in well with Lincoln's personal policy. When Thomas J. Pickett, editor of the *Rock Island Register,* proposed earlier in the year to organize Illinois editors for a simultaneous endorsement, Lincoln had written in reply, "*I really think it best for our cause that no concerted effort, such as you suggest, be made.*"

Reluctant to declare himself a candidate for the presidency, Lincoln nonetheless welcomed the chance to make known his point of view. In the summer of 1859, he went on a tour of western states, responding to his many invitations to speak. The *Press and Tribune* occasionally sent along Robert Hitt to provide verbatim reports. When Lincoln appeared in Cincinnati in September, there was a six-column report in the *Press and Tribune* and an editorial congratulating Cincinnati for inviting Lincoln: "Well done, Cincinnati. You are paying merited respect to an honest man." The paper called the speech one of Lincoln's ablest and most penetrating. "The popular sovereigns," Lincoln said, thrusting at the Douglas supporters, "are blowing out the moral lights around us; teaching the Negro is no longer a man but a brute; that the Declaration has nothing to do with him; that he ranks with the crocodile and the reptile; that man, with body and soul, is a matter of dollars and cents."

In October abolitionist fanatic John Brown outraged the South, shocked the North, and brought the nation closer to open civil warfare. On the 16th, Brown, shaggy of hair and beard, wild-eyed, armed to the teeth, led 21 deluded followers, 16 whites and five blacks, against the Federal arsenal in Harper's Ferry, Virginia (now West Virginia), swiftly capturing it. Brown and his band held out for two days against Virginia militiamen but capitulated when Col. Robert E. Lee arrived with a detachment of regular troops. Ten of the raiders were killed, and Brown and most of the other survivors were taken prisoner. The country's abolitionists hailed him as a martyr, the Southern press denounced him as insane, and most Republicans disavowed him.

The *Press and Tribune* published a series of dispatches on Brown's raid, and on October 19 commented:

> Osawatomie Brown . . . figures not unexpectedly to us in this purposeless and senseless riot. Since the death of his son Frederick, who was shot down at his own door in Kansas, by a Missouri mob tenfold more revengeful and bloody than that which now fills Virginia with terror, and since the old man witnessed, on the same occasion, the destruction of the property he had been a life time in accumulating, he has been a monomaniac. He has supposed himself divinely appointed to free all American slaves by some violent and decisive movement.

Two days later the paper editorialized, "Let the Democracy of the North—particularly of the Northwest—who, under the lead of Douglas, have stopped at nothing to degrade Freedom and elevate Slavery, bear the burdens which their causeless criminality had imposed upon them. Republican skirts are clear."

On November 19, 1859, the *Press and Tribune* went informally on record for Lincoln for president. Taking notice of a suggestion in a Pennsylvania newspaper that Sen. Simon Cameron, Pennsylvania's Republican boss, should be the candidate, with Abraham Lincoln for vice-president, the *Press and Tribune* said: "We fancy the Republicans of the Northwest will insist upon turning it end for end, so that it may read Lincoln for President and Cameron for Vice-president. We make these suggestions not to insist that the Republican party shall nominate Mr. Lincoln for the Presidency, but to state what sort of ticket we should prefer."

Shortly after John Brown was hanged on December 2, at Charlestown, Virginia, the paper reported on a Lincoln speech in Kansas. Brown had shown exceptional courage, said Lincoln, but his lawlessness was indefensible. Then, addressing his proslavery listeners, he added, "[*You say*] if the Black Republicans elect a President . . . you will break up the Union. That will be your act, not ours. . . . Old John Brown has just been executed for treason against a state. . . . If constitutionally we elect a President, and therefore you undertake to destroy the Union, it will be our duty to deal with you as old John Brown has been dealt with."

In December, 1859, Joseph Medill returned to Washington as correspondent and to "preach" Lincoln among the congressmen. In addition, he was to urge Chicago as a site for the Republican convention. Medill found that national leaders of the Republican party were receptive to Lincoln for second place, but not for president; Seward was the favored man. Chicago, however, was easily ahead as a convention site, and on December 22 the *Press and Tribune* reported that the Republican National Committee, meeting at the Astor House in New York, had chosen Chicago over Indianapolis and St. Louis. The *Press and Tribune* was jubilant. Chicago had won, said the paper, because it had the facilities—excellent transportation and fine hotels. But a proper meeting hall would have to be built. The city was in an ideal situation to play host to a national convention, for business was good, the earnings of the railroads had trebled (and thus could be levied upon for some of the convention costs), and the city of 110,000 was well qualified and able to care for its distinguished guests in a proper way.

Medill was sending daily dispatches to his paper signed "M" and also "Chicago." Katherine, left at home with the girls, wrote:

> I am grateful for your letter and ten pages of remembrance. It is pleasant to know one is not forgotten. You send your letters [to the paper] under differing names. Doesn't that diminish the credit you receive for your work? . . . It is a pity that Scripps is not here to tone [Dr. Ray] down. He is so rough and hateful I really can't endure him. . . . For pity sakes don't write the office that you plan to stay for six or eight weeks, my beloved. Are you demented?

THE PEOPLE'S
CANDIDATE

6

Despite Joseph Medill's efforts among the congressmen, and Chicago's success in obtaining the Republican National Convention, Lincoln's backers knew well enough that it was Thurlow Weed, Republican boss of New York, who was making progress for his candidate, William Seward. Weed sent an emissary to Illinois to size up Lincoln, possibly for second place on a Seward ticket. Norman Judd and what opponents derisively called "the *Chicago Press and Tribune* clique" knew that Lincoln needed to get some personal, firsthand attention in the East. Jesse Fell, a downstate leader, made a small but important move when he induced the *Chester County Times* in Pennsylvania to print an autobiographical sketch he had persuaded Lincoln to write, after months of cajoling. Fell thought a Lincoln self-portrait placed in an Eastern paper might be picked up rather widely in the East, and he was right. Of even greater importance was the invitation Lincoln received to lecture before a forum of Henry Ward Beecher's Plymouth Church in Brooklyn. There could hardly be a more prestigious podium, but Lincoln hesitated. He had delivered a few lectures, on scientific discoveries, and he was no good at it. His style was politics. He inquired of the committee on arrangements if he might speak on a political subject, and, on receiving an affirmative answer, accepted the invitation, vastly pleasing his Illinois strategy group.

Medill, in Washington, continued "preaching" Lincoln among the congressmen and began to feel he was having some success in persuading them that Lincoln had the ability to win in the doubtful states. He informed his *Press and Tribune* colleagues that the time had come for the

111

Republican newspaper leading public opinion in the Northwest to make known its own opinion. Scripps was instructed to complete a 4,000-word Abraham Lincoln biography, which the *Press and Tribune* would print, holding the type for reissuance in booklet form. Dr. Ray prepared an editorial that appeared on February 16 and, like Scripps's biography, was widely reprinted. The editorial began:

> Of the three or four States [*Illinois, Indiana, Pennsylvania, New Jersey*] . . . believed to constitute the debatable ground in the next Presidential campaign, and whose electoral votes will determine the result, Illinois is universally conceded to be one. It appears to be a foregone conclusion that the nomination of the Chicago Convention will be conferred upon no one who does not unite in himself the essentials of requisite qualification, devotion to the distinctive principles of the Republican party, and availability [*ability to win*] in the States alluded to above. We have no hesitation in saying that . . . Abraham Lincoln, of Illinois, is the peer of any man yet named in connection with the Republican nominations. . . . His memorable canvass with Mr. Douglas in 1858, gave Republicans throughout the Union an opportunity of becoming familiar with his admirable personal qualities, his entire devotion to the distinctive principles of the party, his rare abilities, and his broad, statesmanlike views. . . . We briefly sum up some of the elements of his popularity and strength:
>
> 1st. A gentleman of unimpeachable purity of private life. His good name is not soiled by a single act, political, social, moral or religious, that we or his friends need blush to own as his. In all his relations to his fellows . . . he is the peer of the most unspotted man in the Republic—the living likeness, full length size, of the best of the eminent characters who laid the foundation of the government.
>
> 2d. A man of, at once, great breadth and great acuteness of intellect. Not learned, in a bookish sense, but master of great fundamental principles, and of that kind of ability which applies them to crises and events. . . . One of the ablest political thinkers of his day.
>
> 3d. Right on the record. An Old Line Whig of the Henry Clay school, originally, he came early into the Republican movement. . . . He has that radicalism which a keen insight into the meaning of the anti-slavery conflict is sure to give; but, coupled with it, that constitutional conservatism which could never fail in proper respect for existing institutions and laws. . . .
>
> 4th. A man of executive capacity. Never garrulous, never promising what he cannot perform, never doing anything for show or effect, laboriously attentive to detail, industrious and conscientious. . . .
>
> These are some of the reasons why we favor the nomination of Mr. Lincoln for the first place on the National Republican ticket. We do not know, however, that he has any aspirations for the position. . . . But he is no doubt at the disposal of his friends; and we feel very confident that Illinois will present his name to the Chicago Convention, as the man, above all others, who will be most likely to lead the Republican party on to a glorious victory. . . . Should the Convention give him this position, then the honor

which he has not sought, but which his admirers have hoped he might attain, will, like ripe fruit, fall into his hands. Abraham Lincoln will never be President by virtue of intrigue and bargain.

Medill, reporting under the name "Chicago," wrote from Washington that the editorial was well received. In a letter published February 26, 1860, he asserted, "I hear the name of Lincoln mentioned for President in Washington circles, ten times as often as it was one month ago. The more the politicians look over the field in search of an *available* candidate, the more convinced they are that 'Old Abe' is the man to win the race with." He added that the prospects of his old friend William Seward were slipping because Seward was "too radical" and could not carry the doubtful states. When the issue of the *Press and Tribune* carrying Medill's letter reached Washington, Senator Seward, the perpetual New York candidate, was infuriated. "You have stunned me," Seward told Medill privately. "You advocate Lincoln in preference to me, giving reasons that are wide of the truth; saying that I haven't the strength Lincoln has . . . and that your man Lincoln out there on the prairies can carry the essential states. . . . I consider this a personal insult. I had always counted on you as one of my boys. Henceforth you and I are parted . . . I defy you to do your worst. I know three papers in your town that are with me, and I shall never trust you again."

En route east for his Brooklyn appearance, Lincoln stopped off in Chicago to discuss his proposed remarks with Medill, who had just returned from Washington, and Dr. Ray. Lincoln explained that he had researched the constitutional issues of slavery with great care, reading Elliot's *Debates on the Federal Constitution,* studying the *Annals of Congress* and the *Congressional Globe.* Now he desired the criticism and counsel of his good newspaper friends. Medill and Ray read the speech together, praised it highly, to Lincoln's evident pleasure, then divided it and took the parts home, where, upon second thoughts, they inscribed their criticisms and comments in the margins. Lincoln accepted the notations provided by the *Tribune* men and went on to New York. There he learned that his address would be sponsored by the Young Men's Central Republican Union of New York City and that he would speak at Cooper Union in Manhattan instead of Beecher's church. It was not until a week later that Ray and Medill saw the complete Cooper Union text, as published in Horace Greeley's *Tribune.* "Well," said Ray sourly after reading it, "he must have thrown our suggestions out of the train window!"

Lincoln had not used any of their ideas; nevertheless the speech was well received in New York and highly praised by such journalists as Henry J. Raymond of the *New York Times* and William Cullen Bryant, the learned editor of the *New York Evening Post.* Though Lincoln was regarded as a country bumpkin by some New Yorkers, his oratorical style and the erudition of his remarks impressed the 1,500 Republicans who attended upon him at Cooper Union, and he was welcomed warmly in New England towns on his way to Phillips Exeter Academy in New Hampshire, where his son Robert was a student. The *Press and Tribune* editors decided to reprint the text of his address in the paper and to reissue it as a pamphlet, to be sold at cost.

There were other political preparations. Chairman Norman Judd named Medill to the Republican State Central Committee, giving him the task of assigning speakers and financial aid to needy counties in central Illinois, a post of responsibility and power. The *Press and Tribune* urged each of the Republican county organizations in the midwestern states to form Wide Awake marching clubs—oil-cloth-garbed, torch-carrying young men who were to parade at the rallies and in the Chicago streets as the national delegates began arriving, and who would pack the auditorium seats of the convention hall in a crucial tactical hour. Dr. Ray commissioned Chicago's noted sculptor Leonard Volk to prepare a bust of Lincoln to be reproduced for sale to help raise campaign money, $10 full-size, $4.50 for a smaller version. Lincoln posed for Volk's "life mask" in Ray's office, stripping to the buff above the waist. When the plaster cast had been removed, Lincoln suddenly remembered an appointment and quickly donned his shirt and coat, forgetting that the top of his union suit was still dangling unbuttoned around his thighs. Derisive cries of newsboys awaiting their papers in front of the *Press and Tribune* building sent Lincoln bounding back up the steps, two at a time and double quick.

Despite the efforts of his supporters, Lincoln was not yet convinced that he should seek the presidential nomination. On at least one occasion, recalled Medill, Lincoln approached him and said, "See here, you *Tribune* boys have got me up a peg too high. How about the vice-presidency—won't that do?"

"We are not playing second in this dance to any musician," Medill replied. "Start in for the vice-presidency, you have lost all chance of the higher place. If you must 'come down a peg,' as you say, it will be mighty easy later on. The Seward fellows would jump at such a chance to get rid of you. But now it is president or nothing. Else you may count the *Tribune* out. We are not fooling away our time and science on the vice-presidency."

The state Republican convention, which met in Decatur on May 9–10, 1860, was considered routine, but it named the next governor of Illinois, Richard Yates, picked other candidates who would win state offices in November, and approved committal of the Illinois delegates to the national convention to the unit rule—an important tactical maneuver by the Lincoln backers. It also dramatized an exploitable facet of the developing Honest Old Abe Lincoln legend. Early in the proceedings, Richard Oglesby, also destined to become an Illinois governor, suspensefully informed the delegates that an "old time Democrat from Macon County has requested a chance to make a contribution to this convention." The expectant delegates watched two old men, one said to be John Hanks, a country cousin of Abraham Lincoln, circle the convention hall, carrying two split rails and supporting a banner that read: "ABRAHAM LINCOLN. The Rail Candidate for President in 1860. Two. Rails from a Lot of 3,000 Made in 1830 by Thos. Hanks and Abe Lincoln—Whose Father was the First Pioneer of Macon County." As the import of the message grew—Lincoln allowed he must have cut some rails just like those on display—men shouted, cheered, wept, stamped on the floor, and caused such pandemonium that part of the awning roof fell on their heads.

Abraham Lincoln was formally acclaimed Illinois's favorite son and thereafter he was also "Abe Lincoln, the rail splitter." The nomination of Yates ended a long, grim struggle with Norman Judd, who also aspired to the governorship, and who had joined the Chicago newspapers early in the spring in an unsuccessful attempt to block the renewed mayoral aspirations of Long John Wentworth, both being fights that required Lincoln's intervention. At the 11th hour, literally, Judd and the *Press and Tribune,* still reluctant, supported Wentworth, giving Chicago, host city to the Republican convention, a Republican mayor, and giving Lincoln a spate of peace in Illinois, now made complete by Judd's acceptance of Yates for governor.

*   *   *

Chicago, ninth city of the land in 1860 with a population of 110,000, boasted 15 railroads, the world's largest railroad station, seven first-class hotels, such as the Tremont, the Richmond, the Briggs, and the sleek new Sherman, charging $2.50 a night for their sumptuous accommodations, 50 more hotels at $1.50 a night and a hundred at a dollar, plus almost innumerable rooming houses at moderate prices! Such a magnificently endowed host city looked eagerly to the Republican National Convention and maintained, quite credibly, that no other metropolis in America could receive with equal elegance and panoply the expected 30,000 visitors—delegates, alternates, honored guests, marching clubs, singing groups, and the merely curious. There were many cities claiming to be the birthplace of the National Republican party, but Chicagoans knew that the party had been nurtured to maturity in the Queen City of the Lakes. Now the city, especially its politicians and newspaper editors, was prepared to teach the new party a thing or two about political infighting.

There was to be much more to the Republican convention than the demarcation and proscription of slavery, or the naming of candidates, or the metamorphosis of a political party, of course. Also at issue were the prospect of free western lands, a proposal dear to farmers, tradesmen, mechanics, and immigrants alike; the Homestead Act, which President Buchanan threatened to veto and soon did; and a protective tariff, which, as Joseph Medill had pointed out years before, would help farmers sell at better prices to factory workers earning higher wages. River and harbor improvements had to be considered, as well as the compelling necessity for a railroad to the Pacific coast, built with government help if not at government expense, to haul gold and grain to the eastern ports and processed goods west. Where better than Chicago to dramatize these problems and the great opportunities for solution? Where was the small farmer more conscious of the threat posed by the aristocratic Southern plantation owners, an awareness heightened since the revolutions of 1848 by the influx of tough, skilled European peasants and artisans seeking a few acres of their own to till, or a place to build a town? And which would be a better market, the thousands of small farmers needing McCormick reapers and steel plows and cast-iron stoves and sewing machines and those newfangled phosgene lamps—or 300,000 slave owners, who bought and sold in England and required for their workers only a darkened cabin, a brick oven, a shift or pants, a hoe, and a cotton bag?

In Chicago, the newspapers told the country, there were now more than 500 factories, one of them the famous reaper works employing more than 4,000 mechanics; there were beautiful retail stores, fronted with pink Chicago marble; theaters, dime museums, 56 churches, a canal pumping station regarded as one of the wonders of the world, and more ships, barges, railroad cars, packinghouses, and grain elevators than could be found in New York, Boston, New Orleans, and Cincinnati put together. Here was the city of the future, looking directly into the America of the future. Here was the booming Northwest, the partner of the great manufacturing and banking Northeast, linked together by bands of railroad steel, with Chicago as its capital. Here the slave-holding oligarchy would be given the ultimatum, this far and no farther. And what city would best tell the Republican story to the nation? Chicago, of course, with eight daily newspapers, 15 weekly papers and magazines, and telegraph lines to every important city east of the Rocky Mountains.

Not without cause had Chicago won the name "Windy City," used by envious rivals to describe both its atmospheric turbulence and the excesses of its boosters. Years later, Ida M. Tarbell, in her *Life of Lincoln*, observed:

> The audacity of inviting a national convention to meet there, in the condition in which Chicago chanced to be at that time, was purely Chicagoan. No other city would have risked it. In ten years Chicago had nearly quadrupled

its population. . . . In the first flush of youthful energy and ambition the town had undertaken the colossal task of raising itself bodily out of the grassy marsh, where it had been originally placed, to a level of twelve feet above Lake Michigan. . . . When the invitation to the convention was extended, half the buildings in Chicago were on stilts; some of the streets had been raised to the new grade, others still lay in the mud; half the sidewalks were poised high on piles, and half were still down on a level with the lake. A city with a conventional sense of decorum would not have cared to be seen in this demoralized condition, but Chicago perhaps conceived that it would but prove her courage and confidence to show the country what she was doing; and so she had the convention come.

Chicago, the Garden City, prepared itself for the convention's arrival. The city council, led by Republican Mayor Long John Wentworth, appropriated money for a convention hall, 100 by 180 feet, at Lake and Market streets, a two-story pine-board structure that was promptly called the Wigwam. The Wigwam was simply heavy scantlings and deal sheathing around a vast speakers' platform big enough to hold the more than 400 convention delegates, with alternates, newspapermen, and telegraphers on a lower platform and the honored guests and the ladies accommodated in wide balconies on three sides of the hall, allowing seating and standing room for 10,000 on the main floor. It was built at low cost, and it did not look like much. The *Press and Tribune* expressed satisfaction that city tax dollars were employed in the construction, since that forced pro-Southern sympathizers to participate, and, by *Press and Tribune* admission, there were a number of them in Chicago. Two large reception rooms placed at the off-street sides of the Wigwam could also be used for caucuses. The whole was roofed with pinewood and tar paper, with the cupola strengthened to mount a brass cannon that would boom out when the convention had chosen a candidate. A few days before the delegates were to convene, the Republican ladies of Chicago draped the Wigwam inside and out with buntings, flags, flowers, and greeneries and hung the walls with allegorical paintings and the coats of arms of the various states. Wise old Thurlow Weed, always the courtly diplomat, visited the gleaming Wigwam, pronounced it the finest political convention hall in the United States, and rented it for a Seward rally the night before the convention was to begin.

The Pennsylvania, Ohio, Indiana, and Illinois delegations had already been in town two days before Boss Weed arrived aboard the Seward special train from New York. So the town was jumping with Illinois and Indiana Wide Awake marching clubs, their ingenious torches protected by glazine coverings. Pennsylvania and Ohio, too, had steamed in with resplendent bands and marching clubs, but it remained for the Sewardites to detrain with more magnificent splendor that awed the estimated 30,000 visitors who were now taxing even Chicago's vast housing facilities.

There were bands, dragoons in red and green uniforms and gleaming epaulets and tall beaver hats, artillerists with brass cannon, and countless "Irrepressibles," pro-Seward marching clubs from the East that overwhelmed by their numbers and their brilliance the friendly Illinois clubs come to meet them and to escort them to their headquarters at the Richmond House. The thousands of visitors, sated by two days and nights of marching and thumping and blaring brass and flying pennants and bunting and banners, were awed to near silence at the sight of the Irrepressibles, marching to the commands of Tom Hyer, a noted New York pugilist.

But there was a further thrill for the spectators before Weed's delegation was safely lodged in the Richmond House that afternoon. As a signal honor, the New York delegation was treated to a special demonstration by Col. Elmer Ellsworth's Zouaves, a Chicago drill team that was about to reform political parades and even dress military maneuvers and uniforms in the United States for a generation by its fantastic success. Ellsworth was a handsome lad with long, black, curling hair, a neat beard, trim waist, and lean limbs. He had hoped to attend West Point, but his health was not good, so he studied law and drill manuals instead. He got hold of some European magazines with color plates showing the brilliantly costumed French Zouaves, then consulted his fencing master, Dr. Charles A. De Villers, who was from Algiers, and from him obtained a drill manual used by the Zouaves. Ellsworth soon created a troop resplendently garbed in beaded blue jackets, red vests, yellow sashes, white pantaloons and gaiters, and blue cadet caps. In 1859 he acquired a drill hall where his men lived during intense training periods, and, under the formidable Ellsworth discipline, his troop quickly achieved a wide reputation. It was Elmer Ellsworth's Zouaves who now awed the brilliant New York Irrepressibles and won their admiration and cheers. The Irrepressibles were being honored, and outdone. Soon after their Chicago convention appearance, Ellsworth's Zouaves went on national tour. Abraham Lincoln, who called young Ellsworth "the greatest little man I ever saw," invited him to come to Springfield to study law with him and Herndon, an invitation Ellsworth accepted following his tour. When the Civil War began, hundreds of Zouave companies, all copied from Ellsworth's, were called into the Federal army, where they made superlative targets for Confederate sharpshooters.

*   *   *

William Seward's awesome power was fully as great as *Press and Tribune* editors and Lincoln supporters feared. It seemed that the entire East now was for Seward. Since Weed's agents had gone about reasoning with editors and proprietors, scarcely a seaboard newspaper mentioned

Lincoln's name, except for the autobiography that had been planted by Jesse Fell. The machinations of Thurlow Weed were obvious; his experienced hands reached, grasped, and twisted everywhere. His candidate, the egotistical Seward, who once described Weed as "the tyrant I love," was able enough and fully qualified by experience, though somewhat lacking physically as a presidential hopeful. Henry Adams described him as "a slouching, slender figure with a head like a wise macaw, a beaked nose, shaggy eyebrows, red hair, a free talker, a perpetual smoker." Weed and Seward might easily have smashed the efforts of "the *Tribune* clique" to nominate Lincoln, had it not been for one major mistake—after a quarter of a century of close collaboration, the two had turned their political partner Horace Greeley into a vengeful, implacable enemy. The Syracuse Republican convention, mostly Whigs by another name, had not even chosen Uncle Horace as a delegate to Chicago. So the moon-faced editor, unpredictable and eccentric and yearning for the presidency himself, got an appointment as a delegate from the new state of Oregon, and went to Chicago to seize control of Missouri's Edward Bates delegation and to plot the ruination of his former cronies. "Anybody but Seward!" was Greeley's cry.

Boss Weed, a tall, suave, gracious man, held court in the Richmond House, receiving the various delegations. He warned Iowa not to repeat the mistake it had made at Philadelphia, helping to nominate Frémont, a sure loser. Iowa was inclined toward Lincoln, but where could Lincoln find votes east of Illinois? Where would the campaign money come from? With Seward as the Republican candidate, said Weed, he could raise money from big business, especially those seeking water, transportation, and gas franchises. William Cullen Bryant reported to his newspaper, the *New York Post,* that Weed had a pork barrel of nearly half a million dollars for the support of Seward. Carl Schurz, the German educator who had once favored Seward, declared that Weed was making deals that could not be carried out with honor. George Schneider of the *Staats-Zeitung,* once a Lincoln man but later for Seward as a candidate who could be elected, was impressed by Schurz's revulsion. Schneider was wavering. Greeley, out to undo Weed's efforts, could buttonhole only a few old cronies in behalf of Bates of Missouri. Not many politicians wished to pay close attention to cherubic Uncle Horace, yet they could not afford to ignore his *New York Tribune.* He was still popular with the crowds in the streets, and a *Press and Tribune* reporter followed him about to ask his opinion of Lincoln. "The trouble with Lincoln is that he has no experience in national affairs," said Greeley. "He is too risky."

On the night prior to the convention opening, both Greeley and Murat Halstead of the *Cincinnati Commercial* telegraphed their newspapers that Seward appeared unbeatable for the nomination. More than

10,000 people accepted the New York delegation's invitation to a rally at the Wigwam that night. But Thurlow Weed's plan to use the meeting to whip up enthusiasm for Seward was foiled by Pennsylvania's William D. ("Pig Iron") Kelley, who, on pretense of offering a routine motion, gained the floor and then refused to relinquish it, his harangue lasting until nearly midnight, by which time the weary audience had dwindled to fewer than a thousand.

While Pig Iron Kelley's stentorian voice filled the Wigwam, the Lincoln strategists were operating a busy intelligence and command post at the Tremont House under the direction of Judge David Davis, 300 pounds of political wisdom, persuasion, and ruthless force, all of it totally dedicated to Abraham Lincoln. Dr. Ray and Joseph Medill shared with Davis some responsibility for the Ohio, Indiana, and Pennsylvania delegations, with Medill, of course, expected to have important influence within the Ohio group. The *Chicago Press and Tribune* had published a special edition, summarizing its many arguments and exhortations in behalf of Honest Old Abe in an editorial confidently headed "The Winning Man." Nevertheless, the editors were extremely worried by Seward's strength. They spent much time in Judge Davis's back room witnessing his efforts to capture votes and soon were themselves involved in Davis's intrigues. Medill commented years later, "There was more management of the nomination of Lincoln than has been set down in history."

In anticipation of some of the political necessities, Charles Ray had written a note to Lincoln, who remained in Springfield throughout the convention.

> Your friends are at work for you hard, and with great success. Your show on the first ballot will not be confined to Illinois, and after that it will be strongly developed. But you need a few trusty friends here to say words for you that it may be necessary to be said. Dare you put yourself in the hands of Judd, David Davis, and, if there is no better man, Ray? A pledge or two may be necessary when the pinch comes.

At the Tremont House Judge Davis struggled for every possible erg of Lincoln leverage. Working with him almost without sleep were Norman Judd, Jesse Fell, Stephen T. Logan, Isaac N. Arnold, Leonard Swett, John Palmer, Medill, and Ray, with Billy Herndon hovering on the fringes, though in no official capacity. Before the convention opened, Davis himself hog-tied the Indiana delegation with a promise that Lincoln would name Caleb B. Smith secretary of the interior. Dr. Ray accompanied him, and later told Medill, "By the Lord, we promised them everything they asked." Medill visited his friends on the Ohio delegation. Near midnight he returned to the Tremont House feeling somewhat optimistic but lacking a commitment.

All of the men had been scurrying for votes and trying for deals when a telegram arrived from Lincoln on the second day of the convention, saying: "I AUTHORIZE NO BARGAINS AND WILL BE BOUND BY NONE." Norman Judd swore fervently. The others stared blankly at one another, until the imperturbable Judge Davis gruffly gave them guidance: "Lincoln ain't here, and don't know what we have to meet." And so, on the eve of the balloting, Davis went calling on the Pennsylvanians. In the early hours of May 18, the big man returned to Lincoln headquarters, grinning triumphantly. "Damned if we haven't got 'em!" he exclaimed. Someone asked, "How?" "By paying their price," Davis replied. Medill and Dr. Ray didn't learn the price until later, and it appalled them: the treasury post for Simon Cameron. Yet Ray was said to have called it "a small price when playing for the presidency." If so, Ray recanted, for the *Tribune* later fought bitterly against the appointment of Cameron, accusing him of dishonesty. (Cameron, a Pennsylvania newspaper publisher, financier, and canal and railroad builder, was said to have defined an honest politician as "one who when bought, stays bought.")

The efforts of Lincoln's supporters were not limited to behind-the-scenes dealing, for convention seating arrangements were in the hands of Judd and Medill. Years later, Medill described the strategy:

> It was the meanest trick I ever did in my life. New York was for Seward, and the isolation of its delegates was desired by the Lincoln men. Pennsylvania was the most important doubtful State. It followed that the New York delegates were seated at one end of the vast hall with no State for neighbor that was not hopelessly for Seward. At the other end of the hall, so far away that the voices of the Seward orators could scarcely be heard was placed Pennsylvania. Between Pennsylvania and New York were placed the Lincoln delegates from Illinois, also those of Indiana and New Jersey.

The Lincoln strategists passed out hundreds of lower floor convention tickets to the members of the Wide Awake Lincoln clubs. Judd, the Rock Island Railroad attorney, arranged with the various railroads to sell cut-rate tickets to any Lincoln supporters who wished to visit Chicago. These visitors were not needed the first two days of the convention but were instructed to report hours early on the third day. Consequently, when the Seward Irrepressibles and other convention guests reached the Wigwam on the third day, they found it packed to the doors with howling Lincoln enthusiasts.

It was showdown time on May 18. Thurlow Weed had spread about money and promises, but also his reputation for New York political dealing, a kind not appreciated in the West, where the ethics were different if not better. The more Weed spent, the more his gold-braided bands and Irrepressibles paraded for Seward, the better Lincoln looked as the "rail splitter" and man of the people. Seward had done himself no good by once declaring that an "irrepressible" conflict lay ahead for the nation. Lincoln had outlined a safer way, to let the slave states continue in slavery, which seemed a solution if one did not recall his "House Divided" speech. A ruckus over convention tickets—it turned out that Jesse Fell had printed extras, and it was these that were distributed to the Wide Awakes—delayed the opening of the convention for nearly two hours. Chairman George Ashmun of Massachusetts got the proceedings under way at noon, and following prayer and routine announcements, recognized William Maxwell Evarts, a New York lawyer noted for his florid and prolix manner of speech. Evarts took the podium, glanced malevolently at the thousands of Lincoln supporters packing the floor before him, and began and finished in a single sentence, "Mr. Chairman, I take the liberty, sir, to name as candidate to be nominated by this convention for the office of president, William H. Seward, of New York." There was a stunned silence at Evarts's restraint, then a shout from the Seward supporters, who were numerous among the delegates and alternates if not among the visitors and guests.

Norman Judd was equally succinct: "I desire, on behalf of the delegation from Illinois, to put in nomination as candidate for president of the United States, Abraham Lincoln of Illinois." Special shouters, one reputedly able to yell across Lake Michigan, had been placed about the hall, but even their yells were drowned in the turmoil. Indiana seconded the nomination, and other nominations followed—Cameron, Bates, Chase. The roll call began, and Seward quickly pushed ahead, until it was Seward 123^1/$_2$, Lincoln 102, Cameron 50^1/$_2$, Chase 49, Bates 48. Needed to nominate, 233.

On the second ballot the big Pennsylvania delegation broke for Lincoln with 48 votes, a result of the deal by Judge Davis to insure a cabinet seat for favorite son Cameron. Lincoln gained a total of 79 votes, while Seward picked up only 11. The tension grew fierce in the steaming hall, the Lincoln backers unruly as the clerk began the roll of states on the third ballot, but Ashmun obtained order and the roll call resumed. Lincoln was picking up, until his total reached 231^1/$_2$, one and a half short of the nomination. Joseph Medill was seated among his former neighbors in the Ohio delegation. He whispered to chairman David Cartter, who had placed Salmon Chase's name in nomination: "If you can take Ohio to Lincoln, Chase can have anything he wants." "How do you know?" Cartter demanded suspiciously. "I know and I wouldn't promise if I didn't," Medill answered. Cartter, who stammered when excited, shot up, signaling for attention: "Mr. Chairman! I-I-I a-arise to announce a ch-change of f-f-four votes, f-f-f-rom Mr. Ch-Chase to Mr. Lincoln."

There was a second of silence, then the vast Wigwam literally shook with sound as men yelled and stomped; women in the balcony screamed their delight and tossed down upon the crowd handkerchiefs, scarves, and flowers; and the cannon on the Wigwam roof was fired. Soon boat whistles screeched and moaned along the river, the courthouse bell sounded, and church bells about the city responded. According to the *Press and Tribune:*

> The scene [*was*] absolutely impossible to describe. It is equally impossible for one not present to imagine the scene in the Wigwam when Lincoln was nominated. Without attempting, therefore, to convey an idea of the delirious cheers, the Babel of joy and excitement, we may mention that strong men wept like children, that two candidates for gubernatorial chairs of their respective states, who looked to the nomination of Honest Old Abe to carry the Republican cause at home through the storm, sank down in excess of joy.

The Illinois delegates, especially Medill and Dr. Ray, took enormous pride in the accomplishment; they felt that their strategy and tactics had taken the nomination away from the man who had come to Chicago seeming certain of victory. There could be little doubt that the steady embellishment of Lincoln's name, and the highly skilled maneuvers of the Illinois politicians on the scene, deserved much credit, but there was also the influence of another man, a delegate from the new state of Oregon who gained vengeance that day for slights and insults visited upon him while the Weed, Seward, and Greeley triumvirate endured. Horace Greeley held 48 Bates votes from Seward through the second ballot, and when the tally was announced, John Defrees, chairman of the Indiana delegation, telegraphed Schuyler Colfax at South Bend: "GREELEY HAS SLAUGHTERED SEWARD BUT HAS SAVED THE REPUBLICAN PARTY." Said Thurlow Weed: "I have done with Greeley." Hannibal Hamlin, of Maine, was nominated as Lincoln's running mate, and a moderate Republican platform was adopted.

That night Chicago celebrated, as did Springfield. The *Press and Tribune* building was illuminated "by the glare of a thousand lights." From the split rails the paper had been displaying now hung banners reading, "For President—Honest Old Abe—for Vice President—Hannibal Hamlin." A procession of Wide Awakes paraded along Clark Street and stopped at the *Press and Tribune* offices to cheer. In Springfield, Abraham Lincoln had received the news in the offices of the *Journal* and went home to report to Mary. That night neighbors and friends called at his house to congratulate him. The *Press and Tribune* on May 19 published an editorial widely reprinted, "The Man of the People." It extolled Lincoln, compared him with the great men of history, and concluded:

> No fact stands out more clearly than this—that Abraham Lincoln is indebted to the people—not to the politicians—for his nomination. From every part of our country where freedom is cherished, the voice of the

people came up in unmistakable tones, calling for the nomination of honest old Abe. Neither personal effort, neither private pledges, neither promise of office nor of patronage, were used to secure the end. They are wholly ignorant of the character of Abraham Lincoln who suppose him to be capable of any of these things. Men peculiarly fitted for great occasions are sought for and called to their work by the spontaneous, unbought suffrages of the people; and never was the fact more signally illustrated than in the nomination of Abraham Lincoln. And now that he stands before the country as a candidate of the people's own choosing, it requires no gift of prescience to foretell the result. As surely as the sun shall rise upon election day, just so surely will the people of this nation place the man of the people at the head of the government.

It was said that Dr. Ray wrote the editorial. If so, he forgot in his enthusiasm and excitement some of the details of the convention maneuvers, which caused Lincoln later to complain, "They have gambled me all around, bought and sold me a hundred times. I cannot begin to fill all the pledges made in my name."

*   *   *

Nearly three weeks before the Republicans convened in Chicago, the Democrats had attempted to nominate a national ticket at Charleston, South Carolina, on April 23. Stephen A. Douglas, 47 years old that day, seemed the sure candidate for the presidential nomination, and Murat Halstead, of the *Cincinnati Commercial,* reported that Douglas delegates from the East and Northwest were making progress in their efforts to conciliate the South, though they also were "brim full of the sound and fury of boastfulness." The convention began quietly enough, and both Douglas supporters and opponents agreed that the platform should be adopted before nominations could be considered. It was a fateful decision for the Douglas men; the convention became hopelessly split on the popular sovereignty issue, and after protracted debate, eight Southern states walked out. The remaining delegates adopted a platform they hoped would placate the absent states, then attempted to select a candidate. Douglas received a majority of votes on the first ballot, but a two-thirds vote was required, and after two days and 57 ballots the Little Giant was still short of victory. On May 3, the convention adjourned without a nomination, agreeing to reconvene in June.

On May 10, the Constitutional Union party, mostly former Whigs and Know-Nothings, nominated John Bell of Tennessee for president and Edward Everett of Massachusetts for vice-president. Douglasites were pleased, since Bell's candidacy would make inroads into the strength of Republican front-runner William Seward, and Seward himself would drive moderates to support Douglas. But when the Republicans met in

Chicago, the "availability" argument prevailed, and Lincoln, not Seward, was nominated.

The Democrats reconvened in Baltimore on June 18. From a convention marred by credentials challenges, platform disputes, and the withdrawal of more Deep South delegations, Stephen Douglas emerged the presidential nominee. His original running mate withdrew from the ticket, and Herschel V. Johnson of Georgia reluctantly became the candidate, writing to a friend, *"I was literally forced to take the V. Pret. nomination."* Commented the *Press and Tribune,* "Yesterday we witnessed the expiring throes of the Democratic party in the United States. It has long been suffering from delirium tremens and at last it 'fell headlong and burst asunder and all the bowels gushed out.'" On June 28, the dissident Southern Democrats nominated John C. Breckinridge of Kentucky for president and Joseph Lane of Oregon for vice-president.

The *Press and Tribune* was cheered by the results of the four conventions, calling the Constitutional Union party the "Do-Nothings" and forecasting that Douglas would have to run against Lincoln in the North and Breckinridge in the South, a forecast of considerable prescience.

*   *   *

The *Chicago Press and Tribune,* having obtained the nomination of Abraham Lincoln, as it would repeatedly assert, and having made itself the leading newspaper in Illinois and a dominant influence in the Northwest, was not about to have its laurels filched by the miscreant press of the misled East. To the seaboard newspapers attributing Lincoln's victory to Horace Greeley, the *Press and Tribune* responded angrily on May 25: "It is the stupidest blunder into which . . . responsible newspapers could possibly have fallen. The truth is, Mr. Greeley opposed Lincoln down to the last moment with just as much earnestness as he opposed Seward, and Mr. Thurlow Weed, though working industriously no doubt, failed so far as we know to win a single vote."

Lincoln's nomination was no fortuitous chance, the *Press and Tribune* insisted. "The Illinois unit rule was important to the planning. Then Indiana was won over. Lincoln's conservative record, his ability displayed against Douglas and his honesty known to the world formed a happy combination for which the country is looking." The *Press and Tribune* took no breather but at once resumed its activist thrust. Within days of the nomination it republished John Scripps's biography of Lincoln, which it later issued as a pamphlet of 32 pages. A *Press and Tribune* campaign special was announced, to be sold at cost to individuals and at even less than cost to such organizations as the Wide Awakes. A series of campaign pamphlets was prepared by the *Press and Tribune* writers and editors and printed on *Press and Tribune* equipment.

The *Press and Tribune* gave strong support to the Republican platform, which actually said much less about slavery than did the paper: It emphasized free western lands for settlers ("Vote yourself a farm," some politicians urged), the construction of a railroad to the Pacific at government expense, and a protective tariff. On June 7, the paper felt required to justify its extensive campaign coverage and enthusiasm for the Republican candidate: "It is expressly understood that the *Press and Tribune* is in no sense Mr. Lincoln's organ. We have never consulted him about what was said or unsaid in this paper. That we in some sort aided his nomination is true, but our poor service in that regard gives us no claim to speak for him." After this lapse into modesty, the paper lashed out against a new enemy, James Gordon Bennett and his *New York Herald.* "Old Man Bennett . . . is again at his stupendous lies, calling Lincoln a ferocious John Brown abolitionist," the paper said. It then reprinted remarks Lincoln had made during the debate with Douglas at Charleston, Illinois, wherein he promised not to disturb slavery.

*   *   *

Though much preoccupied with the political campaign and the ominous secessionist rumblings from the South, the *Press and Tribune* did not neglect the multifold other interests of its readers. There were commercial reports, general Chicago and Northwest news, fascinating stories from the western goldfields, especially those of the Pikes Peak area, and dispatches from Europe, as well as timeless oddments snipped from British newspapers, features to please the ladies, and nods to cultural needs, such as poetry, travel letters, book reviews, book serializations, and Sam Slick essays reprinted from the Dublin University magazine and other literary publications. The news wherever it occurred was well covered. When a tornado swept through Iowa and northern Illinois, killing at least 100 persons, the *Press and Tribune* continued the columns of reports for days, until every destroyed village and farm was accounted for. Then the paper launched a special benefit concert in the Wigwam to raise funds for the storm victims. The date chosen, June 12, turned out to be the Reverend William Patton's prayer meeting night. When he objected, the *Press and Tribune* editorialist informed him crisply that the paper felt the Lord would overlook the infraction because of the nature of the cause.

Adelina Patti sang in Bryan Hall that summer, winning the praises of the young *Press and Tribune* critic George P. Upton, and the town was agog when Mayor Wentworth, after a quick trip to Montreal, succeeded in inducing the Prince of Wales, later Edward VII, traveling as Baron Renfrew, to change his plans to include Chicago in August. The event was a smashing social success, of such elevation that Mrs. Roxanna

Wentworth came to town for the banquet honoring the young prince and remained at the Tremont House for several weeks.

In the predawn hours of September 8, there was a major disaster. As the passenger steamer *Lady Elgin,* a 1,000-ton side-wheeler owned by Gurdon S. Hubbard, was returning from Chicago to Milwaukee with nearly 400 excursionists aboard, it was rammed amidships by the lumber schooner *Augusta,* running without lights. There were 297 lives lost when the boat went down off Winnetka, despite heroic rescue efforts by a group of Northwestern University students.

But it was politics most of the time throughout the summer and fall. "The prairies are on fire," the *Press and Tribune* reported, predicting that Lincoln would carry Illinois by 20,000 votes. Everywhere in the state the Republican rallies were most enthusiastic, the paper said, and more than 75,000 called on Lincoln for an "at home" in Springfield, with 50 Wide Awake clubs in the procession, which was reported to have stretched for ten miles. Said the *Press and Tribune* on August 10, "We are very sure that this gathering was never surpassed in the West, if, indeed, any part of the Union." There were worrisome days, too. Though he had been snubbed by Norman Judd at the national convention and continued to be ostracized by his journalistic peers, Long John Wentworth persisted in claiming to be a Republican and a friend of Lincoln, and this was causing problems. Medill wrote to Lincoln in mid-summer, warning him that Long John was up to no good. *"His plan is to pretend that he is your devoted friend; that you are an ultra abolitionist who will if elected put down slavery in the South. He professes to adore the spirit of liberty. John Brown is worshipped by him. . . . If he can make people in the North believe that you are a radical ultra fanatic he expects that it will drive the conservative moderate voters away from you."*

Wentworth had indeed praised John Brown as a martyr in his *Chicago Democrat,* and there were others besides Medill who doubted the sincerity of his conversion to Lincoln and Republicanism. Some thought that he hoped a Lincoln defeat would mean the defeat of the forces in the state legislature that had elected Trumbull to the U.S. Senate, and that Wentworth himself wanted to acquire a Senate seat. The *Press and Tribune* attacked the Republican mayor almost daily—for failure to clean up crime, for associating with gamblers and consorting with women of low repute, for general malfeasance in office. Medill wrote letters denouncing him to Eastern editors, and it was suggested in the *Tribune* that if Wentworth's portrayal of Lincoln in his paper as a radical abolitionist was not malevolent and calculated duplicity, then the only acceptable explanation was Wentworth's insanity. Lincoln refused to repudiate Long John despite all criticism, and Wentworth did not, in the end, disappoint him.

In the last days of the presidential campaign, the *Press and Tribune* proprietors announced that henceforth their paper would be known as the *Chicago Daily Tribune,* though they themselves referred to the paper simply as "the *Chicago Tribune.*" The final efforts in behalf of Lincoln were prodigious. The paper denounced the canard that Lincoln was a radical bent on stamping out slavery in the South. At the same time it attacked the Southern states as extremists ready to smash the Union for the sake of immoral slave exploitation. It printed excerpts from Lincoln speeches, the Republican platform, and its array of special pamphlets, and it declared that the real issue was the preservation of the Union: "This fight is for the rescue of free principles, for good, honest, economical government, and for perpetuity of the Union."

On election day, November 6, the paper exhorted all to vote. "New York and Illinois will decide. The labor of six years centers in this day." The paper said that election returns would be received and displayed at the *Tribune* office as well as the Wigwam, the Tremont House, and the Briggs House.

"THE GREAT VICTORY" was announced in five columns on page one on November 7. "REPUBLICANS TRIUMPHANT OVER FRAUD, FUSION, COTTON, DISUNION AND TREASON. HONEST OLD ABE ELECTED . . . REJOICE AND BE GLAD." Two hundred guns were fired in salute from the Randolph Street bridge. The paper said that some 10,000 Wide Awakes celebrated the victory with "a procession ten miles long," and on the night of November 8 other thousands, 16 abreast, paid tribute to the *Chicago Tribune* by performing their evolutions at 51 Clark Street.

The *Tribune,* triumphant, dominant, powerful, and nationally influential, chose a posture of caution and forbearance:

> Now while in the flush of triumph achieved after years of waiting and working, while the smoke of the conflict is in our garments, it will be wise and discreet of Republicans to avoid all causes of additional irritation and to convince the people of the South by our words and acts that we are not half so fierce and ravenous as we have been represented—that we are still their countrymen—bound to them by a thousand ties, which we would not rupture if we could!

CHICAGO DAILY TRIBUNE.

WHEELER, STEWART, & SCRIPPS—Editors.

OFFICE, 159 LAKE STREET.

CHICAGO, ILLINOIS.

VOL. II.

MONDAY, APRIL 23, 1849.

12½ CTS. PER WEEK

Above: Newspaperman Joseph Medill as he appeared in 1855, when he decided to sell his interest in the *Cleveland Leader* and seek his fortune in the West, purchasing a share in the struggling *Chicago Tribune*.

Opposite page: Joseph Medill's brothers accompanied him to Chicago, where they worked for the *Tribune* as printers. James (top left) and William (bottom right) died while serving in the Union Army during the Civil War. Samuel Medill (top right) became *Tribune* managing editor in 1875, a position he held until his death in 1883. Another man making the journey from Ohio was Alfred Cowles (bottom left), who had worked for the *Cleveland Leader*. Cowles was the *Tribune*'s business manager for over 30 years and for a time was the paper's major shareholder.

Opposite page: Dr. Charles Ray (top left), former editor of the *Galena Jeffersonian* and an ardent abolitionist, was Joseph Medill's associate in purchasing an interest in the *Tribune.* (HUNTINGTON LIBRARY) Horace White (bottom left) joined the staff in 1857 and was assigned to accompany Abraham Lincoln during his 1858 senatorial canvass. After the Civil War, White engaged Medill in a struggle over editorial policy and for nearly a decade exercised effective control of the paper. When the *Tribune* merged with the *Democratic Press* in 1858, John Locke Scripps (top right) and William Bross (bottom right) became co-proprietors of the *Chicago Daily Press and Tribune,* renamed the *Chicago Tribune* in 1860.

Below: On a visit to Chicago in 1858, Lincoln posed for an itinerant daguerreotypist, holding a copy of the *Daily Press and Tribune.* (THE LOUIS A. WARREN LINCOLN LIBRARY AND MUSEUM, FORT WAYNE, INDIANA) The letter was written by Lincoln in 1859 to renew his subscription and to thank the paper for its support in his campaign against Stephen Douglas. The *Tribune* would claim a large share of the credit for Lincoln's election to the U.S. presidency in 1860.

Chicago Tribune.

VOLUME XV. CHICAGO, TUESDAY, FEBRUARY 18, 1862. NUMBER 190.

THE OCCUPATION OF SAVANNAH.

PART OF THE
COAST OF S. CAROLINA

The Seat of War on the Southern Coast.

THE LATEST NEWS
BY TELEGRAPH.

DAY OF GREAT EVENTS.

Fort Donelson Taken

SAVANNAH OCCUPIED

Reported Evacuation of Columbus.

Three Rebel Generals and 15,000 Troops Prisoners.

THE FT. DONELSON VICTORY.

Latest and Most Complete Particulars.

SAVANNAH CAPTURED!

THE TWO FLAGS.

This is the glorious old banner that now floats in triumph over Fort Donelson.

THE STAR SPANGLED BANNER

And here is the emblem that slunk away before the resistless valor of our Illinois boys, and will hurry to hide itself in the closest fastnesses of Whippy Swamp.

THE RATTLESNAKE FLAG.

Citizens, study these two emblems in the light of the stern conflict on the Cumberland. Did they die in vain and for a worthless prize who laid down their lives at Donelson that the starry flag might float again over a re-united land?

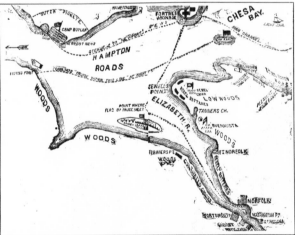

The *Tribune* was heavily involved in the Civil War and became nationally known for both its staunch support of the Northern cause and its excellent news reports. In addition to the editors, who wrote articles critical of the way the war was being prosecuted, more than a score of correspondents covered the action for the paper.
Opposite page: The *Tribune* of February 18, 1862 (top), exulting over the capture of Savannah and General Grant's victory at Fort Donelson, shows the paper's new type dress and makeup and the excellent map service developed during the war. The chart at bottom right appeared on March 11, 1862, to illustrate the setting for the battle of the *Monitor* and the *Merrimac,* which inaugurated the era of ironclad warships.
Below: The end of the Civil War, announced in the *Tribune* of April 10, 1865, was greeted with great joy, the paper illuminating its building with fireworks for vast crowds.

Chicago Tribune.

VOL. XVIII.   CHICAGO, SATURDAY, APRIL 15, 1865.   NUMBER 280.

NEWS BY TELEGRAPH.

JEFF. DAVIS ON THE SITUATION.

HE ISSUES AN EDICT AT DANVILLE.

He Thinks that Lee can now Strike the Enemy in Detail.

And will never Abandon a foot of Territory.

Graphic Details of the Surrender of Lee.

SHERMAN LEFT GOLDSBORO ON THE 10TH.

REPORT THAT HIS FORCES ARE AT RALEIGH.

GEN. SHERIDAN REPORTED TO BE IN DANVILLE.

Important Union Movement in Alabama and Mississippi.

GEN. MAURY'S CHIEF OF STAFF KILLED AT MOBILE.

GEN. WEITZEL RELIEVED OF HIS COMMAND.

POSTSCRIPT.

TERRIBLE NEWS

President Lincoln Assassinated at Ford's Theater.

A REBEL DESPERADO SHOOTS HIM THROUGH THE HEAD AND ESCAPES.

Secretary Seward and Major Fred Seward Stabbed by Another Desperado.

THEIR WOUNDS ARE PRONOUNCED NOT FATAL.

Full Details of the Terrible Affair.

UNDOUBTED PLAN TO MURDER SECRETARY STANTON.

Very Latest—The President is Dying.

On April 15, 1865, the *Tribune* proclaimed the "TERRIBLE NEWS" of President Lincoln's assassination.

"THE WIND BLOWS
FROM THE NORTH"

7

The nation's president-elect was a man who sought above all to preserve the United States as one Union, rejecting radical and divisive philosophies. Even before the campaign ended, however, his opponent had expressed to friends his fears for the future of that Union. "Lincoln is the next president. We must try to save the Union. I will go south," Senator Douglas told his secretary, James Sheridan. The Democratic candidate was thinking neither of himself, nor his party, but of his country, and he did go south and spoke conciliatory words, as Lincoln did in Springfield after the election. But the details of Lincoln's victory presaged troubled times, for though he had won a clear majority of the electoral votes, in ten Southern states he received not one popular vote.

The time for compromise was past, though Sen. John J. Crittenden, of Kentucky, attempted it by proposing constitutional amendments. On December 20, 1860, the day a Senate committee gathered to consider Crittenden's proposals, South Carolina, by a vote of 169 to 0 in a special convention, chose to secede from the Union, an action President Buchanan had said no state could legally take—nor the government of the United States legally prevent. In the various Southern states, the Federal forts and arsenals were manned by forces too small to hold them for the Union should the surrounding populace prove hostile. On December 27, while other Southern states were calling secession conventions, the South Carolina militia occupied Fort Moultrie and Castle Pinckney after the small Federal garrison under Maj. Robert Anderson abandoned Moultrie for safer Fort Sumter, in Charleston Harbor.

Neither the Crittenden committee nor a similar committee in the House of Representatives could agree on any plan for compromise, and President Buchanan remained unwilling to act when South Carolina seized the Federal arsenal at Charleston. On December 28, 1860, the *Chicago Tribune* denounced "the hoary headed traitor in the White House" and called for his impeachment. "The question of the hour," it said, "is—shall the Union be preserved?" And on January 1, 1861: "In view of the miserable spectacle which the country now presents—treason and rebellion in the South, treason and scheming in the Cabinet, and indignation filling the hearts of the people, energetic patriotism, which holds self and party as nothing if they stand in the way, is demanded." Two days later a *Tribune* editorial said:

> What a sight! The leading politicians of a great and once liberty-loving and patriotic party, the chief executive offices of the government, a full half of the people of one section of the Republic, all plotting and conspiring against the perpetuity of the fairest political fabric ever built by human hands, and provoking civil war between brothers—for what? That the representatives of a little Oligarchy of 374,000 slave-holders may have the privilege, not authorized by the Constitution, of buying, selling, working without pay and whipping at will, men, women and children in the Territories which God made free. . . . We are not the advocates of a policy which will bring slavery to a sudden end at the point of a bayonet, [*but*] we insist *that the Union and the supremacy of the Constitution be maintained.*

Joseph Medill was again in Washington, keeping a *Tribune* pledge that it intended to maintain one of its editors in the national capital during such perilous times. His dispatches were pessimistic, forecasting seizure of arsenals, the secession of six more states, an attack on Fort Sumter, and an invasion of Washington in March to prevent the inauguration of President-elect Lincoln. Charles Ray was spending much of his time in Springfield, where he consulted regularly with Abraham Lincoln, who was receiving delegations, considering cabinet appointments, discussing his problems with friends and former adversaries alike, and granting a few newspaper interviews. Horace Greeley, of the *New York Tribune*, got three hours of his time, but a Missouri newspaper that had fought Lincoln throughout the campaign aroused his ire when it demanded his statement on secession and possible civil war. *"Please pardon me for suggesting that if the papers like yours, which heretofore have persistently garbled, and misrepresented what I have said, will now fully and fairly place it before their readers, there can be no further misunderstanding. . . . The Republican newspapers now, and for some time past, are and have been republishing copious extracts from my many published speeches, which would at once reach the whole public if your class of papers would also publish them,"* Lincoln told the Missouri editor. *"I am not at liberty to shift my ground—that is out of the question. If I thought a* repetition *would do any good I would make it. But my judgment is it would do positive harm. The secessionists,* per se *believing they had alarmed me, would clamor all the louder."*

As the year drew to a close, Medill wrote a brief letter to President-elect Lincoln, warning him that the anti-Unionists intended to have an army in Washington within five weeks. Then Medill entrained for Chicago. On New Year's Day, despite the grim national news, the *Tribune* was in a relatively cheerful mood. Business was good; the paper's circulation stood above 24,000. "The prospects of Chicago becoming the leading commercial center of the great Northwest were never so flattering as now," the paper said. The winter weather was beautiful, with sleighs and bobsleds in the streets and skaters on the river. Medill, home for a few days, called at the office to see if preparations had been made for the new Hoe press that had been ordered, and read in print his recent letter from Washington, saying in part, "Civil war is on the eve of breaking out. Treason is stalking forth in the light of day and comforted by the administration itself. The men in power, from the President down, are busy sapping and mining the foundations of the Union."

At some time during the day, the *Tribune* editors had a conference on an issue that agitated them all, Lincoln's intention to name Simon Cameron, Pennsylvania political boss, senator, and a general in the Pennsylvania militia, to a cabinet post. They also were incensed that Ebenezer Peck, the longtime silent partner in the *Chicago Democrat,* and Charles Wilson, editor of the *Journal,* both dared to request appointment as Chicago postmaster. The patronage position, which would have to be approved by Senator Trumbull, traditionally went to a newspaper official, and Medill, Ray, and Bross were determined that it must go to a *Chicago Tribune* man. They chose Scripps for the honor. Scripps ultimately was named postmaster by Lincoln, but the president-elect's insistence on honoring the promise made by David Davis to Cameron at the Republican convention threatened to end the support of the *Tribune,* and to alienate much of the Middle West. *"Dismay reigns among our friends at the capital tonight,"* Congressman Washburne wrote Dr. Ray on January 2. *"The confirmation of the report that Cameron goes into Lincoln's cabinet literally appalled them. . . . If you have any influence* [with Lincoln] *for God's sake, use it!"*

Two days later Medill, back in Washington, directed an angry letter to Horace White: *"White, this appointment fills the hearts of our Senators and Representatives with apprehension. . . . This awful appointment . . . installing the Harrisburg lobby and the 40 thieves."* As he learned more of the nature of the proposed cabinet over the next few days, Medill wrote anguished letters to his other *Tribune* colleagues. *"If reports from Springfield are true, there will not be one* original Lincoln *man in the Cabinet. It will be made up from his many competitors and enemies. . . . Thank heaven we own and control the* Trib. *We made Abe and by G— we can unmake him."* Medill suggested not only that Davis was responsible for *"pushing Cameron on Lincoln,"* but that he was *"one of Weed's gang."*

"We feared Lincoln was indebted to certain factions and now it is proved," Medill wrote to Ray, conveniently overlooking his and Ray's connivance in the convention deals made to insure Lincoln's nomination. *"Lincoln is a failure. Perhaps it is best to let disunionists take Washington and let Lincoln stay in Springfield."* Yet at the same time, Medill was writing for publication, "Abandon all idea of having the oath administered to Lincoln in Springfield or anywhere else, save on the east portico of the Capitol. The American people will listen to no other suggestion. The wind blows from the North this time. Any attempt to seize the capital, or the archives of government or to prevent the inauguration of the President-elect, will be resisted by a million men in arms."

Medill's jeremiads about Lincoln's appointments and actions would go on throughout the war, but only in private correspondence. His public support for Lincoln never wavered, nor did Medill hesitate later to discuss frankly those occasions when Lincoln chastised him, sometimes severely. Lincoln too wrote angry letters, though he rarely mailed them. In both cases, the letters have become public knowledge only in history. During the long crisis, Lincoln, Medill, and Ray were often critical of one another, but they worked together. When Medill's concerns about Cameron excited Congressman Elihu Washburne, for example, it was Ray who kept cool, writing Washburne, *"Keep your shirt on. Cameron has no place in the cabinet and will not get one—that's sure."* The treasury post went to Salmon Chase, but Cameron was named secretary of war—Judge Davis had promised—and in January, 1862, following army contract scandals, Cameron was sent as minister to Russia. Thus Lincoln kept the word of his friends and forged a working force needed to govern the North and wage war, a force composed mostly of men who had sought to defeat him but who represented the required elements for a Northern consensus, and victory.

Early in January, 1861, the *Tribune* sponsored a mass meeting to rally support for the Union. There was ominous news from southern Illinois: Southern sympathizers had stopped 30 river barges at Cairo and threatened to close the Ohio and Mississippi rivers to Northern traffic. The *Tribune* noted strong Southern sympathy in Indiana as well and spoke of fears that if secession continued to spread, Indiana could be lost to the Union.

Dispatches to the *Tribune* were alarming. On January 8, writing under the pen name "Chicago," Medill disclosed a Southern plot set for February 15, the day the presidential electoral votes were to be officially counted. Guerrillas from Southern states would raid Washington, stop the voting, and take over the government. However, Medill added, Gen. Winfield Scott, commander-in-chief of the Federal forces, was making preparations to protect the capital. On January 9, South Carolina guns fired on the unarmed U.S. ship *Star of the West,* which sought unsuccessfully to resupply Fort Sumter. That same day Mississippi became the second state to secede from the Union; Florida, Alabama, Georgia, Louisiana, and Texas would follow within a month. Forts, arsenals, and other Federal properties were seized, as expected, by the seceding states. In St. Louis, it was feared that Southern sympathizers might take the guns in the Federal arsenal. In New York, Mayor Fernando Wood proposed that the city declare itself free and neutral in event of hostilities between North and South.

On January 21, Medill reported gloomily that President Buchanan would take no action against the rebels, regardless of provocation. "He says that if there is to be any fighting, his successor will have to do it. He will give no other pledge than to preserve peace in this district on March 4. The imbecile old creature has completely shown the white feather since the '*Star of the West*' was cannonaded by the insurgents. But the country has only to endure six weeks more of this miserable cowardice, incompetence and disloyalty."

The *Tribune* helped to organize another rally, this one for the younger men who would be expected to do the fighting in the event of war. It began publishing a daily column on the "Progress of Treason" in the South, and it reviewed the Chicago and Illinois military organizations and found them wanting in both training and arms. "No more than 100 men could be turned out fully equipped—this in a city of 100,000!" the paper stormed. Some political progress was being made, as well-known Democrats were taking prominent part in the war rallies in northern Illinois and Indiana. But in central and southern Illinois there was strife—clashes between rival Democratic factions in Springfield, mob violence against abolitionists, and reports that the secessionists planned to seize Cairo, thus gaining control of both the Mississippi and Ohio rivers. Richard Yates, the new governor, took office breathing fire. "The foot of the traitor has never yet blasted the greensward of Illinois," he proclaimed, and in several thousand impassioned words, he promised it never would.

On January 29, the *Tribune* stated its war views in its annual Prospectus. They were in part:

> The Fire-Eaters of the Cotton States have undertaken to break up the American Union, because they are not allowed forever to rule it. . . . Demands of the Fire-Eaters—1st, That the people of the North shall give up their conviction that Slavery is wrong, and profess to believe that it is morally and politically right. 2d, That the Constitution shall be so construed

as to recognize property in Man, and thereby Nationalize the institution of American Slavery. 3d, That the Free States shall pay for all fugitives from labor who may escape. 4th, That all State laws against kidnapping shall be repealed. 5th, That Slavery shall be extended into all the Territories. . . . 6th, That the Slave traffic shall be re-opened in the District of Columbia. 7th, That a law shall be passed granting the right to slaveholders to travel and sojourn in the Free States accompanied by their slaves.

Insisting that the "Fire-Eaters" intended to secede, to found "a great slave-holding empire," including Mexico and Central America, and to expand the slave trade, the *Tribune* called upon "every sound patriot and friend of the Union and Constitution to stand by Lincoln's administration. . . . The free North must not be bullied nor frightened by the arrogant oligarchy into a base surrender of its dearest rights and most cherished principles."

Medill reported sympathetically from Washington on the compromise proposals of Cassius M. Clay, of Kentucky, and enthusiastically on the introduction of the Pacific Railroad Bill, which, of course, could be expected to make Chicago a main transfer point on a route from the Atlantic to the Pacific coast. But the paper declared that further compromise on the slavery problem was not really possible, saying on February 8: "Seven states have gone beyond reach of compromise, a population of six millions, half slaves. . . . The New Orleans custom house and mint have been robbed of one million dollars by the rebels. What will Buchanan do? Nothing. The execrable old villain should be taken on the 4th of March and hanged to the nearest lamppost, as a warning to traitors. . . . What will happen to the hoary old wretch? Nothing." On February 9, the Confederate Provisional Congress, meeting at Montgomery, Alabama, elected Jefferson Davis president and Alexander H. Stephens vice-president.

Despite the hot and hateful words and threats of war on all sides, it did not appear that any newspaper or responsible politician really thought that widespread civil violence was imminent. The polemics had gone on for a long time; there had been bloodshed for some years in Missouri and Kansas without spreading the conflict. Yet, the new challenges, especially the seizure of the arsenals and the creation of the provisional Confederate government, had to be met, and Lincoln would have to meet them.

Sometime in January, the president-elect had spoken to a member of the *Tribune* staff, probably Ray, to clarify his position. This statement was published on February 12, the day the *Tribune* reported Lincoln's departure from Springfield. "I will suffer death before I will consent, or advise my friends to consent, to any concession or compromise which looks like buying the privilege of taking possession of the Government to which we have a Constitutional right; because whatever I might think of the merit of the various propositions before Congress, I should regard any concession in the face of menace as destruction of the Government itself." Lincoln's friends genuinely feared that he would be in grave personal danger during the two weeks' journey east for the inaugural. Nevertheless, many stops for personal appearances and speeches had been planned, and the schedule could not now be changed; no sign of fear could be shown.

The temperament of the country was vividly demonstrated to Chicagoans when Congressman William Kellogg of Illinois, resentful of a *Tribune* editorial critical of his proslavery stand, charged down upon Joseph Medill in the National Hotel and began beating him. Medill, vulnerable because of his spinal rheumatism and surprised by the attack, might have been badly injured if Kellogg had not been driven off by his colleagues. In Chicago there were demonstrations against the *Tribune*'s "refusal to compromise" on the slavery question, including a protest meeting in Bryan Hall claiming to represent dissident Republicans. Along Lake Street, some of the merchants were said to have signed petitions promising to boycott the *Tribune* if it did not change its stand. The paper replied that it would not change its position "one iota" under any kind of threat, denied that it was obdurate or unreasonable in its antislavery, pro-Union stand, and continued to report daily on Lincoln's progress eastward in "copious and we may say costly dispatches." The *Tribune* also pointed out that its circulation now exceeded the total of all other English-language dailies in the city. The *Tribune* feared no man, it stated, and proved this by scolding the town's ministers for their "excessive" pacificism.

The *Tribune* continued to cover politics thoroughly and well, but, of course, from its own oracular viewpoint. It also provided local and international reports, printed reviews of literary materials, initiated a "Farm and Garden" column, and serialized such authors as Charles Dickens, Bayard Taylor, and Emerson Bessnett, the latter specializing in books about the West. There were travel reports—"Life in Naples" and "The Hayes Arctic Expedition"—science articles, and verbatim coverage of lectures by Ralph Waldo Emerson, Henry J. Raymond, editor of the *New York Times,* and the Reverend T. W. Higginson. Mary Howett's *History of America* was reviewed at length and favorably, and the paper took note of a new edition of Walt Whitman's *Leaves of Grass.*

On February 18, 1861, The Tribune Company was incorporated by an act of the Illinois legislature, with a capital stock of 2,000 shares at a par value of $100. The stock owners were John L. Scripps, 420 shares; Charles H. Ray, 420 shares; William Bross, 430 shares; Alfred Cowles,

300 shares; and Joseph Medill, 430 shares. At a stockholders meeting on March 2, Scripps was elected president of Tribune Company and Cowles became secretary.

*   *   *

President-elect Abraham Lincoln, grown even more patient and kindly and worn in the few months since November, was being well received as he traveled east, talking to and talking with the American people. He had grown a beard, partly because his advisors had been recommending it for some time, believing it would add to his dignity, and partly because 11-year-old Grace Bedell of Westfield, New York, had written a letter during the campaign suggesting that all ladies liked whiskers and would *"tease their husbands to vote for you."* His Eastern reception was by no means entirely kindly; there were hate merchants who called him an ignorant backwoodsman, even a baboon. But there were those who even then could glimpse the special kind of man who was to become president, who seemed to be drawing spiritual sustenance from the people and from his renewed relations with the traditions of his country. Many who heard him speak, without a prepared text, in Independence Hall in Philadelphia long remembered his words:

> I am filled with deep emotion at finding myself standing here in the place where were collected together the wisdom, the patriotism, the devotion to principle, from which sprang the institutions under which we live. . . . All the political sentiments I entertain have been drawn, so far as I have been able to draw them, from the sentiments which originated, and were given to the world from this hall in which we stand. I have never had a feeling politically that did not spring from the sentiments embodied in the Declaration of Independence. . . . Something in that Declaration [*gave*] liberty, not alone to the people of this country, but hope to the world for all future time. It was that which gave promise that in due time the weights should be lifted from the shoulders of all men, and that *all* should have an equal chance.

Amid such noble and poetic thought came the crassest of political realities. Chicago detective Allan Pinkerton, a squat and burly Scot with a reputation for hard-nosed investigative work, requested a secret meeting with Norman Judd, who was heading Lincoln's entourage. Pinkerton had learned of a plot to assassinate Lincoln on his way through Baltimore, a report made credible by many extremist elements there sounding threats. Lincoln made a scheduled speech in Harrisburg, then reluctantly consented to an elaborate charade that took him through the suspect city incognito and placed him safely in Washington. Both Medill and Ray had been sending dispatches from Washington. They approved of the Pinkerton-Judd secrecy arrangements for the president-elect. "Thank God, the country has at last got an honest, brave and true MAN for President," said the paper prayerfully on February 27. "The people will stand by him to the end of the chapter, come what may. . . . Old Abe is now here. . . . All hail the national regeneration!"

On March 5, the paper gave three columns to President Lincoln's inaugural address and other columns to the details of the affair, including approving paragraphs concerning Sen. Stephen A. Douglas, who not only accommodatingly held Lincoln's hat during the inaugural oath and address, but was proving the fullness of his patriotism by seeking to rally all possible loyal Democrats behind the new Republican administration.

"Thank God that this is the day of deliverance," said Dr. Ray's editorial, telegraphed from Washington. "It is Israel looking on the Promised Land . . . the Pilgrims on the Mayflower straining their eyes to the distant shore. . . . The struggle has been long and fearful, but this day repays all. Justice, Humanity and the Consequences of Freedom are in the ascendant." The paper even professed to be content with Lincoln's cabinet appointments, though only one *Tribune* recommendation, Salmon P. Chase for secretary of the treasury, was honored. "We believe that Lincoln has sought to make the Cabinet harmonious on all vital questions, and yet has sought to satisfy the largest number of those who gave him the votes," the paper said. "In this he has done the right thing."

*   *   *

Joseph Medill had not changed his opinion of Washington. He was eager to return to Chicago to be with Kitty and his growing daughters, to savor his beloved Garden City in the spring, and to supervise the installation of another Richard Hoe four-cylinder press, which, more than even Medill realized, would soon be working to capacity. "Some people love to live in Washington," Medill had written to his paper. "Your correspondent is not one of this class. To him it is always an irksome place of abode." In a private letter he added, *"Too many people are coming here wanting help. . . . I knew you in Ohio, when you edited the* Leader, *or, everybody knows the* Tribune *brought out Lincoln. So, now. . . ."* Before departing, Medill went to pay his respects to President Abraham Lincoln in the White House.

Medill was glad to be back in Chicago, to see the growing and increasingly pleasant city, with wide, tree-lined boulevards, and huge oaks on the hummocks surrounding the marshlands. The town was spreading to reach the forests, and downtown the effort of proud residents was at last winning out against the squalor of the past, as the city continued to lift itself out of the mud. Medill took Kitty and their daughters, eight-year-old Katherine and six-year-old Elinor, on long afternoon drives, joining other carts and surreys and broughams drawn by glistening sorrels or blacks or spanking bays.

Chicago was passing elegant Cleveland in size and gaining in beauty, its 120,000 hardworking people bringing in wealth that paved streets and built new homes and grand business blocks. From the cupola of the blue limestone courthouse at Randolph and LaSalle, Medill could look down upon Lake Street and its new five-story stores of pink Chicago marble; at the corner of Clark and Randolph the elegant Sherman House, six stories of brick, stood across the street from the *Tribune* building. Spread for miles were the bright mosaics of greening lawns and groves and the outlines of formal gardens that would be budding soon.

The networks of railroad lines extended in every direction, and towns could be seen along them, such as Hyde Park to the south, from which people could ride the Illinois Central to work and home again six days a week. Commuters were coming to work in Chicago on the Burlington and the North Western and the Rock Island, too.

Looking to the west, Medill could see the old Bull's Head Tavern, where Matthew Laflin had started Chicago's first stockyards. To the southeast, along the lake near the city limits, John B. Sherman had recently established newer yards, close to the packing plants and railroad lines. Too much wood construction everywhere, Medill noted, and the *Tribune* would soon begin its long campaign for fireproof construction, a largely ineffectual fight in the midst of the world's largest lumber market.

The most thrilling sight in the West, Medill thought, and the *Tribune* so said editorially from time to time, was gained by looking slightly north by east from the courthouse cupola toward Lake Michigan and the mouth of the Chicago River. There the great Illinois Central station and train yards were situated, and across the river the McCormick Reaper Works. Barges plied the river and high-masted schooners drifted in from the lake, the bridges turning to let them pass. The huge Sturges and Buckingham grain elevators poured their stores into holds bound for New England, New York, and Europe. There, felt Medill, was the strength of Chicago shown; there were created the fortunes responsible for many of the magnificent new mansions in their luxurious parks occupying entire blocks on the Near North Side.

But look anywhere—Cottage Grove Avenue, Wabash Avenue, the hundreds of hummocks among the sand marshes—the editor could see greening lawns and trees. There was really no city like Chicago, and Medill, still somewhat crippled by his rheumatism and the beating from Congressman Kellogg, was glad to be back with Kitty and the girls. On March 15, 1861, a *Tribune* editorial, probably not written by Medill, surely reflected his sentiments on returning to the Garden City:

> Spring is coming. The trees have caught a hint of it and are quietly busy with their buds. In little sunny nooks, patches of turf wax fresher and greener day by day. Yellow daffodils in the gardens are getting impatient in their imprisoned folds, and the first kiss of sunshine will bring them out. The

other day we heard a frog. . . . Nature goes right on, year after year, not in the least mindful of the fortunes of States and plots of statesmen. . . . Buds burst in their season, whether human governments burst or not. . . . Thank Providence this was all kept out of the hands of free and independent voters.

*   *   *

Early on April 11, Gen. Pierre Gustave Toutant Beauregard, commander of the new Confederate force at Charleston, sent three officers to call upon Maj. Robert Anderson to surrender. The demand refused, Beauregard waited a day. Then, at 4:30 A.M. on April 12, the first cannon shell of the Civil War was fired by Edmund Ruffin, an old secessionist from Virginia. The bombardment of Fort Sumter was under way.

The news of the outbreak of hostilities appeared in the early *Tribune* editions on April 13: "WAR INAUGURATED." A one-column "cut" of the Stars and Stripes was shown on page one, an illustration that would reappear to signal major national news for years to come. Editorially, the *Tribune* said: "The bombardment of Sumter is going on. The issue is in doubt. Our fathers fought for seven long years that the Constitution might be framed. We, the descendants, can afford any sacrifice, any exertion, that their labor may be preserved to the world for the blessing of mankind. Now, men of the North, for the struggle!" The paper announced a rally to be held in the Metropolitan Hall "for all in favor of maintaining the government. We call on the Republican guard. Let them come up to the work before them." The *Tribune* apologized for its poor news coverage of the Sumter attack, forbearing, for once, to blame the New York Associated Press and its cabal of treacherous monopolists: "Just at the moment when the country needs the special dispatches for which we bargained on Tuesday last, they fail to come, probably suspended, as Jeff Davis ought to be, somewhere on the poles between here and Washington."

Major Anderson surrendered Fort Sumter on April 13, and President Lincoln conferred with congressional leaders in Washington, including an ailing Senator Douglas. Lincoln proposed to issue a call to the states for 75,000 volunteers to serve for three months. Senator Douglas urged 200,000, since the regular army of 16,000 was scattered in small garrisons throughout the country, only a part readily available. Except for its navy, the North was almost defenseless. But Lincoln stayed with his 75,000 total, probably for the reason that more men could not be trained and equipped with the resources available. The South, too, lacked an army of consequence, but it did have the captured Federal arsenals, and many of the Federal army's best career officers were Southerners who even then were beginning to say their good-byes to Northern comrades they would soon be opposing in battle.

On the 15th, the news of Fort Sumter's fall covered most of page one of the *Tribune,* which printed all the information it could assemble. Labeled *"BY TELEGRAPH,"* the leading dispatch was headlined: "THE ATTACK ON SUMTER. THE BOMBARDMENT AND DEFENSE. EFFECT OF THE NEWS IN WASHINGTON. PRESIDENT LINCOLN'S PROCLAMATION. ACTION OF THE STATES. THRILLING WAR NEWS. THE VERY LATEST." The dispatches came from Charleston, Washington, New York, and various state capitals. Michigan was promising 50,000 men if needed; Indiana had doubled its quota; Horace Greeley said the country could raise 500,000 men. Governor Samuel Kirkwood of Iowa, receiving in a cornfield the War Department's telegram asking for men, made the most sensible response of the day: "FOR GOD'S SAKE SEND US ARMS. WE HAVE THE MEN."

The country was aroused; mass meetings were held, but few people seemed quite sure what should be done. President Lincoln knew that the national capital must be made secure. In the various states militiamen were being called up, and soon some Eastern contingents arrived at Washington or were reported on the way. In Chicago young men appeared at recruitment centers, militia prepared to mobilize, and bankers offered loans to the government. Senator Douglas issued a strong statement supporting the Union and made plans to come to Illinois to talk down the fire-eaters in the southern part of the state. There appeared to be a real possibility that both Illinois and Indiana could be split by war.

Chicago was in a state of almost transcendental excitement. No one could think or speak of anything but the attack and the probable war. There was an unprecedented outpouring of patriotism. On April 16, the *Tribune* published an editorial that would soon be reprinted throughout the North: "War—Every Man's Duty—Read." It began: "Lenity and forbearance have only nursed the viper into life—the war has begun! It may not be the present duty of each one of us to enlist and march to the sound of bugle and drum; but there is a duty not less important, which is in the power of every man and woman in Chicago, and in the North, to perform—it is to be loyal in heart and word to the cause of the United States."

A bipartisan meeting of citizens was held on the 19th in Bryan Hall to decide on the best means of supporting the government in the crisis. Before the night was over, the citizens were starkly aware of the defenseless situation of their city and state, as had been charged by the *Tribune* some weeks before. Militia companies existed in name only. The army forts and arsenals were mostly along the western frontier and at coastal and river locations. General Richard K. Swift, commanding the Chicago military district, had some 500 partly trained men, including an artillery unit. Citizens at the meeting pledged $30,000 for Chicago militia supplies and set up a committee of 28, headed by Augustus Harris Burley and Julian Rumsey, the new Republican mayor. This group resolved itself into a smaller Committee of Safety, empowered to recruit patrols to safeguard powder magazines, docks, ships and barges, railroad yards and trains, warehouses, elevators—all possible targets of guerrilla bands that might be organized in southern Illinois and Indiana, or might move up from south of the Ohio River, or across from Missouri.

There was a more immediate and much graver danger, and on April 19, Secretary of War Cameron sent a telegram to Gov. Richard Yates in Springfield. Yates immediately telegraphed General Swift, who, as it turned out, had no practical military experience whatever, but was nonetheless a man to get things done: "AS QUICK AS POSSIBLE, HAVE AS STRONG A FORCE AS YOU CAN RAISE, ARMED AND EQUIPPED WITH AMMUNITION AND ACCOUTREMENTS, AND A COMPANY OF ARTILLERY, READY TO MARCH AT A MOMENT'S WARNING. A MESSENGER WILL START TO CHICAGO TO-NIGHT. RICHARD YATES, COMMANDER-IN-CHIEF."

Next morning Yates's messenger advised General Swift that he was to occupy Cairo, stressing that his destination must be kept secret. Getting a satisfactory number of men together was one thing—many volunteers had to be turned away—but arming them was another. The force borrowed 50 muskets from a Milwaukee militia company; otherwise, according to Burley, it was largely armed with "squirrel-rifles, shotguns, single-barreled pistols, antique revolvers, and anything that looked as if it would shoot, that could be obtained from the gunstores, second-hand stores and pawnshops."

General Swift's force of 500 Cook County volunteers left on a special Illinois Central train at 11 P.M. on April 21. Despite the secrecy of the destination, all Chicago knew of the planned entrainment. Thousands of relatives, friends, and well-wishers were at the Illinois Central station that Sunday night to cheer the men on. Enthusiastic Illinois Central engineers tied down their locomotive whistles; factory and boat whistles responded, and the courthouse bell was rung. Slowly, the train of 26 cars, drawn by two locomotives, crawled along the Illinois Central railroad pier, the crowds of citizens along the lakefront cheering. The cooperation of railroad and telegraph authorities was enlisted to preserve the secrecy of the operation, at least insofar as the southern part of the state was concerned. Late on April 22, the expedition secured the railroad bridge over the Big Muddy River, and early next morning, said Burley, "rolled into Cairo to the astonishment of all, and rage of many of its citizens."

The Chicago force was soon to be supported by other troops from northern Illinois, northern Indiana, and Wisconsin and before long would receive modern guns. (Some of these weapons were the result of another bit of pro-Union derring-do. Captain James A. Stokes, a representative of Governor Yates, spirited 23,000 stand of arms out of the

St. Louis arsenal the night of April 25–26 without being detected by the thousands of secessionist sympathizers then surrounding the place.) The North, in effect, had won the first important strategic move of the war, for Cairo was the key to controlling traffic on the Ohio and Mississippi rivers. It was also a salient into the South and later became a staging point for Federal forces engaged in the river war in the West.

On April 23, the *Tribune* reported what had been taking place in Chicago since the Cairo expedition's departure. "The streets were alive all day with the movement of volunteers. Everything gives way to the war and to its demands. Workmen from their shops, printers from their cases, lawyers from their offices, clerks and bookkeepers from counter and counting-room. . . . Enlistments are marvelously rapid. . . . Incidents of loyalty and sacrifice press upon us in such numbers that we do not attempt their narration." Hundreds of details were reported, however. Courts were closed; managers of companies such as Sturges grain elevators and Titsworth clothing manufacturers, banker J. Young Scammon, steamship line owner Gurdon S. Hubbard, the Chicago Gas Light Company, railroad president Henry Farnam, and a score of others were listed by the paper as promising to equip militia companies with guns and uniforms or to donate cash for other supplies. Railroads offered free passage to militiamen and volunteers. The city's survey office organized an Engineer, Sapper and Miner Corps in a day. "They are noble-looking men and will do splendid service," said the *Tribune*. "The German residents, married men, of the ages of 25 to 45 years, organized a reserve corps yesterday, a battalion of four companies, electing officers who have served in European armies." A splendid-looking Zouave company from Waukegan marched through the city and entrained for Springfield, the paper said, and five other suburban units set off for various training camps. "The 'Union Rifles,' a corps of German sharpshooters, armed with the Enfield rifle, are to leave for Springfield this morning. . . . Irish citizens are vying with all other classes in pressing forward into the ranks." Seven recruiting offices were announced. More were planned, since any citizen able to raise and equip a company had an excellent chance of being elected its commanding officer.

The *Tribune* concluded its April 23 story on Chicago's war activities: "It is now permitted to transpire that the first detachment of Chicago troops were destined for Cairo, and reported as near there last evening. They have a battery of eight pieces, and are well supplied with ammunition and camp equipage, and the detachment is under the command of army officers of high reputation. These troops . . . are located at a most important position, and are worthy of the trust."

*　　*　　*

The early months of the war saw the end of the journalistic career of John Wentworth. After years of political strife, it was a business controversy that laid Long John low. Through his *Democrat* Wentworth had attacked certain Chicago bankers, asserting that they were defrauding the public by issuing worthless wildcat currency. He was not precisely alone in criticizing the bankers—many papers had done so, including the *Tribune*—but the others had questioned the value of the wildcat money rather than implying larceny on the part of the bankers. On April 29, 1861, the *Democrat* accused a group of bankers of taking advantage of wartime conditions and illustrated its charges with what was probably Chicago's first truly imaginative newspaper cartoon demonstrating some artistic pretensions. Under the caption "The Wild Cat Bankers in Council," five disreputable-looking felines were depicted sitting about a table discussing ways "to flood the state with any quantity of irredeemable currency." One cat, which had a number of rodentlike characteristics, was easily recognizable as J. Young Scammon, president of the Marine Bank. Scammon sued. Wentworth, a man of wealth and the sole proprietor of the *Democrat,* realized that at last he had gone too far. His *Democrat* was losing money and circulation. He began negotiations with two men who he knew had influence with the bank president—Joseph Medill and Charles Ray.

On July 25, 1861, the *Tribune* informed its readers that it would absorb Chicago's first newspaper, the *Democrat.* In announcing the discontinuance of his paper, Wentworth gave no indication that any money was to change hands, nor did the *Tribune* reveal details of the transaction. Apparently the *Tribune* simply took over *Democrat* subscription lists, while Wentworth retained his building and equipment but promised not to publish a newspaper for three years. There was no further word about the Scammon libel suit.

The *Chicago Tribune* sent Horace White to Cairo to cover the activities at that staging area for a time, and it assigned leading editors, including William Bross, to report on the headquarters of General Frémont in St. Louis, where it would soon be found that Frémont had set up a kind of imperial court but was getting little done about waging a war in the West. The *Tribune* urged from the start that the West should be cut off from the South by closing the Mississippi to rebel traffic all the way to New Orleans. "Let us advance!" it cried. "The people burn with impatience to meet the enemies of the Republic and open a way down their river to the sea." There were a few difficulties in that way, of course. The Federal government had no river navy, nor trained men to carry out such an operation, though the *Tribune* did boast that the troops of the First Minnesota, parading proudly through Chicago in their dusty green uniforms and black slouch hats, were "the finest body of marching men we have seen." They were, in fact, about the finest body of men anyone would see throughout the Civil War, but they were en route east, to the Army of the Potomac.

The Confederate Congress had recognized a state of war as existing since May 6, and the U.S. Navy had established a blockade of Southern ports. By May 20, Virginia, Arkansas, Tennessee, and North Carolina had joined the Confederacy. In many parts of the North there was dissatisfaction with Lincoln for his seeming failure to act. But the *Tribune* was not yet one of the papers to join Horace Greeley in crying, "Forward to Richmond!" The editors knew well enough that the defenses of the country were in deplorable condition, and it simply would not do to assume that the South would be equally ineffective. The *Tribune* welcomed the appointment of Gen. George B. McClellan as commander of the army's Department of the Northwest. "He will commit no mistakes. We congratulate the Northwest that the conduct of her armies is confided to such a man." The paper conceded that private subscription would be needed to equip the 11 Chicago companies reported to be in training. At the moment, men were no problem. Dozens of students had come down to recruiting stations from Northwestern University in Evanston only to be told they were not needed. The *Tribune* suggested that militia drill with wooden guns.

On May 25, the *Tribune* reported that 10,000 Federal troops had invaded Virginia. It also disclosed the first Northern casualty that truly brought the war home to Chicago—none other than the brilliant, dashing Col. Elmer Ellsworth, whose Chicago Zouaves had so impressed the nation a year earlier. The glamorous young officer, a personal friend of Abraham Lincoln, had died needlessly. At Alexandria, Virginia, Ellsworth had resented the flying of a secessionist flag by an innkeeper. When he personally went to take it down, the irate Southern patriot shot him dead. In Washington, President Lincoln wept.

On June 3, there was another poignant Illinois death. Despite illness and exhaustion, Sen. Stephen A. Douglas had been campaigning without cease through the early months of 1861 in his efforts to hold elements of his party and some of the border states to the cause of the Union. He had come to Chicago on May 1, and there he remained until his death, at the age of 48. On June 4, the *Chicago Tribune* filled three columns with details of Douglas's colorful life, and three more with the text of his last speech. On July 8, another three columns reported his funeral. Two editorials acknowledged that Douglas had been a longtime *Tribune* adversary but solemnly asserted that he had been a patriot who loved his country and who, in fact, had died for it. "He whom we place in the sepulchre will live long in his country's history," the paper said.

The *Tribune* announced that it would publish a Sunday edition as an extra wartime service and invited the public to visit its pressroom to watch the newly installed Hoe press in operation. It published a report from Washington that claimed Gen. Winfield Scott, the plump and phlegmatic commander of the armies, intended to put down the rebellion in 11 months, with the "Western army" expected to be in Memphis by July, and in New Orleans by February. "Not so fast," said the *Tribune* editorial. "The enemy should not be under-rated. The war is not to be ended by a single campaign."

President Lincoln summoned a special session of Congress to deal with the rebellion, and the Confederate Congress met in Richmond, making that city its capital. Now, in late June, the *Tribune* joined the Eastern press in crying, "Forward to Richmond!" It criticized General Scott for failing to move in the East although, ironically, Scott proposed first to close the Mississippi to Southern shipping all the way to New Orleans, exactly the *Tribune*'s own policy. Scott, however, was not going anywhere in the *Tribune*'s view, and his army of 65,000, many of whom were over halfway through their three-month enlistment, was losing morale because of idleness.

* * *

In July, 1861, Charles Ray briefly took over as the *Tribune* correspondent in Washington, and before he returned to Chicago he had produced one of the finest stories of the war, though it dealt with a Union disaster. Ray first established himself in Willard's Hotel, then called on his old friend Abraham Lincoln. The president gave him a letter to General Scott, who, it was rumored, was to move at last against rebel forces entrenching along Bull Run, a creek about 25 miles west of Washington. Possibly Lincoln told Ray that on June 29, at a meeting of his cabinet attended by Scott, he had strongly urged his commanding general to turn back these forces before they seriously threatened the capital. When Ray sought Scott, he found that the portly general, six feet five inches tall and weighing 300 pounds (too big and heavy to bestride a horse, it was said), was in the field. Ray took to the field himself, joining a group of newsmen invited by Gen. Irvin McDowell to visit the camps. Some friends of the Chicago editor were in the group—Murat Halstead, editor of the *Cincinnati Commercial,* and Henry Raymond, of the *New York Times.* On July 17, Ray filed a dispatch to the *Tribune,* reporting that five divisions under Mc-Dowell had advanced into Virginia, reaching Fairfax Court House. McDowell's orders, Ray learned, were to find and crush the forces of Confederate General Beauregard, which were massing near Manassas Junction, an important railway crossroads. The *Tribune* had just arranged to pay German-born correspondent Henry Villard $15 a week for his letters, but Ray, like several other editors in Washington, was not about to miss the story of his lifetime. He informed the paper that he himself would cover the forthcoming engagement between McDowell and Beauregard.

At some time prior to the battle, the editor had an opportunity to discuss politics and the war with old Illinois friends, Senators Lyman Trumbull and Orville Browning and Congressmen Isaac Arnold, Owen Lovejoy, and Elihu Washburne. They agreed that General Scott commanded the largest and best force ever assembled on American soil, and they did not accept his excuse for inactivity, that his troops were poorly trained. No one doubted that Scott could defeat the rebels and end the threat to Washington if he would simply make the attempt. All were sanguine concerning the coming battle. The elite of the capital, especially the senators and representatives, were planning to spend Sunday somewhere near Manassas Junction to watch the rebels run. Congressman Arnold, an aide to Gen. David Hunter, would be involved in the fighting himself, but Ray was invited by other friends to share a carriage to the battlefield.

Early Sunday morning, July 21, Ray left his hotel, taking with him a telescope, notepaper, pencils, and a box lunch. He previously had checked the telegraph station at Fairfax Court House, as any good war correspondent should, since a news story possessed value only if transmitted promptly to the newspaper, and the probable battlefield was near the courthouse. Most of Washington, it appeared, was going to the battle. Parties of congressmen with honored guests, foreign observers, newspapermen, and carriage-gowned women riding in landaus, surreys, and buggies crossed Long Bridge into Virginia, hoping to enjoy an outing and a picnic lunch on the hot July day while watching the battle.

Ray found General McDowell's field headquarters in the Grigsby house, at the intersection of Centreville and Warrenton pikes. Mounted couriers and officers sped by bringing messages or carrying orders. A group of newspapermen had collected. There was a sound of intermittent firing ahead, as Federal skirmishers began to make contact with the rebel advance guard. Ray learned soon enough that the incoming reports were not good. Union Gen. Robert Patterson, in the Shenandoah Valley in western Virginia, had been ordered to keep pressure on Confederate forces under Gen. Joseph E. Johnston so that Johnston would be unable to detach any troops to aid Beauregard. Now it became clear at staff headquarters that Johnston had eluded Patterson to reinforce Beauregard's right. From the Grigsby house vantage point, smoke puffs indicated a distant battle line. The Northern advance appeared to have stopped, but if troops were falling back it was in good order, and then it seemed that the Union advance resumed.

Other correspondents came up, Halstead and Raymond and a newcomer, William Howard Russell, the elegant and experienced reporter from the *Times* of London, whose dispatches from the Crimean War had so impressed General Scott that he had invited Russell to dinner with some of his generals. The men borrowed Ray's telescope to study the scene and all agreed that the Union forces were moving again, which meant they were winning a victory. Details of the action, even through the glass, were unclear, but the heavy cannonades, followed by musket fire, indicated a hot engagement was in progress.

Raymond, of the *New York Times,* was the first to leave, convinced that a Union victory was imminent. He had an earlier deadline than Ray, who stayed on. It became apparent to Ray that some of McDowell's forces were moving back, but in good order. What was not observable was that up ahead, near the fighting, retreating troops were colliding with the advancing rear of the army. The Union artillery, ambulances, and supply wagons had moved too far forward, and when green Federal troops broke before heavy gunfire from the Confederates' protected entrenchments, the turnpikes were blocked. Unaware of the growing chaos near the front, Ray looked about for Russell, who had been complaining that his buggy and driver were missing, but Russell had departed. Ray obtained a ride to Fairfax Court House. There it was evident that the telegraph lines were jammed, but Ray got a brief message through, indicating that the Federals had suffered early reverses, yet were regrouping for an ultimate victory.

As he headed back to Washington, Ray had cause to review what he had written. Deserters from the Union army were on the Centreville road, fleeing the rebels. They in turn had caused others to turn back, and the roads around the battlefield were choked with panicked men, frightened horses, and broken equipment. Foot soldiers had overrun artillery and field hospitals, and able men were climbing into carriages with the wounded in their attempt to escape. Back in Washington, Ray hastened to correct his earlier dispatch. "A GREAT BATTLE! FIRST VICTORY—THEN DEFEAT. DISASTROUS RETREAT OF OUR TROOPS. PANIC AMONG THE FEDERAL TROOPS."

On July 26, after Ray had an opportunity to learn the full extent of the disaster from officers and men returned to Washington, the *Tribune* published his full report, some 3,000 words, which began:

> The battle is lost. The enemy have a substantial victory. The result, so unexpected, dangerous and mortifying, is due to causes that the country will bye and bye discuss. Men who have been inattentive observers of the field of operations and of the tendency of the popular mind, will say that popular clamor has outrun military preparation; but this is not true. The well-appointed and magnificent army that is now coming back broken and disorganized into the entrenchments on the opposite side of the river, ought never to have been beaten. It was known here, or at least so strongly

suspected that not to have been guided and controlled by the fact would have been madness—known that Patterson . . . had permitted the rebel general, Johnston, to outwit him and get away, carrying the greater part of his force down to Manassas—leaving in his camp only men enough to maintain appearances. . . . That I say was known. It was known also that Beauregard's position was very strong, and that his army, before Johnston's column came, was equal in number to our own.

Dr. Ray recounted the early stages of the battle and explained his early, incorrect dispatch, referring to the beginning of the retreat:

I was at that time on the left of the line as it was formed, and the passage of shell and shot in the air over my head compelled me and all the civilians of the party to beat a quick retreat. Capt. Ayer brought up his battery and returned the fire; but by some means the fact of McDowell's retrograde movement becoming known, the troops left their position and fled. I was not there to see, as I will soon explain, but I do not hear that a retreat was ordered; but it is certain that when made, the officers were far in advance of the men. The panic was communicated to the crowd of civilians on the ground, and the scene that followed in which soldiers, officers, Congress-men, editors, distinguished citizens, camp followers, teamsters and baggage guard took part, beggars description. As I have explained, I had returned, going up the hill a mile. I then heard news which made it apparent that we had won a great victory—that Hunter's column had silenced all opponents on the right, that [*Gen. Israel*] Richardson was triumphant on the left, and that the center was in retreat. In a haste to communicate the news to your readers by telegraph, I exchanged my seat in the carriage, in which I went out, for a mount on Senator [*James Alexander*] McDougall's horse, took a lunch and started up the Centreville road.

Then Ray described the scene from the various hill positions he had paused at as he rode toward Fairfax Court House, when each sign he saw had seemed an implication of victory, though the Federal forces actually were trying to retreat. What he saw and heard on Sunday, Dr. Ray continued, was "but little of what occurred. . . . To-day I have seen perhaps a hundred men who remained on the field to the last." After detailing the grim facts thus gathered, the chastened editor concluded: "The main question is—who ordered that fight without bringing Patter-son's forces down? That the country must know. CHR."

Ray's report appeared in 36,000 *Tribunes,* the largest edition of the paper published up to that time. The victorious Southern forces were unable to exploit their triumph. Washington was still well protected, or so it seemed to General Lee and Jefferson Davis. Ray and the other editors returned to their home offices, leaving battlefield correspondence to younger men. When the official accounts of the Battle of Bull Run were in, it was found that McDowell's army was smaller than supposed, 28,452 men, and that it had indeed met a larger as well as an entrenched force of 32,232 Confederates. The Federals lost 481 killed, 1,011 wounded, 1,216 missing; the Confederates, 387 killed, 1,582 wounded, 12 missing.

The nature of the retreat and the evidence of unpreparedness shook the North and roused the Copperheads, as the Southern sympathizers came to be called. The soldiers had learned something about war at the Battle of Bull Run, and now it was time for the civilians. Both the Union and Confederate governments imposed heavy taxes and raised large loans to finance what promised to be a long war. The consequences of the defeat at Bull Run, said the *Chicago Tribune* with assurance, "will only be a mightier uprising of the people on behalf of their beloved Union and Constitution, a firmer resolve to conquer the traitors, a more gigantic preparation and a more nervous energy for the work to be accomplished. . . . Mortification may well mingle with our sorrow for the dead and wounded, but despair never. . . . Let vast camps of instruction be organized forthwith. Let educated and competent officers be appointed to command our soldiers."

The *Tribune* poured two columns of scalding wrath upon General Patterson (a "miserable old man sipping mint juleps at leisure near the Pennsylvania border"), who not only failed to hold back the Confederate General Johnston but also locked up some war correspondents who dared to criticize his inactivity; and it responded to the *Chicago Times* and other Illinois newspapers that had sought to blame the *Tribune*'s exhortations to action as a primary cause of the Bull Run disaster. The *Tribune* hailed the appointment of General McClellan as commander of the Army of the Potomac. The "Forward to Richmond" call would be responded to by "the star of hope," McClellan. But, pleaded the paper, "do not spoil McClellan. He is already made a candidate for the Presidency by enthusiastic journalists. . . . In Heaven's name, let him alone. If there is good in him let the country profit thereby."

It was Russell of the London *Times,* however, who aroused the *Tribune* to truly thunderous wrath when his report of the retreat reached the United States in mid-August. "The scene had now assumed an aspect which has not a parallel in any description I have ever read," wrote the man who presumably had witnessed the ultimate in military disasters in the Crimea. He went on:

> Infantry soldiers on mules and draught horses, with the harness clinging to their heels, as much frightened as their riders; negro servants on their masters' chargers [*Russell's own servant had fled with his carriage, leaving the eminent reporter temporarily stranded*]; ambulances crowded with unwounded soldiers; wagons swarming with men who threw out the contents in the road to make room, grinding through a shouting, screaming mass of men on foot, who were literally yelling with rage at every halt.

Russell concluded that the Northern soldiers had dishonored their Anglo-Saxon heritage, and asserted that even General Hunter escaped by riding in an ambulance, escorted by a major who had deserted his battalion.

Ray responded in high anger and withering scorn. Correspondent Russell had departed the scene of battle before Ray did, so he could not have witnessed the events he described. General David Hunter was in fact wounded, and the "deserting major" was none other than the general's staff aide, Isaac Arnold, one of Chicago's most distinguished citizens. Ray interviewed various correspondents who, like himself, had left the scene after Russell. All agreed with Ray—none had seen the rout because it had not yet developed. Ray concluded:

> The truth is probably this. The imaginative correspondent left the battle-ground before any confusion occurred, and when the retrograde movement was ordered, hearing the exaggerated stories of what came to be a flight, after he got into Washington, on Monday, while excitement was at its height, he wove them into his letters as facts of his own observation. The rout was disgraceful enough to make any man's blood run cold in his veins; but it was not what Mr. Russell describes. As we have asserted, he did not see it.

The North welcomed this defense of its forces and especially Ray's documented and conclusive attack on Russell's credibility as an eyewitness, which vitiated his insults. Ray's critique was widely praised and reprinted. Some Northern honor had been restored and the detestable pro-Southern foreigner and his scurrilous mendacity had been fearlessly exposed. A cartoon on the cover of *Vanity Fair* magazine, published in New York, depicted Russell being pinned down as a specimen in an insect collection by Ray's report. "The great humbug of the London *Times,* nailed to the wall by C. H. Ray, of the *Chicago Tribune*," read the caption.

THE BOHEMIAN BRIGADE

8

The impatience of editors and the ingenuity of reporters did not make up for the fact that there was a limited amount of battle news to be published during the early months of the war, for the reason, as demonstrated by the first battle of Bull Run, that neither side was ready or able to fight a major engagement. The *Tribune* had understood the situation and counseled patience when Gen. George B. McClellan took command of the Army of the Potomac. Nonetheless, the paper continued to demand action in the West, where Maj. Gen. John C. Frémont, the Republican presidential candidate in 1856, was in command of the Union forces, with his headquarters in St. Louis.

The paper had been intensely pleased by Frémont's appointment, but its enthusiasm for the general diminished after August 16, when it published a report on a Union disaster at Wilson's Creek, near Springfield, Missouri, in which Gen. Nathaniel Lyon, one of the leaders credited with helping to keep Missouri in the Union, was killed. General Lyon had been ordered by Frémont to search out and defeat a contingent of 11,600 Confederates, regulars and guerrillas, under Generals Benjamin McCulloch and Sterling Price, the latter a former governor of Missouri. Lyon had only 5,400 men but had been promised reinforcements and supplies. Neither had arrived, the story said, when General Lyon found the guerrilla armies camped along Wilson's Creek, but he nevertheless attacked. While rallying an Iowa regiment to meet an enemy charge, the impetuous Lyon, already wounded, was killed by a rifle slug in the stomach. Lyon's troops were defeated, though they exacted heavy casualties from the enemy, including General McCulloch, who was also killed. The Confederates now owned the cornfields in which the battle was fought, and they continued to control southwestern Missouri.

The *Tribune*'s report of the Battle of Wilson's Creek, the fiercest engagement since Bull Run, was reprinted from the *Missouri Democrat,* which had picked it up from the *Dubuque* (Iowa) *Herald.* The reporter, unsigned, was 29-year-old Franc Bangs Wilkie, formerly the city editor of the *Herald.* He had gone to Missouri to cover the war, joined General Lyon's force, and was the lone correspondent with the Iowa troops as the battle began. Wilkie, destined to become one of the best known of the Civil War correspondents and a leading member of the "Bohemian Brigade," as the Union war reporters came to be called, wrote vividly of the encounter between Iowa and rebel soldiers in which General Lyon was killed:

> Gen. Lyon now desired the Iowa boys, whom he had found so brave, to prepare to meet the next onset of the enemy with the bayonet immediately after firing. They said: "Give us a leader and we will follow to death." On came the enemy, in overwhelming numbers, confident of victory over such a meagre force. No time could be lost to select a leader. "I will lead you," exclaims Lyon. "Come on, brave men!" and placing himself in the van, received a fatal bullet just at the pit of the stomach, which killed him instantly. The Iowas delivered their fire and the enemy retired, so there was no need of charging bayonets. . . . The battle raged for two hours more, the command devolving upon Major [*Samuel D.*] Sturgis. The enemy made repeated attempts to retake the heights from which they had been driven, but were gallantly repulsed each time. The Kansas regiments behaved with a bravery seldom or never equaled, forming ambuscades for the benefit of the rebels by lying flat on the ground until the enemy came near enough for them to see their eyebrows, when they would pour a deadly volley into their opponents and again remain in possession of the field.

But the ammunition soon ran out, and the Federals were forced to retreat.

The valor of Lyon and his men was made even more apparent when Wilkie described what had transpired before the battle, when Lyon had complained of the failure of the War Department (i.e., Frémont) to reinforce him, saying: "Well, I begin to believe our term of soldiering is about completed. I have tried earnestly to discharge my whole duty to the Government, and appealed to them for reinforcements and supplies; but, alas, they do not come, and the enemy is getting the advantage of us." Lyon held a council of war, and his officers voted almost unanimously in favor of evacuating Springfield. But one of his generals, said Wilkie, "plead eloquently against such a course, declared it would be the ruin of the Union cause in that quarter of the State." This argument won Lyon's approval, and later, having been asked when the Federals would leave Springfield, "General Lyon replied, 'Not before we are whipped.' This was the proper course to pursue," the young correspondent noted.

In addition to publishing Wilkie's report of General Lyon's despair at his lack of support, the *Tribune* also printed the young reporter's comment that "with two more regiments we should have driven the enemy entirely from the valley, and with a proper cavalry force, could have followed up such a victory with decisive results." Criticisms of Frémont appeared frequently in the news columns thereafter, although the paper also continued to praise him on the editorial page. Over the next few weeks all four editors, Bross, Medill, and later Ray and then Scripps, went to St. Louis to investigate ugly rumors concerning Frémont's competence. The general was accused in news stories of living in exotic splendor, like a Persian satrap, concerning himself with trivia of rank and precedence and planning a grand campaign against New Orleans while losing the battle in Missouri.

The *Tribune*'s seeming ambivalence indicated a split between Medill and Ray, since the criticisms of Frémont in the beginning appeared in the news columns, which Medill controlled as managing editor and superintendent of editorial, while Ray's editorials were as friendly as ever to the autocratic general. When, on August 30, Frémont issued a proclamation invoking martial law and freeing the slaves within his military purview, the *Tribune* gave him unqualified support. Lincoln, however, was acutely embarrassed. He needed desperately to hold the border states, and such an emancipation order not only was impracticable in Missouri, but it would alienate other areas that the Union still had a chance to hold. The abolitionists rallied to Frémont, until it seemed as though the North would break apart before the war was fairly begun. "Frémont's proclamation is our platform henceforth to the end of the war," the *Tribune* declared editorially. "Attach no credit to the report from Kentucky that the President disapproves." Soon the paper was forced to retract. Lincoln gave Frémont an opportunity to modify his order, and when the general refused, the president published a letter commanding him to do so.

While the *Tribune*'s editorial page continued ardently to support Frémont's emancipation position, the paper also remained one of the general's principal detractors in its news columns. On September 15, 1861, page one of the *New York Times* published both Lincoln's letter rescinding Frémont's edict and a recent column from the *Chicago Tribune* detailing "Some of the Personal Complaints Against Gen. Frémont."

> We fear that the military service in the Western Department is suffering seriously from the extreme exclusiveness of Gen. Frémont. A few days since the Hon. Isaac C. Wilson . . . was sent to St. Louis by Gov. Yates, to consult

with Gen. F. on important business connected with the efficiency of the Illinois troops. Judge Wilson remained three days making vain efforts to get an audience with Gen. Frémont, when, learning that it was not unfrequent for persons on equally important errands, to wait a whole week and then fail of getting into the sacred penetralia, he came away without seeing the General.

The *Tribune* column went on for two more paragraphs, adding sarcastically, "If General Frémont's time is too much occupied . . . let us have two major generals." This item, and others, angered the abolitionist press in the East, which in turn attacked the *Tribune*.

The country was dangerously divided by the Frémont controversy. The president's countermand antagonized radical Republicans and widened the breach between Ray, who clung to his strict abolitionist position, and Medill, the pragmatist, who backed Lincoln. The *Tribune* admitted that it was confused by Lincoln's position and predicted the day would come when the slaves would be freed. "The people can be trusted," it said on September 28. "They see ahead of government, press and pulpit. The march of human development sweeps grandly over the worst obstacles of ignorance and wickedness."

Events in Missouri, meanwhile, were further eroding Frémont's standing in the eyes of the president and of the *Tribune*. And back in the thick of things was Franc Wilkie, recently engaged as the Western correspondent of the *New York Times*. Wilkie was accompanying Sam Sturgis, now Brigadier General Sturgis, who had been ordered to take a division up the Kansas River to rescue Col. James A. Mulligan, the colorful Chicago politician whose Irish brigade, raised in Chicago, was trapped at Lexington. Mulligan's force of fewer than 3,000 was cut off by an estimated 20,000 to 30,000 rebels under General Price, who controlled the river at Lexington. The rescue expedition was "most miserably planned," according to Wilkie.

> The idea of sending a regiment and a half of men forty miles across a hostile country to raise a siege conducted by thirty times that quantity of men, is one of those preposterous ones that strikes a thinking mind only for its outrageous absurdity. Nor will its character in this respect be diminished when it is known that not a single piece of artillery accompanied the expedition, not a single cavalry soldier, and that all the troops were raw volunteers who had never been under fire, and would be quite as likely as not to fall in their initiation. However, the business of a soldier is principally to obey orders. Gen. Sturgis was ordered to go, and he went.

Not surprisingly, Sturgis could approach no closer than six miles from Mulligan's beleaguered brigade. No correspondent was with Mulligan in Lexington, and the *Tribune* had no reporter of its own with Sturgis's troops. But the paper had arranged to receive correspondence of the *New York Times*, which meant it would have the reports of Franc Wilkie. The young Iowan, frustrated at being separated from the battle scene by Price's army, challenged Confederate guards at a river crossing and promptly disappeared into the rebel lines, not to be heard of again for several days. He had decided to get the story from the rebel side!

First reports of the Lexington disaster, in which Colonel Mulligan was finally obliged to surrender himself and all his troops, came to the *Tribune* from official dispatches to Frémont's headquarters in St. Louis. The paper also learned that Wilkie, as a Confederate prisoner, had witnessed the final hours of the Lexington battle by courtesy of General Price, who then freed him on parole. When Wilkie reached St. Louis, a *Chicago Tribune* reporter met him to get an interview on the Battle of Lexington, which ran in the *Tribune* several days before his detailed account of the siege and its conclusion appeared in the *New York Times*.

The loss of a second battle in the West and the capture of Mulligan and his men caused the *Tribune* to abandon all support for Frémont. It said editorially on September 24:

> Our Washington dispatch intimates that this disaster terminates Gen. Frémont's career as commander of the Western department. So far as we are able to judge at this time, *we think it ought to.* The inhabitants of Nova Scotia have been discussing Gen. Price's advance upon Lexington for more than a week. What was this Major-General of the United States Army doing meanwhile? Keeping, as we are told, Col. Mulligan's messengers *waiting three days* cooling their corns on his vestibule, unable to gain an audience to deliver their dispatches. And when they were delivered, what action was taken? Heaven knows!

Colonel Mulligan's men were almost immediately released on parole, and Mulligan, wounded and held as a prisoner, later escaped and reformed his brigade of Irish, who performed ably throughout the war and became Chicago heroes.

The abolitionist newspapers had continued their assault on the *Tribune* throughout September. Greeley's *New York Tribune* and William Cullen Bryant's *New York Post* assailed the paper, as did its Chicago rivals, the *Times,* the *Journal,* and the *Post.* Downstate, the *Illinois Register* declared the *Chicago Tribune* should be suppressed. Responding to its critics, the *Tribune* on October 3 published a statement on the responsibilities of newspapers in time of war, which said in part:

> The country is engaged in a war upon which hang momentous consequences, not alone to our government . . . but to every man, woman, and child living beneath our country's flag. . . .
>
> Our interest in it is not less than our neighbor's. Our feelings are as vitally concerned, our property is as seriously imperiled. . . . But we cannot

regard it alone from an individual and selfish standpoint. We have duties to the public which we must discharge.

By their own assumptions, or by quasi-popular consent, leading and influential journals like our own are in some sort regarded as watchmen on the walls, to look for approach of danger toward what their readers hold dear. They have had thrust upon them the duty, not always pleasant, of acting as conservators of the public good, often at the expense of their private interests. Men look to them not only for facts but for opinions. They do not often create, but they shape and give direction to public sentiment. They are the narrators of facts, the exponents of policy, the enemies of wrong.

Their office, in time of war, is not a whit less responsible, though infinitely more delicate, than in a period of peace. They deal with excited opinion, with passions painfully aroused, and with fears that know no reason. . . . On that account they should not shrink from the responsibilities of their position. As dangers thicken, their courage should rise to meet them. To avoid expression of what high public interests demand, because of probable offense to this class or that or because of prospective loss of peace, would be to cowardly abandon duty and float with the current for safety. . . .

We know of no reason that exempts the military man from criticism and, if necessary, vigorous denunciation, that does not apply to the civil servant in public life. . . .

It would be as recreant and cowardly not to speak out plainly as on the field of battle to refuse to fire at the foe. The country, we say, is in danger. Its salvation is the first duty of every man who loves it. Parties, private interests, personal safety are nothing when they stand in the way of the one grand object to be accomplished. We know our duty in the emergency and intend honestly and fearlessly to do it.

Editors of the *Tribune* ever since have called the editorial a classic statement on the role of newspapers in time of war.

Late in October, following investigations by Secretary of War Cameron and others, President Lincoln resolved to relieve Frémont of his command. The president sent a special courier, who assumed a disguise in order to get through Frémont's lines and deliver the letter of dismissal personally to the general. Frémont gave up his command on November 2, bringing a new storm of protest from antislavery radicals, including mass meetings in New York and Boston. In Chicago, the *Tribune* again defied its detractors, reprinting in a five-column summary its own charges against Frémont. While troops were without food and medicine, said the *Tribune*'s report in part, "Frémont, behind his barricades, is debating shall the color of the horses of my bodyguard be dark or light bay? Shall I have white kid military gloves or wash leather? . . . We would wish that things were otherwise—that Gen. Frémont were all that we hoped he would prove to be. But we must tell the truth. If no other number of the *Tribune* is ever printed; if we lose all we have; if our lives are forfeit for our words, we must speak. Our country demands it and we cannot be silent."

General Henry W. ("Old Brains") Halleck was dispatched from Washington to take command in the West. "No more foolish advance praise of a man," the *Tribune* said. "Halleck is untried. Let him demonstrate his worth by his works."

*   *   *

Thus the *Tribune* learned its lesson early in the war. Popular politicians do not necessarily make good generals, untrained forces should not attack solely to fulfill political necessities, and the war could not be won swiftly by either side. The paper had been among those calling Gen. William Tecumseh Sherman, the Federal commander at Louisville, Kentucky, "insane" for his reticence about either engaging troops or discussing his plans with the newspapers. It had joined others in crying "Forward to Richmond" and "Open the Mississippi" at a time when, as General Sherman pointed out, it was still an amateurs' war, with no plan or strategy and little capability on either side. The *Tribune* was now ready to wait for the professionals to get organized, and it liked one who seemed to be getting things organized around Cairo, Illinois, and later in Kentucky, a shuffling, taciturn, red-bearded West Pointer who had been dropped from the service but had been brought back by Governor Yates to train Illinois troops—Ulysses S. Grant.

The army did not become fully professional for two years, until Gettysburg and Vicksburg, according to General Sherman, but the navy moved swiftly to clamp a highly effective blockade on the South, and the ragtag group of newspapermen who became known as the Bohemian Brigade proved that they were professionals in their craft from the start.

The men of the Bohemian Brigade were a breed apart, a fantastic, unpredictable group who, in addition to writing eyewitness accounts of the action, published battle plans on the apparent theory that no Southern commander knew how to read, criticized and attacked generals they regarded as inadequate, and praised their special heroes, one of whom was Grant, who did not talk but did make news. ("In the two years I was with Grant," Franc Wilkie wrote years later, "I spoke often to him but he never said one word to me.")

Louis M. Starr, in *Bohemian Brigade: Civil War Newsmen in Action*, credits the *Chicago Tribune* with having the largest string of war correspondents in the West. The *Tribune* itself claimed it had 27 correspondents covering the war, though it is unlikely all were in the field at a time. Among them, in addition to the austere and businesslike editors, who never really qualified for the Brigade, were Irving Carson, a silent, sinewy man who crossed Confederate lines on scouting missions for Grant and was killed when a cannonball took off his head as he rode beside Grant at Shiloh; Joseph K. C. Forrest, one of the *Tribune*'s founders, who wrote letters to the paper while carrying out his mission of looking after the welfare of Illinois troops in the field as a militia colonel and aide to Governor Yates; Dr. Frank Reilly, an army surgeon who sent occasional dispatches to the paper, one of them a two-column description of the Battle of Shiloh, written after he himself was wounded; George P. Upton, who covered the Mississippi flotilla and later became the *Tribune*'s music and drama critic; and Horace White, who covered the Cairo headquarters before becoming Washington correspondent late in 1861.

But the *Tribune*'s most dynamic and irrepressible contribution to the Bohemian Brigade was Albert Holmes Bodman. As modestly portrayed in his unpublished memoirs, only recently discovered, the *Tribune* correspondent was a solemn, reclusive young man, unswervingly devoted to his craft. Franc Wilkie agreed that Bodman was a hardworking reporter, but he insisted that Bodman was also a prodigious poker player and was sometimes called "the cotton broker" by peers who admired his successful trafficking in the permits necessary to ship cotton from occupied areas of the Confederacy. Wilkie pointed out that Bodman, after only five months on his $16-a-week salary, was able to return on furlough to Chicago and invest $22,000 in real estate. Short, plump, and sleepy-eyed, Bodman had "the sleek, well-fed air of a caterer in a first-class restaurant," noted Wilkie. Bodman, from Milwaukee, was publishing a guide to Chicago when the *Tribune* hired him as its regular correspondent. Just when he began covering the war is uncertain; many of his early dispatches were merely signed "B" and some have been attributed to William Bross. But ultimately he began signing himself "Bod," and under this cognomen many of his accounts can be identified.

Others who reported the war for the *Tribune* were J. A. Austen, Llewellyn Curry, Richard J. Hinton, Ralph Kaw, Henry Martyn Smith, Joseph A. Ware, and T. Herbert Whipple. Many of their individual dispatches have never been traced. While each correspondent occasionally saw his initial or code name in the paper, all of them were relatively unknown as individuals, working virtually anonymously to make the *Tribune* outstanding in the West for its coverage of the war and, according to many accounts, the most popular paper among the soldiers in the western armies.

*   *   *

As the western campaigns began, Medill, Ray, and Bross, except for a sortie to St. Louis or Cairo and visits by Medill and Ray to Washington, left the riverboats and battlefields to the reporters, for they were occupied in Chicago with more than publishing a newspaper. All served on various civic and political committees concerned with the war effort, but the chief interest of each was Augustus Burley's Committee of Safety. Under the governor of Illinois and the mayor of Chicago, this committee had responsibility for obtaining money with which to raise and equip troops required by the calls of the Federal government. When Lincoln issued a call for 500,000 men in July, 1861, the *Tribune* proprietors had responded by recruiting a company for the Eighth Illinois Cavalry, led by Col. John F. Farnsworth. Medill supervised the recruiting, and the *Tribune* announced that 12 of its staff had volunteered on the first day. Among them were two of Medill's brothers, William and James; Samuel Medill, considered too young, joined the company later. Within a few months, John Scripps, who had been named Chicago postmaster by Lincoln, financed the organization of an infantry company called the Scripps Guards. Still later in the war, William Bross assisted in the formation of a Negro brigade, in which his brother, John, was an officer.

In the beginning, men for service were no problem. They volunteered in greater numbers than could be accepted. Midway in the war, enlistment fervor would die, and the Committee of Safety would raise money to pay bonuses up to $402 a man for enlistment and reenlistment. But through 1861 and early 1862, the problem was uniforms and equipment. "Begin to drill," the *Tribune* exhorted the new companies of troops constantly being formed. "Don't wait for guns. Use oak staves."

The *Tribune,* recognizing the injustice of a system that permitted men with money to hire others to do the fighting for them and foreseeing the day when volunteers would be insufficient, urged a draft. "Let the government draft 300,000 without delay and march them to camps of instruction," the paper said on September 11, 1861. But the draft suggestion got little attention. The *Tribune*'s campaign for medical supplies and other aid for the men serving the colors fared better. At a meeting held in the Tremont House to discuss aid for Union soldiers and sailors, William Bross made the motion to organize Chicago's Sanitary Commission. The U.S. Sanitary Commission, founded in July, 1861, became the Red Cross of the North during the Civil War. Thousands of Sanitary Fairs were held throughout the North, those in Chicago designated the top social benefits of the year. The money raised enabled the Sanitary Commission to send doctors, nurses, ambulances, and medical supplies to the various fronts and to organize hospitals, aid stations, and recreational centers, called "shebangs" by the soldiers. Women were able to serve the cause of the North through the Sanitary Commission, which became an important morale force in carrying on the war effort on the home front.

The *Tribune* did not shirk its own responsibility to arouse the enthusiasm of its readers for every aspect of the war, with editorials, service articles for the women telling them how to help, and, above all, extensive reports from the fronts, the sea, and the rivers. From time to time it looked to political and commercial concerns at home, and reminded its advertisers that the best way to prosper was to invest in the *Tribune*'s brand of printer's ink. "Foreign nations have paid us $36,000,000 for the products of our industry," the paper said in its January, 1862, commercial report. "To share in this general wartime prosperity, and to enlarge business, advertise in the *Tribune*. Our terms are below what they ought to be. Travel through the West anywhere and you will find the *Tribune*." At the same time, the paper admitted that the military outlook was not good. "The arms of the Republic are broken and disorganized. The enemy is defiant and jubilant." The paper called for an "active war," and was pleased that General Grant, in Cairo, was gathering troops to seek out the Confederate armies in Kentucky and Tennessee. Why did the Army of the Potomac not move?

When President Lincoln on January 12, 1862, at last got rid of one of the *Tribune*'s favorite targets, Secretary of War Simon Cameron, making him minister to Russia and naming Edwin M. Stanton his successor, the paper wondered whether Stanton would be any improvement. Such conjecture may have been justified. Cameron, despite the opposition to him by the *Tribune* and others, had got forces into position to protect Washington and other parts of the nation's vitals, even if he did not successfully attack. Stanton, a big, bandy-legged man with a fierce shaggy beard and a fiercer myopic stare through his thick-lensed glasses, was notoriously uncooperative and a malicious critic of Lincoln. But he was an extremely hard worker, and he was honest.

On January 27, President Lincoln issued General War Order No. 1, calling for the advancement of all forces. General Grant was ready. General George Brinton McClellan, named November 1, 1861, to succeed Scott as general-in-chief, and fondly called "the Little Napoleon" by his troops, was not.

*   *   *

The flanking movement by Grant, intended to clear the West and to open the Mississippi River to the Gulf of Mexico, made immediate progress as Grant pushed his troops along the Mississippi and Tennessee rivers, backed by ironclad gunboats built by the Eades Company in St. Louis and commanded by Commodore Andrew H. Foote. Fort Henry, on the Tennessee, capitulated on February 6 after a pounding by Foote's gunboats. Many of the troops escaped to nearby Fort Donelson, but among those captured was the commander of Fort Henry. The *Tribune*'s Bodman was in the front rank of the correspondents as General Grant received the surrender of Brig. Gen. Lloyd C. Tilghman, haughty and resplendent in his fresh uniform, epaulets, and sash, in contrast to Grant, with his sweat-brined blues, a slouch hat, and only his shoulder straps to denote his rank. "Sir," cried Bodman, proving himself a good newsman by attention to the simplest of detail, "how do you spell your name?" "Sir," replied Tilghman frostily, glaring down his nose at the plump newsman, "if General Grant wishes to use my name in his official dispatches, I have no objections; but, sir, I do not wish to appear at all in this matter of a newspaper report." Wilkie, who witnessed the scene, swore that for once Grant's eyes twinkled, but otherwise he remained imperturbable as usual. Brigadier General Tilghman provided the correct spelling of his name for the official records. The newsmen, said Wilkie, were so impressed with the Tilghman name that they made sure he received special prominence in all their dispatches.

It was a day's march across to the Cumberland River and Fort Donelson, but Grant moved slowly because of heavy weather and to give Foote's gunboats time to reach the fort via the river route. Grant himself reconnoitered the positions. He remembered that he had known one of the commanders, Gen. Gideon J. Pillow, in the Mexican War, and he planned his strategy accordingly. Pillow had 23,000 men and a strong position. Grant desired reinforcements from General Halleck at St. Louis, but they did not arrive. "I felt that 15,000 men on the eighth would be more effective than 50,000 a month later," said Grant in his report after the battle. "I asked Flag Officer Andrew H. Foote, therefore, to order his gunboats still about Cairo to proceed up the Cumberland River and not to wait." While Foote pounded Fort Donelson from the river, Grant's troops prepared to close the trap. He did not entrench, however, relying on his conviction that General Pillow would not order a sortie from the fort.

But Grant was wrong. The gunboats sustained considerable damage, and on February 15, while he responded to a call for a conference from Flag Officer Foote, who had been wounded, the Confederates attempted a breakout, overrunning the Union right and sending Gen. John A. McClernand's division into full retreat. General Lew Wallace, later the famed author of *Ben Hur,* decided in the absence of Grant to counterattack, preventing a total rout and halting the rebel advance. When Grant returned, he saw the near disaster as an opportunity and ordered an assault by the Union left. The counterattack was so successful that the two ranking Confederate officers fled with some of the rebel troops to Nashville. General Simon Bolivar Buckner was left behind to ask Grant for terms and got them: "No terms except an unconditional and immediate surrender. . . . I propose to move immediately upon your works."

The *Chicago Tribune* had published a detailed biography on the relatively obscure Grant a day before Fort Donelson. Now Bod's telegraphed dispatch, filling two columns of the paper, which was displaying its new, ultramodern dress, made the general a hero. Said the joyful headlines: "THE FORT DONELSON VICTORY! LATEST AND MOST COMPLETE PARTICULARS. INCIDENTS OF SIGNAL VALOR!" The *Tribune*'s new makeup, copied by many newspapers well into the 20th century, included an excellent map three columns wide. The front page also displayed two flags, an American flag above a rattlesnake flag, and explained the symbols: The American flag was "the glorious old banner that now waves in triumph over Fort Donelson." The rattlesnake flag was "the emblem that slunk away before the resistless valor of our Illinois boys." Bodman reported 15,000 prisoners captured, a remarkably accurate estimate, since the actual count, days later, showed that the Confederates had lost 2,000 killed and wounded, 14,623 missing and captured; the Federals 500 killed, 2,108 wounded, 224 missing. It was a great victory, an Illinois victory, a day long to be remembered, said the *Tribune*. The first dispatch, "FORT DONELSON IS OURS," reached the office at 10:00 A.M., the paper recounted. A bulletin was posted, and Clark Street in front of the *Tribune* building was soon filled with a crowd that blocked traffic. "The dispatch was read. It was followed by a pause whose hushed stillness might be felt, and then broke out such a cheer as men do not often hear in a lifetime. . . . Humanity will bless God for a great work accomplished, Liberty avenged and triumphant, while Treason totters to its crumbling base." The *Tribune* referred to General Grant as "Unconditional Surrender Grant" and to his forces as "General Grant's Grand Army." It urged subscription lists to provide care for the many wounded and the prisoners.

Other papers, including the *Richmond* (Virginia) *Examiner,* agreed that Grant's victory was a heavy blow against the South. It would open up Tennessee, force the evacuation of Nashville, and clear the way for the attack on Pittsburg Landing and the investment of Vicksburg. Lincoln promoted Grant to major general of volunteers. But enemies said Grant was drunk the day of the battle and charged that he was away from the battlefield because of it. Dr. John H. Brinton, the army surgeon who rode with Grant at Fort Henry and Fort Donelson, asserted that there was no liquor in the party, at Grant's order, and the records showed that Grant was indeed summoned by Flag Officer Foote, who besides being wounded at the time outranked him, though Grant was not excused for failure to entrench or to avert surprise.

The *Tribune,* like Lincoln, continued loyal to Grant and pointed out that all his generals were from *Tribune* territory: John A. McClernand, a Springfield lawyer; Richard J. Oglesby; and John A. Logan, a Douglas Democrat who had raised his troops in the midst of Southern sympathizers in Illinois's "Egypt." General Lew Wallace was from neighboring Indiana.

During February the *Tribune* had other good news to present to its growing flock of readers, now numbering 30,000 paid subscribers, the paper said, with an estimated 10,000 more buying the *Tribune* on the streets. General Ambrose E. Burnside captured Roanoke Island, North Carolina, for the North, and the people of northwestern Virginia voted to form a free state supporting the Union. The Legal Tender Act, for which the *Tribune* had been campaigning, was approved by Congress, and the paper soon noted that Federal greenbacks were valued at 98.7¢ in gold and were in demand in the South.

On March 8 came news of another sort: The ironclad ship *Virginia* (*Merrimac* in prewar days) sortied into Hampton Roads, destroying two Federal warships and running another aground. Official Washington was sent into a panic. The ironclad might indeed have turned the tide for the South by destroying the Federal wooden navy, but on March 10 and 11 the *Tribune* was able to publish a series of stories and maps on a great Union naval victory. The recently launched *Monitor*, the "iron pot" invented and built by a Swedish immigrant named John Ericcson, met the *Merrimac* in an ironclad battle that would change the world's navies. The *Monitor* drove her adversary back to Norfolk, maintaining Northern naval superiority.

The *Tribune* provided an ample quota of news from the South, which it called Secessia, including the annual message of President Jefferson Davis and a biography of Robert E. Lee when he was appointed commanding general of the rebel army. It covered the Chicago and Illinois news and maintained a lethal duel with the *Chicago Times*, designated as a "scurrilous, pro–slave holder sheet." Said the *Times*, on one occasion, "There is a strong disposition in the public mind in this city during the last few days to shell the morning abolition newspaper concern out of its habitation." Replied the *Tribune:* "The *Times* has mistaken its theatre. Paragraphs like this might do in Charleston, but in Chicago, a city preeminent for its observance of law and attachment to order, in which toleration of opinion is so broad that the *Times* can daily spout its treason and go unharmed, such incitements to violence should not go unpunished."

On March 21, the *Tribune* published three full columns from correspondent George Upton, covering the five-day shelling of Island No. 10, in the Mississippi River; General Burnside was moving in North Carolina; in Arkansas, Gen. Samuel Curtis led 11,200 Federals against 15,000 Confederates at Pea Ridge and won the victory; and a stretch of the Mississippi was cleared when troops under Gen. John Pope captured New Madrid, Missouri. Grant, suspended by General Halleck for failing to forward requested reports to St. Louis, resumed command of the Tennessee River forces on March 23, the day Chicago was hit by a 12-inch snowfall that caused the roof of the *Times* to collapse and prevented it from getting out that day's editions. The *Tribune* expressed its sympathy.

Correspondent Bodman had joined Upton in covering Island No. 10 and was with Grant's forces for the Battle of Pittsburg Landing, later called Shiloh after the little church on the battlefield. Bodman wrote of the unprecedented number of casualties at Shiloh; the Federal losses were 1,723 killed, 8,012 wounded, 959 misssing. Dr. Frank Reilly provided two columns of details. Neither writer mentioned the death of Irving Carson, which would have been a matter of importance whether or not he represented the *Tribune,* since he was in Grant's retinue, so evidently they lacked knowledge of the event. The fact that his army had been surprised and the news of heavy casualties again put Grant under a cloud, and some called him a butcher. Lincoln, urged to dismiss the general, who according to rumor had been drunk again, refused: "I can't spare this man. He fights."

Wilkie, the irrepressible Iowan, missed Shiloh, but he talked with troops after the battle and conducted one interview that may have been unique. Mrs. William Hall had arrived in camp to visit her husband, a colonel in the 11th Iowa, and from her Wilkie learned some of the details of the battle. "Is it true," the reporter asked her, "that you were surprised?" "Well," responded Mrs. Hall, "we were in our tent and not prepared to receive company. In fact, we were both *en dishabille* when a big cannon-shot tore through the tent. A caller at that early hour, considering its unexpectedness, and our condition, may possibly be regarded as a surprise."

The *Chicago Tribune* did not waver in support of General Grant, who, the paper said, "exhibited the most heroic bravery at the battle of Pittsburg." With victory "trembling in the balance" Grant himself led a charge across the field. "The General and his legion fell upon the rebels like a destroying avalanche; they fled before the resistless shock of cold steel, and the day was won. In all Napoleon's career there is nothing to exceed this charge in gallantry and daring." Such support, along with Lincoln's helped to dissuade the much-disparaged general from resigning his commission. The *Tribune* printed a letter in which Grant said, "I will go on and do my duty to the very best of my ability without praise, and do all I can to bring this war to a speedy close."

But General Halleck, commander of the western armies, arrived at Pittsburg Landing to take active field command, and he would not move on the enemy at Corinth, Mississippi. Grant had scorned trenches at Shiloh and had been mauled, so Halleck entrenched. The Federals under Halleck moved 20 miles in 25 days, allowing General Beauregard to extricate his entire army from Corinth before they arrived. The *Tribune* criticized Halleck "for letting 30,000 rebels escape" by his slowness and urged consideration of Grant as commander-in-chief in the West.

Though there was frustration on the home front, since Democrat Francis Sherman was elected mayor of Chicago against *Tribune* advice, other *Tribune* campaigns were successful. A majority of 20,000 voters supported the *Tribune*'s position in June by defeating a proposed new state constitution. The *Tribune* had urged the establishment of a Federal arsenal in Illinois and in July announced that one would be located at Rock Island. The paper also demanded Federal aid in developing the port of Chicago and the Chicago River, and it urged support for the Sanitary Fair, to be held in a giant tent on the lakefront.

In June the *Tribune* hailed Lincoln's signing a bill to prohibit slavery in the territories, which it saw as a move toward the goal of emancipation. "The morning is breaking," it said, "and the long night of the domination of slavery in our national councils has ended." The river war was going well, as New Orleans, Fort Pillow, and Memphis were taken by Federal naval forces. On June 7, the *Tribune* got out its flags again: "This is the flag that now waves in triumph over New Orleans and Memphis and will shortly be carried in triumph the whole length of the Mississippi," the paper said.

But news from the East in late June and early July was grim. General George McClellan, despite his reputation as an organizer and his popularity with the troops, had failed in his peninsular campaign against Richmond and in fact had been forced back to the protection of James River gunboats by Robert E. Lee's Army of Northern Virginia. Federal losses were 1,734 killed 8,062 wounded, and 6,053 missing, as against Lee's losses of 3,478 killed, 16,261 wounded, and 875 missing. The clamor for McClellan's ouster as commander of the Army of the Potomac intensified. On July 4, 1862, President Lincoln issued a call for 300,000 more men, raising the upper age limit to 45, and authorized using freed blacks in the military services. "For the first time since secession showed its head, the Republic is in real danger," the *Tribune* said. "The President has appealed . . . the people will respond promptly and with zeal."

On July 11, Halleck was named general-in-chief of all the Northern armies, and on July 17, Grant resumed command of the Army of the Tennessee.

*   *   *

The *Tribune* relied largely on its editor correspondents, other newspapers, and the New York Associated Press for its coverage of the war in the eastern theater. Medill continued to be dissatisfied with the dispatches provided by the Associated Press and called again for an alliance of Western newspapers. At a meeting in Indianapolis, he was made chairman of an organization committee, a move causing the New York Associated Press to offer improved service. The frustrating news from the East arrived more promptly and in greater quantities, and the *Tribune* continued to give most of its attention to the war in the West and to Chicago news.

Another war rally was held in Chicago on July 26. "Shall the Republic live or perish?" the *Tribune* demanded. "Three hundred thousand more for Uncle Abraham. Uncle Abe is calling us. Come and act for the Union!" As usual, William Bross of the *Tribune* was one of the chief speakers. "For no holier cause can ever patriot lay down his life than this," said Bross. "Shall we yield? Never, so long as patriot hearts breathe in American bosoms." The *Tribune* reasserted its support of "Old Abe" and declared that "in what makes a powerful if not a popular journal, the *Tribune* will remain unsurpassed—the great newspaper and leading organ of opinion in the West."

In this hour of adversity, the *Tribune* drew attention to the need for a proclamation of freedom for the slaves. Speaking of President Lincoln's policies on July 28, it said: "He is not afraid *himself* of a radical course, but he fears that the great body of the loyal men are not ready for it. . . . Were the next news dispatch to be the President's Proclamation of Freedom to every slave who would take up arms against the enemies of the Union, it would be received with one shout of joy from the Atlantic to the Rocky Mountains."

But Lincoln did not respond to this modified proclamation proposal. He did respond, with a strong negative, three weeks later on August 19 when Horace Greeley published his "Prayer of Twenty Millions," which declared it preposterous to continue the war without a proclamation freeing the slaves. Lincoln's reply appeared August 24 on the *Tribune*'s front page: "My paramount object in this struggle is to save the Union and is not either to save or destroy slavery. If I could save the Union without freeing any slave I would do it, and if I could save it by freeing all the slaves I would do it; and if I could save it by freeing some and leaving others alone I would also do that." In an editorial a few days later, the *Tribune* suggested that Lincoln was waiting for a Union victory before issuing an emancipation proclamation. Perhaps the editors knew that the president had prepared a draft proclamation and read it to his cabinet in July.

Meantime, Medill wrote to Schuyler Colfax, saying that he understood Lincoln was ready to issue the proclamation, but had been prevented by a member of the cabinet. This could only be Seward, Medill said. *"He is Lincoln's evil genius . . . who keeps a sponge saturated with chloroform to Uncle Abe's nose."* Publicly, the *Tribune* praised Lincoln: "His unselfishness, his unambitious, unpretentious, undoubted patriotism, his logical ability and his pure character, give him a strong hold on the hearts of the people." It cautioned the people to be patient.

During the summer of 1862 Richard Jordan Gatling demonstrated his new machine gun on the lakefront, and a company of troops led by John Brown, Jr., saluted the *Tribune* with maneuvers in Clark Street, singing the song that was sweeping the North, "John Brown's Body Lies A-Mouldering." A version of the song, sung to a Southern gospel tune, had been popular in the army from the beginning of the war, and for a time some Illinois troops sang it using the name of Ellsworth. The lyrics that eventually spread through the army had first appeared in print in the *Chicago Tribune* on December 16, 1861, as "The New John Brown Song." Not long afterward, Julia Ward Howe wrote other lyrics, entitled "The Battle Hymn of the Republic."

It was during 1862 that the paper published an exposé of the Illinois activities of the antiwar secret society known as the Knights of the Golden Circle, based on investigations made by Joseph Forrest. Medill, as usual, was writing letters to Northern politicians, this time urging the right of soldiers to vote, and to one of his favorite correspondents, Senator Trumbull, he boasted a little: *"I meet men daily from this and adjacent states. They all talk one language. The* Tribune *is read by a quarter million men in the West, and it simply indicates as the dial finger the sentiment of the people."*

In September, Lee was finally stopped in his intent to invade Maryland at the Battle of Antietam, in which each side lost more than 11,000 killed and wounded. It was not a decisive victory, since Lee's army was allowed to escape across the Potomac, but it was the victory that Lincoln needed for his proclamation, which he presented to his cabinet on September 22. The cabinet now approved. The *Tribune* had greeted Antietam as a great triumph, illuminating its building with fireworks while a band played for the crowd. "The demonstration was perhaps premature," said the paper a day later. "Our army has achieved decided advantages, if not a victory. . . . The real victory is to come and come it must." The real victory was the Emancipation Proclamation for which so many Northern men and women had struggled, not the least of them the proprietors and staff of the *Chicago Tribune*. On September 23, 1862, the paper said:

> President Lincoln has set his hand and affixed the great seal of the nation to the grandest proclamation ever issued by man. He has declared after the first day of January next all the slaves in the then rebellious States *shall be free*. . . . So splendid a vision has hardly shone upon the world since the day of the Messiah. From the date of this proclamation begins the history of the republic as our fathers designed to have it—the home of freedom, the asylum of the oppressed, the seat of justice, the land of equal rights under

the law, where each man, however humble, shall be entitled to life, liberty and the pursuit of happiness. Let no one think to stay the glorious reformation. Every day's events are hastening its triumph, and whosoever shall place himself in its way it will grind him to powder.

*   *   *

The proclamation of emancipation had been achieved. Now the *Tribune* demanded action to win the war, in the face of strong attacks against it by peace forces and the Southern sympathizers. The *Times* lashed out against the "Black Republicans" as dangerous radicals led by "the *Tribune* clique." Medill traveled to Washington and came back pleased with the discussions there. "All men who have made the journey to Washington return with the conviction that Old Abe is master of the situation," said the paper on October 1. "We reaffirm our determination to stand by the government. The proclamation of the President on September 22 has our hearty approval as we advance toward the overthrow of the rebellion by dealing sternly at once with its cause."

Possibly Medill had urged Grant upon Lincoln as supreme commander in the West, for the *Tribune* had printed in its editorial column: "Wanted—a Man!" It went on to explain that the army in the West consisted of 200,000 men, "as good fighting material as there is in the world. . . . Here are the conditions precedent for a great and successful campaign, which shall carry our arms in triumph to the Gulf—all the conditions save one: A Man! That army wants a leader. . . . Grant is to-day under the immediate command of Gen. Halleck [*and*] receives his orders from a captain in St. Louis. . . . We wait impatiently for the march to begin." Medill, too, might have boasted to the president of the Illinois and Chicago contributions to the Federal cause. The state had 27 regiments in the field, and 17 more in training.

Many of Chicago's 500 factories had overnight become war processors. During three months of 1862 the city killed 300,000 hogs and packed more pork than Cincinnati. Grain shipments for the year jumped from 16 million bushels to 65 million, sent to the needful troops and to various states or to Europe, where a drought had occurred. Thirty beef packing plants worked day and night, and the brewery output increased by 300 percent as the city supplied thirsty soldiers and factory workers. McCormick reapers, now with binder attachments, rolled out by the thousands and were pronounced by Secretary of War Stanton to be worth more than an army in the field. New factories were erected, expanding Chicago by 20 square miles, and the city soon was employing over 3,000 workers in a new boot and shoe industry, more than St. Louis manufacturers in their best prewar days. Chicago's matchless railroad system, which had proved its worth as well as its patriotism during the

Cairo crisis period and now provided free passage to militia forces en route to their camps, was demonstrating that Chicago had become the new transportation capital not only of the Northwest, but of the nation, including the secessionist parts.

Down in southern Illinois, secessionist sympathizers were reported to be threatening to send 500 contrabands (blacks) to the *Tribune* "as a present." "Send them," urged the paper, which asserted it could "locate them where they might demonstrate to the doubters in negro humanity, that chattels as they were . . . a negro owning himself and his children, is of more and better service to the State than the same colored person bought, sold and driven to his unwilling task."

The *Times* blamed the *Tribune* for starting the war. The *Tribune* spoke bitterly of "a Tory editor of this city who has served Jeff Davis long enough."

On October 6, the *Tribune* reported a victory at Corinth, Mississippi, where Union forces under Gen. William S. Rosecrans turned back a Confederate assault. But Rosecrans failed to follow up the victory, and when the *Tribune* learned that the Union had again missed a chance to crush the Southern force, it renewed its cry: "We move that Grant be let loose. He can take Chattanooga in a month and before winter rains set in will be on his way to the Gulf." Lincoln had somewhat the same idea. On November 25, the paper said: "We are glad to chronicle the fact that Grant has been let loose." McClellan, arrogant and ineffective but beloved by his troops, was removed from command at last, and Gen. Ambrose Burnside replaced him as head of the Army of the Potomac. Grant was given more discretionary power in commanding the Army of the Tennessee. Albert Bodman had the "exclusive" story for the *Chicago Tribune,* which indicated the editors believed their paper was first, in the West at least, to learn the news. But Grant was dealt a chastising defeat on December 20 when the Confederates seized his supply depot at Holly Springs, in northern Mississippi, and it would be a year, rather than a month, before Union forces took Chattanooga.

As Grant continued his campaign to clear the Mississippi River southward, Bodman covered much of the action. One of Bod's major stories of the river war, concerning an attempt to run the Vicksburg blockade, appeared in the *Tribune* on March 3, 1863. It was datelined "Steamer *Era No. 5,* In Red River, February 15, 1863," and began:

> The career of the gallant *Queen of the West* is ended. Her crew are dispersed; some are wounded, some are killed, and more are taken prisoners. A small remnant, so far escaped from death and capture, are now about twenty miles from the mouth of Red River, moving as rapidly as Providence permits, from the scene of one of the most thrilling incidents of the rebellion, towards the far-famed old city of Vicksburg. . . . We had intended

> to leave on Monday, but certain repairs were, at the last moment, found
> necessary. . . . Captain Ellet decided to run the batteries [*on the Vicksburg
> bluffs*] by star light.

The *Queen of the West* slipped past the Confederate guns without a shot
being fired, but short of her goal, a river depot for rebel supplies, the
vessel was attacked by shore-based guerrillas. According to Bodman, this
so angered Captain Ellet that he landed his force and burned their
headquarters, a cotton plantation. The *Queen* captured *Era No. 5*, loaded
with corn for the Confederate army, plus 15 Texas cavalrymen and four
officers, who were made prisoner. Then the *Queen of the West* ran
aground.

> The pilots tried to back her off, but we were immovable. Shots were flying,
> shells bursting and worst of all we could not reply. Three huge 32 pounders
> exploded on deck, in between the smoke stacks, not 20 feet from our heads.
> Soon we heard a crash among the machinery below . . . another crash and
> we learned that the escape pipe was gone—then another and the steam
> chest was fractured. The whole boat shook with the rush of escaping steam.
> The engine room was crowded with engineers, firemen, negroes, prisoners,
> who had sought that place under the impression it was the safest. Now the
> shells penetrated the hull. The *DeSoto* came near and sent her yawl to pick
> up survivors. I was sitting on the rudder of the *Queen* and was picked up. On
> the way to the *DeSoto* we passed Captain Ellet and Captain McCullough of
> the *Commercial* riding on a cotton bale. Then three boatloads of Confeder-
> ates reached the *Queen* and our boys remaining there became their prisoners.

On the way back past Vicksburg aboard the *Era No. 5*, the Union men
no longer had the benefit of darkness. "We took 100 shots in 35 miles,
which is pretty good for an old steamer," Bodman noted.

*   *   *

Historians would later demonstrate that economic forces produced the
Civil War and made the defeat of the South inevitable even before the
conflict had begun. But as the war continued, it was the zeal and determination of the idealists, especially the ardor of self-proclaimed radicals
such as the *Chicago Tribune,* that forced political and military action and
kept the pressure on the South. The paper was ecstatic about the proclamation of emancipation that would become effective on January 1, 1863.
Dissenters were not far away, and they became menacing. All who
opposed the war were usually lumped together under the label Copperhead or secessionist, though there were some in central and southern
Illinois who wanted the Union preserved but opposed the freeing of
slaves. Early in 1863, Joseph Medill helped to counter the influence of
the Southern sympathizers by aiding in the organization of Union League

clubs, loyal to the Federal government. (One such club is still extant and powerful in Chicago, another in Philadelphia.) The paper pushed hard for the work of the Sanitary Commission, and it generally covered the news in a sprightly way. It even changed its Puritanical ideas about prize-fighting, publishing the results of the Jem Mace-Tom King battle in England for the heavyweight championship of the world on a Sunday! Jem Mace was the winner in the 43rd round. There was no recorded complaint from *Tribune* readers.

Throughout the war the *Tribune* was a formidable, implacable, and hated enemy of Congressman Clement L. Vallandigham of Ohio, a leader of the antiwar movement in the North, a prime obstructionist to Lincoln's policies, and the reputed dictator of the Knights of the Golden Circle and other Copperhead organizations. The *Tribune* kept up a steady fire on the congressman, even after he had been banished to rebel territory, whence he went to Canada to direct his activities. Other *Tribune* targets were the *Times* of London, which the paper regarded as the most noisome foreign enemy of the North ("the lying *Times,* with money its god"), and the *Chicago Times,* its local counterpart. In autumn, 1862, the *Tribune* published a series of articles demonstrating the real danger of a prosecessionist movement becoming effective in Northern areas, especially in Ohio, Indiana, and Illinois, charging that the Knights of the Golden Circle intended to start civil war in these states if they won the November elections.

The *Tribune* gave special support to Congressman Isaac Arnold, running for reelection from the Second District in Chicago, a spare, spade-bearded former Democrat who was proving especially loyal to the Union and effective as a Lincoln supporter. In addition, as a member of the House committee on railroads, he had made sure that Chicago would have a connection with the proposed Union Pacific Railroad. His opponent was the ubiquitous Francis Sherman, builder and owner of the Sherman House, Democratic mayor of Chicago despite *Tribune* opposition, and, said the paper, "a senile tool of Tory Democrats. Who votes for Sherman? Every disloyal man."

On November 4, 1862, Arnold won reelection, decisively walloping Sherman. "A glorious victory," crowed the *Tribune.* But results were not glorious elsewhere. Radical Republicans in some parts of the country were dissatisfied with Lincoln's handling of the war and thought his emancipation statement on September 22 did not go far enough. Other opponents of the president pointed to his suspension of the privilege of *habeas corpus* and the arbitrary arrests of suspected seditionists. Determined Democrats won in New York, Pennsylvania, Ohio, and Indiana, all states that had supported Lincoln in 1860. The Democrats also won control of the state legislature in Illinois. As this result became known, the

Tribune grew apprehensive. Insurrection in Illinois and Indiana was not unthinkable, and the editors watched the situation closely. It promised its readers that it would keep a vigilant eye on the officially elected Copperheads in Springfield.

The paper never ceased, in between criticisms of some of his policies, to reiterate its esteem for "Honest Old Abe," saying characteristically on October 15, 1862:

> It is with patriotic pride, with heartfelt satisfaction, that we can now, with deeper impressiveness than ever before, say to the public that whatever may be the faults and deficiencies of our President, in the sum and completeness of his character, his fitness for his position, his present stand before the bar of the civilized world . . . he is more nearly what a great and noble people desire . . . in a chief magistrate than anyone . . . since the first president.

Such acclamations would appear with increasing frequency as the war went on, and as the temper of the populace turned against the conflict.

The *Tribune* was much interested in the welfare of the farmers, demanding lower shipping and elevator rates in their behalf. When the farmers held an agricultural convention in Dixon, the paper provided two and a half columns of coverage and happily reported that its own campaign for the manufacture of sorghum molasses to replace supplies once received from New Orleans had been endorsed by the convention; it called for greater attention to the possibility of increased iron production in Chicago, pointing out that the city was the natural meeting place for Lake Superior ore and Illinois coal; looked into the possibility of using wood pulp for the manufacture of newsprint; hailed the arrival of a new 19-inch refractor telescope in the city; and described the progress of the new State Street railway, which now had expanded and was carrying an average of 15,000 passengers a day in a city with a population of 135,500.

On January 8, 1863, the *Tribune* published what it said was the longest telegraphic dispatch ever carried in a newspaper in the Northwest, a four-column report on the Battle of Stones River (Murfreesboro), in which Braxton Bragg, the Confederate general, lost to Rosecrans in the struggle for the Nashville and Chattanooga Railroad and the Nashville Pike after having won the battle on the first day. The *Tribune*'s narrative, probably written by Bodman, filled the four columns, and the casualty list printed two weeks later filled six columns more. General Rosecrans had moved forward in his march on Chattanooga, though he seemed temporarily checked, at a cost of 1,677 killed and 7,543 wounded, while Bragg's losses were 1,294 killed and 7,945 wounded. The Federal flanking movement in the West was in progress, helping to offset the disastrous defeat of Burnside at Fredericksburg, Virginia, in December.

More than 3,800 Confederate prisoners arrived for internment in

Camp Douglas, a barracks located south of Chicago, but while these men inspired some direct concern, the *Tribune* was more worried about the possibilities of insurrection among the people of southern Illinois. When the state legislature organized, the Copperheads were in fact in a majority, and they threatened to pass a resolution calling for the impeachment of Lincoln, "the usurper." The *Tribune* recognized the dangers and thundered against them. "Abraham Lincoln a usurper?" it yelped. "Abraham Lincoln the tyrant whose hand is destroying the liberties of this country? Abraham Lincoln, himself a creation of our institutions, the enemy of popular liberty? You lie, you scoundrels, you know you lie!" Governor Yates, a loyal Republican, maintained tight control of his contingent in Springfield, and frequent no-quorum sessions kept the Copperheads from passing any prosecessionist resolutions, except one calling for an armistice, before the legislature adjourned in February.

But the danger to Illinois and neighboring states persisted, and Medill and the *Tribune* pressed the campaign for the formation of Union League clubs throughout the state. Reporters on all fronts sent in stories describing the revulsion of the soldiers against secessionist sentiment in Illinois. By March, the paper reported that 500 Union League clubs had been formed to help defend the state against any Copperhead strikes.

In April, the paper had to deal with the pestiferous Mayor Sherman again. "Let the Union League boys remember today," urged the *Tribune* on April 21, election day. "The Knights of the Golden Circle will be as busy as Old Nick in a gale of wind." Again Sherman defeated the *Tribune*-endorsed candidate, Thomas Bryan, but only by 150 votes. "We make no attempt to conceal our disappointment and mortification," the paper mourned. "A bad day's work has been done. The city is dishonored."

In June, Gen. Ambrose Burnside, whose luxuriant side-whiskers inspired the term "sideburns," added to his fame, or notoriety, by ordering the suppression of Wilbur F. Storey's *Chicago Times*. Burnside, who had been removed from command of the Army of the Potomac and was headquartered in Cincinnati as commander of the Army of the Ohio, dispatched soldiers from Camp Douglas to shut down the presses. Crowds hostile to the action and to the *Tribune* gathered in Courthouse Square. Speakers called for the destruction of the *Tribune,* and an armed guard was set up at the *Tribune* building. The paper did not comment on Burnside's action other than to assert it was not soon enough. It said of the crowd demonstrating in behalf of the *Times* that half of them were Republicans who, "under the pretense of defending free speech, met to assail the government. . . . Let us hope that in all future gatherings . . . Union men may not give dignity to the proceedings." The paper described the agitators in the crowd as "refuse and offscourings of the

Copperhead party," and suggested that the Knights of the Golden Circle had inspired the cries and threats against the *Tribune*.

President Lincoln revoked General Burnside's order on June 4. Said the *Tribune* the following day: "That action was as unexpected as the action of Burnside. . . . Yesterday, before the revocation of the Order was announced, there was a clear majority of our citizens not only in favor of Order 84, but resolved that it should be enforced against any mob opposition." But a meeting of responsible citizens, including some friendly to the *Tribune,* such as Senator Trumbull and former mayor Ogden, had passed a resolution asking Lincoln to revoke the Burnside order. The *New York World* printed the *Chicago Times*'s claims that those with "interests in the *Tribune*" had inspired the meeting to save the paper from destruction. "This is a point blank fabrication," declared the *Tribune*. "No living human being that owns a dime's interest in the *Tribune* had anything to do with the meeting, or knew that such a dispatch was prepared, until after it was sent. . . . The proprietors and friends of the *Tribune* felt perfectly confident of their entire ability to repel any number of Copperheads that might attempt its destruction."

Later, on June 7, the *Tribune* exculpated President Lincoln from all blame for revoking Burnside's order and gave further indication of its own readiness in the emergency. Lincoln, said the paper,

> had probably not seen or read a copy of the sesesh *Times* since he was inaugurated. . . . The President rarely reads any newspaper. . . . On Thursday night, when all prudent men knew that serious trouble was expected, our business office was protected against rebel bullets by a proper barricade. . . . Now that [*the* Times] again has free license to belch its treason . . . let its dupes remember that when they see fit to attack our office, they will find the *Tribune* fully prepared to welcome them with sharp sounds and sudden illuminations. We know no fear.

VICTORY AND TRAGEDY

9

The effective date of the Emancipation Proclamation, January 1, 1863, was an occasion of joy and triumph for the *Chicago Tribune,* and abolitionists everywhere, but freedom for an estimated 3 million slaves was a long and bloody distance from realization. "We have the Proclamation," the *Tribune* said, "a late but grateful recognition of the finger of God in the affairs of nations as well as individual man. There need be no fears as a result of what Mr. Lincoln has done." But there were fears, grave fears. It was not yet clear that the South, grower of cotton and tobacco, was to collapse from shortages of food, money, and war materiel—the ability and valor of Southern fighting men effectively obscured that fact. It was not yet clear that General Grant, beginning his sanguinary struggle to open the Mississippi, would succeed not only in seizing Vicksburg, but in sending Sherman from Chattanooga through the Southern heartland, before crushing Lee. In January the capital of the United States was threatened, the South appeared capable of breaking the Federal blockade, and there was even danger that the Confederates and their Copperhead supporters would carry the war into Illinois and Indiana.

Spring brought no improvement. In April Gen. Joseph Hooker, who had replaced Burnside at the head of the Army of the Potomac, confidently set off on yet another Union attempt to take Richmond. In early May, the Army of the Potomac was put to flight by Robert E. Lee's much smaller forces at Chancellorsville, Virginia. Richmond seemed farther away than ever. The outlook was just as bleak in the West, where Grant

183

appeared bogged down in the swamps and wilderness of Mississippi as he applied his python pressure to Vicksburg.

Lee, seeking a decisive victory to break the North's will to continue the war, took the offensive in June. On June 28, 1863, President Lincoln, still trying to find a winning commander for the Army of the Potomac, turned to Gen. George Gordon Meade, a quiet, hardworking, lean and long West Pointer. Meade's troops sometimes called him "the damned old goggle-eyed snapping turtle." The *Tribune* cautiously reserved judgment until Meade proved whether he would fight. It developed that Meade would have to fight, for Lee had come out of his trenches in home terrain to force the action at Gettysburg. On July 1, Lee's troops mauled the badly outnumbered Meade forces on Seminary Ridge, and might have turned defeat into a rout and total disaster for Meade if the South's Gen. Richard S. Ewell had pressed home the attack. But Meade's army was rallied by Generals Winfield S. Hancock and Oliver O. Howard, and on July 2, greatly reinforced, occupied the crest of Cemetery Ridge and Little and Big Round Tops. Lee attacked, sustained heavy losses, and achieved no gains. On the third day the Confederates renewed the attack, and the disastrous charge of Pickett became history. On July 4, Lee's defeated army moved back toward Virginia. The casualties at the crucial Battle of Gettysburg were appalling. The Union lost 3,155 killed, 14,529 wounded, and 5,365 missing; Confederate losses totaled 3,903 killed, 18,735 wounded, 5,425 missing.

Meanwhile, in the western theater, Vicksburg at last fell to Grant on July 4. The *Tribune* had a full page on the Gettysburg triumph on July 7, and the next day another page on the Vicksburg victory. Its own writers covered Grant, but the paper relied on press services and other newspapers for the Gettysburg report. A world "scoop" was won by the *New York Herald,* which had eight reporters on the scene and had set up its own telegraph line to the Gettysburg battlefield.

The joyous news of the twin triumphs was marred by personal tragedy for Joseph Medill. His brother William, a major in Gen. Elon J. Farnsworth's cavalry, a force raised in Chicago with Joseph Medill's aid, had been gravely wounded. Farnsworth's Eighth Illinois, engaged in an attack as dismounted skirmishers, struck the Confederate rear near Williamsport, Maryland, on July 6. General Farnsworth was killed in the fighting, and William sustained a critical stomach wound. Joseph hurried east to be at his side. For days, almost without rest, Joseph helped to care for his brother in a military hospital near Fredericksburg. Katherine Medill wrote him that she would come east soon to help. *"I will nurse him,"* she wrote. *"I will talk him back to health."* But then Joseph's telegram was delivered: "TELL MRS. MEDILL TO REMAIN. THE MAJOR WILL BE NO MORE BEFORE SHE COULD ARRIVE."

Medill's diary indicates that William died on July 16 at 10:20 A.M. The funeral was held from Joseph Medill's home on Washington Boulevard on July 22. Two companies of the 15th Illinois regiment from Camp Douglas and representatives of the Chicago Typographical Union escorted the body through downtown Chicago, past the *Tribune* building on Clark Street, and north to Graceland Cemetery. William Medill had led his regiment, the paper said, in 19 battles, and while in Virginia the regiment had killed or captured nearly 2,000 rebels, liberated 5,000 slaves, and once approached within three miles of Richmond.

The *Tribune* meantime hailed the twin Union victories, printed columns of details, compared Vicksburg with other famous sieges in history, and taunted its enemies. "How will the London *Times* take the Vicksburg and Gettysburg victories?" it asked on July 20. "All that our great unseen enemy, the master of the *Times,* could do has been done to damage us with the English people. It was only on April 29 that the *Times* said the Northwest must give up any hope of seeing the Mississippi open again. All that is now smashed like a dream." And, of Grant: "The laurels of Grant are green and flourishing. He has more work to do. With this and the crushing of Lee's army, patriots may hope to see the winding up of this wicked and causeless rebellion. . . . Let the peace terms embrace freedom to all slaves in the rebellious states, pardon and amnesty to the people and death to Jeff Davis and his infamous conspirators."

The paper sent a reporter to Niagara Falls to cover the strange campaign of Vallandigham, running for governor of Ohio from exile in Canada. It predicted that the New York draft riots would not be repeated elsewhere in the country, and especially not in Illinois. "Only 9,000 will be needed at this time [*in July*] for the Illinois draft as we have sent more than the required number," the paper said. "Let no one fear riots here." The *Tribune* had long urged the draft, but it viewed dimly the provision that substitutes could be hired by the payment of $300. It was true that many men had taken the places of others in the militia at prices of from $300 to $1,000, but these were private arrangements. The payment plan was unjust, even though sometimes it meant that one brother with obligations at home would pay another who was willing if not eager to take his place. The *Tribune* especially disliked the government's imprimatur on such a system and by fall declared editorially that the draft was a waste of effort, yielding only 35,000 men out of 250,000 called up in 12 states. The War Department exemptions left "a hole as big as a barn door," the *Tribune* said. "We warned the Secretary of War when we first saw the Leiber [*exemptions*] list that the draft would be a failure."

Now President Lincoln called for 300,000 volunteers for three years. States could supply the men by forming and filling militia companies by any means they chose. If men did not volunteer in the required numbers, the state would have to draft. Chicago remained unworried. It had raised funds to pay an average bounty of $400 per volunteer, and expected to continue to do so.

*   *   *

The war went on. Joseph Medill was depressed since the death of Will and drained by the wartime struggle, and he was having differences with Dr. Ray. He returned reluctantly to Washington. At home the *Tribune* was fighting for the election of Republicans to state offices, and William Bross was helping to raise the 29th U.S. Colored Regiment, which was to be commanded by his brother, John. There was heavy coverage of local news and much criticism of the way the booming city was being run. On September 25, the paper said:

> Though Chicago may boast rapid and wonderful metropolitan advances in population, prosperity and civic power, we are very far behind every other locality in the country in matters of public taste. Our growth has been a rude, uncultivated one . . . there is not a single park or drive in the city. True, we have cow pastures and rotten plank roads dignified with these names and a shame to the reputation of the city. Dearborn park [*at Michigan and Randolph*]—a few shriveled trees without a flower, overgrown with rank weeds, the receptacle of tin cans, dead animals and rubbish. The Court House is a standing disgrace to the city. Let us have trees and flowers and walks.

On September 19–20, Union General Rosecrans and his Army of the Cumberland suffered a costly defeat at Chickamauga Creek. Pursued by Braxton Bragg's Confederates, Rosecrans's shattered force withdrew to Chattanooga. Bragg entrenched on high ground overlooking the city, and the Army of the Cumberland found itself trapped between the Confederates and the Tennessee River.

When it became clear that Rosecrans was in genuine trouble at Chattanooga, the *Tribune* urged that Grant should take charge in the West, a suggestion frequently reiterated. But Grant was under a cloud again. It was reported that he had been drinking, and this time the report was totally true. The little, taciturn general, who reputedly ordered thousands of men into battle with a cold eye and a cold heart, had gone on a two-day spree during the siege of Vicksburg while he was aboard the U.S.S. *Diligence* for a reconnaissance up the Yazoo River. The general spent much of his time in the vessel's bar, emerging with staggering gait and slurred speech. Sylvanus Cadwallader, though a war correspondent for the *Chicago Times,* the notorious Copperhead paper that consistently attacked the Northern cause, had nonetheless won Grant's confidence and become his friend. He sought now to get the general's aides or the boat's captain to turn off the whiskey supply, but they declined until

Cadwallader threatened to report them to a higher command. The bar was closed, and Cadwallader undertook to minister to General Grant.

"I then took the general in hand myself," he recalled years later, "enticed him into his stateroom, locked myself in the room with him (having the key in my pocket) and commenced throwing the bottles of whiskey which stood on the table through the windows . . . into the river." Grant ordered Cadwallader out, and when the newsman refused he unsuccessfully attempted to open the door, shouting orders for it to be opened. Finally, Grant settled down and slept.

Charles A. Dana, formerly of the *New York Tribune* and then a special agent for the War Department, was aboard the *Diligence* specifically to investigate drinking charges against Grant. He learned nothing from Cadwallader and in his reminiscences wrote, "Grant was ill and went to bed soon after we started."

In the morning, Dana recalled, Grant appeared for breakfast "fresh as a rose, clean shirt and all, quite himself." But at a subsequent stop that evening, Cadwallader returned from news hunting to find Grant aboard another craft, drunk again. He lured him ashore, where Grant leaped onto a horse appropriately named Kangaroo. "Grant literally tore through and over everything in his way," Cadwallader recalled. "The air was full of dust, ashes and embers from camp fires; and shouts and curses of those he rode down. . . . I took after him as fast as I could go, but my horse was no match for Kangaroo."

Cadwallader finally did catch up and seized the reins of the general's horse. There was a struggle in the dusk. "Fearing discovery of his rank and situation [*I took him to*] the foot of a bluff. Here I helped him dismount, secured our horses . . . and induced the general to lay down on the grass with the saddle for a pillow. He was soon asleep." After his nap Grant returned to camp and bade his waiting officers good-night "in a natural tone and manner, and started to his tent as steadily as he ever walked in his life." Cadwallader's aid in covering up the incident cemented his relationship with Grant. Later, in response to continuing rumors that Grant had a drinking problem, Lincoln summed the solution neatly: "What kind of whiskey does he drink? I'll send a barrel of it to my other generals."

In addition to urging Grant as commander of the western armies, the *Tribune* was encouraging Lincoln to get rid of Old Brains Halleck and take an active role in the war in the East. Lincoln, said the paper on October 16,

> has more horse-sense and more practical information about military matters, especially in relation to the Army of the Potomac, than any other man. . . . If he would put out that beetle-headed Halleck, whose study is how not to do it, unless it is done according to the traditional policy of the

ancients, when shield and buckler, catapults and boiling oil were the weapons of warfare; and . . . put himself actively in command of the forces about the Capital, he would achieve the victories for the attainment of which all his policy has been shaped. . . . Let Old Abe order and mount his horse, and unsheath his sword.

On October 16, Lincoln named Grant general of the armies west of the Alleghenies and instructed him to save the Army of the Cumberland. The *Chicago Tribune* was pleased, congratulating both Lincoln and Grant. Sylvanus Cadwallader, who had suppressed a great opportunity to embarrass the Federals in his Copperhead-oriented newspaper, changed jobs, becoming a correspondent for Bennett's *New York Herald,* and followed Grant to Chattanooga. The *Tribune* also had a correspondent on the scene, the ubiquitous Albert Bodman.

Bodman had been with Grant at Holly Springs, according to family accounts, and probably did not precede the general to bleak Chattanooga by many days, but, wherever he might be, he seemed to enjoy life and to communicate that enjoyment to his readers. En route to the besieged city he wrote:

Night overtook us at the house of a genuine East Tennessean, and we were compelled to crave his hospitality for the night. The family consisted of a farmer, his wife, an infant, two marriageable daughters, a grown son and four younger ones. Nine [*sic*] altogether, besides the two of us. About nine o'clock the husband who had been watching the glittering coals in the ten-foot fireplace, waked up with a snort. "Wall, strangers, you kin peel."

I started, and looked enquiringly. "You kin peel," he repeated. "Me and th' old woman wants to tumble in."

Here was a fix for a modest man. Should I disrobe before the old man and his wife, not to speak of the marriageable daughters, or should I tumble in, regardless of white dimity and feathers? I turned down the coverlid [*sic*], pressed my hand upon the downy pillows and glanced at the sheets, white as driven snow. No. It would never do to anger this good housewife, and, reflecting that if she could stand the pressure, I ought, I deliberately kicked off my boots and spurs, laid aside my vest, drew off my nether integuments and leapt so rapidly my shirt described an angle of 90 degrees. I landed in the center of the bed of down. Captain Steele followed ditto.

The husband and wife and the marriageable daughters piled into another nearby bed, I believe. How they slept and who slept with me I never knew. I dreamed of a large family and two marriageable daughters who hovered over the bedside on large white cotton wings, until they finally flitted to the live coals in the fireplace. I slept well and was the last up in the morning. We had a breakfast of milk and corn bread and feed for our horses.

On November 20, as Grant's armies made final preparations to break the siege of Chattanooga, the *Tribune* printed a 300-word dispatch from

Pennsylvania on the dedication of the Gettysburg battlefield. "The oration of the Hon. Edward Everett, the solemn dirge of the choir, and the dedicatory remarks of President Lincoln will live long among the annals of war," the paper said. The *Chicago Times* declared that Lincoln acted the clown, with "silly, flat and dishwatery utterances." The following day the *Tribune* printed Lincoln's remarks in full, saying: "More than any other single event will this glorious dedication nerve the heroes to a deeper resolution of the living to conquer at all hazard."

As if to underscore their "deeper resolution," Union forces at Chattanooga almost immediately began their assaults on the entrenched Confederates. On the second day of battle, November 24, while Gen. William Sherman challenged the Confederate right, Gen. "Fighting Joe" Hooker's forces stormed mist-shrouded Lookout Mountain on the left, in an action often called "the Battle above the Clouds." Bodman was attached to Hooker's army and so was able to report on what turned out to be a visually spectacular but militarily unremarkable operation. The mountain was lightly defended and was soon secured. The action nevertheless was an exciting one, and Bodman as usual provided a graphic account. The end of the Battle of Chattanooga came unexpectedly on November 25, when what was intended as a diversion to aid Sherman's progress developed into a spontaneous surge that carried Gen. George Thomas's forces nearly 500 feet up the steep inclines of near-impregnable Missionary Ridge and routed the center of Bragg's line. The siege was broken, the rebels were driven from Tennessee.

President Lincoln confided to close associates after the Tennessee victories that he had made up his mind about the general he needed to command all the Union armies, but more than three months would pass before he announced his choice. The *Tribune,* meantime, was making clear whom it would support for president in 1864. On November 3, 1863, in an editorial entitled "A Look Ahead," the paper said:

> [*Abraham Lincoln*] is making his way nearer and nearer to the people's heart . . . the most popular man in the United States, not alone among the Radicals with whom we labor, but among the classes who are pleased to call themselves Conservatives—among the soldiers and officers as well as among the civilians, among men of the East as well as among men of the West. . . .
>
> We do not know what a year will bring forth but the political outlook . . . tells us . . . that our old fashioned Illinoisan will continue to rule the country after March, 1865, with the same vigor, wisdom and success that have marked his administration since March, 1861. . . . Though our zeal may sometimes have outrun his motions since the war began; and though we, with only a partial and limited view of the vast field of operations, have often

chafed against the delay of him who saw and comprehended the whole, we have never for a moment doubted that Mr. Lincoln, in whom there never was an impulse of unlawful ambition, a shadow of dishonesty, a wish that was not for the welfare of his country . . . is, his errors and faults all included, the wisest, the safest, the most unselfish—the man most fitted for the time in which he lives, and for the desperate dangers against which he contends.

The Eastern papers were already speaking of rewarding Grant with the presidency, and once again the *Tribune* had to ward off an Eastern attack to safeguard Lincoln. This time the potential candidate himself helped. "Gen. Grant is a great strategist," the paper reported with satisfaction on December 23. "He has headed off an attempt of the *New York Herald* to kill him by advocating him for the presidency." On January 5, 1864, the paper repeated its conviction about Lincoln: "The public generally means to elect Mr. Lincoln . . . God meant him for President or the nation is deceived." The *Tribune* warned the *New York Herald* to keep its "Copperhead slime" off General Grant and said of former friend Uncle Horace of the *New York Tribune,* who sought peace at any price and was a "no two terms" advocate: "Greeley is in the main honest but is addled by the pertinacity of brazen women who think they have a mission and long-haired baboons who delude themselves with the notion they are philosophers and the whole tribe of reformers."

During the spring of 1864 there was a great outpouring of letters from Medill to political leaders such as Trumbull, Colfax, and Washburne. Medill appeared to be reasserting himself not only as a proprietor and editorial superintendent of the *Chicago Tribune* but also as a founder and leader of the Republican party. His letters indicate that he had an excellent grasp of needed strategy and that, in the course of the war, he had put away his customary shyness and forbearance and had grown tough. Though Grant had put off the effort by Eastern Republicans to tout him for the presidency, Medill and others began to fear that the Copperheads might manage to make Grant the Democratic nominee. Could Grant be counted on to resist such temptation? In May, Medill wrote to Washburne, one of the general's most trusted advisors:

> *If Grant will . . . calmly apply himself to closing up the war and putting out the last embers of the rebellion he will have all he can attend to for a couple of years. He will in the meantime have the administration with him and the great party of freedom on his side and four years hence will be their candidate and president for eight years. Nothing more certain surely. . . . Now let me whisper a word in your private ear. How would you like a seat in Lincoln's Cabinet? The Postmaster General's place? There you would control an immense patronage. . . . Now sir, if you keep Grant clear of copperhead temptations and out of their hands Lincoln must give you that seat in the Cabinet if you want it. He dare not refuse it. . . . Once in the Cabinet you would*

be the master spirit of the administration. . . . The Old Trib is popular among the
"peeps" when you get right down to the bone about it. A good many swear at it, but
swear by it notwithstanding as it does a good deal of their political thinking for them.

Medill's actions may have been triggered in part by his conviction that the beleaguered Lincoln was in serious political trouble. Some opponents objected to Lincoln's announced intention to continue the war but to deal leniently with Southern states and their citizens when the rebellion was over; others were opposed to breaking with the nearly 30-year tradition of a president serving a single term. Medill must also have been influenced by the fact that he could no longer rely on his principal editorial associates for active policy leadership at the *Tribune.* Scripps had long since departed to become postmaster; William Bross, heavily involved in civic and political affairs, soon would be nominated and elected lieutenant governor, and he had a penchant for travel and exploration; and Ray, following Lincoln's announcement of the Emancipation Proclamation, seemed to have lost interest in the war and the paper.

Charles Ray, the crusader, had achieved the goal toward which he had thrust ever since leaving Galena, the dedication of Northern power to the freeing of the slaves. Like Medill and the other proprietors, he was weary. His wife, Jane, had died during the summer of 1863, and his own health was precarious. He sent the children to live with relatives in New York State, but he could not conquer his despondency and sleeplessness. Ray and Medill had had their differences over the years, and of late the bickering, disagreement, even signs of jealousy over credit for the selection and election of Lincoln had increased. Ray let it be known that he wished to sell his stock, and the last of it was purchased by the other proprietors in late November, 1863.

Ray's departure was the most significant of several changes taking place at the *Tribune.* When it became evident that Ray would be leaving the paper, his protégé, Horace White, had resigned his position as the Washington correspondent and worked briefly for the War Department. Early in 1864, White joined with Henry Villard, formerly a *New York Tribune* correspondent, in forming a news service agency. He was able to take the *Chicago Tribune,* of which he was a minor stockholder, to the agency as his account. Bohemian Albert Bodman returned to Chicago after covering the Tennessee campaign for the *Tribune;* he served for a time as city editor, then went into politics and was elected Chicago's city clerk.

Bodman was succeeded as city editor by quiet, scholarly George Putnam Upton, another former war correspondent. Upton, born in Roxbury, Massachusetts, was a highest honors graduate of Brown University. He had contributed to literary magazines before coming to Chicago, in the fall of 1855. His second day in town he was hired as a reporter for the *Daily Native Citizen,* an obscure journal of Know-Nothing opinion owned by Simon Buckner, the same Buckner who later commanded Confederate forces at Fort Donelson and was given responsibility for the surrender. Upton joined the *Tribune* in 1860, taking "the local chair." In 1862 he covered the war on the Mississippi, reporting on the capture of Island No. 10, New Madrid, and Fort Pillow. Upton became music and drama critic of the paper in 1868, preferring that duty to the chores of news editor, to which position he had been promoted. He concluded his career as an editorial writer, a confidant of Medill, and a Tribune Company director.

Medill now undertook to perform the triple duties of proprietor, editor and policy maker, and superintendent of the editorial, or newsgathering, department, responsible for the general mechanical operations, circulation, and advertising. He had the role of the modern publisher and editor but did not assume that title. Medill shared the business responsibilities of the paper with Alfred Cowles and William Rand, who had become a minor shareholder late in 1863, possibly by purchasing some of Ray's stock. Rand had joined the *Tribune* in 1859 as superintendent of the job printing operations, bringing with him as his foreman young Andrew McNally. Ray's resignation left the execution of editorial policy solely in Medill's hands, though the determination of policy would continue to be by vote of all of the proprietors, including absentees Bross and Scripps. That all did not run smoothly was indicated a year later, when some of the stockholders, among them Horace White, became dissatisfied with Medill and wanted to invite Ray back as chief editor. Richard Oglesby, the new Republican governor of Illinois, learned of the schism, and, desiring stability at the *Tribune* for the good of the Northern and Republican cause, wrote to President Lincoln. Dr. Ray was interested in traveling and in the opportunities becoming available for trade with the Southern states, Governor Oglesby suggested. Lincoln acted promptly, and in February, 1865, Ray was given credentials for travel in liberated Southern areas under Federal control and a "trade with the enemy" permit. The former editor, supplied with capital from his recent success in real estate speculation, left for the South.

*   *   *

On March 9, 1864, Ulysses S. Grant was commissioned lieutenant general and given command of all the Union armies. The appointment was greeted with restrained optimism by the *Tribune:*

> What may be said with safety is that Gen. Grant has earned his way to his present position. . . . The manner in which Grant has thus come to his laurels gives us good hope that he will keep them. The man who won't make a speech, even if he is treated to a good dinner; who has no itching for the

presidency that betrays itself under the blandishments of sycophants; who suffers the mosquitoes of criticism to bite him without a wince; and only looks grave and smokes on, gives good assurance that he will keep his balance and do work yet worthy of the public expectation.

By May, Grant and Meade were beginning the campaign to crush Lee's Army of Northern Virginia and take Richmond. The Army of the Potomac crossed the Rapidan River and moved into the Wilderness, near Chancellorsville. News from Grant reached Washington slowly, and there was indecision and worry about the 122,000 men he had taken into the forbidding terrain that had stopped Gen. Joe Hooker the year before. There were rumors of fierce fighting, great loss of life, but then came word that after two days' battle in the Wilderness, Grant had resumed his southward march, surely an indication of victory. "We have won the first round," exulted the *Tribune* on May 10. "For the first time in the war all our available forces are concentrated into one grand movement upon the rebel hosts."

"Our very hearts seem to pause in their beating as we listen, breathless, for the most meager news of the conflict," the editors said on May 13. Then, the day following, "There is a general advance by Grant. We are confident the road to Richmond is now open." To the *Tribune* and Chicago, victory seemed imminent. "We have seen this city excited, but never to that degree as yesterday." As the dispatches came in giving indications of Grant's victory, the city celebrated:

> Cheers and shouts began to go up on the corners of the streets, wherever a dozen were gathered. The saloons were visited, and many men who never before had indulged in excesses became joyous and hilarious as the veriest roisterer in the city. . . . A grand display of fireworks was given at the *Tribune* office in honor of the success of our armies. The Light Guard band discoursed excellent music and, for more than an hour, the whole central portion of the city was ablaze with rockets and Roman candles.

But the "victory" was illusory, and there was no celebration when the casualty lists began to appear—17,666 Federals killed, wounded, or missing in the terrible carnage of the Wilderness, where 10,000 of Lee's force of 62,000 were casualties. At Spotsylvania, Grant lost 10,000 men in a single day, May 12, trying to smash the rebel salient called "Bloody Angle," a square mile of scraggly, tortured earth. Again, heavy rumblings against Grant were heard, but his defiant telegram to Halleck, now chief of staff in Washington, told of his determination: "I PROPOSE TO FIGHT IT OUT ALONG THIS LINE IF IT TAKES ALL SUMMER." In June came Cold Harbor, on the James River, where the Union army lost 7,000 men in a half hour, and 5,000 more before the battle ended in defeat for Grant. But Grant would not retreat, as had happened to the Army of the Potomac in the past. Instead he continued pressing southward and outmaneuvered Lee to approach the nearly impregnable fortifications at Petersburg, 20 miles south of Richmond.

*   *   *

Following Lincoln's call for 500,000 more men in February, 1864, the *Tribune* had heard rumors that Copperheads and "peace sneaks" were again about to attempt insurrection in southern Illinois. The paper dispatched its redoubtable Albert Bodman to investigate, since he had returned from the western front after covering the Tennessee campaign. Joseph Forrest, an aide to Governor Yates, probably arranged for the loan of Bodman's services by the paper. Bodman was to prepare a secret report for the governor as well as to obtain stories for the *Tribune,* and he disappeared into the rural areas of Copperhead country. In March the paper's fears were partly realized when insurrectionists, including the sheriff, attacked the Circuit Court at Charleston, about 160 miles south of Chicago. Yates, who had been alerted to the danger by Bodman, sent in the 54th Illinois Regiment to restore order after several persons had been killed. In midsummer, Bodman prepared his final report for Governor Yates. Bodman wrote that he had visited 11 counties in central and southern Illinois, and said in part: "I am irresistibly led to the conclusion that there is imminent danger of outbreak, unless steps are taken immediately to prevent such a contingency." Bodman declared that armed men were drilling in the various towns of southern and central Illinois, sometimes openly parading in military formations; traitors were sworn into the Confederate service, and irregulars aiding the Confederate cause were looting in some areas. "Citizens cheer for Jeff Davis and promise to shoot an abolitionist on sight. There is armed rebellion in Jasper, Montgomery and Moultrie counties." Bodman urged Governor Yates to consider using the state militia, or to seek the assistance of the Federal government. Yates acted swiftly and decisively. In August he called out 2,000 militiamen and sent them into the Mattoon area, where Bodman had indicated a large camp of irregulars existed. The militia surrounded a group of 700 men, who declined to fight and obeyed orders to disperse. The *Tribune* said the leaders should be caught, tried, and hanged. Bodman's stories on the incipient insurrection in southern Illinois and Indiana ran in the paper through July, August, and September.

The *Tribune* was having Copperhead problems in Chicago, too. The paper attacked Francis Sherman, whom it described as the Copperhead mayor, nor did it spare the Copperhead city council or the Copperhead *Chicago Times.* A week of heavy rains left the city knee-deep in mud, and the *Tribune* said it was the fault of incompetent Copperhead city employees, who failed to repair the plank roads and drainage facilities. It asserted that Chicago policemen heard expressing loyalty to the Union were promptly fired. The paper declared that crime was rampant, much of it fostered by criminals from the South who were running the river blockade. The *Tribune* maintained a daily barrage against the criminals, prosecutors, and police, reporting murders, robberies, swindles, gambling, thuggery, and vile traffic in the bodies of young women. Criminals swarmed into the city, seeking a share of the new wartime prosperity. Michael Cassius McDonald was rising as the crown prince of the underworld, where former riverboat gamblers, army deserters, and smugglers swelled the criminal ranks. Challenging McDonald and George Trussell, the reigning ruler of the hoodlums, was "Captain" Hyman, a swaggering lout who carried a six-shooter in the streets and once captured the Tremont Hotel lobby and held it against the police for several hours. Trussell, probably the most successful among the new breed of underworld rulers, ended his career abruptly when Molly Cosgriff, his mistress and a brothel madam, shot him dead. McDonald would win the struggle for power, becoming a political strong man as well as a boss of crime. The gamblers and whores infested wide areas of downtown Chicago, and, said the *Tribune,* they were protected by the mayor.

While the editors were unhappy about the alliance of crime and politics and the low state of municipal management, they were pleased with economic conditions and the growth of Chicago to a population of 156,000. Chicago was, despite the presence of many Copperheads, intensely loyal to the war effort, with leading businessmen contributing funds to the cause as the city regularly exceeded its army enrollment quotas. The city continued to raise and equip troops. Colonel John Bross's black regiment was raised to full strength and in May marched to the *Tribune* building before departing for the East. When the Board of Trade and several Chicago bankers agreed to buy and sell only in legal tender treasury notes, the *Tribune* was pleased, since it had long campaigned for such action. The paper provided a new feature, called "The Voice of the People," where letters received from its readers were printed; it also continued the Medill policy of publishing interesting new books and articles, despite the abundance of war news. One piece of fiction displayed on page one, "The Man Without a Country," by Edward Everett Hale, became a minor classic. The paper thus looked after the general needs of its readers while it also retained sufficient space and energy to continue its daily battle with the pesky *Times.* The feud sometimes descended to odiferous depths: "It is evidence of the strength of the government that it can afford to let alone such malignants as the *Times.* A strong man may carry boils that would kill a weak one. Swine enjoy their own perfume. Nobody cares now for that paper's venom since the rebels are bound to be put under at any rate."

The *Tribune* blamed the *Times* in part for inviting the national Democrats to hold their convention in Chicago, a move it considered insulting impudence. "This party has plunged the nation into war," it fumed. "Its chief strength and power is in the Southern states. War Democrats of the North are denounced as abolitionists. The only states that seceded are Democratic." But the Democrats insisted they were coming to Chicago in August, welcome or not.

As May gave way to June, Grant had not found the way to trap and grind up Lee's armies. Radical Republicans denounced Lincoln's failure to unconditionally abolish slavery, then crush the rebels and confiscate their property. The war seemed as far from conclusion as ever, and President Lincoln appeared to be abandoned by his party and by the country. Nonetheless, the *Tribune* predicted that Old Abe would win the presidential nomination by acclamation when the Republicans met at Baltimore. He almost did, except that 22 Missouri votes were cast for Grant on the first ballot. The vice-presidential nominee was a former Democrat, Andrew Johnson, the military governor of Tennessee. Said the *Tribune* on June 9:

> The nomination of Mr. Lincoln by the National or Union party ⌊*names substituted for Republican to attract prowar Democrats*⌋ is the expression of the substantially unanimous voice of the entire people of the United States, so far as they favor the preservation of the Union and the suppression of the rebellion. . . . God bless our Honest Old Abe and grant him victory over all the Union foes, whether military or political, to the end that the coming four years of his administration may be over a Union wholly free, reunited and peaceful.

Meantime, the fortunes of the North appeared to crumble during the summer of 1864, and Lincoln's popularity continued to diminish. The gold value of the Union greenback sank to 39¢.

On July 11, Gen. Jubal Early pushed his rebel skirmishers into the Maryland outskirts of Washington after defeating Gen. Lew Wallace's outnumbered forces. There was genuine danger that the Federal capital would fall, since its powerful guns were mostly manned by convalescing wounded, government clerks, and a few experienced cannoneers. Jubal Early, tough, grizzled, and mean, was a former West Pointer turned lawyer who led an army of seasoned, lean veterans. His plan was to disrupt Washington and seize supplies if he could not at least temporarily capture the city. He almost succeeded in all three purposes. But Grant, alerted by Secretary Stanton, sent battle-hardened troops under Gen. Horatio G. Wright to the defense of Washington, and they arrived as the rebel skirmishers were within 600 yards of the capital's boundaries. Old Jube Early was defeated and driven back, and Washington was saved. The *Tribune* professed minor concern about the episode. "It is humiliating to have the shadow of a doubt whether our capital is safe," it commented, but "why should we, away here in Illinois, be distressing ourselves about that town, while the people who live within a day's communication of it . . . are so indifferent to capture as to run away . . . and hide from a few hundred marauders?"

Farther south, Grant was stopped before Petersburg, finding its works impenetrable. On July 30, the North narrowly missed breaking through the massive fortification when coal diggers in the Union army counter-mined the rebel works and blasted a huge gap through which a brigade of troops was supposed to charge. Instead, Gen. James H. Ledlie's brigade literally got lost in the vast crater caused by the blast and could not cross it. General Edward Ferrero's black brigades, including the 29th U.S. Colored Regiment, which William Bross had helped raise, were sent in as reinforcements, but they, too, floundered in the crater and suffered heavy casualties in the hopeless assault. Among the dead was Col. John Bross. "Already in the history of this war, two associates of the Tribune Company have been called to mourn the loss of brothers killed in battle," said the paper. "The *Tribune* will not hate this accursed rebellion and its cause less because its blows have fallen upon hearts in our midst."

Grant's campaign to destroy Lee's army had been extremely costly, and on July 19, 1864, Lincoln issued a call for 500,000 additional troops to be supplied by the states. The Illinois quota was 52,000 men, and Cook County, despite the pleadings of the *Tribune* and the efforts of local officials, was having trouble raising its share. Colonel J. L. Hancock, president of the Board of Trade, went to Springfield to consult on the problem. Hancock took the position that since Chicago and Cook County had regularly provided more than quota in past years, the county should not now be required to meet the new quota, but should have credit from the past surplus. Cook County insisted it had a surplus of 1,400 men, but the Federal government had ruled otherwise: Cook County owed 2,000 men. "There is something wrong here," said the *Tribune*. "This county stands ready to honor all just and equitable drafts on her loyalty, but is not quite prepared to pay other people's debts. All our citizens want is fair play and no favors."

*　　*　　*

In August the *Tribune* published its first full-page advertisement, extolling the multifold virtues of Hemhold's Fluid Extract Buchu and Improved Rose Wash. Hemhold's usual one-column advertisement was simply repeated across the page to fill all nine columns. The paper installed an eight-cylinder Hoe press to meet its growing circulation and advertising requirements and announced that it would again publish a campaign weekly, available at club rates, and, of course, it would support the candidacy of Abraham Lincoln. Joseph Medill journeyed to Detroit, where he urged members of the loosely affiliated Western Associated Press to "mind their machinery," always the first consideration. Then he turned their attention to problems of content, and especially the unsatisfactory amount of news received from the New York Associated Press. It was agreed that a formal association of Western newspapers should be organized, and Medill was named permanent secretary of the committee that would explore the possibilities.

When the Democratic National Convention met in Chicago on August 29, it appeared that the *Tribune* was not far off the mark in predicting that Copperheads would control the assemblage. United principally by the desire to oust Lincoln and bring the war to a quick, negotiated conclusion, the delegates permitted the notorious Clement Vallandigham to have major influence in framing the party's platform. Accusing Lincoln of being more interested in abolishing slavery than in preserving the Union and claiming that a military victory was impossible, the convention named George B. McClellan the presidential candidate and George H. Pendleton of Ohio as his running mate. McClellan accepted the nomination but repudiated the peace plank of the platform, denying that the sacrifices made in the struggle for the Union had been in vain. Nonetheless, the Democrats were confident that the country's dissatisfaction with the protracted war would give them victory in November.

But the tides of war were changing. Even before the Democratic convention, Adm. David G. Farragut had won a victory in Mobile Bay, closing the port of Mobile. On September 2, William Tecumseh Sherman's armies entered Atlanta, and three weeks later, while Northern readers were still thrilling to the details of Sherman's great victory, came the news that Philip Sheridan's Army of the Shenandoah had defeated Jubal Early's invading army and was driving the Confederates from the Shenandoah Valley. Northerners, particularly the pro-Lincoln Republicans, were jubilant.

Another lift to Chicago and *Tribune* spirits came with the unraveling of the plot by Capt. Thomas W. Hines, a rebel spy, to free the 9,000 Confederate prisoners held at Camp Douglas, along South Cottage Grove Avenue, and to use them in seizing Chicago. Two weeks prior to the Democratic convention, William Bross of the *Tribune* had heard about such an escape plot and a cache of arms, and he conveyed his information to Gen. B. J. Sweet, commandant of the camp. Sweet was not surprised; he told Bross there had been many reports of such plots and he knew that the camp was organized for a breakout any time that outside help could be obtained. Originally planned to take advantage of the activities associated with the Democratic convention, the breakout was postponed when reinforcements requested by Sweet arrived and were posted conspicuously about Camp Douglas and the city. But the conspirators did not give up, deciding instead to release the rebel prisoners in time to take possession of Chicago on election day, November 8. Again Bross learned of a hidden supply of guns, which he reported to General Sweet.

As election day approached, there were signs that the outside help Sweet feared was about to appear. "Delegations began to arrive from Fayette and Christian counties," Bross wrote years later. "Bushwhackers journeyed north from Missouri and Kentucky. Some came from Indiana, and rebel officers from Canada." On November 7, Sweet's officers and agents descended on the locations they had kept under surveillance since August. At the elegant Richmond House they arrested Col. George St. Leger Grenfell, adjutant to General Morgan of the Confederate army, who had been sent to Chicago to direct the outside forces; J. T. Shanks, an escaped Confederate prisoner; Col. Vincent Marmaduke; Brig. Gen. Charles Walsh, a wealthy Chicagoan and a leader of the Sons of Liberty; Capt. George Cantrill; and others. At Walsh's home, near Camp Douglas, the Federal officers found "two cartloads of large-sized revolvers, loaded and capped, and two hundred muskets and a large quantity of ammunition." By evening, more than 100 men had been arrested. Those conspirators not caught sent telegrams to Confederates outside the city, telling them the trap had been sprung. "The plan," said Bross, "was to attack Camp Douglas, to release the prisoners there, with them to seize the polls, allowing none but the Copperhead ticket to be voted, and to stuff the boxes sufficiently to secure the city, county, and State for McClellan and Pendleton, then to utterly sack the city, burning and destroying every description of property except what they could appropriate to their own use and that of their Southern brethren— to lay the city waste and carry off its money and stores to Jeff Davis's dominions."

The *Tribune* lauded General Sweet for his prompt action, without indicating Bross's role. "The praises of this vigilant, untiring officer are on every tongue," the paper said. "Those whose homes have been saved from midnight pillage and conflagration, whose families have been rescued from a perfect carnival of horrors, by his promptness and energy, will hold the name of General B. J. Sweet in everlasting gratitude."

The irresistible pressure of Grant on Lee, timely victories by Sherman and Sheridan, and the intense loyalty of Lincoln supporters such as the *Chicago Tribune* brought the president victory on November 8: Lincoln 2,203,831 votes to McClellan's 1,797,019, which translated into an electoral vote of 212 for Lincoln and Johnson and 21 for McClellan and Pendleton. The Illinois majority for Lincoln was more than 30,000, and five congressional seats had been gained. Republican Richard Oglesby was elected governor and William Bross lieutenant governor. The *Tribune* was elated. "THE PEOPLE TO THE ARMY—GREETING: SHERMAN CARRYING ELECTION RETURNS TO CHARLESTON. THE LAST ACT OF THE DRAMA OF THE REBELLION BEGINS."

*   *   *

The *Tribune* turned to Chicago and its own affairs. In the midst of the bitter dispute with the government over the Illinois troop quotas, it took time and space to acknowledge some plaudits from its peers. In Michigan, the *Grand Rapids Eagle* called the *Tribune* "beyond dispute the leading paper of the Northwest." In Illinois, the *Jacksonville Journal* said, "The *Chicago Tribune* is decidedly the ablest, most sterling paper in the West and we think the United States." And according to the *Rockford Reporter,* "The *Tribune* is a power in the Northwest and probably . . . has been as effective against the rebellion as an army corps in the field." The Federal government, however, continued to insist that Cook County owed more troops of the kind to carry guns. Replied the *Tribune:* "We claim we are called on for 37 per cent more men than we really possessed." The situation was intensified by a new call for 300,000 more men announced on December 21, the day the *Tribune* finally could report some news of General Sherman, who had been largely incommunicado during his march to the sea: "The great march has ended and has been in all respects a successful one." Then, on December 26, "SHERMAN'S CHRISTMAS GIFT TO THE PRESIDENT, SAVANNAH HAS FALLEN." Medill, in Washington, talked with President Lincoln. "He is in splendid spirits, feeling fine, overflowing with good humor and the milk of human kindness." No mention of the draft.

Any miscreant politicians in Chicago or Illinois assuming that the *Tribune* was so preoccupied with Washington and the war that it would fail to keep an eye on local scandals and scoundrels grossly misjudged. On January 28, 1865, the paper published a report and a map alleging an immense theft from the taxpayers via "a horse railway swindle" that would empower the city council to surrender the rights to certain Chicago streets for 99 years instead of the 25 initially contemplated under a franchise arrangement that, said the paper, was not too good in the first place. It was the beginning of a struggle to continue almost without interruption for 70 years, through the eras of horse railroads, cable cars, and steam, electric, gasoline, and diesel propulsion, finally summarized by cynical reporters as simply "traction."

The 99-year franchise measure passed overwhelmingly in the state legislature. Rival papers sneered at the *Tribune*'s petty efforts and pointed out that Lieutenant Governor Bross, presiding over the Senate, had failed to stop the street railway swindlers. The *Tribune* came back fighting. It called on Governor Oglesby to veto the Horse Railway Bill. When he did so, the editors led the city in a celebration on February 6, supplying the fireworks, torches, red flares, and rockets. "Rockets were sent up in the air copiously, the people shouted their joy in the streets," the paper exulted. "Men shook hands with each other and all felt happy except those pecuniarily interested in the passage of the bill." There was a two-column editorial threatening grievous political harm to anyone voting to pass the bill over the governor's veto. But, as one ravenous senator suggested, "They could smell the meat a-cookin'," and a day later the *Tribune* mourned. "The deed is done," wrote its Springfield reporter. "The horse-railway bill with all its odious features passed both houses, the Senate by 18 to 5 and the House by 55 to 23. Chicago is bound hand and foot and delivered over to an unscrupulous and never ending monopoly." Said the *Tribune* editorial: "The public knows that a given sum in greenbacks will pass any bill in Springfield that can be named, and pass it over a veto."

More woe lay ahead. Colonel Hancock had gone again to Springfield on the draft problem. He returned defeated and dejected, for Governor Oglesby had informed him that the Federal government was inflexible: Cook County owed 5,200 more men, and the number would grow to 6,000. The *Tribune* said no such number could be obtained: "Even if the men could be had, the bounties would total over $3,000,000." Cook County was well ahead of past quotas, the editors insisted. A draft meeting of the wards was called for, and Joseph Medill was among the speakers on the injustice of the thing. He was chosen to head the committee that went to Washington to present the plea to Lincoln and Secretary Stanton.

When the chastened and determined committee members returned from the capital, they divulged none of the details of their meeting with President Lincoln, and no report appeared in the *Tribune*, other than a statement of the president's decision and a promise that the quota somehow would be met. "Happily this does not mean any man will be dragged from his home," the paper said on March 2. "There are men enough willing to go voluntarily if sufficient pecuniary provision is made for them." Illinois and Cook County set about raising the money, with the state issuing bonds to repay those who pledged funds. A few weeks later, news from the battlefield made the draft crisis a thing of the past.

*   *   *

Sherman had ravaged Georgia and reached the sea. Sheridan had burned out the Shenandoah Valley, depriving Lee's armies of supplies. Grant continued the inexorable pressure. "Sherman and Grant," said the *Tribune*, "like the opposing jaws of a terrible vise, are nearing one another. . . . Richmond will be ours by surrender or by evacuation. . . . The end is near." The page-one flag appeared on April 3, under the headline: "VICTORY." The triumphant dispatches from City Point, Union army headquarters, were signed "A. Lincoln." General Sheridan, wild, rampaging, with an entire corps given to his command, smashed and pulled apart the reeling rebels at Petersburg and Grant pushed the pursuit. The Army of Northern Virginia was beaten, demolished. On April 7, Abraham Lincoln walked in the streets of Richmond, holding his little son Tad by the hand.

"Richmond is ours," the *Tribune* reported. "Lee has gone toward Danville with Grant in pursuit. . . . The rebellion is among the things of the past. From the ashes of the rebel capital will rise a new life in the United States. Freedom will henceforth be the crown and glory of the Republic." The paper described the receipt of the news in Chicago:

> Business was in great degree suspended. . . . The city was ablaze with the banner of beauty and the symbol of freedom waving from every available staff, from the spires of our vessels, from all our principal public buildings, mercantile houses and private residences. Processions of workingmen and teams filled the streets, bands of music discoursed their stirring and eloquent strains; artillery and other "pomp and circumstance of glorious war" patrolled the streets. . . . The day rivalled the Fourth of July. . . . Certainly yesterday has no rival in the history of Chicago.

On April 10, the day following the surrender of Lee at Appomattox Court House, the *Tribune*, in an editorial entitled "A Rich Man's War," talked of reconstruction: "We have, from the first, branded the rebellion against the Union as a war of aristocracy against democracy, of slave-holders against workingmen, of oligarchs against the people. . . . Shall we reconstruct the Union on the principle of the aristocracy, which has overthrown it, or on the broadest possible basis of true democracy?" The *Tribune* printed 53,000 papers providing the news of the surrender. This, it said later, was the largest single edition of a newspaper issued in the Northwest, 9,000 more than average *Tribune* editions. There were 20,000 people celebrating before the *Tribune*'s offices, the paper estimated, and an impromptu parade took four hours to pass the building. The entire city showed its joy, flooding the streets "to shout, sing, laugh, dance and cry for very gladness."

On Saturday, April 15, the *Tribune* headlined: "TERRIBLE NEWS . . . PRESIDENT LINCOLN ASSASSINATED IN FORD'S THEATER. A REBEL DESPERADO SHOOTS HIM THROUGH THE HEAD AND ESCAPES." A brief page-one editorial explained, "The news reached us just as we were going to press and we held the form open to the latest moment. The mournful, terrible dispatches explain themselves . . . we cannot write more. The news is too fearful, the blow has fallen too suddenly almost to comprehend. . . . Our latest dispatch reports no material change in the President's condition, but alas there is no hope."

The *Tribune* editorial following President Lincoln's death extolled him and bemoaned his loss:

> He was so great where men are rarely great, in his simplicity, his integrity, his purity of patriotic purpose, his kindliness of heart, especially toward the class of offenders before whose malignity he falls a martyr. . . . Already the complaint was on the lips of the nation that he was in danger of sacrificing justice and security to leniency, when he is struck down by those whom he was lifting up. He is murdered by those whom he would have spared and reconciled.

President Andrew Johnson had come under *Tribune* attack following his inauguration as vice-president in March when word spread that he had been drunk during the ceremony. The paper on March 14 had called his conduct a national disgrace and demanded that he resign. "Who can measure the calamities that would befall the country if the Presidential chair were filled by a person who becomes grossly intoxicated on the gravest public occasion?" But now the paper was lenient. "Let us have confidence in Andy Johnson," it said, suggesting in its editorial that on the day of the inauguration in March, Johnson may have been ill, as he claimed, and had taken some brandy "for his stomach's sake."

While the stunned, grieving North mourned its murdered president, the *Tribune* reported in lugubrious detail the slow passage of the funeral train to Chicago. At last the flag-draped engine and cars, shrouded in black crape, drew at five miles an hour over the Illinois Central trestle across the Lake Michigan shoreline, where an estimated 100,000 Chicagoans watched. Forty thousand of them escorted the cortege to the Courthouse, where, on May 2, President Lincoln lay in state while some 125,000 citizens passed by, paying their final respects.

THE HEGIRA
OF JOSEPH MEDILL

10

The war's end and the assassination of President Lincoln left the North emotionally spent. As the mourning eased and the nation took cognizance of the problems ahead, both North and South prepared for continuation of the unequal struggle on the political and economic fronts. The death of Lincoln aroused cries for vengeance in the North from those who had a week before urged conciliation, including the *Tribune*. The South, devastated and in economic ruin, feared the Northern carpetbaggers and the blacks who had been shut out by Southern laws from any educational advantages, forces soon to be in control of some of the legislatures.

The *Tribune*'s response to Southern cries for aid and forbearance now became harsh:

> Let them [*the former rebels*] work or die—it is to us not much matter which. We know that they are many; and that hunger will pinch and that they are proud; but there is the spade—dig or starve! We do not mean to be hard-hearted nor to ignore the claims of women to sympathy and commiseration; but if Mrs. Davis is in want, let her take in sewing, as many a better woman whom her husband's crime has first deprived of a protector and then beggared, is doing to-day. . . . General Lee is receiving rations, too, from the Government whose citizens he has slain by tens of thousands. We are in favor of . . . feeding him in some penitentiary. . . . But if he prefers liberty, we will hire him to tote paper in the *Tribune* press rooms, provided no Union soldier applies for the place.

There were great problems for the North as well: Reconstruction, wartime inflation and debt, the presence of a French army in Mexico.

205

The financial drain of the war, which the *Tribune* estimated at $4 billion for the North and $2 billion for the South, would bring on panic, especially as prices declined and government scandals were exposed. A struggle raged among gold, greenback, and free coinage advocates. While the South needed to be almost totally rebuilt, the industrial North needed to convert to a peacetime economy. But opportunities in the postwar years were also immense: the possibility of extending U.S. hegemony over North America, a dream of Medill and Senator Douglas alike; the development of the West; the exploitation of energy and mineral resources; the growth of cities; the markets to be found in a new and reconstructed South.

All these opportunities, it appeared to boosters like the *Tribune*, centered in Chicago, already the transportation and neural center of the nation and hoping to become the industrial and economic hub as well. The immediate market for Chicago was impressive. Much of the 242,000 square miles of land granted to the nation's railroads, a region larger than France or Germany and most of it tributary to Chicago, was already filling with settlers and towns. The Union Pacific and the Northern Pacific would link Chicago to the West Coast, and no one doubted that the Illinois Central would soon go to the Gulf as initially planned. The Western Union telegraph monopoly followed the railroads and thus made Chicago a communications center. The *Chicago Tribune* could collect news and ideas from the world's capitals at night and have them on the breakfast tables of thousands of subscribers more than a hundred miles from Chicago the following morning.

The outlook for Chicago and the *Tribune* appeared optimistic in the spring of 1865, but for Joseph Medill it was grim. Though editorial control of the paper had devolved upon him with Ray's departure, his fellow proprietors were not entirely satisfied with Medill, and now he was in danger of being virtually ousted from active management. In April, 1865, John Scripps elected to sell his interest in the paper to Horace White, making the Washington correspondent a real power in the company. White shared the liberal ideas of Dr. Ray and as a minor stockholder had consistently supported him in his disputes with the relatively conservative Medill. Now, fortified with Scripps's stock, White was intensely eager to take effective control of the Northwest's leading newspaper.

White's career with the *Tribune* had been spectacular almost from its onset in 1857, when he joined the staff at the age of 23. Born in Colebrook, New Hampshire, in 1834, White moved to Wisconsin as a child. His father, a leading physician in his New England community, had come west seeking home and farm sites for a group of prospective New England emigrants. Dr. White chose an area in the Rock River Valley, and soon a colony of New Englanders had gathered there, including White's pregnant wife and two small sons, Horace, age four, being the elder. Before long the cluster of log houses had become the village of Beloit. Five years later, Dr. White died. His widow married Deacon Samuel Hinman.

In 1849, Horace entered Beloit College, known at the time as a Whiggish school, and he was graduated in 1854. He was handsome and personable but was considered a somewhat wild youth in Beloit, since on more than one occasion he smoked tobacco. This reprehensible behavior came to the attention of the Reverend David Root, father of the comely Martha, whom Horace was courting, and the father undertook to break up the romance.

Horace set off for Chicago in 1854, and there he found a low-paying job as a reporter for the *Chicago Daily Journal*. He shortly disclosed to Martha that he had been named city editor, over two other members of the three-man editorial staff. Within the year, he left the *Journal* to become the agent of the New York Associated Press in Chicago. In 1856, he became assistant secretary of the National Kansas Committee, an abolitionist organization that had established its national headquarters in Chicago. Young White's acquaintance with the abolitionist movement gave him a new purpose in life and led him to abandon his carefree ways. Soon he was selected to join one of the expeditions of armed men being sent into Kansas to aid the Free State settlers, forces termed by the Southerners as guerrillas and bushwhackers. The party of 75 men was stopped by Missouri vigilantes and turned back. Early in 1857, White did get into Kansas, where he filed claim to 160 acres of land.

White's abolitionist activities failed to impress the Reverend Mr. Root, who was a wealthy owner of Wisconsin land, a patron of Beloit College, and a former agent of the Massachusetts Anti-Slavery Society, as well as a man of the cloth. He sourly observed that Horace appeared to be a young fellow of few religious convictions and no discernible profession. White was too busy organizing forays into Kansas and attempting to get rich by the exploitation of Illinois coal to immediately press his pursuit of the beauteous Martha. In later years, White referred to his harrowing days in Kansas and to his friendship with John Brown of Osawatomie. However, Joseph Logsdon, in his readable and well-documented biography of White, says that the young man never shouldered a gun in the border state, though he helped send in many Sharps rifles, and that he met John Brown in Chicago.

His divergent interests caused White difficulties in 1857, when he found that his investment in Illinois coal properties, which failed to produce a return and could not be sold, deprived him of needed capital for building on his Kansas land. So he sought a job again. Dr. Charles

Ray, who had become acquainted with him through his abolitionist activities, offered White a place on the *Tribune*. (He had sent Ray some letters for publication while he was in Kansas.) The Panic of 1857, which frustrated his land plans, also deprived him of this job after a few months, but White stayed on without pay. His loyalty was rewarded when the *Tribune* merged with the *Democratic Press*. He was assigned to travel with Abraham Lincoln in the 1858 canvass.

A medium tall, intense young man with warm brown eyes and an engaging personality, White quickly made a friend of Lincoln. He covered the Lincoln-Douglas debates and became one of Old Abe's most partisan admirers. Following the election, in which Republicans won the popular vote but Douglas retained his Senate seat, Horace White traveled to Connecticut, where Martha had moved with her parents. The Reverend Mr. Root agreed that his daughter's suitor now had a recognizable profession and assented to the marriage. While the nuptials and honeymoon were taking place, White's alleged friend John Brown raided Harper's Ferry and was captured. White was called to Washington to testify in February, 1860, though he had not seen Brown in months. He was pleased to be accounted a pro-Kansas leader of such importance, and, in addition to testifying before the Mason Committee investigating Brown and his raid, he wrote a letter to the *Chicago Tribune,* disagreeing with its editorial position that John Brown was insane. The Republican party sustained severe criticism because of Brown's activities, but most of the witnesses called before the Mason Committee, including White, were exculpated from any responsibility for the raid.

White obtained a position as secretary of the Illinois Republican State Central Committee, an appointment made by Chairman Norman Judd, who years before had helped Charles Ray become clerk of the Illinois Senate. He took part in the preparations for Lincoln's presidential drive, and he let it be known that he despised those real or alleged Lincoln enemies, Horace Greeley of the *New York Tribune* and Long John Wentworth of the *Chicago Democrat.* When Lincoln was nominated for president, White promptly sent him a letter promising to write his biography. He contributed a chapter to such a campaign document, but it was John Scripps who wrote the biography later circulated by the *Tribune.* When, despite the strong opposition of Medill and Ray, Lincoln indicated that he would appoint Simon Cameron to his cabinet, White was even more furious than his mentors, and he wrote Dr. Ray: *"If Cameron goes into the Cabinet I go out of the party."* He soon became resigned to the appointment, however, and wrote a letter to Lincoln providing him with political guidance from the viewpoint of young men, whom, said White, he was particularly qualified to represent, being 27 years of age himself. When the Civil War began, White remembered his promise to the president-elect that if Lincoln stood firm against slavery, the young men of the country would respond. He enlisted in a volunteer company being formed but withdrew because of the entreaties of his bride. Instead he became a war correspondent of the *Tribune,* spending the early months of the war in Cairo.

As early as 1861, Charles Ray began thinking about leaving the *Tribune,* probably because of his frequent disagreements with Medill. In the fall of that year Horace White went east to visit his father-in-law and while there received a letter from Dr. Ray suggesting that the Reverend Mr. Root might put up sufficient funds for White to buy Ray's shares, but the minister was not so inclined. White, on returning to Chicago, was able nevertheless to buy a few shares from Ray. He also learned that Medill was weary of Washington and that the job of correspondent in the capital was open, and he was eager to go. Through Elihu Washburne, the longtime friend of Medill, Ray, and the *Tribune,* but without Medill's knowledge, White obtained a Treasury Department position that would supplement his income from the *Tribune,* and he and his lovely young wife set out for the national capital.

White hoped to conquer Washington, and he had a gorgeous ally in Martha. She became a favorite of the senators and congressmen who resided in the rooming and boarding house where the Whites lived, and soon she was a much-sought belle of Washington political society. In his first correspondent's letter to his paper, White wrote with the kind of authority only a proprietor might assume. He was no "trimmer or compromiser," he warned. He developed excellent news sources and did a thoroughly good job of covering Washington news and political speculation and gossip. But when Medill learned that White held a patronage job while working for the paper, he demanded that he give it up. White simply changed government jobs. He angered Medill further with letters attacking Schuyler Colfax of Indiana, Medill's valued friend. Colfax protested to the exasperated Medill, but White, with the support of Ray, was able to stay on in Washington.

In March, 1863, White's letters to the *Tribune* from Washington ceased, though he continued to own stock in the paper. White was aware that his mentor, Dr. Ray, was again trying to sell his interest in the *Tribune.* Ray's departure, White knew, would return full charge of the editorial department to Medill, who did not share Ray's esteem for the young radical. White took a patronage job in the War Department and turned to Henry Villard, whom he had met while they were covering Lincoln in Springfield. Villard refers to White in his memoirs as "my life-long friend," and he proved his friendship by offering White a chance to join his newly organized Independent News Service. White, despite his troubles with Medill, was able to acquire the *Chicago Tribune* as one of the agency's clients. The news agency brought White some prosperity. In addition, he and several friends, learning of new taxes to be imposed, bought whiskey warehouse receipts and made a large profit on them.

By late 1863 White again was sending special correspondence to the *Tribune*. Ray's resignation in November, 1863, had not ended the bickering in the executive area, and with the important 1864 campaign approaching, White returned to Chicago, seeking to negotiate a settlement of the difficulties by inducing a majority to vote for Ray's restoration as editor of the editorial page. On September 29, 1864, he wrote to Ray:

> We had a stockholders' meeting a couple of weeks ago at which Bross proposed your name for editor-in-chief at a salary of $3,000 a year. . . . Medill thereupon remarked that he had anticipated this for some time . . . he knew the experiment would have to be made —he was confident it would fail (you not possessing the qualifications to conduct a newspaper without his help). He desired it should be now —for that reason he would give you his vote cheerfully. . . . But he would not assist you. . . . [If necessary] he would retire.

A decision was temporarily averted in February, 1865, when Lincoln arranged with General Grant to provide Ray with a Federal permit to travel and trade in the liberated areas of the South. But Ray's speculations were unsuccessful and he was soon back in Chicago. White in the meantime had considerably strengthened his position on the paper by acquiring Scripps's stock, and he had formed an alliance with Cowles and Bross, who succeeded Scripps as president of Tribune Company. The three men controlled a solid majority of *Tribune* stock, so that White soon was able to supplant Medill as managing editor, though not immediately as superintendent of editorial. In late May, 1865, the proprietors, without the concurrence of Medill, brought back Charles Ray as editor of the editorial page. The paper's policy problem was not solved, however. White and Ray soon clashed over President Johnson's Reconstruction programs, and in August Ray again departed the paper. He joined the noted sculptor Leonard Volk in organizing a Chicago Academy of Design and in time returned to journalism as an editorial writer with the *Chicago Post,* a position he held at the time of his death in September, 1870.

Joseph Medill was still a stockholder and superintendent of editorial following White's coup, but he lacked real power. His beleaguered situation was worsened by the establishment of a new evening paper, the *Chicago Republican,* said to be financed by a group of Republican politicians who intended to break the power of the *Chicago Tribune.* They employed as editor Charles A. Dana, the New York journalistic genius who had helped to guide Horace Greeley's *New York Tribune* to national influence and dominance. Another who joined the *Republican* staff was James W. Sheahan, the brilliant editor whom Senator Douglas had brought to Chicago to establish the *Times*. Dana sought to entice newsmen from the *Chicago Tribune*. He came up with an astonishing catch, Joseph Medill's brother Samuel, a defection Joseph would have been powerless to prevent had he wished to do so. Despite such talent, and its promising initial prospects, the *Chicago Republican* did not do well. Charles Dana returned to New York after little more than a year. Sam Medill went back to work with his brother, having evidently made his point, for he was soon named *Tribune* city editor. James Sheahan joined, of all papers, the *Chicago Tribune*, as an editorial writer. In 1871 the *Republican* merged with the *Post*.

*   *   *

Managing editor Horace White, a liberal free trader, soon invaded the editorial page realm, where he and Medill differed sharply. Joseph Medill was obviously weary. He was only 42 in 1865, but it was a day when many men accounted themselves old at such an age, and he continued to be troubled by rheumatism and his hearing impairment. The loss of two brothers in the war, the murder of Lincoln, and the prolonged struggle to shape *Tribune* policies and to sustain the paper's economic survival had left him drained. When the indefatigable White formed his alliance with Bross and Cowles, the former often away, the latter preoccupied with the financial affairs of the paper, he quickly made clear that Medill was no longer in control of the *Tribune*, nor even much listened to, despite his ownership of more than 20 percent of the stock. White took over the editorial page completely and struck a sensitive Medill nerve by attacking the protective tariff. Medill had favored the tariff since his days as owner of the *Coshocton Republican*, and his position was indelibly known. He continued to believe, as he always had, that the tariff safeguarded factory workers' jobs, enabling them to buy more of the products of the American farms. Medill wrote Elihu Washburne that he *"could not control White,"* but he retained an editorial chair and stayed on, under what must have been near-humiliating conditions.

The *Tribune* supported President Andrew Johnson immediately after Lincoln's assassination, predicting, relative to the South, that "Johnson's little finger will prove thicker than were Abraham Lincoln's loins. While he whipped them gently with cords, his successor will scourge them with a whip of scorpions. . . . Nothing will be done vindictively, nor from a spirit of revenge; but justice must be meted out."

During the interregnum, as Medill and White struggled to control policy, it appeared that both agreed at least on the need to change policy toward President Johnson. Medill wrote his friend Hugh McCulloch, the new secretary of the treasury, on June 23:

It gives me great pain to be obliged to differ with Mr. Johnson and especially on so vital an issue. On the question of the power of the President to concede or withhold suffrage to the colored people, I enclose our editorial which I think fully covers the point. The President has just as much power to confer suffrage as to deny it, and I think more. If the result of the Presidential policy shall prove unfortunate and we hold our place while it was being perpetuated into law, could we look a reader in the face? We have always tried to be true to our convictions of right and duty.

He enclosed an editorial attacking the Johnson administration for failure to support black voting rights, asserting that the president was permitting a reign of terror against Southern blacks.

As White's editorial powers grew, the paper turned farther from Johnson and from its traditional Republican policies. It also tended to alienate the business community, with which Medill and Bross had maintained close and cordial relations. Still, the paper was prospering as Chicago grew, and superficially all continued to seem well. The *Tribune* boasted that its circulation was double that of any of the other dailies in town, 46,999 daily and 18,000 Sunday, and listed its annual revenues, evidently the combination of advertising and circulation, as $393,600. The nearest competitors, said the paper, were the *Times* and the *Journal*, with total revenues of $100,000 each. "The *Tribune* is read by nearly everybody but a few Copperheads and the majority of these read it clandestinely," the paper asserted. "It circulates in profusion throughout the Northwest and thousands who do not fully agree with its views patronize it for its boldness and independence and patriotism and because it is the leading business paper of this section and they cannot do without it." The paper announced that it was enlarging to ten columns, eight pages daily and 16 pages Sunday, at a cost of $100 a day for added newsprint.

The *Tribune*'s boast that it was the "leading business paper" was undoubtedly true. Medill had given special attention to business news when he was in Cleveland and continued this policy in Chicago, and both Bross and Scripps were expert in this field before Medill arrived. Despite the departure of Scripps, and Bross's involvement with politics and travel, the *Tribune* continued its excellent commercial coverage, a policy especially effective at a time when Chicago was fast rising to second place among the country's commercial and industrial towns. On July 15, 1865, the paper declared that it had set a record for a business dispatch, receiving 6,800 words on a commercial convention in Detroit, sent in three hours and 15 minutes.

On July 25, the *Tribune* published a telegraphic summary of crops throughout the Midwest, requiring considerable planning and effort as well as expense. It printed one of the first detailed maps of Chicago ever to appear in a newspaper in an effort to promote the Illinois state fair, which was being held on the South Side of Chicago near the site of the present Douglas monument. At the same time, the paper continued to be lax in its attention to advertising and continued to vilify the "bummers" who solicited advertising for the *Chicago Times.* Like other newspapers, the *Tribune* accepted and published many columns of advertising for patent medicine nostrums and quack doctors. The leading merchants were not yet big daily advertisers, although Marshall Field and Levi Leiter, having taken over Potter Palmer's dry goods store, were beginning to show the way, together with Mandel Brothers and Willoughby & Hill, clothing merchants. Solicited or not, those interested in advertising wished to appear in the *Tribune,* so that its receipts from that source totaled $190,000 for the year ending May 31, 1865, as compared with $69,950 for its nearest competitor, the *Journal.* The *Tribune* also had the bulk of the legal notices, though it charged $24 a card, as compared with $7 by the competing papers.

In its September 5 Prospectus, the paper again envisioned the goal that so often had been proposed by Medill and Bross: "The newspaper is the great educator of the age and if conducted in the interests of public virtue is the principal safeguard of liberty and law." Part of that education, Medill decided, would include a new system of simplified spelling. Not many examples of his proposed simplifications got into the newspaper, but the *Chicago Evening Journal* commented: "Our friend Medill of the *Tribune* has had much to say lately about a new system of spelling. About as bad a spiel as any man has ever made was his recent spiel as a bolter of the Union nominations." The non sequitur appears to have referred to Medill's refusal to back the straight Republican, or Union, ticket in the November county elections because it failed to include the names of Civil War veterans he wished to support. The bolters, including Medill, went down to defeat, which must have particularly rankled Medill since the *Tribune*'s editorial page, now dominated by White, had backed the straight ticket.

The gibe of the *Journal* brought from the *Tribune* a partial explanation of its internal difficulties. The paper explained that Joseph Medill had resigned from the managing editorship some six months previously but that he "maintained a chair in the *Tribune* office and his pecuniary interest." This, presumably, entitled him to suggest simplified spelling but not to dictate political endorsements. On November 14, the *Tribune* addressed a highly self-serving editorial to a growing concern of its newspaper rivals. According to its critics, said the editorial:

> It was the *Tribune* which produced the war; it was the *Tribune* which moved the army to Bull Run; it was a *Tribune* man that led it back again; it was the *Tribune* which appointed all the Generals; it was the *Tribune* which laid half of them on the shelf . . . it was the *Tribune,* in short, which was responsible for

everything that happened, and everything that was going to happen. The people came, very naturally, to the conclusion that a newspaper possessing such tremendous executive powers as the *Tribune* must be a great institution. . . . Just now the brood of cacklers are tremendously agitated on the great question who edits the *Tribune?* . . . No question except that of original sin has excited so much turmoil and anxiety. It is in fact the great question of the age.

The editorial concluded by offering sympathy—but no answer. White may have been in a sardonic mood, telling the *Journal* in effect to mind its own business. The *Galena Gazette* answered the question directly and succinctly: "The managing editor is Horace White, who has been connected with the paper nearly ten years. He is a ripe scholar with a wide knowledge of politics."

White now had the power and the will to change the course of the *Tribune*. He began with a renewal of his attacks on the protective tariff. Medill responded at once through letters to the editor written under the pseudonym "Protection," but soon he concluded that such obfuscation was ridiculous and thereafter he signed as Joseph Medill. The astonishing battle between the editor of a newspaper and one of his chief stockholders and proprietors went on for months. White and Charles Ray, who had not yet joined the *Post,* assumed leadership in forming a Free Trade League, and White issued free trade ultimatums to congressional leaders. Medill responded by calling for a mass meeting on the protective tariff in Bryan Hall on February 22, 1866, and more than 5,000 attended. Medill's speech filled three and a half columns in the *Tribune*. He was elected president of a new organization, the American Industrial Union "for the defense of home labor against the raids of foreign free trade."

The wartime coalition formed by the Republicans under Lincoln and with the aid of the *Tribune* broke apart as demoralized politicians ran for cover. White attacked the so-called Black Codes passed by Southern legislatures to restrict the freedom of blacks, saying, "We tell the white men of Mississippi that the men of the North will convert the State of Mississippi into a frogpond before they will allow any such law to disgrace one foot of soil in which the bones of our soldiers sleep and over which the flag of freedom waves." When he learned that Andrew Johnson might veto a bill to enlarge the powers of the Freedmen's Bureau, White lashed out, calling the president a reactionary and editorializing, "The simple question is . . . whether the Union shall be reconstructed for the profit of Andrew Johnson or the American people."

Even Dr. Ray was alarmed at the vehemence of White's attack on President Johnson. He visited White to protest and wrote to Senator Trumbull, urging caution in the matter of demanding black voting rights. Both the *Evening Journal* and Dana's new *Republican* were delighted by

White's editorial course; they turned their guns on the *Tribune* and began picking up the subscribers that paper was losing. "We are Radicals and we don't quarrel with the name," the *Tribune* said on February 10, 1866. "One must be something less than a man, who would not be radical now." On February 20, Johnson did in fact veto the Freedmen's Bureau Bill as White had predicted, and it appeared that White had won a position in the ideological vanguard of the postwar Republican party.

*   *   *

In Chicago, conditions continued good. The city's population passed 200,000 in 1866, and the *Tribune* bragged that the financial difficulties reported elsewhere in the country had not affected the Queen City of the Lakes. The paper was under attack from the city's ministers for publicizing the various features in its Sunday paper, which had appeared during the Civil War, lapsed briefly, and now had been resumed. The *Tribune* demanded to know if the Scriptural laws applying to the Hebrew Sabbath could be construed as applying to the first day of the week. George Bancroft, the historian, spoke before Congress on the thesis, "That God rules in the affairs of men is as certain as any truth of physical science," and the *Tribune* published five columns of his address, but this did not appease the preachers. When the *Tribune*'s new eight-cylinder Hoe press broke down on a Saturday afternoon, forcing the paper to print on *Journal* presses, and to miss much of the Sunday edition, it was said that some ministers ascribed the mishap to an act of God.

Medill was traveling now. In New York he had an interview with Alexander H. Stephens, former vice-president of the Confederacy, who of course favored the readmission of rebel states on a white-only voter basis. Medill responded, said the *Tribune*'s correspondent, "that the Black Republicans of the South must be allowed to vote as an offset to the ex-Rebel Democrats." Later, Medill, writing from Washington, accused Johnson of betraying the Republicans who had elected him vice-president and of sympathizing with the Copperheads. "Now Congress is master of the situation and the Johnson policy of reconstruction will be summarily set aside." When Congress passed the Civil Rights Bill over President Johnson's veto, Medill wrote that the foundation for Reconstruction had been laid. "All men are now equal before the law in their civil rights. It only remains for Congress to secure to them their political rights." The report of the Joint Committee on Reconstruction, however, was not all the *Tribune* had hoped, for it failed to recommend universal manhood suffrage. "A freedman without a vote is no freedman. This disfranchisement of labor is a libel on our Republican form of government." The paper sent correspondents into the South. From New Orleans came the report that General Sheridan insisted it was necessary for troops to remain in New Orleans and Texas. Outrages against blacks were reported, and riots in Memphis. General Grant was interviewed. "He does not see things in the rose colored light of Johnson and Seward. He thinks the Rebels regard themselves as masters of the situation. Their leaders think that treason will triumph by politics if not by war. This change was brought about by Johnson."

President Johnson was planning a trip west and would stop in Chicago to dedicate the city's monument to Stephen A. Douglas. The *Tribune* warned him not to use the trip for any electioneering and predicted that the Republicans would nominate Gen. Ulysses S. Grant for president in 1868. When a new Freedmen's Bureau Bill was passed over Johnson's veto in July, 1866, the *Tribune*'s editorial said: "Let the President resign." Medill now left the paper temporarily to become secretary of the Republican Central Committee, with the reelection of Senator Trumbull its primary goal. Almost daily, the *Tribune* fulminated against Johnson, "dictator, usurper and despot." The paper's new chief editorial writer, James Sheahan, is credited with writing the September 4, 1866, editorial, "Coming to the Funeral," referring to Johnson's impending arrival in Chicago for the Douglas monument ceremonies.

> The President is coming to the funeral. He comes with music and banners and fireworks and cannon. He comes with speeches and processions. He comes vaunting his own glories, shouting his own praises, singing his own paeans, threatening honest officials who do not swear fealty to him, and holding out bribes in the way of public offices to other men to do violence to their consciences. He is coming to the funeral distributing his advertising cards. He is coming to the funeral of a patriot, and on the way is threatening civil war; he is coming to the funeral of a Senator, threatening to dissolve the Senate by the sword. He is coming to the funeral of a freeman, asserting how easily he may declare himself a dictator. . . . He is coming to the funeral of a statesman, belching forth at every station the duty of the nation to accept his acts as law. He is coming to the funeral of one of the people, proclaiming as he comes, that there is tyranny in the rule of the many, freedom only in the rule of the one.

General Grant, Adm. David G. Farragut, and Secretary of State William H. Seward were among those accompanying the president, and Chicago received Johnson with the honors due a president, the Knights Templar band escorting him to the Sherman House. The *Tribune* filled ten columns with details of the eulogy and tributes to its sometime enemy, Senator Douglas. Then Johnson departed grandly, aboard the newest Pullman Palace car, the "Omaha," well provided with viands by H. M. Kinsley of the Opera House restaurant. But, as the trip wore on, the *Tribune* reported that Johnson was frequently incensed by the crowds cheering for Grant. Grant and Farragut, meantime, let it be known that

they were on the presidential trip under orders, and not by choice. Soon
after Johnson's trip, Medill himself went west aboard one of the new
Pullman cars. He described the fabulous interior and the meal provided
by the caterer Kinsley, which, said Medill, was the finest ever served on a
railroad train, and included game, fish, fowl, meats, salads, jellies, grapes,
pears, and wines.

The *Tribune* reported "Magnificent Republican Victories" on November 7. Republicans had swept Illinois by 40,000 votes, posting a 5,000
gain in Cook County, and were victorious in Michigan, Wisconsin, New
York, and Massachusetts. "Chicago is now the banner Republican city of
the Union," crowed the *Tribune*. White was especially overjoyed, for his
policies seemed vindicated. After a further report indicated that the
Republican majority in Illinois was actually more than 50,000, he wrote:
"The elections are over and if any external proposition may be said to
have received popular approval, it is that the impeachment of Andrew
Johnson has been authorized by the American people." Republicans
would have a majority of 81 in the House of Representatives, with ten
states unrepresented. The Congress could now do as it wished about
impeachment, the paper pointed out, but it cautioned full observance of
the law and the requirements of proof.

The November election triumph catapulted White to giddy political
heights, but to maintain his leadership among the radicals, he found
himself forced into increasingly extreme postures. He demanded that
Congress set aside all Johnsonian provisions for the South and reorganize
the rebel states without consideration of their constitutional rights, which
they had forfeited by rebellion. When the U.S. Supreme Court seemed
about to check congressional plans to reorganize the South under military
rule, White called upon Congress to pack the court, without explaining
just how Congress would make the appointments. He also found himself
demanding universal suffrage, without regard to educational qualifications. Universal suffrage did not, of course, include the right of women to
vote; not even White would go that far. "Universal suffrage," he wrote, "is
in accordance with the genius of our institutions as remoulded by the war.
It is the destiny of this nation, as inevitable as the war itself."

When the basic Reconstruction Act finally passed on March 2, 1867, it
was a compromise the *Tribune* found necessary to accept. "It is a peace
and Union measure. It is a law that will put an end to anarchy and restore
constitutional Union and freedom to the people of the Rebel states."

White hoped that the Southern problem was at last settled, for there
were other problems close to home. The new and growing labor movement staged a mass meeting of 5,000 in downtown Chicago, and laboring
men were writing letters demanding that the *Tribune* take a stand on the
eight-hour day. White did, pointing out that the *Tribune* was "the enemy

of oppression and wrong everywhere; but it does not believe that eight is the same as ten." When labor riots occurred, White urged that the strikers be "reduced to obedience by the bayonet." This stand put White into a difficult position. He had called for the impeachment of Andrew Johnson. Should Johnson be impeached, the man in line for the presidency was Sen. Benjamin Wade of Ohio, since there was no vice-president. And what were Wade's views on major issues? He favored a high tariff and an eight-hour day.

Medill and White were not always on opposite sides. In December, 1866, they joined forces in a new attempt to break the New York press monopoly, which Medill had been battling for nearly a decade. The *Tribune* assailed the "arrogant New York Associated Press," charging that New York papers published a page of Washington news each day but sent only half a column westward, and special dispatches cost the *Tribune* $800 a week. Western papers, the *Tribune* said, could achieve prosperity only "by freeing ourselves from the tyranny of a monopoly in telegraph news." Medill addressed a meeting of the Western Associated Press in the beautiful new Crosby Opera House, asserting that the New York papers must "open their eyes to the fact that if the sun does rise in the east it does not set there, but in the west." Horace White was named to the committee to organize a United States Associated Press.

*   *   *

Following the war, Chicago took advantage of its opportunity to relax a bit. The parks and lakefront attracted not only residents of the city, but people from all over the Middle West, who came to Chicago to shop, see a play, visit the new dime museums, and ride the horsecars. Baseball, popularized by the soldiers, was rapidly becoming the national sport. In July, 1867, Chicago hosted a tournament in which some of the nation's top teams participated. The final game, pitting the Chicago Excelsiors against the Washington, D.C., Nationals, was expected to determine the relative superiority of eastern and western teams. Since the Nationals had lost earlier to a Rockford team, the Excelsiors were heavily favored. Instead, they were annihilated by the Nationals 49 to 4. The *Tribune* devoted two and a half columns to an inning-by-inning account of the game, and in an editorial commented on "Base Ball as a Confidence Game." The Nationals' victory should have surprised no one, the *Tribune* explained, for the Nationals were professional athletes. "The catcher, Alsted, receives a regular salary of $1,500 per annum besides what he can make by betting. . . . The victory of the Rockford club . . . was a regular confidence game . . . an operation intended to induce the sporting men of Chicago to venture their money. They did so and the Nationals have pocketed it. It is estimated that $20,000 changed hands . . . . The *Tribune* was the only paper which was not deceived by this simulated defeat."

In October, a 44-round fight between two heavyweights named Davis and Gallagher received page-one coverage, but that did not mean the *Tribune* approved of prizefighting, in which, it said, "one brute pounds another for the benefit of a gang of other brutes." Walking, however, was considered a fine sport, and the paper gave columns of space to the plans of Edward P. Weston, who hoped to trek from Portland, Maine, to Chicago in a month to win a wager of $10,000. Weston's progress frequently was reported on the front page. He arrived in Chicago, footsore but perky, on November 30, having walked 1,326 miles in 26 days. Mounted reporters met him and escorted him into the city. The *Tribune* covered his arrival in four columns, but it remained inflexible against prizefights. Reporting another boxing match in Indiana, it said the sheriff should in future deputize enough men to arrest anyone who might come to see such an exhibition, and it demanded a state law to make prizefighting a crime. "Anything is preferable to barbarism growing up among us," the paper said.

*   *   *

The struggle between executive and legislature continued in Washington. President Johnson demanded the resignation of Secretary of War Stanton, who refused to give up his office. The president suspended him and named General Grant interim secretary; also he removed General Sheridan from his command in New Orleans. The *Tribune* responded on August 21: "The country has endured Andrew Johnson as long as endurance can be counted a virtue. There being reasons now in law as well as in fact, why he should be impeached and ejected from office, and rendered incapable of holding office hereafter, we hope that Congress will resolutely take hold of the work at the coming session and put him out."

After many false starts, the conflict between Congress and President Johnson reached the impeachment stage in February, 1868, when the president removed Stanton from office in violation of the Tenure of Office Act. An impeachment resolution was carried in the House by a vote of 126 to 47, and the North became inflamed. The Chicago City Council voted for impeachment 20 to four. The *Tribune* reported the action of the council and a demonstration for impeachment at Library Hall in nearly a page of type. Meantime, the paper had announced its support of General Grant for president. Once again political news dominated the paper. Johnson's trial in the Senate began in March, with Chief Justice Salmon P. Chase presiding, and the Grant campaign advanced. However, there were now more columns for editorial material; and general news, literary and religious coverage, and articles of special interest to women received added space. The *Tribune* announced it would publish a special campaign edition, starting in May and continuing through election day, in support of Grant for president and John M. Palmer for governor.

In May, the *Tribune* acquired a new Washington correspondent, one of the most popular newspaper writers of his time, and one of the best in the history of the paper. Gangling, genial, unforgettable with his bowler and cane, he would later be praised by Mark Twain, Henry W. Longfellow, and Oliver Wendell Holmes as the best newspaper writer of his time. He was George Alfred Townsend, the rangy, six-foot son of an itinerant Methodist preacher, who learned to appreciate good writing by reading three chapters of the Bible each day as a child. Townsend became a reporter on the *Philadelphia Inquirer* the day he was graduated from high school, and a war correspondent for the *New York Herald* when he was 20, in 1861. He wrote as "GAT" until he joined the *Tribune*, then changed to "Gath," explaining in his first letter: "I'm tired of writing GAT. So, I made a monogram of it, it's a Philistine city . . . it's written in the Scriptures, 'Tell it not in Gath,' so I'm writing it Gath."

Whether Medill acquired Gath while he was in Washington or White signed him up for the *Tribune,* the paper now had a reporting specialist who was recognized for his writing skill on both sides of the Atlantic. Gath was granted the privilege of covering part of McClellan's ill-fated peninsular campaign from T. S. C. Lowe's military balloon and caught a glimpse of Richmond before Confederate fire obliged a hasty descent. Suffering an illness while with the Army of the Potomac, Gath went to England to recuperate and to study. While there he also wrote for *Cornhill* magazine and penned much of the material for his book *The New World Compared with the Old,* which sold 80,000 copies in the United States. His wartime book, *Campaigns of a Non-Combatant,* was equally successful, enabling the poor preacher's son to begin a palatial estate in Maryland, not far from Washington, that was an early San Simeon and attracted politicians, writers, even presidents when it was completed. Ultimately Gath's work, which appeared in the *Tribune,* the *Cleveland Leader,* and scores of other publications, became a column, "Washington Outside and Inside." David Donald, author of *Lincoln's Herndon,* wrote of him: "As the columnist 'Gath,' he went everywhere, met everyone, saw everything, and told it all and more to his newspaper audience. He thrilled American readers with poignant tales of Civil War daring and heroism; he reported the dramatic, the unique, the personal. Human interest was Townsend's business."

Gath was quickly into the Johnson impeachment. Horace White was in Washington to aid him for a time, and so was a reporter not further identified who signed himself "Nix." White's editorials vacillated as the trial wore on. First he was ardently for the impeachment, then he urged caution, to make sure that no illegal steps were taken. One of the reasons for White's indecision was disclosed in an editorial. He had learned that a meeting of tariff protectionists had taken place in New York on April 28, to plan action to take advantage of the anticipated ascension of Senator Wade to the presidency.

A visit to Washington in early May convinced White that moderate Republicans' fear of Wade made acquittal almost certain. He endeavored editorially to prepare his readers for the vote: "Better the acquittal of Johnson, than his conviction upon grounds that would not endure scrutiny in the coming presidential election." Other Republican newspapers did not agree with White, however, nor did many readers, and the *Tribune* suffered. When at last acquittal was voted, Joseph Medill wrote his friend Washburne: *"Horace continues to blaze away against the impeachers. The paper has lost many subscribers and worse still has lost a great degree of its influence with the radical masses who are deeply offended at White's course; but I am unable to do anything. Trumbull and Grimes* [Republicans who voted against impeachment] *are of more importance in W's eyes than the power and friendship of the Republican patrons of the paper. It is a deplorable blunder."*

The *Tribune* was jubilant on May 22, 1868, when it announced that the Republican National Convention had nominated Ulysses S. Grant for president and Schuyler Colfax of Indiana for vice-president. Both men were old friends of the paper, and the *Tribune* felt sure that they would carry out policies it favored. The news was not printed on the front page, however; that was covered with advertising. On May 25, the *Tribune* said of the ticket: "Never since the Republican party was organized has the response of the country to a presidential ticket been so cheering, so enthusiastic, so unanimous. Four years ago the Republicans were not waked up until the first of August . . . . This year, if we are wise, we shall have our organization perfected and put in thorough working order before our enemies shall have got out of their muddle and selected their candidate." The *Tribune* was also pleased to report that suffrage for blacks had been established in eight of the rebel states, and was soon to be established in three more, "making eleven states in which freedom and manhood have been made the standard of political right instead of complexion."

General Grant and the Republicans won a narrow victory, with a popular majority of 309,594 over Democratic candidate Horatio Seymour, but Grant and Colfax received 214 of the 294 electoral votes. One of those named to Grant's cabinet was Elihu B. Washburne, the longtime confidant and correspondent of Joseph Medill. Another proposed member, as secretary of the treasury, was A. T. Stewart, New York department store tycoon, importer, free trader, and friend of Horace

White. But Stewart was found to be ineligible for the treasury post. White pleaded in vain. Stewart was dropped and in his place Grant named George Boutwell.

*   *   *

Women were seeking the right to vote in 1869, but no paper was giving their pleas serious attention. Woman had her own sphere, said the *Tribune* patronizingly in February. "She must not come down to the lower level where men wrangle. Her kingdom and power is simple faith and goodness, the greatest power on earth." This attitude did not please Mary Livermore, leader of a movement for a constitutional amendment permitting women to vote. "We are tired of chignons and husband-catching," she told the *Tribune*. "We want to have equal right with men to vote and hold office." When resolutions for universal suffrage—including women—were passed at the Chicago Sorosis Convention, the *Tribune* provided a full report. But the paper's Springfield correspondent probably left readers wondering why any woman would want the right to serve in the Illinois state legislature. He wrote on March 12 that the legislature was incompetent and dishonest.

> It is not a pleasant thing to have the fact forced upon your attention that a man is venal, nor is it agreeable to see a member behave like a ninny. . . . Men of doubtful character sit upon the floor, and are tutored by the representatives of monopolies. Women of doubtful character sit in the galleries, and throw notes to Senators. If she is not expert with the pencil she besieges with smiles, and he capitulates with a nod. He bargains with the lobby and he bargains with the gallery. And one is not expected to mention all this, because it hurts the feelings of members.

In April, 1869, the *Tribune* moved into its own handsome four-story building of Joliet pale marble, built at Dearborn and Madison streets at a cost of $250,000 on land leased from the Chicago school board. The building not only housed the most modern printing plant in America, said the paper, but it was also fireproof and had space for quality tenants. White and Cowles planned and financed the building, White, according to his biographer, putting in $100,000 of his own money. Since the building was fireproof, the owners decided not to take out fire insurance, as previously had been the custom. Again the paper invited the public, especially the ladies, to visit its new premises, and it described the facilities that made it the finest newspaper in America: $5,000 a month spent for wire services and special dispatches; $800 a week paid to employees; circulation and advertising greater than those of all the other Chicago papers, published in English, combined. The market value of the paper, it was estimated, had risen from $200,000 at the beginning of the war to more than $1 million. The paper also suggested that its circulation was

near its wartime high of 50,000. However, in November the figure had
been announced at 42,240, and that included election specials.

Joseph Medill provided his prescription for the making of a good
newspaper in addressing editors and publishers at Indianapolis in May.

> Be very particular with the mechanical execution of your paper, charge fair
> living prices for your work, and stand by them; do cash business, as nearly as
> practicable, refuse long credits . . . devote your main editorial efforts to the
> discussion of home topics and furtherance of home interests. Let each issue
> be a photograph of the doings of your county for the previous week, and a
> foreshadowing of the week to come. Preserve your independence of all
> demagogues and place-hunters and never submit to their dictation; write
> boldly, and tell the truth fearlessly; criticize whatever is wrong, and de-
> nounce whatever is rotten in the administration of your local and State
> affairs, no matter how much it may offend the guilty or wound the
> would-be leaders of your party. . . . Make an earnest and conscientious
> journal; establish its reputation for truth and reliability, frankness and
> independence. Never wilfully deceive the people, or trifle with their confi-
> dence. Show that your journal is devoted to the advocacy and promotion of
> their temporal interests and moral welfare.

The *Tribune* itself was spreading its wings beyond its county and state,
Horace White spending money freely on staff coverage when he thought
he could get good, exclusive stories. In July, 1867, the *Tribune* had
published a series of brief reports of gold strikes in the South Pass area of
Dakota Territory, later Wyoming. In November there was a further
report of "a gold stampede" into the rugged Wind River country in the
Big Horn Mountains. Editor White, recalling the gold strike stories of
Bret Harte, Mark Twain, and others, decided the *Tribune* should send its
own correspondent. He hired James Chisholm, a slender, flute-playing
young Scot, from the staff of the *Chicago Times*. Chisholm promised to
report from the wild West for at least a year.

The Union Pacific Railroad reached Cheyenne, D.T., in November,
1867. Chisholm's first *Tribune* story came from that roaring frontier town
in March, 1868, detailing the invasion of a Cheyenne dance hall by 15
masked vigilantes who seized a notorious badman and hanged him "with
a piece of bed cord." The *Chicago Tribune* gave more space to the event
than did the *Cheyenne Leader,* notes Lola M. Homsher, who edited
Chisholm's journal 92 years later, but then, shootings and hangings were
almost daily occurrences in Cheyenne and Chisholm was easily impressed, having covered nothing in Chicago more exciting than a drama
or a charity ball. Chisholm continued to provide excitement for *Tribune*
readers with his Cheyenne dispatches, signed "J.C." A former Civil War
general was killed in a fight over a prostitute, one of "the 200 fair but
frail" women plying their trade in Cheyenne. "The 'Vigilants' are still at

work," said a letter signed "Western," published in the *Tribune* in April. "Two men were hung in the streets a week ago. Street fights are almost of daily occurrence. Four men have been shot within six days." Chicagoans were so impressed by the reports from Cheyenne that the vilest part of their own notorious red-light district came to be called "Little Cheyenne."

Chisholm sent another dispatch about a great new gold find in the Wind River range. Then, except for a letter to the mother of his sweetheart, Mary Evelyn Garrison, he was not heard from again in Chicago for several months. He reached South Pass after weeks of hardship, panned and dug gold himself, and returned to Chicago with his carefully kept journal in December, 1868, as agreed. He outlined in his journal the stories he planned to write for the *Tribune*, but no stories appeared. The Wind River and Sweetwater gold mines had run out fast. Chisholm wed Miss Garrison, was assigned to write dramatic criticism, and covered a part of the reelection campaign of President Grant. When the *Tribune* withdrew support from Grant, Chisholm angrily resigned and became a columnist for the *Chicago Inter-Ocean*. His journal, compared with the works of Robert Louis Stevenson and Mark Twain by some critics, was published for the first time in 1960.

Despite Chisholm's unproductive Big Horn trip as a special correspondent, the *Tribune* did have excellent western adventure accounts in 1868–69. It published regularly the dispatches of explorer-geologist Maj. John Wesley Powell, whose party explored the gorges of the Green and Colorado rivers by boat, becoming the first men to traverse the Grand Canyon.

The *Tribune*'s own editors and writers were no stay-at-homes. Upton, using the pen name "Peregrine Pickle," covered a music festival in Boston; writers were traveling through the South, reporting on political and social affairs; Deacon Bross was writing along the California-bound route of the Union Pacific; Horace White sent dispatches on life among the Mormons in Utah, then wrote from California; and Medill described his arrival in Salt Lake City by stagecoach. A total eclipse of the sun, to take place on August 7, 1869, was described in advance by commercial editor Elias Colbert and illustrated with charts. Colbert, also a writer, an astronomer, and a lecturer at the first University of Chicago, joined a scientific expedition to the Southwest to observe and report on the phenomenon. Four columns were carried on the actual eclipse, which lasted one hour, 58 minutes, and two seconds over Chicago.

The *Tribune* gave excellent coverage to the convention of the Western Female Suffrage Association in Chicago, which was attended by Lucy Stone, Susan B. Anthony, Mary Livermore, and other feminist leaders. If Negroes could vote, why not women? the suffragettes wanted to know. The *Tribune* repeated what it had said previously: "Woman's sphere is the home"—then added "nursery, kitchen, schoolroom, church," so that there would be no misunderstanding. "We should not point to the plow, the steamboat, the army, the navy or the legislature. . . . When the sex generally demand the right of suffrage they will obtain it. That demand is not general now." Livermore told her friends the *Tribune* had treated the women fairly, but she had hoped for better than that since she had taken a bouquet of flowers to the editors.

On his return from California, White plunged into a study of economics, reprinting excerpts from the works of European theoreticians in the *Tribune*. The works selected always supported his own free trade ideas. He edited a new translation of Frederic Bastiat's *Sophisms of Protectionism,* which was issued in book form as well as appearing in the paper. White was moving now beyond economics in his liberal apostasy. He demanded that the Republican rule of Chicago be terminated for corruption and inefficiency and helped to organize a Citizens' Ticket. The committee running the campaign for the bipartisan slate was headed by none other than Long John Wentworth. Mayoral candidate on the Citizens' Ticket was Col. Roswell B. Mason, a civil engineer who had directed construction of the Illinois Central Railroad. Running against Mason as the candidate of the regular Republicans was George Gage.

The victor in this, Chicago's first autumn mayoral contest, would govern a booming city with a population of 289,000, almost triple that of the year prior to the war. The 500 manufacturing establishments at the beginning of the war had more than doubled to 1,176, employing 27,000 workers and turning out products valued at $83 million. The city hall and the county building were being expanded, and the city was constructing ingenious tunnels beneath the river at Washington Street and LaSalle Street to relieve the overcrowded bridges, and to avert the delay of bridge openings. Chicago's exports totaled $182,743,578. The voters heeded the *Tribune*'s advice, and Mason and the Citizens' Ticket swept into office.

The success of White's new movement in Chicago did not go entirely unheeded in the national capital. In April, 1870, White journeyed to Washington, where he met with a group of Eastern liberals who promised to use their best efforts to elect congressmen friendly to tariff and revenue reform regardless of party. They especially sought the reappointment of David Wells as special revenue commissioner. White volunteered to write to President Grant, but Grant was unmoved. He refused to take steps to lower the tariff, and he indicated that his secretary of the treasury, Boutwell, did not care to retain Wells. By June 30, 1870, Wells was out of office.

The defeat of a number of high-tariff Republicans by low-tariff candidates in the fall congressional elections seemed to confirm White's belief that tariff reform was gaining impetus and that he was once more

in the forefront of an important political trend. Anxious to avoid splin-
tering the Republican party, Speaker of the House James G. Blaine, a
man with presidential aspirations, came to Chicago to see what White
wanted. He agreed to let White and his friends name two members of the
Ways and Means Committee, where tariff measures originated. He also
asked White's advice on who should chair the committee. White suggested James A. Garfield of Ohio. With the two members, an anti-
protectionist alliance could be formed with Democrats to control the
committee.

Joseph Medill, meantime, had been elected in November, 1869, to the
Illinois state constitutional committee and offered the chairmanship,
which he declined because of his defective hearing. For months he would
labor on the new constitution of 1871. One of his goals was to provide for
state improvement of the Illinois River and canal connections in order to
restrain the railroad monopoly. Medill was also chairman of a Chicago
committee on electoral and representative reform. He occasionally visited
the *Tribune* newsroom, much to the annoyance of White, who would stop
a conversation in mid-sentence and change the topic when Medill appeared. The chasm between the men widened.

Not all the controversies in the *Tribune* were serious, however. Peregrine Pickle, whose columns were now issued in booklet form at Christmas, in February, 1870, started a disputation as to whether blondes had
any dramatic ability. None of them displayed the needed spark, he
averred. Special articles were published on working girls in the big city.
The editor of the *Times,* Wilbur F. Storey, himself became a subject of
discussion when he publicly criticized Lydia Thompson and her "Black
Crook" burlesque troupe, and two of the enraged young ladies of the
troupe caught him in the street and horsewhipped him. When the Black
Crook blondes were brought to trial, the *Tribune* printed six columns of
detail. The girls were fined, but they received an ovation that night from
the 3,000 persons who packed into Crosby's Opera House to see them.

The *Tribune* increased its quota of articles aimed at women and articles
of a cultural nature, among them a translation of the *Iliad* by William
Cullen Bryant, editor of the *New York Post.* The paper spoke frequently of
its dominance in the advertising field, particularly in want ads. They were
highly read, such as the "Personals": "Will the little young lady with light
dress and dark eyes who noticed two gentlemen on Lake Street and
afterwards as she was going out of a drugstore on Clark Street on Friday
noon, please send her address to Sojourner, Box 22."

The *Tribune* declared on June 21 that visitors were coming to regard
Chicago as one of the wonders of the world for "our tunnels, our cribs [*in
the lake*], our water works, our Board of Trade, White Stockings, and
Court House, marble palaces, lovely women, energetic men, suicides,

murders, divorces, pig killing, Historical Society, one-horse cars, etc."
Joseph Medill wrote letters to the paper, urging citizens to vote for the
new state constitution. He particularly commended the sections on
railroads, warehouses, the canal, and minority representation. The
people of the city were now driving in the park of an evening, and the
Tribune called attention to the 2,000 or more fastidiously dressed Chicagoans who participated in the "fashionable airings." Nearly all were
capitalists, the paper commented.

Medill went to Nantucket on vacation and Gath followed President
Grant to Long Branch, where he wrote articles critical of the president
and his cronies. The new state constitution was approved in July, 1870,
and Medill returned to Chicago late in August to give city councilmen
guidance in complying. The *Tribune* had given excellent coverage to the
Franco-Prussian War from the beginning, and on August 24 it published
a detailed map of Paris and environs as that city prepared for siege. Soon
the thousands of Germans in Chicago celebrated as news of the surrender
of the French army at Sedan was reported over the *Tribune*'s cables. There
was a fire on Wabash Avenue September 5 that destroyed a block of
stores, at a loss of $3 million. "This is the third time that Chicago has been
visited by such a calamity," said the *Tribune*. "Shall it be the last? The walls
of one building had been condemned. Economy of construction was
pushed to penuriousness. Mansard roofs, high buildings, weak walls, are
not dispensations of Providence. The community will find it has new
reasons to demand the enactment of a more rigid system of public
supervision over architects and builders." The *Tribune* stated that its own
building was fireproof.

The *Tribune* Prospectus for 1871 said in part: "The *Tribune* is the
enemy of monopoly and tax thieves in national and state politics and
always the champion of the people." Some of the words reflected Medill's
own views, but the frustrated proprietor did not agree with Horace
White's ventures into Republican party reform, his tariff stand, or his
failure to become concerned about the rising labor radicalism in Chicago,
a movement Medill believed to be spawned by the growing Communist
movement in Europe. Some friends thought that Medill would depart
Chicago in disgust, but he denied a report in the *New York Sun* that he was
buying a plantation in Louisiana, and he continued to provide his services
to the Chicago community. He soon would be called upon for a major
public service.

"I HAVE 'MET THE ENEMY AND THEY ARE OURS'"

11

Horace White continued his editorial barrage against the entire conservative segment of the Republican party throughout 1870 and into the year following, seemingly unaware that Joseph Medill was not the only one at the *Tribune* dismayed by his editorial course. To escape some of the annoyance and humiliation, Medill traveled extensively, sending correspondence back to the paper for publication and writing letters to his fellow proprietors that expressed his exasperation: *"I bitterly regret this schism in our office and would give thousands of dollars (if money could cure it) to heal the breach and place the* Tribune *in sympathy with the Republican party,"* he wrote to Alfred Cowles. Significantly, the letter carried the salutation "Dear Mr. Cowles," rather than the "Dear Alf" characteristic in prior years. *"But as I have explained to you,"* Medill continued, *"the trouble is fundamental—it is as broad and deep as that which separates* conservatism *from* radicalism *and can only be ended by unconditional surrender of the convictions of Mr. W. or my own. . . . We have tried the compromise business and it has failed utterly. Mr. W. fully appreciates the source of the difference. He knows that in mental structure we are greatly unlike, which in executive management of political matters renders harmony of views utterly impossible."* Medill explained in detail that although his own views represented *"those of 99 percent of the Republican party . . . the prejudices and notions of one member of our firm are allowed to over-ride the platform, the sentiments of the party and the interests of the* Tribune, *to say nothing of the views and wishes of the Senior Editor."*

William Bross and Cowles continued to support White, however, though Bross was preoccupied with politics and travel. Cowles normally confined his interests to the efficient operations of the business department, where conditions appeared excellent despite reduced circulation as a result of White's policies. Newsprint and labor prices had risen, so that circulation no longer returned the profits of the past; in some geographical areas an increase in readership could actually cause profits to fall. But advertising revenues were growing, partly because of generally improved economic conditions and also because White was content to devote his premium front-page space to advertising rather than news and features. Thus the paper was published at less cost and earned a greater net return. Bross and Cowles found this bottom-line result comforting.

Medill, on the other hand, saw disaster ahead. The *Tribune* was losing influence. Fewer readers inevitably would mean less advertising. The apparent financial gains were illusory since they were temporary. Medill sought to force his views upon his fellow proprietors by offering to sell his stock, setting off a flurry of interoffice notes early in 1870. On January 5, Medill wrote to Bross, who was president of Tribune Company, offering his stock at $500 a share (par value $100). Bross did not panic but replied formally and crisply to Medill later that day:

> *I have yours of this morning. As to the office buying your stock at anything like 500 I think it is out of the question. On the other hand, to consummate what you proposed . . . it seems to me that the best thing is for you to buy White out. I presume you would have to give 550. . . . As to Cowles, he is a good newspaperman and for myself I would like to retain him where he is. If you insist on buying White out and he will take $5.50 [sic] in order that matters may be lovely and the goose hangs high, I suggest this—you take 150 shares, Cowles 50 and I 100, if I can arrange with White for payment. That would give you and me 60/200 of the stock [sic]. I have nothing to advise and leave it to you.*

Bross wrote in haste, responding in the afternoon to a note received from Medill in the morning, which might explain his confusion relative to stock ownership. At the time Bross wrote, he owned 500 of Tribune Company's 2,000 shares and Medill had 456, a total of 956, already more than a "60/200" interest. Probably Bross meant to say that adding 250 of White's shares to theirs would give him and Medill control of 60/100 of the stock. In any case, Medill was not likely to forget that Bross had proposed restoring Charles Ray to the *Tribune* hierarchy, and he must have been shocked by the suggestion of $550 a share for 150 of White's 300 shares, even if Bross was willing to buy 100 at that price himself.

In mid-January, Bross again wrote Medill, who was away on one of his trips for news and recreation, indicating his increasing disenchantment with White.

> *At our meeting of the stockholders today I did some scolding. . . . The only item that will interest you was the remark of Mr. White that he should be content if you or I were elected in his place* [as managing editor and superintendent of editorial]. *He seemed to feel pleasant, whatever turn the matter should take. As to myself, you know that I do not want it. You do. But if you or others think I should have it for a time, I should do so, in consultation with you on important matters. . . . I am willing to do anything to restore the* Trib. *to its former prestige and power.*

About a month later, Bross wrote further, probably referring to a new offer by Medill to sell his stock: *"I slept almost none coming home last night. The result of my thinking then and today is this. I want you, if you please, to consider yourself bound to sell my stock if your offer is likely to be accepted. I don't want to be in the paper when you go out. I want to retire if you do."*

Medill had earlier received another assurance of support, this from William Rand, who continued to own his *Tribune* stock after leaving the paper in 1868. By agreement with the other proprietors, Rand and Andrew McNally had taken over the job printing contracts, such as those for railroad tickets, to form Rand McNally & Company. On January 13, 1870, Rand wrote to Medill:

> *You have not heard from me for the reason that until today I have not had an opportunity of conversing with Messrs. Cowles and Bross. I have now seen them both and we have canvassed* Tribune *matters pretty thoroughly. Mr. Cowles is dissatisfied with Mr. White's management in some respects, though I believe that he would vote for his retention as editorial superintendent. Mr. Bross is very much dissatisfied with the present status. I left him with the impression upon my mind that he would vote to reinstate you as editorial superintendent if you would take the position and devote your energies to the management of the paper.*

Two weeks later, Rand wrote that he regretted Medill had not come to the stockholders' meeting and that he understood Bross had written him about it. Rand reminded Medill that

> *you have not yet written me that you would accept the office of editorial superintendent. On the contrary, you say that you will sell if possible. Then you have written to Mr. Bross that you will vote for him rather than Mr. White. Now that mixes things, for Mr. Bross has got it into his head that he is about the right man for the position and he is making efforts to get it. Mr. Bross has told me that you shall have his vote. I have made up my mind that you will have mine. And don't stuff Mr. Bross any more or the fat will be in the fire. If you want the editorial superintendency say so, and stick to it. You can be elected in my opinion, if you will come up and cast your own vote.*

The struggle for control continued throughout January and into February, when it took a somewhat unexpected turn. On the 28th, White wrote: *"J. Medill, Esq. —Dear sir: Your letter of the 7th inst. offering to sell me 400 shares of* Tribune *stock at $525 per share was duly received. Mr. Rand had* *previously offered his at $550 but he subsequently reduced the price to 525 at which figure Mr. Cowles and myself have bought it together with a portion of Mr. Upton's. . . . The time which you gave me to consider your offer expires tomorrow. I think I shall not be able to purchase it. Yours truly, Horace White."*

White had triumphed temporarily in the internecine conflict due to his alliance with Cowles and Rand's decision to sell, a decision evidently made by Rand because he was disappointed by Medill's failure to drive for reelection as editorial superintendent. Also on February 28, Bross had written Medill:

> I have news for you. White and Cowles have bought Rand's stock and $500 of George Upton's giving them that majority of the whole. When we came together this morning, Rand's letter was read, offering to sell to the company. Of course I was unwilling that the company should buy. Cowles then said that he and White had bought Rand's at $5.25 and Upton's at $5.00 [sic]. I told them that I thought you would give more, intending to telegraph you, Cowles replied that you could not get it if you would. Seeing that the whole thing was fixed I subsided. Those are the facts as they occurred.
>
> Now as to the Tribune future. Of course C & W have the matter within their own grasp. I am perfectly cool and I hope that you will keep so. If we flounce it will only do our property harm and depreciate its value. We have too much at stake for that. I shall bide my time and do my best for the paper and I hope you will. C & W have too much property in it now to run it for any considerable time on the wrong track. I think they will feel their responsibility more than ever, and be glad to avail themselves of our knowledge, judgment and experience. As they must have gone heavily into debt, they will be as much disposed to make money as we can be. The whole purchase is $131,500. Of course White must make money pretty rapidly or be carried by Cowles. . . . N.B. I think Rand sold for more than any one else will, perhaps in our life time.

White's success in office politics was paralleled for a time on the national scene. He suffered a brief setback in late spring, 1870, when he and his Eastern liberal friends failed to persuade President Grant to reappoint David Wells as special revenue commissioner. But then came the victories of low-tariff candidates in the fall congressional elections and James G. Blaine's trip to consult White on the chairmanship of the House Ways and Means Committee. White and his group got three low-tariff men on the committee, and, while they were unsuccessful in getting the chairmanship for James Garfield, they could and did dominate the committee. White, exulting in his own prominence within the growing liberal Republican movement, took occasional editorial potshots at President Grant's policies. By March 23, 1871, the question of civil service reform, intraparty controversies arising from Grant's proposal to annex Santo Domingo, and a struggle over the correct policy for the conquered South led White to conclude that the time was right for a massive stroke against the president.

That afternoon, White wrote an editorial detailing President Grant's mistakes and shortcomings. Unfortunately for White, he acted at the very time that Grant, responding to widespread complaints about Ku Klux Klan violence in the South, issued a brief statement calling for legislation to empower the federal government to crush the Klan. Since 1867, the position of White and other liberals had been that the Reconstruction Act made further federal attention to the South unnecessary. Instead, they urged, the country should concentrate on economic matters, especially the tariff. Thus Grant's recognition that certain elements of the South continued to resist federal authority destroyed the liberals' position.

"Within a single day, the political plans of Horace White virtually collapsed," notes his biographer, Joseph Logsdon. "He had firmly committed his paper to nonintervention in the South. . . . Grant's speech isolated White and other discontented Republicans almost instantly."

White's editorial response to President Grant's action was to feebly suggest that high-tariff diehards were acting against the Ku Klux Klan simply to divert attention from the financial problems of the country. When this response was read in the House of Representatives, Logsdon reports, "the words drew a shout of laughter." Even one of the free-traders chosen by White and his friends to sit on the Ways and Means Committee voted for Grant's Ku Klux Klan laws. But White was spared further humiliation by an even greater disaster, this one at home.

*   *   *

Repeatedly that summer and fall, the *Chicago Tribune,* like an Old Testament prophet, thundered its warnings of imminent disaster unless the city would change its ways. The paper was not alluding this time to continued crime and vice, but instead assailed the city council and businessmen for failure to take proper precautions against the perils of fire. The *Tribune,* published in its new four-story fireproof building, insisted, as it had been doing for years, that Chicago, more than 90 percent wood construction, was an enormous firetrap, made more flammable because it lacked proper fire-fighting equipment and laws. To emphasize the threat, all through the dry summer and fall the paper printed almost a column a day about fires throughout the Northwest. Towns, cities, forests, prairies, all contributed their testimony to the danger. "There has been no rain for three weeks," the paper said early in October. "We will continue to print these stories on conflagrations until the common council acts." Then, on Saturday, October 7, the dire prediction of a holocaust came to pass. As the Sunday editions were about to go to press, flames breaking out in the Lull and Holmes planing mill on Canal Street near Van Buren were spread swiftly by a strong wind, and soon the city's fire department was alerted by a second alarm from Box

No. 248, with four steam engines responding. The dry wood of the surrounding lumberyards threw up flames that attracted thousands to the scene, interfering with the work of the 200 firemen. Soon coal yards, stores, and homes were being devoured, and the avid crowds were driven back by the heat and by police attempting to aid the firemen.

When the fire was struck out at 3:30 on the morning of October 8, four blocks had been burned over, with losses estimated by the *Tribune* at nearly $1 million. The paper reminded its readers of its warnings and noted that there had been 30 blazes within as many days. "For days past alarm has followed alarm, but the comparatively trifling losses have familiarized us to the pealing of the Courthouse bell, and we had forgotten that the absence of rain for three weeks had left everything in so . . . inflammable a condition that a spark might set a fire which would sweep from end to end of the city." And the same day the paper was asking editorially, "Shall we have another great fire? The common council fails to enact the needed laws or to recommend ordinances."

That night, shortly after nine o'clock, the weary men serving the steam fire engines "America" and "Little Giant" were responding again on the Southwest Side. They had seen flames, though no alarm had been sounded, and when the alarm was given at last, it was at the wrong box, No. 342. The watchman in the courthouse cupola saw a fiery reflection in the southwest and assumed it was some flaring embers of the prior night's fire. At the *Tribune* offices downtown, the staff was busy, under city editor Samuel Medill, putting together the Monday paper. Horace White had come in to prepare his Monday editorials, one on the iniquities of the Grant administration and another on fire dangers, and at some time during the night Joseph Medill and Elias Colbert, the *Tribune*'s astronomer-in-residence, arrived. Colbert took his telescope to the roof of the four-story building as he often did for a bit of stargazing. This night he observed that a new blaze had evidently flamed up to the southwest. He watched, then summoned a reporter and began dictating notes on the outbreak of another fire. Sam Medill, thus alerted, looked about for a reporter to send to the scene. Gustav Percy English, the *Tribune*'s night police reporter, had completed a second-day story on Saturday's fire and was leaving the Tribune Building when he heard alarm bells. He reported to city editor Medill, who told him to jump into a hack and take a look. When he returned to the office to write for the Monday paper, Sam Medill asked where the fire was. "Everywhere," said English.

Atop the Tribune Building, Colbert was getting an excellent view of the spread of the flames, which began jumping entire blocks of buildings as hot gases and winds formed "fire devils." It was clear soon that an even worse disaster than that of Saturday night was in the making. But the downtown area, with its "fireproof" structures surrounding the "fire-proof" Tribune Building, seemed safe. "The faith of every employee of the *Tribune* in the fire-proofness of the structure was sublime," George Upton wrote. It appeared that the fire had passed beyond the Tribune Building when he left his office early on the morning of the 9th, so Upton merely locked the door, not troubling to remove any of his papers and manuscripts. But the fire doubled back. Colbert grabbed up one of the half-printed papers of the Monday edition and went to get the bound files. Others aided him, but those who attempted to carry away files lost them in the heat and confusion. There was a tremendous crash as a wall of McVicker's Theater collapsed, falling against the Tribune Building and ripping it open to the flames, and soon it, too, was afire. The entire building was gutted, only some financial papers in the vault surviving, plus a linen coat that had in its pocket a packet of matches unexploded by the heat.

The story of those last hours was told later in the *Tribune* of February 15, 1873:

> When the gas gave out, candles were procured, and the work went on. The staunch building was fire-proof, and so seemed the *Tribune* workers. . . . Here follows the last "take" set in the old *Tribune* composing room by the light of the burning city . . . "and the wind raging, and the fire burning, and London, and Paris, and Portland outdone, and no Milton, and no Dante on earth to put words together! A group of men on the fourth story of this office all write at once on the spectacle, and hand sheet after sheet of 'copy' to the faithful compositors, who have not forsaken their posts." [*The forms of type were locked up and sent down to the press.*] The first pages were worked off. . . . But there the work ended. The fire cut a new swath across the city at Taylor street, and swept like a prairie-flame up State street. The stately Palmer House came down like a castle of cards. McVicker's Theatre put on its last spectacular effect, and, thus attacked in the rear, aided by the treachery of a rear wall, the Tribune Building succumbed.

When Joseph and Samuel Medill left the Tribune Building they were able to get safely to their homes down Madison Street. After a quick breakfast Joseph Medill began a search for a small printing plant he remembered along Canal Street. He found the Edwards Job Shop at No. 15 Canal and bought it. He knew of a four-cylinder press for sale in Baltimore and dispatched Sam to send a telegram buying it. Within hours the press was on the way to Chicago. The *Journal's* building had been hit by fire but the presses were in good condition, and Charles Wilson offered to share his presses with the *Tribune* as long as they were needed. Murat Halstead of the *Cincinnati Commercial* sent a font of type, distributed in cases, and the *Missouri Democrat* sent a supply of paper. Other newspapers offered aid including the *Aurora Beacon,* which said it would print the *Tribune.* The printing offers were gratefully declined. Sam Medill rounded up his news staff, finding that no one of the *Tribune* organization had been hurt, and the paper prepared to go to press Tuesday night, October 10. By the time William Bross and Horace White had discharged their family obligations, arranging for temporary homes for their families, they found that the Medills were ready to print.

There was an awesome story of devastation to be told. The fire, which had started in a barn at 137 De Koven Street, a poverty patch near Halsted and 12th streets, had progressed northeast without touching the home occupied by the barn's owners, Patrick and Catherine O'Leary. Swept by strong winds and whipped on by fire devils, the flames had desolated the entire downtown area, after jumping the South Branch of the Chicago River and then the east-west confluence. The fire burned out early Tuesday morning, leaving a three-and-a-half-square-mile area from Harrison Street to Fullerton Avenue, between the North and South branches of the Chicago River to Lake Michigan, a mass of charred ruins. In the business district only three structures still stood, the almost unscathed Lind Block at the river at Randolph Street, the castellated water tower and pumping plant on Pine Street (Michigan Avenue), and the Nixon Block, partly finished, at LaSalle and Monroe. Property damage was $200 million, more than 250 lives were lost, 17,450 buildings were destroyed. The correspondent of the *New York Herald* said the fire began when Mrs. O'Leary went out to milk her cow, which kicked over a lantern. English, the *Tribune* reporter, never believed that story, and Mrs. O'Leary denied it under oath at the official inquiry, according to the *Tribune.* But there seemed no doubt that the fire did begin in the barn, on the site now occupied by the Chicago Fire Department's training academy, perhaps started by someone who left a party next door to the O'Learys to get milk for a milk punch.

The *Tribune* published a brave editorial in that first postfire edition of Wednesday, October 11, which began:

CHEER UP.

In the midst of a calamity without parallel in the world's history, looking upon the ashes of thirty years' accumulations, the people of this once beautiful city have resolved that CHICAGO SHALL RISE AGAIN.

With woe on every hand, with death in many strange places, with two or three hundred millions of our hard-earned property swept away in a few hours, the hearts of our men and women are still brave, and they look into the future with undaunted hearts.

The day following, another *Tribune* editorial explained why Chicagoans could face the future with optimism:

REBUILD THE CITY.

All is not lost. Though four hundred million [*sic*] dollars' worth of property has been destroyed, Chicago still exists. She was not a mere collection of stone, and bricks, and lumber. These were but the evidence of the power which produced these things; they were but the external proof of the high courage, unconquerable energy, strong faith, and restless perseverance which have built up here a commercial metropolis. The great natural resources are all in existence; the lake, with its navies, the spacious harbor, the vast empire of production, extending westward to the Pacific; the great outlet from the lakes to the ocean, the thirty-six lines of railways connecting the city with every part of the continent—these, the great arteries of trade and commerce, all remain unimpaired, undiminished, and all ready for immediate resumption. . . . Let us avail ourselves of the liberal spirit which the country has shown in our calamity. There are no relentless creditors pressing us for payment, foreclosing mortgages, or demanding the full measure of their bonds. On the contrary, the world is asking us to take money,—unlimited credit, and go ahead, leaving the past to be taken care of in the future, when Chicago shall have resumed her power and glory.

Let the watchword henceforth be: CHICAGO SHALL RISE AGAIN.

The slogan caught on. George F. Root wrote a song about the Chicago fire incorporating it. The city at once began the tremendous task of rebuilding as gifts and offers of help arrived from rival cities and small communities from "Maine to Omaha," as the *Tribune* put it. The first postfire edition of the paper carried a few routine advertising cards, but soon the advertising of merchants such as Mandel Brothers and Field and Leiter, who had reestablished themselves in structures south of the burned area, appeared. The *Tribune* published daily an eight-column, four-page paper sold at 5¢. For years, Joseph Medill has been accredited personally with authorship of the "Cheer Up" editorial, but biographer Logsdon presents White's claim, supported by a witness. Whoever penned the words, it was possible to publish them because of Medill's quick action in obtaining a printing facility. White lost $100,000 of his personal fortune because the building he owned with Cowles was uninsured. White and Bross also lost their homes. The *Tribune* losses, however, were much less, $50,000 to repair the presses and to replace other equipment. Preparations were made to erect a new, five-story building on the site and to add equipment at a total cost of $300,000.

Chicago began its reconstruction tasks under military rule. Mayor Mason proclaimed martial law on the 11th and Gen. Phil Sheridan was ordered to bring in soldiers to protect the stricken city from looters. Sheridan summoned the Fifth U.S. Infantry under Col. Nelson A. Miles, much to the annoyance of Gov. John Palmer, who insisted that the rights of the state of Illinois had been violated. Governor Palmer was technically correct, but few cared. Like Bross, most Chicagoans were "delighted to see the boys in blue." The *Tribune* also editorially approved. Medill arranged with Bross to go east to procure supplies for the paper and to assure businessmen, especially bankers, that Chicago would surely rise again. Bross, the indefatigable booster, enthusiastically urged the East to take advantage of a rare new opportunity to make money in Chicago. "Go to Chicago now!" cried Bross. "Young men, hurry there! Old men, send your sons! Women, send your husbands! You will never again have such a chance to make money! . . . Now is the time to strike. A delay of a year or two will give immense advantage to those who start at once. . . . The fire has leveled nearly all distinctions." And, finally, booster Bross provided his prophecy:

> I tell you within five years Chicago's business houses will be rebuilt, and by the year 1900 the new Chicago will boast a population of a million souls. You ask me why? Because I know the Northwest and the vast resources of the broad acres. I know that the location of Chicago makes her the center of this wealthy region and the market for all its products. What Chicago has been in the past she must become in the future—and a hundredfold more! She has only to wait a few short years for the sure development of her manifest destiny.

Thousands took the advice of Bross. The Illinois legislature appropriated $3 million to help Chicago rebuild, Eastern bankers loaned money, and Queen Victoria and her subjects sent a gift of 8,000 books to help start the city's first public library. Joseph Medill was called upon to become candidate for mayor on the "Union-Fireproof" ticket, a request made by a nonpartisan committee led by Norman Judd, who had been prodded by Horace White's suggestion that there should be no partisan rivalry under the circumstances. Some people, including Governor Palmer, complained that the *Tribune* was assuming dictatorial powers, but it was generally recognized that the need for a strong leader was compelling, and it also was clear that Medill accepted the candidacy reluctantly. He was elected over token opposition and assumed the responsibilities of the reconstruction mayor. White, meantime, was free to begin new adventures in liberal politics.

*   *   *

Beginning with his anti–Ku Klux Klan statement in March, 1871, President Grant had by a series of political moves reasserted a large measure of control over the Republican party. Yet Republican insurgents, particularly those dedicated to revenue reform, remained dissatisfied. Early in 1872, the anti-Grant movement gathered momentum when Liberal Republicans in Missouri drafted a platform on national affairs and called for a convention of like-minded reformers to meet in Cincinnati on May 2.

Horace White already had indicated to friends that he was leaning toward Sen. Lyman Trumbull for president, but when Trumbull urged White to throw *Tribune* support to the Missouri plan, the editor's public utterances were guarded. Any pronouncements aligning the traditionally Republican paper with the Liberal bolters would require substantial agreement among the proprietors. William Bross was inclined to back White, but the key to control of *Tribune* policy resided with major stockholder Alfred Cowles. Leonard Swett, a former Lincoln supporter who was now active in the anti-Grant politicking, explained Cowles's position to Judge David Davis: *"Coles* [sic] *looks at the paper from a money standpoint purely. The establishment is making more money than ever before. . . . Still, it cannot afford to lose its present subscribers. In its editorials it is one day for the administration and the next shadows a support of the opposition."*

Cowles, of course, was not alone in his concern for *Tribune* finances. White, still smarting from the embarrassment inflicted by the Ku Klux Klan episode, and Bross wanted to be sure of their ground before risking financial loss and political opprobrium by embracing the Liberal movement. The only proprietor who seemed sure of where he stood with respect to the Republican bolters was Joseph Medill, who despite his onerous duties as mayor and his responsibilities as a Grant-appointed civil service commissioner, found time to visit the *Tribune* offices occasionally to register his dissatisfaction with White.

On March 16, 1872, he addressed a long letter to "Mr. A. Cowles" marked "Confidential," in which he expressed alarm concerning *Tribune* policies, specifying the following:

1. *Mr. White hates Mr. Grant. Why I never knew nor had explained. Grant himself does not know the cause of this daily hatred. . . .*

2. *But that is no good reason for putting the paper in a false position before its patrons. He* [White] *owns but 20 per cent of the property; is the smallest shareholder of the four owners and has no right to damage my property or yours to gratify animosity toward the president—has no right to do it in law or equity.*

3. *Gen. Grant is sure to be nominated at the Philadelphia convention—almost by acclamation. He can only be defeated by defeating the Republican party of the United States.*

4. *Judge D. Davis will be the candidate of the Democrats,—ex-Rebels, sore-head Republicans. . . . Then comes the "tug of war"—the glorious old Republican party on one side and its enemies and deserters on the other. On which side of the fight will the* Tribune *be? I have been identified with the* Tribune *for 17 years. In all that time it has claimed to be a Republican organ. It cannot now change into a Democratic sheet without serious pecuniary injury, nor with my legal consent. . . . There is not room in the Democratic party for the* Tribune. *The* Times *fills that space. . . .*

Does Mr. White want to organize a new party? No new party can be constructed of better materials than the Republican party. . . . One of the Tribune's *hobbies has been revenue reform. Have you thought how much of a revenue reformer Judge Davis is or has been? He was a high-tariff Whig and no man ever heard him declare he had changed his notions one iota.*

Does it occur to you that the Democratic party since the destruction of slavery has ceased to be a free trade party? It is a fact.

After several further paragraphs of political and philosophical discussion, Medill wrote: *"My proposition is this: that you buy me out and I will purchase the* Times *and convert it to a Republican paper while the* Tribune *can take its place as a Democratic paper. You don't want a new, powerful Republican paper started here, as there will be soon unless it is prevented in the way I suggest. I don't care a button about the mayoralty and am ready to resign if you accept my offer."* The letter breaks off abruptly and is not signed, but it is unquestionably in Joseph Medill's handwriting, the pressure of the pen indicating his anger as he wrote. Medill's demands for policy changes and his proposal to sell evidently were not considered at that time by the directors, who allowed him to fume in frustration.

As Medill indicated to Cowles, David Davis, the man who had masterminded Lincoln's nomination in 1860, was taking advantage of White's indecision to make his own move for the presidency. Davis, who was now a Supreme Court justice, felt that he could win support from Democrats as well as the insurgent Republicans. Swett, one of Davis's managers, wrote an open letter to the *Tribune,* urging support for the Cincinnati convention and backing Davis. Still White hesitated. Using the *Tribune* to back a Liberal Republican was a dangerous but possible course, but support for a coalition with the Democrats would be likely to deprive the paper of the bulk of its Republican subscribers. White solved his dilemma in early April by declaring that the Democratic party was dead; splitting the Republican party could not prove harmful since no opposition party remained! White then went to Springfield to join Trumbull supporters in endorsing Trumbull for the presidency on a Liberal Republican ticket. An urgent meeting of the directors of the *Tribune* was arranged, as Medill sought to stop this new defection, but he and the other proprietors were compelled to recognize White's fait accompli.

White enjoyed considerable prominence at Cincinnati, where he served as a representative of the *Tribune,* reporting the proceedings; as chairman of the important committee on platform; and as a behind-the-scenes kingmaker, one of the self-styled "Quadrilateral," a stop-Davis cabal of four of the nation's top editors: Samuel Bowles, of the *Springfield* (Massachusetts) *Republican;* Murat Halstead, of the *Cincinnati Commercial;* Henry Watterson, of the *Louisville Courier-Journal;* and Horace White.

Closely allied with them was U.S. Sen. Carl Schurz, of the *St. Louis Westliche Post,* who with the aid of the Quadrilateral was named permanent chairman of the convention.

As the convention got under way, two other candidates began to show power against the Illinois contenders Trumbull and Davis—one the New York favorite, the unpredictable perennial Horace Greeley, whom White had criticized a few years before as "ambitious and vindictive, an eccentric and ill-balanced mind"; the other Massachusetts's Charles Francis Adams, a dark horse with powerful New England support. To keep the New York delegates from throwing their votes to Davis, who was their second choice, White found himself maneuvered into accepting the strongly protectionist Greeley as a vice-presidential nominee on a Trumbull ticket. In addition, the Quadrilateral, confident that it could elect either Adams or Trumbull, both prominent revenue reformers, agreed to support a platform that was ambiguous on the tariff issue. Many Liberals were shocked, and Joseph Medill, who had been read out of *Tribune* policy-making partly on the tariff issue, was furious at White's opportunistic turnabout. Worse was to come.

On the convention's crucial last day, 10,000 shouting delegates and visitors packed the hall as the Liberals assembled to adopt the platform and select their candidate. The platform drafted by White's committee was swiftly accepted, the nominations were chanted, and the balloting began. On the first round the austere Adams led the serious contenders, receiving 205 votes to 147 for Greeley, 110 for Trumbull, and only 92 for Davis. The Quadrilateral had stopped Davis, all right, and the race quickly narrowed to Adams and Greeley. During the sixth ballot, while the Illinois delegation was paralyzed by a caucus fight, Alabama, Arkansas, and California cast their votes for Greeley, starting a stampede. Before the Illinois delegation could get back to the floor to vote, Greeley had 318 votes, Adams 292. The Illinois vote made little difference— Greeley's momentum was too great—and Uncle Horace became the nominee for president, with Gov. Benjamin Gratz Brown of Missouri his running mate. The Quadrilateral was demolished. Wrote Greeley's biographer, Henry Luther Stoddard, "No political boss ever planned control of a convention with greater zeal than these leaders of the independent press of the country, nor ever planned so futilely." It was the last great concatenation of newspaper editors and proprietors who aspired to take over the duties and obligations of politicians.

Though Greeley's candidacy and the Cincinnati platform were given the near-unanimous endorsement of the Democratic convention in July, the Greeley campaign was a shambles. Early in September, Greeley himself decided he could not win. His personal affairs were in disarray, his wife was gravely ill, his newspaper was in financial difficulty. Writes Stoddard, "Tortured by her [*Mrs. Greeley's*] sinking condition, astounded by the virulence of the attacks upon him, wearied by anxieties for the *Tribune* and his own personal affairs, the last two months of the campaign were a race for the grave by both wife and husband far more than a race for the presidency by one of them." Mrs. Greeley died during the final weeks of the campaign, and on November 4, two days before the election, Greeley wrote his friend, Mrs. Margaret Allen, *"I am not dead but I wish I were. My house is desolate, my future dark, my heart is a stone."*

Horace White had explained to his staff at the *Tribune* that "the nomination of Mr. Greeley was accomplished by the people against the judgment and strenuous efforts of the politicians." But, despite the best efforts of White and his editorial writer Sheahan, the people did not respond to the Greeley campaign. The *New York Sun* broke the Crédit Mobilier scandal, and the *Chicago Tribune's* Gath provided the lurid details of the special arrangement putting Crédit Mobilier stock in the hands of congressmen and high officials of the Grant administration to promote favorable railroad legislation. One of those named, Schuyler Colfax of Indiana, was Grant's vice-president. "A smooth career has been broken," said the *Tribune* sadly. Yet Grant himself was not directly involved, though he had, in other instances, unwisely accepted big gifts, ranging from a horse to a house and library that he indicated were rightfully his due. The public did not seem to object. The *Tribune* heard that Greeley would do well in some southern and border states and dispatched reporters to send back optimistic tidings. They were quite correct, but on election day President Grant carried Chicago by 6,000, Illinois by 55,000, and the country by 763,000 votes, more than double the victory margin of his first presidential campaign. Horace White undertook to explain the phenomenon in a *Tribune* editorial: "The first thing that occurs to the reflecting mind in reviewing the recent campaign is that the business men of the country took an early dislike and almost an alarm at Mr. Greeley's candidacy." White wrote to Greeley to ask his plans, whether he intended to return to the regular Republican party, but received no reply. Horace Greeley was in Dr. Choate's sanitarium in Pleasantville, New York. On November 29, he died there.

*   *   *

Following the Greeley disaster White was hard-pressed by circumstances both within and outside the *Tribune*. During the campaign, the normally reticent Alfred Cowles had written an angry letter to Whitelaw Reid, Greeley's managing editor at the *New York Tribune,* making it clear that he had not favored support of Greeley in the first place, and promising that if Greeley did not have enough sense to *"keep his mouth shut . . . I will swing the* Chicago Tribune *around for Grant so quick that it will make your head swim."* Now Cowles was pressing White to pay his share of the *Tribune* rebuilding costs. White attempted to borrow from Villard, who was in Germany, but was refused when his friend declared that he could not borrow for his own needs, even at 16 percent. In January, 1873, White's wife, Martha, died suddenly. Her husband was distraught and left the paper for a rest. He returned in a short time, however, and attempted by hard work to assuage his grief and to improve his relationship with the other proprietors. There is no record that he was requested to change course. The paper's financial situation seemed satisfactory; costs were down, advertising revenues increased. Cowles and Bross were apparently willing to remain estranged from the regular Republicans, and Medill was busy with his job as reconstruction mayor of Chicago.

Chicago was rising again, and in great beauty. In the first year after the fire, Chicagoans borrowed and spent an estimated $40 million on new retail establishments and homes and warehouses. Since few industrial plants had been destroyed in the Great Fire, the new construction could be devoted largely to stores, office buildings, theaters, homes, and churches, greatly enhancing the entire downtown area. The city was now safer also. The council had approved several of the fire protection ordinances proposed by Mayor Medill and supported by the *Tribune* and the other newspapers. Chicago had become the commercial showplace of the Northwest, with dry goods emporiums unmatched outside New York and Philadelphia, and hotels, such as the new Palmer House, Grand Pacific, Sherman House, and Tremont House, unmatched anywhere.

But Mayor Medill was beginning to find that supervising the reconstruction of Chicago was an easier task than conciliating the various special interests and ethnic groups within the city. Like mayors before him, he had the pleasure of cutting ribbons at the opening of new business and cultural projects—he experienced the special joy of opening Chicago's first public library, containing 30,000 books—and also the frustration of the Sunday saloon closing problem. Medill chose to go with the Protestant preachers and their congregations, who demanded that the Sunday closing laws be enforced, and against the foreign-born, especially the Germans, who wanted the saloons open. He fired his police department officials when they refused to obey Police Superintendent Elmer Washburn's closing orders, and succeeded in losing the German vote, the *Staats-Zeitung* labeling him "Joseph I, Dictator." Mayor Medill responded by backing an 11 o'clock closing law; he ordered the enforcement of the Sunday closing measure and threatened to call out the militia if needed. The mayor was clearly disenchanted with the petty aspects of his job and in July, 1873, announced that he would not be a candidate for reelection. He had, in fact, indicated to his family that he would not finish out his term but would leave in the fall to take them on a grand tour of Europe, where he intended to study accomplishments of European cities. For a while he considered the possibility of buying the *Inter-Ocean* from J. Young Scammon, who had established the paper early in 1872 with the intention of making it the dominant Republican paper in Chicago, as Medill had predicted might happen. However, while he could not endure the new *Tribune* policies, neither could Medill bring himself to finally cut all ties with the paper. He would hold his stock, write letters from Europe, and bide his time.

In August, Medill designated Ald. Lester Legrand Bond as acting mayor and departed with his wife, Katherine, and their three daughters (Josephine, the youngest, was born in 1866). Mayor Medill, supported by the Committee of Seventy, had waged war against saloon and liquor interests and the criminal elements with considerable success, but in the mayoral campaign that fall it became clear that many Chicagoans would never opt for the closed town Medill had envisioned. The Mike Mc-Donald election machine backed Harvey D. Colvin, who was an easy winner. The *Staats-Zeitung* rejoiced that the elements represented by Joseph I, Dictator, had been crushed. King Mike McDonald was again the ruler. "The underworld was at last getting organized in a big way," Virgil Peterson records in his history of Chicago crime.

In September, the failure of Jay Cooke & Company, heavily involved in the financing of the Northern Pacific Railroad, signaled the arrival of the economic panic that had been threatening throughout the year. President Grant rushed back to Washington from his vacation but could do little. The New York Stock Exchange was closed for ten days. Before the year ended, there would be 5,000 business failures, rising to more than 10,000 in the two years following. Yet as 1873 drew to a close, Chicago business appeared relatively strong. Medill, in Europe with Kitty and his daughters for an extended tour, was soon sending travel articles on Ireland and Switzerland to the *Tribune,* then discussions of political, social, and fiscal management of cities from Germany, England, and France. In a speech in Paris, Medill said, "I came abroad to study the institutions, methods and customs of the Old World. I expect to return home much changed and modified in previous estimates of men and things, methods and manners. Not a little conceit already has evaporated. It has not modified, however, my love for America, the freest, happiest and most glorious country on earth."

Through the winter and spring, Medill spent much time in Paris with his old and dear friend Elihu Washburne, minister to France, with whom he had corresponded over many years, and who appears to have been his most trusted confidant outside his own family. During the summer of 1874, the Medills were in Switzerland, the baths particularly benefiting

Joseph, the Swiss climate congenial to Katherine. In Chicago, meantime, economic conditions had worsened as the Panic of 1873 continued to run its course, and the *Tribune* itself appeared to be in trouble. Medill's prediction that a sound Republican paper would win readers from the *Tribune* was proving accurate, as Scammon's *Inter-Ocean,* with its strong conservative Republicanism and its protectionist tariff policy, made gains at the *Tribune*'s expense. At one point Scammon had publicly declared that the *Tribune* was "only 18 months away from bankruptcy." Messages from Alfred Cowles were reaching Medill as he summered in Europe, via an undisclosed intermediary whom Medill declined to identify even to Washburne. On September 25, 1874, Medill wrote a joyful eight-page letter to Washburne, who was out of the capital on a holiday, announcing the developments in Chicago and his own hopes of reassuming control of the *Tribune.*

> *I greatly regret I will not see you before leaving for home. I start for London Sunday morning and sail on the* Baltic *Oct. 1.*
>
> *Shortly after my arrival in Paris from Switzerland I received a letter from home saying it was important—essential in fact—that I be back by the middle of October—Mrs. Medill and the girls will return later as soon as they can arrange passage. I think I told you last summer that I had received a hint from a "mutual friend" that perhaps I could purchase a controlling interest in the* Tribune. *The information, however, was very vague. I wrote back for full and definite information and facts. While at Wiesbaden taking the baths for my old rheumatic troubles an answer came detailing the substance of a long series of interviews with Mr. Cowles, the business manager and largest stockholder. He said in brief, "Tell Medill that the recent course of the* Tribune *has been wrong and impolitic—that he was right in his policy and that White erred, etc. That when he returns he can get controlling interest in the concern if we can agree on terms, but he should return in September if possible."*
>
> *To this letter I wrote a cautious reply, rather cold, saying that the mischief had already been done, the usefulness and influence of the paper greatly impaired, the volume reduced and the political outlook to me dark and discouraging, that I had much rather sell out than buy in deeper, etc. This was written on Aug. 8. On the 18th of September came the answer thru the "mutual friend" urging me to come home to close the matter up one way or the other. . . .*
>
> *"Say to Medill," says Cowles, "that he is the dissatisfied party, who has protested the management and the course of the paper. Let him say what he will give or take; we will either sell him what stock he wants at his offer or buy his interest."*
>
> *I don't believe that Cowles is serious in saying he will buy my stock if I don't purchase his. He wants to sell me control, he wants me to take charge and restore the* Tribune *to the old relations with the Rep. party and White to step out,—go abroad for a year or two. Cowles' pocket nerve has been touched and that is bringing him to a realizing sense and comprehension of the mischief that White has done.*

Medill discussed political considerations and suggested that White had Cowles "*mesmerized.*" He said that he had withdrawn to await the denouement of that situation. He was happy that now Cowles *"wants the old man back to set things right."* Medill declared that he intended to *"stop defections from the party"* and even to reestablish peace with the *Staats-Zeitung*. *"If I get control of the* Tribune *it will not be long until we will again have a Republican paper in Chicago,"* he added.

On Medill's return to Chicago, he found that the opposition forces were not so ready to capitulate as he had assumed. Alfred Cowles was not prepared to concede that his alliance with White had been a mistake, nor that it was imperative to have "the old man" lead the charge that would crush J. Young Scammon's "I.O.," as Medill called it. Also, there was the problem of the proper financial valuation of the paper. While the negotiations had been continuing, the outlook had somewhat improved, partly because of a new, handsome *Tribune* format, and partly because some "preacher scandals," which the *Tribune* exploited vigorously, had increased circulation. Medill was indignant at his cool reception and sent a memorandum marked *"For Your Private Eye Only,"* with no salutation or date, but obviously directed to Cowles.

> To show you how widely I was in error as to your and Mr. W's intentions, I supposed before I came home that Mr. W. desired to retire from the firm, if he got a good price for his stock, and that you and the "Deacon" intended to sell me ten [100?] shares each, leaving you a quarter and he a fifth interest, and us three then to run the concern—putting it back where it was three or four years ago politically, and making it a vigorous and independent sort of Republican paper, and regathering about us its thousands of old but lost friends, and speedily killing off the I.O. which would naturally follow . . . or that Mr. White, for the purpose of removing my discontent and strengthening his own position, desired to purchase a large "chunk" of my interest and you and "Deacon" the remainder. But it appears I was in error on both guesses. However, some solution to the problem must be found—the present status cannot continue, so I do not intend to remain passive in the future.

On October 24, Joseph Medill made his formal proposal to Cowles, the secretary of Tribune Company. Medill said he would sell his stock at $440 a share, up to the amount of $200,000, or he would purchase 600 shares of *Tribune* stock at $440 a share, *"paying $96,000 in money and my five-acre lot of land in Hyde Park situated at 45th Street and Cottage Grove Avenue. In regard to existing debt of the Tribune Co. the purchaser shall assume the pro rata liability of the stock, all credits and assets to belong to the firm."*

Alfred Cowles evidently responded on the 27th, since Medill on October 28 referred to *"your communication of yesterday"* and *"its novel proposition."* *"In making my proposition to you I was seriously influenced by your notification that it must include an offer for a half interest in the whole concern."* Medill then made his offer $500 a share, or $300,000, which would purchase enough stock to make his total holdings 1,056 shares. Marshall

Field, the merchant prince, had advanced him the necessary funds. This offer was accepted. Later Medill acquired four additional shares, giving him 53 percent of Tribune Company ownership.

At some point during the negotiations, Medill also had made clear his concept of how the newspaper should be run, and would be if he acquired control. In one of his series of memoranda, directed to the proprietors generally, he stated:

> You all know that I hold the opinion inflexible, that the editorship of the Tribune is radically defective, in this, that it lacks unity . . . and that there must be an executive head to a newspaper whose decision is supreme though he shall consult his associates . . . all experience shows the soundness of this view. The managing editor of this paper has too much power for a legislative form of government and too little for an executive form . . . Mr. White deems himself competent to conduct the editorship of a newspaper. I possess the same qualities to at least an equal degree [but] his views and mine of men and policies and details constantly and at times radically differ.
>
> Holding many decided notions as regards newspaper management I find it impossible to subordinate my will to that of another and at the same time I have no rights under the by-laws to demand that the managing editor shall adopt my views rather than his own. Hence my editorial contributions to the Tribune have been [diminished] and my usefulness as an editor greatly [impaired]. I see no way to effect an escape from this except by selling my interest and retiring, or purchasing sufficient stock to entitle me to the editorial control of the paper, and I am willing to pursue either course and to leave it entirely to you to determine which it shall be. You must consult your own interests, and not mine.

On November 1, 1874, Joseph Medill dispatched a jubilant message to his friend Washburne:

> I have "met the enemy and they are ours." Once more the dear old Tribune of former days will be itself again. The spirit of Ray, tho dead in the body, and much of Medill, tho long speechless, will again be felt and heard thru the columns talking to old families and friends. Poor Ray is dead and his eloquent, powerful periods cannot be reproduced but his spirit will live again in the Tribune. Both sides meant business and it was give and take. . . . As Old Abe said, "it must be all one thing or the other." [There were four days of haggling over price.] . . . Finally I offered them $300,000 for 60 [sic] shares, the balance in three years at ten percent. In 36 hours they accepted.
>
> The paper passed into my hands forever during this mortal life and that of my family after me. On the 9th inst. Mr. White retires and on that day one Medill resumes his old "throne and sceptre" in the Tribune "kingdom."
>
> I hear a good deal of talk of E.B.W. for the next Presidency.
>
> Horace W. is about to marry a girl of 24 or 26 and good looking.

Medill was now in full control.

*   *   *

During the long summer and autumn of negotiations, *Tribune* readers were being treated to some new departments and features, in addition to the easier-to-read format, and, to their obvious delight, to news of a sensational nature provided by two ministers of the Gospel. These stories pushed politics off the front pages for months at a time, and rather obscured the political reports, which Medill had remarked on to Washburne, that the American minister to France indeed was being mentioned as a possible Republican candidate for the presidency in various parts of the country.

The local pastoral contribution to the news, entirely ecclesiastical in nature, was provided by Professor David Swing, described by the *Tribune* as "Chicago's most popular preacher," a minister at Fourth Presbyterian, who was accused of heresy by the Reverend Francis L. Patton, Presbyterian leader and editor of the *Interior*, a Presbyterian journal owned by Cyrus H. McCormick, the multimillionaire Reaper King. Swing responded by asserting his individual right to interpret Scripture, since "he was first a Christian and then a Presbyterian," and claimed to be one "of the new school." The Swing ecclesiastical trial opened on May 5, 1874, and was given thorough coverage by the *Tribune,* though the testimony consisted largely of theological involutions ordinarily not understood or savored by the general public. The *Tribune* made it clear from the start that it was sympathetic to Professor Swing. When it was asserted at the trial that Swing was sympathetic to atheism, since he had praised John Stuart Mill, the *Tribune* took offense. It had published some of Mill's work and he had joined in the tariff debate on the side of free trade, having an occasional letter printed in the *Tribune.* The paper said that Mill had stated that the origins of life were unknowable, which was not atheistic.

The *Tribune* was quite consistent. It had published articles on Darwinism, its editors William Bross and Elias Colbert lectured on scientific topics at the Academy of Sciences, and the paper was generally friendly to scientific thought. Yet its editors were also basically religious, and, for the most part, puritanical. Professor Swing was acquitted by the Chicago Presbytery 48 to 15, then withdrew from the Fourth Presbyterian Church, although his congregation asked him to remain. "He is so much of a Christian," said the *Tribune* on May 16, "so little of a pettifogger, so abounding in his love of good and beautiful in every creature, so little skilled in the trickeries of theological finesse, that, if he be not a good Presbyterian, the misfortune is not his but that of the Presbyterian church." Years later the *Tribune* supported Professor Swing when he joined Henry Ward Beecher of New York in asserting that there was no such place as an orthodox hell.

It was Dr. Beecher who provided the sensational news of 1873–75, which helped to gain back circulation for the *Tribune* and many other daily newspapers. Scandal had been simmering since November, 1872, when *Woodhull and Claflin's Weekly* intimated improprieties in the relations of Beecher and a Mrs. Theodore Tilton. By June, 1873, Beecher felt impelled to make public denial of the rumors circulating about him. Then, in March, 1874, it was hinted that Dr. Beecher had been called before the Congregational Council in New York and had failed to deny certain charges made against him, charges not made known to the press. "While our sympathies have been with Mr. Beecher right along," the *Tribune* said on March 27, "they have been so on the presumption that an investigation would do him no harm. That is our present belief, but we do say that to longer resist an investigation will bring a reproach upon the Congregational Church in the person of its most distinguished representative." On July 22, 1874, the *Tribune* published five columns on "the Beecher Explosion." The rumors and innuendos had become allegations, for Theodore Tilton formally charged the minister with "criminal intercourse with his wife." It was said that she had been under the sway of Dr. Beecher and did not think that she was doing wrong, the *Tribune* reported. Both Beecher and Mrs. Tilton denied the charges.

Gath, George Alfred Townsend, the *Tribune*'s Washington correspondent, was vacationing at Saratoga, and he was ordered to New York City to investigate. He had a long conversation with Tilton, concluded that Tilton was "a bigger man morally than Beecher," and induced him to part with the correspondence between Beecher and Mrs. Tilton that supported his charges. The *Tribune* had a major and highly sensational scoop and used nearly five pages on August 13 to publish some of these letters, which detailed the lives, and especially the love life, of Elizabeth Tilton and Henry Ward Beecher.

The New York newspapers had missed what some editors and readers thought was the most readable story of the year, and the *Chicago Tribune* telegraphed back to both the *New York Tribune* and the *New York Sun* a great part of the content of the letters. Gath had a further interview with Tilton concerning details of Mrs. Tilton's confessions, and the account of this interview appeared on August 15. On August 17, the paper printed comment by other newspapers on the *Tribune*'s scoop and published a further interview by Gath with Frank Moulton, a friend of Tilton, who said that Beecher had discussed his relations with Mrs. Tilton over a period of years. The New York papers attacked Gath's story, and Gath responded by obtaining a second exclusive interview with Moulton. In Chicago, a reporter confronted Susan B. Anthony, in town for a women's rights congress, concerning reports that she once sat on Theodore Tilton's lap. "Why should I not sit on Mr. Tilton's knee?" she demanded.

"All the men said that Susan was so sour she couldn't get a husband and I thought I would show them I could sit on a young man's knee just like any foolish girl." On August 20, Tilton filed a charge of adultery against Beecher, asking $100,000 damages. The country was divided in its opinion of the case during the six months the trial proceeded and so was the jury, which was unable to reach a verdict, deadlocked at 9–3 for the defendant. A year later, a Congregational church council completely exonerated Beecher.

*   *   *

On November 9, 1874, a notice appeared on the *Tribune*'s editorial page, signed by Joseph Medill, one of the few ever signed by an individual:

> To the Readers of the Tribune
>
> With this issue of the *Tribune* I resume its editorial control. Having within the past fortnight purchased enough shares, added to what I previously owned, to control the majority of the stock, the responsibility of the future management of the *Tribune* will necessarily devolve on me. With what degree of ability and success I shall discharge the new obligations, time alone can make known. . . .
>
> A few words of explanation may not be inappropriate. . . . Shortly after the close of the Great Rebellion I was obliged by ill-health, caused by overwork, to resign the managing editorship of the *Tribune,* first to the late Dr. C. H. Ray, and, after he vacated his post, to Mr. Horace White, who has since then had chief control of the paper. After a brief rest I took an editorial chair and wrote for its columns for several years.

Medill described his political disagreements with White, adding that their differences "were always political and not personal." He then acknowledged that the readers would want to know the probable line of conduct of the new management and suggested that he was not ready for a definitive statement.

> But this much may now be safely promised: the *Tribune* will hereafter be, as it formerly was, when under my direction, an independent Republican journal. It will be the organ of no man, however high; no clique or ring, however influential; or faction, however fanatical or demonstrative. While giving to the Republican party and its principles a hearty and generous support, it will criticize the actions and records of Republican leaders as freely and fearlessly as in days of yore. But it has seemed to me unwise for a great representative journal, for the purpose of correcting some alleged abuses of administration, to desert its party organization and turn its guns on old friends, or help into power and places the leaders of the organization whose political records and whose official conduct show that they are insincere in their professions of desire for administrative purification.

There were hundreds of words more, summarized by Medill himself when he reiterated, "Hence, the *Tribune* will be conducted as a Republican journal."

Horace White was to keep some of his stock and would write for the paper. However, after a journey to England, White found the writing arrangement uncongenial. He retained his stock but rejoined his friend Henry Villard in financial ventures; then, with the aid of Villard, he acquired control of the *New York Post,* becoming its editor.

THE MEDILL YEARS

12

It was not until after I had been home several months that I fully comprehended the extent and depth of the injury inflicted on this city and the surrounding country by the panic of 1873. . . . I slowly awakened to the painfully realizing sense that I had gone too deeply into debt, that the former rate of profits could not by any human effort be restored, chiefly because the advertising business had dropped off and could not be gained back until there was a revival of trade. The panic following the fire had left this city in a sad plight . . . so you may imagine that I felt a little blue.

The stultifying effects of the Panic of 1873 endured for nearly five years, chastening even Chicago and the *Chicago Tribune*. Joseph Medill's letter to his friend Washburne, written in June, 1875, indicated that his jubilation over his victory in the power struggle with White was short-lived. Now in full control, Medill had to shore up the *Tribune*'s sagging finances in a period of severe economic depression. Medill's personal finances suffered an immediate setback; despite his greater ownership of shares, his income from the paper in 1875 was 50 percent less than it had been in 1874, since he allowed himself only $100 a week in salary in addition to the 8 percent he received on his stock.

Medill, who liked big open spaces for the display of his news and special articles, especially on page one, had all the space he could comfortably use, but at greater cost than he cared to pay. The cold hand of panic had touched Chicago's retail trade, which also had been the chief sufferer from the Great Fire, and newspaper advertising declined. Frequently through 1875 there were four columns of news space on page

253

one, and Joseph Medill and his brother Sam, the new managing editor, made good use of them, displaying somewhat piquant, robust news of general interest, while relegating the customary news fare of the past, usually politics, to inside pages except when major events decreed otherwise. Thus the Beecher-Tilton adultery trial found a home on the *Tribune*'s front page almost daily, except Sundays, for nearly six months in 1875. The Whiskey Ring scandal, which broke early in the year, usually had a fixed position on page two, but sometimes intruded into the Beecher scandal area, as did politics and religious controversy.

On Sundays the advertising situation was somewhat better than in the daily edition, so that less page-one space was available for editorial material, almost always on religious topics. The Sunday edition grew to 16 to 20 pages before the panic had run its course, with classified advertising contributing importantly to its success, and the *Tribune* soon asserted that it had the biggest and best Sunday paper in the United States, with the possible exception of the *New York Herald*. Frequently the Sunday front page was entirely filled with advertising, leading the proprietors to try such a display on weekdays. The procurement of advertising was not yet a recognized profession at the *Tribune*, but Medill and Bross evidently made known the availability of the page-one position, since the front page was completely filled for a few days in April and May; then daily classifieds had to be pulled to the front to supplement the ads of retail stores and patent medicine nostrums, and soon the experiment was abandoned.

Medill believed in a provocative kind of journalism that questioned not only the actions of politicians, businessmen, and religious leaders, but also of other publications. The new struggle with the *Inter-Ocean* was perhaps as vituperative as the long-standing, noxious feud with the *Times*. Even the *Interior*, the Presbyterian journal owned by Cyrus McCormick and edited by the Reverend Francis L. Patton, did not escape the *Tribune*'s occasional wrath, but both McCormick and Patton asked for it. Mc-Cormick was a professed Democrat who supplied money supporting his party's causes, and some critics said he felt that he owned both the Democratic party and the Presbyterian church. Dr. Patton, Cyrus's pastor, greeted Medill's return to the *Tribune* with an impertinent editorial, which the paper reprinted.

"Now that Mr. Medill is in charge of the *Tribune*," said the *Interior*, "would it be too much to ask, very respectfully, that the wholesale and retail slander of the ministry in the columns of that able paper be stopped? Clergymen do not like to rush into print against unseen assailants of their reputation and honesty." The editorial continued with more of the same, to which Medill replied in kind: "As the editor has been absent for some time, he cannot conscientiously or intelligently agree with the above. Whose character has been assailed? Of what do those faults consist? What are the facts in the case? If there have been assaults, what was the provocation offered? Has Professor Patton, the editor of the *Interior,* been hunting Prof. Swing, a clergyman in whom we feel a lively interest? Prof. Patton, whom we only know by report, which is not very flattering." Within a few months, Professor David Swing was a weekly contributor to the *Tribune,* whose editors appeared to welcome various evidences of his unorthodoxy. Together with some 50 other leading Chicagoans, Medill and William Bross became contributors to Swing's new nondenominational church, which met in McVicker's Theater.

By early 1876, the editorial techniques Medill had used previously in the *Tribune* and the *Cleveland Leader* could be observed reappearing. The decline of advertising in the eight-page paper allowed a large editorial space commitment, so bigger headlines were used, a more open format was developed, and regular departments were established in a pattern to be followed a century later by news magazines: Washington, National, Foreign, City, Financial and Commercial, Books, Theater, Religion, Sports, Women, even Humor. The humor column was mercifully brief, offering such items as "Hard Drinking,—chewing on ice," and "It is said that Digger Indians are never known to smile. They are grave diggers." Since news was somewhat bland after the war years, Medill garnered books, articles, and special stories, including travel reports by Mark Twain, to enhance the paper's appeal to the general reader. He especially strengthened the business coverage. Said the paper on May 1, 1876:

> The *Tribune* is a business man's newspaper. It is taken and read by all classes of people who have any property or anything to sell, lease or loan, or any money with which to make purchases or investments, or any useful services to hire or engage. Its circulation is not of the back alley sort nor dependent upon occasional sensational or scandalous articles. It is the character of the constituency that determines the quality of circulation and its corresponding value as an advertising medium. . . . Readers in the slums and back alleys who occasionally invest a nickel in a newspaper are not the class whom advertisers desire to reach.

Despite its disclaimer of sensationalism and its self-designation as a businessman's newspaper, the *Tribune* under Medill showed marked interest in both scandal and a special appeal to women. There were columns on homemaking; a woman fashion writer described the new styles displayed by the leading Chicago stores; columns frankly labeled "Gossip" covered such tidbits from Chicago, and gossip appeared also in special columns datelined Washington, London, and Paris. All these, presumably, had a feminine appeal. The paper launched a series, "How to Get Married," which it hoped would appeal to both sexes, and did. One article, on a young couple's house-hunting, related that a cottage could be obtained for $12 a month, or $25 a month furnished, a hired girl for $12 a month. Travel articles by staff reporters were instituted, a *Tribune* writer disclosing from Jacksonville, Florida, in January that the weather was "like summer." The cost to Jacksonville by Pullman, round trip, $66.

The *Tribune*'s interest in religion and religious personalities was intense. At least one sermon in each church was covered at some time during the year, a full page of sermons appearing each Monday. In addition there were many articles on religious fads. When it was learned that Wilbur F. Storey, the erratic editor of the *Times* and the new *Telegraph*, had embraced spiritualism, a *Tribune* reporter interviewed him and then consulted a Dr. Isaac Redfield on the subject. "An insane delusion," said Dr. Redfield. Dwight L. Moody and Ira D. Sankey opened their first Chicago revival in October, 1876. The *Tribune* covered the occasion with four columns of reports and continued coverage throughout the revival campaign. More than 7,000 Chicagoans attended the services the first night, hundreds standing in line outside the hall to gain admission. Some Chicago matrons, the *Tribune* said, sent servants or hired messengers to stand in line to assure their wealthy patronesses a place inside the hall. Moody was so pleased with his Chicago reception that he returned to the city in the late 1880s to found the Moody Bible Institute.

The pages of the *Tribune* also contained reports on religious controversies and on the clash of science and religion. The editors were sympathetic to the science advocates but cautioned, "Science should just make the facts available, don't try to make science a religion." Medill was fascinated by the experiments and inventions of Thomas A. Edison, and a *Tribune* article on Edison's phonographic experiments accurately predicted the vast recording developments of the future. "Mr. Edison says that upon a disc of copper or tin foil . . . the entire contents of an ordinary novel can be recorded," the paper reported. Why not get an outstanding actor to read a book onto a record? it suggested, predicting that thousands of such records could be sold. Medill, sharing scientific interest as well as a hearing impairment with Edison, became a lifelong friend and supporter of the inventor and his ideas.

One of the most successful Medill innovations of the period was the home service department, which appeared on Saturdays. Women writers—among them Jane Grey Swisshelm of the *Tribune* staff, Julia Ward Howe, and a contributor calling herself Fern Leaf—wrote for the section on subjects that went beyond mere household hints. Swisshelm, in an article on coeducation, counseled girls to avoid corsets, garters, and high-heeled shoes. Howe contributed her reports on women's activities in

Europe. Books on women's rights received intelligent and sympathetic reviews.

All these changes helped the *Tribune* to regain circulation, which had declined under the White regime. The Saturday women's columns and the book reviews appear to have had special appeal. By early 1877 the daily circulation of the *Tribune* was stated at 31,331, while the Saturday circulation was over 40,000 and Sunday slightly under the daily. Nonetheless, revenues continued to be meager.

* * *

As Medill had stated upon resuming control of the *Tribune*, he intended to swing the paper back on course politically, and to him that meant returning it to mainstream Republicanism. Nationally the Republicans were having their difficulties. Investigations following the exposure of the Whiskey Ring by Treasury Secretary Benjamin H. Bristow appeared to lead directly to the White House and to many high Republican officials. In May, 1875, Bristow revealed that distillers in St. Louis, Chicago, Milwaukee, and other cities had for years been falsifying their production records to cheat the government of taxes. Politicians, revenue agents, and other government officials had become involved in the far-flung conspiracy, which also included raising campaign funds and distributing hush money to hide the fraud. The *Chicago Tribune* devoted countless columns to the thievery and was not disappointed when Anthony C. Hesing, the local *Tribune* enemy, turned out to be one of the malefactors. The Whiskey Ring trials continued on into 1876. Dozens of conspirators pleaded guilty, and others, among them Hesing, were found guilty and given jail sentences.

The *Tribune* commended Bristow's investigative tenacity and honesty and proposed that the Republicans nominate him for president, as "the all sufficient and at the same time only answer . . . to the Democratic [*charges*] of official Republican corruption and extravagance." But President Grant, who was entertaining unrealistic hopes of being nominated for a third term, turned on Bristow, forcing him to resign. Grant's personal secretary, Col. Orville Babcock, had been linked with the ring, and Babcock's acquittal was brought about largely on the basis of Grant's testimony.

Joseph Medill himself went to Cincinnati in June to cover the Republican convention. Though Bristow was among the leading contenders, the presidential nomination went to reform candidate Rutherford B. Hayes of Ohio, with William A. Wheeler of New York as his running mate. Medill, who wrote the lead story, was satisfied. "Let us all rejoice and give thanks," said the *Tribune* on June 17. "The government is not about to pass into the hands of those who strove to destroy it. The work of official purification will go on, revenue thieves will be hunted down and driven from public life, and honest men will be put in their places. We have no fears for the result of the election of 1876."

When Samuel J. Tilden of New York was nominated by the Democrats as Hayes's opponent, the *Tribune* warned, "The Republican party now has knowledge of whom they have to deal with—a desperate, unscrupulous foe, armed with immense wealth, controlling a legion of agents skilled in the machinery of fraud elections." The campaign was hard-fought, as the Democrats hammered away at Republican scandals while the Republicans tried to resurrect Civil War issues. Tilden's popular vote exceeded Hayes's, but Hayes won the electoral vote 185 to 184, though due to disputed returns from four states the decision was not announced until March 2, 1877, only two days before the inauguration.

Medill also faced a local political battle of major proportions, arising in large part from his own term as mayor. Hesing, under attack for his connection with the Whiskey Ring, was a part owner of the *Staats-Zeitung*, which had labeled Mayor Medill "Joseph I, Dictator." When Medill had declined to seek reelection in 1873 and the Hesing-supported candidate, Harvey Colvin, was victorious, the German leader sent an exultant telegram to Medill in Paris, announcing that the Prussian flag would be flown over the *Staats-Zeitung* in a victory celebration. Medill had indicated in a letter to Washburne that he intended to overlook that gratuitous insult and make peace with the *Staats-Zeitung* in order to increase Republican influence among Chicago's Germans.

Nonetheless, he welcomed the opportunity to get a bit of his own back. In 1875, a new city charter changed the date of city elections from fall to spring; supporters of Mayor Colvin engineered the implementation of the new charter in such a way as to extend the mayor's term of office until April, 1877, nearly 18 months beyond the term to which he had originally been elected. Needing little urging from the *Tribune*, Chicago citizens registered their outrage by voting overwhelmingly Republican in the spring, 1876, aldermanic elections, and the aldermen promptly endorsed the victory of Thomas Hoyne in an unofficial write-in vote for mayor. "The bummers are outwitted," chortled the *Tribune*. Colvin refused to give up his office, and the Circuit Court agreed that Hoyne's election was illegal, but it ordered that a special mayoral election be held. Thus, in July, 1876, the *Tribune* not only ranged itself against Mayor Colvin, giving its support to Republican Monroe Heath, but did so with its old-time vigor and vehemence. Heath, a businessman and manufacturer, was the winner by a solid majority, and when he was handily reelected in 1877, Joseph Medill could boast that Chicago indeed was a Republican town.

Meantime, the city was $4.5 million in debt, and city workers received only half to three-quarters of their pay.

*   *   *

With the brief but bloody episode of the Paris Commune of 1871 still fresh in their minds, Chicagoans were gravely concerned about the labor discontent arising from the widespread unemployment and wage reductions that followed the economic panic. The *Tribune* shared such fears. It rejected the rumors that Communists had started and spread the Great Chicago Fire, but it blamed them for agitating among the workers and suspected German laborers in particular of being associated with Communist or anarchist movements. As the decade of the 1870s unfolded, Medill came increasingly to believe that chaos would result from labor unrest, but for a time he defended the workers' right to organize. Considering unfair practices by employers at least partly to blame for labor agitation, he leveled his heavy guns at big business, especially the railroads, the grain elevator trust, and the Standard Oil Company. His most expert artillerist, who became known as the country's first and greatest muckraker, leading the way for Ida M. Tarbell and Upton Sinclair a generation later, was already on the staff when Medill returned from Europe. He was to rise to sudden heights at the paper under Joseph Medill, first as financial editor, then as chief editorial writer. His name was Henry Demarest Lloyd.

Born in New York City on May 1, 1847, Lloyd was the son of Aaron, a rigidly Calvinist minister of the Dutch Reformed church, and his wife, Maria. The boy demonstrated writing talent early, and also a penchant for caustic criticism of the establishment, but his energies were channeled into orthodox scholastic pursuits. He was graduated from Columbia College in New York in 1867 and began the study of law, being admitted to the New York bar in 1869. The young lawyer joined a series of reform movements, rose to leadership in each, and was a passionate and skilled polemist for free trade and the Young Men's Municipal Reform Association, which opposed the corrupt political machine of William "Boss" Tweed and in 1871 succeeded in administering an election defeat to powerful Tweed-controlled Tammany Hall.

Lloyd wrote occasionally for William Cullen Bryant's *New York Post* and edited two monthlies, *People's Pictorial Tax-Payer* and *Free-Trader*. He met fellow Liberal Republican Horace White at the 1872 Cincinnati convention, which dismayed them both by nominating protectionist Horace Greeley for president. During the Greeley campaign, Lloyd called on White at the *Tribune*'s temporary Canal Street quarters, seeking a job. Since White had been forced to let members of his staff go because of curtailed funds and newsprint shortages resulting from the previous year's Great Fire, he felt compelled to reject Lloyd's application.

Henry Lloyd had traveled to Chicago with his good friend Henry Francis Keenan, a political reporter for the *New York Tribune*. Keenan much admired a liberated young Chicago woman who was a leader of South Division society, presided at literary salons, was a vice-president with Frances E. Willard of the Chicago Philosophical Society, and was fond of literature and appreciative of writers. She was Jessie Bross, a handsome, vivacious girl who had her father's auburn hair and love of scholarship, and her mother's empathy for the needy and sense of humor. Jessie was the only surviving child of William Bross, who had lost four sons and three daughters. Because of her mother's ill health, it was Jessie, 27, who had accompanied her father on tours of Europe and America, and who acted as his hostess and companion at cultural events. Bross guarded her as closely and proudly and jealously as Aaron Burr ever watched over his precocious Theodosia, and it was well known in Chicago that Jessie's father considered no young man good enough for her. But when Lloyd was introduced to Jessie at the Brosses' rented house—their Terrace Row home had burned and their new mansion on Calumet was incomplete—it became clear at once to both Keenan and William Bross that Jessie and Henry Lloyd were in love, totally and undeniably.

In something of a state of shock, Henry Keenan left Chicago and took a job with the *Indianapolis Sentinel*. Horace White, after seeing some samples of Lloyd's unquestionably brilliant writing, decided that he needed him at once on the *Chicago Tribune*. Young Mr. Lloyd was placed on the night shift as night city editor, writing paragraphs and making up the paper. He did this work extremely well and for good measure sometimes improved White's and Sheahan's editorials, which created no difficulties until the night Lloyd inserted an editorial of his own, one attacking protectionism in severe and sardonic language. The editorial reflected the paper's policy, but White found it expedient to find a new job for Henry Demarest Lloyd, as literary editor. It was a virtually perfect job, for it afforded the young journalist free evenings to call on Miss Jessie, enabling them to study Italian and German together and to improve their appreciation of the lessons by attending the opera in the brief Chicago season. They also took in concerts and lectures, and Henry Lloyd found that he shared Jessie's enthusiasm for the philosophy of Ralph Waldo Emerson, and her opinion that George Eliot was the greatest novelist writing in English. As a social reformer in good standing, Lloyd reflexively agreed with Jessie's ideas on women's rights.

Henry Demarest Lloyd was an ideal suitor. He came of good family, as

William Bross took the precaution to check out, and in addition to his intellectual qualifications he was an attractive man of medium height, with a slightly broad forehead, a beaked, inquisitive nose, and hair combed in the new pompadour fashion. When Jessie was required to go to Boston for several weeks, she left with Henry a portrait of herself and her favorite George Eliot novel, *Adam Bede*. In a few weeks Henry Lloyd followed her, after first visiting his mother and father in New York, to declare his love. She, too, was in love, yet felt that she was too old for Henry, who was 25. But she promised "to leave it up to God." Henry could ask no more. Anticipating the heavenly verdict, he asked Deacon Bross for his daughter's hand and Bross assented. The wedding took place Christmas night, 1873.

The *Inter-Ocean* lured away the *Tribune*'s financial editor and Joseph Medill assigned the chair to Lloyd, greatly pleasing his associate, father-in-law William Bross. The promotion of Lloyd completed a series of changes made by Medill soon after his return to control of the *Tribune*. His brother Sam became the managing editor; Elias Colbert remained as an assistant, responsible for special editorial projects and aide to Lloyd in preparing the paper's annual financial review; Frederick H. Hall was made city editor; and Henry A. Huntington succeeded Lloyd as literary editor. Joseph Medill was in charge of all the paper's activities, including the editorial page, where he was assisted by Sheahan. William Bross at this time gave Henry Lloyd 100 shares of *Tribune* stock, at the suggestion of Jessie, and Lloyd found himself in the best of all possible worlds—a loving wife (and, within the year, a child, William Bross Lloyd), an approving father-in-law, and a chief editor who "hated the high tariff robbers and professional tax eaters." Medill now favored a moderate protective tariff, and clearly indicated to Lloyd that he could go after greedy capitalists whenever he felt obliged to do so.

His work for the *Tribune* by no means expended all of Henry Lloyd's energies. When Joseph Medill suggested editorially that Chicago ought to have a downtown Sunday afternoon discussion club, Lloyd at once enlisted his friends the Reverends Robert Collyer and Charles Wendt and led them in forming the Sunday-Afternoon Lecture Society; he soon became its president. He also welcomed the efforts of Melville E. Stone to start an afternoon penny newspaper in Chicago, and in early 1876 brought his brother, John Lloyd, from New York to help. Henry wrote for the new paper himself in his spare time, and underwrote the deficits. He went to William Bross to seek a loan to expand these efforts, explaining that he had always wanted a crusading liberal newspaper. There was a highly vocal and acrimonious confrontation as the astounded Bross brought in Medill. The Lloyds were induced to withdraw from the

Chicago Daily News, John returning to New York. Stone quickly found another collaborator, and in July, 1876, Victor Lawson became a *Daily News* proprietor.

Briefly dejected by being forced to end his association with the *Daily News,* Lloyd nonetheless found his editorial freedom on the *Tribune*'s financial page exhilarating, and he swiftly learned the technicalities of his craft. Soon he was demanding free silver coinage at 16 to one and campaigning for Chicago Board of Trade reform, which led Philip D. Armour, a major trader, to complain ineffectually to Medill. Others found, as Armour did, that the new financial editor was not merely exercising a youthful exuberance in attacking the financial establishment, but was carrying out *Chicago Tribune* policy, as decreed by Joseph Medill. Medill for years had favored unrestricted coinage of silver at a ratio of 16 to one, 16 ounces of silver having the value of one ounce of gold. This ratio of silver to gold had been established by Congress in 1837, but actually few silver coins had been minted, and by 1873 new coinage laws placed the country on the single gold standard. The discovery of new silver lodes in the West in the mid-1870s led silver men to demand a return to a bimetallic standard. This demand was echoed by many of the common people, especially the debtor farmers, who thought that the free coinage of silver would increase the money supply and thus help them recover from the effects of the financial panic. Medill would eventually abandon his devotion to free silver, but for now financial editor Lloyd was pitted against Wall Street in this and other matters. He joyously took up the battle.

Lloyd studied economics voraciously. He received suggestions and help from Professor Edmund Suess of Vienna and Ernest Seyd of Göttingen, two leading European economists, and he quoted frequently the editorials favoring bimetallism in the *London Economist.* The *Tribune* sounded repeated demands for agrarian reform and for government regulation of railroads and the telegraph. The paper also called for government supervision of grain elevators, a goal achieved when the U.S. Supreme Court, in the landmark case *Munn* v. *Illinois,* upheld the states' power to regulate business "clothed with a public interest." In February, 1878, Congressman Richard P. Bland, "Silver Dollar Dick," finally got the Bland-Allison Act passed over President Hayes's veto. The act required the government to purchase at least $2 million worth of silver bullion monthly and coin it into dollars. Though the bill fell short of the *Tribune*'s goal, free coinage of silver at 16 to one, the paper said it was acceptable. The *Tribune* was widely recognized, especially in the West, for its strong stand against "the special interests." The *Des Moines Register,* Iowa's leading paper, declared, "The *Chicago Tribune*'s splendid fight on the money question is one of the ablest, strongest, most powerful, and most effective contests ever engaged in . . . by any journal in America."

.   *   *   *

His long sojourn in Europe had made Joseph Medill keenly sensitive to the dangers of radicalism. And now the continuing hard times created a ready audience for the radicals' call for action to improve the lot of the workers. Laborers had flocked to Chicago to rebuild the city after the Great Fire, and they swelled the ranks of the unemployed when construction projects came to a stop. The railroads, for years engaged in cutthroat competition, were especially hard hit, and they reduced wages and discharged workmen as receipts fell. In July, 1877, a strike by railroad workers in Pittsburgh broke into riots, and on July 22, the *Tribune* carried a half-column list of dead and wounded. The paper said editorially that mob rule must be stopped, but also that the railroads should pay their men a living wage.

The news from Pittsburgh caused many Chicagoans to fear their city would be next. Mayor Heath was urged to prohibit mass meetings, but he declined, citing the American right of free speech. On Monday night, July 23, Albert R. Parsons, a printer, was one of the Chicago Socialists who addressed some 5,000 men at a rally called to encourage labor solidarity. By July 24, the railroad strike had become nationwide. Bands of strikers roamed Chicago, urging others to stop work, and soon they were joined by "idlers, thieves and ruffians" who were eager for an excuse to riot and loot. "There must be no parley or temporizing with rioters," the *Tribune* said. "Mob rule is a weed to be torn up by the roots." The paper added that $5 million worth of property had been destroyed in the East and that Communists were responsible for the turmoil.

The police department of 841 men was unable to maintain order, and Mayor Heath requested assistance from the Illinois militia. On July 25, federal troops were brought into Chicago, and an estimated 20,000 men were under arms. Rioters attacked the McCormick Reaper Works, packinghouses, and the Burlington and Quincy roundhouse, where they smashed even locomotives. Several men were killed in armed clashes along the Halsted Street viaducts. By week's end, when order was at last restored, hospitals were filled with wounded, between 25 and 35 people had been killed, and 300 of the rioters who had rampaged in the downtown streets had been arrested.

The *Tribune,* which was commended by union groups for its "decent pay stand," supported the workers' wage demands; but it attributed the riots to the incitements of "Communist rabble." The paper set the financial loss in Chicago at $7 million, urged an increase in the national army, and said on page one, July 28: "The *Tribune* is in favor of one more strike, and it ought to be made today. . . . This strike should be against the villainous scoundrels who have incited the mob and who at the same time have been too cowardly to lead or take part in it."

The paper urged the unemployed to attempt to go back to the land, saying there were a million unemployed. "Seek the country, go to work, be sober and industrious and other things will follow as a matter of course." Like Horace White, the Medill editorialists did not accept the eight-hour day, and they bitterly assailed the Chicago Communists, who held a meeting on August 21: "A loaf for every loafer. If the chief end of man is to become a lazy lout, a shiftless vagabond, a pestilent putrefaction, a brawling, long-haired idiot, a public nuisance and an enemy of his race, let him turn Communist."

Though he abhorred the violence associated with labor agitation, Medill nonetheless realized that the workers did have legitimate grievances. He and Lloyd felt that the accelerating process of consolidation taking place in American business would lead to greater exploitation of consumer and worker alike and would result in the spread of Communism and chaos. The *Tribune*'s antimonopoly campaign thus took on greater urgency following the railroad strike of 1877. At the same time, Medill recognized that industry needed a boost, and he somewhat changed his tariff views. The *Tribune* now declared that the tariff needed thorough revision and advocated the repeal of all taxes on foreign articles used in manufacturing. "Remove all laws which limit or restrict or prohibit production."

*   *   *

In a speech before the Ohio Editorial Association at Toledo, Medill described the technical improvements making newspapers useful and powerful in America, including the telegraph, which brought information, and the railroads, which distributed it via the press. He was critical of the lack of specialized education for journalists. "The profession that is overshadowing all others in influence and power has no colleges, no professors of journalism—strange, is it not?" He denied the assertions of "many politicians, office holders and office seekers who declared it [*the press*] is becoming dictatorial and overbearing, and is wielding a dangerous influence among the people." These charges were "inspired by jealousy and resentment," said Medill. "The press interferes with slates and programs having selfish aims and aspirations, and hence these tears and fears." He warned newsmen, "Let it be the ambition of every editor to contribute toward elevating the tone and standard of journalism; to make the profession more honorable as well as useful."

The paper continued its support of freedom of thought. Following a debate on evolution at a meeting of the Philosophical Society, it said:

> The mysteries of the origin of life, of the spanless abyss of the past, the viewless future, which religion, with its fables of Genesis and Gehenna, has failed to make clear, must yield to the universal solvent of science. There is complete absence of any connection between man and any other vertebrate animal, whether ape or ass. What shall science teach? Only actual knowledge. Today science must not teach doctrines of universal evolution, of the protoplast soul, of spontaneous generation, of mental physiology, of the animal origin of man. Some day it may find them true.

It also supported the practical scientist, and on April 8, 1878, published a full-page life of Thomas Edison, written by George H. Bliss.

The Beecher scandal erupted again, along with Mount Vesuvius in Italy, on April 16, when the newspapers acquired a letter written by Mrs. Tilton to her lawyer, Ira B. Wheeler, saying that she was guilty of adultery with Dr. Beecher and wished to return to her husband. The *Tribune* editorialists merely counseled Mrs. Tilton to keep quiet, suggesting that all minds had been made up about the case. It devoted its attention instead to the threat of Communism, saying, "One of the most alarming dangers which threatens the future safety of this Republic is Communism. Its growth during the past 25 years has been so rapid that its disciples are found not only in the large cities, but in almost every town and village in the Union." The *Tribune* suggested that bad government, such as the graft-permeated ring headed by Boss Tweed of New York, who had stolen $6 million from the people before he was convicted and imprisoned, encouraged Communism. But popular violence was no solution, said the paper, and recalling the days of the Paris Commune, it reminded the workers that the Paris rising "led to the shooting of 20,000 [*sic*] Communists and the exile of a thousand more." In excoriating Communists the paper made clear that it meant also Socialists, anarchists, and "bummers" in general.

*   *   *

Joseph Medill was one of the few newspapermen of his time who appeared to recognize that he was a manufacturer as well as an educator and communicator. The newspaper proprietor undertook to gather news locally and worldwide (the *Tribune* opened its London bureau in 1877), and then to process it and deliver a finished product to thousands of consumers within each 24 hours at a cost to the individual reader of a few cents a day. When Medill entered newspapering, as a weekly publisher, the business was still largely based on handicraft processes. Rag paper was handmade, type hand-set, presses hand or foot operated or both, papers hand wrapped. Circulation was limited. Richard Hoe enabled publishers to provide a better product in less time and at less cost when he improved upon the cylinder press being imported from England, and later, in 1845, invented his own "10-feeder type-revolving machine." Such a press was expensive to buy and required much manpower in addition to steam power, but it could process thousands of papers per hour. The cylinder press inked sheets of newsprint across a moving flat bed of type, each sheet introduced by a pressman and printed one side at a time. In the late 1860s Hoe and others made available a true rotary press; the type bed was stereotyped into curved plates that could be bolted to the cylinders, providing the printing surface. Such presses could produce so many papers per hour that they glutted the mailing process, still done by hand.

In 1878, the *Tribune* announced that a member of its production department, Conrad Kahler, superintendent of the pressroom, had received a patent on a mechanized folder and paster that was synchronized with the press, allowing papers to be folded and wrapped at press speed. Shortly thereafter, other innovations accelerated the printing process, one of the most important of which was Ottmar Mergenthaler's invention of the Linotype machine in 1885, which permitted casting a full line of type at a time via a keyboard operation rather than picking out and arranging the characters by hand. The International Typographical Union, one of the first unions in America to attain national scope, felt the machine would be a threat to jobs, a fear shared even by Medill for a time, but the process actually helped to proliferate newspapers, to increase their size and circulation so that it increased the number of jobs.

But each new process also added to the requirement for heavy capital investment. The day was past when a printer possessing only a genius for expression and great motivation could launch his own mass circulation newspaper against established competition. Medill foresaw that the *Tribune* would require an influx of capital for its highly competitive and exquisitely demanding manufacturing process, and it also would need the ability to engage in auxiliary processes such as paper making. Medill and his associates had anticipated such future requirements in 1861, when Tribune Company was incorporated, its charter providing that the company might "manufacture in the city of Chicago or elsewhere, paper and other such articles as they may use in the business of printing, publishing and binding . . . and shall have power to purchase and hold so much real estate and water power as may be necessary."

During the Civil War there was a shortage of the rags required for the production of newsprint, and the costs went to 28¢ a pound. It was said that the problem was partially solved by an importer who bought up

Egyptian mummies, then plentiful, and unwrapped them, but this seems to be an apocryphal story. By the late 1880s, the *Tribune* would be using newsprint made from a mixture of wood pulp, straw, and rags. Not until 1913 would Tribune Company have its own mill, made possible by the incorporation charter and built at a cost of $1 million, which would provide wood pulp newsprint for 21¢ a pound, at a rate of 30,000 tons a year, supplying nearly all the paper's needs.

The development of a process for making wood pulp newsprint in huge rolls enabled the press industry to create a method for printing on continuous webs, or rolls, of paper instead of sheets, enormously speeding up press production. Thus the modern metropolitan newspaper became possible, culminating in the romantic but expensive and ultimately futile competition of papers to beat one another to the street with the latest news. With rare exceptions, such costly news beats, or scoops, endured no more than a few minutes or hours, and the advantage usually was lost in transit time to home-delivered and mail subscribers. Still, for 50 years, papers in fast-paced cities with vast populations close to the point of newspaper production did engage constantly in the cutthroat competition that kept wits and reflexes sharp, and taught the public to expect split-second decisions and actions from the daily newspaper industry. Conrad Kahler moved the *Tribune* ahead in this competitive situation, and Medill never ceased to search for ways to sharpen the *Tribune*'s productive capability. His paper was now 12 pages daily and 16 to 20 on Sundays, and would grow ever larger.

*   *   *

During the summer of 1878, the *Tribune* began its attack on the faction of Republicans encouraging former President Grant, then touring Europe, to seek a third term in 1880. The paper also sought to strike down radicals, such as labor agitator Denis Kearney of San Francisco, who was speaking in Chicago, and Ben Butler, who was running for governor of Massachusetts. Both of the latter, the paper suggested, subscribed to the philosophy, "Corral the capitalists, and when you've got 'em corralled, grind 'em, God damn 'em"—a quotation from Kearney. The paper sent a reporter to describe the horrors of the yellow fever epidemic in the South. He found that in Memphis 2,000 people were prostrated by the disease in a day, 2,250 dying before cold weather helped to end the plague. The paper took part in starting a fund for Southern fever victims, and Chicago raised $92,000. The *Tribune* looked with favor on James Garfield of Ohio and James Blaine of Maine as possible Republican presidential candidates.

The *Tribune* had been without a formidable favorite Chicago enemy since the decline of Long John Wentworth and Anthony C. Hesing, but that need was soon supplied, and in good measure, by a former congressman whom the paper had been attacking in desultory fashion for most of the four years he served. The ex-representative was Carter Henry Harrison, born in Kentucky, a suave, courtly Democrat who frequently carried a stuffed eagle with him when he campaigned. "Our Carter" was popular with the working masses. He declared whenever he had the opportunity that the Democratic party was the party of the people, but he also asserted to the thousands of Chicagoans who welcomed him with a band and lighted tar barrels when he returned from Washington, that he would never hold office again by his own will. The *Tribune* was not deceived. "It was a put up job, arranged in advance, and his talk of never again running for office meant nothing," the paper said. It was quite right; the Democrats nominated Harrison for mayor in 1879, and he was elected over the opposition of the *Tribune* by a 5,000 majority. "Our Carter" would continue to win over *Tribune* opposition most of his remaining years and then his son, Carter Harrison, Jr., would take over, serving five terms as mayor between 1897 and 1914.

In the beginning, the *Tribune* was exceptionally mild in its criticism of Harrison. "His views on politics . . . are somewhat erratic, [*but*] he is a man of pure personal character, justifying the belief that he will not only be honest himself in office but will require others . . . to be equally honest." The truce was of short duration. A few days later the *Tribune* renewed its attack on Chicago crime. "Bold faced vice has never been so rampant," the paper said. There were dives of every sort on State Street, and no man could walk in the afternoon along Harrison Street "without being compelled to hear the solicitations of the vile women who inhabit the unsavory thoroughfare." The mayor, it turned out, was a frank advocate of the wide-open town, and the candidate of King Mike McDonald, boss of gambling and vice.

Said the *Tribune* on July 21, "Mayor Harrison has become a spoilsman. He has run his brief course as the patriotic citizen-mayor. He now enters the second act . . . a puppet in the hands of a gang of desperate politicians bent upon the restoration of the Democratic party to power in the whole country through the aid of spoils." But the Republicans won the next election for Cook County, and on November 5, 1879, the *Tribune* celebrated by publishing one of its first editorial cartoons, a woodcut of the American eagle shaking a plucked chicken.

The *Tribune* continued its opposition to a third term for Grant, "Not for personal reasons but as a matter of principle," Medill made clear. A few of Joseph Medill's spelling ideas were tried out, such as "favorit" for "favorite," but most of his orthographic thought, as he had expounded it in a monograph published in 1867, "An Easy Method of Spelling the English Language," was not practical. Medill called it phonotypy, and a sample sentence from his booklet stated, "Lerning tu spel and red the Inglish langwaj iz the grat elementary task ov the pupol." But he recognized, "The reflectiv organz hav not yet cum into ful pla." Years later, Medill's grandson Robert R. McCormick would try similar spelling ideas and make them work, at least for a time.

The Republican National Convention met in Chicago in June, 1880. The Grant third-term bid was defeated, as the *Tribune* had predicted it would be, and James A. Garfield emerged as a compromise candidate to win the presidential nomination on the 36th ballot. Chester A. Arthur was the nominee for vice-president. "THE BATTLE WON. THE LONG AGONY OVER AND THE REPUBLICAN PARTY SAVED FROM DESTRUCTION," read the headlines on June 9. Page one was comfortably filled with four columns of advertising and three columns of news of the Garfield victory. The Democrats met in Cincinnati, selecting Gen. Winfield Scott Hancock as their presidential candidate. The *Tribune* predicted that he would not carry a single northern state. In Garfield, the paper said, "The Republicans have a magnificent standard bearer, at once a statesman, scholar and soldier."

The political campaign was a mild one, with only Mayor Harrison's threat to institute a $50,000 libel suit against the *Tribune* to enliven it in Chicago. Garfield won and the *Tribune* crowed: "VICTORY. THE GREAT BATTLE DECISIVELY WON. GLORY HALLELUJAH! THE SOLID SOUTH BATTERED AND SCATTERED AND SHATTERED BY THE SOLID NORTH." Thus the headlines on November 3. On July 2, 1881, President Garfield was shot in a Washington railroad station by a Chicago lawyer named Charles J. Guiteau. He died on September 19, making Chester Arthur president. The *Tribune* predicted that James Abram Garfield would live forever in history, and pointed out that he had died on the anniversary of the Battle of Chickamauga, where he won his rank as major general. Page one of the *Tribune* by now had yielded almost completely to advertising, but on September 26, the day of the state funeral, it was devoted to President Garfield. The printers' rules, which normally separated the columns with thin black lines, were turned, thus printing broad bands of black between the columns, a newspaper's traditional sign of mourning.

The *Tribune* was cautious in its praise of Arthur. He had been dismissed from his job as collector for the Port of New York in 1878 for allowing political considerations to influence his appointments, and it had been said that he was put on the ticket by Republican spoilsmen expecting to line their pockets. Medill now expressed skepticism about Arthur's planned cabinet appointments. *"I am apprehensive as to the effect of placing the national treasury under Wall Street influence,"* he wrote to another Illinois journalist, L. W. Reavis. But the fears were not warranted. President Arthur, once known as a spoilsman, turned his back on machine politics and became a determined advocate of civil service reform. He also ordered an overhaul of the tariff, recommending a 25 percent general reduction, although only 5 percent was actually achieved. His main financial problem was a treasury surplus of $100 million.

In the spring of 1881, the *Tribune* accomplished one of its most memorable scoops, publishing the full text of the freshly revised New Testament in the single edition of Sunday, May 22, 1881. The "Revised New Testament Edition" appeared as a 16-page supplement. The idea was that of Samuel Medill, the managing editor; it had come to him years before, when the *Tribune* was debating with theologians over the sacredness of the King James version. The paper had reported that American and British scholars were working on a revision, and insisted that the King James translation, far from being sacrosanct, actually contained errors. Ninety-two compositors set the type of the Revised New Testament in 12 hours. "No other newspaper in the world will have a standard edition of the New Testament like this one, a perfect reproduction of the original print, free from typographic or telegraphic errors, and in large type," the *Tribune* claimed. The edition was authorized, it was noted, by the American Committee of Revision. The complete Sunday paper was 36 pages. "The *Tribune* is not inclined to boast of its present achievement," it said. "It believes in doing thoroughly what it undertakes to do at all." The newspaper that Sunday, a subsequent editorial asserted, was the largest ever issued in Chicago. "It was an epitome of the world's news, both of this world and the world to come. . . . It was the most remarkable newspaper ever issued on this continent." The *Tribune* quite evidently performed a feat serving a public need, for in New York the Revised New Testament sold 200,000 copies the first week of its appearance.

Chicago and the country and the *Tribune* prospered under the Arthur regime, and advertising crowded the paper's pages. Celebrities visited Chicago, among them Oscar Wilde, who angered the city by calling its celebrated Water Tower a "castellated monstrosity," and Lillie Langtry, "the Jersey Lily." Chicago ladies emulated the Langtry hairstyle, men sneered at Wilde's shoulder-length curls. The *Tribune* compared Wilde's art with that of John L. Sullivan, the pugilist, and found Wilde generally lacking, though it was not fond of fighters either. Joseph Medill lectured on Irish history, and Mayor Harrison ordered all Chicago gambling shut down.

*   *   *

Henry Demarest Lloyd and his family had moved to Winnetka in 1878 when his health failed under the heavy schedule he set for himself. He was soon fully recovered and eager to resume the fight against big business. Joseph Medill left no doubt that Henry Lloyd spoke for the *Tribune*, for on January 2, 1880, Medill made him chief editorial writer of the paper, with business and finance, railroads, and labor as his special fields. In addition Lloyd would continue to direct special publications. Elias Colbert succeeded Lloyd as commercial editor.

The enemies Medill and Lloyd chose were impressive: men like oil industrialist John D. Rockefeller and railroad magnates William H. Vanderbilt, Collis P. Huntington, and Jay Gould. Lloyd preceded Thorstein Veblen in criticizing conspicuous spending by the rich, called the speculator oligarchy arising after the Civil War a major national evil, and proceeded to detail business abuses, including those of the Chicago packers, who often acted in concert with the railroads in fixing shipping rates or arranging for special rebates, forcing smaller concerns out of business. Gustavus F. Swift, who had developed the refrigerator car, Nelson Morris, and Philip Armour felt that they should have been commended for contributing to the expansion of the packing industry rather than criticized for their business methods. Joseph Medill ignored their complaints.

The railroads were accused of stealing a $300 million profit from western shippers by agreeing to hike freight rates from $3 to $8 a ton. The Vanderbilt-Gould combination threatened the trade of most of the country, the *Tribune* said. The paper called Gould "a colossal thief." It cited the strong national railways acts passed by European countries and urged such legislation for the United States. The *Tribune* also took note of legal action in Pennsylvania against the Standard Oil Company, alleging that the company received secret rebates from the railroads. Henry Lloyd wrote an article attacking Standard Oil for *Atlantic Monthly*, edited by William Dean Howells. "The Story of a Great Monopoly" appeared in March, 1881, and was hailed throughout America and England; the *Atlantic* issued six reprintings due to its popularity. According to Lloyd biographer Chester Destler, "Lloyd's term, 'the octopus,' stuck to Standard thereafter, like the barnacles on the hulls of tankers."

Lloyd's antimonopoly crusade continued with a noted editorial, "American Pashas," published in December, 1881. A few months later Lloyd took another editorial swipe at "Pasha" Jay Gould. Estimating that Gould was worth about $100 million, the paper said: "There is something radically wrong in a system that enables one man to plunder tens of thousands of people to the extent of 100 millions of dollars within a dozen or fifteen years. It is only the contemplation of such monstrous pillage which makes Communism comprehensible." In his famous analytical article "Making Bread Dear," published in the *North American Review* in August, 1883, Lloyd charged "the criminal rich" of market rigging and grain adulteration.

A number of causes were forwarded by Lloyd's frequent articles and editorials, including the movement that ultimately led to pure food legislation. The paper also called for conservation of forests, a cry taken up by Theodore Roosevelt years later; attacked the gas monopoly; and declared that the tariffs had become too high, enabling the Bessemer steel rail pool to raise the price of rails 100 percent in seven months. Lloyd, in the *Tribune* and in magazines, went on to attack the match trust and the copper and coal monopolies, always asserting that politicians were in league with the robber barons. "Scratch a monopoly and you will find the Government underneath," he wrote.

Industrialists who were attacked by Lloyd's editorials generally shared the feelings of John Archbold, elegant lobbyist for the new Standard Oil trust, who said, "Men like Lloyd do no good to anyone and simply serve to raise the final cost of political privilege." More outraged foes of the *Tribune*'s liberalism protested to Joseph Medill, calling Henry Demarest Lloyd himself a Communist, though all editorials were unsigned and no names appeared in the editorial page "flag." Medill refused to yield to the critics. Another ineffective protest of a *Tribune* editorial position would later be registered by Marshall Field, whose loan had made it possible for Medill to buy control of the paper. Frank A. Vanderlip, *Tribune* financial editor in the early 1890s and later editor of Chicago's *Economist*, recalled the incident:

> Marshall Field, the greatest merchant and prodigal advertiser, let it be known that he was much put out with the way I was dealing with financial news. He had come in to kick, and I was sent for . . . to the office of the editor, Joseph Medill . . . who was old, deaf and shuffled in his stride. This day, greeting me with nice dignity, he explained Mr. Field's objection to what I'd written. Mr. Field was a beautifully groomed man. As I listened to his complaint, I was aware he was no ordinary person. Then I expressed my viewpoint, gratefully aware that the dim-eyed old man was listening as judicially to me as to Marshall Field. . . . Mr. Medill did not truckle. He simply stood up to the situation . . . Mr. Field had the right of any reader to make a protest, but Mr. Field was mistaken. The *Tribune* would proceed.

*   *   *

The year 1883 was a grim one personally for Medill, though the paper was prospering as never before. His brother Samuel, the capable managing editor of the paper and an extremely popular man in Chicago, died on February 20 at the age of 42. James Sheahan, the brilliant editorial writer who was entirely amenable to his employer's suggestions and enabled Joseph Medill to express himself in writing when he lacked the time to actually compose the editorial himself, also died in 1883, on June 17. Yet the course of the paper held steady. Despite occasional expressions of favor for James G. Blaine, who was looked upon as a friend of Jay Gould and others of the "wealthy predators" of the time, Medill continued the paper's attacks on monopoly, especially that of the railroads. Not only were editorial pages employed, but the financial and news pages kept up the assault. On March 17, 1883, the *Tribune* ran its first width-of-the-page map, seven columns wide, at the top of page 12 to show the land grants that had been made by the government to the railroads. A two-page article detailing how the people's land had been given away, sold too cheaply, or stolen in some instances, accompanied the map. So strong was the paper's antimonopoly stand that when an antimonopoly convention met in Chicago on July 4, attracting delegates from 20 states, it was assumed by many that the *Tribune* was an official sponsor. The paper disclaimed this, but urged the convention to demand a congressional investigation of monopoly abuses. The convention instead voted to form a third party, and this policy the *Tribune* rejected. Medill intended that his paper be steadfast in its support of the Republican party, and he continued to look upon James G. Blaine as the man who could best serve as the party's standard-bearer.

This was a position Henry Lloyd found difficult to accept due to his growing distrust of the partnership between government and big business and of the Republican business establishment, of which Blaine was a prime representative. As the 1884 campaign approached, Medill asked Lloyd, his chief editorial writer, not to write on politics but to confine himself to financial subjects.

Blaine, a presidential aspirant in 1876 and 1880, at last received the Republican nomination in June, 1884. He was, it developed, among the worst of candidates, unable to show needed strength even against a relatively colorless and unknown man such as Grover Cleveland, his Democratic opponent. Both men were plagued by scandal, but the charges against Blaine were well known. In 1876 a congressional committee investigating railroad graft had accused Blaine of receiving equities in the Little Rock and Fort Smith Railroad at rock-bottom prices in return for favorable legislation, and his attempt to exonerate himself in a speech on the floor of the House had been far from successful. The public had not fully accepted his explanation then, and his opponents made sure that in the public mind he continued to be associated with the graft and corruption that had flourished during Grant's administration.

Someone resurrected an old Algonquin word from John Eliot's 17th-century Indian Bible to describe the Republicans who not only repudiated Blaine but actually campaigned for Cleveland. The term *mugquomp* became "Mugwump" and was used by the popular press as the designation for Republican independents. The desertion of the Mugwumps doomed Blaine.

Grover Cleveland had a scandal of a different sort, a mistress and an illegitimate child. In addition, Cleveland was said to have been a saloon brawler and a ward heeler in his younger days. Nonetheless, as sheriff of Erie County, mayor of Buffalo, and governor of New York, he had discharged his responsibilities so honestly and well that Tammany Hall opposed him. He was elected president after a close, bitter campaign.

Cleveland turned out to be largely conservative, though he favored a tariff-for-revenue-only. The *Tribune* began reporting and commenting favorably on the statements of young Theodore Roosevelt, who was denouncing "the wealthy criminal classes" in New York. It continued to attack monopolies, in oil, barbed wire, coal, telegraph, and railroads. When the *Chicago Journal* assailed the *Tribune*'s moderated tariff stand, the paper replied that the people should not be taxed for the benefit of the few. Murat Halstead's *Cincinnati Commercial* upbraided the *Tribune* for suggesting that the telegraph monopoly should be broken or totally regulated by the government. "If we propose to remain Republicans in this country we must confine the government to indispensable public business," the *Commercial* said.

Despite the closeness of views of Joseph Medill, editor-in-chief, and Henry Demarest Lloyd, chief of his editorial page, there was evident dissension within the *Tribune* family over Lloyd's campaigns. Growing disapproval would before long lead William Bross, who had given his son-in-law 100 shares of *Tribune* stock, to change his will so that the remaining Bross stock would not go to his only daughter, Jessie, but to his grandchildren. And early in 1885, Alfred Cowles made known his intention to play a greater role in formulating *Tribune* policy. Editorialist Lloyd declined to accept Medill's suggestion that the editor and Cowles would henceforth designate targets for *Tribune* criticism. Medill then agreed that Lloyd could have a long leave of absence to spend some time abroad. The Lloyds departed for Europe in March, 1885, and did not return to the United States for several months. Lloyd did not write again for the *Tribune*'s editorial pages, but he continued to hold stock in the paper and later served on the board of directors. Though his career as a *Tribune* writer was over, he continued his muckraking attacks in articles and books that were influential in Europe and America. One of his most famous books was an analysis of the Standard Oil monopoly, *Wealth*

Against Commonwealth, in which he sounded the warning, "A small number of men are obtaining the power to forbid any but themselves to supply the people with fire in nearly every form known to modern life and industry. . . . You cannot free yourself." But Lloyd's pen provided powerful help. Four decades later, economic historian Harold U. Faulkner wrote, "The heaviest guns in the antitrust agitation were fired by Henry Demarest Lloyd in his unsparing denunciation of monopoly."

The Republican party was at last out of power, after 24 years, but Medill viewed the change with equanimity. Cleveland would be inaugurated "with complete and cheerful acquiescence of every Republican as well as every Democrat," the *Tribune* said. "Principles are more important than men, and the fundamental principle on which our institutions are founded, namely:—that the majority must rule—has never found more respectful and constant vindication than in the ranks of the Republican party. . . . No patriotic citizen will ever be willing that any lasting harm should come to the country, whichever party may be in power."

THE EIGHTIES,
YEARS OF CHANGE

13

Following the deaths of Samuel Medill and James Sheahan in 1883 and the departure of Henry Lloyd in early 1885, Joseph Medill increasingly felt the lonely pressures of his ownership-management role at the *Tribune*. He was over 60 years old and weary, his back ailment troublesome, his newfangled hearing device an annoying boon. He might have tossed it away, as his friend Tom Edison had done, except that in the newspaper business he had to listen to what people wished to say. But he grew aloof and spoke of himself as an old man, as Abe Lincoln once did when he was 45. Now Medill was sought out for interviews about his association with Lincoln, his role in the election of the Great Emancipator, his experiences in the Civil War and the early days of newspapers. Medill spoke freely. He believed that the press and the public had a right to know, and he was generous in sharing credit with former colleague Charles Ray; but he made it clear that it had been Joseph Medill who ran the *Tribune* then as now. One of the interviews was with Gath, a scintillating star of journalism now appearing in other papers across the country as well as in the *Tribune*. It was Gath who publicly disclosed Medill's use of a hearing aid, which did not disturb "the Chief," as many of his staff now called him, half as much as Gath's comment about Chicago: "It is 100 years behind Cincinnati as a civilized city, though 100 years ahead as a driving force in the West." Published interviews appearing in the country's newspapers and magazines, and later Ida M. Tarbell's books, referred to Medill as a distinguished journalist and "chief owner and editor" of the *Chicago Tribune*. He was indeed the complete boss, though he continued to consult regularly with Alfred Cowles and Deacon Bross until their deaths. Medill at last accepted the title of editor-in-chief, a designation given to him by the Chicago city directory as far back as 1882. He was successful, powerful, and influential, but a lonely man, especially after the marriage of two of his daughters in the late 1870s.

In 1875, Medill's firstborn, Katherine, whom he called Kitty, fell in love with Robert Sanderson McCormick, the son of William McCormick and a nephew of Reaper King Cyrus McCormick, relationships fully qualifying him for the Copperhead category as far as Joseph Medill was concerned. The McCormicks had come to Chicago from Virginia and were Democrats, and in the early 1860s Robert's uncle Cyrus had briefly owned the detested *Chicago Times*. Despite the fact that the young man, born July 26, 1849, was a member of Chicago society and had inherited a modest fortune when his father died, the *Tribune* editor and publisher found Robert McCormick totally unsuitable for his slender, red-haired daughter. Kitty was his favorite, who shared his confidences and was fond of riding about town with him behind the matched bays. Kitty also had a temper to match her father's. She had tormented many a prior suitor, but she found the tall and suave Robert, a graduate of the University of Virginia, to be completely acceptable, and made that fact unmistakably clear to her parents. The wedding took place on June 8, 1876, and the McCormicks set up housekeeping in an apartment on Ontario Street just east of Pine (now Michigan Avenue), not far from the new home of the Medills at Cass and Ontario. Robert invested his small inheritance in a brokerage firm, which failed. He was induced to take a job with the *Chicago Tribune* as literary critic, a position of considerable prestige. Joseph Medill McCormick was born to Robert and Katherine on May 16, 1877, and Kitty decided at once that he was certain to become the editor-in-chief of the *Tribune*. A second son, Robert Rutherford McCormick, was born in the Ontario Street apartment on July 30, 1880. Rutherford was for the family of his great great grandmother, the wife of Thomas Medill.

Robert S. McCormick was not happy at the newspaper and Kitty sometimes yearned for the life she had learned to love in Europe, when she was on the year's tour with her parents in 1873–74. But not until 1889 did McCormick enter the field to which he aspired. Robert Todd Lincoln was the paper's lawyer at that time, and when Benjamin Harrison became president he appointed Lincoln U.S. minister to Great Britain. Lincoln then helped McCormick to obtain the position of second secretary in the American embassy in London. It was an excellent arrangement. McCormick would soon distinguish himself as a diplomat, and the high-spirited and ambitious sisters Katherine and Elinor, who had become bitter rivals, were now separated by an ocean and half a continent.

Unmarried Josephine Medill, who lived with her parents and attempted to keep the peace between her sisters, died while she was visiting Paris with Katherine in 1892.

The second candidate for admission into the family was Robert Wilson Patterson, Jr., a member of the South Division social set who had joined the *Tribune* staff in 1873 and had proved himself to be an excellent newspaperman without especially coming to Medill's attention. In January, 1878, he asked for the hand of Elinor, Joseph and Katherine Medill's second daughter, and also was summarily rejected. Some said the couple eloped, but if so they did not run far, for they were married at 10 Park Row in Chicago. Medill may finally have relented, perhaps remembering that Judge Patrick of the *Tuscarawas Advocate* had not thought much of him as a son-in-law either, and had been wrong.

Robert Wilson Patterson, Jr., was born in Chicago on November 30, 1850, the son of the pastor of Deacon Bross's Second Presbyterian Church and Julia Quigley Patterson. The Pattersons were social as well as religious leaders of Chicago's fashionable South Division. The elder Patterson had accepted the call of the newly founded Second Presbyterian Church in 1842 and had been its only minister until his retirement 32 years later. The Pattersons were close friends of the Bross family, but since Robert Patterson, Sr., had been born and raised in Tennessee, Medill had regarded them as Copperheads. Young Patterson was a quiet man, fond of literature and skilled as an editor and a writer. Following his education in the Chicago public schools, he attended Lake Forest College and then Williams College in Massachusetts, where he received his degree in classical literature. On his return to Chicago he studied law, but newspaper work appealed to him more. He obtained a job as a reporter for the erstwhile Copperhead *Times,* then became managing editor of the *Interior,* a *Tribune* enemy from the days when it had attacked Professor David Swing for heresy. That Patterson, with such a background, could obtain a job with the *Tribune* as night telegraph editor in 1873 was evidence of the high value his peers in the business placed on his talents. Within two years he was night editor, charged with "putting the paper to bed"—laying out the stories and checking headlines and the general format. His romance with Elinor Medill began a year later despite the curtailment of his social evenings by these new duties.

A year after their marriage, on January 6, 1879, the Pattersons became parents of a boy, Joseph Medill Patterson, and on November 7, 1881, Elinor (Cissy) was born. She would later spell her name Eleanor. The Medills had become fully reconciled to their new son-in-law, and when Samuel Medill died in 1883, Patterson was made *Tribune* managing editor and was carefully coached in that job by the Chief himself. Patterson was an experienced journalist, the only man on the staff, it was said, who could say no to Joseph Medill. When he was given the added title of editorial superintendent, the title held by Joseph Medill all but nine years since 1855, and later, following the death of Alfred Cowles, made secretary and treasurer of Tribune Company, there was no doubt as to who was heir apparent at the *Tribune*.

Patterson was put in general charge of the paper whenever Medill chose to be away, and Medill so chose with increasing frequency. He and Katherine traveled widely, in search of articles and ideas for the *Tribune*, or in the interest of their health. Wherever he might be, Medill bombarded Patterson daily with memoranda on the conduct of the paper, including such details as the correct use of punctuation and modifiers on the editorial page. When Medill was in Chicago he increasingly worked in the library of his new home on Cass Street, where he had placed his favorite rolltop desk. He either wrote or dictated editorials when he was in town, following a morning conference with Patterson and Fred Hall or George Upton, his editorial writers.

Medill lived a somewhat austere life, allowing himself a cigar once a week and a valet as his chief luxuries. His valet had little to do, since Medill liked old things and rarely paid any attention to his wardrobe, which had not changed much from what he found comfortable in post–Civil War years—congress gaiters, a white shirt and dark trousers and frock coat, and a black string tie. In summer he wore a black alpaca coat. Food interested him moderately. "I eat what is put before me," he liked to say. He was interested in the news, hour by hour—and almost minute by minute, some despairing editors thought. If he forgot that a story he had ordered had appeared in the paper and he demanded again to see it in print, it usually was republished, unless Patterson undertook to make an issue of it, and then even Patterson was likely to lose, Medill telling him, "Anything that hasn't been printed for three weeks becomes news again." When his wife was on a trip or at their summer home in Elmhurst, their youngest daughter, Josephine, would frequently stay in town with her father, to accompany him on drives through the city he loved.

Robert Patterson closely followed the Medill editorial policies. He was fond of the production department and was beginning to know it as well as Medill did, and he was a diligent editor. Since Patterson shared Medill's political philosophy, there was no policy problem, but there were occasional clashes nevertheless, as when Patterson succeeded in overcoming Medill's initial opposition to acquiring Linotype machines, which functioned from typewriter-like keyboards, for the composing room. It was highly unusual for Medill to object to any mechanical improvement. The *Tribune* was traditionally proud of its ready acceptance of technical innovations. It had been one of the first businesses in Chicago to subscribe to the services of the Chicago Telephone Company in 1881. Electricity required by the Linotypes had been introduced into the *Tribune*'s composing room in 1888 by the Chicago Edison Company shortly after it opened its Chicago plant. Medill appeared to welcome any device that could help him to produce a better paper—except the newfangled typesetting machines, possibly because they seemed to threaten the jobs of his beloved printers. The Linotypes nevertheless were installed, they worked well, and their speed and efficiency helped the paper to grow in size and circulation.

*   *   *

The decade of the 1880s was one of excellent growth for Chicago and the *Tribune,* a growth remarkably steady despite the severe economic problems that continued to afflict the country. It was a time of troubles for Chicago, too, especially labor troubles, which came to a head in the Haymarket Riot in 1886, the event that turned Joseph Medill of the *Tribune* away from many of the liberal ideas he had adopted and supported over the years. His attacks on monopolists would continue, but his tentative support of the eight-hour day for some industries and his friendliness to labor organizations changed abruptly after May 4, 1886, and anarchists and Communists increasingly became the targets of the *Tribune*'s editorial wrath.

In the beginning of 1886 it was clear that the *Tribune* was prospering as never before, despite the proliferation of competition. The daily paper was 12 to 16 pages, the Sunday as many as 28 pages. Daily circulation was above 60,000 at the first of the year and gained 6,000 by March, while Saturday and Sunday totals reached 78,000. The newcomer in the evening field, the *Daily News,* which Medill and Bross feared as potential competition when Henry Demarest Lloyd was befriending it, turned out to be exactly that. The Chicago newspaper environment had changed. For decades, most newspaper proprietors had wanted a morning paper, so that it could be sent by railroad at night to subscribers throughout a wide trade region. The *Tribune* had won that circulation battle, even though there were, in the eighties, five English-language competitors in the morning field, the *Inter-Ocean,* the *Morning News,* the *Herald,* the *Times,* and the short-lived *Globe.* As Chicago gained in population, an evening paper could also find the circulation potential it required within the city and suburbs, a highly concentrated population totaling well over 750,000. Medill had introduced book serializations, special articles, and personal service items to increase readership; his rivals emulated him and went on to bring to their own staffs the most popular writers they could find, such as Eugene Field of the *Daily News.* The *Journal* and the *Inter-Ocean* continued to limit themselves to politics as usual, while the

Post gave special attention to women's interests and literary subjects. In 1886, the afternoon *Daily News* claimed a circulation of 160,000, said by proprietor Victor Lawson to be the largest in the country. Lawson gave meticulous attention to content, especially that intended to appeal to women readers who could be reached quickly by the largest boy carrier organization in town, and the advertising linage grew.

Chicago Tribune advertising also continued strong, but Medill decided the time had come to go after mass circulation, especially since Lawson's *Morning News* claimed to have taken the lead among morning papers. Circulation at the time was not officially audited, but still such claims had to be countered. Medill began calling the *Tribune* the "People's Paper" and boasted that it had the largest morning circulation in the West. To meet the competition of the *Morning News,* which sold at 2¢, he reduced the price of the *Tribune* from 5¢ early in 1886 to 3¢. Circulation immediately spurted throughout the Northwest, but the *Tribune* did not for many years achieve undisputed leadership in Chicago circulation.

Politically, the *Tribune* modified its tariff position away from protectionism to one more in keeping with its "People's Paper" policy, leaving maximum protectionism and other conservative positions to the *Inter-Ocean,* which never swerved from its orthodox conservative Republican line. Medill again called for the redemption of currency in both gold and silver, continued his attacks on monopolistic big business, and assailed the railroads, packers, and oil companies for their practices limiting competition. The railroads, the *Tribune* said, continued to make rebates to favored shippers as before, and to conspire to share the available business in order to control and increase shipping rates instead of bringing them down.

The paper took another hard look at the activities of the town's leading meat-packers, Philip Armour, Nelson Morris, and Louis Swift. They were accused of forming a combination to the disadvantage of producers, who were paid low prices for their livestock, and consumers, who paid high prices for the processed meats. A U.S Senate committee was formed to investigate possible collusion between packers and shippers, and when the committee met in Chicago in 1889, the three packers arrogantly refused to obey its subpoena. The *Tribune* denounced them. The paper also found the Union Stock Yard an inviting target; it too engaged in allegedly monopolistic practices, and the filth that accumulated there, especially in the hog pens, gave Chicago a "Porkopolis" odor and endangered public health. The world's largest livestock enterprise, the stockyard company was owned and controlled mainly by out-of-towners; its president, Nathaniel Thayer, resided in Boston, and four of the ten members of the board of directors lived in London, England.

Despite *Tribune* disapproval of its methods and alien ownership, the company persisted in its ways and became a city to itself, including a bank, a daily newspaper, and a hotel, in a square-mile area at 40th and Halsted streets.

As Chicago itself evolved into big business, many businessmen, recalling the days when European capital helped to finance the town's railroads, joined with New York and European capitalists to increase the scope of their operations. A group of Chicagoans and New Yorkers acquired control of much of the Minnesota iron range country, intending to link it with Illinois coal and to process steel in or near Chicago. The rulers of the barbed wire trust often attacked by the *Tribune,* John W. Gates and Col. Isaac Ellwood, brought their headquarters to Chicago. They recruited lawyer Elbert H. Gary to help them invade Wall Street and to form a series of manufacturing trusts. Within a decade the trio had created Illinois Steel Company, with five major works, 12 blast furnaces, four Bessemer steel plants, an open hearth plant, two rail mills, and rod, billet, and plate mills. In addition, the company controlled a railroad connecting its South Chicago and Joliet plants. In time Gary would turn against Gates, his fellow townsman from West Chicago, to join J. Pierpont Morgan, the New York financier, in organizing the biggest industrial complex then known, United States Steel, which would establish its chief works in the sand dunes along the south shore of Lake Michigan, creating the town of Gary, Indiana. As early as 1880 Chicago was third in the nation, after New York and Philadelphia, in wages paid to industrial labor, $34,646,812 to 79,391 employees, and in 1890 it ranked second to New York in gross value of manufactured products, $664,567,923.

While the *Tribune* continued watchful and critical of the powerful new business combinations in its area, it hailed with uncritical pride the city's fantastic growth as a printing and publishing center. In addition to 15 daily newspapers, including specialized papers such as the *Drovers' Daily Journal* and ethnic publications, Chicago had become a leading printer of mail-order catalogs and book publisher. The inexpensive Lakeside Library and Fireside Library produced by R. R. Donnelly & Sons were widely sold, and included works by such authors as Wilkie Collins, Jules Verne, and Anthony Trollope. Rand McNally boasted over 200 separate titles in its paperbound Globe Library and Rialto Series, with H. Rider Haggard, George Meredith, and Bertha M. Clay among the authors represented. Belford, Clarke & Co. reprinted special editions of Ruskin, Bulwer-Lytton, George Eliot, and Thackeray. Its special 15-volume set of Charles Dickens, issued in 1885, sold 75,000 sets. Book wholesaler A. C. McClurg & Co. was one of the largest firms of its kind, sending salesmen throughout the West. The company also published a distinguished literary review, the *Dial.* Fleming Revell, whose authors included his brother-in-law Dwight L. Moody, was one of the country's biggest publishers of religious books, and the school textbook field was well filled. "Chicago," said the *Tribune,* "has many of the largest publishing houses in the United States. . . . It has become the Leipsic of the United States."

Chicago aspired to be a "Leipsic" (Leipzig) in more ways than one. The German city, like many others in Europe and Asia, had grown great in part because of its famed expositions and trade fairs. In the mid-1880s, Chicago leaders began to talk about hosting such a fair, a mighty world's fair to commemorate the 400th anniversary of Columbus's landing in the New World. The idea was put forward at a meeting of the Inter-State Industrial Exposition directors in November, 1885, said the *Tribune.* It would result in the World's Columbian Exposition of 1893, one of the most significant world's fairs of all time.

*   *   *

In 1886, Chicago, a major manufacturing center as well as a transportation hub, possessed a labor force numbering over 300,000 in a city whose population would exceed 1 million by 1890. The skilled worker received $4 a day, unskilled labor $1. Labor discontent had been general throughout the country for years, and Chicagoans recalled vividly the week of violence that had shocked the city in 1877. In the intervening years, Chicago had become a center for labor agitation as relatively moderate groups such as the Knights of Labor vied for adherents with trade unionists, socialists, and anarchists. The radicals were almost as repugnant to the Knights of Labor as to the capitalist establishment, since they impeded orderly labor progress and gave the employers excuse to refuse to bargain. Unrest among the workers was exacerbated in 1884, when a severe recession increased unemployment and reduced wages, and by 1885 skirmishes involving strikers, strikebreakers, and policemen were commonplace in Chicago's streets.

By that time it was estimated that perhaps 3,000 anarchists had gathered in Chicago. Among their spokesmen were Albert R. Parsons, of the Socialist Labor party; Michael Schwab, on the staff of the anarchist *Chicagoer Arbeiter-Zeitung;* Samuel Fielden, a former Methodist lay preacher; Oscar Neebe, organizer of the Beer Wagon Drivers; Adolph Fischer, a printer; George Engel, a toymaker; August Spies, editor of the *Arbeiter-Zeitung;* and Louis Lingg, a Carpenter's Union organizer.

The anarchists brought fear to most of Chicago by their repeated threats of violence during the tense days of 1885–86. Harry Barnard, whose biography of John Peter Altgeld, governor of Illinois from 1892 to 1896, provides a highly readable account of the period, suggests that newspaper publishers like Joseph Medill and Melville E. Stone printed the most horrendous of the anarchists' threats in efforts to discredit both the radicals and the labor movement. Though the *Tribune*'s dialogue with the anarchists was usually violent, as its dialogue with Copperheads had been in prior years, a reading of *Tribune* editorials does not support his contention of antilabor bias. The paper in fact approved many of labor's goals, and Medill himself had excellent relations with the unions at the *Tribune*. It had often acknowledged the deplorable working conditions in some industries, especially those employing many women, and it agreed with the position of its former chief editorial writer, Henry Demarest Lloyd, who denounced industry and society as a whole for the exploitation of child labor. Over the years, Medill's *Tribune* had attacked monopoly in every visible form, incurring the wrath of wealthy industrialists both in Chicago and in the rest of the country, especially the East. More recently, the *Tribune* had frequently expressed the expectation that the eight-hour workday, which had become the nationwide focus of the labor movement in 1885–86, would eventually be achieved.

Certainly the radical rhetoric easily matched any press commentary, as Barnard suggests in quoting from a speech made by Lucy Parsons, the wife of Albert, as reported in the *Tribune:* "Let every dirty, lousy tramp arm himself with a revolver or knife and lay in wait on the steps of the palaces of the rich and stab or shoot the owners as they come out. Let us kill them without mercy, and let it be a war of extermination without pity. Let us devastate the avenues where the wealthy live as Sheridan devastated the beautiful valley of the Shenandoah."

For more than a year the battle of words went on, with the Socialists making little progress. An English-language Socialist newspaper was started, and soon closed. The anarchist *Arbeiter-Zeitung* and the *Alarm* published by Parsons had small circulations. There were no more than 5,000 Socialist families in Chicago in 1886, according to estimates, but the moderate labor movement, the Knights of Labor, had experienced a phenomenal rise in membership and prestige since a series of successful strikes against Jay Gould's rail system.

Early in 1886, a year that became known as "the year of strikes," Medill appears to have believed that he could maintain his moderate position. The *Tribune* scored the telephone company for its "exorbitant charges" and ascribed the strike against Gould's entire railroad network to the practices of the owner. "Jay Gould's wire-pulling is largely responsible for the violence in the Southwest." The paper was commended at one point by an official of the Knights of Labor for its reasonable position regarding wages. When the *Tribune* addressed this organization on May 3, 1886, it was in measured tones. Commenting editorially on the May 1 general strike that had been called to emphasize the workers' demand for the eight-hour day, the paper said:

> The best advice that can be given to the Knights of Labor is to go slow, and to those who thoughtlessly suppose that ten hours pay can be given for eight hours work not to go at all. To define eight hours as a day's work in every channel of industry will not succeed. There are many in which eight hours are entirely practicable, if the Knights of Labor continue to confine their movement to channels in which it can be made to run. Provided the reduction of hours from 10 to 8 be not accompanied by pay for the two hours after quitting time.

The anarchists, although they had supported the call for the nationwide strike, held other grievances to be more important. Said Fielden: "We do not object to it, but we do not believe in it. As to whether a man works eight hours a day or ten hours a day, he is still a slave."

The *Tribune*'s attitude appeared to be paying off in the accounting room. On May 2, it published one of its early full-page retail advertisements, Smyth's offering of furniture, which began by chirping in a headline across the page, "Blue Birds and Robins Are Singing in the Land!" Other advertisers—Mandel Brothers, Schlessinger and Mayer, Marshall Field, Carson and Pirie—were also using greater space. There was even a display advertisement saying: "Eight Hours a Day's Work at City of Paris," a leading Chicago dry goods store.

The moderation exercised by the *Tribune* drastically changed after the events of May 3 and 4, 1886. It had reported as early as March 1 on the dangerous state of affairs at the McCormick Reaper Works, which had been closed for two weeks due to labor difficulties and was planning to reopen using nonunion workers. "WILL BLOOD BE SHED? EXTENSIVE PREPARATIONS TO OPEN MCCORMICK REAPER WORKS THIS MORNING. THREE HUNDRED FIFTY POLICE TO BE ON THE GROUNDS." The feared bloody confrontation did not occur on March 1, but as the weeks wore on, the situation at the McCormick plant had become ever more volatile.

On May 3, the day the *Tribune* published its conciliatory editorial urging labor to "go slow," there were some demonstrations in the streets by both men's and women's strike groups. The Lumber Shovers Union held a mass meeting on the "Black Road" not far from the McCormick works on Blue Island Avenue. August Spies arrived to address the meeting, though he was not invited, and some of the union members sought to keep him from speaking. While Spies was exhorting the crowd to greater labor solidarity, the noon bell sounded at the McCormick works and hundreds of strikebreakers issued through the gates, surrounded by union pickets. Fighting broke out, and police riot squads rushed in. The police opened fire. Spies now hurried to the *Arbeiter-*

Zeitung office, where he produced a broadside in English and German that read in part: "REVENGE! WORKINGMEN, TO ARMS!!! Your masters sent out their bloodhounds—the police—; they killed six of your brothers at McCormicks [*sic*] this afternoon. They killed the poor wretches, because they, like you, had the courage to disobey the supreme will of your bosses. They killed them because they dared to ask for the shortenin [*sic*] of the hours of toil." There was more denunciation, and a final "To Arms!" By that evening half of the 2,500 circulars had been distributed. The next day another circular in German and English called for a meeting in Haymarket Square, on Randolph between Halsted and Desplaines streets. "Workingmen Arm Yourselves and Appear in Full Force!" it urged. That morning, May 4, the *Tribune* devoted its front page and most inside pages to the harvester works fighting: "A WILD MOB'S WORK. TEN THOUSAND MEN STORM M'CORMICK'S HARVESTER WORKS. WROUGHT UP TO A FRENZY BY ANARCHISTIC HARANGUES THEY ATTACK THE EMPLOYEES AS THEY COME FROM WORK. TWO HUNDRED POLICE CHARGE THE RABBLE AND USE THEIR REVOLVERS. RIOTERS AND POLICEMEN WOUNDED."

That night Mayor Carter Harrison, anxious to prevent any further outbreak of violence, went to the Crane Brothers factory on Desplaines Street near the Haymarket. There Spies was speaking to a crowd that had totaled about 3,000 but began dwindling as rain fell and the listeners obviously became bored with him and Albert Parsons, the second speaker. Both men were denouncing the capitalists, using a dialectic evidently confusing and irrelevant to the bystanders. By the time Samuel Fielden had an opportunity to speak, only 500 persons remained. Mayor Harrison listened a few minutes, noted the apathy of the remaining audience, then walked to the Desplaines Street Police Station, where 180 policemen under Inspector John Bonfield awaited emergency orders. Harrison told Bonfield that the crowd was quiet and it did not appear that police action would be needed. Nonetheless, soon after Harrison departed, Bonfield and Capt. William Ward lined up the police and marched to the scene of the meeting. Captain Ward ordered Fielden to stop speaking and the crowd to "peaceably disperse." As Fielden protested, a bomb was thrown into the ranks of police and exploded. Shooting started as police drew their revolvers and men in the crowd opened fire. Policeman Matthias J. Degan and one civilian were killed on the spot, 66 police and 12 civilians were wounded. Six of the wounded policemen and an unknown number of civilians died later. The crowd was in panic.

The day following the *Tribune* used all seven columns of page one and much of the rest of the paper to provide details of the story, which shocked and sickened Chicagoans and many other people throughout the country. As compared with those of May 4, the *Tribune*'s headlines on May 5 were restrained: "A HELLISH DEED. A DYNAMITE BOMB THROWN INTO A CROWD OF POLICEMEN." There was a small diagram of the scene, fashioned with printer's rules. During the course of the story, the paper reported that following Mayor Harrison's departure from the scene a speaker had said: "You have nothing more to do with the law except to lay hands on it and throttle it until it makes its last kick. Throttle it, kill it, stab it." A runner had taken that report to Bonfield, which led the inspector to order out his men. The *Tribune* called for a public meeting, saying, "The time has now come when it must be for the interest of all who believe in American principles to take a stand in defending them against attacks of an incendiary and alien rabble. . . . The people of Chicago must overcome Communism or it will ruin them."

The reaction across the country to the Haymarket violence was immediate. In Chicago, the publication *Knights of Labor* denounced the anarchist perpetrators as "cowardly murderers, cutthroats and robbers," deserving "no more consideration than wild beasts." The press generally reflected horror and fear of "foreign rabble rousers." The *New York Times* urged death for the "cowardly savages," the *Philadelphia Inquirer* recommended the repression of anarchy by the "mailed hand," and the *New York Tribune* declared that "these brutal creatures can understand no other reasoning than force and enough of it to be remembered for generations."

As suspects were rounded up, including the entire staff of the *Arbeiter-Zeitung*, the *Tribune* found itself calling the participants in the Haymarket Riot anarchists, Communists, or Socialists, and finally settled for anarchists, explaining "a Socialist makes a bomb, an Anarchist throws it." A few days later the paper published a history of the anarchist movement in Chicago, illustrated with a four-panel cartoon, the first panel showing a whiskered, gesticulating radical shouting "Kill the law!" and the last panel a row of gravestones on which were printed the initials of some of the arrested anarchists. The paper said that freedom of speech was consistent with liberty, but not license. The grand jury moved swiftly and on May 27 indicted eight of the anarchists for the murder of Officer Degan. The *Tribune* commented: "The people of Chicago will tolerate no interference with the course of justice in this case either by the cranks who are half in sympathy with the murderers or by pestilent politicians catering to the murder element of the community."

The details of the trial occupied the *Tribune* and other papers of Chicago and much of the world during the summer. A jury was selected after 981 men had been examined. The trial began on July 15, and the jury reached a verdict following three hours of deliberation on the afternoon of August 19. The next day Judge Joseph E. Gary sentenced Parsons, Spies, Fischer, Schwab, Engel, Fielden, and Lingg to death, and sentenced Oscar Neebe to 15 years' imprisonment. Rudolph Schnaubelt, the man said to have thrown the bomb, had been picked up by the police and then released on the night of the incident; he was never apprehended. Louis Lingg, who was believed to have made the death bomb, killed himself on the day he was scheduled to be hanged by biting a dynamite percussion cap. On November 10, 1887, the sentences of Schwab and Fielden were commuted to life imprisonment. Parsons, Spies, Fischer, and Engel were hanged the following day. Spies, when permitted to speak, cried out, "There will be a time when our silence will be more powerful than the voices you strangle today!" "DROPPED TO ETERNITY," said the *Tribune* headline on November 12.

*   *   *

Those in the city who thought the Haymarket Riot and hangings would forever besmirch Chicago were proved wrong. Both the city and the labor movement pushed ahead. Samuel Gompers, who said of the Haymarket trial, "Trade unionists had no reason to sympathize with the cause of the anarchists as such," realized his dream, the American Federation of Labor, organized before the end of 1886. Chicago was about to enter its greatest era of growth and prosperity, enabling it to offer generous encouragement to the fine arts and to witness the development of an indigenous architecture and literature.

It was in the 1880s that Chicago began to find leaders and money to provide permanent homes for its hitherto somewhat peripatetic culture, and the Chicago school of architecture began to arise. Ten years before, orchestra leader Theodore Thomas had said that, outside New York, Chicago was the only city "where there is sufficient musical culture to enable me to give a series of fifty successive concerts." In the mid-decade, Chicago vowed at last to build a permanent home for his great orchestra. With Ferdinand W. Peck leading the way, and the newspapers cooperating, a committee including Philip Armour, William E. Daggett, Potter Palmer, Levi Leiter, and Marshall Field undertook to raise $2 million to construct the magnificent Auditorium Building on Michigan Avenue at Congress.

Chicago had for years endured the taunts and censure of visiting celebrities who deplored the city's appearance and provincialism. English writers, among them Oscar Wilde, Charles Dickens, and Robert Louis Stevenson, had recorded Chicago's ugliness for all the world to know. Even Chicago's own savant and critic, James Weber Linn, looking back on his hometown of the 1880s, later commented, "Few visitors did like it. . . . It was probably the meanest-looking prosperous big city in the world."

And the *Tribune* itself, from time to time, had added a few disparaging words.

The city's boundaries enclosed 23,000 acres of land, but of these fewer than 800 acres were devoted to parks. Except for the "Crystal Palace," the Inter-State Industrial Exposition Building created mostly of iron and glass in 1873, the lakefront along the Illinois Central Railroad's piers and tracks was a mass of fire rubble. The beauty Joseph Medill had admired on his drives through the West Side following his return from Washington in the prefire years was largely gone. The rich who had lived west now lived south, beautifying Prairie Avenue and Terrace Place with stately homes, or north, where Potter Palmer was building his huge new castle on the lakeshore, as well as a row of magnificent graystone houses that he would offer for sale to those of wealth and taste who might wish to become his neighbors. There was beauty on State Street and along other downtown streets rebuilt after the fire, but conversion of much of the lakefront and riverfront from industry and warehousing to residential districts and parkland was yet to come, together with the downtown skyscrapers that would bring Chicago architectural fame.

Dankmar Adler and Louis Sullivan were commissioned to design the Auditorium Building, a massive structure that would have one of the world's finest theaters, called acoustically perfect, as well as commercial office space to help provide financial support. Adler and Sullivan had worked in the office of William Le Baron Jenney, who in 1885 changed the world's urban architecture by designing the first steel-skeleton skyscraper, the Home Insurance Building at LaSalle and Monroe streets. He used steel and glass curtain walls in a structure to be served by elevators and electric lights. It has been said that an anonymous *Tribune* writer was the first to call the ten-story building a "skyscraper." The Auditorium, begun in 1887 and completed two years later, was one of the first Chicago structures to use a "floating raft" foundation to sustain its massive tower. The restored building, now housing Roosevelt University with its auditorium used for public performances, continues as one of Chicago's glories. Others of the "new school" of Chicago architects were John Wellborn Root and Daniel H. Burnham, who designed the beautiful, still extant Rookery Building, erected in 1884–86, also with a floating foundation. Root's 20-story Masonic Temple at State and Randolph streets was the tallest building in the world at the time of its construction in 1892.

The *Chicago Tribune* kept pace with its city, the paper's daily circulation passing 70,000 by the end of the decade, with greater numbers on Saturday and Sunday, and a heavy schedule of advertising. The *Tribune* displayed its awareness of the cultural revolution with a handsome redesign of its own pages, clean, clear, easy to read, with lightface one-column headlines and effective use of pen-and-ink art. Advertising, which had cluttered the front page for years, was relegated to the inside pages of the daily paper in 1886, though it remained on the Sunday front page till 1889. Still calling itself the "People's Paper," the *Tribune* established a "People's Page." This included controversial articles as well as letters from readers, which continued to appear under the heading "The Voice of the People." Great attention was given to news of religion, as before. Solid pages were devoted to Sunday's sermons, and when Sam Small and Sam Jones, the Georgia evangelists, opened in Chicago, the *Tribune* published the text of the Reverend Mr. Small's sermon, totaling 12,000 words. Reader interest justified this, undoubtedly, for when the evangelists had completed five weeks of services, the *Tribune* estimated they had been heard by 260,000 persons! The paper did not limit itself to Protestant affairs, as had Henry Fowler's *Tribune* of the early 1850s. When Archbishop James Gibbons of Baltimore was made cardinal by Pope Leo XIII, the *Tribune* ran a full-page story of the announcement, illustrated with pen-and-ink sketches of Pope Leo and the new prince of the church, James Cardinal Gibbons. Editorially, it recommended to His Holiness that the next cardinal should be a Chicagoan.

The paper increased its sporting news content, covering baseball almost every day in the summer, college boat racing, and also horse racing at Washington Park, which usually appeared on page one. It even took note of golf, remarking that golf was a game "requiring a servant to play." Baseball was more popular in Chicago than in any other city of the country, the paper said, possibly because Adrian C. "Cap" Anson and his White Stockings won the National League championship five times from 1880 to 1886. Generally 3,000 to 5,000 fans would see a ball game at the diamond on the lakefront, paying 50¢ each for the privilege, but 40,000 attended a four-game series between the "Chicagos" and the "New Yorks" in 1888. "This proves," said the *Tribune*, "that Chicago is a city of baseball maniacs." When horse racing meets were scheduled, the *Tribune* doubled its sports space, from a column and a half to three columns. Nearly everyone rode a horse, or hoped to, and had an appreciation of horseflesh. In addition, betting was widespread. Late in the decade attention was given to such participation sports as biking and swimming.

The "women's interest" items, which appeared first on Saturdays, then increasingly on Sundays and finally throughout the week, were mostly concerned with fashions, gossip, society news, and various "special services," such as meal planning. In the late 1870s, the Saturday paper's circulation exceeded that of the Sunday paper and the rest of the week by several thousand, and the different ingredient that day was women's and literary features and news. Society stories increasingly appeared on Sundays as Medill sought to build up Sunday circulation and advertising. Bertha Honore Palmer, "the queen of Chicago society," and Nannie Scott

Field, whose husbands had revolutionized the dry goods business, were leaders whose parties and balls sometimes made the front page. The *Tribune* also gave special attention to women who devoted their lives to reform and welfare work, among them Frances Willard, Julia Lathrop, Jane Addams, and Florence Kelley; and to the rising professional women, such as lawyers Myra Bradwell and Catherine Waugh McCulloch and physicians Sarah Hackett Stevenson and Julia Holmes Smith. Men, especially newspapermen, tended to express snide views of the women's columns, but owners of newspapers who watched the circulation figures knew their value.

Besides, there was little doubt that many articles especially slanted to women were also read by men. On September 1, 1886, the *Tribune's* women's page fare included "The Shop Girls of Paris, Their Trials and Temptations in a City of Pleasure," "Advice about Marriage," "The Young Women of Today—All Wrapped Up in Themselves and Their World," "Queen Victoria Was Jealous," "Some Strange Hands" (an interview with a palmist), and "The Man Who Married His Mother-in-Law." And news coverage was not slighted. World, national, regional, and state events were thoroughly reported, as well as local politics, court proceedings, and board meetings. And in case men overlooked the women's pages, there was usually lively scandal to be found among the news stories, such as "Maidens Lured to Ruin. Canadian Girls Enticed into Life of Vice in the United States."

By 1886 the *Tribune* had two cable services in addition to its own, one from the *New York Herald* and the other from the *New York Times;* it also leased four telegraph lines to New York and two to Washington. In 1887 the paper set up its own engraving shop, so that it could more readily obtain the zinc etchings of the pen-and-ink sketches that now graced its pages. The shop was established by D. La Pointe, with Louis Racicot as his apprentice. Under Racicot, the engraving department would grow to become one of the largest of any paper in the country.

The paper obtained rights to many books and special articles, and with pride announced the serialization of *Ramona* by Helen Hunt Jackson, one of the most popular novels of the decade. The world's leading writers were almost as well represented in the *Tribune* as they were on book publishers' lists. In addition, visiting literary notables were regularly interviewed, as were preachers, politicians, and other dignitaries.

As the battle for morning circulation heated up, the *Tribune* added more service columns—"Gastronomical," "Household Hints," "Woman and Her Ways," "Farm and Garden," "Field and Stables." The *Inter-Ocean* continued its dull adherence to the format of a staid political journal with a reactionary viewpoint, and offered little competition. But the *Times*, though it had begun faltering even before Wilbur Storey's death in 1884 and was in gradually worsening financial condition, still fought the *Tribune* and Lawson's *Morning News* for morning leadership.

The *Tribune* was pleasing both readers and advertisers to the extent that its Sunday paper of March 18, 1888, was the biggest regular issue in the paper's history, 32 pages with 137 columns of advertisements, and had a circulation of 78,000. While the *Tribune* was battling the *Times* to the death, however, Lawson's *Morning News* moved ahead of both in circulation, since Lawson had cut his price to a penny. In July the *Tribune* lowered its price from 3¢ to 2¢, saying it hoped "to include among its new readers many who have been tempted by low prices to subscribe to inferior newspapers."

Until the return of Joseph Medill in 1874, the *Tribune* had permitted its correspondents to inject their own viewpoints into reports as readily as if they were writing for the editorial page. Medill discouraged that practice. Reporters were not prohibited from expressing an opinion, but the opinion had to be compatible with the editorial page, and that page represented the thought of Joseph Medill. He made clear his position on matters of policy in an editorial responding to a suggestion by a reader that every report in the paper should carry the name of the writer. The *Tribune* replied that such an idea was not practical because more than 200 men and women worked for the paper every day. "The Editor assigns half a dozen subjects a day with a memorandum of points he wishes made, sometimes the framework of the article. The editorial page represents the sentiments of the chief. It is only by inspiration of this kind that it can preserve anything like unity or consistency. But who should sign, the editor-in-chief or the directed writer?" The era of personal journalism was nearing full flower, and Medill, together with James Gordon Bennett of the *New York Herald* and Victor Lawson of the *Chicago Daily News,* was among the brightest blooms. Journalism as practiced in Chicago at the time was the best in the United States, according to Henry R. Elliott, writing in *Forum* magazine in March, 1888.

Chicago's rival editors fought one another hard, but they were able to get together occasionally, when self-interest required. They formed the City News Association to gather local news for all members in the early 1880s; however, for a time they could not agree on the matter of a national press association. The feud that had gone on for nearly 30 years between the Western Associated Press and the New York Associated Press continued well into the 1890s. In 1893, under the leadership of Victor Lawson, the Western Associated Press became the Associated Press of Illinois, forerunner of the modern Associated Press. Melville E. Stone, formerly of the *Chicago Daily News,* was named general manager of the new organization, which proposed to end the East's monopoly of national news service. Medill, instrumental in founding the Western Associated

Press back in 1865, now perversely chose to continue the *Tribune*'s relationship with the United Press (not related to today's United Press International), which had absorbed the New York Associated Press. Not until early 1894 were all of Chicago's newspapers brought into the new Associated Press. Competition between the two services was fierce but of brief duration. The United Press expired in 1897, and for a decade national news service was the province of the Associated Press.

*   *   *

The Republicans in the fall of 1886 won their greatest Cook County victory since the Civil War. Perhaps because of this unfavorable portent, Democrat Carter Harrison, Chicago's mayor since 1879, refused to seek reelection in the spring of 1887, giving Republican John Roche an easy win. Delighted to report the Democrats driven from office, the *Tribune* soon had news of another victory, this time over King Mike McDonald's cohorts. McDonald was not merely a gambler; he speculated in securities, he was building an elevated railroad, and he had control of the construction companies that obtained most of the county and city jobs, including that of renovating the combined county building and city hall. The *Tribune* carried daily reports on a grand jury investigation of county "boodle" methods. One of the most startling and interesting of the discoveries was the sale of a special preservative for the outer walls of the county building that had been invented by no less a genius than Mike McDonald's patronage factotum and former croupier, Harry S. Holland. The city and county had purchased $128,250 worth of this secret formula, which, upon analysis, turned out to be mostly colored water. A number of boodlers were indicted, and some went to prison, though Holland and McDonald were not among those punished.

It seemed a propitious time for Republicans to reassert their leadership in Illinois. Medill, wintering in St. Augustine, Florida, decided that the time had come also for Illinois to dominate the national scene as it had in 1860, by the same method, announcing the "availability" of a totally pure, Lincoln-like character for the presidency. He picked for the role Judge Walter Quintin Gresham, federal judge of the seventh Indiana district, and directed the *Tribune* to popularize the good judge and to strike down the opposition, which included Gresham's longtime Indiana rival Benjamin Harrison and U.S. Sen. John Sherman of Ohio. Judge Gresham had much to recommend him, but also some liabilities: He was not well known nationally and there would be no Lincoln-Douglas type debates to popularize him; and he had won only a single election in his life, that in 1860 when at the age of 28 he was elected to the lower house of the Indiana legislature by a margin of 60 votes.

Far from being a practical politician in the accepted sense, Judge

Gresham was a fearless reformer who had antagonized hack politicians and some of high status by being honest and efficient and an enemy of spoils politics in the appointive federal offices he had held. As a colonel in Grant's western army, Gresham had been directed to smash a ring of smugglers and cotton profiteers; he did it so fearlessly and vigorously that Grant nominated him for brigadier general. In 1883, President Arthur pleaded with Gresham to enter his cabinet as postmaster general. In 18 months Gresham had achieved an astonishing record, cutting postage from 3¢ to 2¢ a letter while increasing the allowable weight to one ounce, improving foreign mails and carrier delivery—and returning a post office surplus to the government! Medill loved him for his enemies, especially Gresham's most powerful foe, Jay Gould, the financier and railroad tycoon.

The *Tribune*'s campaign for the nomination of Judge Gresham for the presidency was being opposed by Gould and Wall Street, the paper said. Medill, in an interview on the eve of the Republican convention in June, 1888, declared that Gresham was the man who could be elected, if nominated. The people were for him, Medill insisted. On June 11, the *Tribune*'s headline was reminiscent of 1860: "HE IS THE WINNING MAN." That headline helped Lincoln, but Judge Gresham got only 107 votes on the first ballot to 229 for Senator Sherman, while Benjamin Harrison was in fourth place. On the eighth ballot, Harrison received the nomination, to run against Democrat Grover Cleveland. The *Tribune*, of course, bowed to the wishes of the Republican convention delegates, although without enthusiasm. It noted that Harrison appeared ready to uphold "cardinal Republican principles," and said it would give "such support to the nominee as his record shall justify. Further than this an honest party journal is not bound to go."

Harrison lost the popular vote by nearly 100,000 votes, but he received 233 electoral votes to 168 for Grover Cleveland and was inaugurated on March 4, 1889, with Levi Morton as vice-president. The *Tribune* was well satisfied with the outcome of the election and published a Harrison souvenir edition on March 5. When the *Manchester Guardian* in England declared that the return of Republicans to power could please no liberal in the world, the *Tribune* retorted that the British were unhappy because Harrison stood for American rather than British interests.

Editor-in-chief Medill continued to stand by his America first principles, but he had changed his views on the press and patronage. When Lincoln was president, Medill had worked hard to help obtain the job of Chicago postmaster for *Tribune* proprietor and editor John L. Scripps. Now the *Tribune* observed with disapproval that newspaper editors were seeking diplomatic positions and patronage jobs with the new administration. Said the paper on March 6: "Let us suppose, for instance, that the chief editor of a metropolitan daily accepts a postmastership or a collectorship of customs. While he retains it his paper really belongs to the appointing power. He might as well execute a deed for his journal at once for four years to the secretary of the treasury or the postmaster general. He has sunk his personal freedom and every right of political criticism."

Near the close of the year and a few weeks later, the *Tribune* lost two officials who were early proprietors with Medill and had shared leadership with him for many years. Alfred Cowles, secretary-treasurer of Tribune Company since 1861, died following a stroke on December 20, 1889. On January 27, 1890, William Bross, president of Tribune Company, succumbed after an illness lasting two years. Despite his ill health, he had attended a stockholders' meeting the week before.

Descendants of Cowles and Bross would serve on Tribune Company's board of directors in succeeding generations. But Joseph Medill was more than ever a leader much alone. He consulted with his old editorial associates George P. Upton and Elias Colbert, who had been made company directors; and he relied increasingly on his son-in-law Robert Patterson, the new secretary and treasurer, and Patterson's aide, Alfred Cowles, Jr., who had joined the staff. A heart condition and other ailments caused Medill to sometimes work at home or to seek a warmer climate in winter months. He seemed more and more distant and occasionally explained his growing isolation to Upton or Colbert, "A good newspaperman can't have friends." Yet he graciously responded to those who sought him out for interviews, and he warmly welcomed his grandchildren, who spent vacations with him and Kitty in Chicago or Elmhurst or one of their winter residences. And he left no doubt that the Chief continued in full control of the *Chicago Tribune*.

THE GAY AND GRIM NINETIES

14

Despite the loss of valued leaders, the *Tribune* began the final decade of the 19th century with excellent prospects. The company was prosperous, reporting an annual income of $1.5 million. It had stabilized under the congenial direction of Medill and Patterson; the editorial unity Medill desired was achieved, and the paper spoke with a single, powerful voice. The *Tribune*'s typography was sedate and tasteful, befitting a morning newspaper that had no need to clamor for attention in the streets. The format was visually pleasing, clear, well organized, and easy to read; appearance was enhanced by pen-and-ink drawings almost photographic in their quality, which could be used readily as art and engraving techniques improved. The paper reached all the way to Paris for excellent fashion plates to dazzle the ladies and employed its own artists to graphically report news and illustrate feature articles. It also attracted advertising from retail establishments eager to exploit its excellent art facilities, so that the retail displays rivaled the editorial pages in soliciting the attention of the readers. The daily paper was usually 16 pages long, while the Sunday paper frequently ran 48 pages. Special color art supplements for the Sunday editions were obtained from one of the many outside lithographing establishments that were helping to make Chicago the nation's printing capital.

On February 24, 1890, Chicagoans were elated by the news from Washington that the House of Representatives had chosen their city to host the 1893 world's fair, the ninth such exposition in modern times.

The victory was especially palatable since New York and St. Louis were second and third in the balloting and they were Chicago's fiercest commercial rivals, at least in the minds of the editorialists of all 15 of the town's newspapers. Chicago, now with a population of 1,200,000, was second in size among American cities, passing Philadelphia in the 1890 census, and it claimed to be first in most commercial categories. The city's selection was by a margin of three votes over the 154 required to win, but this slim victory did not diminish the *Tribune*'s satisfaction: "The moment it was decided the Fair should be American, not foreign; National, not provincial; depending for its success on the citizens of the New World, and not of the Old, the selection of any other place than this became a practical impossibility." Since the foreign-born population of Chicago was almost 40 percent, nearly all from the Old World, the rationale of the editorial may have eluded some readers.

The *Tribune*'s satisfaction with the decision to give Chicago the planned world's fair was somewhat marred by national political developments that accompanied the Harrison administration. When the McKinley Tariff was proposed in the spring of 1890, the *Chicago Tribune* denounced it. Joseph Medill had been a protectionist from the time he was editor of the *Coshocton Republican,* but his position had gradually moderated. The McKinley Tariff provided for the highest levies on manufactured products in the country's history and, said the paper, it would increase prices for consumer goods while big business reaped unconscionable profits. The *Tribune*'s position shocked the orthodox Republican establishment, including Congressman Robert M. La Follette of Wisconsin, who would later become known as the "insurgent Republican." A member of the House Ways and Means Committee in 1890, La Follette said that the McKinley Tariff would increase the sale of U.S. farm products abroad by $75 million a year, thus enabling farmers to pay more for the goods produced by factory workers, who in turn could pay higher prices for their necessities. But the *Tribune* insisted that the protectionists were out of hand. When the tariff measure passed in October, it predicted disaster for the Republicans. "It will precipitate a financial debacle and bring down the party," the paper warned.

The conservative *Inter-Ocean* chided Medill for being unfaithful to the Republican cause. The *Galveston News* in Texas demanded to know why the *Tribune* did not bolt the party, and got a stinging reply:

> During the 43 years of the life of this paper it has been a steadfast supporter of the Nation and the Union idea and will continue to be so, at least as long as its old editors are above ground. Who then but an idiot would expect it to bolt the Republican Party on a dispute regarding an economic question and support the candidacy of the State supremacy organization? Who but a

fool would think the duty on pig iron, or tin, or crockery of more importance than the question as to which of the two vital schools of thought shall rule the destinies of the American Republic?

Good news emanated from the world's fair planners. Lyman J. Gage, of the First National Bank, became chairman of the fair board of 45 leading Chicagoans, including Joseph Medill. Gage and his directors moved swiftly into action. They decided to call the fair the World's Columbian Exposition and began preparations for its opening, scheduled for 1893. George R. Davis was named the fair's general director, and he employed Daniel H. Burnham and John W. Root, leading Chicago architects, and Frederick Law Olmsted and his partner Henry Sargent Codman, nationally known landscape architects, to draft the general plan for the fair.

There was an initial squabble over the site, with the South Division of the city emerging as the victor since nearly 1,000 acres could be cleared there, along the lakefront, by combining Washington and Jackson parks, the latter largely swamp and marshland with a few oak-crowned hummocks. Burnham and his architects made the most of the liabilities of the Lake Michigan site, using swamp water and hydraulics as the ancient Romans did to create a handsome environment for the fair from the otherwise dismal scene. They drew upon the Greco-Ionic experience for the architectural theme. The *Tribune* followed the planning closely. Answering critics of the fair board, who felt that the exposition should open in 1892, the paper explained that the 1893 date was set by Congress, to the exact hour, to allow individual communities to celebrate the 400th anniversary of the discovery of America in their own way. No one need worry, the World's Columbian Exposition would open precisely on time.

Among the committees named by Chairman Gage and his directors was the Board of Lady Managers, led by Bertha Honore Palmer, president, and Susan Gale Cooke, secretary. This committee, whose name one contemporary fair historian called "a palpable blunder in taste" due to the use of "the artificial term ['*Lady*'] instead of the broader and more noble designation 'Woman,'" was one of the most significant and successful of the entire fair panoply. The Woman's Building was designed by 22-year-old architect Sophia G. Hayden; women participated in the selection of exposition subjects and displays; and the fair's Congress of Representative Women was among the most impressive of the international forums conducted in 1893. It attracted such world-famous feminist leaders as Maud Ballington Booth and the Countess of Aberdeen from England and Scotland, Polish-born actress Helena Modjeska, physician Mary Jacobi, poet and reformer Julia Ward Howe, lawyer Myra Bradwell, social worker Jane Addams, and scores of others. The Board of Lady

Managers also helped to obtain employment for women in the creation and conduct of the exposition, and several women painters, sculptors, and writers received their first recognition at the fair, among them the poet Harriet Monroe, who wrote the dedicatory "Columbian Ode," published in the *Tribune*.

By April 1, 1891, Lyman Gage was able to announce that $17,625,453 had been committed to the fair, $3 million of this amount from 29 states that intended to be represented. The South was missing, and it was questionable from the beginning whether southern states could be induced to participate in any way. The Chicago newspapers undertook to make them welcome. Nineteen foreign nations, including France, Great Britain, Germany, Spain, Japan, and China, had indicated that they would participate, and more were interested. The committee offered Robert Sanderson McCormick, of the U.S. embassy staff in England, the position of the fair's American commissioner in London, and he took leave from the embassy to accept the post. Gage anticipated that the total investment in the fair might reach $40 million, six times that of the Vienna fair of 1873 or the Paris fair of 1889. The actual total was $30 million.

The *Tribune* published a full page of sketches showing the planners' conception of the forthcoming exposition. A magnificent Court of Honor, consisting of the main exposition buildings, would be constructed around a vast Grand Basin in which splendid fountains would play, the whole to be surveyed by Daniel C. French's Statue of the Republic, serenely commanding a scene that would be part Roman forum, part Parthenon, and part a bit of Venice. Root created the initial plans, and when he died suddenly, Burnham named Charles B. Atwood of New York as chief designer. Atwood had provided the architectural proposal for the fair's Palace of Fine Arts, which sculptor Augustus Saint-Gaudens later would describe as the greatest architectural achievement since the Parthenon, and which appeared to George Warrington Stevens, the English journalist, as "surely as divinely proportioned an edifice as ever filled and satisfied the eye of man." The classic structure, with its grave and graceful caryatids, continues to beautify Jackson Park, housing the Museum of Science and Industry. The park also has a replica of the gilded Statue of the Republic and of the modest monastery La Rabida, where Columbus dwelled when he was seeking funds for his first journey. La Rabida, much expanded, is now a children's hospital.

That spring of 1891, Joseph Medill and the *Tribune* were greatly pleased that the voters supported their choice of Hempstead Washburne for mayor. There were scoffers who said that Washburne, the son of famed Illinois politician and diplomat Elihu Washburne, had done nothing useful in life, and never would. But he turned out to be one of

Chicago's better mayors, cleaning up much of the graft and crime as well as scrubbing the city physically in preparation for the great exposition. Vacant lots were rid of weeds and trash, alleys scoured, 117 miles of streets paved, 603 miles of sidewalks built, new sewage and water facilities constructed. There were new piers and breakwaters on the lakefront and new slips along the river, enlarging Chicago's harbor to an estimated 400 acres. The 5,346-foot-long breakwater, ten feet higher than Lake Michigan's high-water mark, was created in months, an engineering marvel, and some 30,000 buildings, from cottages to mammoth hotels, were completed weeks ahead of the fair's scheduled opening. Mayor Washburne undertook to close down the city's gambling dives and brothels by conducting police raids on the realm of King Mike McDonald and his lieutenants, Harry "Prince Hal" Varnell, Ike Bloom, Johnny "Fix 'em" Condon, Billy "The Clock" Skakel, and George Hankins, the tidy little group that elected "Bathhouse John" Coughlin and Michael "Hinky Dink" Kenna as First Ward aldermen and fixers for the Levee, the red-light district in the south end of the business area. Washburne's raids on the gambling hells, dance halls, barrel house saloons, and brothels had mixed results. He drove much of the vicious element from the city, but this turned out to be a temporary achievement; most came back to relocate near 22nd Street, a site more convenient for visitors expected to the fair. So Hempstead Washburne's anticrime efforts accomplished little, except to unite King Mike McDonald's forces against him.

The *Tribune* sent a reporter and photographer over the proposed fairgrounds, a bleak stretch of shoreline extending for two miles along Lake Michigan. Nearly 1,000 men with horse-drawn scrapers were at work on drainage and lagoons. The paper predicted the fair would be such an attraction that southerners would attend, and urged readers to ignore the carping of New York newspapers, which said Chicago was not ready for a major cultural event.

While the Columbian Exposition activity moved forward, the cornerstone for the new Chicago Public Library was laid in Dearborn Park, on Michigan Avenue; the building would be dedicated some five years later. Meanwhile, Charles L. Hutchinson, the grain trader, aided by Martin Ryerson and Cyrus H. McCormick, Jr., directed a campaign to raise funds for a permanent home for the Art Institute of Chicago, which had developed from the Chicago Academy of Design started by Charles Ray and Leonard Volk. Ground was broken for the new building, to be erected at Adams and Michigan on the site of the Crystal Palace exposition building, in 1892. After serving as a meeting hall for the international congresses that would be part of the world's fair, the structure would revert to the Art Institute.

John D. Rockefeller disclosed that he would underwrite a new University of Chicago, with William Rainey Harper, the brilliant professor of Greek and Hebrew from Yale University, as president. "A soul has been found even in the Standard Oil octopus," the *Tribune* commented. The paper had sour notes for labor as well. When a Labor Day parade was held downtown on May 1, 1891, the *Tribune* declared that most participants were Socialists. The marchers sang the "Marseillaise" and chanted slogans urging an eight-hour day. "To be successful," the paper commented, "the eight-hour day must be adopted in competing cities and countries," and even then there would be a question of whether fewer hours of work would reduce productivity and thus increase the cost of living. The directors of the fair refused to fix minimum wage scales for the labor unions at work on the site, and the *Tribune* supported the directors.

*   *   *

The massive preparations for the fair enabled Chicago to surmount for a time the economic problems that would lead to another nationwide panic in 1893. The city was in a construction boom, jobs were created, money was plentiful. The *Tribune* undertook improvements intended by Medill and Patterson to make the paper the finest in the nation. The headlines no longer descended halfway down the page telling all the story; instead, for the most part, they sought to "sell the news," an idea Patterson may have derived from his new assistant city editor, James Keeley, a young Englishman who was to become the *Tribune*'s managing editor. It was Keeley's thesis that "news is a commodity and for sale like any other commodity." The most ultramodern aspect of the *Tribune* was its full-page use of pen-and-ink sketches, which were only slightly less detailed than photographs and had the advantage that they could portray a scene before it was in being. Thus *Tribune* readers saw the World's Columbian Exposition as it would appear prior to a cornerstone being laid, or the Grand Basin dug. Soon the paper would be reproducing actual photographs.

Patterson also improved the news-gathering effort of the paper. A New York editorial office was opened, with four leased wires available. Correspondent Alex C. Kenealy was assigned to sail from New York with Robert E. Peary's latest expedition to the Arctic. Another reporter was sent to interview Thomas Edison, who was completing his "kinetograph," the forerunner of the motion picture, which would be demonstrated at the fair. The Medill influence continuing to pervade, the work of leading writers was obtained for publication in the *Tribune*, mostly in the Sunday paper, among them Robert Louis Stevenson, Mark Twain, Bret Harte, Sir Edwin Arnold, Lord Randolph Churchill (and later his son, Winston Churchill), Rudyard Kipling, and Theodore Roosevelt.

Patterson introduced page-one bulletins, which called attention to the most important stories in the paper, and he gave increasing space to sports, so that the paper had a full page of sports reportage, illustrated with drawings most days of the week and Sunday. Football received growing linage, with the play of eastern schools being reported, as well as contests between the Chicago Athletic Club and eastern clubs. The game was somewhat a mystery to some of the sportswriters in the beginning. When the new University of Chicago fielded a team that beat Lake Forest College 18 to 16, there was no explanation of the play, only a few descriptions of long runs and assurance to the readers that "Captain Stagg [*Alonzo Stagg*], leader of the Chicagos, employed strategy like the wizard he is." The game between Chicago A. C. and Boston on Thanksgiving Day, November 24, 1892, was given exceptional advance notice, including a roster of the players, but no report on the outcome appeared in surviving Friday editions, which were largely devoted to accounts of Thanksgiving Day sermons in many of the town's churches.

The paper campaigned for clean water and clean milk. It gave attention to the work of Jane Addams and Ellen Starr, who were maintaining a settlement home on South Halsted Street to aid the foreign-born of that area. It was an experiment modeled after Toynbee Hall in London, the paper said, then published an excellent report on the Toynbee Hall accomplishments. The Hull House effort launched by Misses Addams and Starr, the *Tribune* noted, "could be greater than any charity."

There was much attention also to the work of Dr. Leslie Keeley, formerly of Rush Medical College, who had developed his "gold cure" for alcoholics, which greatly interested Temperance-minded Medill. When Dr. Keeley spoke in Chicago, the *Tribune* published 8,000 words of his text. The paper over the years supported Keeley's "inebriety" institute at Dwight, Illinois, with Medill's financial contributions, editorials, and sometimes by proffering an erring member of the staff to undergo a period of treatment, which consisted principally of injections of double chloride of gold. The paper's attention to religion continued. On Sundays a page of space would be devoted to the upcoming church events of the day and week; on Monday at least a page would be allocated to sermons.

In the summer of 1892, the paper gave full coverage to the strike of the Amalgamated Association of Iron, Steel, and Tin Workers against the Carnegie Company in Homestead, Pennsylvania, its reporter saying on one occasion that he was scribbling his notes "under the whizzing fire of many bullets." The *Tribune* suggested that anarchists were responsible for the violence, a position supported when the Russian immigrant who shot and stabbed Henry C. Frick, manager of the works, proclaimed himself an anarchist. The strike was broken, with the Pinkerton company of

Chicago sending in hundreds of detectives to Carnegie's support.

In the fall of the year, fear chilled the city when it was reported that steerage passengers on the *Moravia* had brought cholera to America from Europe. Chicago had endured a cholera-like "ague" each summer for generations, thousands dying, but now it was feared that visitors to the fair would start an epidemic.

A heroic, unnamed *Tribune* writer in France interviewed Dr. Louis Pasteur, was inoculated by him against cholera, then went to live among cholera victims in Hamburg, Germany, reputed source of the disease in America. The reporter did not become ill and so informed *Tribune* readers. The paper reported also on the construction of sewage treatment works and of a new drainage canal started on September 3 near Lemont, Illinois, which would carry pollution away from Chicago through a massive cut across the drainage divide between Lake Michigan and the Mississippi River system. The result of the tremendous ditching operation, which would require nearly eight years to complete, would be the Chicago Sanitary and Ship Canal. Relying on natural processes to break down the pollutants en route so communities downstream would not be endangered, the canal would reverse the flow of the Chicago River, taking water from Lake Michigan to flush it down the Des Plaines, Illinois, and Mississippi rivers, all the way to the Gulf of Mexico.

Daily reports and illustrations extolled the wonders of the upcoming fair, with particular attention to Thomas Edison, whose incandescent lights by the thousands were to illuminate both the interior and the exterior of the great "White City" that was arising on the lakefront. Other marvels were promised: electric boats that would carry sightseers in the Grand Basin; fish tanks specially heated, made of glass so that fish could be seen hatching; the world's largest cannon, to be shipped by the Krupp works in Germany; and replicas of Columbus's caravels, soon to be en route from Spain. A full foretaste of the future was promised. The *Tribune* said it would be the "electric age," but along with the managers of the fair and other Chicago papers, would miss two seemingly minor but highly significant possibilities for the future. In Springfield, Massachusetts, in 1893, Charles Edgar Duryea drove around town in a gasoline-powered buggy, the first automobile built in America, and in Detroit Charles Brady King soon did likewise in the first automobile built in Detroit, while Henry Ford rode beside him on a bicycle. King did come to the fair, to exhibit his pneumatic hammer rather than his car, and in 1895 both King and Duryea participated in America's first auto race, from downtown Chicago to Evanston and back.

The formal dedication of the grounds and buildings of the World's Columbian Exposition on October 21 constituted the culmination of

Chicago's 1892 observation of the Columbus 400th anniversary celebration. The festivities had lasted six days. The *Tribune* published a souvenir edition, decorated with drawings of the great carbon spotlights that would be used to illuminate the buildings of the White City, and pictures of various structures garlanded with electric lights.

*   *   *

The *Tribune*'s year was good not only in format improvement and circulation progress, but in the paper's counting room as well. Advertising was never better. A great influx of new merchants increased the retail advertising clientele of the paper, and these newcomers invested in large display ads, illustrated with drawings produced by the *Tribune*'s etching department. In addition to the big advertisers of prior years, such as Marshall Field & Co., Carson and Pirie, and Mandel Brothers, The Hub took a full illustrated page to advertise men's overcoats at from $10 to $15, ladies' coats at $8.98, and ladies' shoes and men's hats at $1.98. In a single issue the Boston Store, Siegel Cooper, Alexander H. Revell & Co., Charles A. Stevens & Brothers, the Fair, J. S. Walker, Frank Brothers, Rothschild Brothers, Tobey Furniture, John T. Shane, and Bell Clothing presented their appeals via major displays, some full-page, while hundreds of other merchants, manufacturers, inventors of appliances and nostrums, banks, insurance companies, and real estate dealers clamored for public attention, in addition to the 2,300 classified advertisers.

The editorial department, too, made good use of the etching room to illustrate the news and to produce cartoons to comment on it. On November 15, 1892, when the *Tribune* was campaigning against the Consolidated Gas Company for ripping open the downtown streets, then failing to properly repair them, page one contained eight illustrations to accompany the text. A three-column picture of State and Madison streets depicted women trying to cross on narrow footbridges, no more than strings of planks, over the mud and water for which Consolidated Gas was held responsible. Pictures of blamable company and city officials were shown. On November 23, the city council revoked all Consolidated Gas construction permits, pending restoration of the torn-up streets.

In November, Grover Cleveland was again elected president, receiving 277 electoral votes to 145 for incumbent Benjamin Harrison, and the Democrats took charge of both houses of Congress, a victory that the *Tribune* had anticipated following passage of the unpopular McKinley Tariff. The national political loss was distasteful to the *Tribune,* but the Democratic victories in Illinois were regarded as a disaster, especially John Peter Altgeld's election as governor. A friend of Carter Harrison and the late publisher Wilbur Storey, Altgeld was said to associate with radicals and to represent them in his law practice, despite the fact that he had made a modest fortune in Chicago real estate. The *Tribune* promised grimly that it would "watch" Governor Altgeld. The paper, however, had not changed its antimonopoly, antitrust position, despite its abhorrence of radicals. It hailed an Ohio Supreme Court decision breaking up the Standard Oil trust, and when Jay Gould died, the paper flouted the tradition that of the dead nothing ill should be spoken. "Jay Gould was one of the richest men on earth," the editorialist noted. "He got that way building his fortune on the misfortunes of others."

*   *   *

Early in 1893, Carter Henry Harrison, then 68, concluded that he alone could fittingly represent Chicago at the World's Columbian Exposition receptions, dedications, and other festivities. He announced his availability for mayor, declaring to a badly split Democratic party, "I am a candidate and all the newspaper liars in Chicago cannot hold me back." Harrison for some months had been a newspaper owner himself, having acquired the *Chicago Times* in 1891 as his personal political organ. Harrison was elected and on April 17 took the oath of office as Chicago's mayor for the fifth time.

It was a year to be remembered, 1893, the fair an accomplishment almost beyond individual comprehension. The World's Columbian Exposition opened on May 1, the date set by Congress three years before. The *Tribune* reported that more than a half million people greeted Grover Cleveland and his retinue as the president of the United States arrived at the Court of Honor to push the electrical control that opened the White City. The *Tribune* devoted more than six pages of its May 2 editions to text and pictures showing the presidential activity, and it brought back to Chicago one of the country's leading correspondents, the great Gath, who used the arrival of the exposition's honored guest, Spain's Duke of Veragua, said to have been a descendant of Christopher Columbus, as his opening theme: "The blood of Columbus has reached the heart of the Great Lakes, following Marquette and La Salle. Veragua, his posterity, has seen the arts and fabrics of the world piled on the further shore of Lake Michigan, heard engine whistles which go to the furthest reaches of the Grand Khan." Possibly Gath was referring to the ultimate destination of many of the fair's exhibits, which were already sold and would be shipped as far as China when the fair closed at the end of October. Gath said that not since the beginning of the evolution of nature, through thousands of millions of years, had there been a more magnificent collection of the examples of the creative ingenuity of man.

The exposition was, in fact, tremendous, from the glorious Palace of Fine Arts to the demure Japanese teahouse on the Wooded Island and the quiet modesty of La Rabida. Even the public comfort station, designed by Atwood, looked like a European palace. From the farms and ranches of the West, the cotton and peanut patches of the new South, the factory towns and cities of the East, and scores of foreign nations, visitors by the thousands came to Chicago. They rode the cable cars, the new steam-powered elevated railway, the commuter trains, or horse-drawn omnibuses to the fair gates; then they walked or used rolling chairs or naphtha-propelled boats or gondolas, to see the great extravaganza. Yokels and intelligentsia alike were spellbound by the newly created city that projected the arts of the ancients into the future world of science. They saw the new and the traditional, boarding replicas of the *Niña, Pinta,* and *Santa Maria,* or the imitation U.S. battleship *Illinois,* 348 feet long, built on piers on the lakefront. The warship was a mock-up, but it was fully armed with four 13-inch breech-loading rifle cannon, eight eight-inch breech-loading cannon, twenty six-pounder rapid-firing guns, six one-pounders, two Gatling guns, and six torpedo tubes. Additional machine guns were mounted in the sharpshooters' masts, 76 feet above the deck.

Distinguished visitors came, among them Ignace Paderewski, the great Polish pianist, to dedicate the Hall of Music; the Countess of Aberdeen; and the haughty Infanta Eulalia, representing the royal family of Spain, who was entertained by Mrs. Palmer and the rest of Chicago's society. Chicago sighed in relief when Her Difficult Royal Highness departed but felt it had answered the question posed by Ward McAllister, New York's social arbiter, "Why should an exposition honor Columbus? In a social way he was an ordinary man." The *Tribune* pointed out that it was not the leaders of Chicago, or Illinois, or foreign visitors or the great art and exhibits that were making the fair a success, but the people. They rode the new electric train, which received its power from a third rail, marveled at the electric lights, heard concerts from New York on the Bell telephones in the Electricity Building, saw refrigeration methods by which Chicago meats were shipped abroad, watched the fish hatch in the Romanesque-style Fisheries Building, attended concerts, looked at paintings from over the world, and goggled at the big Krupp gun, a ten-ton cheese from Canada, and the giant telescope that Traction Baron Charles Tyson Yerkes was giving to Yerkes Observatory. But the marvels that appeared to excite them most were the gigantic wheel invented by G. W. G. Ferris, its 36 cars rising 265 feet in the air, and a diminutive Armenian terpsichorean, Fahreda Mahzar, who did a belly dance in the Midway's Streets of Cairo. She was called "Little Egypt," and she usually danced clothed from toes to chin, but her gyrations set men's hearts beating faster, and Little Egypt, as much as the Ferris wheel, became a symbol of the World's Columbian Exposition.

During the final days of the exposition, all Chicago hoped and expected to eclipse the attendance record of the Paris exposition of 1889. On October 8, prior to "Chicago Day" on the 9th, the rush of visitors completely jammed the city's hotels. Cots were rented, and people slept in chairs; some slept outside the hotels and rooming houses in parks and parkways. The *Tribune* recalled the fire of 22 years before, pointing to the great development of the city in only two decades in its special Chicago Day issue of 24 pages, called "Canoes to Skyscrapers." The Chicago Day paid attendance was a stunning 713,646, a figure disbelieved by the New York newspapers, so that the *Tribune* later published an audited breakdown, 682,587 adults at 50¢ each, 31,059 children at 25¢ each. In addition, the paper said, there were 37,380 free passes. The exposition grounds were so congested that many women and children and some men fainted. The *Tribune* announced that it had printed 208,671 copies of its special edition, saying "every copy was paid for." Prince Otto von Bismarck was quoted as commenting in Germany that he regretted not visiting the fair. Chicago, he said, was the one city of the world outside Germany he wished to see.

The final days of the fair were saddened by tragedy. On October 28, a few hours after he had delivered a speech to a meeting of mayors in Chicago, Carter Harrison was resting and reading in the library of his Ashland Avenue home. There was a knock, Mayor Harrison responded, and Patrick Eugene Prendergast, a frustrated office seeker, fired three shots that fatally wounded the mayor. Fifteen minutes later, "Our Carter" was dead. The *Tribune*, noting their quarrels and differences, praised him. "The sorrow is universal," the paper said. There was a public funeral, and the last days of the exposition were somewhat muted, in respect to the martyred mayor. But there was bedlam the final day. The grand total of visitors to the fair was reported at 27,529,400, slightly below the Paris total of 28,149,353. The *Tribune* blamed Chicago's failure to win on the petty mistake of a clerk in the Library of Congress who had fixed the time of closing at October 30, rather than the 31st as the congressional act intended.

Even New York newspapers praised the fair in its final days. Forty years later historian Arthur Meier Schlesinger, in *The Rise of the City*, gave his evaluation of the exposition: "While the Panic palsied the country's industrial energies and turned hordes of jobless into the streets, an extraordinary outburst of philanthropic relief effort attested to the essential humaneness of the American character, and the Columbian

Exposition on the south shore of Lake Michigan revealed to a wondering world the summit of American accomplishment in the fine arts and the graces of life."

*   *   *

The great exposition brought the Chicago school of architecture to international attention. The men who were designing the new skyscrapers and functional factory and warehouse buildings had proved that they knew classical architecture as well. Daniel H. Burnham was called upon to advise a federal architectural committee in Washington, and he received a commission for the Flatiron Building, as it came to be called, in New York. Later he designed the Chicago Plan of 1909, which was basically responsible for the city's beautiful lakefront and Wacker Drive, though his plan was much modified over the years. Chicagoans built skyscrapers throughout the world, and Chicago city designers made urban plans and created buildings in Japan and Australia and in Europe.

The new fame of the city helped to attract those who would over the next 30 years establish what became known as the Chicago school of writing. Among the first to arrive was Hamlin Garland, later famous for his stories of the "Middle Border," whose novel *Rose of Dutcher's Coolly* won him recognition even among the Boston Brahmins. Theodore Dreiser worked briefly for the grubby *Chicago Globe* before going east, where he would write *Sister Carrie, Jennie Gerhardt, The Titan,* and other novels drawing upon his Chicago experiences. Frank Norris's *The Pit,* Will Payne's *The Money Captain,* and Robert Herrick's *The Memoirs of an American Citizen* also looked to Chicago for inspiration, as did many of the muckrakers, most notably Upton Sinclair, whose *The Jungle* shocked the nation with its depiction of conditions in Chicago stockyards and packinghouses. Young poets, such as Edgar Lee Masters and Carl Sandburg, would find encouragement in the Windy City, especially from Harriet Monroe, who launched *Poetry: A Magazine of Verse* and would later appear in the *Tribune* as an art critic. Newspapers also contributed to Chicago's literary renown. Eugene Field's "Sharps and Flats" column delighted *Daily News* readers until his death in 1895. George Ade and John T. McCutcheon arrived from Indiana to do their "Stories of Streets and Town," also for the *Daily News,* while Finley Peter Dunne created the incomparable "Mr. Dooley" for the *Post.* A second wave of young writers, among them Susan Glaspell, Edith Wyatt, Edna Ferber, Sherwood Anderson, Margaret Ayer Barnes, Willa Cather, and Floyd Dell, would work in Chicago in the early 1900s, most of them finding temporary shelter in the city's new advertising businesses.

The Chicago school of writing grew, cultivated by young men and women who celebrated rural virtues and working ways, yet found the city congenial. Dreiser and Sinclair would attack the injustices of the day, Dunne's "Mr. Dooley" would lampoon the foibles of the politicians, but generally the writers were apolitical, adjusted to middle-class values, and dealt with social problems, if at all, with sardonic humor. Their readers were the people, not the intellectuals, and the writers were deeply appreciative of the common man.

While the exposition occupied the attention of most Chicagoans, business continued at a rate higher than that in the rest of the depression-struck country, and the city's cultural leaders moved ahead with their special projects. In December, 1893, scarcely a month after the last world's fair congress had met on its premises, the Art Institute of Chicago was formally opened as a museum; Chicagoans for years after would seek to provide it with old masters, as well as to offer incentives to new American painters and sculptors. Marshall Field gave money for a splendid museum of natural history, to be built on the lakefront; meanwhile the Field collection was housed in the former Palace of Fine Arts. An Academy of Science was planned for Lincoln Park; Newberry Library was completed on the Near North Side; and a number of Chicagoans, including Joseph Medill, decided that the town was deficient in statuary. Medill's contribution was a statue of his lifelong hero Benjamin Franklin, given to Lincoln Park in honor of Chicago's printers.

Even before the world's fair ended, the cessation in Chicago construction and the halt in railroad building that accompanied the Panic of 1893 had created unemployment problems, but labor disturbances were moderate. The *Tribune*, looking ahead to cold weather, said that the city must better prepare to take care of its poor. Meantime a book the *Tribune* denounced turned out to be the one most Chicagoans wanted to read: *If Christ Came to Chicago* by William T. Stead, a London editor and reformer who had spent months investigating Chicago crime, graft, corruption, and vice. Stead's description of political boodling, vice, and gambling was not unfamiliar to *Tribune* readers, since most of these problems had been attacked in the paper's pages over the years. Stead's book, however, and his lectures, provoked city leaders to action. They formed the Civic Federation to fight corruption. On June 22, 1894, Joseph Medill addressed the federation, urging it to concentrate on Chicago crime, not national politics as some had urged. He said that Chicago needed civil service and a single term for mayors. The *Tribune*, of course, supported the federation and its various crusades through the years, but it continued to insist that much of Stead's book was little more than a guide to gambling hells and brothels, and it especially scoffed at his statement that Vina Fields, one of the madams he interviewed, conducted her parlor house according to rules of "decorum and decency . . . which could hardly be more strict than if they were drawn up for the regulation of a Sunday School."

*   *   *

On June 26, 1893, Gov. John Peter Altgeld committed the unthinkable act: Claiming they had been victims of an unfair trial, Altgeld pardoned the three Haymarket anarchists who remained in prison, Fielden, Neebe, and Schwab. Altgeld immediately took precedence over all others in the *Tribune*'s gallery of enemies. "Governor Altgeld has apparently not a drop of true American blood in his veins," the paper fumed. "He does not reason like an American, feel like one, and consequently does not behave like one." Thereafter he was "Viper" Altgeld in the *Tribune*'s lexicon. When the Republicans won five of six judgeships in the superior court, four in the circuit court, and the entire slate of candidates for the Cook County Board, including the president, in the ensuing county election, the *Tribune* jubilantly credited the triumph to the malfeasance of Altgeld, now expelled "into outermost political darkness . . . with his mob of Socialists, anarchists, single-taxers, and office-holding louts at his heels."

It took Eugene V. Debs but a single year to achieve an eminence almost equal to Altgeld's in the *Tribune*'s enemy category. Debs had organized the American Railway Union (ARU) in Chicago in 1893. By 1894, the spare, tall labor leader had 150,000 members in his union and felt sufficiently powerful to challenge the Pullman Palace Car Company. In May, 1894, shortly after "General" Jacob Coxey's army of unemployed had marched on Washington only to be dispersed by mounted police, with Coxey and two aides arrested, the Pullman company's refusal to negotiate allegedly unfair pay cuts and dismissals led more than 2,000 ARU members to go on strike. According to the strikers, the famous Pullman company town, just south of Chicago, was far from being the laboring man's utopia it had sometimes been designated, and while wages were being cut because of the panic, rents and company store prices were not reduced a penny. In mid-June Debs was in Chicago for an ARU convention. When the Pullman company rejected his offer to help negotiate a settlement, Debs undertook to demonstrate labor's power by calling for nationwide action, in this instance a sympathy move to support the strikers by an ARU boycott of all the western railroads hauling Pullman cars. The railroads discharged the boycotters and attempted to run without Debs's followers. Strikers responded by attacking trains, overturning freight cars and wrecking locomotives. Signalmen were taken from their towers in the Chicago railroad yards, beaten, and killed. Three persons were killed in a Grand Avenue bomb blast. Mobs of men roamed Chicago streets, burning buildings whose owners were not connected with the strike. On July 4, 1894, President Grover Cleveland ordered federal troops to Chicago to restore order. Governor Altgeld called out the state militia to trouble spots at Danville and Decatur.

"No despot ever conducted himself with more brazen and insolent defiance of popular rights than this man Debs," the *Tribune* said. "Seeking for some pretext to make war upon society he found it in this Pullman strike and then declared war upon 21 railroads which had nothing to do with that labor dispute, seeking to paralyze the business of the whole country." When U.S. Judges W. A. Woods and P. S. Grosscup issued an injunction against interference with the trains, a *Tribune* reporter went to the Blue Island yards to hear it read to some 2,000 strikers. He was given a guard of federal marshals as he phoned in his story. "The workers yelled, 'To hell with the courts and the government,' when the injunction terms were read," the *Tribune*'s man declared.

By this time infantry, cavalry, and artillery from Fort Sheridan and four companies of infantry from Fort Leavenworth had arrived in Chicago to take up their stations in Blue Island and other violence-ridden areas. John P. Hopkins, Chicago's new Democratic mayor, chosen to succeed the late Mayor Harrison in a special election, ordered out 1,000 police, and Governor Altgeld sent five regiments of militia to Chicago at Hopkins's request. By July 8, the law forces numbered 10,000, the *Tribune* estimated.

The paper restored the American flag to page one for the first time since the Civil War. Editorially, it declared that George M. Pullman was wrong to refuse to negotiate with his striking men. At the same time it attacked "Viper" Altgeld as a "lying, shameless politician," because he initially had sympathized with the strikers. When the strike collapsed, the *Tribune* took some satisfaction in pointing out that it had "repeatedly warned" the strikers that failure would be

> the inevitable outcome of their short-sighted action and for this it was roundly denounced by the salaried agitators, some of whom were asses enough to propose that [*the* Tribune] be included in [*the*] boycott. . . . The *Tribune* persistently has been the friend of the working classes. Through a long course of many years it has set before its readers statements of the conditions which are essential to plenty of employment at good wages. The *Tribune* has a policy of fair and adequate protection to home industry as the best means of enabling employers to hire many workers at fair wages, and insists that the coercive strike is the very worst remedy the workers could possibly apply to a depressed business and labor market. . . . When the workmen are able to see from the disastrous results of the Debs and other strikes that their professional agitators have been their worst enemies, they will come to understand that the *Tribune* has been their best friend.

The troops left Chicago on July 19 and Debs was jailed for violation of the injunction. The *Tribune* proposed a labor pension plan for railroad employees and urged that in the future labor and management should keep the paid anarchist agitators out of the action. It sent reporters to investigate conditions in Pullman and reported that 1,000 families were in urgent need. It contributed $200 to a fund to aid such families and provided a page of space detailing the individual needs that might be supplied by money or gifts of food and clothing.

*   *   *

The *Tribune* called for a modified tariff as the proper antidote for the depression, and the response by Congress was the Wilson-Gorman Tariff Act, which established protectionist tariffs at some levels but put wool, copper, and lumber on the free list. To boost revenues, to replace free list losses, the Wilson-Gorman Act provided for a 2 percent federal income tax, the kind of tax that had been used temporarily to help finance the Civil War. No one appeared to be happy with this total package, including the *Tribune* and President Cleveland, who berated his own party for its passage but allowed it to become law without his signature. The income tax feature was declared unconstitutional in 1895. Cleveland's anger with his party was justified in the November elections, when Republicans won both houses of Congress.

Joseph Medill had been away from the *Tribune* for long periods of time because of the ill health of Mrs. Medill and his own indisposition. On October 1, 1894, the woman who had helped to bring him into the newspaper business, and who had been his beloved companion and confidante for 42 years, Katherine Patrick Medill, died in their summer home in Elmhurst. Medill now grew increasingly remote from the actual operations of the paper. There was some talk among Republicans of nominating Medill as a candidate for the U.S. Senate, but he declined. The policies of the paper continued unchanged: attacks on City Hall boodlers and corruptionists, attacks on "Viper" Altgeld and Democrats generally, attacks on the Standard Oil "octopus"—its monopoly of the oil business east of the Mississippi was documented in the issue of April 17, 1895—and general attacks on most other newspapers in town. One morning competitor derided by the *Tribune* was the *Inter-Ocean,* which called itself "Republican in everything, Independent in nothing," a slogan and policy Medill found particularly obnoxious. Doubtless Medill viewed with some satisfaction the demise of the *Tribune*'s longtime foe the *Times,* which in 1895 merged with the *Herald,* leaving Chicago without a Democratic organ. The *Times-Herald* was owned by Herman H. Kohlsaat, a former baking company executive who not long before had been proprietor of the *Inter-Ocean.* (Within a few years the *Times* would cease to exist in name as well as in fact, when Kohlsaat purchased the *Record* and created the *Record-Herald.*) The loss of their traditional partisan paper symbolized the Democrats' troubles in Chicago. In the city election that spring, Republican George B. Swift won the office of mayor, and Republicans emerged with a 50–20 margin in the city council. But a few of the "Gray Wolves," as the boodlers sometimes were called, survived, among them First Ward Ald. Bathhouse John Coughlin, and Democratic council boss John Powers won reelection as usual.

It appeared for a time that the *Tribune* might bring about serious division in Republican ranks nationally when it opposed a strong movement by Eastern business interests in support of William McKinley, now governor of Ohio, for the 1896 presidential nomination. Regular Republicans about the country criticized the *Tribune,* as they had when it opposed the McKinley Tariff, and the paper responded: "Some advocates of McKinley say the *Tribune* is behaving badly. The *Tribune*'s only interest is in a good man, who will leave the party in good shape in 1901. We wonder if McKinley is that man." By the time McKinley was nominated in St. Louis in June, the *Tribune* seemed reconciled; and all doubt was dispelled in July, when the Democrats convened in Chicago and were captured by the young silver-tongued supporter of free silver, the "Boy Orator from the Platte," William Jennings Bryan, transplanted from Illinois to Nebraska where he had won his way into the House of Representatives and achieved some national political prominence. Said the *Tribune* of the famous "Cross of Gold" speech:

> Then Bryan took the stand and with the masterful oratory for which he has become famous soon wrought up the crowd to a spirit of wildest enthusiasm. The Nebraskan is young in years, but aged in the wiles of the politician and the demagogue, and eloquent as are all his speeches, he never fails to inject into them a sufficient amount of claptrap to capture his hearers. . . . When he closed with a rather profane appeal that the crown of thorns could not be placed on the head of the honest laboring man, he lighted the spark which touched off the train of gunpowder, and the Bryan boom, which was only inchoate the night before, as told in the *Tribune,* suddenly seized upon the convention and carried everything before it.

The *Tribune* thereafter gave its full support to McKinley. McKinley was also the choice of the voters in November, and Republicans seized control of both houses of Congress. Cook County went Republican by 65,000 votes, Illinois by 125,000.

The *Chicago Tribune* prospered right along with its party. Daily editions sometimes ran as many as 24 pages, Sunday issues 48 pages, and packed with advertising. Circulation increased also. Robert Patterson, like Medill, constantly sought the kind of exclusive materials that would help to sell the paper, especially the Sunday editions. These included the special art supplements; new "departments," mostly intended for women, such as the dress pattern department and the offer of material to help children with their studies; special stories of general interest, such as a series on Chicago's ethnic neighborhoods; and more of the work of the world's outstanding writers, among them Arthur Conan Doyle, George Bernard Shaw, Stephen Crane, Hamlin Garland, Margaret Deland, and Richard Harding Davis, the last covering major news events in Europe for the newspapers of William Randolph Hearst. Walter Camp was employed to explain football to *Tribune* readers. When Mary Leiter, daughter of Levi Leiter, the former Marshall Field & Company executive, married George N. Curzon, heir to an English title, the *Tribune* sent an unnamed female reporter to travel with the happy couple to India, where Curzon was to command the British forces, and to send back stories on the "Cinderella princess."

The bicycle boom hit Chicago, requiring special garb called "bloomers." The *Tribune* employed Frances E. Willard to write "How I Learned the Bicycle," and ran bloomer patterns and drawings of women clad in bloomers. Thus the garment introduced by Amelia Bloomer in 1851, which had been laughed at and sneered at by some men as a symbol of suffragettes, came at last into its own as sports garb. "It is highest folly," said the *Tribune* editorially on August 12, 1895, "for men to lay down the law on what the other sex shall wear—or shall not wear." But elsewhere in the same issue it was suggested that women cyclists ought to wear bloomers. Some of the attention to women was quite negative; the paper had many articles on their fate in white slave rings and brothels, and the leading scandal story of 1895 concerned "Dr." H. H. Holmes, reported to have been marrying, insuring, and murdering comely young women, then burning their bodies and burying their bones in the basement of his "murder castle" in Chicago. Holmes, said to have murdered 11 women in Chicago, was arrested and convicted in Pennsylvania on similar charges and sentenced to die for his crimes.

Also in this period, on August 1, 1895, the *Tribune* began occasional publication of four pages of "comics." These were not the "Yellow Kid" type of comic soon to be popularized in New York as Hearst and Joseph Pulitzer battled for circulation leadership, for the *Tribune*'s early comics were not in color, nor did they center around a continuing character. Rather, they consisted of caricatures and sketches of odd news events, printed in black and white. At the same time, the Sunday paper introduced a "highbrow" page, devoted largely to educational and scientific subjects, one of the articles reporting on Wilhelm Roentgen's discovery of X rays, with a drawing that showed how a human hand would appear in a picture made by the rays.

*   *   *

During the 30 years the *Tribune* had occupied the corner of Dearborn and Madison, it was attacked repeatedly by its enemies for alleged failure to pay adequate rentals to the Chicago Board of Education for land it held under a 99-year lease. These attacks exasperated Joseph Medill. The lease had been acquired and the building erected while he was out of power at the paper, and he insisted Tribune Company had a bad bargain. The original lease provided that the property be appraised every five years, with the rental being established on the basis of that paid on private land in the area. An amended lease in 1888 lengthened the interval between appraisals to ten years. On February 24, 1894, in answer to renewed attacks from its critics, the paper published the terms of its lease and an accounting of moneys paid to the school board. Said the *Tribune* editorially: "The Tribune Company made a most unfortunate move when it began to occupy the site of its present building a generation ago. If it had gone almost anywhere else in the business district it would now be in possession of a fine property bought for a small sum in fee simple and it would not pay rent to anybody nor be subject to all the exasperating circumstances of a revaluation every ten years under the stress of hostile political feeling." The paper invited all readers to peruse the terms of its amended lease, which would not expire for another 90 years. "The *Tribune* only desires a fair rental," it said. "That much it is willing to pay without contest or objection, and it will pay no more unless compelled."

Since the company's lease on such valuable property had so many years to run, Patterson convinced Medill that a new skyscraper building should be erected on the site, to obtain best and highest use of the land. Patterson began preliminary plans for such a building. He concluded that the presses should be placed in the basement, to eliminate the intense vibration throughout the extant building. Since the huge presses would require a basement 33 feet deep to provide adequate headroom, architects and builders sought to convince Patterson that such a move would not be possible. The high-rise buildings in the downtown area were mostly set on floating foundations. Should a 33-foot basement be dug, some leading architects claimed, the foundations of the surrounding buildings would be disturbed, and it was believed that they would fall into the Tribune Building's excavation. Patterson persisted. Injunctions were sought to prevent the work, but Holabird & Roche, the *Tribune* architects, and George A. Fuller, contractor, were sure that such a basement could be dug and maintained successfully. It was, after months of planning and legal wrangling. A new 17-story Tribune Building at Madison and Dearborn would eventually be erected, but too late for Joseph Medill to see it.

During the last half of the decade, Medill and Patterson totally abandoned the concept of a limited circulation newspaper and undertook price reduction in conformity with the policy of the "People's Paper." The price of the daily paper, which had gone from 3¢ to 2¢ in 1888, dropped to 1¢ on November 11, 1895, while the Sunday paper sold for 5¢. The first day of the 1¢ price, the circulation increased by 25,000. The paper said it wished to extend the benefits of cost reductions to the general public. The use of wood pulp newsprint, along with more modern machinery, had lowered costs. The management also may have been influenced by the fact that Victor Lawson was claiming morning circulation leadership in Chicago, and the rumors that West Coast publisher William Hearst, who had recently bought the *New York Journal,* might be ready to invade Chicago as well. But no special reason was required. Competition in the morning was especially intense, and each newcomer hoped to be the one that would at last take the measure of the *Chicago Tribune,* especially since persistent rumors of office warfare and family struggle made the task appear, to an outsider, relatively easy.

318

Below: The first issue of the *Tribune* was published June 10, 1847, from a third-floor room at LaSalle and Lake streets. Fire destroyed the small plant in 1849, and the paper was printed for a time on a borrowed press in a loft over J. H. Gray's grocery store at Clark and Randolph streets.

Bottom: From 1850 to 1852, the paper shared offices with two religious publications in the Masonic Building at 171½ Lake Street. The illustration shows part of Lake Street as it appeared in 1860, after Chicago had begun the arduous process of lifting itself out of the mud, raising the grade of its downtown streets. (CHICAGO HISTORICAL SOCIETY)

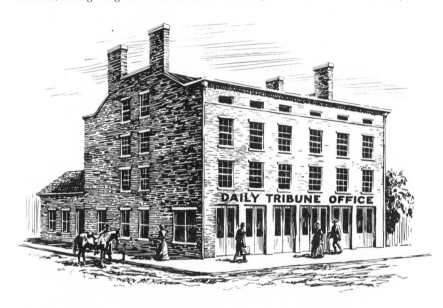

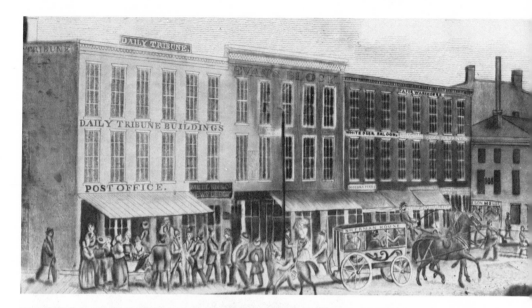

Top: Newspapers of the period sought to be as close as possible to the post office, and in 1852 the Chicago directory listed the *Tribune*'s address as 51 Clark Street, "over the post office." Other papers were clustered nearby, so that Clark Street between Randolph and Lake became known as Newspaper Row. (CHICAGO HISTORICAL SOCIETY)
Above: In 1869 the paper occupied the first building designed especially for it, at the southeast corner of Dearborn and Madison. This four-story "fireproof" building was destroyed in the Great Fire of 1871, an event depicted by artist James Sessions.

Right: The Tribune Building in ruins. Joseph Medill, on the morning after the fire, leased a print shop on Canal Street, and on October 11 the paper issued its first postfire edition, which expressed the resolve that "Chicago Shall Rise Again."

Below: The *Tribune*'s new five-story building, on the site of the burned structure, was ready for occupancy in 1872.

Above: Aftermath of the Great Fire, which destroyed more than 17,000 buildings and left some 2,200 acres of smoldering ruins. This view looks north from Congress Street, along Wabash Avenue. (CHICAGO HISTORICAL SOCIETY)
Below right: In 1902 Tribune Company constructed on the Dearborn and Madison site a 17-story publishing plant and office building.
Below left: Joseph Medill in 1880.

In December, 1887, the *Tribune* acquired its own etching facilities, and the paper blossomed with zinc engravings of pen-and-ink sketches—news events, fashions, advertisements, maps, and cartoons.

Below: Some of the sketches illustrating the news reports on June 17, 1888, the eve of the Republican National Convention, hosted by Chicago. The *Tribune* campaigned vigorously but unsuccessfully for the nomination of Judge Walter Quintin Gresham, and the party chose Benjamin Harrison instead.

Opposite page: The advertisements of major department stores were even more profusely illustrated than the news pages.

ONE OF THE DELEGATES.

GEN. HASTINGS.

INTERIOR OF THE GREAT AUDITORIUM.

The Chicago Daily Tribune.

VOLUME LVII—NO. 122.   MONDAY, MAY 2, 1898—TWELVE PAGES.   PRICE

THEY REMEMBERED THE MAINE!

GREAT SEA VICTORY FOR AMERICA!
VENGEANCE FOR THE MAINE BEGUN!
SPAIN'S ASIATIC FLEET BURNED AND SUNK!

Washington Aflame with Joy Over the Reports of the Royal Victory Won by Commodore Dewey's Fleet.

NOTABLE COMPANY HEARS THE NEWS.

Additional Credence Lent to the Dispatches from Madrid Because They Emanated from Distinctively Spanish Sources.

THINK THE DEFEAT HAS BEEN DECISIVE.

General Deploring That the First Real Engagement of the War Should Have Been So Triumphant for the American Cause.

ENTHUSIASTIC COMMENT OF GUESTS OF PRESIDENT M'KINLEY.

HERO OF THE BATTLE OF MANILA.

COMMODORE GEORGE DEWEY,
Commander of the Victorious Asiatic Fleet of the American Navy.

KNOWN CASUALTIES OF THE FIGHT.

Spanish cruiser REINA MARIA CHRISTINA, Admiral's flagship, burned.

Spanish cruiser CASTILLA, said to be completely burned.

Spanish cruiser DON JUAN DE AUSTRIA, blown up.

Several Spanish ships sunk.

Cadarso, Captain of the Spanish flagship, and crew of 370, who perished with the vessel.

Commanders of the Spanish cruisers Castilla and Don Juan de Austria, with their crews of about 500 men all told.

American losses are unknown.

SUMMARY.

United States vessels lost (Madrid admission)	0
United States vessels damaged (from best information)	0
Spanish cruisers totally lost (Madrid admission)	3
Spanish gunboats damaged (Madrid admission)	2
Spanish Captains lost (commanding lost cruisers)	3

SHIPS THAT FOUGHT OFF MANILA.

UNITED STATES FLEET.	SPANISH FLEET.
OLYMPIA, flagship; first-class cruiser, Capt. C. V. Gridley.	REINA MERCEDES, cruiser.
	REINA CHRISTINA, cruiser.
BALTIMORE, protected cruiser, Capt. N. Dyer.	ISLA DE CUBA, cruiser.
	ISLA DE LUZON, cruiser.
BOSTON, protected cruiser, Capt. Frank Wildes.	DON ANTONIO DE ULLOA, cruiser.
	DON JUAN DE AUSTRIA, cruiser.
RALEIGH, protected cruiser, Capt. J. B. Coghlan.	VELASCO, cruiser.
	ELCANO, gunboat.
CONCORD, gunboat, Commander Asa Walker.	GENERAL LEZO, gunboat.
	MARQUIS DEL DUERO, gunboat.
PETREL, gunboat, Commander E. P. Wood.	QUIROS, gunboat.
	VILLALOBOS, torpedo gunboat.
McCULLOCH, dispatch boat.	GENERAL ALAVA, transport.
NANSHAN, collier.	CEBU, transport.
ZAFIRO, collier.	MANILA, transport.
	ISLA DE MINDANAO, converted cruiser.

Commodore Dewey Crushes the Spanish Squadron in a Terrific Battle Off Cavite, Near the Capital of the Philippine Islands, Sunday Morning.

ONE OF THE GREAT NAVAL ENGAGEMENTS OF THE AGE.

Admiral Montejo's Flagship, the Reina Maria Christina, and the Cruiser Castilla Are Burned, While the Don Juan de Austria Is Blown Up.

OTHERS ARE SUNK TO SAVE THEM FROM BEING CAPTURED.

Captain Cadarso Is Among the Killed on the Spanish Side, and the List of Fatalities Is a Large One. Though the Particulars on This Point Are Slow in Coming to Hand.

LOSS TO AMERICA'S WARSHIPS AND SAILORS IS NOT BELIEVED TO BE HEAVY.

Commodore Dewey's squadron won a decisive victory over the Spanish fleet yesterday.

The battle was fought off Cavite, ten miles southwest of Manila. It lasted for several hours and resulted in a crushing defeat for Spain.

The American squadron arrived off the Philippines on Saturday night, taking advantage of the darkness to gain a favorable position. The attack on the Spanish fleet began soon after daylight yesterday morning.

It was a terrific battle, undoubtedly one of the fiercest and most brilliant in the history of naval warfare. The nine ships of the American fleet were outnumbered by those of Spain, but the Americans were superior in armament.

The heavy fire from Commodore Dewey's guns was effective from the outset. Admiral Montejo's flagship, the Reina Maria Christina, was burned and its commander killed. The Don Juan de Austria was blown up and the Castilla was burned.

The Spanish sailors fought bravely, and refused to leave their burning ships when ordered to do so. Commander Cadarso of the flagship went down with his vessel, and many of his crew perished with him.

Others of the Spanish fleet were badly damaged, and were sunk to prevent their falling into the hands of the Americans.

There was considerable loss of life on the Spanish side.

The American losses are not stated. As most of the news was sent by the Governor General of the Philippines it is certain that if Commodore Dewey's squadron was materially damaged the fact would not be minimized.

Admiral Montejo cabled to Madrid admitting the defeat of his squadron.

One Spanish report says that the American commander retired after an hour's fighting to land his wounded.

The battle took the form of a double engagement, according to the somewhat indefinite reports on this point. Presumably these reports are based on the maneuvers of the American squadron. The statement is made that Commodore Dewey's ships withdrew for a time and then returned to the attack. As the advantage was all on his side from the first, it is not believed that he at any period in the fight withdrew from action, though his ships may have changed positions.

The news of the Spanish defeat was fully confirmed in Lisbon last night, where the early reports gave Spain the victory.

Madrid officials profess to consider the battle a brilliant page in the nation's history, and the Minister of Marine telegraphed praise and congratulations to Admiral Montejo.

The feeling in London is that Commodore Dewey's job cannot be considered complete until he has captured Manila, and that he will be in an awkward position unless he succeeds in taking the city.

There was wild enthusiasm in Washington when the news of the victory arrived.

STORY OF THE BATTLE.

Spain Admits the Disaster in Which the Fleet Was Routed at Manila.

REINA MARIA CHRISTINA, SPANISH FLAGSHIP, BURNED.

The Reina Christina was 290 feet in length, had a displacement of 3,090 tons, a natural speed of fourteen knots, and a crew of 420 men. Its armament consisted of six 6.2-inch Hontorias, two 2.7-inch, three 2.2-inch rapid fire guns, two 1-inch, six machine guns, hull, steel.

Though the newspapers of the world were filled with reports of the great sea battle that had taken place between Commodore Dewey's fleet and the Spanish fleet at Manila Bay on May 1, 1898, their only information had come from Spanish sources before the cable from Manila was cut. The world waited, breathless, for some word from Dewey.

The Chicago Daily Tribune.

VOLUME LVII—NO. 127.   SATURDAY, MAY 7, 1898—SIXTEEN PAGES.   PRICE

POPE MOVES FOR PEACE.

Be Telegraphs to the Queen Regent of Spain Advising Her to Ask for the Mediation of the European Powers to End the War.

IMPOSSIBLE FOR THE DONS TO COPE WITH AMERICA.

Emperor Francis Joseph Is Using His Influence to Secure Intervention and His Course Is said to Be Indorsed by Officials in France.

NO COMMUNICATION WITH THE UNITED STATES THUS FAR.

Christina Reported to Be Checkmated by Her Spanish Advisers in Her Previous Efforts to Avoid and Terminate Hostilities.

ISOLATED POSITION OF ENGLAND WITH RESPECT TO INTERVENTION.

SEE THE SPANISH SHIPS

What Is Believed to Be the Cape Verde Fleet Is Sighted Off the Island of St. Thomas.

FIGHT MAY SOON OCCUR.

Harbor at San Juan, Puerto Rico, Is Cleared of Non-Combatants and Merchantmen Seek Shelter.

PEOPLE ARE IN A PANIC

Work on the Fortifications Is Pushed Forward While Famine and Terror Reign Supreme.

CANARY ISLANDS FEAR ATTACK.

4:30 A.M. EXTRA 4:30 A.M.

DIRECT NEWS FROM DEWEY!
NO AMERICAN SHIP LOST!
NOT ONE AMERICAN KILLED!
ONLY SIX AMERICANS INJURED!
ELEVEN SPANISH SHIPS SUNK!
300 SPANIARDS ARE KILLED!
400 SPANIARDS INJURED!

From Our Own Correspondent.

On Board the United States Flagship Olympia.
Manila, Luzon Island, Philippines.
By Dispatch Boat to Hongkong.

(SPECIAL CABLE.)

(BY E. W. HARDEN OF CHICAGO.)

Hongkong, May 7.—(Copyright, 1898, by the Press Publishing Company, New York World.)—The victory of the American fleet in the bombardment of Manila on Sunday was complete and overwhelming.

Of the Spanish ships eleven were sunk. The fleet was completely destroyed.

The Americans did not lose a single man, and the ships came through the battle uninjured in the least by the Spanish fire.

The Spanish lost 300 men killed and 400 wounded.

On the American fleet only six of the entire number of men engaged were injured.

These are not serious, the wounds being only slight.

The results are a great tribute to the daring and skill of the men in the American navy.

It seems almost incredible that the ships and men should have come through the ordeal without a scratch.

The guns were served with admirable precision, and the ships were maneuvered in so clever a manner that the Spaniards were not able to do any execution.

The enemy's fleet was of course outclassed, but, that even being so, it is a cause for the highest gratification and even wonder that the American men and fleet should have emerged from the conflict comparatively unharmed.

I have just arrived here on the United States boat McCulloch from Manila.

PUERTO RICO TO BE TAKEN

Importance of Sampson's Operations in Attacking the Islands—Battle with the Armada Imminent.

QUESTIONS OF THE HOUR

Where is Admiral Sampson

Where is the Cape Verde fleet

What is Dewey doing at Manila

When will Puerto Rico be taken

When will Havana be bombarded

When will the Flying Squadron sail

When will the troops start for Cuba

?

James Keeley's insistence that the *Tribune*'s news staff be on constant alert paid off with a fantastic news beat on May 7. The *New York World* received a dispatch from its correspondent with Dewey's fleet too late for its final edition, but at the *Tribune,* men were ready to produce an Extra when the news came in from the *World*'s press service. After sending the *Tribune* to press, managing editor Keeley called the White House and got the president out of bed to tell him the first news from Dewey.

Below: The first map known to have appeared in the *Tribune,* published on March 31, 1860.
Bottom and opposite: In the 1880s and 1890s, the *Tribune* lured readers with special graphic effects, including halftone engravings. The paper also offered four-color reproductions obtained from specialized printers, which usually appeared on Sundays and depicted children, animals, and flowers, though occasionally an artistic nude was represented. The starkly prescient air battle appeared as a halftone on March 13, 1898.

MAP AND DESCRIPTION OF THE PIKE'S PEAK GOLD REGIONS.

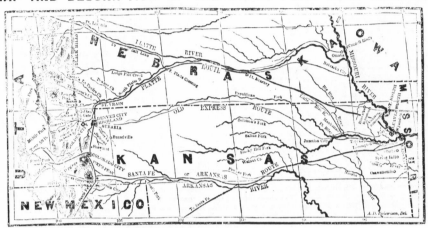

328

Above: An early *Tribune* comics feature page.

Opposite page: The *Tribune* used its color premium pages to present views of the world's fair of 1893, the stupendous World's Columbian Exposition. Top: "Along the Plaisance." The great Ferris wheel became a symbol of the fair, as was the dancer Little Egypt. Bottom: "Looking East in the Grand Court." A replica of the gilded Statue of the Republic is still to be seen in Jackson Park.

"STAND-AND-DELIVER" POLICY OF THE ADMINISTRATION WITH CITY EMPLOYES.

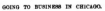

GOING TO BUSINESS IN CHICAGO.

Opposite page: One of the *Tribune*'s earliest editorial cartoons appeared on April 5, 1891 (top), and was directed against Mayor DeWitt Cregier, who was defeated for reelection two days later. In 1892 the paper used cartoons on page one to attack the gas company for tearing up streets and leaving them in disrepair (bottom left). The campaign was successful, and the repairs were soon made. In 1903 the *Tribune* acquired John T. McCutcheon from Victor Lawson's *Record-Herald,* and in his more than 40 years with the *Tribune* McCutcheon became known as one of America's greatest editorial cartoonists. He drew for seven editions a week, alternating political work with thematic drawings, most celebrating youth and the joys of a simple life. When Pope Leo XIII died on July 20, 1903, McCutcheon's globe in mourning (bottom right), appearing the following day, won international admiration.

Below: In the 1912 presidential campaign, the *Tribune* threw full support to Theodore Roosevelt's Bull Moose party, McCutcheon's pre-election cartoon predicting "Tuesday will be Mooseday." Roosevelt finished second to Democrat Woodrow Wilson, polling nearly a million more votes than Republican William H. Taft, which prompted McCutcheon to classify the G.O.P. as extinct. (McCUTCHEON CARTOONS COURTESY OF THE NEWBERRY LIBRARY, CHICAGO)

Top left: George P. Upton, Civil War correspondent, music and drama critic, the puckish "Peregrine Pickle," and editorial writer. He became a director and vice-president of the *Tribune* in 1891 and was a confidant of Joseph Medill. **Top right:** Henry Demarest Lloyd, first and perhaps greatest of the muckraking journalists. He became the *Tribune*'s chief editorial writer under Medill and lashed out at such capitalist giants as John D. Rockefeller, Cornelius Vanderbilt, and Jay Gould. **Above left:** Elias Colbert, city editor and science editor, was also close to the editor-in-chief until Medill's death. **Above right:** Robert W. Patterson, Jr., Medill's son-in-law. The only man who dared say no to Medill, he did so on rare occasions. Patterson served the paper as general manager and editorial superintendent in Medill's final years and became president of Tribune Company following the Chief's death.

Tribune editor-in-chief Joseph Medill surrounded by his grandchildren not long before his death in March, 1899. Clockwise from left: Robert R. McCormick, Eleanor Patterson, Medill McCormick, Joseph M. Patterson. Medill McCormick served for a time as a *Tribune* executive, then entered politics and was elected a U.S. senator. Eleanor Patterson became owner and publisher of the *Washington Times-Herald,* later purchased by Tribune Company and ultimately sold to the *Washington Post.* Joseph Patterson and Robert R. McCormick shared direction of the *Tribune* from 1914 until 1925, when Patterson departed for New York to devote full time to his *Illustrated Daily News,* leaving the Chicago paper increasingly in his cousin's hands.

19 PARTS

The Chicago Sunday Tribune.

19 PARTS

VOLUME LXVIII—NO. 6.　　　194 PAGES.　　　FEBRUARY 7, 1909.　　　194 PAGES.　　　★ ★ ★ PRICE FIVE CENTS.

"The Greatest Issue of the World's Greatest Newspaper."

THE LINCOLN OF FORTY YEARS FROM NOW.

Somewhere in this country today there is an unknown boy who will be the country's greatest living man forty years from now.

CONCERT OF BLOWS AT THE PRESIDENT

Raymond Sees Conspiracy to Discredit the Roosevelt Administration as Its End Draws Near.

CITES THE PANAMA CASE.

Tennessee Coal and Iron Merger Another Instance of Hostile Unanimity Without Basis of Evidence.

ATTACK SHERIFF'S PROFIT ON FEEDING

Citizens' Association Alleges Official Nets $30,000 in a Year on Poor Meals at the Jail.

'BLACKMAIL,' HIS RETORT

Strassheim Courts Inquiry and Secretary Singleton Says Complaint Will Be Pressed.

LINCOLN'S SPIRIT DOMINATES CITY.

Week of Celebrating Centenary of the Birth of the Great Emancipator Begins.

PEOPLE JOIN IN HOMAGE.

Patriotism for a Time Blots Out Differences in the Politics and Religion of Citizens.

REFUSES PLACE IN CABINET

G. M. Reynolds Declines to Be Secretary of Treasury.

WILL WAIT FOR HONORS.

Continental National Bank Raises His Salary $15,000 a Year.

RACE 1,800 MILES FOR MINE AND RAID CHICAGO OFFICE.

REAR ADMIRAL EVANS HERE.

"Fighting Bob" Stops Over Between Michigan and Wisconsin Points on His Lecture Tour.

BRYAN HURT IN AUTO WRECK

Motor Car Strikes Bridge Crushing Commoner Against.

BONES SAID TO BE INTACT.

Injuries Serious Enough to Expel Consolation of Speaking Dates.

POLICEMAN SHOT IN HEAD WHILE LEADING A PRISONER.

SHIPPY GETS BACK TOMORROW.

The *Tribune* of February 7, 1909, was the largest edition of the paper published up to that time, 194 pages, including seven special sections in honor of the centenary of Lincoln's birth. In addition to the Lincoln sections, the paper offered its usual assortment of items appealing to a wide range of interests, from fashions to electric carriages to humorous political commentary. The phrase "The World's Greatest Newspaper" caught managing editor Keeley's fancy, and it was used in advertising from time to time. The phrase was later registered as a trademark, and on August 29, 1911, it began appearing regularly on the paper's masthead. The use of the slogan was not discontinued until January 1, 1977.

"Report at five o'clock to swim acrost th' Pottymack."

THE CHICAGO SUNDAY TRIBUNE: FEBRUARY 7, 1909.

Lincoln and The Tribune

ABRAHAM LINCOLN

JOSEPH MEDILL

Medill McCormick (top left) succeeded
Robert Patterson in directing the *Tribune*,
but in the uncertain days of family
factionalism, it was James Keeley (top
right) who often managed the paper's
affairs. After Medill McCormick went into
politics, Robert R. McCormick (left) and
Joseph Patterson (above left) agreed to
share direction of the paper, but they did
not actively do so until Keeley quit to
head the rival *Record-Herald*. McCormick
concentrated on business matters of the
burgeoning Tribune Company, and
Patterson oversaw daily features and the
Sunday department. As assistant Sunday
editor he chose Mary King (above), whom
he later married.

A LONDONER
TAKES CHARGE

15

Since the day in January, 1865, when the *Tribune* turned from its preoccupation with the Civil War and national affairs to discover that the horse railway monopoly, the city council, and the state legislature were in the midst of a conspiracy to steal the rights to Chicago's streets, Joseph Medill sought to make sure that there would never again be any lack of vigilance by his newspaper over Chicago municipal affairs, nor any failure to attack ugly monopoly wherever it might be found. The editor ranked monopoly as the country's second-worst enemy, after slavery, and in the years following the Civil War his guns seemed mostly trained on wealthy predators in the East. In January, 1881, Medill issued a dire warning, saying in a *Tribune* editorial: "These monopolies threaten the commerce of the country and the peace of the country, for America is not to be relegated to a reign of feudalism peaceably." That editorial was speaking of Gould and Vanderbilt again, men who had created vast telegraph and railroad empires and sought to levy extortionate prices upon the public. But the paper was just as heavily engaged at home, against equally formidable antagonists—the meat-packers, the grain speculators and elevator entrepreneurs, the railroad tycoons, and most especially the newcomers planning to use Chicago's streets for their private gain, the gas trust, the power trust, and the street railway trust. It was a war that appeared without end.

The Traction Barons were especially difficult to check and seemingly impossible to destroy. Led first by King Mike McDonald, the gambling and political boss who helped to build the first elevated railroad, then by the redoubtable Charles Tyson Yerkes, the Traction Barons bought and sold city and state politicians and had indeed created a feudal system in Chicago. Small local tyrants, aldermen or ward committeemen, were allowed to establish their limited fiefdoms in exchange for money supplied by the Barons, who were granted rights to operate, usually in, under, and over the city streets. The monopolists, whether they were interested in gas or electrical power franchises, cable car or electric trolley rights, or the right to string wires or construct elevated tracks, were willing to pay the elected public servants well for cheap, exclusive privileges. The city charter adopted in 1875 authorized the city council to grant franchises of no more than 20 years' duration, far too short a period to satisfy the Traction Barons, who continually sought ways to improve their position. The *Tribune* and other newspapers, always vigilant, had returned endlessly to the fight, with Henry Demarest Lloyd early showing the way. The papers pointed out the stringencies of city charters in Europe, where 20 years was the maximum length of a franchise, and where in some instances private ownership of such services was not permitted at all.

Many of the newcomers seeking rights for their new power, propulsion, heating, and lighting techniques were honest businessmen with needed capital and skills that they were ready to provide for a proper return. They, as much as the general public, became victims of the predators and were either driven out or felt required to engage in graft themselves to survive. Most of the Chicago newspapers, except those owned by the bribe-passers, fought and fought hard for the rights of the public. Medill paid tribute to the efforts of these competitors in an address before the Chicago Press Club, saying in part:

> [*The Chicago press*] is not afraid to criticize or censure what it deems inimical to the public interest or general welfare. The press of Chicago despises pretentious humbugs. . . . It speaks its mind freely on all subjects and reports everything that transpires without fear, favor or affection. It attacks the wrongdoings of the strong and the high as fearlessly as it defends the weak and helpless. Every class of grasping, overreaching men in business or politics comes in for its exposure and stings, and political bosses are its especial aversion, and on them the press of Chicago wages a war of extermination.

In the 1890s such a war was waged against King Mike McDonald, Roger Sullivan, boss of the gas trust, and Charles Tyson Yerkes, the most powerful of all. Only Yerkes was actually driven from power at the peak of his career. The son of a Philadelphia bank president, Yerkes had come to Chicago in 1882 after serving seven months of a two-year prison sentence on charges of embezzlement. Philadelphians backed him with funds to acquire traction lines, and within a few years he organized the

North Chicago Street Railway, which he electrified and otherwise improved. Gradually, Yerkes acquired rights to trolley lines in many of the city's streets by shrewd bargaining with other street railway owners who lacked connecting links. Other rights he obtained from the city council, and there was not much attention paid to the newspaper cries of boodle payoffs because a unified streetcar system was needed by working people, who were not that much concerned about how it was obtained. Yerkes's tactics were emulated by seekers of gas and electrical franchises—they paid off the aldermen. Similar steps were taken by those desiring access to the streets for loading docks or driveways, or who wished to avoid paying for safety requirements, such as street elevations by the railroads, a costly but effective way to protect grade crossings. The boodlers among the aldermen, denounced daily in the newspapers, grew ever more callous and rich. Some squirmed under the attack, a few sought occasionally to reply, and at least two, Bathhouse John Coughlin and Hinky Dink Kenna, appeared to glory in the notoriety. The Bath protested only once, because the Municipal Voters' League erroneously listed his birthplace as Waukegan rather than Chicago.

But even Yerkes at last went too far. In 1895 the Traction Barons went to Springfield to plump for the Crawford Bill, which would authorize the city council to grant 99-year franchises rather than the 20-year limit then in effect. Though the bill had little difficulty gaining passage, the newspaper outcry and public outrage were so great that some legislators had second thoughts and refused to override Governor Altgeld's veto. By the time the Barons were ready to try again, two more formidable opponents had entered the fray: The Municipal Voters' League, which began in 1896 to investigate Chicago's aldermen and to publicize its findings; and Carter H. Harrison, Jr., who based his successful campaign in the 1897 mayoralty race on an antigraft platform. Despite his claim to be a reformer, Harrison wooed a motley crew of aldermen, including such worthies as Bathhouse John and Hinky Dink, for he knew their support would be needed if the genuine reformers were to defeat the unregenerate phalanx of Gray Wolves and the financial largesse of the Barons. Some people said the Bath and the Hink stuck with Harrison only because Yerkes was not offering a big enough bribe. But Harrison was aware they were struggling with Johnny de Pow Powers for race track revenues, and the mayor shrewdly exploited this split to the benefit of the public.

Yerkes meanwhile, deciding to give the reform spirit in Chicago a chance to die down, renewed his attack in the Illinois legislature. The slavering Springfield Gray Wolves howled happily. Not one, but two measures were introduced to insure that Chicago streets could be sold for as long as Yerkes deemed satisfactory, and at bottom price. His representatives introduced the Humphrey Bill and when that was defeated, rebounded with the Allen Bill. Both bills were denounced by the *Tribune*, which declared the Allen Bill to be "the most odious steal in Illinois history." John R. Tanner, a Republican, was now governor, and Republicans were in control of the legislature, but it was clear that, as in the days of the horse railway steal, money was prevalent in Springfield to buy the necessary votes regardless of party. The Allen Bill, authorizing the city council of Chicago to grant 50-year franchises, passed easily and was quickly signed by Governor Tanner after Yerkes reportedly told him, "The newspapers do not express the sentiment of the people of Chicago." The *Tribune* suspected that Tanner listened also to the voice of U.S. Congressman William Lorimer of the Second District, the rising "Blond Boss" of Republican committeemen in Chicago.

The Allen Bill became law on June 9, 1897. The newspaper clamor was so horrendous that Yerkes decided to postpone petitioning the city council to renew his franchises under the new 50-year limit. Surely the public furor would soon subside; and besides, the delay would give him time to buy a few more aldermen to insure a clear majority when the matter came up for a vote. The struggle for advantage, ranging the boodlers and the Barons against the mayor, the newspapers, and the Municipal Voters' League, continued until the historic council meeting of December 19, 1898. Citizens' groups packed the galleries early, dangling hemp and leather nooses menacingly over the railing, while the Gray Wolves ignored them, walking smugly to their seats and smirking at one another in anticipation. Again Carter Harrison held his coalition together, with the help of Bathhouse and Hinky Dink. As the vote progressed it became clear that if Harrison and the people were to win, it would be by a slim margin; and it was, 32 to 31. Not long after, the Illinois legislature repealed the Allen Law.

The *Tribune* exulted, reporting that Yerkes blamed his defeat on "Socialists, anarchists and newspapers." The paper promised that it would remove from the public payroll the next-most-dangerous rascal in Illinois, Congressman William Lorimer, "the hired agent of Yerkes & Co. . . . who should be thrown out of the Republican Central Committee as a Jonah to his party." Over a decade would be required for the *Tribune* to make good on that promise, but Yerkes quit Chicago in disgust, going to England, where he built London's first subway system.

*   *   *

Joseph Medill did not permit his readers at any time to forget that the *Tribune* was fighting for them, providing the news, and affording them the country's most interesting newspaper while matching the country's lowest price, 1¢. "It has not been an accident that the *Tribune* has grown into the hearts of the people," the paper noted. "It has not been the result of a single or several exploits. . . . It has been by the steady and unremitting championship of the right at any cost and at all times in obedience to deliberate and sincere judgment. It has been by publishing each day the history of the world as it was made the day before, unbiased by prejudice. It has been by unflagging loyalty to the best interests of the whole people of Chicago."

The *Tribune* celebrated its 50th birthday on June 10, 1897, with a special Golden Jubilee edition that included a four-color outer cover decorated with patriotic symbols, highlights of Chicago history, and a poem written for the occasion by James Whitcomb Riley. The *Tribune* suggested that newspapers in the future would use color regularly, though the June 10 color cover was almost certainly printed outside its own plant. The paper reported that its engraving department was experimenting with a new halftone process that would soon enable it to reproduce the various shades of gray in black-and-white photographs and paintings with great fidelity and at high press speeds. One of the early halftones appeared in the Sunday *Tribune* on March 13, 1898, depicting "How the Battles of the Future May Be Fought." It showed an air attack being repulsed over a city, with airplanes and dirigibles crisscrossing their cannon fire, an imaginary scene chillingly accurate as wars of the future developed.

Along with its new ability to reproduce halftones, the paper continued to obtain from commercial plants in Chicago large four-color prints that it offered as premiums suitable for framing. The *Tribune* searched for excellent artists to supplement the work of its reporters and writers in bringing the news of the world to its readers. One of the early choices was Frederic Remington, well known for his scenes of the American West, who had been commissioned by Hearst to accompany correspondent Richard Harding Davis to Cuba, where since 1895 insurgents had been struggling to free the island from Spanish rule. Among Remington's first contributions to the *Tribune* was a tragic moonlit scene of a young Cuban farmer being shot by Spanish soldiers. It was given a five-column display across page one in February. By April, Remington's work was appearing regularly in the Sunday *Tribune*.

There were other international events to occupy the news columns and the attention of *Tribune* readers. In April, 1897, Hawaii asked for a U.S. warship, asserting that Japanese ships of war were maneuvering in a threatening way in the vicinity of the islands. The *Tribune* declared that Japan must be recognized as a menace in the Pacific as a result of its occupation of Formosa, and the paper urged that Hawaii be annexed to the United States, an extension of the Manifest Destiny policy popular in America since the 1840s, a policy supported by Senator Douglas and one of the few Democratic ideas adopted by Medill. *Tribune* correspondent Charles Pepper was sent to Havana. In May, Stephen Crane, whose *Red Badge of Courage* was to become a classic, was reporting on the Greco-Turkish War. During the summer, a *Tribune* delegation under Professor Elias Colbert, now the paper's science editor, attended the meetings of the British Association for the Advancement of Science in Toronto, and three pages were devoted to its reports on controversial papers relating to the ages of the earth and man. When gold was found in the Klondike, the paper sent William J. Jones and two assistants to the Chilkoot Pass, while three other *Tribune* writers, Hal Hoffman, Bertha Craib, and Sam W. Wall, also sent reports from Alaska and northwestern Canada. Joaquin Miller, "poet of the Sierras," wrote on his impressions of the gold camps for Hearst, and these letters, too, appeared in the *Tribune*. Correspondent Pepper traveled to the Pacific but soon returned to Chicago. The Hawaii crisis receded after President Sanford B. Dole of Hawaii appeared in Washington to plead for annexation and Congress threatened to send the entire American fleet to Pacific waters.

*　　*　　*

Joseph Medill increasingly relinquished control of the *Tribune* to the capable hands of his son-in-law Robert Patterson. Patterson had assumed new duties as general manager early in 1890, after serving as managing editor for seven years, and had appointed William Van Benthuysen his successor. While Patterson continued to manage news matters and to oversee editorials in Medill's absence, he was also responsible for supervising production, planning a new building, dealing with the complaints of advertisers, and handling the general public relations and civic obligations of newspaper management. Van Benthuysen was managing editor until March, 1898, when he took a similar job with the *New York World,* but he was so dominated by the family hierarchy as to remain obscure in *Tribune* history.

Not so the brash young man who came to the *Tribune* shortly before Van Benthuysen was named managing editor. James Keeley possessed no Chicago acquaintances and no knowledge of the city, but he had been a reporter in Memphis and in Louisville. He proclaimed himself an orphan with a modicum of British education, but it was Keeley who would be raised by Patterson to the job of city editor when he was only 27, and who would demonstrate to Chicago journalists just how well news could be written, exploited, and sold. His habits, practices, and decrees, both as city editor and as successor to Van Benthuysen in 1898, would force a change in the habits and practices of morning newspaper editors and their staffs for decades.

James Keeley was born in England, but the rest of his life remained somewhat a mystery to his associates, since he was as able at concealing his past as he was in probing that of others. According to his biographer, James Weber Linn, Keeley's father had deserted his mother after five years of marriage so his mother, Elizabeth Rawlings Keeley, taught school to support her two sons, James and Charles. James attended Wesleyan School, Colchester in Essex, where he was reported to be an excellent student. He left school at 14 to take a job with an uncle in a London bookstore. On Sundays he could visit his mother who, says Linn, was "sternly religious and ruthlessly right." At the age of 16, Keeley was sent by his mother to live with friends in Leavenworth, Kansas.

Keeley was called "Bird" as a boy, since he had sharp, darting eyes and a habit of carrying his head to one side, bird-like. This nickname he carried from England to Leavenworth. His alienation from his mother was such that for years he insisted he had no mother nor father. In Leavenworth he worked in Hirschfield's jewelry store until he got a job as a train "butcher," selling newspapers, chapbooks, and candy. He had no further formal education after leaving England, but he learned much by reading the books and newspapers between his trainboy rounds; also he learned what kind of content and titling of such popular literature was easiest to sell. Keeley wrote some news items himself, sending them to the *Kansas City Journal*, which occasionally bought and published one. The lad was offered a steady job as a reporter and worked for the *Memphis Commercial* for a year, then went on to the *Louisville Commercial*. In the summer of 1889 he appeared in Chicago. He was 21 years old when he was hired by the *Tribune* as a night police reporter, competing against the representatives of the morning *Herald, Times, Record, Inter-Ocean,* and *Globe.*

The young reporter wrote well and succinctly, and he could outwork everyone else on the police beat. Keeley guarded his exclusives, won the confidence of good news sources, and, it was said, did not hesitate to disrupt a rival's telephone if that would help him get a beat on a story. His first big story came in 1892, after he had been made a general reporter, and was not based on a Chicago incident at all. Rather, it resulted from a tip from one of the news sources he had developed. There was going to be a cattlemen's war in Johnson County, Wyoming, said Keeley's tipster, and 150 deputies had been recruited to meet an expected invasion of hundreds of rich stockmen and their hands. The *Tribune* editors agreed that the situation had possibilities. Keeley was given $300 and sent to Wyoming. His first story came from Buffalo, Wyoming, and reported a battle at the KC ranch between stockmen and "rustlers." Four rustlers had been killed, Keeley wrote; later he revised the death toll to two. But there was much action, and though it was Easter Sunday, which the *Tribune* usually devoted to accounts of church services and other non-criminal and peaceful interests, Keeley's story was spread over page one. It involved what might happen more than what had happened. Keeley envisioned a "war" with stockmen and U.S. cavalry from Fort McKinney attacking the rustlers, who some said were really small-time cattlemen trying to avoid being swallowed up by the big ranchers.

Keeley's stories of the impending war excited other newspaper editors as well as readers, but they were unable to get any news from the center of the trouble. Meantime, the *Tribune* was receiving correspondence regularly from its man on the scene. At last came a dispatch datelined Brown Springs and transmitted "via *Tribune* courier," reporting that the conflict was coming to an end and that the cavalry was on its way back to Fort McKinney with the invading stockmen under escort. Notwithstanding the fact that the range "war" was over before a major battle could be fought, Keeley's story was tremendous and totally exclusive. It was especially difficult for rival editors to check out since Brown Springs, too small to appear on any map, was temporarily without telegraph service. Only later did they learn how the resourceful correspondent had achieved and guarded his scoop. Eager to be nearer the anticipated battle, Keeley had gone to Douglas, where he hired a guide to take him to Brown Springs, 40 miles away. The pair had become lost in a raging blizzard, but Keeley noticed a telegraph line and pulled down the wire with his companion's lasso. The two men followed the wire into Brown Springs, yanking wire off the poles as they went along. When at last they reached their destination, they encountered the cavalry and the stockmen, delayed by the same storm. Sending his guide back to Douglas to transmit his exclusive to the *Tribune,* Keeley went along with the stockmen as far as Cheyenne, where he filed another report.

Historians and Keeley's biographer have never been sure whether the destruction of the telegraph line was actually caused by the weather or the reporter. More important, observes Linn, was that Keeley had managed to provide for the *Tribune* "eleven first-page stories in two weeks, on a matter which turned out to involve no more than the killing of two inconspicuous ranchmen, Nate Champion and Ray Kelly, over a line-fence quarrel two thousand miles from Chicago in a country almost worthless for ranching." In the *Tribune* editorial offices it was apperceived that the young man from Kansas had exceptional potential; he was soon made assistant city editor, and in 1895 Patterson awarded him the job of city editor.

James Keeley meanwhile had married Gertrude Small, a *Tribune* reporter. At the time, says Linn, he was a handsome young man, with long hair "roached back from a high forehead," unusually bright eyes, set far apart, and obviously an extremely winsome personality. In his later years the good-natured smile would harden to a somewhat thin, cynical smirk, and he was frequently called "brutal" or "ruthless" by his workers. Keeley believed in hard work, the total exploitation of any news incident, the absolute dedication of every reporter and editor to his job, and complete disavowal of ordinary human relationships, such as friendship. "A good newspaperman has no friends," Keeley liked to say, a belief he shared with Joseph Medill. "A good newspaperman is always on the job. He never rests." Keeley himself did not rest. Prior to his ascent to the position, city editors generally would end their day in the early evenings and go home to their families, leaving final decisions and the display of stories to the night editor and his staff. Keeley remained on the job until 4 A.M. if little was happening, longer if there was reason for it. Sometimes he played poker from midnight until early morning at a nearby hotel or club, making it clear to his staff that he was to be summoned back to the office if there was the slightest need. He worked six and sometimes seven days and nights a week and generally, wrote a new reporter, Burton Rascoe, displayed "the unpleasant aspects of a particularly vicious bulldog."

Keeley's taut discipline and alertness pleased Patterson, however, and when Van Benthuysen left the paper in March, 1898, Keeley was made managing editor, in time to preside over the biggest scoop in the history of the paper up to that time. It was in fact one of the greatest scoops in newspaper history, and though coincidence played a part, much of the credit was due to the inflexible system of checks and controls Keeley had imposed upon his local staff as city editor and then expanded to include the entire news-gathering staff of the paper. It continued 24 hours a day, seven days a week, and applied to all the paper's bureaus and correspondents. The system was virtually failure-proof. It kept track of personnel wherever they might be, and even while they slept, for reporters and correspondents were required to keep "the office" apprised of their availability by telephone even during vacations. The system that paid off so handsomely in 1898 remained standard operating procedure at the *Chicago Tribune* for decades.

The news event harvested by Keeley's discipline was Commodore George Dewey's great victory over the Spanish fleet in Manila Bay, the first action of the Spanish-American War, and the *Tribune* had Dewey's story before the president of the United States got his official report. In fact, the managing editor of the *Chicago Tribune* got President McKinley out of bed to tell him the news and then thoughtfully placed a second call, giving the same information to the secretary of the navy.

Almost from the beginning, the Cubans' struggle for independence had provided a new battleground for the circulation war being waged in New York by Hearst's *Journal* and Pulitzer's *World.* Their coverage of the guerrilla fighting, and the stories of Spanish oppression and reprisals, aroused strong American sympathies for the rebel cause and in time worked up a war fever that demanded intervention on the side of the Cubans. During this period the *Tribune* had not been heavily preoccupied with the Cuban situation, concentrating its attention instead on possible troubles in Hawaii. Prior to the arrival of the U.S. battleship *Maine* in Havana on a good will mission in February, 1898, and the return of Charles Pepper to Cuba, the *Tribune* relied on the Associated Press and the dispatches of Hearst correspondent Richard Harding Davis. The paper was strongly sympathetic to the rebels, but it showed no interest in the sensational display of Cuba news that characterized coverage in New York, a sensationalism that caused opponents of American intervention to charge Hearst and Pulitzer with misrepresenting the nature of the rebellion and overemphasizing Spanish misrule.

President McKinley had resisted the pressures of those in the East clamoring for war, and as reports of Spanish atrocities grew, the *Tribune* became increasingly critical of this stand and began urging action to aid the suffering Cubans. On February 15, 1898, the *Maine* was sunk in Havana Harbor by an explosion whose source has never been determined; but most newspapers and the general public in turn believed it was deliberately caused by the Spaniards. There was an American loss of 260 men, and war fever raged. Charles Pepper wrote that the explosion "unquestionably was from an outside source," a conclusion he reached without waiting to learn the findings of the U.S. Navy's Court of Inquiry. On February 28, the *Tribune* reproved the court's dilatory tactics. "If the Court of Inquiry has received an intimation that delay will be acceptable, is the motive back of that advice commendable?" the paper asked. It suggested that the "commercial spirit" took precedence over patriotism among those who opposed war with Spain. In the *Tribune* offices, Joseph Medill was overheard dictating to an editorial writer, "There is no price on the lives of murdered American seamen." On March 9, the paper declared, "The country is unanimous that the sword be drawn against Spain." In April, President McKinley sent an ultimatum to Madrid that the Spanish government accepted, but too late. On April 25, Congress declared war; the war would last only 113 days, but it would propel the United States into an era of expansionism and world influence.

Commodore George Dewey was in Hong Kong with elements of the American Pacific fleet when he received his orders to attack: "You must capture vessels or destroy them. Use utmost endeavors." The *Tribune* had urged that the Philippines should present one of the first opportunities to weaken the Spanish and sent correspondents to the Pacific, but meantime it took the precaution of arranging with the *New York World* for its services. The new managing editor of the *World*, Will Van Benthuysen, had no correspondent in the Pacific either, but he knew that former *Tribune* reporter Edward Harden, now on the *Chicago Post*, was accompanying

John T. McCutcheon of the *Chicago Record* on a round-the-world cruise aboard the cutter *McCulloch*. Van Benthuysen reached Harden by cable in Hong Kong, asking him to accompany Commodore Dewey for the *New York World*.

Dewey steamed for Manila and found the Spanish fleet in Manila Bay. When his flagship, the U.S.S. *Olympia,* was within 5,000 yards of the enemy, Dewey issued his about-to-be-famous order to Capt. Charles Gridley: "You may fire when you are ready, Gridley." Seven hours later the Spanish ships were burning or sunk, the guns of the forts were silenced, and not a single American had been killed. The cable from Manila to Hong Kong had been cut, so the correspondents had to wait until Dewey sent the dispatch boat to Hong Kong, carrying his own official report and the eager newsmen. Harden took the extra precaution to mark his cablegram "Urgent," which cost an extra $5 a word to New York but qualified it to be the first sent, right after Dewey's own report. As military procedures required, the commodore's message was repeated to the sender at each intermediate station to prevent mistakes; but Harden's report went straight through.

James Keeley had made it a rule at the *Chicago Tribune* that all night personnel in the editorial department would remain on duty until the paper was off the presses, and as usual he remained available nearby. He knew that the *World* had reached Harden and that no one could report by cable from Manila. So he especially cautioned his New York correspondent to remain in the offices of the *World* to examine all dispatches until Harden had been heard from. At 4:20 A.M. May 7, Harden's cable began to come in. The *World* had gone to press and only a skeleton staff remained, but the *Chicago Tribune* man present read the first words of the cable and telephoned Keeley in the *Tribune* offices at 3:22 A.M. Chicago time. Keeley ordered the presses stopped, Manila bulletins set, and page one remade. The *Tribune* had learned how to use banner headlines during the early days of the war, and it used them now:

4:30 A.M.   EXTRA   4:30 A.M.

DIRECT NEWS FROM DEWEY!

NO AMERICAN SHIP LOST!

NOT ONE AMERICAN KILLED!

ONLY SIX AMERICANS INJURED!

ELEVEN SPANISH SHIPS SUNK!

300 SPANIARDS ARE KILLED!

400 SPANIARDS INJURED!

The dispatch was credited to E. W. Harden of Chicago, "Our Own Correspondent, On Board the United States Flagship Olympia, Manila, Luzon Island, Philippines, By Dispatch Boat to Hongkong." It was datelined Hong Kong, May 7, and copyrighted 1898 by the Press Publishing Company, *New York World*. Though the action described had taken place on May 1 and early reports from Spanish sources had received front-page coverage for days, this was the first confirmation from Dewey to be published. The prior edition of the *Tribune* was recovered from downtown newsstands and railway stations and the Extra papers substituted. Then Keeley learned that not even the dispatch from Dewey had arrived ahead of Harden's cable. He telephoned the White House and demanded to speak to President McKinley, saying he had an urgent message from Commodore Dewey. He was put through at once, and the president was grateful.

*   *   *

The entire war was a debacle for Spain. And it was almost a tragedy for the *Tribune*'s H. J. Whigham, who was sent to Cuba to search for the insurgent General Gomez, inform him of the American declaration of war, and find out his needs, which, it was promised, would be transmitted to President McKinley. Whigham found the guerrilla camp on the north coast of Cuba, interviewed Gomez, and set out through Spanish lines to send the story to the *Tribune* and a message to President McKinley. Then Whigham and two other correspondents were captured by the Spaniards, who chose understandably to regard Whigham as a spy. The early end of the war saved the correspondent's life. The second big story of the war, the exploit of Lt. Richmond P. Hobson, who sank the collier *Merrimac* in Santiago Harbor in an effort to bottle up Admiral Cervera's fleet, was received from the Associated Press, proof that all news-gathering facilities were required to give readers top service, the *Tribune* pointed out. When the war ended on August 12, the *Tribune* urged that the United States consider Cuba and Puerto Rico for naval bases to defend the proposed canal across the Isthmus of Panama, and suggested that the Philippines be annexed despite the objections of insurgents there under Emilio Aguinaldo.

The American victory had been quick and obtained without great cost or casualties, but the *Tribune* soon was publishing reports of mismanagement and graft in army affairs. Chicago packers and others had sold rotten beef, there was a lack of medical supplies, uniforms and equipment were poorly made, and army depots were full of moldy munitions. The sanitary facilities in training camps and forward bases were shocking, the paper said. Nearly 5,000 soldiers died of disease and wounds, as compared with fewer than 400 killed in action. The navy, more professional, lost only 20 men during the entire war. When Gen. Nelson Miles, the Civil War veteran and Indian fighter, complained specifically about rotten beef from Chicago, the *Tribune* backed him and hearings were ordered. General Miles was sustained, but no one was punished, the war was over.

A strike of stereotypers closed up all Chicago papers for five days, saddening Medill, who prided himself on his good relations with his workers. His health was deteriorating. He wrote to a friend that his rheumatic ailment had been incorrectly diagnosed for years, and that now he knew he had kidney infection and ought to return to Wiesbaden for treatment, but he did not feel up to it. Several of his letters in the last years of his life were to George Upton, who appeared to be handling some of his personal financial affairs.

At some time during 1898, Joseph Medill posed for a photograph with his grandchildren, Robert McCormick, a student at Groton School; Eleanor Patterson, a student at Miss Porter's School, Farmington, Connecticut; Medill McCormick, a Yale junior being groomed to take over management of the *Tribune;* and Joseph Patterson, a sophomore at Yale. All would enter the newspaper business. *Tribune* general manager Robert Patterson was in Europe, and Keeley was running the paper, assisted by his city editor, Edward S. Beck. A story was published in a rival paper predicting that Patterson would soon resign his position as secretary of Tribune Company and that Alfred Cowles, Jr., would replace him. This was denied. Patterson and Cowles were excellent friends, the *Tribune* said, implying that someone was attempting to start trouble.

Medill's home in Los Angeles burned in November, 1898, and Medill wrote Upton of his close escape from the flames. He then journeyed to San Antonio to live for the winter in the Hotel Menger. His editors and managers in Chicago had the impression that he was again in good health, for almost daily they received telegrams, letters, and memoranda concerning the paper, suggesting editorial ideas, stories to be covered, mechanical changes to be considered, and complaints about the content of the paper. Medill told his family that he did not need anyone to visit him, but his grandson Robert went to San Antonio during the holidays and remained. On Friday, March 17, 1899, the *Tribune* reported that the death of Joseph Medill, age 76, had occurred the previous morning. His personal physician, Dr. Toras Sarkisian, stated, "The immediate cause of death was heart failure, underlying which was an organic heart lesion. Up to ten days ago Mr. Medill was doing as well as could be expected, but although confined to his room he was not, strictly speaking, a sick man. Since last Sunday, however, his indisposition grew. . . . On Wednesday morning Mr. Medill's condition was not encouraging. [*On Thursday morning*] he had his coffee and read his morning paper with his usual interest. The end was sudden, but not unexpected." Medill's last words, it was reported, were, "What is the news this morning?"

The death of Joseph Medill was a major news event not only for the

Tribune and other Chicago newspapers, but throughout America and in foreign cities. Interviews were republished, Lincoln stories reexamined. Medill was hailed as a leader in the development of modern journalism. He had been influential in politics as well and was always alert to his country's needs. Just a few hours before his death, he had sent President McKinley a telegram urging retention of the Philippines as a Pacific Ocean bastion.

Many years earlier, on June 16, 1882, Medill, on completing his will, had written to his wife and daughters, telling them his wishes for the paper: *"I want the* Tribune *to continue to be after I am gone as it has been under my directions: an advocate of political and moral progress, and in all things to follow the line of common sense. I desire the* Tribune *as a party organ, never to be the supporter of that party which sought to destroy the American Union or that exalts the State above the nation."*

Tributes flooded into the *Tribune* offices from newspapers, magazines, politicians, and business and civic leaders, and the estimates of the famous editor were summarized by the *Journalist:* "Mr. Medill is almost the last of the great editors who have impressed their personalities upon their papers and through them upon the American people. He stood beside Greeley, Raymond and Dana, and in many ways he wielded a wider influence and surveyed a larger public. The *Chicago Tribune,* which is one of the few papers in the country, outside the *New York Herald,* which has an international reputation, is an enduring monument to his sagacity."

Joseph Medill's estate, estimated at $2 million, was bequeathed in equal shares to his two daughters, Mrs. Elinor Patterson and Mrs. Katherine McCormick. His stock in Tribune Company, which at this time amounted to 1,050 shares, was left in trust to his sons-in-law Robert W. Patterson and Robert S. McCormick and his attorney William G. Beale, who were given full power to vote the stock and manage it or to sell it as a block. In addition, gifts were left to a number of *Tribune* employees. The will and the trusteeship arrangement did not provide for the kind of unified management of the paper that Medill had called for in 1874, and it was not long before attorney Beale was complaining that as a trustee he was called upon to settle family fights. With Medill's death the presidency of Tribune Company and the post of editor-in-chief passed to Patterson, though his own ill health would cause him to rely increasingly upon Keeley and Beck in the editorial area.

*   *   *

Edward Scott Beck was a student of both Keeley and Joseph Medill techniques, the latter as carried out by Robert Patterson. But Beck's interests remained concentrated in the editorial areas, whereas Patterson had become a business and production man as well as an editor; and as Patterson's surrogate, Keeley also handled many of the paper's business and advertising interests. The Keeley–Beck partnership was a youthful and effective one. When Patterson named Keeley managing editor, Keeley was not yet 31; Beck, the new city editor, was 29. Keeley perfected the image of a hard, demanding, often mean editorial executive, presenting a cigar-chomping, glowering image that daunted his reporters and deskmen. Beck, called "Teddy" by his friends, was understanding and compassionate, closing rifts created by his superior, undoubtedly with Keeley's secret approval.

Edgar Sisson, one of the reporters and later the editor of *Cosmopolitan* magazine, described the procedure of the Keeley–Beck team. Sisson had interviewed a reluctant Marshall Field, who finally talked for publication after being promised he would not be quoted directly. The reporter wrote up the story and carefully explained the promise to the substitute city editor. "He grunted, and I went home," recalled Sisson. "In the morning I read my story . . . and all but the first paragraph in quotes. To the bull-headed substitute, all interviews meant quotes. He had edited to suit himself." Field was furious. Sisson was summoned to the office. "Teddy Beck held out the order dismissing me. Of course, though, being Beck, he was willing to listen to my explanation."

A recheck demonstrated that Sisson had kept the agreement with Field, and Beck took the young reporter to see Keeley. "When pressure was high," Sisson later said, "Keeley didn't light his cigar but kept biting it until it was a third gone, then threw it away and took another." Keeley sent Sisson to explain the misunderstanding to Field, but he was refused admission to the office of the merchant prince. Certain of his doom, Sisson reported his failure to Keeley. On this occasion Keeley consulted Patterson before his final decision. When Keeley emerged from Patterson's office he turned to Sisson. "Well, get to work," he said. "That was all," Sisson concluded. "A weaker man would have sacrificed me in a minute. . . . The substitute city editor was let off with a tongue lashing, but in a few months he quit."

Managing editor Keeley insisted that the editorial department of the *Tribune* should be completely separate from the paper's other departments, and he barred anyone involved in advertising from even entering the editorial rooms. However, Keeley himself talked to advertisers about their complaints, at least when Patterson was away, and he also ignored his own credo, that a newspaperman should have no friends. He had a number of friends, from Samuel Insull, the utilities baron, and Dr. William Rainey Harper, president of the University of Chicago, to poker cronies and Levee bums, these last mostly tipsters from his police reporting days. And his ultimatum against advertising men was issued in a day when the *Tribune* had no advertising men in the modern sense. But the separation was perpetuated after the advertising department was formed in 1905, strictly enforced by Beck in later years, and continued by Col. Robert R. McCormick.

Keeley had no favorites among his staff other than Beck, with the possible exception of James Durkin, the world's oldest and most famous copyboy, according to *Tribune* lore. Keeley, who continued to insist that he was an orphan, hired Durkin from an orphanage in 1895. "Durk" was astonishingly quick in mind and body. He soon knew the answers to reporters' questions, details they ordinarily would search for in the paper's "morgue"; he could deliver copy faster and more accurately than any other boy and was made chief copyboy. Before he died in 1928, Durk's fame in journalistic circles was worldwide. As a promotional stunt, Lord Northcliffe, the London publisher, sent Keeley a note by special messenger and announced in his *London Daily Mail* the exact moment of the departure of his man, who reported his delivery time when he appeared in Chicago a few days later. Whether the stunt was prearranged neither His Lordship nor Keeley explained, but Keeley, reading the note, calmly called Durkin, told him to draw $500 cash and to take a reply to Northcliffe as rapidly as possible. Durkin raced to London, having no passport problems that were noted, and both newspapers boasted of their efficient copyboys, though it was not clear who won the race, if there was one. Then Durkin returned to Chicago, reappearing as unobtrusively as if returning from an errand across the street. Keeley noticed him, and his eyes glittered. "All right, Durk," he said.

*   *   *

In 1896 William R. Hearst ran the circulation of his *New York Journal* to 995,000 copies by supporting William Jennings Bryan, "the Great Commoner," for president; by calling for war with Spain; and by publishing reeking scandal, ingeniously illustrated pseudoscience news reports, and droll comics that began with the portrayal of a nameless street urchin in a triangular yellow gown who became known as the "Yellow Kid" and soon lent his name to an entire era and style of newspapering, "yellow journalism."

When Hearst was reported ready to invade Chicago in 1900, his potential competitors quaked. Hearst seemed better able to practice sensationalism than Joseph Pulitzer, who invented it, and he raided rival staffs for talent that he would buy at inflated prices. Hearst's *Chicago American* first appeared on July 2, 1900, with an evening edition. Hearst supported Bryan, free silver, and the eight-hour day, and quickly captured segments of the labor population. The new paper promptly undertook to carry out orders to make news as well as to report it. If there was violence to report, the *American* made the most of it. Some news took a pixie form, as when the paper brought Carry Nation from Kansas to Chicago to smash up saloons. Hearst's Chicago news department was called "the Madhouse on Madison Street" by people who worked there.

Hearst was determined to seize circulation supremacy in Chicago. He promised to send Arthur Brisbane to take over as editor of the *American,* but it soon became evident that Brisbane's occasional appearances were not enough and eventually Victor Watson, who had directed exposé work for Hearst in New York, was sent to Chicago. Watson was as tough and resourceful as Keeley, and soon a headline war for readership was on. At times Hearst had two managing editors simultaneously, as when Arthur L. Clarke, later managing editor of the *New York Daily News,* was sent to replace Moses Koenigsberg before someone thought to inform Koenigsberg that he was being relieved, but such complications did not impede Hearst as much as the total refusal of other Chicago publishers to allow the *American* on the crowded Chicago newsstands. Hearst circulators under Max and Moses Annenberg responded with rocks and clubs in an effort to intimidate vendors into cooperating. The circulation struggle in the streets was on and would continue for years, growing more vicious when Hearst came out with the *Morning American,* later designated the *Chicago Examiner,* and vowed to conquer the *Tribune.*

The guerrilla activity among the circulators in the field, including truck drivers, corner men and vendors—and, some said, a few specially hired sluggers—continued for years. It was almost never discussed publicly, however, until Robert R. McCormick took notice of past rumors in a WGN radio address. Speaking about his newspaper experiences on May 29, 1954, Colonel McCormick mentioned the "circulation wars," disavowing *Tribune* responsibility for them:

> While you can't write an ideal bill of health for the circulation departments of the newspapers concerned, the fundamental reason for the disturbances lay deeper than anything over which they had control. . . . Newsboys were being eliminated by the immigrant adolescent and adult. The fight was more between the incoming foreigner and the outgoing American than it was between newspapers.
>
> In 1912, the Chicago newspapers went through a strike of union employees. It grew out of a technical dispute in the pressrooms. When it spread, the teamsters and newsboys took it up and it became a bloody affair. Of course the newspapers employed men of violence at the time. Some of them afterward achieved criminal records. This fact has led to reports . . . of the Chicago newspaper wars, which were supposed to resemble the vendettas of early Italy.

Whatever may have been the causes of the newspaper struggle that extended through two decades, the *Chicago Tribune* from the beginning let its readers know it was not to be intimidated by Hearst, nor his political candidate in the 1900 presidential election, William Jennings Bryan. The *Tribune* had never cared for President McKinley, but it liked his running mate, New York's young governor Theodore Roosevelt. The paper detested Bryan, and it was not much better pleased with Adlai Stevenson for vice-president, though he was from Illinois. McKinley won by nearly 1 million votes over Bryan in the popular vote. Less than a year later, on September 6, 1901, McKinley was shot by Leon Czolgosz, a confessed anarchist, at the Pan American Exposition in Buffalo, and the ebullient Teddy Roosevelt became president. He pleased the *Tribune* with his initial message, promising to regulate the trusts and big corporations, and within a few months his trust-busting activities began.

Meantime, Keeley proved that he could out-Hearst Hearst in pleasing readers. Chicago's crime provided a rich lode, especially in the Levee district, where there were nightly shootings, robberies, kidnappings, and occasional scandals involving playboys, from a Prussian prince to a scion of a leading family who allegedly was shot to death in the famous Everleigh Club, one of the most elegant bordellos in the country. The papers were beginning to treat the peccadilloes of the red-light district, short of murder, as amusing recreational reading. This was especially true of the antics of Bathhouse John and Hinky Dink and their strumpet and hoodlum friends, particularly their annual First Ward Ball, the cotillion where madams and wine merchants exhibited their finest wares not only for habitués of the demimonde, but for many of the town's business, civic, and political leaders. Bathhouse John Coughlin, who led the grand march clad in a dress coat of billiard-cloth green plus lavender pants and mauve vest, was nationally known for his escapades, as well as his "poetry," most of which was actually written by *Tribune* reporter John Kelley.

The *Tribune* continued to maintain its supremacy in coverage of business news and in personal service features. And when a big news story broke, its superior facilities and the ingenuity of its staff prevailed. There was such a story—a tragic one—the Wednesday afternoon of December 30, 1903. Hundreds of children were present in the Iroquois Theater for a performance of *Mr. Bluebeard* when Eddie Foy, in his grotesque costume, stepped forward on the stage to call out, "Please be quiet. There is no danger." The applauding audience was unaware that a strip of gauze on the proscenium arch had caught fire and ignited the scenery in the "fireproof" theater. The orchestra played at Foy's nod, but the crowd panicked when some of the burning fragments floated into the auditorium. Soon flames raged across the orchestra pit and into the theater dome. It was later learned that the asbestos fire curtain, which might have protected the crowd, jammed on its way down. Within 15 minutes hundreds were dead, scores of them children.

All of the Chicago papers covered the story with the kind of journalistic skill that was the trademark of Chicago publications, but it was Keeley who most effectively evoked the true horror of the tragedy. "I want the names," he told city editor Beck, "I want all the names." It seemed an impossible assignment. The hundreds of dead and injured were in a score of morgues and hospitals. Most of the victims were women and children, less likely to have personal identification with them, and many were from out of town. But the entire editorial staff of the paper participated in the effort to obtain names and addresses while also obtaining the details of the fire, interviews with survivors, pictures, and a dozen side stories. On December 31, the impossible had been done. Under a page-wide headline, "FIRE IN THE IROQUOIS THEATER KILLS 571 AND INJURES 350 PERSONS," most of the names of the known dead, with addresses and, in many cases, ages, were listed. The paper devoted six full pages to the tragedy and two part pages. Other newspapers covered the Iroquois fire well, but none matched the emotional impact of the *Tribune*'s stark list of names. In the same issue an editorial offered its sympathy to the kin of the victims and began a campaign for fireboxes in the theaters—the Iroquois had none—and more efficient fire curtains and fire prevention installations.

The constant alertness of Keeley to news opportunities was well demonstrated by one of the paper's major local scoops, appearing the morning of December 18, 1905. The *Tribune* was a longtime enemy of John R. Walsh, an entrepreneur and exploiter who was a close friend of Yerkes and had bought the evening *Chronicle* in an effort to help the traction and other monopoly interests. Walsh also owned two banks. On the night of December 17, Keeley, having worked late as usual, saw lights in the office of the First National Bank Building. Inquiring of a friendly policeman at the bank's door, he learned that a business meeting was in progress. Keeley decided to include himself, entered the bank's boardroom, and found several of Chicago's leading financiers present. A few, knowing him to be a *Tribune* editor, regarded him with suspicion, but Keeley conducted himself as if he had been sent for, and they soon resumed their discussion, which concerned Walsh's troubles and the imminent closure of his banks. After a time, Keeley excused himself to go to the washroom. There he found a bucket and slouched past a guard. "They want some coffee," he explained. Back at the *Tribune*, Keeley stopped the presses, dictated his story, and had a scoop on the failure of the Walsh banks. The *Chronicle* collapsed also and Walsh, convicted on embezzlement charges, went to prison.

Keeley had his own list of tipsters whom he paid from his contingent account. Often he would instruct a reporter to "be there"—a certain place at a certain time—without divulging the action to be expected. Usually there was news, sometimes of a violent sort, as when a persecuted wife shot her husband. Keeley believed it was a newsman's duty to report what happened, not to attempt to intervene, but he also barred the publication of some stories on the grounds that they would injure a reputation needlessly, or cost a life.

In 1906 one of his tipsters launched Keeley into a fantastic adventure, and the managing editor would himself intervene to pull off yet another scoop. Paul Stensland, a leader in the Norwegian community and a prominent Chicagoan who had been a director of the World's Columbian Exposition, was president of the Milwaukee Avenue State Bank, with $5 million in assets and 20,000 depositors. When Stensland, considered one of the city's most honorable men, and George Hering, the bank's cashier, disappeared along with more than a million dollars, all Chicago was stunned. A Keeley tipster told him where Hering was hiding, and Keeley found the cashier on the verge of suicide, obtained his confession, and turned him over to the police. Hering was convicted and sent to prison. He had told Keeley that Stensland intended to go to North Africa. Keeley followed some leads fruitlessly, then assigned men to keep watch on Stensland's son, Theodore, who was not suspected in the bank case. When Theodore received a cable in Norwegian from Tangier, signed Paul Olson, Keeley became convinced that it was from Paul Stensland. He obtained copies of the indictments, and letters from the state's attorney and governor requesting the return of Stensland. Then he told his friends and family that he was going to Canada on a fishing trip. Keeley sailed for Europe from Montreal, took an express from Paris to Gibraltar, and was soon in Tangier. But he was unable to find Stensland.

Keeley learned that Stensland had gone to Spain. He acquired a guide, Mohammed Hamdushi, who, after prowling the criminal hang-outs, reported that Stensland was in Gibraltar. It was Sunday, but Keeley induced a captain of a small boat to take him to Gibraltar, where he learned that Paul Olson had gone to Mogador, about eight days' journey down the coast of Africa. But Olson had left only an hour before, on the German vessel *Oldenburg*. "Well, the fat was in the fire!" Keeley said later. "In Tangier and on the boat I was so sure of my man I had written 3,000 words, with an introduction saying a *Chicago Tribune* reporter had found the fugitive." Before sending his cable back to Chicago, at a cost of $1,200, he changed his story to say the *Tribune* reporter was close on the trail of Stensland. Keeley now hired a small Spanish steamer with a crew of ten to pursue the *Oldenburg*. "I could see that the captain was a born kidnapper," he remarked. There was a storm, and the *Oldenburg* put in at Tangier. Keeley went ashore, found his guide, Hamdushi, and induced him to pay the port health officer to board the *Oldenburg* and take Hamdushi along to see if Stensland was aboard.

Hamdushi soon returned from the *Oldenburg* to report that Stensland was indeed aboard. Now all Keeley could do was wait; if Stensland came ashore during the layover, Keeley would not have to trail the *Oldenburg* to Mogador. Shortly, a small boat put off from the German vessel and pulled alongside the pier; among those who clambered ashore was Stensland. Keeley followed him to the post office, where Stensland claimed the mail for Paul Olson. As he was signing, Keeley stepped up. "Write your own name, Stensland," Keeley said, "and make your next address Chicago, not Mogador." Stensland surrendered meekly, and Keeley had his story. Since there was no extradition treaty, Stensland could not be forced to leave, but after several days Keeley talked him into going back. "He was a fine, fascinating old chap who fell among thieves and fled, foolishly, when his bank was solvent," Keeley wrote. Though Stensland was convicted, he was soon paroled, since Keeley persuaded Samuel Insull to give him a job.

*   *   *

James Keeley, whose formal education had ended at the American equivalent of eighth grade, was among the first newsmen to actualize Joseph Medill's belief that the industry should encourage the establishment of schools of journalism. He lectured occasionally at Notre Dame University in South Bend and for a time was honorary dean of the journalism department. He set forth his own credo in his first lecture at Notre Dame. After quoting Arthur Brisbane's assertion that a newspaper mirrors its public, Keeley said:

> I believe, however, that the real newspaper has outgrown the looking-glass stage as the sole object of its existence. . . . The editor of a paper who conceives his whole duty to be the printing of the news and commenting sagely or foolishly thereon, according to the viewpoint of his readers, probably would shiver with disgust and repel with indignation some of my suggestions. . . . The big development of the modern newspaper will be along lines of personal service. The newspaper that not only informs and instructs its readers but is of service is the one that commands attention, gets circulation, and also holds its readers after it gets them.

Keeley practiced what he taught. In his 15 years as managing editor and then general manager of the *Tribune* he started many new "personal service" features, most of which endured for years, some still being used. He induced Dr. William A. Evans, Chicago health commissioner, to write a daily "How to Keep Well" column, which later became widely syndicated and imitated, so that such a column appears in most American newspapers today, and many abroad. Recognizing the high value of the column, the *Tribune* made sure that it continued to be conducted by distinguished medical men, Dr. Irving S. Cutter, and, following Dr. Cutter's death, Dr. Theodore Van Dellen. Keeley hired Bert Leston Taylor to conduct "A Line O' Type or Two," a highly popular column of humor, verse, and quips, most of which was submitted by readers. He engaged Lillian Russell, the buxom, famed American actress, to write on charm and beauty care; and Laura Jean Libbey, a widely known writer of stories for women's magazines, to edit an "Advice to the Lovelorn" column. Keeley told a friend he had to pay each woman "more than a justice of the United States Supreme Court," but their columns brought in readers and vast quantities of mail. He declared to his Notre Dame audience in 1912 that Libbey had received 50,000 letters in two years. "Over 200 young women have written and acknowledged that her words of warning saved them from taking the irretrievable false step which often confronts the friendless girl in a large city," he claimed. Another department, Marion Harland's "Helping Hand," helped people exchange used household articles, including those of a medical nature, such as trusses, abdominal supports, and crutches. In addition, said Keeley, "Over a dozen orphans have found homes through Mrs. Harland's efforts." The column continued for many years under the name of Sally Joy Brown.

The *Tribune* department Keeley thought epitomized the personal service concept was "The Friend of the People," where readers could write in their complaints, what Keeley called "the simple annals of a broken sidewalk, street lamps that fail to light the way, insanitary alleys, unlighted halls in tenements, uncollected garbage . . . the petty burdens of the poor and uninfluential. . . . It would astonish you to observe the celerity with which 'The Friend of the People' gets results."

Service features appearing seasonally included "The Good Fellow" campaign, launched in 1909 to provide Christmas baskets for the needy. In 1899, the Keeleys' daughter Dorothy was critically ill, and her physician told the family the girl's life was endangered by the uproar of fireworks accompanying Chicago's Independence Day festivities. The following year Keeley began a crusade for "a Sane Fourth," which after more than 30 years helped achieve the outlawing of the general sale of fireworks in most states. The *Tribune,* like most other newspapers, had for years published the advertisements of "doctors" making fraudulent claims, especially appealing to victims of venereal disease. Keeley sent out reporters pretending various illnesses, including VD, helped to convict a number of quack doctors, and caused their advertising to be barred from the paper. It cost the paper $200,000 a year in lost revenue, actual and potential, he declared.

Since columns and special services were successful elsewhere in the paper, Keeley decided to try them in the sports pages. He launched an "In the Wake of the News" column, something like Taylor's "Line O' Type" column, but relating to sports; its first editor was Hugh E. Keough. Harvey Woodruff was hired as "sporting editor"; Walter Eckersall, a former University of Chicago football star, was employed to help the reader understand the popular new sport; John T. McCutcheon, the brilliant young cartoonist and writer, was lured away from the *Record-Herald* at a price higher than editorial cartoonists had previously known; and Burton Rascoe became the *Tribune*'s knowledgeable and acidulous drama critic, whose most venomous attacks did not appear in the paper but were directed at James Keeley, a man he professed to detest.

*   *   *

Keeley, respected by the Tribune Company directors and recognized as an editorial genius by his peers, was both a beneficiary and a victim of the confused ownership situation that followed the death of Joseph Medill. The directors considered providing stock options to Keeley, but dared not disturb a delicate balance of power resulting from strife between Joseph Medill's daughters. Katherine (Aunt Kate), wife of trustee Robert S. McCormick and the mother of Medill and Robert, had ambitions for her sons, as did her sister Elinor (Aunt Nellie), wife of trustee and editor-in-chief Robert W. Patterson, for her son, Joseph. The third trustee, Beale, refereed and generally determined the voting of the Medill stock. So intense was the antagonism between the two sisters, noted John McCutcheon, that the *Chicago Tribune* paymaster had a standing order to keep each sister informed as to the whereabouts of the other so that there would be no accidental confrontation, and especially not in Chicago. Elinor bitterly resented criticisms of the paper's editorial policies by Katherine. Aunt Kate, in turn, saw Aunt Nellie's animadversions as a personal attack on her candidate for dominance over the paper's affairs, her firstborn, Medill McCormick. The embattled sisters frequently communicated through their sons Robert and Joe after the young men had graduated from college and returned to Chicago, always warning them that they should not allow any criticism from the family to reach the ears of James Keeley. So while the family wrangled, outsiders such as Beale and Azariah T. Galt, also an attorney and a trustee of the Bross estate, were elected to preside over Tribune Company affairs when Robert Patterson and later Medill McCormick found it necessary to seek refuge in European spas from time to time to regain their health.

It had been anticipated from the day of his birth that Medill Mc-Cormick would be the family representative who in time would lead the *Tribune.* He was the first of the Medill grandsons to attend Groton School in Massachusetts and Yale University and to join the staff of the paper. This he did immediately following his graduation from Yale in 1900, starting out as a police reporter, then serving for a time as correspondent in China and the Philippines. On a visit to Grandfather Joseph Medill at Thomasville, Georgia, Medill met and wooed Ruth Hanna, daughter of the Ohio Republican boss Mark Hanna. They were married in 1903, and young McCormick soon thereafter obtained an interest in the *Cleveland Leader,* founded by his grandfather, and became a co-publisher of the *Leader* and its afternoon paper, the *News,* at the same time serving as a corporate officer of the *Chicago Tribune*—he was elected treasurer in 1904. Medill McCormick gave up his Cleveland interests in early 1907 for full-time work in Chicago, where he did well in the business department of the paper, to which he was restricted since Robert Patterson continued to be the editor-in-chief. Medill McCormick decided that the *Tribune* no longer could disdain advertising solicitors, as it had done under Joseph Medill. He set about reorganizing the business and advertising departments.

On May 6, 1907, Medill's hard work was rewarded. He was made vice-president, secretary, and treasurer of Tribune Company, and his salary was set at $20,000 a year, considerably more than Patterson's $15,000. Patterson, of course, shared income from his wife's fortune, while Medill McCormick owned a single share of *Tribune* stock. An executive committee, with advisory functions and chaired by Beale, was formed. The directors appeared to be preparing for the departure of Patterson, who was away frequently for long periods because of illness or fatigue. In 1908 Medill's services again were recognized by the board. He continued as vice-president, secretary, treasurer, and in addition was made auditor and assistant editor-in-chief. Patterson, however, did not retire as anticipated. Instead he raised the rancor between the two Medill sisters by intervening when he learned that Katherine wanted the *Tribune* to help her husband obtain a new ambassadorship. In early 1907 Robert S. McCormick had resigned as U.S. ambassador to France, where he had been transferred—some said demoted—in 1905 after two and a half years in Russia. In August, 1908, Patterson wrote Republican presidential nominee William Howard Taft that his brother-in-law in no way represented the *Tribune,* nor was the paper interested in obtaining a new diplomatic appointment for him.

Patterson's position with the *Tribune* was abruptly strengthened by the nervous collapse of Medill McCormick. On November 18, 1908, a special meeting of the directors was called to receive Medill's request for a two months' leave of absence. Three directors attended, Beale, Cowles, and Galt, with Galt presiding. Medill McCormick's need for a rest was recognized, and the young editor and his wife left almost at once for Europe. Patterson was vacationing in Cuba, so pending the return of McCormick or Patterson, Keeley, by resolution, was placed in charge of all company affairs, subject to the approval of the board, which in that period supervised the smallest details of company business. Patterson and Beale were soon approached by Victor Lawson, offering to buy the *Tribune,* and throughout 1909 the negotiations cautiously continued.

*   *   *

In February, 1909, Medill McCormick was back at the paper, seemingly in excellent health and prepared to resume his arduous work schedule. The new advertising department, which he had reorganized, was developing rapidly under the able but erratic Harrison Parker, the paper's full-time advertising director. It helped to power the Sunday paper of February 7, 1909, which, with seven special sections prepared in honor of the centenary of Abraham Lincoln's birth (February 12, 1809), totaled 194 pages. This was the largest issue of the *Tribune* to that time, and in a page-one boxed banner it styled itself "The Greatest Issue of the World's Greatest Newspaper." Managing editor Keeley and the promotion department picked up the phrase "The World's Greatest Newspaper," using it in advertising from time to time. The phrase was later registered as a trademark, and on August 29, 1911, it became a fixture on the masthead every day. The widely known promotional slogan was not discontinued until nearly 66 years later, on January 1, 1977.

In addition to covering the news and including regular *Tribune* features, among them a McCutcheon cartoon on page one, the Lincoln centenary issue showcased most of its new writers and artists, presented a detailed biography of Lincoln, offered the most complete display of Lincoln photographs to appear in print up to that time, and presented a history of the Civil War period and numerous Lincoln anecdotes. Lincoln's centennial was obviously of local interest, for the paper noted that more than 200 Chicago meetings and observations in honor of the Great Emancipator would take place during the ensuing week. Clifford Raymond wrote from Washington on the national significance of the occasion, and there were dispatches on the subject from other cities and cables from foreign capitals. The close association of Lincoln with the *Chicago Tribune* was, of course, thoroughly documented.

That Sunday issue of February 7 exemplified the technical perfection of the Keeley–Beck editorial regime, establishing basic journalistic patterns that would be changed in the *Tribune*, and then moderately, only by "the Great War" and the advent of Robert R. McCormick and Joseph M. Patterson into full power. The typography was clean, sedate, attractive. The banner headlines and wildly mixed typefaces of the Spanish-American War period were gone, not to be reintroduced until 1913, at which time banner headlines became a permanent fixture. Halftone printing had been perfected, and photographs were profusely used, with accent on action, especially on the sports pages. In addition the editors showed imagination: A report from Philadelphia saying that Paderewski, the great Polish pianist, could not play because of a split fingernail on his right hand was illustrated with a photograph of the master playing vigorously, his right-hand fingers striking the keys, the injured finger indicated. That slight but unfortunate accident, the paper said, would cost an insurance company $5,000.

There was other news of less than universal significance, but evidencing the touch that led the *Tribune* to a circulation of a million in a later era. Women's suffrage was a hot issue of the day. The *Tribune* reported from New York that the eminent society personage, Mrs. Stuyvesant Fish, had told the National League for Civic Education for Women that women were not the equal of men and never would be. Nor should they have the vote. "I think too well of women," said Mrs. Fish, "to imagine that they can be benefitted by mixing in the mire of politics." The paper published rebuttals from Chicago suffrage leaders and also carried a report of their unique suggestion for combating smoke pollution. The *Tribune* had started a long-range campaign against polluters that was restraining some belching smokestacks during daylight hours, but, said the women, the offenders were burning their worst pollutants by night. Why not use some of the giant searchlights developed for the world's fair to light up the offending chimneys? The idea was a good one, the paper said, but there was no evidence of searchlights being used by the *Tribune* until 1912 when the paper employed them for promotional purposes.

The Lincoln issue included the paper's annual automobile show sections, which advertised half a hundred cars, tires, and other automotive equipment. The *Tribune* was not among the early supporters of the automobile, and for a time it had urged that autos should be barred from roads and parks, or at least limited to a speed of eight miles an hour. In 1900 there were only 90 automobiles in the city, but for the 1909 motor show in the Coliseum and the First Regiment Armory, 92 motor car manufacturers were listed as exhibitors, and more than 200,000 persons were expected to attend the six days and nights of showings, a total actually surpassed. The paper was by that year completely in support of the new industry. The auto section opened with a full-page halftone picture of a pert motorist in a duster, bonnet, and veil, standing before her vaguely outlined motor car. Inside there were endless pictures of autos, American and foreign makes, electric and gasoline-propelled, and a few steam cars. The automobiles, from the French Alco to the American Woods Electric, were with few exceptions open models and included such popular makes as the Stearns, Simplex, Locomobile, Mitchell, White Steamer, Rambler, Marmon, Packard, Cadillac, Stevens-Duryea, Babcock Electric, Chalmers, and Ford. Prices ranged from $850 for the Ford four-cylinder entry, later known as the "Tin Lizzy," to $10,000 for the big touring cars. It was the first exhibition of Ford's new Model T, which had gone into the production line in 1908. The few closed cars were the electric runabouts. Some autos boasted running boards and most had left-hand steering, both introduced by Charles Brady King. A few manufacturers still said their machines had "bonnets" over the engines, later called hoods.

That the automobile really had arrived was demonstrated by a news item on the front page, a report from Tampa, Florida, that William Jennings Bryan, the perennial Democratic presidential candidate, had been injured when the auto in which he was riding crashed into a bridge. Another item in the paper of an auto-age nature described the campaign of New York women to obtain segregated space in the new autobuses and the elevated cars to save them from crushing and leering stares as they were closely packed into public transportation among men.

That Sunday the *Tribune* announced that construction was beginning on the new Chicago and North Western Railway station at Madison and Canal streets, estimating it would accommodate 300 trains arriving and departing each day. *Tribune* sporting editor Harvey Woodruff telegraphed from California that Frank Chance, of the famous baseball double-play combination, intended to return to Chicago to fulfill his four-year contract with the two-times world champions, the Chicago Cubs. The sports department now had four pages of space each Sunday, complete with banner headlines, photographs, and its own cartoonist, Clare Briggs. Hugh Keough was conducting the "Wake of the News" column, to be followed in later years by Ring Lardner, Woodruff, Westbrook Pegler, Arch Ward, and David Condon. There were eight sections of the paper, of from four to 16 pages each, preceding the sections about Lincoln. One contained three and a half pages of comics, "Danny Dreams and Lil Silly Sally," drawn by Briggs; "Economical Bertie," a title destined for banishment; the highly popular "Mama's Angel Child"; "Old Opie Dilldock's Stories," a combination of cartoons and text; and "Pranks of the Four Paws," with animal characters. All, including the half page of advertising, seemed totally directed to children.

Part Seven of the special issue opened with a near orgy of Oriental art, replete with gems and harem girls, displayed against the porcelain towers of Bangkok, illustrating an article entitled "How to Manage a Wife as Told by the Royal Husband of 600." The article was based on British traveler Hartley Wentworth's interview with King Chulalongkorn, who as a young man was trained by a redoubtable English governess on the subject of women. His Royal Highness asserted that it was not at all difficult for him to get along with his 600 wives, nearly all young and beautiful, once he learned to understand them. The rest of the section covered entertainment, including the new motion pictures, many of which were being made in Chicago. The combination magazine–entertainment section was racy and bold. Not the least provocative of the illustrations was that portraying the beautiful Lillian Russell, who that week was appearing in *Wildfire* in a Chicago theater. There were 20 or more legitimate theaters, downtown and in the growing neighborhoods, and almost as many of the new nickelodeon and motion picture theaters. The February 7 paper carried two score of theater and film production advertisements, including a full page by the Selig Polyscope Company, showing a studio building that filled an entire block at Irving Park and Western avenues. Selig boasted that it made not only the world's best dramatic films but also fine adventure movies, and announced that it had a crew on location in Panama filming the visit of President-elect Taft to canal construction sites. It listed a number of successful pictures made in Chicago and "shown throughout the world," among them *The Squaw Man, The Squaw Man's Daughter, The French Spy, Rip Van Winkle, East Lynne, Tale of Two Cities,* and *The Road to Ruin.*

Finley Peter Dunne's "Mr. Dooley" occupied the front page of the editorial section, with a dissertation on the outgoing administration of President Theodore Roosevelt and his prospects for the future. The editorial page and "page opposite" presented the paper's tribute to Lincoln leading the editorials, religious news, and "guest editorials," the equivalent of the popular personal opinion columns of later years. Guests on February 7 were Ada May Krecker, Helen Oldfield, and London editor William T. Stead, who had been condemned by the *Tribune* a few years past when he published *If Christ Came to Chicago.* All wrote on general topics. The Marquise de Fontenoy, a fixture on the *Tribune* editorial page for two decades, delivered her usual commentary on European politics and gossip. The section closed with pseudoscience articles of the kind Hearst and Pulitzer had popularized in New York: "Are You Ticklish?" plus diagrams of brain and nervous centers; "If Bugs

Were the Size of a Man," with illustrations that would have delighted Kafka; a special article on money by Professor Frederic Starr of the University of Chicago; and one asking "Are You Married to Your Affinity?" dealing with astrology. In addition to the special Lincoln sections, the history of Chicago filled four pages of the Business and Financial section, "From Trading Post to Central Market."

The advertisements in the 194-page paper, many of them full-page size, reflected numerous developments in American life. No longer did the linage consist chiefly of classified advertisements, retail display ads, and ads for patent medicines. Following *Tribune* campaigns against patent medicine nostrums and quack doctors and dentists, most such advertising had disappeared from the paper's columns. But solicitation, research, and advertising promotion were paying off, contrary to the notions of Joseph Medill, who insisted until his last days that no respectable paper would actively seek to sell its space to advertisers. Major advertisements now related to automobiles, Goodyear and Goodrich tires, motion pictures, telephones, and Edison's phonograph, all new consumer items. Among the new, rich accounts were land companies and state governments lured by *Tribune* research that showed the paper's readers were relatively wealthy and could afford to buy city lots and western farms.

Section 19, Classified Advertising, closed the paper. The *Tribune* had led the Chicago classified market for years, soliciting want ad linage even in the days of Joseph Medill. It was, the paper boasted frequently, the biggest people's market in the country. Thousands of ads were obtained through the paper's front-page promotions and by salespeople calling on commercial accounts in person or by telephone. Over-the-counter sales at the *Tribune*'s public service office and through more than 30 agents in groceries and drugstores accounted for still more customers. Anyone in Chicago and its suburbs with access to a telephone could place a want ad in the *Tribune* simply by calling Central 100.

The week following the appearance of its special Lincoln issue, the *Tribune* proudly reported details of its achievement. The editorial staff had worked an entire year developing the product. The advertising department sold 1,355 columns of advertising. The production department set type for six weeks and cast 2,704 stereotype plates that impressed five tons of ink on 11,000 miles of newsprint. Twelve black-and-white presses and one color press were used. More than a hundred Lincoln portraits were examined for the illustrations used in the paper. Rare pictures and Lincoln manuscripts were found during the course of the historical preparation. The individual paper, which sold for 5¢, weighed three and a fourth pounds. Thousands of telegrams had been received from around the country, ordering extra copies. For days the

Tribune printed congratulatory messages from admiring newspaper editors and publishers.

Later in the year the *Tribune* would capitalize on its ability to attract land advertising by sponsoring a great land show to be held in the Coliseum, an exhibition which, during its brief life, attracted more people than the auto show. Harrison Parker, the advertising manager, devised the land show. Held in the Coliseum in late fall of 1909, it attracted thousands, but created a deficit of $40,000, which the *Tribune* paid. Though the paper was not too much harmed, since it sold thousands of lines of extra advertising to the exhibitors, the directors were reluctant to take the risk again, and Parker proposed that he should take the show over, together with a group of businessmen. At first the directors declined, but later they relented, accepted Parker's resignation, and allowed him to continue the land show, using the *Tribune* name.

The 1910 show was successful, but not sufficiently so to satisfy Parker. In 1911, to encourage ticket sales, he offered Michigan "town lots" in a lottery. The *Tribune* was embarrassed and its directors were furious when hundreds of "lucky winners" complained to the paper that their "town lots" were only 25 feet wide and located miles from any railroad. In a court action by the paper, Parker and his associates were put under bond to make restitution to the winners of the lots, and Parker was forbidden to use the *Tribune* name further. The *Tribune* resumed control of the show, continuing it in 1912 and 1913, running deficits both years despite large crowds. The bitter feud between the paper and its former employee lasted almost half a century, until Parker died in Washington, D.C., in 1961.

* * *

At a meeting of the board of directors on February 21, 1909, the appreciative and grateful *Tribune* proprietors voted their aggressive managing editor an annual raise of $5,000 and elected him a second vice-president of the company. But Keeley held no *Tribune* stock, he was not a company director, and even after his election as second vice-president, he continued to be outranked in the corporate hierarchy not only by Robert Patterson and Medill McCormick, but also by George P. Upton, the veteran editorial writer, Joseph Medill confidant, and former drama critic who owned ten shares of stock and had been a vice-president since 1891.

In addition, with Patterson's health not improving, the directors determined that the time had come for Medill McCormick to take active charge of the paper. Despite the fact that Keeley had worked closely with him and knew that his elevation was inevitable, and seemingly was himself admired by young McCormick, something must have snapped when the new acting editor moved into the former office of Robert W. Patterson. Things went smoothly for several months, but in September Keeley abruptly called city editor Beck before him, told Beck he was to take orders from McCormick, and announced that he, Keeley, was going on an extended vacation to Japan.

Introspective Medill McCormick did not appear happy in the newspaper business, but as the eldest grandson of Joseph Medill he felt required to undertake *Tribune* management duties and was eager to prove himself. He continued to be interested in upgrading the business and advertising departments and brought to the paper as business manager a Yale University classmate, Vermont-born William H. Field, recruited from one of the country's most successful magazine publishers, the Munsey Company in New York. McCormick promised Field $18,000 a year, then found to his consternation that the directors declined to authorize any such amount. Medill stormed until he won out, a fortunate victory, because Field's business genius matched Keeley's ability in the editorial area. Medill's relations with the directors obviously continued to be good, for his own pay was raised to $30,000 a year.

An ardent follower of Theodore Roosevelt and a Progressive, Medill McCormick had nonetheless been as shocked as the rest of the family when his cousin Joe Patterson announced that he was a Socialist. Nor had he approved of Keeley's sometimes amused coverage of the city's red-light district. Instead, Medill McCormick directed Beck to assign the staff to dig up the names of all respectable persons and business institutions in Chicago or elsewhere who derived income from lands or structures used for prostitution and gambling or other illegal activity. It was a large order. The reporters dug and probed for weeks, and Teddy Beck, fearing such a crusade would spell disaster for the *Tribune* and hoping for Keeley's reappearance to put a stop to the plan, allowed them ample time to make sure their information was correct and complete. Day by day new names and addresses and data were added to a thick red book that, one reporter suggested, read increasingly like Chicago's *Bon Ton* social directory.

Beck, having received word that Keeley was about to return, delayed printing the hundreds of names he had gathered. When Keeley asked to be brought up to date, Beck showed him the book. It was late at night, and Keeley was standing near Beck in the composing room, somewhat apoplectically turning the pages and grinding down a series of cigars, when Medill McCormick came in, in opera cape and hat. According to Keeley's biographer Linn, McCormick laid down his hat and stick on a composing stone, put his arms around Keeley, welcoming him home, and laughed. The following day Medill McCormick left Chicago for Switzerland; the fate of the red book was never known. Keeley was again in effective charge of the paper, and after Robert W. Patterson died on April 1, 1910, James Keeley took over as general manager of the *Chicago Tribune* by order of the directors. Meantime, he had already begun to uncover the biggest story of his career.

*   *   *

It began simply enough. In March, 1910, not long after Medill McCormick's departure left him in charge of the *Tribune,* Keeley was talking with State Representative Charles A. White about a manuscript White had offered via one of the Keeley tipsters. White wanted $50,000 for the document, which he claimed would prove that in 1909 certain Illinois legislators had been bribed to vote for William Lorimer, the "Blond Boss" of Republican politics and a top *Tribune* enemy, as U.S. senator. After thoroughly investigating the charges contained in White's manuscript (for which he paid $3,250), Keeley ordered out the paper's biggest type to play the story on April 30: "DEMOCRATIC LEGISLATOR CONFESSES HE WAS BRIBED TO CAST VOTE FOR LORIMER FOR UNITED STATES SENATOR."

Keeley wrote the headlines and dictated most of the story. The rise of Lorimer from streetcar conductor to political boss was described, as well as his political relations, associations, and sources of money and power. He had seemed a quiet, virtuous man to most when in May, 1909, after a five-month deadlock, the legislature named him to the Senate on the 95th ballot. Lorimer promptly responded to Keeley's charges by asserting that the *Tribune* ran the exposé because Washington correspondent Raymond Patterson, brother of Robert, wanted to be a U.S. senator himself, and because the *Tribune* did not like Lorimer's recent vote on a wood pulp tariff. The U.S. Senate was shocked, as were most Illinois Republicans and even the reform newspapers, which of course did not have documentation to support or deny the *Tribune* story. Keeley's story said that the *Tribune* possessed the proof and would submit it to proper authorities. The documents included the sworn confession of Charles White, asserting that he had received $1,900 in bribes, and naming others.

Lorimer insisted that White, also a former streetcar conductor, but in East St. Louis, had tried to blackmail him of $75,000 with the story. He threatened a libel suit. A leading national magazine had turned the story down. James Keeley owned no part of the *Tribune* and would not be endangered if Senator Lorimer sued for libel, but the McCormick and Patterson families, as well as Cowles and other stockholders, were highly vulnerable. The case dragged on for months without action, the *Tribune* demanding daily an investigation by the Senate and learning how difficult it would be to obtain any such action by "the world's most exclusive club." Robert McCormick and Joseph Patterson also had company positions, McCormick as treasurer and Patterson as secretary of Tribune Company. Their property and careers were at stake, but both stood by Keeley.

The *Tribune* would not be silenced. It had information that a wealthy lumberman had put up some of the bribe money and that meat-packers also were involved. Daily it asked: "Who put up the money for Senator Lorimer's election?" "Who furnished the sawdust?" "Who provided the grease to lubricate the wheels of the senatorial chariot?" McCutcheon's first cartoon on the Lorimer affair showed the senator in a huge chair covered with dollar signs, behind a desk papered with $1,000 bills. When Lorimer declared he was a victim of a conspiracy, McCutcheon returned with a drawing of the "conspirators," including President Taft, Theodore Roosevelt, William Jennings Bryan, and a massive book labeled "The Evidence." Papers about the country came to the support of the *Tribune.* Lorimer attempted to resurrect the school board lease scandal, but that issue had been thoroughly ventilated. *Tribune* circulation boomed.

Lee O'Neil Browne, one of the legislators charged with handing out bribes, went on trial June 8, 1910, but the judge barred his confession and there was a hung jury. The *Tribune* offered $5,000 for legal proof against Browne that would stand in court, but none was obtained, and in a second trial the legislator was acquitted. A juror told a grand jury that he had been bribed to vote not guilty; Lorimer's lawyer was tried twice, and acquitted. Despite all Keeley's efforts, it appeared that Lorimer might in fact weather the storm, and in March, 1911, the U.S. Senate voted to allow Lorimer to retain his seat. Then Herman H. Kohlsaat, publisher of the *Record-Herald,* came up with his own scoop when he revealed that Clarence Funk, general manager of International Harvester Company, had confided that he had been asked for $10,000, part of a $100,000 fund "to put Lorimer over." Funk named the representatives of the alleged bribe committee, which included packers and lumbermen and involved tariff considerations.

The libel suits against the *Tribune* piled up. The U.S. Senate at last was prodded into action by the Illinois legislature and by Senator La Follette of Wisconsin. More than 5 million words of testimony were taken in the Senate investigation. Keeley himself was called before the Senate on July 24, 1911. "What is your present employment?" he was asked.

Keeley—I am editor of the *Chicago Tribune.*
Q.—Are you the chief managing editor of that publication?
Keeley—I am general managing editor.
Q.—What is your authority and duty?

Keeley—My authority is absolute.

Q.—In all departments?

Keeley—In all departments.

Q.—Do you direct the editorial policies?

Keeley—Now I do, yes.

Q.—What was your authority in the year 1910?

Keeley—The same as now.

Q.—Throughout the year?

Keeley—About the latter part of February, 1910, or the first of March, I should say, I was placed in control of the property. Before that time I was managing editor—subordinate to Mr. Medill McCormick.

Q.—And since that time?

Keeley—I repeat, my authority is absolute.

Finally, on July 13, 1912, the U.S. Senate voted to unseat William Lorimer. On July 15 the *Tribune* published a quietly triumphant editorial:

> So far as Mr. Lorimer is concerned, he is no longer a United States Senator. . . . The *Tribune*, which presented the first disclosures by publishing the narrative of Charles A. White, April 30, 1910, did not need the justification of the senate vote which declared the seat vacant. No justification was needed for publishing the truth and insisting upon it in spite of discouragement and malice.
>
> The public knows little of the methods adopted by the defense in efforts to stop not only the *Tribune*, but other newspapers, public officials, and citizens from doing their duty in the matter. . . . It is the belief of the *Tribune* that the whole miserable story will come out some day. . . . The crimes committed to protect the men responsible for the crime of May 26, 1909 [*the day of Lorimer's selection by the Illinois legislature*], have been as low and despicable as the original crime itself. Some of them have revealed a far lower morality than that of the briber and bribe taker.
>
> A great deal of good already has come out of this fight against organized corruption. Citizens who have been patient to follow as complications were unravelled and as men were dragged out from shadows are better equipped to understand the relations of corrupt politics and corrupt business. When the secrets were opened up the stench offended and disgusted many people, including some respectable people who wished for the sake of their own peace of mind they might have been spared the knowledge.

The paper then commended those who persevered in the case against Lorimer, who appeared in courts before the Senate, and finally those who voted for his unseating. And it reiterated that the importance of the case was the ability of an American newspaper to print the truth so the people might know, a right seemingly threatened many times during the course of Lorimer litigation and the voting in the U.S. Senate, a vote that supported the election of Lorimer though it had been taken before all the evidence was in.

The action of the Senate richly enhanced the *Tribune*'s reputation as a guardian of the public interest and a defender of the free press, and it was in many ways a personal triumph for James Keeley. He had acted without consulting his superiors, thus causing the financially liable stockowners many anxious months as lawsuits were instituted. But he had turned out to be right in his judgment of the Lorimer case evidence, the legal actions against the paper were dismissed, and the senator was driven from office and from political leadership in Illinois, thus realizing *Tribune* threats made in the days of the Allen traction legislation. Nonetheless, even as he testified before the Senate in 1911, Keeley perhaps more than anyone else must have realized that his "absolute authority" over the paper's affairs and policies was only temporary. The heirs of Joseph Medill were preparing to make the *Tribune* again a family affair.

THE YOUNG
PROGRESSIVES

16

Medill McCormick, his brother Robert, and their cousin Joseph Patterson were to bring a new way of thinking into the *Chicago Tribune* and Tribune Company after a long period of difficulties and family strife following the death of Joseph Medill. The young men reflected in part the liberal posture of many sons of the newly rich and powerful who had the advantages of education in the country's leading seaboard colleges. The McCormicks additionally spent much of their early lives abroad. They accompanied their parents to London in 1889, when their father was appointed to the American legation, and both entered Ludgrove, a preparatory school in Middlesex. Contrary to later assertions by some of his critics, Robert McCormick was happy there. His grades were good, he acquired an English accent, learned to play cricket, and seemed much like the average upper-class English schoolboy. It was Medill, a quiet, thoughtful young man, less interested in sports than his younger brother, who appeared anxious to leave England. The brothers later went to Paris, where they were tutored, and they lived briefly with their parents in the austere but stimulating atmosphere of the American diplomatic communities of Vienna and Petrograd, as Robert S. McCormick was named minister and later ambassador to the elegant courts of the Hapsburgs and Czar Nicholas. The young men returned to America to enter Groton, which "Bertie," as Robert was called by the family, disliked. He was not sorry when he contracted pneumonia, getting the opportunity to spend much of the winter with Joseph Medill in Thomasville, Georgia. Thereafter McCormick absented himself from school whenever possible to accompany his grandfather, and he was with him at the time of Joseph Medill's death in 1899. Later that year McCormick entered Yale, graduating in 1903. He traveled to Central America, then thought briefly of entering the newspaper business. But he felt his presence at the *Tribune* would be coolly received, so he studied law at Northwestern University instead.

At the time some of Chicago's political leaders were finding it useful to support sons of wealthy families in so-called blue stocking wards for minor public office. George F. Harding, rising Republican boss on the South Side, had backed William Hale Thompson, well known as an athlete but a newcomer to politics, for the city council in 1900. In 1904, Fred Busse, the Republican North Side boss, induced young Robert McCormick, a first-year law student, to run for the council from the 21st Ward, and McCormick was elected. He discovered that he liked politics, and he was quite aware that his family and newspaper connections made a career in Illinois politics feasible. Deciding that he could become governor of Illinois, he ran for president of the Sanitary District of Chicago as a step up and won the election in 1905. It was a highly potent political job with extensive patronage and responsibility. The district's vast drainage and disposal system, which combined with various sewage disposal plants completed later to form one of the modern wonders of the world, was carried forward under McCormick's direction. He drove himself and other men hard. When contractors appeared about to fail to meet deadlines for a North Shore canal and a dam and power plant at Lockport, McCormick found legal ways to cancel the contracts and to complete the work with Sanitary District workers, engineers, and foremen, one of them Edward J. Kelly, who later became mayor of Chicago. This experiment in semisocialism McCormick preferred to ignore in later years when he became the country's leading anti-Socialist.

That McCormick had worried about the affairs of the *Tribune* while he was engaged in his political and law career was indicated in letters to his parents. Reporting still another rumor of Robert W. Patterson's anticipated retirement, he wrote to his parents:

> The report is RW is about to retire. I find my feelings are not unmixed with anxiety. . . . I do not care who shall hold office of president or title of editor. . . . I am interested only in how we are going to see that that man conserves the property. I gave up my journalistic ambitions some years ago when I saw that I would not be welcomed in the office and that my presence there would cause friction. . . . Since then I have journeyed far enough on my own two feet to know that the editor of a paper is not the only big man in the world. . . . Your loving son, Bertski.

And later, in an undated letter with only 1907 showing in the postmark, Robert R. observed, "*If old quarrels can be forgotten, present necessities will soon cause an entente between the two families."* He began to talk with his cousin Joe Patterson about the property and to think of his own potential role as a peacemaker. Aunt Nellie, especially, seemed to welcome Bert's good offices. She was ready to sell the paper, however, since it appeared that her son Joe was not about to disavow his unacceptable political views.

*   *   *

Joseph Medill Patterson preferred to be called Joe and superficially appeared to be the exact opposite of Robert Rutherford McCormick. Joe was affable, democratic, a free thinker, and he seemed to enjoy the company of common people more than the social and club life into which he had been born. Both Joe and Robert shared Joseph Medill's tough stubbornness, his flair for new ideas of a pragmatic nature, and his idealism, though the two grandsons differed almost completely when it came to their ideas concerning economics, government, and the social system. Joe Patterson, like the McCormicks, attended Groton and was graduated from Yale, traveled during vacations—Patterson to work as a cowboy in Mexico and Wyoming—and like his cousin Bert, Joe entered politics young. Patterson started as a reporter on the *Tribune* in 1901. He soon was promoted to assistant editorial superintendent, a potent title from Medill days, and assistant Sunday editor.

Patterson was an able writer and editor. He felt he knew what the readers wanted and he frequented one-armed lunchrooms and work- ingmen's bars to keep in touch. Early in 1905 he and Keeley launched the *Tribune*'s *Workers' Magazine.* A subtitle said the supplement was "For the Man Who Works with Hand and Brain," but after a few do-it-yourself issues it concentrated attention on livelier subjects. His somewhat lurid approach to the Sunday magazine and other Sunday sectional articles was an advance on the Keeley technique that Keeley subsequently retained, but it did not at all please Joe's father, Robert Patterson, the editor- in-chief, nor his mother, Elinor, so Patterson was transferred to the news department. Meantime, in 1903 he had been elected as a Republican to the Illinois legislature.

In the state legislature Patterson demonstrated his political independ- ence by joining a group of public ownership men supporting the Mueller Bill, authorizing Chicago to buy out the public transportation lines. The methods of the traction lobbyists and their political friends to block the bill exasperated Patterson and his friends to the point that they created a near riot in the legislature, tossing chairs and inkwells. The Mueller Bill passed. Judge Edward F. Dunne, Democratic candidate for mayor of Chicago, said he would use the act to enable the city to take its first step toward municipal ownership. That was good enough for Joe Patterson. On a March day in 1905, while his father was in Washington for the inauguration of Theodore Roosevelt, Patterson appeared at a rally for Dunne. "Capitalism has seen the end of its days as we have known it," said young Patterson as one of the speakers. He turned his back to the crowd and pointed to imaginary handwriting on the wall and intoned the Biblical words foretelling the doom of Babylon, "Mene, mene, tekel, upharsin" ("Thou art weighed and found wanting."). Then Patterson said a few good words for some capitalists, explaining that they were unaware of the evils of the system. He declared himself for Dunne for mayor.

The shock waves reached Robert Patterson in a hurry, and spread all the way to Paris. Patterson hurried to Chicago, called a special meeting of the *Tribune*'s board of directors, and presented Joe's resignation, which was accepted at once. On March 21, Ambassador Robert McCormick, a director and trustee, cabled William Beale, chairman of the executive committee: "WHAT MEANING JOE RETIREMENT. HOW AFFECTED FATHER. WRITE FULLY." Before Beale could respond, a letter followed, indicating that McCormick had further facts. "*I have received a brief and laconic letter from Rutherford,*" he wrote, using the name Robert R. disliked.

> [It] *says no more than that Joe has resigned his position on the* Tribune *and taken the stump for Dunne and municipal ownership. Knowing the latter's extreme opinions on social economy as well as I did, I must confess that this extreme step nevertheless surprises me very much and I regret it deeply on the boy's account. . . . It seems to me that this extreme step of Joe's should settle once and for all the question of who shall be the one man to assume the management of the* Tribune, *directing its policy and keeping a hand on business policy as well, when Robert Patterson retires from that position.*

The man Ambassador McCormick had in mind was of course his son Medill, and the next several pages of the letter to Beale recited Medill's qualifications and suggested that Medill should be made a vice-president, as eventually was done.

Joseph Patterson was not quite finished, however. After serving ably for a year as Chicago public works commissioner under Mayor Dunne, ousting bureaucrats and grafters he said were trying to cheat the city, Patterson surprised Dunne with his decision to quit. On February 28, 1906, while he was in Washington, Commissioner Patterson dispatched a letter of resignation to Dunne that also proclaimed his personal political manifesto:

> *It was through a common belief in the cause of municipal ownership of municipal utilities that I first became acquainted with you, and I desire publicly to express just how my views on this subject have changed.* They have not diminished. They have enlarged. *I used to believe that many of the ills under which the nation suffers*

and by which it is threatened would be prevented by the general inauguration of the public ownership of public utilities. But my experience in the department of public works has convinced me that the policy would not be even one-fourth of the way sufficient.

Patterson discussed at length the progress of political and social reforms in various European countries, especially Great Britain and Germany; he praised Mayor Dunne but pointed to his deficiencies also, and concluded: *"In other words, as I understand it, I am a Socialist. I have hardly read a book on Socialism, but that which I have enunciated I believe in general to be their theory. If it is their theory, I am a Socialist. . . . You will find, and other advanced liberals and radicals who believe as you do also will find that you are merely pottering around with skin deep measures when you stop short of Socialism."*

The Patterson letter jolted *Tribune* editors and owners alike. His credentials as a Socialist were such that Eugene V. Debs, the Socialist candidate for president, sought the young man's services as a national campaign manager in 1908. Patterson meantime had entered the School of Agriculture at the University of Wisconsin for an intensive short course on modern farming methods. After the 1908 election he returned to his farm near Libertyville, where he had moved with his wife, the former Alice Higinbotham, daughter of a Marshall Field & Company executive, and their two children. His neighbors included Samuel Insull. Patterson farmed and produced a series of books, tracts, and plays. Three of his four plays were for the eminent actress Pauline Fredericks and were performed on Broadway. His first novel, *A Little Brother of the Rich,* won critical and public acceptance. He retained some *Tribune* ties in addition to those with his cousin Bert, for James Keeley was a collaborator on one play, *The Fourth Estate.* When Paul Thompson of the *Chicagoan Magazine* went to the farm to interview Patterson, he found the young author happy with his writing and boasting that he was doing farm labor as well. "Plowing is a better exercise than polo," Patterson said. Thompson remarked that Joe was prouder of his Percherons than he had been of his polo ponies.

*   *   *

Robert R. McCormick never accepted the social justice notions of Joe Patterson, though he was an independent thinker and something of a maverick himself. McCormick was the aristocrat, shy, aloof, fastidious, served by London tailors and bootmakers; Patterson, the democrat, gregarious, understanding, as little concerned about his clothes and food as Joseph Medill had been. McCormick, too, liked some people but usually lacked the ability to show it. He demonstrated an astounding understanding of the wants and interests of those with whom he had no close association at any time in his life, the common citizens. He had a sense of *noblesse oblige* that led him to fight for what he conceived to be the cause of the people, as Joseph Medill had done before him, and he was an intense student of American history, from which he derived a strong sense of patriotism. McCormick was remote, sometimes eccentric, and except for Carter Harrison, Jr., and a few University of Chicago professors, was probably the truest cosmopolite who lived in Chicago in his time. He had an astringent sense of humor, and once summarized his aloofness and somewhat autocratic bearing, "Having been brought up in England, I knew how to brow beat the lower classes." He was, in fact, very much an English gentleman in the ducal tradition. He was tall, six feet four, and handsome, with a somewhat impish smile that he showed rarely; brown, almost hazel, eyes; and a trace of Medill russet in his hair.

Patterson was the commoner. He was totally at ease with ordinary people, and completely unfastidious. These traits he retained throughout his life. John Chapman, in his informal history of the *New York News*, which Patterson founded in 1919, presented a typical portrait of the man as he appeared in the 1930s: "One early afternoon on a hot July day I encountered him heading west on Forty-second street, eating an Eskimo Pie and wearing rumpled wash trousers and a short-sleeved shirt opened at the collar. 'Where are you going?' I asked. 'To the Paramount Theatre to see if they'll let me in without a jacket,' he answered." Patterson was bound for a movie, which he would see while his editorial writers worked on his ideas for that day. Then he would return to edit them and some parts of the news and features. "If he wanted to make changes," recalled Chapman, "he did so with a dull pencil stub; he would have no truck with mechanical pencils or pencil sharpeners." Joe Patterson had an almost mystical sense of what ordinary people wanted to read, acquired through association and patient study and understanding. Robert McCormick knew that his cousin had the instincts of a good newspaperman and was a creative editor, and Robert did not share the family's dim view of some of the innovations Joe had brought to the Sunday paper. He wanted to get Joe off his farm and back at the *Tribune*.

Early in 1909, Robert McCormick, in Boston to visit his ailing father, who had been supplanted by his mother Katherine as a trustee and director, showed himself almost ready to assume his own place in *Tribune* affairs. He wrote his mother:

> The Chicago situation is extremely complicated. Joe and A.N. [Aunt Nellie] and R.W. [Patterson] all have different points of view. Joe fears Beale's [continued] connection [with his law firm] will ruin the goodwill of the property. A.N. resents his (R.W.'s) loss of importance. Beale is beginning to pay the penalty of greatness. [Beale was somewhat pompous and dictatorial, it was said.] The editor-in-chief

[Joseph Medill] has passed away, nor will there be another until a man comes along who commands implicit confidence of a majority of the stockholders. It might be possible to have J. Keeley hold one of the minority positions . . . I doubt the Pattersons would allow the majority to be held by two McCormicks.

McCormick proposed that Keeley should become a director.

Three weeks or so later, Robert wrote to his mother concerning the February 21 meeting of the board of directors. Robert W. Patterson had been reelected president of the company and editor-in-chief of the paper; Azariah T. Galt was named chairman of the board, and George Upton vice-president. James Keeley became second vice-president, Joseph M. Patterson secretary, and Robert R. McCormick treasurer. Medill McCormick continued as a vice-president, auditor, and assistant editor-in-chief. Beale retained the chairmanship of the executive committee, and McCormick noted with satisfaction that he had worked out an arrangement with Beale to become informed on the paper's inner affairs.

During the several conversations which preceded this meeting I talked with considerable frankness about the local policy of the paper and the effect on the public of Beale's double position. I do not believe that the result of my frankness will cause the paper to run along those lines I believe to be correct. I have talked with Nellie about the property and tried to impress on her the necessity of mutual confidence and mutual good will and good faith on the part of the majority stockholders . . . but I cannot say that I made any impression what-so-ever. The situation today is that I am treasurer without any power or duties, but with the right to study the paper from the inside, and the personal promise of the chairman of the executive committee that I will be consulted in the newspaper affairs. If Medill . . . wishes to resign his position as director, I will be elected in his place.

*   *   *

In the months following the triumphant Lincoln centenary edition the *Tribune* management situation deteriorated, with Medill McCormick departing for Europe, leaving Keeley to run the paper. Then, the night of April 1, 1910, Robert W. Patterson died in his room in the Bellevue-Stratford Hotel in Philadelphia. Robert R. McCormick was in his law office in the Tribune Building when his secretary informed him that Anna Garrow, chief telephone operator, urgently wished to see him. McCormick recalled the scene at an advertising department dinner in 1949, when Garrow was still with the company:

She is the head of our telephone company and knows all that goes on. She told me Robert Patterson had just died. I had seen him a few days before. He had not seemed ill to me. I went down to his office to find out what was going on and there were all the principal stockholders of the Tribune Company and they were there to consummate the sale of the *Tribune* to

Victor Lawson. That seemed a terrible thing to me. The *Tribune* has always been much more to me than either a newspaper or a source of revenue. . . . I talked them out of it and Alfred Cowles made a condition that I should go into the *Tribune*.

But Lawson was tough and advised McCormick to prepare for a price war if he was not ready to sell the paper. McCormick worried about Medill, too. On March 19, Robert had written his mother that he had invited Dr. Carl Jung to visit Chicago during the eminent psychiatrist's American tour. McCormick wanted to discuss the situation of his brother, then staying at Jung's Zurich sanitarium, and to assess the ability of the doctor, but Jung did not reply. *"My present opinion is that Dr. Jung's influence has been very bad,"* McCormick said. *"From his grip on Medill and the way he has forced his personality upon you I can readily recognize the great strength of this man. Whether he is using his strength to the good of the patient is a question upon which I am willing to be convinced. . . . If he returns to Europe without coming to Chicago it will be hard for me not to consider him a charlatan."* Robert was genuinely fond of his brother and, in a somewhat boyish gesture, offered him half his polo ponies and the use of all of them if Medill would quit the sanitarium and return to Chicago. *"I am delighted to hear of your improvement,"* he wrote. *"I cannot agree with you that the* Tribune *is a particularly hard paper to run under present conditions. The family rows are disagreeable and detrimental to all members . . . but they are infinitely preferable to other control."*

Meantime, a barrage of criticism of the *Tribune* from his mother and Aunt Nellie was largely directed at Bertie. Aunt Nellie wrote, *"I wish the* Tribune *would let up for a while on the rich malefactors and tell some wholesome truths about those foreign-born murderers and anarchists that are drawing our country, possibly, to a frightful revolution. . . . I am not criticizing Keeley, not at all! Don't tell your mother about this or she would say I'm criticizing Keeley's policy."* In another note to Bertie about his mother, Aunt Nellie said:

> *She has forcefully, belligerently & most blindly insisted that Medill, only, was capable of being head of the* Tribune, *made the* Tribune, *etc. . . . As for keeping the paper for the boys—both you boys can take care of yourselves and make your own careers. Keeley might have a little stock—do you think a man of his decision and will power wishes to be an employee of two ladies who are well known to be usually disagreeing? Your mother and I have no respect for each other's capacity as business women . . . and no man cares one penny for their [sic] opinions; this is necessarily the case.*

On April 6, 1910, a few days following the death of Robert Patterson, there was another meeting of Tribune Company directors, and another blow to the company. Katherine McCormick had become a member of the board the year before because of the serious illness of her husband. Now it became her duty to request indefinite leave without pay for Medill

McCormick. She sent younger son Robert to present the resolution to the board, which passed it unanimously. Medill would soon leave Dr. Jung's sanitarium, but he would never return to the *Tribune*'s corporate staff, preferring instead a career in politics. On May 15, the directors passed a further resolution, "that Second Vice President James Keeley take entire charge of the affairs of the corporation until further action by the board."

*   *   *

The situation was far from satisfactory, but Robert R. McCormick had at last established communication among the family, Keeley could hold for a time, and McCormick was beginning to realize that he himself was emerging as the "conserver" he had described as needed for the paper. He obviously talked with his cousin about the two of them acting together, since Joe Patterson soon wrote his mother indicating that he had seen her letter to Bertie and that they had been having discussions:

> *Bertie and I are perfectly capable of safeguarding your interests in the paper and seeing that it produces for you, as long as we take an interest in it, a larger income than you could secure in any other way, also a more secure income. . . . I know not a little about newspaper work from inheritance, environment and active work. . . . As far as your saying you and Aunt Kate are not capable of managing a newspaper, that is perfectly true. Nobody expects you to manage a newspaper. You can't do it. Bertie and I can manage this property for you. Your suggestion that Bertie and I will quarrel—we shall not because we are too selfish.*

In November, Aunt Nellie wrote Bertie: *"Your mother says you came up to say that Keeley and Field are nervous. I am concerned by reports to Keeley of her complaints . . . I wonder who has talked? I have said to Joe once or twice over the telephone that I thought the editorial page wasn't much and I didn't care for the Sunday supplement."* She added a postscript: *"Joe told me your mother already has begun to oppose stock for Keeley, and that worries Joe."* Then a second angry letter in which Aunt Nellie charged Katherine of accusing her of driving her husband away. *"Dear Bertie . . . I enclose your mother's latest outburst. It was this kind of violence that finally wrecked your poor father and keeps Medill away from her. Aunt N."*

On April 16, 1910, Robert R. McCormick was ready to bring the dissident factions together. He had indicated to Lawson that he would oppose the sale of the paper, and had received from Lawson's intermediary, Herman Kohlsaat, the warning that the street sale price of the *Record-Herald* would be reduced. He wrote to his mother on the stationery of his law firm, Shepard, McCormick and Thomason:

> *Yesterday I accidentally ran into Alfred Cowles and the conversation naturally drifted into the topic of selling the property. I retold all my arguments against it without success. He said in the absence of somebody vitally interested being in charge of*

the property, it must decline. He said this was Horace White's opinion and the opinion of the Lloyds. Also, Horace White had arrived in town with the idea of accomplishing the sale. I said, "Be explicit. What do you mean by somebody vitally interested?" He replied, "Some one with a large financial interest in the profits which interest would be larger than any other he might have." I then said, "Would it make any difference in your feeling if I should take an active part in the property?" He replied, "It certainly would. If you would take charge of the property I would then change my position because I would see a great future in it, one much greater than any other investment." He then made an appointment with me to meet Horace White and said he would talk with him and Beale and A.N., and oppose the sale.

White has taken the same position, only less emphatically. I have told them, that if my staying out of the property would prevent the sale, I would do that; that if taking partial management and becoming a director would prevent the sale, I would do that; that if it were necessary for me to give up my present occupation and my political and legal prospects and take charge of the property to prevent a sale, I would do that. I have since seen Joe and Lloyd together, both of whom favor the plan.

The plan favored was obviously No. 3—McCormick to take full charge—since he added, *"I suppose the resentment of Medill might be life-long."* Then he continued:

The step means for me, the total abandonment of my prospects for a political career, whatever they are, and they are as high as any man of my age in this city. I have, since your departure, been offered practically unanimous support for renomination [as president of the Sanitary District] and also given a fair prospect if I desire it, to have the nomination for Congress in our district, which prospect in case of a sale, can become a certainty if I say so. Mr. Kohlsaat has sent word that Mr. Lawson will support me for any position I desire to seek.

Be all these things as they may, the retention of the property in its present form far out-weighs everything, unless it be the breaking up of family ties. If I can prevent the sale by any act which will not make it necessary for me to take charge of the property, I will do so with a cheerful heart. If the condition of retaining the property shall finally depend upon my taking charge of it, I will put the decision up to you and abide by your conclusion.

*   *   *

In mid-June, 1910, Victor Lawson through Herman Kohlsaat gave formal notice to the *Chicago Tribune* directors that he had determined to cut the price of the *Chicago Record-Herald* to 1¢, beginning July 1. Under a publishers' agreement, the *Chicago Tribune* was to be notified so that it might also reduce its price, which had been raised to 2¢ after the Spanish-American War. Robert McCormick branded Lawson's move a threat and continued to urge rejection of his offer to buy the paper. He was authorized to transmit formal rejection to Lawson. McCormick was extremely nervous about the prospective encounter. He smoked a package of cigarettes early in the day of his scheduled interview, and, in disgust, vowed to stop smoking. Never again did he have a cigarette.

Finally, having marshaled his thoughts on the situation, and with assurance that Lawson was expecting his call, McCormick telephoned the formidable publisher. "I told him of the change of plans," McCormick recalled years later. "He was very angry and said that unless we carried out the sale, there would be a newspaper war; that he would reduce the price of the *Record-Herald* to one cent, and that his great experience in newspaper publishing and our disorganization would destroy the *Tribune*."

There was indeed great disorganization, as McCormick acknowledged. "Mr. R. W. Patterson was dead; my brother, first vice president, [*had been*] in a sanitarium. . . . All three trustees were now in Europe. . . . Mr. Lawson suggested that, before reaching an irremediable conclusion, I [*convey to*] them a somewhat better offer than he had made before. This offer I agreed to take to the trustees, not expecting to have it accepted, but wishing to gain time for Keeley and Field to organize the *Tribune*."

The directors authorized McCormick to travel to Europe to confer with the trustees, and on June 27, McCormick dispatched a cable to William Beale in Paris: "GOING EUROPE. WHERE FIND YOU JULY TWENTI-ETH." Earlier he had sent a telegram to Medill McCormick, who had left Jung's sanitarium and was with his wife, Ruth, at Sea Harbor, Maine: "GOING EUROPE JULY SIXTH. JOIN CRUISING AUGUST EIGHTH. LETTER FOL-LOWS." McCormick had made a tentative agreement with Joe Patterson that they would join forces in directing the *Tribune,* but the agreement was vague at the time. It was becoming evident to all the trustees that Robert McCormick was the man who could bring the family together.

Characteristically, McCormick wanted to get as much return as possible from any expenditures he might make, whether they were company or his own funds, so while in Europe he visited the Manchester Ship Canal and the Berlin sewage disposal plant, thus benefiting the Chicago Sanitary District, since it was involved in both canal construction and sewage disposal problems. Also, the British and German phases of the journey provided a cover for his real purpose—it would be highly disadvantageous under the circumstances for talk of sale of the *Tribune* to grow more widespread.

McCormick was successful in his mission to Europe. "When I returned and gave Mr. Lawson the final answer, he immediately cut the price of the *Record-Herald* to one cent." On October 3, 1910, the *Tribune* followed suit. James Keeley had taken the prudent step of hiring Max Annenberg away from Hearst. "Annenberg," said McCormick, "later assisted by his brother-in-law, Louis Rose, proved to be much the best circulation manager in town. It was the *Tribune* that gained circulation at the expense of the *Record-Herald* and Hearst's *Chicago Examiner*." Rough methods were employed by all sides, despite the fact that the Hearst circulation manager was Max Annenberg's brother, Moe. Vendors were threatened and beaten. At least some of the drivers and dispatch riders employed by the newspapers later found employment with gangsters in the Prohibition era—one of them being Dion O'Banion, who had worked for the *Examiner*. But it was the editorial content of the rival publications and their promotion and services that in the long run would determine the victors in the circulation struggle.

* * *

Robert R. McCormick had helped to precipitate a renewal of the circulation war by blocking Lawson's offer for the *Tribune,* but he had not yet made the decision to take over a share of the *Tribune* management, though he and Patterson had a tentative agreement and Keeley was willing to work under them. But his mother, Katherine, who had great power as a company director and a trustee of the Medill stock, persisted in her refusal to authorize stock for Keeley. She had not given up her ambitions for Medill to return to the paper, despite the fact that her elder son had gone into politics and was happily serving in the Washington headquarters of the Wisconsin Progressive senator, Robert M. La Follette. Robert wrote to Medill:

> The situation as to you, me, Joe and Cissy is the same. We are potential owners of ½ plus of the stock. This interest cannot be changed by force. Attempts along this line have hurt all equally. Your interest in the property is as great now as it was any time you were working for it. It is supporting you now as then and it represents ninety percent of your political expectations—or mine. I imagine you have seen enough of political life in the last few months to recognize it as pleasant, or even tolerable only if carried on in connection with some regular gainful occupation. We are all in the same boat. No one can get in, or get out. It would be folly to buy control at this time, or to sell.

Robert McCormick's assessment that no one could get in or get out was entirely correct. Nonetheless, Medill had no intention of returning to the *Tribune* after his involvement in politics. Robert himself intended to remain in politics at the time he wrote. He was a candidate for reelection as president of the Sanitary District in the fall of 1910. McCormick's record at the district was an excellent one, so good that Edward J. Kelly, the Sanitary District foreman whom McCormick admired and a rising young Democratic politician, declined to run against him. But McCormick was swamped in a Democratic sweep of Cook County and became totally available to the needs of the *Tribune.* He had his understanding with Joe Patterson, and his mother and aunt and the directors were ready for a permanent resolution of the squabbles, recognizing that a family peace must be effected.

Early in 1911 the arrangements were made for what would lead to a highly successful resolution of the company's management problems. Joseph M. Patterson would become chairman of Tribune Company, free to seek his own role in the editorial department or elsewhere in the paper, but paying special attention to the Sunday paper and to daily features. Robert R. McCormick would be named president and, in effect, chief executive officer. His immediate missions were to upgrade the business department of the paper and to insure an adequate supply of newsprint at reasonable prices by building a mill to produce it. McCormick retained his position of treasurer and Patterson continued as secretary. Vice-president James Keeley would continue to manage the daily paper. The settlement was approved by the directors on March 1, 1911.

Keeley meantime was fighting a brilliant circulation battle with both Lawson and the Hearst papers, not only acquiring Annenberg to reorganize the circulation department but creating an editorial staff that produced excellent content. In addition to its own John McCutcheon the paper continued to present such outside talent as Finley Peter Dunne and Jack London, the popular novelist. Reporter James O'Donnell Bennett, editorial writer Clifford Raymond, and chief editorial writer Tiffany Blake were among the men Keeley hired for the *Tribune* who stayed with the paper long after he was gone. Others spent a relatively short time at the *Tribune,* such as Sunday editor Burns Mantle, who left after three years to go on to New York, where he became a well-known theater critic, and sportswriter Ring Lardner, who conducted the "Wake of the News" column for six years before joining the Bell Syndicate. Bennett, Raymond, Blake, Mantle, and Lardner all were skilled writers who became known for their books and essays as well as their newspaper work. Yet another Keeley recruit was a young reporter from Minneapolis, Floyd Gibbons, who acquired fame covering the Battle of Cameron Dam in Wisconsin, a frontier conflict somewhat reminiscent of that described by Keeley in Wyoming but considerably more bloody and authentic. Keeley not only knew good writers and writing, he could exploit the news, and he maintained his popular list of service features.

On Sundays the paper made some circulation gains attributed to the magazine, a publication that turned strongly toward light feminine appeal: "The Most Beautiful Women in Chicago," profusely illustrated with photographs; "Scent Your Hair if You Would Be Up-to-Date"; "A Kentucky Wife Sells Her Husband for $1"; "Mary and Her Lamb Brought Up-to-Date"; "The Mermaid Dress," showing the latest hourglass figure for women; and "Little Arthur Meeker Owns the Smallest Mule in the World," with a picture of little Arthur astride the diminutive beast. (As an adult Meeker became a well-known novelist and a *Tribune* travel writer.) There were science stories such as "Do You Know You are a Living Telephone Exchange?" and garishly illustrated pseudoscience articles, definitely slanted to men, like "The Greatest Prize Fight the World Has Ever Known," showing two 36-ton dinosaurs meeting in deadly combat, with the text describing the reign of such creatures millennia ago.

To increase sales on the streets, Keeley enlarged headlines and concentrated on local news as well as his precious features. He achieved an excellent public response from his war on vice, recounting in rich detail the evils of the Levee district and the streets nearby. "A man cannot walk a few yards by night without being accosted by a dissolute woman," the paper noted. The licentiousness of the brothels, saloons, and concert halls was described, and the paper took special offense at a brochure issued by the elegant and notorious Everleigh Club, which delineated the charms of the boarders and the luxury of the house, and photographically illustrated some of the special rooms, Japanese, College, Copper, and Gold, depicting their elaborate decor, including the beautiful brass bedsteads and the gold-plated spittoons. The public cry for the closure of such resorts of ill-fame and the suppression of prostitution and gambling finally forced action by Mayor Carter Harrison, and late in 1911 he ordered the Everleigh Club closed. Proprietors Minna and Ada Everleigh took the action graciously, packing their bags and going off on a six-month jaunt to Europe.

The *Tribune* did not have leadership in either circulation or advertising in Chicago—those records were held by Victor Lawson, dour, taciturn, and forbidding in his dark Prince Albert garb, whose morning *Record-Herald* outdistanced the *Tribune* until 1911, and whose afternoon *Daily News* would lead it for a decade more. Lawson, said Robert R. McCormick in 1952, was the greatest publisher of his time. He had one fault, McCormick noted—his penuriousness led him to lose his best editorial talents to the *Tribune*. Hearst's *Examiner* also took part in the circulation battle, using the slogan, "Exit *Tribune*, Enter *Examiner*." But it was the *Tribune* that triumphed. In 1912 there was a strike of stereotypers, pressmen, wagon drivers, and newsboys, which arose from a dispute at the *Examiner*. All papers were hit and profits depressed. "At this time," McCormick later reported, "the *Tribune* circulation department was so much better organized that it not only held a great proportion of its circulation during the strike but obtained a large number of readers who had read other journals."

*   *   *

Neither McCormick nor Patterson had any desire to interfere with the attempts of Keeley and Field to improve *Tribune* circulation and advertising prospects. Nonetheless, when they began to take an active role in the paper's operations, the young proprietors privately were dismayed by some of the conditions they encountered. The counting room was "chaotic," McCormick later told the directors, and the circulation department had not yet fully responded to the reorganization efforts of Max Annenberg. McCormick demanded a tightening of business procedures, bringing in Daniel M. Deininger from the Sanitary District as auditor. Patterson studied the Sunday paper and the operations of a news bureau and features syndicate, which returned a profit the following year. It was McCormick who presided over the meeting of the directors on July 17, 1911. He urged consideration for a paper mill to be built in Canada and was authorized to proceed with preliminary studies and plans. McCormick arranged with George W. Wisner, an engineer with the Sanitary District, to act as his consultant, and began looking around for an expert on paper mill siting and construction. McCormick had observed that Hearst got his newsprint at $5 less per ton because of his chain of newspapers, plus his threats to build a mill at contract negotiation time. A few publishers had attempted to construct their own mills without success. But McCormick was convinced that such a plant could succeed if built in Canada near a major power supply, close to raw materials, and with adequate transportation available. The passage of a reciprocal trade agreement with Canada, which removed part of the tariff on newsprint imported into the United States, made such a plan more attractive.

William Field, returning from a Canadian fishing trip, told McCormick that he had met in Canada a pulp mill engineer named Warren Curtis, Jr., who had just completed a newsprint plant and was available for a new project. McCormick reached Curtis at once, obtained some cost projections, and induced his directors to authorize him to spend $1 million to construct a mill. Considering McCormick's inexperience, age, and the history of failure of newspapers in the newsprint business, it was a fantastic demonstration of persuasive powers. McCormick and Curtis worked hard and fast. They decided that Thorold, Ontario, near Niagara Falls, would provide the best site; it had ample electrical power and rail facilities, and it was convenient to the pulp forests. McCormick and Curtis desired 300 square miles of timber limits to insure a steady supply of pulpwood but were repulsed by the Canadian minister of Crown Lands. They decided to go ahead with the plant anyway, and on March 15, 1912, little more than a year after McCormick had been elected president of Tribune Company, the directors authorized Stuart G. Shepard, McCormick's law partner, to negotiate a lease for 30 acres of Thorold pastureland as a plant site. On June 5, 1912, McCormick sent Curtis a note, *"Go ahead with the construction of the mill. Before finally locating same, please send me a blueprint showing the layout. I may run down Sunday night."* The letter was on the stationery of McCormick's law firm. Soon he would use stationery of the Ontario Paper Company, Ltd. McCormick was heavily occupied on the mill project for the next two years. Two paper machines, vast rolling mills that pressed cooked wood pulp and groundwood into glistening sheets of newsprint, were contracted at a cost of $184,000. McCormick hired another Chicago Sanitary District engineer, George S. Brack, and sent him to Thorold to help Curtis, while he personally continued to supervise the work, dividing his time between Chicago and Thorold, when he was not in New York or seeking northern timber limits.

*   *   *

The bellow of the Bull Moose was heard in the land that tranquil summer of 1912. Former president Roosevelt, trust buster, conservationist, advocate of physical fitness, and exemplar of virile American manhood, a man who read and understood two books a day when he was not in office or running for one, had returned from his world travels in a rage. President Taft was not carrying out his mandate to press the attack on the malefactors of great wealth, and Roosevelt's young, ardent supporters, such as Medill and Robert McCormick, were urging him to consider candidacy for the presidency on a Progressive Republican ticket. There was a question about Roosevelt's health, for, in addition to having bad eyesight, his early life in the West had not completely corrected his essential frailty. But, questioned about his ability to campaign for the presidency, Teddy Roosevelt had cried, "I'm as fit as a bull moose!" When he appeared in Milwaukee and was wounded by an insane gunman, Roosevelt insisted on making his speech, saying, "You can't stop a bull moose," and thereafter it was the "Bull Moose" campaign.

Nowhere was Teddy Roosevelt and his Republican-party-shattering Bull Moose campaign supported more enthusiastically than in the younger echelons of the McCormick family. Medill McCormick became a national campaign director for the Progressives and Roosevelt. Robert R. McCormick was chairman of Chicago's Committee of 100, dedicated to the election of Roosevelt. The *Tribune* of course gave Roosevelt all-out support. The mothers and trustees were not pleased, but William Bross Lloyd, now a director, agreed with the young McCormicks, as did Patterson.

Teddy Roosevelt, the opinions of Katherine McCormick and Elinor Patterson to the contrary, had moved a long way toward carrying out policies of Joseph Medill during his tenure, especially after he had been elected on his own. The Sherman Anti-Trust Act of 1890, passed following long campaigns in which the *Tribune* was credited with important contributions, had been much ignored later until Teddy Roosevelt revitalized it. He and his attorney general, Philander C. Knox, thoroughly trounced the forces of great wealth when they brought suit against the Northern Securities Company put together by J. P. Morgan, John D. Rockefeller, Edward H. Harriman, and James J. Hill, and the order to dissolve Northern Securities was upheld by the U.S. Supreme Court on March 14, 1904. Roosevelt pushed through the Reclamation Act of 1902, which promoted and assisted the irrigation of arid lands, the Pure Food and Drug Act of 1906, and established the Bureau of Corporations in 1902; except for a lapse when he permitted the strengthening of trust combinations during the panic of 1907, he had a record that could be generally supported by the young Republican reformers. Medill McCormick had gone with the Progressives as a Senator La Follette campaign official in the fall of 1910, when the Progressives sustained defeats generally, but he was not dismayed. All that was needed, Roosevelt's young men believed, was Teddy to lead them, and on August 7, 1912, the Progressives in convention in Chicago nominated him for president and Gov. Hiram Johnson of California as his running mate. Medill McCormick signed on to direct the Bull Moose campaign in the Middle West.

"The *Tribune* threw its whole weight behind Teddy Roosevelt," wrote McCutcheon in his memoirs. "My cartoons were 100 percent for him." The *Tribune* had supported President Taft, who actually had been harder on the trusts than Roosevelt, warmly endorsing his reciprocity treaty with Canada, which Robert McCormick later found highly useful in his newsprint quest. However, its support of the Progressives, said the paper editorially, was a natural continuation of past campaigns against "invisible government," the trusts and special interests, and the kind of Republicanism symbolized by William Lorimer. Progressivism, said the *Tribune*, was the logical repudiation of "bossism" and was needed to make government responsible not to special interests, but to the people.

The Committee of 100 entered the pro-Roosevelt campaign with an impressive list of Republican reformers among its directors. The officers were: president and chairman, Robert R. McCormick; vice-president and chairman of the executive committee, Dr. Harry Pratt Judson, president of the University of Chicago; treasurer, A. W. Harris, of the Harris Bank; secretary, John J. Abbott of the Continental Bank; among the directors were Frank J. Loesch, who later founded the Chicago Crime Commission, Judge Harry Olson, and Col. Nathan W. McChesney. The committee, in backing Roosevelt, called for revision of the tariff act and enforcement of the civil service laws. It did not exclude all regular Republicans from support, and as the campaign progressed, it backed Gov. Charles S. Deneen for reelection. During the course of the campaign, a curious division between the young McCormicks occurred, so that *Tribune* readers were urged in full-page advertisements signed by Robert R. McCormick and his associates to vote for Roosevelt for president and Deneen for governor, while on another page, via an ad signed by Medill McCormick, they were exhorted to vote for Roosevelt for president and Clarence Funk, a Progressive and one of the men who helped to expose the Lorimer plot, for governor. The latter ad quoted Teddy Roosevelt himself as endorsing Funk as the true "Bull Mooser." The Tribune editorial page backed Roosevelt and Deneen, while Medill McCormick was given space for an article opposing Deneen, whom he called "a reluctant reformer."

In its final appeal for Roosevelt, on November 2, the Tribune said:

> For many years, though we have talked much about the trust evil, the anti-trust law has been enforced only feebly, half-heartedly, and with little substantial effect. When Roosevelt was elected president, a new energy was injected into the enforcement and suits multiplied and were pushed with zeal and considerable success.
>
> Roosevelt and the Progressives propose to get results. We demand a strong regulation of interstate corporations. The corporation is an essential part of modern business and the concentration of modern business in some degree is inevitable and necessary for national and international business efficiency. But the concentration of vast wealth under a corporate system, unguarded and uncontrolled by the nation, has placed in the hands of a few men enormous, secret, irresponsible power over the daily life of the citizen—a power insufferable in a free government and certain of abuse.
>
> The power has been abused in monopoly of national resources, in stock watering, in unfair competition and unfair privilege and finally in sinister influence on the public agencies of the state and nation. We do not fear commercial power, but we insist that it be exercised openly, under publicity, supervision, and regulation of the most efficient sort, which will preserve the good while eradicating and preventing the evils.
>
> The Progressive plan does not propose the elimination of competition. It does not propose the acceptance of monopoly. It proposes by regulation in the public interest to make the one profitable and the other useless or beneficial.

The Tribune demonstrated its new promotional flair, developed by the advertising department, on election night. During the week the paper installed giant searchlights at strategic points around the city, stating that varying patterns of light would reveal the election winner to the populace. A rainbow movement signifying that Teddy Roosevelt and his Progressives had won was the signal first given, but on November 6 the final vote showed that Democrat Woodrow Wilson, former Princeton University president and incumbent New Jersey governor, had received 6,293,454 votes to 4,119,539 for Roosevelt and 3,384,980 for Taft. The paper also set up seven reception centers where the public could follow the returns and listen to band concerts. More than 13,000 persons in the

Coliseum watched as the returns received by telephone from the *Tribune* offices were projected onto giant screens. The crowds in all seven viewing stations totaled more than 47,000.

Roosevelt appeared to have a chance of carrying Illinois, but his Cook County lead was reduced downstate and in the final count his apparent victory by 10,000 votes became a defeat by Wilson, by a margin of 13,855. Progressives carried Cook County, where the vote for president was 78,340 for Taft, 134,828 for Wilson, and 172,506 for Roosevelt. Thomas R. Marshall of Indiana was elected vice-president with Wilson; he later would become famous for stating that what the country needed was "a really good five cent cigar." Edward F. Dunne, the former Chicago mayor, was elected governor of Illinois.

The paper in its postelection editorial declared:

> The Progressives are triumphant in defeat. Theodore Roosevelt is not to be our next President, but considering what he has had to overcome he has achieved something like a political miracle. The great vote rolled up by his party is at once a noble tribute to him and an assurance that Progressivism is in the flood and will yet carry the day. To have brought forth a new party and developed this strength in a three months' campaign is the most remarkable feat in our political history. It could not have been accomplished even under the leadership of Theodore Roosevelt if the cause were not ripe, if the forces for political progress had not been running deeply in the nation's political life, if the people had not been ready for forward leadership.

The editorial was published when the Progressive cause appeared to have done better than was finally recorded in the canvassed returns. Cartoonist McCutcheon assessed the outcome with his usual incisive analysis, showing a crowd in the great hall of the new Field Museum viewing an elephant labeled "G.O.P. (elephas antiquas). This rare species now extinct. Fatally wounded by Taft . . . and put out of its misery by T. R."

*   *   *

As *Tribune* president Robert McCormick labored to get Teddy Roosevelt elected and the paper mill into operation in 1912, *Tribune* sales were expanding to 230,000 daily and 304,000 on Sunday, as calculated by a new process of audited circulation. The paper boasted that its various categories of advertising linage—classified, display, and general—as well as total linage, exceeded the combined totals of its morning rivals, the *Examiner,* the *Record-Herald,* and the *Inter-Ocean.* James Keeley and E. S. Beck continued their policy of displaying sound political and financial stories against the somewhat dull competition of the failing *Record-Herald* and *Inter-Ocean,* and lurid crime and divorce accounts to counter the appeal of Hearst's *Examiner*. The editors continued to seek outstanding writers well known to Chicagoans. The *Tribune* published the work of Chicago poet Harriet Monroe, as well as special articles such as that by James A. Patten, the wheat speculator, telling all interested "How to Become a Millionaire." Jane Eddington joined the cooking staff, Percy Hammond was music critic, Glen Dillard Gunn, drama critic.

The Sunday paper, "the flagship of the fleet," was always expected to be far in front of the daily paper in circulation and advertising revenues. It was recovering well by 1912, after having deteriorated to the point, McCormick would say in a letter to his mother, where it could have brought down the entire paper. He and Joe had decided that the Sunday edition must become the major Patterson mission, and Patterson turned out to be exactly the right man for the job. Patterson assigned himself the duties of Sunday and features editor and caused the paper to begin the reviewing of motion pictures. He gave the critic a house name, Mae Tinee. He was also taking a look at the *Tribune* comics, a field in which he would prove himself a creative genius.

Patterson reorganized the Sunday department and found new artists and writers, including a young Baltimore editor who contributed regularly to the Sunday *Tribune*, H. L. Mencken, and such eminent British and Irish contributors as George Bernard Shaw, H. G. Wells, G. K. Chesterton, and T. P. O'Connor. The quiet, attractive blonde secretary to Burns Mantle, the Sunday editor who had departed for New York, demonstrated an aptitude for acquiring the new kind of Sunday features Patterson sought, and he appointed Mary King as assistant Sunday editor. Her artists showed modern Chicago women how to do the "Ingenue Crouch," a dance or walk brought on, the paper said, by the new craze for tight skirts. Patterson brought Herbert Kaufman, a liberal writer, into the Sunday magazine, but under King's supervision the magazine increased its feminist slant, in a popular vein. One of its stories depicted in grisly detail the activities of "The Greatest Bluebeard of All Time." Egyptologists from Chicago had just dug up a mummy that they identified as King Amunoph (1450 B.C.), who was said to have thrown wives who displeased him to the crocodiles. Science was no longer pseudoscience under Patterson, and the paper ran an excellent in-depth report on Dr. Alex Carrell's experiments in heart and artery surgery. "Ex-attache" wrote that there was danger of a major war in Europe. Said the subheadline: "He Thinks Austria-Hungary and Russia Likely to Clash."

Meantime, Patterson had been examining the possibility of an alliance between newspapers and the new motion picture, which was enormously popular with the public, showing in hundreds of nickelodeons and theaters throughout the country. He at last came up with the promotional idea he had been seeking and worked out an arrangement with the Selig

Polyscope Company, Chicago's largest film producer and one of the biggest in the nation. The *Tribune* began publishing each Sunday for 26 weeks chapters of a romantic thriller, *The Adventures of Kathlyn*, illustrated with still photographs from the two-reel film that would be shown in Midwest theaters the following week. The story was written by Harold McGrath, and the star was Kathlyn Williams.

The success of the joint serialization was immediate and tremendous. *Chicago Tribune* Sunday circulation jumped almost 80,000, while the motion picture theaters showing *Kathlyn* were packed. Patterson and his assistant King began looking for other stories suitable for the cooperative venture. A second serial, *A Diamond in the Sky,* was even more popular than the innocent adventures of Kathlyn and continued to appear in theaters nationally for years. Patterson and King became convinced that motion pictures were one of the compelling natural interests of the public, that newspapers should publish reports on the activities of the stars and writers in the new medium, and that newspapers also should publish fiction daily. This the *Tribune* did for the next half century.

*　　*　　*

The No. 1 machine at the Ontario Paper Company's Thorold mill began operation on September 5, 1913, prompting McCormick to write an optimistic letter to his mother a few days later: *"The paper mill started making paper in a commercial way today. I was down there two weeks getting it started. I can attribute the delay partly to the month I had blood poisoning, and partly to the month Keeley was away. The mill is going to take a lot of management, but I am confident it is a sound investment and will prove quite profitable."* Then he referred to the bitter circulation fighting with the Hearst papers:

> I did not like to invite trouble, but I felt the fight must be made. . . . These papers have sued for peace. I believe this is the first time that has happened.
>
> The paper is doing extra-ordinary well. The daily circulation is over 260,000, and the Sunday back to 380,000 and I am confident it will go over 400,000 before the end of this year. . . . I am stale and it is plain to me that who carries the responsibility of the continued success of the Tribune has little time in the way of public activities or private enjoyment. He must be constantly looking around for a weak spot and protecting it. If I had not noticed that the Sunday paper was failing to keep up with the daily . . . we would have been weakened in that section of the paper which is our chief source of revenue.
>
> As to a newspaper taking marked leadership in political affairs, that is dead for the present. Hearst failed to do this on a large scale. Where other newspaper men have tried it recently they have hurt the newspaper without accomplishing anything.

The papermaking enterprise almost immediately ran into mechanical difficulties, though McCormick and Curtis were convinced that the problems could be solved. The No. 2 machine started on November 14; it too had trouble, and by year's end output of the mill was only about half of what was expected. Nonetheless, McCormick and Patterson continued to be optimistic. Canada indicated that timber limits could be acquired, the *Tribune* was doing well, and the young proprietors briefly considered acquiring a New York paper, the *Herald,* which was reported to be in trouble.

In Mexico, revolution, which had erupted in 1910, continued. The United States had refused to recognize the provisional government of Victoriano Huerta when he seized power early in 1913, and on November 4, President Woodrow Wilson delivered an ultimatum for which the *Tribune* broke out its biggest condensed Gothic type: "UNITED STATES ULTIMATUM ORDERS HUERTA TO RESIGN: CAN'T NAME SUCCESSOR." The bold, black headline used by Hearst and Pulitzer in New York became a *Tribune* contribution to Chicago morning journalism. The headlines stimulated street sales and incited the news department to match them with suitable news stories. Huge banner headlines had come to stay. So had a new *Tribune* policy, demanding national preparedness. The United States was not ready to back up its diplomacy with arms, the paper said, in approving Wilson's Mexico policy. More trained men and more modern guns were needed for the armed forces.

The year 1913 closed on a positive note for the *Tribune,* with profits surpassing the greatest previous annual profit by $54,000. Prospects for the paper had never seemed better. So smooth were the Sunday operations that Patterson could go to Mexico in April, 1914, to cover the occupation of Vera Cruz by U.S. Marines seeking to prevent Huerta's forces from obtaining German arms. He started a Mexican edition of the *Tribune* for the troops and took with him a *Tribune* photographer, Edwin F. Weigel, who soon was given other duties in addition to those of taking news photographs. Patterson instructed Weigel to bring along a motion picture camera and film and ordered him to film U.S. Navy and Marine operations in Mexico. The newsreels were only moderately successful, since there was little action, but they got a showing as a *Tribune* promotional device, and Weigel obtained useful experience.

McCormick meanwhile had traveled almost to Labrador seeking timber limits that would provide an everlasting supply of pulpwood for the *Tribune* paper mill. Patterson was still in Mexico and McCormick in the Canadian wilds when seeming disaster struck their paper in Chicago.

*   *   *

In the spring of 1914, McCormick and Curtis had made progress in negotiations with the Canadian Crown Lands authorities for the acquisition of timber rights, and the two men, accompanied by William Carter, an experienced timber cruiser, began exploring along the Saguenay River about 200 miles north of Quebec City. The area was remote—on one trip McCormick was caught in a storm and spent the night on the earth floor of an Indian hut with a chief and his squaw and children—and although McCormick had left instructions for reaching him in case of emergency there was no practical way to do so, except by dispatching a courier by sled or snowshoes. Curtis, who was somewhat pudgy, collapsed after a long day tramping across the crusted snow. McCormick sent Carter back to the nearest town on the railway for a doctor. Returning with the medic, Carter brought along a Quebec paper. While Curtis was being success-fully treated, McCormick, who read French, perused the paper and discovered that James Keeley, general manager of the *Chicago Tribune*, had resigned to take control of the morning *Record-Herald*.

McCormick hurried to the end of the railroad where the switch engine that had brought Carter back with the doctor was waiting. He was taken to the nearest railroad station and asked if there was a message from Keeley. There was none. He envisioned the entire *Tribune* editorial department deserting with Keeley, especially since Patterson was not in Chicago to take action, but he hoped that William Field, his business manager, was on the job. He telegraphed Field, urging him to try to keep managing editor Beck, circulation manager Annenberg, and other key men. Then he rode the switch engine to the main line where he boarded a train for the 48-hour journey to Chicago.

Keeley had hired many important men for the *Tribune* over the years, and McCormick expected to find they were gone, but none of the key men had followed Keeley. His erstwhile general manager had been less perfidious than he first supposed, McCormick later admitted. Keeley had indeed attempted to take Annenberg and the others with him, but his departure without warning resulted because a sudden opportunity to obtain and merge the *Record-Herald* and the *Inter-Ocean* was linked to an availability of funds to be supplied by Samuel Insull and others. The deal had not been completed until the day it was announced, and Keeley had been pledged to secrecy.

McCormick was ready for a new circulation battle. "We began our fight—the *Tribune* and its reputation against the *Record-Herald* with Keeley's reputation. We felt we had a tremendous struggle ahead of us. We bent every energy to the task," McCormick said. "The loyal staff members felt that disaster might lie ahead," McCutcheon reported. But the *Record-Herald* had been going downhill for some time, and the *Inter-Ocean* was stodgy and tottering. Victor Lawson wrote to the busi-nessmen who were backing Keeley, some of them department store owners, *"There is every prospect, in my judgment, that Mr. Keeley will make a great success of the new, combined paper."* But he was wrong. War in Europe soon boomed the American economy and newspaper circulations, but it also boosted the price of newsprint from $43.60 a ton in 1914 to $63.78 in 1917. Noncontract purchases were often repudiated, and prices doubled if the publisher went into a black market. By 1916, the *Tribune's* mill was producing 35,889 tons, within 5,000 tons of the paper's total needs although circulation had increased by 33,000. Keeley continued to be an able newspaper editor, but he could not cope with the management problems. Within four years he had failed his backers and lost his paper, which was taken over by Hearst, who combined it with his *Examiner*.

THE RETURN
OF THE FAMILY

17

Following Joe Patterson's return from Mexico in 1914, McCormick and Patterson completed a private compact for the direction and control of Tribune Company that would result in a lifelong partnership. It provided that the cousins would share responsibility for management and policy making, and that they would call in an arbitrator if they ever quarreled. They never did, McCormick wrote years later to editorialist Clifford Raymond. A portion of the agreement, in McCormick's handwriting and signed by both, was found years after the deaths of the two men by Tribune Company archivists. It concludes, *"The ironbound agreement lasts until we both are dead."*

This unique arrangement for the management of the *Chicago Tribune* was contrary to the belief of Joseph Medill that only one voice should direct a newspaper, and it was said by some to be doomed from the beginning. The division of the spheres of influence and management by the cousins that had been in effect since 1911 was logical enough, with McCormick working on the financial problems of the paper and for provision of adequate newsprint supplies at reasonable prices, and Patterson overseeing the Sunday *Tribune* and daily features. But one provision under the new agreement seemed completely absurd—they would share authority over the editorial page. They found they could accomplish this only if they alternated control from month to month. So this was done, McCormick, the Progressive Republican, directing editorial policy one month, and Patterson, formerly an avowed Socialist, taking the helm the next. This unusual practice continued until 1925, when Patterson turned

397

his full attention to the *New York News,* the company's new paper in the East, leaving McCormick in Chicago to follow an editorial policy of his own.

The separation of powers agreement worked well, even at the start. Although both men were strong-willed and had divergent views in many areas, they put together a tough, apparently unified editorial policy, sometimes hastily patched over by Raymond or Tiffany Blake, but solid and unflawed to public view. Each man regarded the other with genuine fondness and admiration, and they were tolerant with one another. Also they were determined that the disruptive family differences would be ended. McCormick, in any event, felt it was not the time for the *Tribune* to be attempting political leadership. The Progressive movement had proved a disaster for the Republican party. McCormick's goals in 1914 were to maintain *Tribune* support for Republicans of all persuasions and to mend party breaks, while attempting to please the members of his own family, his conservative mother and aunt, the moderately liberal Medill McCormick, plus Joe Patterson and his ultraliberal director, William Bross Lloyd.

Patterson was amenable. While he continued to hold his public ownership views, he no longer had illusions about the immediate potential of the Socialist party. He grew interested in a more acceptable form of political activism, the women's suffrage movement (by late 1913, Illinois had granted women full voting rights), and took himself away from Chicago for extended periods with self-selected assignments. He kept McCormick informed of his views wherever he happened to be. While in London, Patterson wrote of the suffrage movement, concluding his letter with an encouraging comment, *"The* Tribune *looks good to me."* Again, in New York, he noted the importance of the suffrage drive, predicting that it would achieve its goal of a constitutional amendment, and he described to Bert some of the comely leaders of the movement in the East. *"When you come to New York I'll arrange for you to have dinner with them,"* he wrote. *"If you don't want to talk, you can look."* As a correspondent with American troops on the Mexican border, Patterson indicated he was also keeping track of events elsewhere. *"I'd be pleased if it would please you to approve the President's policy of government ownership of railroads in Alaska,"* he wrote to McCormick. At another time he suggested a "Legal Voice of the People" column to aid those who could not afford lawyers, and the new service feature was soon instituted.

The *Tribune* gave extensive coverage to the women's suffrage movement, with McCutcheon's cartoons showing enthusiasm for the cause, while the editorials were friendly but somehow bemused. There were almost daily stories, and the meeting of more than 10,000 Chicago members of the Women's Trade Union League to hear Emma Steghoves of New York exhort them into partisan politics was given almost full-page coverage. The women in the movement, the paper noted, included waitresses, clerks, shoemakers, glove makers, and representatives of 25 other trades and professions, as well as housewives. The *Tribune* commented that the paper employed more than 150 women.

When President-elect Woodrow Wilson came to Chicago on January 11, 1913, to explain his "New Freedom" program, it was not difficult for the *Tribune* to be warm, for he appeared to have written his speech from the paper's Progressive editorials. "The business of the United States," Wilson told the conservative Commercial Club members, "must be set absolutely free of every feature of monopoly." The president-elect attacked the perfidious tariff lobby, called for new banking laws, promised action against the trusts, and spoke well of free competition, as the *Tribune* had done under Joseph Medill, Medill McCormick, and again under Robert R. McCormick and Joseph Patterson. Wilson also promised strong action to bring order back to Mexico, where American citizens and property were being menaced by the revolutionaries. None of this was repugnant to McCormick, who later had an interview with Wilson's secretary of state, William Jennings Bryan, and wrote his mother that he had even made peace with that old enemy. *"I told him that political and journalistic partisanship should not enter the realm of foreign affairs."*

McCormick's diplomatic handling of the family problems brought favorable responses from Aunt Nellie, and, evidently, editorial assistance from his mother, for he wrote her early in 1913: *"Dear Mother . . . Your editorial on divorce is by far the best contribution we have had on the subject, both as to the statement of principles and as to the phrasing of it. I agree with you that it is better as you wrote it than as it was printed. As far as rewriting goes, every editorial is copy-read. Joe told me long ago that this practice was established by your father, who had his own editorials read over and changed."* Mrs. McCormick had urged that uniform marriage laws were more needed than uniform divorce laws. Her son clearly was a match for both her and Aunt Nellie.

Joe Patterson's suggestion that probably did the most to weld relations with his cousin had been written early in their new relationship, April, 1911, when he sent a note to each of the directors of the company, proposing that Robert's salary of $5,000 a year be doubled. *"He has assumed practically the entire responsibility for finance of the paper as well as building the mill,"* Patterson pointed out. The suggestion received a favorable vote. On another occasion, in describing his own activities for the paper on the Mexican border, Patterson displayed his boyish affection for his cousin in a postscript: *"You are my best friend. Sniff! Sniff!"* And when he departed to cover the war in Europe late in 1914, Patterson left a confidential memorandum for McCormick, requesting the latter to handle his personal affairs, *"if I should get bumped."* On August 14, 1914,

Patterson wrote attorney Beale, chairman of the executive committee, *"The* Tribune *has done very well under Bert and myself and I don't hesitate to attribute the major part of this success to him."* Even Aunt Nellie at the time set down in writing her favorable thoughts about her nephew Bertie.

* * *

McCormick and Patterson had done well prior to the departure of James Keeley, but they recognized the enormity of their editorial loss. In a note to McCormick, Patterson admitted he did not know all he should about the newspaper business, and McCormick was equally candid about his own lack of experience. (McCormick would later explain his accession to the *Tribune* presidency by saying, "The family knew I didn't know anything about the newspaper business, but also they knew that I wasn't a Socialist.") The two began their regime by announcing the departure of Keeley on page one May 13, saying in part:

> He takes with him to his new venture profound newspaper experience and conspicuous native ability and he leaves behind him permanent results of many years of faithful and brilliant work. . . . We have no doubt that he will give to the combined properties [*the* Record-Herald *and the* Inter-Ocean] a high moral and editorial tone for he is that kind of man. . . . We wish him Godspeed in his new enterprise.
>
> There will be no change in the *Tribune*'s staff. As in the past the vacancy will be filled by the next in line. . . . The family of Joseph Medill will continue to conduct the *Tribune* as it has done since 1855, with a brief intermission from '71 to '74 [*sic*]. The policy will be guided in the future as in the past by the ideals of that great man—freedom, courage and justice.
>
> Robert R. McCormick   Joseph M. Patterson
Editors and Publishers

Obvious improvement at the *Tribune* was almost immediate. The new managers had feared that Keeley would attract much advertising from the paper, since several owners of large downtown stores were investors in his new *Herald.* Also they feared that Keeley's ingenuity would take circulation away from the *Tribune,* despite the fact that he had failed to lure circulation manager Max Annenberg. Both fears were unrealized. Keeley had trouble running against his own editorial formula, carried out capably at the *Tribune* by managing editor Beck and the new city editor, Walter Howey. Since the *Tribune* was concerned about street sales, they increased the use of banner headlines and attempted to improve the appearance of the paper with lively photographs and excellent maps and charts. Keeley had given his young successors valuable experience when he went to Europe in 1913 in search of comics for the paper, and again, just before his departure, by taking a long vacation, another European voyage. And the new proprietors were not total neophytes.

Robert McCormick had spent much of his youth with Grandfather Medill, and knew his thoughts about the newspaper business. Joseph Patterson had been schooled by his own father, before politics took Joe away from the newspaper office. The cousins found themselves easily adapting traditional *Tribune* policies from the Joseph Medill era. They attacked the Democratic mayor, again a Carter Harrison, and they went after monopolies and trusts, calling for approval of the Clayton Act and the Federal Trade Commission Act to help eliminate nefarious business practices. A major campaign against the "trust politicians" produced page-one banner headlines exposing a "secret lobby" in Washington. This turned out to be an agency of the National Association of Manufacturers. The *Tribune* continued its attack, charging the association with attempting to rig the tariff laws and railroad legislation. Soon the "insurance trust" came under *Tribune* guns for other economic offenses. The editorial pages in many respects resembled those in the days when Henry Demarest Lloyd, the first of the muckrakers, was in charge.

The paper also was hospitable to new ideas for improving city government, and it sent reporters about the United States and Canada searching for examples. It found that the municipal operation of street railways was highly successful in Winnipeg. Toronto and Montreal were effectively removing and incinerating garbage. Henry M. Hyde, who was the chief author of the series, which adopted a "We Will" identification symbol, traveled to London to find the best example of effective police protection. London methods, he said, might enable Chicago to better protect its 70 miles of waterfront, which was hardly policed at all.

That summer of 1914, in response to increasing newspaper and public outcry against Chicago vice and crime, Mayor Harrison directed his new police chief, tough, incorruptible Capt. James Gleason, who had earlier smashed the notorious "car barn gang" of bandits, to shut down the entire red-light district. Gleason chose as his field marshals former army major M. C. L. Funkhouser and Detective W. C. Dannenberg, who were put in charge of a task force called the Morals Squad. Funkhouser and Dannenberg rampaged through the Levee, first closing Big Jim Colosimo's restaurant and vice headquarters to show that Colosimo and his nephew, Johnny Torrio, had lost their immunity. Next to go were houses of prostitution, saloons, gambling joints, and panel dives controlled by Colosimo and Torrio with the assistance of Aldermen Hinky Dink Kenna and Bathhouse John Coughlin and their police captain, Michael "White Alley" Ryan, known around town as Chief of Police of the First Ward.

It was the first all-out drive against the crime lords in Chicago since the forays of Long John Wentworth. The *Tribune,* the citizens' Committee of 15, other civic groups, and preachers claimed credit for the massive onslaught on the Levee. Rival newspapers sought to outshout the *Tribune*'s coverage, banner headlines, and indignant editorials, but did not succeed. The *Tribune* printed reports on "secret" meetings of the Colosimo–Torrio forces seeking ways to stop the raids—attempts to buy off Dannenberg and to kill him both failed—and *Tribune* men were present when the Levee gangsters fought Dannenberg's police on July 16, 1914, in a street battle in which one policeman was killed and four were wounded. Newspaper reports of that fight and the *Tribune*'s assertion that the gang gunmen had used dumdum bullets aroused Chicago.

The *Tribune* blamed corrupt politicians and citizen indifference as well as criminals for the Levee evils, saying in its editorial the day after the battle in the Levee streets:

> There are three reasons why the tragedy of the Levee could not have been avoided. First, in order of importance, is Ald. "Hinky Dink" Kenna, the absolute overlord of Chicago vice. . . . The Levee exists because it is by the denizens of the Levee that he rolls up the voting power that causes such men as Carter Harrison and Roger Sullivan [*the Chicago and Illinois Democratic boss*] to consult him as a political peer; and County Judge [*John*] Owens to have him as a trimmer.
>
> Second is "Bathhouse John" Coughlin. He it is who rubs elbows with that powerful source of graft and revenue, the red-light district. Coughlin takes his orders and does not fear to rush in where Kenna fears to tread.
>
> Third is Captain Michael Ryan of the Twenty-second street Police Station. He is Chief of Police of the First Ward. The "Hink" put him there. The "Hink" and the "Bath" keep him there. He has been denounced as either notoriously corrupt or incompetent, but Funkhouser, Dannenberg, Gleason and Hoyne [*State's Attorney Maclay Hoyne*] cannot budge Ryan from that station. They have all tried and failed.
>
> In other cities the one "ring" has been found to be a clique of gambling kings who ruled the situation; in Chicago the ring is extended to the formation of a complete wheel. Ryan is the hub. His plainclothes policemen, his confidential men, are the spokes. . . . But more important than any of these parts . . . is the axle . . . and this axle is "the little fellow" to every denizen of the district, or "Hinky Dink."

John McCutcheon, whose cartoons had become a page-one feature of the *Tribune* seven days a week, trained his pen on the elements of corruption. The demands for reform increased; the ministers preached angry sermons; and at last Mayor Harrison removed White Alley Ryan from the First Ward and assigned a determined, honest German police-man, Capt. Max Nootbar, to the vice district. For the first time a red-light area of a major world city was permanently closed. The women scattered, the vice lords set them up in hotels and flats in other parts of Chicago, or retreated to their roadhouses in a few wide-open suburbs, and the segregated district was gone. Big Jim Colosimo had failed the first duty of a vice lord, to protect his own. He was arrested and jailed for the first time in his life; his tight hold on the underworld was shaken.

The *Tribune* grudgingly gave Mayor Harrison credit for the successful action against the Levee. "The respectable elements of Chicago will thank His Honor, Mayor Harrison," the paper said. "Chicago will take a long step toward good government." McCutcheon's page-one cartoon praised the mayor, but the gangs were far from defeated.

*   *   *

One of the important developments in the newspaper circulation wars in New York had been the color comics. Another, brought from Europe, was the use of rotogravure supplements. The *Tribune* had experimented with comics since zinc etchings were used on newspaper presses, but few had survived long. After Hearst established his papers in Chicago, sending in such Eastern favorites as "The Katzenjammer Kids," James Keeley had been sent to Europe to find adequate competition. It appeared that a German artist would be needed to match the Katzenjammer Kids' popularity, so Keeley brought back Lionel Feininger, who drew "Der Kinder Kids." The *Tribune* promotion department printed notices and distributed posters hailing Feininger as a genuine German artist, a campaign expected to especially aid circulation in the large German community. Keeley had ascertained Feininger's skills, but not his motivation and ambition, which was to become Americanized as speedily as possible and to win recognition in the fine arts. Feininger drew a page of gag cartoons with incorrigible children as the chief characters for a time, but then insisted, with Teutonic obduracy, on doing a page to be called "Wee Willie Winkle" or nothing. Keeley and the *Tribune* surrendered and Wee Willie appeared, but Feininger shortly departed for a career in the fine arts. When Patterson took over, the *Tribune* had a four-page comic section, mostly gag comics, with "Mama's Little Angel," a kind of antidote against the Katzenjammer Kids, getting top billing, and Sidney Smith's "Old Doc Yak," concerning an old goat and his humanized son, in second place.

Even before the departure of Keeley, Patterson began pushing the artists toward his goals. He wanted story lines for the comics, and real people involved, and he urged Smith to think about substituting a man, a common man, for his goat. He joined Keeley in looking about for tested work. Rudolph Dirk, who had been drawing the Katzenjammers in imitation of the originator, Wilhelm Busch, for Hearst's *New York Journal*, left the *Journal* to do a similar strip, called "Hans und Fritz," for the *New York World*, and the *World* made it available. Thus the *Tribune* got the

German comic it wanted, renaming it "The Captain and the Kids" after the United States entered the war against Germany in 1917.

Patterson's greatest achievements were not represented in print until after the war, since comic artists always have been slow to change. Sidney Smith's "Old Doc Yak" became "The Gumps" under Patterson's direction, carried a story line, and introduced characters newspaper readers learned to love—chinless Andy Gump and his wife, Min; Chester, their son; Uncle Bimbo, Andy's multimillionaire uncle from Australia; and the Widow Zander, who wanted Bim and his money as much as Andy did. The comic appeared in color on Sundays and as a strip daily, and it became a prime property of the fledgling Chicago Tribune Newspapers Syndicate (later the Chicago Tribune–New York News Syndicate), which burgeoned under Patterson and sold rights around the world. Smith and Patterson involved the public so deeply in the comic strip characters that newspaper buyers often asked for "the Andy Gump paper." In 1923 they were able to do the unthinkable, dooming the lovely Mary Gold, a heroine in the strip, to die. When this horrid fate was foretold, hundreds of readers appeared before the Tribune Building to protest, and thousands of calls jammed the telephone switchboards, so that extra operators had to be brought in to handle the traffic. But Mary Gold was committed to die. After the solemn moment was portrayed, thousands more called the *Tribune* and other newspapers carrying "The Gumps" to express their outrage, and more hundreds showed up before the Tribune Building as mourners. Earlier, on a happier occasion, when Uncle Bim was saved from marrying the scheming Widow Zander, the Minneapolis Board of Trade stopped action long enough for the joyful news to be read on the floor, news greeted by wild masculine cheers.

Other artists were similarly inspired by Patterson, who assembled them regularly in his "bull pen" to discuss ideas, characters, and story lines. He acquired and directed Carl Ed in the development of "Harold Teen," the story of a mooning youth and Lillums, his girl friend, which created its special teen argot and fashions. He was also responsible for "Winnie Winkle," by Martin Branner; "Smitty," the office boy, by Walter Berndt; "Moon Mullins," by Frank Willard; and the seemingly ageless and imperishable "Little Orphan Annie," by Harold Gray. Precocious Annie, taken from the James Whitcomb Riley poem, started in 1924 as a zero-eyed waif whose sole possession was her beloved dog, Sandy. Like Andy Gump she had a rich relative, a mysterious Daddy Warbucks who appeared with his magical servant Punjab when the plot became too complicated for any other quick solutions. In later years, Annie and Daddy Warbucks turned into ultraconservative symbols, so pleasing to the establishment that when Sandy disappeared in 1933 and Annie was as hysterical as she ever became, a Detroit motor tycoon telegraphed the Tribune Syndicate: "PLEASE DO ALL YOU CAN TO HELP ANNIE FIND SANDY. WE ARE ALL INTERESTED. HENRY FORD."

In 1931, Patterson, in New York, opened a package of drawings from Chester Gould, who was drawing a "Film Fables" strip for the *American* in Chicago. Gould had created a plainclothes detective, called "Plainclothes Tracy." Patterson liked what he saw and arranged at once to put Gould under contract, provided that he would change the name of his proposed strip to "Dick Tracy" and would agree to consult with Patterson on the story line. "Dick Tracy" started in the *New York News* on October 12, 1931, moved into the *Tribune* on March 22, 1932, and has been the front-page Sunday comic for both papers for years, as well as a daily strip. Tracy, drawn by a man whose imagination and inventiveness matched Patterson's, was the first to glamorize police work on the basis of careful research and has been one of the most successful strips in cartoon history. But it was Robert McCormick who claimed credit for another of the famed Tribune–News comics, "Gasoline Alley." It existed as a panel cartoon created by Frank King and ran in the editorial section, McCormick's special domain. McCormick urged King to make it a strip, following the customary Patterson story line. A big event in the life of bachelor Walt Wallet, hero of the strip, occurred on February 14, 1921, when a valentine left on Walt's doorstep turned out to be a foundling whom "Uncle Walt" named "Skeezix." Third-generation Gasoline Alley characters continue to appear more than half a century later in newspapers throughout the world.

Patterson became an acknowledged genius in the world of syndicated strips. He insisted that the characters depict the lives and dreams, hardships and accomplishments of the kind of people who could be found in mass newspaper readership. He suggested ideas, coached the artists, and provided promotional stunts and campaigns to sell the comic wares. His formula was simple: "Youngsters for kid appeal, a handsome guy for muscle work and love interest, a succession of pretty girls, a mysterious locale or a totally familiar one." All these ideas came together in "Winnie Winkle," the story of a working girl, and in Patterson's formula masterpiece, "Terry and the Pirates," initially devised by Milton Caniff, who was lured from the Tribune Syndicate following Patterson's death.

Only once did Patterson show disdain for a strip that became successful, Dale Messick's "Brenda Starr," which was launched in the *Tribune* and did not appear in the *New York News* until after Patterson's death. When Brenda got into difficulties, Ardis M. Kennedy, Sunday editor of the *Tribune,* did the coaching. Brenda has proved as ageless and enduring as Annie, enjoying a public relations triumph in 1976 when she married her eye-patched boyfriend, Basil St. John, after 31 years of platonic friendship. The wedding and reception in Washington, D.C., were reported by national news magazines and world press services, and inspired Ann Landers, columnist of the rival *Chicago Sun-Times,* to comment: "Brenda has been 23 years old for 36 years and still a virgin. That's pretty nigh impossible." The *Sun-Times* covered the Washington reception, which Landers herself attended, with a news account and a three-column picture.

Patterson's interests were by no means limited to comics and special features. Although McCormick had charge of the *Tribune*'s foreign correspondents, Patterson suggested assignments for them. He also was involved in the importation of a rotogravure press from Germany shortly before the outbreak of the war. He had revised the format of the *Workers' Magazine* to become a general interest Sunday magazine, and he started the *Chicago Tribune Pictorial Weekly,* a rotogravure publication. Mary King, meantime, in addition to being assistant Sunday editor, had taken over the women's features as women's editor and she aided Patterson in the purchase of fiction to run Sundays and in the daily paper as well. Patterson, in developing special *Tribune* Sunday sections, told writer Burton Rascoe that he wanted a Sunday magazine so excellent no one would feel an urge to buy one of the national weeklies.

*　　*　　*

Plans changed abruptly for Patterson and McCormick, as they would shortly for all Americans and most of the rest of the world. In the summer of 1914 stability appeared to have been restored in Mexico, thanks to Wilson's firm policy. The *Tribune* banner on July 16, 1914, announced: "HUERTA ABDICATES: CARRANZA INVITED TO THE CAPITAL." Provisional president Victoriano Huerta, whose revolution had cost American lives and property, was forced to make way for President Venustiano Carranza. But more spectacular events were soon to preoccupy the world. On June 28, 1914, as American suffragettes marched in Washington, Archduke Francis Ferdinand, heir to the Austrian throne, was killed by a Serb nationalist at Sarajevo. The assassination got little immediate attention in the *Tribune* or the Chicago press generally, but it was the beginning of a new era for America and for the world, an incident that did more to speed national suffrage and a new way of life for American women than all the marching that had taken place in a century.

Austria declared war on Serbia on July 28. Russia mobilized the next day; the New York Stock Exchange closed temporarily to avoid panic;

Germany declared war on Russia on August 1, prepared to move into Belgium, and declared war on France on August 3. The United States proclaimed its neutrality on August 4, the day Britain declared war on Germany.

On August 2, the *Tribune* published its most remembered editorial in the first quarter of the 20th century, written by Clifford Raymond:

The Twilight of the Kings

Before establishing hell on earth the pietistic kings commend their subjects to God. Seek the Lord's sanction for the devil's work.

"And now I commend you to God," said the kaiser from his balcony to the people in the street. "Go to church and kneel before God and pray for His help for your gallant army."

Pray that a farmer dragged from a Saxon field shall be speedier with a bayonet thrust than a winemaker taken from his vines in the Aube; that a Berlin lawyer shall be steadier with a rifle than a Moscow merchant; that a machine gun manned by Heidelberg students shall not jam and that one worked by Paris carpenters shall.

Pray that a Bavarian hop grower, armed in a quarrel in which he has no heat, shall outmarch a wheat grower from Poltava; that Cossacks from the Don shall be lured into barbed wire entanglements and caught by masked guns; that an innkeeper of Salzburg shall blow the head off a baker from the Loire.

"Go to church and pray for help"—that the hell shall be hotter in innocent Ardennes than it is in equally innocent Hessen; that it shall be hotter in innocent Kovno than in equally innocent Posen.

And the pietistic czar commends his subjects to God that they may have strength of arm in a quarrel they do not understand; that they may inflict more sufferings than they are required to endure and the name of Romanoff be greater than the name of Hohenzollern, that it may be greater than the name of Hapsburg, that its territories shall be wider and the territories of Hohenzollern and the territories of Hapsburg less.

The pietistic emperor of Austria commends his subjects to God, to seek divine assistance to crush the peasants of Serbia, dragged from the wheat field when it is ready for the scythe and given to the scythe themselves.

This is, we think, the last call of monarchy upon divinity when Asmodeus walks in armor. The kings worship Baal and call it God, but out of the sacrifice will come, we think, a resolution firmly taken to have no more wheat growers and growers of corn, makers of wine, miners and fishers, artisans and traders, sailors and storekeepers offered up with prayer to the Almighty in a feudal slaughter, armed against each other without hate and without cause they know, or, if they know, would not give a penny which way it was determined.

This is the twilight of the kings. Western Europe of the people may be caught in this debacle, but never again. Eastern Europe of the kings will be

remade and the name of God shall not give grace to a hundred square miles
of broken bodies.

　　If Divinity enters here it comes with a sword to deliver the people from
the sword.

　　It is the twilight of the kings. The republic marches east in Europe.

Newspaper circulations shot up; so did newsprint prices and the price
to subscribers. A paper shortage would soon develop despite the company's elaborate provision for its own supply. Boats chartered by
McCormick were taken over by the Canadian government for the war
effort, and there was a shortage of men to work in the Canadian woods
and the mill.

The *Tribune* had already ordered John T. McCutcheon to Europe
from the Mexican border, and James O'Donnell Bennett, in London
when the war began, was also directed to provide coverage. The British
and French were almost totally uncooperative with correspondents,
directing their activities, feeding them propaganda, and severely censor-
ing their dispatches. The Germans, guilty of violating Belgian neutrality
and later of conducting unrestricted submarine warfare, unpredictably
allowed more freedom to the reporters than any but Belgium of the
Allied powers.

The Allied restrictions led some correspondents to forage on their
own. This was highly dangerous but generally rewarding, taking some of
them further into the action than they had intended. In August, 1914,
McCutcheon and several of his peers found themselves frustrated in
Brussels as they sought battle news and verification of the atrocity reports
being released by the French and British, which depicted the raping of
women and the killing of women and children by German infantry and
cavalry. Failing to get permission from Allied authorities to go out toward
the German advance, McCutcheon and three others hired a taxicab.
Armed only with documents attesting to their American citizenship, they
passed through checkpoints and outposts until they had reached the city's
edge and were on their way to Louvain. They soon encountered columns
of fleeing refugees, and their driver balked. So the correspondents
proceeded on foot. Before long they realized the Germans were nearer
than they had expected, but when they tried to return to their cab they
found themselves cut off by a column of marching troops.

"We waited until we saw an especially jovial-looking German officer
and then reported to him, explaining in some trepidation how we
happened to be there. Instead of ordering us to be shot immediately, he
laughed heartily," McCutcheon wrote in his memoirs. The correspondents were soon released and allowed to travel with the German forces.
They saw wanton artillery destruction of the famed library at Louvain but
none of the alleged savagery against civilians. Their stories continued to

reflect the correct behavior of the German soldiery, though the troops undoubtedly were in Belgium in violation of a "scrap of paper," as the German foreign minister contemptuously termed the treaty that guaranteed Belgium's neutrality.

Later, McCutcheon and Bennett were among five American newsmen who prepared a joint statement that they had seen no evidence of the alleged German atrocities and sent it to the United States. "Even though none of us was pro-German in his sympathies, it was the unanimous opinion of all that the atrocity stories were being tremendously and intentionally exaggerated," wrote McCutcheon. When he arrived in Chicago in November, McCutcheon found that Germany was receiving good press and that the *Tribune,* in particular, was being criticized as a pro-German newspaper.

*   *   *

Both Patterson and McCormick made plans to cover the war themselves. Patterson embarked for France in August, taking with him Edwin Weigel, his motion picture cameraman. He immediately had problems with French and British censors, and, like other correspondents, decided that he would get more news by covering the German army in Belgium, where he reported on the Battle of Alost and before returning to the United States covered the fall of Antwerp, which Weigel filmed.

McCormick, some months later, was presented with an unusual opportunity to gain exclusive coverage for the *Tribune* on the Russian front. Since his father had served as U.S. ambassador to Russia, the family had friends in the czar's government and diplomatic corps. McCormick's father was ill, but his mother had kept in close touch with the Russian ambassador to the United States, George Bakhmeteff, and she was eager to help. She induced Ambassador Bakhmeteff to have her son invited to inspect the Russian army as "a distinguished foreigner personally known" to Grand Duke Nicholas Nicolaievitch, commander-in-chief of the Russian armies.

This arrangement would be possible, Bakhmeteff warned, only if McCormick possessed the military rank of colonel, as a minimum. It would be futile to go as a mere correspondent, Bakhmeteff said, since the Russian army would not permit reporters within miles of the front. McCormick was eager to act. Patterson was also hoping to return to Europe, but the cousins could be away from Chicago simultaneously if necessary. McCormick had made sure that newsprint was on hand or in prospect for the time he might be away. The *Tribune* had an efficient business office under William H. Field, business manager, and Daniel M. Deininger, controller. Managing editor E. S. Beck and assistant Sunday editor Mary King had the news and features departments well in hand, as did Tiffany Blake and Clifford Raymond the editorial page.

From a former *Tribune* enemy, Illinois Gov. Edward F. Dunne, McCormick obtained a commission as colonel of cavalry in the Illinois National Guard. He acquired the proper uniforms, including a swagger stick and a monocle, and, on the advice of Ambassador Bakhmeteff, white tie and tails for his expected audience with Czar Nicholas II. The new Colonel McCormick was now ready for the kind of travel coup that would become typical for him: He would interview government leaders—British at least, since some of his former schoolmates in England now occupied high office—and he would inspect the Russian army and send back occasional correspondence to his newspaper.

He would also have a honeymoon of almost regal status, for, as usual, McCormick had a double purpose in his trip. He intended to marry Mrs. Amie de Houle Irwin Adams (Amy by McCormick's spelling), a divorcée whose decree was to become final under Illinois law in March, at which time she could remarry. Colonel McCormick sailed for England on February 10, 1915. Mrs. Adams, daughter of a U.S. Army surgeon and former wife of McCormick's cousin, Edward Adams, sailed a week later. McCormick had occasionally resided with the couple in their Chicago and Lake Forest homes, where a romance began that ended in Amie's divorce. He and Amie were married in London on March 10.

McCormick's advance arrangements for his news-gathering tour in England were productive. He lunched twice with British Prime Minister H. H. Asquith, who asked him about the attitude of the American people toward the war. McCormick explained that while an elitist part of American society appeared to be definitely pro-Allied, or at least pro-British, most ordinary American citizens were against any kind of involvement, and many were pro-German, especially in Chicago. The young American colonel was briefed by Foreign Secretary Sir Edward Grey, met First Lord of the Admiralty Winston Churchill, beginning a lifelong friendship, and had discussions with newspaper magnate Lord Northcliffe about British censorship and propaganda, which Northcliffe, England's leading publisher, vehemently deplored. McCormick's dispatches to the *Tribune* indicated his friendliness toward the Allied cause, but his effort to obtain permission to visit the British lines in France was rebuffed. McCormick was determined to go to France, nonetheless. He had accepted as true and transmitted to the *Tribune* some of the atrocity stories made available by the British press office. Now he wanted to make sure about the reported shelling of hospitals and churches.

In France, Colonel McCormick was more successful. He obtained a pass to visit the ruins of the cathedral at Arras, destroyed by the Germans. Since he found that he was near the headquarters of Sir John French, commander of the British Expeditionary Forces, he promptly had his driver take him over and bluffed his way into the presence of General French by allowing the officer to assume he had been approved by the British War Office. That evening Colonel McCormick had dinner with French and his staff.

For the next several days he was shown about by Lord Brook, a colonel, like himself, or Maj. Charles Grant of the Coldstream Guards, and saw various units in action, including the Canadians at Ypres. There he acquired grist for commenting in his book *With the Russian Army*, "The British Expeditionary Force . . . without a whimper, without protest . . . went to its destruction in defense of the nation which had neglected it, just as our regular army must go some day unless by Grace of God we may learn preparedness in time."

McCormick, in his book, demonstrated that he had some of the writing talents of his cousin Joe: "One day Major Charles Grant of the Coldstream Guards took me to the front. He was the only one of seven officers of his company to be on his feet at the end of a day at Aisne. He had two bullet holes through his arm, and his tunic had been scorched by a shell that had blown him several yards. Only seven of his men out of 230 remained." After describing Major Grant's clear and calm issuance of orders under a heavy barrage, McCormick continued:

> From him I received a lesson in conduct under fire. . . . The men were not afraid. I was. I was very much afraid, and did not resist by a large margin the desire to ask my conductor to move to some safer place. This confession is not pleasant to make, but it is put down with a hope that other boys will be instructed in courage as I never was. . . . Physical courage varies with the individual, but the natural tendency in that direction can be improved like piano playing and polite conversation. It is a more desirable accomplishment for a man than either of these.

*   *   *

Following his news coverage of the British and Canadians in France, McCormick and Amie left London for Russia by way of the Balkans and Greece, McCormick carrying with him, at the request of the Russian Embassy and with the approval of the British War Office, a mysterious black box, which he was to deliver to a Russian official in Odessa and which he guarded carefully throughout the voyage.

McCormick had interviews with government officials en route to Russia and was received by an official Russian party at a border town on the Dneister, where he was told to carry his precious box to Petrograd, rather than Odessa. This he did, delivering it to Russian Assistant Minister of Foreign Affairs D'Artusnovich, without ever learning precisely what was inside; but he assumed it was a set of naval codes, to enable Russian and British fleets to coordinate their movements. Shortly he was ordered to Tsarskoye Selo, where he was presented to Nicholas II, czar of all the Russias. The czar was gracious during the brief audience, desiring McCormick to tell him about his observations on the western front.

Colonel McCormick was eager to go forward into the Russian lines, and he finally received the needed papers from the headquarters of Grand Duke Nicholas. He and Patterson had agreed that he too should have a motion picture cameraman, if he could find one—Patterson planned to take Weigel with him to France. In Petrograd, McCormick discovered a free-lance photographer from Kansas, Donald F. Thompson, who had a "cinema" camera, and arranged with him to go to the front as McCormick's aide. Thus prepared, they boarded a military train to a point in Galicia, where Colonel McCormick was invited to dine with Nicholas Nicolaievitch. Then he and Thompson were at last allowed to go to the front lines.

McCormick's reports mingled his desire to acquaint readers at home with military life in an especially exotic area with his need to maintain the military responsibilities he had assumed. He paid special attention to the technical aspects, since he was officially there, after all, as a military observer: "The cannon wheels rest on a central wooden platform, and, to get the requisite elevation, the trail is let down into a circular excavation cut around the platform. To obtain the exactitude of range necessary for wing shooting, a 'jack-knife' method has been devised, indicative of a high state of originality in the Russian artillery arm." On trench warfare: "The trench winds continually to prevent enfilading fire and to limit the effect of a fortunately placed shell." But McCormick, like newsmen generally, was at his best with the human side of the war. In an army hospital in Poland he saw a young soldier beaming at him and guessed that he spoke English. "He said that he had worked in the steel mills in South Chicago," McCormick wrote. "Thinking to cheer him up, I said we would be glad to see him in Chicago after the war, and he replied—'Oh, I can never go back to America.' 'Why?' said I, and in answer he lifted the bedcovers, showing two stumps where his legs had been and over his face came an expression that I would not describe if I could." And, of a blind soldier: "I stopped spellbound at his misery. I was told that I might photograph him, as he would not know it. Nothing could have made me do so. It is enough that his expression should be seared upon my memory forever."

Donald Thompson, who often tried to go beyond the trenches for better photographs but usually was stopped by the Russians, was praised for his bravery by his employer. The pair also observed the fighting in the Carpathians, about which McCormick wrote:

Mountain warfare is the only warfare these days where anything can be seen. . . . A mile away a Russian battery was planted in the open to cover some strategic ground. The Austrians were firing upon it with shrapnel, and other Russian batteries firing to protect it. The horizon was fairly dotted with puffs of darkened smoke, but my neighborhood was in the sleepy quiet of a spring noonday.

Modern guns are protected with armored shields and modern gunners are quick to build shrapnel-proof homes; so that while the Austrians have shelled this battery until more bullets than grass can be seen in its vicinity, its losses for a month have not much exceeded one man a day.

McCormick wrote of champagne and caviar with the officers and of his surprise that the Cossacks, whom he had seen only in Wild West shows in America, looked and behaved like the rest of the Russians. He paid his respects to the well-trained Russian fighting men and to that other ingredient of trench warfare, the lice. He concluded his Carpathian experience on a somber note:

Our regiment had a splendid searchlight, or projector, as they called it. It was mounted on a collapsible structure that could be put up or taken down and transported without difficulty. While I was standing looking through a loop-hole the light was turned on, and quite halfway between the opposing trenches I saw a German scout. He was less than 100 yards away and as clearly defined as a shooting gallery bull's-eye. I shrank a little, as I do not like to see men killed, and this scene was as dramatic as a play. As the seconds passed, my nervousness increased; I felt that some sure marksman was drawing a steady bead.

No shot was fired and the man was suffered to withdraw to the shelter of a rifle pit.

I could not understand why the man was allowed to escape. If he had been picked up by the searchlight during a period of absolute calm, failure to shoot might have been explained on the ground of a desire not to start a fusillade, but at this time the enemy were firing not only with rifles but with machine guns.

As we returned to the regimental headquarters I mentioned the subject to one of the officers. His answer was "À quoi bon tuer le pauvre malheureux?" [*What good would it do to kill the poor fellow?*]

There is a strange psychology about the Russians that is hard to fathom. Their military tradition and military success are founded upon an ability to undergo a greater butchery than their enemy, and yet they would not take a life as clearly forfeited as the one I had just seen. I do not believe any other nationality of men, under the same circumstances, would have allowed an enemy to escape.

En route home, Colonel McCormick stopped in Norway, where he met James O'Donnell Bennett, who was rated by McCormick as the best correspondent on any battlefront. He covered the German army on the eastern front at the time McCormick was with the Russians. His dispatch on the fall of Novo Georgievsk appearing in the *Tribune* on August 27, 1915, is exemplary of his excellent writing, which survived military telegraph, cable, and the copy editors:

> NOVO GEORGIEVSK (By Courier to Warsaw and by Military Telegraph to Berlin)—The fortress of Novo Georgievsk is a roaring furnace. The hamlets around the forts are bedded with live coals, and the barracks, chapel, bake houses and armory buildings, stretched along the heights a hundred feet above the waters of the Narev and the Vistula, are in flames.
>
> The fire has already reached the munitions chambers and the stores the Russians could neither remove nor destroy are exploding in ceaseless volleys. Bullets are thrown a hundred feet from the windows by these explosions and come swishing and pattering down among the trees along the river like a hailstorm.
>
> The fire is raging for blocks behind walls seven feet thick and the chill night wind is driving the flames steadily forward and is forcing them in crimson streams through the sally ports, ventilators and chimneys.
>
> Already some of the walls have begun to melt and are sinking slowly into the craters created by the fire of the Austrian thirty and a half centimeter mortar batteries. . . . [*After further description of the destruction and the flames menacing the wounded and the stretcher bearers, Bennett continues.*] Taking one of these passages I penetrated to the great paved court before the garrison church. Just before the chapel lies a dead Russian soldier. . . .

While in Norway, McCormick also talked with the famed explorer Roald Amundsen, whom he later engaged to write on polar explorations for the *Tribune*. In Montreal he and Joe Patterson conferred about *Tribune* affairs. Patterson was on his way to the battlefronts. McCormick had been away six months, Patterson would be gone for two.

* * *

Unlike McCormick and characteristically, Joseph Medill Patterson elected to cover the war as an ordinary newspaperman, which, in the beginning, caused him some problems. The British and French had not relaxed their censorship, but Patterson made his way to the front lines in France despite such harassment and scored a first by persuading a French pilot to take him on an airplane flight over the French lines in Flanders, Nieuport, and Woester. He also arranged for an excellent aerial photograph of the stark ruins of Ypres, shattered by German shelling, which appeared as a full-page roto print in the Sunday *Tribune Pictorial Weekly*.

Accompanied by Weigel, Patterson again covered the German army and received excellent cooperation from the Germans. Patterson, like McCormick, wrote a book about his wartime experience, *Notebook of a Neutral*, which appeared serially in the *Tribune* in the fall of 1915. In it he praised German efficiency and declared that France and England could win the war only if they adopted similarly effective military methods.

By September, 1915, the *Tribune* could boast that it had more correspondents at the fronts than any other Chicago morning paper—Joe Patterson, John McCutcheon, James O'Donnell Bennett, Carolyn Wilson, and Oscar King Davis—and also the complete world services of the Associated Press and the United Press and the correspondence of several New York and European newspapers. In addition, each European country was covered by one or more stringers, writers paid for dispatches only if they appeared in print. It was said that Robert R. McCormick was the only American correspondent to send wartime reports from the Balkan countries.

The *Tribune*'s reputation for news coverage benefited also from the motion picture documentaries produced by McCormick and Patterson and their photographers. McCormick's documentary, *With the Russian Army*, was shown at the downtown Studebaker Theater for weeks, beginning at 10 A.M. each day, until it was moved to the Midway Gardens Theater to make room for Patterson's documentary, *The German Side of the War*, taken by Weigel, who returned to Chicago to deliver the commentary. Block-long crowds awaited their opportunity to view the action scenes of trench warfare and battle areas and the lives of people at war, paying 25¢ each, half the profits going to the Fund for the Blind and Crippled Soldiers. The *Tribune*'s war films later had equal success in New York theaters.

*   *   *

Few travelers boarding the British Cunard liner *Lusitania* on a May morning in 1915 had read a somewhat obscure notice placed by the German consulate in the New York papers to warn them against taking passage on that particular ship. On May 8, the *Tribune*'s banner was black and bold: "1,400 DEAD ON LUSITANIA: SAVED 658." The final death toll was nearly 1,200, including 128 Americans. A list of the Chicago passengers aboard was provided and there were five pages of text and pictures. Said the *Tribune* editorial: "To the slaughter of innocents in Belgium and Poland has been added the slaughter of innocents on the *Lusitania*. Whether the American government will acquiesce to this new German law of the sea is a question that will agitate all American hearts today and all days until the decision is announced." The decision referred to was a proposed U.S. ultimatum, following past ineffectual American protests. When President Wilson made public his protest note, which was no stronger than the paper had anticipated, it said on June 1: "An ultimatum must not be followed by a slap on the wrist. An ultimatum which involves nothing more than breaking of diplomatic relations will accomplish nothing except to impress the world with our futility and to invite further aggression." Then, referring to a speech Wilson had made only three days after the *Lusitania*'s sinking in which he had said, "There is such a thing as a man being too proud to fight," the *Tribune* remarked, "If we are too proud to fight let's be too proud to talk as if we were ready to fight."

In July, Dr. Heinrich Albert, director of German propaganda in America, carelessly left his briefcase on a New York subway train. It was recovered by the U.S. Secret Service and found to contain documents signed by Ambassador Johann von Bernstorff and military attaché Capt. Franz von Papen among others, revealing plans for espionage and sabotage activities against the United States. The *New York World* obtained copies of the documents and they were supplied in its service to the *Tribune,* which also published them.

*   *   *

Chicago that summer was having its own problems. The city had recovered from still another national recession, but a building boom that was lining Lake Michigan with apartment skyscrapers and was expanding both the residential and industrial suburbs was stopped abruptly by a series of building trades strikes. The *Tribune* called on Chicago's new mayor, William Hale "Big Bill" Thompson, to bring an end to the labor strife. Thompson, a former ranch cook, cowboy, and football hero, had won the Republican nomination for mayor in the spring following a vigorous campaign. Working 18 hours a day seven days a week in the primary, he had attracted favorable attention from the *Tribune.* "He has great physical vitality and a fighting spirit," wrote Henry M. Hyde, the paper's specialist on urban affairs. "Good or bad, there will always be something doing if William Hale Thompson is elected mayor."

Opposing Thompson for the mayoralty was Democrat Robert M. Sweitzer, whose pro-German appeal encouraged Big Bill to assume a strongly pro-German stance himself. The *Tribune* at the time was running a series of articles expressing skepticism regarding the atrocity charges the British and French were making against the Germans. Thompson quoted from the articles and in turn got *Tribune* headlines: "THOMPSON SAYS BRITISH DIPLOMACY STARTED THE WAR!" "THOMPSON DENOUNCES ATROCITY PROPAGANDA!" "THOMPSON SAYS GERMANS FIGHT FAIRLY AND BRAVELY!" Fred Lundin, Big Bill's mentor and campaign manager, then reprinted the headlines in German for the estimated 600,000 Germans and Austrians in the city.

Thompson won easily, defeating Sweitzer by 139,189 votes and carrying with him Progressive party candidates for lesser city offices. Colonel McCormick, who was abroad, was not displeased to learn that his erstwhile boyhood hero had won the election. McCormick as a youth had admired Big Bill's athletic prowess but had been disillusioned when he heard Thompson himself boast of his exploits in the Levee. Nevertheless, the two men had been on friendly terms when both were members of the city council.

By mid-June, labor troubles had spread to the streetcar and elevated lines, until more than 11,000 workers had walked away from their jobs. The night of June 16, the mayor finally responded to calls from the *Tribune* and others that he end the strikes that were disabling the city. He summoned both union and management leaders to City Hall and informed them that none would leave until the public transportation strikes were settled. During the next 16 hours Thompson, his shirt sleeves rolled and his collar open, scuttled between the negotiating and conference rooms, exhorting both sides to modify their position. The union leaders were stubborn; the cost of living had jumped, and they had the support of many civic leaders and political progressives, including Medill McCormick and his wife, Ruth. But, by midday on the 17th, Mayor Thompson called in newsmen to announce that the strike was over.

The *Tribune* praised Mayor Thompson with a front-page McCutcheon cartoon, "Saved by the Mayor," and an editorial that said in part: "Mayor Thompson had the power and he had the sand. He took a masterful shortcut to victory and the honors are his. . . . The community owes him a substantial debt of gratitude. The situation called for iron hands, and Thompson had them."

The building strikes ended, giving Chicago a taste of the prosperity Thompson had promised in his campaign, but the crooks, whom he had threatened to drive from the city, were still around. In fact, suggested the *Tribune*, there seemed to be more of them. There was talk around the country of William Hale Thompson as the Republican candidate for president. The *Tribune* preferred to talk of the crime wave. Abruptly, Mayor Thompson announced that he intended to enforce the saloon Sunday closing law, an action that had caused trouble for Chicago mayors back in the days of Joseph Medill and Levi Boone. A young Bohemian named Anton J. Cermak, secretary of the United Societies for Local Self-Government, led a demonstration against such action, and Thompson petulantly demanded to know why there was so much fuss. "I'm no reformer," Thompson insisted. Was the drive against the saloons triggered by his presidential hopes? "No," said Thompson, "I acted because Charles Deneen, supported by the *Tribune*, intends to have me indicted for failing to enforce the Sunday closing law."

The *Tribune*, however, seemed far from taking the bluenose attitude claimed by Thompson. It ran a page-one article telling Chicagoans how to enjoy a dry Sunday, by attending church or visiting museums, parks, libraries, and theaters, under the heading "Entertainment for a Dry Sunday." There was an implication that there would not be many of them. The first dry Sunday, Mayor Thompson's police chief, Charles C. Healy, closed 28 saloons. Healy's men also raided a soft drink parlor operated by George "Cap" Streeter, an eccentric squatter on the lakefront who claimed most of Chicago's northeast downtown area, which later became its "Gold Coast," the domicile of the wealthy. Streeter called his domain "The District of Lake Michigan." His wife, "Ma" Streeter, shot and wounded one of the raiders, an action starting a series of legal steps that eventually achieved the ouster of Cap and Ma from the wrecked houseboat from which, with a shotgun or two, they had ruled their waterlogged empire for nearly 30 years. The saloon raids ended, and Mayor Thompson, who had observed that most of the United Societies demonstrators were German, though their leader was a Czech, became first among Chicago's pro-Germans as the war engulfed Europe. He was soon known as "Kaiser Bill."

*   *   *

In late July, 1915, Chicago was shocked by its worst tragedy since the Iroquois Theater fire. On a Saturday nearly 2,000 workers from the Western Electric Company boarded the excursion steamer *Eastland* for their annual outing on Lake Michigan. The overloaded vessel, docked in the Chicago River, slowly sank until its keel touched river bottom, then listed and turned over, drowning 812 men, women, and children. Throughout the afternoon and evening, police, firemen, Coast Guard, and volunteer rescuers saved hundreds of survivors who were in the water or had climbed atop the broached hull, while the hundreds of dead were carried to morgues improvised among the sheds and warehouses lining the river. At the *Tribune,* managing editor Beck remembered his experiences organizing the Iroquois fire coverage under Keeley. He and city editor Howey marshaled their forces: The *Tribune* reporters and photographers found and identified corpses, talked to grieving kin, interviewed ships' officers arrested for negligence, and provided 11 pages of text and photographs, including again an almost complete list of the dead and missing, with their addresses. The *Tribune*'s eight-column photograph of the *Eastland* on its side, with victims clinging to its hull and lines, dramatically highlighted the paper's excellent coverage. The investigations of the disaster continued for years, without precisely establishing a cause. The *Tribune* was proud of the fact that Dr. William Evans, its health columnist, headed the coroner's blue ribbon jury in the first of the investigations.

*   *   *

On February 21, 1916, President McCormick was able to present a triumphant report to Tribune Company directors on the progress made since he and Patterson had become actively involved in the paper's operations. He detailed the circulation gains being made at the expense of the *Tribune*'s competitors, the reorganization of the business department, the revitalization of the Sunday paper, and the improved profits during the years preceding the outbreak of war in Europe.

Among the *Tribune*'s achievements in war correspondence that he cited were the cabled description of the German entry into Brussels by James O'Donnell Bennett; letters from Bennett and John T. McCutcheon recounting their experiences as prisoners of the Germans; letters from Joseph Patterson describing the Battle of Alost, followed by a presentation of motion pictures taken under his direction; the first interview with the British cabinet by a special correspondent of the *Tribune;* the first correspondent to visit the British army at the front and to interview Sir John French; the only American war correspondent to visit the Russian army, and to obtain motion pictures of the Russian army; letters from a foreign correspondent first suggesting that Bulgaria would enter the war on the side of Germany; the only American paper to have a special correspondent in Serbia at the time of its conquest by Germany; special correspondence from China, Japan, and the Philippines. McCormick himself accounted for the majority of the firsts he claimed for the paper.

McCormick noted that "all the present methods of war reporting are losing their interest for the public and new methods must be found. Plans are in process which, if successful, will equal the successes of last year." McCormick paid tribute to Patterson's film serial triumphs and disclosed an arrangement by which the *Tribune* received $1,100 a week to make war documentaries that Selig released, paying the *Tribune* an additional 40 percent of net profits.

Profits of over $1 million were reported for 1915, "the largest profit made by a newspaper enterprise, $164,630 of that amount coming from the newsprint mill, $132,064 from the new building, and $751,327 from the *Tribune* itself. The *Tribune* now is infinitely too large for control by one man in power," McCormick noted. "Its management must be a highly complicated machine, the efficiency of which depends upon the harmonious working of many parts. As long as this condition can maintain, and I see no reason why it should not maintain for many years, the *Tribune* will be indestructible and unassailable. It will increase in profit, in power and in value to this community."

In March, 1916, the *Tribune* sent one of its most colorful reporters, Floyd Gibbons, an eager, lean, toothy young Irishman, to the Mexican border. Gibbons was to accompany Gen. John J. Pershing, commanded to capture Francisco "Pancho" Villa, the Mexican rebel whose forces had attacked Columbus, New Mexico, the night of March 8–9, killing 17 Americans. Gibbons charmed Pershing, as was his custom, but found the general much too restrained for his editorial needs. He set out on his own to find Villa, whose reputed hatred for journalists failed to daunt him. Gibbons's fast talk, though in a language Villa only haltingly understood, won him an exclusive interview. He stayed on to cover the man called an outlaw in the United States, occasionally serving as a kind of unofficial press adviser. It is said that on one occasion Villa held up an attack because Gibbons convinced him he would not get good U.S. press during the week of the World Series.

The presence of American forces in Mexico put an even greater strain on the already tense relations between the two countries, but the Wilson administration claimed great progress in the attenuated exchange of diplomatic notes with Germany relative to the sinking of the *Lusitania*. Secretary of State William Jennings Bryan had resigned early on to protest the severity of President Wilson's demands, but Wilson continued to press for an end to submarine attacks on noncombatant vessels. Though Germany eventually agreed to make reparations for the *Lusitania,* submarine attacks did not cease, and American ships and American lives were lost. A clamor for war began to be heard, but Wilson insisted that diplomacy could solve the problem. A final, stern note issued by the president in April, 1916, at last, on May 4, brought a German pledge that merchant ships "shall not be sunk without warning and without saving human lives unless they attempt to escape or offer resistance."

Wilson's supporters hailed this pledge as a diplomatic coup, but the *Tribune* was less enthusiastic.

> The *Tribune* during negotiations has discussed all phases of the problem without fear or favor. Especially it has tried to keep before its readers the realities which much of the public discussion has tended to obscure rather than reveal. . . . Now that the case is closed for the United States, if the note is to be deemed to have closed it, the duty of all citizens is best expressed, we believe, by the much abused, much mis-read sentiment of Stephen Decatur which the *Tribune* prints daily at the head of its editorial page: "Our country! In her intercourse with foreign nations may she always be in the right, but our country, right or wrong!"

The *Tribune* saw itself as pro-American and for preparedness, and on June 3 its position was supported when 130,000 Chicagoans marched in a preparedness parade. The paper then turned its attention to a brace of national conventions scheduled for Chicago in June. It supported Charles Evans Hughes of New York for president, and the Republicans nominated him on the first ballot, naming Charles Warren Fairbanks of

Indiana as his running mate. At the Progressive party convention on June 7, Theodore Roosevelt was nominated for president, but he at once withdrew and gave his support to Hughes. The Democrats gathered in St. Louis from June 14 to June 16 and renominated President Wilson and Vice-President Marshall by acclamation.

On June 22, 1916, the paper reported a defeat for Pershing's Punitive Expedition in an encounter with Mexican government troops at Carrizal: "FIRST U.S. MEXICAN BATTLE." War with Mexico seemed imminent. It was recorded that 6,000 Illinois national guardsmen had been called into service, and the *Tribune* announced what was happening to its editors in a page-one notice:

> In consequence of the mobilization of the National Guard, the editors of the *Tribune,* Robert R. McCormick and Joseph Medill Patterson, are in the service of their respective organizations the First Illinois Cavalry, and Battery C, First Battalion of Artillery. During the period of this service they will have no connection with the editorial management of the *Tribune.* For such time the Board of Directors has designated William H. Field, second Vice President of the Tribune Company, and Edward S. Beck, Managing Editor, to have editorial charge of the *Tribune.*

National guardsmen from the *Tribune* would continue to receive their pay and to keep their jobs. The paper initiated a drive for money to provide family benefits for men less fortunate than *Tribune* workers and published an item from Detroit under the heading "Flivver Patriotism," which stated: "Ford employees who volunteered to bear arms for the United States will lose their jobs."

The following day there was an editorial, "Henry Ford Is An Anarchist." It quoted from the *Tribune* story that no job security had been provided for any Ford employee called into service. The editorial stated that the paper did not know how many men would be affected since "information was refused as to the number of American soldiers unfortunate enough to have Henry Ford as an employer." The editorial concluded that "anywhere in Mexico would be a good location for the Ford factories."

Henry Ford issued a denial that his men called into service would be refused jobs on their return, said the *Tribune* had libeled him by calling him an anarchist, and sued for $1 million. The action remained to haunt McCormick and Patterson after World War I, during which time Ford sent his peace ship, *Oscar II,* to Europe, loaded with idealists, in an ineffective effort to stop the fighting. He established his credentials as a sincere pacifist, but he was not ready to drop the fight with the *Tribune.* Gaining a change of venue to Michigan after first filing his action in Chicago, Ford in 1919 won a favorable verdict, the jury fixing the damages at 6¢. During the course of the trial, Ford's advertising men asserted under oath that the *Chicago Tribune* was among the most influential newspapers in the country, a charge the *Tribune* obviously did not wish to dispute. Years later, on July 30, 1941, Ford and McCormick's birthday, McCormick sent an apology: *"It occurs to me on this, our birthday, to write and say I regret the editorial we published about you so many years ago. I only wonder why the idea never occurred to me before. It was a product of war psychology which is bringing out so many familiar expressions today. I am not planning to publish this myself, but you are perfectly welcome to use it in any way you wish."* Later, McCormick met Ford in the automaker's private railroad car in Chicago. "We agreed the whole thing was a mistake, that we should never have let our lawyers get us into it," McCormick said.

*   *   *

In June, 1916, however, Robert R. McCormick, newly elected a major in the Illinois National Guard, was far too busy with military affairs to be concerned about his paper's editorial problems. His cavalry force was being mobilized at Springfield, Illinois, and would soon be on its way to the Mexican border. McCormick found it lacked almost everything needed for war except a few polo ponies and milk horses that had been contributed. McCormick designed a mobile field kitchen of the type he had seen in Russia and had it built at a cost of $750, and he was buying some horses, but what he particularly required was machine guns. It appeared that neither the National Guard nor the regular army had any of the improved type being used in Europe. McCormick wrote and telephoned state and national government officials demanding such guns, and, failing to get satisfaction, he turned to his newspaper, which said editorially on June 22, the day he and Patterson officially left the paper: "The Illinois troops were utterly without machine guns. These may be had in less than a week from either the Colt, the Remington or Savage Arms companies—in less than a week if the government demands. Illinois regiments may be in battle next week. A competent critic has said that a machine gun is worth a hundred men."

The paper announced that a special committee headed by Charles Gates Dawes, later vice-president of the United States, would raise money to buy modern machine guns, and J. Ogden Armour, a member of the committee, made the first gift of $2,500. McCormick meantime was sending telegrams to the arms companies. He found that, contrary to the editorial, it was not at all that easy to get guns within a week. Savage Arms, for example, had its entire output contracted for, presumably to the European combatants. But, persisting, McCormick was able to buy five machine guns from Colt's Patent Fire Arms Company, a feat that caused him years later to write that he had introduced machine guns into the American army, which was correct in the sense that the five guns used in training his federalized Illinois National Guard unit in Texas were probably the first of their type to be used by federal troops.

Like his cousin, Joe Patterson went with his National Guard unit almost immediately to the Mexican border. But unlike Major McCormick, Patterson insisted on serving as a private, and he declined the offer of a commission from his old friend Governor Dunne. According to the men in his artillery company, Patterson could cuss and push mules aboard cattle cars with the best of them. By early 1917 he had attained the rank of lieutenant.

*   *   *

The *Tribune*'s dissatisfaction with the Wilson administration had been growing for some time. On September 17, 1916, the paper at last broke with the president, citing not only his failure to deal firmly enough with the Germans, but also his dilatory policy relative to Mexico (despite the fact that troops under General Pershing had invaded that country) and his failure to take a strong stand for national defense. Said the paper's editorial: "The *Tribune,* just as many other Rooseveltian agencies [*Progressives*], resolved every doubt in favor of Mr. Wilson for nearly two years. . . . [*But*] Wilson is agile in words and sluggish in deeds." A later editorial asserted, "Most Americans, we believe, who have given thorough, unprejudiced consideration to the problems of our national defense are convinced that some form of obligatory military service is desirable, if not necessary."

President Wilson defeated Hughes in November's election, but so narrowly that the *Chicago Daily News* declared Hughes the winner in a banner headline, an embarrassment the *Tribune* would know years later in the Truman–Dewey campaign.

Despite the increasing conviction of the *Tribune* that the nation should prepare for war, Chicago and the Midwest surrendered slowly their reluctance to accept the atrocity stories the British had tried vainly to sell early in the war. The *Tribune* itself vowed it would never be deceived by the propaganda machine, asserting in an editorial and full-page advertisements: "The *Tribune* will give you honest war news, no faking. Its special writers and cameramen are at the center of the trouble. First and most important of all, the *Tribune* will print nothing as fact until it has made certain that the information is authentic. Its chief concern will be to avoid misleading its readers with false and terrible rumors. When such rumors and unconfirmed reports are printed, they will be printed as such."

*   *   *

Early in February, 1917, as Germany pursued its newly announced policy of unrestricted submarine warfare and the British were finally turning back the Germans with their breakthrough in the Somme, using new war machines modeled after the Caterpillar farm tractors made in Peoria, Illinois, the *Tribune* dispatched its own secret weapon to France. Floyd Gibbons, the frenetic, fast-talking beanpole who had charmed Pancho Villa into an interview and who seemed to have the Mexican situation well in hand, was en route by sea to his customary rendezvous with glory. On February 27, 1917, the *Tribune* got out its biggest headline type for its Extra edition: "TWO CHICAGOANS DIE ON LINER. GIBBONS WIRES THAT HE IS SAFE; SENDS STORY TO TRIBUNE." It was a second-day story on the sinking of the *Laconia*, and, characteristically, Gibbons had found himself precipitated into the midst of the news even before he arrived at the point where he expected to find it. A German submarine had sunk the Cunard liner *Laconia* off Scotland, and Gibbons was one of those rescued. "The *Tribune* received word that Gibbons is safe and his story is on the way. As soon as the dispatch arrives it will appear exclusively in the *Tribune*." The headlines and readout were based on a cable, "QUEENSTOWN, FEB. 27 AM CABLING THREE THOUSAND LACONIA SINKING. TWO CHICAGO WOMEN VICTIMS. PLEASE EXPEDITE WITH WESTERN UNION THROUGH NEW YORK. GIBBONS." Even for the Extra edition, the paper's researchers were able to identify the two women victims and to find in the *Tribune* morgue pictures of the women and of the *Laconia*.

On February 28, the paper prepared special banner type to display its exclusive story. "HOW LACONIA SANK. FLOYD GIBBONS CABLES FIRST COMPLETE STORY OF LINER TORPEDOING":

> Queenstown, Feb. 26 (Via London Feb. 27) I have serious doubts whether this is a real story. I am not entirely certain it is not all a dream. I feel that in a few minutes I may wake up back in Stateroom B 19 on the Promenade deck of the Cunard *Laconia* and hear my cockney steward informing me with an abundance of "and sirs" that it is a fine morning.
>
> It is now a little over thirty hours since I have stood on the slanting decks of the big liner, listened to the lowering of the lifeboats, heard the hiss of escaping steam and the roar of ascending rockets as they tore lurid rents in the black sky and cast their glare over the roaring sea.
>
> I am writing this within thirty minutes after stepping on the docks here in Queenstown from the British minesweeper which picked up our open lifeboat after an eventful six hours of drifting and darkness and bailing and pulling on the oars and of straining aching eyes toward that empty, meaningless horizon in search of help.
>
> But dream or fact, here it is. . . .

Gibbons proceeded with the needed details: "*Laconia*, 18,000 tons, 73 passengers, men, women and children torpedoed without warning by a German submarine." The *Laconia* carried war matériel. Two passengers and one crew member were lost, 71 passengers and 252 crewmen rescued.

President Wilson ruled that the sinking of the *Laconia* was another of the German "overt acts" that might force America to take drastic measures to protect herself, and a cry for armed merchant ships was heard. James O'Donnell Bennett reported from Berlin on the German concept of the psychological effect of unlimited U-boat warfare. There were six pages of text and photographs. When the president at his inaugural on March 5, 1917, spoke of "armed neutrality," the *Tribune* snapped, "All we can say of armed neutrality is that it is not neutral and it is not armed." The paper called for a special session of Congress to deal with the nation's unpreparedness, a proposal supported on page one with a cartoon by the new editorial cartoonist Carey Orr, who would back up McCutcheon. Yet another *Tribune* editorial demanded: "Prepare! Prepare! Prepare! . . . When American merchantmen engage German submarines the distinctions of International Law will not protect us. It is the duty of Congress to see that the nation is able as soon as possible, for the present and the future, to defend itself from the consequences of a resort to hostile acts. . . . We cannot longer drift unless we are ready to die as an independent nation."

*   *   *

Events moved swiftly in April. On April 2, President Wilson asked Congress, in special session, to declare war on Germany. The Senate acted 82 to 6 for such a declaration on April 4, and the House concurred 373 to 50 at 3 A.M. on April 6. That same day, in addition to the headlines and the war stories on almost all the main news section pages, a unique full-page advertisement appeared in the *Tribune:* "VOLUNTEERS NEEDED" said the eight-column headline. Cavalry volunteers were invited to apply to Maj. Robert R. McCormick on the main floor of the Tribune Building between the hours of 9:30 A.M. and 6 P.M. Artillery volunteers were invited to call at the same address, same hours, and to seek out Lt. Joseph M. Patterson. McCormick had been released from duty on the Mexican border in November, while Patterson was more recently returned to Chicago. Both men would soon be on their way to Europe.

The advertisement calling for volunteers ran for a week, being reduced to one-third page size after the fourth day. On the second day the paper reported that 135 recruits had responded and been sworn in, and three days later the total was 245. The unique advertising campaign thus brought in an astonishing 10 percent of the total number of recruits for the entire state of Illinois in the first 20 days of the statewide recruiting effort, which yielded 2,427 men. On April 12, recruiting officers at the Cubs baseball park failed to get a single response, Gov. Edward Dunne reported in his history of Illinois. Yet, Dunne noted, Illinois led the nation in per capita final recruiting totals.

A prize catch of the *Tribune* recruitment advertising was "the richest young man in the United States," Marshall Field III, who enlisted as a private in McCormick's cavalry regiment. Young Field was photographed taking his oath, and the picture was published together with a *Tribune* editorial praising Field, commending him especially for his decision to serve as an enlisted man. The editorial concluded: "When the call to duty leads the country's richest young man into service, other young men should follow his example."

The paper was not pleased with the general response to the state's volunteer appeals, saying on April 16, "While 16,000 Chicagoans, more or less able-bodied, watched yesterday's contest at the baseball park, the struggle with Germany was of keen interest to something less than 200 men." And on Tuesday the paper noted bitterly that there was a rush of young men to marry, 1,126 obtaining Cook County marriage licenses. Yet the state and the country did respond, not in high emotion but with the slogan, "We're going to do our bit."

As the *Tribune* undertook to cover the war and to "do its bit" on the home front, it also established, on July 4, 1917, its Army Edition, intended to boost the morale of American troops in Europe. The five-column, eight-page paper, with offices in Paris, was under the supervision of Joe Pierson, the *Tribune* editorial staff member who suggested it, basing his idea on the paper Patterson had published in Mexico.

THE __TRIBUNE__
HAS THE TREATY!

18

As the *Tribune* had repeatedly warned, the nation was not prepared for war, with one exception. Plans for conscription were ready, and the paper agreed that this was the correct and fair procedure. The military strength of the United States totaled 196,000 men, 77,000 in the regular army. The Selective Service Act of May 10, 1917, enrolled 10 million men, of whom 4 million were drafted. It would take months to train the forces and to manufacture needed weapons and supplies. The Mexican war scare and war orders from Europe had helped, yet only a few U.S. munitions plants were ready to meet the demands that American participation required.

The paper's war policy was simple and stated almost daily: "Universal training; only trained American troops to Europe; no separate peace . . . no American force to be sent abroad until our main army is trained and fully equipped." It was a policy coinciding with President Wilson's, and though the *Tribune* was less than pleased with the Wilson administration's performance, the paper's demands were met, largely because most troops in training had neither guns nor bullets. The average American dough-boy received six months' training in the States and three months' in Europe, then spent a month on a quiet sector of the front before he saw heavy action. Meantime, the Allies, near collapse, were required to hold. The Germans pressed on Paris and failed, and the hostilities subsided into static trench warfare, made triply miserable by machine guns, grenades, and poison gas and stabilized by an Illinois invention, barbed wire.

While Lieutenant Patterson accompanied his own 149th Field Artillery, 42nd (Rainbow) Division, to the Mexican border for training,

McCormick was detained in Chicago. On May 18, President Wilson named Brig. Gen. John J. Pershing to command the American forces in France, and shortly thereafter McCormick received a letter from Pershing's chief of staff, asking that Major McCormick be mustered into the service and sent to his headquarters in France, the only National Guard officer so chosen. The move was a logical one. A serious problem for General Pershing was effective liaison with the Allied forces while he strove to get his own troops into the field as an autonomous army. McCormick spoke French, knew leaders in the Allied governments and the military, and was familiar with action on both the western and eastern fronts; soon he was involved in unraveling the intrigues of the British and French staffs, who were attempting to take over the American force and integrate it with their armies. Major McCormick reported directly to General Pershing on these matters.

*   *   *

In Chicago William H. Field was in general charge of the *Tribune,* with Edward S. Beck responsible for the editorial department. Under their direction the paper kept up civilian morale and maintained its coverage of the war despite severe censorship of war-related news at home and the dwindling amount of news from abroad caused by the stalemate along the fronts. Yet, regardless of the scarcity of action and officious censors, Floyd Gibbons kept some war news flowing to readers of the *Tribune.*

Gibbons was always in the thick of things, even when little newsworthy was happening on the battlefield. So of course he was in Liverpool on June 8, 1917, to welcome General Pershing and the first American troops to land on foreign soil in a major war. British security guards attempted to fend off Gibbons, but he was recognized as an old friend by "Black Jack" Pershing, who remembered the resourceful reporter from the Mexico campaign. Gibbons joined Pershing's personal retinue for the trip to Paris, which went wild when the Americans arrived on June 13. Gibbons wrote emotionally of the excitement and the significance of the occasion: "Gray-haired fathers of French fighting men bared their heads and with tears streaming down their cheeks shouted greetings to the tall, thin, gray-moustached American commander who was leading new armies to the support of their sons. . . . Women heaped armsful of roses into the general's car and into the cars of other American officers who followed him. Paris street gamins climbed the lamp posts and waved their caps and wooden shoes and shouted shrilly."

After a brief period with the First Division in its French training camp, Gibbons began his personal search for trouble. He covered the French and British sectors of the front, impatiently awaiting his chance to go forward with the Americans. He rode the European cattle cars with U.S. soldiers and their horses and mules, eight horses and four men to a car. His description breathed life into the boredom of the war: "Then the train moves. If the movement is forward and sudden, as it usually is, the four horses in the forward end of the car involuntarily obey the rule of inertia and slide into the central space. . . . On the whole, night life for the men in the straw on the floor of the central space is a lively existence, while 'riding the rattlers with a horse outfit.'" He at last was allowed to join an American force in a quiet sector of the front.

> With all lights out, cigarettes tabooed and the siren silenced, our overloaded motor slushed slowly along the shell-pitted roads carefully skirting groups of marching men and lumbering supply wagons that took shape suddenly out of the mist-laden road in front of us. . . . Although it was not raining, the moisture seemed to drip from everything. . . . In the grayness of the night sight and smell lost their keenness, and familiar objects assumed unnatural forms, grotesque and indistinct. . . . From somewhere ahead dull, muffled thumps in the mist brought memories of spring housecleaning and the dusting out of old cushions, but it was really the three-year-old song of the guns.

Usual Gibbons luck put him on the scene when the cannon of the American side were first fired with intent to kill. Assuming that Battery A of the Sixth Field Artillery would be first into the artillery line, he obtained permission to accompany Battery A. He was wrong; Battery C was the outfit that opened fire. But C was a close neighbor, so close that Gibbons had his "first" anyway. He and Raymond G. Carroll of the *Philadelphia Public Ledger* were the only American correspondents to witness the initial salvo blasting away at 6:05 A.M. on October 23, 1917.

Seven months later, Gibbons was with his beloved First Division when it attacked and took the village of Cantigny. (It was there that McCormick, detached at his request from Pershing's staff to rejoin the artillery, served and received his lieutenant colonelcy.) The First was then moved to the Soissons sector, and Gibbons joined the Second Division, which included a detachment of U.S. Marines, who were ordered to counterattack through Belleau Wood. Gibbons, through his friend Lt. Oscar Hartzell, the field press censor, was granted permission to participate in the attack, and the two of them went forward with the Fifth Marines. Led by Maj. John Berry, they were advancing across an oat field when German machine guns opened up. Men fell like mowed grain. Gibbons heard Major Berry cry, "My hand's gone," and saw the wounded officer gazing at his bleeding left arm, trying to staunch the flow. The bullet had struck near Berry's elbow, torn through the flesh along the bone, and lodged in the palm of his hand, shattering the bones. "Wait until I get to you," Gibbons cried, "then we'll get up and make a dash for it."

"I started forward, keeping as flat on the ground as it was possible to do so and at the same time move," Gibbons wrote.

> I pushed forward by digging in with my toes and elbows extended in front of me. It was my object to make as little movement in the oats as possible. I was not mistaken about the intensity of the fire that swept the field. It was terrific. And then it happened. The lighted end of a cigarette touched me in the fleshy part of my upper left arm. That was all. It just felt like a sudden burn and nothing worse. . . . There was nothing to indicate that the bullet had gone through the biceps muscle and come out on the other side. . . . I glanced down at the sleeve of my uniform coat and could not even see the hole where the bullet had entered. Neither was there any sudden flow of blood.

The pain was less than one endures sometimes when a dentist drills a tooth, Gibbons averred. A second bullet struck him a glancing blow on the top of the shoulder that, like the first, he barely felt. But then a third slug ricocheted off the ground, entered his left cheek, went through his left eye socket, and emerged through his helmet. His personal story had come to a temporary halt.

Rescued by Hartzell, Gibbons awakened in an army hospital. He had suffered a compound skull fracture and had lost his left eye. As he lay in bed, he dictated a letter to his mother: *"I am perfectly easy and without pain and have everything in the world that I could want or wish for. I have had a most remarkable experience which has cost me not a single regret."* Thereafter, Gibbons wore a white eye patch, probably the most famous journalistic symbol of recent times.

Gibbons barely missed a step despite the seriousness of his wounds. He wrote dispatches from the hospital and soon was back in action. On July 5, 1918, only a month after being wounded, he was covering the Allied advance at Amiens. On July 21, he was the only reporter at Chateau-Thierry. Soon afterward he returned to the United States, where he undertook a lecture tour. Thus it was that Gibbons missed the final campaign of the war, the 47-day-long Meuse–Argonne battles, in which the American army, employing over 1 million troops, provided the preponderance of power in the Allied drive that smashed the Germans' western front.

By the beginning of 1919, Gibbons was back in Europe as head of both the Paris bureau, which was headquarters for the *Chicago Tribune*'s European correspondents, and the Army Edition of the *Tribune,* which McCormick and Patterson would soon decide to continue as the European Edition. Correspondents operating out of the Paris bureau at the close of the war included Farmer Murphy, Henry M. Hyde, and Frederick A. Smith, Paris; Percy Hammond, former music critic, Belgium; Frazier Hunt, who had covered U.S. naval operations, Russia; and Parke Brown, Germany. Arthur M. Evans and John T. McCutcheon were occasional members of the staff, for which Smith acted as assistant director. Whenever McCutcheon was abroad acting as a correspondent, Carey Orr's political cartoons appeared on page one of the *Tribune*. The Paris office received correspondence from throughout Europe by courier, then transmitted it to Chicago via special cable.

*   *   *

Throughout the war the *Tribune* kept up its strident demands for greater war effort, attacking slackers, pacifists, and pro-German textbooks in the Chicago public schools, while citizens abolished German names of buildings and sauerkraut appeared in restaurant menus as "liberty cabbage." On November 15, 1917, the paper detailed its dissatisfaction with all aspects of the nation's fighting stance:

It Is High Time For This Nation To Get Fighting Mad

It is high time for this nation and this nation's government to wake up to the fact that it is in the center of the world war—

It is high time we stop compromising with ourselves and others and put our teeth into this job, the very biggest we have ever tackled. For months we have been bogging morally, mentally and in our practice. The trouble with our war work is that we haven't yet got the *war mind*. We have let ourselves be infected with the sentimentalities of the pacificism which was having its own way before the war. We still want to make war without making war. We want to fight without hurting anybody. We are afraid to use the bayonet.

In certain phases of the war we have done well. The adoption of the conscription at the beginning was a triumph of common sense over false reasoning, false sentiment, and traditional prejudice. The operation of the draft was a moral triumph for the nation.

The paper continued to enumerate other credible war works, conceding that some of the people called into Washington were doing well, but then added:

For anyone who can see the actual situation from without and who counts the precious months lost, with countless lives and the world at stake, conditions at Washington are challenging. We have withheld criticism and protest patiently. We have realized the staggering difficulties in the path of war organization. We have admired the splendid devotion shown by men of all parties and all conditions of life who have gone to Washington to give themselves to their country. But the fact remains that while we have admirable examples of creative organization in some branches, there has been no such articulation and concentration of authority as it is the duty of the government to achieve, and there is apparently even now a deplorable failure to realize this paramount necessity.

This at bottom is an expression of our lack of fighting spirit. We have not yet achieved the passionate energy in whose white heat is beaten the steel of effective accomplishment.

The paper concluded: "The first duty of the President at this moment is to take up the problem of articulating organization and establishing an efficient authority."

This and some other involved editorials may have puzzled many *Tribune* readers, who were accustomed to more succinct and simple statements. But the paper's stance was clear enough to young, liberal director William Bross Lloyd, one of the country's leading opponents of any war involvement whatever. On December 27, 1917, Lloyd, the grandson of William Bross, submitted his resignation. Pointing out that he and the majority stockholders had long been in disagreement over policy and politics generally, Lloyd wrote:

> *I have found it embarrassing at times as I pursued my course in the world outside the Board Room to be associated with a group who differed so radically with me on the questions of the day. And I have no doubt that the group have found it at least as embarrassing. The* Tribune *has no control over me, nor I over the Tribune Company, and yet, at least in the eyes of our friends and the public at large . . . it appears so. This mutually embarrassing situation I desire to terminate.*

Lloyd's resignation was at once accepted by unanimous vote, without comment. His brother Henry D. Lloyd continued the family representation on the board.

*   *   *

While nations fought and newspaper editorialists squabbled, Chicago exceeded all past records in growth, production, and prosperity. The city's economy boomed with war orders. Shoes and uniforms were needed; field telephones, artillery fire control systems, and parts for ships, trucks, and weapons were required in endless numbers. Labor, too, was in short supply as the wartime demand for agricultural products, infantrymen, and sailors used up the supply of farm boys who previously had hearkened to the call of the city. Women increasingly took jobs in retail shops and along the assembly lines that had been popularized by Ford; 50,000 blacks moved into Chicago from the South within two years. As the British and American navies found ways to break through the German submarine packs at sea, grain ships and refrigerated vessels from Chicago carried millions of tons of foodstuffs abroad.

William Field and Eugene Parsons, his advertising manager, verified this unprecedented prosperity. Relying on the research supplied by their unique merchandising bureau, they had begun publishing a compendium of up-to-date information about the region served by the paper so that potential advertisers could easily see why the *Tribune* was one of the best advertising investments in the country. First issued in 1916 as *Winning a Great Market on Facts,* which title was changed to *Book of Facts* in 1918, the publication gained rapid acceptance as an authoritative advertising tool and was distributed annually until 1964.

Taking cognizance of the zoning of the United States into 13 census areas, with Illinois, Iowa, Indiana, Michigan, and Wisconsin comprising Zone 7, the *Tribune*'s research people mined and processed all possible information on Zone 7, showing its resources, production and consumption statistics, the economic status of its citizens, their education, social background, family size, housing patterns, and shopping habits. The story of Zone 7 was told to advertisers from year to year, while the paper's name for the zone changed from "*Tribune* Town" and "*Tribune* Territory" to "Retail Trading Area."

Companies in Chicago and throughout the United States began to use the *Book of Facts* not only for guidance in the placement of advertising, but also for predetermining product acceptance in the *Tribune*'s circulation area and for planning the location of retail outlets. The *Tribune* studies limned the paper against its own economic and sociological environment and against all other newspapers and all magazines, but dealt especially with the particular viability of morning newspapers in general.

> When the world wakes up and has breakfast, things begin to happen, *and not until then.* During the following six hours, from 9 to 3, the afternoon newspaper must gather its news, write it, edit it, print it, and distribute it in several editions. A large proportion of the news, big news events of every nature, come to a head too late in the day to be adequately treated in an afternoon paper. . . . The morning newspaper starts its news gathering at the same time as the afternoon paper, but works more than twice as long, during which time twice as many things happen, before it needs to begin to get ready to print its first edition. No wonder its news is more comprehensive, more authentic, better written, better edited, better presented.

In a manuscript study of the *Tribune,* James Cleary, a member of the advertising and promotion department during this period, later wrote, "Campaigns created by *Tribune* salesmanship resulted in large volumes of copy being placed in morning and Sunday newspapers throughout the country."

The *Book of Facts* showed the *Tribune* of the wartime years to be a national leader in the advertising field and Chicago to be a leader of cities. The *Tribune*'s figures were impressive, its circulation and influence reaching well beyond Chicago and its growing suburban communities. The five-state area served by the *Tribune* comprised a population of 16,500,000, double the population of the six northeastern states and greater than that of all the states west of the Mississippi, excluding Texas. With a daily circulation of over 400,000 and a Sunday circulation exceeding 650,000, the *Tribune*'s distribution was the greatest of any newspaper in the Midwest. On the average, 29,500 Sunday *Tribunes* were purchased in Michigan and nearly 50,000 each in Indiana, Iowa, and Wisconsin. The *Tribune* served so significant a market that even national advertisers sought space in the paper's pages, making it a competitor of national circulation magazines.

The facts about Chicago, many of which were derived from Census Bureau reports and government production statistics, were equally impressive. The *Tribune* designated the intersection of State and Madison streets as the world's busiest corner and cited a *National Geographic* article on Chicago in which the Rush Street bridge was described as the world's busiest, carrying more traffic than London Bridge; the post office was said to handle 2 billion pieces of mail annually, with receipts greater than those of any other post office in the world; and the "amazing Loop district," with an area of barely a quarter of a square mile, was reportedly "entered daily by twenty-odd thousand street-cars and more than 130,000 vehicles."

Said the *Tribune*'s *Book of Facts:* "Chicago's preeminence as a food metropolis is generally recognized, but the extent of its manufacturing is sometimes not appreciated. During 1918 products manufactured in Chicago approximated $4,000,000,000 in value." Chicago's heavy industry had tripled its production in a score of years, a consequence at least in part of the fact that the city was uniquely linked to ore and coal resources and to consumers via the greatest inland water system and railway network in the world. The Chicago rail system was said to total 46,980 miles in the five states of "*Tribune* Territory," more than England, Ireland, Scotland, Wales, France, Germany, Holland, Sweden, and Denmark combined. "Thirty-eight railroads which terminate in Chicago operate 109,000 miles of track." More than 2,500 freight cars loaded with manufactured goods left the city every day, and, in the navigation season, thousands of ships and barges brought in grain, lumber, and coal for transshipment to the East and Europe, in addition to the iron ore bound for the south shore of Lake Michigan. The *Tribune,* noting the growth of the city and its industries, was proud of the fact that in "Chicago Territory" there was one automobile to every 12 persons, as compared with one to 19 in the East and one to 31 in the South. Chicago's subscriptions to Liberty Loan drives were the highest in the country. "The Chicago Market," declared the *Tribune*, "is the greatest and most desirable market in the world."

Chicago's prosperity had been the consequence of steady growth since the turn of the century, but it stood in particular relief during the war years. While there was a shortage of consumer goods, there was no shortage of goods or customers in the town's saloons, nightclubs, theaters, and dance halls. And while churchmen deplored the decline of morality evidenced, they felt, by the land-office business being done in the town's unsavory establishments, there was clearly a new freedom, and it was not only for the young men and women who were in such great demand in the job markets. The foreign-born, too, were better off than ever before. They suddenly had the money to move where they chose within the city or the suburbs, which previously had been the refuge of the wealthy. A score of suburban areas, from Waukegan to Elgin to Joliet, doubled in population from 1900 to 1920. Other suburbs remained the preserves of the wealthy but reflected dramatic growth nonetheless: Oak Park to the west, Evanston to the north, and Beverly to the south also doubled. Even more dramatically, Gary, Indiana, one of the country's great producers of steel, jumped from zero in 1900 to 55,378 by 1920, and Hammond, its neighbor, grew from nothingness to 36,004.

The wartime prosperity was only briefly reflected in Chicago's newspapers, however. Newsprint costs rose, consumer items disappeared from store shelves, taxes jumped, and millions of dollars were diverted from the consumer economy by four Liberty Loan drives, which the *Tribune* strongly supported with publicity, editorial exhortation, and its own purchase of bonds. Contrary to public belief that newspapers welcomed America's participation in the war as a spur to profits, all Chicago papers found profits declining. Although the *Tribune* led the other Chicago papers in total advertising linage by a wide margin, nearly 55,000 columns in 1918 compared to 42,000 columns for the second-place *Daily News*, both papers had lost linage since the previous year. The *Tribune*'s circulation exceeded that of the *Daily News* by 40,000 in November of 1918, but with advertising revenues down and costs up, increased circulation only meant greater losses.

*   *   *

The entry of the United States into the war in Europe did not diminish the pro-Germanism of Big Bill Thompson. The Rotary Club expelled him; the Illinois Athletic Club, which he had helped to found, removed his picture from its wall; and Floyd Gibbons, in France, always alert to an exploitable situation, sent his paper excerpts from letters of indignant servicemen who denounced their mayor for giving aid and comfort to the enemy. Clergymen seemed to be the most upset by Thompson's attitude. "Anyone who questions the justice of America's part in the war," said Dean Shailer Mathews of the University of Chicago Divinity School, "must be idiotic, blind, pro-German, or—the mayor of Chicago." Texas Bishop George Herbert Kinsolving said succinctly, "I think that Mayor Thompson is guilty of treason and ought to be shot." The Chicago press, except the Hearst papers, sometimes referred to Mayor Thompson as "Kaiser Bill," "Burgomaster Bill," and "Wilhelm der Grosse."

Gleefully the *Tribune* published reports of the attacks on Thompson and leveled additional criticisms, assailing his conduct of Chicago affairs. The paper asserted that the mayor was packing the city payrolls with his political workers, approving illegal fees for condemnation and construction work on the widening of 12th Street (a project that the paper had urged and continued to favor), and encouraging graft in school board contracts. On September 17, 1917, Thompson filed a libel suit against the *Tribune* and another against the *Daily News*, which was attacking him with equal vigor. This was the first volley in more than a decade of legal skirmishes between Thompson and the *Tribune*.

As 1918 approached, Illinois politicians prepared for the upcoming campaigns. For the second time since 1913, when the 17th Amendment was ratified, the Illinois electorate would be voting directly for a U.S. senator. Medill McCormick, who had been serving as a U.S. congressman since 1917, offered himself as a candidate. McCormick had supported war measures in the House of Representatives, and he decided the time had come to demonstrate that Progressive Republicans, Republicans generally, and citizens of Chicago and Illinois were loyal to the government of the United States. The *Tribune*, of course, pledged its support. Big Bill Thompson yelped with pleasure when he learned the news. He himself would challenge McCormick in the Illinois primary, thereby crushing McCormick, humiliating the *Tribune*, and reproving his newest enemy, Gov. Frank O. Lowden, in a single act. But Thompson and political adviser Fred Lundin had underestimated the pro-Allied feeling in downstate Illinois. Momence barred him at the city limits with a sign: "ALL AMERICANS HERE. THOMPSON NOT WANTED. THIS WAY OUT." Jeering crowds tore the banners from his caravan in Kankakee, he was stoned and reviled in other towns, and he was denounced by Teddy Roosevelt at a McCormick rally in Springfield.

Medill McCormick was an easy victor in the primary and went on to oppose the Democratic incumbent, James Hamilton Lewis, a former congressman from Washington State who had moved to Illinois and promptly won election to the U.S. Senate. Pink-bearded J. "Ham" Lewis, immaculately dressed like McCormick, offered relatively mild opposition to his opponent, and during the course of the quiet and gentlemanly campaign the *Tribune* was satisfied to call him a carpetbagger who did the bidding of President Wilson. In support of Medill McCormick, the paper said on November 1, 1918:

> Mr. McCormick was born in Illinois. He has grown up in Illinois. He represents historic Republicanism in Illinois. He has served Illinois at home and in Washington and will continue to serve her interests and to express her will in the national councils if the people of Illinois elect that he do so. . . . Mr. McCormick may not have the confidence of the present executive, his cabinet or his administration—apparently the only way he could win it would be by supporting the purposes and policies of the administration. But Illinois, we believe, wants a senator who will represent the purposes and policies of Illinois.

The following days were filled with good news for the *Tribune,* its readers, and the country as a whole. The Sunday paper exceeded 700,000 circulation, selling at 10¢ in the country, 7¢ in the city. No other Sunday newspaper at those prices matched the *Tribune* in numbers, said the full-page promotion advertisement on November 3. Daily circulation was announced to be 440,000, and the *Tribune* declared that this was 40,000 greater than that of the next weekday paper, an evening paper, which of course was the *Chicago Daily News.* The Sunday edition, the *Tribune* claimed, was the largest in the United States except for the *New York Journal,* which sold for less.

On November 4, the *Tribune* used its biggest headline type: "AUSTRIA QUITS WAR." The day following, the headline read: "TERMS TO BERLIN." And on November 6: "McCORMICK WINS: 60,000." The Republicans gained control of both the U.S. Senate and the House. Senator Lewis had carried Chicago by 51,000 votes but lost "downstate and in the country towns," a historic pattern for Democrats in Illinois politics. Said the *Tribune* editorially: "At the election, the American people gave Republicanism one of the most remarkable tributes of confidence in the history of the party."

Chicago and the nation went wild on the morning of November 8, 1918, when false news of an armistice was released by the United Press Association. The *New York Times* printed the story, which was denied by President Wilson that evening. However, the *Tribune* and citizens generally knew that the collapse of Germany was but days or hours away, and editors readied their forms for a quick Extra when the genuine news should come.

Three days later, the Associated Press's telephoned "flash" was received at the *Tribune* telegraph desk at 1:55 A.M. central time, November 11: "ARMISTICE SIGNED." Within minutes the presses were rolling, and the first "Peace Extra" was selling on the street corners by 2:25 A.M. The editors also gave the signal for the *Tribune*'s electric sirens, which were wailing within five minutes of the "flash." The signals of the other papers, factories, fireboats, and suburban plants soon joined in. "Chicago Gets Out of Bed; Bedlam Reigns in Loop," announced one of the *Tribune's* page-one headings. Hundreds of sailors from the Great Lakes Naval Training Station were in town, awaiting transportation. They piled from their beds, hotel lobbies, and train stations to improvise a parade in Madison Street. Soon bands had formed. The crowd continued to grow during the early morning hours until, the *Tribune* estimated, more than a million persons were milling, marching, shouting, and singing in the Loop.

"Before 3 o'clock the downtown streets were taking on the aspect of madness which ran riot on Thursday when the country went crazy over a rumor," the paper reported. But the activity on the 11th was "as a tornado is to a summer storm. . . . The wild celebration ended in hysteria, delirium and license." Women, emancipated by their war jobs and the knowledge that the long campaign for suffrage was at last bearing fruit, asserted their freedom by rushing into the bars, opened early for the celebration, drinking with the men, and, noted the paper, "hugging and kissing anyone with whom they drank." In the streets, "disheveled girls led the fun, seizing men's coats and capes and hats, charging through the streets." Men in uniform were the beneficiaries of the new ardor. City police and shore patrol and military police watched happily as the crowds celebrated, or restrained hoodlums from excesses.

While the celebration proceeded, the *Tribune* produced Extra editions: "GREAT WAR ENDS."

> Washington, D.C., Nov. 11, 3 A.M. (by Associated Press.)—Armistice terms have been signed by Germany, the State Department announced at 2:45 o'clock this morning.
>
> The world war will end this morning at 6 o'clock, Washington time, 11 o'clock Paris time. The armistice was signed by the German representatives at midnight.

Later editions provided unofficial armistice terms, described the joy and celebration in London and Paris, and reported on the reception of the catastrophic news in Germany, where red flags of the socialist government that had deposed Kaiser Wilhelm were said to be flying on the public buildings of Berlin and all other major cities. The kaiser had fled to Holland. The *Tribune* published photos of the royal family in better days, together with pictures of the palace the Hohenzollerns would occupy in exile.

The *Tribune's* editorial on the 12th was sedate: "The great drama is ended. For the first time in four years the sound of giant cannon cannot be heard anywhere along the long line from the channel to the Adriatic; the deadly rattle of the machine gun is stilled; no gas fumes poison the winter air, no clouds of burning cities darken the sun. . . . Better than all, no life blood flows, the fighting men rest in their lines, the bayonet is sheathed, the bullet sleeps harmless in its clip. . . . This, at last, is peace." The paper paid customary tribute to the victorious armed forces and to the sacrificing people, and warned, "We have with us the tremendous task of restoration." America was relatively fortunate and should consider sympathetically the plight of the Allies, and even of the Germans. "If our war experience has proved anything," the paper concluded, "it has been the soundness and beneficence of American institutions and the life they make possible. . . . Let us resolve to strengthen these institutions for our children . . . and for the sake of our heroic dead."

The casualty lists ended. Throughout the war the *Tribune* had published names and addresses of all Midwesterners killed, wounded, or missing, the agate type filling an entire page during the days of the fierce fighting along the Meuse.

*   *   *

The armistice had been signed, but Europe was still not at peace. In Russia, civil war raged on. The bloody conflict between the White Russians and the Red Russians, or Bolsheviks, had taken on international dimensions in March, 1918, when a separate treaty with the Central Powers formally ended Russia's participation in the world war. In April, 1918, British and Japanese troops landed in Russia, ostensibly to protect Allied supply lines and to reopen a second front against Germany. In August the United States sent its own forces, officially for the same reasons. Yet, after the November, 1918, armistice the Allies stayed on in Russia, and for a time the U.S. Senate debated the advisability of sending large numbers of American troops to aid the White Russians in the continuing struggle with the Reds. Although the level of intervention never achieved major proportions, the last of the Allied troops would not leave Russia until 1922, when Bolshevik control of the entire country was at last established.

Tribune correspondents were on the scene from the first to cover the action in Russia, with Frazier Hunt providing the most exciting accounts. During the war Hunt had done for the American sailor what Gibbons did for the infantryman, sending dispatches from an unnamed base on the French coast that reported experiences with convoys and minesweepers. In 1918 he traveled to Archangel to report on the American mission against the Bolsheviks. On December 15, 1918, he wrote:

> Early this morning an American patrol of seventeen men led by a Serbian scout returned to our lines with a story of gallant work against the Bolshevik outposts. Sent on a mission to burn a partly completed blockhouse they ambushed an enemy patrol, killing seven out of twelve and injuring three others. Not an American received a scratch. . . . Through the desolate,

trackless forests, with a foot of snow on the ground, walking is most difficult. It is always zero weather here these days and the enemy is tireless. Daylight lasts only four to five hours, but when the earth is lit up now and again with the northern lights it is never black, and when full moon is here it is almost as light at midnight as at noon.

At six o'clock last night the patrol of seventeen Americans tracked off through the woods on a long flanking tramp to the enemy lines. A majority of the men had been fighting here for a month or more, but none were old soldiers, and they were going through a no-man's-land. The patrol commander, a smiling, red-cheeked Serbian lad of 19 had been fighting since he was 14, a member of the famous Serbian mountaineer outlaw band called the Komitadgis. He is now in British uniform with three honor stripes on his left sleeve.

Hunt described the long march and the appearance of an enemy patrol, walking into an American trap. "A dozen Bolsheviks came strolling up the path with rifles slung over their shoulders and within thirty yards the Serbian threw a hand grenade and the Americans opened up with their rifles and a Lewis gun. The first burst of fire killed five, the rest turned and ran. Two more dropped within the next few seconds, and three were wounded." It was an exciting moment of the strange Archangel campaign. But most of the time, Hunt reported, the Americans were scared and bored and kept asking, "What are they going to do with us now that we are in Russia?"

Hunt, meanwhile, knew what *he* was to do in Russia. He was directed to "proceed Petrograd" to report on the Communist government and to check out the rumors of a great famine. His first dispatch from Petrograd, sent to Paris on March 23, 1919, appeared in the *Tribune* two days later with a lead-in by Paris bureau chief Gibbons, describing Hunt as the first correspondent to enter Petrograd in six months. "Last eyewitness accounts," said Gibbons, "were brought out by refugee Europeans, who reported that the life of a non-Russian traveler was not worth a kopek within the borders of unholy Russia." With American troops engaged in fighting the Bolsheviks, he went on, Hunt's "daring presence in Russia is that of an enemy within the lines. For moral and physical courage in risking his life to present news to the world his latest achievement is unsurpassed in the journalism of the war." Hunt's dispatch followed:

Petrograd, March 23, via Paris March 25—Bread and fuel—these today are the title slogans in the present phase of the Russian revolution. Before, peace and land; at this time food and wood are the new watchwords.

Here in Petrograd 90 percent of the 900,000 population are underfed, probably 5 percent actually dying of starvation. All the rest through under-nutrition are having their resistance to sickness and epidemics broken down.

Three thousand nine hundred typhus cases are officially listed in the hospitals. The official figures show fifteen dying daily of typhus. There is a smallpox epidemic, but it is not malignant [*sic*]. In the whole city from 200 to 500 are dying daily.

The birth rate has fallen off because of malnutrition. [*Government rations were too small to really sustain life. Black market dark flour cost $2 a pound.*] People who were rich have had their businesses, stocks, bonds, bank accounts, everything taken from them. . . . The Red Army has taken part of the surplus of young men but there are thousands of unemployed despite the city and government work which has been handed out. . . . No one in the city except the Red Army gets enough to eat.

Hunt's stories and, later, those by Gibbons, reporting pogroms, decimation of the kulaks, government inefficiency, famine, and hideous suffering, shocked *Tribune* readers, as had the stories in the wake of the Haymarket Riot. McCormick, reviewing some of them, remembered the dark days of Communist threats feared by his grandfather in 1886. He warned his staff to be unceasingly alert to the Communist danger.

*   *   *

While giving a great deal of attention to the conflict in Russia, the *Tribune* also reported on the increasingly rancorous debate over foreign policy that was raging at home. The vitriolic exchanges that echoed through the nation's legislative chambers concerned Versailles, France, where President Wilson was attending the postwar peace conference. Even before the world war ended, the president had enumerated Fourteen Points he said should serve as the basis for the peace settlement. One of the points urged formation of an international association, a League of Nations. This proposal was highly unpopular with the Progressives and most other Republicans in the Midwest, who opposed greater U.S. involvement in world affairs, a position largely shared by the *Chicago Tribune*.

Wilson's Fourteen Points had also called for "open covenants of peace openly arrived at," yet the Versailles negotiations seemed to be veiled in secrecy and intrigue. *Tribune* correspondent Henry Wales's reports about the proceedings heightened the dark suspicions in the *Tribune*'s editorial offices, as well as in the U.S. Senate, that there were secret agreements and hidden clauses not included in the official summary of peace terms that had been released to the peoples of the world on May 8, 1919. Had agreements been made which, by the nature of their punitive terms and general failure to correct the mistakes of the past, would lead inevitably to another war? How deeply was the United States being committed to foreign entanglements and intrigues?

Several U.S. senators demanded a complete copy of the treaty, insisting on their right to review the text and study the proceedings. After all, they asserted, the governments of all the warring nations and most of the neutral countries had been informed of the treaty's terms, and the German government had been given an ultimatum to sign. If the Germans refused, rumor said, hostilities would resume, though Germany had been shattered and could no longer fight. The implication was obvious: Germany was being forced to accept unjustly harsh terms, and the United States was being committed to treaty provisions that, by their very nature, would provide fuel for another world conflagration in the future. In addition, it was said that Wall Street insiders already had copies of the complete treaty and were using the information to manipulate the bond market. Since so many people did have the treaty, what justification could the president give, his critics argued, to withhold it from the Senate of the United States? The American people had a right to know what was being negotiated and promised in their name.

The text that the U.S. Senate, the *Chicago Tribune,* and many of the people wished to see, President Wilson steadfastly declined to disclose, explaining that he was bound by his promise to keep the conference's decisions secret until the official release of the treaty. Also, tradition was on the president's side, for past presidents or their representatives had always carried out treaty negotiations, and it was at the president's initiative that a treaty was then submitted to the Senate for ratification. But the president's obduracy implied that he had other reasons for not making the treaty public.

Wilson was, indeed, motivated by other concerns. Less than a year earlier, Republicans had gained control of the Senate, so, in purely partisan terms, the outlook for ratification was not promising. Also, the president was well aware of the opposition to the treaty, particularly to provisions concerning the League of Nations. He wanted to present the full text in his own way and at his own time in order to win maximum support for its terms, especially the League, and to have an opportunity to explain the treaty to the public as well as to the Senate. The controversy grew in intensity, and Republican Sen. William E. Borah of Idaho, a leading opponent of American involvement in European affairs and a member of the Senate Foreign Relations Committee, proclaimed that somehow he would get one of the secret copies of the treaty and make it public.

On Monday, June 9, 1919, the *Chicago Tribune* jolted Washington, Wall Street, and the capitals of the world with its full disclosure of the terms of the Treaty of Versailles. The paper's banner headline that morning read: "TRIBUNE HAS TREATY." Another headline read: "PEACE TERMS BROUGHT TO U.S. BY FRAZIER HUNT." The complete text of the treaty, the paper said, had been delivered to Sen. Henry Cabot Lodge and other members of the Senate Foreign Relations Committee, who selected Senator Borah to present it to the Senate for publication in the *Congressional Record*. Borah was doing so that morning, at approximately the same time that the treaty was appearing in the *Tribune* and the *New York Times,* which had received permission from the *Tribune* to share in the publishing feat. The *Tribune* explained that it had obtained an original copy, which was in French and English, "from a legitimate and confidential source."

The *Tribune* declared that all Washington recognized the delivery of the treaty to the Senate as one of the great events of the war era and one of the most important scoops in journalistic history. Years later, some critics of the newspaper and writers on foreign affairs would assert that the publication of the treaty helped to keep the United States out of the League of Nations. Whether providing public access to the document before President Wilson had his opportunity to sway the senators was the decisive factor is moot, but the stunning impact of the *Tribune*'s accomplishment on world attention was at once obvious.

Senator Borah promptly telegraphed: "THE EDITORS OF THE TRIBUNE: WE ARE DEEPLY GRATEFUL TO YOU AND BELIEVE THAT THE COUNTRY WILL APPRECIATE YOUR PATRIOTIC SERVICE." The president's reaction was considerably different. "ANYONE WHO HAS POSSESSION OF THE OFFICIAL ENGLISH TEXT HAS WHAT HE IS NOT ENTITLED TO HAVE OR TO COMMUNICATE," he said in a cable from Paris. The *Tribune* of June 9 remained silent as to the source of the leak, and Frazier Hunt's cryptic summary of his activities offered little enlightenment. On Tuesday, June 10, his account appeared in the paper: "On May 26 I left Paris for Brest, France, sailing from there on the 29th of May. On June 7 [*sic*] I landed in New York. The following day I was in Chicago and handed over the valuable document to the publishers of the *Tribune*."

Although numerous accounts of the treaty publication appeared in magazines and newspapers throughout the world, the full story was not told until three decades later, when the man who had helped trigger the leak, Henry Wales, provided the details in an account for the *Tribune*'s *Graphic Magazine*. The source of the leak had not been the Germans, as was widely believed at the time, but a Chinese delegate, Eugene Chen. Many of the smaller powers, China among them, had resented the autocratic behavior of the "Big Four," Britain, France, Italy, and the United States. Wales had made many friends among representatives of the smaller nations for his honest and courageous job of reporting the proceedings of the conference for the *Tribune*. Chen was one such friend. The *Tribune*, Chen decided, could be trusted to do the right thing with a copy of the full treaty, but the Chinese delegate did not want to get his friend Wales in trouble with conference authorities. So on the afternoon of May 25, Chen appeared at the *Tribune*'s Paris offices at 420 Rue St.

Honore and asked to see the editor in charge. He handed a large, unmarked envelope to Spearman Lewis, who was running the office during Floyd Gibbons's absence, and left without saying a word. When Lewis opened the package, he found an official, numbered copy of the Versailles Treaty.

Frazier Hunt, returning from assignment in Archangel, was sitting in the Paris office at the time. He would be leaving for the United States the next day, and agreed to smuggle the document out of France. Hunt reached New York on Friday, June 6, and the next day he was in Chicago, presenting the exclusive copy of the treaty to the *Tribune*'s publishers. McCormick and Patterson agreed that the treaty should immediately be given to the Senate Foreign Relations Committee, even at the expense of losing their scoop. They directed Hunt to Washington.

On Sunday, Hunt and Arthur Sears Henning, the *Tribune*'s Washington correspondent, met with Senators Lodge and Borah. After the senators examined the text, they agreed to return it briefly to Henning and Hunt so that the *Tribune* could publish it the next morning and thus get the reward for its accomplishment. Henning leased 25 extra wires to telegraph the treaty to Chicago, but the Chicago editor told them he could publish only 25,000 words of the 75,000-word text. Henning and Hunt finished the massive job of editing and cutting by 3:00 A.M. and at 9:45 A.M. on June 9, returned the document to Senator Borah, who presented it to the Senate that morning shortly after it appeared in the *Tribune* and the *New York Times,* which on Sunday had leased 50 additional wires and published the complete text.

Spearman Lewis had known that Wales would be suspected of violating the ground rules laid down for reporters covering the peace conference, so he never told Wales about the delivery of the treaty. When Wales was called before angry Versailles officials, he was able to honestly deny any knowledge of how Hunt came to have a copy of the document. More than a year passed before Wales learned that Chen was the source of the leak and that his reporting had been the reason the *Tribune* had been chosen.

While the shock waves of the unofficial publication of the treaty reverberated, Senator Borah was leading the fight in the Senate to have it published in the *Congressional Record.* The debate, which began on Monday morning, was bitterly partisan. Only one Republican, Porter J. McCumber of North Dakota, joined the phalanx of Democrats who were determined to prevent the publication of the text and who demanded an investigation of the *Tribune*'s acquisition of the treaty. Nine Democrats joined the majority insisting on publication, won over, possibly, when Republican Sen. Hiram Johnson of California sent a shock of surprise through the galleries by bringing into the open the charges that the secrecy was being continued to help insiders in Wall Street.

Senator Johnson pointed out that copies of the treaty had been widely distributed to the governments of the world, including neutral countries. "Then it has developed that there were copies of this treaty in this country and among certain individuals or gentlemen of financial interests. . . . All these are admitted facts. . . . Then, upon what theory, when every country on earth has a copy of this treaty and it is in the hands of the financial men of New York . . . upon what theory, if you believe in democracy, do you keep it from the people of the United States?"

Johnson's reference, it developed, was to a report, later established as a fact, that a copy of the treaty had come into the possession of Henry P. Davidson, of J. P. Morgan & Company.

Nebraska Senator Gilbert M. Hitchcock, the minority leader, accused publication proponents of acting in cooperation with the German government. He implied that the treaty had been made available by the Germans, and that those who were supporting publication wished "to throw a monkey wrench into the peace machinery."

George W. Norris, Nebraska Republican, shouted angrily in reply: "Instead of throwing a monkey wrench into the peace machinery, the publication of this text will carry out a doctrine of which we have heard much lately, 'open covenants, openly arrived at.'"

Senator Miles Poindexter, Republican from Washington, was also incensed by the pro-German insinuations of the Democratic leader. He charged that those in the forefront of the fight against publication included senators who had voted to embargo shipments of war supplies to Allied nations, and who therefore were the real pro-Germans.

Vice-President Thomas R. Marshall, presiding, cautioned the senators not to go beyond the rules, but then softened his comment by allowing that no such violation had yet occurred, whereupon a red-faced Frank Brandengee (Republican, Connecticut) challenged him: "I disagree with the chair. . . . I think we already have gone too far. However, I do agree that when Senator Hitchcock stood up there and accused members of this senate with being pro-German, he did not mean it."

"I meant exactly what I said," yelled Hitchcock. "I do not need the senator to vindicate me."

"Then," said Brandengee evenly, "the senator is crazier than I thought."

Georgia Democrat Hoke Smith gained the floor, charging, "Someone came into possession of this treaty illegitimately." He demanded an investigation by the Senate "to see who has been guilty in this crime against humanity."

Senator Henry Ashurst (Democrat, Arizona) brought the senators back to Senator Johnson's Wall Street statement, which evidently had swayed him to the defense of the *Tribune*'s action: "The financial interests have control of a few copies of this treaty and, knowing what bonds would be stabilized and what bonds would not be stabilized, began a system of flotation and speculation and gambling to the tune of millions of dollars, and, by the nine gods, what Wall Street is entitled to have, the people are entitled to have! That is my reason for voting to make the treaty public, and I have no excuse to offer here or elsewhere and I would slap the face of any man outside the Senate who challenges me for that vote!"

The intemperate debate continued throughout the day. On the roll call motion to publish the treaty, 38 Republicans and nine Democrats voted "aye"; opposed, Republican McCumber and 23 Democrats. It was the beginning of defeat for President Wilson's foreign policy and his dream of American participation in the League of Nations.

Several London newspapers commented on the *Tribune*'s achievement. The *Daily News*, organ of the Liberal party, predicted that publication of the full text "would create an angry flood which may swamp the covenant of the League of Nations." Said Lord Beaverbrook's *Express*, "President Wilson has got himself, so to speak, up a gum tree."

The New York newspapers acknowledged the *Tribune*'s beat, but some sniffed at it. They pointed out that disclosure of the full text did not show anything contrary to what had been in the officially released summary. The *Times* emphasized that critics who feared diabolical terms not disclosed in the official summary had been proved wrong. The *Post* asked whether the peace conference had been ashamed to lay its decisions before the public, and urged readers to study the text "now given to the public through the enterprise of Frazier Hunt of the *Chicago Tribune*." Said the *Sun*, "The publication of the full text is a matter of great popular interest. . . . Full publication of the text has several obvious effects of a beneficial character." The *Standard Union* of Brooklyn called the *Tribune*'s feat "a magnificent public service."

Said the *Seattle Times*, "A more extraordinary episode probably never was witnessed in American history. Never previously was a peace treaty furnished Congress by a newspaper after a copy had been denied Congress by a president. Mr. Hunt has scored the most sensational newspaper beat of recent years."

The *Tribune*'s Versailles Treaty triumph did not preclude the signing of the document by the countries involved in the war. President Wilson signed for the United States, yet it was already clear from the Senate vote concerning publication in the *Congressional Record* that prospects for ratification were dim. The official signing of the treaty on June 28, 1919, prompted this *Tribune* response:

President Wilson has taken the occasion of the signing of the Treaty of Versailles to send to the American people a message upon that much mooted instrument. We should like to share Mr. Wilson's enthusiasm for the treaty. We wish that it might prove to be all that he claims for it. But we are not as much impressed by his confidence as we might be if our observation of the course of events at the conference gave his eloquent periods more support. The Treaty of Versailles will prove to be "a great charter for a new order of affairs in the world," there can be no doubt of that, a new order in the Adriatic, in the Balkans, in Asia Minor, in central Europe, in Shantung and Siberia and Africa. But what the new order will be lies in the bosom of Providence.

Mr. Wilson's aspirations are likely to take in public utterance the form of assertions having more the tone of certitude than, perhaps, he intends. This is a familiar device of leadership, but it is not a basis of cool judgment in public opinion or in the formulation of policy.

For example, when Mr. Wilson declares that the treaty "ends, once and for all, an old and intolerable order under which small groups of selfish men could use the peoples of great empires to serve their ambition for power and dominion," we must beg leave to take the assertion in a poetic if not a Pickwickian sense. . . .

Examined with neither cynicism nor evasive optimism, the Treaty of Versailles must seem to most of us to promise an order of affairs which is indeed new in its rearrangement of power, but which is in many essentials as old as Europe. It is important, if there is any considerable measure of truth in this view, that the American people, unused as we are to old world problems, look straightly at the facts of the new order rather than accept blindly any zealous claims of Utopian accomplishment.

ON THE HOME FRONT

19

William Field and Edward Beck struggled to maintain a taut ship in the absence of the owners, and while the *Chicago Tribune* sometimes ran a zigzag course, usually it arrived on schedule at the proper ports. Field and Beck were determined not to change the format left behind by the young proprietors, and this attitude prevailed long after McCormick and Patterson returned in 1919, for the front page on any day in 1947 looks almost exactly like one on a day in 1917. Beyond such limitations, however, the new managers achieved major improvements, reorganizing the business and editorial staffs and upgrading the paper's content, so that Burton Rascoe, the paper's iconoclastic critic and assistant Sunday editor until he departed in a huff in 1920, would later write: "It was not far from living up to its boast, *then,* of being The World's Greatest Newspaper." But even the editorial refinement was based on ingredients of past years, and the superb advertising and research organization had been started in the days of Medill McCormick.

Edward Scott Beck, Indiana-born and a graduate of the University of Michigan, was described by the hard-bitten Rascoe as one of the finest newspapermen of his day, "a man of education and natural refinement, conservative, tactful, mild-mannered." Beck's only fault, in the opinion of Rascoe, was that he had been beaten down too much by James Keeley. It was in Beck's editorial area, Rascoe reported, that the mothers of the cousins in France, Katherine McCormick and Elinor Patterson, concentrated their interference with the paper's affairs. Despite such problems, the *Tribune*'s editorial department flourished under Beck's leadership.

Veteran correspondents James O'Donnell Bennett, Floyd Gibbons, Frazier Hunt, and John T. McCutcheon were winning readers for the paper with their dramatic coverage of European events. In Chicago, Beck, aided by Sunday editor King, moved the *Tribune* ahead of the *Daily News* in the areas of excellent writing, good cultural features, and sound foreign reporting, while he outdid Hearst in the coverage of local news and the concoction of wildly readable localized features.

Beck, himself a literate man, and his editors assembled a talented staff of writers. In addition to Rascoe, there were Courtney Riley Cooper; Edwin Balmer, the novelist; Lucian Carey; Bert Leston Taylor; George T. Bye; Marquis James, who would win a Pulitzer prize in history; Mark Watson, later to become editor of the *Ladies' Home Journal;* Percy Hammond; Vincent Starrett; and Robert Herrick.

Rascoe, a middle-sized, introspective scholar whose working schedule kept him out of much of the social life of the Chicago writers of the period, got his first job with the paper by consistently scooping his rivals while he was the *Tribune*'s campus correspondent at the University of Chicago. His method was simple, yet one rarely emulated by other news reporters. He regularly read the output of the University of Chicago Press, including *Journal of Sociology, Biblical World, Journal of Archaeology, Journal of Philology,* and the *Classical Journal.* He also became acquainted with professors in the research departments and at Yerkes Observatory. All of this activity was directed at finding studies that could be rewritten as news stories. Academicians, he reasoned, usually did not appreciate the popular appeal of their investigations and discoveries, and the soundness of his theory was borne out by many unusual articles. His story on cheating among high school students, based on information reported in the *American Journal of Sociology,* particularly impressed city editor Walter Howey and Beck, and Rascoe was hired as a full-time reporter in 1913. Mary King soon discovered his multifold talents and drafted him into the Sunday department.

In one of his autobiographical books Rascoe complained that King, the shy but tough Sunday editor, grossly overworked him, a not uncommon grievance of assistant Sunday editors. Rascoe listed the jobs he already held when he got a raise from $50 to $60 a week and was made assistant Sunday editor as well: drama critic, literary critic, editor of the Saturday book page, editor of the "high-brow" page, and roto magazine editor. In addition, Rascoe translated from French, German, and Latin works as the editorial department required. He said he accomplished these duties by working from 8 A.M. to 3 A.M. six days a week. Rascoe conveniently forgot, however, that he had aid with his book reviews and literary page from Fanny Butcher, and he got no sympathy when he talked with city editor Howey about his bereft wife and children in Rogers

Park, since Howey insisted that anyone who worked for a morning newspaper should not get married in the first place.

Rascoe brought brilliant outside talent to the pages of the *Tribune,* supplementing the fiction writers obtained by Mary King. In addition to H. L. Mencken, Joseph Conrad, and George Bernard Shaw, Rascoe published articles by Edith Wharton, H. G. Wells, Vicente Blasco-Ibañez, Harold McGrath, Hal Crain, and George Jean Nathan, writers generally proscribed as too daring and advanced by a group of women who called on King to protest the wanton cultural pages of the *Tribune.* Rascoe, supported by his young editor, went on to greater excesses, campaigning for recognition for James Branch Cabell, whose work appeared to be pornography, and for Theodore Dreiser and Sherwood Anderson. He backed the judgment of Harriet Monroe, whose *Poetry* magazine was publishing such iconoclasts and radicals as T. S. Eliot, Conrad Aiken, Maxwell Bodenheim, Rabindranath Tagore, Ezra Pound, and Alfred Kreymborg, and he championed the work of Carl Sandburg, Edgar Lee Masters, Vachel Lindsay, and Louis Untermeyer. Rascoe and Butcher did not have a literary criticism monopoly, however. Floyd Dell produced an excellent page in the *Chicago Post,* as did Harry Hansen in the *Daily News.* Also, Margaret Anderson was publishing her *Little Review,* and Ben Hecht and Max Bodenheim were putting out their raunchy *Literary Times.*

It was a great age of writing in Chicago, though the *Tribune* scoffed that newcomers "were trying to get up a school of literature overnight." Sir Walter Besant, the British critic, told his readers, "There exists in this city of a million inhabitants . . . a company of novelists, poets, and essayists who are united, if not by associations and clubs, at least by the earnest resolution to cultivate letters." Hamlin Garland returned from Boston and started two literary groups, the Cliff Dwellers and the Society of Midland Authors. And on the South Side, Harriet Moody, widow of young poet William Vaughan Moody, created what Herman Kogan would later call "the foremost literary salon in the country," attracting many of the world's most famous prose writers and poets.

On October 28, 1917, Mencken, writing in the Sunday *Tribune,* paid his respects to the flourishing Chicago literary renaissance. "All literary movements that have youth in them, and a fresh point of view, and authentic bounce and verve of the country . . . come out of Chicago. . . . Find me a writer who is indubitably American and has something new and interesting to say, and nine times out of ten . . . he has some sort of connection with the abattoir by the lake." Three years later Mencken would repeat his view in the *London Nation* under the title, "The Literary Capital of the United States." Chicago writers and critics have sought to defend Mencken's view ever since.

Rascoe's schedule eventually proved to be too much. He left the

Tribune in December, 1920, insisting that he was exhausted from over-work, and took his wife and children back to the farm in Oklahoma from which he came. Later he joined the Chicago literary exodus to New York, where he became literary editor of the *New York Tribune* and the author of numerous books of criticism and reminiscence.

*   *   *

While managing editor Beck and Sunday editor King were taking the measure of the *Daily News* on the cultural front, the *Tribune* sports department also was rising to a high level of performance. There had been sports coverage in the paper almost from the beginning. On July 4, 1847, the paper reported a race "at Merrick's race track," witnessed by 5,000, between "a white man on a horse," an Indian named White Foot, and the town's black barber, Louis Ishbell. The race was a half mile, to a turning stake and back, and the Indian and the black easily outdistanced the rider, "as the horse could not turn the stake so quickly as its human rivals." The rider was "rods" behind when Ishbell beat White Foot, "by one foot."

A few months later, however, the *Tribune* took an entirely different view of racing. On October 8, 1847, an advertisement was sent to the paper with the money to pay for it enclosed, giving notice of a horse race to take place on a wager. The editor acknowledged the receipt of the money and the advertisement but returned them to the sender, saying: "Horse racing on the whole is a bad business—it neither aims at or accomplishes any good end, while the evils that attend it are many and manifest."

The paper's attention to sports was somewhat indifferent until base-ball gained popularity after the Civil War, and for many years thereafter the news department reluctantly gave up space to sports when there were major events to be covered. By 1919, however, sports had equal space with the business news department, generally three pages weekdays and four pages Sundays, though part of the space on Sunday was taken by three or four comic strips and some advertising. Joe Davis covered golf, Walter Eckersall covered football and trapshooting, Larry St. John covered "Woods and Waters," and there were anonymous race handi-cappers and reporters. Boasting the largest sports staff in the nation, the department also covered auto racing, baseball, boxing, billiards, bowling, horse racing, polo, tennis, track and field, and wrestling.

The big sports news in Chicago in the fall of 1919 was the upcoming World Series between the Chicago White Sox and the Cincinnati Reds. Sporting editor Harvey Woodruff was not given extra space, even though the football season was also under way, but he did lead a formidable staff to Cincinnati to cover the first game of the Series on October 1. Jack Lait conducted the "Wake of the News" column, I. E. Sanborn wrote the lead story, and James Crusinberry submitted a side story. Carey Orr provided special cartoons, and there were excellent action pictures by a *Tribune* photographer. Ring Lardner's syndicated column was also carried by the paper. The *Tribune,* always promotion-minded, erected a giant electric scoreboard in Orchestra Hall, where Chicagoans could follow the games.

White Sox fans were stupefied by what the scoreboard showed. Their team played miserable baseball, though they managed to stretch the best-of-nine Series to eight games before losing. Said William "Kid" Gleason, the Sox manager, "The Reds beat the greatest ball team that ever went into a World Series. . . . But it wasn't the real White Sox. They played baseball for me only a couple or three of the eight days." How could the "greatest ball team" have lost so badly? About a year later, the truth came out.

Rumors of a payoff had been circulating as early as the third game of the Series and had persisted through the winter and the following summer. White Sox owner Charles A. Comiskey had taken the rumors seriously enough to hire private investigators. In July, 1920, Crusinberry prepared a story about an impending baseball scandal, based in part upon a conversation he had overheard between two gamblers about the fix of the 1919 Series, but Woodruff held the story, feeling there were not enough facts available. By late August, although no new information had surfaced, there was talk of initiating a grand jury investigation. In early September, Crusinberry, convinced that matters were moving too slowly, persuaded Fred M. Loomis, a Chicago businessman and baseball fan, to sign a letter to the *Tribune* that he, Crusinberry, had written. Was there any truth to rumors that the White Sox lost the World Series because of "an alleged conspiracy between certain unnamed members of the Chicago White Sox and certain gamblers?" the letter asked. Woodruff printed it on page one of the sports section on September 19, 1920.

On September 22, Judge Charles MacDonald of Chicago was named to conduct a grand jury investigation of the matter. The grand jury convened the following day and the *Tribune* began its story of "the most gigantic sporting swindle in the history of America," based on affidavits by players who had wagered that the Sox would lose the Series. Pitcher Eddie Cicotte, who had won 29 games in 1919, and outfielder Joe Jackson, considered one of the greatest hitters of all time, confessed to receiving bribes. They and six other players were indicted. The *Tribune* published thousands of words of the sordid testimony; small boys who loved baseball wept. "Say it isn't so, Joe," a boy cried to Jackson as he stood on the courthouse steps.

But it was so. Even though the jury felt there was not sufficient evidence to warrant conviction, the eight men, who had been Chicago heroes, were barred forever from organized baseball by Commissioner Kenesaw Mountain Landis, who said: "Regardless of the verdict, no player who throws a ball game, no player who entertains proposals or promises to throw a game, no player who sits in a conference with a bunch of crooked players and gamblers where the ways and means of throwing games are discussed and does not promptly tell his club about it, will ever again play professional baseball."

Comiskey paid the other members of his team $1,500 Series money each, declaring that they had played their hearts out and deserved to have first-place money even though they had been denied the glory.

*   *   *

Acting publisher William Field, whose sound management organization matched Beck's editorial and news staff in every way, was a tense perfectionist, quiet-spoken, looking older in 1917 than his 40 years. He ate little and slept less, allowing himself only the luxury of rolling his own Bull Durham cigarettes. Hired as business manager in 1909, he had helped Medill McCormick to organize the new advertising department and quickly assumed increasing importance in the *Tribune*'s administrative affairs. He listened well and got action in a deceptive, self-effacing way, for he was tough as steel, the only man who could oppose Joe Patterson and make it stick. Field, always dressed in a gray suit, paid the postage on his personal letters sent from the office and scrupulously paid for personal telephone calls, idiosyncrasies long remembered by his peers. He occupied Patterson's office, in which he posted a sign: "This is Joe Patterson's office. He is fighting in France. I am sitting in his chair for a little while until he comes back."

Field drove the advertising department hard, gaining more national linage than any other publication save the *Saturday Evening Post*. His famous *Book of Facts* would become the prototype for similar publications throughout the country. Elected chairman of the committee on advertising standards of the World Advertising Council, he imposed tough standards for any advertiser wishing to place copy in the *Chicago Tribune*. He pioneered rotogravure advertising, as the *Tribune* pioneered the roto picture magazine in America. At the same time Field managed the newsprint division of the company, the Tribune Building, and the other developing company interests. The strain was great, and in June, 1918, with the approval of McCormick, Field brought Samuel Emory Thomason to the paper from the Shepard, McCormick and Thomason law office to fill the role of business manager. Thomason proved himself the equal of Field in newspaper management techniques. Born in Chicago, he was graduated from the University of Michigan and had studied law at Northwestern. His supposed temporary stint as business manager became permanent when the weary Field went into semiretirement in January, 1919, handling only perfunctory duties as Tribune Company's "eastern representative."

Other key Field subordinates included Eugene Parsons, who became advertising manager, and William E. McFarlane (former secretary to Harrison Parker), who became manager of classified. The *Tribune* had seized circulation leadership from the *Chicago Daily News* in 1918, and Field was determined that the paper would now gain dominance of retail display advertising, which included the lucrative and prestigious department store ads. The *Daily News* had for years led in this advertising category and would continue to do so into the mid-1920s. McFarlane, in his quest for preeminence, increased the advertising personnel to nearly 100 salespeople, mostly women recruited for telephone work. Over the years claims and counterclaims of advertising superiority would be asserted by the *Tribune* and the *Daily News,* being based on seven days versus six, full run of the paper as contrasted with zoned editions, and other specialized considerations. But whatever the measuring stick, the *Tribune* in time would gain superiority over all other Chicago newspapers.

The paper, which once refused to solicit advertising and in 1905 had a total advertising staff of eight, became one of the largest and most aggressive marketers of advertising in the country. The concern of *Tribune* management for the growing department was indicated by the fact that its third-floor quarters were the first in Chicago to become air-conditioned. Included in the advertising establishment were the research and marketing group and a company postal force that, said the promotion ads, handled nearly 3 million responses to the "blind" want ads published by the paper in the course of a year.

Under Parsons's direction McFarlane developed an extraordinary staff. There were star salesmen, such as Daniel Francis McMahon, who later became retail advertising manager. According to James Cleary, McMahon "started as a clerk in 1908 and rose because he was flamed with the conviction that he was representing the world's greatest newspaper and performing a great civic and economic service by showing merchants and manufacturers how they could win profits from associating with this unique enterprise." Another such figure was Ted Blend, who dealt with the automotive industry, which was considered fast and high living. Blend was the only *Tribune* employee allowed to put liquor on his expense account. And there was "Full Page Donahue," William Donahue, who in his enthusiasm for his work was said to shout at passing merchants from a *Tribune* window, "How about a full page for your basement sale?" suiting his pitch to his knowledge of the merchant's incipient needs. Donahue soon became a divisional manager.

Increasingly more women were employed by the paper. During the first quarter of the 20th century, their progress was remarkable. In 1896 the paper listed four women in the accounting department and 12 others in the circulation department. By 1915 there were 156 women, and by 1925 the number had increased to 369, the circulation department alone claiming 46. Under Anna Garrow, women were responsible for the paper's telephone switchboard. They also did the telephone selling in the classified advertising department, and they comprised a major part of the staff of Sunday editor Mary King. The war improved their opportunity, but most obtained their jobs through King's conviction that women were better judges of women's true interests than men, and a consensus in the advertising office that women were much more expert with the newfangled telephones than men.

Although women conducted telephone sales, men were preferred for direct selling of the classified ads and were sent out in teams to canvass a neighborhood, each man receiving $6 a week, his captain $11. An advertisement cost $1.05 a line for seven days, cash on order. The teams mostly obtained "rooms for rent" and "help wanted" ads. The best salesmen were assigned to special accounts that used classified display advertising and later were permitted to sell and service the major retail establishments, where good salesmen in time became as familiar with and as concerned about the business as its owners and managers. No advertising man could rise, nor for a time enter the department, except as a classified salesman. This was true even for a company director, Henry D. Lloyd.

In addition to the *Book of Facts,* Parsons developed a customer service for advertising clients. Large department stores and other major businesses had their own advertising copy departments or could afford to employ advertising agencies to prepare their selling copy and artwork. The smaller buyer lacked such expert advice and craftsmanship until the *Tribune* decided to provide it. Parsons hired Oscar Brodfueher from Northwestern University and H. C. Olson, an artist, to establish the paper's copy and art department. Parsons also created a system of zoned advertising that enabled a big advertiser to change his copy for various neighborhoods and the small buyer to use the *Tribune* to saturate his immediate neighborhood with his messages. Zoned advertising did not have the full circulation of the paper, and thus obtained lower rates. To make the zoned sections more attractive to readers, the paper eventually printed neighborhood news in them. The *Tribune* also increasingly perfected sections to appeal to the special interests of its readers. These sections, usually appearing in the Sunday edition, dealt with such topics as women's features, culture and arts, sports, and business; eventually nearly a score of interest divisions were represented.

The *Book of Facts* explained the use and cost of the various zoned sections as well as of the paper's merchandising and research services and its copy and art department. On a milline basis (cost per 1 million circulation), the *Tribune*'s rates were compared with those of other newspapers and of magazines. There were glowing letters describing the results of advertising in the *Tribune*. Jason Rogers, publisher of the *New York Globe*, studied the *Tribune*'s techniques and wrote: "For years this newspaper has rendered wonderful service in showing all newspapers how to make distant manufacturers visualize the great opportunities for marketing their goods in Chicago. Its survey and statistical data regarding Chicago are without question in advance of anything ever attempted by a big city newspaper. . . . From my standpoint, the *Tribune* is the soundest model on which to shape a morning newspaper enterprise." Later, in his book *Building Newspaper Advertising,* published in 1919, Rogers wrote, "The *Tribune* can do things that probably no other newspaper can do."

The proper treatment of advertising was the concern not only of the department responsible but of everyone involved in the production of the paper, especially Robert R. McCormick. Since Tribune Company owned its paper mill, McCormick was involved in the control of quality from the selection of woodlands in Canada to the final printing impressions. He worked so closely with all phases of *Tribune* operations that he was able to recommend improved press designs.

A major contributor to the *Tribune*'s superior advertising displays, copied by most other newspapers, was Leo Loewenberg, who joined the paper as a compositor in 1893 and became superintendent of the composing room in 1906. American newspapers had followed the British style of running advertising in full columns along the outer sides of a page and filling inside columns with news. The first full-page advertisements in the *Tribune* were simply nine of these filled columns ordered by a single advertiser. In time the ads were two or more columns wide, but they continued to be stacked vertically. This arrangement created a dull page and lessened the impact of individual ads. Loewenberg proposed placing large advertisements at the bottom of each page toward the inside margin, with progressively smaller ads stacked atop one another along the fold, creating a half pyramid on each page. When the paper was fully opened to a two-page spread, the ads formed a pyramid in the center. James Keeley and Teddy Beck held off this notion of Loewenberg's for years, fearing it would interfere with their editorial layout concepts. At last, however, Loewenberg was given a chance to try his plan in a single edition. The edition at once attracted the attention and admiration of Medill McCormick, then in charge, and he ordered the pyramid system used regularly.

By 1920, the scientific approach to selling was well established in the *Tribune* advertising department and was widely copied. The *Book of Facts* enjoyed wide acceptance, and what it had to say about postwar Chicago was impressive, especially as to the *Tribune*'s own preeminent position. No place on earth, according to the *Book of Facts,* could match Chicago as a consumer market. It cited the consumption statistics of the 500,000 prospering families in the immediate trade area and demonstrated that it could identify them as to ethnic background, education, income, and store and brand preferences. The entire range of consumer goods was covered, from breakfast cereal to motor cars. Questionnaires distributed to *Tribune* subscribers in Iowa, Michigan, Wisconsin, Indiana, and Illinois showed that millions of residents of those states visited Chicago from once to a dozen times a year, buying everything from baby rattles to farm tractors.

The *Tribune* itself was flourishing, with its circulation of 424,026 daily and 693,895 on Sundays (down slightly from a wartime high) now leading the *Daily News*'s 386,498 daily and the *Herald and Examiner*'s 289,880 daily and 597,789 on Sundays. The *American* with 330,216 daily was in third place; the *Journal*'s daily circulation was 116,807 and the *Post*'s 51,023. Equally important, and increasingly more so as newsprint costs continued to rise, the *Tribune* printed 29.6 percent of all daily newspaper advertising in Chicago. The *Daily News* ranked second with 25.2 percent, followed by the *Herald and Examiner* with 18.2 percent, the *Journal* with 8.9 percent, the *American* with 8.4 percent, and the *Post* with 6.1 percent. In automotive advertising, the *Tribune* had 30.2 percent of the market; for trucks and tractors it had a remarkable 40 percent. The *Tribune* continued far behind the *Daily News* in department store advertising, 20.1 percent to 31.5 percent, but it led in grocery and food products. The *Daily News*'s dominance in department store ads, the *Book of Facts* pointed out, was in the basement departments of the various stores. But Marshall Field & Company; Mandel Brothers; Carson, Pirie, Scott & Company; and Charles A. Stevens placed 37.1 percent of their "upstairs" advertising in the *Tribune* compared to 14.5 percent in the *Daily News.*

While Field and Parsons were pushing the development of the advertising department, they were also responsible for the upsurge in the *Tribune*'s promotional efforts—the activities and statements by which the paper advertised itself, usually in a cause generally beneficial to its readership and the community. The impetus they provided established a tradition that lasted long beyond their tenures with the paper. During the 1920s the paper supported such events as the Silver Skates Derby (initiated by *Tribune* sportswriter Walter Eckersall). The series of boxing benefits known as the Golden Gloves, which was started in 1928 by the *New York News,* grew from a *Tribune*-sponsored boxing benefit for charity held in 1923. The *Tribune* began sponsoring Golden Gloves contests as Chicago-area benefits in 1930. Two inspirations of sports editor Arch

Ward, the All-Star baseball game, first played in 1933, and the College All-Star football game, played yearly from 1934 to 1976, became national sporting traditions under the paper's guidance. The *Tribune* also sponsored an all-star bowling tournament, the Chicago air races, and a wrestling show. When admission was charged for these events, the proceeds were given to charity via Chicago Tribune Charities, Inc. The total paid attendance for such shows from 1928 to 1946 was 3,379,633, not including participants, which included thousands in the Music Festival, or recipients of passes. Scores of special events were arranged or supported by the *Tribune* and related to almost every field of interest, from kite flying to horse racing to fashion shows to a "share your lilacs" campaign, in addition to civic promotions and events supported by all the media.

*   *   *

Colonel McCormick and Captain Patterson returned from France to home front wars that would outlast their lifetimes. Both cousins retained their military titles, which seemed appropriate to their embattled civilian roles, McCormick keeping also his military moustache. Long, lean, immaculate, Colonel McCormick appeared aloof and austere, as forbidding, *Fortune* magazine once remarked, as "a guardsman for Frederick the Great." Patterson continued relaxed as usual, buddying with the circulation drivers, taking his lunch where he could overhear what the ordinary people were saying, and paying minimum attention to what he wore. The cousins worked well together, and for a time were usually, but not always, on the same side.

They were completely in accord during a major attack that came from the detested William Hale Thompson in the fall of 1918, while Patterson was yet in Europe. Following his defeat by Medill McCormick in the Republican senatorial primary, Thompson responded to a call for his reelection as mayor, put forth by Fred Lundin, his political adviser, and announced his candidacy on November 30. Colonel McCormick had returned stateside, and although he would not be discharged from the army until December 31, his assignment to Fort Sheridan permitted him to meet with the directors of the *Tribune* to plan the anti-Thompson campaign. The paper pounded Thompson hard, pointing to rampant crime, corruption and inefficiency in public office, the rape of the fragile civil service, graft in construction projects, and interference with the schools. Big Bill's pro-German record had destroyed him downstate and had cost him the nomination to the Senate, but it continued to do him no harm in Chicago. Though his Democratic opponent, again Robert Sweitzer, was equally pro-German, Thompson appeared strong in the German wards as well as in the black wards controlled by George F.

Harding. The *Tribune* chose to back State's Attorney Maclay Hoyne, a Democratic maverick who was running as an independent. Hoyne had been attempting, without much success, to expose some of the alleged Thompson malfeasance and graft.

There were Republicans who feared that, by dividing the party's vote, the *Tribune* would repeat the debacle of 1912, when the split between Taft and Roosevelt made Woodrow Wilson president, but the paper rejected any such idea. "Some staunch Republicans are considering whether to hold their noses and vote for Thompson," said the paper on March 24, 1919, "though they are disgusted with the waste and spoils politics of the Thompson administration." The editorialist enumerated the many and justified reasons for disgust, pointing out that the man guilty of such political iniquities had been totally rejected by the Republicans in the recent senatorial race. But, even more heinously, Thompson was a rascal besmirching the Republican name nationally. Could a decent Republican vote for Thompson? Obviously not. "The opposite is true. We could better recommend that Democrats vote for Thompson, since they might be glad to wreck the Republican party. The reelection of Thompson would be the worst possible black eye for the Republican party throughout the nation, the worst possible start for the campaign of 1920. . . . Vote for Hoyne."

Maclay Hoyne ran a poor third. Mayor Thompson defeated Sweitzer by 21,000 votes. Thompson chortled that he was a better Republican than the editors of the *Chicago Tribune*. Fred Lundin rubbed his hands and smiled his Uriah Heep smile. He dictated an editorial for the *Republican,* the weekly newspaper he had started and was directing for Thompson: "The people of Chicago have won a great victory. It spells the defeat of newspaper control." Commented the *Tribune:* "It is our hope that Mayor Thompson's second term is more useful than his first term was."

*　　*　　*

While the *Tribune*'s directors were not happy with the outcome of the election, other concerns were receiving their attention. On March 15, 1919, at the peak of the fight against Thompson, Patterson was in Chicago and out of uniform, presenting his plans for the tabloid newspaper he wanted to publish in New York.

Shortly before leaving France, Colonel McCormick had paid a visit to Captain Patterson at the 42nd Division headquarters near the front. En route to the meeting, McCormick borrowed a helmet and a gas mask from a friendly young brigadier general named Douglas MacArthur. "If I had known how famous he would become," McCormick noted in his memoirs, "I would have begged him to give them to me." In order to speak privately, McCormick recalled, he and Patterson "went through a window and sat on a straw pile where we could also watch enemy shells. It was at this time Patterson said he would like to found a picture newspaper after the war." Years later, especially when he spoke at *New York News* parties and dinners, McCormick liked to say that he and Patterson were sitting on a manure pile when the hatching of the *New York News* took place.

Captain Patterson, before returning to the United States, inspected the methods employed by Lord Northcliffe in building his successful tabloid, the *London Daily Mirror.* In February, 1919, Colonel McCormick urged the directors of the *Chicago Tribune* to authorize William Field, the company's eastern representative, to prepare for Patterson's venture. It was an assignment Field happily accepted, for the new project offered an exciting alternative to the doldrums of retirement.

At the March 15 meeting, the directors approved Patterson's appointment of Arthur L. Clarke as the managing editor of the New York paper, yet unnamed. Also at that meeting, S. E. Thomason, the *Tribune*'s business manager, was elected a director of Tribune Company. On May 10, McCormick presented the following resolution for approval of the directors: "That the officers of the company be empowered to take the steps necessary in their discretion to institute a subsidiary pictorial newspaper enterprise in New York City." The resolution was unanimously adopted. Captain Patterson was elected president of the new company, though it was understood that he would continue to provide half his time and energy to the *Tribune.* Patterson borrowed other talent from the *Tribune* in addition to Field to start the *Illustrated Daily News* (more commonly called the *New York News*), which went to press on June 26, 1919, and in time acquired the biggest newspaper circulation in the United States.

Other such ventures would follow. In 1924, the board of directors authorized the establishment of the Coloroto Company to publish a weekly national magazine. Ultimately called *Liberty,* it also drew from the *Tribune* staff, taking Harvey Deuel, the paper's assistant city editor, for managing editor. *Liberty,* designed to compete with the *Saturday Evening Post* and *Collier's,* was printed on the *Tribune*'s coloroto press and, under the direction of McCormick and Patterson, sold nearly 2½ million copies, passing *Collier's* in circulation. It could not, however, obtain the needed advertising and was sold to Bernarr Macfadden in 1931, whereupon Deuel became city editor of the *New York News.*

Another *Tribune* executive to leave the paper for the *New York News* was Sunday editor Mary King. During the absence of McCormick and Patterson, King had assumed leadership in creating the kind of feature package she and Patterson envisioned, one supplied with excellent fiction by able and popular writers purchased at prices competitive with those paid by the national magazines. King called it "Blue Ribbon" fiction, for which she commissioned some of the country's leading writers. In 1920, she departed Chicago for New York, where she continued her career as women's editor of the *New York News,* fiction editor of *Liberty* magazine, and fiction editor of the Chicago Tribune–New York News Syndicate, supplying high-quality original fiction and other features to the *Tribune.* In 1938, following Patterson's divorce, she became Mrs. Joseph Patterson.

Expansion was not the only reason for loss of *Tribune* employees. Many came and went—Rascoe, for instance—seeking their fortunes elsewhere. But one of the departures of the war years became a source of considerable exasperation to the *Tribune.* Walter Howey, the paper's frenetic city editor, who became the prototype for tough newsroom bosses in Ben Hecht and Charles MacArthur's play *The Front Page,* had quit in anger in 1917 when Patterson upbraided him for being too free with *Tribune* space for a Hollywood producer, D. W. Griffith. Howey had a standing offer from Hearst for double his *Tribune* salary, and he accepted, becoming managing editor of the *Herald and Examiner.* There he plagued the *Tribune* with scoops and his peculiar brand of diabolism. Did Howey's alert competitors note an item in an early edition of the *Herald and Examiner,* reporting the arrival of a rich heiress from South Bend, and conclude that Howey had muffed a good feature story? They did, and worked fast. The girl, given a few months to live, sought expert advice in Chicago on the best way to dispose of her $10 million fortune. The *Tribune* played the feature and picture of the heiress on page one. In later editions of his paper, Howey thanked them for advertising the new serial, "The $10,000,000 Heiress," starting the following Sunday in the *Herald and Examiner.* The actress he had hired played her part well. On another occasion, Howey employed Eleanor "Cissy" Patterson, the ex-Countess Gizycka, to write a series of articles on Chicago society, and he added a few words to her by-line: "Sister of Joseph Medill Patterson of the *Chicago Tribune.*"

*   *   *

During the 1919 mayoral campaign the *Tribune* had warned its readers that reelection of Big Bill Thompson would be of disastrous moment for the Republican party at both the local and national levels. After his victory, Thompson acted self-righteously indignant. "I've been maligned," the mayor shouted to his jubilant supporters. "I've been misunderstood. I want to make Chicago a great city, a summer resort of the United States. I want to build her lakefront, to widen her streets and build bridges. I love this city."

The mayor's plans for Chicago, at least as far as the *Tribune*'s editors were concerned, sounded suspiciously similar to the exhortations that had been appearing on the paper's editorial pages since the beginning of the year, calling for ambitious works for the city: "1. A South Shore park plan, improvement of the lakefront according to the Burnham plan and expansion of a belt of parks, which would join with boulevards to be constructed along Sanitary District canals." Since McCormick's friend Edward J. Kelly was president of the South Park board, this plan appeared to have a good chance of success. "2. Modernize the Chicago water department." Mayor William Hale Thompson was eager to modernize and expand any and all city departments, even if it had to be done under the watchful eye of the press. "3. Extend the Chicago plan, Ogden Avenue, 12th Street and Michigan Avenue." The 12th Street and Michigan Avenue projects were proceeding so handsomely that the paper soon would be able to charge Thompson's cronies with stealing millions from them and make it stick legally, at least for a time. "4. Complete terminals under way and build new ones." This was a reference to the railroad terminals that soon would be built by private enterprise. "5. Lessen the smoke horror." Such an ecological campaign had been launched by the *Tribune* years before, was slowly succeeding, and was being helped by Mayor Thompson's espousal of the Illinois Central electrification ordinance.

The *Tribune*'s platform for America, while not included in the editorial flag, was spelled out in various editorials. Two major items were stated repeatedly: Get wartime government regulation off the back of business, and prevent, at all costs, any further involvement of the United States in European affairs. The paper's stand opposing the League of Nations was popular among its readers. Midwestern representatives and senators described the enormous profits made from the world war, and even President Wilson, taking the stump to defend his proposals for American adherence to the Versailles Treaty, and membership in the League, was forced to admit that the war had been for crass profit and commercial advantage. Speaking on August 5, 1919, he said:

> Is there any man here, or any woman, let me say is there any child here, who does not know that the seed of war in the modern world is industrial and commercial rivalry? The real reason that the war we have just finished took place was that Germany was afraid her commercial rivals were going to get the better of her, and the reason why some nations went to war against Germany was that they thought Germany would get the commercial advantage of them. This war in its inception was a commercial and industrial war. It was not a political war.

The *Tribune* and the Midwest and its senators supported Sen. Henry Cabot Lodge of Massachusetts in the attack on the Covenant of the League of Nations, particularly Article X, which required "members of the League to respect and preserve against external aggression the territorial integrity and existing political independence of all members of the League." President Wilson's attempt to gain the support of the American people for the League failed. In Pueblo, Colorado, on September 26, 1919, he sustained a stroke that left him almost totally incapacitated for the rest of his term. On March 19, 1920, the Senate rejected the treaty 55 to 35. Then Congress passed a resolution declaring the war to be at an end, and President Wilson, though physically helpless, vetoed it. U.S. involvement in "Europe's war" did not officially end until August, 1921, during the Harding administration, when the United States signed separate treaties with Austria, Germany, and Hungary.

From time to time the *Tribune* also introduced into its editorial masthead a platform for the Midwest, generally calling for the development of waterway transportation to carry farm products to market, especially to port terminals, and demanding an end to "Pittsburgh Plus." The latter was the policy of pricing all rolled steel at the Pittsburgh mill price plus the cost of transportation from Pittsburgh, regardless of where the mill was located. The practice harmed the Chicago area steel industry and was especially obnoxious to farmers, who were forced to pay more for steel products. In 1922 the paper would make "Abolish Pittsburgh Plus" a new plank in its Chicago platform, saying editorially on April 22: "The manufacturing business of Chicago is placed under a tremendous handicap. The entire prosperity and development of the city is impeded. We gain nothing from our proximity to the great steel mills of the Calumet district." In 1924 the Federal Trade Commission ordered an end to Pittsburgh Plus, an important victory, the *Tribune* said, for Midwestern manufacturers and consumers alike, and for free enterprise as a whole.

* * *

During the summer of 1919 grim tragedy and terror stunned the city. Over the years Chicago had seen frequent ethnic disturbances as immigrant groups sought to adjust to one another in the harsh environment. Germans were sometimes killed when they pushed their libertarian ideas too hard and too fast; Irishmen fought for their neighborhoods with clubs and stones; and Jews and Bohemians battled the Irish and one another. Heads were broken, and some people died. During the war more than 50,000 blacks had migrated to Chicago, doubling the city's black population in less than five years. The rapid expansion of black neighborhoods had caused occasional racial conflict, but nothing in the past equaled the numbing news of Sunday, July 27. Whites on the 29th Street beach drove a black youth back into the water as he attempted to swim to a raft that was within the area the whites had arrogated to themselves. The boy was drowned. The news of his death, and of fighting on 29th Street, raced through the black and white neighborhoods. There was further fighting; homes of blacks were burned. On July 28, a streetcar strike, unrelated to the racial incident, tied up police as strikers fought along the picket lines, making it even more difficult to keep the peace.

The race riots, among the worst in Chicago's history, continued on the South Side for five days. Reporters and photographers from all the city's newspapers risked their lives in covering the disorder. On the sixth day Gov. Frank O. Lowden sent 6,000 state militiamen to patrol the black neighborhoods, and the rioting ceased. The commission that Lowden appointed to investigate the riots reported that the Chicago police had failed to restrain white hoodlum gangs in the area and had failed to protect blacks or their property. It found also that blacks were being exploited by the bosses of vice and "numbers" gambling, that brothels and gambling resorts were forced upon the people, and that they were left without recourse. The coroner fixed the death toll at 23 blacks and 14 whites; 500 people had been injured.

*   *   *

In the spring of 1920 the *Tribune* and Mayor Thompson ran a collision course en route to the Republican National Convention, scheduled to be held in Chicago in June. The *Tribune* in 1919 had reprinted an editorial from the *New York Post* that suggested that Lowden might be an excellent candidate for the U.S. presidency. The *Tribune* agreed. Lowden had been an effective governor, and he was a good friend of the *Chicago Tribune*. He had once been a good friend of Big Bill Thompson, too, but he had not backed the mayor's bid for the senatorial nomination in 1918, a dereliction Thompson would not forgive. Lowden had compounded his sins by refusing state patronage to the Thompson–Lundin political machine. Besides, in Illinois it was no longer possible to be a friend of both William Hale Thompson and the *Chicago Tribune*.

Thompson set out to wreck the Lowden–*Tribune* plans for the national convention. From the Illinois advisory primary and the party's state conclave, Lowden emerged with 38 delegates, but Thompson managed to capture 16 in addition to being a delegate himself. These votes would have to be reckoned with. Meantime, the *Tribune* did what it could to dilute Thompson's influence. Thompson was a national committeeman and, as the convention approached, the paper warned, "If Mayor Thompson is reelected for Illinois on the Republican national committee, it will indicate to the rest of the country that Illinois approves Thompson's views on the war."

The warning was sufficient. At the Illinois preconvention caucus on June 7, the delegates chose U.S. Sen. Lawrence Y. Sherman, not

Thompson, for the national committee. They also rebuffed two Thompson proposals. The first, to withhold support from any candidate criticized by U.S. Senate investigators for excessive spending in the primaries, was obviously aimed at crippling the Lowden candidacy. Lowden had spent heavily, though it was his own money and that which his wife received from her father, George Pullman. The proposal was defeated 38 to 17, as was a second, opposing U.S. affiliation with the League of Nations. Thompson, undaunted, waited for his chance to settle the score.

As the Republicans gathered in Chicago for the convention to be held in the Coliseum, Mayor Thompson let it be known that he and his followers would never support Lowden, for "moral reasons." One-third of the convention's delegates were pledged to Frank Lowden for president and one-third to Gen. Leonard Wood. Thompson joined forces with his friend and ally William Randolph Hearst, who had come to town to push the candidacy of Sen. Hiram Johnson of California. In the background hovered a fast-talking politician from Ohio, Harry Daugherty, who was extolling that state's handsome but little-known favorite son, Sen. Warren G. Harding. To convention visitors who called at Mayor Thompson's suite in the Congress Hotel, Big Bill cautioned: "Look out for that Lowden. His word is no good."

On June 11, the *Tribune*'s banner read: "NOMINATE TODAY. SUPREME TEST. LOWDEN WOOD IN FIRST VOTE." Lowden and Wood led the first six ballots, alternating the number one position, but no winner emerged. Every time that Lowden appeared sure of victory, Bill Thompson's 17 votes and Senator Harding's Ohio contingent stood in the way. Lowden was Ohio's second choice, and some of the politicians said that if Thompson would allow his delegates to vote for Lowden, Harding would follow suit and the Illinois governor would win. But Big Bill relished his spoiler's role. Finally, to insure that no deal could be made with the Lowden forces, Thompson and his delegates took a walk. To avoid a hopeless deadlock and destructive party infighting, Lowden finally released his own delegates.

That night there was a meeting in the suite of Col. George Harvey, a former Democrat and an experienced political manipulator. With him was the ubiquitous Harry Daugherty. Leaders came to the smoke-filled room, got their promises, and departed. Shortly after 2 A.M., Senator Harding was called in. He was told that he would be the Republican nominee. "Well," said Harding to Daugherty, "looks like we drew to a pair of deuces and filled." That afternoon Warren Gamaliel Harding was nominated on the tenth ballot, and Calvin Coolidge of Massachusetts was named for vice-president. There were some who would agree with the opinion of Edward F. Dunne, who wrote in his history of Illinois that if Thompson's 17 votes had gone to Lowden, the Illinois governor would have been the nominee and probably president of the United States.

Thompson was elated. He would have preferred Senator Johnson, but the defeat of the detested Lowden and the *Tribune* was satisfying. The *Tribune* printed a somewhat labored editorial indicating how little it knew about Senator Harding. It began: "A convention as freely deliberative as a great political assembly can be, but as nearly unbiased as a party organization ever has been, a convention without a steam roller and free to express its own judgment and honestly considered free will, has decided in the best interests of the country and nominated Warren G. Harding for President of the United States." The paper then observed that Harding had served in the U.S. Senate, that he was a "four square American," and "a man without blemish . . . who had worked himself up from low position to a high position. . . . As President, Mr. Harding will bring to the government firmness and breadth."

The *Tribune* praised Lowden and urged him to seek reelection as governor. Lowden decided not to run and backed instead his lieutenant governor, John G. Oglesby, for the post in the Republican primary in September. Lowden's plans again were frustrated, however, for Len Small, the Thompson-backed candidate from Kankakee, was victorious over Oglesby. Disillusioned and angry, Lowden announced that he would retire to his Sinissippi farm, though, he declared, he would do whatever he could to defeat the "Thompson Tammany."

Big Bill's Illinois victory in November was almost total. The Harding–Coolidge ticket won by a landslide, but more important to Thompson were the state and local returns. Len Small was elected governor; Robert Emmett Crowe, another Thompson candidate, was elected Cook County state's attorney; and Frank Righeimer, also a Thompson man, triumphed over Francis X. Busch, a leading Chicago attorney, in the contest for Cook County judge. Righeimer, whose father owned a saloon across from City Hall, could be counted on to run the county election machinery properly.

"The lid's off!" Thompson yelled to his cronies as the returns came in. "We ate 'em alive with their clothes on!" Only a single avowed Thompson enemy survived, Edward J. Brundage, elected attorney general of Illinois. Big Bill found himself at the peak of his power, with only the *Tribune* and *Chicago Daily News* standing in the way of his absolute control of Cook County.

Flushed with the thoroughness of his victory, Thompson turned his attention to other matters. At midnight on January 16, 1920, the 18th Amendment to the Constitution and its enforcement provision, the Volstead Act, had become the law of the land, thus crowning the long crusade by proponents of Temperance to prohibit the manufacture, sale, and transportation of intoxicating liquors. While city police and federal agents took months to close down all the formerly legitimate saloons, a great thirst arose in a town that had been wet since its founding, and Johnny Torrio and his deputy, Al Capone, were ready to slake it. The Genna brothers, Capone followers, set up alcohol-cooking operations on the city's West Side, and the Torrio–Capone syndicate arranged for the importation of liquor from eastern ports and Canada. "Needled beer," a method of introducing liquor into legal "near beer," was invented. Battles for booze-selling territory began.

Since the days of the Maine liquor laws, Chicago had voted dripping wet on all local liquor options, so it was clear to hoodlums and politicians alike that huge profits could be made if enforcement were ineffective. Enjoyment of the lucrative rum revenues depended in great part on control of the enforcement machinery—not that all officials planned actually to enforce Prohibition. Rather whoever controlled enforcement could demand payment for nonenforcement and could harass, even destroy, those who would not pay tribute for license to ignore the law.

In November, Mayor Thompson appointed his secretary, Charles Fitzmorris, a former Hearst city editor, as police superintendent. Fred Lundin fumed because he had not been consulted about the appointment, but Big Bill ignored Lundin's pout while Fitzmorris launched a demonstration of power that won general newspaper approval. Some 800 men and women were arrested in various notorious dives within 24 hours, though most were freed because of faulty warrants or lack of evidence. A few were fined $25. Mayor Thompson praised Fitzmorris, but State's Attorney Robert Crowe, who had intentions of setting up his own enforcement organization, like Lundin was irked because he had not been consulted about the Fitzmorris appointment. The *Tribune* attempted to encourage a split between Crowe and Big Bill and lauded a trio of Thompson enemies, Attorney General Ed Brundage, Secretary of State Louis L. Emmerson, and State Sen. Otis Glenn of Murphysboro. All seemed well in Big Bill's political world, yet the first crack in the Thompson machine had appeared.

*   *   *

While Joseph Patterson was busy with the *New York News,* Robert McCormick was supervising plans for a new manufacturing plant on the north bank of the Chicago River, east of Michigan Avenue at St. Clair Street, where an office building for the paper would later be situated. He also was directing the construction of a wharf at Shelter Bay, Canada, which eventually would permit shipments of wood pulp to Thorold for processing, and still later, shipments of newsprint to the planned *Tribune* pressroom on the Chicago River. As this work progressed, McCormick's father, the former ambassador, died in Hinsdale on April 16, 1919, after an extended illness. Robert R. McCormick had for some time been handling family finances, and he now had the details of his father's estate in his care. His burdens were eased when he acquired, during this period, an invaluable supervisor of the Canadian properties. One of his outstanding lieutenants in France had been a young Princeton graduate, Arthur Schmon. Following the war, McCormick offered Schmon a job as supervisor of operations at bleak Shelter Bay, in the wilderness of the Quebec north shore. Schmon accepted, taking his bride to a log cabin on Shelter Bay. Now McCormick extended Schmon's responsibilities to the Thorold plant and the transportation problems. Ultimately Schmon would become president of the Canadian properties and a director of Tribune Company.

Plans for the publishing plant in Chicago moved swiftly, but those for the office tower would await the construction of the Michigan Avenue bridge, which would link North Michigan Avenue with double-decked Wacker Drive and South Michigan Avenue, also under construction. The *Tribune*'s interest in the speedy completion of those projects did not keep the paper from criticizing the way the work was being done. It dropped frequent hints that the state's attorney ought to look into the high costs and waste being allowed by the Thompson administration. But no such investigation transpired. On May 14, 1920, the mayor dedicated the Michigan Avenue bridge and took note of his newspaper critics: "They'll be building big skyscrapers here with this bridge finished. And some of 'em that will build them will be the very ones that are hollering at me now."

Big Bill was right, of course. McCormick had already acquired the land needed for the office building as well as the new printing plant and on October 15, 1919, had reported to the board of directors on the progress of plans. They included not only provision for "the biggest and most efficient newspaper printing establishment in the world," but a massive 35-story office building, which would be "the world's most beautiful office tower," a structure intended to follow the plant by a few years.

On June 7, 1920, Colonel McCormick and Captain Patterson were present for the laying of the cornerstone for the manufacturing plant. McCormick, familiar with the crowded pressroom problems of the paper's Loop location, worked with engineers on the proposed press layout and developed a system so successful that he obtained a patent on it. The subbasements of the new plant would provide for newsprint storage, reel rooms, space for a line of 30-ton press units and folders a city block long, and machinery for automatically carrying folded newspapers to the loading docks on the ground floor. McCormick's arrangement alternated folders between some of the press units, so that more than one press could be coupled to a folder. There would be six 4-unit presses, each printing a 32-page paper; five 5-unit, printing 40-page sections; and four 6-unit presses, printing 48 pages each. Room was provided so that in 1923 a second line of 30 press units could be added. All the presses were to be Goss high-speed units, rated at 30,000 per hour press speed.

The newspaper plant, rising seven stories above ground, six above the present Michigan Avenue level, was completed in astonishing time, six months. The location was excellent. The property was on a railroad line, important since nearly all the paper's newsprint from Canada was shipped by rail at the time. The *Tribune* would soon acquire an adjacent site on the river for a newsprint unloading dock and warehouse, with a tunnel for utilities linking it to the plant. McCormick planned that eventually newsprint would be loaded on shipboard at docks in Canada and unloaded at the St. Clair Street docking area. Then, by gravity feed, the giant newsprint rolls would travel to the storage area under the pressroom, whence they could be lifted by machinery to the presses.

John Park, production manager, was placed in charge of the formidable moving operation. Once the huge presses were in place and tested, the *Tribune* would have to move all of its Linotypes, stereotype furnaces, steam tables, steel storage cabinets, steel chases and turtles (heavy makeup tables), and the other cumbersome equipment of the printing industry down the stairs and freight elevators of its Madison and Dearborn building, through the city streets, across the river, and into the new plant. All of this had to be accomplished between the final run of the Sunday paper of December 12, 1920, an edition of 760,000 copies, and the first edition of the Monday paper, 450,000 copies. Each piece of equipment was marked and its location keyed to maps of the new building. So efficient was the operation that not a deadline or a mail car was missed. Nine steam tables weighing seven and one-half tons each, 57 Linotype machines, scores of steel type racks, and hundreds of steel turtles, office desks, filing cabinets, typewriters, and telephones were carried through the city streets by motor trucks and wagons during the early Sunday hours. Electricians were ready to hook up the metal pots of the Linotypes as well as the motors (gas heaters were being abandoned); telephone men wired 100 main lines and 275 extensions, without disturbing service. The telegraph lines connecting the home office with Washington and its worldwide bureaus were made ready.

By evening the reporters, rewrite men, and copy editors were in their places on the fourth floor. Below them the compositors, seeming to cover a half city block of area, were checking their headline type or preparing their Linotypes for action. Soon copy was flowing, telegraph instruments were clicking, Linotypes chattered, the compositors were locking their chases for the stereotypers to plane and mold, and 125 pressmen and hundreds of mailers and distributors were ready. The rheostats started the huge presses; the pressmen checked web tension, adjusted the ink fountains, monitored the folding equipment and conveyers and stackers. Outside, the trucks lined up for their bundles, newsboys and distributors in autos were ready, and the big metropolitan newspaper was in almost flawless operation in its new home. So smooth was the move that there were few complaints about late delivery or lost subscription lists. There had been only one small mistake: No one thought to write and print a news story about the tremendous accomplishment!

*   *   *

Despite political disappointments, the *Tribune* was increasingly prosperous and expanding. The paper had not led the way to victory against the Thompson machine in the elections, but it was the city's solid newspaper of record, providing the vital data required by the community for its existence, regardless of expense to the *Tribune* and, sometimes, even at the cost of boring its readers. Generally, competitors did not match the *Tribune*'s detailed coverage of all news and vital statistics, although some, such as the *Chicago Daily News*, occasionally exceeded *Tribune* coverage on a selective basis. *Tribune* editors searched the pages of opposition papers, seeking bits and pieces that might have escaped their own vigilant reporters. Any reporter or rewriter or copy editor missing a detail would be called to account. The paper began to acknowledge its own mistakes, publishing corrections under a "Beg Your Pardon" headline. It increased its reach for news and circulation throughout the Midwest, employing part-time correspondents and carrier delivery persons in more towns and cities. As in the days of Joseph Medill, the *Tribune* regarded itself as the voice not only of a city, but of a large section of the nation.

The grateful Tribune Company directors increased the salaries of McCormick and Patterson to $50,000 a year each. They earned the money. They were responsible not only for two large daily and Sunday newspapers in Chicago and New York and the properties under Schmon in Canada, but also for a growing number of Tribune Company subsidiaries (some 30 of them eventually). Among those directed by McCormick and Patterson in the early 1920s were Ontario Paper Company, Ltd.; Franquelin Lumber and Pulpwood Company; Daily News Paper Corporation (later the Tonawanda Paper Company); Coloroto Company, publisher of *Liberty* magazine; Pacific and Atlantic Photos, Inc., Newspaper Supply Company, and Chicago Tribune–New York News Syndicate, all three supplying photos, news and features copy, and production materials to the *Tribune*, the *News*, and other newspapers. Later, a transportation company would be organized to operate 19 freighters used to haul pulpwood, newsprint, and grain.

In addition, at war's end, Tribune Company built a radio receiving station at Halifax, Nova Scotia, to handle transatlantic traffic for a group of American newspapers; in 1929 this was superseded by the Press Wireless system. In late 1921 negotiations were under way with KYW in Chicago to broadcast *Tribune*-sponsored radio programs, leading in 1924 to Tribune Company ownership of radio station WGN, the call letters, of course, standing for "World's Greatest Newspaper."

Increasingly McCormick took over the news-gathering activities of the *Tribune,* especially those abroad, since Patterson was occupied with features and the procurement of photographic coverage for his picture newspaper. In France, the Army Edition of the *Tribune* became the European Edition, a seven-column, eight-page daily paper published in Paris but seeking subscribers throughout Europe. Floyd Gibbons had been placed in charge of the Paris *Tribune* as well as of the *Chicago Tribune*'s European correspondents at the close of the war. The foreign correspondents continued to provide reporting triumphs. During the summer and fall of 1920, Gen. Henry J. Reilly covered the struggle of the Poles against the Russian Bolsheviks, an effort aided by Allied forces. Reilly's rank gained him entry to the French general staff headquarters just as the Russian forces were within a few miles of Warsaw, when most correspondents were predicting the city's fall. General Reilly, in an analytical dispatch to the *Tribune,* declared that the Bolshevik forces were actually weak and spent, that the Polish army was fighting intelligently and bravely, and that Warsaw would not be taken. Reilly was right, to the great relief not only of Chicago's 250,000 Poles, but of most of the Western world, which had acquired a deep and lasting fear of the Red armies. The *Tribune*'s Thomas Ryan covered the situation in Fiume, where the flamboyant poet and ardent fascist Gabriele D'Annunzio had seized the Yugoslavian port for Italy. Ryan's stories so enraged the Fascisti that they broke into his hotel room and threatened to kill him; he was saved only by the presence of an American army officer.

When, in 1921, the USSR finally admitted what the *Tribune* had been printing—that famine was threatening millions—and requested American aid, the *Tribune* cabled four of its correspondents to get the total story of the disaster and an estimate of the aid needed. Floyd Gibbons, Larry Rue, and John Clayton converged on Russia from the West, and Charles Dailey entered from China. The *Tribune*'s men estimated that 20 million Russians died of hunger. The grim reports of disorganization, inefficiency, and death won the *Tribune* no friends among those who regarded socialism and communism as the hope of the future, but it did help speed the work of the American relief mission, organized by Herbert Hoover, to bring U.S. aid to the starving millions.

John Steele, another *Tribune* foreign correspondent, produced a major scoop when, because of the confidence placed in him by the British foreign office and the Irish Sinn Fein leaders, he was able to bring them together to a peace agreement in meetings held in the *Tribune*'s London office in mid-1923, a success providing him with a page-one exclusive and winning him praises in the *Tribune*'s editorial columns.

During the 1920s, several reporters who were later to win worldwide fame as correspondents and authors could be found working for the Paris *Tribune*. Pay was low, but the young writers were eager to become a part of the expatriate colony in Paris, and there was the possibility of a better job with the *Chicago Tribune*'s foreign service. David Darrah succeeded Floyd Gibbons as editor of the Paris *Tribune* in 1927. A taciturn young intellectual, Darrah worked closely with Henry Wales, the correspondent responsible for the *Tribune*'s Versailles Treaty scoop, who took over as chief of *Tribune* operations in Paris. One of the new recruits to the foreign staff was Vincent Sheean, who scooped the world by breaking through the French lines in Morocco to interview Abd-el-Krim, the Riff leader. Another was William L. Shirer, a Cedar Rapids, Iowa, newsman who got a job on the Paris *Tribune* by going to Paris and writing to Darrah. Shirer has described his life on the Paris *Tribune* in his memoirs, *20th Century Journey*. He was put to work on the copydesk, where his associates were James Thurber, Elliot Paul, Alex Small, a cum laude graduate of Harvard, the poet Eugene Jolas, and unofficially, F. Scott Fitzgerald, who occasionally came in sloshing drunk just to have the companionship of the desk.

Chief duty of the night staffers was to rewrite items from the Paris newspapers and Havas, the French news agency, and to interpret and expand the laconic cable dispatches from Chicago, which were limited to ten words (at $1 a word) but often filled an entire column of the Paris *Trib*'s eight pages as rewritten. Best of the rewriters, according to Shirer, was Thurber, who specialized in Calvin Coolidge news and could provide a speech report, replete with quotations, simply from a ten-word sentence giving the subject of Coolidge's address and the site of its delivery. A Coolidgism invented by Thurber: "The man who does not pray is not a praying man." Usually, when the Coolidge speech arrived in Paris in American papers, no one could discern much difference between the original and the Thurber version.

Colonel McCormick continued the European Edition of the *Tribune* in the belief that it was wanted by homesick Americans. He even established a winter edition for the Riviera. However, the Paris *Trib*'s staff was largely preoccupied with the activities of the artists and writers working in Paris, and the paper's popularity, Shirer believed, resulted from its appeal to those who were living happily in France and had little interest in home. Shirer, made a reporter, kept the Paris colony apprised of the activities of

Ernest Hemingway, Ezra Pound, T. S. Eliot, Gertrude Stein, James Joyce, and F. Scott Fitzgerald. Staff members raised funds to get a Paris show for young Iowa artist Grant Wood, though he received little popular recognition until his *American Gothic* was later purchased by the Art Institute of Chicago and became a sensation of A Century of Progress.

Shirer made the switch from the Paris *Trib* to the foreign service after he had collaborated with Henry Wales in reporting the triumphant arrival of Charles Lindbergh at Le Bourget airport following his transatlantic solo flight. Shirer soon became a leading writer for both the Paris and London bureaus. He was reprimanded only once, he recalled, and that was when he simply put a lead on a speech at Oxford by American Ambassador Charles Gates Dawes, a close friend of Colonel McCormick. When Dawes's remarks appeared in the *Tribune* with some of the quotation marks missing, McCormick fired an angry cable: "SHIRER. YOUR PIECE ON DAWES OUTRAGEOUS . . . STOP TOADYING TO BRITISH. BE AMERICAN. MCCORMICK." McCormick was pleased with other Shirer dispatches, however, and when the young Iowan returned to the Midwest for a vacation, he was summoned to the Colonel's aerie in Tribune Tower. Shirer nervously lighted a cigarette and was ordered to put it out. McCormick pointed to a large map. "I want you to go there," he said. Shirer was elated. McCormick was pointing to Vienna. He would have his own bureau. "You're a little young," the Colonel said—Shirer had admitted to 26—"but on the *Chicago Tribune* it doesn't make much difference. If you're good enough to make the paper, you're good enough to take on any assignment." Shirer had a few beautiful months in Vienna, then came a Colonel McCormick cable, "FLY INDIA." Mohandas Gandhi was beginning his nonviolent movement to free India from British rule.

The Paris *Tribune* ended its freewheeling ways in the Depression days of the 1930s, when the executives in Chicago terminated unprofitable and marginal ventures. The *New York Herald* had begun its own Paris edition, and it absorbed the Paris *Tribune* in 1934.

TAKING THE MEASURE
OF BIG BILL

20

Charges and countercharges had arisen from the *Chicago Tribune*'s strictures against Mayor Big Bill Thompson over many years, beginning with allegations of his failure to support the war effort, and culminating in assertions that Thompson's political machine was looting the city treasury. On September 17, 1917, Thompson had filed a personal libel suit against the paper, seeking $500,000 damages. By August 31, 1918, when the mayor filed a fourth suit, total damages sought reached $1,350,000. The suits asserted that the *Tribune* had damaged Thompson personally by calling him pro-German and by impugning his integrity, and it was further claimed that the paper had damaged the good name of the City of Chicago as well.

The *Tribune* had continued its attacks, accusing the mayor and his officials of inefficiency, incompetence, corruption, and graft. Thompson's actions, the paper declared, had brought Chicago to the brink of bankruptcy. Big Bill, acting on the advice of Fred Lundin and Samuel Ettelson, his corporation counsel, on December 10, 1920, instituted a $10 million libel suit against the *Tribune* in the name of the City of Chicago. The action constituted the biggest demand for libel damages in U.S. history up to that time. It asserted that the *Tribune*'s charges of corruption and malfeasance against city officials had maligned Chicago's good name and credit.

The *Tribune* was prosperous and strong, but legal actions for a total of $11,350,000 presented a lethal threat. No newspaper could pay such damages and survive. McCormick and Patterson saw an even more menacing aspect to the suit in the city's name. If a newspaper could be sued for libel by a municipality and if the press could be made liable for criticizing public officials in the discharge of their office, all public criticism could be outlawed. Freedom of the press and, soon thereafter, of speech would cease to exist. Self-defense was obligatory, the ideal of a free press compelling, and, equally important, Thompsonism, which the *Tribune* defined as corruption arising from Lorimerism, had to be crushed. McCormick and Patterson decided they had to fight Thompson's actions to the finish, regardless of the cost. The Tribune Company directors concurred, and McCormick discussed legal strategy with Weymouth Kirkland and Howard Ellis.

The *Tribune* responded by filing its own lawsuits, based on investigative work by Oscar Hewitt, the paper's City Hall reporter, which tended to show that thousands, perhaps millions, in graft had been obtained by Mayor Thompson's officials in the course of the building of Wacker Drive, South Michigan Avenue, the widening of 12th Street, and other major construction projects. The *Tribune*'s actions named Mayor Thompson; his Irish leader, Michael J. Faherty, president of the Board of Local Improvements; George Harding, South Side Republican leader and city controller; and Frank H. Mesce and Austin J. Lynch, two Thompson cronies. The initial action, filed on April 19, 1921, sought the return of $1,065,000 paid by the city to Mesce and Lynch for their appraisal fees in condemnation suits connected with city improvements. In June a second suit was filed, asking the return of $1,700,000 paid to Mesce and Lynch and three others, Edward C. Waller, Jr., Ernest H. Lyons, and Arthur S. Merrigold. Here again, the actions portended far more than was stated in legal language. If the *Tribune* could require Thompson and his friends to be personally responsible for misused city funds, millions more could be recovered from "expert fees" alone, since scores of Thompson ward leaders and cronies had been paid from hundreds to thousands of dollars each during the mayor's six years in office. The bill for the return of such sums could ruin Big Bill Thompson, though he was a wealthy man.

The first legal battle to come to trial was the city's $10 million suit. No American politician had previously been sufficiently malevolent and ingenious to sue a newspaper in the name of a municipality, as the *Tribune*'s lawyers, Weymouth Kirkland and Howard Ellis, pointed out. Their demurrer asserted that the City of Chicago had sustained no harm and could not maintain an action because, as a municipality, it could not be libeled. To allow recovery, they argued, would be to violate the constitutional guarantee of freedom of the press.

Judge Harry M. Fisher in the Superior Court of Cook County upheld the *Tribune*'s position on October 15, 1921, ruling that there was no cause of action. The *Tribune,* the judge noted, had indeed accused city officials of inefficiency and incompetency and of bringing the City of Chicago to the point of bankruptcy, but the court took cognizance of the defendant's contention that the statements mentioned were not libelous, and it noted the various examples provided in the demurrer of press responsibility and acts of criticism both in times of peace and times of war.

In sustaining the demurrer, Judge Fisher said, "This action is not in harmony with the genius, spirit and objects of our institutions. . . . It fits in rather with the genius of the rulers who conceived law not in the purity of love for justice, but in the lustful passion for undisturbed power. It will, therefore, be unnecessary to consider the other questions involved." Judge Fisher went on to say:

> The press has become the eyes and ears of the world, and, to a great extent, its voice. It is the substance which puts humanity in contact with all its parts. It is the spokesman of the weak and the appeal of the suffering. It tears us away from our selfishness and moves us to acts of kindness and charity. It is the advocate constantly pleading before the bar of public opinion. It holds up for review the acts of our officials and those men in high places who have it in their power to advance peace or endanger it. It is the force which mirrors public sentiment. Trade and commerce depend upon it. Authors, artists, musicians, scholars and inventors command a hearing through its columns.

Judge Fisher listed other attributes of the press, then commented that the performance of such services resulted in corresponding power, power sometimes abused by the press. He added, "But fortunately, while the good the press is capable of rendering if unafraid, is without limit, the harm it can do has its own limitations. The press is dependent for its success, for its very existence, almost, upon public confidence."

The *Tribune* gave page-one publication to Judge Fisher's ruling and noted that Chester E. Cleveland, named special counsel for the city administration, promised that an immediate appeal would be taken. The paper fervently hoped that the case would be carried to the Illinois Supreme Court, since the principle of the freedom of the press was involved. Said the paper editorially on October 17:

> The private consequences, through the infliction of confiscatory damage, in a lawsuit against the *Tribune* could interest the public only in the degree that it threatened the public service of a newspaper. But the $10,000,000 libel suit instituted in the name of the municipality against this newspaper involves an issue of vital importance to the body politic and the whole people of the United States.
> The opinion is a lucid and forceful statement of constitutional law and its principle, dealing with the issues fairly and with exceptional grasp of the fundamentals of American political philosophy. . . . Judge Fisher holds that

a suit for defamation, that is, libel, does not lie against the municipal corporation, being an infringement of the constitutional guaranty of a free press.

The editorial recited the points of the demurrer and the judge's opinion, and concluded: "If such a suit, hitherto unheard of in this country, were sustained in law, all criticism of public administration would rest under the paralyzing threat of an exhausting and completely destructive attack by politicians in power. No more fatal assault upon the liberties of the individual could be devised."

The dismissal of the city's suit was hailed by the press of America as a successful blow for the freedom of the press, as it undoubtedly was, despite the uniqueness of the case. Three Chicago newspapers, the *Journal,* the *Daily News,* and the *Post,* ran editorials praising the court's decision, but the Hearst papers, Thompson supporters, were silent. For the next several days the *Tribune* published editorials and telegrams from newspapers across the country expressing appreciation of Judge Fisher's ruling and gratitude to the *Tribune* and its lawyers.

The legal fighting resumed in May, 1922, when Thompson's personal libel actions went to trial before Judge Francis Wilson. Again the *Tribune* was the winner. Thompson was called as a witness by Weymouth Kirkland. He admitted opposing food conscription during the war, that he opposed sending troops to Europe, and that he had declined to issue Red Cross and Liberty Loan proclamations when requested to do so by the government. As the trial neared an end, two jurors fell ill. The *Tribune* counsel said their client was ready to proceed with ten jurors, but Thompson exercised his privilege to ask for a mistrial. The case was never reinstituted.

The Illinois Supreme Court upheld Judge Fisher's ruling in the city's suit on April 23, 1923. Said the court:

> Prosecution for libel on government is unknown to American courts. A prosecution, civil or criminal, for libel on the government has no place in the American system of jurisprudence, as the people have a right to discuss their government without fear of being called to account for their expression of opinion.
>
> Where any person by speech or writing seeks to persuade others to violate existing law or to overthrow by force or other unlawful means he may be punished, but all other utterances or publications against the government must be considered absolutely privileged against civil as well as criminal prosecutions.

*   *   *

Thompson had appeared politically unassailable following the election of 1920, with Len Small in the statehouse, Robert Crowe as Cook County state's attorney, and Frank Righeimer in control of county election machinery. But during the years of litigation with Thompson, the *Tribune* had continued to investigate his regime and to publish charges against it, among them assertions that officials employed by the school board, which Thompson dominated through Fred Lundin, his patronage chief, had played fast and loose with funds, paying added money for building sites after a Thompson associate had acquired the land, for example. By 1923, State's Attorney Crowe felt compelled to investigate the school graft charges, which the *Chicago Daily News* also was publishing. Thompson angrily declared that his former friend Crowe had been seduced by the press. In truth, Crowe had been pushed into the investigation by a political friend of the *Tribune*, Illinois Attorney General Brundage. If Crowe failed to act, Brundage intended to invoke a law that would enable him to summon a special grand jury.

Lundin left town to avoid involvement in the proceedings, though he soon was required to return to stand trial. George Harding and Sam Ettelson advised Mayor Thompson that, though he could not be directly implicated, the scandal might ruin his chances for reelection against a strong Democratic candidate, expected to be Judge William E. Dever, who was known as an honest man. Thompson withdrew from the 1923 mayoral race. The Republicans nominated Arthur C. Lueder, Chicago's postmaster, and the Democrats named Dever. Clarence Darrow defended Lundin and his alleged conspirators. Days were spent detailing the alleged graft in school board purchases and business, but in the end, Lundin and his fellow defendants were acquitted. Nonetheless, Thompson had lost his opportunity to try for reelection.

The *Tribune* declined to endorse a mayoral candidate, but it allowed Sen. Medill McCormick space to state reasons why Lueder, whom he had recommended for postmaster and for the mayoral nomination, should be elected. The election, on April 4, resulted in a landslide for Judge Dever, who defeated Lueder by 103,748 votes. J. Loy Maloney, the *Tribune* reporter covering the City Hall side of the story, wrote that the most powerful allies of Big Bill Thompson had been defeated and that no "simon-pure Thompsonites" remained in city government. The *Tribune* accepted the result as joyfully as if Dever had been an acceptable Republican:

> A new era should open for Chicago today. The election of Judge Dever as mayor of the city by a majority of more than 100,000 prepares the way for accomplishments within the next four years such as has never before been known in any period of the city's history.
>
> The old regime is crushed. The machinery of demagogy, graft, fraud, and trickery has been destroyed and its builders and operators have been thrust out into the cold world.

Since the return of McCormick and Patterson from the war, the *Tribune* had gradually altered its position on Prohibition. The paper had at one time published strong editorials attacking the liquor industry for excesses, saying in 1917, for example, that the "inherent corruption" of the liquor industry had "extended even to the so-called decent saloon. . . . We are speaking of the decent saloon; the other variety is almost unspeakable." But as the evils of Prohibition became manifest, both publishers of the paper said privately that the approval of the 18th Amendment had been a mistake, and in 1921 the *Tribune* began its movement toward an outright demand for repeal. In the spring primary of 1924, U.S. Sen. Medill McCormick, seeking renomination, ran against State Sen. Charles S. Deneen, a former foe of Thompson who had decided to take advantage of the strife between the Thompson–Small forces and the *Tribune*. In a close primary race, Deneen was the winner. McCormick blamed his defeat not on Thompson and Small opposition, but on the *Tribune*'s stand against Prohibition. On the following February 25, 1925, shortly before his term of office was to end, Senator McCormick was found dead in his Hamilton Hotel suite in Washington, the victim of hemorrhages. The Senate adjourned in respect to its departed member, and President Coolidge attended the services of the former *Tribune* editor in the Fourth Presbyterian Church in Chicago.

*   *   *

During the summer of 1924 politics were forgotten for a time, and citizens had difficulty concentrating on baseball, Mah-Jongg, and the adventures of Rudy Vallee, Helen Kane, and Rudolph Valentino while Chicago's newspapers demonstrated their superiority in covering sensational crime news by exploiting a story that became known as "the crime of the century." On May 21, 1924, Bobby Franks, a quiet, dark-haired 14-year-old pupil in the Harvard private school on Chicago's South Side, failed to return home after classes. Bobby, son of wealthy realtor Jacob Franks, was last seen at 47th Street and Ellis Avenue at 5:15 P.M. That night the worried parents received a telephone call indicating that the boy had been kidnapped, and the following day there was a long, detailed ransom note. But before any ransom could be paid, police found the body of the lad in a culvert on the South Side. The *Tribune*'s banner story, "KIDNAP RICH BOY: KILL HIM" appeared on May 23 without a by-line. Similar sensational headlines would continue to appear almost daily on page one through the summer.

The Bobby Franks murder case was extraordinary not only because it was a bizarre crime but also for the degree to which police and reporters cooperated in tracking down the slayers, Nathan "Babe" Leopold and Richard "Dickie" Loeb, two University of Chicago students. The day after the discovery of the Franks boy's body, James Doherty, the *Tribune*'s big, bluff police reporter who wrote most of the page-one stories about the case, pointed out that the wording of the ransom note was similar to one in a detective magazine, a copy of which, it was later learned, had been bought by Loeb. James Mulroy and Alvin Goldstein of the *Chicago Daily News* found the typewriter on which the ransom note had been written. Their stories on the case would win them the Pulitzer prize.

The arrest of Loeb and Leopold on May 31 created a sensation. It was the kind of continuing shocker that Chicagoans found irresistible: Wealthy, decadent young men sought to commit the perfect crime but failed because they could not outsmart ordinary policemen, prosecutors, and police reporters. Young men who confessed they killed for "kicks," while dark suggestions of perversion and the sexual mutilation of the victim were circulated. Assistant State's Attorney Berthold A. Cronson was the man who really broke the case with his questioning of the suspects, but Robert Crowe took the credit and emerged a Chicago hero.

The trial received worldwide publicity as correspondents not only from Chicago but from the rest of the country and from Europe covered the story. Eminent labor lawyer Clarence Darrow, who was beginning to acquire a reputation in Chicago as a criminal lawyer as well, defended the two boys. He insisted that his clients plead guilty, a strategy most observers believed would mean their certain execution. But during the sentencing phase of the trial Darrow, a firm opponent of capital punishment, took the novel step of presenting expert testimony about the psychological state of his clients in an effort to save their lives.

Despite the publicity and confusion, Judge John R. Caverly kept the trial in orderly process, cooperating with the avid press to the point that he delayed the sentencing over the weekend so that it would not interfere with the wedding of Genevieve Forbes and John Herrick, two *Tribune* reporters who spent so much time together covering the investigation and trial that they decided to get married. Even so, Mrs. Herrick did not write the *Tribune*'s lead story. City editor Robert M. Lee wrote it, as he frequently did when he judged that a news event merited the scope of his talents. On September 10, Nathan Leopold and Richard Loeb were sentenced to life in Joliet prison by Judge Caverly, who ended speculation about mutilation of the Franks boy by stating that there had been none. The bailiffs and police held back the crowd pushing forward to congratulate Darrow for his brilliant defense and Leopold and Loeb on escaping the death penalty.

*　　*　　*

In June, the Republican convention in Cleveland chose as its nominee for president Calvin Coolidge, who had acceded to the presidency when Harding died on August 2, 1923. Charles Gates Dawes, the Chicago banker who had helped McCormick buy his machine guns during World

War I, was nominated for vice-president. The paper devoted itself enthusiastically to the support of the national ticket. But it was also determined to exterminate the remnants of the Thompson–Small political machine, so it vigorously supported the Democratic gubernatorial candidate, Judge Norman L. Jones, from downstate Illinois. Many Republicans questioned such a schizoid political policy, but the *Tribune* repeatedly insisted it would be entirely possible to obtain the requisite number of split ballots. Just prior to the election, the paper went to the unusual length of printing a full-page ballot, with a cross in the Republican circle and a cross opposite the name of Jones, explaining that this was the correct way to split the ballot.

The paper on November 1 also printed the results of its intensive investigation of charges that the Ku Klux Klan was supporting Len Small for governor and Progressive Robert M. La Follette of Wisconsin for president, its page-one banner reading: "LINK SMALL, KLAN AND BOB." Strong support was given to the women's Independent Jones for Governor clubs, led by Mrs. Roy Dickey of Chicago, and the Republican and Democratic women's clubs for Jones.

The campaign was exemplary of the kind Robert R. McCormick would wage against powerful political opponents the rest of his life. Every publishing tool was employed, old political philosophies abandoned. McCormick, the former Progressive and ardent Republican, did not hesitate when the objective was to crush Small–Thompson power. In the future he would continue to seek out and print whatever intelligence could be procured to blunt the political efforts of the candidates opposed by the *Tribune,* with a single pragmatic criterion: The material was to be accurate and provable and, thus, believable. Also, there were areas into which politics could not intrude. When J. Howard Wood was made financial editor, on his way to becoming chief executive officer of the *Tribune* empire, Colonel McCormick instructed him: "Don't pay any attention to what I say on my editorial page. Your job is to obtain and print the facts. I'll do the interpreting in the editorials."

Coolidge and Dawes carried Illinois by 875,000 votes and nationwide received almost double the popular vote, 15,725,016 to 8,386,503, of Democrats John Davis and Charles W. Bryan, while La Follette received under 5 million votes. Len Small was reelected governor of Illinois. The *Tribune* could only point out that he received 300,000 fewer votes than did Coolidge, showing that a large number of voters had followed the *Tribune*'s ticket-splitting advice.

The man who demonstrated top vote-getting power in Cook County was State's Attorney Crowe, the squat, wide-eyed, bandy-legged hero in the prosecution of the Leopold–Loeb case. Crowe was an erratic ally of Thompson, and his ambition could lead him away from the new and powerful Thompson–Small machine, especially if he should be given a few more nudges by Attorney General Brundage. The *Tribune* undertook to cultivate Crowe and to lead him along the path of righteousness by reporting his special efforts to turn back the attempts of Johnny Torrio and his chief aide, called by the *Tribune* Alphonse Capone, alias Al Brown, to take over vice, gambling, and the illicit liquor trade in all of Cook County.

Al Capone had come to Chicago from Brooklyn in 1920 at the request of Johnny Torrio, chief lieutenant and nephew of Big Jim Colosimo, the overlord of Chicago vice. Capone's fortunes rose with those of his boss, who took over operations when Big Jim was gunned down in his café at 2126 South Wabash on May 11, 1920. With Colosimo's passing—at Torrio's direction, it was said—Torrio inherited his uncle's holdings and with his tough assistant began to expand his operations into beer and liquor, an activity little hindered by police under Big Bill Thompson's administration.

In 1923 the election of Mayor Dever cheered the anticrime forces in the city. Dever and his police chief, Morgan Collins, attempted to enforce the law, cooperated with federal agents, and sought to create an inhospitable climate for "doing business." But it was a losing battle; gangland operations continued to grow. Torrio and Capone strengthened their power in April, 1924, by taking over the suburb of Cicero in an election-day raid carried out by carloads of armed gangsters. Capone's brother Frank, killed in the fighting, was given the most spectacular funeral since that of Big Jim Colosimo, a total of $20,000 being spent for flowers in the shop of Chicago gangster Dion O'Banion.

Torrio and O'Banion were partners in a Cicero gambling joint, the Ship, and evidently had an agreement on beer territory as well. But the chubby O'Banion, a former altar boy, had ambitions of his own, and most members of the Torrio–Capone gang held O'Banion responsible for Torrio's being caught when police raided a South Side brewery in May. Nonetheless the partnership continued for several more months, though with Torrio still waiting to stand trial his domain came more and more under the control of Al Capone. O'Banion finally went too far when he threatened to kill Angelo Genna, chief of Capone's alcohol cookers, for failing to pay a gambling debt at the Ship, a debt Capone wanted to cancel. On November 10, 1924, three gunmen hired by Capone went to O'Banion's flower shop at 738 North State Street and shot him dead. The killing announced to the hoodlums if not to the public that Capone was on the way up as the new boss of gangland and Torrio was on the way out.

The *Tribune*'s second-day banner on the O'Banion slaying read: "GIRL AN O'BANION DEATH CLUE," the story theorizing that

O'Banion and a Torrio–Capone henchman, Mike Carrozzo, had fought over a woman. Years later newsmen would come to realize that the mobsters rarely killed over the plentiful women in their domain; they killed to protect territory and to maintain discipline.

O'Banion's wake and funeral affected the spectacular grandeur that would characterize obsequies for mob chiefs in ensuing years. To cover the wake, the *Tribune* sent Maureen M'Kerman and also a reporter named Jake Lingle, who reputedly knew most of the gang bosses, politicians, and police officials on sight. Lingle did not write for the paper and never received a by-line, but he was probably responsible for identifying the judges, city aldermen, and state legislators who were named in the paper as having attended O'Banion's wake and funeral. M'Kerman wrote the color story: "Last night Dion O'Banion lay in state. His couch was a casket priced with a touch of pride at $10,000 (and brought to Chicago by special freight). There were candles at the head and candles at the feet, a rosary lay in his soft, tapered hands that could finger an automatic so skillfully. . . . In the soft light of the candles at the head of the $10,000 casket sat Mrs. O'Banion, a picture of patient sorrow."

The funeral and its procession eclipsed even that of Frank Capone. George "Bugs" Moran, Hymie Weiss (real name, Earl Wajciechowski), and Vince "Schemer" Drucci saw to that. The rival barons were required to demonstrate their power, and the lavish trappings accomplished it. There were 2,000 red roses in the funeral decorations, the *Tribune* reported, including a seven-by-ten-foot floral blanket of roses and orchids. There were again judges, politicians, and police in the mammoth procession.

The O'Banion slaying marked the beginning of major gang warfare in Chicago, for Moran, Weiss, and Drucci vowed to avenge O'Banion and, incidentally, to preserve their beer territory. On January 24, 1925, just before Torrio was to begin serving a nine-month sentence for the brewery arrest, rival gangsters believed to have been Moran, Weiss, and Drucci seriously wounded him. They also went after the Gennas, and within a six-week span of time Angelo, Michael, and Anthony Genna all died violently, at least two of them the victims of O'Banion's avengers.

In the meantime, Weiss and a parcel of gunmen went after Capone on the South Side of Chicago, but they succeeded only in wounding the mobster's chauffeur. Torrio had known that the O'Banion chieftains were after him, but believing that it would be good psychology to walk around unprotected—and unafraid—he had declined to hire bodyguards or even to arm himself. "The flaw in his reasoning," observed Judge John H. Lyle, an important figure in the eventual downfall of Capone, "was that Hymie Weiss and Bugs Moran had never cracked a book on psychology." Capone avoided his boss's near-fatal logic. After the attack, he promptly purchased a $20,000 armored car and increased the number of his bodyguards. When Torrio recovered from his wounds, he served his time in the Lake County Jail, and when he got out he went to New York City, leaving Chicago and its suburbs to Al Capone.

*   *   *

Following the wartime boom, both circulation and advertising proved more difficult to get, especially during the financial recession from 1921 to 1922. But Eugene Parsons, the *Tribune*'s advertising manager, was a most resourceful man. The marketing, research, and sales methods he had developed with Field were taking the measure of all competition, and in 1921 he convinced his recession-ridden associates that they too could conquer hard times. Parsons coined a slogan, "1921 will reward fighters," sold it in full-page advertisements, and had the satisfaction of seeing it repeated around the country. More solid than his slogan, however, was the fierce selling campaign conducted by his staff. *Tribune* president McCormick, impressed by the paper's advertising advance under difficult circumstances, informed Parsons that if he could continue the gains in 1922 he would receive a special bonus, based on the amount of gain. Before the year was well under way, it became clear to McCormick that Parsons's aggressive methods, including a rate hike, would net him a bonus of a million dollars. Such a bonanza, said McCormick, should properly be shared by others who had helped make it possible— Thomason, the business manager; Beck, the managing editor; and Annenberg, the circulation manager. If Parsons would agree to share his bonus, McCormick would extend it for six years. Parsons, of course, agreed. Thus began a system that was the envy of less fortunate newsmen everywhere. Yet, although they were becoming millionaires, Thomason and Annenberg left the *Tribune,* the latter in 1926 to become circulation manager of the *New York News* as well as general manager of *Liberty* magazine. Thomason, complaining that he was given too little to do (though by the time of his departure he had become a vice-president and general manager), left the *Tribune* in 1927. In 1929 he founded the *Chicago Times,* Chicago's first tabloid and predecessor of today's *Sun-Times.* Late in the 1920s, a modest bonus, based on a salary scale and tenure, was extended to all *Tribune* employees, and in 1932 they were enabled to purchase beneficial interests in nonvoting employees' trust units, which shared in company stock dividends.

The competitive situation in those difficult postwar years not only produced unusual bonus arrangements, but also precipitated the wildest circulation promotion efforts in Chicago newspaper history. Early in November, 1921, Hearst's *Herald and Examiner* launched a highly successful and costly campaign to add readers by circulating "Smile" coupons about Chicago. These coupons could be redeemed for cash by lucky holders if the coupon matched a number printed in that day's *Examiner*. Such coupons could be had free from every grocer's counter, and they were stuffed into almost every mailbox in the city and suburbs. The result was thousands of added readers scanning the lists of lucky numbers that politicians, led off by Gov. Len Small and Mayor Big Bill Thompson, Hearst's allies, selected through daily drawings.

The *Tribune* held the circulation leadership in Chicago and had no intention of losing it. Its own lottery, which promised to give away $200,000 in prize money, was announced in a double-page advertising spread on November 25, and the distribution of *Chicago Tribune* "Cheer Checks" began that day. The results of the first public drawing were announced on Sunday, November 27. By the following Sunday $76,625 in prizes had been paid out to 2,373 lucky ticket holders.

"Cheer Checks take Chicago by storm," wrote the *Tribune*'s promotion man. "Two of the largest railway ticket printing houses in the world worked 24 hours a day printing 25 million Cheer Checks!" It was a fantastically successful promotion. Groceries, banks, industrial firms, even churches and Sunday schools participated, and the clamor for tickets could not be met. The *Tribune*'s daily circulation, already the largest of any morning paper in the country, increased by 250,000, and the Sunday circulation by 200,000. There was only one thing wrong with the promotion: It was almost ruinously successful. "Did We Fall, or Were We Pushed?" the paper asked in an editorial. It was clear that neither the *Tribune* nor the *Herald and Examiner* could for long sell papers at below cost and spend tens of thousands of dollars in prizes for the privilege of doing so. Someone said to have represented both newspapers visited the office of Postmaster General Will Hayes in Washington to ask plaintively if the Chicago newspaper lottery might not be illegal. Hayes ruled that it was. Both papers stopped promptly when the eight days of the "Cheer Checks" announced by the *Tribune* were up.

Circulations settled back to normal, the *Tribune* pushing a half million, at 499,725 daily and 827,028 on Sunday. The *Herald and Examiner* totaled 396,871 daily and 731,010 on Sunday. The *Chicago Daily News,* once Chicago's daily leader, had fallen behind Hearst's *American,* 397,584 to 415,056, with the *Journal* fifth at 117,493 and the *Post* a poor sixth, 42,219.

*　　*　　*

Since the days of Joseph Medill, the *Tribune* possessed the capacity for excellent production work. It published useful maps during the Civil War, printed finely detailed drawings in the 1880s, and in 1898 claimed to be the first newspaper to print photographic halftones on a rotary press. The halftone, an acid-engraved metal plate, had followed woodcuts and lithographs in the printing process but was not adapted to the curved plates of the new, fast rotary presses until Charles D. Stewart, a *Tribune* engraver, accomplished it in 1898, a first, he reported, after checking with other newspapers. The paper also was a leader in color printing. In the 1890s the *Tribune* began frequent use of four-color reproductions obtained from outside lithographing plants as a circulation gainer for its Sunday paper. It first did its own color printing, in red and black, on June 17, 1900, and in 1901 installed a special color press for printing comics. On September 23, 1903, the *Tribune* employed "run-of-paper" color for a John McCutcheon cartoon. It carried its first color advertisement that same year, in two colors, for Mandel Brothers department store. *Tribune* production personnel became extremely sophisticated and creative in the use of color. Right after World War I, John Yetter, superintendent of the rotogravure pressroom, and Otto Wolf, assistant production manager, designed a press able to print color rotogravure on a continuous web, or roll, of paper. The press, said to be the first of its kind in an American newspaper plant, enabled the paper to provide the color quality then found in national magazines.

On March 29, 1929, the *Tribune* carried its first three-color advertisement, for Allied Florists Association. Thereafter there were rapid color developments, with the paper carrying three- and four-color advertisements and page-one cartoons almost daily, the American flag in color, and three- and four-color feature and spot news engravings. The first three-color editorial feature, a fashion page, appeared on March 6, 1932. That same year cartoons appeared in three and four colors, and on April 17, 1934, run-of-paper color was used in the sports section. Generally, it was not yet possible to use run-of-paper color for fast-breaking news events, since much time was required to filter colors in special cameras, etch plates, and provide for correct register so that the colors would not improperly overprint. The pictures for the sports pages, team photos of the Cubs and Sox, could be prepared in advance. The first spot-news color picture, of a burning $4 million grain elevator, appeared on May 12, 1939, representing a high degree of teamwork between the news photography department, the engravers, stereotypers, and pressmen. Later that year, the paper published the first color photo transmitted by wirephoto, from Washington, D.C. It showed the reception of King George VI and Queen Elizabeth of England by President and Mrs. Roosevelt.

Color has remained an integral part of the *Tribune,* used widely by advertisers both on newsprint and roto presses. The huge press runs at high speed present special printing problems, for paper must be of a precise quality, presses carefully regulated, camera and engraving work extremely accurate, stereotyping as near perfection as possible, and "make ready" on the presses done by experts. Even the temperature of the pressroom can affect the printing quality. The *Tribune* over the years has been the recipient of many awards for its color work. The production department also has provided the *Chicago Tribune* with top executives. Joseph Medill was essentially a production man, as was Robert R. McCormick, both continuing their close association with production work while they were editors and publishers. Harold Grumhaus, president and chairman of Tribune Company and publisher of the *Tribune* from 1967 to 1974, rose to those positions from the production department, as has Stanton R. Cook, publisher of the *Tribune* since 1973 and president of Tribune Company since 1974. The Joseph Medill slogan, "First the machinery must work," continues effective.

*　　*　　*

On July 6, 1925, the *Tribune* opened to the public its soaring Gothic tower on Michigan Avenue, a skyscraper whose flamboyant grace would be the subject of controversy for months ahead. In 1922, two years after the *Tribune*'s manufacturing plant began operations in what was once pioneer Antoine Ouilmette's bean field, the directors of the company announced a worldwide architectural competition for an office tower to symbolize the *Tribune* and to provide space for company workers and outside tenants. There was a single requirement: It was to be "the world's most beautiful office building." The paper offered $100,000 in prizes, promising in an editorial that "the world's greatest architectural competition" would be exactly that, opened to architects everywhere. Some 300 responded, 115 from foreign countries, submitting 285 designs for consideration of the jury, which consisted of Alfred Granger of the American Institute of Architects, chairman of the contest committee; McCormick, Patterson, and Beck; and Holmes Onderdonk, *Tribune* real estate manager. John Mead Howells and Raymond M. Hood, associate architects of New York, won the first prize of $50,000. Second place, worth $20,000, went to Eliel Saarinen of Finland, whose modern setback design would influence urban high-rise structures in the years to come. The third prize of $10,000 was awarded to Holabird & Roche of Chicago. Ground was broken on May 23, 1923.

James O'Donnell Bennett, the paper's leading writer, was selected to invite the public to come to visit, and to tell the story of the tower:

> It has been under construction two years and a month, a Gothic tower rising to 473 feet on a plot of ground formerly 431–439 North Michigan Avenue, but by unanimous action of the city council, now called Tribune Square. . . .
> The building (tower and plant) comprises nine and one-half acres of floors

and 36 stories. It is to house 4,000 persons, which was one fourth the population of Chicago when the *Tribune* made its first appearance 78 years ago.

Half the 4,000 would be *Chicago Tribune* employees.

Bennett described the exterior, except for the steel window frames, as "good old Gothic materials—limestone and lead. . . . The interior fabric comprises travertine marble, solid mahogany and oak, statuary bronze, cork for much of the floor surfacing, and antique plastering." The cost of the tower was $8,500,000, "exceeding by 40 cents per cubic foot the cost of any other skyscraper in the world."

The winning architects were influenced, it was said, by the famous Tour de Beurre of the Rouen Cathedral in France, and the Tower of Malines in Belgium. The somber beauty of the flying buttresses and delicate traceries and the vaulting grandeur of the symmetrical stone were admired by many grateful letter writers to the paper but fetched also wrathful criticism from those who objected to medieval connotations in the city that had given birth to modern skyscraper architecture. As the structure was rising, the *Tribune* published news stories on the controversy, citing those who were enchanted by the idea of mingling 12th-century concepts with the high-rise creations of William LeBaron Jenney, and giving equal space to those who believed that the medieval mass would sink to its flying buttresses in Michigan Avenue mud. "Mostly the criticism rages at the Art Institute," the paper said.

It was generally agreed by Chicagoans that Tribune Tower and William Wrigley's twin towers gleaming white on the other side of Michigan Avenue were worthy of Chicago. They exemplified, as did the other construction of the period, the untrammeled individual cultural ideas of owners, architects, and builders who were under no legal or traditional restriction, as were inhabitants of the capitals of Europe.

Paradoxically, Chicago had been given a unique opportunity to build imaginatively when it was freed from the very guidelines that had made the new architecture possible. For years, the city felt itself under guidance of the plan promulgated by famed world's fair adviser Daniel Burnham, who uttered the remembered words, "Make no little plans. They have no magic to stir men's blood." The Burnham Plan inspired Chicago to seek architectural greatness, but the goal was achieved only after the Burnham Plan was modified and almost abandoned in detail, though not in concept.

Tribune Tower was only one of the construction projects that helped to glorify Chicago in the 1920s. Charles H. Wacker's unstoppable push for a double-decked drive along the Chicago River, the raising of Michigan Avenue, and A. Montgomery Ward's and the *Tribune*'s watchful guardianship of the lakefront also made possible new beauty along the lake and river. Big Bill Thompson, too, had a part in it. There were many indigenous geniuses who carried Chicago to further architectural greatness as the face of the city changed, when the London Guarantee Building, the thin, graceful, spire of the Mather Tower, the domed Pure Oil Building, the Civic Opera House and Theatre, the *Chicago Daily News* building on the river, the new United States post office, Union Station, and the vast Merchandise Mart rose to make Chicago one of the world's most beautiful cities.

Sculpture, painting, and the performing arts flourished also, as Chicago's wealth increased. Mary Garden gave worldwide fame to Chicago's opera, endowed by Samuel Insull, the utilities czar. Sculpture, somewhat neglected since the day of Leonard Volk's statue of Stephen A. Douglas, showed new signs of life. To the John A. Logan equestrian statue in Grant Park and the seated Lincoln in Lincoln Park, both by Augustus Saint-Gaudens, Lorado Taft added his beautiful *Fountain of Time* in Washington Park and the *Spirit of the Great Lakes* to the Chicago Art Institute grounds. Ethnic contributions were added in the various parks. Kate Buckingham gave to the lakefront the Clarence Buckingham Fountain, modeled after the *Latona* at Versailles, and Ivan Mestrovic created his romantic Plains Indians, astride Arabian stallions, at Michigan Avenue and Congress Street.

*   *   *

The ugly side of the city expanded as well. Despite plentiful jobs and prosperity, the slum areas began to surround the downtown complex. The rise of gangs fighting for the rich profits of the illicit booze trade was vigorously reported by the Chicago press. The city's reputation grew black as gang forays and killings increased. It was the time of the Roaring Twenties, the Jazz Age, the years of the Lost Generation, emancipated women (the 19th Amendment was finally ratified in 1920), and uprooted farm boys finding their way to the city. The recession of 1921–22 was followed by a period of prosperity unmatched in degree and duration, and Chicago "made whoopee" with the rest of the country and wallowed in wickedness unmatched since the aftermath of the Civil War or the gaudy days of the Gay Nineties. Big Bill Thompson had created a wide-open town. Now, under honest Mayor Dever, the city continued to be wide-open, since Democratic boss George Brennan, not Dever, was running the party and dealing with the vice and rum lords.

Young men back from the wars, off the farm, in from the West, up from the South, and down from the North swarmed to the new jobs on assembly lines and the new high-rise construction projects, made money fast, and spent it faster on needled beer, speakeasies, dime-a-dance girls, and the Torrio–Capone brothels. Daughters, and sometimes their mothers, smoked cigarettes, daubed lipstick, bobbed their hair, rolled their stockings, and wore short skirts showing a flash of thigh. Atlantic City titillated the country with its first bathing beauty contest, and soon there were young women in similarly skimpy suits on the Chicago beaches, and eager policemen going about with tapes to determine whether epidermis exposure exceeded the limits set by the park board.

Many of the city's young men and women, of course, went to church, joined the "Y," took out library cards, attended college and night school, held down jobs, and used their income to aid their families. But the 1920s, by consensus, were dissolute and degenerate. Boys and girls might go to college, but they also drank bathtub gin from hip flasks, dressed like bummers and floozies, read bad books, and listened to the radicals in Bug House Square. Women swooned over a film star named Rudolph Valentino, while men and boys gloried in Babe Ruth, the Sultan of Swat, but also admired Al Capone, the smart ex-pimp who was making millions, it was said, from illicit booze and broads. It was a time of gang fighting in the streets, but a time also of solid building, expansion, increasing wealth and culture, and scientific learning as Chicago became a center of growing universities, colleges, seminaries, medical institutions, laboratories, and museums as well as railroads and factories.

On October 12, 1925, the *Tribune*, having identified many of the numerous evils arising from the Prohibition amendment, reasserted its opposition to that law.

> Something over four years ago this newspaper took its stand against prohibition by constitutional amendment. The decision was not an easy one to take. The *Tribune* had never been a wet newspaper, and it did not want to be considered a wet newspaper in the sense which that phrase was understood at the time. The editors of the *Tribune,* then as now, believed liquor was bad for men and women. We feared that if we attacked constitutional prohibition and the rigors of the Volstead Act we should inevitably be accused by many of our readers as advocating the use of intoxicants. How thoroughly justified that fear was the readers of the Voice of the People column know.

The paper went on to say that though it had aroused many critics by its stand, it had by no means suffered financially nor in loss of prestige. Its circulation, in fact, had grown from 480,000 daily and 800,000 on Sunday to 658,000 daily and 1,020,000 Sunday in the four years, proving that "the prohibition cause is not dear to the hearts of the people of this community." The *Tribune*'s experience, the paper said, should provide a lesson "for the politicians who vote dry but drink wet. They can vote as they drink and they will not suffer for their sincerity."

*   *   *

Until 1925, when he departed for the East to devote full time to the *New York News,* Captain Patterson in addition to co-directing *Tribune* editorial policy with Colonel McCormick gave close and continuing attention to the features area and so-called "women's news," including society news. After India Moffitt left the news department to become society editor, Patterson sought to persuade her that the reverence shown by her department for those in the social world tended to dullness for *Tribune* readers. Mrs. Moffitt disagreed, and society news continued unchanged for several days, whereupon Patterson offered his rebellious editor the opportunity to resign and appointed to her place Mildred Jaklon, who had joined the paper the year before, following her graduation from the University of Wisconsin. Thereafter the *Tribune's* society news had a brighter aspect. Mrs. Jaklon, wife of Proel Jaklon, *Tribune* promotion executive, later developed a daily crossword puzzle for the paper, which was introduced to *Tribune* readers with such success that it sold to hundreds of newspapers throughout the world via the Tribune–News syndicate. After Captain Patterson's departure to New York, Moffitt returned as society editor of the *Tribune* until she left to become the assistant national committeewoman of the Democratic party.

The *Tribune* of the 1920s was proud of its women's staff, boasting in a promotional advertisement that there were 25 women writers and editors, among them Antoinette Donnelly (beauty), Mae Tinee (films), Doris Blake (lovelorn), Kate Weber (clubs), Jane Eddington (food), Eleanor Jewett (art), Anita de Campi (home decoration), Corine Howe (fashion), Maude Martin Ellis (staff artist), and in addition, in the news department, Kathleen McLaughlin, Carol Krum, and Genevieve Forbes Herrick. Herrick became the first woman reporter to interview Al Capone. "The people want booze and I sell 'em what they want," he told her. Some female members of the staff held two or more jobs. Fanny Butcher, book critic, also was a society columnist. She was screened, she recalled in her memoirs, *Many Lives, One Love,* by none other than Katherine McCormick, who, even in 1925, was continuing to aid her son in his editing chores.

Philip Kinsley, veteran *Tribune* reporter and later author of a history of the paper, also discharged two jobs simultaneously, when he covered the John Thomas Scopes trial in sweltering Dayton, Tennessee, in 1925. Scopes, teacher of mathematics, biology, and chemistry in the Dayton high school, was accused of violating state law by "denying the story of the Divine creation of man as taught in the Bible and teaching instead that man has descended from a lower order of animals." The story might not have made the front pages of the metropolitan newspapers regularly except that William Jennings Bryan, the three-time Democratic candidate for the presidency, was chosen to prosecute the case, and Clarence

Darrow, Chicago's free-thinking liberal lawyer, was selected by the defense. Kinsley arranged for the *Tribune* to enter into a unique contract with the court, providing for daily, live radio broadcasting of the proceedings. Telephone tolls alone for the broadcast totaled $1,000 a day, but Colonel McCormick advanced a theory that, far from detracting from Kinsley's coverage, the radio report would lead more people to want to read the *Tribune*'s published dispatches.

McCormick was right. The *Tribune* enjoyed a twin triumph that muggy summer, when salable news was hard to come by. Unlike the David Swing religious trial in 1874, the Scopes affair was dealt with lightly by the *Tribune*. When the young teacher was found guilty and fined $100, the paper said: "The defense wanted to lose the case to carry it up for final decision on the issues. . . . In its essence it was a religious trial. Technically Mr. Scopes was not on trial because he had any particular belief or opinion, but he was on trial because Mr. Bryan and the people influenced by him had a particular belief and opinion." The real victim of the proceedings was Bryan himself, who, on July 26, died in Dayton of apoplexy induced by the tension and the heat.

*   *   *

During the fall of 1925, the *Tribune* took time to show its concern about education for journalists, a Joseph Medill dream half a century previously. On October 19, 1925, on motion of Alfred Cowles, seconded by Colonel McCormick, Tribune Company directors voted to provide funds to a new school of journalism that had been started in 1921 at Northwestern University. Northwestern named the institution the Joseph Medill School of Journalism, which continues conducting classes both on the downtown campus of the university and in Evanston. In recent years the school has added a teaching laboratory in Washington, D.C., and the Frank E. Gannett Urban Journalism Center, which offers midcareer training for professionals. The *Tribune* and other newspapers have supplied some of the teachers to the Medill School, which ranks among the most prestigious journalism schools in the country and boasts over 5,000 graduates.

The value the *Tribune* placed on writing talent was daily evidenced in its own pages. In addition to book critic Butcher, critics included Percy Hammond, Edward Moore, and Charles Collins on music, drama, and the dance. The paper also carried Burns Mantle's column of dramatic criticism filed from New York. *Tribune* columnists were such as Bert Leston Taylor and Richard Henry Little, and, in sports, Westbrook Pegler and Harvey Woodruff. Political cartoonists McCutcheon and Orr continued to bring a wry smile to readers' faces. The brilliant crew of editorial writers, headed by Tiffany Blake and Clifford Raymond, included Leon Stolz, from the University of Chicago and the Paris *Tribune;* Baker Brownell, a George Santayana disciple from Harvard University; and a bright new Princeton graduate, Levering Cartwright.

The editorialists were content with anonymity—and with good reason. On July 18, 1926, one of them commented on the fact that a Chicago ballroom had just installed in its men's room a powder dispenser and pink powder puffs. "It is time for a matriarchy," the *Tribune* declared. "Better rule by masculine women than by effeminate men. Man began to slip, we believe, when he discarded the straight-edged razor." Warming to his task, the editorialist dipped deep into his tub of venom. "Rudy, the beautiful gardener's boy, is now the prototype of the American male. Why didn't someone quietly drown Rudolph Guglielmi alias Valentino years ago?"

Valentino, of course, had nothing whatever to do with the effete ballroom; despite the fact that he wore slave bracelets from time to time, he was known by intimates as a considerable man. Arriving in Chicago the day after the "Pink Powder Puffs" editorial appeared, Valentino challenged the author to a duel, with boxing gloves. There was no response whatever from Tribune Tower, where someone suggested the whole thing was a publicity stunt for Valentino's new picture, *The Son of the Sheik,* which opened in Chicago on July 20. The *Herald and Examiner* wrote a sneering story about Valentino's unanswered challenge, but the writer of the *Tribune* editorial did not disclose himself. He was Clifford Raymond, a scholar and the author of mystery novels when he was not writing editorials. He rarely attended motion pictures and possibly had never seen a Valentino film. Eighteen hours later, Valentino departed, stating to the *Herald and Examiner* in a Caesarean manner, "I came, I challenged this man to fight. My honor has been cleared." The wisdom of Raymond's discretion was confirmed three days later in New York. Frank O'Neil, boxing expert for the *New York Journal,* went two rounds with Valentino and wrote that the actor was quite good.

The Chicago Daily Tribune. FINAL EDITION

THE WORLD'S GREATEST NEWSPAPER

VOLUME LXXVI.—NO. 80. C.   TUESDAY, APRIL 3, 1917.—TWENTY-FOUR PAGES.   ★ ★ PRICE ONE CENT.

U. S. AT WAR: WILSON

U-BOAT SINKS AZTEC, ARMED U. S. STEAMER

Americans in Crew Are Believed Victims of Blow in Dark.

AMERICANS ON BOARD

CAUGHT BY SURPRISE.

SUNK WITHOUT WARNING.

PARIS REPORTS REWARDS.

NOW FOR THE DEEDS

(Copyright 1917; by John T. McCutcheon.)

THE WEATHER.

DEFENSE BODY LAYS PLANS FOR 3 YEARS OF WAR

REPORTS MEXICO PLANS TO LEASE ISLAND TO JAPAN

VOTE TODAY! CITY ELECTION

FOR ALDERMEN

BOTH HOUSES HASTEN WORK ON PROGRAM

Resolution Will Be Passed at Once—Universal Service Aided.

BY ARTHUR SEARS HENNING.

Washington, D. C., April 2.—[Special.]

SENT TO COMMITTEES.

FOR UNIVERSAL SERVICE.

GIVES SCATTERING INDICTMENT.

THE DECLARATION

A JOINT resolution prepared by the president and introduced last night in both houses of congress, and referred to the foreign affairs committees for consideration today, follows:

THE WAR PLAN

PRESIDENT WILSON'S address to congress last night told what the war program of the United States will be. On this Mr. Wilson said:

RESOURCES.

THE NAVY.

THE ARMY.

FINANCE.

MUNITIONS.

COLT ARMS CUTS $3,500,000 MELON

Hartford, Conn., April 2.—[Special.]

"WE MUST FIGHT FOR JUSTICE AND RIGHTS"

President Tells Joint Session of Congress That German Monarchy Is Threat to All Mankind.

WASHINGTON, D. C., April 2.—(Special.)—President Wilson's epochal address to congress, calling for action against Germany, delivered tonight, follows:

"Gentlemen of the Congress: I have called the congress into extraordinary session because there are serious, very serious, choices of policy to be made, and made immediately, which it was neither right nor constitutionally permissible that I should assume the responsibility of making.

HOPED FOR MODIFIED WARFARE.

RELIED ON LAW OF NATIONS.

CHALLENGE TO ALL MANKIND.

Right: One of the full-page recruiting posters published in April, 1917, by McCormick and Patterson to raise their National Guard companies to strength after the United States declared war on Germany. The recruit they were proudest of snagging was Marshall Field III, "the richest young man in the country."

Below: McCormick (left) and Patterson (right) both served with the American Expeditionary Force in France, McCormick for a time attached to General Pershing's staff. By war's end, McCormick had been promoted to colonel, Patterson to captain, titles they retained throughout their lives. Patterson was a lieutenant at Fort Sheridan when this photo was taken, and the picture of the helmeted McCormick was taken in France.

(PATTERSON PHOTO COURTESY OF NEW YORK NEWS)

Left: Floyd Gibbons, the *Tribune*'s most famed World War I correspondent. Always eager to be in the thick of things, Gibbons had first shown his potential in Mexico, where he charmed even the notorious bandit Pancho Villa, once persuading Villa to postpone an attack on the grounds that he would not receive good press coverage in America during the World Series. En route to cover the war in Europe, Gibbons came up with a fine exclusive story when the ship in which he was traveling was sunk by a German submarine. Gibbons was severely wounded while covering action in France and lost his left eye; the white eye patch he adopted became a widely known journalistic trademark.

Below: While McCormick and Patterson were overseas, the *Tribune* was left in the capable hands of managing editor Edward Scott Beck (left) and business manager William H. Field (right). Beck guided the *Tribune*'s editorial department for 26 years, stepping down as managing editor in 1937. Field left the paper in 1919 to go to New York to aid in the establishment of Joe Patterson's tabloid *News*.

Above: After the 1918 Armistice, the *Tribune* turned its attention to treaty negotiations in Versailles, France. The paper scored a world beat by obtaining a copy of the full treaty text before its official release, turning the document over to forces in the U.S. Senate who were determined to keep the country out of the League of Nations.

Below: Following his return from France, Colonel McCormick led the *Tribune* in attacks on Chicago's Republican mayor, William Hale Thompson, who had opposed the war and was accused of corrupt city building practices. One Thompson achievement that had *Tribune* approval was the Michigan Avenue bridge, shown here at dedication ceremonies in 1920 (the view is southeast, toward buildings of the Illinois Central Railroad). The bridge provided access to riverfront property owned by Tribune Company.

Within months of the opening of the Michigan Avenue bridge, the *Tribune* had built a printing plant on the north bank of the Chicago River, and on December 12, 1920, the paper moved its manufacturing facilities into the new structure (right) without delaying an edition. Tribune Tower was opened to the public on July 6, 1925.

THE GUMPS

GASOLINE ALLEY

MOON MULLINS

HAROLD TEEN

DICK TRACY

LITTLE ORPHAN ANNIE

Although some *Tribune* comics were developed by artists working closely with Joe Patterson in the years before and during World War I, his greatest successes came following the war, most of them after he had gone to New York to concentrate on running the *New York News.* The strips were also made available to other newspapers across the country through the Chicago Tribune–New York News Syndicate.

Opposite page: Sidney Smith's "The Gumps" was among the most successful of the early strips. "Gasoline Alley" by Frank King, converted in 1919 from a panel cartoon to a strip, is one of the few comics in which characters have grown with the years; the family story is now in its third generation. Frank Willard began to draw "Moon Mullins" for the *Tribune* in 1923; Patterson wanted a rough and ready character with whom most men could identify. "Harold Teen" by Carl Ed portrayed a swinging cat back in the days before a youth culture dominated the American scene; Harold the sheik and his sheba Lillums enjoyed great popularity for a time but nevertheless expired, one of the few comic casualties in the Patterson era.

Top and above: Two of Patterson's greatest successes. "Dick Tracy" by Chester Gould was renamed and given a story line by Patterson when Gould came to the *New York News* and the *Tribune.* Harold Gray's "Little Orphan Annie" is shown meeting her benefactor, Daddy Warbucks, who grew much less tough as the strip progressed.

7 CENTS PAY NO MORE

Chicago Sunday Tribune
THE WORLD'S GREATEST NEWSPAPER

FINAL EDITION

VOLUME LXXXVI. NO. 21   MAY 22, 1927.   A **** SEVEN CENTS — TEN CENTS ELSEWHERE

LINDBERGH LANDS IN PARIS

"Am I Here," He Asks, as City Goes Wild with Frenzy of Joy

WILD REJOICING IN CHICAGO AT FLYER'S VICTORY

Armistice Day Scenes Repeated in Loop.

NEWS SUMMARY

THE BOND SALESMAN

"BUT IF THE INTEREST LAPSES, THE BONDS ARE NO GOOD??"

FLIES ATLANTIC ALONE; 33 HOURS 29 MINUTES

3,600 Miles at Over 100 Miles an Hour.

BY HENRY WALES

HERO OF EPOCHAL FLIGHT

CAPT. CHARLES LINDBERGH.

Lindbergh, in Pajamas, Tells His Story

BY HENRY WALES

TRAIN AND AUTO CRASH; 2 DEAD; 2 IN HOSPITAL

Paris Flight Brings Tears, Joy to Mother

Lindbergh's Full Story Tomorrow

LINDBERGH'S LOG

How He Found Paris.

But He Keeps Smiling.

THE WEATHER

TEMPERATURES IN CHICAGO

Lindbergh's solo flight across the Atlantic in 1927 captured the imagination of millions of people the world over and perhaps spurred Colonel McCormick's lifelong interest in flying. Lindbergh and McCormick were later allies in the America First movement, which sought to keep the United States out of World War II.

Above: Al Capone, king of Chicago's underworld in the late 1920s and early 1930s, chats with Cubs player Gabby Hartnett. The *Tribune* helped to bring about the federal investigation that led to the gangster's imprisonment.
Below: Robert M. Lee (left), managing editor from 1937 until 1939. Lee was city editor when reporter Jake Lingle was the victim of an apparent gangland slaying. J. Loy Maloney (right), managing editor from 1939 to 1950, was severely shaken in 1942 when the Justice Department sought to prove that a *Tribune* exclusive on the Battle of Midway violated the espionage act.

The Tribune
Shadow

From their point of view —
"Chicago's Greatest Curse"

Above: The *Tribune* vigorously worked to break the power of Mayor Thompson's Republican machine, which had the direct support of gangster Al Capone. By 1931 the "Tribune Shadow" was stretching long indeed, for Thompson was defeated in his bid to retain the mayoralty and Capone was on his way to Alcatraz, convicted of income tax evasion.

Left: These unemployed men, victims of the Depression of the 1930s, contemplated a grim winter after police burned the shack they had erected in Grant Park. Late in the decade the Depression began to lift as U.S. industry geared up to fill the armaments orders of European nations preparing for war.

A WISE ECONOMIST ASKS A QUESTION

"I DID"

"BUT WHY DIDN'T YOU SAVE SOME MONEY FOR THE FUTURE, WHEN TIMES WERE GOOD?"

VICTIM OF BANK FAILURE

Left: The cartoon for which John T. McCutcheon was awarded a Pulitzer prize in 1932.
Below: December 5, 1933. Bartenders worked overtime as Chicagoans celebrated the repeal of Prohibition. From the days of Joseph Medill, the paper had been Temperance-minded. But as early as 1921, when it was perceived that gangsters were making millions from illicit booze, the *Tribune* began voicing disapproval of the "noble experiment," and repeal met with hearty *Tribune* approval.

506

The battle between the *Tribune* and the New Deal was long and bitterly fought. Among the weapons in the *Tribune* arsenal was the pen of cartoonist Carey Orr.

10 CENTS PAY NO MORE

Chicago Sunday Tribune
THE WORLD'S GREATEST NEWSPAPER

FINAL

VOLUME. XCIV.—NO. 32   AUGUST 11, 1935.   A ★★★PRICE TEN CENTS

VOTE TAX TO SOAK EVERYBODY

NEW DEAL LOSS AT POLLS BARES ILLS OF REGIME

Rhode Island Vote Repudiation.

BY ARTHUR SEARS HENNING

[Chicago Tribune Press Service.]

Providence, R. I., Aug. 10.—[Special]—The political earthquake in Rhode Island last Tuesday has revealed the structural weakness of the New Deal throughout the England and other predominantly industrial parts of the country.

NEWS SUMMARY
Of The Tribune
(And Financial Scrap Book.)
Sunday, August 11, 1935.

WASHINGTON.

Senate committee rebels on soak the rich program and decides to soak everybody.   Page 1.

New Deal's revenue act puts in Rhode Island to satisfy structural weakness of regime in industrial areas.   Page 1.

DOMESTIC.

WPA strikers in New York decide they'll not bow to Roosevelt administration.   Page 1.

Two hundred veterans build New Deal and croaks for tons of 2,000, half colored.   Page 2.

Passion Play is presented by townsfolk of Sussex, Wis.   Page 2.

Pennsylvania now far Virginia troops from army maneuvers as a mob of paraplegia epidemic.   Page 2.

A kindly wizard knows as the case of men solves a maze of problems for G. of I. students.   Page 4.

FOREIGN.

Nazi official rebukes Jacoti infant for praising God and not mentioning Hitler.   Page 1.

Pan-American Clipper clears from U. S. to Honolulu to record time of third trans-Pacific trip.   Page 1.

Five men arrested in bid to assassinate Mexican president.   Page 1.

Japan threatens to oust China's dictator, Chiang Kai-shek, unless suppression of Foreign Wang Ching-wei is overhauled.   Page 11.

Premier Mussolini reviews army and pushes Ethiopian war plans.   Page 10.

Tribune writer tells events upon which Italy bases Ethiopia claim.   Page 10.

LOCAL.

Strange, empty home demands in pots of drain silk, quizzical.   Page 1.

Illinois manufacturers assail pension bill's cost, fearing tax load will cause increases in unemployment.   Page 4.

Halts to seek trial of Mandeville Dance next month.   Page 1.

Police departmental calls bid recruits for training this week.   Page 5.

Federal Works Progress administration is alert men to work in eleven Illinois counties tomorrow; no state over wage scale expected at present.   Page 5.

American localities will be in hot spots of the sixth and greatest Chicago-land Music Festival.

Movement gains strongly among Democrats to run Michael L. Igoe for governor in 1936.   Page 5.

It was just an old Evanston custom to but warrants are out lest three city officials.   Page 5.

Death notices, obituaries.   Page 6.

SPORTS.

Detroit beats White Sox, 4 to 0; St. Louis trims Cubs, 4 to 3. Part 2, Page 1.

All-Americans football squad starts training tomorrow.   Part 2, Page 1.

Slim Bink's early speed wins Cubs brothers.   Part 2, Page 3.

Moms to defend Joan Owens in A. A. U. pro open.   Part 2, Page 3.

Discovery wins at Saratoga under loomst of 120 pounds.   Part 2, Page 3.

Glenna and Paraline girls in June and affaults fight.   Part 2, Page 5.

Yankees gain on Tigers; defeat Athletics, 18 to 3 and 7 to 2.   Part 2, Page 4.

Colored All-Star teams meet in Comiskey park before.   Part 2, Page 4.

James Marker, All-Star game winner in 1934, pitches apprenticeship of his station.   Part 2, Page 4.

Markham wins Glee Amateur golf championship.   Part 2, Page 4.

EDITORIALS.

Where the New Deal's Big Money?   Door, Ethiopian Dope Show. After in the United States.   Part 1, Page 14.

FINANCE, COMMERCE.

Hurley Iarvisters' bonus cut for New Deal's easy money policy; sees confidence to offset market returns from actual bonds.   Part 3, Page 1.

Nation's biggest bank drops portions of suspicious New Deal difficulties; sale of supervisory New Deal ABA's undue safe of sites.   Part 3, Page 2.

Broad buying pushes stocks to new high levels.   Part 3, Page 2.

Tax on big corporations hits basic small stockholders.   Part 3, Page 2.

Money trade to be ruled by Half Coordinator Statement.   Part 3, Page 8.

Wheat prices break after tax to new export.   Part 3, Page 8.

July hog slaughter at record low level in sixteen years.   Part 3, Page 8.

Part 3—Automobiles; real estate.
Part 4—Women's and children's features; society; business.
Part 5—Society; art; travel and resorts.

Rotogravure section—Right pages.

Graphic section—stage and screen, music. Illustrated news on half page.

Article: "The Day Joe," serial by Booth Tarkington.

Comic section—Twelve pages.

WPA STRIKERS HURL DEFIANCE AT WHITE HOUSE

'We Will Not Bow,' Say Workers.

[Picture on Page 4.]

New York, Aug. 10.—[Special.]—Convincing President Roosevelt's bars against use of federal money for relief of striking Works Program administration workers as a scare of starve sector, George Meany, president of the New York State Federation of Labor, today deemed the union members would not bow to it.

Mayor F. H. La Guardia, on whom rests the decision as to whether the strikers may be led by city relief money, had not made up his mind which course he would pursue. He did not go to city hall but it was understood that he was still conferring with members of the emergency relief board about the problem.

First Test Monday.

The first test of the strike was brought for Monday when Langdon W. Post, tenement house commissioner, declared that the state free cost looking pockets on the lower east side, on which work has been stopped by the walkout, would be resumed with other workers from the national re-employment service and contractors' staff.

While collar workers, also associated with the wage program headquarters by the WPA, staged a demonstration in front of Administrator Hugh R. Johnson's office on Eighth avenue today. They sent a delegation of three up to see Col. Brehon Somervell, deputy assistant administrator in charge in the absence of Gen. Johnson, who was in Washington, and who has declined to see a picket at the East Harlem Post office on Eighth avenue which had been on strike for two weeks.

Mr. Meany, who is also connected with the national program of the Central Trades and Labor council, was asked for comment on the executive affirmation of Harry L. Hopkins' ruling that strikers could not go back on relief where federal money was used.

Interprets Roosevelt's Ultimatum.

"That means work or starve." he said. "Do you think we are going to bow to anything like that?"

In New York City half of the 11,-118,769 home relief budget for August is made up of money supplied by the federal government.

Mr. Meany declared that the strike activity would be resumed in telephone booth on Monday and that the strike now would stop the workers in all jobs we haven't reached yet."

Work so practically all WPA projects were stopped when the strike week and were checked in on the three weeks would continue to be laid whether work was done or not. "They," he went on, meaning the WPA, "may be able to get enough men to report in that way to make it look like the job is resumed, but if they try to put them to work they won't work."

Mr. Meany, in regard to the general thesis of the newly formed coalition work and were checked in on the three week cold continue to be on the relief whether work was done or not. And I am informing you all WPA officials to go out there to work they won't work."

Mr. Meany, in regard to the general theory of the newly formed association with the trade union which declared that such an affiliation would be against the policy of the American Federation of Labor.

Green Stands By.

Atlantic City, N. J., Aug. 10.—[Special.]—President Green of the American Federation of Labor, said tonight he stood ready to help settle the New York relief strike, if called upon to effect of the unions concerned.

Green declined to discuss, however, what he might do. Inasmuch as the White House, he said, would be the one in charge of 2600 Broadway accounts.

There are two sides. One of whom interposes against the federal relief policy, which permits the business council a substantial spread of about four units on 2000. To save the business the property is in a small twelve-hour power order. The strike minimize in significant conclusions but—

Brushelle leads the industric fifteen sooner workweek by started hight engaged and keeping for tests on the side decreased at the semi-radioactive speed and asserting the scan that share the horizontal propeller, by deemed be magically arrested and that sort the speeds arrested twin must shaped and proofed and asserted the fundamental propeller in the narrow direction formed. There was no regret that it went when he knew half the homenite party settle in the flow, was frozen from her chair.

DAVID AND GOLIATH

ROOSEVELT'S FIVE BILLION DOLLAR CAMPAIGN FUND

IF I COULD ONLY FIND A ROCK

GOP SEARCHING FOR THE RIGHT CANDIDATE

McCUTCHEON IN BRAZIL

Cartoonist Files North; Plane Conquers Fog Along the Coast.

[Chicago Tribune Press Service.]

PORTO ALEGRE, Brazil, Aug. 10.—A glimpse of sunset tipped the snow in favor of continuing our journey from Montevideo, Uruguay, which two airplanes that fairest ascent to be by gasoline, to say. The others seeming slight bit blot-smooth. I found 50 Montevideo airman to be

He maintain the fog returned with viciousness. This morning it was clear and a-roses' there we visited the Pan American fleet to be far-best but a soft wind blew up, warned up the sea, and cleared the fog. We took off at 7 a.m.

Freak Storm Hits Here and There; 3 Hurt

[Picture on Page 3.]

Summer squalls of unusual intensity, accompanied by high winds, thunder, and lightning, blew up suddenly yesterday afternoon in parts of the north side and sections of several western and northwestern suburbs. Three persons were injured by lightning, and two houses were struck by lightning.

Although huge sections of the north side and the Logan Square section to the north, no rain fell in the Loop area of Chicago or in the Loop area. The storm was brief.

GIRL, 21 MONTHS, USES 400 ENGLISH WORDS; KNOWS ITALIAN, TOO

Rochester, N. Y., Aug. 10—[A.P.]—A chubby little 21 months old, but yet, was too, can use correctly 400 words, her mother declared today.

While 5 months in his life, Mrs. Carpino knows the Italian equivalent of most of the 400 words her mother usually heard as home, a music teacher disclosed today.

Prince-Priest Lauds God, Not Hitler; Chided

BY SIGRID SCHULTZ

[Chicago Tribune Press Service.]

BERLIN, Aug. 10.—Father George of the home of Jesuits, who is the former crown prince of Saxony, has received the displeasure of the Nazi authorities by urging world war victims to be "faithful to God and the flag" without reminding them to be true to National socialist Hitler and the state.

SENATORS ACT TO HIT INCOMES FROM $800 UP

Expect a Revenue of 400 Million Yearly.

BY CHESLY MANLY

[Chicago Tribune Press Service.]

Washington, D. C., Aug. 10.—[Special.]—Revolting in disgust from President Roosevelt's scheme to soak the rich in a purely class social reform scheme to the senate finance committee today voted against the tax of both their incomes down to $800.

THE WEATHER

SUNDAY, AUGUST 11, 1935.

TEMPERATURES IN CHICAGO

Mounted in the depths of the Depression, the Chicago world's fair of 1933, "A Century of Progress," was so successful that it was repeated in 1934. The fair drew nearly 28 million visitors in 1933 and over 21 million the following year. Among the major attractions was fan dancer Sally Rand. (AIR CORPS PHOTO)

THE LAST DAYS
OF CAPONE

21

Chicago and the *Tribune* had recovered from the recession years of the early 1920s. By January, 1926, the paper noted that a new building boom was under way as multimillion-dollar apartments were announced for the North, West, and South sides in the wake of the commercial construction that had immediately followed the war. The *Tribune* itself was doing well, its daily circulation over 700,000, its Sunday circulation more than 1,100,000, and advertising totaling more than 100,000 columns in 1925. "We continue to regard the *Tribune* as having the largest morning circulation in the nation," the paper said in an editorial on January 3. It allowed that circulation figures were not everything—the quality of the numbers counted, too. Still, the editorialist said, "it's nice to have a comfortable surplus of numbers."

But citizens looking forward to a great new year of growth and economic expansion, as they were advised to do by the business leaders interviewed by the *Tribune* in its early 1926 editions, found themselves shortly facing a far worse scourge than economic panic. Al Capone, having inherited the overlordship of the old Colosimo gang from Johnny Torrio, had been moving to expand his domain. In the first four months of 1926, gang wars erupted throughout the city, 29 men falling in street shootings, others dying by torture in gang dungeons such as that maintained by Capone under his Four Deuces Saloon at 2222 South Wabash Avenue.

On April 27, 1926, Assistant State's Attorney William H. McSwiggin was slain. He had been successful in obtaining the death penalty in a gangland case, and it was whispered about that he intended to prosecute Capone for the murder of a small-time hoodlum named Joe Howard. No precise motive for the McSwiggin killing was established, however, as the newspapers repeated the question in their headlines: "Who Killed McSwiggin?" As far as gang chiefs were concerned, the murder of a law enforcement officer was a minor incident, but Chicago was thoroughly aroused. The newspapers, aware at last that Al Capone, alias Al Brown, used furniture dealer, had the power and the determination to attempt to take over Chicago, called it war. Alluding to Bugs Moran's claim that "we only kill each other," the *Tribune* said, "We can no longer comfort ourselves with the thought that they are only killing one another. This is a war in which we all are involved." Before the decade ended, more than 1,000 combatants would be killed, victims of machine guns, sawed-off shotguns, knives, and baseball bats in bloody battles fought mostly in the Chicago streets.

Chicagoans were discovering that Al Capone, who helped trigger the gang warfare, was not the Robin Hood he was earlier reputed to be in some Chicago neighborhoods, where he also was known as "kind-hearted Al Brown." The newspaper stories of warfare showed Capone to be a cruel killer and terrorist. Judge John H. Lyle, who became a close ally of the *Tribune* in the fight against Capone, was to see him at close range before his bench, and would describe the hoodlum as "a sloppy, gross person, five feet eight inches, 190 pounds. He had a large, flabby face with thick lips, and coarse features. His nose was flat, his brows dark and shaggy, and a bullet-shaped head was supported by a short, thick neck. His favorite expression was 'Ya keep ya nose clean, ya unnerstand?'"

Capone rarely carried a gun since he was surrounded by armed bodyguards, but he sometimes attacked trussed-up enemies with a baseball bat before his minions threw the battered bodies on the door-steps of rival gang headquarters or stuffed them into the rumble seats of autos. Capone was a coward, his fear of physical pain such that he refused medical treatment when he first learned of the venereal disease that led ultimately to his death. In his early days, as a Torrio bodyguard and pander, Capone carried a gun, once using it to pistol-whip an injured taxi driver whom he crashed into when driving while drunk. At another time he had shot and killed Joe Howard. Capone's right cheek was scarred, a war wound he sometimes said, but actually he was cut up in a barroom brawl.

The departure of Torrio from Chicago left Capone in charge of the Torrio gang at a strategic time. Income from the illicit booze trade was exceeding anything realized from vice and gambling. The next mayoral election was only a year away, and a highly favorable political alliance with Big Bill Thompson was possible. Torrio's had been the voice of moderation, admonishing his associates that negotiation could provide enough for everyone. Since no one was left to preach restraint to the gangs, the struggle for power and profits grew increasingly violent.

On September 20, 1926, Hymie Weiss struck again at the main enemy, Al Capone. Weiss led a force of 11 carloads of gunmen into Cicero, Capone's headquarters town. At noon, when 22nd Street was filled with strollers and shoppers, they raked the Hawthorne Inn, Capone's Cicero base, with fire from machine guns, pistols, and sawed-off shotguns. Capone, having lunch in a restaurant next door, was pushed to the floor by Frankie Rio, his bodyguard. Windows, glasses, and dishes in the restaurant were smashed by bullets, but Capone and Rio were unhit. Bullets pockmarked the Hawthorne Inn walls, furniture was ripped apart, but only a single Capone gunman, Louis Barko, was wounded. A car in the street in which an innocent victim, Mrs. Clyde Freeman, sat holding her small child, was struck 30 times, and Mrs. Freeman was seriously wounded. Al Capone, it was said, later sent $10,000 to pay her medical bills.

Chicago waited in dread. The gangsters were gunning for one another, but the terrorist tactics now threatened anyone near the scene. The revenge attack by the Capone gang was neat and professional. On October 11, as Weiss and four associates got out of their car near Dion O'Banion's old flower shop, they were cut down. Weiss and Patrick Murray, a beer peddler, were killed instantly; their associates were seriously wounded but survived.

The newspapers erupted, and this time it appeared that gangland was as frightened as ordinary citizenry over the wanton bloodshed. The *Tribune* reported a gangland truce established at a meeting of leaders on October 21. Beer territory was divided, Capone retaining the area south of Madison Street, Moran and Drucci getting the 42nd and 43rd wards on the North Side. All gambling chiefs anywhere, however, were to continue to report and pay tribute to Al Capone. To insure good connections with the Democratic hierarchy, Capone placed Dennis Cooney, Hinky Dink Kenna's bagman, in charge of the town's brothels. The understanding with Hinky Dink was clear enough: Capone was the boss. Mike Carrozzo, ruler of the street cleaners' union, was another link to the Democratic political machine presided over by George Brennan. Now Capone moved to cement direct and satisfactory connections with the Republicans—through Big Bill Thompson, who was planning his political comeback.

*   *   *

Al Capone had strengthened his grip on Chicago's underworld and even extended his empire despite the fact that an honest Mayor Dever was in

City Hall in 1926. But the takeover of Chicago was far from complete. There were still labor unions and legitimate businesses to be seized and additional political graft to be divided. Big Bill Thompson chose now to run again for mayor, and he looked to Capone for aid. His alliance with Fred Lundin was broken; his No. 1 critic, the *Chicago Tribune,* was more powerful than ever; but with Capone's support and a neutrality arrangement with Gov. Len Small, Thompson needed only to repair the rupture with State's Attorney Robert Crowe. And Crowe was agreeable. Thompson chose as his campaign slogan, "America First." He also advertised himself as "Big Bill, the Builder," responsible for Chicago's renewed prosperity and architectural renaissance. He promised what everyone expected, a wide-open town, and Al Capone's forces responded by raising more than $100,000 for Thompson's primary campaign. Capone pledged that his men would be in the streets on election day to protect Thompson's interests.

Fred Lundin, considered Chicago's keenest political tactician, somehow forgot his experience and training and entered Dr. John Dill Robertson, once Thompson's health commissioner, into the primary campaign. Thompson's assault was vicious. He appeared on the stage of the Cort Theater with two rats in a cage, calling them Doc and Fred. He described Doc Robertson's disgusting eating habits. Robertson did not finish the campaign, and Thompson won the primary by 180,000 votes over his other opponent, Edward R. Litsinger. Concerning the victory, the *Tribune* said:

> Thompson is a buffoon in a tommyrot foundry, but when his crowd gets loose in City Hall, Chicago has more need of Marines than any Nicaraguan town. No one is obliged to guess as to Thompson or as to Dever. The city has had experience with both and knows exactly what to expect. It is not exploring unknown territory. Both regions are mapped and sign-posted. The issue is between common sense and plain bunk. It is between decency and disreputability, between sensible people and political defectives, between honesty in administration and the percentage system.

The 1927 mayoral campaign was as vicious as any Chicago had seen. Thompson accused the *Tribune* of plotting his death and threatened that if anything happened to him, Colonel McCormick would be slain. Thompson's charge was absurd and treated as such by the press. McCormick ignored it, continuing his practice of walking about the downtown area, until one night he was pursued, escaping his potential assailants by fleeing down an alley. Back at the newspaper he informed circulation manager Max Annenberg, in town on a brief leave from the *New York News,* about his experience, and another McCormick sortie into the Loop was arranged. This time he was trailed by his own men. "The hoodlums followed me down an alley," McCormick recalled later. "They didn't get far and some ended up in a hospital. After that I got an armored car and a bodyguard, Bill Bockleman."

Both Mayor Dever and the *Tribune* found it impossible to force Thompson into a head-on confrontation. Big Bill instead poured his venom on the king of England and insisted on fighting what became known as the Battle of the School Books, denouncing pro-British influence in the public schools. "How can I campaign against a mind like that?" Dever complained. Then Big Bill turned truly diabolical by adopting as his own almost the entire platform for Chicago which the *Tribune* published daily under its editorial page flag.

The platform had changed from time to time, but it had remained fixed since January 1, 1926: "Make Chicago the first city of the world. Start building the subway. Electrify the railroads. Abolish the smoke pall. Build safe streets and highways. Re-establish constitutional representation." Big Bill Thompson was for all of that and for the *Tribune*'s platform for the Middle West as well: "A highway system adequate at all points to the demands of traffic. Purchase of the western railroads by western investors. National and state legislation to encourage the growth of our forests. Build a nine-foot waterway from Chicago to New Orleans." Thompson especially liked the waterway plank and promised, as mayor, to lead an expedition to New Orleans to study the matter.

Mostly, however, Big Bill ran against George V. "I wanta make the King of England keep his snoot out of America," he told his dazzled crowds. "I don't want the League of Nations. I don't want the World Court. America first, last and always. That's the issue of this campaign." Thompson accused Mayor Dever and Superintendent of Schools William McAndrew of introducing pro-British books into the Chicago schools, ignoring the fact that many of the books being used were first purchased during his own administration. But he persisted in his attack, "This fellow McAndrew . . . teaching un-Americanism! By God, you elect me mayor and I'll fire him!"

For a time it appeared that Thompson was in trouble. Fred Lundin continued to control some state of Illinois patronage in Cook County. There appeared to be rebellion in the black wards, which in the past had obeyed George Harding's commands, because a few blamed Thompson for the 1919 race riots. But the Capone organization was hard at work, aided by some of Hinky Dink Kenna's Democrats, who had no liking for the honesty of Mayor Dever. So confident of the outcome was Capone that he moved his headquarters from the Hawthorne in Cicero to the Metropole Hotel at 2300 South Michigan Avenue and took 50 rooms. Yet the Dever forces continued to be optimistic. On April 3, two days before the election, the *Tribune*'s page-one banner proclaimed: "I'LL WIN BY 158,000—DEVER SAYS." "City's Maddest Ballot Fight Rages to the

End," read a secondary headline. The following day the paper reported on its own straw poll, which continued to show Dever leading: "BIG SWING OF VOTES TO DEVER." The swing occurred in the straw poll, but it did not represent voting intentions in wards being worked by Capone men. The *Tribune* promised its usual superior election coverage to the public, special editions, returns telephoned from *Tribune* election headquarters to 135 motion picture theaters, where they were projected onto the screens, and bulletins and interviews on its own radio station, WGN. On the morning of April 6 the paper's banner blared the depressing news: "THOMPSON VICTOR BY 83,072." As later returns came in the result proved even worse: Thompson won control of the city council as well. His victory was complete.

The *Tribune*'s editorial indicated some puzzlement over Thompson's ability to win, considering the inanities of his campaign. The paper failed to recognize the effectiveness of Al Capone's activity. "The *Tribune* would have preferred Dever for the sake of the city," it said. It noted that Chicago was a wet town, and that Thompson promised a wide-open town, but then, Dever also was wet. Did Chicagoans really want rampant gambling, vice, and graft? Certainly the citizens who voted for Thompson would deserve what they were about to get. "He is elected. The *Tribune* is well satisfied to have opposed him. If his impending term shall prove to have no relation to the other two, the *Tribune* will be glad to accept it for what it is. . . . The *Tribune* is carrying on no feud. It is doing what it can for the general welfare."

The enormity of the election disaster became clearer each hour. Capone, already snug behind newly placed steel doors in the Metropole, did not lose a minute. His armed thugs roamed the streets, giving orders to operators of the beer flats, brothels, and gambling dens not previously under Capone's "protection." It was clear that the destruction of rival gangs would occur as swiftly as it became evident that any would dare to balk the new order. A reporter for the *London Daily Mail* visited Chicago and wrote: "Three thousand hooligans are carrying on a campaign of brigandage and murder. Machine gun bullets sweep the streets." The *Tribune* declared that the report was exaggerated, but essentially true. "A Chicagoan will soon be regarded as a person who is alive because of a particular hardihood, courage and marksmanship," it commented.

*   *   *

As the nature of the new alliance became clear, the *Tribune* resumed its attack on crime, now called organized crime, holding Thompson responsible. His victory had promptly led Gov. Len Small and State's Attorney Robert Crowe to pledge anew their alliance with the mayor. But it was Al Capone who loomed as the new supreme boss, the man who fought with terror, ordering his enemies killed. Colonel McCormick also sought alliances for the resumption of warfare. He had a staunch ally in former alderman Judge John H. Lyle, and others in reform leader Frank Loesch and a group of businessmen who insisted on anonymity and became known as "the Secret Six." Big Bill Thompson was no longer Chicago's major problem. He was traveling around the country ostensibly seeking support for flood control, but his real purpose, to win support for his candidacy for the presidency, was believed to be too ridiculous for genuine concern. What was needed was a way to deal with Alphonse Capone.

Judge Lyle and the Secret Six made a careful study of the gang in an effort to find ways to defeat it. In 1923, Lyle learned, Capone and Torrio had received $7 million from 25 brothels, scores of gambling dens, 65 breweries, and several distilleries. By the end of 1926, Chicago had an estimated 20,000 speakeasies, 3,000 brothels, 300 large gambling houses, and 2,000 handbooks taking bets. In 1927, federal authorities put Capone's income, as sole chieftain, at $110 million: $60 million from illicit beer, whiskey, and alcohol cooking; $25 million from gambling and dog tracks; $10 million from vice; and $15 million from a new criminal field, labor racketeering. Thus, while he had enormous expenses, paying his gunmen, accountants, distillers, and brewers, and paying off politicians and police, Capone's income and power dwarfed those of his predecessors.

The *Tribune* undertook to obtain detailed coverage of the vast illegal enterprise that was taking over Chicago and could be expected to engulf all of Illinois if it continued unchecked. Reports of murders were daily routine, and the lead "Gangland guns roared again last night" became a cliché. Some labor leaders, such as Big Tim Murphy, a tough Irishman who had muscled into the labor movement himself in earlier days, tried to fight Capone. Murphy, of course, was killed, as were others who failed to learn from example. Police who arrested suspects in the gang and labor killings found them promptly released by judges asserting there was lack of evidence. Prohibition agents looked hard for stills, but mostly the stills of hardy outlaws who tried to live beyond the gang law—they refused to pay protection to the mob or to the agents. Chicago was becoming a city of cynics, unable and unwilling to fight the forces of crime and corruption. McCormick, Judge Lyle, and members of the Secret Six sought a strategy that might bring down even the all-powerful Capone.

*　　*　　*

There was good news, too, in 1927. On May 21, a Saturday, the *Tribune*'s banner read: "LINDBERGH OFF IRISH COAST." On the following day, "LINDBERGH LANDS IN PARIS." The story of the flight of the youthful "Lone Eagle" from New York to Paris in 33 hours and 29 minutes was told by *Tribune* correspondent Henry Wales, an account reprinted in anthologies of great news stories. After describing the enormous crowds at Le Bourget Air Field and the thrilling sight of the Ryan monoplane circling in for a landing, Wales related his own adventure getting through police lines to the plane. "Am I in Paris?" asked the weary young flyer. "You're here," Wales told him. William L. Shirer, the Paris *Tribune* reporter who accompanied Wales, in recalling their wild push to the plane, could not remember words being spoken. Later, Jay Allen of the Paris office supplied interview material to bureau chief Wales, who pounded out the *Tribune*'s story.

Lindbergh was so cramped from his hours of sitting that he could not stand after he was helped from the plane. The French crowds went mad with enthusiasm as Lindbergh was assisted to the car of U.S. Ambassador Myron Herrick, and Wales, caught up in the crowd, almost missed his deadline. On Monday the *Tribune* banner blared: "CAPTAIN LINDBERGH—HIS STORY." The personal narrative of the pilot had been arranged with the *New York Times*. More important for the *Tribune* were its wirephoto experiments conducted by Joe Patterson for the *Tribune* and *New York News*. This system, the Bartlane system, produced a full page of excellent pictures for the Monday paper. A page-one story told how the photographs taken at Le Bourget were flown to London, cabled to New York by the Bartlane system, and then sent to Chicago over American Telegraph Company wires.

The paper's editorials did not immediately recognize the significance of Lindbergh's flight in popularizing aviation but hailed it as a kind of sports achievement: "There was everything in young Lindbergh's flight to give his countrymen one of the thrills of their lives. He is young, engaging, bashful. He went alone. As a sporting event it hasn't many equals for the United States." Then, the day following, the importance of the flight grew: "Apparently French and American relations are more cordial now than any time since the war. The warm-hearted admiration of the French has had a response in the United States and everybody seems a bit more amiable because a brave young American had the skill, endurance and good fortune to fly from New York to Paris." Finally there was an added thought, without much doubt from Col. Robert R. McCormick: Chicago must take steps at once to build an airfield adequate for the coming air age. That campaign would not cease until Meigs Field was built during the 1930s on a man-made island just southeast of downtown. The air age would be much vaster than even the *Tribune*'s air-minded publisher could imagine. Meantime, McCormick acquired a twin-engined Sikorski amphibian for his personal use, and his pilot, Bob Gast, landed it on the Oak Street beach, on Chicago's Near

North Side. McCormick named the plane the "Untin' Bowler."

On June 4–6, two weeks after Lindbergh landed in Paris, U.S. pilots Clarence Chamberlain and Charles A. Levine flew from New York to Eisleben, Germany, in 43 hours, a new record for nonstop distance and amount of flight time; on June 28, Army Air Corps pilots Lester Maitland and Albert Hegenberger flew from San Francisco to Honolulu. The *Tribune* tried its own pioneering aviation adventure on July 3, 1929, when Gast, Parker Cramer, and *Tribune* aviation editor Bob Wood took off in the "Untin' Bowler" to establish a new air route to Europe. The first two steps on the flight were uneventful after a publicity blast in Chicago. At Port Burwell on Ungava Bay, Canada, however, there was a violent storm while the plane was moored, and the "Untin' Bowler" went down. No one was hurt, and McCormick's enthusiasm for aviation was undimmed by this failure. He became chairman of Chicago's first National Air Races and bought a new Sikorski amphibian, which also got an English cockney name, "Arf Pint." McCormick had decided to leave air route pioneering to others, but he would help establish and name airfields in Chicago, and in one four-year period, from 1948 to 1952, he flew 1,500 hours, 265,000 miles, to 80 countries.

*   *   *

Late in 1927 Big Bill Thompson understood that he was not to become president of the United States. He ended his political travels and roared back into Chicago, vowing to carry out his campaign promise to rid the schools and the library of pernicious British influence. J. Lewis Coath, proud of his nickname "Iron Handed Jack," had been made president of the Board of Education and was ordered now to throw out School Superintendent William McAndrew. Coath enlisted former congressman John J. Gorman, a rabid Anglophobe, who searched the school texts for evidence of lies and subversion and ended up charging McAndrew with insubordination. The school board ordered a formal hearing.

The trial was as weird as Thompson's campaign, prompting Professor Charles Merriam of the University of Chicago, intellectual, Thompson foe, and former alderman, to comment, "This is very funny, but I find the comic strips more amusing." Coath brought to the trial a hand-sewn silk flag with the words "America First" that he flew above the American flag, thereby drawing the wrath of American Legionnaires. Frederick Bausman, once a Washington State Supreme Court justice, was Coath's special prosecutor. He never mentioned the insubordination charges against McAndrew, but summarized Gorman's findings that there was no pro-Americanism in the schools. He stormed at English perfidy, asserting the British were conquering America "not by shot and shell, but by a rain of propaganda." The *Tribune*'s editorials chortled at the daily revelations.

"Mr. Gorman tells Mayor Thompson he has uncovered a plot to feed the American eagle to the British lion," the paper said. "Is there no end to absurdity?"

No end seemed in sight. During the school trial, Thompson ordered an attack on the public library, which had been started by a gift of books from England following the Great Fire. Thompson may well have been unaware of this beginning in ordering Urbine J. "Sport" Herrmann to "get rid of the British books." Herrmann, a Thompson yachting crony who had won local notoriety by sailing into Midwestern yacht clubs clad only in his athletic supporter, was eager for the battle. "I'm going to burn every book there that's pro-British!" he disclosed. "Will you seek the help of an historian?" asked a precise *Tribune* reporter. "Hell no!" Sport cried. "I'll be my own judge, and Mayor Thompson will help me." Herrmann seized scores of books but could find no one who would burn them on the lakefront as he had intended. Finally Sport limited his Index to four volumes by eminent historians: *The American Nation,* by Harvard's Alfred Bushnell Hart; *Practicer of American Ideals,* by Hart and C. H. Van Tyne; *The Causes of the War of Independence,* by Van Tyne; and *The Story of American Democracy,* by Willis Mason West. How did those books become suspect? "A feller tipped me off," Herrmann told the reporters. "I don't have time to read 'em myself." The books were not burned, however. Carl Roden, the librarian, suggested putting them in the library's "Inferno," along with Joyce's *Ulysses* and other "obscene" volumes unfit for general circulation. But the story of the book burning had gone around the world, adding ridicule to the already blackened Chicago reputation. Few noticed in 1930 when Sport Herrmann and his business partner, Eugene McDonald, contributed $250,000 to the library to buy books without restriction.

While offers poured into Chicago from librarians in Canada and Europe to rescue the endangered "pro-British" books, the school board trial continued to its dismal denouement. Mayor Thompson furnished his own list of Revolutionary heroes, mostly Irish, German, and Poles, a roster calculated to please the city's major ethnic groups. Dour Frank Righeimer, Thompson's personal attorney in the case, enlivened the proceedings when he confused Ethan Allen with Nathan Hale in his statement to the board, but he continued, unabashed by the laughter: "When a man teaches that the Revolutionary soldiers were smugglers, bums, pettifogging lawyers and loafers, the Board of Education should refuse to be cowed." Just who Righeimer was talking about was not clear, for McAndrew was not a teacher. However, on March 21, 1928, the Board of Education formally voted eight to two to oust him. It was the day that hoodlums gunned down Diamond Joe Esposito, political leader for the Deneen Republican faction in the Italian community, pumping 58 bullets into his body, a slaying reported to have been directly ordered by Al Capone. A few hours later John Infantino, a witness to the Esposito slaying, was killed, and the infamous "Pineapple Primary" of 1928 replaced the school and library follies in the news.

The Esposito murder took the banner headline. Editorially, the *Tribune* twinned the stories of new Chicago shame and obliquity. "McAndrew Goes One Way, Diamond Joe Another," read the editorial headline. "With each explosion of a bomb and with each coroner's report of a man killed by persons unknown, the people of Chicago are threatened and shamed," the paper said. "Mr. Thompson requested the populace to step up and observe the iniquities of the school superintendent engaged in the British service in the public schools. Mr. McAndrew is fired. The schools will be run by such politicians as can dodge bombs and keep out of the way of shotguns. . . . As Mr. Thompson marked Mr. McAndrew off one scorecard, gangland marked Joe Esposito off another."

The paper began a series of articles on Chicago's besmirched image throughout the world, under the headline "'CHICAGO' WORD OF TERROR ALL OVER THE WORLD." As the grim series ran, the Pineapple Primary, another bloody battle, roared on in the struggle of Capone and Thompson for domination of Chicago and Illinois.

*　　*　　*

The Pineapple Primary began as a gambling war early in 1928, according to Virgil Peterson. Capone put Jake Guzik in charge of his gambling division, with Jimmy Mondi as his enforcer, and demanded higher financial returns. When Mondi summoned the resort owners to the 16 South Clark Street headquarters of the mob and told them the Capone organization wanted from 25 to 40 percent of the take, trouble erupted. Within the next six months there were 62 bombings in Chicago, two damaging the homes of Thompson followers Charles C. Fitzmorris, former police commissioner and current city controller, and Dr. William H. Reid, city smoke inspector. Other attacks wrecked the homes of U.S. Senator Deneen and his candidate for state's attorney, John A. Swanson. Mayor Thompson insisted that the bombing outrages were ordered by the Deneen Republicans and even charged that Deneen had ordered himself and Swanson bombed as a cover. Deneen, said Big Bill, was attempting to break up the mayor's reforged alliance with Governor Small and State's Attorney Crowe.

It was true that the Deneen forces, strongly backed by the *Tribune*, were attempting to defeat both Small and Crowe. Only with an honest state's attorney in office was there any possibility of smashing the Capone–Thompson alliance. That effort could best succeed with the corrupt state machine, run by Small, out of power. The *Tribune* asserted that the bombings were the work of the Capone mob, and redoubled its efforts to elect Swanson. On April 10, Judge Swanson defeated Crowe, and Secretary of State Louis L. Emmerson, also backed by the *Tribune,* took the gubernatorial nomination from Small. The *Tribune,* grimly satisfied, said on April 12 that the decent people were beginning to win the war.

> The *Tribune* feels that there has been a political reassociation of it and its readers and that it took place in time to avoid an intolerable situation and avert unendurable consequences.
>
> It should be apparent that this newspaper and the citizens have in the main the same purposes with respect to public life and government. The object is the maintenance of praiseworthy administration and honest legislation. It is not of primary importance what particular persons shall be given authority and responsibility, but that the persons so trusted shall be competent and willing to conduct public affairs honestly with regard to public funds and successfully with regard to public security.

The editorial dissected the cancerous situation of the city and state governments. Names were named: Small had obtained passage of legislation enabling him to avoid being charged with the mishandling of state funds; utilities baron Samuel Insull had invested $158,000 in the senatorial campaign of Frank L. Smith, chairman of the Illinois Commerce Commission, which regulated utilities. The revelation of this and other utilities contributions to Smith resulted in his being denied his U.S. Senate seat. Insull's office also had drawn up bills providing for perpetual franchises for streetcar interests and had sent them to Sam Ettelson, Thompson's corporation counsel. When the bills failed in the legislature, Small promised to call a special session to pass them.

Small, Thompson, and Crowe, said the paper, had formed a combination that controlled police activities, limited criminal prosecutions, and dispensed pardons when convenient. The combination had made lucrative arrangements with the public utilities as well as with crime and vice. "The campaign was to be terrorized. It was to be dominated by machine guns and bombs. Precincts were to be carried by killers, gamblers, procurers, and male brothel house keepers. They were to take their profits out of the degradation of city morals. They were to intimidate the decent citizenship. They were to keep the people from the polls."

The *Tribune* confessed that it had failed for almost 12 years in helping the people to understand "the frightful consequences they were bringing down upon themselves by their refusal to protect themselves in their elections. People even took some satisfaction in seeing the failure of just newspaper criticism and of self-evident facts. If that was to continue, the immunity of reptilian politics was found in the very exposure of criminal acts and it was the critic who was in danger and not the criminal." The paper discussed the nature of the thugs and criminals menacing Chicago and indicated that it feared for the lives of its staff members if the public should again fail to stand up to the outlaws.

"It was against this that the voters arose in a storm of indignation, in a return to old-time savvy in voting, in protection of themselves and their institutions," the editorial concluded. "With this accomplished revolt of Illinois citizens, Illinois seems a cleaner state and certainly is a safer one."

Some perspective indicates that the *Tribune*'s assessment of the situation was accurate. The Illinois electorate was almost completely demoralized, it had appeared, during the course of the campaign. During the primary period, Sen. George W. Norris of Nebraska had called upon President Coolidge to send Marines to Chicago to restore order. The paper's analysis of the problem was correct, but its optimism for the future turned out to be wrong. The Al Capone–Big Bill Thompson combination was far from finished—Capone simply had risen to the status of senior partner. The *Tribune* and the *Daily News* continued to assume that Thompson's police department could effectively control the gangs and daily demanded action against them. While the mayor was out of the city, corporation counsel Sam Ettelson, acting for him, boosted Deputy Commissioner William Russell to the position of commissioner of police, replacing Michael Hughes. He made the announcement in Thompson's name.

Russell's promotion caused little surprise, for he obviously was a man Big Bill could count on. Shortly after the mayor's election, the then deputy commissioner had told reporters, "Mayor Thompson was elected on the 'open town' platform. I assume the people knew what they wanted when they voted for him." But the appointment of John Stege as deputy commissioner was difficult to fathom. Stege was known to Judge Lyle as a fearless enemy of hoodlums and had brought many mobsters before him.

After Russell's appointment was announced, there was a short flurry of police activity. Then the city settled back into its old ways. In August, 1928, George Brennan, the Democratic boss, died, and Anton J. Cermak, president of the Cook County Board of Commissioners, took his place. On September 7, Antonio Lombardo, who had been placed at the head of the Unione Siciliana by Capone, was shot down during the rush hour, half a block from the intersection of State and Madison streets, known as the world's busiest corner. Joseph Ferraro, one of Lombardo's two body-guards present, also was killed. The other, Joseph Lolordo, escaped.

So supine was the city by October that Frank Loesch, the respected reform leader who worked with Judge Lyle and the Secret Six, asked for an interview with the archcriminal Capone, to see if some kind of peace, or at least a truce, could be negotiated. He was instructed to come to the Lexington Hotel on Michigan Avenue, Capone's new headquarters. Loesch went there, hot with shame that such an errand was necessary. The Lexington itself was frightening. Tough young men in neat, dark business suits, their shoulders bulging with muscle, padding, and guns, guarded the lobby and corridors, some of them lounging near the door, wearing the wide-brimmed pearl-gray hats that completed the uniform of Capone gunmen. Two efficient bodyguards opened and closed the steel door to the Capone suite, where Al Capone sat in a soft light beneath three huge portraits of Presidents Washington and Lincoln and Mayor William Hale Thompson. Capone nodded, spoke softly, indicated a chair. Loesch, ashamed but determined, came directly to the point. Would it be possible for Chicago to have an orderly election in November? Capone seemed surprised and relieved that no more was wanted. "Sure, I'll give you a square deal," he said. Loesch gritted his teeth, said his friend Lyle, to whom Loesch gave his verbatim report of the meeting. The gangster, obviously alluding to the violence of the Pineapple Primary, said such things would not happen again; he would order his own men to behave and they would see that the others did. Then he added, "I'll have the cops send out squad cars the night before the election. They'll throw the punks in the cooler and keep 'em there until the voting's over."

Loesch left the meeting shaken. The quiet assurance of Capone was more ominous for Chicago's future than he had expected. It had been asserted that Capone controlled the police; that his pal Daniel Serritella, who had been appointed city sealer, looked after Capone interests in City Hall; that his subaltern Mike Carrozzo, boss of one labor union, the street cleaners, was moving in on others, which could tie up city services. Now Capone himself was casually indicating that the least documented of the charges was true: He controlled the police directly and from the top.

The election was calm, no violence. Capone himself had little to lose in it—Crowe and Small had already been defeated in the primary, and, besides, Thompson and his cronies still controlled the city. *Tribune*-supported candidates Louis Emmerson and John Swanson were elected governor and state's attorney, respectively. Republican presidential nominee Herbert Hoover was swept into office over New York Gov. Al Smith by more than 6 million votes and left on a goodwill tour of South America aboard the battleship *Maryland*.

Colonel McCormick, who had learned the details of Loesch's visit to Capone from Loesch and Lyle, vowed he would go to Washington to talk with Hoover about ways to deal with Capone as soon as the new president was inaugurated. Despite the editorial optimism occasioned by the earlier ouster of Crowe and Small, McCormick had concluded that Capone could not be defeated without the aid of the federal government. But which federal laws might prove effective? The Volstead Act, seemingly, but there was no chance of nailing the gang chief personally for the misdeeds of his minions. In 1927 the Supreme Court had upheld the conviction of Manley Sullivan, a small-time bootlegger, for income tax evasion. Al Capone, very probably, had violated the federal income tax laws. McCormick's determination to discuss the problem with the new president was sharply spurred shortly by a new outrage in Chicago.

$$*\qquad*\qquad*$$

On that cold, clear St. Valentine's Day in 1929 even the toughest newsmen were shocked by the carnage in the S.M.C. Cartage Company garage at 2122 North Clark Street. Seven of Bugs Moran's men, caught by what must have appeared to them to be a police raid, had turned to face a brick wall, then were mowed down by machine gun fire, their bodies falling to the bloody, oil-soaked floor. Witnesses saw several men, two of them in police uniforms, race to their automobile, ostensibly a police squad car, following the sounds of shooting. Since the story broke on afternoon paper time, the *Tribune* carried a second-day banner: "SEVEN KILLED: DOCTOR AMONG THEM," exploiting the fact that its reporters had identified one of the dead men as an optometrist, Dr. Reinhardt H. Schwimmer, whose presence among gangsters added to wild speculation about the killings. The *Tribune* advanced the police theory: "It is police belief that the gangsters who were killed paid the penalty for being followers of George Moran, successor to Dean [*sic*] O'Banion. The historic antagonist, as history goes in the swift careers of gangsters of the O'Banion–Moran crew, is Alphonse Capone, otherwise Al Brown."

Police under Commissioner Russell and investigators for State's Attorney Swanson were hunting evidence, and a special coroner's jury was impaneled by Coroner Herman N. Bundesen. The *Tribune* in various editions suggested that the killings were over beer rights or an attempt to take over the treasury of the Laundry and Dyehouse Chauffeurs Union, a theory advanced since the Moran gang had been hired by some laundry owners to protect them from the Capone racketeers. One witness thought he could identify one of the men fleeing the garage as Joseph Lolordo, one of the bodyguards who had escaped the State Street ambuscade of Antonio Lombardo six months earlier. Had the Moran gang assassinated Lombardo?

Al Capone had taken steps to make sure of his alibi and was in Florida at the time of the St. Valentine's Day Massacre. Machine Gun Jack McGurn was sought as a likely contract killer. Members of Detroit's

Purple Gang also were suspected. No one doubted that Capone had issued the orders, and few doubted that his all-out war for dominance of Chicago had been resumed.

On February 15, both the *Tribune* and State's Attorney Swanson supported the beer rights motive for the slaying. Swanson called together Police Commissioner Russell, his deputies, and 50 captains and ordered them to shut down all Chicago liquor supplies as the only way to break the power of the gangs. He promised to prosecute any officer who failed to act. The *Tribune*'s page-one story reporting Swanson's action read almost like an editorial: "Prohibition was ordered into effect in Chicago by State's Attorney Swanson—ordered into effect ten years late—but within 36 hours after seven men were slain in a beer runner's nest."

Although the *Tribune* frankly supported Swanson's action, no one on the *Tribune*'s editorial board, especially not Colonel McCormick, assumed that the state's attorney's orders to the police would dry up Chicago and drive out the gangs. On February 16, the *Tribune*'s leading editorial reflected the considered views of the paper as well as Chicago's despair:

Is the City Helpless?

> It would have been imagined difficult for gang warfare, reprisal, and murder to give Chicago a shock, but the killing of the Moran gangsters did it. The criminals have been defiant and successful in their apparent immunity, but these murders Thursday went out of the comprehension of a civilized city. . . . The worst of it is that throughout the years of gang warfare and murder there has been plenty of evidence to indicate who had reason to do it and no proof discoverable of who did it.
>
> A good many citizens have been consoling themselves with the reflection that after all the gangsters are only killing each other. That's a deadly consolation. . . . The interlocking activities of the gangs and racketeers have already affected considerable of the city's life. Citizens have been buying protection for themselves and their business.
>
> Can the various authorities of the city break up these organizations? Can they penetrate into the headquarters of them and find the leaders and agents? It is probable that there are few of the killers who are not known to the police of Chicago and other cities . . . arrests can be made, they are made, but what proof can be brought in with them? The criminals believe that it cannot be done, or that it will not be done. . . .
>
> The butchering of seven men by open daylight raises this question for Chicago: Is it helpless?

Al Capone came storming back to Chicago in May. Capone's man Pasqualino Lolordo, head of the Unione Siciliana, had been murdered, as had his predecessor Antonio Lombardo nine months earlier. Capone gave a dinner in his Hawthorne Inn headquarters for Joseph Guinta, who had succeeded Lolordo. As the dinner was ending, his gunmen jerked Guinta, John Scalise, and Albert Anselmi to their feet and held them fast. Capone, raging, accused the trio of plotting to kill him, threw wine in their faces, then grabbed a baseball bat ready for the occasion and pounded the helpless accused traitors until they crumpled and dropped to the floor. They were then dragged away, Capone pursuing the lifeless bodies to land final blows. They were found the day following near the Indiana state line, knifed and shot.

*   *   *

The *Tribune* increasingly blamed national Prohibition and the Volstead Act for abetting the evil situation in which organized gangs amassed vast war chests, enabling them to corrupt public officials, law enforcement officers, and judges. In the days when gangsters like Big Jim Colosimo depended on vice and gambling, their powers and ability to corrupt were limited; in the Prohibition era there appeared to be no limit. In 1928, the paper, estimating that Capone controlled well over $100 million of revenue a year, pointed out that all freedoms and all aspects of economic welfare were threatened. As astonishing as this amount must have seemed to most readers, it was quite close to the figures that subsequent investigations disclosed. A year later, in 1929, the *Tribune* published an estimate of the Employers Association of Chicago that 91 different kinds of rackets had developed in the city, costing inhabitants $136 million a year, a figure which, according to the Chicago Crime Commission, reached $200 million by 1931. By seizing control of labor unions, Capone men could control business as well. Scores of honest businessmen were being forced to pay "protection."

The paper had fought supposedly law-abiding predators of great wealth for decades and expected to continue doing so. But now the concentration of money and power in the hands of admitted outlaws presented an even greater threat, since illicit liquor and beer profits enabled Capone to become greater than the most powerful monopolist before him. When President-elect Herbert Hoover, answering critics of Prohibition, called it "a noble experiment," the *Tribune* replied sharply: "More of Volstead merely will be more of what we have, growing worse as the experiment, no longer noble, continues."

The *Tribune* consistently attacked the dry forces, especially the Anti-Saloon League, which it charged with bribing and corrupting Congress in the same ways monopolists had bribed and corrupted Congress, city councils, and state legislatures in other days. Earlier, when the *New York World* asserted that many congressmen were on the payroll of the Anti-Saloon League, the *Tribune* agreed: "The facts constitute one of the outstanding scandals of the year," it said. "It remains for someone to discover just how many congressmen are paid to vote dry, how much they get and who they are."

In a later editorial, the *Tribune* answered a correspondent who recalled that the paper had denounced brewers and distillers back in 1917:

> The *Tribune* was the first metropolitan newspaper, if not the first of all American newspapers to expel liquor advertisements from its pages. [*Yet,*] the paper did not believe in prohibition. It advocated effective control by the states, with effective control of interstate transport by the federal government. It did not believe in the efficacy or propriety of federal prohibition, but it did not oppose the experiment. . . . In this course, the *Tribune* was mistaken. If it had foreseen more clearly the results of the experiment, if it had considered the constitutional issues involved more thoroughly, it would have fought with all its power against the adoption of the prohibition amendment. But, like most Americans, the *Tribune* was preoccupied with the great war and its editors were in the army. It preferred to wait, though not with confidence in the results. We waited until the conditions created by prohibition convinced us that it was a major error of American policy.

Colonel McCormick's determination to talk with President Hoover about the Capone situation did not necessarily indicate that he placed any great reliance upon the new Republican leader. The *Tribune* had given his campaign only half-hearted support, and while Arthur Sears Henning was writing the report of Hoover's inaugural address that soggy March 4 in 1929, he was astounded to receive a telegram: "THIS MAN WON'T DO. MCCORMICK." But the Colonel felt he had to talk with someone in Washington, since he had become convinced that Capone and the other big-time gangsters could be successfully attacked by nothing less than the power of the federal government.

McCormick was not alone in his desire to place the woes of Chicago before President Hoover and to urge action against Al Capone. He had spoken to Judge Lyle of his plan, and Lyle worked closely with Frank Loesch. According to President Hoover's recollection, in March, 1929, he saw a committee of Chicago businessmen headed by Loesch and Walter Strong, publisher of the *Chicago Daily News*. The names of the other committee members are not recorded. The committee wanted the attorney general to act against Capone. Hoover informed them that federal action was limited to income tax and Prohibition violations.

On April 8, George Akerson, secretary to the president, sent McCormick a telegram at his vacation home in Aiken, North Carolina. "THE PRESIDENT WOULD LIKE TO HAVE YOU STAY AT THE WHITE HOUSE SUNDAY AND MONDAY. IF THAT IS NOT CONVENIENT HE WOULD LIKE TO HAVE YOU TAKE LUNCHEON WITH HIM SUNDAY AT ONE O'CLOCK." Hoover's engagement book indicates that McCormick "and 3" joined him for lunch on Sunday, April 14, and that on Wednesday, April 17, the president canceled three appointments to make time for McCormick. At the

April 17 meeting, McCormick recalled, he urged the president to send the Treasury Department after Capone. The gangster, in his ostentatious manner of living, clearly spent vast sums. Agents of the Internal Revenue Service and special Treasury agents could determine whether Capone had reported and paid taxes on the income he obviously had received. He could be prosecuted for income tax violations since charges based on the Volstead Act could not be made to stick.

Colonel McCormick communicated the results of his meeting to Judge Lyle and members of the Secret Six, including Col. Robert Isham Randolph. President Hoover had instructed Secretary of the Treasury Andrew Mellon to go after Capone with his Treasury agents. There would be a two-pronged attack: Special Prohibition agent Eliot Ness and his men would set about wrecking Capone's bootlegging operations while Elmer Irey, chief of the enforcement branch of the U.S. Treasury, would build a tax case against the gangster. Ness and his agents had plenty of experience in busting up stills and speakeasies, and Irey had a precedent in the 1927 Supreme Court decision in the Sullivan income tax evasion case. If Irey prepared his case against Capone properly, conviction was assured. Once Irey and Ness began their attack, it would be only a matter of time.

Judge Lyle wrote that the Secret Six subsequently gave Irey $75,000 to assist in the work of investigating Capone. Some of the money, Lyle recalled, was spent in the card games running in Capone's headquarters at the Lexington. Irey had recruited an out-of-town agent he called Pat O'Rourke, alias Mike Malone, alias Michael Lepito, who posed as an Eastern gunman. O'Rourke took a room in the Lexington and became acquainted with Capone's men. The investigation moved ahead, time passed, but Hoover did not forget his promise to McCormick and Strong. Each morning at the medicine ball exercise session in the White House, Irey told Lyle, the president would ask Secretary Mellon, "Have you got that fellow Capone yet?" And, when the exercise ended, Hoover would admonish Mellon as he departed: "Remember now, I want that man Capone in jail."

*   *   *

There were bleak days ahead for the country, the Republican party, Chicago, and the *Tribune*. Throughout 1929 rumbled warnings that the wild financial speculation in which the country was engaged could only end in panic. The Federal Reserve Board had resorted to an easy money policy in 1927 to head off a new recession and to attract foreign gold. Stock market gambling raged, there was a fantastic land boom in Florida, and in Chicago thousands of people from charwomen and shoeshine boys to corporation presidents bought on margin, bought dime and dollar stocks, bought shares in the Insull utilities, bought bonds on the new

apartment buildings—bought anything that looked like a stock certificate
or a bond. There were groaning creaks along Wall Street in the spring
and summer and a sharp fall on October 24, "Black Thursday."

The *Tribune's* first report was optimistic. "STEM 12,880,900 SHARE
RUN," said the paper's banner of October 25. "Record Slump Checked:
Key Stocks Rally." O. A. "Cotton" Mather, the paper's financial editor,
said Chicago stock prices were "nervous." He also quoted bankers and
investment analysts who found reason to be hopeful, but the expected
rally did not occur. On Tuesday, October 29, 1929, there was another
precipitous drop, the worst ever in the history of Wall Street. The markets
continued to plunge until nearly 50 percent of values had been lost.
President Hoover undertook steps to halt the general panic following the
stock losses, presenting many ideas subsequently adopted by President
Franklin Roosevelt, but in the opinion of much of the public and much of
the Eastern press, Hoover could do nothing right. The country was soon
caught in the worst and most extended depression in its history. Jobs
vanished, small and large businesses closed, many businessmen ruined by
the market crash and the depressed economy committed suicide, thousands were cold and hungry during the next several winters. Except for
the Reconstruction Finance Corporation, established to make loans to
strapped railroads and banks, Hoover's early plans failed to get launched,
and Hoover himself, according to historian W. E. Woodward, "appeared
to be completely bewildered."

On November 10, 1929, Albert B. Fall, secretary of the interior under
President Harding, was sentenced to a year in jail and fined $100,000 for
his part in the Teapot Dome oil lease scandal. The *Tribune* considered this
one of the worst crimes in American history, noting that Fall was "the first
member of a President's cabinet to be found guilty . . . for a crime
involving his official position and duty." The paper blamed Harding and
"the entire Ohio gang." For good measure, it also blamed the Anti-Saloon
League, which had its headquarters at Westerville, Ohio. The League,
said the *Tribune,*

> had produced a school of politics which perfumed rascality with the odor of
> sanctity which found protection in the political pew. . . . This scheme of
> combining the lip service of religion with the expert use of burglar tools had
> the approval of Ohio moralists and prohibitionists, because it enabled them
> to use the politicians for the one purpose they had in mind, the coercion of
> government. . . . These considerations may be taken into account in the case
> of Mr. Fall, the only cabinet minister ever convicted of a crime committed in
> office.

Tribune editorial writers did not always succeed in capturing Colonel
McCormick's ideas, as expressed in cryptic notes and telephone calls
when he was out of town. The theory that Fall's troubles arose from

Anti-Saloon League contamination must have astonished the former interior secretary as much as the prison sentence itself.

*   *   *

On a warm June day in 1930, a round-faced, curly-haired Chicago police reporter of middling age and height tucked the *Racing Form* and the early afternoon papers under his arm, relit his cigar, and turned to the Randolph Street steps leading down to the Illinois Central station. Three men in a car parked near the entrance on Michigan Avenue waved to Alfred "Jake" Lingle, one calling out, "Don't forget Schneider in the third!" Jake grinned. "I got him," he answered; then he went down the steps, headed for the race special to Washington Park. A trim, tall blond man followed him. Lingle had reported a few minutes earlier to Police Sgt. Tom Alcock, "I'm being tailed," but he seemed unconcerned now. He loved the races and was free for the afternoon. As the *Tribune*'s street expert on crime, Jake Lingle had had a busy week—at least one shooting every night, holdups, and a kidnapping. Earlier that afternoon, Lingle called J. Loy "Pat" Maloney, day city editor of the *Tribune*, to see if anything was doing, and the answer was negative. But both of them knew that wherever Lingle might be something could be doing—at the track, at Postl's where he had been working out lately, and in the gang hangouts that Jake haunted by night. Lingle had never written a line for the *Tribune* since joining the staff in 1912, but the information he supplied was superb.

Lingle was born and went to elementary school in a West Side area called "The Valley," where many of the hoodlums prominent in the postwar years grew up. He played semiprofessional baseball and was office boy in a surgical supply house before he got an office boy job in the *Tribune* editorial department. He knew policemen as well as hoodlums from his school and baseball days, chummed with them as a *Tribune* copy boy, and was known in police stations and the cheaper gambling joints. He brought in tips to the newsroom and finally was put on the street as a police reporter, specializing in the private detective bureaus. Soon he became one of James Keeley's most effective informants.

When Keeley departed, Beck retained Lingle, turning him over to the new city editor, Robert M. Lee, who found Jake's knowledge of the rising gang chiefs fascinating and highly useful and his horse race sense, to hear Lingle tell it, uncanny. Lingle usually knew where a story was going to break and, most important, when. These were qualities Lee prized as much as Keeley, so that sometimes reporter Lingle went on vacation trips with his city editor, an unusual occurrence in the newspaper business. Lingle, a man of mystery among his fellow newsmen, lived well for a $65-a-week police reporter, betting as much as $1,000 on a single horse race. In addition to the family home on the West Side, he had a summer home in Long Beach, Indiana, and a suite at the Stevens Hotel. According to Al, as his oldest friends called him, or Jake, as he was known professionally, he had received a $50,000 inheritance from his father's estate. Other times he said that he had made a bundle in the bull market, some stocks he had bought tripling in value. Yet frequently he was reduced to borrowing from his colleagues. Now and then, but not often, Lingle provided profitable tips on the market to a favored friend or a superior, implying that he got the information from a wealthy investor. If the market was up when the friend sold, Lingle brought him his profit, in cash; sometimes, of course, the market went down.

There was no doubt that Lingle could provide excellent news stories and tips despite the fact that Big Bill Thompson ordered his staff to give the *Tribune* nothing. After William Russell was made police commissioner, Lingle's pipeline to the most interesting City Hall stories was excellent, since Russell was a good friend and sometimes sat in on meetings of Thompson's cabinet. What Lingle could not get in the way of crime beats from Russell he got through another friend, Al Capone, whom he had known since the days when Capone was one of Torrio's pimps. Capone, like Lingle, enjoyed playing the races. It was said that Capone had given Lingle a diamond-studded belt estimated to be worth more than $1,000 as a mark of his high esteem.

With Capone and Russell in power, Jake Lingle had a monopoly on major crime news, unless the hoodlums were not under Capone persuasion. His news tips were always accurate, and usually first, so that, as in the Keeley days, the *Tribune* would often have a reporter and photographer on the scene when the news began to happen. Many of his *Tribune* colleagues believed that Lingle got his information directly from Capone. Scarface Al could not, however, have been the source of Lingle's racing tips. One of Lingle's first front-page stories on Al Capone, unsigned, said the gangster had lost an estimated $1 million on the races since coming to Chicago.

The tall, blond young man caught up with Lingle in a space between the hurrying noontime crowds in the middle of the IC underpass. There was a single shot from his .38 police special, striking Lingle behind the left ear. The assailant dropped his gun and fled through the crowd toward Randolph Street. He jostled a woman whose angry husband pursued him up the steps, where he disappeared into the traffic. Dr. Joseph Springer, who knew Lingle and had been walking a few steps ahead of him, turned at hearing the shot and rushed to Jake's aid. The newsman was dead. It was the 11th Chicago murder in ten days.

The afternoon papers had the jolting story in big headlines, and the *Tribune* banner on June 10 covered the second-day aspects of the murder

that shook Chicago and reverberated around the country: "OFFER
$30,000 FOR ASSASSIN." Said the *Tribune* story:

> Alfred J. Lingle, better known in the world of newspaper work as Jake
> Lingle, and for the last 18 years a reporter for the *Tribune,* was shot to death
> yesterday in the Illinois Central subway at the east side of Michigan Boule-
> vard at Randolph Street.
>
> The *Tribune* offers $25,000 as a reward for information which will lead to
> the conviction of the slayer or slayers. . . . An additional reward of $5,000
> was announced by the *Chicago Evening Post.* The Press Club of Chicago
> issued a statement it stood ready to pay a reward of $10,000.

The *Tribune,* the other newspapers of Chicago, and newspapers
generally throughout the country termed the murder of Jake Lingle an
assault on the press to punish it for carrying out attacks on gangdom and
racketeering and to deter it from further such revelations. The Chicago
newspapers were united in their defiance. On June 11, the *Tribune*
announced that the *Chicago Herald and Examiner,* its arch rival, had posted
a $25,000 reward for information leading to the conviction of the Lingle
killer or killers, putting the story under its banner: "$55,000 PRICE ON
KILLER." The Press Club's emotional pledge evidently had not been
taken seriously. Most of Chicago pledged aid, although there was silence
from the mayor's office. But Police Commissioner Russell, probably
Lingle's closest friend, declared, "I'd give my two eyes to solve the murder
of Al Lingle." And Deputy Commissioner John P. Stege, known to Judge
Lyle and the Secret Six as Chicago's most fearless and honest cop, was
quoted: "I knew Lingle for ten years. He was honest and courageous and
with greater knowledge of the underworld than any [*other*] man known to
me." Frank J. Loesch, now president of the newly formed Chicago Crime
Commission, State's Attorney Swanson, and U.S. District Attorney
George E. Q. Johnson each promised special efforts to solve the case and
to make it clear that the gangsters had at last gone too far. "UNITED
WAR ON GANGS" proclaimed the *Tribune:*

> The meaning of the murder is plain. It was committed in reprisal and in
> attempt at intimidation. Mr. Lingle was a police reporter and an exception-
> ally well informed one. His personal friends included the highest police
> officials. . . . What made him valuable to this newspaper made him dan-
> gerous to his killers.
>
> The *Tribune* accepts this challenge. It is war. There will be casualties, but
> that is to be expected, it being war. The *Tribune* has the support of the other
> Chicago newspapers. . . . The challenge of crime in the community must be
> accepted. . . . Justice will make a fight, or it will abdicate.

Fred Fuller Sheed, editor of the *Philadelphia Bulletin* and president of
the American Society of Newspaper Editors, declared, "It is our duty and

that of the entire newspaper profession to answer this challenge and to stand beside the *Chicago Tribune*." In Los Angeles, Harry Chandler, publisher of the *Los Angeles Times* and president of the American Newspaper Publishers Association, called Lingle "a first line soldier" who had fallen in the war on crime. "The nation's press will support the *Tribune* and the people of Chicago not only to capture and punish the killers but to permanently end the conditions which made the atrocity possible."

Never was the war on the gangs pressed more fiercely by united enforcement officials. Al Capone himself got involved, sending word to State's Attorney Swanson that he, Capone, was innocent and wanted to prove it by aiding in the search for the Lingle killers. Later it was reported that 50 men Capone had assigned to find clues had come up empty-handed. Colonel McCormick assigned a staff of reporters and Charles F. Rathbun, a *Tribune* attorney and the Colonel's favorite investigative attorney, to work on the case under State's Attorney Swanson's direction.

The investigators learned unpleasant truths, which appeared under a banner line in the *Tribune* on June 29, 1930: "LINGLE'S MONEY DEALS BARED. BANK DEPOSITS AND RACE TRACK CHECKS LISTED." The lead story told of the records in banks used by Lingle. His inheritance was $500, not $50,000 as he had claimed, and he had lost it in the stock market debacle of 1929. But, on his $65-a-week salary from the *Tribune*, he had continued to bank thousands of dollars. The paper published the complete list of Lingle's bank deposits and checks, and it detailed his payment for the home in Long Beach. The story revealed how Lingle used his friendship with Capone and with Commissioner Russell to serve as middleman for those who desired privileges such as opening illicit enterprises, or wanted policemen and police captains transferred. In some gangland areas Lingle was known as "the unofficial police chief of Chicago." City editor Robert M. Lee was assigned the task of explaining how Lingle kept this secret life and power from the paper, which pointed out that it had never ceased to attack Capone and the gangs. Lee's story was written in almost telegraphic style:

> During his 18 year career, Lingle worked under four city editors. A newspaper is the least likely to hear bad news about its own. During the 18 years there was no lack of accuracy, nor did he ever show lack of zeal for his work. Prior to the gangster era Lingle worked with detective agencies for stories. He knew Colosimo and Torrio. He had an easy and pleasant affability. Much has been made of the diamond studded belt Lingle wore. . . .

Lee went on to say that when Lingle was asked about evidence of wealth he claimed to have inherited the money. The now-famous belt was indeed from Al Capone, probably costing the gangster $300, not

$1,000—but still a big item in Depression days. Lingle only grinned when he was questioned by his curious friends, said Lee, and kept his life "mysterious." He had furnished materials for columns exposing Capone and his gangsters. He was a frequent borrower in the office. "Now it is known," Lee wrote, "that Lingle had deals with Police Commissioner Russell."

City editor Lee's explanation appeared one day, the *Tribune*'s editorial the next, June 30:

> When Alfred Lingle was murdered the motive seemed to be apparent. He was a *Tribune* reporter and when he was shot, the newspaper saw no other explanation than that his killers either thought he was close to information dangerous to them, or intended the murder to serve as notice given the newspapers that crime was ruler in Chicago. It could be both, a murder to prevent a disclosure and to give warning against attempts by others. . . .
>
> Alfred Lingle now takes a different character, one in which he was unknown to the management of the *Tribune* while he was alive. He is dead and cannot defend himself but many facts now revealed must now be accepted as eloquent against him. He was not and could not have been a great reporter. His ability did not contain these possibilities. He did not write stories, but could get information in police circles. He was not and could not be influential in the acts of his newspaper, but he could be useful and honest and that is what the *Tribune* management took him to be. . . .
>
> The murder of this reporter, even for racketeering reasons, as the evidence indicates it may have been, made a breach in the wall which criminality has long maintained about its operations here. Sometime, somewhere a hole may be found and the Lingle murder may prove to be it.

Police Commissioner Russell resigned when the story of his deals with Lingle appeared. Even John Stege took a leave—to work on the case in his own way, he said. There was terror in the *Tribune* news department as the wrath of Col. Robert R. McCormick was felt. McCormick had stood up for his man as long as he believed him innocent. Now he ordered staffwide investigations. He stormed into the news department to let executives know that each would be held responsible for the correct behavior of his subordinates. McCormick assigned his personal aide, West Point graduate Maxwell M. Corpening, to keep an eye on things in the news department, and the Colonel himself took a small office in the area but rarely visited it. McCormick trusted Corpening, who was without doubt totally honest, but he also lacked knowledge concerning the operations of a news department. His task was to determine why no one suspected Lingle and whether others were involved. In addition to investigative attorney Rathbun, McCormick assigned Daniel Deininger, the controller, to check out the financial affairs of editors who dealt directly with Lingle. Pat Maloney, characteristically, was able to account for every nickel he had received in the newspaper business. Another editor was heavily in debt. Deininger, like Corpening, cleared the staff members he checked. Yet now the *Herald and Examiner* began to suggest in print a possible coverup, angering McCormick. On July 6, he wrote State's Attorney Swanson: *"We have given every assistance in our power and through the endorsements on the paychecks of Lingle found where he had been banking and with the public spirited cooperation of the bank secured . . . the clue which will capture his murderer. . . . It is natural that during such an investigation a multitude of rumors, some of them imagined, should have arisen, some of them very definite and strongly supported. In fact the names of certain suspects have been provided."*

McCormick's order to the editorial staff was to publish all the facts brought up in the investigation. John Boettiger, the reporter who had been first on the scene following the slaying of Lingle, led the force engaged in the probe and subsequently wrote a book about it. Boettiger had found $1,400 currency in Lingle's pocket and turned it in, a somewhat unique development in a Chicago murder case and an act commending him for the investigative job.

Some of the news about Lingle was benign. He had received stock market tips from Arthur S. Cutten, one of Chicago's most successful investors, since Cutten knew Lingle from good work in a burglary case. Intruders had trussed up Cutten and left him to die. Lingle, first reporter on the scene, helped to free him and then followed through on the case until the culprits were captured. Cutten had been grateful. A few *Tribune* men had profited on the tips, together with Lingle, but, in the end, Lingle was wiped out on the market's Black Thursday like everyone else.

There was no finding that the *Tribune* had withheld news of gangster activity at any time. Harry Brundige, a writer for the *St. Louis Morning Star,* came to Chicago to conduct an investigation and named several newsmen who had been receiving money for moonlighting in public relations jobs, some mob-controlled. The *Tribune* published Brundige's series because, the *Herald and Examiner* asserted, no *Tribune* men were named. The *Tribune*'s rejoinder was obvious: None was named because no one was involved except Lingle. Brundige interviewed Al Capone, among others, and established that Lingle was, indeed, a friend of Capone's "right up to the day he died." "How many reporters are on your payroll?" Brundige asked. "Plenty," Capone was said to have responded. When the *Tribune* and the *Morning Star* published the stories, Capone said Brundige was lying.

Concerned that the outlaws had managed to infest even the newspapers, *Tribune* city editor Lee called Judge Lyle to ask if some means could be found in the law to move against the mobsters, including Al Capone. Lyle knew federal agents were working toward that objective, but their

success was far from certain. Lyle went to his law books and came up with
a simple but effective method of harassment: the vagrancy law. Gangsters
arrested by the police and brought before Lyle could be sent to jail for
having no visible means of support. The seemingly petty legal stratagem
not only would enable Judge Lyle and the police to arrest the gangsters, it
would also force the crooks to go on record about their earnings. Vagrancy warrants for Frank Nitti, Capone's chief executioner, and Jake
Guzik, his business manager, wrote Lyle, "would place them in the same
sort of cross-fire I visualized for their chief."

*   *   *

While Lyle proceeded with plans to pester leading underworld figures,
progress was being made in the Lingle case. The government's secret
agent, Pat O'Rourke, living in the Lexington Hotel, overheard Al Capone
tell Jake Guzik that he knew the real murderer and had no intention of
betraying him. Others were convinced that Capone was behind the
killing. In October, 1930, Rathbun, Patrick T. Roche, chief investigator
for State's Attorney Swanson, and the police hired a former bank robber
and small-time crook named John Hagan to join the informers prowling
gangland. Hagan, through another hoodlum named Pat Hogan, came up
with a lead. A thug called Leo Bader was rumored in the underworld to
have been Lingle's killer. He needed money and wanted a partner for a
bank robbery attempt. On December 21, Patrick Roche, Rathbun, four
police detectives, and John Boettiger raided the Lake Crest Drive apartments and seized Bader. He was tall and blond, and his real name was
Leo Vincent Brothers. He had come to Chicago from St. Louis, where he
was a member of the "Egan's Rats" gang and was wanted on several
charges, including murder.

Brothers was indicted for the murder of Lingle. Arraigned before
Chief Justice John P. McGoorty in Criminal Court, he stood mute. The
Tribune was satisfied that Hagan had come up with the right man and paid
him the promised $25,000 reward. Other newspapers were skeptical.
Why Brothers? What was his motive? Over the years police reporters
would come to know that a gunman wanted for murder in one town
would hire out for a "hit" in another without having a motive and without
knowing the identity of his victim. He would simply be provided with a
description and the movements of his man, and possibly someone he
did not know would "finger" the doomed victim. Thus Brothers, hot in
St. Louis, might have killed a man in Chicago on contract without
knowing who the target was, why the man was to be killed, or even who
paid for the murder.

However, the case against Brothers was not conclusive. Of 14 witnesses, seven positively identified Brothers as the man seen fleeing from

the IC tunnel; seven did not. He was prosecuted by a young assistant state's attorney, C. Wayland Brooks, in a trial lasting from March 16 to April 2, 1931, and the jurors, out 27 hours, took the unusual step of recommending a 14-year prison sentence when they found Brothers guilty. Normally, the death sentence would have been demanded. Brothers had not taken the stand and had not talked. Told after sentencing that he might be freed in six years for good behavior, he finally broke his silence. "I can do that standing on my head," he observed. He served ten years and died in 1950.

There were angry articles in rival newspapers, especially the *Herald and Examiner,* and the analysis of the Lingle case has continued since in books and magazine articles. John Boettiger discounted one theory, that the man who called to Lingle, "Don't forget Schneider in the third," was actually fingering him for the killer. Boettiger said the young man was a respectable bank employee who liked to play the races. Four months after Brothers was in prison, Mike "de Pike" Heitler, a former Capone brothel manager, was gunned down. He had left a note with his daughter, which was to be given to Patrick Roche if Heitler should be killed, as Al Capone had threatened. The note stated that eight gunmen conspired to kill Lingle, acting on Capone's orders.

*   *   *

Using a Chicago Crime Commission publication as a guide, Judge Lyle had drawn up plans to issue vagrancy warrants for 28 of Chicago's most vicious gangsters, called "public enemies" by Col. Henry Barrett Chamberlin, operating director of the crime commission. Heading the list was Al Capone. Detective Roy Van Herik, a fearless, street-wise policeman, appeared before Judge Lyle to swear that "Alphonse Capone, alias Scarface Al Capone," was an idle and dissolute person. "I signed the vagrancy warrant and instructed Van Herik to proceed forthwith to arrest the mob chief," said Lyle. The presses began to roll. "Scarface Al Capone, Public Enemy No. 1, sought for vagrancy," the *Tribune* reported. Other vagrants were similarly named: Nitti; Guzik; Machine Gun Jack McGurn, suspected in the St. Valentine's Day Massacre; Joe Aiello, pretender to Capone's throne and said to be Chicago's toughest gangster; Frank McErlane, sadistic killer; Frank Maritote (alias Diamond), mobster and kidnapper; Frank Rio, Capone bodyguard; Edward "Spike" O'Donnell, bootlegger; George "Red" Barker and Three-Fingered Jack White, labor racketeers. At the suggestion of James Doherty, *Tribune* reporter, and Orville Dwyer, another Chicago newspaperman, Lyle and Chamberlin nominated 35 more public enemies, and Judge Lyle issued warrants for them as well.

The results, though not permanent—except for Joe Aiello, whose new prominence got him 50 steel-jacketed bullets into his body—were seemingly miraculous. The previously glamorized whoremongers, bootleggers, thugs, and killers were now hounded as bums without visible means of support, and if they attempted to prove they had incomes Treasury agents beset them for tax evasion. The gang chiefs, possessing big money they could not explain, fled to the Wisconsin woods and to Florida, but only to discover that the federal law could reach across all 48 states. The government men, soon called "G-men," were genuinely feared. They could be neither bought nor intimidated.

In June, 1931, Elmer Irey was ready with the income tax cases prepared against Capone, Nitti, and Guzik. Capone was the first to go to trial. Irey told Lyle that Capone emissaries had offered him $1,500,000 to drop the action, but in such a way that he could not press bribery charges. The Capone income tax case, however, was solid. The federal grand jury returned indictments charging that Capone failed to pay $215,030.48 on income totaling $1,038,654.84 over a five-year period. The government was so fearful any Chicago jury would be bribed or intimidated into freeing the gangster that for a time a plea bargaining arrangement was considered, whereby Capone would plead guilty and receive two and a half years in prison. Federal Judge James H. Wilkerson rejected the arrangement and ordered Capone to trial. U.S. Attorney George E. Q. Johnson conducted the government's case, assisted by Dwight H. Green. During 11 days in October, the story of Capone's life-style was described by tradesmen and government undercover men: his living expenses, his $35 shirts, $15 silk underwear, $150 suits, the $3,000 in telephone bills for his Florida home. The defense contended that Capone had not willfully violated the law—he simply had not known that revenue from illegal enterprise was taxable! The gangster was found guilty, sentenced to 11 years in prison, fined $50,000, and ordered to pay court costs of $30,000. Public Enemy No. 1 at last was retired from the Chicago scene, and his chiefs, Nitti and Guzik, soon followed him to federal prison on similar charges.

Colonel McCormick promised Dwight Green, assistant prosecutor of Capone, and C. Wayland Brooks, prosecutor of Leo Brothers, that they would have the support of the *Chicago Tribune* should they choose political careers. A more enticing invitation to public service would be hard to imagine. Despite Democratic landslides in the years ahead, Green was elected Republican governor of Illinois (1941–49), and Brooks Republican U.S. senator (1940–49).

*   *   *

From time to time, ever since the end of the war, readers would write to the *Tribune* chiding it because, they said, the Stephen Decatur toast to patriotism used in its editorial flag was irrationally chauvinistic. Whenever such a letter appeared in print, the public was reassured that Decatur's immortal words would never disappear from the *Tribune*. But they did. On June 24, 1931, words from an address by Col. Robert R. McCormick were substituted, and they have remained in the paper's editorial flag ever since:

> THE NEWSPAPER is an institution developed by modern civilization to present the news of the day, to foster commerce and industry, to inform and lead public opinion, and to furnish that check upon government which no constitution has ever been able to provide.

These were the words of a man about to prove that the era of personal journalism was far from ended.

THE FIGHT
FOR A FREE PRESS

22

While the fight against Capone raged on, it appeared that the *Tribune* had crushed another hateful enemy, Mayor William Hale Thompson. Victory had come on June 20, 1928, when Circuit Court Judge Hugo Friend ruled in the "expert fees" cases that the paper had filed more than seven years before. Mayor Thompson, George Harding, now Cook County treasurer, and Michael Faherty, president of the Board of Local Improvements, were ordered to repay to the City of Chicago $2,245,604 wrongfully paid out in a conspiracy to divert taxpayer money to Thompson's political machine and certain of his followers. In nearly two years of legal motions and trial, the court had heard more than 100 witnesses, had recorded 11,000 pages of testimony, and had inspected 3,000 exhibits. Judge Friend found that the so-called experts not only were unqualified, but they increased their appraisals on property the city contemplated buying or condemning in order to boost their fees, which were fixed on a percentage basis. In addition, Judge Friend ruled, there were fake names on the city payrolls, allowing workers to pocket as much as $1,500 a day, so long as they remitted part of the money to the mayor's political machine.

Big Bill became hysterical when he learned of the decision. "They've ruined me!" he wailed. "They're going to take everything I've got! The sons-of-bitches have ruined me!" Harding, a man of wealth, quickly scheduled $3 million in real estate to provide bond covering an appeal for himself and Thompson. The mayor, however, was not comforted. He broke down mentally and physically, drank excessively, spoke irrationally, called old friends by wrong names, and finally was led off to the estate of trusted friend Carter Blatchford, in northern Wisconsin, for a long rest. There Thompson slowly recovered his health, while corporation counsel Sam Ettelson served as unofficial mayor.

In September, Thompson returned to Chicago, tanned and fit and momentarily quiet. He told John Dienhart, of the *Herald and Examiner,* that he intended to clean up and rebuild Chicago, but he dodged other newsmen. He expressed pleasure when President Coolidge signed a $300 million Mississippi flood control measure, which he and the *Tribune* both supported, yet he remained listless and shunned publicity. Even in the spring of 1930, when Ruth Hanna McCormick, the widow of Medill McCormick, announced that she would challenge Sen. Charles Deneen for the Republican senatorial nomination, Thompson made no move. When she defeated Deneen, the mayor's advisers pointed out that he could now take vengeance on the *Tribune* by announcing for the Democratic contender, James Hamilton Lewis. But Big Bill, who had no liking for the diminutive, pink-whiskered former senator, declined to act.

On October 23, 1930, came the news Thompson had been awaiting. The *Tribune*'s victory in the expert fees cases, it turned out, was temporary. Michael Faherty had entered a separate appeal from Judge Friend's ruling. The Illinois Supreme Court absolved Faherty of all conspiracy charges, holding that he had not received any of the misused money personally and that the experts who had contributed to the Thompson organization had a legal right to do so. Two days later the court issued a similar ruling in the appeal of Thompson and Harding. "Truth crushed to earth shall rise again!" cried the jubilant mayor as he permitted himself a highball with his friends. "I'm ready to go now!"

Time was short. Thompson dictated a speech he intended to make at the Apollo Theater in announcing his support of Lewis. When Ettelson learned the nature of the charges Big Bill intended to hurl at Colonel McCormick and the *Tribune,* he urged him to change his mind. Thompson persisted. At 11:45 A.M. on the day of the proposed theater appearance, he was felled in his hotel room by an appendicitis attack but refused to be taken to a hospital until Richard Wolfe, his flamboyant commissioner of public works and composer of his theme song, "America First, Last and Always!" promised he would read the speech. Then the mayor was put into an ambulance and hauled to Passavant Hospital, while vehicles bearing signs and shouters with megaphones rolled through the city announcing that Mayor Thompson would pay his respects to the *Chicago Tribune* at the Lewis meeting in the Apollo that night.

Mayor Thompson underwent surgery at 1:00 P.M. and was found to be suffering from peritonitis, an inflammation of the abdominal wall. His speech, read by Wolfe as the mayor's "deathbed statement," was a wild, rambling diatribe that no paper published in full. It accused the *Tribune* of responsibility for the assassination of President Lincoln, charged the paper's managers with plotting the death of Thompson himself, attacked Colonel McCormick personally, and generally recapitulated most of the allegations Thompson and his spokesmen had aired over the years.

The Thompson precinct machinery creaked into operation. Workers swept through the South Side wards, where they were expected to turn the black vote to Lewis. Thompson, recovering, was certain he had given a mortal blow to the *Tribune* and ordered his speech printed and sold to the public at 10¢ a copy. The *Tribune* ignored the charges but respectfully covered the mayor's illness in detail. When his recovery became a probability, it suggested that his support was a burden not even J. Ham Lewis deserved.

The *Tribune* gave Ruth Hanna McCormick headlines throughout the campaign, but its editorial endorsement was restrained. Mrs. McCormick, conceded the paper regretfully, was a dry, as was Mrs. Lottie O'Neill, the independent candidate supported by the Anti-Saloon League. Lewis was dripping wet. "The *Tribune* does not consider Mrs. McCormick's position on prohibition as correct as that of Mr. Lewis," it said. "In other respects, the *Tribune* does not find Mr. Lewis as well qualified as Mrs. McCormick." But the voters of Illinois elected J. Hamilton Lewis by a plurality of 720,000 votes. "COUNTRY GOES DEMOCRATIC" said the headline on Wednesday, November 5. The *Tribune* could find no salvage until final returns showed that its friend and ally Judge John H. Lyle had been reelected to the Municipal Court, carrying three Republican judicial candidates with him. Later, a comforting analysis was evolved. The election, said the paper, was a revolt against Prohibition, and it also indicated support of the position the *Tribune* had adopted as its sixth plank for a better Chicago: "End the Reign of Gangdom." Upon further reflection, the paper added that hereafter the Democrats, having accepted Thompson's support, would have to bear the odium of Thompsonism: "It is a burden no party can carry. Thompson is a 100 percent liability." This conclusion was deduced from the report that Lewis had failed to carry the black neighborhoods after Thompson's representatives had made a special appeal there.

The following spring, Mayor Thompson, fully recovered, vowed that he would become Chicago's mayor yet once more. But his enemies, led by the *Tribune,* were prepared. Judge Lyle, who was putting gangsters in jail, at least for a day, or sending them scurrying, sought the Republican nomination with *Tribune* support. The Deneen Republican faction picked a city council foe of the mayor, youthful Arthur F. Albert, who entered the primary backed by the *Chicago Daily News.* Thompson charged into town from one of his frequent vacations to astonish his divided enemies with his fiery vigor. "I'm not dead yet and I'm not sick any more," Big Bill cried. "I have 250,000 loyal friends in Chicago. Dead or alive, they'll vote for me!" "Give 'em hell, Bill!" cried leaders in the estimated crowd of 5,000 men and women gathered to hear him. Big Bill, appearing fit in a neat gray suit, tan shirt, and red tie, his hair graying a bit but his jowls firm, relished the cheers. He reached for a halter on a table beside him. Swinging it, he called out, "Tell me the name of the candidate who won't take orders from a newspaper!"

"Bill Thompson," they chorused.

"Who's the man who won't wear a newspaper collar?"

"Bill Thompson!"

"Where would this cheap judge be without newspaper publicity?"

"In the sewer!"

"Where will this halter lead if Lyle's elected?" He dangled it provocatively.

"To the *Tribune*!"

Then, pretending to pick up another halter: "Here's one for Lil' Arthur. If he's elected, he'll put this halter around his neck, and where will it lead?"

"The *Daily News*!"

Throughout the campaign, Thompson ran his circuses and sideshows, using animals, barkers, and actors at noontime theater political rallies. He issued special newspapers and magazines because he said no paper would give him a fair shake, though both the *Tribune* and *Daily News* were scrupulous in reporting fully Thompson's utterances and meetings. One of his booklets was entitled, "The Tribune Shadow—Chicago's Greatest Curse." In it was a statement by Daniel A. Serritella, Thompson's city sealer, president of the Newsboys' Union, and the alleged Capone liaison man in City Hall, asserting that in 1929 Al Capone helped to prevent a strike of newspaper delivery men and that Robert R. McCormick thanked him for it.

Serritella was a "close personal friend" of Capone, according to Virgil Peterson, a careful historian of Chicago crime, and there undoubtedly was a publishers' meeting at which Serritella, as president of the newsboys, would likely be present. He evidently was accompanied by his friend the gangster chief. Serritella declared that Max Annenberg brought in Robert McCormick and introduced him to Capone. "McCormick thanked Capone for calling off the strike," his statement said. Then, according to Serritella, McCormick told Capone: "We can't help printing things about you, but I will see that the *Tribune* gives you a square deal."

McCormick's own account, for his memoirs 25 years later, recalled the meeting differently. "I arrived late," he said. "Capone brazenly had invaded the meeting with the aim of terrorizing those present. I ordered

Capone to leave, and to take his plug-uglies with him. I knew his reputation but I also knew he never killed anyone himself and I didn't think he'd start then. . . . He didn't muscle in on the newspapers. We continued to expose him." Colonel McCormick may have exaggerated his posture before the gangsters, as some of his critics have asserted. But since Capone was regularly attacked by the *Tribune* thereafter and ultimately sent to prison by strategy McCormick helped to devise, it is doubtful that the version of the meeting provided by Serritella, the longtime associate of Capone, is reliable.

Mayor Thompson defeated Judge Lyle by 70,000 votes. And now he was challenged by a thick-set, well-muscled former saloon gang leader and wily politician, Tony Cermak, president of the Cook County Board of Commissioners and new boss of the Democratic party, about whom Richard Wolfe, Thompson's chief jester, penned a song lyric: "Tony, Tony, where's your pushcart at?"

The Thompson backers who jeered at Anton Joseph Cermak soon found themselves against a superb political strategist with formidable organizing ability. The death of George Brennan had left a shattered Democratic machine, which Cermak patched up by forming an alliance with Jacob Arvey's Jewish Democrats, who controlled the 24th Ward on Chicago's West Side; Patrick Nash, the Irish leader; Edward J. Kelly, Irish too, and the power on the South Park Board; and the remnants of the Brennan crowd. Only the Sherman Hotel Democrats, who held their City Hall jobs by sufferance of the Thompson organization, failed to follow Cermak, so he simply ignored them. Cermak showed campaign skill and organizational power from the beginning, inspiring even Republicans with hope that he could eradicate Thompson. The *Tribune*'s tentative support and the disgust of the citizens generally with Thompson machine politics led most Chicagoans to welcome Tony Cermak with relief.

Almost from the day he arrived in Chicago from his mine job in Braidwood, Illinois, Cermak had been attuned to politics. For a time he drove a beer truck, calling on saloon accounts in the Bohemian neighborhood in Lawndale and supplying the 750 Czech societies, lodges, and Sokols in Chicago their club and festival needs. When Cermak learned that the clubs had problems getting the city licenses they required to serve beer and spirits, he helped organize the United Societies for Local Self-Government and in their second year of existence was elected secretary. So effective were the United Societies in obtaining licenses and keeping the town wet when local options came up that Irish and German groups were glad to join.

In 1902 Cermak was elected to the state legislature, where he voted for William Lorimer for U.S. senator. The 12th Ward sent him to the city council in 1909, and he became president of the Cook County Board in

1922. Since Big Bill Thompson dominated the Chicago scene, Cermak was content to remain "Mayor of Cook County," especially after the Thompson machine had obtained his indictment on corruption and fraud charges in 1917 while he was the chief bailiff of the Municipal Court. Cermak was acquitted, following six months of hearings. With the death of George Brennan, Cermak became chairman of the Democratic Central Committee, thus controlling the party patronage both in Chicago and the Cook County country towns. Over a period of two years, he consolidated his control of the party, being aided by the troubles of Edward J. Kelly and other Irish leaders who were indicted in connection with Sanitary District and Park District payroll scandals. Like Cermak himself in the bailiff scandal, Kelly and his associates were acquitted, but by 1931 Cermak's power was such that he was unopposed for the mayoral nomination in the Democratic primary and piled up 234,258 votes, 56,000 greater than the Dever total in 1923.

The *Tribune,* ignoring Cermak's vote for Lorimer in the past, if indeed anyone remembered, promptly announced its support for the Democrat. The paper was determined that Thompson should be driven forever from Chicago politics and mounted its most powerful political campaign since the era of Abraham Lincoln. Daily editorials sought every possible appeal to the sanity and self-interest of the voter. Civic leaders, especially Republicans, who could be induced to speak up for Cermak, were given news display, and there were daily cartoons by McCutcheon and Orr, pages of marked ballots, and columns of editorials. Alex Gottfried, Cermak's biographer, measured the support quantitatively and reported that 22 marked ballots, 297 column inches of cartoons, and 106 inches of editorials were published. These were pro-Cermak totals. The anti-Thompson display was considerably greater. Only on April 1 did the paper give up its page-one political headlines, to report that Knute Rockne, Notre Dame football coach, had been killed in an airplane crash in Kansas.

Big Bill Thompson, with only desultory support from the Hearst press, campaigned viciously, seemingly unable to realize that his flamboyant style had become obsolete. He undertook to renew the sideshows; to run against the papers and the king of England ("The *Chicago Tribune* has sold out to the king of England to get 1,200 acres of Canadian land"); to use ethnic slurs ("I won't take a back seat to that Bohunk, Chairmock, Chermack or whatever his name is"). Again and again he lambasted the paper: "The *Chicago Tribune* called Tony a horse thief—now they say, 'Elect a thief.' . . . The *Chicago Tribune,* the greatest curse Chicago has ever had . . . lies about me with dribbling idiot pictures. . . . Wrote my obituary when they thought I was dying—wouldn't they like to know how I got it? . . . Called me an international figure always on the front seat of the Great American bandwagon—not a garbage wagon like Tony." Thompson did indeed have a copy of a *Tribune* editorial that made favorable comments about him in observance of the ancient injunction, *De mortuis nil nisi bonum* (say only good of the dead). But he had lost his closest followers, including George F. Harding.

Cermak, wise and well-advised, ran a dignified campaign, promising to clean up crime, to keep politics out of the schools, and to provide jobs for unemployed Chicagoans.

On Monday, April 6, 1931, the *Tribune* pleaded with Chicagoans to "bury Thompsonism." On Tuesday, April 7, election day, it published a unique exhortation, an eight-column banner on page one: "VOTE FOR CERMAK TODAY!" Cermak polled 671,189 votes to Thompson's 476,922, and Big Bill Thompson was at last finished as a political power in Chicago, as was the Republican party, which would not elect another mayor for at least the next half-century. To insure that there would be no misunderstanding of its final appraisal of William Hale Thompson, the *Tribune* said:

> For Chicago Thompson has meant filth, corruption, obscenity, idiocy and bankruptcy. . . . He has given the city an international reputation for moronic buffoonery, barbaric crime, triumphant hoodlumism, unchecked graft, and a dejected citizenship. He nearly ruined the property and completely destroyed the pride of the city. He made Chicago a byword for the collapse of American civilization. In his attempt to continue this he excelled himself as a liar and defamer of character. He's out.
>
> He is not only out, but he is dishonored. He is deserted by his friends. He is permanently marked by the evidences of his character and conduct. His health is impaired by his ways of life and he leaves office and goes from the city the most discredited man who ever held a place in it.

*   *   *

The destruction of the Thompson machine and the imprisonment of Capone were exhilarating victories for the *Tribune* and for all who had participated in the fight against civic corruption. Rival newspapers, especially the *Chicago Daily News,* had been sturdy in the struggle against Capone, and the civic leaders, politicians, and judges who dared to oppose the gangster had literally risked their lives. William Randolph Hearst's *American* and *Herald and Examiner* supported Thompson and were with the *Tribune* only briefly in the early days of the Lingle case. Yet there was total and enduring cohesion on matters of mutual benefit. The papers had united in McCormick's campaign for a free American press; in the efforts to establish high advertising standards for newspapers, originally instituted by William Field; and in the verification procedures of the Audit Bureau of Circulations. Again in 1929, despite competition and political strife, they had joined McCormick, via the American Newspaper Publishers Association, when he led a new fight for the freedom of the press and was rewarded with a major triumph, a landmark decision in the U.S. Supreme Court.

Near v. *Minnesota* began inconspicuously when a small Minneapolis scandal sheet called the *Saturday Press* published a series of attacks on the city's police department. J. M. Near, the publisher, had been a ubiquitous gadfly stinging Minnesota officialdom for years, but usually his accounts were considered to be sensational lies and half-truths, and his paper was described in one lawsuit as a "malicious, defamatory and scandalous" publication. The Minnesota legislature passed a law providing that such a newspaper could be suppressed as a public nuisance. When Near began his highly accurate assault on the Minneapolis city government and the police, asserting that a gangster was ruling the city, the state's attorney of Hennepin County invoked the new gag law, seeking to enjoin the *Saturday Press* from publication.

Near's editors had heard of the *Chicago Tribune*'s battle against the Thompson stratagem, the libel suit by the city for $10 million. They called the attention of the *Tribune* to their plight. McCormick, too, regarded the *Saturday Press* as a scurrilous publication, but an investigation by the *Tribune*'s law firm, Kirkland, Fleming, Green, and Martin, convinced him that the principle involved in the *City of Chicago* v. *Tribune* was again at stake. If the press was not free to criticize government, there would be no freedom for anyone. McCormick retained Charles F. Rathbun of the law firm to study the legal aspects of the case. He agreed to underwrite the costs of the legal action but appealed to the Newspaper Publishers Association to join him. The association unanimously pledged its support in April, 1929, but by this time the Minnesota Supreme Court had sustained the constitutionality of the gag law. McCormick, now honorary chairman of the Freedom of the Press committee, determined to carry the cause to the U.S. Supreme Court. The *Tribune* assumed the burden of the cost, spending $35,000; the association contributed a modest $5,000.

The case was argued before the high court by Weymouth Kirkland, who drew upon the researches of Rathbun and Howard Ellis. The ruling was forthcoming on June 1, 1931. On the morning after, the *Tribune* had a banner headline: "DECISION ENDS GAG ON PRESS. MINNESOTA ACT QUASHED BY U.S. SUPREME COURT." The story was written by Arthur Sears Henning, the paper's Washington correspondent: "The United States Supreme Court handed down today (June 1) a decision that constitutes a great charter of freedom for the American press. In a five to four decision the court held unconstitutional the Minnesota law authorizing the suppression of newspapers and other periodicals publishing matter deemed by the authorities to be defamatory of public officials or other persons or institutions."

Chief Justice Charles Evans Hughes read the majority opinion, in which associate justices Oliver Wendell Holmes, Louis D. Brandeis, Harlan F. Stone, and Owen J. Roberts concurred. The majority took the position "that freedom of the press to criticize public officials is one of the bulwarks of our institutions, that for any abuse of this freedom there is adequate redress under libel and other laws." "The decision is a sweeping victory for the American press," Henning wrote. Associate Justice Pierce Butler read the dissenting opinion, with Justices Willis Van Devanter, James Clark McReynolds, and George Sutherland concurring. The dissenters in summary held that the libel laws were inadequate to restrain unscrupulous publications.

The *Tribune* published both the majority and minority opinions, noting without comment that Justice Butler was from Minnesota, where presumably he had obtained his peculiar ideas about press freedom. In its June 3 editorial, the *Tribune* covered the history of press freedom, noting that the colonial press took the first steps toward the American Revolution by challenging the right of the crown government to control the press, notably in the John Peter Zenger case in New York.

"The *Saturday Press* was not suppressed for the lies that it told," the *Tribune* said. "It was suppressed for the true stories it printed of official perfidy." Concluding, the paper referred to Thomas Jefferson's assertion, "No government ought to be without censors, and where the press is free, no one ever will."

The victory was unanimously hailed by the press of the nation, so far as the *Tribune* could discover. Colonel McCormick, "leader of the fight against the Minnesota gag law," was asked to preside at ceremonies at Monticello honoring the memory of Jefferson on October 21, 1931. Before dignitaries representing the press and government, with the gathering enlivened by the landing of an autogiro on the Monticello lawn bringing a message from President Hoover, McCormick spoke of the fight for liberty of the press:

> Our struggle for liberty was fostered by a press freed from control by our revolutionary arms. The great principles of human relationship to governments, frequently stated by revolutionary leaders, were immortalized by Thomas Jefferson in the Declaration of Independence and were further guaranteed to the citizens of the republic by the first amendment to the Constitution, the acceptance of which was made a condition precedent to the acceptance of the Constitution itself.
>
> That when the Federalist party, degenerated from its days of greatness, passed the Sedition Act to protect its corrupt members from well earned criticism, the courts should have declared the act unconstitutional is now well

understood. This the Federalist judiciary refused to do, and, harking back beyond the Declaration of Independence, assumed that royalist attitude appearing from time to time in all branches of the Washington government and one conspicuously prominent in the dissenting opinion of Near v. the State of Minnesota.

The great fight that Thomas Jefferson led against the abuses of the Sedition Act, against the corruption of the Federalist Party and the tyranny of the Federalist judiciary, ranks as high in the array of his noble achievements as the Declaration of Independence and the abolition of primogeniture. It re-established by political action that freedom which a few years before had been won by arms.

The speaker closed, quoting Jefferson: "'The fact that the liberty of the press may be abused by miscreant purveyors of scandal does not make less necessary the immunity of the press from previous restraint in dealing with official misconduct.'"

*   *   *

The Great Depression wore on, with the *Tribune* publishing relatively cheerful and optimistic editorials despite the fact that the economic news seemed endlessly bad. "The present period of depression, we are reminded repeatedly, differs from its predecessors in the fact that this time there is no credit stringency," the paper said on October 25, 1930. "Money is plentiful and cheap. Likewise, though there has been a marked decline in commodity prices, individual houses have not suffered severe losses on inventories which marked the depression of 1921. . . . The outlook is far from hopeless." Some of the optimism persisted, possibly, because Chicago had been among the first to recover from panic in the past, and the city's industry was largely consumer oriented, except for the steel mills, and had not been the first to feel the slowdown of the world economy. But in 1932 heavy industry was of greater importance than in the prior decade. Jobs disappeared in steel and light industries alike, the price of a bushel of wheat fell from $1.82 in 1928 to 38¢ in 1933, the export of agricultural products almost ceased, and the manufacture of agricultural implements and supplies declined. The ultimate consumer could no longer afford to buy. This time the Great Depression included Chicago.

Despite the optimistic editorials, Colonel McCormick was taking precautions against hard times. In 1925 he had predicted the stock market crash, which occurred in 1929. Such prescience now helped him to make sure his paper would be ready for the new economic storm. Projects that failed to pay their way, such as *Liberty* magazine and the wire picture service and communications ventures, were cut away. Cash reserves mounted. Consequently, as the Depression worsened, the *Tribune* was relatively stronger than its competitors. Even so, in 1932 the paper failed to pay the bonus that had been instituted for employees in the 1920s, wages were reduced, and the staff diminished by attrition. That same year Chicago applied to the Illinois legislature for permission to sell bonds and to issue tax anticipation warrants in order to pay police, firemen, and teachers; the city's unemployed scoured the streets and alleys for firewood and scraps of garbage, and thousands of jobless men slept under double-decked Wacker Drive and Michigan Avenue, which became known as the "Hoover Hotel." By mid-1932 Samuel Insull, whose utilities empire crashed, had fled to Europe to evade state and federal investigations, stock prices were down to 10 percent of their former values, desperate war veterans were preparing to march on Washington to demand payment of a bonus for their military service, and disillusionment with President Hoover, the Republican party, and the American economic way of life was pervasive in city and rural areas alike.

In March, 1932, came the worst of the year's grim news, with the *Tribune*'s banner on March 2 reporting: "LINDBERGH BABY IS STOLEN." Charles Augustus Lindbergh, 19 months old, child of the couple who had been accepted emotionally as America's first family, was taken from his crib in a lonely house in New Jersey to which his parents had retreated after too much national adulation. The baby would not be returned alive. The ensuing investigation, seizure of suspects, and trial revealed the United States at its maudlin worst, and, following their ordeal, the Lindberghs escaped from their homeland to live for a time in England. Tom Pettey covered the Lindbergh case for the *Tribune,* while Philip Kinsley traveled to Hawaii to report another major crime story, which involved the rape of a naval officer's wife and the lynching of a native suspect. There were 42 lynchings of blacks in the United States that year.

But there was news other than crime reported adequately and displayed well in the *Tribune* in 1932. The paper was especially proud to announce that John T. McCutcheon had been awarded a Pulitzer prize for his cartoon "A Wise Economist Asks a Question," published August 19, 1931. Hattie Caraway of Arkansas was elected to the U.S. Senate. Dr. C. C. King, of the University of Pittsburgh, succeeded in isolating vitamin C. Congress authorized the Reconstruction Finance Corporation (RFC) to aid distressed agriculture and industry, and the Federal Farm Board was directed to give 85 million bushels of wheat to hungry Americans. It was in 1932 that Japan created the puppet state of Manchukuo, ignoring the protests of China, the League of Nations, and the United States; and in Italy, Benito Mussolini's fascist regime, the first modern totalitarian state, marked its tenth anniversary. Also in 1932 the *Tribune* again attempted a "bring back the horse" campaign. It did not succeed. Americans wanted automobiles, and the United States, already short of oil reserves, had to search for oil and deal for it in other parts of the world, both to power automobiles and tractors and to provide fertilizer for horseless farms.

*   *   *

For a time Colonel McCormick continued the largely progressive policies of Joseph Medill, Robert W. Patterson, Medill McCormick, and Joseph Patterson—policies progressive to the extent that they demanded restraint of monopoly and a "fair deal" for the farmer. At times while Medill McCormick and Joe Patterson were influential, the *Tribune* favored municipal ownership of street railways and power resources. Robert McCormick himself had pioneered a government power project. As president of the Chicago Sanitary District he pushed construction of the power plant at Lockport, Illinois, with the intention of selling its electricity to the City of Chicago. The contract was signed in 1910, incurring the hostility of the private utility interests, which attempted to defeat the move in the city council. But McCormick, like Joseph Medill, did not carry his antagonism to monopoly, high tariffs, and "Pittsburgh-plus" railroad rates so far as to tolerate those who wanted to take over private enterprise completely. Like Medill, McCormick distrusted, feared, and hated the forces of communism, socialism, and anarchism. He was aware of Lenin's dictum that a revolution, to succeed, must control the press, and, as the Depression continued, he was alert for signs of anarchy and Communist plotting. Yet, when the time approached for the Republican National Convention to meet in Chicago in June, it was not the economic situation or Communist threats that preoccupied the *Tribune,* but Prohibition. The first three items in the paper's "Platform for America," which it published under the editorial page flag on the eve of the convention, dealt with that subject: "1. Repeal the Eighteenth Amendment. 2. Repeal the Volstead Act. 3. Stop appropriations for the Prohibition Tyranny." The other points: "4. End tax confiscations. 5. Half government expenses. 6. Free the railroads. 7. Establish 12-foot navigation from New York to New Orleans. 8. Adopt an American foreign policy."

The *Tribune* admitted at last that the country was in a dreadful economic situation, but it expected that the RFC, headed by McCormick's good friend, Chicago banker and former vice-president Charles Gates Dawes, along with other measures taken or planned by President Hoover and the Congress, would prove adequate. The paper declared, however, on June 13, that the soldiers and the unemployed had every right to go to Washington to demand aid. "The unemployed should go there and camp," said the paper's editorial. "It is their equitable privilege. Washington has put them in the condition in which they find themselves. It should take care of them."

McCormick's policy, thus enunciated, must have confused some Republican leaders. As the convention got under way on June 14, the paper patiently explained that while the unemployed required aid, the country on the whole was sound economically and a laissez-faire attitude would, in the long run, straighten out business problems. But the *Tribune* had no patience whatever with the Drys, on whom it blamed the country's crime problem. When the Prohibition forces backing Hoover for re-nomination obtained a compromise platform plank by proposing to allow the states to choose their own kind of Prohibition enforcement, if any, McCormick was as angered as Joseph Medill had been by Douglas's popular sovereignty compromise of the slavery evil. The *Tribune* printed a black page-one banner on June 16, "GOP STRADDLE PLANK WINS," and under it a two-column page-one editorial excoriating those who pushed through the so-called compromise. "The plan is a fraud!" the paper raged. "It is an offense to the Republican party and to the American people. It is a declaration of political bankruptcy upon this great issue, for it is as futile as it is fraudulent." On June 18 the paper continued its attack, contending that "prohibition is a federal problem and the states can't cure it." But there was bitter defeat: "HOOVER FORCES DEFEAT WETS IN WILD BATTLE," the headline reported. The Republicans would again be dry and the *Tribune* would support Hoover, but with no more enthusiasm than it showed in 1928 when McCormick sent his best writer, James O'Donnell Bennett, to cover Al Smith, while his editorialists spoke softly for the Republican nominee, Hoover.

The renomination of President Hoover and Vice-President Charles D. Curtis on a dry platform was a disaster compounded when remnants of the Thompson machine, allied with the downstate forces of Len Small, were able to reslate Small as the party's candidate for governor. The *Tribune* promptly pledged its support to Democrat Henry Horner, a Chicago Municipal Court judge. On July 1, the Democrats held their national convention in Chicago and named Franklin Delano Roosevelt, governor of New York, as their presidential candidate, and John Nance Garner of Texas as his running mate. The Democratic platform de-manded immediate repeal of the Prohibition amendment, labor legisla-tion, farm and unemployment relief, federal regulation of holding companies and utility rates, government control of security exchanges, and a sound currency. Governor Roosevelt, once a schoolmate of McCormick at Groton, flew to Chicago to accept the nomination and to promise "a new deal for the American people."

*   *   *

In later years, when President Franklin Roosevelt and the *Chicago Tribune* were locked in fierce battle over most aspects of the New Deal and foreign policy, editorialists, radio commentators, and later still some historians would assume that McCormick and Roosevelt had perpetuated a personal vendetta from school days, abetting irreconcilable philosophical differences. Actually, the two men engaged in friendly exchanges both before and following Roosevelt's nomination and in the early days of the New Deal.

Prior to the national conventions, *Tribune* editors sent telegrams to all candidates for nomination, requesting, "400 WORDS YOUR ATTITUDE ON GOVERNMENTAL EXPENDITURES. HOW MUCH SHOULD FEDERAL EXPENSES BE CUT. WHAT YOUR PLAN FOR ECONOMY—CHICAGO TRIBUNE." Roosevelt had replied directly to McCormick, rather than to the editors. He was not ready to provide an exclusive statement to any newspaper on the complex subject, said his telegram, but "FOR YOUR PERSONAL INFORMATION AND NOT FOR PUBLICATION PRELIMINARY SURVEY LEADS ME BELIEVE FEDERAL EXPENDITURES CAN BE CUT TWENTY PERCENT BY ELIMINATING FUNCTIONS NOT ABSOLUTELY ESSENTIAL AND BY COMPLETE REORGANIZATION OF MANY DEPARTMENTS. I HAVE BEEN GIVING DEEP STUDY TO THIS THE PAST MONTH AND HAVE EXCELLENT BASIS OF COMPARISON OF PRESENT DAY WITH STATUS OF EXPENDITURES IN NINETEEN FIFTEEN. SHOULD LIKE TO TALK THIS OVER WITH YOU SOME DAY. FRANKLIN D. ROOSEVELT."

Colonel McCormick responded immediately with a letter:

Dear Frank:

The telegram asking you for four hundred words on economy was identical to those sent to the other candidates for nomination. I was away at the time . . . but was called back because of the bank crisis that precipitated Thursday.

I am glad you entertain these views on public expenditures, although I doubt there will be enough money in the country to meet half the present budget by March fourth next.

Yours sincerely,
Robert R. McCormick

After Roosevelt's nomination, Colonel McCormick assigned his favorite writer, John Boettiger, to cover Roosevelt and sent the candidate a personal, friendly note introducing Boettiger. Later that summer, McCormick had his opportunity to discuss expenditures and other issues when he was a guest of Governor Roosevelt at Hyde Park, the Roosevelt ancestral home. He wrote on August 6, 1932:

A line to thank you for your hospitality to me. I enjoyed every minute of it.

Your general's driver took me to Peekskill very cleverly. I told him I thought he ought to become a racing car chauffeur. We made the train by seconds.

Presumably you will want some relaxation from the strenuosity and monotony of the campaign. I am therefore sending you under another cover a copy of John Boettiger's book on the murder of Jake Lingle. You will find it interesting, and also get an insight into the author.

As my eyes struck the enclosed clipping I recalled your remarks about the people who wish to tax corporation surpluses in order to force their distribution.

Booth Tarkington in The Magnificent Ambersons *ascribes the money hoarding proclivities of that generation to their sharp recollection of want in the pioneer days. I imagine that the impulse back of big corporate surpluses is the outcome of similar experiences. Such, at least, was the case in my small company.*

With us it had always been customary to divide the earnings every month — the rule, I suppose, among partners. No sooner had I entered the business than, with no nest egg in the bank, I ran into cut rates in circulation, a strike, a depression, and the war. From that I reacted to a big surplus for us, none of which was loaned on call. That became too great a responsibility during the bank panic, so I distributed it. Now that the panic is over, I might like to have some of it back in the treasury.

But whatever my successes or failures, or those of anybody else running a business, I am sure I can do it better than any outsider, whether his motives be good, theoretical, or hostile to our form of government.

*   *   *

Throughout the campaign it was clear that the *Chicago Tribune* found it onerous to obey the injunction of Joseph Medill that it should never support the party of rebellion. The paper gave President Hoover his fair share of news coverage, assigning Arthur Evans and John Herrick, two of its better writers, to his entourage, but of editorial page support for Hoover there was almost none. There were daily editorials backing other Republican candidates, notably Otis F. Glenn for reelection to the U.S. Senate and C. Wayland Brooks for state treasurer, and the paper urged election of a Republican Congress. Daily the newspaper smote Len Small, the Republican candidate for governor, demanding his defeat and the election of Democrat Henry Horner.

On November 4, the paper said: "Many of Mr. Hoover's tendencies in government have not had the sympathy of the *Tribune*. His prolonged satisfaction with the operation of the Volstead Act under the 18th amendment has been regarded by this newspaper as stubborn in the face of the facts and in consideration of the country's moral and financial condition. With other members of his party, he has changed position and has announced himself as unwilling to tolerate such conditions. Much of his foreign policy has been regarded as dubious and downright unsatisfactory."

The *Tribune* went on with criticisms, said that Hoover was at heart a bureaucrat, and noted that the operations of Hoover's Farm Board were costly and mistaken. But, the *Tribune* concluded, it had to admit that President Hoover was the only one in Washington openly against radicalism. "We see no other place for a conservative in this election. Mr. Hoover is their man. He is at the present moment such a candidate as the Republican party would be expected to present." Such lukewarm enthusiasm might well be construed as an invitation to vote for Roosevelt.

On Sunday, November 6, the *Tribune*'s biggest circulation day prior to the election, the editorial providing guidance for voters the ensuing Tuesday began: "Governor Roosevelt in his speeches says very little to which the average American can take exception. He's a high-minded man with a desire to advance the well-being of American citizens, to bring his party into power, and to be of service to the United States. Whatever may be the opinion of the chances of his success of this, no fair critic will doubt his intentions." After extensive discussion of the issues, the editorial concluded, "Even if we prefer as conditions now are and as prospects are to be viewed that President Hoover and the Republican party should continue in administration, we are not, because of that, justified in anticipating the election of Governor Roosevelt as a calamity. Whether Mr. Hoover or Mr. Roosevelt there must be a change in the attitude of the federal government to the citizens of the United States."

Roosevelt and the Democrats swept the country in a landslide, Hoover and Curtis carrying only six states. The *Tribune* did not comment editorially on the national verdict, but it took satisfaction in the victory of Henry Horner in the gubernatorial contest, destroying the last of the Thompson–Small forces. "Illinois is particularly fortunate to have voted itself out of a nightmare, and to get Judge Horner," the paper said. "No other electorate in the Union can be congratulated as heartily upon the results of its state election." The paper was pleased also to report its largest daily circulation in history, having sold 1,075,000 copies of the election editions.

During the campaign the waning Hoover administration had initiated some constructive moves: the Home Loan Bank Act, a moratorium on mortgage foreclosures, the provision of $1.8 billion by the RFC to states for relief and public works construction. The country, however, seemed paralyzed by fear as Roosevelt declined to reveal his own plans for combating the Depression, and Hoover's aid program was regarded as too little, too late. There seemed no end to bad news. In December the nations owing money to the United States defaulted, with the exception of Finland. On February 14, 1933, Gov. W. C. Comstock of Michigan ordered the closing of the state's banks, among the first of a wave of such closures. And on the following day there was a shocking tragedy in Miami, Florida: "MANIAC FIRES ON ROOSEVELT. CERMAK SHOT, WOUND GRAVE."

*　　*　　*

John Boettiger, traveling with the president-elect, telephoned the story, reaching the *Tribune* city desk shortly after 8:00 P.M. on February 15. Managing editor Beck was out of town and city editor Lee was in charge. He telephoned circulation manager Louis Rose, who had not yet made his daily visit to the news department to see what headlines were being prepared for the final editions. "We've got the story of the year!" Lee told Rose. "A nut just shot at Roosevelt down in Florida. He missed, but he hit Cermak."

The press run of the evening bulldog edition was ending. "Get everything together as fast as you can," Rose urged Lee. "We'll go Extra." He picked up another phone. A siren screamed in the pressroom, stopping the presses. Boettiger's dictated story was being edited and sent in short "takes" to the composing room to be set in type. The headlines were written and the pictures of Roosevelt and Cermak engraved before the story was fully in type. The printers made up the pages and trundled them to the stereotype department, where a matrix was made from which curved plates could be cast. These were locked in the rotary presses and the Extra edition rolled. Within 20 minutes the Extra *Tribunes* were on the street. That night the *Tribune* sold 188,602 additional papers, a total of 956,031. Later editions provided more details from Boettiger, eyewitness side stories, a report from the hospital, a diagram showing the course of the bullet that wounded Mayor Cermak, and a psychological profile of Giuseppe Zangara, the "anarchistic gunman" who not only shot Cermak but also wounded four bystanders.

The paper carried Cermak's reported statement, "I'm glad it was me instead of you," uttered to Roosevelt en route to the hospital according to Chicago Ald. James Bowler. On the following day Carey Orr's cartoon showed Cermak in his hospital bed, speaking to the president-elect those memorable words. The *Tribune* editorial had high praise for the mayor, not only for his selfless sentiment, but for the fine leadership it credited him with providing to Chicago. The paper wished him a quick recovery, but Mayor Cermak succumbed at 5:57 A.M. on Monday, March 6, with the *Tribune* receiving the story in time for its final edition. Later there were rumors that Cermak was the intended target of the assassin, that he had obtained a bulletproof vest because of fear of Chicago gangsters but had failed to take it to Florida.

There was an immediate struggle for the succession and control of the party and the city. Alderman Frank J. Corr (17th Ward) served temporarily as mayor until the inner-party strife could be settled and some state laws amended, whereupon Edward J. Kelly, president of the South Park Board and former chief engineer of the Sanitary District, was elected by the Chicago City Council. Colonel Robert R. McCormick was highly pleased, for he and Kelly had been friends for years. Kelly was a Democrat and would be a loyal supporter of President Roosevelt and the New Deal. The *Tribune,* when it turned on Roosevelt, would remain a friend of Mayor Kelly, though not for all time. But while it lasted, Kelly's rapport with McCormick was nearly perfect.

There is evidence that McCormick and Roosevelt intended in the beginning to maintain their own cordial relations. Following the assassination attempt, McCormick let it be known that he would like to talk with the president-elect. He was invited to Hyde Park for lunch. On February 22, 1933, he wrote, *"I'll be there."* Then, likening Roosevelt to a soldier about to charge from the trenches, *"I feel you are going over the top, and the least I can do is wish you well."*

A few days later, McCormick again wrote the president-elect, suggesting that the United States might be making a mistake in its proposed Canadian water treaty. *"The connection between the Great Lakes system and the Mississippi river system and Chicago, the transportation center of the nation, is just opening,"* McCormick wrote. *"Nobody can know how much water will be needed to make this waterway practically successful. If the amount set up in the Canadian treaty turns out to be insufficient, we will never be able to have it increased without paying some great international price for it."* McCormick included maps and rainfall data. McCormick was an expert on inland waterways, having studied them both in North America and abroad when he was president of the Sanitary District. This Roosevelt did not know, and since he was engaged in more urgent matters after his inauguration, he sent the letter and enclosures to Harold L. Ickes, his new secretary of the interior. Ickes knew McCormick's qualifications well enough—he had served with him on the Committee of 100 during the Bull Moose campaign—and he was aware of Chicago's waterway needs. But he returned the letter to Roosevelt on April 4, 1933, saying, *"I am not in a position to answer the general objection raised by Colonel McCormick to the treaty, so I am sending his letter back to you."*

If anyone had been put down in the exchange, it would appear to have been Roosevelt. But McCormick was miffed. Thereafter Ickes was handled with increasing coolness by the *Tribune.* Despite the secretary's lack of knowledge of waterway problems, the new deep channel in the Illinois River, the Illinois Ship Canal, was officially opened in June, 1933, and the *Tribune* sent through the first boat from Joliet to Cairo, the motorship *Sea King,* with Arthur Evans, the paper's acerbic, British-born correspondent, aboard to cover. "The *Tribune* today took the first boat, the first passengers, the first cargo over the new Illinois waterway," Evans wrote. He described the importance of the new 12-foot channel, which would eventually link the Great Lakes to the Gulf. The channel would make Chicago one of the world's great inland ports, and during World War II it would enable the United States to send steel, ships, and armaments from the interior of America to the Gulf as readily as to the Atlantic.

*   *   *

President Roosevelt took his oath of office on March 4, 1933, and in his inaugural address told the people, "The only thing we have to fear is fear itself." The following day he issued a call for a special session of the Congress and proclaimed a holiday for all the national banks. The *Tribune* responded with a glowing editorial lauding the president both for the wisdom of his plans and for his prompt action, while on page one Carey Orr's cartoon depicted the Ship of State about to pull off the "Shoals of Depression," to glide into the oil-slicked waters of "Confidence in Roosevelt." Said the editorial:

> The President has acted with admirable promptness. He has seen the immediate situation truly and has taken emergency measures required to meet it. But now, as always, the final responsibility rests upon the American people. If, as we have every reason to believe, they will meet the crisis in the spirit in which the President has met it, there will be a minimum of disruption of industry and commerce. If the people yield to fear, resumption of normal business conditions may be needlessly delayed. . . .
>
> What is needed above all else is the calm assumption on the part of the American people that the crisis is temporary and that the proper course of conduct is the normal course. Normal buying, normal credit extensions and normal confidence in the future will do a maximum of immediate good. Conduct born of fear can only hamper the President, the treasury, and the banks in their task of restoration.
>
> The firmness which has been displayed in Washington is most reassuring. If Mr. Roosevelt had not issued his decree suspending specie payment and placing an embargo on gold there would have been something to worry about. The fact that he acted without shilly-shallying indicates as plainly as anything can that he knows what it is all about and is not afraid to take drastic action for the protection of the people of the United States. . . .
>
> The confidence which the President engendered with his decree was reinforced by his summoning of Congress to meet before this week is out. This provides a measure of Mr. Roosevelt's political astuteness. He is not afraid that Congress will get out of hand.

It was a time when calls for confidence and courage were needed. The bank holiday, closing all the nation's banks temporarily, was probably the most frightening aspect of the Great Depression to citizens generally. The *Tribune*'s reports on the situation were written by J. Howard Wood, a tall, good-looking business reporter from Harvard University Graduate School who had taught at Middlesex School in Massachusetts and at Northwestern University. Young Wood seemed to have the confidence of the leading bankers, since he generally had been first with the developments in the banking crisis situation as they were about to occur. Now, on March 6, he wrote an optimistic story that appeared on page one, predicting that 32 of the Chicago banks would shortly reopen. He was conservative; 34 banks were back in business by the 13th, as the Roosevelt administration moved into action, with the *Tribune* approving Roosevelt's new banking laws.

Meantime, Colonel McCormick was taking a careful look at Wood, his young financial reporter. Dominance in the business news field was as important to the Colonel as it had been to Joseph Medill. Soon Wood was a financial page columnist, called to frequent conferences with Mc-Cormick. Then he was informed that he would become the new financial editor, succeeding O. A. Mather. *Tribune* financial editors generally moved up in the company. Wood was not to be an exception.

*   *   *

Despite the economic distress, Chicago had moved ahead with its plans to host a world's fair to commemorate the city's centennial. The site was again the Chicago lakefront, the theme "A Century of Progress," especially progress in the sciences during the period Chicago itself had developed from a frontier village to one of the world's leading cities. Rufus C. Dawes, Chicago banker and brother of Charles Gates Dawes, was president of the fair board, and McCormick was one of the board members, as his grandfather had been for the World's Columbian Exposition.

Chicago's 1933 world's fair was not planned to the grandiose scale of the World's Columbian Exposition. Contemporary architecture predominated, rather than the classical style of the earlier exposition. The buildings again stretched along the lakefront, surrounding two giant lagoons formed by man-made islands. During much of 1932 there was a question whether the fair would open at all. Major Lennox R. Lohr, general manager and director of construction, said he almost literally built sewer lines, walks, and streets as the money came in to pay for them and could never be sure that the next day's construction would resume. Toward the end, however, there was an influx of cash as it appeared that the fair would actually open. Some of the money came from the gangster elements, who chose to run the village concessions, which had been so successful in 1893. According to the *Tribune*, more than 10,000 workmen got jobs in the final rush toward completion of the exposition.

On May 7 it was announced that President Roosevelt would come to Chicago to open the fair on May 27. The preceding day, Colonel McCormick addressed an invitation to the president:

> *Dear Frank:*
>
> *It would give my wife and me great pleasure to have you and Mrs. Roosevelt stay with us when you come to Chicago to open the World's Fair.*
>
> *My house was a present from my mother, who held all the mansion ideas of her generation, and it therefore is so much too large for us as to contain room for you and at least a considerable part of your staff.*
>
> *It seems to me that you are making very good weather of it in the storm.*
>
> > *Yours sincerely,*
> > *Robert R. McCormick*

President Roosevelt found he could not come to Chicago and replied:

Dear Bert:

It is fine of you to ask me to use your house while I am in Chicago but, as you know now, I shall not be there. I have been a long time in writing to thank you but I was waiting to see how it turned out in order that I might know definitely whether or not I could get away. However, I would have only been in Chicago for a few hours and would not have had any time for a visit.

It was more than generous of you to offer to let me share your home. Do let me know when you are coming to Washington.

Very sincerely yours,
Franklin D. Roosevelt

Postmaster General James A. Farley came to open the fair, another dazzling Chicago extravaganza. The glowing electrical and moving exhibitions were activated by light from the star Arcturus captured by four astronomical observatories about the country to make sure that cloud cover would not obstruct the signal. James O'Donnell Bennett, still the *Tribune*'s top reporter when it came to describing man-made wonders, hand-penned the leading stories, both preceding and at the official opening: "This morning wonders upon wonders will be unveiled to an expectant nation at the World's Fair." And, following the event: "The seventh great World's Fair in United States history opened brilliantly and auspiciously yesterday." Philip Kinsley wrote the color story on the Arcturus ceremony: "Starlight 225 million miles from earth, after a journey through the depths of galactic space for forty years at 9:15 o'clock last night furnished the impulse which turned the Chicago World's Fair into a glittering fairyland."

Nearly a score of other *Tribune* writers described the opening and the marvels of the great exposition, which, while it did not equal the world's fair of 1893 with which it was compared, did brilliantly display modern science and 20th-century materialism, art, and culture in a spectacular manner that proved again that Chicago, of all cities, could provide stimulation and leadership to a faltering nation in difficult times.

The *Tribune*, in connection with the great exposition, launched a campaign reminiscent of its editorial after the 1871 fire, "Chicago Shall Rise Again." "Chicago Will Come Back First" was the new cry sounded by the paper to challenge its city and the rest of the nation. A Carey Orr page-one cartoon and an editorial were followed by pages upon pages of advertisements trumpeting the theme. The *Tribune* predicted that A Century of Progress would eclipse the 27.5 million total attendance record of the fair of 1893. The vaulting Skyride over the northern lagoon to Northerly Isle; the Enchanted Island, a fairyland that was to give Walt

Disney inspiration; the great Hall of Sciences, the Communications and Transportation exhibits, the rows of modern homes, the temple of Jehol, the colony of houses of the future, and the streets of foreign villages—all of these enthralled the visitors of the more sophisticated world of 1933 as much as such exhibits had moved the bumpkins who had flocked to the exposition of 1893.

Using plans drafted by Capt. John Whistler, the original designer of Fort Dearborn, Major Lohr recreated the fort much as it had appeared in 1803. He also built a pioneer village, which included replicas of the cabin occupied by black fur trader Jean Baptiste Point du Sable, Chicago's first permanent settler; the Father Marquette cabin, where the Jesuit explorer wintered in 1673; and the cabin in which Abraham Lincoln was born. There were a Hall of Religion, a reconstructed Egyptian temple, a Siamese temple, and the pavilions of 17 foreign countries as well as the Federal Building and the Hall of States. *The City of New York,* the vessel used by Richard E. Byrd on his voyage to Antarctica, was moored nearby, as were a prison ship and a U.S. submarine. An oil company created a fossil zoo of prehistoric animals; Dr. John Wesley Kelchner erected a replica of what he said was King Solomon's temple, destroyed some 3,000 years previously in Jerusalem. Most popular of the places to frequent were the restaurants and nightclubs of the foreign villages, especially the Streets of Paris. There were also pay toilets, greatly irking most of the visitors.

The fair was a magnificent success from the start. It soon acquired its symbol, fan dancer Sally Rand, who quickly outstripped Little Egypt of the World's Columbian Exposition in her fame. Special trains, planes, and autos brought millions of visitors. An attendance record was set on September 3, when 367,737 people packed the grounds so thickly that it was impossible for them to enjoy, or even to see, many of the exhibits. By this time there was a clamor among Chicagoans for a renewal of the exposition in 1934, since the fair was lifting the city out of the Depression doldrums.

At the exposition grounds the *Tribune* maintained a news bureau run by a happy young reporter named Earl "Moon" Mullin, who not only had a private supply of passes from Major Lohr but provided a favorite retreat for Sally Rand, where she could rest from her fan-swishing labors and meet various newspaper escorts, most of them from the *Tribune* staff, who desired to show her "the other Chicago." Toward the end of September, the *Tribune* began to foresee that A Century of Progress would pass the world's fair of 1893 in attendance, and it began to publish daily comparative totals. The new record, 21,480,141 paid, was achieved at 1 P.M. on October 30, at which time it was disclosed that the fair would open again in 1934. The exposition drew 27,703,132 (including 5 million free) in 1933, and 21,066,095 (including nearly 4,600,000 free) in 1934, thereby becoming the largest fair in history. Major Lohr estimated that it brought $200 million in fresh capital to Chicago.

*   *   *

One of President Roosevelt's campaign promises, repeal of the Prohibition amendment, was well on its way to being fulfilled by the fall of 1933 (the "noble experiment" would officially end in December), and to this the *Tribune* gave hearty approval. But other aspects of Roosevelt's presidency were less well received, and on October 7, 1933, the *Tribune* indicated that its patience with the New Deal was running out. During the first 100 days of the new administration, the special session of Congress had enacted a flurry of measures that created agencies to take over or regulate almost every phase of the American economy. Beginning with the bank acts, which the *Tribune* praised, and a measure reducing the pay of federal employees, to which the paper did not object, New Deal legislation went on to create such agencies as the Civilian Conservation Corps (CCC), the Agricultural Adjustment Administration (AAA), the Tennessee Valley Authority (TVA), and the Federal Emergency Relief Administration (FERA). One of the last pieces of legislation of the Hundred Days—and probably the most controversial—was the National Industrial Recovery Act (NIRA), which established the Public Works Administration (PWA) to help alleviate unemployment through public works programs, and the National Recovery Administration (NRA) to supervise the drafting of codes of fair competition by various industries and to protect the rights of organized labor.

Much of the NIRA legislation had already been drafted under the Hoover administration; public works construction had been a Hoover policy, and Hoover had first suggested fair practices codes while he was Coolidge's secretary of commerce. Regardless of origin, the *Tribune* opposed the NRA, especially as it was directed by dour, tough Gen. Hugh Johnson. McCormick did not want the government to control his newspaper, as he felt was threatened by the agency's imposing codes of business conduct. Agencies and regulatory bodies proliferated, and bureaucracy burgeoned. McCormick saw much of the legislation as creeping socialism or worse, intended to destroy American private enterprise. Only the Security and Exchange Act of 1934, in a later outpouring of New Deal legislation, would win the paper's warm approval.

Although the days of editorials favorable to Roosevelt ended with the advent of the NRA, the *Tribune*'s first attack was quite temperate. It took note that a top NRA official, Donald Richberg, had publicly declared that not only was a revolution intended, it was under way.

Said the paper on October 7, 1933: "Many ardent supporters of the New Deal feel that the constitution, both as a framework of government and as a declaration of rights, is obsolete, but the real issue is whether we shall continue to maintain our free society or exchange it for one based on the principle of authority. This is the revolution which one of the leading members of the administration, Mr. Donald Richberg, declares has taken place."

A new correspondent was needed in Washington to back up Arthur Sears Henning, who seemed inadequate alone before the New Deal onslaught. City editor Lee chose John Boettiger, who had traveled with Roosevelt but was regarded by Lee as strong enough to resist Roosevelt's wiles. Boettiger was soon enticed to the Sunday musical soirees and political discussions in the White House. There he met Anna Roosevelt Dahl, the president's daughter, and his usefulness to the *Tribune* seemed to be nearing an end. Boettiger saved *Tribune* management from any decision-making by resigning from the paper. He arranged a divorce, as did Mrs. Dahl, and in 1935 they were married. Boettiger later became publisher of a Hearst paper in Seattle. Chesly Manly was sent to the Washington bureau, and, although he appeared to be a match for Roosevelt, he was reinforced by two able assistants, Willard Edwards, described by Pat Maloney of the paper's editorial department as "the *Tribune*'s best all-around reporter," and the equally brilliant Walter Trohan, who had the added capacity to so infuriate bureaucrats with his questions that he could lead them into outbursts against their own interests.

In foreign affairs, a Roosevelt thrust that especially upset the *Tribune* was the establishment of diplomatic relations with the USSR in November, 1933, following a conference with Maxim Litvinov, Soviet commissar for foreign affairs. Such traffic with the devil convinced McCormick that Roosevelt was hell-bent for a Communist dictatorship, based on that people's revolution Donald Richberg kept talking about. It was not until months later, however, that he printed the charge that President Roosevelt "was creating a half-way house for some stronger man to move to some other location, either Fascist or Communist."

Meantime the paper pounded away at the domestic aspects of the New Deal. The TVA was denounced as an outrageous socialistic boondoggle that would cost billions while it crushed private utility enterprises with their own tax money, a position not dissimilar to that of the Utility Barons who opposed Robert McCormick when as president of the Chicago Sanitary District he sold electricity from the Sanitary District power station at Lockport to the City of Chicago. The FERA, authorized to distribute $500 million to the states for unemployment relief, was under the supervision of Roosevelt's aide and confidant, former welfare worker Harry L. Hopkins, a man of whom even a friend once said, "Harry never had the faintest conception of the value of money." Hopkins, the *Tribune*'s candidate for King of the Boondogglers, was soon engaged in a struggle for control of spending with Secretary of the Interior Harold Ickes, who as director of the PWA had over $3 billion at his disposal. Ickes rarely failed to voice his contempt for the *Tribune* and was in turn regarded by the paper as nearly as incompetent as the chain-smoking, nerve-racked Hopkins.

In 1933 more than a million corn and hog producers signed contracts with the AAA to reduce acreage by approximately 25 percent, and the government bought and slaughtered 6 million pigs in an effort to bring up farm prices. The killing of the pigs became symbolic of the waste, inefficiency, and possible insanity of the New Deal, so far as the *Tribune* was concerned. Secretary of Agriculture Henry Wallace, of Iowa, appeared to be a schizoid who decreased farm production overall while at the same time increasing it by developing hybrid seed. McCormick obtained some of the seed and planted it on the *Tribune*'s experimental farm with excellent results.

But it was another Iowan, Hopkins, who received the paper's maximum scorn with Walter Trohan of the Washington bureau portraying him in devastating reportorial prose: "A lean, gangly figure with thinning brown hair and dandruff made his way with his face twisted by a sardonic grin through an ill-assorted group of representatives, crackpots, senators, bums, governors, job-seekers, political leaders, and toadies. . . . In the person of Harry Lloyd Hopkins, son of an Iowa harness maker, Santa Claus had come to town. He emptied his hands of other people's money." Elsewhere in the article Trohan compared Hopkins to the mad Russian monk, Rasputin. The president's aide was furious and wanted to sue, but friends dissuaded him. Even then a political figure could hardly win, and Hopkins, who was busy putting the country's 4,700,000 distressed families into useful government work, as his friends saw it, or squandering billions on the dole, according to the *Tribune*'s version, could not be spared for courtroom appearances.

Roosevelt, in responding to a question about Richberg's statement concerning the impending American revolution, had once drawled sarcastically to correspondent Boettiger: "John, you tell Bertie he's seeing things under the bed." Nonetheless, by July 2, 1934, the *Tribune* could no longer endure what was happening in Washington. Its editorial that day likened Roosevelt's New Dealism to the fascism Mussolini had imposed on Italy and to the totalitarianism of Adolf Hitler's Germany, which was being exposed in the paper almost daily in dispatches from correspondent Sigrid Schultz in Berlin. The editorial began by referring to the most recent reports from Germany, of the summary execution of a number of alleged conspirators among Hitler's storm troopers:

> Enemies of Hitler will speak of the events of the week-end in Germany as murders and assassinations. Apologists for Hitler will reply that he has been obliged to take strong measures to preserve order. Students of political history will regard the argument as fruitless. They will recognize what has happened in Germany as the expectable consequence of any dictatorship and the inevitable consequence of a dictatorship which has disappointed or angered a considerable number of people subjected to it. They will recognize, also, that the killing has only begun. Bloodshed begets bloodshed.

After detailing the means Hitler had used to rise to power, recalling that among his first acts were those to take over newspapers as well as the radio, the paper pointed out that all opposition parties were proscribed. "Religious tolerance ceased. Suspected opponents were jailed without being told why and in hundreds of instances without the barest formality of a trial." It then described the futile nature of the remaining opposition and asserted that Hitler was following the way of Mussolini. The fate of the press was sealed in both countries. "When the press is fettered, the machine gun and the bomb replace it as organs of opinion." Then came the point of the dissertation.

It was time, said the editorial, for the American people to understand that the trend toward dictatorship was fast running its course in America.

> In the light of events in Germany, the American people dare not defer a candid appraisal of our administration. The preservation of the republic demands an examination of official pronouncements and official acts to determine our government's attitude toward freedom of expression. Such an examination will show that the government has sought to prevent opponents from enjoying the use of the radio. The government, not content with its control of the radio, has just taken over the control of all other forms of electric communication, with all that that implies of control of opinion. The government did seek by every means in its power to keep out of the newspaper code a clause specifically reserving the constitutional freedom of the press. When this effort failed because of the foresight and determination of editors and publishers throughout the country, the President expressed his intense irritation in words scarcely less vehement than those of his subordinate, Gen. Johnson.
>
> It should be unnecessary to add further items to the record. There is no lack of them. The evidences of trend are as unmistakable as they are ominous. This nation has received its warning. Will it apply the brakes in time to avoid the precipice?

*   *   *

The *Tribune*'s all-out assault on the Roosevelt administration had begun. The conflict was fought on principle, but the obviously deep philosophical differences between McCormick and Roosevelt led to bitter personal antagonism. Colonel McCormick could not forget the personal distrust and fear he had known since childhood for radical movements, whether symbolized by the Haymarket rioters, whose terror he had known on that grim day when they were hanged, the recollections of Grandfather Medill's reports of the excesses of the Paris Commune, or the experiences of his own Russian friends, whose families were liquidated by Lenin's followers. Nor did McCormick ever change the opinion he formed during World War I that America had wasted the lives of its young men in attempting to impose democracy upon Europe. The *Tribune* had been among the first to point to the inadequacies of the Versailles Treaty, and when Hitler tore it up with impunity, McCormick was convinced that he and the *Tribune* had been right from the beginning.

Not without reason did the Colonel consider himself well suited to the task of opposing the president. McCormick was emerging as the country's toughest fighting editor and publisher, the last of the effective practitioners of personal journalism in America. William Randolph Hearst, who also had backed Roosevelt in the beginning, was losing power, the time of Joseph Pulitzer and James Gordon Bennett was past, Horace Greeley was almost forgotten. The *New York Times* had grown in stature not so much as the personification of Adolph Ochs, but as a total newspaper, speaking for a unified staff. McCormick was in his prime, a powerful, athletic man, six feet four inches tall. He seemed austere with his military moustache and aloof manners, yet he was a man whose eyes twinkled when he laughed or smiled, and these evidences of good nature occurred more often than many supposed. McCormick was widely traveled, educated abroad and at Yale and Northwestern in America, experienced in politics and war. He had lived in the courts of Vienna, Petrograd, and Paris, had been hardened by conflict with Mayor Big Bill Thompson and Gov. Len Small as well as with the likes of Al Capone. A victor in the Thompson libel suits and in *Near* v. *Minnesota,* McCormick regarded himself as a top guardian of the free press, and so did his peers, who had made him the permanent chairman of the Freedom of the Press committee of the American Newspaper Publishers Association. He was also, in his own mind, a foremost antagonist of the spread of communism in America, which it appeared to him the Roosevelt administration was encouraging. He was equally firm in his determination to prevent American involvement in Europe's quarrels or quarrels anywhere that need not involve the United States.

Whatever his opinions, bias, knowledge, and insights, Colonel

McCormick was totally monolithic in his rule of the *Tribune* by 1934. His mother, Katherine, one of the directors of the company and his adviser through the 1920s, died in Versailles, France, on July 4, 1932. Mrs. Elinor Patterson, "Aunt Nellie," also a director, died on September 5, 1933. On May 5, 1932, the McCormick–Patterson Trust had been established to hold the 1,050 Medill shares controlling the company, to which were soon added 20 shares from other sources. Joseph Medill's other heirs shared beneficial interest in the trust, while Joseph Patterson and Robert McCormick as trustees voted the stock jointly. Otherwise, each cousin went his own way, Patterson completely controlling the *New York News*, which supported Roosevelt through his second election, and McCormick in full charge of the *Tribune* and the Canadian operations.

Not even death would end the fight between publisher and president, for the *Tribune* continued to condemn Roosevelt's works long after his demise, and the liberal supporters of the president have never ceased to attack McCormick and the *Tribune*. In the beginning the fire of the Roosevelt forces was directed entirely at Colonel McCormick, since Joseph Patterson and the *New York News* supported the president. Later it was aimed at the "McCormick–Patterson Axis," a slurring allusion to the Hitler–Mussolini Axis, in recognition that Patterson had at last turned on the president and had been joined by his sister, Eleanor, who took control of the *Washington Times-Herald* in 1939. Alone or with allies, McCormick showed no fear even when he was under heaviest personal attack, and, a few months after the death of Cissy Patterson in 1948, the *Tribune* bought the *Times-Herald* from the employees to whom she had left it and Colonel McCormick took over the fighting on the Washington front himself.

In 1934, McCormick, the *Tribune,* and anti-Roosevelt forces generally were heavy losers. In the fall elections, the Democrats captured two-thirds of the Congressional seats. "The completeness of the Democratic victory in the Congressional elections leaves the party unopposed in both chambers of Congress," Chesly Manly wrote from Washington. The *Tribune*'s editorial was brief, concluding: "The voters have said it should be so and whatever comes of it, so it is."

THE COLONEL
VERSUS THE PRESIDENT

23

Those few people who believed that McCormick would be chastened by the 1934 election results were soon proved wrong. His attacks on Roosevelt, the Democrats, and the New Deal increased in number and violence: Roosevelt's paternalism was destroying American freedom and property rights; the future was being mortgaged; the people had been subverted; there were hints that many in the New Deal were of the same political persuasion as those running the Communist dictatorship in Moscow. Enraged liberals rose to defend Roosevelt, who, with his fireside chats over most of the nation's 900 radio stations to most of the owners of the nation's 52 million radio sets, did a rather good job of defending himself.

Colonel Frank Knox, former chief executive officer of the Hearst papers in Boston, acquired control of the ailing *Chicago Daily News* and came to Chicago to do battle with McCormick, since Hearst seemed no longer willing to meet the *Tribune* head-on and Thomason's tabloid *Times* had not won strong acceptance. Hearst's Sunday *Herald and Examiner,* which carried the popular Hearst *American Weekly,* had Sunday circulation leadership in areas as far away as Kansas and Saskatchewan, where the *American Weekly* advertiser was well served, but the Chicago retail advertiser was not. The Sunday *Tribune* and daily *Tribune* claimed a smaller Midwestern area as *Tribune* Territory. Knox sneered at it as "Scatterville" and set out to make the *Daily News* again supreme in the immediate Chicago trade territory. So Chicago had the pleasure of watching at first hand the war of the "Morning and Evening Colonels" in addition to McCormick's assaults on President Franklin D. Roosevelt.

567

In 1934 also, McCormick initiated another campaign to stimulate his readers, the reactivation of the simplified spelling reform attempted unsuccessfully by his grandfather Joseph Medill. The Colonel assigned the preliminary work for the experiment to distinguished writer and scholar James O'Donnell Bennett. An initial list of 80 words was offered in simplified form, beginning on January 28. It started with "advertisment" for "advertisement," and included "fantom" for "phantom" and "monolog" for "monologue." Bennett provided attractive explanations for the proposed changes, and he drew upon his erudition for examples and rationale. There were memorable contributions, such as "herse" for "hearse" and "frate" for "freight." The paper published letters from readers praising and denouncing the simplified spelling project, which was abused even more by members of the paper's editorial staff in their private conversations. The paper did not seem to take the experiment too seriously, for an editorial on the subject was headed, "To Phyllis Who Might Spell it Phreight." Changes were made in the simplified spelling list from time to time, and the experiment continued until after the death of Colonel McCormick. In 1955, W. Donald Maxwell, the editor of the *Tribune*, ended the project. "Teachers were having trouble with it," he explained. "They'd tell a child a way to spell a word and he'd bring in a *Tribune* to prove the teacher wrong. That didn't help us with the teachers." On August 21, 1955, the *Tribune* revealed in an editorial that the experiment was over; that, in fact, it had ended the prior Monday. "To our surprise, not one reader, so far as we are aware, noticed the change last Monday," the editorial admitted.

*   *   *

The combat between the *Tribune* and the New Deal was vicious, but the purposes of the antagonists, according to their lights, were lofty. McCormick was fighting for the preservation of an American society of individuals he considered fully able to manage their economic affairs with minimal government supervision. It was the system envisioned by Jefferson, whom he much admired; it had worked until the early 1930s, and he believed it would work again. Roosevelt's partisans sought a strong central government to correct the evils allegedly brought on by predatory capitalists under a laissez-faire system that demonstrated its inadequacy in the Great Depression. *Tribune* editorials charged Roosevelt and his aides with perverting the American way. The result, as in Europe, would surely be anarchy, then dictatorship. Years later, Harvard historian Daniel Bell concluded that "from 1910 to 1930 we had built a national economy, but didn't have the institutions to manage it. President Roosevelt, in his fumbling way, was creating institutions to match the scale of management necessary to deal with the national economy." Robert Sherwood, himself of the New Deal, wrote that some of Roosevelt's methods seemed insane but added, "they worked," while historians Samuel Eliot Morison and Henry Steele Commager evaluated the New Deal as socializing the United States but, in the long run, saving the system by forcing it to get rid of its abuses.

The *Tribune*'s attacks appeared calculated to enrage its opponents and enemies, and they did. A neutral, Robert Ardrey, in his delightful, scholarly book *The Territorial Imperative*, described the views of some not unfriendly readers: "When I was a young man in Chicago we used to say that the secret of acknowledged Chicago vitality was the *Chicago Tribune*. We read it at breakfast, we hit the ceiling in rage either for or against it, we hit the street on a dead run, and we could not survive without it." Ardrey was comparing the matinal habits of Chicagoans with those of the callicebus monkeys, who inevitably interrupt breakfast to dash to their periphery for a good fight with their neighbors, a catharsis enabling them to survive serenely the rest of the day.

Others were less kind, especially former employees of the paper who turned on it and on Colonel McCormick. Burton Rascoe called McCormick "the greatest mind of the 14th century." The irascible Harold Ickes, who once worked as a *Tribune* reporter, wrote of "reactionary McCormick, noted for Toryism and personal vindictiveness." Ickes accused the *Tribune* of garbling the Douglas debates with Lincoln, a charge even Douglas did not make, and asserted that McCormick worked with great success to disprove the *Tribune*'s motto, "World's Greatest Newspaper." Later, in his autobiography, Ickes recalled his days as a reporter prior to the *Tribune*'s "disgrace" under McCormick. He once sat beside McCormick at dinner, he said, and now regretted not poisoning his soup, humor somewhat typical of Ickes, who styled himself "the curmudgeon." In the end, however, Ickes admitted to having voted for McCormick for president of the Chicago Sanitary District and having worked with him and Medill McCormick in the Bull Moose campaign. His feud with "Misanthropic Mac" he called "the happiest and most satisfying of my career."

One example of the extremes of overstatement, misstatement, half-truth, and innuendo that issued from both sides appears in a book written by George Seldes, who was a *Tribune* correspondent from 1918 to 1928. In *Lords of the Press,* published in 1938, Seldes declared that, with the possible exception of the fascist newspapers, the *Tribune* was the most hated paper in the world. This, of course, was a matter of opinion, but to Seldes can also be attributed a falsehood that has been re-used by critics of the *Tribune* since his book was published. To back up his assertion that no other newspaper could match the *Tribune*'s antagonism to labor and the poor, Seldes cited an alleged "editorial" in the July 12, 1877, issue of the paper, which, he wrote, disclosed the policy of Joseph Medill and the *Tribune* that tramps should be put to death with poisoned food. Seldes's allegation was picked up and reprinted by others, including John Tebbel as recently as 1974 in his *Media in America*. Tebbel called it an "unbelievable editorial" that presented Medill's "recipe for dealing with the unemployed," thereby enlarging upon Seldes's original misrepresentation.

The item in the paper, which unquestionably should not have been printed, was not an editorial, as Seldes or any other newsman would know. The *Tribune*'s editorials were so labeled and were published on page four in July, 1877. The item referred to by Seldes and Tebbel was at the bottom of a column headed "The City/General News" on page eight. The column contained oddments supplied by *Tribune* reporters and stringers in the country towns and suburbs, which were of insufficient importance to merit headlines. The item in question began:

> A suburban correspondent wants the *Tribune* to inform its readers in the outlying districts how to get rid of tramps, some of whom, the writer says, are still prowling around, barefooted and ragged, begging for one thing and another, and stealing what they can lay their hands on. The correspondent believes that the law, which went into effect on the 1st inst., on the subject of vagabonds, will give him some relief, and asks to be informed just what consolation he can get from that source.

After explaining the difficulties of finding a constable and establishing a case, the item continued:

> The law, while an improvement on the old one, is not of much use for suburban districts, where officers are scarce and Justices of the Peace hard to find. The simplest plan probably, where one is not a member of the Humane Society, is to put a little strychnine or arsenic in the meat and other supplies furnished the tramp. This produces death within a comparatively short period of time, is a warning to other tramps to keep out of the neighborhood, puts the Coroner in good humor, and saves one's chickens and other portable property from constant depredation.

The suburban reporter, or stringer, and the copy editor responsible for "The City/General News" that July night were guilty of what they evidently intended as grisly humor. Seldes perverted the execrable joke into a statement of policy and his error was perpetuated by Tebbel, whose explanation has been that he did not see the item but relied on a researcher, who provided him with the wrong year, saying it appeared in 1884, as well as wrong information concerning the so-called *Tribune* editorial.

In spite of the acrimony, both principals, Roosevelt and McCormick, appeared to relish the battle. McCormick also took to the radio, via WGN and the Mutual Network, to increase his exposure to the public. He accepted speaking engagements about the country, and his statements, editorials, and articles were reprinted widely. The main artillery continued to be the *Tribune,* since the *New York News* supported Roosevelt into his second term. Generally, shorn of polemics and vituperation, the *Tribune* simply held that Roosevelt should keep his hands off business and farmers and allow the laws of supply and demand to restore prosperity and jobs. In the realm of foreign affairs, the paper believed that the United States should do everything possible to avoid involvement in any foreign war, a position it had consistently maintained since 1919. Roosevelt, the paper insisted, had doubled government expenditures after promising to reduce the budget by 25 percent during the campaign. His administration cultivated radicals, socialists, and communists, and it sang the litany ascribed to Hopkins: "Tax and tax, spend and spend, elect and elect." One reader who followed the *Tribune*'s line avidly was Franklin D. Roosevelt, who read the paper each morning in bed. But unlike the callicebus monkeys, he did not screech out his anger. Rather he gleefully plotted revenge.

Meanwhile, the *Chicago Tribune* was flourishing. "Those who don't like it read it," *Fortune* magazine reported in May, 1934, noting that there was no simple explanation. "The sheer dominance of the *Tribune* is one cause for its unpopularity, no doubt. People question its motives because it is so powerful. They read it for the same reason, perhaps." *Fortune* proceeded to describe the *Tribune* as highly readable. "Its typeface was evolved after long research, it has by far the most popular comics, prints more news from special correspondents than any other paper except the *New York Times,* sex is not glorified but not barred. . . . The *Tribune* is read by those who dislike it but have no other choice." Or, as Joseph Medill had noted when remarking to Elihu Washburne on the paper's readership back in 1864: "A good many swear at it, but swear by it notwithstanding."

The *Tribune* was disliked by more, and read by more, and subsidiary companies were prospering. In 1933, despite the Depression, the paper had a daily circulation of 771,190, far behind the *New York News*'s total of 1,428,908, but well ahead of the *Chicago American*'s 424,719 and the *Chicago Daily News*'s 399,891. Net earnings of the *Tribune* for 1933 were estimated by *Fortune* as $2,900,000, not far from the correct total of $3,232,000. The consolidated earnings of Tribune Company, including all subsidiaries, were $6,700,000 net in 1933 and would climb to $8,400,000 by 1936.

*   *   *

On August 14, 1935, President Roosevelt signed the Social Security Act, which the *Tribune* reported with text and photograph but did not evaluate editorially, its editorial page being largely devoted to a series on the ominous economic outlook for the country and Roosevelt's "soak-the-rich" Wealth Tax Bill. Carey Orr was drawing most of the paper's cartoons at the time, McCutcheon having taken his genial good humor on a trip to South America. As the *Tribune's* anti-Roosevelt campaign increased in ferocity McCutcheon drew less and less, returning to the paper when the antiwar campaign was in full cry. On August 4, Orr's cartoon showed Uncle Sam riding in a rowboat labeled "Roosevelt Regime" and about to grab an overhanging branch called "1936 Election" to avoid going over a waterfall into a vortex of "Communism"—a sharp contrast to the calm pool "Confidence in Roosevelt" depicted a few years previously. Another drawing showed Roosevelt, his cigarette holder tilted maliciously, trundling out a bag that was marked "1936 Campaign Funds" but contained a $5 billion appropriation for the recently established Works Progress Administration (WPA), directed by the hated Harry Hopkins.

Colonel McCormick and his *Chicago Tribune* were far from alone in battling President Roosevelt's New Deal, especially in the attack on the National Industrial Recovery Act and its offspring, the National Recovery Administration. Opposition to that measure was, in fact, quite general. Various commissions studying the codes found that they hindered small business by fostering monopolies, while big business resented the labor relations provisions, consumers objected to the price increases, and liberals disliked the suspension of antitrust laws. Even labor was dissatisfied. For once, liberal magazines such as *Nation* and *New Republic* were on the same side as the *Tribune,* which applauded the Supreme Court decision declaring the NIRA unconstitutional on May 27, 1935. The Agricultural Adjustment Act, which was seen by the paper as a scheme to win political control of the farmers, was invalidated by the high court on January 6, 1936. But the "socialistic" Tennessee Valley Authority was upheld by the court in February.

Some of the New Deal measures swept away by the Supreme Court in 1935–36 were soon replaced by other legislation. Many of the benefits farmers lost when the AAA was abolished were almost immediately restored by the Soil Conservation and Domestic Allotment Act; more were restored in 1938 by the second Agricultural Adjustment Act. Labor unions found that the Wagner-Connery National Labor Relations Act of July, 1935, gave them even more protection than was offered under the NIRA. Thus encouraged, organized labor moved swiftly ahead, especially the Committee for Industrial Organization (later the Congress of Industrial Organizations), known as the CIO, planted and nurtured by bushy-browed John L. Lewis, the tough, bulky boss of the United Mine Workers, who had his headquarters in Illinois. It was Lewis who devised the vertical union and the sit-down strike in which workers refused to leave a plant, thus insuring its shutdown more effectively than pickets could. The American Federation of Labor had no liking for Lewis and his CIO, and to the *Tribune* he was a noisome enemy, possibly the creature of Russian Communism itself.

An alliance between Lewis and the USSR was suggested by Donald Day, a fervent anti-Communist and the *Tribune*'s correspondent at Riga, Latvia. In 1936 Day wrote that William Foster, presidential candidate of the American Communist party, had reported to the Communist International Executive Committee that President Roosevelt favored the CIO politically, and later Day asserted that Moscow favored Roosevelt. Both stories were denied by the White House. Day, after serving through Finland's war with Russia, was dismissed from the paper without returning to America, so his allegations against Lewis and Roosevelt were neither proved nor repudiated by the paper. Ironically, after the outbreak of World War II, when it became clear that President Roosevelt was determined to aid Britain and France at the risk of U.S. involvement, both Lewis and the *Tribune* were on the same side as antiwar leaders, and Roosevelt was as eager to crush Lewis as the *Tribune*.

Harry L. Hopkins continued to be the *Tribune*'s favorite target, ahead even of Ickes and Wallace, and the president seemed to set him up for a few choice shots from time to time. At a dedication of Boulder (Hoover) Dam, Roosevelt praised Hopkins for planning useful ways to spend the $5 billion Congress had appropriated to the WPA to put the country back to work. The *Tribune* snorted:

> There is a saying in Washington that if you can't find a way to spend all the money, call in Harry Hopkins. President Roosevelt has called in this expert, and within ten days Hopkins showed his reputation does not rest upon a false foundation. Having shown the President how to allot the money at a rate of $125 million a day . . . Hopkins required just ten days to dispose of the billion and a quarter which so distressed the President. Now, having previously succeeded in spending two dollars of public funds for every dollar spent by any other peacetime president, he will manage to spend an extra $5 billion, all of it by November, 1936.

Hopkins, firmly backed by Roosevelt, did indeed spend $4 billion prior to the 1936 elections through the WPA. The WPA "pump-priming" effort, called a "leaf-raking boondoggle" by the *Tribune,* produced good and bad results. Appraising the activities in their *Growth of the American Republic,* published in 1950, Morison and Commager commented: "The task of carrying through this gigantic program of public works was attended with inevitable confusion and waste. Some of the projects were ridiculous, some were useless, many were so ill-directed as to be worthless. Administrative costs were high, construction was often shoddy, and politics influenced the choice of the work, the hiring of workers, and the appropriation of money." Yet by the end of 1936, the historians point out, 1,497 waterworks, 883 sewage treatment plants, 741 street and highway improvements, 263 hospitals, 166 bridges, and 70 municipal power plants had been built, while almost half a billion dollars had been spent on school buildings and $150 million on slum clearance.

The *Tribune* did not disapprove of all WPA activities, nor of Civilian Conservation Corps endeavors, which put young men to work; but the mistakes and wastage were constantly being brought to the paper's attention by its own reporters and by angry taxpayers. After these negative stories had been printed, not much news space remained to deal with the constructive side of the government's program. But positive aspects were reported, especially on the financial pages, where improving prosperity was regularly recorded. The news pages, too, often reflected federal projects benefiting the community and the state; but they were almost always transmogrified by local politicians, including Gov. Henry Horner and Mayor Edward J. Kelly, into their own achievements. The *Tribune* knew perfectly well where the money came from: the taxpayer, of course. It was gathered in by the hungry New Deal and then disgorged for political purposes to the cities and states. The paper scolded the Democrats it supported but did not cease to show pictures of Governor Horner and Mayor Kelly cutting ribbons at highway projects, schools, state police headquarters, and firehouses.

The *Tribune*'s attacks on the New Deal grew more and more strident. There were Communist plots to be found in extreme corners of the United States. McCormick habitually referred to Roosevelt officials as "commissars." After printing charges by Dr. Hugh Magill's American Federation of Utility Investors that it was spied upon by the government, the paper said: "All forms of despotism rely on the spy system. The Cheka and the GPU were the Russian form of terrorism." The implications were clear. The paper suggested with greater frequency that the country was headed for a dictatorship in the great age of dictators; it published a series of editorials, "Come the Revolution—and How," which described the forms of totalitarianism prevalent in Europe and found parallels in Roosevelt's rule.

*   *   *

In 1919 the *Tribune* had predicted that the Versailles Treaty would some-day be unceremoniously torn up by the despot it would create. Adolf Hitler, dictator of Germany since 1933, fulfilled that forecast, declaring that Germany would no longer be bound by the terms of the treaty. From Berlin, indefatigable *Tribune* correspondent Sigrid Schultz was somehow able to transmit details of Nazi oppression of the Jews, and the progress of German rearmament, without herself being tossed out of the country.

Her dispatches appeared almost daily in the *Tribune,* warning of the dangers of Nazism, while *Tribune* editorials condemned both Hitler and Mussolini, the bellowing Duce of Italy, and warned that their virulence would infect all of Europe.

In May, 1935, McCormick perceived that the border disputes between Ethiopia and Italy's colonies in East Africa might result in a full-scale invasion of Ethiopia. He ordered Wilfred Barber of the paper's London bureau to the forbidding land of Emperor Haile Selassie, where he would await the coming of the Roman legions. Barber, the first foreign correspondent to arrive in Ethiopia, conducted an exclusive interview with the emperor and was the first American correspondent allowed to visit the Ethiopian front in the Ogaden Desert.

Barber was back in the capital, burning with malarial fever, as Selassie, "King of Kings," finally was ready to mobilize his mountain defense forces. Barber was taken by his friends past the palace and to the Seventh Day Adventist hospital in Addis Ababa, from which on October 3 he dictated a dispatch to be cabled to the *Tribune:* "TO THE ROLLING THROB OF A FIVE-FOOT LION'S HIDE WAR DRUM, ECHOING THE EXPLOSION OF ITALIAN BOMBS WHICH FELL ON THE TOWNS OF ADOWA AND ADIGRAT IN NORTHERN ETHIOPIA, EMPEROR HAILE SELASSIE TODAY ORDERED A GENERAL MOBILIZATION, TANTAMOUNT TO A DECLARATION OF WAR UPON ITALY."

The dispatch reported the eagerness of the primitive war chiefs to fight, noted sadly the bombings of villages and hospitals, told of women and children killed, and described the ferocity of the Italian ground attack, which was almost unopposed on the Ethiopian flatlands and had not yet reached the mountains where the capital was situated. Returning to the mobilization, Barber said:

> THE LONG AWAITED MOBILIZATION ORDER SENT THE CROWD OF CHIEFTAINS AND WARRIORS GATHERED IN FRONT OF THE OLD PALACE INTO A FRENZY OF HATRED AGAINST THE ITALIANS AND ALL FOREIGNERS. FOREIGN NEWSPAPERMEN, HERETOFORE TREATED WITH UNFAILING COURTESY ON ALL OCCASIONS, WERE SWEPT OFF THE PALACE STEPS BY A MOB OF WARRIORS AS THEY STRUGGLED FORWARD TO HEAR THE CALL TO ARMS.
>
> "SOLDIERS, GROUP YOURSELVES UNDER YOUR CHIEFS," THE PROCLAMATION SAID. "OBEY THEM WITH ONE HEART. REPULSE THE INVADER . . . THE OPINION OF THE WHOLE WORLD IS REVOLTED BY THIS . . . AGGRESSION AGAINST ETHIOPIA."

"ITALY HITS WITH FOUR ARMIES," read the *Tribune*'s October 4 banner. The modern war machine of Il Duce rolled across the flatlands and over Selassie's primitive warriors, armed with spears, bows, and antique guns, while Count Galeazzo Ciano, Mussolini's son-in-law, led air attacks on defenseless Ethiopian villages and destroyed the few hospitals and schools in the hinterland. On October 5, 1935, President Roosevelt announced that a state of war existed between Italy and Ethiopia.

On the following day, October 6, the *Tribune* received another cable from Addis Ababa, from Robinson Maclean, correspondent of the *Toronto Telegram:*

> WILFRED COURTENAY BARBER, CORRESPONDENT OF THE CHICAGO TRIBUNE, THE FIRST AMERICAN NEWSMAN TO REACH ETHIOPIA TO REPORT THE PRESENT CONFLICT, DIED AT 12:45 O'CLOCK THIS AFTERNOON. THE CAUSE WAS HEART FAILURE DUE TO TOXEMIA COMBINED WITH INFECTED KIDNEYS AND MALARIA. HE WAS 32 YEARS OLD. . . . BARBER SCOOPED THE WORLD WITH HIS FIRST STORIES FROM ETHIOPIA LAST JUNE AND AGAIN BY GOING INTO THE YELLOW HELL OF THE OGADEN DESERT TO GET THE STORY OF ETHIOPIA'S FRONT LINES. . . . HIS LAST STORY, DICTATED FROM HIS SICKBED, TOLD HOW THE WAR DRUMS CALLED THE ETHIOPIANS TO MOBILIZE FOR THE WAR HE CAME TO COVER.

Will Barber was buried in the Gulaly foreign cemetery on a hilltop overlooking Addis Ababa. A notice in Amharic posted on the palace walls on the orders of Emperor Haile Selassie read: "He was a great friend of your country. Show him honor." In 1936, Barber was posthumously awarded the Pulitzer prize for foreign correspondence.

The *Tribune* editorially denounced the invasion of Ethiopia and observed that Mussolini was following in the evil path of other European powers: "The trouble with Mussolini is that he insists on doing what others have done and doing it at a time when they don't want him to do it. There is, however, a just complaint against Mussolini—his methods are outrageous." The editorialist added sarcastically that Mussolini should study the methods used by the Germans, French, British, Belgians, and Portuguese in the past and closed with a dire and accurate prophecy: "Mussolini is insanely shaking the peace of Europe. He is an exhibit of absolutism such as most of Europe has made its master in recent years. This absolutism is the plague of humanity, and its works have not as yet been accomplished."

When President Roosevelt proclaimed American neutrality and an embargo in the Italo-Ethiopian war, the *Tribune* approved and published a page-one McCutcheon cartoon captioned: "That proclamation in 1914 would have kept us out of war." The editorial writer was more cautious, however, noting that "we must remember that the President who by his note writing was supposed to keep us out of war later demanded of Congress a declaration of war, and got it."

*   *   *

The skirmishing with Roosevelt filled many columns of the *Tribune* with rancorous political news each day, mostly reports from various sectors of the electorate dissatisfied with local manifestations of the New Deal. But it by no means fully occupied either the paper or Colonel McCormick.

Although the *Tribune* did not dramatically revise its appearance, changes and improvements were constantly being made. On August 16, 1935, the day its banner proclaimed "SENATE PASSES TAX TO SOAK THE RICH," the paper introduced a larger body type, 7 point Regal on an 8½ point slug, a more open and easy-to-read design. That same day the paper, taking note of a new tax measure that would drain off capital to the government, asked rhetorically: "Maybe a democratic republic could discover it turned out to be a communistic corporation. Who knows?"

Typographical changes were few, but coverage of local and national news was expanded, and the content of the features pages increased, largely with materials from the Patterson-run syndicate in New York. Patterson also continued developing comics, so that the *Tribune* was presenting 20 colored comics each Sunday in a section that averaged 12 to 14 pages in length, depending on the amount of advertising space sold, usually four to six pages. During this period city editor Robert M. Lee took on the added title of assistant managing editor and some of the Sunday editor duties. A Sunday magazine called the *Graphic* (for a time spelled *Grafic*) had been launched on September 20, 1931. At first it appeared only in the country edition, but it was so successful that it was included in the city editions beginning on October 15, 1933. The color cover was John T. McCutcheon's popular "Injun Summer," which had first appeared in the paper on September 30, 1907, had been reprinted annually since 1912, and would appear on *Tribune* Sunday magazine covers for many more years. Inside, the so-called magazine was simply a continuation of the paper's older entertainment and Sunday features section, laid out in newspaper style. In time a change was made to a magazine style of typography, and Lee introduced photo essays, consisting of a single picture and a few hundred words of text, an effort to enliven the magazine without competing directly with the paper's popular rotogravure *Pictorial* magazine. He also began a news of the week review section. Specialized departments were introduced in the *Graphic:* science, pets, photography, beauty, astrology.

Remembering the success Patterson had achieved by coordinating stories in the Sunday paper with motion picture serials, Lee sought to use another medium, radio. He wrote his own fiction, "The Return of Peter Quill," which appeared in the *Graphic* magazine to great promotional fanfare, then was supplemented in a WGN radiocast. The idea failed to attract readers to the magazine or listeners to the station, so it was dropped, together with the costly news review. Lee's daily features were highly successful, however. After FBI agents ambushed and killed the country's most-wanted criminal, John Dillinger, on July 22, 1934, Lee anticipated intense reader interest in exploits of the government men, who were proving to have better brains and reflexes than the criminals. He launched a series of stories relating the experiences of G-men in outwitting gangsters and other felons. A particular hero of the series was Melvin Purvis, agent in charge of the Chicago office of the FBI.

Lee, flamboyant and imaginative, relied upon day city editor J. Loy "Pat" Maloney to find and motivate exactly the right reporter in the execution of a Lee idea. Reporter Virginia Gardner, who appeared deceptively frail, visited quack doctors and exposed their fraudulent practices. Marcia Winn tracked down the odd and bizarre, including a hobbyist named Duncan Hines, who himself tracked down good restaurants, providing lists for his friends. Hines later made a business of it, thanks in part to *Tribune* publicity. Kay Hall consented to spend a few days unobtrusively in a nudist camp, which provided her with grist for a series of articles as well as with the novel experience of a chance meeting with the Reverend John Astley-Cock, assistant religion editor of the *Tribune,* and his wife, confirmed nudists, who happened to be spending the summer in the camp.

Robert Morton Lee was a tough, hard-driving city editor who wore vivid shirts, trim, shoulder-padded jackets, and tight-fitting trousers, giving him the appearance of a charging fullback as he came scowling into the newsroom, juggling a chain of glistening keys. New reporters told one another the plastering would crack if Lee smiled, and they assumed the keys were from honorary fraternities, but they were wrong on both counts. Lee, born near Estherville, Iowa, was self-taught, and late in the evening, when he had peeled down to his purple-and-gold-striped silk shirt and was happily rewriting some cub's copy, he was affable and almost kindly. Lee, whose hobbies were the study of Napoleon and interesting actresses, wrote well himself and appreciated good writing. He built an excellent reportorial staff that performed ably for his deputy, Pat Maloney, who won the love and admiration of reporters and photographers by his own example of utter devotion to his creed: Get the news first, get it right, tell it pithily. Maloney's chief of photographers was dour, worried Lyman Atwell, whose lensmen were the most numerous and best in town. But Atwell endlessly mourned his lot as ideas from Lee and Maloney beat upon him, the intricacies of new color photography projects plagued him, and unfeeling editors tossed away prize photographs to accommodate a few more takes of dull type.

Maloney's staff in the 1930s included some of the top writers in the paper's history; James O'Donnell Bennett, Philip Kinsley, Arthur Evans, and Parke Brown remained active and were joined by younger reporters and rewriters, Wayne Thomis, Thomas Morrow, Percy Wood, Joseph Ator, Seymour Korman, Harold Smith, and Lee's favorite rewrite men, William Shinnick and William Moore. Religion news was covered by two men, the Reverend John Evans and the Reverend John Astley-Cock, both

INJUN SUMMER

Yep, sonny, this is sure enough Injun summer. Don't know what that is, I reckon, do you?

Well, that's when all the homesick Injuns come back to play. You know, a long time ago, long afore yer granddaddy was born even, there used to be heaps of Injuns around here—thousands—millions, I reckon, far as that's concerned. Reg'lar sure 'nough Injuns—none o' yer cigar store Injuns, not much. They wuz all around here—right here where you're standin'.

Don't be skeered—hain't none around here now, leastways no live ones. They been gone this many a year.

They all went away and died, so they ain't no more left.

But every year. 'long about now, they all come back, leastways their sperrits do. They're here now. You can see 'em off across the fields. Look real hard. See that kind o' hazy, misty look out yonder? Well, them's Injuns—Injun sperrits marchin' along an' dancin' in the sunlight. That's what makes that kind o' haze that's everywhere—it's jest the sperrits of the Injuns all come back. They're all around us now.

See off yonder; see them tepees? They kind o' look like corn shocks from here, but them's Injun tents, sure as you're a foot high. See 'em now?

Sure, I knowed you could. Smell that smoky sort o' smell in the air? That's the campfires a-burnin' and their pipes a-goin'.

Lots o' people say it's just leaves burnin', but it ain't. It's the campfires, an' th' Injuns are hoppin' 'round 'em t' beat the old Harry.

You jest come out here tonight when the moon is hangin' over the hill off yonder an' the harvest fields is all swimmin' in the moonlight, an' you can see the Injuns and the tepees jest as plain as kin be. You can, eh? I knowed you would after a little while.

Jever notice how the leaves turn red 'bout this time o' year? That's jest another sign o' redskins. That's when an old Injun sperrit gits tired dancin' an' goes up an' squats on a leaf t'rest. Why, I kin hear 'em rustlin' an' whisperin' an' creepin' 'round among the leaves all the time; an' ever' once'n a while a leaf gives way under some fat old Injun ghost and comes floatin' down to the ground. See—here's one now. See how red it is? That's the war paint rubbed off'n an Injun ghost, sure's you're born.

Purty soon all the Injuns'll go marchin' away agin, back to the happy huntin' ground, but next year you'll see 'em troopin' back—th' sky jest hazy with 'em and their campfires smolderin' away jest like they are now.

(ILLUSTRATION COURTESY OF CHICAGO HISTORICAL SOCIETY)

scholars as well as reporters and writers. The paper's other specialists, Hal Foust, automobile editor; Al Chase, real estate; and Larry Wolters, radio, knew their people and beats so well that they held a virtual monopoly on the news, as did William Fulton, the handsome young school board reporter. A former University of Illinois gymnast, Fulton covered board meetings by day and prowled the city at night with his close friend James B. McCahey, president of the Board of Education. This was Maloney's idea of how his reporters should cover a beat, by working at it 18 or so hours a day. Fulton maintained excellent relations with the teachers also, and when Chicago proved unable to pay them in cash, he and Maloney led the *Tribune* into a successful campaign in Springfield and Washington to obtain the needed money.

The reporters generally would submit to any sacrifice Maloney required, knowing that he would offer himself were he not chained to a desk. Earl "Moon" Mullin subjected himself to the ministrations of the young women in Chicago's massage parlors in order to write a first-person exposé of that social evil. The owners of the parlors had been advertising in the morning *Herald and Examiner,* advertising the *Tribune* refused to accept. When Mullin's experiences were recounted in print, the *Examiner*'s advertising, if not the massage parlors, disappeared.

Not all *Tribune* campaigns of the period went as well. Following the arrival onto the Chicago newspaper scene of the other colonel, Frank Knox, who took over the *Daily News* after the sudden death of Walter Strong, a new enmity was engendered. In addition to criticizing Mc-Cormick's longtime friend and political associate, Mayor Edward J. Kelly, Knox showed signs of coveting McCormick's leadership of Illinois Republicans. The McCormick counterattack began as an innocent editorial appearing on October 9, 1935, when summer daylight time ended, suggesting that Chicago ought to have daylight time year round. There were excellent reasons for the suggestion—for example, it would save energy and reduce auto accidents in the evening when drivers were weary—reasons that caused the entire country to move to "fast time" during World War II. Also, the *Tribune* showed, existing time zones had been created by railroads for their schedule convenience, and Chicago should have been in the Eastern zone from the beginning. The editorial was followed by a news story stating that Ald. Berthold A. Cronson would introduce an ordinance to give Chicago daylight time throughout the year, and the next day ten suburban mayors were quoted as approving the move, which would, of course, affect the entire metropolitan community.

There were belated yelps from the other newspapers, especially the afternoon papers, and most especially the *Chicago Daily News.* The *Daily News* competed strongly with the *Tribune* in the area of financial and market news, and it saw that daylight time would deprive it of an hour's Eastern market report five days a week, nine months of the year, handing that hour to its morning rival. Since Hearst's *Herald and Examiner* did not attempt to fully compete with the *Tribune* and the *Times* carried almost no market reports, it appeared quite clear to Col. Frank Knox whom the Eastern time ordinance was aimed at. So the *Tribune* was alone in the fight, except for a secret pledge of aid from Mayor Kelly. The *Tribune*'s City Hall reporter was detached to write daily stories on the merits of daylight time. He traveled through western Michigan and Indiana, which actually wanted Eastern time, reporting in the *Tribune* and, by remote control, broadcasting over WGN the benefits to be expected. Both Detroit and Cincinnati had moved into Eastern time years before and were delighted with it, their mayors said.

Ultimately the Interstate Commerce Commission was drawn into the daylight time controversy. It ruled that western Indiana and Michigan should, indeed, move into the Eastern time zone, but not nearby Chicago. Not until the spring of 1936 did the battle end. By that time Colonel Knox yearned for a spot on the Republican presidential ticket. In a visit to McCormick's Astor Street apartment, an accommodation was arranged. If Knox could win the nomination for vice-president, the *Tribune* would continue to support the ticket. The citizens of Chicago would receive an opportunity to vote in referendum on whether to have Eastern time year round or daylight time from early April to late October. In the referendum, only one follower of Mayor Kelly, Ald. Jacob Arvey, was able to carry his ward for Eastern time. While the rest of the city rejected the year-round proposal overwhelmingly, the 24th Ward approved it by an 82 percent vote, demonstrating to both Kelly and McCormick Arvey's masterly control of the ward organization. So summer daylight time was continued, extended by two months in Chicago. The controversy was over.

During this period, Colonel McCormick was frequently occupied with problems in Canada. He was required to make the decision on the site for a paper mill and town in Quebec Province, on the north shore of the Gulf of St. Lawrence some 75 miles west of the company-owned pulpwood limit and plant at the mouth of the Rocky River. McCormick, with inspiration, had christened the Rocky River site "Shelter Bay," a name much more acceptable to ships' captains. Now he joined Arthur Schmon, director of the Canadian properties, and Leonard F. Schlemm, a Montreal expert in town planning, in seeking a location that would provide a year-round port, serve as the manufacturing center for pulpwood limits stretching 200 miles to the north, offer rivers and creeks to float logs to the mill for 100,000 tons of newsprint annually, and at the same time provide a townsite for a planned model city. The town became Baie

Comeau, 250 miles northeast of Quebec City and not too far from a power plant built in 1928 on the Outardes River. Throughout 1935, the staff at the Thorold mill employed its skills to plan a new power plant, mill buildings, the wharf, a railroad to the wharf, water supply and river improvements for logging, holding areas for the logging operations, and the town itself.

Specifications were drafted for all equipment—the paper machines (each long enough to stretch the length of a football field), groundwood mill, sulphite digesters, steam plant, and other machinery. McCormick, who often pushed his people to top speed, this time urged them to go slow. "Make no mistakes," he advised. He did not want Baie Comeau to be the usual company town. "We should encourage our employees to build and own their homes and own the land upon which the homes are built," he told Schmon. Construction began in the spring of 1936, with the men living in a log village, an improvement over Shelter Bay, site of the earlier operations, which in 1931 had consisted of two tar-paper shacks. Tribune Company directors went to Baie Comeau in the fall of 1937 and held their meeting aboard the company's M.S. *Franquelin.* On December 24, 1937, months ahead of schedule, No. 1 paper machine was turned on for a trial run. Forty years later there would be two towns at the site, Baie Comeau and Haute Rive, with a total population of 30,000, in an area once called by Canadians "the land that God gave Cain," and the company's timber limits would total over 12,500 square miles.

*   *   *

Tribune Company had become an international corporation that in later years would have 25,000 employees. Long before, McCormick had said it was too big for one man, but the Colonel made his will effective upon most of the vast organization most of the time, whether he was in the Canadian wilderness, in New York or Chicago, or on one of his vacation trips. McCormick appeared to spend all his waking hours thinking about some phase of Tribune Company operations and was prone to summon anyone at any time for a question or a conference. He ran his organization with an erratic kind of military precision. He was thoroughly acquainted with military staff work and "through channels" procedure, yet was enough of an autocrat to breach any and all regulations whenever he chose, which was frequently. A *Tribune* worker, especially in editorial, might be summoned without notice into the presence of the Colonel for a brief conference—to receive an order, to answer a question, or simply to be inspected. On such occasions the employee invariably donned a jacket. He appeared before whichever secretary he assumed had called him, Miss Genevieve Burke, whose office was to the left of McCormick's as a visitor approached, or Miss Dorothy Murray, who had an office to the right.

Since McCormick did not keep both secretaries informed of his frequent summonses, there was confusion at times, but the system generally worked well, possibly because the good secretaries feuded and rarely spoke to one another.

Inside the vast paneled office, with a fireplace at the right and McCormick's enormous marble-topped desk at the left, the publisher would be at work as a visitor arrived. A newcomer would be left standing until he was surreptitiously eyed, whereupon McCormick would sometimes smile, ask his question, issue his order, and watch with amusement as the visitor turned to leave. There were no doors visible inside the office, and the trapped visitor had to wait until McCormick freed him by pushing a hidden button. Generally, before his next summons, the visitor would find out how he could touch a footplate that would swing open the door. If the Colonel was on familiar terms with the visitor, he might come from behind his desk, indicate a chair, and sit informally for a chat among the huge armchairs and divans in the center of the room.

McCormick arrived in Tribune Tower at 10 A.M. By this time he had thoroughly read that morning's editions. It could be professionally fatal for an editor to appear before him without knowing the answer to a question about any story in the paper. Usually McCormick devoted his mornings to the business affairs of the company, discussing matters with the department heads, receiving the few outsiders admitted to his presence, and getting his staff of librarians and consultants to work on the various projects in which he was endlessly engaged. At 11 o'clock, or whatever time he chose, McCormick would hold a conference with his editorial page staff, without much doubt the pleasantest time of his day. Personnel changed, but the system did not. In the late 1920s and early 1930s, the venerable Tiffany Blake was the man who led the editorial writers into the meeting and gently guided McCormick now and then. Blake, who wrote his editorials in longhand while standing at a high desk, was the only *Tribune* editorial man to call McCormick "Bert." Present at that time were Clifford Raymond, veteran editorial writer and a former Washington correspondent; Leon Stolz, son of a rabbi and a University of Chicago graduate, sometimes called "the Rabbi" in this group; Levering Cartwright, who would go on to make his fortune in the investment business; and Baker Brownell, who soon departed to become a professor of contemporary thought at Northwestern and to write books on philosophy and religion. McCormick, though a world traveler and former dweller in exotic courts, was essentially a shy man; he never quite lost his awe of the gentle-voiced Brownell and seemed less comfortable when "the Professor" was present, though his other occasional editorial adviser, Reuben Cahn, a former professor at Northwestern, discomfited him not at all. In 1931, McCormick yielded to Brownell's insistent invitation to lecture to his class at Northwestern, where he spoke to a hostile audience on the responsibilities of the press and ownership of a large corporation. He was studying ways to best perpetuate the *Tribune*, he said, and cited the corporate structure of the University of Padua, which was 700 years old. In the question period he was asked, "Colonel McCormick, what is the primary duty of a newspaper?" He replied, "To return a profit."

Typically in the editorial meetings there was animated talk, even debate, with McCormick by his own announced rules being required to hold his own. By 1935, however, he was testy about the New Deal and inclined to be oracular. Frequently the cartoonists, John McCutcheon, Carey Orr, and newcomer Joseph Parrish, would be present, McCutcheon sometimes mildly taking issue with the Colonel, while Orr was always in enthusiastic agreement. As the heavy fire of criticism from Roosevelt's supporters increased, McCormick's editorial meetings sometimes became strained, curt orders were issued, and the policy of the paper became increasingly monolithic. Inevitably, McCormick got what he wanted. Later in the day he would read copies of the editorials with relish, but sometimes, irked, he would send for the chief editorial writer and begin brusquely, "Can't I get it through your head . . . ?" Such occasions were rare. Generally, a single phrase from the Colonel could generate not only an editorial pleasing to him but a campaign of months' duration.

Following the editorial conference, Colonel McCormick took lunch with his business department heads, and sometimes an editorial writer or two, in what was called the Overset Club on the 19th floor. As few as six or as many as 20 might be present. They were to begin eating as soon as they were served. McCormick might arrive at any time, eat in ten or 15 minutes, then vanish, or he might remain for an hour or more of discussion. Whichever he chose, there was an invariable rule: No one left before he did. Occasionally a dignitary would accompany McCormick to lunch, at one time Herbert Hoover, at another, Winston Churchill, who complained that the Scotch served him was ruined by the ice in it. Drinks were provided only when special guests were present. Usually McCormick departed early to exercise, practicing polo in a special cage of wood and wire netting built for him by John Park. On a rooftop beneath the flying buttresses, Colonel McCormick, in T-shirt, jodhpurs, and boots, bestrode a wooden horse within the wire cage, where he could whack a polo ball into the netting, the concave floor bringing it back to his mallet range.

After lunch and noontime recreation, McCormick pushed vigorously into a new round of work. There were speeches to write, correspondence to answer, and business staff conferences. McCormick never ceased to have a special interest in the presses, the mills, the Tribune Company fleet, the foreign correspondents, the Sunday department, and the financial pages. Consequently he met quite regularly with John Park, production department superintendent; Elbert Antrim, his business manager; J. Howard Wood, financial editor; any visitor from the Canadian properties or any visiting correspondent; A. M. Kennedy, Sunday editor; and Lee, who became the managing editor on January 1, 1937. There were conferences with the new advertising manager, Chesser M. Campbell, who was reorganizing one of the few areas in which McCormick did not profess special expertise, and an occasional meeting with Louis Rose, the circulation manager, who arrived late in the afternoon. Frequently there were visits from the company's legal representatives, Weymouth Kirkland, Howard Ellis, and Keith Masters. C. Wayland Brooks, who eventually became a U.S. senator, was an occasional visitor, and, more rarely, Mayor Kelly called. Miscellaneous persons constantly sought an audience with the Colonel but rarely were received, and none without excellent references and prior preparation.

Possibly the most important regular meeting of the afternoon was with the managing editor. It began precisely at 2 P.M., at least in the days when Pat Maloney held that position. Each day Maloney, who became managing editor in 1939, would wait in the office of Miss Burke for admittance, and he was seldom delayed. There would be a discussion of the possible news stories, McCormick handing Maloney a sheaf of notes he had saved up during the earlier hours of the day. Many would be written on scraps torn out of that morning's *Tribune*. Some of them, written as McCormick traveled to town in his armored car, and in later years by plane to Meigs Field, were almost indecipherable. Maloney and Miss Burke could usually solve that day's scrawl but not always, in which case they simply hoped that the Colonel would not remember everything he had suggested. On at least one occasion, McCormick himself could not read what he had written. Since it was on a Washington topic, he sent it off to Walter Trohan in the Washington bureau with a further note asking, *"What do I mean?"*

It became evident that the younger men who were regular visitors to McCormick's office were bound for top company jobs. Chesser Campbell would succeed McCormick as chief executive officer of Tribune Company and publisher of the *Tribune*. Campbell would be followed by J. Howard Wood, who, on retirement, was succeeded by Harold Grumhaus. Grumhaus in 1934 was the *Tribune*'s new insurance executive, responsible for all the company properties in the United States and Canada. None were "yes" men, and all were striving to bring new business methods to a paper that in the past had usually rejected outside influence. When Wood, who had made negative reports and recommendations in his private meetings with McCormick while he was financial editor, attended his first Tuesday meeting of department heads as the newly appointed auditor, he sat unobtrusively in the back row among the 40 present. McCormick immediately spotted him. "Come up front, Howard," he invited. "I want a 'no' man in the front row." There was rarely dissent at the general Tuesday meeting, however. McCormick led the discussion. If he had criticism, he asked the department head affected to remain behind, and they would talk privately. Once he objected to a change of typography Maloney had instituted in his absence. "I want you to change back to the way we were," he said. Then he added, "But take two weeks doing it, Pat. I don't want anyone to know I corrected you."

Tribune editors and executives endlessly marveled at McCormick's inexhaustible supply of ideas on every possible subject. A central desk in the office was covered with books and magazines McCormick was then pursuing. Usually two or three librarians were searching for data for his memorandums, speeches, and articles. His interests were totally catholic, covering the universe and the full span of time. He was generally pragmatic, and the *Tribune* rarely ran an editorial if it had not been determined in advance that the idea was practical. In the early days of Wood's visits, McCormick especially relied on his young editor's knowledge of the city's business leaders. "He'd get ideas and I'd carry them out," Wood recalled. On one occasion McCormick wondered why milk companies did not use cardboard containers instead of bottles. Wood visited milk company executives. Most scoffed in the beginning, but ultimately the idea was tried and widely adopted. Another time, McCormick, who had campaigned against smoke pollution, wanted Wood to find out why trains should turn around in downtown Chicago. Why not simply back them out? The Chicago and North Western agreed it should be done, and the practice became general.

McCormick knew how to give orders, and on one occasion at least showed he knew how to accept an assignment as well. One late Sunday afternoon, shortly before the first edition was to go to press, he telephoned the newsroom and was put through to the day city editor, as was the custom. A young substitute was in charge, harried by the fact that he had no "speed" story to go with the *Tribune*'s "massacre clock," part of a campaign against reckless driving. A story a day was mandatory, and a fatal accident often took the clock to page one. There was no "speed" story in sight as the day editor responded to Colonel McCormick, expecting any kind of an order, but acutely aware that the Colonel's wishes or whims had total precedence. "There's an accident here," McCormick rumbled, phoning from somewhere southwest of Wheaton. He provided last names of victims and most of the needed details. The day editor took notes, and then a deep breath: "Colonel, this is the story we need. But we can't go without all the facts—names, ages, addresses of the victims . . . We've got five minutes. Only you—" "Yes," McCormick agreed promptly.

In three minutes he called back, providing full information on the one dead and several injured in the crash. The story and the massacre clock ran on page one. The following Monday the substitute day editor was invited to Colonel McCormick's office. After a brief and pleasant chat McCormick unloosed the secret door with a slight chuckle. Neither mentioned the car crash story.

*   *   *

In 1936 the *Tribune* led an exasperated and angry Midwestern constituency that agreed that Franklin Delano Roosevelt was moving the nation into bankruptcy and then into the hands of the radical left. The leading editorial on January 1, 1936, was a ringing exhortation to readers to rise against the New Deal tyranny that was threatening the doom of the country. Colonel McCormick initiated the battle cry, and it was hoisted that morning to the topmost position beneath the editorial page flag: "TURN THE RASCALS OUT."

"There is a new plank this morning in the *Tribune*'s Platform," began the editorial. "It is probably the most imperative of them all for the year 1936: 'Turn the rascals out.' The opportunity to get rid of the dangerous and unsavory conditions used by countless predatory politicians is offered this year in the campaign and the election. The people can vote the rascals out of office, out of Congress, out of the alphabetical administrations, out of important missions, boards, and commissions, and out of the affairs of the nation."

The editorial indicted the New Deal and Roosevelt, with its style and rhetoric embodying the high moral purpose of Thomas Jefferson arraigning King George III. It charged the Roosevelt regime with suppressing freedom of speech and press, enriching the gold and silver producers while robbing the citizens of their savings, encouraging Socialists to organize government corps to run private businesses, imposing ruinous taxes, and leading the country toward bankruptcy and communism.

> Get rid of the men who have broken faith, been false to their word, untrue to their promises, and dishonest with the American people. Turn out the wasters who have hoisted the national debt to the 30 billion dollar mark. Turn out the men who have abused their diplomatic immunity, traded secret information for profit, treated desperate situations vaingloriously and in high spirits dealt lightly with the miseries of their fellow countrymen.
>
> Turn out the men responsible for the reduction of the country's food supply, for the boosting of its costs, for the weeds that grow on fertile acres, for the impairment of honorable obligations, for the silly schemes for robbing those who have and giving it to those who envy.
>
> Turn out the men who buy elections. Turn the rascals out. Clean house.

Stop the spoliation and destruction. Call a halt while there is yet something to be saved and in time to save it. Restore the national honor. Return the national sanity. Give the people back their faith in government. Time still remains and the opportunity is at hand. It cannot be the destiny of the United States to run like the Gadarene swine violently down a steep place and perish in the sea.

The editorial provided a rallying cry for millions of angry Middle West voters, from farmers who had laid siege to Chicago rather than sell at abysmally low prices, to disgruntled Democrats. The Midwest appeared to McCormick as sure a center for revolt against Eastern seaboard control and malign foreign influence as it had been against the Southern slave oligarchy in the days of Grandfather Medill. McCormick dedicated the *Tribune* to the cause as Medill had done. In addition he undertook personally to organize "The Volunteers," a nationwide Republican strike force similar to the Wide-Awakes of Lincoln's day. Shortly after the new plank and the editorial appeared, a daily exhortation was added to the editorial page flag: "Only 231 days to save your country. What are you going to do about it?" Each 24 hours, of course, a day was torn from the prophetic calendar, and as election time neared, the Cassandra-like warnings proliferated throughout the paper, even into the society and sports pages, and *Tribune* telephone operators responded to callers: "Only xx days to save your country."

It appeared that the Midwest really was about to spring to arms. Although the New Deal had put thousands to work, other thousands observed the waste and ineptitude of the WPA, the CCC, and other alphabetical creations. They saw farmlands removed from cultivation and pigs slaughtered to be burned or buried; they perceived taxes rising faster than wages and profits and the national debt growing endlessly. Yet there were other signs, which the *Tribune* editorials could not ignore. On January 2, the paper noted in its lead, "Business the year just ended was in the largest volume in a number of years." Still there was discontent among the little people. Forty percent of the farmers were tenants in the Midwest, and they saw soil bank and other government benefits going to the owners, not to the field workers. In the city, men who worked in factories felt they were little better off than the "loafers" seen leaning on shovels or rakes in the parks and streets. Where there had been bleak despair in early 1933, before the New Deal began, there was now dissent and resentment, and McCormick believed it was deep and general. The America of Joseph Medill's day was still wanted and would work if given a chance.

Colonel McCormick momentarily considered making himself available for the presidency, then rejected the thought. But the idea recurred constantly to the colonel across town, and Frank Knox, publisher of the

Daily News, announced his availability for the top of the Republican ticket and began his campaign. McCormick, meantime, had learned of the good works of Gov. Alfred Landon of Kansas and sent reporter Joseph Ator to investigate. Ator, a lean, grumbling cynic who professed hatred for most politicians, wrote a series of approving articles on Alf Landon. On January 24, while Colonel McCormick was vacationing in Miami, the Associated Press asked him to name his candidate for the Republican nomination for president, and he replied without hesitation, Alfred Landon of Kansas. Governor Landon, said McCormick, was an outstanding conservative who could win.

Having so early announced his choice and excluded Frank Knox, McCormick began his Landon campaign shortly after returning to Chicago. There were more stories and editorials. By March, McCormick was sending letters and telegrams to Landon, offering counsel and warning against unwise political associations, i.e., William Randolph Hearst. Hearst had arrived in Topeka to visit Governor Landon, a visit not suggested by McCormick, and the Colonel was disturbed. Will T. Beck, a publisher and Kansas Republican state chairman, assured McCormick that Hearst had not been invited but simply dropped by. "Hearst will have no hold on Governor Landon," McCormick was told. McCormick's protest was effective, however; he was invited to be Landon's guest and was given a chance to expound his own campaign ideas.

On May 11, Landon wrote McCormick thanking him for an offer of WGN facilities to broadcast his campaign messages. Although he was himself becoming heavily involved in the Landon cause, McCormick nevertheless sent a note to managing editor E. S. Beck, directing that the *Tribune* should be completely unbiased in the forthcoming campaign. The note, posted on the newsroom bulletin board, was not, however, totally unequivocal:

> *Dear Teddy:*
>
> *When Roosevelt came into power he immediately tried to control the correspondents and to over-awe the newspapers. We reacted against this and have led the fight ever since. The fact that Roosevelt was trying to dominate the newspapers was recognized even by his followers, and our demonstrated independence did us more good than our bias did us harm.*
>
> *With the nomination of the tickets I think this will change. One organized group will oppose another organized group and people will want to read all about each side. We will therefore aim to keep the balance as even as possible.*
>
> *There will be so much Roosevelt news created by his commissars that it will be necessary to see that Landon gets a fair share of that total. But the Roosevelt stories must be adequate and must be written without any animus towards him. As far as interpretive sentences and paragraphs are used, they must be real interpretations and not hostile arguments.*

In the spring of 1936, McCormick acquired a new Sunday editor, Ardis M. "Mike" Kennedy, son of a Sault Ste. Marie, Michigan, minister and brother-in-law of Chesser Campbell, the *Tribune*'s advertising director. Kennedy, a World War I flyer and graduate of the Columbia University School of Journalism, came to the *Tribune* with experience on Minneapolis papers and the *Chicago Herald and Examiner*. He had studied color photography at Campbell's suggestion, and the two men foresaw great developments in that area for the Sunday supplements under Kennedy's charge and for run-of-paper color to enhance editorial and advertising pages. Colonel McCormick's first interest at the time, however, was the use of color in the political fray. He instructed Kennedy to ready a color portrait of Governor Landon for the front page of the *Tribune*'s magazine. He also ordered a straw poll conducted in Illinois, in which Landon drew 56 percent of the Republican votes against Knox, Ohio Sen. Robert Taft, and Sen. Arthur Vandenberg of Michigan. "What is true of the sentiment in Illinois is true of other states," said the June 7 editorial, entitled "Who But Landon?" Two days later the page-one banner blazoned: "STAGE IS SET FOR LANDON. BORAH REFUSES TO JOIN PLOT TO STOP KANSAN." A page-one editorial was headed: "Republicans at the Hour of Decision."

A large *Tribune* staff was sent to Cleveland to cover the anticipated victory. McCormick himself attended as a delegate. His sister-in-law, Ruth Hanna Simms, the widow of Medill McCormick, was present as chairman of New Mexico's delegation. (She had married Albert G. Simms, a former New Mexico congressman and a member of the Republican National Committee, in 1932.) William O'Neill was covering Landon in Topeka, and Walter Trohan traveled with President Roosevelt, who was on a speech-making tour of six states—an unconscionable move, the paper said, designed to distract attention from the Cleveland proceedings.

The *Tribune*'s coverage of the 1936 convention in Cleveland almost matched that of the 1860 convention in Chicago's Wigwam, which nominated Lincoln. The daily eight-column banners were exhortations to the delegates in Cleveland as much as news reports to readers in Chicago, while page-one editorials and cartoons all pointed to the inevitability of the party's choice. On June 10, the editorial was titled: "Landon Can Beat Roosevelt." On June 11, the paper urged that the ticket be made Landon and Vandenberg. It conceded that Vandenberg did not want the job but urged that he be drafted. On June 12, the eight-column banner proclaimed: "LANDON CHOSEN! UNANIMOUS." A subhead predicted: "Senator Vandenberg May Be Picked Today as Running Mate."

But the selection for vice-president was to be Col. Frank Knox, publisher of the *Chicago Daily News*. The *Tribune*'s June 13 headline read: "LANDON IS READY FOR CAMPAIGN," while the subheadline disclosed, "Knox Is Chosen Candidate for Vice President." In its page-one editorial, the paper admitted its dislike of Knox, but it gamely accepted the ticket:

Republicans Are Ready for the Enemy

The Republicans have their platform and their candidate. No honest minded person can deny that the party has been moved by a spirit of devotion to the common country and has done what it could in this hour of decision to raise itself to the need of the day.

Having made the wisest choice possible in nominating Gov. Landon to head the ticket, and having received Senator Vandenberg's final word on second place, the convention thought it expedient to conciliate elements in the party which, having opposed Landon, responded to the popular urge and accepted him. Col. Frank Knox, the Chicago publisher, who had been a candidate for president, was nominated to complete the ticket.

These elements thus conciliated have been opposed by the *Tribune* for many years, but it can be said for Col. Knox that he is a better man than *[Vice-President John]* Garner, who does not believe in one particle of the New Deal, which might be to his credit, but dare not open his mouth against it, preferring to keep his place, his salary, his automobile with the loss of his own self-esteem. Col. Knox believes in what the Republican party says.

The *Tribune* continued to say it was satisfied with the actions of the convention, that the platform was adequate, and that a fair fight on principle was to be expected. Then it added its estimate of what the campaign would be all about: "The Republican candidate will carry the nation back to the older and higher standards of government conduct in which service of country is placed above service of self."

On June 18, Colonel McCormick was able to send to the Republican nominee his printed color portrait as it would appear on the cover of the paper's magazine. *"I stopped the press and had the quotation from your May 7th speech etched on the cylinder,"* McCormick wrote. *"It seems to me an excellent slogan for the campaign."* He had indeed stopped the press. The preparation of a color cover on a 16-page rotogravure cylinder ordinarily required three weeks. McCormick had the color cylinders ready in advance. On June 15, he had sent Sunday editor Kennedy a note: *"Dear Mike: On the Landon picture put that quotation—something to the effect that 'I am dedicated to the cause that Americans will not have to sell their votes for bread!'"*

Governor Landon promptly thanked McCormick and asked his advice on the selection of a press secretary, a request McCormick relayed to managing editor Beck, though whether such advice was offered is not known. On June 24, McCormick wrote Landon warning him that *"J. P. Morgan and Company has gone New Deal"* and thanked the governor for his hospitality. Beck, meantime, sent five men to Topeka to do interviews and arrange for more color pictures, in addition to William O'Neill, already on the scene. When Landon formally accepted the nomination, the *Tribune* captured the scene in color, which was also published as a cover of the magazine and offered for sale "framed and under glass."

On June 27, while Landon was taking a brief rest on the McGraw ranch at Estes Park, Colorado, McCormick wrote him: *"There is a whispering campaign that you are a far western man with no knowledge or sympathy for Jews. . . . The opposition is also capitalizing on Americanism as an added foreign fascist movement."* He warned Landon that he had to make a speech somewhere in the East to demonstrate his sympathy with minority problems and his abhorrence of religious intolerance. On July 8, he urged Landon again to *"get right with the Jewish community"* and sent suggestions as to what might be said, adding, *"Leon Stolz has read and agrees."* Stolz was the *Tribune* editorial writer whom associates called "the Rabbi." On July 14, an editorial by Stolz on the subject of racial and religious prejudice and persecution was sent to Landon for his guidance.

Landon's obstacles were formidable. He was unknown to most of the country, and his opponent was discovered to be one of the most popular presidents in history, a man who could use radio and manipulate much of the press with superlative skill. Because of the New Deal, or despite it, the economy was constantly improving, and not even the rejection of the president by Alfred E. Smith at the Democratic convention in Philadelphia slowed down Roosevelt and his campaign. His luck seemed always good. His most unpopular measures were abolished by the Supreme Court, decisions for which Roosevelt felt no gratitude whatever. He vetoed a bill to pay off claims of war veterans, but it was passed over his veto; the payments began in June, 1936, aiding prosperity and good feeling, which in turn somehow reflected favorably upon Roosevelt.

Colonel McCormick fought desperately for his candidate. He pushed the organizing of the Volunteers, which had headquarters in Tribune Tower with Chauncey McCormick, the Colonel's cousin, as president and Ruth Simms as one of the national speakers. He ran scores of stories and editorials and sent exhortations to Landon. On July 23, Landon formally opened his campaign, saying, "I intend to approach the issues fairly, without rancor or passion. If we are to go forward permanently, it must be with a united nation—not with people torn by appeals to prejudices and divided by class feeling. The time has come to pull together." McCormick telegraphed: "ACCEPTANCE SPEECH WELL RECEIVED EVERY-WHERE I HAVE BEEN. HEARTY CONGRATULATIONS." Landon replied that he was delighted with the praise. He promised to follow up on McCormick's written suggestions. The two men were friendly, but somewhat more distant than McCormick and Roosevelt had been in their correspondence during the campaign of 1932.

On August 16, the *Tribune*'s leading editorial, in its first paragraph, set forth the situation faced by the Republicans: "Business has now attained its highest level in five years, and, in some respects, the highest since 1929. Employment has increased, wages are up, a larger dollar volume of business is being done. There can be no question that there has been a substantial recovery from the low point of the depression." The editorial then went on to attack Roosevelt and the New Deal on other than economic grounds, and three days later the paper felt required to say: "Some people think there is a bewildering inconsistency in what appears in the political columns and the financial columns."

The people most bewildered were those in the Landon camp, it appeared. The campaign was slow to begin, while Roosevelt, as the incumbent, campaigned every time he made an inspection trip or signed a measure for disaster relief, as he did for flood-stricken eastern states. Colonel McCormick wrote letters and sent telegrams suggesting speaking dates, urging the candidate to write a personal letter to key people who were working hard for him. On one occasion, the Colonel acknowledged his own inadequacy: Referring to troubles with the Volunteers organization in California, McCormick said his offer to help was received coldly. *"I am beginning to think they do not want me in California,"* he wrote. He again urged Landon to speak on the subject of *"racial and religious equality,"* saying this had been urged by Jewish leaders in New York, and recommended that Landon *"must appeal to immigrant workers"* and use the report that *"Communists are urging votes for Roosevelt."*

When Roosevelt repudiated various accounts of Communist support, the *Tribune* replied: "The question is not whether Mr. Roosevelt repudiates or accepts communism. It is whether he has done and proposes to do things which Communists recognize as their own."

On September 21, McCormick telegraphed Landon: "THE COMMUNIST ALLIANCE IS PRETTY WELL PROVED ALSO CORRUPTION IN THE ALPHABETICAL AGENCIES. IN THE CURRENT EXCHANGE OF THE HOSTILITIES IS THERE NOT ROOM FOR A NOTE OF IDEALISM, LOVE OF COUNTRY AND ITS PEOPLE. I LEAVE THE SUGGESTION WITH YOU." Landon replied the same day: "YOUR OBSERVATIONS RELATIVE TO THE PROGRESS OF THIS CAMPAIGN ARE WELCOME AND I SHALL GIVE EVERY CONSIDERATION TO YOUR SUGGESTIONS FOR THE INJECTION OF COMMENT ON IDEALISM, LOVE OF COUNTRY AND ITS PEOPLE." The governor rather pointedly omitted reference to the Communist alliance approach. Thereafter much of the communication was handled by aides and secretaries. On September 23, McCormick wrote that he was ill in bed, but noted that Louis Rose, circulation director, *"has been working among his co-religionists"* for Landon. He also suggested that since the governor's scheduled speech in Chicago would be on the anniversary of the Chicago Fire, on October 9, he should take note of it.

Throughout the campaign McCormick sent editorials, several on the subject of prejudice, which he always indicated were written by Leon Stolz. The Asheville (North Carolina) Conference on Religious Tolerance in late August, with Catholic, Jewish, and Protestant leaders in attendance, was especially hailed.

> Against the dark and stormy background of Europe, with its incorrigible and sanguinary hatreds and rivalries, its wars of atheism against religion, its tragic conflict of anarchy and tyranny, this American conference shines like the returning sun. . . . We have cherished religion without intolerance, liberty without fatal disorder, unity without tyranny. . . . The statement of Asheville is of special value, a great service of wise and honest men to their fellow Americans in a time of momentous crisis.

Roosevelt supporters attacked the *Tribune* for the viciousness of its anti-Roosevelt campaign, though Joseph Parrish, the new *Tribune* cartoonist, was depicting Roosevelt as a handsome, charismatic individual, and Walter Trohan, with the president, was sending objective dispatches. There were injections of poison from both sides, however, and as the invective descended, the *Tribune* was increasingly recognized as the leader of the New Deal foes. On October 8, the National Broadcasting Company wired McCormick for his views. Would Landon carry Chicago? McCormick replied:

> LANDON WILL CARRY CHICAGO. CHICAGO IS AS HONEST AS MAINE AND CANNOT BE BOUGHT OFF BY FARLEY AND HOPKINS BY GROSS CORRUPTION. THE REVELATIONS THAT THE RUSSIAN COMMUNISTS ARE BACKING ROOSEVELT AND THAT ROOSEVELT HAS ACCEPTED THEIR SUPPORT IN MINNESOTA, THAT TUGWELL IS PREACHING THE IDENTICAL DOCTRINES OF KARL MARX AND LENIN, THAT COMMUNISTS HAVE BEEN ACCEPTED AS ROOSEVELT ELECTORS IN NEW YORK STATE HAVE PROFOUNDLY SHOCKED HUNDREDS OF THOUSANDS OF TRADITIONAL DEMOCRATS WHO WILL PUT THE SALVATION OF THEIR COUNTRY ABOVE PARTISAN HABIT.

During the final days of the campaign, McCormick sent to Landon information from a confidential letter written by Sigrid Schultz in Berlin, whose dispatches detailing the nature of the Nazi movement had been given prominence in the *Tribune* for some time. Now she told McCormick of rumors that Landon forces were attempting to deal with the discredited German regime. McCormick wrote to Landon:

> *Sigrid Schultz writes me confidentially:* "The Nazis are convinced that Mr. Landon, after his election, will see to it that they get American credits and American lard and copper. [She indicated her sources.] These Nazis belong to a very small group that we have never caught lying. This conviction, a high Nazi official claims, is based on promises made by the former ambassador to Germany, Mr. Jacob Gould Schurman, and 'other unofficial representatives' of Mr. Landon.
> "Promises of credits, etc., may seem like a good policy to an old gentleman like Mr. Schurman who has never gotten over his student days in Heidelberg. Past expe-

rience has shown that even an empty promise of help to dictatorships strengthens their positions. They know how to make a tremendous amount of capital out of mere promises."

I will not intrude upon your time with the rest of the letter, which is of no importance to the campaign.

Foreign policy was discussed relatively little during the campaign, the issue instead being the respective responsibilities of the federal government and the states. On October 28, McCormick sent his penultimate message of advice: "IT IS NOW MOST IMPORTANT THAT THE THURSDAY NIGHT NEW YORK SPEECH CHALLENGE ROOSEVELT ON EVERY PARTICULAR OF HIS PROGRAM FOR THE FUTURE RECALLING THAT HE SAID NOTHING OF HIS INTENTIONS FOUR YEARS AGO AND IS SAYING NOTHING NOW." Landon's Madison Square Garden address eminently satisfied McCormick, who telegraphed on October 30: "YOUR MADISON SQUARE SPEECH WILL GO DOWN AS ONE OF THE GREATEST IN POLITICAL HISTORY COMPARABLE WITH LINCOLN'S COOPER UNION."

McCormick had a final opportunity to advise on November 2, and he called Philip Kinsley, who was with Landon, to pass along his counsel "in re your speech tonight." At about that time Arthur Sears Henning, who each presidential year covered most of the states to report trends, was indicating in his dispatches that Landon could lose. *Tribune* staff members were summoned and questioned, including a reporter covering the campaign in Illinois. "How is Landon doing in Illinois?" the Colonel asked. "He is sure to lose," the reporter told him. McCormick frowned but brightened when Ruth Simms, who was present, assured him: "Landon will win by a landslide."

The landslide was for President Roosevelt, who received 27,751,597 votes to 16,679,583 for Landon, and 523 electoral votes to eight for Landon, who carried only Maine and New Hampshire. On November 28 Governor Landon wrote McCormick, thanking him for his support, and on December 5 McCormick replied: *"While I am disappointed with the result, I am anything but stunned. Seventeen million people voted for you—a cohesive army bound up by some principles. . . . I cannot think of anything that would have changed the results. . . . If we had not fought a vigorous campaign the election would have been so one-sided that a Republican form of government would have fallen apart."*

*   *   *

Following the Republican defeat, the *Tribune* was enraged anew when President Roosevelt presented his plan to reorganize the Supreme Court on February 5, 1937, seeking authority to appoint additional justices, which was understood to mean liberals who would outvote the "nine old men" who had derailed the NIRA. The paper withheld comment until it could speak calmly, it explained, then on February 7 said of the plan:

> Its objective is to enable Mr. Roosevelt to command a majority of the
> Supreme Court. The question raised . . . Shall the Supreme Court be turned
> into the personal organ of the President . . . is fundamental because, if
> Congress answers yes, the principle of an impartial and independent
> judiciary will be lost in this country. In all probability it will be abandoned
> for all time. . . . Mr. Roosevelt . . . places his immediate objectives above
> everything. . . . Tomorrow Mr. Roosevelt's successor may be the creature of
> a Ku Klux Klan party, with all the fanatical belief in racial and religious
> intolerance which goes with it. Racial and religious minorities in this country
> may well tremble at the prospect which Mr. Roosevelt has presented.

This time Roosevelt lost, both to public opinion and the Congress.
The Senate Judiciary Committee voted 10 to 8 to reject the president's
proposal, and it died, "the most stinging rebuke of his political career,"
according to Morison and Commager. But, with his usual luck, Roosevelt
won in the long run: Senior justices retired, and the president soon had
the liberal court he craved. Yet the *Tribune* and its admirers, having tasted
victory, were renewed in their determination to battle the New Deal to the
finish.

By the beginning of Roosevelt's second term the ground for controversy began to shift as the international situation increasingly intruded
upon the lives of Americans. In the Orient, Japan persisted in its efforts
to turn China into a client state. When the League of Nations protested,
Japan responded by withdrawing from the League and continuing its Far
East conquests. Mussolini's invasion of Ethiopia had brought only ineffective League of Nations sanctions, and these were formally abandoned
on July 4, 1936. Two weeks later, a military revolt led by Gen. Francisco
Franco plunged Spain into civil war. Spain's left-wing Republican forces
had the support of the Soviet Union, while Italy and Germany came to
the aid of Franco's nationalists. Hitler, having repudiated the Versailles
Treaty, denounced the Locarno Treaty in 1936, and Germany occupied
the demilitarized Rhineland, arousing only feeble protests from other
European nations. By the fall of 1936 the aggressor nations were openly
banding together. Italy and Germany announced formation of the
Rome–Berlin Axis, and Germany and Japan signed the Anti-Comintern
Pact, to which Italy soon adhered. Europe appeared to be on the edge of
war, and it was clear to the *Tribune* that Roosevelt was determined to
involve the United States.

*   *   *

When the president was scheduled to come to Chicago on October 5,
1937, to deliver a major foreign policy speech while dedicating the Outer
Drive bridge, McCormick noted that Roosevelt, in facing his crowd,
would be looking directly at the *Chicago Tribune*'s block-long newsprint
warehouse on the north bank of the river. The address turned out to be

the famous "quarantine" declaration pledging the United States to join with the peace-loving nations for its own protection: "Let no one imagine that America will escape, that America may expect mercy, that this Western Hemisphere will not be attacked." Roosevelt issued his challenge at the center of American isolationism, and Colonel McCormick was ready for him. As the president glanced up from time to time he could hardly fail to see McCormick's response in letters five feet tall, painted across the warehouse: "UNDOMINATED. CHICAGO TRIBUNE." And in smaller letters under the name: "THE WORLD'S GREATEST NEWSPAPER."

Said the *Tribune* editorially of the bridge address:

> Mr. Roosevelt announced a new foreign policy for the United States. It would be more accurate to say that he readopted the foreign policy of Woodrow Wilson, the policy which brought the United States first into armed conflict with Mexico and then into the world war, the policy which was overwhelmingly rejected by the American people after the war.
>
> Mr. Roosevelt, like Mr. Wilson, believes it is the mission of the United States to maintain the sanctity of international treaties; that it is our duty to side against the nation which our government deems to be the aggressor in war. Specifically, he indicates that the United States is in duty bound to take action of some sort against Japan for her war in China as well as Italy and Germany for their participation in the Spanish Civil War. He did not name these countries, but the inference was unmistakable in his reference to the nations which broke the league covenant, the nine-power treaty for the protection of China and the Kellogg-Briand treaty for the preservation of peace everywhere.
>
> We signed two of those treaties, he said, and having signed them we have assumed a duty to see that they are observed . . . Mr. Roosevelt went a step further. He plainly indicated the line of action he intends to pursue. We are to associate ourselves with the powers that abide by their word. He did not name *[them but]* they are to be Britain, France, Russia.

The *Tribune* then cited the possible consequences of Roosevelt's policy. China had asked for League of Nations action against Japan. What will happen, it wanted to know, if a boycott is attempted against Japan? "If the boycott is adopted and it doesn't work; if, while it is in progress, Japan's conquests continue, then what will Mr. Roosevelt do? The moment came when Mr. Wilson found himself with no alternative but war. Does not Mr. Roosevelt's policy invite the coming of the day when he, too, may have no alternative but resort to arms?"

The editorial concluded: "At the dedication of the new bridge Mr. Roosevelt repeated his declaration that he hates war. The crowd applauded. The crowd also applauded Mr. Wilson when he campaigned on the slogan, 'He kept us out of war.' They accepted his word and did not examine the meaning of his diplomatic acts. A month after his inauguration America was in the war." It was an editorial some would remember on December 7, 1941.

Tribune enemies asserted that because the paper was antiwar it was pro-Nazi, but in fact the paper opposed Hitler as strongly and as consistently as it opposed Stalin, and in similar terms. "The truth of the matter is that in most essentials the Nazis and the Communists think alike," the paper had said on September 26, 1933. "They both deify a central government. Both prevent free criticism and the organization of a political opposition. Both exercise a rigid control over the printed and spoken word. Both deny that the individual has any rights either of life or property which must be respected. The principal difference between them is that Stalin speaks Russian and Hitler speaks German."

The *Tribune*'s position also was consistent relative to Asia: America should stay out of Sino-Japanese troubles. The paper looked with revulsion upon Japan's invasion of China, but it also acknowledged that other foreign powers were there, including the United States. They were there by treaty, a legality and slight moral justification, but a posture that made further involvement likely. After the Japanese had seized American shipping at Shanghai, the paper said on December 4, 1937: "The United States and Japan are said to have friendly relations. If that were the actual truth they would be able to negotiate. . . . We have threatened indirect war. The countries which have hostages in Shanghai have done everything they could to make the position critical and the condition of the Chinese desperate. Real statesmen should see things down the road."

On December 13, the *Tribune* headline announced an unprovoked attack by the Japanese on the American gunboat *Panay* in the Yangtze River: "JAPANESE SINK U.S. GUNBOAT." The story was covered in detail with text, maps, pictures, and charts during the next two days, the wire services being used since the paper's two correspondents in China, John B. Powell and Capt. Maxwell M. Corpening, were not at the scene. On December 14, a McCutcheon cartoon portrayed a worried Japanese saying, "We are becoming the most hated nation." On the following day the *Tribune* editorial said: "The bombing of the gunboat *Panay* brought a delicate situation not exactly to a critical moment but at least to the point of alarm. Neutral rights are unusually precarious in China because of treaty conditions permitting the presence of foreign warships. There are methods for settling for damage to private property which are less satisfactory when the dignity and sovereignty of a nation are involved."

After thus counseling calm, the paper conceded that the attack might have been a deliberate insult and approved the effort of the Roosevelt administration to carry a demand for an apology directly to the emperor, though it also predicted that the Japanese people would never know of it if the sequestered monarch were actually approached. What the United States should do as a practical matter, the paper proposed, was "get its ships out of indefensible places . . . start building a bigger navy."

The position of the *Tribune* was for peace, the avoidance of foreign involvement, the strengthening of defenses, and for the condemnation of dictators who threatened war, destroyed individual liberties, and abused religious minorities. It was a position maintained at considerable cost. When the *Tribune* rejected the suggestion made by President Roosevelt at Queen's University, Kingston, Ontario, that Canada was being menaced by the Axis powers, the Canadian newspapers attacked McCormick personally to the point where he no longer cared to visit the Canadian towns and timber limits that he had pioneered. In the United States some portrayed McCormick as anti-Semitic, but the record then and since, public and private, proved the opposite. *Tribune* editorials condemned ill treatment of Jews, and McCormick's private letters similarly denounced such treatment. He was proud of the fact that his father, as ambassador to Russia, and later, had sent letters of protest to the Russian government for its oppression of Jews. McCormick and the *Tribune* were also said to be bitterly anti-British. The Colonel, of course, was the complete British gentleman himself and appreciated as such by Winston Churchill, who had been McCormick's house guest when he was in Chicago in 1932. McCormick and his associates at the *Tribune* defined their policy as pro-American.

*   *   *

The years 1937 through 1939 brought major adjustments for McCormick and the *Tribune*. Edward S. Beck sought to retire in 1937 after 26 years as managing editor and 45 years with the paper. McCormick persuaded him to remain as assistant editor and to begin the study of company letters and documents, some of which have been used in the preparation of this book. But Teddy Beck was weary at last of strife in the newspaper business and the prospect of another war. After directing the reporters covering the 1940 presidential campaign, he completed his retirement in January, 1941. Following his death on December 25, 1942, his widow, Claire, established the Beck Awards in his memory, awards for excellence given annually to *Tribune* editorial people.

Robert Lee followed Beck as managing editor on January 1, 1937, having served in that capacity whenever Beck was absent in his later years, as well as presiding over the Sunday and features department. Lee's official tenure as managing editor was brief, however. He died suddenly of a heart attack in his Lake Forest home on January 8, 1939, at the age of 55. At the time, Pat Maloney, then city editor, was on vacation in Florida. He was summoned to Chicago, rode with Colonel McCormick to the funeral, and learned on the way back that he was to become the new managing editor. McCormick also indicated that he was pleased with Sunday editor Mike Kennedy and financial editor J. Howard Wood. The Colonel would deal directly with them, leaving Maloney free to concentrate on the news department. In August, 1939, a Chicago morning newspaper died, the *Herald and Examiner*, which Hearst merged with his afternoon *American*, taking the *American* also into the Sunday field, continuing the *Herald and Examiner*'s Sunday morning editions. The *Tribune*'s daily circulation moved up to pass the 900,000 mark, and the Sunday paper held its own at 1,040,000.

*   *   *

Sigrid Schultz continued to report from Berlin on Nazi storm troopers smashing windows of Jewish shops, raiding civilians by night, and closing up churches. When Hitler led his mechanized forces into Austria on March 11, 1938, she telephoned her report from Vienna, the first full-length dispatch received by the *Tribune* via transatlantic telephone. Then came the Munich agreement, signed by Hitler, Mussolini, Neville Chamberlain of England, and Edouard Daladier of France on September 30, 1938, which permitted Hitler to seize the Sudetenland from Czechoslovakia. Yet Americans responding to a poll for measuring public opinion devised by Professor George Gallup of Drake University registered 52 percent in favor of the Munich Pact. On January 5, 1939, and again a week later, President Roosevelt finally sent to Congress two measures requesting nearly $2 billion for armaments, which the *Tribune* approved. In March, Hitler broke the Munich Pact and invaded Czechoslovakia. When, on April 14, Roosevelt sent identical notes to potential belligerents asking for a ten-year guarantee of the peace, he was, the *Tribune* declared, following the Wilson policy—too little and too late on the defense front while meddling in the affairs of other nations.

On August 23, Germany and Russia signed a nonaggression pact, torpedoing the Anti-Comintern agreement and abruptly turning about the American Communists who had been calling the *Tribune* pro-German. The paper summarized its views of the international situation in an editorial that appeared on September 1 but which had to be written prior to the events of that day, since it was in editions on the street the night of August 31. The *Tribune* reiterated its belief that Nazis and Communists were equally evil and jeered a bit at the Japanese, who were learning the hard way:

> The Japanese have discovered they have been slapping the wrong people. Nazi Germany's desertion of the anti-Red front stunned the Japanese more than Russia's flipflop did the British and the French. . . . People who have been trying to say that Stalin was a good despot and Hitler a bad one and trying to deny that they were two peas in the same pod have had a shock of their lives.
>
> Japan's policy in China is an Asiatic question. It does not affect this hemisphere. It does not fall within the police duties of the United States. If we refrain from intervention in Asia, Japan will refrain from hostility to America. . . . We threaten to break off trade relations with Japan. For what

purpose? To help China? China is an old hand at fending for itself against invaders. It is big enough for it. To help Great Britain and France? That's not our white man's burden. They are big enough to help themselves. If they cannot remain in China or other parts of Asia they will have to retire.

The Nazi-Soviet pact freed both countries to strike at Poland. That same day, September 1, the *Tribune*'s banner read: "WAR! BOMB WAR-SAW." "EUROPE'S WAR IS ON!" cried the banner on a later edition. Sigrid Schultz sent the chilling story of new conquest from Berlin. The *Tribune* circulation the day before was stated at 900,000. Under the impact of war it would swiftly pass 1 million daily and 1,200,000 on Sunday. The *Tribune*'s editorial on September 2 said:

> The morning headlines told the story the world has dreaded to read. Europe's war is on. Hitler answered the question whether he would take the one step which would be fatal. Would he go over the brink? He has and Europe is now confronted with the event which many of its wise men said it could not survive.
>
> Europe will survive. Its germ of life has resisted history and its history has been a record of great wars growing in intensity of passion, employing increasingly millions of men and weapons of increasing destructiveness. Physically the survivors will be alive. Culturally and intellectually they will have preserved their heritages. But that will not tell the story. . . .
>
> Hitler may have pronounced the death of totalitarian states. . . . He may have ushered in the Red revolution. He may have pronounced the extinction of European bourgeois society and the death of a social order. The survivors will be prostrated with debts which cannot be paid. Their available wealth will be destroyed. Some peoples may go under the yoke. Their masters may themselves be brutalized by the conditions they impose upon the people they defeat. . . .

Could war have been avoided? the paper asked. It recalled Munich, Hitler's perfidy on other occasions:

> Hitler has given *[Munich]* the significance and meaning it has. It spells betrayal. . . . Another Germany, governed by less brutal men, might have presented a good cause to world opinion. . . . But the Germany which made the demands is the Germany which persecuted the Jews, oppressed people because of race and religion, denied them the free exercise of their beliefs in their cathedrals, churches, and synagogues, imprisoned their priests, ministers, and rabbis, denied freedom of opinion and expression, made the purge and the concentration camp instruments of domestic policy, glorified force and might, and ridiculed liberty. These vices obscure the faults and errors of the opposition. They give Germany's enemies the glamor of a crusade against evil, against oppression, and tyranny.

The editorial concluded with the reminder that the United States entered into such a crusade in 1917 "to make people free, to give them hope. With that illusion America entered the conflict. How can we have the illusion again?" Thus, in two concurrent editorials, the *Tribune* had stated its position relative to both a European and a Pacific war, a conviction that war could not solve the problems of Europe or Asia or those of the individual countries involved.

Great Britain and France declared war on Germany on September 3. The American people were aroused. The *Tribune* was criticized much more harshly than in 1914, although President Roosevelt in a fireside chat stated that "this nation will remain a neutral nation."

It was a bleak year for the people of all the nations and especially so for Colonel McCormick. While he was undergoing one of the heaviest assaults of his career both in the United States and Canada, his wife, Amie, was gravely ill. She died on August 14, 1939, and was buried at Cantigny. McCormick, a lonely man, spent his days with his horses and dogs at Cantigny until he recovered sufficiently to plunge fiercely back into newspaper work. He could not bear to go into Canada, however, and sent J. Howard Wood, his young controller, to Thorold, Montreal, and Baie Comeau, where the work of the company was conducted, with Arthur Schmon in general charge and Fred Byington responsible for transportation. The new Baie Comeau mill was operating, but other problems arose. Canada, into the war with England, needed Tribune Company ships. Of those requisitioned, the *Colabee* was soon torpedoed off the coast of Cuba, and the *Thorold* was sunk in the English Channel. Wood and Byington used remaining ships and a string of barges to get newsprint to the *New York News* via the Erie Canal, the paper being transferred to barges at Oswego. On the return trip, the barges carried bauxite for the Canadian war effort.

Colonel McCormick now turned his full attention to the struggle to keep America out of trouble. The paper would long insist that Britain had no need of American aid. Yet McCormick was friendly with the British in a personal way. Lord Lothian, the new British ambassador, came to Chicago for a visit, and the Colonel proudly showed him about the *Tribune* news, press, and composing rooms. In demeanor, speech, and appearance, McCormick appeared as precisely British as his lordship. But *Tribune* editorials did not in the slightest diminish their admonitions against America's involvement in any foreign war.

"OUR WHOLE EFFORT
IS TO WIN THE WAR"

24

The *Tribune*'s fears for Europe under the dictatorships were swiftly realized. The USSR completed the dismemberment of Poland, invading on September 17, 1939, and attacked Finland on November 30. Finland astonished the world with its ability to fight back, and the paper had excellent correspondence from Donald Day, who was almost continuously at the front above the Arctic Circle, sometimes in 40-below temperatures. The Finns daily made top *Tribune* banners. There was little fighting in Western Europe, meantime, and the so-called Phony War continued into the spring. There was action from the first on the high seas, as France and England sought control of the Atlantic and again Germany waged unrestricted submarine warfare.

In April, 1940, Germany began its drive through Europe, invading Denmark and Norway, then blitzing through the Low Countries, moving too swiftly for correspondents to keep up. But when the mighty German panzer divisions at last moved against France, sweeping around the fortifications of the Maginot Line, a wry, wiry, blue-eyed *Tribune* reporter kept up reasonably well, in a borrowed German staff car. He was E. R. Noderer, who had edited the college humor magazine at Penn State and had served as cable editor of the *Pittsburgh Press* before leaving to join the Paris *Herald* when he felt a war coming on. There David Darrah, of the *Tribune*'s London bureau, recruited him. Noderer was perched in Switzerland as the Nazis prepared to move and was sent to Berlin to aid Sigrid Schultz when hostilities began. Noderer soon caught up with the panzers, and he would keep on moving to become the most traveled and experienced of all the *Tribune*'s war correspondents, perhaps of all U.S. World War II writers. When others took a leave to rest, write books, or deliver lectures, Noderer went out to find another theater of war to report, in Iran, Burma, Malaya, the Southwest Pacific, back to Europe, and the Middle East.

As Darrah was preparing to go into France and Larry Rue, also of the London bureau, was reporting British efforts to control the German submarines and to support the French, Noderer described the misery of Belgian refugees again struck down by German power and provided awesome accounts of the blitzkrieg in France. His dispatches told *Tribune* editors and readers in vivid detail of the inadequacy of French and British forces facing a new concept of war developed by German strategists and tacticians and implemented by advanced equipment and well-trained troops. *Tribune* editorials demanded that the American general staff modernize its thinking.

While British dispatches in early June, 1940, hailed the evacuation of 334,000 British, French, and Belgian troops from Dunkirk as an unprecedented accomplishment, enabling England to continue the war, Noderer was seeing it from the viewpoint of the conquerors, so far as he could drive through the rubble or, when that failed, press on afoot:

> With the German Army at Dunkirk, France, June 5—Dunkirk is a pile of rubbish. The wreckage of bomb-shattered buildings chokes its streets. Flames crackle and smoke swirls through the center of town as fires spread unchecked. Dead French soldiers lie where they fell.
>
> I entered this English Channel town, the last foothold of the allied troops in northern France, a few hours after its 40,000 French defenders surrendered to the German army. It presented the scene of utter desolation. With no exceptions every building in the city, the home of 33,000 persons, was destroyed. Nothing was left. . . . I drove into town in a German staff car which we were forced to abandon when we could no longer pick our way through the debris. Buildings, stones and bricks jammed the streets.

Noderer in subsequent stories talked with dispirited French and British prisoners who told him they felt betrayed by their leaders, who did not provide them with proper equipment, training, or tactics for warfare against the German panzers and dive-bombers. British prisoners, he wrote, also blamed their politicians. "These men were not handpicked by the German authorities to be interviewed," Noderer said. "They were part of a contingent of 12,000 to 14,000 British and French troops held in temporary camp while being marched to quarters in Germany. About 4,000 were British. I walked with them talking to whomever I chose." In a June 8 dispatch, Noderer wrote:

The failure of the British and the French to offer serious resistance to the German drive to the English Channel may be attributed in a large measure to the continued use of a world war *[I]* technique by the allied armies, according to neutral military observers. . . . This was the impression also gained by the *Tribune* correspondent in a week's swing through Belgium and northern France as far west as Calais, Boulogne and Dunkirk.

Fundamentally, the allies appear to lack sufficient weapons powerful enough to withstand assault by German tanks, Stukas (dive-bombers), and mechanized infantry. But from Liege to the French coast there was evidence everywhere that the allies also had failed to grasp the principles of the new blitzkrieg sufficiently to form a defense against it.

Tribune editorials would take up the Noderer dispatches, reiterating the warnings of American aviation hero Col. Charles Lindbergh and of Colonel McCormick that America was ill prepared for war and must not become involved. The *Tribune* demanded a strong army and navy; it attacked the chiefs of staff further for possessing a World War I mentality but praised Adm. Harold R. Stark when he recommended to Congress a $4 billion appropriation for a two-ocean navy. The paper suggested that although the rescue of 334,000 troops from Dunkirk was an incredible accomplishment, it was far from the way to win a war. France signed an armistice with Germany on June 22. David Darrah was sent to Paris to cover the occupation, Larry Rue was placed in charge of the London bureau, and young Noderer entered Paris with the German army, where he reported on the occupation until he was sent to Istanbul.

There were other parts of the world and theaters of war to be covered and checked. Sam Brewer was sent to Africa, Maurice English accompanied the remaining French troops in retreat. John O'Donnell of the *New York News* covered British forces for the *Tribune* as well as the *News*. Kempei Sheba, a staff member of the *Asahi Shimbun* in Tokyo, also served the *Tribune*. McCormick dispatched his personal representative, Captain Corpening, on a round-the-world trip to provide confidential reports as well as dispatches for publication. One of Corpening's tasks was to fire John B. Powell, *Tribune* stringer in Shanghai, who also edited his own financial newspaper. McCormick had been dissatisfied with Powell ever since the sinking of the *Panay* by the Japanese, when the *Tribune* cable desk could not find him. After visiting China and presumably informing Powell that his letters were no longer wanted, Corpening crossed Siberia and Russia and eventually reached Egypt. There he aroused British wrath by allegedly violating censorship. He went on to Berlin. Without informing correspondent Sigrid Schultz, Corpening telephoned a message to the *Tribune*'s new Press Wireless transmitting station in Amsterdam, stating that the Germans were secretly attempting to negotiate peace with England, a rumor that had been rampant for some time. The Germans evidently had been monitoring the Press Wireless transmitter, for Schultz immediately was called before the authorities. She knew nothing of the dispatch, but Corpening, learning of her trouble, confessed. He was placed under house arrest in the Hotel Adlon, then ordered to leave the country.

*   *   *

At some time during 1940, the *Tribune* perceived that President Roosevelt was thinking the unthinkable—that he would offer himself for a third term. The idea was equally shocking to many Americans in the beginning, an affront to American tradition, but the president's anticipated decision was attacked so often and so vigorously by the *Tribune* and other newspapers that the public gradually grew accustomed to it. When, in June, Roosevelt nominated two leading Republicans for cabinet posts, Henry L. Stimson as secretary of war and Frank Knox as secretary of the navy, it became obvious to the *Tribune* that the president was moving to scuttle the Republican convention and campaign. Once elected to a third term, he could take America into war, probably under a secret agreement with England.

Meantime, Colonel McCormick had been looking about for a candidate who could frustrate Roosevelt's diabolical plan to become a wartime dictator. Senators Taft and Vandenberg were considered, but Vandenberg appeared susceptible to the president's internationalism virus, Taft too phlegmatic. A superior, fresh personality emerged: the small, dapper, sharp-eyed district attorney in New York who had sent gangsters and Tammany crooks to jail, Thomas E. Dewey. Michigan-born, Dewey had received proper training in a Midwestern school, the University of Michigan, and was vouched for by a fellow alumnus, Chesser Campbell, advertising manager of the *Tribune*. Dewey had narrowly lost the New York governorship in 1938, and he announced his candidacy for the presidency late in 1939. McCormick assigned William Fulton, his personal news representative in New York, the customary situation of the top New York correspondent, to travel with the prosecutor. McCormick liked what he read and heard about Dewey from Fulton. Dewey had adopted the basic position of the *Chicago Tribune* and aviator Lindbergh— America must be kept out of war. In a straw poll conducted by the *Tribune,* Dewey obtained 52 percent of the votes against Taft, Vandenberg, and a New York utilities lawyer, also Midwest-born and reared, Wendell L. Willkie. Colonel McCormick repressed his disdain for short men and agreed that Dewey could win.

As the time for the Republican convention in Philadelphia neared,

Hitler's panzer divisions were pounding through France, and America was seeing the full might of the German blitzkrieg. On June 15, Sigrid Schultz cabled from Berlin, "WITH VERDUN SMASHED AND THE MAGINOT LINE BROKEN ON A LONG FRONT, GERMANS VOWED TONIGHT TO DRIVE ON UNTIL THE FRENCH ARMY IS ANNIHILATED." It appeared that the Germans and their allies would soon possess the entire continent, and possibly North Africa as well, and England's situation was dire.

But Americans had their own future to think about, and Colonel McCormick prepared his defensive maneuvers for Philadelphia, where he perceived that Wendell Willkie was about to launch a political blitz-krieg. Colonel McCormick did not intend to repeat the mistake he had made in the Landon campaign, total involvement. He intended to get his own ideas incorporated into the Republican platform and to fight for Dewey. But the paper would cover the proceedings with a moderate though adequate and competent staff, with E. S. Beck, now assistant editor, in charge, and the paper's best political writers. Arthur Sears Henning was dean of the team, which included Stanley Armstrong, Parke Brown, Arthur Evans, Willard Edwards, Philip Kinsley, Marcia Winn, and Percy Wood. Bill Fulton continued to cover Dewey, and Walter Trohan was with President Roosevelt, as usual.

Colonel McCormick appeared personally before the platform committee to get the kind of foreign policy and defense policy he wanted. He urged that the party promise the country to keep it out of war but, at the same time, to build up its defenses. He referred to the errors of World War I: "It will be a tragic mistake to call away from their work men we are not prepared to equip or train," he said, referring to conscription bills recently introduced in the Congress. America's lack of preparedness was woeful. "You must realize," McCormick said, "that our army is less prepared intellectually to meet the new German tactics and weapons than the armies of Europe which were so easily overthrown. Let us leave the hysterics and bombastics to the administration which has so gravely imperiled the nation, and let us with calm and determination restore the nation to safety."

In New York, Dewey, in his final preconvention statement, charged again that Roosevelt was leading the country into war, and the *Tribune* cheered him. But the paper also recognized that the fall of France and the possible fall of England could place the country in jeopardy, since Germany would undoubtedly attempt to seize the British and French islands in the New World. Thus the need for strong defense. "How can the United States hope to intervene in Europe when it lacks the power to enforce the Monroe doctrine?" the *Tribune* demanded. "The situation would be much better if Canada owned the British islands and we could conclude a defensive treaty with Canada. . . . We do not know how the Canadians would feel about assuming responsibility for those islands." The Canadians felt like ignoring the suggestion.

As the Philadelphia convention got under way, the *Tribune* stated that "the Republicans are for peace." And it concluded that Dewey was right on every essential issue of the campaign:

> Thomas E. Dewey came to the top of the heap by natural processes of selection. At a time when extravagance, waste and corruption were threatening the future of the country, he was a conspicuous fighter for old-fashioned virtues and honesty, thrift and decency. He did it by clear thinking, hard work and careful preparation. He was opposed by the intrenched power of corrupt national and state administrations but couldn't be diverted from his purpose.

But diverted Dewey was when the convention reached its sixth ballot, although on the first ballot he had received 360 votes to 105 for Willkie. On June 28 the *Tribune*'s banner reported: "G.O.P. NAMES WILLKIE." Senator Charles McNary of Oregon was nominated for vice-president. The paper could not yet bring itself to comment editorially on the successful candidates. On the 29th it discussed the excellent platform, giving credit to C. Wayland Brooks, the paper's longtime favorite, now running for the U.S. Senate. On Sunday, June 30, there was finally a statement on Willkie: "There can be no doubt of it; Wendell Willkie is the choice of the Republican party not only in the narrow and obvious sense that he was given the nomination, but in the larger sense that both rank and file and the party leaders favored him." The choice was made freely by an unbossed convention, the paper said, and it ruminated upon the fact that probably three-fourths of the delegates had favored him from the beginning, but were committed to others on the first ballot.

In July, in Chicago, President Roosevelt was nominated for a third term on the first ballot, and, making the misfortune even worse from the *Tribune*'s view, Henry A. Wallace of Iowa was chosen to run with him for vice-president. Said the editorial:

> For the first time in the history of the United States, and at the most dangerous time in which it could be done, an American party has nominated a man for a third consecutive term in the presidency.
>
> This man, in his second term, undertook to make the Supreme Court a ratifying board for his decrees. In his first term he had been accustomed to issue executive orders which he expected Congress to enact into law by acclaim and without study or discussion. . . . He expected that such a congress would ratify his decree destroying the federal judiciary as a separate branch of the government. He demanded that the senators and representatives, without dissent or condition, give him a Supreme Court of Yesmen who would approve any law he issued. . . . When Congress, to his

astonishment, defeated him in that purpose, he resolved that his supremacy would be reestablished by the rejection of the congressional rebels who opposed him. He undertook a great purge, and failed again.

Roosevelt's "purge"—an attempt to rid the Democratic party of its conservative elements in 1938—had been resoundingly defeated. The *Tribune* declared that the presentation of further opportunity for a willful man to take control of the country was shameful and a reproach to all decent Democrats. The Democrats had become the war party. "The Democratic party has nominated for a third term the man who almost established a dictatorship in his second. . . . As the convention adjourns after its great disservice to the Republic the honest public feeling is one of dismay and disgust. The responsible members will hear the reproach for their actions to the end of their days."

*   *   *

The national debate in which the *Tribune* was a leading polemist was the most significant, important, and acrimonious since that of 1860. Motivation differed among the various antiwar and prowar factions, ranging from total hatred, as between CIO leader John L. Lewis and the *Tribune*, to benign dismay, as when *Tribune* editors, preparing to praise Senator Taft for saying: "We want no foreign wars, we want none of our American boys to fight in foreign lands and seas . . ." then heard him add, "I do not know what the Germans will do. . . . We can take the steps necessary to meet the blitzkrieg at the time we find out what it is." Colonel McCormick and the *Tribune* believed they knew what it was, and said so in editorials and on radio, through station WGN and the Mutual Network. McCormick filled his Sunday *Graphic* magazine with articles on German armaments and tactics and the inadequacies of British and French arms. He discussed the world's important battles and the great strategists of the past, but most especially he analyzed the envelopment of Europe and the German movement through France. He urged that the United States restrict itself to defensible perimeters and then defend those boundaries properly. In a special article in the *Graphic,* McCormick discussed the inability of the United States to hold the Philippines and again urged that arrangements be made to take over British possessions in the Atlantic and the Caribbean. On September 3, 1940, President Roosevelt issued an executive order giving Great Britain 50 overage destroyers for 99-year rent-free leases of bases on Newfoundland, Guiana, Bermuda, Jamaica, and other islands in the Caribbean. The paper praised the president for this move.

> President Roosevelt notified Congress yesterday of the agreement between the United States and Great Britain which gives this country leases for naval and air bases in the British-American possessions. . . . The *Tribune*

rejoices to make this announcement, which fulfills a policy advocated by this newspaper since 1922. In spite of much discouragement, the *Tribune* persisted, month by month and year by year, in calling for these additions to the national defense. It may be found, as we think it will be, that this is the greatest contribution of this newspaper to the country's history since the nomination of Lincoln.

The agreement is not in the terms the *Tribune* would have preferred. Nevertheless, any arrangement which gives the United States naval and air bases in regions which must be brought within the American defense zone is to be accepted as a triumph.

But when, on September 26, the president embargoed all sales of scrap metal to Japan, the paper accused him of deliberately provoking the Japanese: "There is no need to examine here the question of whether Mr. Roosevelt should have embargoed the sale of scrap to Japan. The significant fact is that Mr. Roosevelt waited until the last week of September, 1940, to issue his decree. Every moral and legal justification for his action existed as well two years ago as now, five weeks before the third term election. Mr. Roosevelt wanted the crisis when he wanted it and not before."

On September 27, Germany, Italy, and Japan signed the Tripartite Pact, a ten-year military assistance and economic alliance. The *Tribune*, in the light of this move, examined the Roosevelt policy relative to Japan, explaining to its readers that the treaty meant that if the United States entered the war in Europe on the side of England, or in Asia on the side of China, it would fetch an automatic attack by Germany, Italy, and Japan:

> Surely Mr. Roosevelt was not astonished, and, equally surely, he is not displeased by the latest turn of events. His diplomacy resulted precisely as George Washington and every other sensible man in our nation's history said it would. Because we have taken sides in old-world quarrels, we have acquired old-world enemies. For the first time in our history a foreign alliance against us has been perfected. When and if it suits their purpose to do so, they will make war on us.

Philip Kinsley, a top *Tribune* writer, covered Willkie's campaign, while Roosevelt continued to be accompanied by Walter Trohan. Willkie received most of the *Tribune*'s banner headlines, and Harold Ickes estimated that he received 24 times more news space than Roosevelt. Critics assailed the paper for "slanting the news," since it continued the partisan handling of politics it had practiced since the days of Abraham Lincoln. However, there were no formal page-one editorials for Willkie, such as appeared in the Landon campaign. The editorial writers appeared to pay minimum attention to the national candidates, but instead concentrated on the major issues as defined by the Republican platform. The paper devoted much of its political news and editorial space to the Illinois action, where C. Wayland Brooks was running for the U.S. Senate and Dwight Green was the candidate for governor. John T. McCutcheon drew a few cartoons favorable to Willkie. Arthur Sears Henning made his customary swing about the country as the campaign was ending and provided the paper with his first major projection error, forecasting a close election, 280 electoral votes to Willkie, 182 to Roosevelt, with 69 doubtful. The people's verdict was 27,244,160 votes for Roosevelt to 22,305,160 for Willkie, 449 electoral votes to 82. The president had his third term.

"The Solid South and the WPA foremen carried the election for Roosevelt," said the *Tribune*. It foresaw a bad time for the country, quoting Lord Acton, " 'Power tends to corrupt, absolute power corrupts absolutely.' The time to apply it is here. The man has arrived there."

But Colonel McCormick and the paper had much to be happy about. Brooks, called even by the *Tribune* "a perennial candidate," and Green were both elected. By supporting each to victory Colonel McCormick kept the promise he had made nearly ten years earlier, after Brooks obtained the conviction of Leo Brothers in the Lingle murder case and Green assisted in prosecuting Al Capone for income tax evasion. Six Republican congressmen and four other state officials were elected in Illinois. A Carey Orr cartoon showed a Republican patient in bed, the caption saying, "Not so anemic—23,000,000 Red-Blooded Americans."

*   *   *

The *Tribune* was far from alone in opposing Roosevelt's prowar policies. Even after the Scandinavian countries and Greece and Yugoslavia were invaded in 1940, presumably bringing more ethnic groups in the United States to the support of the president's pro-Allied policies, antiwar sentiment continued strong. The America First Committee was growing rapidly under the presidency of Gen. Robert E. Wood. Senators Taft, Vandenberg, Burton K. Wheeler of Montana, and Gerald P. Nye of North Dakota made isolationist speeches about the country, as did former president Hoover. In January, 1941, during hearings held to study the Lend-Lease Bill, Colonel Lindbergh told the House Foreign Affairs Committee that aid to Britain would not change the outcome of the war. Colonel McCormick took a similar stance in testifying before the Senate Foreign Relations Committee in February. Britain's situation was not critical, the Colonel believed. He vehemently opposed Lend-Lease as a further step toward dictatorship in America. The bill, which empowered the president to lend or lease war materiel to Britain and its allies, became law in March.

On May 21, 1941, a German submarine sank without warning an

American-owned freighter, *Robin Moor*. In response to this and other aggressive acts, President Roosevelt proclaimed an "unlimited emergency" on May 27. German consulates were closed; German and Italian shipping in American waters was ordered seized and funds were frozen in American banks. It appeared for a time that the nation would again be revolted by German submarine tactics, but antiwar feeling continued to prevail. On June 22, 1941, the Germans shattered the Nazi–Soviet Nonaggression Pact, invading the USSR. The *Tribune* promptly came under attack from its old enemies, the American Communists. Earl Browder, the Communist candidate for president, came to town especially to work up war spirit among Chicago's radicals and to assault the *Tribune*. "TRIBUNE TREASON EXPOSED AT THE CHICAGO STADIUM" read the headline on a brochure announcing the Browder meeting at the Stadium. The *Tribune* ignored the rally, which featured a speech by Browder and "Broadway entertainers." The highlight was the mass singing of a parody on "Mademoiselle from Armentiers" denouncing Donald Day, the *Tribune,* and McCormick, with verses such as this:

> Colonel McCormick from Illinois, parlez-vous,
> Colonel McCormick from Illinois, parlez-vous,
> Colonel McCormick from Illinois
> Is Adolf Hitler's fair-haired boy
> Hinky dinkey parlez-vous.

American troops occupied Iceland in July to relieve British forces. The *Tribune* did not object, other than to note that the Iceland move could be recorded as an act of war. If Iceland was to be occupied, the paper said, then logistical and strategic sense should require the occupation of the Azores also.

In mid-July the *Tribune* joined the *New York News,* also antiwar, in polling the American attitude toward involvement. Each paper sent out returnable postcards to one voter in ten throughout New York and Illinois. In New York the vote was seven to three against entering the war in Europe, in Illinois it was 74 percent. The *Tribune* was pleased but conceded, "It is not likely that the result of these polls will silence the war mongers." Then came an astonishing rebuff to those who had criticized the *Tribune*'s poll as "probably rigged." A committee led by President Robert M. Hutchins of the University of Chicago, also against the war but as thoroughly liberal as Colonel McCormick was conservative, took a purportedly scientific poll of the entire country. The result was almost exactly that of the *Tribune*'s poll: 74.7 percent against becoming involved in the war in Europe, 19.1 percent favorable, and those undecided 6.2 percent. Said the *Tribune:* "Mr. Roosevelt's record of redeeming his promises is not a good one. Whatever he promised the British people and their leaders either directly or by implication, the polls show that the people of the United States will not tolerate our entry into war!"

*　　*　　*

For a time after Amie McCormick's death in August, 1939, the Colonel withdrew from many of his familiar activities and contacts, except for the paper. But eventually he recovered his spirit and took added interest not only in the affairs of the *Tribune* but also in aviation and social activities. Some of the Hollywood personalities who called at the *Tribune* to inspect the color studios, where Eddie Johnson and his staff were producing superlative portraits of them for the *Tribune*'s *Graphic* magazine and roto picture section, showed interest in meeting one of the country's most talked-about publishers and found themselves welcome in his office. At 60 McCormick was still erectly tall, austere, aristocratic, and in excellent health. His shyness had never interfered with his appreciation of attractive women, and now he found meeting them no trouble at all. The magazine covers featuring Hollywood stars, the unending search for special articles on movie personalities, and McCormick's idea that the United States should take over the world fashion industry following the fall of Paris involved him in many projects with beautiful women. Under the general supervision of Sunday editor Mike Kennedy and Mrs. Grace Pickering, fashion shows were staged in New York, Washington, and Chicago, women's fashions became an important ingredient of the Sunday *Tribune*'s appeal to women readers, and circulation moved up.

McCormick was, in many respects, his own Sunday editor much of the time. His favorite subjects were airplanes, weapons, and ships, but he also was fond of photographs of the English scene and pictures of pretty women, including bare-breasted native girls from the South Pacific. He had a sense of humor about his tastes. When readers wrote complaining that the *Tribune* magazines showed too many naked bosoms and too many English country scenes, McCormick, after selecting several native maidens for publication, tossed out a pair of Shropshire landscapes. "Have to pay attention to our readers," he rumbled.

The editor and publisher of the *Tribune* was as well satisfied with his managing editor as with Kennedy. Pat Maloney was a news-gathering perfectionist who had able assistants in Donald Maxwell, city editor, and Stewart Owen, news editor, both from the sports department. McCormick's every editorial thought, as articulated to Maloney and Kennedy, their assistants, and his two secretaries, became orders and instructions to a growing editorial staff. These orders were translated into type and art and appeared in more than a million *Tribunes*, seven days a week, 52 weeks a year. The impact of "McCormickism," as appreciated by his friends, or "McComicism" as Harold Ickes called it, was tremendous. Only William Randolph Hearst in his prime had surpassed the American journalistic power of McCormick in the 20th century, and Hearst was fading.

The news staff assembled by Maloney was one of the best in *Tribune* history, as were those in the Sunday, financial, and sports divisions. Among its bright young people were Clayton Kirkpatrick, Phi Beta Kappa from the University of Illinois, destined to become editor of the *Tribune;* George Morgenstern, Phi Beta Kappa from the University of Chicago, who would become editor of the editorial page and revisionist historian; William Strand from Brown University in the Washington bureau; Robert Cromie, former Oberlin graduate student; and Herman Kogan, Phi Beta Kappa from the University of Chicago. Both Cromie and Kogan would go on to write books, discuss culture on radio and TV, and edit cultural review magazines, Cromie for the *Tribune* and Kogan for the *Sun-Times*. Others added to his staff of veterans by Maloney— John H. "Jack" Thompson, George Tagge, Frank Hughes, and Tom Buck—were destined for fame as war correspondents or special writers.

The paper was involved with investigative reporting, as it had been since the days of the Whiskey Ring, the horse railway steal, the Lorimer case, and Oscar Hewitt's exposé of the expert fees swindle. In the 1940s James Doherty revealed the continuing spoliation of the city by gamblers and gangsters; Joe Ator wrote of the evils of the rackets; and Gail Compton, farm editor, aided by health editors Dr. Irving S. Cutter and Dr. Theodore Van Dellen, battled the evils of tubercular cattle and unclean milk. In the spring of 1940, the paper exposed the machinations of the former Capone henchman Mike Carrozzo, czar of the street cleaners' and other unions, who was accused of shaking down the city and private business, forcing himself into partnerships in paving companies, and otherwise fleecing the public with his union connections. When Carrozzo and a number of associates, including city officials, were indicted, the gangster snarled, "What this country needs is a Mussolini or a Hitler." Death threats naming Colonel McCormick and the reporter responsible for the *Tribune*'s articles were telephoned to the paper. Colonel McCormick responded with a defiant editorial, promising that the paper would pay $1 million to bring the criminals to justice if the reporter should be harmed but offering no bounty on himself. The *Tribune* guard was increased. Then Carrozzo, who lived in a heavily guarded castle in Lake County, Indiana, surrounded by electrified fence and concrete pillboxes, died suddenly and mysteriously. Strikes against the city ended, and the indictments were dismissed.

Under Mike Kennedy, the *Tribune* Sunday and features sections showed great improvement, returning to the excellence of the Patterson–King days, examples of which Kennedy regularly studied. A Kennedy coup was the recruitment of the incomparable Claudia Cassidy. In 1941 she left the *Chicago Journal of Commerce* to join the *Chicago Sun*. But a year later she was writing music and drama criticism for the *Tribune*. Cassidy shortly became the city's best-known writer in her field, winning praise and denunciation from performers coast to coast. One of Cassidy's predecessors, Charles Collins, took over the "Line O' Type" column in 1938, and Edward Barry, music critic, became a writer for the *Tribune* magazine. The magazine also acquired Norma Lee Browning, author of books and national magazine articles; Louise Bargelt; and Walter Simmons, who joined the veterans John A. Menaugh and Guy Murchie, Jr. The features pages, edited by John Blackburn, continued to use the tested Patterson–King materials with special appeal to women. The financial editor was Thomas Furlong, who had succeeded J. Howard Wood when Wood became assistant auditor and controller in 1939. Furlong became managing editor of the *Washington Times-Herald* in 1952, after that paper was acquired by the *Tribune*. *Tribune* sports, under Arch Ward, burgeoned, as Ward's own promotions made some of the biggest sports news of each year. Wilfrid Smith and George Strickler became Ward's assistants. Each would later become a *Tribune* sports editor.

*   *   *

Throughout 1941 the *Tribune* stepped up its attack on Roosevelt for intriguing with the British and dragging the country into an undeclared war, while failing to adequately prepare in spite of the partial mobilization that put thousands of men in training. In November, the paper began a series of articles quoting American generals in training areas as stating they lacked proper equipment to teach or to fight, a situation the paper had warned of repeatedly. "The United States army is unprepared to meet such an opponent as the German forces," said Lt. Gen. Leslie McNair, who would take over all training operations, in a typical statement. Admiral Stark had pleaded for a two-ocean navy, which was by no means ready, yet his force was under orders to shoot on sight any German submarine or surface warship encountered. "The country is engaged in undeclared war with Germany," the *Tribune* said. "Generals such as McNair must have proper equipment."

On December 1, the paper's banner read: "EXPECT JAP ANSWER TODAY." The readout from the eight-column banner continued: "Two-Ocean War Seen at Stake. F.D.R. Action." The story, by Arthur Sears Henning, related to President Roosevelt's diplomacy, which, the *Tribune* had said, would provoke Japan into attack by shutting off its supplies, including oil. "The issue of whether the United States is to be involved in a war on two fronts will be profoundly influenced by the policy he pursues," Henning wrote. The paper hoisted its new platform on December 2, a single plank in big type, "SAVE OUR REPUBLIC." Even Colonel McCormick's own statement on the role of the newspaper was thrown overboard to make room. Editorially that day the paper said:

> We are facing the possibility that our navy will come to grips with the Japanese in the Far East and that American bombers will be destroying populous Japanese cities, whose flimsy construction will invite disaster. No doubt there are many people who would think this is just retaliation for the fury the Japanese have expended on China, but some undoubtedly will not regard it as the noblest work of American military power, even if it visits on Japan what the Japanese people have permitted the military to do to the Chinese.

The *Tribune* could not foresee that before the war ended bombs would be made that could destroy any city, flimsy or not. Nor did the paper know that President Roosevelt had recently dispatched his son, Col. James Roosevelt, to inform a British intelligence officer in the United States that the Japanese negotiations were going nowhere. On November 27 the British agent, code-named "Intrepid," had sent to Prime Minister Churchill a message: "JAPANESE NEGOTIATIONS OFF. SERVICES EXPECT ACTION WITHIN TWO WEEKS." It was a message signaling a chain of events that would heavily involve the *Tribune*.

*   *   *

The British and President Roosevelt had for some time feared that if the Japanese attacked the United States, the antiwar forces—which included some senators, congressmen, Colonel McCormick, the *Chicago Tribune*, and, according to available polls, a majority of the American people— nonetheless would prevent a declaration of war on Germany, which would not be legally obligated to assist Japan should that nation be the aggressor. In 1940 Winston Churchill had sent William Stephenson to the United States to facilitate his arrangements for secret communication with President Roosevelt, bypassing America's antiwar representative in London, Joseph Kennedy, and Lord Lothian, the British envoy to Washington. Stephenson, working under the code name "Intrepid," established the British Security Coordination (BSC) in New York and aided Col. William Donovan in setting up a similar organization for the United States, later known as the Office of Strategic Services (OSS).

The full extent of Intrepid's activities in the United States did not become public until the restraints of the British Official Secrets Act ended in 1976. According to Stephenson, it was the BSC that originated the idea of creating a secret "war plan" intended to trigger Hitler into a declaration of war against the United States. Once President Roosevelt became convinced that war with Japan was inevitable, the plan was to be brought to the attention of the American people, and thus of Hitler, via the unwitting cooperation of a prominent isolationist.

Over a period of months, British intelligence was aware that a clerk in the American embassy in London had been leaking bits and pieces of strategic information to Berlin. The clerk was quietly arrested and convicted, and the information was incorporated into the 350-page "war plan" to make it convincing to the Germans. Next, President Roosevelt at a Navy Day banquet displayed what he said was a German strategic war map showing how Hitler intended to reorganize South America. Among those present at the banquet was isolationist leader Sen. Burton K. Wheeler, who was convinced that the map was a forgery. A few days later, in early November, 1941, Wheeler demanded to know on the Senate floor, "Where did this [map] originate?" Then he answered his own question: "It originated in the office of Colonel Donovan, in the office of the Coordinator of Information of the United States government. Perhaps I should say it originated in New York, in the minds of gentlemen closely associated with the British government."

In late November, soon after Intrepid's cable informed Churchill that a peaceful solution to America's problems with Japan seemed out of the question, a young officer, variously said to be a U.S. Army or Air Force lieutenant or captain, handed over to Senator Wheeler a large document stamped "Top Secret" and titled *Victory Program*. Despite his prior caution, Wheeler was apparently unsuspicious, and when he realized that the document outlined U.S. plans to enter the war in Europe, he determined to make its contents public. Wheeler turned the *Victory Program* over to Chesly Manly, Washington correspondent of the *Chicago Tribune*.

Managing editor Maloney was especially eager to have a fine, exclusive story for the *Tribune* of December 4, 1941, because that was the day Marshall Field's morning *Sun* was to "rise" somewhat to the southwest of Tribune Tower, from the presses of the *Chicago Daily News*. For months Field's agents had been busy putting together the new paper, raiding the *Tribune* for a part of its staff and generally improving the lot of newsmen, especially editorial people, who suddenly found themselves in demand and able to command raises. The Washington bureau told Maloney that it would have an excellent story for him. The afternoon of December 3 he learned its nature. When he saw Manly's dispatch, he somehow felt queasy about it. A former military man, Maloney knew about contingency plans and secrecy requirements. Yet the summary sent by Manly was such an extensive generalization as to seem a statement of policy rather than the war plan it was apprehended to be by Senator Wheeler. Maloney discussed his misgivings about the dispatch with Colonel McCormick and was given the flat order, "Publish it."

On Thursday morning, December 4, 1941, as the banner on the new *Sun* read: "REVOLT GROWS IN SERBIA," the *Tribune*'s front page proclaimed, "F.D.R.'S WAR PLANS! GOAL IS 10 MILLION ARMED MEN; HALF TO FIGHT IN AEF. Proposes Land Drive by July 1, 1943, to Smash Nazis; President Told of Equipment Shortage." The story was copyrighted by the *Chicago Tribune* and carried Chesly Manly's by-line. It began:

> Washington, D.C., Dec. 3—A confidential report prepared by the joint army and navy high command by direction of President Roosevelt calls for American expeditionary forces aggregating 5,000,000 men for a final land offensive against Germany and her satellites. It contemplates total armed forces of 10,045,658 men.
>
> One of the few existing copies of this astounding document, which represents decisions and commitments affecting the destinies of peoples throughout the civilized world, became available to the *Tribune* today.
>
> It is a blueprint for war on a total scale unprecedented in at least two oceans and three continents, Europe, Africa and Asia.
>
> The report expresses the considered opinion of the army and navy strategists that "Germany and her European satellites cannot be defeated by the European powers now fighting against her." Therefore, it concludes "if our European enemies are to be defeated it will be necessary for the United States to enter the war, and to employ a part of its armed forces offensively in the eastern Atlantic and in Europe and Africa."
>
> July 1, 1943, is fixed as the date for the beginning of the final supreme effort.

The Manly story referred to "the report." It did not contain details that would be found in actual war plans. It also called the report a "war prospectus," saying it was dated September 11, 1941, and had been created in response to a July 29 letter from President Roosevelt to Secretary of War Stimson. The text of the letter was quoted.

Antiwar forces in Congress were in an uproar. Senator Wheeler told *Tribune* correspondent William Strand that he would demand an investigation and was supported by Senators Nye and D. Worth Clark. In the House, Congressman George Holden Tinkham obtained unanimous consent to reprint the Manly report in the *Congressional Record.* Just about everyone in Washington had already read it, either in the *Tribune* or the *Washington Times-Herald,* now published by Eleanor Patterson, or in Joe Patterson's *New York News,* or in other papers receiving the *Tribune*'s press service.

A summary of the story was transmitted to Germany by government radio, according to William Stephenson. One intention of the BSC was to make sure the United States and Germany would go to war; a second was to convince the Germans of the massiveness of the threat and to provide the July 1, 1943, invasion date, thus tying up forces on the western front

Chicago Daily Tribune
THE WORLD'S GREATEST NEWSPAPER

2 CENTS PAY NO MORE!

FINAL

VOLUME C—NO. 290 C   THURSDAY, DECEMBER 4, 1941.—46 PAGES   PRICE TWO CENTS

F.D.R.'S WAR PLANS!

REDS BEGIN NEW DRIVE TO BREAK VISE ON MOSCOW

Strike at Nazi Line South of Leningrad.

BULLETIN.

BERNE, Switzerland, Dec. 4 [Thursday] — A special bulletin from Moscow early today announced Soviet forces had launched a heavy attack along the entire northern line from Kalinin to Leningrad in a terrific effort to crush the German threat against Moscow.

The main fighting was believed to be in the Lake Ilmen district 125 miles southeast of Leningrad where Russian forces were reported breaking thru the German lines on the Volkhov front.

[Maps on Page 17.]

LONDON, Dec. 4 [Thursday] — Russian troops were reported early today to have captured two Italian divisions which the Germans, falling back west of Rostov, had thrown into the path of the soviet steamroller.

The Italians, identified as members of the Union and Tuscan divisions, hardly reached the battle lines before they began giving themselves up as prisoners.

LEIBER TRADED TO GIANTS; CUBS GET BOWMAN

The Chicago Cubs early this morning traded Outfielder Hank Leiber to the New York Giants for Pitcher Bob Bowman and an unannounced sum of cash. The deal was completed at the minor league baseball convention in Jacksonville, Fla. Leiber was one of three Giants sent to the Cubs after the 1938 season in exchange for Bill Jurges, Frank Demaree, and Ken O'Dea.

[Details on sports pages.]

HOUSE ADOPTS DRASTIC BILL TO BLOCK STRIKES

Goes to Senate on 252-136 Vote.

BY WILLIAM STRAND.

[Chicago Tribune Press Service.]

Washington, D. C., Dec. 3 — The house of representatives, by a vote of 252 to 136, today passed sweeping antistrike legislation designed to prevent work stoppages because of labor disputes in war industries.

The final vote was on a complicated measure — introduced yesterday by Rep. Howard W. Smith [D., Va.]. It was regarded as the most drastic of four antistrike measures before the house.

NEWS SUMMARY

of The Tribune

[And Illinois]

Thursday, December 4, 1941.

WAR SITUATION.

LOCAL.

SPORTS.

EDITORIALS.

FEATURES.

COMMERCE AND FINANCE.

[Continued on page 4, column 1]

THE WEATHER

THURSDAY, DECEMBER 4, 1941.

Total average net paid circulation

OCTOBER, 1941

DAILY

1,000,000

THE CHICAGO TRIBUNE

ADMIT FURIOUS BATTLES

THE STRONGHOLD OF PEACE

WAR PROPAGANDA

THE MIDDLE WEST   CHICAGO

Woman Slays Insane Brother as 'Mercy' Act

King's Park, N. Y., Dec. 3 [Special] — An age old ethical and religious problem, whether the snuffing out of human life is ever justified, furnished the background today for the dramatic slaying of George Horn, 36 years old, a patient in the King's Park State hospital.

"YOU KNOW BETTER"

Speaking at Warm Springs, Ga., on April 20, 1940, President Roosevelt said:

"The Republicans are seeking to frighten the country by telling the people the present administration is trying to put this nation into war so that it inevitably is drifting into war.

"You know better than that."

Country Kids Prove Smart as Quiz Kind

Four university youngsters around thru the International Live Stock exposition yesterday.

SCIENCE PINCHES HALF OF AN INCH OFF CLOTHESPINS

New York, Dec. 3 [Special] — Romance, sentiment, and standardization swooped down on the homely hand wooden clothespin today and amputated half an inch of its traditional length.

British Return 17 More Oil Ships, Ickes Reports

Washington, D. C., Dec. 3 [AP] — Petroleum Coördinator Harold L. Ickes announced today that 17 additional oil tankers have returned to American waters from the British shuttle service during November.

Engineers Award Medal to Garand, Rifle Inventor

New York, Dec. 3 [AP] — The Garand semiautomatic rifle John C. Garand, Springfield, Mass., tonight received the Holley medal of the American Society of Mechanical Engineers.

Only **18** shopping days till Christmas

GOAL IS 10 MILLION ARMED MEN; HALF TO FIGHT IN AEF

Proposes Land Drive by July 1, 1943, to Smash Nazis; President Told of Equipment Shortage.

BY CHESLY MANLY.

[Chicago Tribune Press Service.]

Washington, D. C., Dec. 3 — A confidential report prepared by the joint army and navy high command by direction of President Roosevelt calls for American expeditionary forces aggregating 5,000,000 men for a final land offensive against Germany and her satellites. It contemplates total armed forces of 10,045,658 men.

One of the few existing copies of this astounding document, which represents decisions and commitments affecting the destinies of peoples throughout the civilized world, became available to The Tribune today.

It is a blueprint for total war on a scale unprecedented in at least two oceans and three continents, Europe, Africa, and Asia.

REVEAL TURKEY GETS LEND-LEASE GOODS SINCE MAY

BY WALTER TROHAN.

[Chicago Tribune Press Service.]

Washington, D. C., Dec. 3 — President Roosevelt today formalized lend-lease aid, which his administration has been secretly extending to Turkey since last May, by directing the lend-lease administration to look into that country's defense needs.

[Continued on page 6, column 1]

and reducing the pressure on Russia. Both goals were achieved, according to Stephenson.

On December 6, the *Tribune* spoke editorially of the great scoop obtained by correspondent Manly. "It has brought the discussion of national policy down to earth. There can be no doubt of what the administration intends. We can now weigh the probable gains of an adventure in Europe against the probable costs." President Roosevelt declined to discuss the story at his press conference, although Congressman William P. Lambertson and others challenged him to "deny it if it isn't true." Roosevelt said the reporters should talk to Secretary of War Stimson, who said, "The story is wanting in loyalty and patriotism. . . . What would you think of a general staff which did not investigate and study every conceivable type of emergency which might confront it? What do you think of the patriotism of a man or a newspaper which would take those confidential studies and make them public to the enemies of the country?"

The *Tribune* replied that when it had reported recently on President Roosevelt's secret deals with Prime Minister Churchill, the president had caused Sen. Alben Barkley to take the Senate floor to denounce the *Tribune* story as "a deliberate falsehood." Now it had published further proof about the clandestine collaboration of Roosevelt and Churchill, and the president refused comment. The whole truth—that Roosevelt had secretly supported England's war effort for two years—was disclosed by Sir William Stephenson (he was knighted by King George VI on the recommendation of Churchill) in 1976, thus finally vindicating the *Tribune*'s assertions of 1941.

Why did Colonel McCormick insist on publication of the story even though his managing editor had expressed doubts about its authenticity? Was he perhaps privy to the plot? After Stephenson's story of the hoax came out, Maloney provided his own analysis. The idea that McCormick was in on the conspiracy was "nonsense," said the former managing editor. "Colonel McCormick was determined to keep an unprepared America out of war. He was convinced that the Manly story proved the true nature of President Roosevelt's scheming." Since McCormick was an experienced military man and a serious student of military history, he was obviously quite aware of the nature of military contingency plans, however classified. McCormick had no doubt he knew what he was doing, and he accepted the risk. In his determination to demonstrate that Roosevelt was leading the country into war without preparing properly—the gist of the *Tribune*'s campaign—McCormick did not hesitate to provide the American people with information he felt they were entitled to have. There is no evidence to indicate that anyone disclosed to McCormick that the bogus *Victory Program* was a plant to deceive Hitler, but there is evidence that McCormick did cooperate with the U.S. intelligence services in other instances. Prior to Pearl Harbor, he wished to discontinue the lease the Japanese government had on a Tribune Building suite. He was dissuaded by the Office of Naval Intelligence, which had bugged the suite and otherwise placed it under surveillance and was obtaining valuable information. So McCormick silently endured the criticism of those who declared that his antiwar policy was influenced by the rental moneys he received from the Japanese. After Pearl Harbor he was free to kick out his unwelcome tenants, and did.

*   *   *

Sunday, December 7, 1941, was a bright, mild day. The news that morning was routine, the customary dispatches from the various fronts, which were generally quiet; President Roosevelt had sent a note to the mikado in the vexing diplomatic exchanges with Japan; McCutcheon's cartoon concerned the giant cactus in the Southwest; farm editor Gail Compton covered the city's outstanding economic-sports-social event of the year, the International Livestock Show; Marcia Winn was writing a series, "Know Your Chicago," which appeared on page one; and there was an excellent "Books for Christmas" section in the paper. James Doherty continued his series of articles exposing mob control of gambling; Philip Maxwell pleaded for contributions to the Good Fellows, the special *Tribune* charitable effort at Christmastime; and editorially the *Tribune* continued to compare its Manly scoop with the Versailles Treaty scoop of 1919. Many staff members not on duty went to the country on the pleasant day, among them managing editor Pat Maloney. En route home Maloney was stopped by a state policeman, who asked him to call his office. Maloney went to the nearest phone and when he hung up looked pale and even more tense than usual. He drove his family to their house in Flossmoor, then sped downtown. Colonel McCormick and many volunteers from the staff were in the newsroom to aid the regular Sunday crew. McCormick discussed the page-one editorial with writer Joe Ator, Maloney got extra paper allotted, and he and Don Maxwell began scheduling the 16 pages of text, cartoons, pictures, and maps for the late editions. That Sunday evening and through the night, the banners of the *Tribune* Monday editions read: "U.S. AND JAPS AT WAR. BOMB HAWAII, PHILIPPINES, GUAM, SINGAPORE."

On page one were a Parrish cartoon showing a man labeled "Every American" saluting the flag and a brief editorial, two columns wide in 8-point type:

> War has been forced on America by an insane clique of Japanese militarists who apparently see the desperate conflict into which they have led their country as the only thing that can prolong their power.

Thus the thing that we all feared, that so many of us have worked with all our hearts to avert, has happened. That is all that counts. It has happened. America faces war through no volition of any American.

Recriminations are useless and we doubt that they will be indulged in. Certainly not by us. All that matters today is that we are in the war and the nation must face that simple fact. All of us, from this day forth, have only one task. That is to strike with all our might to protect and preserve the American freedom that we all hold dear.

The December 8 editions sold 1,275,000 copies. On December 9, the paper carried war maps in color and biographical sketches of American military leaders, including Gen. George C. Marshall, chief of staff, and Gen. Douglas MacArthur, who commanded U.S. troops in the Philippines and had also taken charge of the Philippine army, which had been integrated into the U.S. forces a short time before. Both men had been guests at Cantigny. Later, Colonel McCormick would write MacArthur, wishing him well and offering his own services, but with the implied understanding that he could not be accepted, though he was only slightly older than the general. Joe Patterson went to the White House to offer his services, where he was kept waiting by President Roosevelt and then told, "Go back and read your editorials." The *New York News,* which had supported Roosevelt for two terms, had turned against him on the war issue.

The editorial on December 9 stated that Americans were completely united by Japanese perfidy. Such editorials continued daily, and McCutcheon, Orr, and Parrish made daily contributions of a patriotic nature. The paper and the country were preoccupied with the assessment of damage at Pearl Harbor, the draft, and the logistical reorganization of the nation—all bleak prospects—but got something to cheer about when Capt. Colin P. Kelly, piloting a dive-bomber, was said to have found and sunk a Japanese battleship. The report was incorrect—it was a near miss—but Kelly became a much-needed American hero.

On December 11, the *Tribune*'s lead editorial discussed the congressional plan for an investigation of the reason U.S. forces had been so totally surprised at Pearl Harbor. The paper approved, noting that "the nation has been told it must wait a long time before the full story can be told." It seemed unperturbed, however, expressing the opinion that "we lost obsolete ships of war called battleships." Then it added, "Before we can win the war in the Pacific and the Atlantic we must win it in Washington." The paper praised the navy and army personnel on the scene, saying, "The heroism displayed by the officers and men in the attack on Pearl Harbor will never be forgotten."

When President Roosevelt took his own action to investigate the Hawaiian debacle, the *Tribune* said on December 18: "To the commission of inquiry, President Roosevelt has named some good men. Mr. Justice Roberts *[of the Supreme Court, chairman of the commission]* is respected by the whole country as an even-handed dispenser of justice." The only lack in the situation the editorialist could discover was that the commission was empowered to investigate only Hawaii and not Washington.

By December 22, the paper had received more reports on Pearl Harbor and its patience ended. A dispatch from Chungking, China, stated that American officials there had been warned on Friday that the Japanese would strike. Why Chungking and not Honolulu? The paper insisted: "KNOX MUST GO. . . . The case for the removal of Secretary Knox is the obvious one that he has failed again. He has been secretary of the Navy two years and hasn't learned that revolutionary changes in sea warfare have occurred. It should be unnecessary to add that Knox's failure as a cabinet officer has been preceded by his failure as a candidate and as a publisher. If Admiral Kimmel *[the navy commander at Pearl Harbor on December 7]* is to be removed, Knox must go also."

Knox's *Daily News* had been engaging in personal attacks on Colonel McCormick, those most effective a series of editorial cartoons by Cecil Jensen depicting "Colonel McCosmic," a takeoff on the cartoons of the bumbling Colonel Blimp in London. The cartoonist took up a letter written by McCormick to a former employee in which he claimed, among other things, to have "introduced machine guns into the army." Jensen detailed other McCormick claims to fame, such as putting the ROTC into the schools, and provided a classic caption, "On the Seventh Day He Rested." McCormick of course had acquired modern machine guns for his federalized National Guard unit prior to America's entry into World War I, but the U.S. Army had used machine guns of various types since the Gatling gun had been introduced back in Civil War times; and the Colonel did campaign for ROTC training in the schools. McCormick's real complaint against Knox, however, was not the cartoons and other personal attacks, but the secretary's failure to respond to *Tribune* demands for a bigger navy, and McCormick's conviction that he was leaking news to the *Daily News*.

* * *

It was soon obvious that the war was not going well. The Japanese had accomplished their purpose of immobilizing the American Pacific fleet, and MacArthur, who lost his air force in the Philippines, was slowly being pressed into a trap on the Bataan peninsula. The *Tribune*'s emotional concern was definitely with General MacArthur. He was the paper's hero. MacArthur photographs appeared daily in color and monotone. The *Tribune* formed MacArthur fan clubs, which bought 222,237 MacArthur pins from the paper in 11 days. The MacArthur Guards were organized.

Colonel McCormick congratulated MacArthur "on your wonderful defense of Bataan," and was pleased when the general responded, "Wish you were here with me." On January 28, however, the paper realized that its hero was facing defeat: "Though General MacArthur's army is out-numbered, it is safe to predict he will hold out as long as he has ammunition to fire. The Japanese, however, have control of the air and the sea. . . . For the long pull the chance of a successful defense of the Philippines is anything but bright. . . . Whether General MacArthur would obey an order to leave is a question to which he alone holds the answer, but certainly our government should make every effort to withdraw him. . . . Our side has need of him."

President Roosevelt did order MacArthur to leave the Philippines with his wife and son and staff members. A rear guard, including Company B, 192nd Tank Battalion, from Chicago's western suburbs, was left to fight on Bataan peninsula. "The garrison on Bataan will be remembered among America's immortals," the *Tribune* said. When Bataan fell on April 9, 1942, with a loss of 36,853 men killed, wounded, and captured, America's worst military disaster, the *Tribune* scrapped all planks and inspirational words from its editorial flag (it had restored Stephen Decatur for a time) to print a single vow in boldface type: "WE'RE GOING BACK TO BATAAN."

By 1942 the *Tribune* boasted circulation of about a million daily, double that of any other paper in Chicago, and greater than any other two. *Herald-American* circulation was reported to be 490,000, the *Daily News* "less than 450,000," the *Times* "less than 400,000," the *Sun* "less than 290,000." The *Tribune* gave generously of its vast resources to the war effort. Almost every day there were color maps of the war areas, paintings of heroic scenes, and facsimiles of coupons relating to sugar, gasoline, and later tire and coffee rationing. "A Friend of the Yanks" column was established. Flags and military insignia were printed in color, and news space was donated to promote bond appeals. The paper printed color pages to spur recruitment and reported that enlistments in the navy were up 500 percent. By April, 252 *Chicago Tribune* and WGN workers were in the armed services; the total reached 861 men and women before the war ended. McCormick began sending monthly checks to the families of employees in service, a practice approved for all Tribune companies by the board of directors in 1944, and one that continued to the war's end, when every employee mustered out of service was guaranteed a job.

The *Tribune* was greatly concerned about the ability of American productivity to win the war. The country had the capacity and know-how and will, said the editorials, but it was feared that politics in Washington would prevent success. When Sen. Harry Truman of Missouri led a

Senate committee into investigations that fully justified the paper's fears and demanded correction of the situation, the paper praised Truman highly in a series of editorials. "Production will be the key to victory," the *Tribune* said, and the paper conducted its own campaign to encourage greater production in war plants, giving gold pins to outstanding workers.

*　　*　　*

Immediately after Pearl Harbor, managing editor Maloney began dispatching members of his war correspondents corps to action areas worldwide, though most of the 21 reporters would remain in the U.S. camps until the Americans were ready for overseas duty. William Fulton initially ventured farthest of the home staff, journeying to an American base in Argentia, Newfoundland, where he reported with characteristic *Tribune* forthrightness that Americans were being overcharged for everything they used. The pre–Pearl Harbor veterans were on various fronts. In Russia, the Germans were pressing on Leningrad and Moscow, and their Finnish allies had entered Russian territory. Donald Day was said to have been fighting with the Finns, an action contributing to his eventual discharge from the *Tribune,* but for now his stories were given top display. Sam Brewer was with the British in Libya, and E. R. Noderer was deep in the jungles of Malaya.

Noderer had left the European war some months past, having received a crisp cable from McCormick: "PROCEED TEHRAN." The British and their Russian allies were having difficulties in Iran, and Colonel McCormick thought some news might develop in that area. Once in Tehran, Noderer soon located the difficulty. The Russians, it appeared, were more interested in obtaining control of the oil resources of Iran than in helping a partner in the war. "The behavior of their Russian allies in the occupied districts of Iran shocks and pains the British, if it does not surprise them. Even the British oil company here is worried now about sending its trucks through the area occupied by the Russians, lest they be seized." Refugees from Kazvin, in the Russian zone, said Noderer, complained that the Communists stole every vehicle and all the foodstuffs within their zone. "During the campaign which was not even a campaign, so far as the British were concerned, the Russians found pretexts to bomb several towns, including the capital, Tehran, Hamadan, and the Holy City of Meshed, a place of pilgrimage for Moslems. . . . At Meshed pilgrims were machine gunned on a road. The wantonness of the act shocked observers."

Moscow promptly denied the Noderer dispatch, and the local Russian commandant demanded that he be ousted from Iran. The reporter remained, however, until it was clear that the British and Russians would

cover over their difficulties, and he informed his paper that he anticipated a scarcity of news. Back came a cable from the strategist in Tribune
Tower: "PROCEED SINGAPORE." Proceeding was growing increasingly
difficult in a worldwide war, but by Christmas Day, 1941, Noderer's
dispatch was datelined: "With Advanced British Forces in Northern
Malaya." The *Tribune* correspondent reported his discovery that the
Japanese were, if anything, as tough and ingenious as the Germans he
had seen smashing through France: "The Japanese, noted for their ability
to adapt the ideas of others to their own use, are doing so with a
vengeance in Malaya. . . . They are waging a war of might—copied
faithfully from the European blitzkrieg model—without overlooking a
single bit of jungle trickery which primitive Malayan fighters might have
used."

In February, Noderer's reports, describing the steady retreat of the
British before superior Japanese power and tactics, suddenly ceased.
Then, on March 5, came a dispatch from Perth, Australia:

> I arrived here today with a number of other evacuees from Batavia after a
> 10-day 2,000 mile trip by ferry boat which had never been out of sight of
> land before in 29 years of service in far eastern waters. . . . We saw no
> Japanese but the trip was not without incident. A mutinous crew of Chinese
> and Malayans was brought aboard in chains and forced to man the ship. . . .
> We escaped two enemy submarines reported in our path and narrowly
> escaped running into a mine field. . . . Our ship had not been able to take
> on food and a water shortage developed. . . . The ship was overloaded and
> 200 tons of cargo had to be thrown overboard on the third day out.

Noderer was soon at U.S. Army headquarters in Melbourne, sending
daily reports on MacArthur and Australian war efforts. He also provided
one of the first accounts of MacArthur's escape from the Philippines by
PT boat. Then Noderer sent dispatches from "Somewhere in New
Guinea," spending three months covering the defense of Port Moresby
and the jungle battle for Buna village, hailed as MacArthur's first engagement "on the way back" to the Philippines. Noderer was one of the
best of the war correspondents, and Colonel McCormick awarded him a
$500 bonus for his reports. Even his datelines were interesting, as for
example from Buna: "By native carrier, boat, airplane, radio—With
American Troops Outside Buna." He wrote of tricky Japanese ambushes
and of a Chicago soldier who, wounded twice, defeated a Japanese in
hand-to-hand combat.

Pat Maloney wanted more of that kind of reportage, and he got it.
McCormick, who for many years had kept close watch over the paper's
foreign correspondents, no longer knew the reporters Maloney was
sending out: Robert Cromie, Seymour Korman, Jack Thompson, Harold

Smith, Tom Morrow, Arthur Veysey. He was sometimes worried, as when Cromie, an irrepressible young man on the battlefield as well as on the golf courses around Chicago, rode atop a tank past enemy lines. "Tell him to stop that," McCormick ordered. "We didn't send him out to get killed." McCormick continued to follow closely the fortunes of MacArthur and thought he saw a presidential candidate emerging. He ordered the paper to run more pictures of the general, and the *Tribune* started a "Life of MacArthur" crossword puzzle series to accompany a biography written by Walter Trohan. There were also stories on new ships, tanks, and guns and on the perfidies of the Japanese as McCormick sought new and better ways to push the propaganda efforts of the paper. President Roosevelt was praised for making General MacArthur commander-in-chief of the Allied forces in the Southwest Pacific.

*   *   *

Stanley Johnston, a correspondent recruited by Larry Rue in London, pulled *Tribune* correspondent Guy Murchie, Jr., from a bombed hotel in England, an act bringing him to the attention of McCormick. Johnston not only proved himself a hero, but, according to Rue, he knew more about German armaments and military tactics than any other newsman in England, and McCormick summoned him to the United States to write a series of articles. It developed that Johnston, a gregarious, grinning moustached young man with popping gray eyes and an infinite capacity for storytelling, was no newspaperman, though he had been almost everything else—a soldier, a sailor, a professional soccer player in Australia, a salesman, an inventor of a hair curler that sold well in Germany, and a man who somehow talked his way into riding in German tanks and examining Hitler's howitzers. A writer was assigned to Johnston, and a series of technical articles poured out. Maloney decided that a man possessing Johnston's talents who had been born in Australia was needed in the Pacific. Navy intelligence checked him out, and he was sent to Hawaii, where he reported on routine naval training activities, then abruptly disappeared.

On May 8, 1942, the *Tribune*'s banner reported: "BIG SEA AIR BATTLE IN PACIFIC." The story was from Allied Headquarters in Melbourne, sent by an Associated Press correspondent. The Japanese, it was believed, were finally making their anticipated lunge at Australia, though actually their target was Port Moresby, New Guinea. Noderer was visiting training sites in Australia and the *Tribune* was without direct coverage. It was not likely that anyone could do more than rewrite the headquarters handouts under the circumstances, but nevertheless, Maloney mourned his bad luck: One of the big battles of the war, and no one there from the *Tribune*! Larry Rue sent a story from London that Japan had invaded India. Sam Brewer, in Libya, reported a minor skirmish, but from the Pacific, nothing. On May 9, Allied Headquarters produced another report, and the *Tribune* banner read: "REPULSE JAP FLEET." The story asserted that a score of Japanese ships had been sunk and implied that U.S. losses were heavy. The *Tribune* quoted from Australian newspapers, which described the battle as "a naval victory" thwarting a Japanese drive on Australia. On May 10, General MacArthur said that major elements of the Japanese fleet had been moving south but after six days of fighting in the Coral Sea had been turned back.

Three weeks later, on June 2, Maloney received a phone call from the West Coast. It was Stanley Johnston. "I have got a great story," Johnston said. Maloney, relieved yet nettled, answered, "Fine, send it, we'll see." But Johnston refused to discuss it. "I can't tell you anything until it goes through navy censorship. I can't tell you where I've been, nor what ship, nor how I got back." Maloney inferred that Johnston was referring to the Coral Sea and that he had not come back on the ship that took him there. Knowing that Johnston would head for San Francisco to see his wife, he sent Wayne Thomis, a skilled, fast writer, to aid with the story. "Telegraph it to Washington, and send a copy to me," Maloney instructed. This was the procedure being observed by the civilian censorship office set up by Byron Price. But Johnston demurred. "This is navy censorship. I can't put it on an open wire."

On June 5, Maloney concluded that he should call Johnston to Chicago. He and Thomis could have an office near the newsroom, and Maloney would know what the story was about and could make plans. He issued the order. That same day there was another big naval fight, and from headquarters at Honolulu came a communiqué furnishing the paper's banner for June 6: "JAPS REPULSED AT MIDWAY." Maloney was frantic for details. Was another great victory being won? The public would be convinced only if there were details, but none were forthcoming. Yet, clearly, momentous events had happened, and the United States was desperately in need of good news.

Saturday night, June 6, Maloney and his editors were putting together the news section of the Sunday paper, their command post being a huge desk in the center of the *Tribune* newsroom. The various editors fetched their dispatches for discussion and evaluation. There was considerable tension at the normally calm cable desk, where numerous bulletins were being moved. Johnston and Thomis had arrived and were busy writing Johnston's series of stories, which Maloney now knew was a first-person account of the Battle of the Coral Sea and the sinking of the U.S. carrier *Lexington*. It was the greatest story of the war, Maloney told McCormick, but it could not be printed until it had passed the censorship. "When it's ready," McCormick replied, "give it to all the papers . . . let all the press services have it. It will be good for the people's morale." Maloney appreciated what the story could do. But give away an exclusive series? The best story of the war? He still marveled, recalling the scene 34 years later.

Johnston described a Coral Sea battle scene to Thomis, and while his writer pounded out the text, he looked over the teletypes at the cable desk. Then he hurried back to the office where he and Thomis were working and fished through a stack of his notes. He began to type a list of ships. Thomis, alerted, went to see Maloney. "Stan Johnston tells me he can give you a good idea of the Jap task force that is being defeated at Midway," Thomis said. Maloney was elated. The story coming in from naval headquarters was good, so was the communiqué of Adm. Chester W. Nimitz, commander-in-chief, Pacific Fleet. But details were needed, exclusive details. "You write it," Maloney commanded.

On Sunday, June 7, the great victory at Midway was reported. "The best front page ever published by the *Tribune*," Maloney exulted. A double eight-column banner read: "JAP FLEET SMASHED BY U.S. 2 CARRIERS SUNK AT MIDWAY." The lead story, occupying the two right-hand columns, was from the Associated Press and began: "United States armed forces have sunk or damaged 13 to 15 warships and transports of the repulsed Japanese invasion fleet at Midway Island. . . . These include the sinking of two, and possibly three, aircraft carriers." In secondary position, set two columns wide in boldface type, was Admiral Nimitz's communiqué, datelined Pearl Harbor, which stated, "A momentous victory is in the making."

The *Tribune*'s exclusive story appeared in column four. The story had been passed by the civilian censorship office in Washington, a step urged by Don Maxwell, Maloney's assistant, although Maloney, after looking through the censorship manual, insisted that this was unnecessary. The Johnston story did not carry a by-line. It was datelined Washington and was attributed to naval intelligence officers, the worst possible attribution, since intelligence officers were sworn to secrecy about even trivial materials passing before their eyes.

Johnston's Midway story, as rewritten by Thomis, ran under a one-column headline: "NAVY HAD WORD OF JAP PLAN TO STRIKE AT SEA. Knew Dutch Harbor Was a Feint." Maloney later took full responsibility for editing the story, putting the Washington dateline on it, and attributing it to naval intelligence. The account, as passed by censorship, began: "Washington, D.C., June 7—The strength of the Japanese forces with which the American navy is battling somewhere west of Midway Is-

10 CENTS PAY NO MORE

Chicago Sunday Tribune
THE WORLD'S GREATEST NEWSPAPER

FINAL

VOLUME CL—NO. 23   [1939, U. S. PAT. OFFICE, COPYRIGHT 1942 BY THE CHICAGO TRIBUNE.]   JUNE 7, 1942.   A   *   PRICE TEN CENTS

JAP FLEET SMASHED BY U. S.
2 CARRIERS SUNK AT MIDWAY

DRAFT DODGERS IN U. S. JOBS HIT BY SENATE QUIZ

Report Urges Move to Induct Them.

BY CHESLY MANLY
[Chicago Tribune Press Service.]

Washington, D. C., June 6.—Sen. Millard E. Tydings [D., Md.], chairman of a special senate committee investigating operations and activities of the federal government, announced today that 3,000 borders have been deferred from military service as "indispensable." He charged that their respective departments and agencies.

Sen. Tydings said the committee had recommended to the selective service system that approximately 1,000 deferments of persons under 38 years of age should be reconsidered. The committee also has recommended reconsideration of the cases of many other federal job holders whose deferments were found to be questionable since the war.

The Tydings committee's records, based on questionnaires filled out by government departments and agencies, show all deferments granted to local draft boards in response to requests made by government departments and agencies in behalf of their employés. The records do not show deferments granted to government workers for other reasons.

Cites Several Examples.

After the committee found that abuses of the deferment privileges have not been general, the statement added that "the abuses we have found exist and like a sore thumb." The statement did not identify agencies or individuals but cited several anonymous examples of apparent draft dodging. It stated that one "agency which has been ordered by the War Production board to cease using critical materials, thereby indicating the value of the agency to the war program, has found it necessary to request deferment for some 52 employés." This statement referred to the Rural Electrification administration.

The statement mentioned one instance in an executive department which attained deferments for 12 men, or 20 per cent of its total clerical force of 63 persons. The committee referred to this agency but not by name. In another case an "agency which has been ordered by the War Production board to cease using critical materials, thereby indicating the value of the agency to the war program, has found it necessary to request deferment for some 52 employés."

The statement contained a defiance of President Franklin Frances Perkins' department of labor:

"These deferments would have been understandable. The committee charges were employed draining our position, stripped deferring a service, not work, but such is not the case. It finally, these deferments are known as permanent officers. Now the deferment of these exceeding 'permanent' officers can be claimed, or glamour because they are indispensable, rare or scarce, is incomprehensible. In the say that the work of this group is so demanding and requires such unusual abilities is ridiculous.

"Let us see what happened these men here which qualifies them for one of the hallowed positions. Here in Mr. X. 31 years old, registered in June, 1941, by the department that month after he became 21 years of age of a salary of $1,800 per annum. Nine months later, he had become such an expert in the field of personnel procedural surveys that he was promoted and his salary raised to $2,600 a year. Further, four months after his appointment he had become such an indispensable cog in the machinations of this department that it was necessary to have him deferred and six months later, not being able to spare this highly indispensable 21 year old expert, it was necessary to obtain a further deferral.

[Continued on page 14, column 5.]

SUMMARY OF WAR NEWS

Latest war developments:

Moscow reported nine German transports in three convoys sunk by Russian flyers in the Baltic, one of them in a raid on a German naval base. Minor fighting was reported on the land fronts.

The RAF continued its offensive by raiding Nazi big guns positions in the Boulogne and Cap Gris Nez areas of France, following a daylight sweep over the channel which London said overshadowed previous attacks. These raids ended a week of air offensive in which 6,000 to 7,000 planes bombed German cities and defensive positions.

Aldbo Tokio claimed the capture of the walled city of Chuhsien, Chungking said the Chinese defenders had thrown back repeated attacks against the city and that infantry and artillery exacted heavy losses from the Japs. American military flyers announced they had killed 200 Japs in attacks on the Salween river and along the Burma road.

Adm. Nimitz reported that "a momentous victory is in the making" in the battle of Wake island, enumerating Jap losses as 13 to 15 warships sunk or damaged, including the sinking of two or three aircraft carriers and their planes. The battle is not over, he said, but "Pearl Harbor has been partially avenged."

[Stories on pages 1, 4, 5, and 6.]

F. D. R. DEFIED ON SALES TAX LEVY

Accept or Fail 2 Billions Short, Says Committee.

BY JOHN FISHER
[Chicago Tribune Press Service.]

Washington, D. C., June 6.—A defiant house ways and means committee has served an ultimatum on the administration that it must accept a federal sales tax or go without 2 billion dollars in additional revenue which the treasury has requested. It was disclosed today.

Such notice was given Secretary of the Treasury Henry Morgenthau, whom the committee ruled over the main earlier in the week for criticizing its progress on the revenue measure. Although the committee refused to entertain a revised statement, reportedly to announce the administration's decision in a written statement, probably next week, it is understood.

According to informed sources, the committee told Morgenthau flatly that it cannot meet the treasury's goal of 8 billion 700 million dollars in new revenue without overriding the opposition of Morgenthau and President Roosevelt to imposition of a federal sales tax.

May Cancel One Year's Tax.

At the treasury, it was learned tonight, no experts are talking of canceling taxes on year's income to put the nation on a pay-as-you-go basis. Treasury figures that this revenue would be lost by remodeling the tax laws would be recovered in later years. Differences between rates could be made up next year. This idea hasn't reached policy-making officials yet, but it has possibilities.

The ways and means committee hasn't acted on a treasury revision for its decision by simple physical deduction on taxes. The tax doubt income taxes from past operation—by payments on the prevailing year's income and tax deductions from current income.

Treasury experts figure that this revenue would be lost by remodeling taxes paid this year on 1941 income as payments in advance on 1942 income. Differences between rates could be made up next year. This hasn't reached policy-making officials yet, but it has possibilities.

The ways and means committee hasn't acted on a treasury conversion dation for compulsory deduction of taxes at the source.

New Sales Levies Planned.

So far the prospective levies asked for committee approval total about 1 billion 300 million dollars, including 1½ billions in new taxes and another 1½ billions in new excise and sales taxes recommended in the treasury's own formal deliberations.

Morgenthau has exerted repeatedly against imposing any further tax burdens, above treasury recommendations, on the "lower income groups," which he defines as those earning $2,000 or less per year. A sales tax on all commodities would be such an imposition on low salaried incomes, in Morgenthau's opinion, and to violate up the needed revenues he favors taxing the rich in the higher income brackets.

The tax bill still faces about a month's study and revision in the ways and means committee, and then action by the house, which usually follows the recommendations of the committee.

Next consideration rests in senate May 1st.

NAVY HAD WORD OF JAP PLAN TO STRIKE AT SEA

Knew Dutch Harbor Was a Feint.

Washington, D. C., June 7.—The strength of the Japanese forces with which the American navy is battling somewhere west of Midway island in what is believed to be the greatest naval battle of the war, was not known to American naval chiefs several days before the battle began, reliable sources in the naval intelligence disclosed here tonight.

The navy learned of the gathering of the powerful Japanese units some after they got forth from their bases. It was said. Altho their purpose was not specifically known, the information in the hands of the navy department was so definite that a fleet of American ships was concentrated to meet any attack. It was possible that some of these wounded ships will not be able to reach their bases.

"One of our carriers was hit and some planes were lost. Our personnel casualties were light.

"This is the balance sheet that the army, navy, and marine forces in this area after their country this morning."

ADM. NIMITZ'S OWN STORY

PEARL HARBOR, Honolulu, June 6 (AP)—Adm. Chester W. Nimitz, commander in chief of the Pacific fleet, tonight issued this communique:

"Thru the skill and devotion to duty of their armed forces of all branches in the Midway area, our citizens can have every reason that a momentous victory is in the making.

"It was on a Sunday just six months ago that the Japanese made their peacetime attack on our fleet and army activities in Oahu. At that time they created heavy damage, it is true, but that aroused grim determination of our citizenry to avenge such treachery and it raised, not lowered, the morale of our fighting men.

"Pearl Harbor has now been partially avenged. Vengeance armed forces have made or damaged 12 to 15 warships in the business. We have made substantial progress in that direction. Perhaps we will be forgiven if we claim we are about midway to our objective.

"The battle is not over. All returns have not yet been received. It is with full confidence, however, that I say this phase of the action the following enemy losses are claimed:

"Two or three carriers and all their aircraft destroyed, in addition to one or two carriers badly damaged and most of their aircraft lost.

"Three battleships damaged, at least one badly.

"Four cruisers damaged, two heavily.

"Three transports damaged.

"One of our carriers was hit and some planes were lost. Our personnel casualties were light.

"This is the balance sheet that the army, navy, and marine forces in this area after their country this morning."

EVEN THO IT'S A REAL GLOCKENSPIEL, THEY STILL LIKE TO SLEEP

[Chicago Tribune Press Service.]

Washington, D. C., June 6.—Government thousands of army recruits who have sworn to murder the Jrspar have been after the wrong man. The trumpeter is the fellow whose blast they're craved.

The war department made this known today when it announced the morale of many recruits was becoming "high" it defined an I, a note from the Latin "reveilles," a young bulbut or steer; 2, a wild companies clip a bulbul, and 3, a horn used by hunters.

The dictionary also says that one type of bugle, apparently something different from the foregoing, is a brass wind instrument used chiefly for giving military signals.

The war department announcement added that there are 41 regulation trumpet calls but that fewer than 20 are in daily use on military reservations. "Sure a new $230 fire cruisers of all of the several days they "reset" and "rage." It's the first and the last ones that give the boys trouble, no soldier having been known to object to the one he loves to hear.

LOOP LID'S OFF as Service Men Jump and Jive

[Pictures on page 7.]

BY MARTHA MURPHY

Jitterbugs jumped and jived in the middle of La Salle street last night. Rug cutting keyed out to pavement prancing as 3,000 girls and men from the Chicago Service Men's center. 176 West Washington street, shagged and lindy-hopped their way up and down the Randolph-Washington block in La Salle street.

In celebration of its anniversary this week, the Greater Chicago Stout association arranged for the street to be blocked off, snagged the services of Lew Diamond and his band and poured coca drinks down parched throats.

Lady Gets Partners.

Red barbecue opened the gates to this dancing haven for more than 1,000 girls. Red crepe paper bows signaled membership to the girls.

"Jersey Bounce! Jersey Bounce!" cried the crowd as Larry Adler, the harmonica virtuoso, stepped before the microphone. Adler "give em" and soldiers, sailors, and marines at most loosened the pavement into putty.

"This sure is a grand brawl," said Sailor Fritz D. Caringgartt of Los Angeles, Cal.

Dagmar Hurlstadt, Evanston, tripped over a street car track at Van Buren, Green Bay, Wis., appreciative assessment her appearing to "Begin the Beguine." "Never mind the tracks," I'll drag down a drill and up to the warring." "too easy."

It's His First Leave.

"Gee whiz, tho," he added, "this is my first leave from Great Lakes and boy, I never had so much fun, hungry asphalt or not. And these rhapsodies oozes up at the moment" Moments.

Even the thaumagast of the jitterbugs turned a circle around Robert Research Messenger, Wheaton, Ill. and Adee Krontz, 2134 South St. Louis avenue, when they exhibited their stuff.

At 9 p.m. happy feet stopped heat to the center and dance dancing. In rugged contrast to the jumps and bounces at La Salle street, most of the next numbers were waltzes.

As slow and dreamy as they had been quick and critical, the service men and their girls drifted around the center ballroom seeking the finale of waltz king sand queen.

13 TO 15 NIPPON SHIPS HIT; PACIFIC BATTLE RAGES ON

Yank Flyers Exact Heavy Toll; Enemy Loses Many Planes.

PEARL HARBOR, Honolulu, June 6 (AP).—United States armed forces have sunk or damaged 13 to 15 warships and transports of the repulsed Japanese invasion fleet at Midway island and "a momentous victory is in the making." These include the sinking of two, and possibly three, aircraft carriers.

Adm. Chester W. Nimitz, commander in chief of the Pacific fleet, enumerated enemy losses tonight in his third communique on the great and continuing battle in the Pacific.

"Pearl Harbor has now been partially avenged," he said. "Vengeance will not be complete until Japanese sea power has been reduced to impotence. We have made substantial progress in that direction."

Announces Victory

ADM. CHESTER W. NIMITZ.

CONGRATULATIONS

Washington, D. C., June 6 (AP).—Adm. Ernest J. King, commander in chief of the United States fleet, today congratulated members of the Pacific fleet "who have so gallantly and effectively repulsed the enemy advance on Midway."

In Adm. Nimitz's message, addressed to Adm. Chester W. Nimitz, commander in chief of the Pacific fleet, said:

"The navy, marine corps, and army guard join in admiration for the American naval, marine, and army forces, who have so gallantly and effectively repulsed the enemy advance on Midway, and we confident that the enemy advance in arms will continue to make the enemy realize that war is hell."

HERE'S BOX SCORE OF JAP LOSSES IN MIDWAY ATTACK

PEARL HARBOR, Honolulu, June 6 (AP).—Here is the latest of Jap casualties as of an hour later:

	Sunk	Damaged
Carriers	2 or 3	1 or 2
Battleships		1
Cruisers		4
Transports		3

And all the airplanes carried by these three to five carriers were lost.

REVIEW OF WAR

Turn to page 14, part 2 for a comprehensive review of the war since the Japs attacked Pearl Harbor six months ago today.

Dizzy Capital Puzzles Lady Hunting Sugar

BY MARCIA WINN

Washington, D. C., June 6.—If there is a single word which best records the impression received by a provincial visitor at the nation's capital at this time the word CONFUSION.

A weary, puddly correspondent, now going the rounds is typical of the Washington of today where bureaucratism, anti, and proved patriotism run to and one often and completely submerged in the confusion mutilating the war effort.

This sadly revealing tale is about a lady who attempted to register for sugar rationing.

Bright and early one morning on the day dedicated to her becomes in our alphabet this lady set out.

Too Value Her Turn.

She waited into a building and saw a long line of people. When her turn came, a warm gridder's got to a table, took samples of her thumb, and then asked her to the room. The lady did and the nurse siphoned out a pint of her blood.

"Thank you very much." The good nurse gently and gave the lady a small lantern emblem denoting that she had contributed to the Red Cross blood bank.

"You're welcome, I'm sure," the lady replied, "and now may I have my sugar card?"

One contradictory incident after another piles up to confound and joined newcomer and veteran alike.

Dispatches to Crosstand Chokes.

And the confusion is not unusual. It is basic. It is as apparent in the manner in which the wartime alphabetical agencies struggle for priority over each other—OCD over OPA, ODWSB over OCD, WPB over OPA, OPA over the war department and all of them over the state department and the department of agriculture—as in the bosoms of the agencies themselves and in the twisted struggle for simple physical survival here.

Despite the surface attempt to decentralize federal agencies, the capital gets more and more crowded each day. The hotels, the buses, the shops, the bars are jammed. Only a hand of American outposts were territories.

Dutch Harbor a Feint.

Ambassador dispositions were made in preparation for the various possible attacks the Japs were believed to be planning.

Up to this time the Japanese had not committed themselves to any action. They were still in position to turn their real thrust against either Dutch Harbor or Midway. By last Tuesday the Americans were able to conclude that a feint was to be made in Dutch Harbor.

Meanwhile preparations among all available American forces in the vicinity of Midway were being rushed in the hope of striking a killing blow against the Japs. The wisdom of this course became apparent last Wednesday when the first code made in its attack on Dutch Harbor. The same day the fleets in the Midway area were reported the Japs making their attack on.

JOHN HERTZ JR., AND MYRNA LOY WED IN NEW YORK

New York, June 6 (P).—Myrna Loy, film star, and John D. Hertz Jr., advertising executive, were married here tonight. The ceremony divorced wife of Arthur Hornblow Jr., film producer, and Hertz were married at the home of the bridegroom's sister, Mrs. Robert Lashan, by Supreme Court Justice Ferdinand Pecora with only members of the immediate families present.

Following a reception the couple left on a honeymoon to an unannounced destination.

Hertz is executive vice president of the Buchanan & Co. advertising agency. He is the son of Mr. and Mrs. John D. Hertz of Chicago. Miss Loy was granted her divorce from Hornblow at Reno last June 2. At the charges extreme mental cruelty.

THE WEATHER

SUNDAY, JUNE 7, 1942.

Sunrise, 5:15. Sunset, 8:25. Moonrise, 1:39 A. M. tomorrow. Yearly to the average daily temperature for this date.

CHICAGO AND VICINITY: Continued cloudiness with occasional thunderstorms today; somewhat cooler. Monday cloudiness.

TEMPERATURES IN CHICAGO.

For 24 hours ended 3 p.m., June 7:

[weather table with hourly temperatures]

Barometer reading at 7:30 p.m., 29.80; humidity, 78%; wind, 12 miles from the southwest.

REVIEW OF WAR on page 14.

[Continued on page 14, column 1.]

land in what is believed to be the greatest naval battle of the war, was well known in American naval circles several days before the battle began, reliable sources in naval intelligence disclosed here tonight."

The story declared that the navy knew of the Japanese sortie soon after the ships left their bases, that it recognized the attack on Dutch Harbor, in the Aleutian Islands, as a feint, and that the Japanese fleet, "the most powerful to be used in this war," was divided into three sections: "First, a striking force; next a support force; and finally an occupation fleet." Admiral Nimitz's strategists in Hawaii had anticipated the Japanese tactics and prepared for them, said the story. "The various forces were made up approximately as follows, according to navy information here," the item went on. It listed the Japanese ships involved by class, and many of them also by name and tonnage; other descriptive details, such as weaponry carried, were also provided.

The Chicago Tribune Press Service carried Johnston's report, and it appeared in the *Washington Times-Herald,* where, that Sunday morning, it was read by Adm. Ernest J. King, commander-in-chief of the U.S. Fleet. King immediately concluded from the reference to "reliable sources in naval intelligence" and the rest of the dispatch that a grave breach of security had occurred. King was aware that Nimitz's knowledge of the planned strike against Midway was derived from one of the most sensitive secrets of U.S. military intelligence: The United States had solved the Japanese machine-enciphered code. Naval intelligence under no circumstances was authorized to disclose anything, and the list of ships in the Johnston article convinced King that the dispatch might lead the Japanese to suspect that their code had been compromised. He demanded action by naval intelligence investigators and got it. That afternoon Maloney was summoned off the golf course at the Flossmoor Country Club and told that the *Tribune* and all concerned were in grave difficulty.

Since the story had been passed by censorship, Maloney was uncertain as to why the *Tribune* might be in trouble. He suspected that Frank Knox, publisher of the *Chicago Daily News* and secretary of the navy, had been giving news breaks to the *Daily News,* and he guessed that Knox was incensed because of the *Tribune*'s exclusive. Maloney did not in the slightest suspect that the real cause for concern involved a secret war code. Nonetheless, he felt instantly that the Roosevelt administration would exploit this incident to do all it could to injure the *Tribune,* and especially Colonel McCormick.

When Maloney learned that he and Johnston would be summoned to Washington, he informed Colonel McCormick and the *Tribune*'s law firm. Both Weymouth Kirkland and Howard Ellis immediately recognized the potential gravity of the situation, and both personally participated in the case. Maloney prepared a statement for the law office in which he characterized the implied censorship violation charges against the *Tribune,* Johnston, and himself as "outrageous and ridiculous. . . . The thought that Stanley Johnston would offer information to the *Tribune* which would be of use to the nation's enemies is just as outrageous." Maloney referred to his own record in World War I and pointed out that Colonel McCormick and the *Tribune* had released to the nation's press its valuable exclusive series on the Battle of the Coral Sea as a contribution to the war effort.

Maloney's statement depended heavily on Stanley Johnston's sworn affidavit as to how he came into possession of the information now being questioned and why he offered it to the paper. Johnston's affidavit stated his background, including his enlistment in the Australian navy at the age of 14 and a half and service in France with the Royal Australian Naval Brigade, then with the artillery and signal service. Following the war, he had entered a mining school in Australia, was graduated, and engaged in engineering activities in Europe. He was employed by *Tribune*-owned Press Wireless in 1939 and then in May, 1940, by the *Chicago Tribune* in its London bureau. He had become a U.S. citizen in September, 1941. Johnston referred to his "lifelong study of military and naval subjects published in the English and German languages. I have made a study of *Jane's Fighting Ships.* . . . I have written articles on the construction of foreign fighting ships." Then he turned to his narrative of events leading to the episode in question:

> I was aboard an aircraft carrier at the Battle of the Coral Sea as a correspondent for the *Chicago Tribune.* . . . After the Coral Sea engagement I returned to a western port, landing June 2nd, arriving in Chicago June 5th.
>
> On my way to and from the Coral Sea engagement, and at many other times, I have discussed at great length the make-up of the Japanese Navy, the construction and type of its war ships and the probable objectives of its naval offensives, the tactics and strategy it would employ and the counter-vailing measures probably to be taken by our navy in response thereto. These matters are discussed not only in navy circles but in military circles everywhere and by armchair strategists. . . .
>
> While at the western port I learned of the Dutch Harbor attack. I considered this a feint. I had previously written a story from Pearl Harbor, passed by military censorship, that the Japanese could not hope to be successful in the Pacific unless they could occupy the Hawaiian Islands, and in order to occupy the Hawaiian Islands they would first have to subjugate the Midway Island outpost. I also wrote in this article that some day we must expect an attempt to invade Hawaii, and that prior to such attempt there

would necessarily be a feint elsewhere before the real attack on Pearl Harbor. This was not only my opinion but that of military authorities throughout the world.

While I was still on the coast there came mention of some engagement in the vicinity of Midway Island. I concluded that this would be the real Japanese attack. I thereupon wrote a memorandum to J. Loy Maloney, Managing Editor of the *Chicago Tribune,* setting up my opinions concerning the situation, to-wit, that the Dutch Harbor attack was a feint; that the real attack would be at Midway Island and the Hawaiian group; that this was the forecast of military and naval circles and that the Japanese fleet would be made up of three sections, first, a striking force, second, a supporting force which would first be used to make a feint, and third, the occupation force. Under each of these three forces I listed the ships in order of their power which in my opinion, and from my studies, would be included.

On Saturday night, after receipt of the official communiqués from Admiral Nimitz claiming that our force had sunk and damaged certain Japanese battleships, cruisers and transports, together with my information that the Japanese force which had attacked Dutch Harbor had not pressed home the attack, I saw the importance of my studies. I thereupon went to Mr. Maloney and handed him my memo. . . .He asked me where I got the information. I said it came from my knowledge of naval affairs, my studies thereof and from the same sources from which I obtained my other stories which had turned out to be correct.

Johnston and Maloney appeared in Washington before Vice Adm. Russell Willson, King's chief of staff; Rear Adm. T. S. Wilkinson, Office of Naval Intelligence; and William Mitchell, a special assistant attorney general representing Francis Biddle, the attorney general and an outspoken enemy of the *Tribune.* Johnston's testimony, as recorded in his affidavit, appeared to satisfy the navy officers except for one particular; his list of the support force ships was not only precisely the same as that which had been transmitted by Nimitz prior to the Battle of Midway, but the misspellings were identical. Johnston offered the following explanation:

During the voyage home aboard the *Barnett,* which was bringing survivors of the *Lexington* from New Caledonia, Johnston and others frequently gathered in the quarters of Commander Mort Seligman of the *Lexington* to discuss task forces, ships, and strategy. During the course of such conversations, charts were drawn, lists were made, memoranda written. When the *Barnett* arrived stateside, explained Johnston, "I was the last but one man who was sick, to leave the ship. I was working in the quarters of Commander Mort Seligman . . . and gathered up my notes. Later I found some of the notes were in handwriting I didn't recognize." Some participant, he said, obviously had brought with him the Nimitz list and left it on the desk. Johnston, not suspecting its provenance and totally unaware that the Japanese code had been broken, proceeded to use the list in working up his story.

The explanation was evidently accepted by the navy officers and, following much hostile questioning, by Assistant Attorney General Mitchell. The Japanese navy, it turned out, was continuing to use its code, so no harm had been done by publication of the list of ships. Byron Price, director of the civilian censorship office, which had cleared the story, was taking no further steps other than to recommend a revision of his procedures to prevent any similar mistake in the future. The navy men made clear to Maloney that his real error was using material obtained at sea without going through naval censorship. Maloney told them of the care Johnston had taken about secrecy on his return, declining to name the battle or his ship until his Coral Sea material had passed naval censorship. Maloney, however, had not realized that the side story on the Midway battle was based on information obtained at sea, and so he had unwittingly submitted it to the wrong censorship.

The incident seemed to be over, but after Assistant Attorney General Mitchell reported to his superiors, the *Tribune* learned that the case was far from ended. Mitchell was upbraided for not pushing the charges more vigorously; he was told that grounds for an indictment must be sought. When this became known on July 15, Maloney wrote Admiral Willson saying that if indicted he would be forced to make his statement public, in his own defense. The navy asked him not to disclose that its investigation related to the breaking of the Japanese code, since this would tell the Japanese exactly what the navy was striving to keep from them. Maloney agreed to make the necessary omissions. Meantime, Mitchell moved to obtain an indictment. According to information sent to Colonel McCormick by Walter Trohan of the Washington bureau, President Roosevelt himself had ordered the Justice Department to proceed.

On August 9, news of the pending indictment was leaked to *PM*, a New York newspaper. "The part played by Colonel McCormick, publisher of the *Chicago Tribune*, and the paper's editors in the publication of Johnston's information has been investigated by the FBI," said *PM*. "If the grand jury returns an indictment it will name, in all probability, several individuals." *PM* also conjectured that "the Navy has persuaded Biddle to proceed in the hope of discouraging any further such flagrant violations of the censorship regulation."

The government in a highly unusual procedure made public the fact that it would attempt to obtain a grand jury indictment of Maloney, Johnston, and the *Tribune* on charges of violating the espionage laws. There were outbursts around the country, with some newspapers attacking the *Tribune* and others rising to its defense. In Congress, *Tribune* friends asserted that the government was going to extreme lengths to smear the paper by announcing its indictment intention. Senator Robert Taft lashed the government for what he said was a highly prejudicial act. Senator Joel "Champ" Clark of Missouri backed up Taft, declaring that the government had assaulted the principle of press freedom. In the House, Rep. Elmer Holland of Pennsylvania had a different idea: "The *New York News,* the *Washington Times-Herald,* and the *Chicago Tribune* consciously or unconsciously under Hitler's orders or their own steam are working for the defeat of the United States and the enslavement of the country." Roosevelt and his friends, it appeared, were exacting a full measure of revenge for criticism they had endured over the years.

McCormick telegraphed Henning: "LET THE SMEAR OF THE TRIBUNE NEWS DEVELOP ITSELF. DO NOT SEEK ANY INTERVIEWS BUT FOR MY OWN INFORMATION I WISH YOU WOULD TELL ME ALL YOU KNOW ABOUT IT AND ESPECIALLY IF THE NAVAL OFFICERS WERE SQUARE OR CROOKED." Walter Trohan provided the answer: The navy had acted when it felt its security had been compromised. When it learned the facts, it dropped charges.

Maloney, proud of his own war record and intensely patriotic, was shaken to the point that his health was breaking, but he was determined to prove Johnston's innocence and his own. Against the advice of attorneys, the two went to the office of a surprised Assistant Attorney General Mitchell and demanded to be heard by the grand jury sitting in Chicago. Such a request was highly unusual, Mitchell demurred. But after telephoning Washington, he agreed that the two principals in the case would appear. The August 19 proceedings before the grand jury were secret, but Maloney and Johnston essentially repeated their earlier statements made in the navy inquiry.

On Thursday, August 20, 1942, the *Tribune* carried an eight-column line: "U.S. JURY CLEARS TRIBUNE. . . . The Federal Grand Jury after extended investigation votes its refusal to indict the *Chicago Tribune* and two of its staff members, J. Loy (Pat) Maloney, managing editor, and Stanley Johnston, war correspondent, who had been accused of violating the espionage act." The paper printed on page one a statement by Colonel McCormick:

> I never had the slightest fear of an indictment. I have known Maloney for 25 years, and when I confided the *Tribune's* honor to him it was with thorough knowledge of his character.
>
> Johnston I have only seen a few times but he has a record of heroism and the impression he made upon all who came in contact with him furnished a complete guarantee of his integrity.
>
> The attitude of the *Tribune* is today what it was before the Grand Jury

investigation was launched and the day after Pearl Harbor. Our whole effort is to win the war and we will not indulge in any factionalism excepting insofar as we are persecuted and have to defend ourselves.

On April 18, 1943, months after charges were made against the *Tribune,* Adm. Isoroku Yamamoto, the Japanese commander at Midway, was killed in a Solomon Islands ambush by the U.S. Air Force. When the war ended, the United Press transmitted a story: "The end of the war permits disclosure of the hitherto undisclosed details of the incident which was one of the most closely guarded secrets of the Pacific conflict." The information permitting the interception of Yamamoto's plane, said the story, "was gleaned from the Japanese military radio. . . . As it turned out, the Japanese never suspected the source of the American information and made no effort to change their code."

Chicago Daily Tribune

2 CENTS PAY NO MORE!
THE WORLD'S GREATEST NEWSPAPER
FINAL

VOLUME XCVIII—NO. 209 C   FRIDAY, SEPTEMBER 1, 1939.—40 PAGES   ★★★ PRICE TWO CENTS

WAR! BOMB WARSAW!

NAZI ARMY ORDER

BERLIN, Sept. 1 (Friday) (A.P.)—Adolf Hitler today ordered the German army to meet force with force. His order of the day to the army read:

"The Polish state has rejected my efforts to establish neighborly relations, and instead has appealed to weapons. Germans in Poland are victims of a bloody terror, driven from house and home. A series of border violations unbearable for a great power show that the Poles no longer are willing to respect the German border.

"To put an end to these insane incitations, nothing remains but for me to meet force with force from now on. The German army will conduct a fight for honor and the right to the life of the resurrected German people with firm determination. I expect that every soldier, mindful of the great traditions of the eternal German military, will do his duty to the last.

"Remember always that you are representatives of the National Socialist great Germany. Long live our people and our reich!"

POLES REPORT ATTACK BY NAZI PLANES, TROOPS

Germany Strikes on Wide Front.

WARSAW, Sept. 1 [Friday] (P)—

Orders Action!

ADOLF HITLER.

London Sends Its Children to Safe Area

BRITAIN, FRANCE TO MARCH WITH POLISH ALLIES

Hitler Speech Fails to Shake Them.

LONDON, Sept. 1 (P)—

WAR BULLETINS

LONDON, Sept. 1 (A.P.)—Reuters [British news agency] said it had learned from Polish sources in Paris that Warsaw was bombed today.

Washington, D. C., Sept. 1 (AP)—Ambassador Biddle telephoned the state department this morning that he had official information that the Polish cities of Warsaw and Cracow were being bombed.

PARIS, Sept. 1 (AP)—The cabinet decreed general mobilization and a state of siege today and called parliament for tomorrow. The mobilization of land, sea and air forces was ordered to take effect tomorrow. The state of siege was decreed throughout France and Algeria.

BERLIN, Sept. 1 (AP)—A radio announcement today from army headquarters said that the German air force was in action over Polish territory. The announcement added that the army was counterattacking all along the German-Polish frontier. It said that Germany had forces were determined to break any possible resistance while the army took over protection of the Baltic sea.

Washington, D. C., Sept. 1 (A.P.)—President Roosevelt directed today that all naval ships and army commands be notified by radio of German-Polish hostilities. The White House issued the following announcement:

"The President received word at 2:50 a. m. [Chicago time] by telephone from Ambassador Biddle at Warsaw and through Ambassador Bullitt in Paris that Germany has invaded Poland and that four Polish cities are being bombed.

ROME, Sept. 1 (9 a. m., transmitted via Berlin)—Italy cannot and remains today. While the nation took resolute measures to be ready in case of war, there were indications she was overwhelmed by events and was not quite sure of her course.

War on Poland Begun, Hitler Tells Nation

BERLIN, Sept. 1 (4:30 a. m.) (P)—

GERMANY TAKES DANZIG; NAVY BLOCKADES GDYNIA

Baltic Sea Declared Danger Zone; All Foreign Shipping Warned Away from Polish Port.

BY SIGRID SCHULTZ.

BERLIN, Sept. 1 [Friday]—Adolf Hitler issued a proclamation to the German people today announcing that Danzig had been incorporated in the German reich.

The outbreak of war in Europe on September 1, 1939, found correspondent Sigrid Schultz (left) in Berlin, from where she had been sending stories to the *Tribune* for most of the 1930s. Schultz spent much of the war in Berlin writing reports that were less than agreeable to the Nazis but not so objectionable as to cause her expulsion. Not until after the war was it revealed that a series of highly critical articles published by the *Tribune* in 1938–39, "The Truth About Nazi Germany," by John Dickson, had actually been written by Schultz.

638

ONCE WAS SOMEBODY ELSE'S FAULT, TWICE WILL BE HIS OWN

The *Tribune* was a major spokesman for the America First movement, strenuously opposing U.S. involvement in World War II. But once the country was at war with the Axis powers, the paper bent every effort toward securing Allied victory.

FROM NOW, UNTIL JUNE EACH DAY WILL LENGTHEN

A longer day to fight the foe,

A longer day to scour the seas,

An earlier dawn to comb the skies,

—And bring the enemy to his knees.

Bottom: Staff artist Gary Sheahan was asked to paint for the *Tribune* the scene at the birth of the atomic age. Scientists who had been present when the historic nuclear chain reaction was achieved provided descriptions of the scene to guide the artist.
Opposite page, top: This *Tribune* news photo of August 14, 1945, shows Chicagoans celebrating the end of World War II.

Chicago Daily Tribune
THE WORLD'S GREATEST NEWSPAPER

★★ FINAL

VOLUME CIV—NO. 196 C   WEDNESDAY, AUGUST 15, 1945—34 PAGES   THREE CENTS—PAY NO MORE

GREAT WAR ENDS!

Japs Will Surrender to Gen. M'Arthur

U.S.S. INDIANAPOLIS SUNK; ALL ABOARD CASUALTIES

Lost in Action After Delivering Atom Bomb Parts

Hundreds Missing

Jury Asks Execution of Petain

Words That Ended War

HIROHITO ACCEPTS ROLE OF PUPPET; AGREES TO CARRY OUT ALLIED ORDERS

EMPEROR SAYS ATOM BOMB MADE NIPPON GIVE UP

Truman to Proclaim V-J Day After Emissaries Complete Signing of Formal Terms

High Commander

Gen. MacArthur

ARMY TO FREE MILLIONS; CUT DRAFT QUOTAS

Allies to Be Represented

Japan's Note of Acceptance

Emperor Assures Signature

End Controls of Man Power; Halt Contracts

JOYOUS BEDLAM LOOSED IN CITY

TRUMAN ORDERS JAPANESE TO CEASE FIRING

Await Signing

Right: Colonel McCormick in his prime, when he led forces opposing the New Deal and later America's involvement in World War II. Although age and ill health forced the Colonel to reduce his activities, he nonetheless continued to direct his vast newspaper enterprise, write books, and keep his hand in politics.

Above: Even during his declining years, McCormick at times visited the newsroom and took a close look at copy being prepared for the paper.

In the late 1940s and early 1950s, the Colonel assembled the management team that would succeed him at the *Tribune*. Clockwise from top left: Chesser Campbell, J. Howard Wood, Frederick Nichols, Walter Kurz, W. Donald Maxwell.

Below: The *Tribune* newsroom in 1951. Standing at the center desk (the news-gathering command post) is Don Maxwell, managing editor. In the foreground, the cable desk. On the right wall, a 24-hour clock reminds the staff that somewhere, day and night without cease, a news story is developing.

Opposite page: One of the *Tribune*'s press lines in the late 1940s.
Above: In the composing room (left), a page is corrected before going to the stereotype room, where the flat bed of type becomes a curved plate. Video display terminals in the newsroom of the 1970s (right) convert writers' thoughts into type.

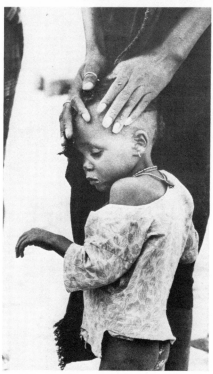

Since the development of the halftone engraving process for newspaper presses, the *Tribune* has published several million photographs. On these and the following two pages are a few of the news photos provided by the paper's photographers, who until recent years remained anonymous.

Opposite page: The grim interior of the Iroquois Theater (top), where nearly 600 people died on December 30, 1903. Bottom: Not all good sports pictures are action shots. The Los Angeles Dodgers trudge off the field after losing the first game of the 1959 World Series to the Chicago White Sox, 11–0.

Above: The February 4, 1977, collision of two trains on the elevated tracks in the Loop resulted in 11 deaths and nearly 200 injuries.

Left: *Tribune* photographer Ovie Carter won national and international prizes for this 1974 picture of a mother in Kao, Niger, comforting her starving child.

Right: Rioting broke out in Chicago and
other major cities in April, 1968, following
the assassination of Martin Luther King,
Jr. This *Tribune* news photo shows
National Guard troops moving into the
ravaged 3300 block of Madison Street after
looting and burning had reduced many
buildings in the area to smoke-blackened
rubble.

Above: One of the most photographed of
Chicagoans was Mayor Richard J. Daley,
who during his two decades in office came
to epitomize the city to the nation and
became one of the country's most
influential politicians. Here, Daley waves in
acknowledgment of the enthusiastic
welcome given him by delegates to the
1968 Democratic National Convention.

"Hippies battling police in disorder in Grant Park," began the *Tribune*'s cutline of August 29, 1968. Police used smoke bombs and tear gas to restore order after violence erupted as the demonstrators gathered to march on the International Amphitheater to protest at the Democratic National Convention.

Tribune photographer Walter Kale catches the beauty of Chicago's lakefront in 1976 as the city welcomes the Norwegian three-master *Christian Radich,* one of the tall ships visiting America for the bicentennial.

Tribune cartoonists in the 1960s and 1970s continued to focus on a wide range of issues, from water pollution to national and international politics. Joseph Parrish joined the *Tribune* during the McCutcheon–Orr era and later became the paper's leading cartoonist, backed by Daniel E. Holland. Wayne Stayskal and Richard Locher were the cartoonists in the 1970s.

Chicago Tribune

THE WORLD'S GREATEST NEWSPAPER

118th YEAR—No. 327 ⓒ Ⓒ 1963 Chicago Tribune   SATURDAY, NOVEMBER 23, 1963   B   5 SECTIONS—TEN CENTS

SPORTS ★★★ | FINAL

ASSASSIN KILLS KENNEDY
LYNDON JOHNSON SWORN IN

35th President

1917 ————— John Fitzgerald Kennedy ————— 1963

GOVERNOR OF TEXAS WOUNDED; MARXIST ACCUSED OF MURDER

President Shot in Head; Wife by His Side

BY ROBERT YOUNG
(Chicago Tribune Press Service)

Dallas, Nov. 22—President John F. Kennedy was assassinated today.

He was killed by a sniper who ambushed the automobile in which the chief executive and Mrs. Kennedy were riding at a motorcade thru the streets of Dallas. Mrs. Kennedy was unharmed.

Gov. John B. Connally of Texas, riding with the President, was seriously wounded by the same shot fired after the bullet which killed the President.

Sworn In on Plane

Kennedy, 46, died at 1 p. m. Chicago time in the emergency room of a Dallas hospital half an hour after he was shot. He never regained consciousness.

Vice President Lyndon B. Johnson was sworn in as 36th President of the United States an hour and half after President Kennedy's death.

Within minutes after he had taken the oath of office, he took off for Washington. His body was aboard the jet plane.

On 2 Day Texas Tour

President and Mrs. Kennedy came to Texas from Washington yesterday morning for a two-day series of speeches and public appearances in San Antonio, Houston, Fort Worth, Dallas, and Austin.

The President was to have gone from Dallas to Austin tonight to end his tour, then spend the night at the ranch of Johnson, 40 miles west of the state capital.

President Kennedy was killed by a bullet from a high-powered rifle with a telescopic sight. There were holes in his throat and the back of his head.

In the short time he was examined

[Continued on page 4, col. 1]

Sniper Fires 3 Times from 6th Floor Window

BY WAYNE THOMIS
(Chicago Tribune Press Service)

Dallas, Nov. 23 (Saturday)—Lee Harvey Oswald, 24, a professed Marxist and Castro follower, was charged late last night with the murder of President Kennedy.

Police Chief Jessie Curry and Homicide Capt. Will Fritz of the Dallas police department made the formal accusation before Justice of the Peace Daniel Johnston. Oswald was held in the grand jury without bail and evidence against him will be presented within the next two or three days.

The action was taken a few minutes before midnight and less than 12 hours after the President was slain in a Dallas street while riding in an open car with the Texas governor, John B. Connally Jr.

Sniper Fires 3 Times

Three shots were fired from the sixth floor of a building facing the street. The President was struck in the head and the neck and died within a few minutes. Connally was also struck thru the right lung, the bullet passing thru his wrist and into his thigh. The governor is expected to recover.

A mountain of evidence, some circumstantial, connected Oswald, a confused turn-coat ex-marine, with the assassination. Earlier yesterday, Oswald had been charged with the murder of a Dallas policeman, J. D. Tippit, father of three children. Witnesses said Oswald fired two shots into Tippit's head when he was stopped on a residential street less than 30 minutes after the Presidential assassination.

Oswald has a long record of Marxist and pro-Castro leanings. He spent nearly three years in Russia after renouncing

[Continued on page 4, col. 1]

36th President

Lyndon Baines Johnson

Judge Sarah T. Hughes, Kennedy appointee to federal court, administering oath of office to Lyndon B. Johnson in cabin of Presidential plane at Dallas airport. Watching are Mrs. Johnson (behind new President's arm) and Mrs. Jacqueline Kennedy (right), widowed only hours earlier by assassin's gunfire.

Blood Stains Tell Tale

Mrs. Jacqueline Kennedy, still wearing blood-stained clothing, with brother-in-law, Atty. Gen. Robert Kennedy, at Andrews air force base, Md., after return from Texas.

MRS. KENNEDY BACK, GOES TO HOSPITAL

2 Children Are in Seclusion

BY LOUISE HUTCHINSON
(Chicago Tribune Press Service)

Washington, Nov. 22—Mrs. Jacqueline Kennedy, 34, again with grief and numbed with shock, walked into the blaze of flashbulbs and television lights at Andrews air force base here tonight and stepped into the hearse bearing her husband's body.

She had sat alone beside the bronze coffin in the Presidential jet on the flight from Dallas to the capital. No one intruded on her vigil.

The navy hearse was battleship gray and the Washington night foggy, but it's doubtful that Mrs. Kennedy, stricken early last August by the death of her infant son, Patrick, noted either.

Goes to Hospital

With Atty. Gen. Robert Kennedy, she rode to Bethesda Naval hospital, where she remained under her physician's care. She was to return to the White House later tonight with the body of the President, and spend the night in her private quarters.

Her two children were whisked from the White House to an unknown hideaway for the night. Whether Mrs. Kennedy would risk telling them

[Continued on page 4, col. 6]

Charged as Assassin

Lee Howard Oswald, accused assassin of President Kennedy and slayer of Dallas policeman, shortly after arrest.

New President Picks Up Reins

BY PHILIP DODD
(Chicago Tribune Press Service)

Washington, Nov. 22—Lyndon Baines Johnson took over the reins as 36th President of the United States tonight after flying into Washington with the body of his assassinated predecessor, John Fitzgerald Kennedy.

After a round of conferences with Kennedy administration and congressional leaders, President Johnson left the White House for his northwest Washington home to spend the night.

Sworn In by Woman

Johnson had taken the oath of office in the front compartment of the Presidential jet as it stood on the runway at Dallas preparatory to taking off for Washington.

With Mrs. Johnson on his

[Continued on page 4, col. 1]

THE WEATHER

SATURDAY, NOVEMBER 23, 1963

CHICAGO AND VICINITY: Cloudy, much colder today, clearing afternoon; high, in 30s; fair, cold tonight, low in 20s; tomorrow cloudy, 35 to 45; w. p. h. Tomorrow: Cloudy, warmer.

NORTHERN ILLINOIS: Cloudy, colder today, low tonight in 20s; tomorrow warmer, 35 to 45; fair.

TV Week Section

Because of the demand for this issue of The Tribune, some copies have been rushed to vendors with the week's TV programs listed in a special section printed in black and white.

Chicago Tribune
THE WORLD'S GREATEST NEWSPAPER

MOON FINAL

ITM YEAR—No. 202 © 1969 Chicago Tribune   MONDAY, JULY 21, 1969   32 PAGES, 6 SECTIONS   10c

FLY U.S. FLAG ON THE MOON

First Picture on the Back Page

Houston, July 20—Man set foot on the moon's surface tonight.

The historic moment came 3 hours and 16 minutes earlier than scheduled when Neil A. Armstrong descended the ladder of the Apollo 11 lunar landing module.

Armstrong's first words on stepping onto the moon were: "That's one small step for man but one giant leap for mankind." Edwin E. Aldrin Jr. followed him out approximately 20 minutes later. The start of the 2 hour 40 minute moon walk came 6 hours and 39 minutes after the tense descent and touchdown on the moon's surface 47 seconds after 3:17 p. m. One of their first acts was to plant an American flag.

The Full Story Begins on Page 2.

On May 9, 1973, Harold Grumhaus (left), chairman of Tribune Company, presented to Dr. Benedict Zobrist of the Truman Memorial Library, Independence, Missouri, a bronze plaque of the front page of November 3, 1948, which carried the famous—and embarrassing—banner "DEWEY DEFEATS TRUMAN." The inscription reads: "Presented with admiration and affection on our 125th anniversary year to Harry S. Truman, whose election victory in 1948 made this one of the most unforgettable front pages ever published by the *Chicago Tribune*."

Tribune and Tribune Company executives who led the paper into the "new era" of the 1970s: Harold Grumhaus (below left), Stanton Cook (below right), Robert Hunt (bottom left), and Clayton Kirkpatrick (bottom right).

The Watergate Conversations

Chicago Tribune

THE WORLD'S GREATEST NEWSPAPER

Section 4

Wednesday, May 1, 1974

Nixon's transcription of Watergate Tapes

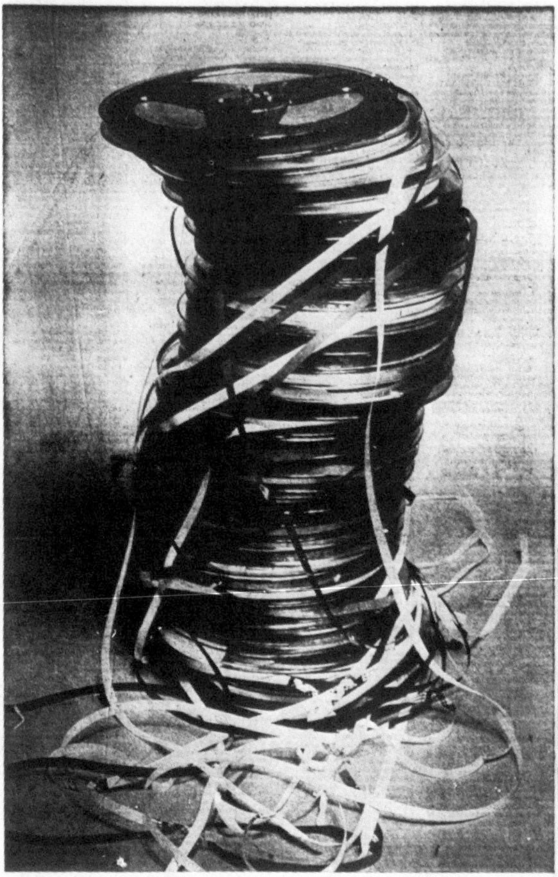

The next question: Will House be satisfied?

The enormous mass of tape transcripts published today by The Tribune were shown in their bindings on television Monday night, stacked by President Nixon's side as he announced to the nation that he would make them public.

The transcripts were contained in 50 volumes, each bound in black leather, and each bearing the gold-embossed inscription:

"Submission of Recorded Presidential Conversations to the Committee of the Judiciary of the House of Representatives. By President Richard M. Nixon."

The volumes bore the date, April 30, 1974. Ironically, that is exactly one year from the date that the President first tried to put Watergate behind him by announcing the resignations of H. R. Haldeman and John Ehrlichman, and the dismissal of John Dean.

"I must now turn my full attention to the larger duties of this office," he said at that time. But the crisis refused to pass, and instead burgeoned to the point where Congress began actively considering impeachment.

It was out of the impeachment inquiry by the House Judiciary Committee that these transcripts arose. The committee, on April 11, subpenaed tape recordings of some 42 conversations and the President, after repeated delays, responded with the transcripts.

However, most committee members were dissatisfied with the offer of transcripts rather than tapes and there were indications that the battle over the tapes is far from over.

The text contains incomplete sentences, sequences that cannot be understood, and confusing syntax. This is the natural result of a full transcription of informal conversation and, of course, it cannot be avoided. The Tribune is publishing the transcript exactly as it was obtained from White House sources, with no additions or deletions. The President's transcript summary has been omitted. He has offered ranking House members access to the tapes.

The participants

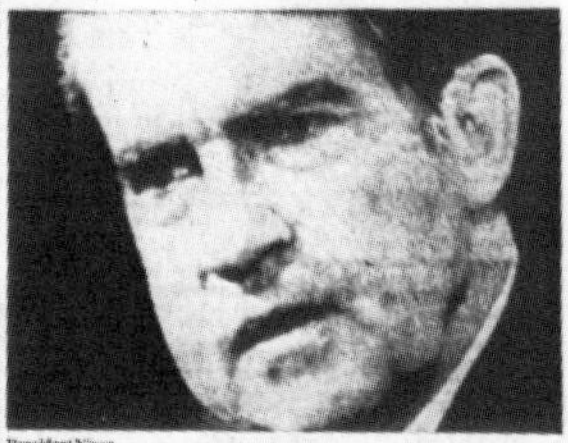

President Nixon

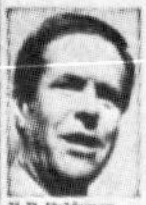

H. R. Haldeman

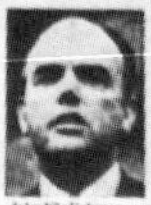

John Ehrlichman

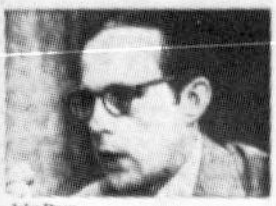

John Dean

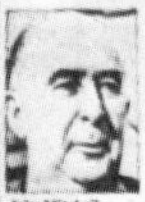

John Mitchell

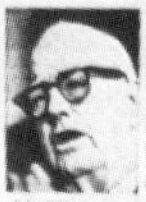

John Wilson

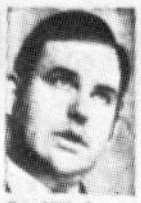

Ronald Ziegler

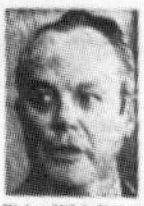

Richard Kleindienst

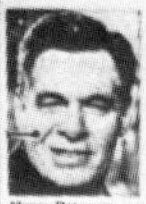

Henry Petersen

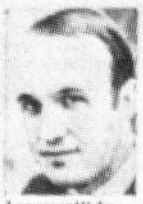

Lawrence Higby

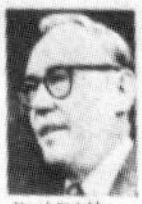

Frank Strickler

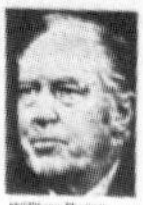

William Rogers

The speakers

P–Richard M. Nixon, *President of the United States*

H–H. R. Haldeman, *former White House chief of staff*

D–John W. Dean III, *former counsel to the President*

E–John D. Ehrlichman, *former chief domestic affairs adviser to the President*

M–John N. Mitchell, *former director, Committee for the Re-election of the President*

Z–Ronald L. Ziegler, *White House press secretary*

K–Richard G. Kleindienst, *former attorney general*

LH–Lawrence Higby, *former assistant to H. R. Haldeman*

HP–Henry Petersen, *assistant attorney general, headed Watergate inquiry in Justice Department*

R–William P. Rogers, *former secretary of state*

W–John J. Wilson, *attorney for John D. Ehrlichman and H. R. Haldeman*

S–Frank Strickler, *law associate of John J. Wilson*

The symbols to the left of each name identify who is talking.

Transcript index

The *Tribune*'s publication of the complete presidential transcripts of Watergate-related tapes on May 1, 1974, was hailed across the nation as a journalistic triumph. On May 8, the paper again made news by calling upon President Nixon to resign.

THE VIEW
FROM THE TOWER

25

The war went on. Maloney's correspondents shone. Robert Cromie, in the Pacific, volunteered to cover the fighting on Guadalcanal, where casualties were heavy, reports of Japanese atrocities numerous, hardships grim, and a general mystery existed about Japanese strength. Cromie wrote of malaria and dysentery and of the misery of jungle fighting, but he never lost his sense of humor or his wonder at the greatness of his fellowmen in adversity. Like all *Tribune* reporters instructed by Maloney, Cromie sought to tell the story of the ordinary soldier, especially the GI from Chicago or Illinois, or, anyway, some place in the Midwest:

> Guadalcanal, Solomon Islands, Nov. 6 *[1942]* (By Airmail)—A gentle-looking little fellow who used to be a greeting card lithographer in Dayton, Ohio, went out this morning with four scouts, hiked 16 miles through the jungle and returned in time for dinner after killing four Japs. . . . The Japs were part of a band of 50 who were separated from the main Jap forces some weeks ago. Fewer than ten are still alive, including a mysterious white man believed to be a German.

Cromie wrote some of the first reports on the U.S. Marine ace Capt. Joe Foss, the fighter pilot who shot down 26 Japanese planes while he led a flight of Grumman Wildcat fighter planes against the superior enemy Zeroes. Cromie could see the air battles only if he dashed out of the jungle and into a foxhole on the beach, where enemy snipers wasted their ammunition on him while he got his story.

Malaria took Cromie out of the Guadalcanal campaign, but after

657

recovering in Australia, he went up to the fighting in New Guinea and took part in a bombing raid on the Japanese stronghold at Rabaul. "Then we were fairly near Rabaul, and I suddenly developed an intense desire to go home. But I wanted to go home after having been to Rabaul—and I still wanted to go to Rabaul—if I make myself clear."

Cromie covered the European war also. He earned an Edward Scott Beck Award for his stories, which included his account of a ride back from a bombing raid in a plane that had lost most of its controls to German antiaircraft fire. Someone asked him why he did not bail out. "How would it look," Cromie answered indignantly, "if a *Tribune* man bailed out and all the others got killed?" Cromie's story told how two Chicago airmen nursed the plane back through flak-riven skies while the tail gunner lay wounded, most controls were out, the tail assembly was hit, and there were still live bombs in the rack. Cromie took care of the tail gunner, pulling him to the center of the plane and cleaning his wounds, while Lt. Col. John S. Samuel of Chicago, the pilot, struggled across France toward the English coast. Cromie, covering the details in a 1,500-word story, described the final stage of the run:

> Samuel, I later learned, was steering the ship largely by means of increasing or decreasing the power of the port or starboard engine, depending upon which way he wanted to turn.
>
> Finally, we reached midchannel and jettisoned our unfused bombs, while the pilot and co-pilot held their breath for fear the lift of the ship when the bombs went away would throw it into a spin. That was always in the back of their minds.
>
> At last I spotted the English coast. In my notes I see I've written "across the channel." "Whew!" I told the tail gunner, who nodded weakly and requested a cigaret. He sat there taking rare puffs between bloody lips adorned with a scraggly mustache that he was too young to grow properly.
>
> We were well into England now. Six P-47s, who had followed us like faithful dogs since we left the formation, went on home, their job well done. We would have been easy prey to any Nazi fighters. . . . Samuel was still using our engines almost entirely for directional changes.
>
> We spotted a field, but it wasn't ours. The tail gunner, finding himself unable to open his right eye, asked me whether he had been hit there. I reassured him, telling him there was only a slight cut.
>
> Then Samuel called, "Pilot to navigator. Keep your eyes wide open. We haven't got much gas." The navigator replied, "We are just about over a field now, sir, but I do not know what it is." It was the first time anyone had said "sir" during our hour-long flight back.
>
> "Roger," Samuel said. "Keep your eyes on it."
>
> The engineer now told those in the navigator's compartment, "We will land according to crash landing procedure." Then he asked me, "Do you want to bail out or land?"
>
> "I'll do whatever the crew does, what the hell," I replied. It was pure

bravado. I would rather have rolled over five times than have pulled that rip cord and waited to see whether it opened.

Samuel spoke again. "Find us an airdrome," he said. "Any one. We'll have to land. We are just about out of gas."

We hurriedly sat on the floor, the wounded man propped against the side against a pillow, with me between his legs and all holding to the back of our necks to prevent snapping in case we hit hard. We made none of the customary circlings and didn't even wait to see which runway we could use. We just came gliding down to little old England, crossed the end of the field at 150 miles an hour, and Samuel greased her in at 130 miles an hour without a bump.

It was a Royal Air Force station, and they met us with an ambulance. On the ground, someone paid me the highest compliment of my life.

"Were you the pilot?" he asked.

In France, Cromie, who fancied himself as a map reader, led an expedition of correspondents into a small French town. They were accosted by an American patrol. "What are you guys doing here?" a tough-looking corporal demanded. "We haven't taken this town yet."

Cromie spent ten months with Gen. George S. Patton's Third Army as it broke the Nazi lines and rampaged through Germany. He wrote of the heroism and the suffering of Midwestern men and their pride in their colorful leader. A fervent believer in the innate goodness of most men, Cromie was shaken when he reported from the concentration camp at Ordruf on April 7, 1945: "Twenty-eight ranking members of the Nazi party in Ordruf visited a place they said they had never seen before—a concentration camp at the edge of town in which the beaten and emaciated bodies of more than 70 men were found four days ago. Colonel Hayden A. Sears of Boston, Massachusetts, leader of Combat Command A of the 4th Armored Division was host." After explaining that the burgomaster and his wife were required to accompany the grisly expedition, Cromie described what they saw among the bodies covered with quicklime in a shed:

> Those too weak to be moved were shot through the jugular vein—according to American medical officers, the most painful death there is. That explains the hideously twisted and contorted bodies we saw. "While you spoke of your culture," Colonel Sears said, "this was going on in your country. You people supported a government that carried on this kind of business."
>
> The next stop was at the pit where between 2,000 and 4,000 men died of starvation, torture or a bullet, then burned. . . . The Nazis examined the "spit" on which the bodies were turned until completely consumed. . . . Two of Colonel Sears's "guests" were elite guards caught after they fled camp. They loudly proclaimed their innocence but one inmate said he had seen them club two men to death.

Cromie got through his European campaigns with only a scratched cheek and a twisted back, received while he pulled a wounded German from a burning ambulance. He returned to the Pacific, flew to Tokyo when General MacArthur moved in to accept the surrender of the Japanese, and was aboard the battleship *Missouri* for the formal ceremonies on September 2, 1945. In Manila he covered the war crimes trial of Gen. Tomoyuki Yamashita, who on December 7, 1945, the anniversary of Pearl Harbor, was convicted and sentenced to death by hanging.

Another of the celebrated *Tribune* correspondents was Jack Thompson, clean-shaven as a plucked duck when he started, but later known as "Beaver" or "The Beard." Thompson began by volunteering to cover the paratroopers who were to fly to the support of the British forces in Africa. He was supposed to have three practice jumps but had none. Since permission for him to fly with the troops was delayed, Thompson went to Algeria by boat and sent an understated dispatch on the landing of the airborne units. A radio correspondent, seeing Thompson on the ground, mistakenly broadcast that he had jumped, a report received in Chicago. Managing editor Maloney was frantic: Where was Thompson's first-person story of his jump? Later Thompson did jump, somewhere on the Tunisian border, but he had not received Maloney's cables and did not realize that he had become big news—news that was not getting through to his paper. On November 5, 1942, the *Tribune* received the story Maloney had impatiently awaited:

> From a personal viewpoint, it was the most exciting moment of my life. I had slept the night before on a concrete floor and was called too late to get my breakfast . . . but I was determined to make the flight.
>
> I had expected to be terrified, but I was not. I was unperturbed, doubtlessly from ignorance, until just the moment for the jump . . . one long ring of the alarm bell. Colonel Raff *[Lt. Col. E. F. Raff]* nodded to the crew chief, "Go." The plane was less than a thousand feet above the field. . . .
>
> Behind me I heard the words of Maj. W. P. Yarborough. "Through the door, Thompy. Through the door." I had expected to shout "Geronimo," the old jump cry of the first parachutists, but I forgot and instead began the prosaic count, "One thousand, two thousand . . . three thousand." If you reach the last of your count without the chute opening you are to pull the release to your emergency chute. But mine opened as I said "two" with a hard yank on my shoulders.
>
> From then on my descent was too speedy to think of anything but Yarborough's instructions. I looked up immediately to see if the canopy was open properly, then grasped the shrouds to guide my descent so I would land facing the wind drift . . . then I saw the man ahead of me in a heap. The next moment my feet, held correctly together, knees bent, jarred against the soft earth. I sat down hard in a perfect three point landing.
>
> The next minutes were spent spilling air out of my chute and unbuckling

my harness while looking over the field . . . some soldiers were laying near their chutes, others moving ahead with their guns ready. Major Yarborough asked if I was hurt and I proudly reported that I was undamaged.

So Thompson finally had his "practice" jump. He was the first correspondent to jump in combat, said the *New York Times,* but there was no shooting. The mission was to secure an airfield expected to come under German attack, and a company of French Zouaves had arrived ahead of the Americans. Colonel Raff, Major Yarborough, and Thompson were greeted by shouting Frenchmen bearing wine. That evening they were each presented with the red fourragère, a French military decoration for valor.

Thompson's next jump, in Sicily, produced his best story. By this time his reputation was such that Maj. Gen. Matthew B. Ridgway, commanding the 82nd Airborne Division, especially asked for him. On July 18, 1943, from 1,200 feet over Sicily, Thompson made his second leap: "A sirocco out of Africa blew the whole armada off course, and we dropped 25 miles from our assigned position as spearhead for the First Infantry Division. . . . I was end man in my plane, and the whole sky exploded with light as I jumped—one of our planes had blown up. I cracked two ribs and tore my knee landing, and as I cut loose from my harness there wasn't a sound. I felt like the only American in Sicily." He found two medical officers and they wandered for two days with only trench knives for defense. Finally they met friendly paratroopers who were cleaning out the Nazi defenders in Sicily. "Now this correspondent is going back to ground fighting fronts and leaving future paratroop missions to other and younger men who had better be rugged," Thompson wrote.

Thompson's 2,000-word story was a classic. Later the *Tribune* learned that he had written it despite painful injuries after refusing to be evacuated with other casualties. He covered the entire Sicily campaign, much of it as the "pool" representative, supplying his material to the Associated Press for general distribution. In September, 1943, Thompson was covering the Italian campaign of Gen. Mark Clark's Fifth Army. Two months later he was in Tehran when Roosevelt, Churchill, and Stalin met to discuss plans for the Allied invasion of Europe. In December, Thompson wrote the story of the reaction to Gen. Dwight D. Eisenhower's appointment as supreme commander, Allied Expeditionary Forces, from the general's headquarters in Algiers. When D day came, on June 6, 1944, Thompson stormed ashore with the First and 29th divisions at Omaha Beach:

> In the face of the cliff was a cleverly concealed artillery observation post which connected by underground cable with a battery inland. . . . Mortars and nebelwerfers, the German multi-barreled mortar, were emplaced on the plateau back of the edge. The cliff was manned by riflemen equipped with

telescopic sights and by machine gun crews. Every strong point was built of concrete and inside were two 75 millimeter guns and one 47. Machine guns protected each strong point. Blocking access to one of the exits from the beach—we had to secure exits to get our equipment off and inland—was a wide anti-tank ditch, with 88 guns guarding the approach to it. And, from inland, the beach could be, and was, swept by fire from many artillery batteries, including a battery of 240 millimeter guns. . . . Topping all this was the fact that on the walls of each pillbox and gun position were charts showing the silhouette of every type of our landing craft, and the exact ranges at which the Germans could fire with best effect. . . . That's what faced the 16th Infantry regiment at 6:30 in the morning on D day, when we came bobbing in over the channel in our little assault boats.

But Thompson, like the other *Tribune* correspondents, mostly wrote about individual American kids who suddenly became men in the fighting—kids like Pvt. Francis S. Currey, 19, who "almost single handedly" stopped a German tank and infantry attack near Malmedy, Belgium. "Currey, firing his Browning, bazookas, rifle grenades, and .30 and .50 caliber machine guns, knocked out at least one tank and immobilized two others as he warmed up. Then he rescued six tank destroyer men. . . . After that, with his knowledge of anatomy, he dressed the wounds of several soldiers and evacuated five on his jeep while under fire." Currey had wanted to be an embalmer before he enlisted.

In the Pacific Theater, meantime, Clay Gowran, Quentin Pope, the paper's Australian correspondent, Tom Morrow, and Harold "Pack Rat" Smith went island-hopping with the marines, mincing through minefields while under fire, following flamethrowers attacking Japanese concrete pillboxes, and crossing jagged coral reefs to reach the wire-strung booby-trapped beaches. Only Smith was slightly wounded. He also fell victim to jungle diseases, which was ironic, because Pack Rat carried supplies adequate for a modest home and medical clinic. Smith's trouble was that he always shared with the less fortunate, thus sometimes exposing himself to fire and plague. When he hit the beach at Makin under heavy fire, he saw a scared marine in a shell hole struggling with a jammed gun. Smith dashed to the lad's aid, fixed the gun, and watched approvingly as his companion shot two snipers from nearby palm trees. Then they dashed through the barbed wire entanglements to a safer shell hole where Smith, now under excellent armed protection, got out his mechanical gear and started to manufacture souvenirs.

Gowran wrote of the Solomons campaigns, receiving the paper's Beck Award in 1943 for his report of a Japanese surprise attack that the marines checked after wading through water up to their necks to stage a counterthrust. Later, from a base in China, Gowran rode in the first American B-29 bombing attack on a Japanese steel works. As the war ended, he covered fighting in Italy and revolutions in Yugoslavia, Greece, Lebanon, and Palestine (now Israel). A quiet, smallish man, Gowran joined the Jewish underground in Jerusalem to get a first-person series of articles on the Stern gang, the guerrillas who helped to establish the state of Israel. Gowran was unhurt until he crashed a glider in the United States while seeking another first-person story, which he had much time to write in a hospital. He then elected a quieter life as associate editor of the *Chicago Tribune Magazine*.

*   *   *

In October, 1944, when General MacArthur returned to the Philippines as he had promised to do, Arthur Veysey, formerly of the *Omaha World-Herald*, who had been island-hopping all the way from New Guinea, landed at rainswept Tacloban, Leyte. He was briefly joined by Pack Rat Smith, Tom Morrow, and Walter Simmons, former city editor of the *Sioux Falls* (South Dakota) *Argus-Leader*. Simmons had joined the *Tribune*'s Sunday department, which produced plastic printing plates for a weekly *Overseas Tribune* published by Don Starr for U.S. troops in Australia and New Guinea. Assigned to the Pacific as a correspondent, Simmons had an extra set of the plates sent to Tacloban, where he hoped to start another edition. When the plates arrived Simmons was elsewhere, but the alert Veysey unpacked them, quickly found a handpress, and went into publication himself.

In January, 1945, Simmons accompanied MacArthur's troops into Luzon, still determined to publish. At Luzon he had no plates, no paper—only a fresh copy of the *Overseas Tribune* flown from Chicago. When he found that the flagship of the invasion force had an offset press aboard, used largely for printing maps, he convinced the admiral that the landing forces needed a newspaper. As for paper supplies, he persuaded an army divisional commander that the invasion's proper moral objective was to liberate both the Filipinos and sufficient Japanese newsprint for the *Overseas Tribune*. The troops soon overran a large cache, which the general presented to Simmons. The paper was the wrong size, but that was immaterial—the pages of the *Overseas Tribune* were reduced photographically to fit it. Simmons presented a copy to General MacArthur, who autographed it, *"To Col. McCormick. The first American newspaper after the Luzon landing. Douglas MacArthur."* For their enterprise both Simmons and Veysey received bonuses from McCormick. On February 11, Simmons and Starr began publication in Manila: "The *Chicago Overseas Tribune,* printed under Japanese shellfire, today became the first American newspaper published in Manila since the entry of General MacArthur's troops eight days ago." Simmons and Veysey each moved on—their job was reporting the war, not publishing—but the new men so impressed McCormick and Maloney that each was assigned a top *Tribune* foreign bureau when the war ended. Simmons went to Tokyo, with his wife, Edith Weigle, as an aide; Veysey went to London, where he was aided by his wife, Gwen Morgan.

Tom Morrow covered some of the hardest fighting of the Pacific war, while Quentin Pope made his way to China by way of Sumatra, producing excellent stories though the action was less fierce. Morrow went ashore at Leyte, covered also by Veysey and Simmons, then on to Iwo Jima and Okinawa. At Iwo, Morrow landed with the Fourth Marines, who, with the Third and Fifth, lost 5,800 men assaulting eight square miles of volcanic rock into which the Japanese had dug their best-protected fighter plane base:

> Iwo Island, March 4 (Delayed)—Hill 382, so costly in lives of the fighting 4th Division Marines, is the most desolate piece of real estate on this nightmare island. A trip to the top of the impossible, eerie terrain, which gained its fame from its height, attested to the unbelievable fighting spirit and courage of the Marine division commanded by Maj. Gen. Clifton B. Cates. Twice the 4th almost won its way to the crest of the hill, which commands a view of most of the Japanese gun positions, only to be forced to retire during three days of bitter fighting. The third time they stormed the ridge they hurled the Japanese back and they held. The way the Marines did it can be seen in the Jap dead strewn in caves and along the incline.
>
> Charred Japanese bodies, cut down by Marine flame throwers, sprawled in concreted and protected cave gun positions. Battered, burned enemy 47s and 75s dotted the hillside. . . . The 4th did it the only way possible, the hard way, with infantry using flame throwers, hand grenades, small arms and mostly courage. . . . Officers believe the capture of Hill 382 broke the back of the Japanese defenders.

There was another hill to be taken, Mount Suribachi, 546 feet, where the famous picture of marines planting the flagstaff was taken. The *Tribune,* at once recognizing it as a classic, was among the first if not actually the first publication to reproduce the photograph in color. The marines and the navy lost 6,137 men taking Iwo Jima, the most costly and savage fighting in marine history. Japanese losses were 20,703 killed and sealed in caves, 216 captured.

The *Tribune*'s correspondents worked for both McCormick and Maloney, the Colonel often forgetting to keep his managing editor informed of his communications. Fortunately, both men sought much the same thing, as explained by Veysey:

> We weren't expected to come up with the main stories, nor exclusives, nor even with first-person narrations. Such things came your way if you were lucky. Generally the press services and the combat correspondents provided the so-called routine news. We were looking for the hometown touch,

hometown for the *Tribune* meaning the Middle West. My work consisted basically of trying to do people-to-people things. The *Tribune* wanted me to tell the individual stories of Chicagoans and others in the Southwest Pacific, later in Europe. That meant going on all kinds of operations to give the names of people there and to tell what they did, be they infantrymen on the first wave, tankers, fliers, warship sailors, submariners, or cooks, divers, unloaders, radiomen, nurses. On my second Pacific tour, most of my stuff ran under a stock heading, "GI Joe in the Pacific."

Managing editor Maloney personally directed the coverage of the Normandy invasion from London, though it was not part of his plan. He had flown to London to acquire the famous Reuters news service for the *Tribune*. Once in London, with Reuters service assured, Maloney could not get out. He set up a command headquarters in Larry Rue's suite in the Savoy, thereby considerably inhibiting Rue's wartime life-style, and attempted to hold conferences on coverage plans while his reporters mysteriously disappeared, one by one. It turned out that they, like their counterparts on the other papers, were being tailed by German agents, who expected to learn the invasion timetable and targets from their preparations. British intelligence was virtually kidnapping them and shipping them out on various secret errands to confuse the Nazis. But all were ready on June 6, 1944: Thompson, Gowran, Cromie, Seymour Korman, Hal Foust, and James Sloan, in addition to the veteran European correspondents, Rue, Darrah, Henry Wales, and Sigrid Schultz.

Schultz was destined for a relatively safe mission, to Paris. Prior to American entry into the war, the Germans refused to let her go to the front because she was a woman and because she had written stories critical of the Nazis. The Germans, however, never knew the full extent of her offenses. In 1938 and 1939 a series of articles appeared in the *Tribune*'s *Graphic* magazine, "The Truth about Nazi Germany," by John Dickson. Dickson was the nom de plume used by Schultz when she crossed the border into Denmark or Norway to send her dispatches from Copenhagen or Oslo. The first articles, appearing in August and September, 1938, exposed the concentration camps, persecution of Jews, secret arrests, labor conscription, and the attacks on churches generally. "Dickson" accurately predicted the Munich agreement between Hitler and Chamberlain and declared that Hitler was fully prepared for war. On July 13, 1939, the most startling Dickson article of all appeared on page one of the *Tribune*. It forecast the German-Soviet pact, which stunned the world less than two months later and opened the way to World War II. "The newest toast in high Hitler guard circles is: 'To our secret ally, Russia,'" Dickson wrote. "Supporters of the theory of Nazi-Soviet cooperation claim that plans for a new partition of Poland, dividing it between Germany and Russia, have been concluded." What Sigrid Schultz was writing from Berlin was bad enough, in the Nazi view—the Germans constantly threatened her with expulsion—but nothing was known of her double role. She continued to work in Berlin until she was wounded in a bombing raid, and finally was permitted to leave.

Noderer also was kept in relative safety this time—in buzz-bombed London—since Maloney felt he had seen enough of combat. Larry Rue was permitted to go with the invasion troops while Noderer ran the bureau. Cromie and Hal Foust drew what turned out to be the prize assignment, General Patton's Third Army, while Thompson and Korman followed the First Army. Thompson by this time had been awarded the Purple Heart and the Medal of Freedom, the first such award ever given to a correspondent. The *Tribune*'s war coverage did not keep enemies from viciously attacking it for editorially criticizing President Roosevelt. On March 1 and 2, 1945, the *Chicago Sun,* for example, published page-one articles declaring, "The *Chicago Tribune* has been the constant darling of Tokyo since a few days before Pearl Harbor. . . . The *Tribune* has also been the darling of Berlin radio." *Tribune* editorials critical of the war effort constituted "a propaganda mating with Axis propagandists," the *Sun* said.

On the night of April 26, 1945, Thompson made his first contact with the Russians at the Elbe. An American lieutenant had glimpsed the Soviet red stars during the day, and, Thompson wrote, "that night I went with a patrol through 25 miles of no-man's-land to reach the river. The Russians ferried us over to their side in a tipsy racing scull, and we all feasted on sardines, cheese and liquor." Thompson had been sure he would have an exclusive story, but a woman reporter whom he did not name talked a pilot into flying her into the Russian lines. His story, nonetheless, was a good one. A woman, Virginia Irving of the *St. Louis Post-Dispatch,* was also one of the first American correspondents into Berlin when the Nazi capital fell in May. The *Tribune* carried her dispatch, together with that of John Groth of the Associated Press. Thompson and Foust, meantime, had come across German records relating to American prisoners of war, and they transmitted thousands of names to the paper for publication as those from Chicago and the Midwest were liberated.

*   *   *

The political situation at home, meantime, had somewhat calmed. On November 7, 1944, President Roosevelt had been elected to his fourth term, with Sen. Harry S. Truman of Missouri as his running mate. The *Tribune* occasionally praised Truman, although it also called him "addle-pated." After another tough fight for Tom Dewey, the Colonel took the fourth term in stride. Soon, in fact, he was taking note of

Dewey's frequent agreement with administration policy and calling him "Me Too Dewey." McCormick had been solaced during the course of the Japanese code case, the war, and the political reverses by a comely neighbor and friend of his first wife, Mrs. Maryland Mathison Hooper, who joined him in picking flowers and pulling weeds in the Cantigny gardens as the Japanese code hearings were under way. They were married in December, 1944, and McCormick looked forward to a round-the-world trip with his bride when the war should end. Meantime, he was planning *Tribune* expansion, seeking ways to build up cash reserves despite the wartime taxes, and trying to discover some way to restore Republicans to power. He liked what Senator Taft had to say against the Democrats, but he liked even better what his friend MacArthur was doing in the Far East.

On April 13, 1945, as the war appeared to be nearing an end in Europe, the *Tribune*'s banner reported the sudden passing of the country's wartime leader and Colonel McCormick's longtime antagonist: "ROOSEVELT IS DEAD." The editors, acting on instructions from McCormick, turned the rules, providing the front page with thick black borders rarely seen in a modern metropolitan newspaper. The story on the death of the president, which had occurred in Warm Springs, Georgia, was from the Associated Press. Arthur Sears Henning analyzed the problems facing President Truman, and Walter Trohan wrote a biographical sketch of the feisty former senator who had been sworn in as president on April 12 at 7:09 P.M. Said the *Tribune*'s editorial, also encased in black:

A Nation Mourns

President Roosevelt is dead and the whole nation is plunged into mourning, those who opposed him in politics no less than those who followed him.

History will appraise his work. For the moment we can only express the deep sorrow all Americans feel at the passing of their chosen leader.

President Roosevelt did not live to see the victory for which he strove but he died in the certainty that the hour of triumph could not long be postponed. He earned his rest.

To his widow and his children, the people of this nation extend deepest sympathy. His successor, President Truman, inherits an immense task at a difficult hour. He will receive the loyal support of all of us.

The *Tribune* covered the story in seven pages, and on the 14th provided an elaborate report on Chicago's and the Allied world's grief. Trohan was aboard the funeral train, bound for New York and the Roosevelt home at Hyde Park. Edward Barry wrote the story of the mourning ceremonies in Chicago. A cartoon by Carey Orr showed the grieving nation backing the new president. Said the lead editorial:

It is needless to stress the difficulties which confront President Truman. A great number of complex problems have been thrust upon him. He must bring the war to a successful conclusion not only in Europe, but in Asia as well, and all the political and economic difficulties of the peace, the demobilization, and reconstruction are to be dealt with.

There is reassurance for him and for all of us in the knowledge that the men who know him best—his former colleagues in the senate—place a high value on his intellect, his good sense, his industry, and his acquaintance with public affairs. They believe he has qualities which will make him fully equal to his responsibilities.

Surely he carries the hopes and prayers of the American people with him. May he lead the nation speedily to victory, to peace and well being.

On Sunday the *Tribune* announced that it would publish a full-page color portrait of President Truman in its picture magazine. The *Graphic* section, still standard page size, carried in color views of the war in Europe as seen by the *Tribune*'s artist Gary Sheahan. A new magazine of books had been added to the paper during the war years, edited by Frederic Babcock, former travel editor. It provided book reviews and special columns by Fanny Butcher, Vincent Starrett, Harry Hansen, and Delos Avery, all skilled and well-known writers. The *Tribune*'s average Sunday circulation was at an all-time high, 1,300,000; the daily 955,000. All editions suffered from a shortage of newsprint, rationed by the government. Following the establishment of Marshall Field's *Sun*, the *Tribune* had sought to prevent him from obtaining an Associated Press franchise, a battle it finally lost in 1945 after a protracted legal fight. The effort was needless from a competitive viewpoint. The *Tribune* had never done better nor dominated the Chicago scene more effectively.

Victory in Europe finally came on May 8, 1945, and while the world read in horror as news of Nazi atrocities became public, the war in the Pacific ground to its conclusion.

On August 8, 1945, the *Tribune*'s banner read: "ATOM BOMB CREW'S STORY. 60% OF JAP CITY WIPED OUT." The description of the first atomic bomb attack in history, directed against Hiroshima on August 6, was as complete as possible from the airmen's view. On August 9, as news of the second attack, on Nagasaki, appeared, the *Tribune*'s editorial foresaw peaceful uses of atomic power that would offset the destruction in Japan. Japan surrendered on August 14.

An early side story by reporter Frank Hughes indicated that the planning of the atom bomb had been done on the campus of the University of Chicago. Later, in its *Graphic* magazine, the *Tribune* would relate full details of the first nuclear chain reaction, which took place at Stagg Field, in a laboratory under the university's athletic stands, on December 2, 1942. Scientists present at the time were interviewed, both for the article on the birth of the atomic age and for a painting by Gary Sheahan depicting the scene.

Following the war Maloney had the problem of finding jobs for correspondents and returning service people without forcing out their civilian replacements. All were cared for. In addition to Veysey and Simmons, who were assigned to choice foreign bureaus, William Fulton, after a tour in London, would become New York correspondent again and then United Nations correspondent; Seymour Korman became West Coast correspondent; Eugene Griffin went to the important Ottawa post; Larry Rue and Alice Siegert to the Bonn bureau; Don Starr to Shanghai; Percy Wood to India. Robert Cromie wrote sports before becoming editor of the *Tribune's* *Magazine of Books* and a columnist; Harold Smith became "Mr. Fix-It," a syndicated columnist; Tom Morrow conducted the "Line O' Type" column; Hal Foust returned to his job as auto editor, enjoying annual trips to Florida and creative expense accounts; Jack Thompson became military editor; and Kermit Holt, following duty in Europe, became travel editor. Wayne Thomis, who served as a navy flier, became *Tribune* aviation editor and one of McCormick's personal pilots. Three other *Tribune* men involved in the military in World War II would rise over the years to top editorial positions at the *Tribune:* John T. McCutcheon, Jr., George Morgenstern, and Harold Hutchings.

*   *   *

War news, including the atomic bomb, did not equal the terror for Chicago that resulted from a series of unsolved murders and assaults that had begun on June 3, 1945. On that morning, the nude and strangled body of Mrs. Josephine Alice Ross, 43, was found on the bed of her apartment on North Kenmore Avenue. When police were summoned, they discovered that the attractive victim also had been slashed and battered, but this had not at first been observed because the killer had carefully washed her body. He had also cleansed the apartment, removing fingerprints. There were other subsequent minor assaults and apartment lootings in the area that might have been the work of the killer of Mrs. Ross, but no useful leads. Then on October 1, Veronica Hudzinski was struck in the shoulder by a bullet when two shots were fired at her as she sat at her desk in her Winthrop Avenue apartment. The police found the revolver on the ground outside her window. Four days later, Lt. Evelyn Peterson, a former army nurse, was beaten into unconsciousness by an intruder who entered her Drexel Avenue apartment through a trapdoor. She was hospitalized with a fractured skull. Her apartment also had been wiped clean, but a partial fingerprint was found.

City editor Don Maxwell urged his police reporters to make every possible effort to come up with a break on the murder and assaults and apartment lootings, all of which were beginning to cause wide public demand for better police protection. However, the crime pattern was inconclusive. On December 5 it varied again, when Mrs. Marion Caldwell was shot and wounded as she sat in the kitchen of her home. Five days later, Frances Brown, a former Wave who had just taken a job in Chicago, was found by a maid in her sixth-floor apartment on Pine Grove Avenue. Her nude body was draped over the edge of the bathtub, the top of her pajamas folded about her neck. When police arrived and removed the pajama top, they found a knife thrust completely through her throat. She also had been shot twice. Again the blood had been washed from the victim's body and again the apartment had been cleaned, but one fingerprint had been overlooked. And on the beige living room wall a grisly message was written in red lipstick: "For heavens sake catch me Before I kill more I cannot control myself."

James Gavin, the *Tribune*'s veteran police reporter, studied these cases, every new apartment burglary and assault report, and kept in close touch with Sgt. Thomas A. Laffey, the police fingerprint expert.

On January 7, 1946, the most ghastly slaying of all was discovered. James E. Degnan, newly arrived in Chicago, went to the bedroom of his blonde, blue-eyed daughter, Suzanne, age six, to awaken her for school. The room was empty. A window was wide open. The bedclothes were neatly folded, and the room appeared to have been cleaned and rearranged since the parents had put Suzanne to bed the night before. The little girl could not be found. The parents called the police, who discovered an oil-soaked ransom note: "Get $20,000 Reddy & Waite For word Do not notify FBI or police Bills in 5's & 10's." And, on the other side, "Burn this for her safty." The police were unable to dust the prints on the oil-soaked paper but sent the note to the FBI, where a single fingerprint and a partial palm print were successfully raised. They checked with nothing in FBI files.

Later that day, two police detectives opened a loose manhole cover near the scene of the crime. There they found the severed head of the child. A further search of the sewers revealed portions of the girl's torso and legs. Her tiny arms would not be found until six weeks later. Chicago was terrorized and frantic with grief and anger. Mayor Kelly called for the biggest manhunt in the city's history, adding several hundred temporary police officers to free experienced men to hunt for the killer of the Degnan child. Joining the other newspapers, the *Tribune* offered a $10,000 reward for clues leading to the murderer; the total offered was $41,000. The *Tribune* also urged all citizens to cooperate with the police in seeking the murder weapon or weapons. It was thought surgical instruments might be involved.

Six months passed without a break in the case. Sergeant Laffey

meticulously checked fingerprints of every possible new suspect against
the fingerprint found on the Degnan ransom note, usually with Gavin of
the *Tribune* at his side. The single, smudged print was of dubious value,
but Laffey by now remembered it so well that he felt he would be alerted
by anything similar.

On June 26, 1946, Detective Tiffin B. Constant was ascending the rear
stairway of an apartment building in response to a routine call on an
apartment intrusion. As he reached the first-floor landing, he saw a
young man leaning over the second-floor railing, pointing a gun at him.
The youth pulled the trigger, but the gun failed to fire. Constant got off
three shots, missing his assailant, who threw his gun at him and then
leaped upon Constant with maniacal fury, knocking the officer's gun
from his hand. A fellow officer arrived as the two struggled and knocked
out the suspect with a heavy flowerpot. The youth was identified as
William George Heirens, 17, a University of Chicago student living in
Gates Hall.

It was soon discovered that the gun Heirens aimed at Detective
Constant was stolen, and a search of Heirens's room yielded two suitcases
filled with pistols, jewelry, watches, and a surgical kit. Meanwhile,
Heirens's fingerprints were routinely sent to Sergeant Laffey. Laffey remembered every whorl from the Degnan case, and as soon as he saw
Heirens's prints he knew he had a match. Nevertheless, he went to his
workroom to confirm what he already knew. With him was James Gavin.

"Why don't you try them on the Peterson case?" Gavin asked. "I'm
going to," Laffey responded. The prints matched. They were dispatched
to the FBI for confirmation and Gavin telephoned his scoop, which
appeared in the late editions of the *Tribune* on June 29, 1946: "Police and
the state's attorney's office early today were working on sensational
developments in the Suzanne Degnan murder case. They have discovered seven points of similarity between the fingerprints on the Degnan
ransom note and the fingerprints of a young University of Chicago
student. He is William Heirens, 17, a husky six footer of Touhy Avenue,
Lincolnwood, and a resident of Gates Hall at the University of Chicago."

Gavin's story recounted all the details of the murders and of the
successful police search. It was, recalled Don Maxwell years later, the
greatest crime case broken by the *Tribune* in his career as city editor. The
Tribune had a publication beat, but Gavin never claimed to have played a
part in solving the case. He had broken the story by being there when it
happened, as a hardworking, conscientious reporter should be. A month
later, Philip Pelos, a Chicago Transit Authority trackwalker, found a
hunting knife not far from the Degnan home on Kenmore Avenue and
brought it to Maxwell's office. The knife turned out to be that used in the
slaying of Suzanne Degnan. It and two guns had been stolen from a

Northwestern University student, and the guns were among those recovered by police from Heirens's room. Within a week, Elgar Brown and John Madigan of the *American* also had a beat, the confession of Heirens to the murders of Suzanne Degnan, Josephine Ross, and Frances Brown, and the shooting of Veronica Hudzinski. In addition, according to the story, Heirens admitted to 125 burglaries. He had confessed to his defense attorneys, who talked to the *American*.

Heirens pleaded guilty to 29 indictments, three for murder and 26 charging assault with intent to kill, burglary, and robbery. Judge Harold G. Ward, chief justice of the Criminal Court, sentenced him to life imprisonment on each of the murder counts, the sentences to run consecutively, and one year to life on the other counts. Heirens was remanded to Stateville penitentiary at Joliet.

*　　*　　*

On May 26, 1946, there was desolate news for Colonel McCormick. His cousin, partner, and friend, Capt. Joseph Medill Patterson, died in Doctor's Hospital, New York. McCormick, instructed by Joe to "take over" more than a quarter-century previously, temporarily assumed the duties of chairman of News Syndicate Company, publisher of the *New York News*. But he soon concluded that the paper was under excellent management, Mary King Patterson continuing active, with F. M. "Jack" Flynn, business manager, and Richard W. Clarke, executive editor, directly in charge. At the annual meeting of the *News* directors on May 19, 1947, Flynn was made president, and Clarke became editor.

During the final days of the war, while the *Tribune* news staff covered the United Nations conference in San Francisco, the Potsdam conference in Berlin, and the fighting fronts and involved foreign areas, McCormick was already preparing for postwar expansion. He informed his directors of his plans and his attempts to salvage capital despite wartime taxes and said that he expected his executives to be early in line for new presses and construction steel that would be available once the economy returned to a peacetime basis.

One major project was a new building, immediately north of Tribune Tower, which would house two lines of presses, other added publishing facilities, and offices and studios for WGN, including a huge new television studio. Since John Park, production manager and veteran of the Tribune Tower construction, was ill, Harold Grumhaus, his assistant, took over the task of coordinating the work. Along with the counsel of Park and Otto R. Wolf, pressroom superintendent, Grumhaus would have the aid of *Tribune* architect Leo Weisenborn and Colonel McCormick himself. Grumhaus at the time, in addition to his other duties, was in charge of labor relations, a full-time job, and he initially protested that he was neither an architect nor an engineer. Colonel McCormick informed Grumhaus that he regarded him as an excellent coordinator and, by working Saturdays, he would be able to include the new building in his schedule. They met Saturdays each week to go over the building plans. Contracts were let to Wieboldt Construction Company, and work started before the plans were completed.

While building was under way, McCormick began to yield to his editors' and advertising manager's desires for changes in the editorial product. A new magazine, *Theater-Music,* issued in tabloid size, had been added during the war, and now, on October 13, 1946, the *Graphic* made its bow in new format, magazine size, printed in four colors on rotogravure presses and stock. As the year ended, the paper was achieving new highs in advertising linage, Sunday circulation went to a record 1,400,000, and McCormick was cheered by auspicious political news. In the November elections Republicans won control of both houses of Congress after 14 years of New Deal control. The Colonel was eager to press his search for a winning presidential candidate for 1948. First, however, the *Tribune*'s 100th anniversary had to be properly celebrated and the cornerstone laid for the WGN Building.

On Sunday, June 8, 1947, some 3,500 invited guests attended a reception after visiting what would become WGN's television studio and were invited to inspect new and old presses in the flag-decked tower and the incomplete WGN Building. On June 9, 1947, a civic committee gave a dinner honoring McCormick and the *Tribune,* to which company directors and executives were invited. The hosts included Gov. Dwight Green and Mayor Martin H. Kennelly, successor to Edward J. Kelly, who was also present. General Robert E. Wood was master of ceremonies. More than 2,000 guests attended, and the committee in charge presented McCormick with a plaque, reading in part: "To you whose life is dedicated to the proposition that fearlessly to inform men is to make men free, your fellow citizens pay tribute on this, the 100th anniversary of the *Tribune*'s founding."

The Colonel was touched. "I could understand the *Tribune* putting on its own show, but I am overwhelmed by this," he told the guests, his eyes misty. He recovered quickly and spoke of his grandfather Joseph Medill, showed his familiarity with Chicago's history, and noted that "two Jews and three heretics" wrote the *Tribune*'s editorials, implying that he sometimes provided assistance. He confided publicly to Mayor Kennelly that his gracious presence might cause the writers to regret, and in the future to soften, some of their comments about him. The dinner demonstrated to McCormick critics that the Colonel was not entirely the ogre he had been represented as in the trying years just past.

In its June 9 issue, *Time* magazine marked the 100th anniversary of the *Chicago Tribune* in a way Colonel McCormick himself could admire. He was on the cover, portrayed by Boris Chaliapin as wearing an admiralty fore-and-aft version of a pressman's cap, the folded front page of the *Chicago Tribune*—first-rate publicity. Inside, the *Tribune*–McCormick article ran 13 columns. It began by describing the anxiety of William Donald Maxwell to please the Colonel with lakefront fireworks and enumerated the details of the planned celebration—5,000 "carefully screened leading citizens to sip punch and nibble cake at a reception," $20,000 spent for radio time on 240 stations of the Mutual Network (in which the *Tribune* owned a fifth interest), a centennial edition "to make his newsboys stagger," and, on the lakefront, "a grand finale" including a fireworks display of Niagara Falls and the A-bomb blast over Hiroshima. Said *Time:* "Of the 1,700 dailies in the U.S., the *Chicago Tribune*, an organ of tremendous vigor and imposing technical virtuosity, is easily the loudest and perhaps the most widely feared and hated. It is also the biggest (circulation 1,040,000 daily and 1,500,000 Sunday) among papers of standard size."

Time employed its usual devastating prose in profiling McCormick, mistakenly describing his hazel eyes as "ice water blue," and correctly appraising his personality as "inordinately shy, insufferably proud." It referred, of course, to Rascoe's remark about the 14th-century mind, adding *Time*'s own appraisal, "It is in some ways a brilliant mind, with some appalling blind spots." *Time* interviewed Colonel McCormick and succinctly quoted him on the reason for the *Tribune*'s success: "It ain't Orphan Annie," he said, "it's the hair on our chest." Did he some day hope to be president of the United States? The interviewer was rewarded with "a withering look." Then the Colonel snapped, "Out of the question. No big publisher has ever held high public office."

"As any fool could see," *Time* concluded, "if a man had a commanding view from the Tribune Tower, what would he want with the White House?"

Colonel McCormick was perhaps even more pleased by the tribute paid him by his respected new Chicago rival, John S. Knight, editor and publisher of the *Chicago Daily News*. On June 9, the lead editorial in the *Daily News* appeared over Knight's signature:

> The fabulous saga of Col. McCormick and the *Tribune* has been told so many times and with such exaggerations of blind prejudice or unrestrained enthusiasm that it need not be repeated here. Suffice it to say on this occasion that under Col. McCormick's direction, the *Tribune*, widely renowned for its enterprise and technical skill, has become one of the most successful newspapers in the world.
>
> While many of us frequently find the *Tribune*'s views and opinions unpalatable and at variance with our own, full credit must be accorded Col. McCormick's courage and singleness of purpose.

Few American newspapers have fought so vigorously to preserve our traditional freedom of expression. No other American newspaper publisher has been the target of so much abuse and character assassination from critics who, in many instances, enter the arena with unclean hands. No slurs upon Col. McCormick's patriotism or journalistic eccentricities can obscure the fact that he has remained true to his convictions, loyal to his country, and held steadfastly to an abiding faith in his own community.

We salute the *Chicago Tribune* and its publisher as they embark upon the second century of exciting, meteoric and controversial journalistic adventure.

On June 10, the *Tribune* published its centennial edition, including a 28-page section on Chicago and *Tribune* history. That evening, to accompany the lakefront extravaganza to which the public was invited, the *Tribune* arranged a dinner party for 500 selected guests atop the Soldier Field east stand, where they could watch the water festival and fireworks. But *Tribune* luck ran out. High winds forced a cancellation of the show and made a shambles of the table settings. Some 30,000 early arrivals were sent home, while the Soldier Field guests went below into a service tunnel lit by an occasional bare bulb, where they had cocktails and dinner amid considerable hilarity.

The *Tribune*'s late editions of June 11 announced that the "epic fete" it had planned for the 10th would occur that night, God willing. The paper said that the high winds would have endangered performers and spectators alike and might have blown the fireworks about to start another Chicago fire. Early on the afternoon of the 11th, crowds began arriving in Burnham Park, until by 6 P.M. an estimated 50,000 were present. Public transportation continued to bring 50,000 more an hour for the next four hours, and 13,500 cars packed the available parking places in the Burnham Park area, while thousands walked from distant lots and their homes on the Near West Side. The *Tribune* estimated that more than 300,000 people sat in the grass of Burnham Park and watched motorboat races, water skiers, army and navy aerial shows; heard a 100-bomb salute; witnessed a helicopter rescue mission; saw a parade of illuminated yachts and high wire and other circus acts; then sang "Happy Birthday, dear *Tribune*" before watching the display of fireworks. Willard Edwards was brought from Washington to write the main story, recalling Gath's presence at the Columbian Exposition 50 years before. So the delayed fete was a success, and the paper sold 1,350,000 of its special issue. There was a report of a party in London, hosted by the American ambassador, honoring the *Chicago Tribune*. The Associated Press and Acme news service sent pictures of the *Tribune*'s June 10 front page on their wires, and the facsimiles were reproduced in front pages of hundreds of newspapers throughout the world.

On June 12, the cornerstone of the new building was laid. It would rise, when completed, four stories above Michigan Avenue in front, nine stories on the eastern side. It would house, the paper said, the biggest and most modern press facility of any newspaper in the world. The WGN Building and press installation project was the largest and most complex in company history, including even the move into Tribune Tower, since Colonel McCormick demanded that both activities should be accomplished simultaneously to make up for the fact that no presses were built during World War II. The press order first contemplated had been gradually expanded by McCormick until it encompassed 39 black press units, eight color units, and seven folders to be built between 1946 and 1949. The first press, consisting of seven units and a folder, was installed while the lower floors of the WGN Building were under construction and operated for the first time on November 11, 1948. The two new lines of presses were mounted on specially designed springs bearing press units weighing 25 tons each, which rested on concrete and steel caissons sunk 110 feet to bedrock. The special mounting was designed to minimize the effect of press vibration on the delicate radio and telecasting equipment being installed on the floors above. Each of the Goss Headliner press units, weighing 18 tons with cylinders removed and measuring ten feet long, six feet high, and five and a half feet wide, was moved into position through a hole cut through foundation walls under Nathan Hale Court, a plaza created between Tribune Tower and the northern wing of the WGN Building. Later a bronze statue of the young Revolutionary War hero much admired by McCormick would be placed at the Michigan Avenue level.

The total project, including replacement of old presses, provided the *Tribune* by 1950 with 126 black press units, 23 color units, and 24 folders in four press rows, each a city block long. The cylinders of the black presses were removed during installation to protect their delicate bearings. The color presses and the folders arrived dismantled and were assembled in the pressroom. While press installations were being completed, the composing room space was increased by 45 percent and 14 new typesetting machines were added, bringing the total to 110. With its 45 percent increase in press capacity, the *Tribune* could print 96-page papers, using four colors, at speeds up to 60,000 an hour. A new kind of stereotype plate locking device insured that the curved metal plates would cling fast to the whirring cylinders without flying free from centrifugal force as had sometimes happened previously.

In addition, the new building provided increased capacity for mail room, stereotyping, circulation, and photography, plus the WGN offices, TV studio, and 12 radio studios. Not the least important, the building was surrounded by loading docks, reached by modern newspaper loading equipment and accommodating scores of *Tribune* trucks. The cost of the building when complete would be $8 million, and Tribune Square would fill the area bounded by Michigan Avenue, Hubbard, St. Clair, and Illinois streets.

*   *   *

On July 21, 1947, McCormick wrote General MacArthur in Japan that he was planning a trip around the world. The general's response was immediate and warm:

> *I am delighted to learn from your letter of the 21st of your trip to the Far East. Tremendous transformations of deepest significance to the future of the world are evolving in the Orient, and it will be good for everyone to have your keen and experienced observations brought to the attention of the American public through the columns of your great newspaper. . . . You can count upon the warmest possible welcome here and the assurance that every facility of the command will be at your disposal while in Japan.*

MacArthur concluded by saying he would arrange details with Walter Simmons, the *Tribune*'s correspondent, as soon as he had McCormick's itinerary.

On August 29, Colonel McCormick responded to MacArthur's hospitality: "*I would be glad to accept any itinerary in Japan you suggest. I do not care to see bombed cities and I presume it would be a humiliation for the Emperor to see me.*" McCormick added that he would especially wish to visit the 24th Infantry, a black combat regiment at Camp Majestic, 250 miles southwest of Tokyo. On September 6, General MacArthur cabled that Colonel McCormick could both visit and review the 24th. The Colonel and Mrs. McCormick departed Chicago on October 25, accompanied by McCormick's secretary, Dorothy Murray, and his personal pilot, Howard West, who flew their leased Lockheed Lodestar to San Francisco, where they joined a Pan American flight.

Colonel McCormick's visit to the Far East was a personal and journalistic triumph. His friendship with General MacArthur, America's proconsul in Japan, was responsible in part for his welcome. Of greater influence with the Japanese was the fact that Emperor Hirohito, still the prime source of authority to his people, granted a rare interview to the American publisher. "The emperor remembered that my father, as ambassador to Russia, looked out for the interests of Japanese nationals during the Russo-Japanese war," McCormick explained in his dispatch to *Tribune* readers. "The emperor made it clear that he looks forward to excellent relations with the United States. He appreciates the splendid conduct of the American occupation forces under General MacArthur."

Thereafter McCormick was a guest of honor at a luncheon given by the presidents of both houses of the Japanese diet; he was interviewed at the Japanese Correspondents' Club by newsmen from over the world;

and he reviewed troops and submitted to interviews by army combat correspondents. Japanese newspapers displayed on their front pages McCormick's statement that world powers should join to resettle displaced persons in potentially productive areas that were at present underpopulated, an idea that appeared to be well received in Japan, as was his declaration that a peace treaty with Japan should not be completed until the Russians were ready to participate. "I don't want to kick up a row with Russia if that can be avoided," the Colonel told the correspondents. "Take five or six years if necessary *[for the peace treaty]*—it's a short time in history." The members of the Correspondents' Club applauded his statements, according to the report of correspondent Walter Simmons.

The Associated Press, United Press, and Reuters carried his dispatches around the world, including his comment that he was skeptical about the plan of Secretary of State George C. Marshall to help rebuild postwar Europe with American funds. "We should provide immediate, short-term relief to end Europe's hunger," McCormick said. "But we can't use our money in an attempt to rule the world." Then he added, characteristically, "American workmen do not want to work 40 hours a week to send help to British workmen who labor only 32 hours a week."

Early in his Japanese visit, the *Tribune* publisher made the 250-mile journey to Camp Majestic to visit the black 24th Combat Regiment. He reviewed the troops and told them: "My only request to General MacArthur was for an opportunity to come to visit you. I have heard so much about what you have done and what you are doing. You have honored your country in war and in peace." Then McCormick and his party visited the housing area of the camp, where 119 black and white families were living in an integrated community. Simmons wrote an account of the visit to the 24th. He described the Colonel's satisfaction at finding that the families were living in complete harmony, sharing recreation, schools, and shopping facilities. McCormick commended MacArthur on the arrangement and told the general that the excellent race relations would provide a good example for Chicago.

Colonel McCormick also sent his own reports to the *Tribune*. He described a visit to Osaka, the "Chicago" of Japan, and wrote of Chicagoan Frank Lloyd Wright's contributions to Japanese architecture. Simmons, managing the tour as well as reporting it, supplemented General MacArthur's efforts for McCormick's comfort by sending over his own seven-foot bed, which was installed in the American embassy apartments where the McCormicks stayed as MacArthur's guests. McCormick never learned of this special accommodation.

Whenever soldiers interviewed him, whether in Japan or China or the Philippines, McCormick was asked whether General of the Army Douglas

MacArthur, supreme commander of the Allied powers, would become a candidate for president of the United States. Colonel McCormick reluctantly admitted that MacArthur would not agree to run. However, shortly after his return to Chicago, the Colonel wrote the general a letter indicating that he had every intention of securing MacArthur's nomination. With Simmons, McCormick and his party flew to Seoul, Korea, where he interviewed Syngman Rhee, the future president. Then McCormick, Mrs. McCormick, and Miss Murray, his secretary, went on to Shanghai, where they were guests of Mayor K. C. Wu; to Peking and Hong Kong, where he conferred with correspondents Starr and Pope; and to Bangkok, where McCormick recorded a broadcast for WGN and Mutual. McCormick dictated several travel articles, some unflattering: "If Hong Kong's airport is not the worst in the world, it is close to it." He returned to Tokyo to record another WGN broadcast. Without using notes, McCormick spoke for 15 minutes on Far Eastern affairs. Before he had left the studio, he was informed that the equipment had failed. Would he try again? McCormick nodded and delivered another 15-minute commentary, this one beginning, "Communism is the most primitive form of property ownership," and going on to expose fallacies of Marxian theory. It was broadcast and printed in the *Tribune*.

Simmons accompanied McCormick to Manila, where he was a guest of President Manuel A. Roxas and visited various army establishments. As they flew about the island, McCormick inquired about surplus B-17 airplanes and discovered they could be had reasonably. He decided to buy one when he returned to the states and to refurbish it as his private plane. In Manila, McCormick yielded to importunities of newsmen for an interview. "Did you say in Hong Kong that you favor Senator Taft over General MacArthur for president?" he was asked. McCormick replied: "I am on my way back. I'm out of touch with American politics." Then, with a tight smile, he volunteered that all present were privileged to be in the Philippines and suggested that the three greatest events in world history were "the birth of Christ, American independence, and the birth of the Philippine Republic." That pronouncement so distracted everyone that the Taft–MacArthur question was not pursued.

Senator Taft clearly was rising in McCormick's estimation, despite the Colonel's secret desire to push the MacArthur candidacy. The Ohio senator was taking a strong stand against the Marshall Plan, while Tom Dewey favored it. At home, the *Tribune* was still reflecting McCormick's thoughts, for it said editorially: "The Marshall Plan, if adopted, will disturb the American economy and disturb it profoundly. Senator Taft opposes the plan because the money costs are too high. President Truman and Secretary Marshall say, 'That's all right,' and Thomas Dewey, the 'me too' candidate, echoes them."

*   *   *

In the weeks prior to Colonel McCormick's departure there were ominous signs that the *Tribune* was about to have the most severe labor problem in its history. Printers employed by Chicago's five general circulation dailies and the *Journal of Commerce* were engaged in a slowdown, and had threatened a strike. At issue was the new Taft-Hartley Act, passed over a presidential veto on June 23, 1947, which limited some of the freedoms unions had previously enjoyed in their relations with management. On November 24 at 9:00 A.M., the printers in Local 16 of the Chicago Typographical Union walked off the job. McCormick, hearing the news in Tokyo, commented, "Good. I hope it lasts a long time." It would. The Chicago publishers, including McCormick, John S. Knight of the *Chicago Daily News,* and Marshall Field III, who had recently acquired the *Times* and would soon merge it with his *Sun,* stood together.

On November 26, 1947, the *Tribune*'s page one had a drastic new look for the first time since 1917, and so did its competitors'. "SIX PAPERS APPEAR IN NEW DRESS" read the headline on the strike story. "Members of Local 16 of the Chicago Typographical Union placed picket lines in front of all five plants in which the city's six daily papers are published. The printers went on strike Monday. During the strike all Chicago papers will be published by the photo-engraving process." The *Daily News* published 34 pages, the *Herald-American* 30 pages, the *Times* 36 pages, and the *Tribune* 24 pages on November 26 but 80 pages on November 27.

By causing a showdown, the printers forced the publishers into developing new printing techniques. News and classified advertising were composed on typewriters; the typed copy, slightly more than a column in width, was reduced in size photographically, then engraved by an etching process so that stereotype mats and plates could be produced. The procedure was slow and crude at first, but it was swiftly improved as the newspapers acquired "varitypers," self-justifying typewriters that permitted neat columns, using a typeface similar to that on a Linotype matrix. When the strike ended 22 months later, the photoengraving process had proved itself in many ways preferable to prior hot-type printing methods.

The *Tribune* scolded its striking employees editorially. "During recent years the management has been aware that a small number of employees have been taking unfair advantage of the *Tribune*'s reluctance to impose any rigid code or set of regulations defining obligations of members of a family whose record of peaceful relationship has been a tradition of journalism." The editorial quoted from a memorial that the union had presented to Colonel McCormick on the paper's centennial: " 'In 1852, the *Chicago Tribune* entered a contractual relationship with the Chicago Typographical Union, No. 16, which has continued until this day without interruption so much as an hour.'" The editorial concluded that since both sides were agreed on wages but the union was protesting an act of Congress, the strike could indeed be a long one.

The burden of the strike fell heavily on the group of executives named to find new ways to solve production, advertising, and editorial problems and to reorganize the work force. The *Tribune* became, in effect, an afternoon newspaper. More than 60 young women operated the self-justifying typewriters. Expert photographers and specialized cameras were required. Engravers labored overtime. Production manager John Park was ill, so his assistant, Grumhaus, took charge of the paper's manufacturing operations in addition to his labor negotiation duties and his responsibilities for overseeing completion of the new building. Managing editor Maloney and news editor Stewart Owen established a new editorial schedule, which Owen, for some unfathomable reason, dubbed "Musk Ox." The schedule required early typewriter composition of news matter, which was then pasted on page forms, photographed, and engraved, a forerunner of printing procedures to be developed a generation later. Frederick Nichols, assistant to advertising manager Campbell, was responsible for advertising coordination with the revised publishing schedule.

Problems were solved in unusual ways, some simple, others highly complicated. Tom Furlong, financial editor, prepared excellent market reports merely by pasting a *Tribune* logo on mint copies of the afternoon *Cleveland News* market pages, from which the *Tribune* made its engraved stereo plates. James G. Paddock, working under Nichols, found technicians on his classified advertising staff who were able to develop a magnetic system for positioning classified ads in page forms in which they could be photographed, so that they could be moved about, removed from some editions, and moved into others. Soon the want ads looked the way they had in prestrike days. Paddock, later manager of the classified department, insisted that the cold-type, magnetic procedure was an improvement over the Linotype techniques, and many agreed with him. Visitors came to the *Tribune* from over the country—editors, managing editors, and publishers who desired to know more about the new system of printing, which steadily showed improvement in readability and gradually made some inroads in reducing the time lag.

* * *

In June, 1948, Colonel McCormick let his presidential views become known to the readers of the paper and the Republican party generally. Since MacArthur would not consider running, the Colonel had switched to Senator Taft. The *Tribune*'s staff at the Republican convention included Arthur Sears Henning, Arthur Evans, Walter Trohan (twice a winner of the Beck Award), Willard Edwards, William Moore, Rita Fitzpatrick, George Tagge, and Tom Morrow, all of them primed to look out for skullduggery on the part of the international bankers and Thomas "Me Too" Dewey. Governor Harold Stassen, the political boy wonder from Minnesota, dropped in to visit McCormick in his Astor Street apartment and went on to Philadelphia in some confusion as to his success in obtaining the Colonel's endorsement. He got it, all right, but not for the office he sought.

On June 22, the *Tribune*'s banner led off by referring to the keynote address by Illinois Gov. Dwight Green. "VICTORY AHEAD—GOV. GREEN. Taft Gains: Col. McCormick Backs Stassen for No. 2 Spot." Colonel McCormick was quoted as saying that Tom Dewey could not be elected. *Tribune* reporters in Philadelphia stated that the convention was "electrified" by McCormick's announcement. Senator Taft said he was glad for any delegate's support but declined to comment on McCormick's choice for vice-president, and Stassen flatly refused to run for the No. 2 spot. So McCormick's scheme for stopping Dewey crashed. Tom Dewey was nominated on the third ballot. Stassen then was prepared to try for No. 2, but no one was interested, and Gov. Earl Warren of California received the nomination. "The international bankers have taken the Republican party for the third successive time," raged the *Tribune*. "We can only hope that Mr. Dewey will not drag down to defeat the congressional, state and local candidates." Then came a bitter addendum: "After listening to the convention speeches we are dropping the word 'internationalist' and using 'America-lasters.'" In July the Democrats met, also at Philadelphia, nominating President Truman for president and Sen. Alben Barkley of Kentucky as his running mate. The pollsters unanimously predicted that the Dewey–Warren ticket would win in a landslide. The *Tribune*'s pre-election editorial on Monday, November 1, warned, "This is no time for over-confidence." On the 2nd its banner read: "GO TO THE POLLS TODAY." The editorial urged the election of Republicans, but Dewey and Warren were not mentioned by name.

That Tuesday, managing editor Maloney faced a new problem. Since the printers' strike required the paper to go to press hours earlier than usual, Maloney had to put together his first postelection issue when even the polls in the East, with a few exceptions in New Hampshire, had not reported results. Nonetheless, as in past years, Arthur Sears Henning made a projection of the winner in the national election, based on his sampling of voter sentiment on his national tour. He had been wrong once in 20 years—not a bad record—and in 1948 everyone agreed with him that Dewey would win. So the *Tribune* went to press with the headline: "DEWEY DEFEATS TRUMAN."

Later in the evening, returns began to indicate a close race. Maloney asked his veteran Washington chief whether he stuck by his projections, based on the returns from certain areas Henning considered indicative of the general ultimate trend, and was reassured. Dewey was still winning, Henning insisted. So, the *Tribune* banner continued to declare: "DEWEY DEFEATS TRUMAN." Still later that night, as West Coast results began to come in, Maloney ordered the lead story rewritten. Dewey still had a narrow lead, according to the *Tribune,* but emphasis was placed on the Illinois races, where Democrat Paul Douglas, a professor at the University of Chicago and a former Chicago alderman, was declared winner of the U.S. Senate seat, and Adlai Stevenson, another Democrat, had been elected governor. Yet the election banner was not changed as Maloney left the newsroom, turning his responsibilities over to his assistant, Don Maxwell. At 11 o'clock, Owen, assisting Maxwell, appeared in the composing room with the new story and the old headline. He was challenged by Grumhaus, who had been following radio returns. The headline had to be wrong, Grumhaus declared. Owen called Maxwell, who rechecked his dispatches and ordered the headline changed: "DEMOCRATS MAKE SWEEP OF STATE OFFICES," read the banner of the two-star edition.

The Dewey gaffe haunted the *Tribune,* especially after the jubilant, victorious President Truman got his hands on a copy. "This is one for the books," Truman exulted, waving the paper to the crowds. Nearly 150,000 copies of the *Tribune* had been published before the headlines were changed, and it indeed was one for the books. The *Tribune* on November 4 grudgingly admitted its error while also accusing the voters of abominably bad judgment, declaring that "for the third time the Republican party fell under vicious influence and nominated a 'me too' candidate." The paper blamed the pollsters for its own mistake. Polling the electorate was an "alleged science," the paper said, adding: "Having been bitten as badly as the next one, we hope to swear off the crystal ball in the future." The paper then congratulated Truman for having made "a valiant fight."

In 1972, as *Tribune* executives discussed 125th anniversary observances, it was decided to make amends to Truman, who, in retrospect, had risen considerably in the paper's estimation. A bronze plaque of the front page with the incorrect headline was prepared for presentation to the Truman Library at Independence, Missouri. Ex-President Truman was ill, but his family was reached and anticipated that he would be delighted to receive the plaque. However, his death occurred before the presentation could be made. On May 9, 1973, Harold Grumhaus, Tribune Company chairman, and Clayton Kirkpatrick, editor of the *Tribune,* presented the plaque to Dr. Benedict Zobrist, curator of the Truman Library. Rose Conway, Truman's secretary during and after his years in the presidency, was present. "I wish he could be here to see it," she said. "He dearly loved that issue of the *Tribune.*" The plaque hangs in a special hall exhibiting memorabilia of Truman's whistle-stop campaign tour of 1948. The inscription reads: "Presented with admiration and affection on our 125th anniversary year to Harry S. Truman, whose election victory in 1948 made this one of the most unforgettable front pages ever published by the *Chicago Tribune.*"

The printing strike continued for almost a year past the election of 1948, but there were no other disasters remotely approaching the Dewey–Truman mistake. In fact, the editorial, production, advertising, and circulation departments all were learning to accommodate to the new technology. Advertisers found they could meet earlier deadlines than they previously had supposed. New, better, and faster photo-typesetting machines were built, and offset printing procedures that could meet the speed and quality requirements of the largest of the metropolitan newspapers were created. Nevertheless, the *Tribune* welcomed the return of its printers, who voted to resume work on September 18, 1949, and within a few days most sections of the papers were "back to normal," using Linotypes and steel chases. But the day of hot-type supremacy was ending. Within two decades, electronic terminal editing, computer memory banks, phototype, and high-speed offset printing would change newspaper technology nearly as much as it had changed in the entire prior century.

*   *   *

The year 1948 brought more than political disappointment for Colonel McCormick; it was also a time of genuine personal sorrow. His cousin Eleanor "Cissy" Patterson, the former Countess Gizycka, after working for some years as editor of Hearst's *Herald* in Washington, D.C., had purchased the *Herald* in 1937. In 1939 she had purchased the *Washington Times* and combined the two papers as the *Times-Herald,* with the largest circulation in the capital. Cissy rarely agreed on newspaper policy with anyone, including Colonel McCormick, yet despite that there was a closeness between them. On July 24, 1948, Cissy died, leaving Robert McCormick as the sole surviving grandchild of Joseph Medill. In February, 1949, Colonel McCormick met with the administrators of her estate. She had given the *Times-Herald* to Frank Waldrop, editor of her editorial page, and six other executives of the paper.

That summer, while McCormick was in Canada with his directors for their annual Canadian meeting, he learned that Eugene L. Meyer,

Washington banker and financier, and his son-in-law Philip L. Graham, publisher of the *Washington Post,* were about to purchase the *Times-Herald.* As part of the proposed deal, they were also offering to buy 202$^1/_2$ units of nonvoting stock in the McCormick–Patterson Trust included in Eleanor Patterson's estate. Colonel McCormick convinced the directors that the trust units should be bought by Tribune Company and existing owners and offered to purchase 45 units himself. The Tribune directors agreed the company should buy 157$^1/_2$ units at $35,000 each, and proposals were made for the absorption of the remaining units. McCormick hastened back to Chicago and dispatched Howard Wood with Keith Masters and Willis D. Nance of the Kirkland law office to Washington to buy both the paper and the trust units. The seven executives of the *Times-Herald* agreed to take ten units each in lieu of full cash payments, and the purchase was made for $4,500,000.

Colonel McCormick, by his action in the Washington situation, had served notice that he did not intend to allow any threat of outside control to menace Tribune Company. Now, he also had a Washington beachhead from which to attack his political enemies. He authorized expenditures for new presses and equipment for the *Times-Herald* and also provided operating capital, which the seven heirs to the paper had lacked. He induced his favorite niece, Mrs. Ruth McCormick "Bazy" Miller, daughter of his brother, Medill, to go to Washington as editor, taking with her as an executive of the paper her husband Peter Miller, Jr. Bazy and Peter had been operating a successful daily newspaper, the *La Salle* (Illinois) *News-Tribune,* which they continued to own. But Mrs. Miller, 28, who swiftly became a social as well as a political leader in the capital and held conservative political views, nevertheless could not accommodate her ideas of Washington newspaper operations with those of her uncle. Nor did McCormick approve her divorce from Peter Miller and her friendship with Garvin E. Tankersley, one of the editorial executives of the *Times-Herald.*

On April 4, 1951, Bazy Miller resigned. "Our differences are intellectual," she told *Newsweek.* She complained that Colonel McCormick had not supported some of her political campaigns. "Perhaps," she said, "Colonel McCormick and I can't agree because of a 40-year age difference." McCormick meantime had induced Tankersley to join the *Chicago Tribune* Sunday staff, evidently with the intention of evaluating him as a potential teammate of Bazy in the management of the *Chicago Tribune,* after they had accumulated some years' experience on the *Times-Herald.* But Bazy's resignation ended any plan, if he had such. Bazy and "Tank" were married, Colonel McCormick forgave them, and Bazy continued as a director of Tribune Company until she was succeeded, at her request, by her husband.

McCormick decided, following Bazy's resignation, that he would have to take over the *Washington Times-Herald* himself. Thomas Furlong, successor to Howard Wood as the *Tribune*'s financial editor, was named managing editor of the paper, with Frank Waldrop as executive editor. E. R. Noderer became chief editorial writer. McCormick instructed Furlong to make the *Times-Herald* as much like the *Tribune* as possible in appearance, and Noderer was supposed to use *Tribune* editorials and columnists whenever possible. Both men, however, found that the *Chicago Tribune* formula simply would not work in the environment of Washington, and they began to modify the paper to meet the wants of a readership that was largely government-employed.

*   *   *

Despite the many demands on his time and energies, Colonel McCormick turned his attention increasingly back to the *Tribune,* to the needs of Chicago, Illinois, and the Midwest. He caused a highly successful railroad fair to be staged on Chicago's lakefront in 1950, with Maj. Lennox Lohr in charge, and endlessly came up with promotion ideas for both the *Tribune* and the city. He personally participated in decisions in all divisions of the paper and frequently spoke of the *Tribune* as a family, sometimes musing that anyone belonging to such a family had little need for other interests. His age and the state of his health no longer permitted him to play polo, but he planned trips to be made when his health bettered. He continued to love horses and dogs, and his English bulldog, Buster Boo, and his German shepherd, Lotta Pups, frequently accompanied him to the office. There Buster showed an especial fondness for Pat Maloney, dashing to his favorite spot under McCormick's marble-topped desk where he could lick the shine off Maloney's shoes as the managing editor conferred with the Colonel each afternoon. Maloney, always frugal but also scrupulously honest, could never bring himself to put his shine bill on his expense account, though he was convinced that he deserved to. McCormick took particular interest in World War II history and set out to memorialize heroes and events by publicizing them in the *Tribune.* He would succeed in campaigns to name Midway Airport for the Battle of Midway; O'Hare International Airport for Edward H. "Butch" O'Hare, navy flier; Waldron Drive for Commander Charles Waldron, leader of Torpedo Squadron 8 in the Battle of Midway; and, honoring a civilian, Meigs Field for Merrill C. Meigs, publisher of the Hearst papers in Chicago, an aviation enthusiast, and a friend of McCormick.

First, however, it was necessary to build Meigs Field. When Commander Wayne Thomis, naval aviator, returned to his job as *Tribune* aviation editor, Colonel McCormick told him, "I want you to fly me." Thomis did, in addition to his work as a writer. On Saturdays Thomis flew about the Midwest picking up sports film from *Tribune* photographers. He would come in low over Northerly Island in Lake Michigan just south of the Loop and drop his film, and a *Tribune* driver would rush it to the paper for processing and publication. Northerly Island, Thomis and McCormick decided, would make an excellent downtown airport for Chicago. Thomis began writing articles urging such a project. Ralph Burke, chief engineer for the Chicago Park District, controlling the island, resisted for a while, but by 1949 a runway 3,000 feet long was paved. There were no lights on the field, only a wind sock. At Cantigny, where McCormick had his own airstrip, built by Bluebird Air Service when he was taking flying lessons, a tall tree was the landmark. McCormick acquired a Cessna 185, which Thomis piloted, and as his flying needs increased, he bought an Aero Commander, the first of three. Often the Colonel needed to fly into or from Northerly Island after darkness, a feat that tested Thomis's skill as a pilot, though for the love of it, Thomis would fly anywhere, any time. If McCormick was aware of the danger of flying through crosswinds into the island strip in darkness, he gave no sign. His comportment was the same on nighttime flights to Cantigny. "We'd take off in darkness and land at the farm with only the house lights to guide us," said Thomis. "The Colonel never said a goddamned word."

Since 1947, McCormick had yearned for a converted B-17 in which he could tour the world. Thomis went to a government airfield in Oklahoma where some 3,000 surplus planes were stored. He found there were two dozen or so B-17s that never had been flown except in tests, and he bought one with 12 hours' time for $7,500. In addition, Thomis acquired 15 new engines and a supply of propellers. "Then I flew it out to Air Research, Inc., in California to have the interior rebuilt for private flying," Thomis said. The *Tribune*'s air fleet was complete, and in the next five years Colonel McCormick would use it to visit 80 countries, in addition to innumerable business trips to New York and Canada.

McCormick never worked harder than when he was in his 70s. As president and chief executive officer of Tribune Company, and chairman of News Syndicate Company, he had basic responsibility for the *Tribune* and the Canadian properties, and his advice was sought relative to the *New York News*. For a time he would continue to have personal charge of the *Washington Times-Herald*. He was president and treasurer of WGN, Inc., which grew from a low-powered, part-time radio station to a clear channel, 50,000-watt station that was developing its own subsidiary operations and included WGN-TV, which had begun operations in 1948. McCormick helped to form the Mutual Broadcasting System. He was a director of the Associated Press and chairman of the Freedom of the Press Committee of the American Newspaper Publishers Association, and he continued to deliver radio addresses, some of which he dictated, and to write books and articles.

The extent of Tribune Company operations required additional executives, new methods, and a team effort by the business department, which left McCormick more freedom for his editorial and political activities and for travel. The management team McCormick was building to take over Tribune Company was led by Chesser Campbell, who became a vice-president in 1951, and included Howard Wood, controller; Harold Grumhaus, assistant production manager; Walter C. Kurz, manager of the sales development division; Frederick Nichols, assistant to Campbell; and Don Maxwell, who was soon to become managing editor. While the team members were not all in charge of major company divisions by 1950, they would comprise the management group succeeding Colonel McCormick and would take Tribune Company into the No. 1 position among Western Hemisphere newspaper organizations following his death in 1955. In the 1940s they were backing up business manager Elbert M. Antrim, production manager John Park, and Chester "Red" McKittrick, who succeeded Campbell as advertising director in 1951.

Campbell was a lithe, quiet-spoken man whose gray-blue eyes were always politely questioning, a Phi Beta Kappa from the University of Michigan, where he had edited the school paper. He was determined to modernize the business side of the *Tribune,* physically and philosophically. Campbell's crisp, analytical style impressed McCormick while the young executive was in charge of the New York advertising office, and under his direction the *Tribune*'s advertising department more than doubled its linage from 1935 to 1939, from 17,854,712 to 41,573,250 lines. Campbell knew how to sell. He had sold subscriptions to the *Tribune*'s Paris edition and classified advertising in Chicago, the latter a mandatory experience for anyone in the *Tribune*'s advertising department. But Campbell's forte was organization, motivation, and the command of research and statistics. He was the one executive in the organization who knew more than McCormick did about his specialty, and, like Wood, he did not fear to say no to McCormick, though he also was often overruled.

Under Campbell, the *Tribune*'s nationwide reputation as a leader in marketing research methods continued. His director of sales development was tall, blond, charismatic Walter Kurz, a University of Illinois graduate who got his beginning journalistic experience publicizing World's Fair villages and entertainment in 1933. Pierre Martineau, specialist in motivational research from the University of Wisconsin and University of Chicago, directed the *Tribune*'s studies in the advertising and circulation research areas, wrote books and articles on the subject, and soon was internationally known for his work. Campbell believed in flawless organization and the use of modern research tools in contrast to the evangelical methods of his advertising predecessors. Consequently, by 1950 the *Tribune* had developed one of the most effective sales organizations in the newspaper business.

Ambitious young *Tribune* executives in training frequently waited years for an opportunity to move ahead, but there was considerable upward motion in the 1950s. Howard Wood, who had assumed increasing responsibilities after Campbell suffered a mild heart attack in 1949, became business manager when Elbert Antrim retired in 1954. Wood also was elected a company director and was given much of the liaison responsibility for the Canadian operations, based on his wartime experience as McCormick's alternate. Arthur Schmon continued in charge of the Canadian companies and his own staff of executives and was also a director of Tribune Company. In 1955 Wood became general manager of the *Chicago Tribune,* president of WGN, Inc., and a director of several subsidiary boards. Chester McKittrick succeeded Wood as business manager, and Kurz took over the top advertising position vacated by McKittrick.

When John Park retired as production manager in 1955, he was succeeded by Harold Grumhaus, expert in labor relations and the man who had helped McCormick put up the new WGN annex to Tribune Tower. Grumhaus's assistant was veteran Lorne M. "Dick" Gossett, an engineering graduate of the University of Illinois. Also a member of the production department was a young man being groomed by Grumhaus for assistant production manager, Stanton R. Cook, an airman in World War II who had received his degree in mechanical engineering from Northwestern University in 1949. Like Grumhaus, Cook was a production man destined to go far in Tribune Company.

As McCormick increasingly absented himself from Chicago, for extended journeys or to rest in Florida, his new management team of Campbell, Wood, and Grumhaus took charge, with Don Maxwell as managing editor following the retirement of Pat Maloney for health reasons in 1950. Maxwell, a shrewd, earthy editorial executive proud of his Hoosier background, liked to say that he went into the newspaper business because he so much admired the big automobiles his mother's cousin, Teddy Beck, the *Tribune*'s former managing editor, drove to the Maxwell home when the Becks were invited down for an Indiana fried-chicken dinner. Maxwell, educated at Depauw University, was on the staff of the college newspaper and had editorial experience in Cleveland before he became a *Chicago Tribune* reporter. When he had been at the *Tribune* a few months, the Tribune–News syndicate sold its editorial services to the *Vancouver* (Canada) *Sun* and the *Sun* requested a *Tribune* editor to go with the deal. Maxwell was offered the opportunity, and he took his young wife, Marjorie, with him to Vancouver for several months. He returned to the *Tribune* as sports editor, and succeeded Maloney after serving as news editor, city editor, and assistant managing editor. Maxwell, under McCormick, was in effect executive editor of the paper much of the time since the publisher's health was deteriorating, and, when he felt well enough, he traveled.

Colonel McCormick had his team of successors chosen, but they were rarely free to direct the editorial policy of the paper. Instead they suffered from the increasingly dictatorial attitudes of McCormick. The advertising and circulation departments found the going rough as McCormick embraced the political right. Businessmen who objected to the *Tribune*'s editorial stand on any issue felt that they should be heard and their views reported back by the *Tribune* advertising representatives, an action rarely tolerated by Colonel McCormick. William Harrison Fetridge, who was trained in the *Tribune*'s advertising department and left to go into business for himself, recalls in his memoirs that McCormick and the *Tribune* were respected if not loved among the space-buyers. "The *Tribune* was a great institution to work for. . . . Its editor and publisher, the renowned, crusty Colonel Robert R. McCormick. It was *his* paper. It reflected *his* views. People did things *his* way. He was of course painted by his adversaries as a sort of Neanderthal man. Perhaps he was, but I never felt so."

Campbell, like all *Tribune* executives, loyally carried out McCormick's ideas when he could not change them. Frequently he sold his own plans to the publisher, and often they acted in concert for differing reasons. McCormick, for example, wanted the *Tribune*'s body type increased in size because, he said, "Chicagoans are growing older." Campbell wanted to increase readership of the *Tribune* among the younger people, and his studies showed that they also would welcome the larger type.

In the end, the Colonel determined all policy, though sometimes major nonpolitical events were launched without his prior approval. Maxwell started the *Tribune*'s Chicagoland Music Festival, and it grew so large that McCormick became interested and attended. Thereafter, the music festival got all the news space anyone could have desired, and Maxwell's brother Philip, who directed the festival, was at last content. Similarly, McCormick became interested in Arch Ward's College All-Star Football Game, brought his friends, and authorized advertising department representatives to bring theirs. Ward got a $10,000 a year raise from McCormick, and in summer much potential news space was devoted to the two major promotions, each of which filled Chicago's Soldier Field, the music festival attracting 90,000 in addition to thousands of participants.

Whatever McCormick desired in those last years of his autocratic reign, he got. And frequently he got too much, especially in editorial areas, where a simple question from the Colonel might result in columns of affirmations of his presumed views. On some occasions, a dissenting report got back to McCormick through the editorial bureaucracy and the subject was dropped, or, rarely, McCormick altered his position. But too often, said one high executive of the paper, "Colonel McCormick asks for a drink of water and someone turns on the hose."

*   *   *

Since the days of the New Deal, the *Chicago Tribune* had repeatedly warned that Communism was gradually penetrating American life at all levels, including the federal government. The *Tribune* was by no means alone in holding this view. In 1938, for example, Rep. Martin Dies, a Texas Democrat, had been authorized to form a special congressional investigative committee whose purpose was to uncover left-wingers and radicals in the federal bureaucracy. In 1945 the committee was given permanent status, and as the House Committee on Un-American Activities it used its broad powers of subpoena to conduct far-reaching investigations.

As America entered the postwar period, the fear of Communism and of Soviet espionage became widespread, even among some presidential advisers. In February, 1946, the Canadian government exposed and expelled a Soviet spy ring said to have been operating within the United States as well. Representative Joseph Sabath, an Illinois Democrat, was so concerned about alleged infiltration of the State Department that in July, 1946, he demanded and got from Secretary of State James Byrnes assurances that the entire department would be investigated. President Truman noted in his diary in September, 1946, that *"the Reds, phonies and 'parlor pinks' seem to be banded together and are becoming a national danger. I am afraid they are a sabotage front for Uncle Joe Stalin."*

Truman knew that the Soviets were plotting a vast expansion of power in war-ravaged Europe, and in Greece and Turkey the situation had become particularly critical. A massive infusion of U.S. aid was indicated, but the president doubted whether he could persuade the Congress and the public that America should shun its former isolationism—that only America's economic resources could prevent the collapse of Europe, and that this was in fact vital to the national interest. Some of the president's advisers, especially Attorney General Tom Clark and Navy Secretary James Forrestal, soon to become secretary of defense, tried to persuade him that the threat of Communism, foreign and domestic, could be used as a prod to obtain defense and foreign aid funds, but President Truman hesitated. Convincing evidence that the Red menace was a viable political issue was not long in appearing. In 1946, Republicans, many of them sounding the anti-Communist alarm, gained 56 seats in the House and 13 in the Senate, taking control of both houses.

Throughout this period, the *Tribune* had supported Sabath and other congressmen who were out to rid the government of alleged Communists and fellow travelers. The election results of 1946 gave additional encouragement to such men as Rep. John Taber, who attacked the problem of Communists in government whenever budgets were discussed before his House Appropriations Committee; Sen. Styles Bridges, who insisted that a "master spy" in the State Department was plotting the downfall of the Nationalist government in China; and Rep. Walter Judd, a former missionary to China who had a similar conviction that leftists were betraying China to the Reds. Congressmen Karl Mundt, Everett Dirksen, John Rankin, and Joseph Martin also won *Tribune* praise, Martin in particular for the excellence of his maiden address as Speaker of the House, when he said, "There is no room in the government of the United States for any who prefer the Communist system. . . . *[Such]* should be, they must be, removed."

By March, 1947, President Truman was ready to use the menace of Communism as a means of mobilizing support for his foreign policy. Speaking before a joint session of Congress on March 12, he enunciated the Truman Doctrine, aimed specifically at obtaining congressional approval of his program of aid to Greece and Turkey, but which implied that U.S. financial aid should be applied anywhere about the globe it was needed to prevent the expansion of totalitarian Communism. On March 21, the president supplemented this action by issuing Executive Order 9835, which required that every federal employee be screened as a potential security risk. Attorney General Clark promptly published a list of subversive organizations, which, writes historian Richard M. Freeland in *The Truman Doctrine and the Origins of McCarthyism*, "was only the most dramatic and innovative effort by the Justice Department to support the campaign for Cold War foreign policy during the summer and fall of 1947. Clark also mobilized the FBI and the Bureau of Immigration and Naturalization for a full-scale program to deport aliens involved in communist activities." The administration continued to raise the specter of a Communist-dominated Europe, and in April, 1948, Congress approved funding for the European Recovery Program, more commonly called the Marshall Plan since it had grown from a proposal advanced by Secretary of State George Marshall. Over a four-year period some $12 billion would be appropriated to aid the reconstruction of Europe.

In the fall of 1948, voters not only gave Truman his stunning victory over Thomas Dewey; they also returned the Congress to the control of the Democrats. But almost immediately, disaster struck, and anti-Red tensions in the United States mounted. Chiang Kai-shek and his Chinese Nationalists were driven from mainland Asia by Mao Tse-tung's Communists in January, 1949, increasing the speculation that fellow travelers in the State Department had engineered America's "loss" of China. In September, it was learned that the Russians had exploded an atom bomb, thus ending America's monopoly. The celebrated Alger Hiss "spy trial," which had been national news for more than a year, ended on January 21, 1950, when Hiss was convicted of perjury for having denied passing State Department secrets to a Communist courier. Two weeks later came worse news. Dr. Klaus Fuchs, an eminent British scientist who had worked on the development of the atom bomb in the United States during the war, had been arrested and confessed to cooperating with a spy ring to betray atomic secrets to the Soviet Union.

Into this dismal scene strode a burly young senator from Wisconsin, one of the 13 new Republicans elected in 1946, a somewhat blustering, bellicose man who appeared contemptuous of both Senate rules and his fellow senators in debate but had kept rather much to himself and a few close friends outside the sedate club. Joseph R. McCarthy had interrupted his term as a small-town judge to serve as a marine intelligence officer in the Pacific in World War II, where he fabricated for himself the reputation of having been a heroic bomber crewman. "Tail Gunner Joe" had returned to Wisconsin a candidate for the U.S. Senate and won an upset primary victory over Progressive Robert M. La Follette, Jr. McCarthy told the voters they could use a tail gunner in Washington, and he promised to shoot down, among others, the Communists who were working against American interests in government jobs.

Senator McCarthy did nothing about Communism during his first years in the Senate, but by 1950 he was casting about for a campaign issue that would help him to overcome the lackluster record he had thus far compiled. He discussed possibilities with friends in Washington. Of the subjects suggested, the one that seemed to have the best potential was Communists in the government. Early in 1950, McCarthy saw in the *Chicago Tribune* exactly the kind of material he needed, a series of articles on Communist infiltration by Willard Edwards of the *Tribune*'s Washington bureau. Edwards was regarded in the capital as an expert on the subject. He had reported on the fight against Reds for a decade, and he had covered the Alger Hiss trial. McCarthy's press secretary asked to borrow some clippings of Edwards's work, including the series then appearing, and he was obliged. One of the stories outlined the 1946 request of Congressman Sabath to then Secretary of State Byrnes for details of the problem in the State Department. At the time, Byrnes had said that of 3,000 persons transferred to the State Department following service in wartime agencies, preliminary security screening had indicated

284 were possibly unfit, and of these 79 had been refused employment. Edwards's latest articles concerned cases of persons actually employed by the government, some 57 alleged to have been card-carrying Communists.

On the night of February 9, 1950, in Wheeling, West Virginia, Senator McCarthy spoke to a dinner meeting of the Ohio County Women's Republican Club and, waving a sheaf of papers at his listeners, he intoned, "While I cannot take the time to name all the men in the State Department who have been named as members of the Communist party and members of a spy ring, I have here in my hand a list of 205 that were known to the secretary of state as being members of the Communist party and who nevertheless are still working and shaping policy in the State Department."

Frank Desmond of the *Wheeling Intelligencer* covered the event, but not until two days later did the press services pick up the senator's charges and send them around the country. A *Tribune* correspondent interviewed McCarthy in Reno, at which time he reduced the number of Communists to 57 and said he would give the names to the secretary of state if the secretary would only telephone him. Two weeks later McCarthy repeated his charges on the floor of the Senate, this time stating that he had 81 verified cases. He denied ever claiming he had 205 names, a figure he later admitted he had obtained by subtracting the 79 people the Byrnes memorandum had said were discharged from the 284 who had been thought suspect. What Byrnes had not said was that even at the time he wrote the memo, only about 60 of the remaining 205, all thoroughly investigated, were still employed by the State Department.

Democrat Millard E. Tydings of Maryland was named chairman of a special Senate committee to investigate McCarthy's allegations, and the senator from Wisconsin had become national news when public hearings began on March 8. He fascinated and frightened his peers and his new national constituency as he strode and rumbled through the hearings, browbeating the committee chairman and several of its members, belaboring witnesses and bureaucrats and consultants called before it. The senator read into the record scores of examples of Communist conspiracy and spying within the government, but for all his bluster he was unable to offer convincing evidence against any individual. Yet in June, when Sen. Margaret Chase Smith, Republican of Maine, sought to obtain a Senate denunciation of McCarthy's methods, she obtained the support of only a handful of her colleagues. The Tydings Committee released its official findings in July. McCarthy's charges, said the majority report, were "a fraud and a hoax." The minority report called the committee's investigation "superficial and inconclusive."

Joseph McCarthy refused to be deterred. He was recklessly, ruthlessly, and effectively using the Red Scare technique the Democratic administration itself had once found useful to cow his enemies in the Congress and to panic anyone, inside government or out, who had ever known a possibly subversive friend or entertained a thought that could be interpreted as hostile to the government. The senator also had given the American people a simple answer to the complex questions about recent foreign policy disasters—the country had been betrayed. The Red Scare, encouraged to gain support for the Truman Doctrine and the Marshall Plan, had created a Republican monster.

* * *

On the clear, bright Sunday morning of June 25, 1950, Walter Simmons, chief of the *Tribune*'s North Pacific bureau, awakened in his room in the Chosun Hotel in Seoul, South Korea, to the "whap, whap, whap" of exploding bombs. He reached his window in time to see high, vanishing Russian-built Yak bombers. Simmons, who had come to Seoul to cover the opening of the assembly under President Syngman Rhee, got into his business suit and civilian shoes and hurried to the American Military Advisers headquarters. There he verified what he already knew—tensions between North and South Korea had at last erupted into war. Simmons sent a brief cable to the *Tribune*, then caught a jeep ride to the front with Capt. Robert Ford. Within minutes they were at the ROK (South Korean) Seventh Division headquarters at Uijongbu, 12 miles north of Seoul. Captain Ford swiftly appraised the situation, then whispered, "Let's get out of here." Minutes more, their jeep wrecked, Simmons and Ford tried to decide which way to run across the desolate landscape, but the approaching Korean troops turned out to be friendly. Back in Seoul, Simmons sent his second dispatch, a side story since he assumed the wire services would report the main news that North Korea had launched a war:

> Uijongbu, Korea, June 26—This is how the Korean civil war looks in the muddy rice fields and slippery mountains where it is being fought:
>
> Two divisions of khaki-clad infantry are pushing north this morning to regain the ground they lost yesterday. Every kind of transport is being used, from modern American trucks to ancient Japanese buses and taxicabs. The road from Seoul is choked with a motley array of vehicles, some broken down. A train-load of troops just pulled in.
>
> Two Russian-built North Korean tanks clanked 25 miles yesterday and almost overran this grim village on the main invasion route. Twenty more Red tanks are approaching today but the enemy has not moved up his infantry.

> More than 60,000 refugees spent last night plodding through the rain toward Seoul . . . their faces are blank with suffering and hunger. Nearly every woman carries a child on her back. . . . A handful of American military advisers is unshaven and exhausted after a sleepless night.

By Tuesday both Simmons and the *Tribune* had learned that he was the only American correspondent on the entire front, and his dispatch of that day appeared as a copyrighted exclusive. Via the Chicago Tribune Press Service, it and his future reports were republished in newspapers throughout the world.

> Seoul, Korea, June 27 (Tuesday)—After two days of furious fighting north of this South Korean capital, military observers today began to doubt whether the republic can hold its own against the vastly superior fire power of the Russian equipped North Koreans.
>
> Monday's developments in the vital invasion corridor north of Seoul all were bad. Near nightfall, a group of American military advisers accompanied by this correspondent were trapped under heavy artillery fire at Uijongbu. We barely escaped in jeeps with a Russian tank in pursuit. Eventually, our group reached Seoul by a narrow, circuitous route after running the gauntlet of small arms and mortar fire.
>
> A tank rumbled unopposed through the headquarters area of the South Korean 7th division—the republic's finest—after the troops had fled. It then crossed to the clubhouse of the American advisers and fired four shells which narrowly missed them as they fled.
>
> In a day's tour of the battlefront as far north as Tongduchin, 25 miles north of Seoul, near the 38th parallel, 1,000 South Korean troops were seen retreating in wild disorder under light artillery fire. South of Uijongbu, an entire regiment was in flight.

Over the next three weeks, as a few American forces landed to temporarily drive the North Koreans from Seoul, General MacArthur arrived to evaluate the situation, and American B-29s began bombing the North Koreans, Simmons cruised the fluid front lines and set up a system for dictating his reports by telephone to his wife, Edith Weigle, in Tokyo. She then typed the stories and cabled them to the paper. Except for the wire services, Simmons had the war to himself. With Seoul under heavy attack, there was no way correspondents in other areas could get to the action. The *Tribune* exulted that this singular good fortune was no accident. Said the paper in a page-one box: "As Tokyo correspondent, Simmons is familiar with the territory. . . . To keep up with events in this hot spot, he has made 16 visits to South Korea. . . . To get the news first every day, read THE CHICAGO TRIBUNE."

The outbreak of hostilities had found a few hundred American military advisers already in South Korea. The *Tribune* by no means supported their presence. In the early hours of the war, it expressed fear that President Truman would attempt to increase the American involvement. Said the paper on June 26:

> The invasion of Korea should warn Congress against giving Mr. Truman the authority he is asking to call conscripts to camp whenever he feels like doing so. The power never should be yielded by Congress to any executive because it is all but equivalent to the power to declare war itself. . . . The majority of Americans have the friendliest feelings toward the Korean Republic, but not one American in a thousand believes the defense of Korea is worth the life of a husband, son, or brother. The members of Congress know this and will bear it in mind.

The United Nations Security Council on June 25 had demanded an immediate cease-fire, but North Korean troops continued their advance. On June 27 the Council called upon members of the U.N. to give military aid to South Korea. President Truman responded promptly, authorizing General MacArthur to use the U.S. Army and Air Force to give Korean troops cover and support. The *Tribune* replied angrily: "Mr. Truman's statement is an illegal declaration of war. . . . Nothing the council of the United Nations has done or may do by the way of pronouncing the invasion of South Korea by the Russian puppets an act of aggression can warrant either the United Nations or the President in throwing the armed forces into the struggle. Only Congress can do that . . . and Congress has not been consulted."

Not even the appointment of MacArthur as commander-in-chief of the U.N. forces on July 7 altered the paper's view. As it expected, President Truman on July 19 asked Congress for a $10 billion war fund and economic controls. Finally, however, the *Tribune* reluctantly admitted, "We are inclined to think that Mr. Truman's undeclared war is popular and that, as matters stand, he has strengthened himself politically. . . . He is promising a cheap war—via air—action similar to that which persuaded Stalin to back away from Iran, Turkey and Greece and which broke the blockade of Berlin. Maybe this experience will be repeated in Korea. All of us hope so." But the paper did not really think so, and in subsequent editorials it pointed out that attempts to push back and contain the Russians, the obvious instigators of the Korean War, would go on until "we run into real trouble." Among the potentials for real trouble, the *Tribune* named French Indochina, where the United States was supplying the French with munitions for their fight with Ho Chi Minh.

*   *   *

When Walter Simmons returned to Tokyo after three weeks on the front in the same civilian suit and shoes, he was 20 pounds lighter after bathing, and his family decreed that his flea-infested clothing must be burned.

Soon Simmons returned to the war. He covered the first American troops to halt the Communist advance, MacArthur's brilliant Inchon landing in September, and accompanied their drive to the Yalu River, followed by disastrous retreat.

MacArthur had become convinced that he could end the war by pushing the North Koreans to the Yalu River, marking the boundary of Manchuria. Only two small units actually reached the Yalu, but it was the signal for 300,000 well-hidden and excellently trained Chinese troops to fall upon the U.N. forces, mostly Americans. The U.S. Marines retreated for the first time in their history. Even the tough Turks, who were among the few U.N. troops aiding the Americans, broke and fled. On December 2, 1950, General MacArthur announced that "a state of war now exists between the Chinese Communists and the United Nations forces."

It was an appalling development. In the north, men fought in temperatures that fell to 32 below, freezing the sweat in their boots, and warmed up to near zero when the sun was out. Half of the many casualties were from frostbite. By Christmas, 105,000 retreating Americans had been evacuated from Hungnam. The Korean retreat was one of the worst ordeals in American military history, and Simmons wrote the long, agonizing story. President Truman threatened to use the atom bomb but then, under international pressure, relented. It was neither a "police action" nor a cheap air war, as had been forecast. American airplanes could not find hidden North Koreans and Chinese to attack in the rugged terrain, and until later in the war they were prohibited by President Truman's order from bombing Chinese bases and supply lines in Manchuria.

The *Tribune*, infuriated by this "no win" policy as much as it had been angered by the U.S. involvement initially, called for the president's resignation:

Truman Should Get Out

General MacArthur says we are in an undeclared war with China. Mr. Truman brought this about in the name of 151 million Americans when he bought himself a war in Korea by executive fiat in disregard of the constitution.

Truman should resign. Under the law of presidential succession, we would be stuck with old Alben Barkley, but though he is not a genius, the country could stomach him more easily than the dishonest nincompoop in the White House who long ago lost his rudder.

On March 24 MacArthur issued a statement declaring that the Red China military forces were near collapse and offering to arrange a field truce with the commander-in-chief of the enemy forces. Since neither Truman nor anyone else in Washington or the U.N. had been consulted, the president was furious. On April 11, 1951, President Truman relieved the general of his command, replacing him with Lt. Gen. Matthew Ridgway, commander of the Eighth Army in Korea. Truman wrote later that his reason was "insubordination." That morning the *Tribune* carried a 120-point banner: "FIRES GEN. M'ARTHUR!" On the 12th the headline read: "TRUMAN TELLS HIS STAND." Walter Trohan reported the president's speech the prior day defending his action, and the text was carried inside. There was also a page-one editorial:

Impeach Truman

President Truman must be impeached and convicted. His hasty and vindictive removal of Gen. MacArthur is the culmination of a series of acts which have shown that he is unfit, morally and mentally, for high office. Mr. Truman can be impeached for usurping the power of Congress when he ordered American troops to Korea without a declaration of war. He can be impeached also, for surrounding himself with grafters and incompetents. Of the grafters alone, there is a list as long as your arm. . . . Every day that Mr. Truman remains in office menaces the safety of the United States and the lives of millions of its sons. The Democrats must put country above party.

"The American nation has never been in greater danger," the editorial concluded. "It is led by a fool surrounded by knaves." General of the Army MacArthur returned to the United States, had triumphal welcomes in several cities, including Chicago, and addressed a joint session of Congress on April 19. Yet, in spite of the adulation he received, MacArthur did not enter political life as McCormick had hoped.

By November, 1951, the fighting had theoretically stopped. According to a cease-fire, which the North Koreans broke repeatedly, hostilities were to end while an armistice could be negotiated. As it turned out, the so-called cease-fire lasted longer than the war, for armistice terms were not agreed upon until 19 months later.

During the war and negotiations, the *Tribune*'s Simmons was relieved from time to time by veteran correspondents Quentin Pope, Hal Foust, Wayne Thomis, and Percy Wood. But, as Wood wrote later, "The Korean war was Simmons's baby. The last day of the fighting, July 27, 1953, found the *Tribune* man on hand, as usual, with a great experience behind him, if much grayer and thinner than he had been three years before. He knows more about the Korean fight than most—if not all—the generals who participated."

*   *   *

Colonel McCormick had resumed his travels. His retinue now included photographer Al Madsen, who would soon become director of the *Tribune*'s photography department. The Colonel and Mrs. McCormick visited points in South America, Liberia, the Belgian Congo, Uganda, the

Sudan, Libya, Malta, and Morocco. Then they proceeded to Paris, where McCormick wished to interview Gen. Dwight Eisenhower, commander of North Atlantic Treaty forces. McCormick was pushing Senator Taft for the Republican presidential nomination, but he also knew that General Eisenhower, who had given up his post as president of Columbia University to take command in Europe, was to be put forward by "Wall Street." The meeting was congenial. As Eisenhower returned from showing the McCormicks out, he found his staff "rocking with merriment." He was told that Mrs. McCormick, departing, archly flipped the lapel of her suit coat to display a large button reading "I Like Ike." Back at their hotel, however, Colonel McCormick told his wife that he had no intention of supporting a man who was backed by Tom Dewey.

The Republicans gathered in Chicago early in July, 1952. General Eisenhower had taken leave of his European command, and the *Tribune* strongly backed Senator Taft. Colonel McCormick was in ill health, but he was ready for the fight. As Dewey, leading the Eisenhower forces, maneuvered to keep the pro-Taft Georgia delegation from being seated, the *Tribune* again used page-one editorials to work its will upon the convention, despite notable lack of success in prior attempts. It said on July 11: "The millions who have made the acquaintance of Gov. Dewey by television in recent days have learned to despise him as a suave and ruthless trickster. He is determined to prevent Mr. Taft, a great mind and a great spirit, from succeeding where Dewey himself failed for lack of mental and moral structure."

The paper suggested that if the 300,000 young men who died in World War II, and the 20,000 dead in the Korean conflict, were alive, they and their parents would make their voices heard against the attempt of Dewey and Wall Street to foist General Eisenhower upon the party. "There is no mystery about why the young people and their parents are for Taft. He is the only candidate who is for them."

Colonel McCormick had little contact with young people, and, it appeared, not much more with the movers and shakers of the Republican party. His editorials jolted the leaders, as did the oratory of *Tribune*-backed U.S. Sen. Everett McKinley Dirksen, but McCormick could only watch the results by television before the morning editions of his paper were delivered. He was hooked up to surgical plumbing in his Astor Street apartment and feeling quite unwell. When General Eisenhower won on the first ballot, after Minnesota switched its 19 votes from Governor Stassen, the Colonel accepted the decision with his thin, drawn smile. "Anyway, I stirred up the animals," he said, recalling a phrase favored by Captain Patterson. Said the *Tribune* editorial: "General Eisenhower is the nominee of the Republican party. Because the people are very generally disgusted with the Truman administration and because it will be difficult for the Democrats to find a candidate who will command support of both the northern and southern factions of their party, the chances of a Republican victory in November can be regarded as fairly bright."

The nomination of Sen. Richard M. Nixon of California for vice-president should have mollified Colonel McCormick somewhat. Willard Edwards had written often of Nixon's leading role in the Alger Hiss case, when, as a young congressman and a member of the House Committee on Un-American Activities, Nixon had made his own reputation as an anti-Communist. "He is the one man on the committee who asks shrewd questions," wrote Whittaker Chambers, accuser of Hiss. Nixon was known to seek Edwards's guidance frequently. But McCormick was nevertheless unreconciled. On August 23, 1952, still ailing and angry, he used his weekly radio broadcast over WGN and the Mutual Broadcasting System to issue a call for a new party, an "American" party, saying in part:

> I swallowed Willkie in '40, Dewey twice in '44 and '48, candidates foisted upon the party by sharp practice, but . . . I will be imposed upon no longer. . . . I can see no benefit in changing "Me Too" Dewey for "I Too" Ike. . . . Do not vote for either of these candidates. Concentrate on voting for patriotic candidates for Congress in both parties. It is time, therefore, that we organized ourselves into another party from which Truman Republicans and Truman Democrats will be excluded. It has been hard for me to reach this opinion because my grandfather founded the Republican party.

The Colonel then endorsed a number of candidates for Congress: "If I were a resident of Virginia, I would vote for Senator Harry Byrd. Every patriot in Wisconsin will vote for Senator Joseph McCarthy. . . ." He continued through the names of 12 other senators he approved and then provided a list of possible representatives.

Colonel McCormick's Saturday night radio speech appeared in the Sunday *Tribune* as was customary. But there was no *Tribune* editorial supporting his new party concept. The paper published eight news stories of comment on McCormick's plan, including disparaging remarks from some of the candidates he had opposed. "Colonel McCormick is whistling in the graveyard," commented one of them, Sen. Ralph Flanders of Vermont. "He refuses to recognize that he is very much in the minority in the Republican party." Some of the candidates approved by McCormick declined any comment.

Despite the dismal response to his call for a new party (it would not be a third party, he insisted), McCormick could find satisfaction in the outcome of the congressional elections if not the presidential campaign. No enemy was purged, but most of the men he had approved by name were reelected, including Senator McCarthy. The Republicans regained control of both houses by a small margin while Eisenhower and Nixon captured 442 of the electoral votes as compared with 89 for the Democratic nominees, Gov. Adlai Stevenson of Illinois and Sen. John Sparkman of Alabama.

Many of the accomplishments of the Eisenhower presidency McCormick found to his liking. Even before inauguration, Eisenhower journeyed to Korea in an effort to end the war, thus fulfilling a campaign promise. The new president cut Truman's budget, removed the American Seventh Fleet from Formosan waters, as the *Tribune* had demanded, and ended wage controls. An arms reduction policy was announced by the president, and his cabinet endorsed plans for a new St. Lawrence seaway and power project that would make Chicago the world's greatest inland port.

*   *   *

In the autumn of 1953, Sen. Joseph McCarthy was near the peak of his power. He had crushed his leading enemies in 1950, helping to drive Millard Tydings from the Senate and aiding Everett Dirksen to defeat Sen. Scott Lucas, the Illinois Democrat who had been the first to dare to challenge McCarthy publicly. McCarthy had gone to the aid of many of his colleagues in the 1952 election, but even some who owed him gratitude for campaign assistance were growing weary of his contemptuous attitudes and bumptious behavior.

The Wisconsin senator now took on the U.S. Army in his anti-Communist crusade, charging that there were subversives in a sensitive U.S. Army Signal Corps center at Fort Monmouth, New Jersey. Hearings by his Subcommittee on Investigations produced inconclusive results. In 1954 the army came back with a counterattack, asserting that McCarthy had sought to influence a promotion for one of his followers, Pvt. G. David Schine. McCarthy accused the military of attempting to "blackmail" him into abandoning a probe into Communist infiltration of the army. New Senate hearings were ordered, to be conducted by a special subcommittee chaired by Karl Mundt, himself noted for his anti-Communist campaigns.

The Army–McCarthy hearings occupied the front pages of all the nation's newspapers for months and kept the public hypnotized before television sets as the proceedings were broadcast nationally from April 22 to June 17. Though the Republican majority report issued in August absolved McCarthy personally, it criticized his chief counsel, Roy M. Cohn, for "unduly aggressive" efforts on Schine's behalf. McCarthy's countercharge of blackmail was dismissed by the Republicans as it was by the Democrats, who felt that the senator, like Cohn, merited "severe criticism."

Meantime, it was becoming clear that McCarthy was losing his ability to terrorize his congressional peers. Even before the army hearings ended, Republican Senator Flanders and five colleagues introduced a resolution to censure McCarthy. On December 2, 1954, Senate Resolution 261, stating that "the conduct of the Senator from Wisconsin is unbecoming to the United States Senate, is contrary to senatorial tradition and tends to bring the Senate into disrepute, and such conduct is hereby condemned," was passed by a vote of 67 to 22. Senator McCarthy's power was then and there demolished.

Throughout all of McCarthy's campaign against the Reds, rarely did the *Tribune* question the senator's tactics. On February 25, 1954, the paper gently rebuked him for his vehement attacks on Brig. Gen. Ralph W. Zwicker during a hearing held by McCarthy's subcommittee: "It seems to us that Sen. McCarthy will better serve his cause if he learns to distinguish the role of investigator from the role of avenging angel. . . . We do not believe Sen. McCarthy's behavior toward Gen. Zwicker was justified and we expect it has injured his cause of driving the disloyal from the government service. That is a great pity because the cause, as Gen. Zwicker himself said, is one which every patriotic citizen must endorse." Later, in the midst of the Army–McCarthy hearings, the *Tribune* paused to wonder about the wisdom of supporting the Wisconsin senator, and then it viewed the matter in partisan terms: "The *Tribune* doubts the McCarthy hearings will hurt the party, but it is too early to tell," the paper conceded on May 17. Otherwise, the *Tribune* staunchly defended him and furiously attacked his enemies. But Willard Edwards himself became disenchanted, since McCarthy flailed foes and critics with charges frequently unsubstantiated by any form of proof. "Senator McCarthy was irresponsible in the way that an overgrown boy is careless when his size belies his years," Edwards said later. "In some respects he never grew up." Edwards recalled that he waited for a telephone call from the *Tribune*'s editorial department as the fight went on. He felt he could have given the editorial writers an appraisal of Senator McCarthy that they appeared to lack. But no such call ever came. "No one of the editorial writers ever sought my advice," Edwards said. "In Colonel McCormick's day, advice on candidates was provided only if sought. This lack of communication was a fault which was corrected when [Clayton] Kirkpatrick became managing editor and editor." Edwards at the same time believed that Senator McCarthy was unduly abused by the liberal front and by the Democrats, and in one of his *Tribune* stories he asserted that most of McCarthy's alleged victims were not harmed but actually advanced in their positions because of the publicity. The senator's opponents, meantime, insisted that he did not, in the nearly five years of his crusade, ever actually prove that anyone employed by the government was a Communist.

Some of McCarthy's critics, writes historian Freeland, employed tactics not unlike the senator's own: "Senator McCarthy has been indignantly reviled by his adversaries in the Truman administration. Their moralism is unbecoming, for it was they who cultivated the public atmosphere in which he thrived. It was the shattering of the illusions they had helped to foster and the existence of fears they had promoted that he exploited, and he did so with a rhetoric they had legitimized for their own purposes."

The *Tribune* continued to defend Senator McCarthy to the end of his days. The senator died on May 2, 1957, and on May 5, after publishing appreciations by various national leaders and by its own Washington columnist Ruth McCormick Tankersley, the paper summarized Senator McCarthy's fight and career in a long and angry editorial, which concluded: "No man in public life was ever persecuted and maligned because of his beliefs as was Sen. McCarthy. All of the phony martyrs of 'ordeal by slander' lumped together never absorbed a fraction of the abuse that was visited upon him. He took it all without a whimper and stuck to his guns. The Republic has lost a stalwart defender."

*   *   *

Colonel McCormick's health continued to deteriorate. He still ran the *Chicago Tribune* and Tribune Company, but his continuous pain from circulatory and other ailments and his lapses of memory caused problems. On one occasion he summoned an executive all the way from Montreal only to forget why he wanted him. But, ill or well, the Colonel missed few opportunities that he might exploit. In Washington the *Times-Herald* had improved its appearance, content, and circulation under Furlong, and in 1954 McCormick decided that the time had come to sell. He sent his good friend Kent Cooper, retired general manager of the Associated Press, to talk with Eugene Meyer. Was Meyer still interested? He was. Howard Wood arranged the details of the sale, resulting in a profit of $4 million for Tribune Company, and the *Times-Herald* was absorbed into the *Washington Post*. Furlong and Noderer returned to the staff of the *Tribune* in Chicago.

Following treatment at Passavant Hospital in January, 1955, McCormick spent some time at his home in Boynton Beach, Florida, where he kept in touch with his *Tribune* offices in Chicago via a special leased wire. Theodore Van Dellen, the paper's health editor and medical director, spent much of his time with the Colonel. In February, following major surgery, McCormick told Howard Wood that he wanted a *Tribune* or WGN staff member with him at all times. Wood named Stanley Johnston, Wayne Thomis, Eddie Johnson, chief of the paper's color photography studio, and Frank Schrieber, manager of WGN radio, to the group. When McCormick departed for his home in Boynton Beach to recuperate, Van Dellen and Johnston accompanied him. Shortly, McCormick summoned Campbell, Wood, and Maxwell to his bedside, told them they were his "lieutenants," and ordered watches especially engraved for them. He also requested his cartoonists to prepare drawings depicting the careers of the three men. It was Colonel McCormick's whimsical way of announcing his successors.

In January, McCormick had his lawyers draft a codicil to his last will and testament drawn the year previously, establishing his successors in Tribune Company and at the *Chicago Tribune*. His long studies of corporate law culminated in a complex trust structure in which he established the Robert R. McCormick Charitable Trust. It would receive his personally owned shares of Tribune Company stock, as well as his beneficial and dominant interest in the McCormick–Patterson Trust, which would continue for 20 years after his death. As trustees of the charitable trust he chose Arthur Schmon, head of Tribune Company's Canadian properties, plus Chesser Campbell, Howard Wood, Don Maxwell, and Stewart Owen of the *Chicago Tribune*. Harold Grumhaus and Walter Kurz were made alternate trustees. To the McCormick–Patterson Trust he named Schmon, Campbell, Wood, Maxwell, and Ruth McCormick Tankersley. The charitable trust was directed to engage in good works. The trustees subsequently voted to establish and maintain at Cantigny a museum memorializing Colonel McCormick's beloved First Division. Since the trustees would vote controlling stock in Tribune Company, they would exercise great power. In addition, Colonel McCormick named Campbell, Wood, and Maxwell as executors of his will.

Despite the gravity of his illness, McCormick kept in touch with his executives by telephone and dictated memos and letters. He wrote testily to Reeve Schley, representing the Yale Alumni Fund:

> *When you put the touch on a classmate, you should know that he has gone thru a very serious operation. . . . I might not have been here to make a gift. However, when I recover, which seems assured now in the not-too-near future, I will look over my affairs and see what I can do for my old alma mater.*

To Bazy Tankersley, still his favorite, he wrote:

> *I am making up the list for my luncheon in April, and of course I will have you on my right. . . . If you prefer to have a table to yourself, just say so.*

To Terry Flahiff, of the Canadian staff in Montreal:

> *We will figure out a time when we can go to Quebec and put on a little shebang. I have forgotten whether ladies can go to the Garrison club. If so, we will have a little mixed party there.*
>
> *There are a few friends of mine in Quebec I would like to see, and I will see them one at a time, and maybe we can have a sea-going airplane and do Quebec from the ground up—magnificent scenery.*
>
> *You have earned a great deal in this world, but you can't have earned Francoise* [Mrs. Flahiff].

Two messages to Keith Capron, Tribune Tower building manager, were both dated February 12: *"Dear Capron: What are you going to do about my swimming pool down here?"* And a separate note: *"Kick the Jung people out immediately."* The latter note referred to the Anti-Communist Bureau, operated from an office in Tribune Tower by one Harry Jung, who depended on an extensive file of clippings to warn his subscribers about possible subversives. Colonel McCormick had asked a subordinate for a report on Jung; when told that the man was considered unreliable by anti-Communist experts in the military services, by the FBI, and by the police department, he obviously decided to take action.

The Colonel continued to offer ideas to his editors. To Sunday editor Kennedy he wrote:

> *I am sure you are taking sufficient care of running pictures from the English magazines. . . . It might be interesting to know how high heels came into use. We know that Cleopatra, who was very vain, had flat heels on her slippers. When the change to high heels came, I haven't the slightest idea.*

And also:

> *I wonder if this spring we can pick out some individual robin on the farm and follow it thru the full growth of the eggs.*

When managing editor Don Maxwell scooped the world by publishing the text of the hitherto secret Yalta Papers, disclosing President Roosevelt's dealings with Stalin, Senator Dirksen wrote to congratulate Colonel McCormick, concluding his letter, *"This was indeed a stellar accomplishment!"* The senator got a formal and perfunctory reply:

> *Dear Senator Dirksen:*
>
> *Thank you for your congratulations.*
>
> *Yours sincerely,*

Late in March, Colonel McCormick indicated that he wished to be taken to Cantigny. His airplane was summoned, and an ambulance stood ready. He reached his Wheaton farm fitfully conscious. On the evening of March 30, he talked with the Reverend Dr. Robert Bowman Stewart, pastor of the First Presbyterian Church of Wheaton, where he had reaffirmed his faith a few months previously. At his bedside that night were Mrs. McCormick; his stepdaughter, Mrs. Ann Hooper Warner; Mrs. Horace Wetmore, a friend and neighbor; Theodore Van Dellen; and Stanley Johnston.

Early on April 1, with Johnston still present, Colonel McCormick died quietly in his sleep, and he undoubtedly would have been pleased to know that he made the deadline of the *Tribune*'s final edition. Said the three-star banner of April 1: "COL. R. R. MC CORMICK DIES. Tribune Editor-Publisher Ill Two Years." The printing rules were turned, and there was a recent portrait on page one. "The gravity of a circulatory ailment from which Colonel McCormick suffered, together with a rapid decline in his liver function, made him weaker day by day. His death came peacefully," the paper said.

On April 2, the *Tribune* recounted the life of Robert Rutherford McCormick in seven and a half pages of text and pictures. Carey Orr's cartoon, showing McCormick and Tribune Tower, with the flag at half-staff, was lettered, "Carry on!" President Eisenhower and Vice-President Nixon led the nation in mourning the death of Colonel McCormick, Walter Trohan wrote from Washington. In Canada, Quebec Prime Minister Maurice Duplessis praised McCormick as a man "who has contributed in a remarkable way to the development of the natural resources of our province, especially at Baie Comeau, in the Saguenay area," and Monseigneur N. E. LaBrie, Roman Catholic bishop of the Lower St. Lawrence River diocese, sent his condolences. Ludgrove School in England lowered its flag to half-staff, and A. T. Barber, headmaster, recalled the publisher's visit to his old school two years previously. "He told me then that the happiest years of his life were spent at Ludgrove," Barber recalled. In London, Sir Christopher Chancellor, manager of Reuters, said, "He was a very great publisher, probably the greatest of his time." L. P. Scott, managing director of the *Manchester Guardian,* was more restrained: "He was best known here as an extreme, if somewhat pleasantly eccentric, anti-British isolationist. Yet it is perhaps typical that his newspapers gave a good deal of space to fair reporting of the British scene."

Private funeral services for Colonel McCormick were conducted by Dr. Stewart at Cantigny on Monday, April 4. Admission was limited to family members, which included many from "Tribune family," as McCormick thought of his employees. Ten officers from the First Division carried the coffin to a temporary resting place. On Tuesday, memorial services for the public were conducted at the Fourth Presbyterian Church in Chicago by the Reverend Harrison Ray Anderson, its pastor, and Dr. Stewart. Some 1,500 persons were in the church, and others were accommodated at the main WGN television studio adjoining Tribune Tower. Memorial services were held also in the towns of Baie Comeau and Haute Rive, brought into being by Colonel McCormick's wood pulp developments in Quebec Province. In time, McCormick was interred near his first wife, Amie, in the exedra at Cantigny. For days and months memorials, editorials, and appreciations poured into the *Tribune*. The tribute of Marshall Field's *Chicago Sun-Times* appeared on April 2. It read in part:

> Colonel Robert R. McCormick's roots were deep in Chicago. He had a paternal affection for the city and its surrounding area, for which he coined the name Chicagoland. . . . Up to the day of his death Col. McCormick was as much a part of the daily life of our city as the beautiful tower he built to house his newspaper is a part of the city's skyline. . . . He will long be remembered as a virile and controversial figure who almost daily proved to the outside world the freedom Americans enjoy to disagree with the government or anything else in our society that is unsatisfactory to the individual.

A TIME OF CHANGE

26

It was the end of an era, the beginning of a new time, for Chicago, the nation, and the world. The *Tribune* was packed with good news under the new editorship and management, a reflection of improved general conditions rather than a different philosophy. Managing editor Don Maxwell, who would decline the title of editor for many months, was determined to follow closely Colonel McCormick's way. But despite this kind of conscious conservatism on the part of the *Tribune*'s editors, the swiftly accelerating changes in the American way of life were of necessity reflected in the news reports. However, the paper's managers neither anticipated nor desired any abrupt revision of the entire editorial format. Maxwell's colleagues were satisfied to see a kind of relaxation in the news and editorial columns, a glint of humor now and then, an emphasis on sports and recreation bespeaking the new life-style of a nation whose cities and suburbs were expanding vastly in a period of relative tranquillity and prosperity.

Following the censure of Senator McCarthy, the public concern with the Communist threat shifted its focus, from ferreting out subversives at home to amassing an arms stockpile that would discourage the Reds from provoking confrontation abroad. As Truman had done before him, President Eisenhower refused to be bullied by the Soviets, and tense cold war battles were waged without the major protagonists firing a shot. The Marshall Plan and then the Mutual Security Agency aided Europe's recovery, and the North Atlantic Treaty Organization expanded until even West Germany was admitted; Americans felt freer to deal with the challenges and opportunities at home.

The opportunities were immense. The country's economy was booming on a scale unmatched in history, and its population was increasing at a record-breaking rate. As in times past, the boom came to Chicago faster and was bigger there than in most other places. Because the city's industry was more pervasive and varied, it could more readily respond to the needs of consumers worldwide than could the industries of rival towns that had specialized in building ships, tanks, airplanes, and heavy weaponry during the war, though Detroit also came back fast with its new, big cars. At the same time, Chicago continued to be the capital of Midwestern agriculture. Despite a great exodus of workers from the countryside, with the help of modern machines, hybrid seed, and synthetic fertilizer, American farmers could produce enough to feed the native population and still meet the needs of the rest of the world.

Even the cold war had a benign effect on business, observed economist John Kenneth Galbraith, who also noted sourly that the prospering American people wasted their money on private consumer goods, being urged on "by the massed drums of modern advertising." Galbraith may have been correct in his assessment, and in any case newspapers were eager to take full advantage of the consumer sales surge. People were spending their money on automobiles, television sets, kitchen appliances, record players, and tape recorders, and on homes in the suburbs that Alvin Toffler would call "instant cities." Around Chicago grew up a huge semicircle of houses clustered about new shopping centers and industrial parks.

Newspapers in general and the *Tribune* management especially saw an urgent need to understand the newspaper's relationship to the new city-suburban-exurban environment. One effect of suburban growth was to force the *Tribune* and other papers to change their patterns of zoned advertising and distribution. The *Tribune*'s circulation department would have to reach thousands of added homes in the suburbs by its own delivery service, but on the other hand it could abandon the expensive process of attempting to maintain high circulation by covering the entire Midwest. An encouraging discovery was that a morning paper could get to those burgeoning suburbs better than afternoon publications, which besides having to fight midday traffic had to contend with evening television for reader time and advertising dollars.

But more than circulation patterns was involved, and *Tribune* president Chesser Campbell asked study groups working under his aides Howard Wood, Harold Grumhaus, and Walter Kurz to come up with specific proposals for exploiting new technologies and for meeting the needs of readers and advertisers. This meant coping with a huge mass of new knowledge and deciding how it might be applied to the business of publishing a newspaper—from new approaches in corporate organization to motivation research to automation, computers, cybernetics, and the possibility that a video display terminal would someday be developed to enable writers and editors to convert their thoughts into type. Not only would the *Tribune* itself have to advance technologically to meet the new conditions, it would have to keep its readers informed and educated and updated in an era in which human knowledge was expanding at a mind-boggling rate.

Some editorial response to the new conditions and the changing interests of readers gradually became evident. The *Tribune* slackened its preoccupation with politics a little. The paper sought more specialists—to write on religion (more churches were built in 1955 than in any other year, it was reported); to look into scientific matters on a practical plane, discussing the uses and popularity of aluminum and plastics, as well as developments in the fields of nuclear energy, mathematics, astronomy, and space science; and to keep up with advances in medicine, such as the new drugs for the treatment of mental patients, thorazine and reserpine, which were pronounced experimentally successful that year. The Salk vaccine, field-tested in 1954, was big news, promising security from one of the world's most dreaded diseases, poliomyelitis, and in Chicago Dr. Herman N. Bundesen, city health officer, decreed that it should be used, despite noisy skeptics. The *Tribune* reported that the general assembly of the Presbyterian church had authorized the ordination of women, but the paper provided the Presbyterians no guidance, as it had in the Reverend Mr. Swing's day. Little discussed but sometimes hinted at was the coming explosion of an enormous new power in the 1960s, that of racial and ethnic minorities, youth, and women.

Managing editor Maxwell was well practiced in the maintenance of the McCormick line. When the Colonel traveled, Maxwell and Leon Stolz, editor of the editorial page, communicated with him on a daily basis, sometimes hourly when McCormick was at the Florida end of the leased telephone line. So during the last days of Colonel McCormick, the *Tribune* had continued its attacks on internationalists, Communists, the brinksmanship of Secretary of State John Foster Dulles, and the profligacy of the big spenders in Congress. When in March, 1955, Dulles warned that the United States might use tactical atomic weapons in case of war, the *Tribune* dissented, even though the threat was directed at Communist China. Several days later, President Eisenhower declared that atomic weapons would not be used in any "police action." By this time the *Tribune*'s editors were launching new attacks on the foreign policy of Franklin D. Roosevelt. The State Department had at last released the Yalta Papers, which revealed new details of the February, 1945, conference during which Churchill, Roosevelt, and Stalin discussed postwar political arrangements. Critics long had charged that the inducements offered to insure Russia's cooperation in the final months of the war had been far too generous, and they considered the release of the full proceedings a victory. Maxwell, using the printing techniques learned in the printers' strike, enabled the *Chicago Tribune* on March 16 to be first to press with the complete Yalta text, beating the rest of the nation's papers by a few hours.

But generally Maxwell sought a quieter, earthier paper than his fastidious and aloof predecessor and mentor had preferred. Norma Lee Browning wrote a series of articles called "City Girl in the Country," which proved so popular that it reappeared as a book. Maxwell dropped most of McCormick's simplified spelling, began including the terminology of the new age, and displayed an enjoyment of rustic humor, as when columnist Tom Morrow roamed Indiana, seeking out atavistic characters for their quaint and piquant lore. (Morrow, elated when he came upon the town of Bourbon, was swiftly dejected upon learning that the inhabitants drank mostly water and milk.)

Whenever Maxwell addressed his editorial staff or any other *Tribune* workers, he made it clear that he would cling to *Tribune* traditions as he had learned them from the Colonel. He quoted often from early *Tribune* editorials, ascribing them all to Joseph Medill, and emphasized a metaphor of the Civil War period, designating newspapers as "watchmen on the walls." Don Maxwell was a pragmatist who tolerated no foolishness from individualistic writers or editors. One of the final assignments given to him by Colonel McCormick was the construction of a vast exhibition center on Lake Michigan. Maxwell intended to carry that assignment to completion as a memorial to the Colonel.

*   *   *

Within the noneditorial areas of the *Tribune*, the desire for change seethed. Under the monolithic rule of McCormick, Tribune Company had become one of the world's most powerful and successful publishing ventures. But McCormick himself, in his final years, had begun to recognize that the management structure was increasingly obsolete and worked well only because of his dominant personality. He established a special study committee under promotion director W. J. "Jerry" Byrnes, which came up with a number of suggestions for changes. But the implementation of such proposals, or of other changes urged by his management team, led by Chesser Campbell, was delayed by the Colonel's ill health. Now his death raised the specter that had almost paralyzed the company 50 years previously, a stockholder struggle for control. When McCormick and Patterson created the pact bearing their names, they provided for 50–50 control of the McCormick–Patterson Trust, which until its dissolution in 1975 would continue to own 1,070 of the 2,000 Tribune Company shares. After the death of Patterson, Mc-Cormick himself had assumed effective control of those majority shares. Now there would be five so-called McCormick trustees, Campbell, Howard Wood, Don Maxwell, Ruth Tankersley, and Arthur Schmon. The Patterson contingent numbered three, Mary King Patterson, Jack Flynn, the tough, capable president of News Syndicate Company, which published the *New York News,* and Richard Clarke, *New York News* editor. All eight would have to agree on a policy to cast the trust votes. Should there be disagreement, it was provided that the senior judge of the U.S. District Court of Northern Illinois would referee.

There were early and ugly rumors that the Chicago and New York trustees would not be able to agree on who should run the company. While the McCormick obsequies were still in progress, Mrs. Tankersley, speaking for the descendants of Joseph Medill, sought to ease the situation with a public statement: "Colonel McCormick made careful preparation for the uninterrupted operation of the Tribune Company and its subsidiaries. . . . I feel extremely confident about the future of the *Tribune*. . . . My uncle, Colonel McCormick, and Weymouth Kirkland, whom I consider the most able attorney in the country, have drawn the blueprint of future management of the *Tribune*."

Mrs. Tankersley praised Campbell, Wood, and Maxwell individually, thus injecting family approval of the men McCormick had selected as executors of his will as well as McCormick–Patterson trustees. There was no statement from the New York group. John S. Knight, publisher of the *Chicago Daily News,* commented to friends, "No metropolitan newspaper can be run successfully by a committee."

Campbell succeeded to the presidency of Tribune Company at a special meeting of the directors in April, 1955. By the time of the annual meeting of the stockholders on May 16, the opposing forces in the McCormick–Patterson Trust had recognized the need for unity, and the slate of company directors was swiftly chosen: Campbell, Alfred Cowles III, Flynn, Henry D. Lloyd, Jr., Maxwell, Mrs. Patterson, Schmon, Mrs. Tankersley, and Wood. They in turn elected the officers of Tribune Company: Campbell, president; Wood and Maxwell, vice-presidents; Paul G. Fulton, retail advertising manager of the *Tribune*, treasurer; and A. M. Kennedy, Sunday editor, secretary. Officers were confirmed for the various Tribune Company subsidiaries: Chicago Tribune Building Corporation; WGN, Inc.; the Ontario Paper Company, Ltd.; Illinois Atlantic Corporation (transportation); Marhill Mines, Ltd. (mineral exploration); News Syndicate Company, Inc.; Chicago Tribune–New York News Syndicate, Inc.; Midwest FM Network, Inc.; Chicago Philharmonic Orchestra (of WGN); and WPIX, Inc. (New York radio and television stations).

The tilt was definitely in favor of the *Chicago Tribune* organization, so Campbell was determined to be as conciliatory and diplomatic as possible in the management of company affairs. The *New York News* was essentially autonomous; Arthur Schmon ruled in Canada, though he was required by his supplier-customer situation to continue an impartial relationship with both sides. Campbell assigned Howard Wood and Fred Byington to continue their close contact with all Canadian operations. Campbell, Wood, and Maxwell divided their areas of *Tribune* responsibility to insure that there would be complete harmony in Chicago.

Not in the best of health since his heart attack in 1949, Campbell nevertheless moved vigorously on his problems, both as publisher of the *Tribune* and as president and chief executive officer of Tribune Company. He ordered a cutback of unprofitable activity in Chicago, curtailing some of the paper's circulation in distant areas, especially on Sundays. He eliminated the thick classified advertising sections from Sunday *Tribunes* outside the paper's eight-county primary circulation area, saving thousands of tons of costly newsprint. Campbell, an advertising man himself, desired a high concentration of *Tribune* circulation in the retail trading area, an economically sound procedure, but one curbing Maxwell, who wished to maintain the paper's widespread political influence. The policy was disturbing also to Charles Corcoran, the new circulation manager from the *Washington Times-Herald*, who, like almost all circulation managers, resented giving up sales of the paper anywhere.

Campbell's program for the *Tribune* went into prompt effect. At the same time, general manager Wood and production manager Grumhaus, working with advertising director Kurz, were proposing new sections of the paper intended to appeal to readers in a concentrated circulation area and to afford added opportunity to sell advertising, especially color advertising, a technology in which the *Tribune* was well ahead of most other papers, including all its Chicago rivals. The popularity of the paper's Sunday magazine, still less than two years old, provided an encouraging precedent for such ventures. The new magazine had been launched after Wood obtained McCormick's approval to merge the *Graphic* and the sepia-inked rotogravure picture section. Grumhaus and Kurz were directed to participate with Sunday department representatives in the planning operation, which was headed by the author of this book, who became the new publication's first editor. The result, appearing on October 4, 1953, was the *Chicago Tribune Magazine*. It received the immediate approval of readers and advertisers, eliminated losses of $1 million a year, and in time earned a profit. These same forces, under Sunday editor Kennedy, created special food and home sections, and a women's interest section for Sunday. Kennedy was at last able to sell to management his proposal for a television magazine, which was put together by the Sunday magazine task force but appeared in the Saturday *Tribune*, increasing its circulation by 90,000.

*   *   *

In the news department of the *Chicago Tribune*, news coverage and the waging of political battles had continued without cease while Colonel McCormick lay ill and dying. A new politician had arisen to seek office as Chicago's mayor: In the March, 1955, Democratic primaries, Richard Joseph Daley, 52, chairman of the Cook County Democrats, had challenged and defeated the two-term incumbent, Martin H. Kennelly. Daley, backed by the powerful Democratic organization and one Chicago newspaper, the *American,* then faced the young Republican nominee, Robert E. Merriam, 36, a World War II combat veteran and son of Charles Merriam, the University of Chicago professor who had battled political bosses and gang corruption as a Hyde Park alderman. Young Merriam, serving as alderman of the same ward, had a similar reputation. Richard Daley was regarded as far from invincible by the *Tribune*, since he had once run unsuccessfully for sheriff, losing in the Republican suburbs. The paper gave Merriam strong support, while conceding that Daley was honest, even if his party was not. Said the Sunday pre-election editorial:

> Ald. Robert E. Merriam has waged an intelligent and effective campaign for mayor. The Republican nominee has posed the issues clearly and has been frank in outlining plans for Chicago. . . . One thing that can be said with certainty of Mr. Merriam is that in office he will be his own man.
> That is one thing that cannot be said with the slightest conviction of Mr. Daley. . . . Mr. Daley bears an equally good reputation for personal integrity, but the issue is machine rule—in fact gangster rule—of this great city.

On Monday, April 4, the day of the Cantigny funeral of Colonel McCormick, the *Tribune* banner read, "TIES MACHINE TO GAMBLING." The paper recounted Merriam's exposé of Democratic organizational links to the crime syndicate, following disclosures by *Tribune* investigative reporter James Doherty and the Chicago Crime Commission that both Democrats and certain Republican elements were tied with the gangsters succeeding Al Capone. The *Tribune* called for a strong Merriam vote, but Daley was elected by a majority of 127,199. It would be his thinnest margin of victory in the longest reign of any Chicago mayor. Said the *Tribune* on April 7: "We congratulate Richard J. Daley upon his election as mayor. As we said more than once during the course of the campaign, he has earned a reputation for intelligence and honesty. We hope, for his sake, as well as for Chicago's, that he will do nothing in the coming four years to sully his good name."

Mayor-elect Daley at once called upon the newspapers and radio stations to help him in a program to repress crime and rebuild the city. He was promised full cooperation by the *Tribune*, which praised Merriam for pointing out the city's needs during his aggressive campaign. It noted sadly, however, that only one Republican, Nicholas Bohling, from the South Shore Seventh Ward, was on the city council's committee on committees, which would determine the council leaders for four years. It was clear that the days of Republican power in the council were ended.

* * *

Daley's victory came as Chicago entered upon its greatest period of economic, physical, and cultural advancement since the World's Columbian Exposition. The Chicago boom continued to lead the country, with factories rising in both the city and the suburbs, creating an industrial complex that would extend from Lake County, Indiana, to Lake County, Illinois, and spread westward 50 miles. *Fortune* magazine, taking a look about America in mid-1955, focused on Chicago:

> Right now the most exciting city in the U.S. is Chicago, Illinois. What is happening in Chicago amounts, in many ways, to a rebuilding of the city. Chicago has needed the rebuilding in the worst way; it is getting it in a big way. . . . All over the city there is a fury of blasting and leveling. And, as the girders go up for the new over-passes, office buildings, factories, apartments, stores, and hospitals, even the most skeptical Chicagoan, hardened against mere rhetoric during the decades of tub-thumping, must now conclude that the city means business.

The *Tribune* was pleased by *Fortune*'s praise, but, having contributed long and loud to the tub-thumping and rhetoric, pointed out that such preliminaries were necessary to action. "*Fortune* is right in saying Chicago is the most exciting city in the U.S.," said the paper on June 3. "Chicago's current boom is largely the result of good leadership, the businessmen who sit on committees and get things done. The characteristic of the new crop of Chicago leaders is they are neither naive, nor cynical."

The paper's part in Chicago's architectural renaissance had begun before World War II, when Colonel McCormick requested Howard Wood to see what could be done to move the city along the road toward slum clearance. Wood sought out financiers, developers, and construction experts. Working within the industry, he helped to found the Chicago Building Congress in 1939. Wood also recruited the aid of then State Sen. Richard J. Daley to obtain passage in the Illinois legislature of the Neighborhood Redevelopment Corporation Act in 1941. This new law permitted the city to invoke the power of eminent domain to clear potentially useful tracts for housing, and to enable private interests to finance housing for middle-income and low-income families. Slum clearance efforts were further strengthened by another law supported by the *Tribune*, the Blighted Areas Redevelopment Act, passed in 1947. These acts, along with major zoning and building code revisions that took place over the next several years, helped shape the city's development.

One result was Lake Meadows, a moderate-rent housing complex on 101 acres south of the Loop, sponsored by New York Life Insurance Company. It cost $23 million and provided housing for 1,600 families. Other inner-city developments included Prairie Shores on the South Side and Sandburg Village, built on the North Side by Arthur Rubloff, the imaginative Chicago developer who gave the city the slogan "The Magnificent Mile" for North Michigan Avenue improvements. Another major project was the West Side Medical Center, on 305 acres, consisting of six hospitals and seven medical schools, costing $45 million. The Michael Reese Hospital complex was also created, new shopping centers sprang up, and from 1950 through 1954 some 65,000 dwellings were erected in Chicago, almost double the number of the previous five years.

The city's banks were expanding and able to finance the building boom, which had been inspired in part by a long period of deprivation and in part by a new school of Chicago architecture, in the forefront of which was an emigré from Nazi Germany, Ludwig Mies van der Rohe, who brought with him an influential segment of the Bauhaus school. Mies van der Rohe had himself been influenced by the work of Frank Lloyd Wright, whose designs in the 1920s were better known in Germany than America. Mies quickly found disciples and associates in Chicago and began construction projects on the South Side, emphasizing natural materials on the exterior with minimal decorative effect and showing some of the concern for mass and horizontal planes that had been exemplified by Wright's James Charnley House, done with Louis Sullivan in 1892; his Robie House, done in 1909; and his industrial buildings.

Chicago's skyline changed. In the 1950s and 1960s, the city would show the world fantastic architectural development of wide variation, but usually with a hint of Mies, and Wright and Sullivan: the University of Illinois Circle Campus; new structures at the University of Chicago and Northwestern University; the immense O'Hare airport complex, mostly the work of C. F. Murphy; the United Insurance Building, an exception to the Bauhaus code; and the Prudential Building.

The new architecture was symbolic of the new prosperity. Chicago was cleaner, no longer the smelly hog butcher to the world, but it continued to be heavily industrialized, challenging new environmental groups. From 1945 to 1955, more than 500 factories were constructed, offsetting the fact that the famed stockyards were broken up and moved to various smaller towns. It was estimated that 20,000 jobs were being created annually, many in the expanding industrial suburbs. The population of Chicago itself declined, but the metropolitan area flourished, totaling nearly 7 million citizens. Nonetheless, hundreds of thousands of people still wanted to live downtown, and the living facilities there proliferated, both in medium-cost and high-cost areas. Mayor Daley and his development experts constructed high-rise garages and underground parking areas at a cost of $27 million to lure motorists back downtown. The improved public transportation system, elevated and underground, completed during the war, helped somewhat, as did the growing network of expressways, which totaled 67 miles in 1955.

The city upheld its reputation as the nation's transportation hub. The completion of the St. Lawrence Seaway in 1959 was promptly followed by the deepening of the Cal-Sag Canal and the construction of huge dock and storage facilities on Lake Calumet, making Chicago, as the *Tribune* had predicted, the world's largest inland seaport. The city continued to ship more agricultural products than any other in the world. Opened in 1956 as a military facility, O'Hare Field in the 1960s was in the process of becoming O'Hare International Airport, the world's busiest. Chicago continued to be the world's largest railroad center and had developed extensive trucking and bus lines as well. In addition, it had become the world's greatest medical center, a powerful banking center, and an important insurance center, while nearby Weston boasted the world's largest atom smasher, a linear accelerator generating 20,000 electron volts and permitting highly sophisticated study of energy and matter. It was named the Fermi National Accelerator Laboratory (Fermilab) in honor of Enrico Fermi, who directed the U-235 experiments that produced the nuclear chain reaction at the University of Chicago in 1942.

The Chicago renaissance included literature as well. Early in the 1950s, Alson J. Smith wrote for the prospering new publisher Henry J. Regnery a book called *Chicago's Left Bank,* in which he asserted that a writing resurgence was at hand. Among those he named were Nelson Algren, Herman Kogan, Meyer Levin, Arthur Meeker, Willard Motley, Karl Shapiro, and Mary Jane Ward. Meeker wrote a column for the *Tribune*, and Kogan had once been on its staff. Smith's list omitted such poets as Gwendolyn Brooks, a Pulitzer prize winner; Elder Olson; and Marcia Lee Masters, daughter of Edgar Lee Masters and later to become poetry editor of the *Tribune*. Some important novelists were also missed—James T. Farrell, Mary Hastings Bradley, Harry Mark Petrakis, Louis Zara, and the temporary expatriate from Chicago, Saul Bellow, whose third novel, *The Adventures of Augie March,* published in 1953, won a National Book Award. Some *Tribune* staff and former staff members who also wrote books were not in Smith's listing either: Baker Brownell, philosophy; Guy Murchie, Jr., *Music of the Spheres,* a well-praised book on space science; Harold Blake Walker, religion; Roi Ottley, *Black Odyssey,* a history of blacks in America; and Norma Lee Browning, books on adventure. Nor did Smith include a number of historians, among them Paul Angle, Bessie Louise Pierce, John Hope Franklin, Virgil Peterson, Daniel Boorstin (later Librarian of Congress), Studs Terkel, the *Tribune*'s Robert Cromie, Harry Barnard, E. B. Long, and Ralph Newman. In addition to the surge of indigenous writing, Encyclopaedia Britannica, Inc., the venerable publishing establishment that had been brought to Chicago, with Robert Maynard Hutchins as editor-in-chief and Mortimer J. Adler as associate editor, issued the 54-volume set *Great Books of the Western World,* encompassing the works of more than 70 thinkers and writers from Homer to Sigmund Freud and including a two-volume Syntopican of great ideas from the history of Western man.

The *Tribune* claimed some credit for providing beneficent influence in the restoration of Chicago's cultural prestige, following its eclipse in the 1920s. Sunday editor Kennedy and McCormick had pioneered in printing reproductions of great works of art on the paper's excellent color presses. The new *Tribune Magazine* attracted Midwestern artists, among them James M. Sessions, James Lockhart, John Doctoroff, Ivan Albright, Aaron Bohrod, Edith Cassidy, Esther Seymour Stevenson, Tom Hill, Thomas Ramsier, Clinton King, and, from the *Tribune* staff, Ray Roland, Gary Sheahan, and Edward Walaitis. Successive magazine editors, Walter Simmons, John Fink, and Robert Goldsborough, published established writers and introduced others.

*   *   *

One of the *Tribune*'s pet projects had over the years consumed what some thought was an excess of printer's ink, and it was continuing to have trouble leaving the drawing boards. Colonel McCormick had long wanted Chicago to have an annual trade fair, like the ones that had given life to many great European cities. Maxwell and his political editor, George Tagge, undertook to carry out the project by inducing the state legislature to create the Chicago Park Fair, a nonprofit corporation authorized in 1952. The Park Fair board would hold annual trade shows, at least in summer months. Such a plan for the lakefront was opposed by many, including conservationists and ecologists and people who owned large exhibition halls elsewhere in the city. Maxwell, however, had obtained the support of Mayor Kennelly and James L. Palmer, president of Marshall Field & Company, as well as other businessmen and leaders in the state legislature. After inspecting the new convention center in Toronto,

Ontario, Maxwell and his associates knew what they wanted for Chicago—an exhibition center, the biggest on earth, to be situated on Lake Michigan near the downtown district.

New legislation was required, laws that would set up an exhibition center board and provide for its financing. Maxwell determined that at least part of the money could be had from a tax on Illinois racetracks, some of the funds going to aid municipalities downstate. This aroused a powerful new enemy, the racing industry. But Tagge got the measure through the legislature in 1953, after Maxwell convinced Benjamin Lindheimer, a major track owner, that the project would actually benefit racing by bringing more people to Chicago. The Chicago Park Fair employed architects and engineers to draft a preliminary study of an exhibition center to be placed on the lakefront at 23rd Street. The report, ready in March, 1955, called for a massive hall 250 feet wide and 1,200 feet long, with an exhibition area of 360,000 square feet and providing for an arena seating 22,000. The air-conditioned building, with adjacent railway facilities and built-in truck ramps and a rooftop helicopter pad, would be the largest and most accessible exhibition hall extant. The cost, $32,282,000. It was estimated that nearly $10 million would accumulate in the racing fund by the time the building was complete. Again new legislation would be required, to raise the rest of the money. Maxwell assigned Tagge to obtain passage of two bills, one to create the Metropolitan Fair and Exhibition Authority, a municipal entity empowered to issue revenue bonds, and a second bill to enable the Chicago Park District to lease 180 acres of Burnham Park to the new authority for 40 years. The campaign was accompanied by some of the *Tribune*'s heaviest editorial thunder. Tagge, by now a seasoned campaigner, maneuvered against powerful opposition, much of it organized by William Wood Prince, who had interests in the Chicago International Amphitheatre. Following the death of Colonel McCormick, the legislation was passed, the authority created, and Maj. Lennox R. Lohr of world's fair fame was selected as general director. Lohr would work with an appointed board of 12 directors. The authority was ready to lease the 23rd Street site, but the Chicago Park District was not ready to let it go, and the *Sun-Times* and *Daily News* campaigned against any lakefront location.

*   *   *

On May 18, 1954, the paper's headlines had read: "PUPIL SEGREGATION BANNED. SUPREME COURT RULES IT UNCONSTITUTIONAL." The full text of the opinion was printed. It was a unanimous decision, based on cases arising from Kansas, South Carolina, Virginia, and Delaware, read out by Chief Justice Earl Warren. Implementation guidance would be provided at a later date. The *Tribune* accepted the decision with equanimity:

> The court left for future determination the question of how soon the change must be made and how the principle announced yesterday is to be enforced. Both the decision and the method of enforcing it are to be commended. In much the greater part of the United States, measured either in area or population, the decision will make no difference at all, for segregation by law in the public schools is largely, though not wholly, a Southern phenomenon. . . . It remains to be seen how the South will accept the court's decision.

The paper evidently assumed that implementation of the segregation decision would be left to the individual states, but on May 31, 1955, the court in its second decision on *Brown* v. *Board of Education* placed the desegregation order under general supervision of the federal district courts. The *Tribune* commented:

> The court was unanimous in finding a year ago that segregation in the public schools is contrary to the Constitution and is unanimous again in insisting that the school boards lose no time in getting started on a program of integration. Time will be allowed, however, to meet the many problems that are foreseen, such as remapping school districts, provision of adequate buildings and transportation for children.
>
> The line the court has taken will be conciliatory. Men of good will everywhere hope the response to it in the South will be equally conciliatory. Many competent observers have said that the people themselves, white as well as Negro, especially in the border states, are prepared to accept the court's decision. The danger is that the southern politicians, seeking an issue to ride to power or to retain power, will seize on this one. We hope this can be avoided.
>
> We expect to be told that Northerners do not understand the problem. That may be true, but it is surely not for lack of acquaintance with Negroes. . . . There are nearly as many Negroes in Chicago as in Virginia. Without segregation, we have a better school system than is usually found in southern states. If the South will make a genuine effort to obey the court's decree, it may find that most of its fears are groundless.

The *Tribune*'s notion that segregation did not exist in Chicago was of course specious. There was no segregation by law, but there was de facto segregation, since the South Side black neighborhoods numbered nearly a fourth of the city's 3,500,000 inhabitants. Nonetheless, the *Tribune* was consistent in its civil rights position. When in 1956 the Supreme Court followed its school desegregation opinion by barring racial discrimination on public transportation and in public places, the paper again approved, harking back to the basic school segregation ruling:

> The Supreme Court said in a unanimous opinion that segregation in the schools deprives Negroes of their constitutional rights. It follows that any Negro anywhere in the United States whose children are sent to a segregated school can enforce his rights in the courts, just as any author or editor can enforce his right to the freedom of the press and a man who wishes to go to the church of his choice can enforce his right but a free government cannot compromise it.

The paper contemplated a further drive by blacks to obtain rights in other areas and told Republican party leaders and delegates about to assemble in national convention in August, 1956: "The Republicans at San Francisco should have no difficulty in writing a civil rights plank that will make sense."

The reference was to the trouble the Democrats were having at that time in their Chicago convention. Southerners in Congress had served notice on March 11 that they intended to use "all lawful means" to overturn the desegregation decision of 1954, and a States' Rights third party was threatened. For the second time the Democrats nominated Gov. Adlai Stevenson of Illinois for president. For vice-president they chose Sen. Estes Kefauver of Tennessee, who as chairman of the Senate Crime Investigating Committee had been a hero of anticrime hearings largely fueled by the investigations of Virgil Peterson and his Chicago Crime Commission staff. Kefauver held off a threat from Sen. John F. Kennedy of Massachusetts, who was backed by Mayor Daley of Chicago. The *Tribune* employed gentle irony in dealing with Stevenson, a Chicago lawyer, whose grandfather had been vice-president of the United States and whose family had interests in the *Bloomington Pantagraph,* one of the state's most respected dailies: "Stevenson is a disciple of Matthew Arnold, apostle of sweetness and light. He endorses fully and sincerely a better world, a world in which poverty does not exist and in which men do not resort to arms to win their aims. . . . We also gather from Mr. Stevenson's remarks this Utopia, and progress toward it, is to be achieved under the aegis of the Democratic party."

The paper, in continuing the McCormick line, had viewed President Eisenhower's first term coolly and said so in accepting the decision of the party at the Cow Palace in San Francisco:

> Make no mistake. The enthusiasm for President Eisenhower was genuine. This newspaper would be something less than candid if it pretended that it approved the Eisenhower record in its entirety. In the course of the campaign, as well as before it, and after it, we intend to call the shots as we see them. . . . We have not admired the New Dealism in the party's economic program and we have regarded the trend toward more involvement and investment abroad as imposing great risks on our country without corresponding advantages.

Don Maxwell led the editorial team covering the convention, which included Washington bureau chief Trohan and political editor Tagge. The three worked hard with the platform committee, as Colonel McCormick had done in his time, especially concentrating on the civil rights plank. On August 21, the paper endorsed the platform it had helped to create: "The Republican platform this year is better than usual. Like the Democrats, the Republicans had difficulty framing the civil rights plank, but unlike the Democrats they resolved their difficulty without double-talk—the plank is strong in the sense that it is forthright and strong also in the sense that it doesn't try to escape the plain implications of the Supreme Court in the segregation cases."

The American people evidently agreed with the paper, for Eisenhower's margin of victory was even greater than in 1952: 35 million popular votes to Stevenson's 26 million and 457 electoral votes to 73.

*   *   *

During 1956, general manager Wood, who also was president of WGN, Inc., invited Ward Quaal, an executive of the Crosley Broadcasting Corporation in Cincinnati, to bring the *Tribune*'s radio, TV, and FM stations out of the red and to make them greater forces in the community. Quaal acted swiftly and effectively, thoroughly revising and reorganizing format to raise ratings and bring the clear-channel radio station and WGN-TV into black figures financially. In time, after acquiring and developing broadcast and telecast subsidiaries, Quaal would become president of WGN and a director of Tribune Company.

Also in 1956, Wood received a telephone call from Stuart List, publisher of Hearst's afternoon *Chicago American,* informing him that the *American* was for sale. Its daily circulation was 523,320, compared with 614,000 for the *Daily News,* and the Sunday *American* had a circulation of 677,709. The *Tribune*'s long advertising dominance, the arrival of television as a competitor for advertising revenues, and generally rising costs had depressed prospects for evening papers, and the *American* was losing money. Wood quickly learned that at least one publisher, John S. Knight of the *Chicago Daily News,* was an eager bidder for the property, and a second bidder, Marshall Field III, was a probability. Wood was quite aware that if Knight should acquire an evening paper monopoly in Chicago *plus* a Sunday paper, he might win back the dominance the *Daily News* had once held over the *Tribune*. Immediate action was indicated, but Tribune Company president Campbell and directors Flynn and Schmon were in London, completing a deal to form the British-Canadian Aluminium Company, which would build a plant at Baie Comeau and draw its power from Tribune Company's huge 442,400-horsepower hydroelectric plant on the Manicouagan River.

Wood consulted the company directors by telephone and was empowered to act. The Hearst Publishing Company was seeking $12 million for its paper, which had absorbed other publications since its founding in 1900. The *Tribune* directors authorized Wood to offer $9 million. By the time the directors could assemble, with the aluminum project successfully completed, Wood had advanced negotiations with H. G. Kern, general manager of the Hearst newspapers, and his associates. In addition to a $9 million cash offer, Tribune Company agreed to assume Hearst's obligations to the *American*'s staff of 1,800, obligations the other bidders declined to accept. On Sunday, October 21, the sale announcement was made in the Sunday editions of the two papers by Campbell and by Kern. Chicago was assured that the *American* would continue publication under Stuart List, executive editor Ted Doyle, and business manager Donald J. Walsh, and the entire existing staff.

Another of Wood's projects was brought to successful completion when James Oates, president of the Equitable Life Insurance Company of New York, accepted Tribune Company terms for the acquisition of property adjacent to Tribune Tower on the Chicago River, where Equitable wished to construct its Midwestern headquarters building. Oates agreed that the skyscraper should rise no higher than 35 floors and that it should be set far back from Michigan Avenue. The companies also agreed to cover loading areas and service entryways for the two buildings and to build and maintain a plaza to beautify the riverfront. The result was a riverfront development on the site of Chicago's first house, built by fur trader Jean Baptiste du Sable. The Equitable Building, designed by Skidmore, Owings, and Merrill with Alfred Shaw, was erected in 1965. The project included Pioneer Court, a plaza along Michigan Avenue connecting Tribune Tower and the Equitable Building and providing a site for a fountain honoring Chicago's founders. Pioneer Court in summer offered facilities for free public entertainment and exhibits benefiting charitable and civic causes.

*   *   *

During the period of transition following the death of Colonel McCormick, *Tribune* editor Don Maxwell had at his disposal an excellent editorial staff, built up over many years by McCormick, Maloney, and himself. Leon Stolz, chief of the editorial page, and George Morgenstern, his first assistant, were brilliant writers, both trained at the University of Chicago. They were politically divided, with Stolz leaning to the liberal side and Morgenstern, author of *Pearl Harbor, the Story of the Secret War* (1947), ably supporting the paper's entirely dominant conservative view. Others on the editorial page staff included Joseph Ator, veteran reporter and political analyst; Carl Wiegman, former reporter and author of *Trees to News* (1953), a history of the Ontario Paper Company; and Alfred Ames, former associate editor of the *Tribune*'s *Magazine of Books,* all graduates of the University of Illinois, where Ames had received his Ph.D. degree. Two of the three cartoonists were veterans, Carey Orr and Joseph Parrish. The newcomer was Daniel E. Holland, who had come to the *Tribune* after four years as a bomber pilot. A new farm editor, Richard Orr, joined the staff. He soon won a Beck Award and was named rural affairs editor. In later years he added to his duties those of editorial writer.

The national news staff included Trohan as Washington bureau chief, with 14 experienced reporters; Harold Hutchings, New York bureau chief, aided by a staff of seven; William J. Fulton, United Nations correspondent; Seymour Korman, West Coast correspondent; plus Hollywood specialists Hedda Hopper, columnist for the *Tribune* and the Tribune–New York News Syndicate, photographer Louis Wolfe, and his wife, writer Frieda Zylstra.

Maxwell's local staff was one of the country's best. Stewart Owen was city editor until 1954, when Thomas Furlong succeeded to that position and Owen was promoted to the post of assistant managing editor. The field forces were directed for more than a decade by day city editor Stanley Armstrong, who in 1958 was succeeded by Clayton Kirkpatrick. Fifteen reporters covered the city beats, and ten more roved the crime front. Suburban reporters, special writers, and assignment reporters, rewriters, and copyreaders raised the local staff to more than 100. In 1956, C. R. Christopherson was senior assistant city editor of the *Tribune*, supervising the local copy desk. He was assisted by Richard Hainey, who later became executive editor of *Chicago's American* and its successor *Chicago Today,* and ultimately a professor of journalism at Northwestern University.

William Clark, business and financial editor, succeeding Philip Hampson, had a staff of three women and 14 men. Clark would become secretary of Tribune Company and its subsidiaries and later director of the McCormick Charitable Trust. Paul Hubbard directed a staff of 25 gathering and editing neighborhood news for the various zoned sections. The women's section, called "Today with Women," showed improvement, with writers Mary Merryfield, Sheila John Daly, Shirley Gould, and Lynn Hurley added to the staff, and Gwen Morgan sending from London and throughout Europe articles thought to be of special interest to women, in addition to her regular cable report. Over a dozen women worked in specialized areas of women's interests: Eleanor Page, society editor and columnist, whose assistants shared the pseudonym "Judith Cass"; Eleanor Nangle, beauty; Evelyn Livingston and Marylou Luther, fashion, succeeding Rhea Seeger; Ruth Ellen Church, who in 1962 became the country's first newspaper wine columnist, and her staff of six, food and home economics; and special writers Ruth Moss and Joan Beck, the latter to become women's editor and later a *Tribune* editorial writer and columnist.

The paper's culture area was well staffed: Claudia Cassidy, music and drama critic; Seymour Raven, her assistant and later business manager of the Chicago Symphony Orchestra; Fanny Butcher, literary editor; Frederic Babcock, editor of the *Magazine of Books;* Larry Wolters, the veteran radio and television critic, and his assistant John Fink, who later became editor of the *Tribune Magazine;* Anna Nangle, film critic (Mae Tinee); William Leonard, nightlife columnist; Marion Purcelli, editor of the paper's new *TV Week;* and John Blackburn and Cornelius Beukema, editors of the features pages, where most of the critics and women writers found lodging. The Sunday *Magazine* had a staff of ten, including some of the paper's ablest writers and editors. Norma Lee Browning, star writer for the magazine, was drafted to write for the daily news sections frequently. John T. McCutcheon, Jr., succeeded Tom Morrow as conductor of the "Line O' Type" column; he later would join the editorial page staff, becoming editor of the editorial page in June, 1971. The personalities column was written by Herb Lyon, who would be followed by Aaron Gold. Veterans Theodore Van Dellen and David Condon conducted two of the paper's oldest and best-known columns, "How to Keep Well" and "In the Wake of the News," and would do so for more years than any other writers in *Tribune* history.

Among the more glamorous jobs in the newspaper business, after war correspondent, was that of foreign correspondent. Maxwell pulled back several of these in the postwar era, thus modifying McCormick policy, but he retained Larry Rue in Bonn, Henry Wales and Paul Ress in Paris, and Arthur Veysey and Gwen Morgan in London, oldest of the *Tribune* outposts. Joseph Cerutti, Mavis Cole, Robert Merry, and Terry Johnson ran the London bureau when Veysey and Morgan were on their widely traveled assignments. Percy Wood covered an Asian beat, first from New Delhi, India, and later from Hong Kong; Eugene Griffin continued as the important Canadian correspondent; Jules DuBois covered Latin America; and Henry Gaggiotini was based in Rome. Don Starr, after serving in Shanghai, returned to Chicago to become cable editor.

Under Maxwell, a former sports editor, the sports area expanded. Following the death of the famed Arch Ward on July 9, 1955, Wilfrid Smith, once a professional football player with the Chicago Cardinals, became editor, heading a staff of 42. It was, said the *Tribune*, the largest sports staff in America, and one of the best. Smith's assistant was George Strickler, a pro football expert who had once served as assistant general manager of the Green Bay Packers. Strickler would succeed Smith and would himself be succeeded by Cooper Rollow.

The shock troops of the editorial department infrequently got their names into the paper, but their work was vital to its success. The 45 photographers were not well known to the public, but they were known to individuals making news. Al Madsen, who in 1954 succeeded Lyman Atwell as chief photographer and director of photography, described his staff: "They must have imagination, think quickly, and plan ahead when possible. They must have courage, for many assignments are dangerous, and they must be able to outsmart criminals intent on avoidance, and officials seeking to interfere with their work." Madsen himself had covered the St. Valentine's Day Massacre and served the army as a motion picture photographer. Tom Johnson and Eugene Powers were Madsen's assistant chief photographers, responsible for many of the assignments and general administration of the department. The *Chicago Tribune* photography department pioneered in color photography for newspaper reproduction. Its color studio, directed by Eddie Johnson, was one of the largest in the country, with Earl Gustie and Ron Bailey as color specialists.

The *Tribune*, describing its staff, referred to its "40 invisible men," the copy editors who safeguarded reporters from error, rendered lax prose succinct and lucid, and wrote headlines intended to summarize the story and win potential readers' attention. Since copyreaders and rewrite men work anonymously, few saw their names in print, though several became editors, such as features editor Blackburn, travel editors Frank Cipriani and Kermit Holt, and Harold Hutchings, who served as city editor and later executive editor.

*   *   *

On October 4, 1957, Russia orbited the satellite Sputnik I around the earth, beginning the space age and sending America into a spasm of self-criticism and investigation of its educational and scientific processes. The *Tribune* was not greatly disturbed: "The U.S. announced first, but Russia did it first, taking propaganda advantage. Yet it cannot be denied that Russia has solved the most pressing of its scientific problems with a speed that is admittedly remarkable. It is a warning to us not to be complacent." On January 31, 1958, four months after Sputnik, the United States launched Explorer I, its first earth satellite, into orbit. The national spirit seemed to lift as well.

Meantime, editor Maxwell continued the fight for the lakefront exhibition hall, and the *Tribune* was battling also, for increased circulation and an even wider margin of domination in the competition for advertising revenues. City editor Furlong and day city editor Kirkpatrick pressed for maximum coverage of city and suburban news. The Furlong–Kirkpatrick staff was tested the afternoon of December 1, 1958, when the worst school fire in Chicago's history occurred. On December 2, the *Tribune* devoted most of eight pages to the tragedy, which took the lives of 53 girls, 34 boys, and three nuns trapped by smoke and flames on the second floor of Our Lady of Angels School. It was a disaster similar to the Iroquois Theater fire, and the reporting basis was the same—page-one prominence of the list of names of 90 dead and 90 injured, with ages and home addresses. The lead story was unsigned, the work of many. Two major side stories, one by Clay Gowran on the grieving parents and relatives awaiting news at the site of the fire, and Robert Wiedrich's description of the charred schoolrooms, where small children were asphyxiated attempting to escape or while huddled at their desks, attested to the poignancy of the event. There were accounts of heroism on the part of nuns, firefighters, and unnamed persons who risked their lives to lead children to safety or caught those who leaped from windows. The fire had started in waste paper at the foot of the stairs leading to the boiler room, it was said. Pictures of the tragic scene appeared on front and back pages of the paper, and individual photos of victims were gathered swiftly from the families involved. As evidence of the improving run-of-paper color technique, a color photograph of the blaze was ready for the late editions. For days the city seemed to slow its frenetic pace to mourn its youthful dead.

The general well-being of Chicago had never seemed better, however, as the business community and the newspapers quickly recognized that in Richard J. Daley they had exactly the kind of mayor a great city needed. Daley brought together business and union leaders, disgruntled partisans, and previously ignored racial and ethnic groups. As the time for his reelection approached, the *Tribune* termed him "an incorruptible man" who could lead all the people. "Mr. Daley runs the whole show," the paper conceded, "bowing to no one but the labor bosses."

The Republicans nominated County Chairman and former Congressman Timothy Sheehan as their token candidate. Some 300 businessmen formed a nonpartisan committee to aid Daley, who appeared to require no aid. On April 5, 1959, the *Tribune* disclosed its views, after giving the mayoral campaign minimum attention. Daley's record was impressive, the paper pointed out: He had seen O'Hare airport through its initial phases and had built the Northwest (later Kennedy) Expressway leading to it; he had made redevelopment of Hyde Park possible; and he had provided improved city services, with only a share of the increased state sales tax to pay for them. As for the Republicans, they faced a dilemma, the *Tribune* said: "Their party has suffered setbacks at the polls and is in danger of being destroyed. . . . The other side is that the Democratic candidate, Richard J. Daley, has a record that deserves respectful consideration—compared to the past, his administration has been almost a paragon of civic righteousness." Mayor Daley was reelected by a majority of 465,000 votes. Only three Republican aldermen remained to rub elbows with the 47 Democrats in the city council.

*   *   *

The paper was covering the news, serializing books, and adding to its features. Mike Kennedy, now the day managing editor, directed the features activity and Stewart Owen was responsible for news, although Don Maxwell himself would work at the "center desk" any day he was in town. The early fall of 1959 lent itself especially to Maxwell's flair for exploitation. When it was announced that Premier Nikita Khrushchev of the USSR was coming to the United States to negotiate with President Eisenhower and to address the United Nations, Maxwell not only prepared for appropriate coverage but he ordered two special series of articles to run during the course of the Communist premier's visit. One, by Chesly Manly, was an extensive biography of Khrushchev, concentrating on the period of his life when he was purging anti-Communists and kulaks in the Ukraine. The series ran through the course of Khrushchev's long stay in September, 1959. "Nikita Makes Good, Becomes Executioner," read one headline over a Manly story; "How Thousands Died as Khrushchev the Executioner Purged the Ukraine," promised another. Larry Rue and Alex Small, both widely traveled in Poland, were commissioned to write another series on Soviet oppression in that unhappy country. If the State Department ever intended to have Khrushchev visit Chicago, the idea was abandoned.

The *Tribune* warned its readers to expect nothing from the Khrushchev visit. "It is foolish to think that men who have spent their whole adult lives in the service of an iron and remorseless doctrine, and by so doing have achieved power and a comfortable life, are amenable to some reform spirit when they breathe the free air of the United States."

Khrushchev was well covered by the *Tribune*. Trohan and Russell Frieburg, later *Tribune* managing editor, reported from Washington that there were some signs of a thaw in the cold war, but that the premier bristled when he was asked questions about Stalin and the Soviets' brutal suppression of the 1956 Hungarian revolt. Joseph Hearst of the Washington bureau accompanied the Russian across country; Seymour Korman soon joined them, and the *Tribune* exulted over stories by the two reporting that labor leaders stood up to Khrushchev, infuriating him. American businessmen should behave as well, the paper said. Back in

New York, after Nikita's trip to an Iowa farm, William Fulton covered him in the United Nations. When the premier visited the Empire State Building, editor Maxwell had a special correspondent ready, his friend Henry Crown, the building's owner. Crown reported that he had given a model of his building to Khrushchev, saying there was no mortgage on it and announcing, "This makes you a capitalist." "I'm with you," Khrushchev answered through an interpreter, and Crown wrote, "I believe I can be the first man to hear him admit to being a capitalist." The incident was played on page one.

Editorially, the *Tribune* allowed that there was some allure in Khrushchev's proposals for total disarmament but asked the question: "Does the USSR intend to withdraw from the satellite countries?" When the Russian leader at last departed, the *Tribune* said: "Khrushchev's visit to America may not have served to educate him, but it should have served to educate the American people."

The paper did not intend to be caught again as it had been in Cuba. Correspondent Jules Dubois had written many favorable dispatches about Fidel Castro during the course of his revolution against the dictatorship of Fulgencio Batista, who resigned on January 1, 1959. But by the time of the Khrushchev visit, both Dubois and the paper's editorialists were describing Castro as a Communist who had betrayed the Cuban people. In Havana the official newspaper printed a cartoon showing Dubois plunging a knife into Castro's back. The *Tribune* took this in good stride:

> Our energetic Latin American correspondent, Jules Dubois, once highly regarded by the Fidel Castro regime in Cuba, now has been downgraded by certain supporters of Mr. Castro to the rank of a bum. Mr. Dubois became known as a hero to the bushy-haired revolutionists while covering their overthrow of the Batista dictatorship. It was his job to cover the news, and he did it well. However, when he continued to do his job by calling attention to some unattractive aspects of the new regime, he was subjected to attacks by pro-Castro elements of press and radio. . . . Mr. Dubois would have to be nuts not to get the hint that he is unwelcome in Cuba.

While the Khrushchev visit, Russian space shots, and congressional hearings on "fixed" television quiz shows were occupying the country generally, Chicago was engrossed in the efforts of the White Sox to win their first American League pennant since the scandal of 1919. The *Tribune* covered the final days of the pennant race with photos and biographies of Sox stars on page one, as well as in the sports section. The Sox succeeded, edging out the New York Yankees and the Cleveland Indians, and on Thursday, October 1, 1959, the first World Series games in Chicago since 1945 opened at Comiskey Park. The entire front page, back page, and page one of Sports were devoted to the Series. Pictures of the wives of Sox players appeared on page one, and Carey Orr's cartoon, showing the White Sox goat butting the Los Angeles Dodgers into oblivion, appeared in the lower right-hand corner of the page. Moving the cartoon from its sacrosanct position near the top of the page seemed a kind of typographical heresy, but it was explained in the paper's editorial: "After forty years of wandering in the wilderness, the White Sox are in a World Series, so that a slight madness afflicts the region." The editorial pointed out that the Los Angeles Dodgers were once Brooklyn's Bums and stated, "The Sox hope to prove that the Dodgers are still bums."

But the Sox lost the Series four games to two, dropping the final game by a score of 9 to 3. The *Tribune*'s editorial on October 10 praised the players for trying, and also praised itself. "The editor of the *Tribune*, having been a sport editor himself, can say that the all-around coverage of this series has been the best in the history of this paper." The editorial appeared well-justified. Ed Prell wrote the lead stories, David Condon, Robert Cromie, and Richard Dozer collaborated on the color, and, while the games were played in Chicago, some of the paper's most skillful reporters, Hal Foust, Robert Wiedrich, George Bliss, and Thomas Powers, aided the sportswriters.

*   *   *

Early in 1960 Sen. John F. Kennedy announced his intention to seek the presidency of the United States. Six days later Vice-President Richard Nixon disclosed a similar ambition. During the winter and spring, "sit-in" civil rights demonstrations began in the South, and a filibuster record of 82 hours three minutes was established in the Senate by anti–civil rights speakers. On May 7 President Eisenhower felt required to accept responsibility for the U-2 plane forced down over the USSR and found to be equipped with intelligence-gathering apparatus. Three days later the U.S.S. *Triton,* a nuclear submarine, circled the globe in 84 days, traveling 41,519 miles, a boost to U.S. prestige. Eisenhower's efforts to achieve a disarmament agreement with the Russians were disrupted by a general worsening of U.S.–Soviet relations crowned by the U-2 embarrassment, and his planned visit to Japan later was canceled by leftist riots.

When the Democratic convention assembled in Los Angeles in July, the *Tribune* had a veteran staff on the scene, editor Maxwell, Trohan, Tagge, Edwards, Robert Howard, Korman, Hearst, and Harold Hutchings. The paper denounced the convention's civil rights plank as "the same old stuff, an exercise in insincerity." "The Democratic platform is the most radical this country has ever seen. It exceeds anything by

Truman or Roosevelt and represents an all-out program of federal beneficences for almost everybody, federal intrusion into every concern of the people, and federal control of those things which so far have escaped government control. It presents a magnificent opportunity for the Republicans."

After Senator Kennedy was nominated on July 13 on the first ballot and made his acceptance speech, the *Tribune* said disparagingly: "The Democratic medicine men always have a 'new' something to explain their ambition to reside in the White House. With Wilson it was the 'new freedom,' with Franklin Roosevelt, 'the new deal.' Now John F. Kennedy introduces 'the new frontier.' He sought to strike an epic note and failed."

On July 10, 1960, Chesser M. Campbell, president of Tribune Company and publisher of the *Tribune*, died of a heart attack at the company's lodge near Baie Comeau. Editor Maxwell was summoned from the Democratic convention by the news, and directors and company officials gathered in Chicago for the funeral. Campbell had served Tribune Company as chief executive officer for only five years, but excellent progress had been made under his direction, both in the United States and Canada, where the development of the aluminum production facility with British partners was a major expansion achievement. Campbell had been most pleased, however, with his accomplishments in improving the Tribune Company pension system, initiating a stock incentive program, and creating the Chicago Tribune–New York News Employees Trust. The trust enabled employees of the two newspapers to share in the profits via a retirement fund, the employees' share being invested in bonds and equities, mostly Tribune Company stock when it could be acquired.

At a special meeting of the directors, Howard Wood was named president and chief executive officer. He had warned that he would not take the job unless the uneasy truce between New York and Chicago interests became an actual peace, and this condition was promptly accepted by the directors and major stockholders. Maxwell was elected first vice-president; Harold Grumhaus, newly appointed the *Tribune*'s business manager, and advertising manager Walter Kurz were elected vice-presidents. Stewart Owen succeeded Campbell as a trustee of the McCormick–Patterson Trust, and Grumhaus succeeded him as a trustee of the McCormick Charitable Trust.

President Wood, who also assumed the post of *Tribune* publisher, directed the attention of his staff toward an expansion and diversification program to employ growing company reserves to strengthen operation facilities, develop existing subsidiaries, and undertake acquisitions. Wood also authorized Grumhaus, his chief aide in all business and production areas, to undertake studies Grumhaus had proposed to provide for the modernization and reorganization of Tribune Company.

Maxwell turned to coverage of the 1960 Republican convention in Chicago. There were few problems. The Republican platform was satisfactory, as was the choice of Nixon as nominee for president on the first ballot. Nixon, meeting in caucus with 32 Republican leaders, proposed U.N. Ambassador Henry Cabot Lodge for vice-president, a choice pleasing to the *Tribune*, which said in commenting on the acceptance speeches: "Mr. Lodge was better than good. Mr. Nixon was outstanding. We say this although we cannot wholly share his ideas of how America should save the world and we are skeptical of his ability to institute many of the social services that he talked about without bringing on inflation." Nevertheless, after having discoursed on the alternatives, the paper insisted, "The Republicans are off to a good start."

The paper gave extensive coverage to both candidates, Joseph Hearst traveling with Kennedy and Willard Edwards with his old friend Nixon. The *Tribune* was firmly against Kennedy for president, and against Illinois Democratic candidates Otto Kerner for governor and Paul A. Douglas for U.S. senator. All three, said the paper, earnestly desired more government, which would mean less liberty for the people, greater spending, and higher taxes. Kennedy especially aroused *Tribune* ire with his foreign policy statements, which proposed to give the Chinese islands of Quemoy and Matsu to the Chinese Communists, criticized President Eisenhower for refusing to apologize to the Russians in the U-2 affair, and described U.S. action against Castro as "too little, too late." The *Tribune* responded that the embargo against Cuba instituted on October 20 was the most that could be accomplished "without dismaying our allies." The paper charged that Kennedy wanted "to openly support anti-Castro forces both inside and outside Cuba." This, it added, "would be in violation of five treaties. . . . The embargo will work only if other American nations will cooperate." It warned Democrats not to assume a smug "I told you so" position on Cuba, lost, at least for the time, to Communism: "The Democrats have lost to Communism half of Korea, half of Germany, Poland, Hungary, Czechoslovakia, Bulgaria, Rumania, Latvia and Estonia, not to mention Gen. Marshall's mission to China." On October 27, the *Tribune* said succinctly, "Kennedy says he will defend the dollar. . . . We wish we could believe his forthright statement but it simply cannot be reconciled with the rest of Kennedy's program."

When Kennedy ended his campaign with a rally in Chicago, the paper devoted an eight-column banner to the upcoming meeting, which attracted 25,000 to Chicago Stadium that night. No Democrat was long beguiled by such kind treatment for the party's candidate, however, since the day following Kennedy's triumphant visit to Chicago, the *Tribune* scoffed:

> Perhaps the biggest fake in the Kennedy campaign, which has been almost all fake, is that America for the past eight years has been "standing still," and that only Jack can "get it moving again." For the record, since 1953, personal income has gone up 48 percent, school classroom construction, up 46 percent, college enrollment, up 75 percent . . . capital expenditures for plants have totaled more in the last 7½ years than in the previous thirty years. The gross national product is up 45 percent, a national system of highways is under construction, we have seen the completion of the St. Lawrence seaway, and inflation, once at a gallop, has been slowed to a hobble. . . . We don't know what makes Jackie run, and particularly to run backwards.

On Monday, November 7, the paper, which had not been especially articulate about the merits of Nixon other than to assert that he would carry out Eisenhower policies and to praise his attacks on Kennedy, urged its readers to vote the straight Republican ticket. "Tomorrow is your day, when you can show that you are a free man or woman, that you value your freedom, and that you mean to do all in your power to retain it for yourself and those who come after you. . . . A vote for Nixon is a vote for liberty."

Kennedy, Douglas, and Kerner carried Illinois, the president-elect by 8,858, less than one vote per precinct, votes the *Tribune* later asserted had been stolen by the Democratic machine; Douglas led the ticket. The paper congratulated Kerner, saying that his worst handicap was his close association with the Chicago machine, plus the fact that Republicans would continue to control both houses of the legislature. As for President-elect Kennedy: "We will not pretend to be overjoyed by the outcome. We are disappointed, and so, too, are just short of half the men and women who went to the polls on Tuesday. They thought Nixon would make a better president. They preferred his ideas or his record or both. But they were out-voted and they now accept the verdict. So do we."

*   *   *

Editor Maxwell, a naturally optimistic and ebullient man, did not let the Nixon defeat or Republican city politics depress him for long. The $35 million convention center he almost personally had created was at last ready for opening to the public. Its name, McCormick Place. The dedication ceremonies for 500 invited guests, including Chicago political and business leaders and 55 editors from over the United States, took place the night of November 18, 1960, in one of the large banquet halls of the new center. Chesly Manly wrote the lead story: "McCormick Place,

Chicago's 35 million dollar lakefront exposition center and convention hall, last night was dedicated to freedom and individual enterprise—the spirit of Chicago." Nearly five *Tribune* pages were devoted to descriptions of McCormick Place, which opened with a 16-day run of the Home and Flower Show.

McCormick Place was soon found to be far too small for the country's larger trade shows and the International Trade Fair held each summer, but that difficulty was solved after the structure burned almost to the ground on January 16, 1967. The *Tribune*'s campaign to build a bigger and better McCormick Place started at once, with Maxwell in charge, aided now by Ed Lee, McCormick Place manager. By 1971 the new center was finished, except for landscaping—a huge exhibition hall and theater complex, 1,360 feet long by 610 feet wide, as compared with the original's 1,095 by 345 feet, a long, low spread of steel and glass that some architects approved as exemplifying the spirit of Ludwig Mies van der Rohe. The cost, an additional $75 million. Said the *Tribune*:

> The new McCormick Place provides 522,000 square feet of exhibition space, has eight restaurants, five theaters and sits under a 10,500 ton roof spanning 18 acres. Computers monitor room temperatures, 24 remote control cameras monitor crowds and guards, some 33,000 electric lights are used, and the building is considered to be fire-proof. The largest hall [*named Don Maxwell Hall*] is 720 feet long by 420 feet wide, with a 50 foot high ceiling resting on eight cruciform columns 150 feet apart. The hall has 32 truck docks and 43 freight doors, and the floor is built to carry a weight of 400 pounds per square foot, sufficient to support the heaviest army tanks made, should a military show be desired.

Editor Maxwell, following his retirement, pronounced McCormick Place his best journalistic achievement, "bringing business to Chicago, providing thousands of jobs, and costing taxpayers not one cent."

*   *   *

On January 20, 1961, Eisenhower stepped down from the presidency, warning his fellow citizens against the creation of a vast military-industrial establishment. But he left behind a hefty budget, which caused the *Tribune* to exclaim angrily: "We have often asked, where is there a party to which the sober majority of the American people can turn for fiscal sanity and conservative example? It is certainly not the Democrats, and now neither is it the Republicans."

President Kennedy immediately came under attack when he presented a welter of measures to the Congress, covering domestic and foreign matters, all promising great expense, during his first 90 days in office. Said the paper on Kennedy's trimester:

> Today is President Kennedy's 90th day as President . . . he predicted the
> first three months of his term of office would be most important. His
> program to build national defense, to "launch an all-out attack on poverty,"
> compares, but not favorably, to President Roosevelt's 100 days.
>
> Mr. Kennedy has rained a bewildering series of messages and requests
> upon Congress, and the Roosevelt confusion looks almost orderly com-
> pared to the haphazard selection of things to be done. He has made stabs at
> defense, foreign aid and anti-recession measures, but their wisdom and
> necessity are equally subject to question.

The paper scored Kennedy for calling on business to increase investment
in plants to create more jobs while, at the same time, he demanded
increased taxes on investment capital. He was criticized for seeking to
control or censor the press, and his proposal for billions to aid Central
and South American nations was called "pounding money down a rat
hole."

The paper also scoffed at Kennedy's assertion that the United States
should be first on the moon and warned once more against efforts in
Laos, involvement in Cuba, and entanglement with the USSR: "It does
not take a Soviet astronaut whirling in space, or the muddy situation in
Cuba, or a cocky Khrushchev, or a Laos to emphasize the vanity of words.
Ninety days has been ninety days, and nothing more. No miracle has been
passed."

But when foreign crises flared, the *Tribune* firmly backed the president. Russia accused the United States of aiding a Cuban invasion
buildup in Central America. On April 18, 1961, Kennedy told the USSR
to mind its own business, and the *Tribune* clucked approvingly: "President
Kennedy's note to Premier Khrushchev was right in content and right in
tone. If Khrushchev thought he could get away with something in Cuba,
he now knows better. We are not guilty of aggression in Cuba, but he
is." Ambassador to the United Nations Adlai Stevenson was praised for
detailing the Russian supplies sent to Cuba, including military tanks. On
April 20, the paper's banner announced the Bay of Pigs debacle: "IN-
VASION CRUSHED: CASTRO." Even so, the paper did not criticize
President Kennedy, possibly because Kennedy, in a shaken press conference appearance, and before a convention of the nation's editors, made it
clear that he blamed himself for the failure of U.S.-supported anti-Castro
rebels to gain a foothold in Cuba.

On August 27, the paper carried the news of the president's "shoot if
necessary" order to the American force in West Berlin. Clay Gowran, in
Chicago, wrote a detailed analysis of the Berlin crisis, asserting it was
triggered by the Khrushchev–Kennedy meeting that had taken place in
Vienna in June. Editorially, the *Tribune* said that Roosevelt and Truman

were really responsible, since each had caved in before Stalin, Roosevelt at Yalta and Truman at Potsdam.

The Congress did not appear unusually fearful of the Russian threat. It accepted Kennedy's "man on the moon" proposal, and appropriated $549 million to get it started. Kennedy himself, after lecturing on "brush-fire wars" in lieu of nuclear confrontation, stepped up aid to South Vietnam and ordered the training of an elite corps of guerrilla fighters, called "the Green Berets."

*   *   *

Chicago, meantime, was seeing at last the denouement of the worst police scandal in the city's history. It had begun the night of July 31, 1959, when Evanston police captured a slight, boastful burglar, who insisted he was the greatest ever to operate in Chicago. He had overestimated the Chicago city limits, evidently, and was handed over to State's Attorney Benjamin Adamowski, once a Democrat, but now a Republican and a fervent enemy of Richard J. Daley. Richard Morrison, the babbling burglar, talked. The *Tribune* assigned one of its aces, Bob Wiedrich, to the story, which unfolded in fantastic episodes. Briefly, Morrison told Adamowski's aides that he had a partnership arrangement with the police in Chicago's Summerdale station on the city's North Side. It began when an officer at the station who knew Morrison to be a burglar arranged to have him steal a set of golf clubs the policeman coveted. Soon Morrison was meeting secretly almost every day with members of the force from Summerdale to take their orders for merchandise to be stolen that night, with police protection.

The story seemed incredible, but it checked out. It would never have been known, Wiedrich wrote, if Chicago police had arrested Morrison, because "Chicago police protect their own." At the same time he suggested that there were thousands of honest police officers who suffered, with their families, because of the Summerdale evils. Lie tests were ordered, and Adamowski prepared to seek grand jury indictments. The *Tribune* pointed out that the Summerdale scandal, revolting though it was, represented only a part of Chicago police venality. "Big time gangsters pay off the police regularly," the paper said. "The *Tribune* has been revealing this since 1953." Actually, the paper had been revealing such payoffs more or less regularly since 1919, and there was much evidence of police-criminal alliances back in the 1880s. "The syndicate payoffs were big time—not connected with some punk burglar," the editorial said.

It was Morrison, the punk burglar, however, who precipitated a major reorganization of the Chicago Police Department. Police Commissioner

Timothy J. O'Connor resigned under fire, and Mayor Daley appointed a committee to select a new police superintendent. The panel first recruited Professor Orlando W. Wilson, a tall, gaunt, quiet-spoken professor of criminology at the University of California, to act as chairman. After months of searching through the United States for a superintendent, the panel members concluded that the job should go to Wilson himself. He was appointed by Mayor Daley on February 22, 1960. Superintendent Wilson, a favorite of the press, shook up police personnel and updated department methods, especially its communication system. When he retired in 1967, he named James B. Conlisk, son of a police officer, as his successor. Only five Summerdale policemen were convicted in the celebrated case, after a trial lasting 57 days. They were sentenced to five years in prison and the convictions were upheld in the Illinois Supreme Court. One officer who pleaded guilty was sentenced to six months, and two others were fined. Morrison, a state's witness, was allowed to leave Illinois.

Wiedrich and other *Tribune* staffers might have won Pulitzer prizes for their journalism, but for many years it had not been the custom of the paper to submit the work of its reporters and writers in "outside" contests. Maxwell decided to change that policy. In 1961, he ordered editorial submissions and Carey Orr won the paper's first Pulitzer since 1936, for his editorial cartoons. In 1962, George Bliss, investigative reporter, won for his exposure of scandals in the Chicago Sanitary District.

*　　*　　*

On Tuesday, October 23, 1962, the *Tribune* told its readers what they had learned the previous night, that the nation appeared again on the brink of war: "QUARANTINE OF CUBA ON! KENNEDY TAKES SEVEN STEPS." Sublines read: "Navy Ready to Sink Red Arms Ships. Russians Held Responsible for Any Aggression." The crisis epitomized the new, tenuous way of life for the American people. Nuclear war was a genuine possibility. The United States could preserve the freedom of the Americas from imminent threat only by its ability and readiness to bring massive power to bear. American intelligence had found Russian missile launchers being erected in Cuba, and the United States and the Soviet Union were finally "eyeball to eyeball," the ultimate confrontation in the prolonged war of nerves.

The people received the news directly from President Kennedy by radio and television the evening of October 22. It was a dramatic example of the way the role of the newspaper had been changed, as many journalists had foreseen for some time. Being first no longer sufficed, nor was it possible when news could be scheduled by the newsmakers. But the role of the newspaper in clarifying a situation and placing it in historical perspective had not changed. That the *Tribune* and other papers were aware in advance of the nature of the emergency—which had called President Kennedy away from Chicago over the weekend, with a story of illness fabricated to explain his sudden departure—was indicated by the depth of their coverage on the 23rd as well as by the *Tribune*'s pre-prepared color map showing the strategic situation. But no newspaper had betrayed the president's secret.

The *Tribune* published the text of Kennedy's address to the nation, and WGN rebroadcast his words throughout the night. Laurence Burd wrote the lead story from Washington, and Philip Dodd a color story, which stated, "The calmest man in the White House is President Kennedy." Four extra pages were allotted to the news department for the story. Said the *Tribune*'s editorial:

> The President has spoken with firmness that can leave no doubt in the minds of Americans, Russians or anyone else about our government's intentions.
>
> The United States is going to stand for no more threats from Cuba. We are not going to let Cuba have arms which menace us, or our neighbors.
>
> The President can count on the support of a united people.
>
> President Kennedy made it clear that if the Russians want war they can have it. We intend to halt the buildup of offensive weapons in Cuba and we intend to use whatever force may be needed to make our will effective. We invite the cooperation of the UN and the Organization of American States, but, whether we get it or not, our course is set.
>
> Most Americans believe that the President's stern declaration should have come sooner, before the military buildup in Cuba got under way. The risks then would be less. Russia would not be challenged to reverse a policy upon which she is fully embarked. . . .
>
> In effect, Mr. Kennedy has once again established the Monroe Doctrine as American policy. Whether we shall have allies or not, we are now wholly committed to stopping the advance of Russian militarism in our hemisphere. Now that ours is, in many respects, the strongest nation in the world, we may hope to be equally successful in achieving our ends without bloodshed. But the risk is real, and great, and there is now no turning back.

The caveat, "Most Americans believe that the President's stern declaration should have come sooner," was followed by *Tribune* criticism of the denouement of the missile crisis, committing the United States to refrain from action against Cuba in the future, and complete dissatisfaction with Kennedy's treatment of the Communist threat generally. The president visited Germany in June, 1963; at Frankfurt he said Americans would risk their cities to save their allies from nuclear attack, and, after seven and a half hours in West Berlin, where he viewed the wall, he exclaimed in high emotion, "Ich bin ein Berliner." The *Tribune* was scornful: "Who, in Europe, would believe Kennedy's bluster against Communism when he does nothing to check Communism in the Americas? Mr. Kennedy may think he's putting up a bold front . . . but Europeans who look over his shoulder and observe the calamities building up in America because of his timidity and inaction will not be taken in." Then, three days later, a considered blast at Kennedy's pledge of all-out support to Europe:

> President Kennedy's blanket pact to the Atlantic allies, "The United States will risk its cities to defend yours," assumes in behalf of his countrymen a willingness to expose them to nuclear attack. The President has spoken in his own authority and we have questioned his assumption that he is equipped with some sort of mandate to engage in any such sweeping undertaking. . . . Mr. Kennedy has asserted a personal initiative as President which is constitutionally beyond his power. . . . Congress and the people should call him to account.

*　　*　　*

By 1961 Maxwell had put his own stamp on the *Tribune*, though he did not alter the McCormick political policy. He at last accepted the title of editor, made Stewart Owen managing editor, in which capacity Owen had been serving for almost six years, and introduced a series of political columns from Washington and Springfield. Letters from correspondents appeared under fixed, hooded headlines, usually on Sunday. The "Editor's Digest of the News," set in 10 point type, was given prominence on page one or page two. The inspirational message on Sundays by Dr. Harold Blake Walker became a daily feature. Owen, on the firing line for the news department as Maxwell increasingly traveled, initiated features also, including a "Voice of Youth" column, inviting participation by the young people of the *Tribune* circulation area. Contributors attended an annual dinner and young people generally were shown more attention than the *Tribune* had previously bestowed.

Editor Maxwell invited New York bureau chief Harold Hutchings to return to Chicago as business editor in March, 1962, joining financial editor William Clark in directing business news coverage. Maxwell contemplated special business reports on Sundays, and Hutchings was placed in charge of a section called "Spotlight on the World," which was initially business-oriented but soon expanded its coverage, receiving the subline "News and What's Behind It." By the time Hutchings was appointed city editor in 1963, "Spotlight on the World" filled much of three pages each Sunday with a wide variety of in-depth reports on foreign and national news, plus abbreviated features. The world news roundup eventually was modified to become the *Tribune*'s "Perspective" section of columns and comment.

In November, 1962, Howard Wood announced that the paper had

contracted with the Goss Company to purchase a block-long line of new presses at a cost of $7,200,000. The new presses were designed to print 56-page papers at the rate of 70,000 an hour; they would print in four colors, could print 112-page papers at lesser speeds, and were designed to print tabloid sections. In making the announcement, Wood noted that since 1954 the *Tribune* had spent $4,500,000 on improving its press lines, giving the paper "the largest pressroom and one of the most modern in the world." The new presses, Wood pointed out, would serve both the *Tribune* and the *American*, which, with the *New York News,* consumed 496,000 tons of newsprint annually, 85 percent manufactured in the company's own plants in Canada. Most of the output of the Baie Comeau mill went to the *News*, that of the Thorold plant to the *Tribune* and the *American*.

The *Tribune*'s vast pressroom and production facility, under the supervision of production manager Dick Gossett, covered a square block with 133 black press units, 24 color units, 24 folders, and 16 color comic press units. Grumhaus, Gossett, and assistant production manager Stanton Cook, together with Fred Paul, *Tribune* mechanical superintendent, were constantly involved in planning, installing, and maintaining the equipment, which published morning and afternoon papers six days a week and two separate papers on Sunday. Eight ships and sometimes railroad cars carried paper to Chicago, 84 Linotype and 29 Intertype machines cast the type, and new dataspeed equipment received market dispatches from New York at a speed of 1,050 words a minute.

While the new presses were being built, the installation of a paper-making machine was in progress in Baie Comeau; it cost almost double the planned $16 million expense and proved inadequate for the ravenous presses in Chicago and New York before it was months old. A fourth machine, costing $70 million, was authorized, with a target completion date of 1971.

At the same time, Jack Flynn, president and chief executive officer of the *New York News,* and Fred Nichols, assistant to Wood, had been representing Tribune Company in searching for newspaper properties, and in June, 1963, an excellent acquisition was made: the Gore Newspapers Company in Fort Lauderdale, Florida, publisher of the *Fort Lauderdale News* and the *Pompano Sun-Sentinel*, purchased from Robert A. Gore for $18 million. Meantime, in New York in October, 1963, the *New York Mirror,* second in the country in circulation only to the *New York News,* collapsed for lack of advertising revenues. The *News* acquired certain of the *Mirror*'s assets for $8 million, and property was purchased for growth in both Chicago and New York. Other acquisitions soon followed. In August, 1965, the Sentinel Star Company in Orlando, Florida, was bought from Martin Anderson for $23,424,000, plus $1,215,000 for the properties of a Sentinel Star trucking subsidiary. The Orlando transaction was concluded shortly before Walt Disney Enterprises announced the selection of Orlando as the site for construction of Disney World, boosting the economy of an already flourishing area. The New York and Florida purchases and others to follow were consummated largely out of Tribune Company reserves and cash flow, only limited short-term loans being required, and no Tribune Company stock involved. Part of the costs were paid by a $4,400,000 profit from the British-Canadian Aluminium venture initiated by Campbell and completed by Wood.

Nichols became chairman of the board and chief executive officer of the Gore and Sentinel Star companies, which soon posted their leading papers, the *Fort Lauderdale News* and the *Orlando Sentinel*, among the top ten in their respective evening and morning fields in total advertising linage. Later the *Sentinel* absorbed the evening *Star* and became a 24-hour paper. Both the *News* and the *Sentinel-Star* continued their prospering Sunday editions. The next major purchases, made in California in the 1970s, were the *Valley News,* based in Van Nuys and serving the San Fernando Valley, and the *Times-Advocate* of Escondido.

*   *   *

On Thursday, November 21, 1963, Robert Young, traveling with President Kennedy in Texas, had a page-one story on the political troubles assailing the young leader in the Lone Star state. The following day Kennedy would be in Dallas, where Texas Gov. John B. Connally was doing what he could to help the president to close the Democratic rift. At 12:30 P.M. on the 22nd, as President Kennedy, his wife, and Governor Connally rode together in a motorcade through Dallas, sounds of gunfire were heard when the procession passed the Texas School Book Depository. Minutes later there were wire service flashes in the newsrooms of the *Tribune* and its sister paper, the afternoon *American*, both now published in the *Tribune* plant. "THREE SHOTS FIRED AT KENNEDY," said the flash. Luke Carroll, managing editor of the *American*, was eating his lunch at the center desk of the *American* newsroom. He at once alerted his news staff. The *Tribune* production force was advised, and, after confirmation that President Kennedy had been killed, the *American* was first in Chicago on the street.

The following morning the *Tribune* itself devoted almost half the paper to the tragedy: "ASSASSIN KILLS KENNEDY. LYNDON JOHNSON SWORN IN." Young wrote the lead story, and the paper's veteran Wayne Thomis, who did not leave Chicago until mid-afternoon Friday, sent a side story from Dallas on the arrest of the man thought to have slain the president and wounded Governor Connally. It was dated

Saturday and began: "Lee Harvey Oswald, a professed Marxist and Castro follower, was charged late last night with the murder of President Kennedy." Philip Dodd covered President Johnson as he arrived in Washington, and Louise Hutchinson wrote of the arrival of Jacqueline Kennedy, widow of the slain president.

The *Tribune* followed the old custom of turning the rules to frame its columns with black mourning lines on page one. Its editorial, "A Nation Mourns," appeared on page three, saying in part: "The tremendous tragedy that has taken Mr. Kennedy in the vigor of his 47th year will have incalculable effects on the immediate future of this country." Johnson, the editorial pointed out, was known to be "an effective political organizer," but his ability to deal with the problems of international relations was "unknown and unproved." There were stories from the paper's foreign bureaus, including one of 60,000 Berliners standing in silence as bells tolled, and Chicago side stories of Mayor Daley weeping at the news of the death of the young president, the city churches packed with mourners, Chicago stunned.

On Sunday, the 24th, the first 14 pages of the paper were almost entirely concerned with the death of President Kennedy, but the editorials were those planned before news of the assassination was received: support for the request of Police Superintendent Orlando Wilson for the funds to run his department, with Wilson candidly admitting that his changes in the department so far had done little to reduce crime; and comment on the formation of Transkei as an independent black state by South Africa, predicting, "A new and explosive element has been injected into the organization of Black Africa."

*   *   *

From the beginning, the *Tribune* did not want the United States to become involved in Southeast Asia. Its editorials had spoken against aid to the French in Indochina before the fall of French power in 1954. In 1952, Colonel McCormick, writing on the subject of foreign policy, had denounced American assistance to interventionists in Indochina: "The United States bears about one-third of the cost of military operations to suppress the people fighting for their freedom there. Fourteen thousand transport and combat vehicles; 228 military planes; 235 naval units; 880 radios; 85,000 small arms and automatic weapons, and 90 million rounds of ammunition, plus mines, mortars, rockets, bombs and other equipment have been delivered." Thus McCormick, criticized as an ultrarightist, was saying in 1952 what millions of liberal and centrist Americans would be saying about Vietnam in 1968.

The paper's stance remained much the same in the years following the

Colonel's death. When, in March, 1964, Secretary of Defense Robert McNamara and Gen. Maxwell Taylor, chief of staff, brought back reports belying the White House view that the war in Vietnam was going well, the *Tribune* commented acidly: "The White House still hits the optimistic note that the situation is not so bad that more dollars won't cure it." Next, the paper predicted, would be a play by the administration to "pass the buck to its man in Saigon, who is being talked up as the Republican candidate for President." The *Tribune* was referring to Ambassador Henry Cabot Lodge and let it be known that it was implacably opposed to his nomination. It demanded to know why, if Americans in Vietnam were simply advisers and trainers, some were getting killed. It estimated that the United States had 15,500 men on such duty. In June, 1964, Philip Dodd wrote a series of articles on the Vietnam War to respond to some of the *Tribune* questions. On June 15, the paper harshly criticized President Johnson for escalating the war: "Some of the truth about Viet Nam is finally getting through despite government attempts to manage the news in Viet Nam and Laos." It drew a distinction between government dispatches and its own reports by Dodd. Then, looking ahead to the fall campaign, it added: "The main concern of Lyndon Johnson in Southeast Asia from now until November is not to win a war, reverse the Communist tide, or to save American lives. It is to save the political skin of Lyndon Johnson."

In early July, 1964, editor Don Maxwell led a staff of 12 to San Francisco, including the new chief of the editorial page, George Morgenstern, to cover the Republican National Convention and to make certain that Sen. Barry Goldwater of Arizona would be the presidential nominee. Others in the traveling staff included Clayton Kirkpatrick, who had been made assistant managing editor in 1963, political editor Tagge, Washington bureau chief Trohan, U.N. correspondent Fulton, and West Coast correspondent Korman. A series of *Tribune* editorials had predicted that new leaders of the Midwest and West were about to wrest power from the Eastern kingmakers who had dominated and ruined the party. The fervor of the *Tribune* matched that of past days when Joseph Medill and his friends captured a convention for Lincoln and when Colonel McCormick did the same in the Landon era. Domination of the platform was the first objective, and parts seemed written to the *Tribune*'s order: The platform rejected the idea that the USSR had abandoned its plan for world domination; it opposed recognition of Red China; it called for eventual liberation of the nations held captive by the USSR; it vowed support for NATO; it pledged support to the SEATO nations in the Pacific; it demanded that the Berlin wall come down before there would be any negotiations on the status of Berlin with the Soviets; and it stated,

"We will move decisively to assure a victory in South Viet Nam."

The Vietnam statement reflected the *Tribune*'s view that, since we were in Vietnam, we should win and get out. Despite its long opposition to foreign involvement, the paper accepted the Republican document, stating, "The platform is one that Mr. Goldwater can accept, and it is one to which all Republicans can subscribe. It offers the springboard for a fighting campaign, and that is what Mr. Goldwater will provide." Senator Goldwater was nominated on July 15 on the first ballot, moving the *Tribune* to publish, in addition to its top banner—"IT'S BARRY ON THE 1ST BALLOT!"—a second, "HE'LL CARRY BANNER FOR GRAND OLD PARTY." Said Trohan's leading story, "Senator Barry M. Goldwater and Rep. William E. Miller (N.Y.), the Republican candidates, opened their crusade to keep America free in ringing acceptance speeches here tonight." The paper's editorial was headlined "Revolt of the People." It said:

> The "liberals" and lachrymose elements of the crape-hanging press can't reconcile themselves to the fact that the people have at last taken over the Republican party. They continue assuring themselves to the end that some vast plot has been unfolding here, and that a devil with horns in the person of Barry Goldwater has risen in a cloud of fire and brimstone to disestablish the old order and replace it with a cult of demonology.

The *Tribune* insisted that the elderly, the college generation, and people of every segment of the electorate had "enlisted for the duration" to elect Goldwater.

On August 2 and 4, two American destroyers were reportedly attacked by North Vietnamese torpedo boats in the Gulf of Tonkin. In response, on August 7 Congress passed the Gulf of Tonkin Resolution, which in effect gave the president a blank check by empowering him to take whatever action he deemed necessary in Vietnam "to repel any armed attack against the forces of the United States and to prevent further aggression." When the Democrats met in convention at the end of the month, their presidential candidate was, of course, Lyndon Baines Johnson, who hearkened to the pleas of Sen. Hubert H. Humphrey of Minnesota to be his running mate. The *Tribune* accused Johnson of "foreign policy inaction, dissimulation, expediency, Roman circuses following the wasteful 'New Frontier,'" and "a disarmament policy which will reduce us to a second class nation. . . . Our embassies are wrecked and burned, our flag is trampled, there is a corruption of morals in every city, the free press is under attack." Johnson and Humphrey were nevertheless elected in a landslide, 486 electoral votes to 52 for Goldwater and Miller, who carried only six states.

So the attacks on Johnson continued, and now the *Tribune* could return to its policy of opposing the Vietnam involvement. Said the paper on February 13, 1965:

> Woodrow Wilson won reelection with the slogan, "He kept us out of war." Franklin D. Roosevelt campaigned for a third term in 1940, promising, "Your sons are never going into any foreign wars." Harry Truman professed to like "Good Old Joe Stalin," but two years later we were fighting in Korea. Johnson claims to be a man of peace, but is embroiled in an undeclared but extending war, and can hardly pretend he is keeping us out of anything.

On the same day, Premier Aleksei N. Kosygin of the USSR declared that "imperialist provocations in Viet Nam" had brought the Soviet Union close to Red China, and it was reported also that Red Chinese troops were crossing into Vietnam. Both reports were exaggerations; the USSR was a rival of Red China in Vietnam, and few Chinese troops crossed over. But both nations provided aid to the Communist North, and Red China sent in thousands of workers to assist the war effort. Meantime, U.S. planes bombed North Vietnamese forces in retaliation for their attack on the American training base at Pleiku. On June 8, the president committed U.S. ground forces to South Vietnam, which almost had been cut in two along a line running through Pleiku. Foreign relations in the Western Hemisphere had not been going well, either. In April, the president had violated agreements with the Organization of American States by sending U.S. troops to quell a rebellion in the Dominican Republic (Santo Domingo).

The news at home had been getting equally grim. The *Tribune*'s assessment of the Supreme Court's desegregation rulings proved to be overly optimistic. In Washington, D.C., on August 28, 1963, Dr. Martin Luther King, Jr., stirred 200,000 supporters of black civil rights with his "I have a dream" speech. But there were nightmarish times ahead. In February, 1965, Dr. King and over 700 others were arrested in Selma, Alabama, while demonstrating against voter registration restrictions. The following month President Johnson sent federal troops to protect a freedom march from Selma to Montgomery, Alabama. Tensions in the South and elsewhere across the nation continued to heat up with the weather; they exploded in rioting in the Watts section of Los Angeles from August 11 to August 16. This period saw the beginning of the youth revolt, the uprising of young people on college campuses from California to the East Coast, and the total turnoff of vast numbers of young Americans who escaped to communes, drugs, offbeat religions and cults, and generally exhibited behavior calculated to outrage their elders. Increasingly, the focal point of the youth revolt was Vietnam, yet, in his

State of the Union message in 1966, President Johnson insisted that the United States would remain in Vietnam as long as aggression continued. Within 11 months, U.S. forces involved there totaled 380,000.

The *Tribune* covered the news and sought to win readers despite the ominous daily reports. On March 1, 1965, managing editor Stewart Owen retired, though he would continue to be a trustee of the McCormick–Patterson Trust and McCormick Charitable Trust until his death in 1970. Clayton Kirkpatrick succeeded Owen as managing editor. In June, 1965, a special section for women readers, urged by Maxwell and devised by Sunday editor Walter Simmons, made its bow as a regular Monday feature, "Feminique." Its wide columns and "rocket" headlines (displaying the lead words of an article in headline type, descending in size to the body type) introduced an entirely new format in the *Tribune*. "Feminique," edited by Marilyn Traum, presented beautiful fashions and models in color and monotone as well as women's interest news. It was an immediate and continuing success with readers and advertisers. Later in the year, its six-column format, but with standard headlines, was introduced to the news pages when a new Sunday real estate page was set in that style. In January, 1966, the daily New York stock exchange table was expanded, adding the year's highs and lows for each stock. On May 19, the paper introduced its "Action Express" column, a consumer service feature.

Book promotions continued to please readers. *The Spy Who Came in from the Cold* by John le Carré was, according to Maxwell, the most successful of his serializations, actually reflecting a circulation upturn. Another success was *A Kind of Anger,* a suspense novel by Eric Ambler. There were new editorial approaches toward coverage of the news, but generally the staples continued—the editor's notebook, the political columns, with Herb Lyon's personality column providing relief, along with the comics. A new column, "Maybe the Week Will Get Better," by an Elmer Muffwinkel, was introduced, but it soon disappeared.

Despite attempts at levity, the view from Tribune Tower was mostly grim. Mayor Daley was acceptable as a leader in Chicago, and Gov. Otto Kerner was tolerable in Illinois, but the Republican outlook was not hopeful. Senatorial candidate Charles H. Percy was by no means a Maxwell choice; Maxwell had encouraged Attorney General William Scott to campaign against Percy in the primary, but Scott, an excellent vote getter as attorney general, had lost. However, Maxwell took solace in Percy's unseating of three-term liberal Democrat Sen. Paul Douglas, a longtime target of *Tribune* criticism. In other parts of the country, there was no brighter side. Riots in Newark and Detroit during July, 1967, caused over 60 deaths, 3,000 injuries, and 3,000 arrests, and left 5,000 homeless from nearly two weeks of burning and looting.

In spite of all the trouble, the *Tribune* tried to strike a constructive note. The paper was publishing one of its most searching and complete series of ecological articles, a study of the pollution of the Great Lakes. Maps and photographs identified those individuals and companies responsible, and interviews with environmentalists suggested solutions. Symbolizing the "Save Our Lake" campaign was a dramatic photograph of a hand emerging from Lake Michigan dripping with muck, illustrating the kind of waste found in the area of steel mill discharges at the lake's southern end. The series was directed by Thomas Moore, who succeeded Kirkpatrick as managing editor on January 1, 1968, and written by Casey Bukro and William Jones. The "Save Our Lake" campaign resulted in the convocation of officials of the Great Lakes states in Chicago in February, 1968. Other newspapers began similar drives, and the *Tribune*'s reprinted series was widely used by ecological groups. Bukro became one of the first reporters to devote his full time to environmental subjects.

Also in February, 1968, the U.S. Riot Commission Report, called the Kerner Report since Illinois's governor was chairman, was issued. The *Tribune* and Kerner were not on the same side, as they had been in the Great Lakes campaign. The paper printed the text, gave the report extensive display, and used three editorials to denounce it. Said one: "The report of the Kerner commission on the 1967 riots is awash with tears for the poor, oppressed rioters. The disorders, they report, were not caused by, nor the consequences of, an organized plan or conspiracy. . . . It is impossible to believe that wholesale arson, gunfire, and looting are spontaneous, unorganized, undirected. Few mobs, whether white or black, are unorganized mobs."

The *Tribune* acknowledged that there was turmoil and division in the country, and it was obvious that the paper was shocked at what the report revealed about growing enmity between blacks and whites. But the subject of the Kerner Report was only one of a list of problems facing the people. When Vice-President Humphrey visited the University of Chicago to attend an awards dinner honoring Sen. William Benton, student protesters caused the police to be summoned. Northwestern University students closed off Sheridan Road and precipitated police action within the campus. Throughout the country there was intense unrest, guerrilla theater, planned demonstrations, and seemingly mindless splinter actions.

There were some signs of possible improvement. When Richard M. Nixon announced that he would again seek the presidential nomination, the *Tribune* was pleased: "Richard Nixon's announcement of his candidacy for President is welcome news, although of course it is no surprise. His intelligence and experience in government are unsurpassed among possible Republican candidates. . . . Our expression of admiration does

not mean, however, that the *Tribune* endorses his candidacy at this time."
By March, after surveying the result of the New Hampshire primaries, in
which Minnesota Democrat Sen. Eugene McCarthy got 40 percent of the
vote with a campaign force of anti-Vietnam college youth called by some
"the Children's Crusade," and after experiencing the Tet offensive in
Vietnam, President Johnson announced that he would not be a candidate
for reelection. The *Tribune* was delighted. It detested Johnson and had
suggested as a campaign slogan for Republicans, "Would you care to be
stuck in an elevator with this man?" But it thought little better of the new
Democratic possibilities, Vice-President Humphrey, Sen. Robert F. Kennedy of New York, and Senator McCarthy. However, none of these
appeared to have a chance against Nixon.

*   *   *

On April 4, 1968, the Reverend Martin Luther King, Jr., was relaxing
with aides on the balcony of the Lorraine Motel in Memphis. A sniper
shot him dead. The country again went into a state of shock, and the
following day riots broke out on Chicago's West and South sides and in
125 other cities. The *Tribune* used the full front page and three additional
pages to tell of the assassination. During the days following, it reported
the rioting of angry blacks, especially on the city's West Side. Nine were
killed, 3,000 National Guardsmen were called out to patrol the streets,
2,000 firemen fought fires reportedly started by arsonists, and 350
persons were arrested for looting. The Reverend Jesse Jackson, an aide to
Dr. King, came to Chicago to address a mourning session of the city
council. He urged citizens to stop demonstrations not only in Chicago but
throughout the nation.

In June, as the California primary campaign was ending, Robert
Kennedy, brother of the slain president, was killed in Los Angeles.
America, long under the stresses of opposing views of the Vietnam War
and the campaign for civil rights that finally brought strife to North as
well as South, seemed to be breaking apart. The *Tribune* had published an
anguished editorial on the death of Dr. King, and when Senator Kennedy
died, it simply republished the King editorial:

> There are not words to express the nation's sorrow when one of its leaders
> is assassinated. All America grieves over the senseless, cowardly, cruel
> slaying. Yes, a day of mourning is in order. The country should repent its
> ways. It should mourn its fall from grace. It should look into its heart and
> abjure the evils to which it has succumbed.
>
> Look about you. Moral values at the lowest level since the decadence of
> Rome. Moral values are scoffed at and ignored. Drug addiction among the
> youth is so widespread that we are treated to a spectacle at great universities
> of faculty-student committees solemnly decreeing that this is no longer a

matter for correction under the law. At countless universities the doors of dormitories are open to mixed company, with no supervision.

Dress is immodest. Pornography floods the news stands and book stores. "Free speech" movements on campuses address themselves to four letter words. Students terrorize faculties and university presidents and assert that they should govern the administration and dictate the curriculum. We are knee-deep in hippies, marijuana, LSD and other hallucinogens. We do not need any of these; we are doped to the point where our standards are lost.

We have spawned a generation raised on the maxims of Baby Doctor Spock that permissiveness is beautiful. If the brat squawks loud and long enough, you can cure him by giving him anything he wants. . . . The same rule has been adopted as a panacea for racial tension.

So goes the fashionable "liberal" reasoning of the day. We have allowed the minority—the worst of us—to take over.

Yes, this nation and its people need a day of mourning—a day in which to look into their hearts, take stock of their conscience, and decide whether repentance is to be their salvation—if any is to be had.

* * *

Upon acceding to the presidency of Tribune Company in 1960, Howard Wood had authorized Harold Grumhaus to proceed with studies intended to bring the family enterprise into the 20th century. Grumhaus had begun the long study and planning procedure with Keith Masters and Willis Nance of the Kirkland law firm, a study not entirely welcomed by the New York interests led by Jack Flynn of the *New York News*. It was feared that any revisions of the broad Illinois charter issued by the legislature in 1861 might impair the rights of the company and the interests of family stockholders. By the late 1960s, Wood and Grumhaus, who became *Tribune* general manager in 1964, were ready to move ahead with the corporate reorganization plan.

Aided in solving the extensive legal complications by Don H. Reuben, who became Tribune Company counsel following the death of Masters, Grumhaus developed a six-stage program for Tribune Company growth. The initial step was sufficiently drastic to almost doom its acceptance by the directors, but Grumhaus was adamant: The obsolete Illinois charter could not be merely amended, it had to be scrapped. On September 22, 1966, four months and three days after the regular board election in May, Tribune Company directors amended the bylaws to create the position of chairman of the board. Wood was elected chairman, and Grumhaus was named president. The choices were reconfirmed at the annual meeting in May, 1967, and on December 19 of that year, the directors passed a resolution "to transfer certain of its assets used in connection with the publication of the newspaper, the *Chicago Tribune,* to the Chicago Tribune Company."

The day following, the Chicago Tribune Company was incorporated at Springfield, Illinois, and on December 21 the directors met again to elect Harold Grumhaus president of the new company. Tribune Company was not dissolved but was being transformed into a holding company, of which the Chicago Tribune Company would be one subsidiary. On March 19, 1968, the certificate of incorporation of Tribune Company was received and filed in the office of the secretary of state of Delaware. Delaware laws provided a more congenial climate for companies planning expansion and diversification, and major companies outside the state had been incorporating in Delaware for more than half a century. On April 10, 1968, a plan and agreement of merger of Tribune Company, an Illinois corporation, into Tribune Company, a Delaware corporation, was entered into by the officers of the respective companies as authorized by their directors. The board of directors of Tribune Company, Illinois, approved the merger plan on May 21, 1968, and the stockholders concurred on May 23. The certificate of agreement of merger was filed with the Delaware secretary of state on June 25, 1968. The original Tribune Company was legally replaced by the Delaware corporation, and the number of shares was increased to 8,000. Tribune Company had become a true holding company and the Chicago Tribune Company was an operations company publishing the *Chicago Tribune*.

In conjunction with the major reorganization, Wood and Grumhaus had initiated management and marketing studies to insure that each of the 26 Tribune Company subsidiaries was effectively involved in the right markets and procedures, and properly staffed. With the reorganization project completed, the next step was to orient executives and employees to it, so it would work. Certainly the vexing command problem had been solved: All executives reported, through channels, to the chairman of Tribune Company, J. Howard Wood, who also retained the position of publisher of the *Chicago Tribune*.

The family and the New York directors were not forgotten. Flynn, a powerful director, was named chairman of News Syndicate Company, with W. H. "Tex" James as president and chief executive officer. Directors of the new Tribune Company included James P. Cowles, president of the Inland Empire Paper Company, and the representative of the Cowles family; Dr. John B. Lloyd, retired physician and the representative of the Lloyd family; James J. Patterson, son of Captain Patterson and assistant managing editor of the *News*; and Robert Schmon, who had become president of the Canadian companies after his father's death in 1964. A new director from the Chicago Tribune Company was the young production director and close associate of Grumhaus, Stanton R. Cook.

*   *   *

In August, 1968, the *Tribune* began its campaign to insure the nomination of Richard M. Nixon for president and a Republican victory in November. It said as the convention opened in Miami Beach, "Richard Nixon is equipped by experience, temperament, and the high qualities of a disciplined mind to be President of the United States." The Democrats, the paper charged, "cannot escape responsibility for violence and terror and insurrection in our cities, a war the Democratic administration cannot solve, uncontrolled spending, which despite crushing taxes that never end, leads to constant deficits, generating an inflation always on the rise." It noted that the Republican platform pledged "a program of peace in Viet Nam—neither a peace at any price nor a camouflaged surrender of legitimate United States or allied interests, but a positive program that will offer a fair settlement based on self determination, our national interests, and the cause of long range world peace." Nixon was nominated on the first ballot, and he chose Gov. Spiro T. Agnew of Maryland as his running mate. The paper said Agnew was little known.

On August 21, as Russian tanks and troops were seizing Prague, Czechoslovakia, an army of young people of the kind the *Tribune* had denounced in its King and Kennedy editorial was moving upon Chicago, site of the Democratic convention. They had been summoned by their leaders—Dave Dellinger, of the National Mobilization Committee to End the War in Vietnam (MOB); Tom Hayden, founder of Students for a Democratic Society; and Jerry Rubin, of the Youth International Party (Yippies). Law enforcement officials were warned by columnists Jack Mabley of the *American* and Bob Wiedrich of the *Tribune*, who had read in the underground press of trouble coming, and the officials prepared. Superintendent James Conlisk ordered his police drilled in riot control, Gov. Sam Shapiro ordered 5,649 National Guardsmen to duty in Chicago in battle dress, 1,000 federal agents entered the city, and 7,500 troops were placed on alert at Fort Hood, Texas, their transport planes ready. "Never before in history has it been necessary to protect a political convention this way," the paper said.

In the days prior to the convention, the *Tribune* had been denouncing Humphrey, who, it said, was called "Pinkie" as a youth. Referring to the fact that Johnson feared to run, it asked, "Why fire the ventriloquist and hire the dummy?" Senator George McGovern of South Dakota and Minnesotan Eugene McCarthy aroused equal ire, and the paper waited to see whether Massachusetts Sen. Edward Kennedy would become a candidate, as Mayor Daley desired. Kennedy again said no. While the hippies, flower children, and many earnest young people, most of them followers of McCarthy, gathered in Lincoln and Grant parks, filled the cheap lodging houses, crowded McCarthy's headquarters, and overran the Democratic headquarters in the Conrad Hilton Hotel, the platform committee labored. The result, said the *Tribune*, "is, as all Democratic platforms are, an offense to reason."

On Monday night, August 26, the Chicago police clashed with the masses of youth who had invaded Lincoln Park and insisted on remaining beyond the 11 P.M. curfew. Police task forces charged the crowds, swinging their clubs. The hard-core dissidents fought back, while others tried to flee. Many newspapermen, several dressed as hippies, attempted to get pictures and the story. Some were struck and knocked down by the police. Tom Hayden and 20 other demonstrators were seized. The action moved to Michigan Avenue, where a march of protesters was stopped at the Michigan Avenue bridge. The crowds in Grant Park attempted to invade the Conrad Hilton. Again the police charged; demonstrators and bystanders were clubbed, and tear gas was used. Guardsmen joined the police to form lines containing the throngs in the park. When television crews came into sight, protesters surged forward to yell insults; bags of excrement, rocks, and, it was said, containers of lye were thrown. Editors of three of Chicago's newspapers and representatives of television networks demanded a session with Conlisk to protest the attacks on the press by the police. The *Tribune* said:

> We have no sympathy with the rowdy demonstrations conducted by the hippies, yippies and other young punks who have gathered in Chicago by the thousands. Their presence is unnecessary for the work of the Democratic national convention, which they apparently are trying to influence. . . . We do have sympathy for the Chicago police, who have been working 12 hour shifts and are tired. . . . Strong security, however, does not require the police to beat up newspaper reporters and photographers who are lawfully trying to cover a news event. At least 24 newsmen were roughed up. . . . Perhaps some looked like hippies and refused to obey police orders to move. If so, the police were perhaps justified in using force. . . . Several editors have asked Supt. Conlisk to make an investigation. We join in that request.

Vice-President Humphrey was nominated and chose Sen. Edmund Muskie of Maine as his vice-presidential candidate. Both men in their acceptance speeches were cool to President Johnson's Vietnam plank. As the convention ended, the *Tribune* said good-bye in a disgruntled page-one editorial, suggesting that Chicago was an excellent place when Democrats did not bring their rowdy friends to town. It accused Hayden, Dellinger, and Rubin of deliberately causing trouble, a position taken later by political historian Theodore H. White, and still later admitted by Rubin. Said the *Tribune*: "The bearded, lawless rabble . . . used every sort of provocation against police and national guardsmen—vile taunts, lye solutions, bricks and rubble. . . . For enforcing law and order, Mayor Daley and his police deserve congratulations rather than criticism." The three leaders and four others, to become known as the "Chicago Seven," in time went to trial, continuing their guerrilla theater tactics for nearly five months in the federal court of Judge Julius Hoffman, and received a split verdict.

On November 5, Richard Nixon won the presidency with a plurality of 250,000 votes, gaining 302 electoral votes to 191 for Humphrey and 45 for Gov. George Wallace of Alabama and his American Independence party. On December 21, the American rocket Apollo 8, with Col. Frank Borman, Maj. William Anders, and Capt. James Lovell aboard, lifted off from Cape Kennedy and orbited the moon ten times, sending a Christmas message of peace and goodwill to all on Earth, then returned safely on December 27. On the 31st of December, the *Tribune* prepared to announce major changes for January 1, 1969.

NEW ERA,
NEW <u>TRIBUNE</u>

27

On New Year's Day, 1969, Harold Grumhaus, president of Chicago Tribune Company, assumed the additional duties of publisher of the *Chicago Tribune;* and Clayton Kirkpatrick, formerly executive editor of the *Tribune,* became editor. Tribune Company chairman Howard Wood, who had increasingly devoted himself to the widespread interests of the new holding company, to industry-wide duties such as the presidency of the American Newspaper Publishers Association and a directorship in the Associated Press, and to various civic and charitable posts in Chicago, had resigned his position as *Tribune* publisher, making way for Grumhaus to take over. Don Maxwell, formerly editor of the *Tribune,* retired from the paper but assumed the position of editorial director of Tribune Company while retaining his directorship and trustee positions.

The January 1 editorial masthead of the *Tribune* signaled major change, since an entire management team was listed in addition to Grumhaus and Kirkpatrick: Walter C. Kurz, executive vice-president and general manager; F. A. Nichols, executive vice-president and treasurer; Thomas Furlong, executive editor; Tom Moore, managing editor; Walter Simmons, Sunday editor; and George Morgenstern, editorial page editor. The lead editorial stated the new policy of the paper, indicating not philosophical or political variance, but a basic difference concerning the means by which policy should be achieved.

"We start 1969 with a new publisher, a new editor and a new masthead leading this page. Readers who have come to regard the *Tribune* as an old friend can expect to see some changes." Then came reassurance:

755

We expect to remain basically conservative. This does not mean that we are opposed to change, but rather that we believe that change must be made in the light of tradition and the lessons of history. Experience, as well as intellect, is essential to wisdom. The conservative is suspicious of untested theory. This has been a basic tenet of the *Tribune*'s conservatism throughout its history. It will continue to be a guiding principle.

We expect to be generally Republican in politics because we believe in the value of the traditional principles of the party, limited government, maximum individual responsibility, minimum restriction of personal liberty, opportunity and enterprise. We fought Republicans when they were wrong. We have supported Democrats when they were right. No political party should take the *Tribune* for granted. . . . We expect to remain dedicated to the future of Chicago. We stand with this inland empire and its people. Their greatness is our greatness. We are confident of both.

Almost at once the editorial character of the *Tribune* subtly changed. It was Republican and conservative on the editorial page, but no longer elsewhere was it a partisan newspaper in the Medill–McCormick style. Managing editor Tom Moore, a graduate of the University of Iowa, where he had captained the football team, had come to the *Chicago Tribune* sports department from the *Des Moines Tribune* in March, 1937. Moore, a big, quiet, persuasive man, had been made managing editor in January, 1968, and now he carried out Kirkpatrick's edict that reporters and writers should not be concerned with the positions taken on the editorial page. Changing the policy was no problem, since most of the staff for years had favored what now was being done. The slanting of news for partisan purposes, the practice of most newspapers in the days when their partisan viewpoints were regularly published in their Prospectus, at last came to an end.

Publisher Grumhaus and editor Kirkpatrick jointly established the *Tribune*'s new posture. "As publisher I felt I was responsible for the policy and voice of the *Tribune*," Grumhaus said in later years. "I insisted that we be right, that we be fair, tell it like it is, be honest and candid. And there were times in the past when I felt we were not as honest and candid as we should have been, that we didn't always print both sides of the story. . . . I felt that we should be able to defend everything we printed." Since Kirkpatrick held similar views, there were no basic problems. Both men referred to themselves as "open-minded" conservatives in public utterances. Grumhaus sought "creative dissatisfaction" among his staff and took special interest in typographical and format improvements. Kirkpatrick, almost evangelical in his journalistic purity, demanded and got pristine editorial content.

Professionals and critics of the press began to take notice. The *Tribune* had really, at long last, changed. In August of 1969, editor Kirkpatrick again made it clear that he did not intend to follow traditionalism in the manner of his predecessors. He introduced a Sunday "Perspective" section, presenting varied editorial comment and in-depth reporting by staff members and outsiders rather than the staff-only letters and reports once used in the "Spotlight" section. Such an allocation of newsprint was made with the approval of the publisher, though the actual content was an editorial responsibility. Some of the new writers were "notorious liberals," and one of the regular staff contributors was Robert Cromie, whose liberal credentials had been established on the book review pages. Some longtime readers wrote wrathful letters of protest, and a few *Tribune* executives, active and retired, sputtered a bit, but Kirkpatrick held his ground. "Perspective," he said, should present a spectrum of opinion for the enlightenment and enrichment of the readers, the news columns should present facts, and the editorial columns would present the *Tribune*'s own point of view.

Lewis Z. Koch of the *Chicago Journalism Review,* no friend of newspaper management or editors, cast a few incredulous glances at the emerging new *Tribune,* then studied several issues and requested an interview with Kirkpatrick. He found the new editor quietly genial in his big, dark-paneled office where he presided over a vast, brightly lighted desk spread with proofs and papers. Koch said Kirkpatrick, 54, had "almost pink cheeks and distinguished gray hair and appeared to be freshly shaven at 3:30 in the afternoon." Possibly he had briefed himself on Kirkpatrick's background: Born January 8, 1915, in Waterman, Illinois; an honor graduate from the University of Illinois; some travel, mostly as a door-to-door salesman, and a job as a radio announcer in Alabama, although his accent was softly but clearly Midwestern. He began his Chicago experience as a reporter for the City News Bureau, covering police and courts, then joined the *Tribune* in 1938 as an assignment reporter. During World War II, Kirkpatrick served three and a half years in the air force, two of them with the intelligence section of the 100th Bombardment Group of the Eighth Air Force, based in England. As a general assignment reporter at the *Tribune* again, Kirkpatrick won a Beck Award for his work, going on to serve as day city editor, city editor, and managing editor. He became executive editor of the paper and a vice-president and a director of Chicago Tribune Company in 1967.

Koch asked about the changes. There would be more, Kirkpatrick told him. But that meant no negative commentary on the past.

> I've lived with this organization for 31 years. I have never lived in any kind of organization for which I have so much respect. I genuinely like the people I worked for all these years. I genuinely like the people I am working for now. . . . There is a great deal of misinformation about the *Tribune* and its history. What many people know about the *Tribune* is from second-hand

sources. . . . We find there is a great deal people *think* they know about the *Tribune*. Myth, partly stemming from the personal character of the journalism that was practiced by the *Tribune* 30, 40, 50 years ago. The Colonel was in his prime and at the height of his powers . . . he injected his personality into the news which gave the *Tribune* this peculiar character.

After a discussion of various stories written in the new, objective style, Kirkpatrick said, "There's a great deal to be said for conservatism. The *Tribune* is a conservative paper. And I'm a conservative, in this sense: that I believe that experience is the most important ingredient in wisdom. . . . I guess I am an 'open-minded' conservative."

"Then what about the dissenters, some of the liberal people the *Tribune* has hired?" Koch asked.

"I like dissenters," Kirkpatrick responded. "My God, you can't be alive if you're not a dissenter. I don't like revolutionaries. My favorite word is 'evolutionary.' . . . You have to keep changing all the time without destroying the things that have demonstrated their values." Koch, in his report of the interview, characteristically questioned whether Kirkpatrick should not engage in "forceful personal journalism . . . without the dishonesty that was inherent in the McCormick *musts*." Then he added, "To a man, the *Tribune* reporters I spoke with said they will remain with the *Tribune* now. They seemed rather exalted by the changes Kirkpatrick has wrought and the changes they see coming."

*   *   *

The new editorial philosophy did nothing to change the paper's approach to an all-too-common local news event: corruption. In the years following the Summerdale scandal, Bob Wiedrich had continued to cover crime and police activities. By February, 1969, he was reporting on another unfortunate connection, asserting that policemen in the Austin district were shaking down tavern owners who were forced to join a $100-a-month club. Such shakedowns were rumored to be going on throughout the city, but in the Austin district Wiedrich had proof, and a new law permitted the FBI to come in. Captain Mark Thanasouras, commander of the Austin district, was arrested and 23 of his men were required to take lie detector tests. Thanasouras pleaded guilty to extorting $275,000 from 30 tavern keepers in the district, was sentenced to prison, and subsequently testified against others in the department. "Thanasouras is a tragic example of what is wrong with the Chicago Police Department," wrote Wiedrich. "He is a man spawned, pampered and sustained by political interference, patronage, and partisan pandering to ethnic and minority groups. His rise has been meteoric—from patrolman to captain in six years. It is a career that does not speak well for the reform regime of the late Orlando W. Wilson."

Other scandals were uncovered by *Tribune* investigative reporting. William Jones, later managing editor–news, won a Pulitzer prize in 1971 for his reports on evils in the ambulance services in Chicago, taking grave risks himself to get the needed facts. The entire *Tribune* editorial staff was honored with the Pulitzer in 1973 for exposing vote frauds in Cook County in 1972.

Although news was covered even more arduously than before, some modern events had become so exotic that not even the most intense managing editor could send his reporters to the source. On July 21, 1969, the *Tribune* published the most unusual front page in its history, a full-page color moonscape with the headline overprinted, "MOON WALK COMPLETED." A replate changed the line to "FLY U.S. FLAG ON THE MOON." The page-one story was distilled from the work of several correspondents:

> Houston, July 20—Man set foot on the moon's surface tonight.
>
> The historic moment came 3 hours and 16 minutes earlier than scheduled when Neil A. Armstrong descended the ladder of the Apollo 11 lunar landing module.
>
> Armstrong's first words on stepping onto the moon were: "That's one small step for man but one giant leap for mankind." Edwin E. Aldrin Jr. followed him out approximately 20 minutes later. The start of the 2 hour 40 minute moon walk came 6 hours and 39 minutes after the tense descent and touchdown on the moon's surface 47 seconds after 3:17 p.m. One of the first acts was to plant an American flag.

Details of the communications between the men on the moon, Michael Collins in the mother ship *Columbia* orbiting the moon, and the ground control station were published on page two, and page three of the "Moon Final" was laid out in the paper's usual page-one style. There were five full pages of moon stories, plus ten more carrying side stories on the space feat. The editorial writer was as succinct as the newsmen were effusive: "No great outpouring of words is necessary to express the feelings of most Americans who are following the grandly successful missions of our men on the moon. 'Well done' and 'Thank God' will suffice for now."

*   *   *

Over his years with the paper, Harold Grumhaus had viewed the management shortcomings of the growing *Tribune* organization, as had Wood and Campbell, without freedom to act unless Colonel McCormick could be convinced that action was necessary. His duties as insurance executive, coordinator for McCormick, labor negotiator, production manager, and director of various management studies had given him a broad view of company activities in both the United States and Canada. Now, as publisher, Grumhaus followed Wood's practice of meeting with operating executives relative to major problems, and he in fact took the process further: In the production department he met periodically with division chiefs, inviting their suggestions and encouraging them to carry on the communicative process with their workers. Thus Fred Brohm, composing superintendent; Erwin Giannoni, stereotype; Pat Bresnahan, engraving; Joe Reed, pressroom superintendent; Harold Maas, roto superintendent; and other divisional leaders regularly provided input received in the old days, if at all, by Medill or McCormick personally on a chance visit to the department. Wood, initially from the editorial department, had had a close relationship with *Tribune* editors, especially since he often was expediting McCormick's orders. Grumhaus now determined to formalize such relationships and to inculcate into editorial executives some idea of newspaper economics. His attempts to obtain workable budgets from the various departments met resistance in the advertising area and stunned disbelief among the editors. "Editorial people are not very knowledgeable about the economics of a newspaper," Grumhaus noted. He demanded budgets and got them.

Grumhaus, much in the Campbell image physically and leveling the same unblinking gaze as a report-laden visitor entered his office, was similarly keen in his ability to analyze a problem and to ask disconcerting questions of anyone appearing without thorough briefing. An expert in the production area in the Medill–McCormick tradition, Grumhaus served as president and director of the Research Institute of the American Newspaper Publishers Association, and he was soon to become president of Illinois Atlantic Corporation, vice-chairman of WGN Continental Broadcasting Company, chairman of the Ontario Paper Company, Ltd., and the Quebec and North Shore Paper Company, Ltd., and a trustee of both the McCormick–Patterson Trust (succeeding Arthur Schmon in 1964) and the Robert R. McCormick Charitable Trust. Grumhaus, educated at the University of Illinois, sometimes described himself as "not a journalist," but, like McCormick, he read the *Tribune* avidly, and his associates quickly learned that he had a keen sense of high journalistic standards.

Early on, his peers recognized in Grumhaus the eventual successor to chairman Wood, and at the annual election in May, 1970, Grumhaus was made vice-chairman of Tribune Company. At that meeting Walter Kurz was elected to succeed Grumhaus as Tribune Company president, a position he held until his death on September 23 the following year. In November, 1970, Wood announced his resignation effective January 1, 1971, and on that date the directors followed Wood's recommendation, electing Grumhaus chairman and chief executive officer of Tribune Company. Grumhaus continued as publisher of the *Tribune* and president of Chicago Tribune Company. Fred Nichols was elected president of Tribune Company in April, 1972, succeeding Kurz. Wood became chairman of the executive committee.

The first of the newcomers to reach top executive ranks was Stanton R. Cook, born in Chicago and educated as an engineer at Northwestern University. He served as a navigator in the U.S. Army Air Corps for two years and worked with an oil company before joining the *Tribune* as a production engineer in April, 1951. He became assistant production manager in 1960 and manager following Dick Gossett's retirement in January, 1965. In May, 1967, when Grumhaus became president of Chicago Tribune Company, Cook was named vice-president and production director, and in 1970 he became executive vice-president and general manager. In April, 1972, he succeeded Grumhaus as president of Chicago Tribune Company and a year later he also became publisher of the *Tribune*.

Another of the new generation destined for a top spot was Robert M. Hunt. Hunt came from a town in Michigan that had given the *Tribune* other executives, Sault Ste. Marie, where his father was the mayor. Educated at Michigan State University, Hunt, like Cook and Kirkpatrick, was early marked for advancement and given a broadly based training program. He began in the classified department, then, in a departure from the usual *Tribune* educational program, spent four years in the circulation department, before joining retail advertising. Later he represented the paper in Detroit, in general advertising, then followed Eugene Strusacker as manager of the New York advertising office. He became manager of the general division in 1966, serving under Edward M. Corboy, who had succeeded Kurz as director of advertising. In 1969, Hunt was made assistant circulation director. Soon Hunt, Corboy, and Joseph F. Burns, who had succeeded Jerry Byrnes as promotion director of the *Tribune,* would be heavily involved in a new problem, arising from the company's evening publication, the *American.*

*   *   *

The problems of the afternoon and Sunday *American* had been of concern to Tribune Company executives from the time of its purchase in 1956, and they increasingly appeared insoluble. Publisher Stuart List had renamed the paper *Chicago's American* and had undertaken massive assaults on the advertising and circulation fronts, but numbers and revenues did not match rising costs. By January, 1961, afternoon circulation had fallen by 73,000 to 450,583, and Sunday circulation by 100,000 to 576,770, declines resulting in part from generally difficult conditions affecting evening newspapers in a television area and, for the Sunday paper, competition with two other Chicago Sunday papers, including, of course, the Sunday *Tribune*. List sought aid from the parent company, which had been underwriting financial losses from the beginning. Sunday editor Lloyd Wendt and assistant neighborhood news editor Richard Hainey were released to become editor and executive editor, respectively, of the *American*, Tom Furlong becoming Sunday editor of the *Tribune*. The new *American* executives joined managing editor Luke Carroll, who had arrived from a similar post on the *New York Herald-Tribune* a few months before, John Madigan, assistant managing editor, and Ernest Tucker, city editor. List, who had complete autonomy, gave his new editors a free hand.

Soon the *American* editorial department had strengthened several weak points, opening a Washington bureau and attracting Jack Mabley, top columnist of the *Chicago Daily News,* to become columnist and associate editor in charge of investigatory journalism, and Vaughan Shoemaker, two-time Pulitzer prize winner, as editorial cartoonist. The editors created an "Action Line" column to aid readers and tossed out existing editorial page columnists to make room for James Reston of the *New York Times* and other *Times* writers.

To cut costs, the paper terminated its Canadian and downstate editions. The circulation losses incurred for these economy reasons initially kept *Chicago's American* from overcoming the *Daily News's* lead of more than 100,000 overall and 50,772 in the city and suburbs, the area designated by the papers as the RTZ, or retail trading zone. But by 1965, the *American* posted a lead of 6,057 in the RTZ, and by 1969 this lead had grown to 11,461. This achievement produced a noisy promotion fight between the *Daily News* and the *American,* each claiming to be No. 1 in circulation in vital areas. Circulation leadership in city and suburbs should have insured advertising increases, but no such gains accrued to the *American*. To further reduce costs, the *Tribune* and *American* advertising departments were merged.

Prior to List's retirement in January, 1969, a marketing analysis was undertaken; it showed that the *American* needed to reach into the suburbs and to appeal to younger, more affluent readers. A completely new format and even a new name were indicated. Two highly talented *American* staff members, Maxwell McCrohon and Scott Schmidt, were appointed to a special task force to help plan the revamped paper, to be called *Chicago Today,* aided by other editorial executives and by Gus Hartoonian, recently named art director. *Chicago Today,* in tabloid format, made its debut on April 28, 1969, and swiftly proved its popularity with readers by taking the overall circulation leadership from the *Daily News* by a margin of 8,273 copies and extending its leadership in the RTZ by 41,291 copies. The Sunday circulation, however, remained static, and late in 1972 it was agreed that publication of the Sunday *Today* should end, since it was in competition with the Sunday *Tribune*. The Saturday paper was also to be abolished and the *Tribune* to be substituted to *Today* readers over the weekend. A secret editorial study envisioning the combination of the Saturday and Sunday editions of the two papers was conducted by McCrohon and Schmidt, assisted by John L. Wagoner, news editor of the *Tribune*. McCrohon, a soft-spoken Australian who had come to the United States as correspondent for the *Sydney Morning Herald* in 1952 and had joined the staff of *Chicago's American* in 1960, had risen rapidly to become managing editor of *Chicago Today* when Luke Carroll became business manager. In January, 1972, he had been invited by Kirkpatrick to become managing editor of the *Tribune* and was succeeded at *Today* by Scott Schmidt.

Meantime, *Tribune* publisher Grumhaus named general manager Cook leader of a task force to work with editors and publishers of both papers in planning the new Saturday–Sunday format and weekend publishing schedule. New sections were created, and a new system of preprinting classified advertising, devised by the committee working with classified manager James G. Paddock, would enable the *Tribune* to issue a much bigger Sunday paper than previously had been possible. The task force also redesigned the *Tribune*'s "Lifestyle" section, created a new "Homes/Leisure Living" section, and redesigned *TV Week* and moved it from Saturday to Sunday. An "Arts and Fun" tabloid guide to entertainment and the arts was designed, to be edited by Larry Townsend, assistant features editor. The staff of the zoned news sections was absorbed into the local staff under city editor William Jones, and metropolitan news pages were introduced into the main news sections of the Sunday paper.

Today ceased weekend publication on January 6, 1973, and the new Sunday *Chicago Tribune* was introduced on the following day, hailed as "Super Sunday" by Joseph Burns's promotional department. The move carried nearly 200,000 Sunday *Today* readers to the *Tribune*. The paper on Saturday and Sunday now offered leading *Today* features, among them "Action Line," edited by Kenan Heise; Jack Mabley; Dear Abby; Dr. Joyce Brothers; and Rick Talley, sports editor of *Today*. The *Tribune*'s own young writers were given added promotion and display, especially in entertainment and fine arts: Aaron Gold, entertainment columnist; Linda Winer, drama and dance critic; Gene Siskel, film critic; Gary Deeb, television critic; and Paul Gapp, architecture critic. Lynn Van Matre, rock and popular music; Jack Hurst, country music; and Harriet Choice, jazz, now supplemented the work of the paper's scholarly music critic, Tom Willis.

While the *Tribune–Today* weekend combination was being readied, editor Kirkpatrick, managing editor Mike O'Neil of the *New York News*, and representatives of the Knight newspapers organized the Knight-News-Wire, a supplemental news service. It began operations in July, 1973, supplying each member paper with specialized news coverage, plus feature materials.

Format changes were not confined solely to the weekend editions. The daily features section of the *Tribune,* renamed "Tempo," appeared in a new magazine format, and the news section generally was reorganized to group news stories in special interest categories, as Joseph Medill had done almost a century earlier. On January 1, 1974, the paper completed a long series of typographical and content changes by introducing "Column 1," an individualized presentation of the news and news-related subjects by the paper's leading writers. The following month, *Time* magazine, in an article evaluating the newspapers of the United States, called the *Chicago Tribune* one of the ten best.

*   *   *

There were other changes, designed as reader services and to attract advertising linage. The *Tribune,* with its extensive financial, production, and newsprint resources, ceaselessly sought to make its leadership in circulation and advertising markets unassailable. The outstanding executive and idea man in this phase of operations was Kurz, the Chicago-born University of Illinois graduate who joined the *Tribune*'s classified department after experience as a promotion and publicity man at A Century of Progress and by the time of his death in 1971, at the age of 63, had risen to become president of Tribune Company. A notable contribution by Kurz, strongly supported by Kirkpatrick, was the development of the *Suburban Trib,* a publication designed as part of the daily *Tribune* but specializing in the editorial and advertising requirements of the various suburban areas. The project began slowly, but by 1976 there were nine *Tribs,* issuing 27 editions each week, published by Area Publications Corporation, a *Chicago Tribune* subsidiary with its own offset printing plant. Byron Campbell, one-time assistant to Kurz and former business manager of *Chicago Today,* became president and general manager of Area Publications after serving also as production manager and assistant to the publisher of the *Tribune.* Campbell reported 20 million lines of advertising for his publications in 1976, earning more than $7 million in revenues.

Projects such as the *Trib* were launched only after intensive marketing studies by the *Tribune*'s marketing and research divisions, brought to a high state of efficiency and creativity by Kurz and directed subsequently by Thomas P. O'Donnell, who, on January 1, 1975, was made marketing director for Tribune Company. He was succeeded at the paper by William Rowe, who thus became responsible for research services, marketing services, public relations, and the creative promotional divisions of the *Tribune*, which issued such special publications as educational editions for schools.

Marketing and research continued to provide the advertising department with specialized studies of aid to *Tribune* clients, the potential market for products, possible locations for new shops and stores, and general demographic data. Information stored in memory banks was kept ready for instant use via computer. Specific problems presented to the advertising department by clients were individually attacked. The division also made digests of market data and maintained information on new store and shopping center openings.

The editorial department in a similar way obtained from the marketing and research divisions information on reading habits, possible new editorial services, and reader responses to innovations. Panels of readers were interviewed, readership traffic studies were conducted, and, from time to time, outside research agencies were employed to do "total market studies" made available to editorial as well as advertising. The resulting information provided useful tools to editorial people in making judgments that involved long-range planning and possible heavy expense. Marketing and research played a major role in determining the final decisions relating to *Chicago Today*, and the techniques have been applied to all phases of Tribune Company operations.

While the research techniques could not extricate *Chicago Today* from a continuing deficit situation, other operations of Tribune Company expanded in the new order of reorganization, research, and change, including the Canadian properties, under Robert Schmon. The Ontario Paper Company, Ltd., in addition to producing 240,000 tons of newsprint in 1975, manufactured 20,000 tons of unbleached sulphite for tissues; 6,200 pounds of vanillin and lioxin for flavoring, perfume, and drug use; 900,000 imperial gallons of ethyl alcohol; and 90,000 tons of sodium sulphate, used by kraft mills for specialty papers. The company operated five paper machines with 1,400 plant employees and 100 men in the Huron Bay and Timmits timber limits in Ontario, cutting 260,000 cunits of pulpwood in 1975. The Q.N.S. Paper Company, Ltd., produced 460,000 tons of newsprint with four machines operated by 1,500 employees, with 1,200 timber cutters felling 400,000 cunits of pulp logs. In total, Tribune Company harvested 4,637 square miles of limits in Ontario and 6,436 square miles in Quebec—a total of more than 7 million acres.

The Manicouagan Power Company, its seven generators possessing a capacity of 442,400 horsepower, supplied not only Q.N.S. Paper Company but also Reynolds Metals' vast aluminum smelting requirements, grain shipping terminals using the harbor facilities created by Tribune Company enterprise, and the towns of Baie Comeau and Haute Rive. It also made power available to the Quebec hydro power grid when such assistance was requested. In addition, Quebec & Ontario Transportation Company, Ltd., operated a fleet of ten ships, from the M.S. *Chicago Tribune,* 5,460 tons, to the M.S. *Golden Hind,* 18,500 tons. In 1976, the Q.N.S. Paper Company announced a partnership with Rexfor Corporation of Canada to build a $14 million sawmill and wood chip complex at Pointe-aux-Outardes, 15 miles west of Baie Comeau. The plant would have an annual capacity of 100 million board feet of lumber and 130,000 tons of chips, the lumber to be exported, the wood chips to be used by the Baie Comeau newsprint mill.

* * *

At the time Stanton Cook became publisher of the *Chicago Tribune* in 1973, many Republican conservatives were of the opinion that editor Kirkpatrick had overextended his parameters in the encouragement of free discussion and dissension on the editorial and "Perspective" pages. The trend, however, continued even faster under the new publisher and appeared to have a general corporate blessing, for in April, 1974, Cook was elected president and chief executive officer of Tribune Company. Cook continued as publisher of the *Chicago Tribune.* Robert M. Hunt was named president of Chicago Tribune Company and a vice-president and director of Tribune Company, and a few months later he assumed duties as general manager of the *Tribune.*

John McCutcheon, Jr., had become editor of the editorial page in 1971, and it and the "Perspective" pages were studded with a collection of brilliant and sometimes acerbic writers calculated to provide a spectrum of political opinion, and often, it appeared, to stimulate the readers with barbs and needles. Cromie, the house liberal, was joined by Vernon Jarrett, an eloquent exponent of civil rights and an occasionally acidulous commentator on the Wasp establishment; Mike LaVelle, a blue-collar workingman turned writer in the Eric Hoffer tradition; and Washington columnist Clayton Fritchey. Protecting the conservative positions were George Morgenstern, newly retired from the editorial page; Bob Wiedrich, a law enforcement loyalist despite his long and effective career in exposing malefactors in the police department; S. I. Hayakawa, former Chicago semanticist and the California college president who dared to stand up to the students in the 1960s; and former aide to President Nixon, William Safire. Another stimulating writer was the *Tribune*'s whimsical Michael Kilian, who joyfully whacked liberals and conservatives alike. The arrival of Nicholas von Hoffman into the "Perspective" precinct, followed by Mary McGrory, turned up the rage of the *Tribune* conservative readers. Kirkpatrick had achieved his goal. Dissenters to someone or something could be found every day in the *Tribune*'s editorial area, and there was healthy dissension among readers as well. While the addition of conservative Patrick Buchanan and gadfly Father Andrew Greeley somewhat altered the balance, total peace with the readers was not restored. But the "Voice of the People" made better reading than ever before.

Tribune watchers waited for pyrotechnics signifying a collision of forces somewhere within Tribune Tower, but no external signs appeared. The new *Tribune* management team appeared to like what its editors were doing, possibly because the mean age of company executives had been reduced from near 60 to nearer 40. The new leaders, Cook, Hunt, and their associates, were less concerned with politics than with bringing the company into closer rapport with the Chicago community, including the ethnic groups, blacks, and the young. With Grumhaus and Kirkpatrick, they supported civic and charitable movements, not only by providing money and newsprint space, as had been the practice in the McCormick era, but by participating personally. The new managers were as determined as McCormick had been to keep the *Tribune* economically strong, and they were as chauvinistic about their city and the Midwest as Medill, Bross, and Ray had been.

The architectural surge of the 1950s and 1960s continued unabated in the 1970s, often pursuing innovative paths. There were the marble-covered Standard Oil Building; the soaring First National Bank Building; the buildings of Illinois Center; architect Harry Weese's new Marriott Hotel, at 45 stories the city's tallest; marble-sheathed, set-back Water Tower Place, housing elegant stores and boutiques and the Ritz-Carlton Hotel, designed by Edward Dart; and the 110-story Sears Tower, at the time of its completion in 1974 both the world's tallest structure and the world's largest private office complex, the work of Bruce Graham and Frazier Kahn of Skidmore, Owings, and Merrill.

With Chicago's new architecture came great new art on a massive scale: Pablo Picasso's enigmatic five-story metal sculpture in Richard J. Daley Center Plaza, possibly a woman but more probably in memory of his Afghan hound; Alexander Calder's stabile in Federal Center Plaza and his mobile in the Sears Tower lobby; Marc Chagall's *Four Seasons* mosaic mural at First National Bank Plaza; Harry Bertoia's *Sounding Sculpture* in the Standard Oil Plaza; Henry Moore's mystical, skull-shaped sculpture *Nuclear Energy*, at the site of the first atomic chain reaction on the University of Chicago campus; and Isamu Noguchi's *Bicentennial Fountain*, commissioned by the Ferguson Fund for the Art Institute of Chicago. To these was to be added the most unlikely sculpture of all, Claes Oldenburg's steel baseball bat, 100 feet tall, commissioned for the Federal Social Security Center on West Washington Street at an estimated cost of $1,000 a foot.

The strength of Chicago's literary renaissance was confirmed in the work of Saul Bellow, who in 1976 received the Nobel prize in literature, after winning a Pulitzer and two National Book Awards. His colleague on the University of Chicago faculty, Milton Friedman, founder of the conservative Chicago school of economics, also won a Nobel prize in 1976, the 25th member of the University of Chicago faculty and the 45th individual associated with the university to be so honored, as the *Tribune* pointed out in extolling the pair.

During the period of literary growth, the Chicago Symphony Orchestra, conducted by Fritz Reiner and then Sir Georg Solti, won international recognition for its excellence, and the Chicago Lyric Opera Company, under the leadership of Carol Fox and the superb conductor Bruno Bartoletti, revived grand opera. And there was a resurgence of "regional theater," with 60 theaters, such as the Organic, Body Politic, Victory Gardens, and St. Nicholas, emerging in Chicago back streets and in the suburbs; four plush theaters maintained for the masses by Anthony DeSantis; and the Goodman Theatre, also a training school, and those at Northwestern University and Barat College, in Lake Forest, producing classic works. Art shows also proliferated, and galleries thrived throughout the Chicago area.

Chicago continued losing population and jobs and accruing problems, but the metropolitan region enjoyed the best prospects of any urban area in the world. So said the Northeastern Illinois Planning Commission (NIPC) in 1975, which forecast 8,750,000 population for northeastern Illinois by 1985. The Chicago Association of Commerce and Industry agreed, crediting the immediate metropolitan area, including northwestern Indiana, with 7,500,000 consumers supplied by 20,000 manufacturers producing $38 billion in goods, much of it sold by 52,000 retailers in the city, suburban, and exurban areas. While the city's population declined, the suburban population had grown, from 887,000 in 1950 to 2,395,000 in 1975. The rapidly growing suburban areas no longer were packed with hard-core conservatives and like-thinking progeny. Liberal Democrats leaving the city now controlled some suburban communities; even the once ultraconservative Tenth Congressional District sent liberal Democrat Abner Mikva to Congress in 1974.

The growth in the suburbs was not merely an increase in bedroom communities. The NIPC forecast 1,193,000 jobs in the suburbs by 1985, not including the heavy industrial areas along the lake in Indiana (double 1965's job rate), and projected 2,600,000 jobs for the entire northeastern Illinois area by 1985, jobs to be held by people of every race, educational level, and political persuasion. Chicago itself lacked some of the discouraging aspects of most large cities, although problems of crime and housing worsened. The city continued to be the world's largest producer of capital goods; it handled 32 million air passengers a year from O'Hare, the world's busiest airport; its trucking centers transported 27 million manufactured tons a year; the railroads, 23 million tons; ships, 81 million tons; barges, 20 million tons. The port of Chicago docked 683 oceangoing ships in a year. The city hosted 6.5 million tourists and convention visitors annually. Chicago possessed the greatest resources of food, fresh water, and workable fuels and ores of any city in the world, according to an eminent geographer, Professor John Garland of the University of Illinois.

The *Chicago Tribune,* firmly believing in the might of the Midwest, as it had since Joseph Medill's day, campaigned to make its capital, Chicago, even bigger and better. The paper supported Mayor Daley's controversial crosstown expressway, which was intended to take through traffic away from the central city and reestablish factories on the periphery; the vast Dearborn Park housing and shopping project, just south of the Loop; and the Regional Transportation Authority (RTA), the first of these projects to be realized. Grumhaus, as publisher of the *Tribune,* had personally led the business establishment in support of the RTA, designed to coordinate city and suburban, public and private local transportation facilities.

The new *Tribune,* veering from partisan politics of the old style and preoccupied with civic advancement and the general welfare of its constituency, continued to be firmly Republican in its editorial stance while it presented its objective news reports and its spectrum of opinion. President Nixon, nominated for a second term at Miami Beach in 1972, had the paper's support, as did the Republican candidate for reelection to the Senate, Charles Percy. Nixon received a whopping 60.7 percent of the popular vote and 521 of the electoral votes to 17 for South Dakota's Sen. George McGovern, while in Illinois, Percy defeated challenger Roman Pucinski in a landslide. The *Tribune* allowed that Chicago was "the city that works" under the rule of Mayor Daley and both praised and criticized him. The paper heavily attacked his top followers, not without reason: Some were sent to jail by U.S. Attorney James Thompson, among them Daley's city council leader and Chicago's No. 2 Democrat, Ald. Thomas E. Keane, who on November 17, 1974, was sentenced to five years in a federal prison on 17 counts of mail fraud. At municipal election time, however, the *Tribune* recalled the mayor's personal integrity and administrative skills. When Ald. William Singer, Democratic maverick, sought to unseat Daley in the 1975 primary, the *Tribune* commented: "Singer has compiled a good record, but if Richard Friedman couldn't do it with an equally good record in 1971, with Republican support, how can Singer expect to do it?" He of course could not. Daley crushed Singer in the primary and his Republican opponent in the election.

*   *   *

The paper continued to disapprove of the conduct of the Vietnam War, now being covered by veteran Wayne Thomis. It ripped into the student dissenters, and sent Bob Wiedrich to cover the crackdown by federal agents on youthful users of marijuana and other narcotics, Wiedrich in time making worldwide trips to the centers of the drug traffic in support of the paper's campaign against drugs. It was skeptical of Nixon's journey to China, but conceded, "Nixon's trip, merely by making it, signifies the abandonment of a policy which was clearly leading to a dead end." The paper hoped, however, that the president would not seek to negotiate with the Chinese. "It would accomplish no more than staying on the Potomac and playing Ping Pong." Yet the *Tribune* was pleased at President Nixon's reception by Chairman Mao: "As we've said many times, and so has Mr. Nixon, the visit is symbolic. And, symbolically, Mr. Nixon's prompt meeting with Chairman Mao Tse-tung is a plus. It reflects China's apparent desire to show its sincerity, but promises nothing in substantive results."

The *Tribune*'s early evaluation of the American détente with China and Russia—that there was little to be gained from negotiations with any Communist powers—was modified later, when there were signs that China and the USSR might bury their enmity. An editorial that would have shaken Medill and McCormick, even in a supernal world, had they not read it to the end. said in part:

> What should be the response to a Chinese-Soviet détente?
> First, we should make ourselves continuously available as diplomatic friends to both, just as we have been doing.
> Second, we should make ourselves indispensable to both through expanding trade in materials they both need.
> Third, we must keep so strong militarily, that even if the Communists should be tempted to launch an attack on us, we would be able to respond with such fury that the attack would be recognized in advance—even to madmen—as insanity.

The new, young *Tribune* correspondents traveled widely. Aldo Beckman, of the Washington bureau, accompanied President Nixon to China. Louise Hutchinson, also of the Washington bureau, went to Moscow with the Nixons, being joined by James Yuenger, Moscow correspondent. William Mullen wrote from the Far East. Philip Caputo covered the Middle East, reporting vividly from Israel and later Lebanon, where he was shot in both legs by Moslem gunmen. Following his recovery, he was assigned to the Moscow post. In 1976, then London bureau chief Yuenger, with reporter Clarence Page and former *Today* photographer Ernie Cox, Jr., covered the new African crisis, in a series widely reprinted.

*   *   *

News stories are sometimes sleeping volcanoes, properly kept so when the volcanologists in government and politics conceal the facts for the clear benefit of society, improperly when social evil is being hidden. The judgment is difficult to make, and the conflict between the press and the newsmakers as to who best serves society never ends. When Dr. Enrico Fermi withdrew his cadmium-coated rods from the atomic pile under the stands at Stagg Field in 1942, no newspaper quarreled later with the secrecy. But through the early 1970s there was a long procession of secrets, found out eventually because the *Washington Post* intently covered what had begun as a seemingly insignificant local news story, a bungled break-in at the Watergate Apartments complex in the early hours of June 17, 1972. The men apprehended at the Watergate were attempting to bug the offices of the Democratic National Committee and were soon suspected of being linked with the Finance Committee to Re-elect the President, which was running Nixon's campaign for a second term. The committee disavowed any connection, while the White House dismissed the break-in as a "third-rate burglary attempt." But *Washington Post* reporters refused to abandon the story, and by February, 1973, fact and rumor about both the break-in and other campaign irregularities combined to lay a trail that seemed to be leading to the White House. Senator Sam J. Ervin, Jr., of North Carolina was named to chair the Senate Select Committee on Presidential Campaign Activities, charged with investigating the 1972 campaign, including the allegation that the Watergate defendants had been bribed or pressured into pleading guilty and refusing to reveal who was behind their activities.

Investigations proceeded, new instances of political malfeasance were revealed daily, press furor mounted. On April 17, in response to growing indications that White House staffers had engaged in a cover-up operation, President Nixon announced that a White House probe of Watergate had been under way since the previous month. On the 19th, White House counsel John W. Dean III stated that he would not be made "a scapegoat." On April 30, President Nixon took to nationwide television.

The *Tribune*'s banner, set in its new lower-case style, read: "Nixon takes 'bug' blame; 3 key aides resign, 1 fired." Aldo Beckman's story detailed the dismissal of Dean, who was talking to Senate Watergate investigators, and the resignations of Attorney General Richard Kleindienst and top White House aides H. R. Haldeman, Nixon's chief of staff, and John D. Ehrlichman, domestic affairs adviser. The president also announced that he would name Elliot Richardson as attorney general and would authorize him to appoint a special Watergate prosecutor. The paper devoted four pages to the text of the president's statement and side stories, including Mayor Daley's defense of President Nixon. The

Tribune's editorial also backed Nixon, assuming that he was not personally involved in Watergate, but it pointed out that he was the one who appointed those presumably guilty:

> The Watergate dam burst yesterday, and four top administration officials were swept out of office in the biggest White House purge in memory. . . . In a television speech last night which was reminiscent of his Checkers apology of 1952, the President took upon himself the blame he could not escape anyway, and sought to drown his Watergate sorrows in a recitation of other and more important programs of his administration.
>
> Despite this havoc, there is a sense of relief; relief that in a large measure the suspense is over, along with the sickening pretenses and the all-too-obvious concealment that have marked the investigation so far. And relief, too, that Mr. Nixon seems to be holding his footing and to be in some measure of control. . . . But to say Mr. Nixon is in control is not to say he will step out of the floodwaters unspattered by mud. Neither the resignations nor the speech answer many questions that have been asked.

Conceding that President Nixon, as head of the government, was responsible for the acts of his subordinates, the *Tribune* suggested that "if this were a parliamentary democracy the whole government would be swept out of office." Fortunately, the paper continued, this was not the case. "Much as we may lament Watergate and much as it may reflect on the White House, we are better off trying to weather the storm in our present ship than allowing it to be sunk and looking for a new one."

On May 17, Senator Ervin's committee began holding televised hearings. On May 25, Archibald Cox was appointed special Watergate prosecutor by Attorney General Richardson. John Dean, testifying before the Ervin Committee on June 25, for the record accused President Nixon of personal knowledge of a cover-up. On July 16, the existence of a taping system, which had secretly been recording conversations in the president's Oval Office and in his office in the Executive Office Building since the spring of 1971, became public knowledge, beginning a months-long struggle by the committee and Cox to obtain the "Nixon tapes." The tapes supposedly would reveal when the president was first apprised of a possible cover-up and whether he was in fact a conspirator.

Vice-President Spiro Agnew had appeared to be untouched by Watergate, but he had a scandal of his own to deal with, and by August the papers were full of charges that he had been the recipient of illegal cash payoffs in his years as a Maryland politician and that such payoffs had continued even after he became vice-president. On October 10, Agnew resigned his office. That same day he pleaded *nolo contendere* to income tax evasion, after conspiracy and bribery charges were dropped, and was fined $10,000. The *Tribune* on the 11th had effective coverage of the event, which had been foreshadowed on the 9th in a story by the Washington bureau's Harry Kelly. Kelly and Beckman had an exclusive story on the pressures brought upon Agnew to quit, and Glen Elasser and Jon Margolis wrote the lead story. All were members of the Washington bureau, which had been reorganized by Kirkpatrick and McCrohon. On the editorial page, the new Louis Harris column, detailing the results of his weekly opinion poll, stated that President Nixon's standing was at an all-time low. There were troubles abroad and at home as well. Philip Caputo with the Israeli forces and Donald Kirk, with the Syrians, were covering the Yom Kippur War, and in Chicago, Superintendent of Police James Conlisk resigned as the result of the latest police scandal.

The *Tribune* on October 12 denounced Agnew: "The letter *[of resignation]* and the circumstances which necessitated it, are testament to the fact that Mr. Agnew is not and was not worthy of confidence. He betrayed the American people. He betrayed his high office, his President, his party. He betrayed everyone who believed in him and the noble principles he professed to stand for." On the Middle Eastern war, the *Tribune* called for aid to the battered nation under attack by Syria, Egypt, and Jordan. "The United States is clearly committed to Israel's survival. We should make every effort short of introducing our own forces and war material necessary to our own survival to insure that end." On the resignation of Conlisk, the paper called him "a man of good character but lacking executive ability." It suggested that Mayor Daley should "act with the statesmanship of which he is occasionally capable" in replacing Conlisk. Daley chose a man from the police force, James Rochford, with general approval of the press. When President Nixon announced the appointment of House Minority Leader Gerald Ford of Michigan as vice-president, the *Tribune* predicted that he would have almost unanimous support in the Congress. "President Nixon's choice was carefully and successfully planned to reassure a country sated with upsetting surprises in political life."

The controversy over the mysterious "Nixon tapes" also came to a head in October. On the 12th the U.S. Court of Appeals upheld Judge John J. Sirica's ruling that the president must turn over subpoenaed tapes of nine conversations to Special Prosecutor Cox. The president proposed instead a compromise: The White House would prepare summaries and partial verbatim transcripts of the tapes in question and Sen. John C. Stennis would verify their accuracy before they were turned over to Cox and the Senate Watergate Committee. This proposal Cox found unacceptable, and he so announced in a televised press conference on Saturday, October 20. What followed became known as "the Saturday Night Massacre": Attorney General Richardson resigned rather than follow

President Nixon's order to fire Cox, and Deputy Attorney General William Ruckelshaus was himself fired when he too refused to carry out the dismissal order, which was finally executed by Acting Attorney General Robert Bork. The fire storm of public indignation was so great that by October 23 the president had backtracked, and he agreed to surrender the subpoenaed tapes. It was then found that not all the tapes were in existence and that part of a tape covering a crucial conversation on June 20, 1972, had been erased. The public, suffering through an oil embargo imposed by the Arab states as a result of U.S. aid to Israel, awaited with impatience some resolution of the constitutional crisis and avidly anticipated the disclosures to be provided by the tapes. None came.

On February 6, 1974, by a vote of 410–4, the House gave its Judiciary Committee authority to proceed with an impeachment inquiry. Again the elusive tapes were sought, the committee on April 11 subpoenaing 42 tapes, to be turned over April 25. Nixon requested a five-day delay, to Tuesday, April 30, which was granted. The *Tribune* stated that impeachment moves should be based on principles, not technicalities:

> By postponing its deadline until Tuesday, the House Judiciary Committee has delayed, not averted, collision. And with each delay there is a growing danger that if impeachment is delayed, the emphasis will be on the technical, the trivial, and the transient issues. . . . If Congress flinches now, the Constitution may be inoperative tomorrow. . . . The refusal to impeach would be as momentous as impeachment itself. It would and could be interpreted only as meaning that Congress does not think Mr. Nixon has done anything to warrant impeachment. . . .
>
> Congress will do neither itself nor the country any good by looking for pretexts on which to impeach Mr. Nixon. It should impeach him on the basic issues that govern the country—issues involving his honesty, integrity, and judgment—or it should not impeach him at all.

On Monday, April 29, President Nixon announced via nationwide television that on the following day he would turn over to the House Judiciary Committee transcripts of all Watergate-related conversations on the subpoenaed tapes, which covered the period from September 15, 1972, to April 27, 1973. At his side were 26 volumes containing 1,308 pages of edited transcripts. He also served notice that he was taking his case to the people and would release the transcripts to the public as well. "The subpoena is not the issue. Watergate is the issue," said the *Tribune* on the 30th. Aldo Beckman reported on Nixon's television appearance. There was a side story by Harry Kelly: "President Nixon pushed his chips to the middle of the table tonight and took a big gamble. He gambled that the nation—and the House impeachment committee—would accept him with all his 'blemishes' as he called them, exposed in his tape recorded conversations." In another side story it was noted that President Nixon had said of an 18-minute gap in one of the tapes, "How it happened is a mystery to me." The full text of the television speech was published by the paper.

*   *   *

Among the millions of viewers that April 29 were two *Tribune* officials, publisher Cook and editor Kirkpatrick. As each listened and gazed at the stack of bound transcripts at Nixon's side, a possibility crossed their minds: To be first to the public with the long-discussed, fought-over mystery tapes would be a stunning publishing feat. Cook, the former production engineer, knew what *Tribune* staff and equipment could do. He telephoned Kirkpatrick as Nixon finished, saying tentatively, "It would be great if we could print the text of those tapes."

"I certainly agree," Kirkpatrick responded. "I think maybe we can get them early. If we print, the sooner the better. I'll make some calls." Thus began a series of late-night phone conversations.

Kirkpatrick first telephoned Frank Starr, Washington bureau chief, and talked to both Starr and Jim Squires, his assistant. The transcripts, two sets, would be needed at the earliest possible time. They were being bound in the Government Printing Office, Squires thought, but both he and Starr averred that it could be done. They called White House correspondent Beckman. Soon Kirkpatrick received a plea for help. "You'll have to call the White House," he was told. Kirkpatrick reached Press Secretary Ronald Ziegler. "I told him we were interested in getting the transcripts at the earliest possible moment," Kirkpatrick recalled. "I said we would send the *Tribune* plane down that evening if we could get copies." Ziegler was noncommittal. The official release to members of the Judiciary Committee and other public officials was scheduled for 11 A.M. on April 30; the press would not be receiving copies until later in the day. Ziegler indicated that the transcripts were not immediately available.

Beckman, Squires, and Starr kept after Ziegler until he authorized a secretary to pick up the transcripts as soon as they were ready. She agreed with the *Tribune* representatives to go to the printing office very early in the morning.

After talking with his Washington staff, Kirkpatrick got back to Cook. "I've alerted our pilot and production people," Cook said. "Every minute will be important."

At 11 o'clock that night, George Cohen, copy editor for the *Tribune*'s book review magazine, received a call from Dick Leslie, then an assistant news editor and later picture editor. Could George be ready for an early trip to Washington? George could. He had been preparing "cold type" for the *Tribune*'s new Mergenthaler 505 typesetting machines. Instead of setting "hot type," created by fixing a line of molten lead into letters via Linotype matrices, the 505 set film type images that, when pasted on a newspaper-size page, could be photographed, engraved, and used to make stereotype mats. The system, using perforated tapes, was faster than hot type, but Cook was hopeful that the transcripts from the Government Printing Office could themselves be pasted up, a procedure used by the *Tribune* to print the Yalta Papers for that scoop. At 12:30 A.M., April 30, Leslie called Cohen again. They would meet at the Monarch aviation hangar at Midway Airport for a 5 A.M. takeoff. Shortly before 5, Cohen met Leslie and Robert Finan, editorial production coordinator; Patrick Ryan, superintendent of the engraving department; and Fred Hemingston, superintendent of the composing room. Pilot Dick Prendergast had the De Havilland jet ready, and the men boarded and were airborne in the darkness.

In Washington there was a brief wait for the arrival of Squires, who had been delivered two complete sets of the transcripts at 6 A.M. Meantime, Leslie, Hemingston, and Ryan had been busy on the telephones alerting their associates in Chicago as to the probable personnel needs. En route back to Chicago, the men read parts of the transcripts and concluded that some of the pages might not photograph well, also noting that they were set in a way that would require maximum use of newsprint space if they simply were pasted up and photographed. By the time the men landed at Meigs Field at 9:30 A.M. to take taxis to Tribune Tower, they had agreed that the type must be reset on the 505s. Leslie and Cohen prepared to instruct copyreaders on the procedure, including the identifying slug ("tapes"), and pagination needed to make sure there would be no mix-up in sequence as the hundreds of pages went to the typesetters.

In Kirkpatrick's office in Tribune Tower, Cook, production director Wayne Perry, and Kirkpatrick awaited the Washington arrivals. They agreed that a typesetting job was needed and that the three-star May 1 deadline that night could be met, although the *Tribune* was also issuing its regular 80-page edition. Perry, a former instructor in printing and journalism at South Dakota State College and ex–production manager of the *Wall Street Journal,* had joined the *Tribune* as assistant production manager in June, 1970, became production director, and had supervised installation of the new equipment.

Hemingston instructed the composing room to prepare for the task of setting the 1,308 pages of transcript as Leslie, Cohen, and eight other copyreaders began editing and numbering pages of the text for the printers. Meantime, managing editor McCrohon assembled a group of editors to work out the problems of format. They organized the materials for easy reading by creating a "transcription index" so the reader would know who was speaking at what time in Nixon's Oval Office. An attractive front page was devised for the section, actually two sections, and a back picture page planned. Throughout the day, the Mergenthaler 505 machines were producing type for paste-up, some 252 columns, equal to 35,380 lines, or 246,960 words. Sixty printers handled the tape perforating, typesetting, and proofreading, and page layouts were prepared by a crew under Dennis Ginosi and art director Gus Hartoonian. The final page paste-up was sent to engraving at 9:45 P.M. The last engraved plates then went to stereotype where matrices were pressed, into which molten metal was poured to create the curved plates that could be locked onto the presses. Since the combination of the 80-page regular edition and the 44-page special section was beyond the 112-page capacity of the regular press lines, extra presses were used. By 11:04 P.M., press time for the three-star edition, the presses were rolling. *Tribunes* were printed, sections assembled, and bundles swept on conveyor belts to mailrooms and the waiting trucks and semitrailers from the company's fleet of 300, recently expanded and reorganized by circulation director Virgil Fassio. Some 2,000 employees would be involved in the publication and distribution of the Nixon tapes transcripts, not including delivery boys and girls and street vendors.

The following morning, *Tribunes* carrying the text of the tapes reached all regular readers throughout the Midwest. Eight hours before the Government Printing Office bookstore in Washington could sell its first bound copy to the general public at $12.25, *Chicago Tribunes* with full text were on sale in hotels and on newsstands throughout the capital. Starr called Kirkpatrick to tell him that "a copy of the paper is the hottest thing in town." In Burlington, Iowa, the alert editor of the *Hawkeye News* called the *Tribune* to ask for permission to engrave his printing plates from the *Tribune*'s pages. Permission was granted. The *Tribune* published 55,000 extra copies of the edition. The afternoon of May 1, Cook and Kirkpatrick appeared before television cameras and reporters to describe the remarkable publishing feat, which was covered by Chicago's four top TV stations, wire services, and radio, and was described as "a publishing miracle" by NBC's John Chancellor. The achievement was detailed also on other network stations and in various national magazines.

*   *   *

Seven days later, in an editorial titled "Listen, Mr. Nixon . . . ," the *Tribune* published its demand for the resignation or impeachment of President Nixon. The paper's policymakers had been studying the tapes and gathering further background material for a week. On Wednesday, May 8, Kirkpatrick telephoned Cook and McCutcheon, editor of the editorial page, urging a decision. McCutcheon checked with Starr and Squires in

Washington on any possibility that Nixon might take some action on his own. The reply was negative. Following a final conference with Cook and the other editorial writers, Kirkpatrick and McCutcheon collaborated on the editorial that was to shake up old-line Republicans throughout the country and serve notice once again that the *Chicago Tribune* had changed. The editorial said in part:

> We saw the public man in his first administration, and we were impressed. Now in about 300,000 words we have seen the private man, and we are appalled.
>
> What manner of man is Richard Nixon who emerges from the transcripts of the White House tapes?
>
> We see a man who, in the words of his old friend and defender, Sen. Hugh Scott, took a principal role in a "shabby, immoral, and disgusting performance."
>
> The key word here is immoral. It is a lack of concern for morality, a lack of concern for high principles, a lack of commitment to the high ideals of public office that make the transcripts a sickening exposure of the man and his advisers. He is preoccupied with appearance rather than substance. His aim is to find a way to sell the idea that disreputable schemes are actually good or are defensible for some trumped-up cause.
>
> He is humorless to the point of being inhumane. He is devious. He is vacillating. He is profane. He is willing to be led. He displays dismaying gaps in knowledge. He is suspicious of his staff. His loyalty is minimal. His greatest concern is to create a record that will save him and his administration. The high dedication to grand principles that Americans have a right to expect from a President is missing from the transcript record. . . .
>
> He thought disclosure of the records would help him. He has had a demonstration that his countrymen are not that tolerant.
>
> And it should be noted here that the transcripts . . . were not the fabrications of his enemies. These were self-created instruments of destruction. . . .
>
> As it stands [the] record leaves no doubt that he lacks the qualities that could edify and inspire his countrymen with confidence in these difficult times. . . .
>
> The balance among the coordinate branches of our government— Executive, Judicial and Legislative—is fragile. It has been established on rather comfortably loose terms by nearly 200 years of experience in practicing the special virtues of American government.
>
> The limits of executive privilege, of congressional power, of judicial authority are not rigidly fixed. We would not relish the prospect of forcing the Supreme Court to make hard decisions in the distorting heat of partisan controversy. This is one confrontation this country does not need and we pray Mr. Nixon will not insist on it. . . .
>
> Resignation of the President would be quick and simple and a qualified successor stands ready to assume office. . . .

The objection to resignation that has been raised—and we have raised it ourselves—is that it would not resolve the issues. It would not answer many of the questions about the President's behavior and degree of complicity. It would leave at least a suspicion that the President had been persecuted instead of properly prosecuted out of office. To some he might remain a martyr. To many it would seem a miscarriage of justice, an example of political exorcism.

The transcripts have changed all that. Though they may clear Mr. Nixon of direct complicity in the Watergate burglary and the early stages of the coverup, nobody of sound mind can read them and continue to think that Mr. Nixon has upheld the standards and dignity of the Presidency. . . .

We urge the House to act quickly on a bill of impeachment. As the impeachment process progresses, as public opinion becomes clear, and as Mr. Nixon sees support dwindling in the Senate, he will have to reconsider his stand and recognize that resignation will spare the country the ordeal of a trial.

By the time the first edition appeared, other media had been alerted. The Associated Press and United Press moved the editorial, and Kirkpatrick was interviewed by Chicago and network television and was called for recorded telephone interviews by broadcast newsmen in England, Australia, and Canada. *Newsweek, Time,* the *Los Angeles Times,* and the *New York Times* gave the event special coverage, and Jiji Press Agency, serving more than 100 Asian newspapers, cabled the story and the full text of the editorial to Tokyo. Anguished cries were raised in the White House, where the *Tribune*'s deed was reportedly considered a crushing blow to any Nixon hopes for political survival. There were angry letters and a few cancellations in the Midwest, but Casey Banas, assistant to the editor, had the staff keep careful account of the letters and telephone calls. By May 14, the *Tribune* had received 2,183 calls supporting the editorial and 2,068 against. Mail was surprisingly light, 322 letters in favor of the editorial decision, 759 against.

*   *   *

On August 9, 1974, Richard M. Nixon became the first president of the United States to resign from office. Vice-President Gerald Ford was sworn in. President Ford called for unity, for exclusion of the Watergate affair from the national consciousness, and for an attack on the vexing problem of inflation. On Sunday, September 8, Ford granted an unconditional pardon to the former president. The *Tribune* was angry:

Pardon Mishandled

Dismay and regret. Those are our two words to best describe our reaction to the manner and timing of the President's announcement of a full pardon for Richard Nixon.

Note that we said manner and timing, not the pardon itself. We can applaud the President's compassion. We agree with him that early resolution of Mr. Nixon's plans is in the national interest; we have made the same argument ourselves when we called, in May, for Mr. Nixon's prompt resignation or impeachment.

The paper went on to assert that President Ford's reasoning about the pardon was in some ways specious, when he might have used instead completely valid arguments for his action. But the main objection was the release of the decision on a Sunday morning as a surprise to the Congress, to the country, and to the Republican party. "Instead of helping Republicans shed the Watergate issue, he has revived it in his own image." The *Tribune* published the news that Ford's press secretary, Jerald ter Horst, had resigned in protest against the pardon, and it promptly acquired ter Horst as one of its editorial page columnists. Ford's visit to the Far East a few weeks later also was displeasing to the *Tribune:* "President Ford's Far East journey seems to be so inadvisable at this moment as to recall the old World War II query, 'Is this trip necessary?'"

*   *   *

"The biggest operational change in the paper's 127 years." So the *Tribune* described the new format and publishing cycle that began on Monday, September 16, 1974. The *Tribune* had become a 24-hour paper, as it once was briefly during the Civil War period, thus issuing new editions throughout the day. *Chicago Today* had ceased publication the preceding Friday, a move that had been studied and debated for more than a year. During that time marketing studies had been completed, futures extrapolated, and a World War II–type operations schedule devised. The planning had proceeded secretly in a locked, windowless "war room" so that action could be suspended or aborted if *Chicago Today* could find a way to change its revenue situation. No such solution was found, D day was set, and on Friday the 13th, *Today* urged its readers to "turn to the *Tribune*" the following Monday.

The task force that a year and a half earlier had merged the weekend editions of the two papers again mobilized under McCrohon and Schmidt. Format and operational procedures were revised to incorporate top *Today* writers and features into the *Tribune* package, to integrate the staffs, and to insure prompt delivery to thousands of new *Tribune* readers who could order the paper on a morning or evening basis. "You'll have the latest any time you want it," said publisher Stanton Cook in a page-one statement. Editor Kirkpatrick on the editorial page described the transformation as "one of the biggest challenges to any American newspaper in this century."

On page one, above the masthead, many of the *Today* stars already part of the Saturday and Sunday *Tribune* were advertised as enhancing the daily paper as well: "Now starting in the new 24-hour *Tribune*—Rick Talley, Maggie Daly, Jack Mabley, Dear Abby, Double Comics. Price 15 cents." Wayne Stayskal's cartoons joined those of the *Tribune*'s Richard Locher on the editorial and "Perspective" pages, also *Today*'s editorial columnists, among them James Reston and Russell Baker from the New York Times Service. Dan Tucker, chief editorial writer for *Today,* became a member of McCutcheon's staff. Scott Schmidt, editor of *Chicago Today,* appeared in the editorial page flag as managing editor–features, and the *Tribune*'s William Jones as managing editor–news, both functioning under editor Kirkpatrick and managing editor McCrohon. Schmidt and Ralph Hallenstein, former managing editor of *Today,* directed the afternoon edition in the early stages, Schmidt later taking over the features area as initially planned. When Schmidt was chosen to serve as president and general manager of Tribune Company's daily and Sunday *Valley News* in Van Nuys, Michael Argirion, formerly of *Today,* became features editor.

There were more steps to be taken to achieve the new *Tribune.* On July 1, 1975, a new format, six columns for the editorial, news, and features sections of the paper and nine columns in the advertising area, was adopted, a revision supervised by production director Wayne Perry. McCrohon and Hartoonian had proved their typographical creativity at *Chicago Today,* where the paper won national awards for typography, and their work on the *Tribune* was similarly recognized. The paper's typography, which had sometimes endured for decades with almost no change, now became drastically different, praised for its beauty and emulated about the country. By September 20, 1976, designated as "Super Monday," the *Tribune* had become almost totally new, the final realization of the format changes begun with the absorption of *Today*'s weekend editions. The *Tribune* was thoroughly departmentalized for easy reading, splashed with color, filled with vivid text under crisp, provocative headlines, and dramatically illustrated with big, closely cropped photographs and maps, charts, and drawings. The lower-case headlines, big pictures, pulled rules, strategic boxes, and the judicious use of summary inserts and precedes, plus news guidelines convenient for the readers, provided a "package" attractive and easy to read, well justifying a "Super Week" promotion, it was believed.

Tribune content as well as format was improved. Kirkpatrick and McCrohon gained added space and added personnel. The editorial staff of more than 500 was increasingly one of specialists who might practice their investigative expertise, political analysis, or sociological insight not only in Chicago, but anywhere in the world. Good writing, responsible reporting, and careful editorial judgments were qualities especially sought by the editors, who afforded the reporters wide range and freedom and who knew the most effective ways to display the gathered news. The paper expanded its local, regional, and national news coverage and organized its foreign correspondents into flying task forces, able to concentrate on major stories worldwide. Some correspondents were kept on in strategic areas—James O. Jackson in Moscow and later London, then on assignment in Africa; Ronald Yates, based in Tokyo; Alice Siegert in Bonn. Managing editor McCrohon dispatched reports from his native Australia, editor Kirkpatrick from China, foreign editor Yuenger from Russia. Ronald Kotulak, an experienced science writer, reported from Antarctica in addition to covering scientific meetings in the more temperate parts of the world.

A full page of news briefs was presented daily "for the busy person who wants all the news in capsule form." New financial pages on Monday and Wednesday provided added coverage of local and Midwestern business news under the paper's new financial editor, Alvin Nagelberg, plus new columnists Myron Kanel and Philip Greer, covering New York and Washington. These writers supplemented columnist Eliot Janeway and a group who had moved to the *Tribune* from *Chicago Today*—William Gruber, former financial editor; Harold Finley; Sam Shulsky; and George Lazarus, advertising columnist.

One of the new page-one columns announced for "Super Monday" was "Close-Up," alternately written by "three of the best human interest writers in the business," Anne Keegan, from the *Tribune*, and Jeff Lyon and Dorothy Collin from *Today*. The "Tempo" pages, thoroughly remodeled, continued largely ornamented with *Tribune* stars, now supported by Dear Abby and Dr. Joyce Brothers from *Today*. The paper offered two pages of comics, in addition to "Peanuts" on the front of "Tempo," sometimes in color, and various panel cartoons. *Today's* original version of "Action Line," edited by Kenan Heise, led off the "Metropolitan" section, while inside were found the *Tribune's* editorials and spectrum of commentators, and the excellent, expanded "Voice of the People," edited by Alfred Ames. McCutcheon's editorial writers, in addition to Ames and Dan Tucker, included Joan Beck, former women's editor; Kenneth Ross, formerly of the financial section; Kenneth L. Simms, specializing on foreign affairs; and Richard Orr, rural affairs. On Wednesday of "Super Week," the paper presented a new section, "Venture," devoted to leisure time activity.

While the paper sought national and international news, it did not neglect sports and local coverage. The staff of 51 editors and writers under sports editor Cooper Rollow continued to be one of the country's largest and best. The revised Sports section, developed under Rollow, offered a new, illustrated scoreboard, more action pictures, and *Tribune* columnists and writers including Rollow himself, David Condon, John Husar, Robert Markus, Bob Logan, Richard Dozer, and Neil Milbert, plus columnists Rick Talley, Ed Stone, Bill Jauss, and Elmer Polzin from *Today*. City editor Bernard Judge directed a local staff of 85 reporters and rewrite personnel and their logistic support, now including former reporters for the *Tribune*'s zoned sections and most of the local staff of *Chicago Today*. Judge had as assistants Don Agrella, first assistant city editor; Sheila Wolfe, day city editor; and seven other assistant city editors to aid in making assignments, maintaining communication with the reporters, assigning rewriters, and generally evaluating material offered for publication. Judge and his staff kept close liaison with the photography staff through Tony Berardi, Jr., formerly of *Today*, who had been named chief photographer. In addition to city editor Judge's large staff, another complete force of editorial personnel reported to Charles Hayes, editor of the 27 *Trib* editions circulated with the *Tribune* in suburbia.

The new approach to coverage and presentation of news and features won recognition for the paper. In May, 1975, reporter William Mullen and photographer Ovie Carter received the Pulitzer award for their 1974 articles and pictures on the famine-stricken people of West Africa and India. That year the *Tribune* amassed 42 national and local awards for writing and editing and 45 for photography. In 1976 there was another Pulitzer, this one given to the newspaper and its entire editorial staff in the category of local reporting for "a distinguished example of investigative or otherwise specialized reporting . . . by an individual or team." The award recognized two *Tribune* investigative projects, the first a series on the Federal Housing Authority, which resulted in reforms, the second investigation exposing unsatisfactory conditions and practices at Von Solbrig Memorial Hospital and the alcoholic treatment branch of Northeast Community Hospital. Reporters George Bliss and Chuck Neubauer were individually cited in the first project, and reporters William Gains, William Crawford, Jay Branegan, and Pamela Zekman were named as the team developing the hospital exposé. Publication of the exposé had led both offending institutions to close voluntarily. That same year Ron Kotulak won awards from the American Medical Association, the American Chemical Society, and the National Society for Medical Research for his science reports. James T. Robinson, religion editor, won the James Supple Award from the Religion News Writers Association. Peter Reich received the citation of the Aviation Space Writers Association for his report on a flight aboard the supersonic jet Concorde. In addition, the

Tribune received the National Press Photographers Association Award for the best use of pictures by a newspaper in the United States, and McCrohon was honored by the association as the country's outstanding picture editor.

Tribune president Hunt explained that the 1976 changes were based on in-depth marketing studies:

> The survey, conducted by a nationally known firm, indicates that a majority of all newspaper readers in a metropolitan area expressed an openness to new ideas, a frankness about sex and controversy, and a rejection of unnecessary complexity. In addition the survey showed that today's readers are self-oriented and involved in personal improvement. . . . These new attitudes mean that readers want a newspaper more closely directed to their own personal needs and interests, and that is what our changes are all about. . . . The improvements will enable us to serve our readers better, and thereby to strengthen our position as the circulation and advertising leader in Chicago.

The paper's advertising department matched the pace of editorial and circulation. In 1976, for the third straight year, the *Tribune* was second among all U.S. newspapers (first, the *Los Angeles Times*) in total advertising linage. *Tribune* executives had additional reasons to look confidently ahead. They had signed long-term labor contracts that included acceptance of laborsaving devices and techniques such as video display terminal editing facilities installed in 1976–77 to bring the paper full-scale into the electronic production era.

*   *   *

Tribune Company president Cook's reports to his directors at the annual meetings reflected general and consistent progress. The new planning and communication procedures, he said in 1975, were effective "without sacrificing a basic Tribune Company policy—decentralized management providing for decisions to be made as close to the point where resultant action takes place as managerial experience justifies. . . . The parent company, freed of day-to-day operational concerns, can stand back and evaluate the industries of which Tribune Company is a part, define overall objectives, and determine what steps should be taken to achieve them." Much of the credit for the management structure thus described by Cook could be traced to the studies carried out under Wood and Grumhaus, which had transformed what had become an unwieldy family enterprise into a modern, multifaceted corporation.

On April 1, 1975, the McCormick–Patterson Trust terminated, the stock reverting to 153 owners of beneficial interests, to executives exercising their stock options, and to the Chicago Tribune–New York News

Employees Trust. Under the new arrangement, the largest block of the 8,000 shares of Tribune Company stock, nearly 20 percent, was held by the Robert R. McCormick Charitable Trust, and other shares were held by the Robert R. McCormick Foundation and Cantigny Trust. *Tribune* executives Hunt and Kirkpatrick were named to serve along with Grumhaus, Nichols, and Cook as trustees. Three families long associated with the paper followed the trusts in share ownership—the Cowleses, the Lloyds, and the Pattersons.

When the original Tribune Company was incorporated in 1861, it had a capitalization of $200,000, representing 2,000 shares of stock. Joseph Medill increased his initial 430 shares to 1,060, or 53 percent, in 1874, an interest that had diminished only slightly, to 1,050 shares, at the time of his death. This block of stock had been maintained intact by the McCormick–Patterson Trust, supplemented by 20 additional shares soon after the trust was established in 1932. By 1974, the net worth of Tribune Company had increased from $386,000 a century earlier to $347 million. That year, on April 9, the issuance of 20 million shares was authorized, but these have not been issued. Minority stockholders sued Tribune Company in an effort to upset the new company arrangement, but the action was defended successfully by Don H. Reuben of the Kirkland law office. (In 1978, Reuben left the Kirkland firm to join Edward G. Proctor in forming Reuben and Proctor, taking the Tribune Company account with him.)

At the board meeting of April 8, 1976, two new directors were named, the first to come from outside family ownership or company management in Tribune Company history. Thomas G. Ayers, chairman of Commonwealth Edison Company, and Robert W. Reneker, chairman and chief executive of Esmark, Inc., both headed Chicago-based companies and were known for their work in civic and charitable activities as well as their business and financial leadership. James Patterson, son of Capt. Joseph Patterson, retired from the board at this time, but there continued to be among the directors representatives of the early *Tribune* families, including James Cowles and Dr. John Lloyd, with Garvin Tankersley representing the Medill–McCormick families. From the middle period there were Fred Nichols, former Tribune Company president as well as chairman of the Florida properties, and Robert Schmon, president of the companies in Canada. And from the newest period, in addition to Cook, there were Robert Hunt and John W. Madigan, formerly vice-president of Salomon Brothers, investment bankers, who on January 1, 1975, became vice-president and chief financial officer of Tribune Company.

While the close interrelationship of Tribune Company and the *Chicago Tribune* continued, Cook ranged far, from northern Canada to Florida and California. Hunt presided over his own Chicago Tribune Company board, which included as directors and vice-presidents editor Kirkpatrick, general manager Harold R. Lifvendahl, production director Wayne Perry, and advertising director Henry K. Wurzer. Named secretary of Tribune Company and all subsidiaries, including Chicago Tribune Company, was John R. Goldrick, also assistant to Cook. William Caplice was treasurer and Donald Christenson controller. Another major *Chicago Tribune* executive appointed in 1976 was Thomas G. Clancy, circulation director, succeeding Virgil Fassio, who departed to become business manager and later publisher of the *Seattle Post-Intelligencer.*

President Cook reported gross revenues of $809,824,000 for 1976 at the April 11, 1977, directors' meeting, compared with $711,373,000 the prior year, and a consolidated net of $42,622,000, compared with $30,411,000—record earnings for Tribune Company and its now 40 subsidiaries for both years. The newspaper and broadcasting groups achieved increases in operating profits of 38 percent and 141 percent respectively, Cook said, the fifth straight year in which earnings advanced. He recalled some difficulties caused by strikes in the Canadian newsprint industry but added that 1976 was "an invigorating year. There was an upbeat quality to most of the important news that contrasted refreshingly with the disquieting nature of such earlier headline fare as Watergate and the recession. . . . Business conditions were better . . . the general economy improved."

The contributions of the *Chicago Tribune* in 1976 were described in general but glowing terms: "Daily circulation began posting steady month-to-month increases in July. According to the report of the Audit Bureau of Circulations for the six months ended September 30, 1976, it was 66 percent above that of the local Sunday competitor. The same ABC report showed circulation topping the morning competition by 32 percent and was more than twice that of the latter publisher's evening-only paper."

(In February, 1978, publisher Marshall Field announced that the *Chicago Daily News* was ending its struggle against the economic maladies and life-style changes menacing evening papers in cities where the competition was fierce. The 24-hour *Tribune* had kept the pressure on in the afternoon, and the *Daily News* gained neither readers nor advertising linage. Said the *Tribune* on February 24: "The *Chicago Daily News* will depart for that journalistic hereafter where it will join a host of other distinguished papers—including our own sister paper, *Chicago Today*—that found themselves unable to overcome the awesome odds that a newspaper must cope with these days. . . . In any account of Chicago journalism, the role played by the *Daily News* will have to be a leading and noble one of long duration." On March 4, 1978, after 102 years and three months of valiant service, in which it won 15 Pulitzer prizes, the *Daily News* succumbed and was merged with the *Chicago Sun-Times,* which also became a 24-hour paper, like the *Tribune.*)

*   *   *

A major crime story handled by the new, young staff began quietly, but the *Tribune* news department, after a slow start, managed to give the story a unique touch. At 9:20 P.M. on February 4, 1974, two men and a woman seized 19-year-old Patricia Hearst, of the famous newspaper family, in her apartment in Berkeley, California, the beginning of the country's most bizarre kidnapping case. The *Tribune* relied on its wire services until February 8, when Ronald Koziol sent his first dispatch. Koziol opened with a straight news report on the search for Miss Hearst, which had taken a radical-political twist when the Symbionese Liberation Army (SLA) assumed responsibility for the kidnapping in a letter to a Berkeley radio station. Soon Koziol was fully in the mood of California news-style and began providing more of the color and flavor of the remarkable crime. He wrote on February 16: "California is the sunny, funny, sad land of drive-in mortuaries and topless massages, of Charles Manson, Mickey Mouse, round-the-world rowboaters, and balloon ascensionists. . . . Sometimes it seems peopled by fanatics, extremists, loony old ladies and acre upon acre of neurotic Loud families. . . . So it was no surprise that America's first radical-political kidnapping happened here in California where the bizarre is commonplace."

Koziol was not overcome by his environment, however, and for months he pursued the Hearst case Chicago-style, a style appreciated by the Hearsts themselves, who gave him occasional leads. On May 12, he reported that FBI agents were beginning to believe that Patty had been a willing victim of the kidnapping. But it was not until after Miss Hearst had been captured, September 18, 1975, that Koziol obtained his major exclusive.

The reporter learned that the FBI had seized a manuscript being written jointly by Patty Hearst and William and Emily Harris, her guards, who had been hiding out in an Anaheim motel when the rest of the SLA kidnappers died in a firefight with Los Angeles police on May 17, 1975. Koziol, besides covering the case for months, had written a special series of articles on it with two other *Tribune* reporters, Michele Sneed and Rick Soll, and had excellent contacts. By January, 1976, Koziol had been assured that he would have an opportunity to study the manuscript. "The thing is dynamite," Koziol was told. On January 19, he met his source in a restaurant down the peninsula from San Francisco. He learned that he could see about 100 pages of what appeared to be a proposed book on the SLA philosophy. His informant said that the manuscript was "under some measure of control," and that Koziol could see it only in a locked room, to which nobody but his contact would have the key. He agreed to the terms. Each day he would call his source to see if there would be a meeting in a hidden place. Once at the rendezvous, Koziol would be given a few sheets of manuscript and sufficient time to take notes in longhand. Then a new set of manuscript sheets would be brought, and those read taken away.

The manuscript, which became known as the "Tania Interview," told a fascinating story of Patty Hearst's experiences with the SLA from the time of her kidnapping, and evidently was in her own words. She described her subsequent "conversion" to the life of an urban guerrilla, signaled by her use of the name Tania, and her close friendship with SLA soldier William Wolfe, who died in the Los Angeles shoot-out. According to the manuscript, the Los Angeles attack strengthened her determination to continue the life of a revolutionary. Other parts of the manuscript related full details of the kidnapping and later events, as seen by her captors, the Harrises. Koziol spent three days taking notes, then informed Steve Lough, national editor of the *Tribune,* of what he had. Lough instructed Koziol to send it late at night via telecopier in order to preserve secrecy.

Patricia Hearst was about to go on trial, and at Tribune Tower the editors decided that the manuscript could not be published until the jury had been selected and sequestered. Koziol was so informed. He pointed out that more than 100 reporters from throughout the world were covering the case and that secrecy of the manuscript story might not be maintained, especially since one of the prosecution staff had alluded to it. But the editors were unmoved. Not until the jury had been picked and locked away on February 4, 1976, was the story printed in the *Tribune*'s afternoon Green Streak edition. It was a major exclusive.

*   *   *

Despite the public's boredom with politics following the interminable 1976 presidential primary campaign, which had begun almost two years previously for former Georgia governor Jimmy Carter, the *Tribune,* like other newspapers and media, felt compelled to cover the national conventions thoroughly. Kirkpatrick himself went to both and sent large staffs, with James Squires, Washington bureau chief, as convention staff director. Jon Margolis wrote the lead Democratic convention stories, with Eleanor Randolph explaining in a side story how nominee Carter happened to pick Sen. Walter Mondale of Minnesota as his running mate. Dan Tucker's editorials were slightly irreverent. "One of the elements

noticeably lacking at this convention," he observed, "along with excitement and suspense—is humor. The amount of comedy and wit in
evidence here might, if concentrated, be just enough to flavor a jelly
bean."

Following the acceptance speeches, the *Tribune* said of Carter and
Mondale: "In sum, the Democrats have fielded what looks like a powerful
team to carry a frayed, hand-me-down ball—the Democratic case for
election in the fall. In terms of personalities, it poses a real challenge for
the Republicans." Then, a day later: "So far, Mr. Carter's great asset has
been that he offers a new face and a new voice at a time when people are
fed up with familiar faces and stale rhetoric. But, in the intense publicity
of a political campaign, no face and no voice can stay new for very long.
What will Mr. Carter have to offer when the novelty wears off?"

The Republican convention, usually drearier than the Democratic, did
have the excitement of a challenge to President Ford by former California governor and perennial presidential hopeful Ronald Reagan. But the
Tribune admitted wearily on August 16, "National conventions really do
not accomplish much. . . . They are unsatisfactory as contests, at least as
far as the nominations are concerned—not since 1952 has any convention in either party gone more than one ballot." And, as for the platform:
"We find the Democrats running on a liberal platform, though the
candidate may be a conservative. . . . The Republican platform is an
equally incoherent mish-mash." As the convention ended, the paper
sought to summon enthusiasm: "With the choice of Sen. Robert Dole of
Kansas as running mate, President Ford has called signals for a fierce,
hard-driving presidential campaign, one that will carry the fight directly
to Jimmy Carter. . . . In some respects this was a high risk choice on Mr.
Ford's part. Senator Dole has a number of liabilities." The liabilities were
Nixon connections, largely, and the paper thought Dole's fighting qualities might overcome them. "The GOP this fall will offer a solidly welded
pair of conservatives," the *Tribune* concluded, "one that even has a built-in
slogan: 'It is better to have a Dole as vice president than as a policy.'"

Neither the slogan nor Dole caught on, but by Tuesday, November 2,
the *Tribune* was truly sanguine. "In the beginning Gov. Carter had what
seemed an insuperable lead; today the race is so close that the polltakers
don't dare predict the outcome. Until recently, it was expected that bored
and frustrated voters would be staying home by the millions and that
barely 50 percent would vote. In the last few days the closeness of the race
has brought new interest and new predictions." Previously, on October
24, the *Tribune* had said flatly, "Ford is our choice," after admitting that
the campaign was a dull one of "potshots and platitudes." It had done
what it could to enliven things by endorsing some Democrats, including
liberal Congressman Abner Mikva in the Tenth District, where he

narrowly won, and by seeking to oust several judges deemed unqualified, including a foe of the press and friend of Mayor Daley, Joseph Power, who was defeated, though the rest were not. Forced to choose between two variously qualified candidates for governor, James "Big Jim" Thompson, the former federal prosecutor whom the paper had praised repeatedly for sending a number of Illinois politicians to prison, and Michael Howlett, Illinois's popular secretary of state, whom it had praised for being a good administrator, the *Tribune* opted for Thompson, the Republican. The paper's poll forecast a close race for the presidency in Illinois and a landslide for Thompson. The poll was correct on both counts.

The *Tribune*, like most other news organs, gave a major part of its attention to the more ponderous aspects of politics, the usually dull speeches, the infighting of special interest to the initiate, the interpretations by specialists and prognosticators. Nonetheless it also saw the lighter side, as when Jim Squires and Eleanor Randolph, both southern members of the Washington bureau, combined to write:

> For some of us the consequences of a Georgian in the White House are at best bittersweet. . . . If America becomes "Southernized," the South can't rise again. It will have risen. As anybody who grew up in the shade of a magnolia knows, this dream of the South rising is far more satisfactory than an actual happening.
>
> The election of Jimmy Carter would simply finalize for the rest of the world what a lot of us already know but won't admit—that the "South" is over. . . . It began to fade 20 years ago when little girls in organdy reached across steamy Southern living rooms to switch on a little magic box called television that had been shipped down from the North. Until then, change had been as lazy as an August day in the delta.

But, wrote Squires and Randolph cheerfully, there might be hope for southerners if not the South. "Finally, now that being Southern doesn't mean much any more, Jimmy Carter is making it fashionable. His presidential campaign has projected the region's new image on the face of the nation better than anybody since Colonel Sanders."

On November 3, the *Tribune* offered its congratulations to President-elect Carter, noting that he had reconstituted the coalition of disparate elements that held the Democratic party together during the New Deal, "the conservative South, the urban liberal North, the labor unions, the blacks, the big city machines and the reformers." After examining what candidate Carter had to say during the campaign, the paper concluded, "He isn't so very different from the Gerald Ford he defeated." It cited Carter as opposing governmental bureaucratic waste, favoring tax reform in the interest of simplification and fairness, not merely to punish business, and said:

He is above all the Jimmy Carter who stands for dignity and integrity in public affairs, for candor with the people, and for preserving the respect of the world.

To the extent that Jimmy Carter who has been elected turns out to be the one with these qualities, he will do a good job and can count on our support. But there were many other Jimmy Carters whom some people voted for on the basis of qualities and policies which could well disrupt our economy for years to come. And if we see any of them around the White House, we shall not hesitate to sound the alarm.

*   *   *

On December 20, 1976, a Chicago political regime coinciding closely with the beginning of the new *Tribune* era came to an end. Mayor Richard J. Daley, 74, died in his doctor's Michigan Avenue office of a massive heart attack. The *Tribune* had supported Daley in four of his six campaigns, though not in the first and not in his last, when it "stood aloof." As Chicago mourned the death of "the last of the big city bosses," the *Tribune* recalled that the political leader who could make a city work had his virtues and his failings. Noting, as all did, that it was the end of an era, the paper continued:

> Many will say that it was an era that should have ended, perhaps long ago. Mayor Daley was the last of the big city bosses. And like other big city machines of the past, Chicago's was one that tolerated things that should not be tolerated—corruption, nepotism, links with crime, and feather-bedding; while refusing to tolerate other things that should be tolerated—notably any sign of real democracy in city hall.
>
> But Chicago is also known, and with considerable reason as "the city that works." Before cheering the end of the Daley machine, it is worth pausing to ask to what extent it has been the city that worked, and to what extent it was the Daley machine that worked.

The *Tribune* concluded in part that Daley had been in many ways effective as mayor because he had excellent communication, with himself at the switchboard, and because Daley, as chairman of the Cook County Central Committee, also had "clout." "In Chicago there has been this communication; there has been some cooperation and there have been sacrifices in the public interest. Policemen and sanitation men have not walked out. . . . Industry has not been in a rush to escape from the city. Taxes have been reasonably steady." These boons accrued, said the *Tribune*, "largely because of threats and promises from city hall. Like most machines, Mayor Daley's centered upon one man, namely himself." The *Tribune* viewed the future grimly, since the machine, being a machine, spawned no heir. "We're left with an assortment of wheels and cogs and bolts and screws—and, we're afraid—some nuts. It is a challenge which all of us must recognize and face, as citizens."

*   *   *

The *Chicago Tribune* by 1977 had changed vastly in typography, in editing processes, in its printing cycle, and in the diversity of its views, news, and features. The paper respected Joseph Medill's injunction "First look to your machines," and Colonel McCormick's belief that the first duty of a newspaper is "to return a profit," but the emphasis was on the responsibility of the press to the people. Believing with Alexis de Tocqueville that the printing press is essential to democracy, and cognizant of Lenin's dictum that those who make revolution must control the press, *Tribune* executives under Cook sought economic viability as a means to insuring press freedom. They built upon the extensive physical resources bequeathed to them by McCormick and expanded by Campbell, Wood, and Grumhaus, finding better inks, faster presses, and improved ways to process pulp, grow more trees, and print more advertising, while editors added content, revised format, and enjoyed full liberty of expression.

Yet the new *Tribune* also continued philosophically to be the *Tribune* of 19th-century political traditions, with a strong Colonel McCormick presence felt not only in the technological and financial areas, but also in its eternal watchfulness for a threat from Communism or a menace to press freedom. It was truly the wary "watchman on the walls" envisioned by Joseph Medill. Said a November 8, 1976, editorial on Red China: "Through the equivocal murk that surrounds nearly everything in Peking, one may detect that Chinese leadership is disillusioned with pure Communism." Then, concluding, "If China and the world can learn from Mao's failure (and Lenin's earlier one) that total equality and even reasonable freedom are incompatible, everyone can make a realistic choice and can then work single-mindedly to obtain the objective which most people regard as more important—namely freedom."

As a representative of a newspaper that since its founding nearly 130 years earlier had made freedom of the press a chief concern, editor Kirkpatrick was named a member of the American delegation to the general conference of the United Nations Educational, Scientific, and Cultural Organizations (UNESCO) at Nairobi, Kenya, in November, 1976. A Soviet-sponsored declaration that the United States contended would reduce press freedom brought Kirkpatrick to the conference podium. "The resolution reflects the views of some nations that regard the mass media as a political arm of the state," he said. Kirkpatrick continued:

> It reflects the view that information media is to be used as a tool or an implement to further the aims and objectives of the state. . . . This view is totally rejected by nations that declare—in many cases by constitutional mandate—that their press, and by extension the mass media, must be free from interference by the state. . . . In these nations the mass media, far

from being a tool of the state, is a counter-balancing force exercising a restraining force to prevent abuse of power by the state. It is more than that, of course. It is an educational and information agency. . . . In these nations mass media is an early warning device to alert the managers of government operating in behalf of the people that the people may desire change and improvement in their stewardship. . . . In these nations mass media is also a safety valve to permit protest to be ventilated before it becomes so explosive that only the destruction of the government can bring relief.

The Soviet declaration was defeated, but Kirkpatrick warned, "The contest is not over, it has just shifted to a new scene." The *Wall Street Journal,* speaking of the possibly transient victory, echoed Kirkpatrick, warning that the United States had indicated to the Third World it would not provide money for subsidized news organizations, presumably of the type owned by the Soviet government. The Third World news organizations "would be nothing more than organs grinding out government press releases," the *Journal* said. In Chicago the *Daily News* congratulated Kirkpatrick and his colleagues "for winning this victory, which affects not only the press and broadcast media, but also, and more important, the right of people everywhere to get closer to the truth."

The new *Tribune* graphically illustrated the process of philosophical and technological change required for newspapers to endure as a vital part of the social order. Longtime critics of the paper voiced approval of the outward evidences of change. *Time,* in welcoming the *Tribune* to its pantheon of the best, found past "raucous eccentricities giving way to a calmer tone and a less polemical approach to events." In the *Columbia Journalism Review,* J. D. E. Bruckner commented, "When the rigid gothic grayness of the *[front]* page went, the old righteous isolationism seems to have gone with it, which is refreshing in a day when righteousness seems to be creeping into the news columns of other papers." *Newsweek* dealt a somewhat mean blow, dubbing the paper "the liberal *Trib*." The *Tribune* struck back in an editorial that said:

> If, in applying liberal to the *Tribune, Newsweek* intends to attribute qualities eloquently described by the great Victorian conservative Cardinal Newman . . . qualities of a cultured, open, inquiring and generous mind, we would not quarrel. . . . However, if we must have a label, we prefer conservative—open-minded conservative in the enlightened sense that we wish to build upon values that have been tested and established and not toss them aside.

A midwestern neighbor, the *Decatur Herald and Review,* published an appraisal by Gerald L. Conner, of the Lindsay-Schaub Newspapers, who wrote: "It is not easy to be an American institution and a daily newspaper at the same time." Conner talked to editorial page chief McCutcheon, who spoke of "the 19th century liberal ideas of freedom, minimum interference by government in the affairs of men, free enterprise and competition, and a sound economy." Conner spoke also with staff members, other executives, and retirees. Most of them, the younger ones in particular, liked what was happening, as when Koch of the *Chicago Journalism Review* had found them "exalted" by the changes. But some detested the new policies. "They're more than modernizing it, they're ruining it," one former copyreader told Conner. He had taken early retirement rather than endure change. "We used to know where we stood, but we don't now," another complained.

Back in Decatur, Conner talked to an octogenarian who had read the *Chicago Tribune* for more than 50 years and who intended to continue. "I suppose there is something they could do to the *Tribune* to make me stop taking it, but they haven't done it yet," he said.

NOTES ON SOURCES

Because many of the issues of the *Tribune* that were destroyed in the Great Fire have never been replaced in the paper's files, a few *Tribune* quotations and references are based on contemporary sources, including the books of Franc Wilkie, memos and letters in the Medill Papers and Ray Papers, and the papers of Albert Bodman. Only limited reference has been made here to Chicago's newspapers, which were consulted extensively.

In addition to the interviews listed in the Preface, basic research was also done in Tribune Company Archives, the corporate files of Tribune Company, and the records of various departments of the *Chicago Tribune*. Periodicals consulted are identified in these notes but are not listed in the Bibliography, where full publication information on the other works cited may be found.

Chapter 1   Joseph Medill of the *Tribune*

Horace White related the incident in which Medill ordered Lincoln's feet off his desk in an interview published in the *Tribune* on February 7, 1909. The description of the telegraph operations room is from Plum's *The Military Telegraph in the Civil War*. "Juno" was one of five code names used for General Grant. Stanton's office is described by Ingersoll in *A History of the War Department*. Medill's recollection of the Chicago draft committee's meeting with Lincoln and Stanton was first published in Tarbell's *Life of Abraham Lincoln*.

The *Chicago Times* mentioned in this and subsequent chapters prior to 1900 is in no way related to the *Chicago Times* founded in 1929, which is one of the forerunners of today's *Chicago Sun-Times*.

Surveys of early Chicago newspaper history may be found in Andreas, *History of Chicago*, and Pierce, *A History of Chicago*. The *Tribune*'s early years are described in the *Chicago Tribune* of August 21, 1864, which devoted a full page to "A Retrospective Survey." Other details of the *Tribune*'s early history appear in Bross's *History of Chicago* and in Kinsley's *The Chicago Tribune: Its First Hundred Years*, which, title notwithstanding, covers the period 1847–1900.

The biographical sketch of Scripps is based on the obituary published in the *Tribune* on September 23, 1866.

All aspects of Chicago's early history are discussed in detail in Andreas's *History of Chicago*, a three-volume work published in the mid-1880s. Another standard reference, highly reliable, is Pierce's *History of Chicago*, also three volumes, published from 1937 to 1957. Also used to prepare the parts of this chapter dealing with Chicago's growth were *The Illinois and Michigan Canal*, by Putnam; Bross's *History of Chicago*; *Reminiscences of Chicago during the Forties and Fifties*, edited by McIlvaine; *The Illinois Central Railroad and Its Colonization Work*, by Gates; and *Main Line of Mid-America*, by Corliss.

Johannsen's carefully researched and documented *Stephen A. Douglas* has been relied on for most of the details of the Little Giant's life. Descriptions of the North Market Hall meeting of September 1, 1854, may also be found in Kinsley and Andreas.

Scripps's response to Dr. Ray's inquiries about business reporting is in the Ray Papers.

Details of John Wentworth's life are based on Fehrenbacher's scholarly and readable *Chicago Giant*. Information on Charles Wilson, Richard Wilson, and James Sheahan may be found in *Biographical Sketches of the Leading Men of Chicago*, compiled by Carbutt.

The discussion of events leading up to Lincoln's Peoria speech and his avoiding meeting with the radicals in Springfield is based on Thomas's *Abraham Lincoln*.

Chapter 2   Chicago, the Meeting Place

No full-length biography of Joseph Medill has ever been written. The richest source of detail on his early life and newspaper career is the Medill Papers, a collection including not only letters and memorandums sent and received by Medill but also the letters of his wife, Katherine, and his brother William. Another unpublished source is Strevey's *Joseph Medill and the Chicago Tribune During the Civil War Period,* a Ph.D. thesis written in 1930. Much of Medill's Ohio newspaper career can be traced in the pages of his *Cleveland Leader* and in Hooper's *History of Ohio Journalism.* Details of the Medill-Cowles-Vaughan partnership on the *Leader* are from the Medill Papers and Bradburn's *A Statement by George Bradburn, of his Connection with the "True Democrat" and John C. Vaughan.* Broader treatments of Medill's life appear in Bennett's *Joseph Medill, a Brief Biography* and in the obituary of Medill published in the *Tribune* on March 17, 1899.

Horace Greeley's remarks concerning the "annihilation" of the Whigs in 1848 are quoted in Stoddard's *Horace Greeley: Printer, Editor, Crusader.* Greeley's letter telling Medill to "go ahead" with a new Republican party was lost in the Chicago Fire, and the citation here is based on Medill's reconstruction of the letter, which appeared in the *Tribune* on March 17, 1899. This is also the case with J. Watson Webb's defense of the label Whig.

The description of the March, 1854, meeting in the *Leader* offices and Medill's summary of the principles of the National Republican party are from H. I. Cleveland, "Booming the First Republican President: A Talk with Abraham Lincoln's Friend, the Late Joseph Medill," published in the *Saturday Evening Post,* August 5, 1899.

Details of the life of Dr. Charles Ray are based on Monaghan's biography, *The Man Who Elected Lincoln,* and the Ray Papers. Ray's *Jeffersonian* editorial "We belong to no clique . . ." is quoted by Kinsley. Ray's letters to Washburne are in the Washburne Papers; many of them are reproduced by Monaghan.

Stephen Douglas's defense of popular sovereignty is discussed at length in Johannsen's biography of Douglas. The senatorial vote in the Illinois legislature in February, 1855, and Lincoln's strategy are related by Thomas in his biography of Lincoln, in which Lincoln's letter to Washburne following his defeat is quoted.

The discussion of the early Medill-Ray relationship and their buying into the *Tribune* follows the lines suggested by Monaghan. Evidence that Medill visited Chicago in November, 1854, and declined Webster's offer to become managing editor is in the Medill Papers. Greeley's role is indicated by Monaghan, and correspondence in the Ray Papers suggests Greeley did indeed bring Medill and Ray together. In later years Medill in one interview agreed with this and in another said that he and Ray met accidentally in the Tremont House Rotunda. Other details appear in the Medill obituary, "A Retrospective Survey" (*Tribune,* August 21, 1864), and Kinsley.

Chapter 3   New Life for the *Tribune*

Chicago's politics are discussed in the Pierce and Andreas histories of the city. Details of the Lager Beer Riots are from Peterson's *Barbarians in Our Midst,* Andreas, and *Tribune* accounts. Other aspects of Chicago are described in Bross's *History of Chicago* and in *Reminiscences of Chicago during the Forties and Fifties,* edited by McIlvaine.

Wentworth's views on the Kansas-Nebraska Act and the Republican party as expressed in his *Democrat* are detailed in Fehrenbacher's *Chicago Giant.*

A memorandum in the Ray Papers notes the April 27, 1855, agreement regarding the sale of the *Tribune* to Medill and his associates. Stewart's farewell to the *Tribune* is cited in "A Retrospective Survey" (*Tribune,* August 21, 1864). Other details of the changeover are discussed by Kinsley in *The Chicago Tribune: Its First Hundred Years.*

Lincoln's visit to the *Tribune* offices to subscribe to the paper was described by Medill in the interview with Cleveland, "Booming the First Republican President" (*Saturday Evening Post,* August 5, 1899). .

The discussion of events and personalities in Kansas relies upon Nevins, *A House Dividing;* Isely and Richards, *Four Centuries in Kansas;* Johannsen's biography of Douglas; and standard references.

The Decatur editors' conference is treated by Kyle in *Abraham Lincoln in Decatur.*

Chapter 4   "The War Has Begun in Kansas"

Katherine Medill's letters to her father and her husband are in the Medill Papers. Monaghan's *The Man Who Elected Lincoln* reports the living arrangements made for his family by Charles Ray. Details of Alfred Cowles's life are from Cowles, *Genealogy of the Cowles Family.* Monaghan suggests some of the causes of friction between Ray and Medill, and a letter from Katherine Medill to her father speculates on the reasons for Vaughan's departure from the *Tribune.*

The *Illinois State Journal*'s description of delegates to the Bloomington Convention is quoted by Cole in *The Era of the Civil War, 1848-1870.* Medill's account of Lincoln's lost speech appears in Tarbell's *In the Footsteps of the Lincolns.* Scripps's description is quoted by Kinsley in his history of the *Tribune.* The activities of Wentworth, including his remarks to Lincoln at the Ogle County campaign meeting, are detailed in Fehrenbacher's *Chicago Giant.* Jim Lane's Chicago mass meeting is described in Andreas's *History of Chicago.*

Medill's letter to Colfax regarding Kansas and Douglas's political situation is quoted by Strevey. Johannsen covers Douglas's repudiation of the Lecompton Constitution. Greeley's attempts to drum up support for Douglas among Illinois Republicans are related by Stoddard. Medill's letter to Trumbull regarding a Democratic split is cited by Strevey. Monaghan quotes Ray's letters to Trumbull about Douglas. David Donald discusses Herndon's trip east in *Lincoln's Herndon.* Ray's letter to Trumbull regarding Douglas's loss of support in Chicago is in the Trumbull Papers. Lincoln's letter to Washburne relating Medill's fears is cited by Kinsley.

The Chicago of the period is described by Bross, Pierce, and Andreas in their histories of the city. The *Effie Afton* case is summarized by Thomas. Robert Hitt's participation in the trial is reported by Kinsley.

Changes in the firm's name are chronicled in the *Tribune*'s August 21, 1864, "Retrospective Survey." The account of the merger of the *Tribune* and the *Democratic Press* is based on Kinsley, Bross, and the "Retrospective Survey." A memorandum of agreement for the consolidation, dated June 15, 1858, is found in the Ray Papers. Details of the life of Bross appear in Carbutt's *Biographical Sketches,* Andreas, and Bross's own *History of Chicago.*

Chapter 5   The Great Debates

Horace Greeley's activities in support of Douglas are detailed in Stoddard's *Horace Greeley.* The preconvention meeting of Judd, Ray, Bross, and Lincoln is described by Beveridge in *Abraham Lincoln, 1809-1858.* The reasons for and significance of Lincoln's endorsement by the Republican state convention are discussed in detail by Fehrenbacher in *Prelude to Greatness: Lincoln in the 1850's.* Herndon's advice to Lincoln about the House Divided speech is cited by Donald in *Lincoln's Herndon.* Angle's *Created Equal? The Complete Lincoln-Douglas Debates of 1858* is the source used for the quotation from the House Divided speech. Douglas's reaction to Lincoln's "nomination" is quoted by Johannsen in *Stephen A. Douglas,* as is Greeley's letter to Medill regarding the nomination. Lincoln's letter scolding Ray is in Tribune Company Archives.

Potter Palmer's career is discussed in Kogan and Wendt's *Give the Lady What She Wants!* Wentworth's activities are detailed in Fehrenbacher's *Chicago Giant.*

Norman Judd's role in delivering Lincoln's challenge to Douglas is mentioned in Carbutt's *Biographical Sketches*. Angle notes the journalistic "firsts" in *Created Equal?*, in which he also quotes the *Tribune* and *Times* accounts of Douglas and Lincoln at Havana. Medill's letter advising Lincoln to take the offensive is in the Medill Papers. Monaghan describes the discovery that Douglas was misquoting the Springfield resolutions at Ottawa and cites Ray's letter to Washburne about the "forgery." The anecdote regarding Hitt's late arrival at Freeport is related in Kinsley's history of the *Tribune*.

Don E. Fehrenbacher, in *Prelude to Greatness,* provides what Douglas biographer Johannsen calls the definitive analysis of the Freeport Question by citing the evidence that Medill and others encouraged Lincoln to ask the famous question, though the final wording was Lincoln's own. Medill's account of events surrounding the Freeport Question and Lincoln's remarks to him after the 1860 election appeared in the *Tribune* of May 19, 1895, as "A Reminiscence of Lincoln. Lincoln's Cunning Question Put to Douglas at the Freeport Debate."

Lincoln's letter to A. G. Henry after his defeat for the Senate is cited by Thomas. In *The Man Who Elected Lincoln,* Monaghan quotes Lincoln's letter to Ray. Medill's letter to Colfax describing the interview with Douglas is quoted by Strevey. Douglas's trip through the South and his other activities during this period are described by Johannsen.

The *Tribune*'s financial problems after the 1858 campaign and the mortgage extension are detailed in "A Retrospective Survey" (*Tribune,* August 21, 1864). Lincoln's June 15, 1859, letter to the *Tribune* is in Tribune Company Archives.

Medill's letters to Chase about his presidential chances are cited by Strevey. Thomas quotes Lincoln's letter to Thomas J. Pickett. Many of Medill's actions in furthering Lincoln's candidacy were recounted in his interview with Cleveland, "Booming the First Republican President" (*Saturday Evening Post,* August 5, 1899).

Chapter 6   The People's Candidate

The actions of *Tribune* editors and others in furthering Lincoln's candidacy are described in Thomas's *Abraham Lincoln*, in Kinsley's *The Chicago Tribune,* and in Monaghan's *The Man Who Elected Lincoln*. In his interview with Cleveland (*Saturday Evening Post,* August 5, 1899), Medill recounted his own activities in Washington as well as Seward's reaction to the *Tribune*'s support of Lincoln.

The February 16, 1860, editorial is one of many included in *A Century of Tribune Editorials* and is considered by Lincoln scholars to be the opening of the public campaign for Lincoln's nomination. The events surrounding the Cooper Union address are described by Thomas, by Monaghan, and by Sandburg's *Abraham Lincoln: The Prairie Years.* Monaghan recounts the anecdote about Lincoln and Volk's "life mask." Medill recorded the conversation in which he told Lincoln the *Tribune* would not "fool away" its time on the vice-presidency in "Recollections of Lincoln, Furnished by Joseph Medill," in the *Tribune* of April 21, 1895. Thomas describes the scene at the Republican state convention.

Details of the setting for the Republican National Convention are from the newspapers; from *Reminiscences of Chicago during the Civil War,* edited by McIlvaine, in which a member of Ellsworth's Zouaves describes the training of the troop and its tours; and from Tarbell's *Life of Lincoln.* Randall, in *Colonel Elmer Ellsworth,* quotes Lincoln on Ellsworth.

Van Deusen, in *Thurlow Weed, Wizard of the Lobby,* describes Weed and his relationship with Seward. Greeley's role at the convention is detailed by Stoddard in *Horace Greeley,* in which Defrees's telegram to Colfax is cited.

Behind-the-scenes activities on Lincoln's behalf are detailed by Kinsley; by Monaghan, who quotes Ray's letter asking Lincoln to trust his supporters; by Medill in his Cleveland interview; and by Thomas, who describes Cartter's crucial vote and quotes Lincoln's complaint at having been gambled away. The Democrats' 1860 conventions are analyzed by Johannsen in *Stephen A. Douglas,* in which he quotes the letter by Douglas's reluctant running mate.

Medill's letter warning Lincoln about Wentworth is in the Lincoln Collection and is quoted by Fehrenbacher in *Chicago Giant*.

Chapter 7   "The Wind Blows from the North"

Douglas's patriotic conciliation is described by Johannsen in his biography of the Illinois senator. Lincoln's admonitory letter to the Missouri editor is quoted by Thomas in *Abraham Lincoln*. The exchange of letters regarding reaction to Cameron's appointment to the cabinet, including Washburne's to Ray, Medill's to White and other *Tribune* colleagues, and Trumbull's to Ray, is in the Ray Papers. Ray's letter advising Washburne to keep cool is in the Washburne Papers.

The progress of Lincoln's entourage eastward is described by Thomas. The president-elect's extemporaneous speech at Philadelphia is quoted in Basler's edition of Lincoln's collected works. Judd recalled the details of the plot against Lincoln and his arrangements with Pinkerton in Carbutt's *Biographical Sketches*.

The activities of Chicago's Committee of Safety and the Cairo Expedition are related by Burley in *Reminiscences of Chicago during the Civil War*, edited by McIlvaine, and by Eddy in *The Patriotism of Illinois*.

Fehrenbacher details the conflict between Scammon and Wentworth in *Chicago Giant*.

Charles Ray's movements in covering the Battle of Bull Run are traced by Monaghan, with additional background information from the *Tribune* and Crozier's *Yankee Reporters*. Battle statistics are from *The Civil War*, by Newman and Long. On August 22, 1861, the *Tribune* reprinted Russell's account of the battle from the London *Times;* Ray's reply ran the day following.

Chapter 8   The Bohemian Brigade

Crozier's *Yankee Reporters* and Starr's *Bohemian Brigade* provide highly readable and well documented overviews of the exploits of the Civil War reporters. Colorful but sometimes inaccurate accounts were written by many of the correspondents themselves. Among the most entertaining are three by Wilkie, *Walks About Chicago, Pen and Powder,* and *Personal Reminiscences of Thirty-Five Years of Journalism*. Other published accounts are in Townsend's *Campaigns of a Non-Combatant* and Villard's *Memoirs*. Bodman's partial memoirs were discovered by his grandson in 1976 and are now in Tribune Company Archives.

Joseph Medill's activities in the Civil War are recounted in the Medill Papers, Strevey's *Joseph Medill . . . during the Civil War Period,* Kinsley's *The Chicago Tribune,* Monaghan's *The Man Who Elected Lincoln,* and the collected papers of Ray, Trumbull, Washburne, and Colfax.

The *Tribune*'s relationship with Frémont is extensively covered by the paper itself, by other contemporary newspapers, and by Kinsley and Monaghan. Bross in his *History of Chicago* states that all four editors went to St. Louis to investigate the general.

Background on the Civil War, descriptions of the individuals involved, and the course of the battles are drawn from Thomas's *Abraham Lincoln,* Catton's *This Hallowed Ground,* the *American Heritage Picture History of the Civil War,* Eisenschiml and Newman's *The Civil War: The American Iliad,* and Newman and Long's *The Civil War*. Casualty figures for major battles are from Newman and Long. The story of Illinois's participation in the war is told by Cole's *Era of the Civil War,* Eddy's *Patriotism of Illinois,* and Hinken's *Illinois in the Civil War*. The Chicago of the period is described by the Pierce and Andreas histories of the city.

Wilkie writes about the Tilghman incident and his interview with Mrs. Hall after Shiloh in *Pen and Powder*. Grant's reports on Fort Donelson and Dr. Brinton's statement on Grant may be found in Eisenschiml and Newman.

Gramling, in *AP: The Story of News*, chronicles the steps leading to the formation of the modern Associated Press.

Kinsley cites Medill's letter to Colfax. Medill's letter to Trumbull is in the Trumbull Papers.

Chapter 9   Victory and Tragedy

The war in the East is recounted vividly in Catton's trilogy, *The Army of the Potomac*. For other works consulted for the course of events during the war, see the citations in the notes for Chapter 8.

Katherine Medill's letter to Joseph relative to his wounded brother and Joseph's telegram are in the Medill Papers. George F. Root, Chicago composer, wrote "There Will Be One Vacant Chair" in memory of William Medill.

Cadwallader's account of General Grant's drunken spree is quoted by Starr in *Bohemian Brigade*. Additional details on Grant are from the *Tribune* and Williams's *Lincoln and His Generals*. Thomas cites Lincoln's tart response to rumors of Grant's drinking problem.

Bodman's movements are sketched in his unpublished memoirs, which include copies of many of his dispatches to the *Tribune* and reports to Governor Yates.

Medill's letter to Washburne to enlist his aid in discouraging Grant from immediate political ambitions is in the Washburne Papers.

Ray's relations with White and his difficulties with Medill are discussed by Monaghan in *The Man Who Elected Lincoln* and Logsdon in *Horace White* and are reflected by the Ray Papers and the Medill Papers.

Upton's career is summarized in Carbutt's *Biographical Sketches* and minutes of Tribune Company. Accounts of Chicago crime are from the *Tribune* and from Peterson's excellent *Barbarians in Our Midst*. Medill's activities in aiding formation of a Western Associated Press are detailed in Kinsley's history of the *Tribune* and Gramling's *AP: The Story of News*.

Bross's version of the plot to liberate prisoners from Camp Douglas is in McIlvaine's *Reminiscences of Chicago during the Civil War*.

Chapter 10   The Hegira of Joseph Medill

The general discussion of the postwar economy is based on information provided by Faulkner's *American Economic History*, Cole's *Era of the Civil War*, and the Andreas and Pierce histories of Chicago.

The story of the policy struggle among *Tribune* proprietors is related in large part in the letters of those involved. The Medill Papers include interoffice memorandums of Medill and Bross. The Ray Papers and Monaghan's *The Man Who Elected Lincoln* provide details from Ray's viewpoint, but only the beginning of the struggle, since Ray departed early. The inside account as Joseph Medill knew it is related via his letters to Elihu Washburne, in the Washburne Papers. Medill's letter to McCulloch is in the McCulloch Papers.

Details of the life of Horace White are mostly derived from Joseph Logsdon's *Horace White, Nineteenth Century Liberal*, a complete, authoritative, and highly readable biography. Additional information is provided by Kinsley's history of the *Tribune*, the White Papers, and White's letters to Ray in the Ray Papers. Henry Villard, in his *Memoirs*, discusses his relationship with White.

Kinsley sketches the *Chicago Republican*'s short-lived challenge to the *Tribune*.

General background on Grant and the postwar reconstruction period is from Hesseltine's *Ulysses S. Grant, Politician* and Stoddard's biography of Greeley. Townsend tells the story of his life in part in *Campaigns of a Non-Combatant*. The experiences of Chisholm are detailed in his journal and the foreword by editor Homsher in *South Pass, 1868*.

Chapter 11   "I Have 'Met the Enemy and They Are Ours' "

General references for Chapter 10, including the standard Chicago histories and Logsdon's excellent biography of White, provide background for the era when Horace White was editor of the *Tribune*. Again the Medill Papers tell the story of Joseph Medill's angry frustration as White turned the paper from the Republican party as Medill and other conservatives knew it. Medill's letters to Washburne describing the progress of the feud are in the Washburne Papers.

The correspondence between Bross and Medill and White and Medill is to be found in the Medill Papers. Corporate records for the period are incomplete, and ownership of Tribune Company stock fluctuated as proprietors traded among themselves or added a few *Tribune* employees to the group of stockholders.

Andreas's *History of Chicago* presents extensive documentation of the Great Fire. The recollections of White and Bross appear in *Reminiscences of Chicago during the Great Fire,* edited by McIlvaine. Elias Colbert of the *Tribune* and Everett Chamberlin of the *Times* wrote a remarkably detailed account for a book published within a few days of the fire, called *Chicago and the Great Conflagration.* Excellent accounts are provided in two recent books, Cromie's *The Great Chicago Fire* and *The Great Fire, Chicago 1871,* by Kogan and Cromie.

The background and denouement of the Liberal Republicans' convention in 1872 are described in *Horace Greeley,* by Stoddard; *Henry Demarest Lloyd and the Empire of Reform,* by Destler; and *Horace White,* by Logsdon, who quotes Swett's letter to David Davis and Cowles's letter to Whitelaw Reid.

Chapter 12   The Medill Years

The Washburne Papers continue to be a valuable source for Medill's views of his political and economic difficulties. Details of the life of Henry Demarest Lloyd are from Destler's authoritative biography and also the two-volume biography by his sister Caro Lloyd. Faulkner's *American Economic History* was relied upon for general economic background.

Chicago politics and economics as well as details relating to the city's labor strife are from Pierce's *History of Chicago,* Currey's *Chicago: Its History and Its Builders,* Peterson's *Barbarians in Our Midst,* and Barnard's excellent biography of Altgeld, *Eagle Forgotten.*

John Archbold is quoted by Josephson in *The Robber Barons.* Frank Vanderlip described the Marshall Field–Joseph Medill encounter in a *Saturday Evening Post* article published November 24, 1934.

Chapter 13   The Eighties, Years of Change

Gath's interview with Joseph Medill is quoted by Kinsley in *The Chicago Tribune.* Other major Medill interviews, cited in the notes for earlier chapters, are those granted to Tarbell for her books on Lincoln and to Cleveland for the *Saturday Evening Post.* Reminiscences published by the *Tribune* are cited in the notes for Chapter 5 and Chapter 6.

Biographical information on Robert S. McCormick may be found in the McCormick Papers, the pages of the *Tribune,* and Waldrop's *McCormick of Chicago,* a biography of Robert R. McCormick. Various phases of the life of Robert Patterson, Jr., are treated in the Patterson Papers, *Tribune* files, Tebbel's *American Dynasty,* and Waldrop. Medill's work habits in the 1880s are described by Bennett's *Joseph Medill, a Brief Biography.*

Pierce's *History of Chicago* provides a wealth of information concerning the city's development in the 1880s, including the growth of newspapers and other publishing enterprises. Dennis's *Victor Lawson* and Kinsley detail the competition between the *Tribune* and the *Daily News.* Labor troubles, culminating in the Haymarket Riot, are discussed in Pierce, Peterson's *Barbarians in Our Midst,* Currey's history of the city, and Barnard's *Eagle Forgotten.* Architectural growth is treated in detail by Randall in *History of the Development of Building Construction in Chicago* and by Mayer and Wade in *Chicago: Growth of a Metropolis.* Linn's disparaging comment appears in *James Keeley, Newspaperman.*

The roles of Medill, Lawson, and other Chicago newsmen in forming the Associated Press are described by Gramling in *AP: The Story of News* and by Dennis in his biography of Lawson.

Chapter 14   The Gay and Grim Nineties

Some of the details of the *Tribune*'s financial status in the 1890s may be found in Kinsley's history of the paper.

The World's Columbian Exposition and its displays are described in Johnson's 4-volume *History of the World's Columbian Exposition*. Statistical information is from the *Tribune* and from Higinbotham's *Report of the President*. Also valuable is Cameron's history of the fair, in which he comments on the inappropriateness of the name of the Board of Lady Managers.

Kogan and Wendt take a close look at the realm of Bathhouse John and Hinky Dink in *Lords of the Levee*, in which they discuss at some length Stead's *If Christ Came to Chicago*. The continuing story of Chicago's construction boom is told in Randall's history of Chicago building and in *Chicago: Growth of a Metropolis*, by Mayer and Wade. Many of the events relating to the Pullman Strike are recounted in Currey's *Chicago: Its History and Its Builders*. The daily reports of the *Tribune* are traced by Kinsley. Chicago's changing newspaper scene is covered by Kinsley, Dennis's *Victor Lawson*, and Linn's *James Keeley*.

Medill's complaints about the *Tribune*'s lease on land owned by the school board are in the Medill Papers. The political and legal struggle over the lease continued for many years. The *Tribune* lease on the Madison and Dearborn property was transferred to a new leaseholder on May 1, 1926. The novel aspects of the *Tribune*'s 17-story skyscraper are described by Randall and by Shultz and Simmons in *Offices in the Sky*.

Chapter 15   A Londoner Takes Charge

The attempts of the city council and the state legislature to sell the city streets in 1897 are detailed in stories in the *Tribune* throughout the year. A brief summary of the traction fight is given by Kogan and Wendt's *Lords of the Levee*. A more definitive treatment is Norton's *Chicago Traction, a History Legislative and Political*.

James Weber Linn, in *James Keeley, Newspaperman*, has written a warmly appreciative account of the life of Keeley. Other information on Keeley's career at the *Tribune* was provided to this author by E. S. Beck and Col. Robert McCormick in interviews conducted a number of years ago. Rascoe's unflattering description appeared in *Before I Forget*. In addition to Linn's account, the story of the paper's coverage of the Spanish-American War is provided by Kinsley's *The Chicago Tribune*, Dennis's *Victor Lawson*, and *Drawn from Memory*, the memoirs of John T. McCutcheon.

The letters Joseph Medill wrote to Upton and Colbert during his later years are in the Medill Papers. Most of the documents relating to Medill's will and the trusteeship arrangement are also in Tribune Company Archives.

The *Tribune*'s operations during the years immediately following Joseph Medill's death are described in part by Linn, who quotes Sisson on the Keeley–Beck team. Additional information was provided by individuals who worked for the *Tribune* at the time, including Irving Crown, a copy boy in 1908, and Harry NMI (No Middle Initial) Cohen, interviewed by the author and Harold Hutchings in 1975, who was employed by Keeley as an office boy, subsequently serving Medill McCormick, Robert R. McCormick, Joseph Patterson, and the *Tribune* advertising department.

The hectic career of Hearst's *Chicago American* is told in Lundberg's *Imperial Hearst*, Tebbel's *The Life and Good Times of William Randolph Hearst*, and *The Madhouse on Madison Street*, by George Murray, top rewriteman on the *American*.

This period in Chicago history has been summarized in two books by Kogan and Wendt, *Lords of the Levee* and *Big Bill of Chicago*.

The McCormick Papers and Patterson Papers record the friction between the Medill sisters. Waldrop tells part of the story in *McCormick of Chicago*. Many details of the frequently changing management situation may be traced in the minutes of Tribune Company directors' meetings.

Keeley's activities relative to the Lorimer case are reported by Linn and by Robert McCormick's Memoirs. McCormick also discussed the case with the author in an interview for *Big Bill of Chicago*.

Chapter 16   The Young Progressives

Some threads of the story of the period of transition eventually leading to McCormick and Patterson's agreement to share direction of the *Tribune* are taken up by Waldrop's *McCormick of Chicago*, Tebbel's *American Dynasty*, Chapman's *Tell It to Sweeney*, and McGivena's *The News*. However, the source of greatest detail is Tribune Company Archives, in which may be found the correspondence of Robert McCormick, Joseph Patterson, Elinor Patterson, and Katherine McCormick quoted here; the minutes of Tribune Company directors' meetings; and the McCormick Memoirs.

Details of the competition between the *Tribune* and the *Daily News* and Lawson's offer to buy the *Tribune* are found in Dennis's *Victor Lawson*, Tribune Company minutes, and the McCormick Memoirs. The cigarette episode was reported by John McCutcheon in *Drawn from Memory* and by Colonel McCormick to the author.

The story of the Ontario Paper Company has been admirably told by Wiegman in *Trees to News;* additional details may be found in Tribune Company minutes. Wiegman describes McCormick's actions upon learning of Keeley's resignation; other information about the event is provided by Dennis, by McCutcheon, and by Linn's biography of Keeley.

Chapter 17   The Return of the Family

The working relationship between Patterson and McCormick is described in the correspondence between them and other family members and in other letters and documents in Tribune Company Archives, including the Patterson Papers, McCormick Papers, Tribune Company minutes, and McCormick Memoirs.

The campaign to shut down the red-light district is described in Washburn's *Come into My Parlor*, the story of the Everleigh sisters; Kogan and Wendt's *Lords of the Levee;* and Peterson's *Barbarians in Our Midst*.

The story of newspaper comic strips and Joe Patterson's contributions to their development is told by Sheridan in *Comics and Their Creators*, by Galewitz in *Great Comics*, and by the McCormick Memoirs.

McCutcheon recalled his experiences as a correspondent during World War I in *Drawn from Memory*. Some of the activities of Patterson and McCormick in covering the war may be traced in Tribune Company minutes. Others are discussed in the McCormick Memoirs, McCormick's *With the Russian Army*, and Patterson's *Notebook of a Neutral*.

The story of Chicago and William Hale Thompson has been told by Kogan and Wendt in *Big Bill of Chicago*.

Floyd Gibbons's career as a *Tribune* correspondent is traced by Guy Murchie, Jr., "The Life Story of a Great Reporter," in the *Tribune*'s *Graphic* magazine, February–March, 1940; Gibbons's own *And They Thought We Wouldn't Fight;* and Edward Gibbons in *Floyd Gibbons: Your Headline Hunter*.

Robert McCormick's note to Henry Ford is in Tribune Company Archives. Because of later controversy over McCormick's machine gun effort, Harold Hutchings, himself an army officer in World War II, made a study of the incident and reported his findings in a research memorandum in Tribune Company Archives. Archibald Cronkite, who served in Battery C Field Artillery of the Illinois National Guard, shared some of his recollections of Patterson with the author.

Chapter 18 The *Tribune* Has the Treaty!

The military records of McCormick and Patterson are in Tribune Company Archives. Floyd Gibbons's activities are detailed by Murchie in his February–March, 1940, articles for the *Graphic* magazine, by Edward Gibbons's biography of his brother, and by Floyd Gibbons's *And They Thought We Wouldn't Fight*.

William Bross Lloyd's resignation from the board of directors is recorded in the minutes of Tribune Company. James Cleary's unpublished manuscript *The Colonel and the Captain Take Command* is in Tribune Company Archives.

The account of the life and times of Mayor Thompson is based on Kogan and Wendt's *Big Bill of Chicago*.

The Versailles Treaty scoop was explained in detail by Henry Wales for the *Graphic* magazine on June 8, 1952. The Senate debate is reproduced from daily reports of the *Tribune*. Woodrow Wilson's actions and attitudes are analyzed in detail by Bailey in *Woodrow Wilson and the Great Betrayal*.

Chapter 19 On the Home Front

Life at the *Tribune* during the war and the immediate postwar years has been described by Rascoe in his autobiographical *Before I Forget*, in which he comments on the paper's excellence under Field and Beck, and *We Were Interrupted*. Besides relating the activities of the editorial and literary departments of the *Tribune*, Rascoe records several of the antics of the legendary Walter Howey. Field's career with the *Tribune* is outlined by Chapman in *Tell It to Sweeney*. The *Tribune*'s own *Book of Facts* and Cleary's manuscript study of the *Tribune* from 1900 to 1920, *The Colonel and the Captain Take Command*, provide considerable insight into the operations of the advertising department. Additional information was given to the author by Henry D. Lloyd.

The account of the Black Sox scandal is based on the reports that appeared in the *Tribune* and on Asinof's *Eight Men Out*.

The events surrounding the founding of the *New York News* are described in Chapman's book, in the minutes of Tribune Company, and in the McCormick Memoirs.

The race riots of 1919 are described by Peterson in *Barbarians in Our Midst*, Heise in *Is There Only One Chicago?*, and Sandburg in *The Chicago Race Riots, July, 1919*. *Big Bill of Chicago*, by Kogan and Wendt, provides the basis for the story of the continuing struggle between the *Tribune* and Thompson and describes Thompson's role in the 1920 Republican convention. Additional detail about the growing alliance between big-time criminals and the political machine may be found in Peterson. Some aspects of the legal struggles between the paper and Thompson are covered in *The WGN*, issued by the *Tribune* in 1922.

Wiegman's *Trees to News* chronicles the operations of the Ontario Paper Company. The McCormick Memoirs provide the background for the construction of the *Tribune*'s new manufacturing plant and for plans for the new office tower. The facilities of the plant and the moving operation were described in a memorandum by Otto Wolf and an interview with John Park; both documents are now in Tribune Company Archives.

The activities of the Paris *Tribune* in the postwar years are described by Shirer in *20th Century Journey*.

Chapter 20 Taking the Measure of Big Bill

The legal battles between Thompson and the *Tribune* are described in detail in *Big Bill of Chicago*, by Kogan and Wendt; *The WGN*, which quotes Judge Fisher's ruling; the McCormick Memoirs; and relevant documents in Tribune Company Archives. *Big Bill* also depicts Chicago politics of the period, including aspects of the growth of organized crime.

Peterson's reliable *Barbarians in Our Midst* chronicles the principal steps in the rise of Al Capone. Judge Lyle recounted his experiences in *The Dry and Lawless Years*. Kobler's *Capone* studies the underworld chief's career in detail.

In an interview with the author, Wood reported Colonel McCormick's injunction not to concern himself with the positions taken on the editorial page. Some of the activities of Parsons and the *Tribune*'s advertising and promotion departments are described in a memorandum by Ted Blend and in interviews with Harry Cohen conducted by the author and Harold Hutchings; the documents are in Tribune Company Archives. *The WGN* relates details of the "Cheer Checks" promotion and also describes some of the paper's color printing accomplishments. Mildred Jaklon told the author of Patterson's difficulties with India Moffitt.

Chapter 21   The Last Days of Capone

The rise of Capone and the battle for control of the city is detailed by Peterson in *Barbarians in Our Midst*, by Lyle in *The Dry and Lawless Years*, and by Kobler in *Capone*. Colonel McCormick told the author about his back-alley encounter with hoodlums and his decision to purchase an armored car.

Politics of the era are described by Kogan and Wendt in *Big Bill of Chicago*. The alliance between Capone and Big Bill is discussed by Kogan and Wendt, by Peterson, by Kobler, and by Lyle, who tells of Loesch's meeting with Capone before 1928's fall election.

Shirer recounts his experiences in covering Lindbergh's triumphal arrival in *20th Century Journey*. Several aspects of McCormick's interest in aviation are revealed in information provided to Tribune Company Archives by Fred Hotson, pilot for Tribune Company.

The activities of Lyle, McCormick, and the Secret Six in combating Capone are related by Lyle, Kobler, and in the McCormick Memoirs. The McCormick Papers contain the Akerson telegram and the Colonel's reply. Hoover's *Memoirs* tell his view of the federal campaign against Capone. His engagement books and pertinent correspondence are in the Herbert Hoover Presidential Library.

John Boettiger's *Jake Lingle* describes the case in detail. The book was published serially by the *Tribune* in 1931. This author in later years discussed the case with Judge Lyle and with J. Loy Maloney. Other recollections of Maloney were recounted to Harold Hutchings for Tribune Company Archives.

Chapter 22   The Fight for a Free Press

Peterson's *Barbarians in Our Midst* provides some background on political events in Chicago, but the most detailed account of the decline of Thompson is that by Kogan and Wendt in *Big Bill of Chicago*. The life and political career of Anton Cermak are described in Gottfried's *Boss Cermak of Chicago*.

The case of *Near v. Minnesota* was followed closely by the *Tribune*. Waldrop summarizes Colonel McCormick's involvement in *McCormick of Chicago*. McCormick's address delivered at Monticello was reprinted by the paper.

A number of the letters and telegrams exchanged by McCormick and Franklin Roosevelt are quoted by Waldrop. The missives themselves are housed either in Tribune Company Archives or the Franklin Delano Roosevelt Library. Ickes's note to Roosevelt regarding McCormick's waterways proposal is in the Roosevelt Library. Sherwood analyzes the teamwork of Hopkins and the president in *Roosevelt and Hopkins, an Intimate History*.

Lohr's *Fair Management: The Story of a Century of Progress Exposition*, depicts much of this highly successful fair. Lohr discussed problems in finding financing with the author.

Documents in Tribune Company Archives and corporate records detail the formation of the McCormick–Patterson Trust.

Chapter 23   The Colonel Versus the President

Harold Hutchings described McCormick's experiments in simplified spelling reform in a research memorandum for Tribune Company Archives. Maxwell discussed his reasons for discontinuing the experiment with the author. The simplified spellings have not been followed in this text in its quotations from the *Tribune*.

The discussion of New Deal policies and agencies follows the lines of most standard references on the period. Bell's analysis of the New Deal was reported by *U.S. News & World Report,* July 5, 1976. Sherwood's *Roosevelt and Hopkins* reports FDR's daily perusal of the *Tribune.* Morison and Commager's evaluation of the New Deal appears in *Growth of the American Republic.* Ickes recorded his opinions of McCormick in *America's House of Lords* and *Autobiography of a Curmudgeon.* Rascoe's comment on McCormick was recorded in *Before I Forget.* In a letter to the author, Tebbel explained how the erroneous statement about Medill's anti-tramps "editorial" came to appear in *Media in America.*

Some of Wilfred Barber's activities in Ethiopia are related by Edwards in *The Foreign Policy of Colonel McCormick's Tribune.* The profiles of Lee and Maloney are based on personal acquaintance and on discussions with other *Tribune* staffers who knew them. The Rev. Mr. Astley-Cock related to the author the chance encounter with reporter Hall. The continued growth of Tribune Company's Canadian holdings is followed by Wiegman in *Trees to News.*

Details of Colonel McCormick's daily routine and work habits are based on discussions with Cartwright, Stolz, Wood, Grumhaus, Park, and Maloney and on the author's personal experience. Many of their accounts were recorded on tape by the author or Harold Hutchings and are in Tribune Company Archives. Trohan related the "What do I mean?" incident in a lecture at Lincoln University, a transcription of which is in the Illinois State Historical Society collection.

Colonel McCormick's numerous letters and exhortations to Landon are in Tribune Company Archives. The precise date of McCormick's note to E. S. Beck is unknown; the text appeared in *Editor and Publisher* under the headline "Col. McCormick Orders Strict Impartiality During Campaign" on June 27, 1936.

Chapter 24   "Our Whole Effort Is to Win the War"

The account of Noderer's activity in covering the war is based on *Tribune* files and on Noderer's recollections as recorded by the author and Hutchings for Tribune Company Archives. Maloney recalled for the archives McCormick's close interest in the work of the correspondents. Edwards, in *The Foreign Policy of Colonel McCormick's Tribune,* traces the movements of some of the correspondents in the early stages of the war. The foreign policy views of Colonel McCormick are discussed by Waldrop in *McCormick of Chicago* and by Edwards.

In *A Man Called Intrepid,* Stevenson relates the secret intelligence activities of Stephenson. The account of how the *Tribune* acquired and published Roosevelt's "war plans" is based on *Intrepid* and on the recollections of Maloney, some of which were shared with the author in private conversations, others of which were recorded for Tribune Company Archives. Chesly Manly never did reveal the source of the report, but Senator Wheeler disclosed his own role prior to his death. McCormick told the author about the Japanese government lease on the Tribune Tower suite. McCormick's exchange of notes with MacArthur is in Tribune Company Archives.

The account of the *Tribune*'s story on the Battle of Midway is based on records in Tribune Company Archives, including interviews with Maloney and Wayne Thomis and the statements made by Maloney and Stanley Johnston for the navy's investigation.

Chapter 25   The View from the Tower

Activities of the *Tribune*'s war correspondents may be traced in their reports to the paper, in the files of the *Tribune,* and in recollections provided to the author or to Tribune Company Archives. Gowran wrote a profile of Harold Smith, which is in the *Tribune*'s research library. Simmons related his experiences during the Philippines campaign to the author; the copy of the *Overseas Tribune* signed by MacArthur is in Tribune Company Archives. Veysey's description of what Maloney and McCormick expected of the correspondents was given to the author. Stein, in *Under Fire: The Story of American War Correspondents,* quotes Sigrid Schultz. Simmons wrote of Schultz's deception of the Nazis for the *Graphic* of December 23, 1945. Stein says Jack Thompson was the first Western correspondent to meet the Russians.

Freeman's *"Before I Kill More . . ."* recounts the story of William Heirens. Maxwell recalled the case and Gavin's role for Tribune Company Archives.

Grumhaus related to the author and to Hutchings information about the construction of the WGN Building.

McCormick's correspondence with MacArthur regarding his trip to the Far East is in Tribune Company Archives. The *Tribune* covered the trip in detail, and Simmons related additional information to the author.

The operations of the paper during the printers' strike is based on accounts provided by the principals involved. The story of the "DEWEY DEFEATS TRUMAN" gaffe was recalled by Maloney for Tribune Company Archives.

Some of the details related to the death of Cissy Patterson and the *Tribune*'s acquisition of the *Washington Times-Herald* are provided by Waldrop in *McCormick of Chicago.* Additional information was given to the author by Wood.

Colonel McCormick's continuing involvement with aviation was described by Thomis for Tribune Company Archives. Background on the management team McCormick groomed as his successors is based on *Tribune* files and the recollections of those involved.

The account of the McCarthy era is based on Cook's *Nightmare Decade,* Freeland's *The Truman Doctrine and the Origins of McCarthyism,* and Matusow's *Joseph McCarthy.* Freeland quotes Truman's diary entry. That the Truman administration encouraged the Red scare as a means of mustering support for the Marshall Plan is suggested by Freeland. Willard Edwards's comments on some reasons for the *Tribune*'s continued editorial support for McCarthy were made to Hutchings for Tribune Company Archives.

Simmons recounted his experiences in covering the Korean War for the author. Percy Wood's comment regarding Simmons's expertise appeared in the *Tribune* on September 8, 1957.

Eisenhower reported the details of McCormick's interview with him in Paris in a letter to Waldrop, who reproduced it in *McCormick of Chicago.*

McCormick's last will and testament, dated December 18, 1954, and codicil dated January 4, 1955, are in Tribune Company Archives, as are the various letters and memorandums the Colonel dictated during his final illness. Accounts of his last days were provided by Mrs. Barbara Johnston (later Mrs. J. Howard Wood), Wood, Thomis, and Dr. Van Dellen.

Chapter 26   A Time of Change

The actions and judgments of *Tribune* executives and others as described in this chapter are based on extensive interviews with the principals involved, many taped by Harold Hutchings and/or the author for Tribune Company Archives. The minutes of Tribune Company also were consulted.

Two influential viewpoints on the changing world of the 1950s and 1960s are those expressed by Galbraith in *The Affluent Society* and Toffler in *Future Shock*. The story of the rise of the new Chicago, the city's architecture and art, is based in good part on research done by Kogan and Wendt for their books and articles about Chicago, among them *Chicago: a Pictorial History*. Additional details are provided by a *Fortune* report on Chicago, June, 1955, and *One Hundred Years of Architecture in Chicago*, by Grube. Banfield, in *Political Influence*, recounts the work of Tagge and Maxwell relative to McCormick Place, as does Maxwell in his interview with Hutchings.

Wood's terms to the directors when they offered him the presidency of Tribune Company were related in an interview with the author. The efforts of Wood and Grumhaus to reorganize the company were recounted by the executives in interviews with Hutchings and the author. The complex series of steps creating the holding company is reflected in corporate minutes and in a chronology prepared by Hutchings, Tribune Company secretary John Goldrick, and communications director William N. Clark for Tribune Company Archives.

Details of Mayor Daley's career are taken from the pages of Chicago's newspapers and *Clout* by O'Connor. The *American*'s assertion that its 31 minutes publication time with news of the John Kennedy assassination was the best among the nation's papers got no challengers. McCormick's denunciation of intervention in Indochina appeared in *The American Empire*.

David English, associate editor of the *London Daily Express,* and seven members of the *Express* staff covered the 1968 Chicago convention and the campaign in a superlative way in *Divided They Stand*. White's observations appeared in *The Making of the President, 1968*.

Chapter 27   New Era, New *Tribune*

Grumhaus and Kirkpatrick have discussed their work and views in interviews with Harold Hutchings and the author, most of which are on tape in Tribune Company Archives. Koch's interview with Kirkpatrick appeared in the *Chicago Journalism Review* of June, 1970. The "musts" Koch referred to were "MUST RRMcC" notices often written on an assignment from Colonel McCormick, usually by the day city editor or a member of his staff. McCormick himself did not provide such a notation.

Details of the Tribune Company reorganization, stock, and corporate activities are from interviews and the corporate records. When Grumhaus retired in 1974, the position of Tribune Company chairman was discontinued. Wood provided information relating to the absorption of *Chicago Today* into the *Tribune;* and the author, as editor and publisher of *Today,* was involved in planning and carrying out the consolidation. Details of Tribune Company's Canadian operations came from Wood, Grumhaus, and records of the Ontario Paper Company.

The description of Chicago's continued architectural and cultural rise is based in part on the sources cited in the notes for Chapter 26. Details on Chicago present and future were provided by *Planning Papers No. 10* of the Northeastern Illinois Planning Commission.

The details of the Nixon transcripts publication were obtained from Kirkpatrick, Cook, Perry, McCrohon, Ryan, Leslie, and Cohen. An excellent account is provided in the *Tribune*'s house magazine, *The Little Trib,* June, 1974.

Kirkpatrick's Nairobi statement was published by the *Tribune* on November 6, 1976; the full text is in Tribune Company Archives. Comments on the new *Tribune* are from *Time,* January 21, 1974; *Columbia Journalism Review,* January–February, 1972; *Newsweek,* July 2, 1973; and *Decatur Herald and Review,* November 14, 1976.

BIBLIOGRAPHY

Unpublished Collected Papers

Bodman Papers. Albert Bodman Papers; an incomplete account of his Civil War experiences. Tribune Company Archives.

Chase Papers. Salmon P. Chase Papers. Library of Congress.

Colfax Papers. Schuyler Colfax Papers. Library of Congress

Douglas Papers. Stephen A. Douglas Papers. University of Chicago Library.

Greeley Papers. Horace Greeley Papers. New York Public Library; Chicago Historical Society Library; Huntington Library, San Marino, California.

Lincoln Collection. Robert Todd Lincoln Collection. Chicago Historical Society Library.

McCormick Memoirs. Autobiographical addresses by Col. Robert R. McCormick broadcast over radio station WGN and reprinted in the *Tribune*, various dates, 1952-55. Tribune Company Archives.

McCormick Papers. Robert R. McCormick Papers. Tribune Company Archives.

McCulloch Papers. Hugh McCulloch Papers. Library of Congress.

Medill Papers. Joseph Medill Papers; also those of Katherine Patrick Medill and William Medill. Tribune Company Archives.

Patterson Papers. Robert W. Patterson memorandums; Joseph Patterson letters and memorandums. Tribune Company Archives.

Ray Papers. Charles Ray Papers. Huntington Library, San Marino, California.

Trumbull Papers. Lyman Trumbull Papers. Library of Congress. Washburne Papers. Elihu Washburne Papers. Library of Congress.

White Papers. Horace White Papers. New York Public Library; Illinois State Historical Society Library, Springfield.

General

Adams, James Truslow, et al., eds. *Album of American History.* 4 vols. New York: Charles Scribner's Sons, 1944-48.

Adler, Mortimer J., gen. ed., and Van Doren, Charles, ed. *The Negro in American History.* 3 vols. New York: William Benton, 1969.

Allen, Frederick Lewis. *Only Yesterday: An Informal History of the 1920s.* New York: Harper & Row, 1931.

Andrews, Wayne, ed. *Concise Dictionary of American History.* New York: Scribner, 1962.

Angle, Paul M., ed. *By These Words: Great Documents of American Liberty, Selected and Placed in Their Contemporary Settings.* Chicago: Rand McNally, 1954.

Ardrey, Robert. *The Territorial Imperative: A Personal Inquiry into the Animal Origins of Property and Nations.* New York: Atheneum, 1966.

Bailey, Thomas A. *Woodrow Wilson and the Great Betrayal.* New York: Macmillan, 1945.

Beard, Charles A., and Beard, Mary R. *New Basic History of the United States.* Garden City, N.Y.: Doubleday, 1968.

Casey, Robert J., and Douglas, W. A. S. *Pioneer Railroad: The Story of the Chicago and North Western System.* New York: McGraw-Hill, 1948.

Chambers, Whittaker. *Witness.* New York: Random House, 1952.

Compton, Arthur Holly. *Atomic Quest: A Personal Narrative.* New York: Oxford University Press, 1956.

Cook, Fred J. *The Nightmare Decade. The Life and Times of Senator Joe McCarthy*. New York: Random House, 1971.

Corliss, Carlton J. *Main Line of Mid-America: The Story of the Illinois Central*. New York: Creative Age, 1950.

Cruttwell, C. R. M. F. *A History of the Great War, 1914–1918*. New York and London: Oxford, 1934.

Dictionary of American Biography. 20 vols. and suppl. 1–4. New York: Scribners, 1928–1974.

Dictionary of American History. 7 vols. and index. 3rd rev. ed. New York: Scribners, 1976.

English, David, et al. *Divided They Stand*. Englewood Cliffs, N.J.: Prentice-Hall, 1969.

Faulkner, Harold U. *American Economic History*. Rev. ed. New York: Harper, 1931.

Freeland, Richard M. *The Truman Doctrine and the Origins of McCarthyism*. New York: Alfred A. Knopf, 1972.

Galbraith, John K. *The Affluent Society*. 2nd rev. ed. Boston: Houghton-Mifflin, 1969.

Gates, Paul Wallace. *The Illinois Central Railroad and Its Colonization Work*. Cambridge, Mass.: Harvard University, 1934.

Graebner, Norman A. *Empire on the Pacific: A Study in American Continental Expansion*. New York: Ronald Press, 1955.

Hendrick, Burton J. *The Age of Big Business: A Chronicle of the Captains of Industry*. New Haven, Conn.: Yale University, 1919.

Hesseltine, William B. *Ulysses S. Grant, Politician*. New York: Dodd, Mead, 1935.

Hibben, Paxton. *The Peerless Leader, William Jennings Bryan*. New York: Farrar & Rinehart, 1929.

Hoover, Herbert. *Memoirs of Herbert Hoover*. 3 vols. New York: Macmillan, 1951–52.

Ickes, Harold L. *America's House of Lords: An Inquiry into the Freedom of the Press*. New York: Harcourt, 1939.

———. *The Autobiography of a Curmudgeon*. New York: Reynal & Hitchcock, 1943.

Ingersoll, L. D. *A History of the War Department of the United States*. Washington, D.C.: Mohun, 1880.

Jaworski, Leon. *The Right and the Power: The Prosecution of Watergate*. Houston: Gulf, 1976.

Jensen, Richard. *The Winning of the Midwest: Social and Political Conflict, 1888–1896*. Chicago: University of Chicago, 1971.

Johnston, Stanley. *Queen of the Flat-tops: The U.S.S. Lexington and the Coral Sea Battle*. New York: E. P. Dutton, 1942.

Josephson, Matthew. *The Robber Barons: The Great American Capitalists, 1861–1901*. New York: Harcourt, Brace, 1934.

Kerner Committee. *Report of the National Advisory Commission on Civil Disorders*. New York: E. P. Dutton, 1968.

Laut, Agnes C. *The Romance of the Rails*. 2 vols. New York: Robert M. McBride, 1928.

Lundberg, Ferdinand. *The Rich and the Super-Rich: A Study in the Power of Money Today*. New York: Lyle Stuart, 1968.

Lyons, Eugene. *Herbert Hoover: A Biography*. New York: Doubleday, 1964.

McGovern, James. *To the Yalu: From the Chinese Invasion of Korea to MacArthur's Dismissal*. New York: William Morrow, 1972.

McMaster, John Bach. *History of the People of the United States: From the Revolution to the Civil War*. New York: Farrar, Straus, 1964.

Martin, Ralph G. *Ballots and Bandwagons*. Chicago: Rand McNally, 1964.

Matusow, Allen J., ed. *Joseph McCarthy*. Englewood Cliffs, N.J.: Prentice-Hall, 1971.

Mee, Charles L., Jr. *Meeting at Potsdam*. New York: M. Evans, 1975.

Morgenstern, George E. *Pearl Harbor: The Story of the Secret War*. New York: Devin-Adair, 1947.

Morison, Samuel Eliot, and Commager, Henry Steele. *The Growth of the American Republic.* 4th rev. ed. 2 vols. New York: Oxford, 1950.

Nevins, Allan. *Grover Cleveland: A Study in Courage.* New York: Dodd, Mead, 1932.

Rose, William Ganson. *Cleveland: The Making of a City.* Cleveland: World, 1950.

Schlesinger, Arthur M. *The Rise of the City.* A History of American Life, vol. 10. New York: Macmillan, 1933.

Schlesinger, Arthur M., Jr. *A Thousand Days: John F. Kennedy in the White House.* New York: Houghton-Mifflin, 1965.

Schurz, Carl. *The Autobiography of Carl Schurz.* New York: Scribner, 1961.

Sherwood, Robert. *Roosevelt and Hopkins, an Intimate History.* New York: Harper & Bros., 1948.

Stevenson, William. *A Man Called Intrepid: The Secret War.* New York: Harcourt Brace Jovanovich, 1976.

Stimpson, George W. *A Book about American Politics.* New York: Harper, 1952.

Sullivan, Mark. *The Turn of the Century 1900–1904.* Our Times: The United States 1900–1925, vol. 1. New York: Scribner, 1926.

Swanberg, William A. *Citizen Hearst: A Biography of William Randolph Hearst.* New York: Scribner, 1961.

Taft, Lorado. *History of American Sculpture.* Rev. ed. New York: Macmillan, 1924.

Taylor, Edmond L. *The Fall of the Dynasties: The Collapse of the Old Order 1905–1922.* New York: Doubleday, 1963.

Thompson, Slason. *A Short History of American Railways, Covering Ten Decades.* New York: D. Appleton-Century, 1925.

Toffler, Alvin. *Future Shock.* New York: Random House, 1970.

Toynbee, Arnold. *A Study of History.* (D. C. Somervell abridgement) New York: Oxford, 1947.

Tuchman, Barbara. *The Guns of August.* New York: Macmillan, 1962.

Wells, H. G. *The Future in America.* New York: Harper, 1906.

Van Deusen, Glyndon G. *Thurlow Weed, Wizard of the Lobby.* Boston: Little, Brown, 1947.

White, Theodore H. *Breach of Faith: The Fall of Richard Nixon.* New York: Atheneum, 1975.

_____. *The Making of the President, 1968.* New York: Atheneum, 1969.

Wilson, Woodrow. *The Public Papers of Woodrow Wilson.* Edited by Ray Stannard Baker and William E. Dodd. 3 vols. New York: Harper, 1927.

Woodward, William E. *A New American History.* Garden City, N.Y.: Garden City Publishing, 1938.

Chicago and Illinois History

Ahern, M. L. *Political History of Chicago, 1837–1887.* Chicago: Donohue and Henneberry, 1886.

Allsop, Kenneth. *The Bootleggers and Their Era.* Garden City, N.Y.: Doubleday, 1961.

Andreas, Alfred T. *History of Chicago from the Earliest Period to the Present Time.* 3 vols. Chicago: A. T. Andreas, 1884–86.

_____. *History of Cook County, Illinois. From the Earliest Period to the Present Time.* Chicago: A. T. Andreas, 1884.

Angle, Paul M., ed. *The Great Chicago Fire.* Chicago: Chicago Historical Society, 1946.

Artistic Guide to Chicago and the World's Columbian Exposition. Chicago: Columbian Art Co., 1892.

Asinof, Elliot. *Eight Men Out: The Black Sox and the 1919 World Series.* Rev. ed. New York: Holt, Rinehart and Winston, 1977.

Banfield, Edward C. *Political Influence.* New York: Free Press, 1965.

Barnard, Harry. *Eagle Forgotten: The Life of John Peter Altgeld*. Indianapolis: Bobbs-Merrill, 1938.

Bennett, Fremont O. *Politics and Politicians of Chicago, Cook County, and Illinois*. Chicago: Blakely Printing, 1886.

Bennett, James O'Donnell. *Chicago Gang Land, the True Story of Chicago Crime*. Chicago: Chicago Tribune, 1929.

Boettiger, John. *Jake Lingle, or, Chicago on the Spot*. New York: E. P. Dutton, 1931.

Bonner, Thomas Neville. *Medicine in Chicago, 1850–1950: A Chapter in the Social and Scientific Development of a City*. Madison, Wis.: American History Research Center, 1957.

Bright, John. *Hizzoner Big Bill Thompson: An Idyll of Chicago*. New York: Cape, 1930.

Bross, William. *History of Chicago. Historical and Commercial Statistics . . . What I Remember of Early Chicago*. Chicago: Jansen, McClurg, 1876.

Browne, Waldo R. *Altgeld of Illinois: A Record of His Life and Work*. New York: B. W. Huebsch, 1924.

Brownell, Baker. *The Other Illinois*. New York: Duell, Sloan & Pearce, 1958.

Cameron, William E., ed. *History of the World's Columbian Exposition*. 2nd ed. 4 parts. Chicago: Columbian History Co., 1893.

Carbutt, J., comp. *Biographical Sketches of the Leading Men of Chicago Written by the Best Talent of the Northwest*. Chicago: Wilson & St. Clair, 1868.

Colbert, Elias, and Chamberlin, Everett. *Chicago and the Great Conflagration*. Chicago: J. S. Goodman, 1871.

Cook, Frederick Francis. *Bygone Days in Chicago: Recollections of the "Garden City" of the Sixties*. Chicago: A. C. McClurg, 1910.

Cromie, Robert A. *The Great Chicago Fire*. New York: McGraw-Hill, 1958.

Cromie, Robert A., and Pinkston, Joseph. *Dillinger: A Short and Violent Life*. New York: McGraw-Hill, 1962.

Currey, Josiah Seymour. *Chicago: Its History and Its Builders: A Century of Marvelous Growth*. 4 vols. Chicago: S. J. Clarke, 1912.

Darrow, Clarence. *The Story of My Life*. New York: Scribner, 1932.

Dobyns, Fletcher. *The Underworld of American Politics*. New York: Fletcher Dobyns, 1932.

Duncan, Hugh Dalziel. *The Rise of Chicago as a Literary Center from 1885–1920: A Sociological Essay in American Culture*. Totowa, N.J.: Bedminster Press, 1964.

Dunne, Edward F. *Illinois, the Heart of the Nation*. 5 vols. Chicago and New York: Lewis, 1933.

Fehrenbacher, Don E. *Chicago Giant: A Biography of Long John Wentworth*. Madison, Wis.: American History Research Center, 1957.

Flinn, John J. *History of the Chicago Police*. Chicago: Chicago Police Book Fund, 1887.

Freeman, Lucy. *"Before I Kill More . . ." The William Heirens Story*. New York: Crown, 1955.

Gilbert, Paul Thomas, and Bryson, Charles Lee. *Chicago and Its Makers*. Chicago: Felix Mendelsohn, 1929.

Goodspeed, Thomas Wakefield. *A History of the University of Chicago, founded by John D. Rockefeller; the First Quarter-Century*. Chicago: University of Chicago, 1916.

Goodspeed, Weston A., and Healy, Daniel D., eds. *History of Cook County, Illinois*. 2 vols. Chicago: Goodspeed Historical Association, 1909.

Gosnell, Harold F. *Machine Politics: Chicago Model*. Chicago: University of Chicago, 1937.

Gottfried, Alex. *Boss Cermak of Chicago: A Study of Political Leadership*. Seattle: University of Washington, 1962.

Grube, Oswald W. *One Hundred Years of Architecture in Chicago*. Chicago: Follett, 1977.

Hamilton, Henry Raymond. *The Epic of Chicago*. Chicago and New York: Willett, Clarke, 1932.

Harrison, Carter H. *Stormy Years: The Autobiography of Carter H. Harrison, Five Times Mayor of Chicago.* Indianapolis: Bobbs-Merrill, 1935.

Heise, Kenan. *Is There Only One Chicago?* Richmond, Va.: Westover, 1973.

_____. *This Is Chicago.* Richmond, Va.: Westover, 1973.

Higdon, Hal. *The Crime of the Century: The Leopold and Loeb Case.* New York: G. P. Putnam's Sons, 1975.

Higinbotham, H. N. *Report of the President to the Board of Directors of the World's Columbian Exposition.* Chicago: n.p., 1892–93.

Hoyt, Homer. *One Hundred Years of Land Values in Chicago, 1830–1933.* Chicago: University of Chicago, 1933.

Hutchinson, William T. *Lowden of Illinois: The Life of Frank O. Lowden.* 2 vols. Chicago: University of Chicago, 1957.

Irey, Elmer L., and Slocum, William J. *The Tax Dodgers: The Inside Story of the T-Men's War with America's Political and Underworld Hoodlums.* New York: Greenberg, 1948.

Johnson, Claudius O. *Carter Henry Harrison I, Political Leader.* Chicago: University of Chicago, 1928.

Johnson, Rossiter, ed. *A History of the World's Columbian Exposition Held in Chicago in 1893.* 4 vols. New York: D. Appleton, 1897–98.

Kirkland, Joseph. *The Story of Chicago: Bringing the History up to December, 1894.* 2 vols. Chicago: Dibble, 1895.

Kobler, John. *Capone: The Life and World of Al Capone.* New York: G. P. Putnam's Sons, 1971.

Kogan, Herman, and Cromie, Robert. *The Great Fire, Chicago 1871.* New York: G. P. Putnam's Sons, 1971.

Kogan, Herman, and Kogan, Rick. *Yesterday's Chicago.* Miami, Fla.: E. A. Seemann, 1976.

Kogan, Herman, and Wendt, Lloyd. *Bet a Million! The Story of John W. Gates.* Indianapolis: Bobbs-Merrill, 1948.

_____. *Big Bill of Chicago.* Indianapolis: Bobbs-Merrill, 1953.

_____. *Chicago: A Pictorial History.* New York: E. P. Dutton, 1958.

_____. *Give the Lady What She Wants! The Story of Marshall Field & Company.* Chicago: Rand McNally, 1952.

_____. *Lords of the Levee: The Story of Bathhouse John and Hinky Dink.* Indianapolis: Bobbs-Merrill, 1943.

Lewis, Lloyd, and Smith, Henry Justin. *Chicago: The History of Its Reputation.* New York: Harcourt, Brace, 1929.

Liebling, Abbott J. *Chicago: Second City.* New York: Alfred A. Knopf, 1952.

Lohr, Lennox R. *Fair Management: The Story of a Century of Progress Exposition.* Chicago: Cuneo Press, 1952.

Lyle, John H. *The Dry and Lawless Years.* Englewood Cliffs, N.J.: Prentice-Hall, 1960.

McIlvaine, Mabel, ed. *Reminiscences of Chicago during the Forties and Fifties.* Chicago: R. R. Donnelley, 1913.

McIlvaine, Mabel, ed. *Reminiscences of Chicago during the Great Fire.* Chicago: R. R. Donnelley, 1915.

Mayer, Harold M., and Wade, Richard C. *Chicago: Growth of a Metropolis.* Chicago: University of Chicago, 1969.

Merriam, Charles Edward. *Chicago: A More Intimate View of Urban Politics.* New York: Macmillan, 1929.

Northeastern Illinois Planning Commission. *Planning Papers No. 10.* Chicago, 1975.

Norton, Samuel Wilber. *Chicago Traction, a History Legislative and Political.* Chicago: A. C. McClurg, 1907.

O'Connor, Len. *Clout–Mayor Daley and His City.* Chicago: Henry Regnery, 1975.

Parsons, Lucy E. *Life of Albert R. Parsons, with Brief History of the Labor Movement in America.* Chicago: Mrs. Lucy E. Parsons, 1889.

Pasley, Fred D. *Al Capone: The Biography of a Self-Made Man.* New York: Ives Washburn, 1930.

Peterson, Virgil W. *Barbarians in Our Midst: A History of Chicago Crime and Politics.* Boston: Little, Brown, 1952.

Pierce, Bessie Louise, ed. *As Others See Chicago: Impressions of Visitors, 1673–1933.* Chicago: University of Chicago, 1933.

————. *A History of Chicago.* 3 vols. New York: Alfred A. Knopf, 1937–57.

Putnam, James William. *The Illinois and Michigan Canal: A Study in Economic History.* Chicago: University of Chicago, 1918.

Randall, Frank A. *History of the Development of Building Construction in Chicago.* Urbana, Ill.: University of Illinois, 1949.

Reckless, Walter C. *Vice in Chicago.* Chicago: University of Chicago, 1933.

Rice, Wallace. *The Chicago Stock Exchange, A History.* Chicago: Chicago Stock Exchange, 1928.

Sandburg, Carl. *The Chicago Race Riots, July, 1919.* New York: Harcourt, Brace, 1919.

Shepro, Richard Warren. *The Reconstruction of Chicago after the Great Fire of 1871.* B.A. Thesis, Harvard University, 1975.

Shultz, Earle, and Simmons, Walter. *Offices in the Sky.* Indianapolis: Bobbs-Merrill, 1959.

Simon, Paul. *Lovejoy, Martyr to Freedom.* St. Louis: Concordia, 1964.

Smith, Alson J. *Chicago's Left Bank.* Chicago: Henry Regnery, 1953.

————. *Syndicate City: The Chicago Crime Cartel and What to Do about It.* Chicago: Henry Regnery, 1954.

Smith, Henry Justin. *Chicago's Great Century, 1833–1933.* Chicago: Consolidated, 1933.

Stead, William T. *If Christ Came to Chicago.* Chicago: Laird & Lee, 1894.

Steffens, Lincoln. *The Shame of the Cities.* New York: McClure, Phillips, 1904.

Stuart, William H. *Twenty Incredible Years, as Heard and Seen by [the author].* Chicago: M. A. Donohue, 1935.

Sullivan, Edward Dean. *Chicago Surrenders: A Sequel to Rattling the Cup on Chicago Crime.* New York: Vanguard, 1930.

————. *Rattling the Cup on Chicago Crime.* New York: Vanguard, 1929.

Thrasher, Frederic M. *The Gang: A Study of 1,313 Gangs in Chicago.* Chicago: University of Chicago, 1927.

Walton, Clyde C., ed. *An Illinois Reader.* DeKalb, Ill.: Northern Illinois University, 1970.

Washburn, Charles. *Come Into My Parlor: A Biography of the Aristocratic Everleigh Sisters of Chicago.* New York: National Library, 1936.

Wilson, Samuel Paynter. *Chicago and Its Cess Pools of Infamy.* 11th ed. Chicago: n.p., 1910.

Zorbaugh, Harvey W. *The Gold Coast and the Slum.* Chicago: University of Chicago, 1929.

Lincoln and the Civil War

American Heritage. *American Heritage Picture History of the Civil War* (Narrative by Bruce Catton). New York: American Heritage, 1960.

Angle, Paul M., ed. *Created Equal? The Complete Lincoln-Douglas Debates of 1858.* Chicago: University of Chicago, 1958.

Beveridge, Albert J. *Abraham Lincoln, 1809–1858.* 2 vols. Boston: Houghton-Mifflin, 1928.

Catton, Bruce. *The Army of the Potomac.* 3 vols. New York: Doubleday, 1962.

————. *This Hallowed Ground. The Story of the Union Side of the Civil War.* Garden City, N.Y. : Doubleday, 1956.

Cole, Arthur C., ed. *Era of the Civil War, 1848–1870.* Springfield, Ill.: Illinois Centennial Commission, 1919.

Donald, David H. *Lincoln's Herndon*. New York: Alfred A. Knopf, 1948.

Eddy, T. M. *The Patriotism of Illinois: A Record of the Civil and Military History of the State in the War for the Union*. 2 vols. Chicago: Clarke, 1865.

Eisenschiml, Otto, and Newman, R. G. *The Civil War: The American Iliad, as Told by Those Who Lived It*. New York: Grosset & Dunlap, 1956.

Fehrenbacher, Don E. *Prelude to Greatness: Lincoln in 1850's*. Stanford, Cal.: Stanford University, 1962.

Hinken, Victor. *Illinois in the Civil War*. Urbana, Ill.: University of Illinois, 1966.

Isely, Bliss, and Richards, W. M. *Four Centuries in Kansas*. Wichita, Kans.: McCormick-Mathers, 1936.

Jaffa, Harry V. *Crisis of the House Divided: An Interpretation of the Issues in the Lincoln-Douglas Debates*. New York: Doubleday, 1959.

Johannsen, Robert W. *Stephen A. Douglas*. New York: Oxford University, 1973.

Johnson, Robert Underwood, and Buel, Clarence C., eds. *Battles and Leaders of the Civil War*. 4 vols. New York: Century, 1887–88.

Johnson, Rossiter, ed. *Campfire and Battle-field: A History of the Conflicts and Campaigns of the Great Civil War in the United States*. New York: Knight & Brown, 1896.

Kyle, Otto R. *Abraham Lincoln in Decatur*. New York: Vantage, 1957.

Lincoln, Abraham. *The Collected Works of Abraham Lincoln*. Edited by Roy P. Basler, et al. 8 vols. New Brunswick, N.J.: Rutgers University, 1953.

Lorant, Stefan. *Lincoln: A Picture Story of His Life*. New York: Harper & Row, 1952.

McIlvaine, Mabel, ed. *Reminiscences of Chicago during the Civil War*. Chicago: R. R. Donnelley, 1914.

Nevins, Allan. *A House Dividing, 1852–1857*. Ordeal of the Union, vol. 2. New York: Charles Scribner's Sons, 1947.

Newman, Ralph G., and Long, E. B. *The Civil War: Picture Chronicle of the Events, Leaders, and Battlefields of the War*. New York: Grosset & Dunlap, 1956.

Plum, William R. *The Military Telegraph During the Civil War in the United States*. 2 vols. Chicago: Jansen, McClurg, 1882.

Randall, Ruth Painter. *Colonel Elmer Ellsworth: A Biography of Lincoln's Friend and First Hero of the Civil War*. Boston: Little, Brown, 1960.

Rhodes, James A., and Jauchius, Dean. *The Trial of Mary Todd Lincoln*. Indianapolis: Bobbs-Merrill, 1959.

Sandburg, Carl. *Abraham Lincoln: The Prairie Years*. 2 vols. New York: Harcourt, Brace, 1926.

_____. *Abraham Lincoln: The War Years*. 4 vols. New York: Harcourt, Brace, 1939.

Scripps, John Locke. *Life of Abraham Lincoln*. Chicago: Chicago Press and Tribune, 1860.

Seitz, Don C. *Lincoln the Politician: How the Rail-Splitter and Flat-Boatman Played the Great American Game*. New York: Coward-McCann, 1931.

Tarbell, Ida M. *In the Footsteps of the Lincolns*. New York: Harper & Bros., 1924.

_____. *The Life of Abraham Lincoln*. 2 vols. New York: Doubleday Page, 1909.

Thomas, Benjamin P. *Abraham Lincoln*. New York: Alfred A. Knopf, 1952.

Williams, Thomas Harry. *Lincoln and His Generals*. New York: Alfred A. Knopf, 1952.

Newspapers and Newspaper People

Beasley, Norman. *Frank Knox, American: A Short Biography*. New York: Doubleday, 1936.

Becker, Stephen D. *Marshall Field III: A Biography*. New York: Simon & Schuster, 1964.

Bennett, James O'Donnell. *Joseph Medill, a Brief Biography and an Appreciation*. Chicago: Chicago Tribune, 1947.

Bradburn, George. *A Statement by George Bradburn of His Connection with the "True Democrat" and John C. Vaughan*. Cleveland, Ohio: George Bradburn, 1853.

Butcher, Fanny. *Many Lives, One Love*. New York: Harper & Row, 1972.

Chapman, John. *Tell It to Sweeney. An Informal History of the New York Daily News.* Garden City, N.Y.: Doubleday, 1961.

Chicago Tribune. *A Century of Tribune Editorials, 1847–1947.* Chicago: Chicago Tribune, 1947.

————. *The WGN. History of the Chicago Tribune, 1847–1922.* Chicago: Chicago Tribune, 1922.

————. *Pictured Encyclopedia of the World's Greatest Newspaper.* Chicago: Chicago Tribune, 1928.

Cleary, James. *The Colonel and the Captain Take Command. History of the Chicago Tribune, 1900–1920.* Unpublished manuscript in Tribune Company Archives, n.d.

Conrow, Robert. *Field Days: The Life, Times, and Reputation of Eugene Field.* New York: Charles Scribner's Sons, 1974.

Cowles, Calvin Duvall, comp. *Genealogy of the Cowles Family in America.* 2 vols. New Haven, Conn.: Tuttle, Morehouse and Taylor, 1929.

Crozier, Emmet. *Yankee Reporters, 1861–65.* New York: Oxford University, 1956.

Dennis, Charles H. *Victor Lawson: His Time and His Work.* Chicago: University of Chicago, 1935.

Destler, Chester M. *Henry Demarest Lloyd and the Empire of Reform.* Philadelphia: University of Pennsylvania, 1963.

Doherty, Edward J. *Gall and Honey: The Story of a Newspaperman.* New York: Sheed & Ward, 1941.

Edwards, Jerome. *The Foreign Policy of Colonel McCormick's Tribune, 1929–1941.* Reno, Nev.: University of Nevada, 1971.

Ellis, Elmer. *Mr. Dooley's America: A Life of Finley Peter Dunne.* New York: Alfred A. Knopf, 1941.

Fetridge, William Harrison. *With Warm Regards–a Reminiscence.* Chicago: Dartnell, 1976.

Galewitz, Herb, comp. *Great Comics, Syndicated by the Daily News, New York's Picture Newspaper, and the Chicago Tribune.* New York: Crown, 1972.

Gibbons, Edward. *Floyd Gibbons: Your Headline Hunter.* New York: Exposition Press, 1953.

Gibbons, Floyd. *And They Thought We Wouldn't Fight.* New York: Doran, 1918.

Gramling, Oliver. *AP: The Story of News.* New York: Farrar and Rinehart, 1940.

Greeley, Horace. *Recollections of a Busy Life.* New York: J. B. Ford, 1868.

Hecht, Ben. *A Child of the Century: an Autobiography.* New York: Simon & Schuster, 1954.

Homsher, Lola M., ed. *South Pass, 1868. James Chisholm's Journal of the Wyoming Gold Rush.* Lincoln, Neb.: University of Nebraska, 1960.

Hooper, Osman C. *History of Ohio Journalism, 1793–1933.* Columbus, O.: Osman C. Hooper, 1933.

————. *Ohio Journalism Hall of Fame.* Columbus, O.: Ohio State University, 1929–32.

Kinsley, Philip. *The Chicago Tribune: Its First Hundred Years.* 3 vols. Chicago: Chicago Tribune, 1943–46.

Linn, James Weber. *James Keeley, Newspaperman.* Indianapolis: Bobbs-Merrill, 1937.

Lloyd, Caro. *Henry Demarest Lloyd.* 2 vols. New York: G. P. Putnam's Sons, 1912.

Lloyd, Henry Demarest. *Wealth Against Commonwealth.* New York: Harper & Bros., 1894.

Logsdon, Joseph. *Horace White, Nineteenth Century Liberal.* Westport, Conn.: Greenwood Press, 1971.

Lundberg, Ferdinand. *Imperial Hearst: A Social Biography.* New York: Equinox Cooperative, 1936.

McCormick, Robert R. *The American Empire.* Chicago: Chicago Tribune, 1952.

————. *The American Revolution and its Influence on World Civilization, A Compilation of a Series of Addresses Broadcast over WGN and the Mutual Broadcasting System, Feb. 24-May 5, 1945.* Chicago: Chicago Tribune, 1945.

————. *The Army of 1918.* New York: Harcourt, Brace, 1920.

_____. *Freedom of the Press: A History and an Argument Compiled from Speeches on This Subject Delivered over a Period of Fifteen Years.* New York: D. Appleton-Century, 1936.

_____. *How We Acquired Our National Territory.* Chicago: Chicago Tribune, 1942.

_____. *Ulysses S. Grant, the Great Soldier of America.* New York: D. Appleton-Century, 1934.

_____. *The War Without Grant.* New York: Bond Wheelwright, 1950.

_____. *With the Russian Army, Being the Experiences of a National Guardsman.* New York: Macmillan, 1915.

McCutcheon, John T. *Drawn from Memory, Containing Many of the Author's Famous Cartoons and Sketches.* Indianapolis: Bobbs-Merrill, 1950.

McGivena, Leo E., ed., et al. *The News: The First Fifty Years of New York's Picture Newspaper.* New York: News Syndicate Co., 1969.

Medill, Joseph. "An Easy Method of Spelling the English Language." Chicago: n.p., 1867.

Monaghan, Jay. *The Man Who Elected Lincoln.* Indianapolis: Bobbs-Merrill, 1956.

Murray, George. *The Madhouse on Madison Street.* Chicago: Follett, 1965.

Patterson, Joseph Medill. *A Little Brother of the Rich.* Chicago: Reilly & Britton, 1908.

_____. *A Notebook of a Neutral.* New York: Duffield, 1915.

Rascoe, Burton. *Before I Forget.* New York: Doubleday, Doran, 1937.

_____. *We Were Interrupted.* New York: Doubleday, 1947.

Robinson, Jerry. *The Comics: An Illustrated History of Comic Strip Art.* New York: G. P. Putnam's Sons, 1974.

Seldes, George. *Lords of the Press.* New York: Julian Messner, 1938.

Sheridan, Martin. *Comics and Their Creators.* Boston: Hale, Cushman & Flynt, 1942.

Shirer, William L. *20th Century Journey: A Memoir of a Life and the Times. The Start, 1904–1930.* New York: Simon & Schuster, 1976.

Smith, Harvey H. *Shelter Bay: Tales of the Quebec North Shore.* Toronto: McClelland & Stewart, 1964.

Starr, Louis M. *Bohemian Brigade: Civil War Newsmen in Action.* New York: Alfred A. Knopf, 1954.

Stein, Meyer L. *Under Fire: The Story of American War Correspondents.* New York: Simon & Schuster, 1968.

Stoddard, Henry Luther. *Horace Greeley: Printer, Editor, Crusader.* New York: G. P. Putnam's Sons, 1946.

Strevey, Tracy Elmer. *Joseph Medill and the Chicago Tribune During the Civil War Period.* Ph.D. Thesis, University of Chicago, 1930.

Tebbel, John W. *An American Dynasty. The Story of the McCormicks, Medills and Pattersons.* New York: Doubleday, 1947.

_____. *The Compact History of the American Newspaper.* New York: Hawthorn Books, 1963.

_____. *The Life and Good Times of William Randolph Hearst.* New York: E. P. Dutton, 1952.

_____. *The Marshall Fields: A Study in Wealth.* New York: E. P. Dutton, 1947.

_____. *The Media in America.* New York: Thomas Y. Crowell, 1975.

Townsend, George Alfred. *Campaigns of a Non-Combatant and His Romaunt Abroad During the War.* New York: Blelock, 1866. Reissued as *Rustics in Rebellion: A Yankee Reporter on the Road to Richmond, 1861–65.* Chapel Hill, N.C.: University of North Carolina, 1950.

Villard, Henry. *Memoirs of Henry Villard, Journalist and Financier, 1835–1900.* 2 vols. Boston: Houghton-Mifflin, 1904.

Waldrop, Frank C. *McCormick of Chicago: An Unconventional Portrait of a Controversial Figure.* Englewood Cliffs, N.J.: Prentice-Hall, 1966.

Wiegman, Carl. *Trees to News: A Chronicle of the Ontario Paper Company's Origin and Development.* Toronto: McClelland & Stewart, 1953.

Wilkie, Franc B. *Pen and Powder.* Boston: Ticknor and Company, 1888.

_____. *Personal Reminiscences of Thirty-Five Years of Journalism.* Chicago: F. J. Schulte, 1891.

_____. *Walks About Chicago. 1871–1881.* Chicago: Belford, Clarke, 1882.

INDEX

ABOUT THE AUTHOR

Lloyd Wendt entered the newspaper business at the age of 16 as a printer's devil for his hometown *Spencer* (South Dakota) *News*, where he subsequently worked as a reporter and columnist. After receiving his bachelor's degree in journalism from Northwestern University, Wendt became telegraph editor of the *Argus-Leader* in Sioux Falls, South Dakota.

With his bride, the former Helen Sigler, Wendt returned in 1933 to Northwestern, where he had a journalism fellowship. He joined the staff of the *Chicago Tribune* as a reporter in February, 1934, and in June received his master's degree from Northwestern. For the *Tribune,* Wendt covered City Hall and wrote on politics, later was assistant to the day city editor, then moved into the Sunday room as a writer for the magazine section.

In the Navy during World War II, Wendt rose to the rank of lieutenant commander and was in charge of a strategic intelligence research unit specializing in amphibious landing beaches and enemy bomb targets. After the war he returned to the *Tribune,* becoming editor of the *Graphic* magazine and, in 1951, assistant Sunday editor. Early in 1953, Wendt was directed to combine the *Graphic* and the picture section of the Sunday paper into a single magazine, and the *Chicago Tribune Magazine* made its debut in October with Wendt as its first editor.

He assumed the position of *Tribune* Sunday editor in 1958 and in 1961 was named editor of *Chicago's American,* later directing the conversion of that paper into *Chicago Today.* He became president and publisher as well as editor of *Today* in 1969. In 1973 he was appointed associate editor of the Saturday and Sunday *Chicago Tribune* to help direct the weekend editions of the *Tribune,* while retaining full responsibility for *Today.*

An editor who likes to go into the field, Wendt has covered the Vietnam War, insurgencies in Latin America, and the Israeli-Arab crisis. He was among the first U.S. newsmen to go behind the Berlin Wall to report from East Germany, Poland, and the Soviet Union during the Berlin crisis in 1961.

Wendt has co-authored five books on Chicago history with Herman Kogan and has written a novel. He taught at Northwestern University and from 1950 to 1953 was chairman of the fiction division of the Medill School of Journalism.

After the *Tribune* and *Today* merged in 1974, Wendt remained with the *Tribune* as associate editor until his retirement in 1977. He now resides in Sarasota, Florida, where he continues active in journalism as editor of the *Pelican Cove News* (circulation 1,000).

PRINTED IN U.S.A.

IN MEMORIAM

RICHARD SWANK

Riverside Public Library
Riverside, Illinois

Presented by

Riverside Democratic
Organization